T0184316

Lecture Notes in Computer Science 11449

Commenced Publication in 1973
Founding and Former Series Editors:
Gerhard Goos, Juris Hartmanis, and Jan van Leeuwen

More information about this series at http://www.springer.com/series/7410

Fuchun Guo · Xinyi Huang
Moti Yung (Eds.)

Information Security and Cryptology

14th International Conference, Inscrypt 2018
Fuzhou, China, December 14–17, 2018
Revised Selected Papers

Editors
Fuchun Guo
University of Wollongong
Wollongong, NSW, Australia

Moti Yung
Columbia University
New York, NY, USA

Xinyi Huang
Fujian Normal University
Fujian, China

ISSN 0302-9743   ISSN 1611-3349   (electronic)
Lecture Notes in Computer Science
ISBN 978-3-030-14233-9   ISBN 978-3-030-14234-6   (eBook)
https://doi.org/10.1007/978-3-030-14234-6

Library of Congress Control Number: 2019932173

LNCS Sublibrary: SL4 – Security and Cryptology

This Springer imprint is published by the registered company Springer Nature Switzerland AG
The registered company address is: Gewerbestrasse 11, 6330 Cham, Switzerland

Preface

The 14th International Conference on Information Security and Cryptology (Inscrypt 2018) was held during December 14–17, 2018, in Fuzhou, China, with more than 170 attendees. Inscrypt is a well-recognized annual international forum for security researchers and cryptographers to exchange their ideas and present their research results, and is held every year in China. This volume contains all papers accepted by Inscrypt 2018. The program chairs also invited seven distinguished researchers to deliver talks. The keynote speakers were Robert Deng from Singapore Management University, Singapore; Jin Li from Guangzhou University, China; Ron Steinfeld from Monash University, Australia; Huaxiong Wang from Nanyang Technological University, Singapore; Yang Xiang from Swinburne University of Technology, Australia; Moti Yung from Columbia University and Google, USA; and Wanlei Zhou from University of Technology Sydney, Australia.

The conference received 93 submissions. Each submission was reviewed by at least three Program Committee members or external reviewers. The Program Committees accepted 31 full papers and 5 short papers to be included in the conference program. The Program Committees selected two papers as the best papers. They are "Cloud-Based Data-Sharing with White-box Access Security Using Verifiable and CCA-Secure Re-encryption from Indistinguishability Obfuscation" by Mingwu Zhang, Yan Jiang, and Willy Susilo, and "Two-Round PAKE Protocol over Lattices without NIZK" by Zengpeng Li and Ding Wang. The program chairs also invited one paper about the analysis of Chinese cryptographic standards to be included in this volume. The proceedings therefore contain all 32 papers revised after the conference.

Inscrypt 2018 was held in cooperation with the International Association for Cryptologic Research (IACR), and was co-organized by the Fujian Provincial Key Lab of Network Security and Cryptology of the Fujian Normal University, and the State Key Laboratory of Information Security (SKLOIS) of the Chinese Academy of Science. Furthermore, Inscrypt 2018 was sponsored by the JUZIX (www.juzix.net/en/index.jhtml).

We would like to thank all 306 authors who submitted their papers to Inscrypt 2018, and the conference attendees for their interest and support. We thank the Program Committee members and the external reviewers for their hard work in reviewing the submissions. We thank the Organizing Committee and all volunteers from Fujian Normal University for their time and effort dedicated to arranging the conference. Finally, we thank the EasyChair system for making the entire process convenient.

January 2019

Fuchun Guo
Xinyi Huang
Moti Yung

Inscrypt 2018

14th International Conference
on Information Security and Cryptology

Fuzhou, China
December 14–17, 2018

Organized and sponsored by

Fujian Provincial Key Laboratory of Network Security and Cryptology
(Fujian Normal University)
State Key Laboratory of Information Security (SKLOIS)
(Chinese Academy of Sciences)
JUZIX Technology Co., Ltd.

in cooperation with

International Association for Cryptologic Research (IACR)

Honorary Chairs

Dongdai Lin	Chinese Academy of Sciences, China
Yi Mu	Fujian Normal University, China

General Chairs

Xiaofeng Chen	Xidian University, China
Changping Wang	Fujian Normal University, China
Li Xu	Fujian Normal University, China

Technical Program Chairs

Fuchun Guo	University of Wollongong, Australia
Xinyi Huang	Fujian Normal University, China
Moti Yung	Columbia University and Google, USA

Organizing Chairs

Wei Wu	Fujian Normal University, China
Shangpeng Wang	Fujian Normal University, China

Publicity Chairs

Rongmao Chen	National University of Defense Technology, China
Zhe Liu	University of Luxembourg, Luxembourg

Publication Chair

Yuexin Zhang   Swinburne University of Technology, Australia

Steering Committee

Feng Bao   Huawei International, Singapore
Kefei Chen   Hangzhou Normal University, China
Dawu Gu   Shanghai Jiao Tong University, China
Xinyi Huang   Fujian Normal University, China
Hui Li   Xidian University, China
Dongdai Lin   Chinese Academy of Sciences, China
Peng Liu   Pennsylvania State University, USA
Wen-feng Qi   National Digital Switching System Engineering
                        and Technological Research Center, China
Meiqin Wang   Shandong University, China
Xiaofeng Wang   Indiana University at Bloomington, USA
Xiaoyun Wang   Tsinghua University, China
Jian Weng   Jinan University, China
Moti Yung   Snapchat Inc. and Columbia University, USA
Fangguo Zhang   Sun Yat-Sen University, China
Huanguo Zhang   Wuhan University, China

Technical Program Committee

Erman Ayday   Bilkent University, Turkey
Mauro Barni   University of Siena, Italy
Donghoon Chang   NIST, USA
Kai Chen   Chinese Academy of Sciences, China
Yu Chen   Chinese Academy of Sciences, China
Ilyong Chung   Chosun University, South Korea
Ashok Kumar Das   International Institute of Information Technology, India
Jintai Ding   University of Cincinnati, USA
Debin Gao   Singapore Management University, Singapore
Dawu Gu   Shanghai Jiao Tong University, China
Feng Hao   Newcastle University, UK
He Debiao   Wuhan University, China
Vincenzo Iovino   University of Luxembourg, Luxembourg
Peng Jiang   Beijing Institute of Technology, China
Dae-Young Kim   Daegu Catholic University, South Korea
Neeraj Kumar   Deemed University, India
Jianchang Lai   Nanjian Normal University, China
Yingjiu Li   Singapore Management University, Singapore
Kaitai Liang   University of Surrey, UK
Joseph Liu   Monash University, Australia
Yang Liu   Nanyang Technological University, Singapore

Zhe Liu	University of Luxembourg, Luxembourg
Florian Mendel	TU Graz, Austria
Jianting Ning	National University of Singapore, Singapore
Kazumasa Omote	University of Tsukuba, Japan
Giuseppe Persiano	Università degli Studi di Salerno, Italy
Josef Pieprzyk	Queensland University of Technology, Australia
Bertram Poettering	Ruhr-Universität Bochum, Germany
Kouichi Sakurai	Kyushu University, Japan
Jian Shen	Nanjing University of Information Science and Technology, China
Chunhua Su	The University of Aizu, Japan
Siwei Sun	State Key Lab of Information Security, China
Qiang Tang	Cornell University, USA
Tian Tian	National Digital Switching System Engineering and Technological Research Center, China
Ding Wang	Peking University, China
Hao Wang	Shandong Normal University, China
Jianfeng Wang	Xidian University, China
Meiqin Wang	Shandong University, China
Wenling Wu	Chinese Academy of Science, China
Shouhuai Xu	University of Texas at San Antonio, USA
Xun Yi	RMIT University, Australia
Ting Yu	Qatar Computing Research Institute, Qatar
Yu Yu	Shanghai Jiao Tong University, China
Fan Zhang	Zhejiang University, China
Fangguo Zhang	Sun Yat-sen University, China
Rui Zhang	Chinese Academy of Sciences, Chian
Yuexin Zhang	Swinburne University of Technology, Australia
Xianfeng Zhao	Chinese Academy of Sciences, China
Cliff Zou	University of Central Florida, USA

Additional Reviewers

Agrawal, Megha
Anada, Hiroaki
Araujo, Roberto
Bag, Samiran
Bao, Zhenzhen
Bi, Jingguo
Biswas, Koushik
Bu, Kai
Chen, Chien-Ning
Chen, Haoyu
Chen, Hua
Chen, Huashan

Chen, Rongmao
Choi, Rakyong
Ding, Ning
Dobraunig, Christoph
Eichlseder, Maria
Erkin, Zekeriya
Fan, Lei
Feng, Qi
Gao, Guanjun
Ge, Chunpeng
Gong, Zheng
Guo, Chun

Guo, Jiale

Hasan, Munawar

He, Yingzhe

Hu, Chunya

Huang, Tao

Huang, Yan

Huang, Zhengan

Jap, Dirmanto

Jianlong, Tan

Kelarev, Andrei

Kim, Kee Sung

Koide, Hiroshi

Krawczyk, Jacek

Kuchta, Veronika

Lee, Jeeun

Li, Huige

Li, Wei

Li, Wenting

Li, Xiangxue

Li, Zhen

Li, Zhi

Lin, Chao

Lin, Chengjun

Liu, Guozhen

Liu, Yunwen

Liu, Zhen

Long, Yu

Lu, Xianhui

Luo, Yiyuan

Ma, Xuecheng

Meng, Weizhi

Paulet, Russell

Poussier, Romain

Pöppelmann, Thomas

Qiu, Tian

Quaglia, Elizabeth

Ravi, Prasanna

Roy, Partha Sarathi

Santoso, Bagus

Sengupta, Binanda

Singh, Ajit Pratap

Singh, Monika

Sun, Ling

Syalim, Amril

Tang, Yongkang

Tang, Zixin

Tian, Yangguang

Wang, Daibin

Wang, Haijun

Wang, Haoyang

Wang, Huaqun

Wang, Jing

Wang, Lei

Wu, Ge

Xiang, Zejun

Xie, Shaohao

Xu, Jiayun

Xu, Ke

Xue, Haiyang

Yang, Wenzhuo

Yang, Xu

Yuan, Lun-Pin

Zhang, Hailong

Zhang, Huang

Zhang, Kai

Zhang, Lei

Zhang, Mingwu

Zhang, Peng

Zhang, Wenying

Zhang, Yinghui

Zhang, Zhenfei

Zhang, Zheng

Zhang, Zhuoran

Zhao, Shengnan

Zhao, Xinjie

Zheng, Yafei

Zhuang, Jincheng

Contents

Invited Paper

Blockchain and Crypto Currency

Lattice-Based Cryptology

Symmetric Cryptology

Applied Cryptography

Information Security

Asymmetric Encryption

Foundations

XIV   Contents

Short Papers

Invited Paper

Security Analysis of SM9 Key Agreement and Encryption

Zhaohui Cheng[✉]

Olym Information Security Technology Ltd., Shenzhen, China
chengzh@myibc.net

Abstract. SM9 is a Chinese cryptography standard that defines a set of identity-based cryptographic schemes from pairings. Although the SM9 key agreement protocol and the SM9 encryption scheme have been used for years, there is no public available security analysis of these two schemes. In this paper, we formally analyze the security of these two schemes in the random oracle model.

1 Introduction

To counter the key replacement attack, in the conventional public key cryptosystems, a certificate is used to prove an entity's ownership of a claimed public key. So such a system has to include an infrastructure to issue certificates, and an entity has to verify peer party's certificate before using the contained public key. This type of system becomes complicated and difficult to manage when the number of users increases. The identity-based cryptography (IBC) offers an attractive alternative. In an IBC system, an entity treats peer party's identity as the party's public key or more precisely an entity's public key can be derived from its identity string through a pre-defined function with a set of system parameters. Hence, in such systems, the public key authenticity problem becomes trivial, and certificates are no longer necessary. Since Boneh-Franklin's pioneering work on identity-based encryption (IBE) from pairings [5], many identity-based cryptographic schemes have been proposed, and several of them have been utilized in practice. Notably, ISO/IEC has standardized some identity-based schemes in [14,15,18].

SM9 is a set of identity-based cryptographic schemes designed during the period between 2006 and 2007. It includes an identity-based signature (SM9-IBS), an identity-based key agreement (SM9-KA), and an identity-based encryption (SM9-IBE). These schemes can be implemented with an efficient bilinear pairing on elliptic curves [16] such as the optimal Ate pairing [20] or the R-Ate pairing [19]. In 2016, SM9 became the Chinese cryptographic public key algorithm standard GM/T 0044-2016 [13], and SM9-IBS has been adopted as part of the international standard ISO/IEC 14888-3:2018 [15]. Although SM9-KA and SM9-IBE have been used for years, there is no public available security analysis of these two schemes. This paper intends to fill this gap. We formally prove the security of these two schemes in the commonly used security models.

© Springer Nature Switzerland AG 2019
F. Guo et al. (Eds.): Inscrypt 2018, LNCS 11449, pp. 3–25, 2019.
https://doi.org/10.1007/978-3-030-14234-6_1

The paper is organized as follows. First, the necessary preliminaries are presented in Sect. 2. The SM9 key agreement is described and its security is analyzed in Sect. 3. In Sect. 4, the SM9 encryption scheme is described and its security is analyzed. Finally, we draw some conclusions.

2   Preliminaries

2.1   Pairing and Related Complexity Assumptions

Without loss of generality, a pairing is defined as a bilinear map

$$\hat{e} : \mathbb{G}_1 \times \mathbb{G}_2 \rightarrow \mathbb{G}_T,$$

where $\mathbb{G}_1, \mathbb{G}_2$ are additive groups and $\mathbb{G}_T$ is a multiplicative group. All three groups have prime order r.

The map $\hat{e}$ has the following properties:

1. Bilinearity. For all $(P, Q) \in \mathbb{G}_1 \times \mathbb{G}_2$ and all $a, b \in \mathbb{Z}$, $\hat{e}([a]P, [b]Q) = \hat{e}(P, Q)^{ab}$.
2. Non-degeneracy. For generator $P_1 \in \mathbb{G}_1$ and $P_2 \in \mathbb{G}_2$, $\hat{e}(P_1, P_2) \neq 1$

To facilitate the security analysis in the following sections, here we list some related complexity assumptions. We follow the approach in [8] to use $i \in \{1, 2\}$ to denote different choices of $P_i \in \mathbb{G}_i$ and an assumption with subscripts such as $\mathrm{BDH}_{i,j,k}$ identifies how the three elements are chosen from the groups for the assumption. Symbol $\in_R$ denotes randomly sampling from a set.

Assumption 1 (Bilinear Diffie-Hellman (BDH) [5]). *For $a, b, c \in_R \mathbb{Z}_r^*$, given $(P_1, P_2, [a]P_i, [b]P_j, [c]P_k)$, for some values of $i, j, k \in \{1, 2\}$, computing $\hat{e}(P_1, P_2)^{abc}$ is hard.*

Assumption 2 (ψ-Bilinear Diffie-Hellman (ψ-BDH)). *For $a, b \in_R \mathbb{Z}_r^*$, given $(P_i, P_j, [a]P_j, [b]P_j)$ for some values of $i, j \in \{1, 2\}$ and $i \neq j$, computing $\hat{e}(P_1, P_2)^{ab}$ is hard if no group homomorphism $\psi: \mathbb{G}_j \rightarrow \mathbb{G}_i$ such that $\psi(P_j) = P_i$ is efficiently computable.*

ψ-$\mathrm{BDH}_{i,j}$ is called BDH-j in [11] without explicit restriction on ψ. Apparently, Assumption 2 is not weaker than Assumption 1 because by calling a BDH algorithm with $(P_i, P_j, [a]P_j, [b]P_j, P_j)$, $\hat{e}(P_1, P_2)^{ab}$ is computed. However, it is subtle to decide the exact relationship between these two assumptions. Depending on the difficulty to compute $\psi : \mathbb{G}_j \rightarrow \mathbb{G}_i$, there are two cases.

– Case 1. For Type-1 and Type-2 pairings [12], an efficient group homomorphism $\psi : \mathbb{G}_2 \rightarrow \mathbb{G}_1$ exists. However, such ψ may not satisfy $\psi(P_2) = P_1$ if P_1 and P_2 are chosen randomly and independently. For example, with a Type-1 pairing and ψ as the identity map, two random generators may be chosen as follows: $P_2 = [c]P_1$ for some random $c \in \mathbb{Z}_r^*$. Similar situation could happen to the Type-2 pairing with ψ as the trace map, and groups are constructed as follows [8]. Let E be an elliptic curve defined over a prime field $\mathbb{F}_p$ with an embedding degree ν. Set $P_1 = \mathcal{P}_1$ and $P_2 = [\frac{1}{\nu}]\mathcal{P}_1' + \mathcal{P}_2$, where $\mathcal{P}_1, \mathcal{P}_1' \in E(\mathbb{F}_p)$ are two random generator of a cyclic group $\mathcal{G}_1$ with order r and $\mathcal{P}_2 \in E(\mathbb{F}_{p^\nu})$ is a generator of a cyclic group $\mathcal{G}_2$ with order r. $\psi(P_2) = \mathcal{P}_1' = [c]P_1$ for some $c \in \mathbb{Z}_r^*$. In this setting, ψ-BDH$_{1,2}$ equals to BDH$_{2,2,k}$. Given a BDH$_{2,2,2}$ problem $(P_1, P_2', [a]P_2', [b]P_2', [c]P_2')$ with $\psi(P_2') = P_1$ (note that in the Type-2 pairing $P_2' = [\frac{1}{\nu}]\mathcal{P}_1 + \mathcal{P}_2$), we can use a ψ-BDH$_{1,2}$ algorithm to solve the problem $(\psi([c]P_2'), P_2', [a]P_2', [b]P_2')$ to get $\hat{e}(\psi([c]P_2'), P_2')^{ab} = \hat{e}([c]P_1, P_2')^{ab} = \hat{e}(P_1, P_2')^{abc}$. Similarly, BDH$_{2,2,1}$ is solvable by ψ-BDH$_{1,2}$.

- Case 2. For Type-2 pairings, there appears no efficiently computable homomorphism $\psi : \mathbb{G}_1 \to \mathbb{G}_2$. For Type-3 pairings, there are no known efficiently computable homomorphisms between $\mathbb{G}_1$ and $\mathbb{G}_2$ [12]. In both cases, there appears no simple way to solve a ψ-BDH problem (ψ-BDH$_{2,1}$ for Type-2 pairings) other than relying on an algorithm like the one for the BDH problem.

More on the role of group homomorphism ψ on cryptographic protocols employing asymmetric pairings can be found in [6].

Assumption 3 (τ-BDHI [4]). *For a positive integer τ and $\alpha \in_R \mathbb{Z}_r^*$, given $(P_1, P_2, [\alpha]P_i, [\alpha^2]P_i, \ldots, [\alpha^\tau]P_i)$ for some value $i \in \{1, 2\}$, computing $\hat{e}(P_1, P_2)^{1/\alpha}$ is hard.*

Assumption 4 (Bilinear Collision Attack Assumption (τ-BCAA1) [7]). *For a positive integer τ and $\alpha \in_R \mathbb{Z}_r^*$, given $(P_1, P_2, [\alpha]P_i, h_0, (h_1, [\frac{\alpha}{h_1 + \alpha}]P_j), \ldots, (h_\tau, [\frac{\alpha}{h_\tau + \alpha}]P_j))$ for some values of $i, j \in \{1, 2\}$ where $h_i \in_R \mathbb{Z}_r^*$ and different from each other for $0 \le i \le \tau$, computing $\hat{e}(P_1, P_2)^{\alpha/(h_0 + \alpha)}$ is hard.*

Note that Assumption 4 is slight different from the one given in [7]. However, the following Lemma 1 together with Theorem 7 in [7] shows that Assumption 4 is equivalent to the one defined in [7]. The proof of Lemma 1 is in the Appendix.

Lemma 1. *If there exists a polynomial time algorithm to solve $(\tau\text{-}1)$-BCAA1$_{i,2}$, then there exists a polynomial time algorithm for τ-BDHI$_2$, if there exists an efficient homomorphism ψ: $\mathbb{G}_2 \to \mathbb{G}_1$.*

Assumption 5 (Decision BIDH (DBIDH) [7]). *For $a, b, r \in_R \mathbb{Z}_r^*$, differentiating*

$$(P_1, P_2, [a]P_i, [b]P_j, \hat{e}(P_1, P_2)^{b/a}) \text{ and } (P_1, P_2, [a]P_i, [b]P_j, \hat{e}(P_1, P_2)^r),$$

for some values of $i, j \in \{1, 2\}$, is hard.

Assumption 6 (Gap-τ-BCAA1 [7]). *For a positive integer τ and $\alpha \in_R \mathbb{Z}_r^*$, given $(P_1, P_2, [\alpha]P_i, h_0, (h_1, [\frac{\alpha}{h_1 + \alpha}]P_j), \ldots, (h_\tau, [\frac{\alpha}{h_\tau + \alpha}]P_j))$ for some values of $i, j \in \{1, 2\}$ where $h_i \in_R \mathbb{Z}_r^*$ and different from each other for $0 \le i \le \tau$, and a DBIDH oracle which solves a given DBIDH problem, computing $\hat{e}(P_1, P_2)^{\alpha/(h_0 + \alpha)}$ is hard.*

The relationship among assumptions can be found in [7]. Note that one of $[a]P_i$ and $[b]P_j$ may be fixed among queries to a DBIDH oracle, and such decision oracle may be called one-sided DBIDH oracle. In this paper, we use the term DBIDH referring to the one-sided DBIDH implicitly.

2.2   Security Model of Key Agreement

The Bellare-Rogaway key agreement model [1,3,8] is widely used to analyse key agreement protocols. In the model, each party participating in a session of a protocol is treated as an oracle. An oracle $\Pi_{i,j}^s$ denotes the s-th instance of party i involved with a partner party j in a session. The oracle $\Pi_{i,j}^s$ executes the prescribed protocol Π and produces the output as $\Pi(1^k, i, j, SK_i, PK_i, PK_j, tran_{i,j}^s, r_{i,j}^s, x) = (m, \delta_{i,j}^s, \sigma_{i,j}^s, j)$ where $r_{i,j}^s$ is the random flips of the oracle; x is the input message; m is the outgoing message; SK_i and PK_i are the private/public key pair of party i; $\delta_{i,j}^s$ is the decision of the oracle (accept/reject the session or no decision yet); $\sigma_{i,j}^s$ is the generated session key and PK_j is the public key of the intended partner j (see [1,3,8] for more details). After the response is generated, the conversation transcript $tran_{i,j}^s$ is updated as $tran_{i,j}^s.x.m$, where "$a.b$" denotes the result of the concatenation of two strings, a and b. An adversary can access an oracle by issuing some specified queries defined in the game below.

The security of a protocol is defined through a two-phase game between an adversary $\mathcal{A}$ and a challenger which simulates the executions of a protocol by providing the adversary with access to oracles. In the first phase, $\mathcal{A}$ is allowed to issue the following queries to oracles in any order.

1. $Send(\Pi_{i,j}^s, x)$. Upon receiving the message x, oracle $\Pi_{i,j}^s$ executes the protocol and responds with an outgoing message m or a decision to indicate accepting or rejecting the session. If the oracle $\Pi_{i,j}^s$ does not exist, it will be created as an initiator, the party who sends out the first message in the protocol, if $x = \lambda$, or as a responder otherwise. Here, we require $i \neq j$, namely, a party will not run a session with itself. Such restriction is not unusual in practice.
2. $Reveal(\Pi_{i,j}^s)$. If the oracle has not accepted, it returns $\bot$; otherwise, it reveals the session key.
3. $Corrupt(i)$. The party i responds with its private key.

Once the adversary decides that the first phase is over, it starts the second phase by choosing a *fresh oracle* $\Pi_{i,j}^s$ and issuing a $Test(\Pi_{i,j}^s)$ query, where the *fresh oracle* $\Pi_{i,j}^s$ and $Test(\Pi_{i,j}^s)$ query are defined as follows.

Definition 1 (fresh oracle). *An oracle $\Pi_{i,j}^s$ is fresh if (1) $\Pi_{i,j}^s$ has accepted; (2) $\Pi_{i,j}^s$ is unopened (not been issued the Reveal query); (3) party $j \neq i$ is not corrupted (not been issued the Corrupt query); (4) there is no opened oracle $\Pi_{j,i}^t$, which has had a matching conversation to $\Pi_{i,j}^s$.*

The above fresh oracle is particularly defined to cover the key-compromise impersonation resilience property since it implies that party i could have been issued a *Corrupt* query.

4. $Test(\varPi_{i,j}^{s})$. Oracle $\varPi_{i,j}^{s}$, which is fresh, randomly chooses $b \in \{0,1\}$ and responds with the session key if $b = 0$, or a random sample from the distribution of the session key otherwise.

After this point the adversary can continue querying the oracles except that it cannot reveal the test oracle $\varPi_{i,j}^{s}$ or an oracle $\varPi_{j,i}^{t}$ which has a matching conversation to $\varPi_{i,j}^{s}$ if such an oracle exists, and it cannot corrupt party j. Finally the adversary outputs a guess b' for b. If $b' = b$, we say that the adversary wins. The adversary's advantage is defined as

$$\mathrm{Adv}_{\mathcal{A}}(k) = |2\mathrm{Pr}[b' = b] - 1|.$$

We use session ID to define *matching conversations*. Two oracles $\varPi_{i,j}^{s}$ and $\varPi_{j,i}^{t}$ have a matching conversation to each other if both of them have the same session ID. Here, we will use the concatenation of the messages in a session (the transcript of an oracle) to define the session ID.

A secure authenticated key (AK) agreement protocol is defined as follows.

Definition 2. *Protocol $\varPi$ is a secure AK if:*

1. *In the presence of a benign adversary, which faithfully conveys messages, on $\varPi_{i,j}^{s}$ and $\varPi_{j,i}^{t}$, both oracles always accept holding the same session key, and this key is distributed uniformly in the session key space;*
2. *For any polynomial time adversary $\mathcal{A}$, $\mathrm{Adv}_{\mathcal{A}}(k)$ is a negligible function of security parameter k.*

If a protocol is secure regarding the above formulation, it achieves implicit mutual key authentication and the following general security properties: the known session key security, the key-compromise impersonation resilience and the unknown key-share resilience [3,8].

Now we consider the forward secrecy property. Informally, the forward secrecy of a protocol requires that the security of a session key established by a party is not affected even if the long-term key of either the party is compromised afterwards.

Definition 3. *An AK protocol is said to be forward secure if any polynomial time adversary wins the game with negligible advantage when it chooses as the challenger (i.e. in place of the fresh oracle) an unopened oracle $\varPi_{i,j}^{s}$ which has a matching conversation to another unopened oracle $\varPi_{j,i}^{t}$ and both oracles accepted and only one of i and j can be corrupted. If both i and j can be corrupted, then the protocol achieves perfect forward secrecy. If in the game, the master secret key can be disclosed, then the protocol achieves master secret forward secrecy. The corruption of long-term keys or the disclosure of the master secret key may happen at any time of the game.*

2.3 Security Model of Identity-Based Encryption

According to Boneh-Franklin's formulation [5], an identity-based encryption is specified by four algorithms:

- **Setup** $\mathbb{G}_{\text{ID}}(1^k)$: Given a security parameter k, the probabilistic algorithm outputs the master public key M_{pt} and the master secret key M_{st}.

$$(M_{\text{pt}}, M_{\text{st}}) \leftarrow \mathbb{G}_{\text{ID}}(1^k)$$

- **Private-Key-Extract** $\mathbb{X}_{\text{ID}}(M_{\text{pt}}, M_{\text{st}}, \text{ID}_A)$: The probabilistic algorithm takes as the input $M_{\text{pt}}, M_{\text{st}}$ and the identifier string $\text{ID}_A \in \{0,1\}^*$ for entity A, and outputs the private key D_A associated with ID_A.

$$D_A \leftarrow \mathbb{X}_{\text{ID}}(M_{\text{pt}}, M_{\text{st}}, \text{ID}_A)$$

- **Encrypt** $\mathbb{E}_{\text{ID}}(M_{\text{pt}}, \text{ID}_A, m)$: The probabilistic algorithm takes $M_{\text{pt}}, \text{ID}_A$, the message m from the message space $\mathbb{M}_{\text{ID}}(M_{\text{pt}})$ as the inputs, and outputs a ciphertext C in the ciphertext space $\mathbb{C}_{\text{ID}}(M_{\text{pt}})$.

$$C \leftarrow \mathbb{E}_{\text{ID}}(M_{\text{pt}}, \text{ID}_A, m)$$

- **Decrypt** $\mathbb{D}_{\text{ID}}(M_{\text{pt}}, \text{ID}_A, D_A, C)$: The deterministic algorithm takes $M_{\text{pt}}, \text{ID}_A$, D_A and C as input, and outputs the plaintext m or a failure symbol $\perp$ if C is invalid.

$$(m \text{ or } \perp) \leftarrow \mathbb{D}_{\text{ID}}(M_{\text{pt}}, \text{ID}_A, D_A, C)$$

Boneh and Franklin [5] formalized a security notion of IBE: ID-IND-CCA2 security, by the following two-stage game defined in Table 1 between an adversary $\mathcal{A} = (\mathcal{A}_1, \mathcal{A}_2)$ of the encryption algorithm and a challenger.

Table 1. IBE security formulation

ID-IND adversarial game
1. $(M_{\text{pt}}, M_{\text{st}}) \leftarrow \mathbb{G}_{\text{ID}}(1^k)$.
2. $(st, \text{ID}^*, m_0, m_1) \leftarrow \mathcal{A}_1^{\mathcal{O}_{\text{ID}}}(M_{\text{pt}})$.
3. $b \leftarrow \{0,1\}$.
4. $C^* \leftarrow \mathbb{E}_{\text{ID}}(M_{\text{pt}}, \text{ID}^*, m_b)$.
5. $b' \leftarrow \mathcal{A}_2^{\mathcal{O}_{\text{ID}}}(M_{\text{pt}}, C^*, st, \text{ID}^*, m_0, m_1)$.

In the games st is some state information and $\mathcal{O}_{\text{ID}}$ denotes oracles to which the adversary has access. In the CCA2 attack model, the adversary has access to two oracles:

1. **Extraction.** A private key extraction oracle which, on input of $\text{ID} \neq \text{ID}^*$, will output the corresponding value of D_{ID}.

2. **Decryption.** A decryption oracle which, on input an identity ID and a ciphertext of the adversary's choice, will return the corresponding plaintext or $\perp$. This is subject to the restriction that in the second phase $\mathcal{A}_2$ is not allowed to call this oracle with the pair (C^*, ID^*).

The adversary's advantage in the game is defined to be

$$\text{Adv}_{\text{ID}-\mathcal{A}}^{\text{ID}-\text{IND}-\text{CCA2}}(k) = \mid 2 \Pr[b' = b] - 1 \mid .$$

Definition 4. *An IBE algorithm is considered to be ID-IND-CCA2 secure, if for all PPT adversaries, the advantage in the game is a negligible function of the security parameter k.*

Following up Cramer and Shoup's formalization of hybrid encryption [10], Bentahar et al. [2] extended the hybrid encryption to identity-based schemes. Their main result is that an ID-IND-CCA2 secure IBE can be constructed from an ID-IND-CCA2 secure identity-based key encapsulation mechanism (ID-KEM) and a secure data encapsulation mechanism (DEM).

Similar to IBE, an ID-KEM scheme is specified by four algorithms as well.

- **Setup** $\mathbb{G}_{\text{ID}-\text{KEM}}(1^k)$: The algorithm is the same as $\mathbb{G}_{\text{ID}}(1^k)$.
- **Private-Key-Extract** $\mathbb{X}_{\text{ID}-\text{KEM}}(M_{\mathfrak{p}\mathfrak{k}}, M_{\mathfrak{s}\mathfrak{k}}, \text{ID}_A)$: The algorithm is the same as $\mathbb{X}_{\text{ID}}(M_{\mathfrak{p}\mathfrak{k}}, M_{\mathfrak{s}\mathfrak{k}}, \text{ID}_A)$.
- **KEM-Encap** $\mathbb{E}_{\text{ID}-\text{KEM}}(M_{\mathfrak{p}\mathfrak{k}}, \text{ID}_A)$: This probabilistic algorithm takes as input $M_{\mathfrak{p}\mathfrak{k}}$ and ID_A, and outputs a key K in the key space $\mathbb{K}_{\text{ID}-\text{KEM}}(M_{\mathfrak{p}\mathfrak{k}})$ and the encapsulation of the key C in the encapsulation space $\mathbb{C}_{\text{ID}-\text{KEM}}(M_{\mathfrak{p}\mathfrak{k}})$.

$$(K, C) \leftarrow \mathbb{E}_{\text{ID}-\text{KEM}}(M_{\mathfrak{p}\mathfrak{k}}, \text{ID}_A)$$

- **KEM-Decap** $\mathbb{D}_{\text{ID}-\text{KEM}}(M_{\mathfrak{p}\mathfrak{k}}, \text{ID}_A, D_A, C)$: This deterministic algorithm takes as input $M_{\mathfrak{p}\mathfrak{k}}, \text{ID}_A, D_A$ and C, and outputs the encapsulated key K in C or a failure symbol $\perp$ if C is an invalid encapsulation.

$$(K \text{ or } \perp) \leftarrow \mathbb{D}_{\text{ID}-\text{KEM}}(M_{\mathfrak{p}\mathfrak{k}}, \text{ID}_A, D_A, C),$$

Consider the two-stage game in Table 2 between an adversary $\mathcal{A} = (\mathcal{A}_1, \mathcal{A}_2)$ of the ID-KEM and a challenger.

In the games st is some state information and $\mathcal{O}_{\text{ID}-\text{KEM}}$ denotes oracles to which the adversary has access. In the CCA2 attack model, the adversary has access to two oracles::

1. **Extraction.** A private key extraction oracle which, on input of $\text{ID} \neq \text{ID}^*$, will output the corresponding value of D_{ID}.
2. **Decapsulation.** A decapsulation oracle which, on input an identity ID and encapsulation of the adversary's choice, will return the encapsulated key. This is subject to the restriction that in the second phase $\mathcal{A}_2$ is not allowed to call this oracle with the pair (C^*, ID^*).

Table 2. ID-KEM security formulation

ID-IND adversarial game
1. $(M_{p\ell}, M_{s\ell}) \leftarrow \mathbb{G}_{\mathrm{ID-KEM}}(1^k)$.
2. $(st, \mathrm{ID}^*) \leftarrow \mathcal{A}_1^{\mathcal{O}_{\mathrm{ID-KEM}}}(M_{p\ell})$.
3. $(K_0, C^*) \leftarrow \mathbb{E}_{\mathrm{ID-KEM}}(M_{p\ell}, \mathrm{ID}^*)$.
4. $K_1 \leftarrow \mathbb{K}_{\mathrm{ID-KEM}}(M_{p\ell})$.
5. $b \leftarrow \{0, 1\}$.
6. $b' \leftarrow \mathcal{A}_2^{\mathcal{O}_{\mathrm{ID-KEM}}}(M_{p\ell}, C^*, st, \mathrm{ID}^*, K_b)$.

The adversary's advantage is defined to be

$$\mathrm{Adv}_{\mathrm{ID-KEM}-\mathcal{A}}^{\mathrm{ID-IND-CCA2}}(k) = \mid 2\Pr[b' = b] - 1 \mid.$$

Definition 5. *An ID-KEM is considered to be ID-IND-CCA2 secure, if for all PPT adversaries $\mathcal{A}$, the advantage in the game above is a negligible function of the security parameter k.*

Apart from the above security requirement, it is required that the ID-KEM has an extra property as follow. In an ID-KEM, for the pair (M_{pk}, M_{sk}) generated by the Setup algorithm and every (ID_A, D_A) where $\mathrm{ID}_A \in \{0,1\}^*$ and D_A is generated by the Private-Key-Extract algorithm using $(M_{pk}, M_{sk}, \mathrm{ID}_A)$, all encapsulations created with (M_{pk}, ID_A) decapsulate properly with (M_{pk}, D_A) (in other words, BadKeyPairs (Section 7.1 [10]) are negligibly few). It is easy to see that SM9-KEM in Sect. 4 has this property.

In the hybrid encryption, a DEM uses the key generated by a KEM to encrypt the message. As the DEM uses a different key derived by the KEM to encrypt each message, a one-time symmetric-key encryption with proper security properties is sufficient for such purpose.

A one-time symmetric-key encryption consists of two deterministic polynomial-time algorithms with the key, message and ciphertext spaces defined by $\mathbb{K}_{\mathrm{SK}}(1^k)$, $\mathbb{M}_{\mathrm{SK}}(1^k)$ and $\mathbb{C}_{\mathrm{SK}}(1^k)$ given the security parameter k:

– **Encrypt** $\mathbb{E}_{\mathrm{SK}}(K, m)$: The encryption algorithm takes a secret key $K \in \mathbb{K}_{\mathrm{SK}}(1^k)$ and a message $m \in \mathbb{M}_{\mathrm{SK}}(1^k)$ as input, and outputs the ciphertext $C \in \mathbb{C}_{\mathrm{SK}}(1^k)$.

$$C \leftarrow \mathbb{E}_{\mathrm{SK}}(K, m)$$

– **Decrypt** $\mathbb{D}_{\mathrm{SK}}(K, C)$: Given a secret key K and a ciphertext C, the algorithm outputs the plaintext m or a failure symbol $\perp$.

$$(m \text{ or } \perp) \leftarrow \mathbb{D}_{\mathrm{SK}}(K, C)$$

The two algorithms satisfy $\mathbb{D}_{\mathrm{SK}}(K, \mathbb{E}_{\mathrm{SK}}(K, m)) = m$ for $m \in \mathbb{M}_{\mathrm{SK}}(1^k)$ and $K \in \mathbb{K}_{\mathrm{SK}}(1^k)$.

The security of one-time symmetric-key encryption is defined by the Find-Guess (FG) game in Table 3 between an adversary $\mathcal{A} = (\mathcal{A}_1, \mathcal{A}_2)$ of the DEM and a challenger:

Table 3. DEM security formulation

FG adversarial game
1. $(st, (m_0, m_1)) \leftarrow \mathcal{A}_1(1^k)$.
2. $b \leftarrow \{0, 1\}$.
3. $K \leftarrow \mathbb{K}_{\text{SK}}(1^k)$.
4. $C^* \leftarrow \mathbb{E}_{\text{SK}}(K, m_b)$.
5. $b' \leftarrow \mathcal{A}_2^{\mathcal{O}_{\text{SK}}}(C^*, st, m_0, m_1)$.

In the game m_0 and m_1 are of equal length from the message space and st is some state information. $\mathcal{O}_{\text{SK}}$ is the oracle that the adversary can access depending on the attack model. In the CCA attack model, the adversary has access to a decryption oracle.

- A decryption oracle which, on input a ciphertext C, returns $\mathbb{D}_{\text{SK}}(K, C)$ with K chosen in Step 3 in the game.

The adversary's advantage in the game above is defined to be

$$\text{Adv}_{\text{DEM}-\mathcal{A}}^{\text{FG}-\text{CCA}}(k) = |\, 2 \Pr[b' = b] - 1 \,|.$$

Definition 6. *A one-time encryption is consider to be FG-CCA secure, if for any PPT adversary $\mathcal{A}$, the advantage in the game above is a negligible function of the security parameter k.*

The FG-CCA secure one-time encryptions are easy to get, such as the one-time pad encryption with a secure message authentication code algorithm [10, 17].

A hybrid IBE construction consisting of the sequential combination of an ID-KEM with a DEM proceeds as defined in Table 4. Here, it is assumed that the key space output by the KEM is identical with the secret key space used by the DEM.

Table 4. Hybrid IBE

$\mathbb{E}_{\text{ID}}(M_{\text{pt}}, \text{ID}_A, m)$	$\mathbb{D}_{\text{ID}}(M_{\text{pt}}, \text{ID}_A, D_A, C)$
– $(K, C_1) \leftarrow \mathbb{E}_{\text{ID}-\text{KEM}}(M_{\text{pt}}, \text{ID}_A)$	– Parse C as $\langle C_1, C_2 \rangle$
– $C_2 \leftarrow \mathbb{E}_{\text{SK}}(K, m)$	– $K \leftarrow \mathbb{D}_{\text{ID}-\text{KEM}}(M_{\text{pt}}, \text{ID}_A, D_A, C_1)$
– Return $C = \langle C_1, C_2 \rangle$	– If $K = \perp$, return $\perp$
	– $m \leftarrow \mathbb{D}_{\text{SK}}(K, C_2)$
	– Return m

Similar to the result of hybrid encryption in [10], Bentahar *et al.* obtained the following theorem concerning the security of hybrid IBE.

Theorem 1 *[Bentahar et al. [2]]. Let $\mathcal{A}$ be a PPT ID-IND-CCA2 adversary of the IBE scheme $\mathcal{E}$ above. There exists PPT adversaries $\mathcal{B}_1$ and $\mathcal{B}_2$, whose running time is essentially that of $\mathcal{A}$, such that*

$$\mathrm{Adv}_{\mathrm{ID}-\mathcal{A}}^{\mathrm{ID-IND-CCA2}}(k) \leq 2\mathrm{Adv}_{\mathrm{ID-KEM}-\mathcal{B}_1}^{\mathrm{ID-IND-CCA2}}(k) + \mathrm{Adv}_{\mathrm{DEM}-\mathcal{B}_2}^{\mathrm{FG-CCA}}(k).$$

2.4   Notation and Supporting Functions

The following list briefly describes the notation used in the scheme descriptions in the following sections. One may refer to ISO/IEC 18033-2 [17] for detailed definitions.

1. $BITS(m)$: the primitive to count bit length of a bit string m.
2. $BS2IP(m)$: the primitive to convert a bit string m to an integer.
3. $EC2OSP(C)$: the primitive to convert an elliptic curve point C to an octet string.
4. $FE2OSP(w)$: the primitive to convert a field element w to an octet string.
5. $I2OSP(m, \ell)$: the primitive to convert an integer m to an octet string of length ℓ.

The SM9 schemes require two supporting functions. The first function is a key derivation function (KDF) which works as KDF2 in ISO/IEC 18033-2 [17]. **KDF2** (H_v, Z, ℓ). Given a hash function H_v with v-bit output, a bit string Z and a non-negative integer ℓ. The second function is a hash to range function **H2RF**$_i(H_v, Z, n)$ which, given a hash function H_v with v-bit output, a bit string Z and a non-negative integer n and a non-negative integer index i, runs as follows:

1. Set $\ell = 8 \times \lceil (5 \times BITS(n))/32 \rceil$.
2. Set $Ha =$ **KDF2**$(H_v, I2OSP(i, 1) \| Z, \ell)$.
3. Set $h = BS2IP(Ha)$.
4. Output $h_i = (h \mod (n-1)) + 1$.

3   SM9 Key Agreement and Its Security Analysis

The two-pass SM9 key agreement consists of following operations: **Setup**, **Private-Key-Extract**, **Message Exchange** and **Session Key Generation**.

Setup $\mathbb{G}_{\mathrm{ID}}(1^k)$. On input security parameter k, the operation runs as follows:

1. Generate three groups $\mathbb{G}_1$, $\mathbb{G}_2$ and $\mathbb{G}_T$ of prime order r and a bilinear pairing map $\hat{e} : \mathbb{G}_1 \times \mathbb{G}_2 \to \mathbb{G}_T$. Pick random generator $P_1 \in \mathbb{G}_1, P_2 \in \mathbb{G}_2$.
2. Pick a random $s \in \mathbb{Z}_r^*$ and compute $P_{pub} = [s]P_1$.
3. Set $g = \hat{e}(P_{pub}, P_2)$.

4. Pick a cryptographic hash function H_v and a one byte appendix hid.
5. Output the master public key $M_{pk} = (\mathbb{G}_1, \mathbb{G}_2, \mathbb{G}_T, \hat{e}, P_1, P_2, P_{pub}, g, H_v, hid)$ and the master secret key $M_{sk} = s$. SM9 standard requires $hid = 3$.

Private-Key-Extract $\mathbb{X}_{ID}(M_{pk}, M_{sk}, ID_A)$. Given an identity string $ID_A \in \{0,1\}^*$ of entity A, M_{pk} and M_{sk}, the operation outputs error if

$$s + \mathbf{H2RF}_1(H_v, ID_A\|hid, r) \mod r = 0,$$

otherwise outputs

$$D_A = [\frac{s}{s + \mathbf{H2RF}_1(H_v, ID_A\|hid, r)}]P_2.$$

Message Exchange

$$A \to B : R_A = [x_A]([\mathbf{H2RF}_1(H_v, ID_B\|hid, r)]P_1 + P_{pub})$$
$$B \to A : R_B = [x_B]([\mathbf{H2RF}_1(H_v, ID_A\|hid, r)]P_1 + P_{pub}), S_B$$
$$A \to B : S_A$$

where random $x_A, x_B \in \mathbb{Z}_r^*$ are picked by A and B respectively and S_B and S_A are the optional session key confirmation parts. The method to generate such optional values is explained later.

Session Key Generation

1. Entity A computes key values

$$g_1 = \hat{e}(R_B, D_A), g_2 = \hat{e}(P_{pub}, P_2)^{x_A} = g^{x_A}, g_3 = g_1^{x_A}.$$

2. Entity A computes ℓ-bit session key

$$SK_A = \mathbf{KDF2}(H_v, ID_A\|ID_B\|EC2OSP(R_A)\|EC2OSP(R_B)\|$$

$$FE2OSP(g_1)\|FE2OSP(g_2)\|FE2OSP(g_3), \ell).$$

3. Entity B computes key values

$$g_1' = \hat{e}(P_{pub}, P_2)^{x_B} = g^{x_B}, g_2' = \hat{e}(R_A, D_B), g_3' = g_2'^{x_B}.$$

4. Entity B computes ℓ-bit session key

$$SK_B = \mathbf{KDF2}(H_v, ID_A\|ID_B\|EC2OSP(R_A)\|EC2OSP(R_B)\|$$

$$FE2OSP(g_1')\|FE2OSP(g_2')\|FE2OSP(g_3'), \ell).$$

Note that entity $A(B)$ should check that $R_B(R_A)$ lies in $\mathbb{G}_1^*$ respectively.

In the following, we show that SM9-KA is a secure AK under the Gap-τ-BCAA1$_{1,2}$ assumption.

Theorem 2. *SM9-KA is a secure AK, provided that* **H2RF**$_1$, **KDF2** *are random oracles and the Gap-τ-BCAA1$_{1,2}$ assumption is sound. Specifically, suppose that there is an adversary $\mathcal{A}$ against the protocol with non-negligible probability $\epsilon(k)$ and running time $t(k)$, and in the attack* **H2RF**$_1$ *has been queried $q_1 + 1$ times, and* **KDF2** *has been queried q_2 times, and q_o oracles have been created. Then there exists an algorithm $\mathcal{B}$ solving the Gap-q_1-BCAA1$_{1,2}$ problem with advantage*

$$\mathsf{Adv}_\mathcal{B}(k) \geq \frac{\epsilon(k)}{(q_1 + 1) \cdot q_o}$$

within a running time

$$t_\mathcal{B} \leq t(k) + O(q_2 \cdot q_o \cdot \mathcal{O}),$$

where $\mathcal{O}$ is the time of one access to the DBIDH$_{1,1}$ oracle.

Proof: Condition 1 of Definition 2 directly follows from the protocol specification. In the sequel we prove that the protocol satisfies Condition 2. We show that if $\mathcal{A}$ exists, we can construct a probabilistic polynomial time (PPT) algorithm $\mathcal{B}$ to solve a Gap-q_1-BCAA1$_{1,2}$ problem with non-negligible probability.

Given an instance of the Gap-q_1-BCAA1$_{1,2}$ problem $(P_1, P_2, [x]P_1, h_0, (h_1, [\frac{x}{h_1+x}]P_2), \ldots, (h_{q_1}, [\frac{x}{h_{q_1}+x}]P_2))$ with a set of pairing parameter where $h_i \in_R \mathbb{Z}_r^*$ for $0 \leq i \leq q_1$ and the DBIDH$_{1,1}$ oracle $\mathcal{O}_{DBIDH}$, $\mathcal{B}$ simulates $\mathbb{G}_{\mathrm{ID}}$ to generate the system parameters $(\mathbb{G}_1, \mathbb{G}_2, \mathbb{G}_T, \hat{e}, P_1, P_2, [x]P_1, \hat{e}([x]P_1, P_2), H_v, hid)$, i.e., using x as the master secret key, which it does not know. Function **H2RF**$_1$ and **KDF2** are constructed from the hash function H_v and are simulated as two random oracles controlled by $\mathcal{B}$.

We slightly abuse the notation $\Pi_{i,j}^t$ to refer to the t-th party instance among all the party instances created in the attack, instead of the t-th instance of party i. This would not affect the soundness of the security model. We also sightly abuse the notation in the proofs without applying element encoding in the corresponding functions.

$\mathcal{B}$ randomly chooses $1 \leq I \leq q_1 + 1$ and $1 \leq J \leq q_o$, and interacts with $\mathcal{A}$ in the following way:

- **H2RF**$_1$(ID$_i$): $\mathcal{B}$ maintains a list **H2RF**$_1^{list}$ of tuples (ID$_i, h_i, D_i$) as explained below. When $\mathcal{A}$ queries the oracle **H2RF**$_1$ on ID$_i$, $\mathcal{B}$ responds as follows:
  - If ID$_i$ is on **H2RF**$_1^{list}$ in a tuple (ID$_i, h_i, D_i$), then $\mathcal{B}$ responds with **H2RF**$_1$(ID$_i$) = h_i.
  - Otherwise, if the query is on the I-th distinct ID, then $\mathcal{B}$ stores (ID$_I, h_0, \perp$) into the tuple list and responds with **H2RF**$_1$(ID$_I$) = h_0.
  - Otherwise, $\mathcal{B}$ selects a random integer h_i with $i > 0$ from the Gap-q_1-BCAA1$_{1,2}$ instance which has not been chosen by $\mathcal{B}$ and stores (ID$_i, h_i, [\frac{x}{h_i+x}]P_2$) into the tuple list. $\mathcal{B}$ responds with **H2RF**$_1$(ID$_i$) = h_i.
- **KDF2**(ID$_i$, ID$_j, R_i, R_j, g_{1t}, g_{2t}, g_{3t}$): $\mathcal{B}$ maintains a list **KDF2**^{list} of pairs in the form $(\langle$ID$_i$, ID$_j, R_i, R_j, g_{1t}, g_{2t}, g_{3t}\rangle, \zeta_t)$. To respond to a query, $\mathcal{B}$ does the following operations:

- If $\mathbf{KDF2}^{list}$ has a tuple indexed by $\langle \text{ID}_i, \text{ID}_j, R_i, R_j, g_{1t}, g_{2t}, g_{3t} \rangle$, then $\mathcal{B}$ responds with ζ_t.
- Otherwise, $\mathcal{B}$ goes through the list Λ built in the *Reveal* query to find tuples of the form $((\langle \text{ID}_i, \text{ID}_j, R_i, R_j \rangle, r^t, \zeta^t, O^t)$ indexed by $\langle \text{ID}_i, \text{ID}_j, R_i, R_j \rangle$ and proceeds as follows:
  * Set $R = R_j$ and $T = g_{1t}$ if $O^t = 1$, otherwise $R = R_i$ and $T = g_{2t}$, query $\mathcal{O}_{DBIDH}$ with $([x]P_1, P_2, [h_0 + x]P_1, R, T)$.
  * If $\mathcal{O}_{DBIDH}$ returns 1 and $g_{3t} = T^{r^t}$, $\mathcal{B}$ removes the tuple from Λ and inserts $((\langle \text{ID}_i, \text{ID}_j, R_i, R_j, g_{1t}, g_{2t}, g_{3t} \rangle, \zeta^t)$ into $\mathbf{KDF2}^{list}$, and finally responds with ζ^t.
- Otherwise, $\mathcal{B}$ randomly chooses a string $\zeta_t \in \{0,1\}^\ell$ and inserts a new tuple $((\langle \text{ID}_i, \text{ID}_j, R_i, R_j, g_{1t}, g_{2t}, g_{3t} \rangle, \zeta_t)$ into the list $\mathbf{KDF2}^{list}$. It responds to $\mathcal{A}$ with ζ_t.

- Corrupt(ID_i): $\mathcal{B}$ looks through list $\mathbf{H2RF}_1^{list}$. If ID_i is not on the list, $\mathcal{B}$ queries $\mathbf{H2RF}_1(\text{ID}_i)$. $\mathcal{B}$ checks the value of D_i: if $D_i \neq \perp$, then $\mathcal{B}$ responds with D_i; otherwise, $\mathcal{B}$ aborts the game (**Event 1**).
- Send($\Pi_{i,j}^t, R$): $\mathcal{B}$ maintains a list with tuples of $(\Pi_{i,j}^t, r_{i,j}^t, tran_{i,j}^t)$ and responds to the query as follows:
  - If $t \neq J$, $\mathcal{B}$ randomly chooses $r^t \in \mathbb{Z}_r^*$ as the random flips of the oracle and generates $[r^t]([\mathbf{H2RF}_1(\text{ID}_j)]P_1 + [x]P_1)$ as the message.
  - If $t = J$, $\mathcal{B}$ further checks the value of D_j corresponding ID_j on the list $\mathbf{H2RF}_1^{list}$ after querying $\mathbf{H2RF}_1(\text{ID}_j)$, and then responds the query differently as below depending on this value.
    * If $D_j \neq \perp$, $\mathcal{B}$ aborts the game (**Event 2**). We note that there is only one party's private key is represented as $\perp$ in the whole simulation.
    * Otherwise, $\mathcal{B}$ randomly chooses $y \in \mathbb{Z}_r^*$ and responds with $[y]P_1$. Note that $\Pi_{i,j}^t$ can be the initiator (if $R = \lambda$) or the responder (if $R \neq \lambda$), and $\mathcal{B}$ doesn't know the random flips of the oracle.
- Reveal($\Pi_{i,j}^t$): $\mathcal{B}$ maintains a list Λ with tuples $((\langle \text{ID}_i, \text{ID}_j, R_i, R_j \rangle, r^t, \zeta^t, O^t)$. $\mathcal{B}$ responds to the query as follows:
  - If $t = J$ or if the J-th oracle has been generated as $\Pi_{a,b}^J$ and $\text{ID}_a = \text{ID}_j, \text{ID}_b = \text{ID}_i$ and two oracles have the same session ID, then abort the game (**Event 3**).
  - Go through $H_1^{list}(\text{ID}_i)$ to find the private key D_i of party i with identity ID_i.
  - If $D_i \neq \perp$, compute $g_1 = \hat{e}(R_j, D_i), g_2 = \hat{e}([x]P_1, P_2)^{r^t}, g_3 = g_1^{r^t}$ where R_j is the incoming message and r^t is the random flips of the oracle $\Pi_{i,j}^t$. $\mathcal{B}$ responds with $\mathbf{KDF2}(\text{ID}_i, \text{ID}_j, R_i, R_j, g_1, g_2, g_3)$ if the oracle is the initiator, or $\mathbf{KDF2}(\text{ID}_j, \text{ID}_i, R_j, R_i, g_2, g_1, g_3)$ otherwise.
  - Otherwise, go through $\mathbf{KDF2}^{list}$ to find tuples indexed by $\langle \text{ID}_i, \text{ID}_j, R_i, R_j, *, \hat{e}([x]P_1, P_2)^{r^t}, * \rangle$ (if $\Pi_{i,j}^t$ is the initiator) or by $\langle \text{ID}_j, \text{ID}_i, R_j, R_i, \hat{e}([x]P_1, P_2)^{r^t}, *, * \rangle$ (if $\Pi_{i,j}^t$ is the responder). $*$ matches any values. For each $(g_{1t}, g_{2t}, g_{3t}, \zeta_t)$ in the found tuples,
    * Set $R = R_j$ and $T = g_{1t}$ if $\Pi_{i,j}^t$ is the initiator, otherwise $R = R_i$ and $T = g_{2t}$; query $\mathcal{O}_{DBIDH}$ with $([x]P_1, P_2, [h_0 + x]P_1, R, T)$.

* If $\mathcal{O}_{DBIDH}$ returns 1 and $g_{3t} = T^{r^t}$, then $\mathcal{B}$ responds to the query with ζ_t.
  - Otherwise (no match is found in the last step), randomly choose $\zeta^t \in \{0,1\}^\ell$ and insert $(\langle \text{ID}_i, \text{ID}_j, R_i, R_j \rangle, r^t, \zeta^t, 1)$ if the oracle is the initiator or $(\langle \text{ID}_j, \text{ID}_i, R_j, R_i \rangle, r^t, \zeta^t, 0)$ into Λ. $\mathcal{B}$ responds with ζ^t.
- Test($\Pi_{i,j}^t$): If $t \neq J$ or ($t = J$ but) there is an oracle $\Pi_{j,i}^w$ which, with the same session ID with $\Pi_{i,j}^t$, has been revealed, $\mathcal{B}$ aborts the game (**Event 4**). Otherwise, $\mathcal{B}$ randomly chooses a bit string $\zeta \in \{0,1\}^\ell$ and gives it to $\mathcal{A}$ as the response.

Once $\mathcal{A}$ finishes the queries and returns its guess, $\mathcal{B}$ goes through **KDF2**^{list} and for each $T = g_{1t}, R = R_j$ from the tuple indexed by ID_i of the revealed oracle, if the revealed oracle is an initiator, otherwise $T = g_{2t}, R = R_i$ for the tuple indexed by ID_j

- $\mathcal{B}$ queries $\mathcal{O}_{DBIDH}$ with $([x]P_1, P_2, [h_0 + x]P_1, R, T)$.
- If $\mathcal{O}_{DBIDH}$ returns 1, $\mathcal{B}$ returns $T^{1/y}$ as the response to the Gap-q_1-BCAA1$_{1,2}$ challenge.
- If no match is found, $\mathcal{B}$ fails (**Event 5**, i.e., $\hat{e}([y]P_1, [\frac{x}{h_0+x}]P_2)$ has not been queried on **KDF2**).

Claim 1. *If algorithm $\mathcal{B}$ does not abort during the simulation, then algorithm $\mathcal{A}$'s view is identical to its view in the real attack.*

Proof: $\mathcal{B}$'s responses to **H2RF**$_1$ queries are uniformly and independently distributed in $\mathbb{Z}_r^*$ as in the real attack. **KDF2** is modeled as a random oracle which requires that for each unique input, there should be only one response. We note that the simulation $\mathcal{B}$ substantially makes use of the programmability of random oracle and the access to the DBIDH oracle to guarantee that the response to the **KDF2** query is consistent with the Reveal query. The responses in other types of query are valid as well. Hence the claim follows.

Note the agreed key value in the chosen fresh oracle $\Pi_{i,j}^t$ should include $T = \hat{e}(R, D_i)$ where $R = [y]P_1$ and D_i is the private key of party j whose public key is $[h_0]P_1 + [x]P_1$, if the game does not abort.

Claim 2. $\Pr[\overline{\text{Event 5}}] \geq \epsilon(k)$.

The proof is similar to Claim 2 in [9]. We skip the details.

Let **Event 6** be that, in the attack, adversary B indeed chooses oracle $\Pi_{i,j}^J$ as the challenger oracle where ID_j has been queried on **H2RF**$_1$ as the I-th distinct identifier query. Then following the rules of the game, it's clear that Event 1, 2, 3, 4 would not happen. So,

$$\Pr[\overline{(\text{Event 1} \vee \text{Event 2} \vee \text{Event 3} \vee \text{Event 4})}] = \Pr[\text{Event 6}] \geq \frac{1}{q_1 \cdot q_o}.$$

Overall, we have

$$\Pr[A \text{ wins}] = \Pr[\text{Event } 6 \wedge \overline{\text{Event } 5}]$$
$$\geq \frac{1}{q_1 \cdot q_o} \epsilon(k).$$

This completes the security proof.   □

SM9-KA is versatile in the sense that it can be instantiated with different choices of system parameters to satisfy different security requirements. SM9-KA can be implemented with both symmetric pairings and asymmetric pairings [12]. If one wants to implement a system with the key escrow property for lawful auditing, he can use a symmetric pairing and set $P_1 = P_2$ when choosing the system parameters. With the knowledge of the master secret key s, one can recover the session key by first computing $R'_A = [\frac{1}{s+\mathbf{H2RF}_1(H_v, \mathrm{ID}_B \| hid, r)}]R_A = [x_A]P_1$ and $R'_B = [\frac{1}{s+\mathbf{H2RF}_1(H_v, \mathrm{ID}_A \| hid, r)}]R_B = [x_B]P_1$ and then computing $g_1 = \hat{e}(R'_B, [s]P_1), g_2 = \hat{e}(R'_A, [s]P_1)$ and $g_3 = \hat{e}(R'_A, R'_B)^s$. On the other hand, if one wants to keep communication to the intended party complete confidential, he needs a protocol without the key escrow property. To serve such purpose, the following security result shows that SM9-KA can also be instantiated to achieve the master secret forward secrecy if the ψ-BDH$_{2,1}$ problem is hard.

Theorem 3. *SM9-KA can be instantiated to achieve the master secret forward secrecy, provided that* **KDF2** *is a random oracle and the ψ-BDH$_{2,1}$ assumption is sound. Specifically, suppose that there is an adversary A with non-negligible probability $\epsilon(k)$ and running time $t(k)$ against the protocol that chooses generators P_1 and P_2 as the ψ-BDH$_{2,1}$ problem, and in the attack* **KDF2** *has been queried q_2 times, and q_o sessions including incomplete ones have been created. Then there exists an algorithm B solving the ψ-BDH$_{2,1}$ problem with advantage*

$$\mathbf{Adv}_B(k) \geq \frac{\epsilon(k)}{q_2 \cdot q_o}$$

within a running time essentially same as $t(k)$.

Proof: Given an instance of the ψ-BDH$_{2,1}$ problem $(P_1, P_2, [a]P_1, [b]P_1)$ with a set of pairing parameter where there is no efficient group homomorphism ψ such that $\psi(P_1) = P_2$. B simulates $\mathbb{G}_{\mathrm{ID}}$ to generate the system parameters $(\mathbb{G}_1, \mathbb{G}_2, \mathbb{G}_T, \hat{e}, P_1, P_2, [x]P_1, \hat{e}([x]P_1, P_2), H_v, hid)$, i.e., using a randomly chosen $x \in \mathbb{Z}_r^*$ as the master secret key. Function **KDF2** is constructed from the hash function H_v and is simulated as a random oracle controlled by B .

Without loss of generality, we use $\Pi_{i,j}^t$ to refer to the t-th session among all the sessions including incomplete ones created in the attack. B randomly chooses $1 \leq J \leq q_o$, and interacts with A in the following way:

- **KDF2**($\mathrm{ID}_i, \mathrm{ID}_j, R_i, R_j, g_{1t}, g_{2t}, g_{3t}$): B maintains a list **KDF2**^{list} of pairs in the form ($\langle \mathrm{ID}_i, \mathrm{ID}_j, R_i, R_j, g_{1t}, g_{2t}, g_{3t} \rangle, \zeta_t$). To respond to a query, B does the following operations:

- If **KDF2**^{list} has a tuple indexed by $\langle \text{ID}_i, \text{ID}_j, R_i, R_j, g_{1t}, g_{2t}, g_{3t} \rangle$, then $\mathcal{B}$ responds with ζ_t.
- Otherwise, $\mathcal{B}$ randomly chooses a string $\zeta_t \in \{0,1\}^\ell$ and inserts a new tuple $((\langle \text{ID}_i, \text{ID}_j, R_i, R_j, g_{1t}, g_{2t}, g_{3t} \rangle, \zeta_t)$ into the list **KDF2**^{list}. It responds to $\mathcal{A}$ with ζ_t.

- Corrupt(ID_i): $\mathcal{B}$ returns $[\frac{x}{\textbf{H2RF}_1(\text{ID}_i)+x}]P_2$.
- Send($\Pi_{i,j}^t, R$): $\mathcal{B}$ maintains a list with tuples of $(\Pi_{i,j}^t, r_{i,j}^t, tran_{i,j}^t)$ and responds to the query as follows:
  - If $t \neq J$, $\mathcal{B}$ randomly chooses $r^t \in \mathbb{Z}_r^*$ as the random flips of the oracle and generates $[r^t]([\textbf{H2RF}_1(\text{ID}_j)]P_1 + [x]P_1)$ as the message.
  - Otherwise ($t = J$. Without loss of generality, let ID_I and ID_R be the identity of the initiator and responder of the session respectively),
    * If $R = \lambda$, $\mathcal{B}$ uses $[a]P_1$ as the message.
    * Otherwise, if $R \neq [a]P_1$, $\mathcal{B}$ aborts (**Event 1**), otherwise $\mathcal{B}$ uses $[b]P_1$ as the message.
- Reveal($\Pi_{i,j}^t$): $\mathcal{B}$ responds to the query as follows:
  - If $t = J$, then abort the game (**Event 2**).
  - Otherwise, compute $D_i = [\frac{x}{\textbf{H2RF}_1(\text{ID}_i)+x}]P_2$, $g_1 = \hat{e}(R_j, D_i)$, $g_2 = \hat{e}([x]P_1, P_2)^{r^t}$, $g_3 = g_1^{r^t}$ where R_j is the incoming message and r^t is the random flips of the oracle $\Pi_{i,j}^t$. $\mathcal{B}$ responds with **KDF2**($\text{ID}_i, \text{ID}_j, R_i, R_j, g_1, g_2, g_3$) if the oracle is the initiator, or **KDF2**($\text{ID}_j, \text{ID}_i, R_j, R_i, g_2, g_1, g_3$) otherwise.
- Test($\Pi_{i,j}^t$): If $t \neq J$, $\mathcal{B}$ aborts the game (**Event 3**). Otherwise, $\mathcal{B}$ randomly chooses a string $\zeta \in \{0,1\}^\ell$ and gives it to $\mathcal{A}$ as the response.

Once $\mathcal{A}$ finishes the queries and returns its guess, $\mathcal{B}$ goes through **KDF2**^{list} to find a set $\mathcal{L}$ of tuples indexed by $\langle \text{ID}_I, \text{ID}_R, [a]P_1, [b]P_1, \hat{e}([b]P_1, [\frac{x}{\textbf{H2RF}_1(\text{ID}_I)+x}]P_2), \hat{e}([a]P_1, [\frac{x}{\textbf{H2RF}_1(\text{ID}_R)+x}]P_2), * \rangle$. $*$ matches any values. $\mathcal{B}$ randomly chooses g_{3t} from $\mathcal{L}$ and returns $X = g_{3t}^{(\textbf{H2RF}_1(\text{ID}_I)+x)(\textbf{H2RF}_1(\text{ID}_R)+x)/x}$ as the answer to the ψ-BDH$_{2,1}$ problem.

Note the agreed key value in the chosen fresh oracle $\Pi_{i,j}^t$ should include $Y = g_{3t} = \hat{e}([b]P_1, [\frac{x}{\textbf{H2RF}_1(\text{ID}_I)+x}]P_2)^{r_I}$ where $[r_I]([\textbf{H2RF}_1(\text{ID}_R)]P_1 + [x]P_1) = [a]P_1$, if the game does not abort. Hence, if the value has been queried with **KDF2** and g_{3t} happens with probability at least $1/q_2$ to be the right choice from $\mathcal{L}$, X is the correct answer to the ψ-BDH$_{2,1}$ problem.

Claim 3. *Let* **Event 4** *be that* Y *along with identities and exchanged messages has not been queried with* **KDF2**. $\Pr[\overline{\text{Event 4}}] \geq \epsilon(k)$.

The proof is similar to Claim 2 in [9]. We skip the details.

Let **Event 5** be that, in the attack, adversary B indeed chose oracle $\Pi_{i,j}^J$ as the challenger oracle. Then, following the rules of the game by Definition 3, it's clear that Event 1, 2, 3 would not happen. So,

$$\Pr[\overline{(\textbf{Event 1} \vee \textbf{Event 2} \vee \textbf{Event 3})}] = \Pr[\textbf{Event 5}] \geq \frac{1}{q_o}.$$

Overall, we have

$$\Pr[A \text{ wins}] = \Pr[\text{Event } 5 \wedge \overline{\text{Event } 4}]$$
$$\geq \frac{1}{q_2 \cdot q_o} \epsilon(k).$$

This completes the security proof.   □

4 SM9 Encryption and Its Security Analysis

The SM9 encryption is a hybrid encryption scheme built from an ID-KEM scheme and a DEM scheme. DEM can be one of those schemes such as DEM2 or DEM3 standardized in ISO/IEC 18033-2 [17]. SM9-KEM scheme consists of four operations: **Setup**, **Private-Key-Extract**, **KEM-Encap** and **KEM-Decap** as follows:

Setup $\mathbb{G}_{\text{ID-KEM}}(1^k)$. Same as **Setup** $\mathbb{G}_{\text{ID}}(1^k)$ of SM9-KA.
Private-Key-Extract $\mathbb{X}_{\text{ID-KEM}}(M_{\mathfrak{pe}}, M_{\mathfrak{se}}, \text{ID}_A)$. Same as **Private-Key-Extract** $\mathbb{X}_{\text{ID}}(M_{\mathfrak{pe}}, M_{\mathfrak{se}}, \text{ID}_A)$ of SM9-KA.
KEM-Encap $\mathbb{E}_{\text{ID-KEM}}(M_{\mathfrak{pe}}, \text{ID}_A)$. Given an identify string ID_A and the master public key $M_{\mathfrak{pe}}$, the operation runs as follows:

1. Set $h_1 = \textbf{H2RF}_1(H_v, \text{ID}_A \| hid, r)$.
2. Set $Q = [h_1]P_1 + P_{pub}$.
3. Pick a random $x \in \mathbb{Z}_r^*$.
4. Set $C_1 = [x]Q$.
5. Set $t = g^x$.
6. Set $K = \textbf{KDF2}(H_v, EC2OSP(C_1) \| FE2OSP(t) \| \text{ID}_A, \ell)$, where ℓ is the key length of the DEM.
7. Output $\langle K, C_1 \rangle$.

KEM-Decap $\mathbb{D}_{\text{ID-KEM}}(M_{\mathfrak{pe}}, \text{ID}_A, D_A, C_1)$. Given an identify string ID_A, the corresponding private key D_A, the encapsulation part C_1 and the master public key $M_{\mathfrak{pe}}$, the operation runs as follows:

1. If $C_1 \notin \mathbb{G}_1^*$, then output $\perp$ and terminate.
2. Set $t = \hat{e}(C_1, D_A)$.
3. Set $K = \textbf{KDF2}(H_v, EC2OSP(C_1) \| FE2OSP(t) \| \text{ID}_A, \ell)$, where ℓ is the key length of the DEM.
4. Output K.

Here, we only present the security analysis of SM9-KEM. The security of the full SM9-IBE follows from Theorem 1, 4 and the security result of DEM [17]. Again, we sightly abuse the notation in the proof without applying element encoding in the corresponding functions for succinct presentation.

Theorem 4. *SM9-KEM is ID-IND-CCA2 secure provided that* **H2RF$_1$, KDF2** *are random oracles and the Gap-τ-BCAA1$_{1,2}$ assumption is sound. Specifically, suppose there exists an ID-IND-CCA2 adversary $\mathcal{A}$ against SM9-KEM that has advantage $\epsilon(k)$ and running time $t(k)$, and suppose also that during the attack $\mathcal{A}$ makes at most q_D queries on the Decapsulation query, $q_1 + 1$ queries on* **H2RF$_1$** *and q_2 queries on* **KDF2** *with ID$_*$. Then there exists an algorithm $\mathcal{B}$ solving the Gap-q_1-BCAA1$_{1,2}$ problem with advantage*

$$\mathrm{Adv}_{\mathcal{B}}(k) \geq \frac{\epsilon(k)}{q_1 + 1}$$

within running time

$$t_{\mathcal{B}}(k) \leq t(k) + O(q_2 \cdot q_D \cdot \mathcal{O}),$$

where $\mathcal{O}$ is the time of one access to the DBIDH$_{1,1}$ oracle.

Proof: Given an instance of the Gap-q_1-BCAA1$_{1,2}$ problem $(P_1, P_2, [x]P_1, h_0,$ $(h_1, [\frac{x}{h_1+x}]P_2), \ldots, (h_{q_1}, [\frac{x}{h_{q_1}+x}]P_2))$ with a set of pairing parameter where $h_i \in_R \mathbb{Z}_r^*$ for $0 \leq i \leq q_1$ and the DBIDH$_{1,1}$ oracle $\mathcal{O}_{DBIDH}$, $\mathcal{B}$ simulates $\mathbb{G}_{\mathrm{ID-KEM}}$ to generate the system parameters $(\mathbb{G}_1, \mathbb{G}_2, \mathbb{G}_T, \hat{e}, P_1, P_2, [x]P_1, \hat{e}([x]P_1, P_2), H_v,$ $hid)$, i.e., using x as the master secret key, which it does not know. Function **H2RF$_1$** and **KDF2** are constructed from the hash function H_v and are simulated as two random oracles controlled by $\mathcal{B}$.

$\mathcal{B}$ randomly chooses $1 \leq I \leq q_1 + 1$ and interacts with $\mathcal{A}$ as follows:

– **H2RF$_1$(ID$_i$)**: $\mathcal{B}$ maintains a list **H2RF$_1^{list}$** of tuples $(\mathrm{ID}_i, h_i, D_i)$ as explained below. When $\mathcal{A}$ queries the oracle **H2RF$_1$** on ID$_i$, $\mathcal{B}$ responds as follows:
  • If ID$_i$ is on **H2RF$_1^{list}$** in a tuple $(\mathrm{ID}_i, h_i, D_i)$, then $\mathcal{B}$ responds with **H2RF$_1$(ID$_i$)** $= h_i$.
  • Otherwise, if the query is on the I-th distinct ID, then $\mathcal{B}$ stores $(\mathrm{ID}_I, h_0, \perp)$ into the tuple list and responds with **H2RF$_1$(ID$_I$)** $= h_0$.
  • Otherwise, $\mathcal{B}$ selects a random integer h_i with $i > 0$ from the Gap-q_1-BCAA1$_{1,2}$ instance which has not been chosen before and stores $(\mathrm{ID}_i, h_i, [\frac{x}{h_i+x}]P_2)$ into the tuple list. $\mathcal{B}$ responds with **H2RF$_1$(ID$_i$)** $= h_i$.

– **KDF2(C_i, X_i, ID_i)**: $\mathcal{B}$ maintains a list **KDF2^{list}** of pairs in the form $(\langle C_i, X_i, \mathrm{ID}_i \rangle, K_i)$. To respond to a query on $(C_i, X_i, \mathrm{ID}_i)$, $\mathcal{B}$ does the following operations:
  • If a pair $(\langle C_i, X_i, \mathrm{ID}_i \rangle, K_i)$ is on the list, then $\mathcal{B}$ responds with K_i.
  • Otherwise, $\mathcal{B}$ looks through list **H2RF$_1^{list}$**. If ID$_i$ is not on the list, then $\mathcal{B}$ queries **H2RF$_1$(ID$_i$)**. Depending on the value of D_i for ID$_i$ on **H2RF$_1^{list}$**, $\mathcal{B}$ responds differently.
    * If $D_i = \perp$,
      · $\mathcal{B}$ queries $\mathcal{O}_{DBIDH}$ with $([x]P_1, P_2, [h_0 + x]P_1, C_i, X_i)$.
      · If $\mathcal{O}_{DBIDH}$ returns 1 and a tuple index by (C_i, ID_i) appears on list $\mathcal{L}_D$ (a list maintained in the Decapsulation specified later), $\mathcal{B}$ returns K_i from the tuple after putting $(\langle C_i, X_i, \mathrm{ID}_i \rangle, K_i)$ into **KDF2^{list}**.

· Otherwise, $\mathcal{B}$ randomly chooses a string $K_i \in \{0,1\}^\ell$ and inserts a new pair $(\langle C_i, X_i, \text{ID}_i \rangle, K_i)$ into $\mathbf{KDF2}^{list}$, and if $\mathcal{O}_{DBIDH}$ returns 1, $\mathcal{B}$ also inserts (C_i, ID_i, K_i) into $\mathcal{L}_D$. It responds to $\mathcal{A}$ with K_i.

∗ Otherwise $(D_i \neq \bot)$, $\mathcal{B}$ randomly chooses a string $K_i \in \{0,1\}^\ell$ and inserts a new pair $(\langle C_i, X_i, \text{ID}_i \rangle, K_i)$ into the list. It responds to $\mathcal{A}$ with K_i.

- **Extraction**(ID_i): $\mathcal{B}$ looks through list $\mathbf{H2RF}_1^{list}$. If ID_i is not on the list, $\mathcal{B}$ queries $\mathbf{H2RF}_1(\text{ID}_i)$. $\mathcal{B}$ checks the value of D_i: if $D_i \neq \bot$, then $\mathcal{B}$ responds with D_i; otherwise, $\mathcal{B}$ aborts the game (**Event 1**).

- **Decapsulation**(ID_i, C_i): $\mathcal{B}$ maintains list $\mathcal{L}_D$ of pairs in the form (C_i, ID_i, K_i). To respond to the query, $\mathcal{B}$ first looks through list $\mathbf{H2RF}_1^{list}$. If ID_i is not on the list, then $\mathcal{B}$ queries $\mathbf{H2RF}_1(\text{ID}_i)$. Depending on the value of D_i for ID_i on $\mathbf{H2RF}_1^{list}$, $\mathcal{B}$ responds differently.

  1. If $D_i \neq \bot$, then $\mathcal{B}$ first computes $g^r = \hat{e}(C_i, D_i)$, and then queries $K_i = \mathbf{KDF2}(C_i, g^r, \text{ID}_i)$. $\mathcal{B}$ responds with K_i.
  2. Otherwise $(D_i = \bot)$, $\mathcal{B}$ takes following actions:
     (a) If a tuple indexed by (C_i, ID_i) is on $\mathcal{L}_D$, return K_i from the tuple.
     (b) Otherwise, $\mathcal{B}$ randomly chooses $K_i \in \{0,1\}^\ell$ and inserts (C_i, ID_i, K_i) into the list $\mathcal{L}_D$. Finally $\mathcal{B}$ returns K_i.

- **Challenge:** At some point $\mathcal{A}$'s first stage will terminate and it will return a challenge identity ID^*. If $\mathcal{A}$ has not called $\mathbf{H2RF}_1$ with input ID^* then $\mathcal{B}$ does so for it. If the corresponding value of D_{ID^*} is not equal to $\bot$, then $\mathcal{B}$ aborts (**Event 2**). $\mathcal{B}$ chooses a random value of $y \in \mathbb{Z}_r^*$ and a random value $K^* \in \{0,1\}^\ell$, and returns $(K^*, [y]P_1)$ as the challenge. For simplicity, if $(\text{ID}^*, [y]P_1)$ has been queried on the Decapsulation query, $\mathcal{B}$ tries another random r.

- **Guess:** Once $\mathcal{A}$ outputs its guess, $\mathcal{B}$ answers the Gap-q_1-BCAA1$_{1,2}$ challenge in the following way.

  1. For each tuple $(\langle [y]P_1, X_j, \text{ID}_* \rangle, K_j)$ in $\mathbf{KDF2}^{list}$, $\mathcal{B}$ queries $\mathcal{O}_{DBIDH}$ with $([x]P_1, P_2, [h_0 + x]P_1, [y]P_1, X_j)$. If $\mathcal{O}_{DBIDH}$ returns 1, $\mathcal{B}$ outputs $X_j^{1/y}$ as the answer to the Gap-q_1-BCAA1$_{1,2}$ problem.
  2. If no tuple is found on the list, $\mathcal{B}$ fails (**Event 3**).

Claim 4. *If algorithm $\mathcal{B}$ does not abort during the simulation, then algorithm $\mathcal{A}$'s view is identical to its view in the real attack.*

Proof: $\mathcal{B}$'s responses to $\mathbf{H2RF}_1$ queries are uniformly and independently distributed in $\mathbb{Z}_r^*$ as in the real attack because of the behavior of the Setup phase in the simulation. $\mathbf{KDF2}$ is modeled as a random oracle which requires that for each unique input, there should be only one response. We note that the simulation substantially makes use of the programmability of random oracle and the access to the DBIDH$_{1,1}$ oracle to guarantee that the response to the $\mathbf{KDF2}$ query is consistent with the Decapsulation query. There are two subcases in the simulation.

- The adversary queries on $\mathbf{KDF2}(C_i, X_i, \text{ID}_i)$. If (C_i, X_i, ID_i) has not been queried before on $\mathbf{KDF2}$, $\mathcal{B}$ should make sure that the response must be consistent with the possible existing response generated in the Decapsulation queries when $ID_i = ID_*$. $\mathcal{B}$ exploits the access to the $DBIDH_{1,1}$ oracle by testing $\hat{e}(C_i, [\frac{x}{h_0+x}]P_2) \stackrel{?}{=} X_i$. If the equation holds, $\mathcal{B}$ returns the response to the Decapsulation query on (ID_i, C_i) if such query has been issued.

- The adversary queries the Decapsulation oracle on (ID^*, C_i). $\mathcal{B}$ cannot compute $X_i = \hat{e}(C_i, [\frac{x}{h_0+x}]P_2)$ (note that if the game does not abort, $D_{ID^*} = [\frac{x}{h_0+x}]P_2$). If $\mathbf{KDF2}(C_i, X_i, ID_i)$ has not been queried, i.e., (ID_i, C_i, K_i) is not on $\mathcal{L}_D$, $\mathcal{B}$ can respond with any random string K_i. Otherwise, $\mathcal{B}$ uses K_i from the tuple on $\mathcal{L}_D$ indexed by (ID_i, C_i) that is inserted by a $\mathbf{KDF2}$ query.

The responses in other types of query are valid as well. Hence the claim is founded.

We now evaluate the probability that $\mathcal{B}$ does not abort the game. **Event 3** implies that the value $\hat{e}(C^*, [\frac{x}{h_0+x}]P_2)$, which is the key value in the challenge encapsulation, is not queried on **KDF2** in the simulation. Since **KDF2** is a random oracle, $\Pr[\mathcal{A} \text{ wins}|\textbf{Event 3}] = \frac{1}{2}$. We have

$$\Pr[\mathcal{A} \text{ wins}] = \Pr[\mathcal{A} \text{ wins}|\textbf{Event 3}]\Pr[\textbf{Event 3}] + \Pr[\mathcal{A} \text{ wins}|\overline{\textbf{Event 3}}]\Pr[\overline{\textbf{Event 3}}]$$

$$\leq \frac{1}{2}(1 - \Pr[\overline{\textbf{Event 3}}]) + \Pr[\overline{\textbf{Event 3}}] = \frac{1}{2} + \frac{1}{2}\Pr[\overline{\textbf{Event 3}}].$$

$$\Pr[\mathcal{A} \text{ wins}] \geq \Pr[\mathcal{A} \text{ wins}|\textbf{Event 3}]\Pr[\textbf{Event 3}]$$

$$= \frac{1}{2}(1 - \Pr[\overline{\textbf{Event 3}}]) = \frac{1}{2} - \frac{1}{2}\Pr[\overline{\textbf{Event 3}}].$$

So, we have $\Pr[\overline{\textbf{Event 3}}] \geq \epsilon(k)$. Note that $\overline{\textbf{Event 2}}$ implies $\overline{\textbf{Event 1}}$ because of the rules of the game. Overall, we have

$$\Pr[\mathcal{B} \text{ wins}] = \Pr[\overline{\textbf{Event 3}} \wedge \overline{\textbf{Event 2}}] \geq \frac{\epsilon(k)}{q_1 + 1}.$$

This completes the security analysis of SM9-KEM.   □

5   Conclusion

In this paper, we have formally proved that SM9-KA is a secure AK in the Bellare-Rogaway key agreement model under the Gap-τ-BCAA1$_{1,2}$ assumption if the used hash functions are treated as random oracles. SM9-KA is versatile and can be implemented with and without the key escrow property. We have proved that under the ψ-BDH$_{2,1}$ assumption, SM9-KA can be instantiated to achieve the master secret forward secrecy. SM9-IBE is a hybrid encryption scheme built from SM9-KEM and a standard DEM. We have proved that SM9-KEM is secure under the Gap-τ-BCAA1$_{1,2}$ assumption in the random oracle model.

A   Proof of Lemma 1

Proof: If there is a polynomial time algorithm $\mathcal{A}$ to solve the $(\tau\text{-}1)$-BCAA1$_{i,2}$ problem, we can construct a polynomial time algorithm $\mathcal{B}$ to solve the τ-BDHI$_2$ problem as follows. Given an instance of the τ-BDHI$_2$ problem

$$(P_1, P_2, [x]P_2, [x^2]P_2, \ldots, [x^\tau]P_2),$$

$\mathcal{B}$ works as follows to compute $\hat{e}(P_1, P_2)^{1/x}$.

1. Randomly choose different $h_0, \ldots, h_{\tau-1} \in \mathbb{Z}_r^*$. Let $f(z)$ be the polynomial

$$f(z) = \prod_{a=1}^{\tau-1}(z + h_a) = \sum_{a=0}^{\tau-1} c_a z^a.$$

   The constant term c_0 is non-zero because h_a's are different and c_i is computable from h_a's.
2. Set

$$Q_2 = \sum_{a=0}^{\tau-1}[c_a x^a]P_2 = [f(x)]P_2,$$

   and

$$[x]Q_2 = \sum_{a=0}^{\tau-1}[c_a x^{a+1}]P_2 = [xf(x)]P_2.$$

3. Set

$$f_b(z) = \frac{z - h_0}{z + h_b}f(z) = \sum_{a=0}^{\tau-1} d_a z^a,$$

   and compute

$$[\frac{x - h_0}{x + h_b}]Q_2 = [\frac{x - h_0}{x + h_b}f(x)]P_2 = [f_b(x)]P_2 = \sum_{a=0}^{\tau-1}[d_a x^a]P_2$$

   for $1 \leq b \leq \tau - 1$.
4. Set $Q_1 = \psi(Q_2)$ and pass the following instance of the $(\tau\text{-}1)$-BCAA1$_{i,2}$ problem to $\mathcal{A}$

$$(Q_1, Q_2, \psi([x-h_0]Q_2), h_0, (h_1+h_0, [\frac{x - h_0}{x + h_1}]Q_2), \ldots, (h_{\tau-1}+h_0, [\frac{x - h_0}{x + h_{\tau-1}}]Q_2))$$

   if $i = 1$, or

$$(Q_1, Q_2, [x - h_0]Q_2, h_0, (h_1 + h_0, [\frac{x - h_0}{x + h_1}]Q_2), \ldots, (h_{\tau-1} + h_0, [\frac{x - h_0}{x + h_{\tau-1}}]Q_2))$$

   to get

$$T = \hat{e}(Q_1, Q_2)^{\frac{x - h_0}{x}} = \hat{e}(Q_1, Q_2) \cdot \hat{e}(Q_1, Q_2)^{-h_0/x}.$$

5. Note that

$$[\frac{1}{x}](Q_2 - [c_0]P_2) = [\frac{1}{x}]([f(x)]P_2 - [c_0]P_2) = \sum_{a=1}^{\tau-1}[c_a x^{a-1}]P_2.$$

Set

$$T' = \sum_{a=1}^{\tau-1}[c_a x^{a-1}]P_2 = [\frac{f(x) - c_0}{x}]P_2.$$

Then,

$$T_0 = \hat{e}(\psi(T'), Q_2 + [c_0]P_2) = \hat{e}([f(x) - c_0]P_1, Q_2 + [c_0]P_2)^{1/x}$$

$$= \hat{e}(Q_1, Q_2)^{1/x} \cdot \hat{e}(P_1, P_2)^{-c_0^2/x}.$$

Finally, compute

$$\hat{e}(P_1, P_2)^{1/x} = ((T/\hat{e}(Q_1, Q_2))^{-1/h_0}/T_0)^{1/c_0^2}.$$

□

References

1. Bellare, M., Rogaway, P.: Entity authentication and key distribution. In: Stinson, D.R. (ed.) CRYPTO 1993. LNCS, vol. 773, pp. 232–249. Springer, Heidelberg (1994). https://doi.org/10.1007/3-540-48329-2_21
2. Bentahar, K., Farshim, P., Malone-Lee, J., Smart, N.P.: Generic constructions of identity-based and certificateless KEMs. J. Cryptol. **21**, 178–199 (2008)
3. Blake-Wilson, S., Johnson, D., Menezes, A.: Key agreement protocols and their security analysis. In: Darnell, M. (ed.) Cryptography and Coding 1997. LNCS, vol. 1355, pp. 30–45. Springer, Heidelberg (1997). https://doi.org/10.1007/BFb0024447
4. Boneh, D., Boyen, X.: Efficient Selective-ID secure identity-based encryption without random oracles. In: Cachin, C., Camenisch, J.L. (eds.) EUROCRYPT 2004. LNCS, vol. 3027, pp. 223–238. Springer, Heidelberg (2004). https://doi.org/10.1007/978-3-540-24676-3_14
5. Boneh, D., Franklin, M.: Identity-based encryption from the weil pairing. In: Kilian, J. (ed.) CRYPTO 2001. LNCS, vol. 2139, pp. 213–229. Springer, Heidelberg (2001). https://doi.org/10.1007/3-540-44647-8_13
6. Chatterjee, S., Menezes, A.: On cryptographic protocols employing asymmetric pairings - the role of ψ revisited. Discret. Appl. Math. **159**, 1311–1322 (2011)
7. Chen, L., Cheng, Z.: Security proof of Sakai-Kasahara's identity-based encryption scheme. In: Smart, N.P. (ed.) Cryptography and Coding 2005. LNCS, vol. 3796, pp. 442–459. Springer, Heidelberg (2005). https://doi.org/10.1007/11586821_29
8. Chen, L., Cheng, Z., Smart, N.: Identity-based key agreement protocols from pairings. Int. J. Inf. Secur. **6**, 213–241 (2007)
9. Cheng, Z., Chen, L.: On security proof of McCullagh-Barreto's key agreement protocol and its variants. Int. J. Secur. Netw. **2**, 251–259 (2007). Special Issue on Cryptography in Networks

10. Cramer, R., Shoup, V.: Design and analysis of practical public-key encryption schemes secure against adaptive chosen ciphertext attack. SIAM J. Comput. **33**, 167–226 (2003)
11. Galbraith, S., Hess, F., Vercauteren, F.: Aspects of pairing inversion. IEEE Trans. Inf. Theory **54**(12), 5719–5728 (2008)
12. Galbraith, S., Paterson, K., Smart, N.P.: Pairings for cryptographers. Discret. Appl. Math. **156**, 3113–3121 (2008)
13. GM/T 0044–2016. Identity-based cryptographic algorithms SM9 (2016)
14. ISO/IEC. Information technology - Secruity techniques - Key management - Part 3: Mechanisms using asymmetric techniques. ISO/IEC 11770–3:2015
15. ISO/IEC. Information technology - Secruity techniques - Digital signatures with appendix - Part 3: Discrete logarithm based mechanisms. ISO/IEC 14888–3:2018
16. ISO/IEC. Information technology - Security techniques - Cryptographic techniques based on elliptic curves - Part 5: Elliptic curve generation. ISO/IEC 15946–5:2009
17. ISO/IEC. Information technology - Security techniques - Encryption algorithms - Part 2: Asymmetric ciphers. ISO/IEC 18033–2:2006
18. ISO/IEC. Information technology - Security techniques - Encryption algorithms - Part 5: Identity-based ciphers. ISO/IEC 18033–5:2015
19. Lee, E., Lee, H., Park, C.: Efficient and generalized pairing computation on abelian varieties. IEEE Trans. Inf. Theory **55**, 1793–1803 (2009)
20. Vercauteren, F.: Optimal pairings. IEEE Trans. Inf. Theory **56**(11), 455–461 (2010)

Blockchain and Crypto Currency

Evaluating CryptoNote-Style Blockchains

Runchao Han[1(✉)], Jiangshan Yu[2], Joseph Liu[2], and Peng Zhang[3]

[1] The University of Manchester, Manchester, UK
runchao.han@student.manchester.ac.uk
[2] Monash University, Melbourne, Australia
{jiangshan.yu,joseph.liu}@monash.edu.au
[3] Shenzhen University, Shenzhen, China
zhangp@szu.edu.cn

Abstract. To hide user identity, blockchain-based cryptocurrencies utilize public key based coin addresses to represent users. However, the user identity can still be identified by linking the coin addresses to the IP address of a user, through network traffic analysis.

Ring Signature based protocols, such as CryptoNote and RingCT, have been designed to anonymize the payers of a transaction, and deployed in leading cryptocurrencies like Bytecoin and Monero. This paper provides a comprehensive evaluation on the performance of Bytecoin and Monero, at both the protocol level and the system level. In particular, our evaluation includes theoretical complexity analysis of the protocols and practical performance analysis of the Bytecoin and Monero implementation. In addition, we also provide an analysis on the existing Bytecoin and Monero transactions, based on the public blockchain data. Our results identify the execution bottleneck and space overhead of generating and verifying transactions, which may encourage the design of more efficient protocols. We also provide insights based on our analysis on the performance of specific cryptographic algorithms, static analysis of the ring size distribution, of the input size distribution and output size distribution, and of the transaction size distribution.

Keywords: Cryptocurrency · Blockchain · Ring signature

1 Introduction

Cryptocurrencies have been very prevalent since the seminal Bitcoin system [9], which targets at democratizing the currency by a decentralized P2P network without governance. However, Bitcoin transactions are accessible for anyone with plaintext senders, receivers and amounts. Although the senders and receivers are cryptographically generated coin addresses, the coin addresses can still be linked to the identity of the real owner via traffic analysis.

In particular, with Bitcoin, a transaction is signed by the transaction sender, broadcasted to peers and verified by peers [9]. The transaction senders and receivers are represented by the explicit addresses generated from the public keys

© Springer Nature Switzerland AG 2019
F. Guo et al. (Eds.): Inscrypt 2018, LNCS 11449, pp. 29–48, 2019.
https://doi.org/10.1007/978-3-030-14234-6_2

which is irreversible and deterministic. Each transaction is signed by the sender's private key and verified by the public key, e.g. ECDSA in Bitcoin [9]. However, because the Bitcoin address is uniquely determined by the corresponding public key and both addresses and public keys are public, the individuals behind the Bitcoin network are traceable. For example, quantitative analyses towards the whole Bitcoin blockchain [7,12] potentially reveal most Bitcoin participants.

CryptoNote [13] has been proposed to improve the anonymity of Bitcoin. In particular, it uses a modified version of traceable ring signatures [3], called One-time Ring Signature, to hide both the payer and payee of a transaction. However, CryptoNote cannot hide the amount of a transaction. Monero[1] proposed Ring Confidential Transactions [10] (RingCT), to further hide the amount by using Pedersen Commitment [11].

This paper aims at providing an understanding on the performance of the above two systems. We evaluate the performance both theoretically and experimentally. We first informally evaluate the algorithms in terms of their security, complexity, and parallelism. Then, we evaluate the systems through experiments.

In particular, we use Bytecoin v2.1.2[2] as the reference CryptoNote implementation, which is a CryptoNote-based and actively maintained cryptocurrency. It has a market cap of more than 432 Million USD to date, and is ranked 25th in the cryptocurrency market cap[3]. We use Monero v0.12.3.0[4] as the reference RingCT implementation, which has a market cap of about 1.9 Billion USD, and is ranked as the 13th in the cryptocurrency market cap[5].

Our analysis includes the performance of the specific cryptographic algorithms (such as time of creating/verifying a transaction with different inputs and outputs), static analysis of the ring size distribution, of the input size distribution and output size distribution, and of the transaction size distribution.

To evaluate the most recent status of the Bytecoin blockchain and Monero blockchain, we crawled more than 200,000 Bytecoin transactions, all Monero V6 transactions (from height 1400000 to 1539500) with the mandatory ring size 5, and all Monero V7 transactions (with the mandatory ring size 7) up to July 28th, 2018 (from height 1539500 to 1626649). Our results give several insights on the two blockchains. Our result shows that while providing a better privacy guarantee, Monero transaction is more time-consuming to create and to verify a transaction. We also observe that with Bytecoin, the average ring size is approximately 3, and the mandatory minimum ring size is 1 (no mixins) in Bytecoin. So it might be vulnerable to "zero-mixin" attacks [4,8]. With Monero, the mandatory minimum ring size has been changed a few times in its earlier versions. Our analysis shows that for Monero V6 where the mandatory minimum ring size is 5, the average used ring size is also 5. Then, when the mandatory ring size is

---

[1] https://getmonero.org/.

[2] https://github.com/amjuarez/bytecoin/tree/frozen-master.

[3] https://coinmarketcap.com/currencies/bytecoin-bcn/. Data fetched on 7th August 2018.

[4] https://github.com/monero-project/monero/.

[5] https://coinmarketcap.com/currencies/monero/. Data fetched on 7th August 2018.

changed to 7 in Monero V7, the mean ring size in Monero is approximately 8. Thus, compared to transactions in Bytecoin, transactions in Monero have a much larger ring in average. This might indicate that Monero users concern more on privacy than Bytecoin users, so they intend to use system with better privacy guarantee and bigger rings.

For the number of inputs and outputs of a single transaction, compared to Monero, Bytecoin users intend to include more inputs and outputs in a single transaction. As for averages, each Bytecoin transactions include approximately 11 inputs and 12 outputs on average, while the average inputs and outputs of a transaction are only 2 and 3 for Monero, respectively. For the number of inputs and outputs, Monero transactions have an upper bound (by practise rather than by pre-defined rules) of 100 inputs and 40 outputs in a single transaction, whereas the upper bounds in Bytecoin are about 10 times as much.

2 Primitives

Ring signature was proposed to hide the real signer in a way that given a signed message, a third party only knows that someone in a particular group of people created the signature, but does not know who is the signer. It provides two anonymity properties [3]:

- Signature Unlinkability: Given two arbitrary signatures σ_a and σ_b, it is computationally infeasible to check if σ_a and σ_b are signed by the same signer
- Signature Untraceability: Given an arbitrary signature σ_a, it is computationally infeasible to determine which public key in the ring is the true signer

Ring signatures cannot be used directly to achieve anonymity of the blockchain transactions, due to a possible double spending attack. In particular, since a third party cannot identify who is the real signer, an attacker can spend the same coin as many times as the size of the group.

To prevent double spending attacks, the ring signature schemes applied to cryptocurrencies must be linkable to eliminate multiple uses of the money. Both linkable ring signature and traceable ring signature can be used to achieve these requirements.

It should be noted that the linkability of ring signature does not imply the transaction linkability. Instead, the transaction utilizes multiple cryptographic techniques including the Linkable Ring Signature to achieve the transaction unlinkability and untraceability, which will be discussed later.

One-time Ring Signature in CryptoNote. CryptoNote utilizes a modified version of *Traceable Ring Signature* [3], called One-time Ring Signature. In One-time Ring Signature, a public key P_π and a Key Image I are derived from a private key x. The private key x and its key image P_π are used to prove that the signer knows at least one pair of public and private keys, while I aims at preventing against the creation of multiple signatures using the same key. Thus,

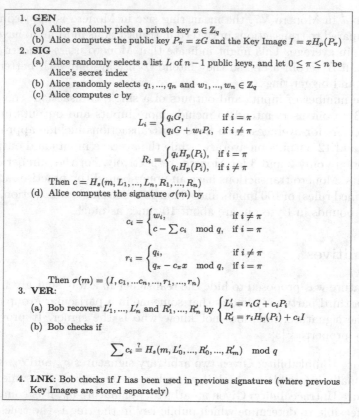

Fig. 1. Signing and verification process of the One-time Ring Signature

it prevents the double spending attack. The detailed process of One-time Ring Signature is shown in Fig. 1.

Multilayered Linkable Spontaneous Anonymous Group (MLSAG) Signature in RingCT. RingCT is based on linkable ring signature, of which the security model is shown in Fig. 2. RingCT defines the Multilayered Linkable Spontaneous Anonymous Group (MLSAG) Signature which extends the Linkable Spontaneous Anonymous Group Signature (LSAG) [5]. Each individual holds a vector of key pairs rather than only one key pair in order to hide the transaction amount by Pedersen Commitment, which will be discussed later. The detailed process of MLSAG is shown in Fig. 3.

Excluding the key vector, the One-time Ring Signature security model is essentially the same as the MLSAG Signature referred to Fig. 2.

1. **GEN**: Generating the private key k_π and the corresponding public key K_π
2. **SIG**: Signing the message m with L, a set of n public keys $K_1, ..., K_\pi, ..., K_n$ and k_π. The signature output is $\sigma(m)$
3. **VER**: Verifying $\sigma(m)$ with an arbitrary public key K_i in L, with an output *valid* or *invalid*
4. **LNK**: Checking if there is a signature using the same set of public keys L, with an output *linked* or *unlinked*

Fig. 2. Linkable ring signature.

1. **GEN**
   (a) Alice randomly picks a private key vector $x_{\pi,1}, ..., x_{\pi,m}$
   (b) Alice computes each corresponding public key $P_{\pi,j} = x_{\pi,j}G$ and Key Image $I_j = x_{\pi,j}H_p(P_{\pi,j})$ where $j \in (1, 2, ..., m)$
2. **SIG**
   (a) Alice randomly selects a list L of $(n-1)$ public key vectors $P_{i,j}$ where $i \in (1, 2, ..., n) \wedge i \neq \pi$ and $j \in (1, 2, ..., m)$. Let $0 \leq \pi \leq n$ be Alice's secret index
   (b) $\alpha_j = rand() \in \mathbb{Z}_q$ for all $j \in (1, 2, ..., m)$
   (c) $r_{i,j} = rand() \in \mathbb{Z}_q$ for all $i \in (1, 2, ..., n) \wedge i \neq \pi$ and $j \in (1, 2, ..., m)$
   (d) Alice computes $c_{\pi+1}$ by

   $$c_{\pi+1} = H_n(m, \alpha_1 G, \alpha_1 H_p(P_{\pi,1}), ..., \alpha_n G, \alpha_n H_p(P_{\pi,m}))$$

   (e) For $i = \pi + 1, ..., n$ and $1, ..., \pi - 1$, replacing $n + 1$ by 1, Alice computes:

   $$c_{i+1} = H_n(m, r_{i,1}G + c_i P_{i,1}, r_{i,1}H_p(P_{i,1}) + c_i I_1$$
   $$, ..., r_{i,m}G + c_i P_{i,m}, r_{i,m}H_p(P_{i,m}) + c_i I_m)$$

   (f) Alice computes

   $$r_{\pi,j} = \alpha_j - x_{\pi,j}c_\pi \mod q$$

   and the signature $\sigma(m)$ is

   $$\sigma(m) = (c_1, r_{1,1}, ..., r_{n,1}, ..., r_{n,m}, I_1, ..., I_m)$$

3. **VER**
   (a) For $1, ..., n$, replacing $n + 1$ by 1, Bob computes:

   $$c'_{i+1} = H_n(m, r_{i,1}G + c_i P_{i,1}, r_{i,1}H_p(P_{i,1}) + c_i I_1$$
   $$, ..., r_{i,m}G + c_i P_{i,m}, r_{i,m}H_p(P_{i,m}) + c_i I_m)$$

   (b) If $c'_1 = c_1$, then the signature is valid.
4. **LNK**: Bob checks if the Key Image vector I_j has been used in previous signatures (where previous Key Images are stored separately)

Fig. 3. Signing and verification process of the MLSAG signature.

3 Protocol-Level Comparisons

This section compares the performance-related metrics between CryptoNote and RingCT at the protocol-level, including the core ring signature algorithm and the approaches of achieving anonymity.

3.1   Algorithm Analysis

We first evaluate the the security, complexity and parallelism of the signature schemes in the context of protocol specifications[6].

Security. Both the One-time Ring Signature and the MLSAG Signature are unforgeable, untraceable and linkable. The unforgeability is a basic requirement for signature algorithms, and the untraceability is key to the blockchain transaction untraceability, while the linkability is exploited to combat the double-spending. Due to the usage of hash functions in both signature schemes, both security proofs are based on the Random Oracle (RO) Model [10,13]. In the context of CryptoNote and RingCT specification, both signature schemes are based on the elliptic curve Ed25519 [1]. Therefore, the security assumption of both schemes is the Elliptic Curve Discrete Logarithm Problem (ECDLP). A tabulated remark on the security is shown in Table 1.

Table 1. The security analysis on One-time Ring Signature and MLSAG Signature

Signature	Proof	Group	Hardness	Forgeable	Linkable	Traceable
One-time Ring Signature	RO	Ed25519	ECDLP	✗	✓	✗
MLSAG	RO	Ed25519	ECDLP	✗	✓	✗

Complexity and Parallelism. Compared to the One-time Ring Signature, MLSAG uses key vectors in its input. We denote the ring size as n and the key vector size as m.

The One-time Ring Signature signing includes computing vectors of L_i, R_i, c_i and r_i where $1 \leq i \leq n$, so the time and space complexity are both $O(n)$. Meanwhile, the One-time Ring Signature verification includes the inverse computation of L_i and R_i, so the time and space complexity are identical to the signing. On the other hand, MLSAG involves similar operations on $m \times n$ keys, so the time and space complexity for signing and verifying MLSAG signatures are all $O(mn)$.

Computations of L_i, R_i, c_i and r_i in the One-time Ring Signature are parallelizable, as no data dependency exists. However, the MLSAG Signature scheme can only be parallelized by vectorizing key vector operations, while operations across n key vectors are not parallelizable due to the iterative data dependency.

As the One-time Ring Signature contains $(c_1, ..., c_n)$ and $(r_1, .., r_n)$, the size of One-time Ring Signature is $O(n)$. Meanwhile, the MLSAG signature involves all $r_{i,j}$ values where $1 \leq i \leq n$ and $1 \leq j \leq m$, the size of MLSAG signature is $O(mn)$. A tabulated remark on the complexity and parallelism is shown in Table 2.

---

[6] CryptoNote Signature specification: https://cryptonote.org/cns/cns002.txt.

Table 2. The complexity analysis on One-time Ring Signature and MLSAG Signature

Signature	Sign		Verify		Signature size	Parallelism
	Time	Space	Time	Space		
One-time Ring Signature	$O(n)$	$O(n)$	$O(n)$	$O(n)$	$O(n)$	Across n
MLSAG	$O(mn)$	$O(mn)$	$O(mn)$	$O(mn)$	$O(mn)$	Across m

3.2 CryptoNote and RingCT Transactions

After comparing the ring signature schemes, we turn to compare the transaction generation and verification between CryptoNote and RingCT.

The cryptocurrency system is basically a currency system, which can be regarded as a ledger recording transactions time-wise. A conventional transaction consists of the sender, the receiver, the amount of money and the signature signed by the sender. Both CryptoNote and RingCT hide the sender address and the receiver address, and RingCT further hides the amount. Similar to the ring signature, the transaction anonymity includes the unlinkability and the untraceability, but with different definitions. Informally,

- Transaction Unlinkability: Given two arbitrary transactions TX_a and TX_b, it is impossible to prove that they were sent to the same person.
- Transaction Untraceability: Given a transaction input, the real output being redeemed in it should be anonymous among a set of other outputs.

The transaction unlinkability is achieved by One-time Public Key, while the transaction untraceability is achieved by the ring signature schemes above. We start from comparing the transaction formats, then we analyse the untraceability and unlinkability provided by different systems.

Transaction Formats. We start from analyzing the transaction formats of CryptoNote and RingCT.

As a generalization of conventional transactions, a CryptoNote or RingCT transaction consists of multiple inputs and multiple outputs. Basically, an input is a spendable deposit in the payer account, while an output is an amount of money that is transferred to the payee. The sum of inputs should equal to the sum of outputs in a single transaction. Due to the space limitation, we refer readers to the original paper for a detailed presentation of creating a CryptoNote transaction and a RingCT transaction.

While the inputs and outputs are similar in CryptoNote and RingCT, the amount of the transferred money is masked in RingCT by using Pedersen Commitment, and each masked amount is with a commitment and the range proof by using Borromean Signature [6]. Moreover, the ring used in RingCT combines amounts besides public keys. Our following analysis will show that the range proof and the ring signature mechanism in RingCT contributes the most overhead, which is a sacrifice for a better privacy, i.e., also hiding the amount.

1. Alice generates the transaction
   (a) Alice chooses a random $r \in \mathbb{Z}_q$
   (b) Alice computes a one-time public key $P = H_s(rA)G + B$
   (c) Alice packs a transaction TX including P and $R = rG$
2. Bob finds TX by scanning the blockchain or by the Payment Proof secretly sent from Alice by other communication approaches
3. Bob judges if the recipient of TX is himself
   (a) Bob computes $P' = H_s(aR)G + B$
   (b) If $P' = P$, the receiver of TX is Bob
4. Bob recovers the one-time private key $p = H_s(aR) + b$, where $P = pG$. Therefore, Bob can spend the money in TX

Fig. 4. One-time public key scheme

Unlinkability by One-Time Public Key. The One-time Public Key mechanism is the same in CryptoNote and RingCT, which is shown in Fig. 4. The design rationale is simple: A temporary public key is generated with random components and the receiver public key which can only be recognized by the receiver and the corresponding temporary private key can only be recovered by the receiver so that the money is spendable for by receiver.

Alice chooses a random $r \in \mathbb{Z}_q$ and mixes r with Bob's public key A and B to produce the One-time Public Key P, then the corresponding transaction TX is committed to the blockchain if verified by the term leader.

In the meantime, Bob finds TX by scanning the blockchain or by the Payment Proof (which will be described later) secretly sent from Alice by other communication approaches. Bob tries to find out if the receiver of TX is himself or not.

To prove this, Bob recovers P again, but by his private key a rather than the public key A which exploited the Elliptic Curve scalar multiplication homomorphism. Bob compares the recovered P' to P, and claims the money ownership if $P' = P$.

Furthermore, Bob needs to prove this ownership to peers without revealing his public key A and B. The One-time Public Key P has an associated private key p which is only recoverable for Bob. As Bob exclusively knows a and b, p can be computed without conducting the computationally infeasible Elliptic Curve scalar divisions. With the exclusively owned One-time Private Key p, Bob can prove the money ownership by digital signatures which is verifiable by anyone.

The One-time Public Key approach indicates that Bob should verify the One-time Public Keys of all new transactions appended to the blockchain, which is similar to claiming the ownership anonymously. However, as a single verification is a fairly time-consuming cryptographic process, the claiming process introduces huge overhead. Monero leverages the overhead by the Payment Proof (also called Transaction Key) which is generated by Alice and unicasted to Bob with other approaches secretly. The Payment Proof is generated from the transaction information cryptographically, by which Bob can easily identify his transaction on the blockchain[7].

---

[7] https://getmonero.org/resources/user-guides/prove-payment.html.

---

1. **GEN**: Alice generates the private key x, public key P and Key Image I
   (a) Alice chooses a random private key $x \in \mathbb{Z}_q$
   (b) Alice computes a one-time public key $P = xG$
   (c) Alice computes the Key Image $I = xH_p(P)$
2. **SIG**: Alice signs the transaction TX with One-time Ring Signature
   (a) Alice selects a random set of $n-1$ public keys P_i
   (b) Alice generates the One-time Ring Signature $\sigma(TX)$ with P_i, x, and I for the transactions TX
3. **VER**: Bob verifies the One-time Ring Signature signature $\sigma(TX)$
4. **LNK**: Bob checks if I was used in previous signatures

Fig. 5. CryptoNote scheme.

Untraceability with Double Spending Resistance by Key Image and One-Time Ring Signature in CryptoNote. While the unlinkability is achieved by the One-time Public Key, the untraceability is achieved by the One-time Ring Signature mentioned in Sect. 2. The process is shown in Fig. 5, which essentially wraps the One-time Ring Signature in Fig. 1 and further fits the signature scheme into the transaction creation.

Firstly, Alice generates a random private key $x \in \mathbb{Z}_q$ and the corresponding public key P and Key Image I. Secondly, Alice grabs a random set of public keys to form a ring and produce the One-time Ring Signature for the transaction TX, in which the inputs store I as the masked sender address. After that TX along with the signature $\sigma(TX)$ is sent to Bob the verifier. Bob verifies the signature with the routine in Fig. 1, unpacks TX to recover I, then checks if I was used in previous signatures. If TX is valid and I is new, TX is treated as valid and broadcasted to more peers by Bob.

The One-time Public Key and One-time Ring Signature are both modular, so easy to fit into a single system in a mutually exclusive manner. However, CryptoNote only masks the sender and receiver, while the amount is visible.

Hiding the Sender and the Amount by Combining MLSAG, Pedersen Commitment and Range Proof in RingCT. The solution, RingCT, mixes the Pedersen Commitment into the ring signature in order to mask the amounts. However, this modification on CryptoNote introduces the Range Proof problem which contributes to significant overhead.

The proposed RingCT scheme is shown in Fig. 6, which integrates the MLSAG scheme in Fig. 3. Instead of "one user one public key", each user has a vector of m key pairs to be compatible with the number of outputs m. Each output amount is replaced by the commitment value which is generated randomly with constraints, and the commitment values are involved in the ring used by the MLSAG Signature. In addition, the message to be signed is a series of commit values rather than the transaction itself.

The Range Proof is utilized in order to determine the range of unmasked amounts. As the amounts are masked and the Elliptic Curve Group is cyclic, a recovered value may have multiple possible values. Therefore, a Range Proof with commitments is conducted again for each output. To make the proof verifiable, a simpler Ring Signature scheme called Borromean Ring Signature is utilized to sign the commitments. However, the Range Proof takes much space in practise. A commitment value takes at least 8 Bytes according to the Ed25519 curve specification, which is 64 bits. For each bit a commitment value is generated in order to form the Ring Signature. In other words, 64 commitment values and a Ring Signature with 128 keys are responsible for only one output amount.

Evaluating Complexity and Transaction Size. We evaluated the computational complexity and the theoretical transaction size against the number of inputs, the number of outputs and the ring size for transaction-related operations. The results are shown in Table 3.

Table 3. The computational complexity of transaction-related operations for CryptoNote and RingCT

		Generate		Verify (+ Link)	
		Time	Space	Time	Space
CryptoNote	One-time address	O(out)	O(out)	O(out)	O(out)
	One-time Ring Signature	O(n)	O(n)	O(n)	O(n)
RingCT	One-time address	O(out)	O(out)	O(out)	O(out)
	Pedersen Commitment	O(in+out)	O(in+out)		
	Fake Transaction Generation	O(n*(in+out))	O(n*(in+out))		
	MLSAG	O(n*out)	O(n*out)	O(n*out)	O(n*out)
	Range Proof	O(out*amount)	O(out*amount)	O(out*amount)	O(out*amount)

Computational Complexity. Obviously, an One-time Public Key is generated for each output in a transaction, so the generation of verification of One-time Public Key is $O(out)$ for both CryptoNote and RingCT.

The Pedersen Commitment generation consists of finding random masked values and masks for each inputs and outputs, so the time and space complexity is $O(in + out)$.

Similarly, generating $(n-1)$ fake key vectors and commitment values involves $n - 1$ One-time Public Key generations, $n - 1$ fake amount and Pedersen Commitment generations. Therefore, the time and space complexity is $n - 1$ times of $O(in + out)$, which is $O(n * (in + out))$.

The verifications of Pedersen Commitments, fake transaction generations, and the MLSAG Signature are all accomplished by the MLSAG Signature verification, as those three processes are deeply coupled. Therefore, we only consider

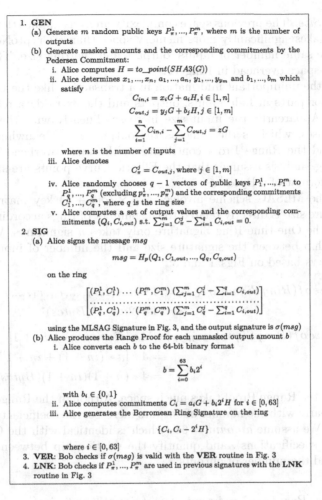

1. **GEN**
   (a) Generate m random public keys $P_\pi^1, ..., P_\pi^m$, where m is the number of outputs
   (b) Generate masked amounts and the corresponding commitments by the Pedersen Commitment:
      i. Alice computes $H = to\_point(SHA3(G))$
      ii. Alice determines $x_1, ..., x_n, a_1, ..., a_n, y_1, ..., y_{y_m}$ and $b_1, ..., b_m$ which satisfy
      $$C_{in,i} = x_i G + a_i H, i \in [1, n]$$
      $$C_{out,j} = y_j G + b_j H, j \in [1, m]$$
      $$\sum_{i=1}^{n} C_{in,i} - \sum_{j=1}^{m} C_{out,j} = zG$$
      where n is the number of inputs
      iii. Alice denotes
      $$C_\pi^j = C_{out,j}, \text{where } j \in [1, m]$$
      iv. Alice randomly chooses $q - 1$ vectors of public keys $P_1^1, ..., P_1^m$ to $P_q^1, ..., P_q^m$ (excluding $p_\pi^1, ..., p_\pi^m$) and the corresponding commitments $C_1^1, ..., C_q^m$, where q is the ring size
      v. Alice computes a set of output values and the corresponding commitments $(Q_i, C_{i,out})$ s.t. $\sum_{j=1}^{m} C_\pi^j - \sum_{i=1}^{q} C_{i,out} = 0$.
2. **SIG**
   (a) Alice signs the message msg
   $$msg = H_p(Q_1, C_{1,out}, ..., Q_q, C_{q,out})$$
   on the ring
   $$\begin{bmatrix} (P_1^1, C_1^1) \cdots (P_1^m, C_1^m) \left(\sum_{j=1}^{m} C_1^j - \sum_{i=1}^{q} C_{i,out} \right) \\ \cdots\cdots\cdots\cdots\cdots\cdots\cdots\cdots\cdots\cdots\cdots\cdots \\ (P_q^1, C_q^1) \cdots (P_q^m, C_q^m) \left(\sum_{j=1}^{m} C_q^j - \sum_{i=1}^{q} C_{i,out} \right) \end{bmatrix}$$
   using the MLSAG Signature in Fig. 3, and the output signature is $\sigma(msg)$
   (b) Alice produces the Range Proof for each unmasked output amount b
      i. Alice converts each b to the 64-bit binary format
      $$b = \sum_{i=0}^{63} b_i 2^i$$
      with $b_i \in \{0, 1\}$
      ii. Alice computes commitments $C_i = a_i G + b_i 2^i H$ for $i \in [0, 63]$
      iii. Alice generates the Borromean Ring Signature on the ring
      $$\{C_i, C_i - 2^i H\}$$
      where $i \in [0, 63]$
3. **VER**: Bob checks if $\sigma(msg)$ is valid with the **VER** routine in Fig. 3
4. **LNK**: Bob checks if $P_\pi^1, ..., P_\pi^m$ are used in previous signatures with the **LNK** routine in Fig. 3

Fig. 6. Hiding the receiver and the amount by MLSAG, pedersen commitment and range proof

the computational complexity of the MLSAG Signature. As the key matrix is $n \times (out + 1)$, the MLSAG Signature generation and verification are all with the time and space complexity $O(n * out)$ according to Sect. 3.1.

As for the Range Proof, for each output in a transaction, a Range Proof is conducted, including the commitment and the Borromean Signature. The commitment value generation for an output is with the time and space complexity $O(out * amount)$ apparently. Based on the Borromean Signature process the time and space complexity is the same. Therefore, for a single transaction with out outputs, the time and space complexity for the Range Proof generation and verification is $O(out * amount)$.

Transaction Size. The previous space complexity analysis implies that a RingCT transaction takes significantly more memory space than a CryptoNote transaction with the same number of inputs, outputs and the ring size. Therefore, we focus on the space overhead in RingCT.

Ignoring the unimportant information in a transaction like the version number, the major parts include inputs, outputs and the extra data related to the verification. Apparently, the input size increases linearly with the number of inputs increases, which is the same as the output size. Meanwhile, the Ring Signature and the Range Proof contribute to the most overhead in RingCT. The following analysis assumes that the Elliptic Curve points are stored in the compressed format of 4 Bytes[8].

Firstly, the MLSAG scheme involves a $n \times (out + 1)$ key matrix, and the Ring Signature size is directly related to the number of rings according to Fig. 3. Meanwhile, the One-time Ring Signature only takes n signatures. We quantify the relationship between the signature size and the number of inputs, outputs and public keys based on Figs. 1 and 3:

$$size\,of(Ring\,Signature_{CN}) = 4 * size(I, c_1, ..., c_n, r_1, ..., r_n)$$
$$= 4 * (2n + 1)(Bytes)$$

$$size\,of(Ring\,Signature_{RCT}) = 4 * [size(ring) + in + 1]$$
$$= 4 * [n * (in + 1) + in + 1])$$
$$= 4 * (n + 1)(in + 1)(Bytes)$$

Secondly, the Range Proof takes much space. Although the Range Proof size increases linearly with the number of outputs increase, the coefficient is quite big in practical. We assume $amount = 64$ (which is identical with the CryptoNote and RingCT specifications), and quantify the relationship between the Range Proof size and the number of outputs:

$$size\,of(Range\,Proof_{RCT}) = 4 * out * [size(signature) + size(maskedValues)]$$
$$= 4 * out * [(size(ring) + 1) + amount]$$
$$= 4 * out * [2 * amount + 1 + amount]$$
$$= 4 * out * [64 * 2 + 1 + 64])$$
$$= 772 * out(Bytes)$$

Table 4 concludes the results above. In conclusion, the approach of RingCT to hide the amount is expensive on the memory space. In the cryptocurrency context, big transactions lead to higher transaction fees[9] and lower transaction throughputs due to the block size limitation [2]. Therefore, leveraging the transaction size while keeping anonymous for cryptocurrencies is a crucial topic.

---

[8] https://crypto.stackexchange.com/questions/8914/ecdsa-compressed-public-key-point-back-to-uncompressed-public-key-point.

[9] The Bitcoin transaction fee specification: https://en.bitcoin.it/wiki/Transaction _fees.

Table 4. The size of Ring Signatures and Range Proofs with different inputs, outputs and ring sizes

	Ring Signature	Range Proof
CryptoNote	$(2n+1)*4$	0
RingCT	$(out+1)(n+1)*4$	$772*out$

4 Performance and Security Comparisons

According to Sect. 3.2, the performance of privacy-related techniques introduces overhead. However, Sect. 3.2 only focuses on the theoretical analysis, which may be different from the real implementation.

In this section, a detailed comparison between the CryptoNote protocol and the RingCT protocol is conducted, including the performance evaluation and the network status of the existing blockchain platforms based on CryptoNote and RingCT (We chose Bytecoin[10] as the CryptoNote reference implementation and Monero[11] as the RingCT reference implementation).

4.1 Experimental Methodologies

Evaluated Metrics. While the privacy is enhanced, the computational and storage overhead is introduced based on our analysis in Sect. 3.2, which may lead to lower transaction throughput and higher transaction fees. To evaluate the performance of privacy-related techniques from the practical perspective, the evaluation task is divided into two subtasks:

- Evaluating the performance of specific cryptographic processes
- Evaluating the blockchain network usage

The first subtask benchmarks the performance of privacy-related cryptographic processes, including:

- Time of constructing a transaction with different inputs and outputs
- Time of verifying a transaction (signature) with different inputs and outputs
- Transaction size with different inputs and outputs

Meanwhile, the blockchain network usage evaluation focus on the actual status of the running blockchains, which represents the true attitudes of network participants rather than the whitepapers. The evaluated metrics include:

- Ring size of signatures
- Transaction size
- The number of transaction inputs
- The number of transaction outs

---

[10] CryptoNote implementation in Bytecoin: https://github.com/bcndev/bytecoin/blob/d3dd3acf0a3113c9801589c6a512ef68a6eabed2/src/crypto/crypto-ops.h.

[11] RingCT implementation in Monero: https://github.com/monero-project/monero/blob/3fde902394946281665531abd742c64bdb23be25/src/ringct/rctOps.cpp.

Experimental Data. The data sources include:

– Results of running official test cases[12,13] with customized configurations.
– The transaction data which can be queried on the blockchain explorers[14,15].

As for performance-related metrics, we chose $1, 2, 4, 6, 8, 16, 32, 64, 128$ as the ring size, the input number and the output number to obtain experimental results from existing test cases.

In the meantime, more than 200,000 most recent transactions are crawled from the Bytecoin and Monero blockchain explorers in order to conduct the network usage analysis.

Experimental Environment

Hardware. The experiments for performance-related metrics were conducted on a laptop with a 64-bit Intel Core i7-6700HQ processor with 8 cores running at 2.60 GHz, 24 GB RAM, one Intel SATA SSD with 210 GB, a Nvidia GeForce GTX 960m GPU with 4 GB DRAM.

Software. We chose Bytecoin v2.1.2[16] as the reference CryptoNote implementation, which is a CryptoNote-based and actively maintained cryptocurrency without modifying the CryptoNote core protocol. Meanwhile, Monero v0.12.3.0[17] was regarded as the reference RingCT implementation, which is the first and the most prevalent RingCT-based cryptocurrency.

The selected blockchain platforms were compiled from the source code with the compiler GCC 5.4.0. The operating system is Ubuntu 18.04.

4.2   Performance of Critical Cryptographic Processes

Constructing Transactions

Results. The time of constructing a transaction with different inputs and outputs is shown in Fig. 7. Constructing a Monero transaction is more time-consuming than constructing a Bytecoin transaction with the same inputs and outputs. Moreover, the number of outputs is the dominant factor of constructing a Monero transaction, while the number of inputs and the number of outputs have similar impacts of the Bytecoin transaction construction.

---

[12] Bytecoin test cases: https://github.com/amjuarez/bytecoin/tree/frozen-master/tests.
[13] Monero test cases: https://github.com/monero-project/monero/tree/master/tests.
[14] https://xmrchain.net/block/1618540.
[15] https://explorer.bytecoin.org/.
[16] https://github.com/amjuarez/bytecoin/tree/frozen-master.
[17] https://github.com/monero-project/monero/.

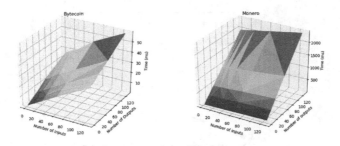

Fig. 7. Time of constructing a transaction with different inputs and outputs

Analysis. The results are expected and consistent to our protocol-level analysis.

As for Bytecoin, the time increases linearly with the increase of inputs and outputs. According to Sect. 3.2, the overhead introduced by the CryptoNote protocol are mainly the One-time Ring Signature which is linearly influenced by the ring size. The rest overhead increases linearly with the increase of the transaction size, which is linearly correlated with the number of inputs and outputs as well. Therefore, the constructing time increases with the number of inputs and outputs increases.

When it comes to Monero, the time is dominated by the number of outputs. According to Sect. 3.2, each output is attached with a Range Proof, and each Range Proof is attached with a Borromean Ring Signature. A Range Proof is considerably expensive, leading to a big overhead. Moreover, the size of a MLSAG Signature is linearly correlated to the number of outputs. Therefore, the number of outputs contributes to the most overhead so dominates the RingCT transaction construction time.

Verifying Transactions (Signatures)

Results. The time of verifying a signature with different ring sizes are shown in Fig. 8. Note that the signature is on an empty transaction with only one input and one output. It is observed that verifying a signature in Bytecoin is faster than in Monero. Also, the consumed time increases linearly with the ring size increases for both Bytecoin and Monero. For example, with the average ring sizes (3 for Bytecoin and 8 for Monero, which will be discussed later), the verification time of the Bytecoin signature is approximately 1ms, while for Monero the verification time is 20 ms.

Analysis. Because the number of inputs and outputs is fixed, the only variable is the ring size. The One-time Ring Signature of CryptoNote has the time complexity $O(n)$, while the MLSAG Signature is $O(mn)$. In Monero context, $m = out$, and $out = 1$ in the test case, so $m = 1$ and the MLSAG Signature time complexity here is $O(n)$ as well. Therefore, the linear increase of the verification time is as expected. On the other hand, the reason why the MLSAG Signature verification time is longer than the One-time Ring Signature is because of the

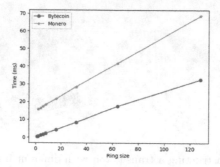

Fig. 8. Time of verifying a transaction (signature) with different ring sizes

space overhead introduced by the iterative hashing process without parallelism for computing $c_1, ..., c_{n+1}$.

4.3   Network Usage Analysis and Potential Threats

Ring Size

Results. The results are represented as histograms with marked average ring sizes, shown in Fig. 11. The average ring size is approximately 3, and the mandatory minimum, ring size is 1 (no mixins) in Bytecoin.

With Bytecoin, the mandatory minimum ring size has not been changed. However, Monero has updated the mandatory minimum ring sizes several times in the history. Monero V6 (Helium Hydra)[18], which hard-forked Monero V5 at the block height 1400000, firstly forced RingCT transactions with the mandatory ring size of 5. Then Monero V7 (Lithium Luna)[19], which hard-forked Monero V6 at the block height 1539500, changed the mandatory ring size to 7. It is noted that RingCT was firstly introduced in Monero V5 (Wolfram Warptangent)[20], but was not mandatory for transactions. The mandatory ring size of Monero V5 is 5 as well. Before Monero V5 the RingCT was not deployed, and the mandatory ring size was even smaller, which is out of our topic.

We conducted ring size analysis on Monero V6 and V7, as we focus on RingCT transactions. With the mandatory ring size of 5, the average ring size is 5.65. After changing the mandatory ring size to 7, the average ring size turns to 7.59. In the meantime, Monero users intend to choose bigger ring sizes than Bytecoin users according to our statistics.

Analysis. The ring size is directly correlated with the anonymity of senders and receivers. With more public keys mixed in a transaction, the identities of senders and receivers will be more ambiguous. Monero chose a bigger mandatory ring size

---

[18] https://github.com/monero-project/monero/releases/tag/v0.11.0.0.
[19] https://github.com/monero-project/monero/releases/tag/v0.12.0.0.
[20] https://github.com/monero-project/monero/releases/tag/v0.10.0.

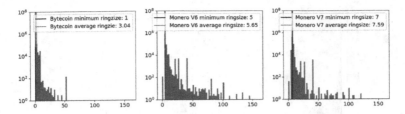

Fig. 9. The distribution and statistics of ring sizes

to strongly guarantee the identity ambiguity, making the Monero transactions harder to trace. As a result, Monero users may concern more on privacy than Bytecoin users, so intend to use bigger rings.

Inputs and Outputs

Results. Similar to the ring size statistics, the inputs and outputs distributions are shown in Fig. 10, with marked averages. Compared to Monero, Bytecoin users intend to include more inputs and outputs in a single transaction. In average, each Bytecoin transactions include approximately 11 inputs and 12 outputs on average, while the average inputs and outputs are only 2 and 3 for Monero, respectively. Furthermore, Monero users never take more than 100 inputs or 40 outputs in a single transaction, but for Bytecoin the corresponding numbers are approximately 1000 and 300.

Analysis. The reason that Monero users intend to take fewer inputs and outputs than Bytecoin users is mainly because of the high transaction fees introduced by bigger transaction sizes. According to the analysis in Sect. 3.2, hiding the output amount sacrifices the transaction size. Moreover, this sacrifice will be greater with more inputs or outputs. The transaction fee in Bytecoin and Monero is directly related to the transaction size[21]. Hiding the amount may not be critical for some Monero users compared to the high transaction fee. Therefore, Monero users intend to include fewer inputs and outputs.

In fact, high transaction fee in Monero is a concerning problem since the RingCT fork[22,23]. Different solutions have been emerging, which will be discussed later.

Transaction Size

Results. The size of a transaction has a direct impact on the transaction fee. We conducted the transaction size statistics like before, shown in Fig. 11. The

---

[21] Monero transaction fee calculator: https://www.monero.how/monero-transaction-fee-calculator.

[22] https://www.reddit.com/r/Monero/comments/7h0i5e/why_is_the_fee_so_high_380/.

[23] https://www.reddit.com/r/Monero/comments/74flal/why_are_fees_so_high/.

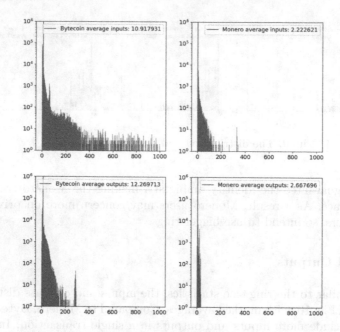

Fig. 10. The distribution and statistics of inputs and outputs

transaction size is 3KB on average for Bytecoin, while 18KB for Monero. In addition, Monero transactions are much bigger than Bytecoin transactions based on the distribution.

In addition, we correlated the transaction size with the number of inputs and outputs directly in Fig. 12. It should be noted that Fig. 12 omitted some unusual data on the blockchains. For example, a Monero transaction contains 2495 inputs, which is a really big number regarding to the RingCT transactions. Apparently, the transaction size of Monero is much bigger than of Bytecoin with the same number of inputs and outputs. Moreover, the number of outputs in Bytecoin is the dominant factor of the transaction size. As for Bytecoin, the relation between the transaction size and the number of inputs and outputs is fairly ambiguous.

Analysis. Based on our protocol-level analysis in Sect. 3.2 and analysis on the ring size, inputs and outputs, the transaction size distribution is as expected: Hiding the transaction amount introduces space overhead which greatly affects the transaction size.

As for the relation between the transaction size and the number of inputs and outputs for Bytecoin, the transaction size is most influenced by the ring size rather than the number of inputs and outputs. In the meantime, due to the MLSAG Signature combining with the Pedersen Commitment, the outputs take the major part of a RingCT transaction, which proves the protocol-level analysis towards transactions in Sect. 3.2.

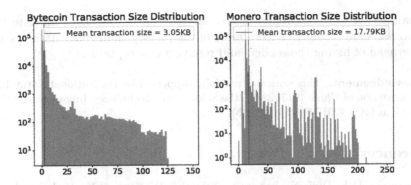

Fig. 11. The distribution and statistics of transaction sizes same scale for all gifures

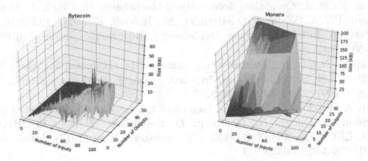

Fig. 12. Size of a transaction with different inputs and outputs

5   Conclusion

In this paper, we analysed the performance of two CryptoNote style blockchains, i.e., ByteCoin and Monero, from the protocol layer and the application perspective. Our protocol-level comparisons started from formalizing the core Ring Signature schemes and the processes of hiding senders, receivers and amounts in transactions. Then we compared the performance of the formalized anonymization processes, including the theoretical time and space complexity and the transaction sizes in depth. The protocol-level comparisons indicate that RingCT hides the amounts with significant space overhead, mainly from the MLSAG Signature and the Range Proof.

We experimented on benchmarking the aforementioned cryptographic processes and analyzing the real transaction data on these two blockchains. The benchmarking results proved our protocol-level analysis that the number of outputs dominate the performance of transaction generations and verifications for RingCT. Meanwhile, our network usage analysis based on the real blockchain data showed that Monero users intend to include fewer inputs and outputs but mix more public keys in a single transaction than Bytecoin users. The fewer inputs and outputs of Monero is because of the high transaction fees introduced by big transactions, implying that hiding the amounts is less concerning than the transaction fees for Monero users. More mixed public keys indicate that Monero users are actually concern more of the privacy than Bytecoin users, and the overhead of hiding the senders and receivers is acceptable.

Acknowledgement. This work was partially supported by the National Natural Science Foundation of China (61702342), the Science and Technology Innovation Projects of Shenzhen (JCYJ20170302151321095).

References

1. Bernstein, D.J., Duif, N., Lange, T., Schwabe, P., Yang, B.Y.: High-speed high-security signatures. J. Cryptogr. Eng. **2**(2), 77–89 (2012)
2. Croman, K., et al.: On scaling decentralized blockchains. In: Clark, J., Meiklejohn, S., Ryan, P.Y.A., Wallach, D., Brenner, M., Rohloff, K. (eds.) FC 2016. LNCS, vol. 9604, pp. 106–125. Springer, Heidelberg (2016). https://doi.org/10.1007/978-3-662-53357-4_8
3. Fujisaki, E., Suzuki, K.: Traceable ring signature. In: Okamoto, T., Wang, X. (eds.) PKC 2007. LNCS, vol. 4450, pp. 181–200. Springer, Heidelberg (2007). https://doi.org/10.1007/978-3-540-71677-8_13
4. Kumar, A., Fischer, C., Tople, S., Saxena, P.: A traceability analysis of monero's blockchain. In: Foley, S.N., Gollmann, D., Snekkenes, E. (eds.) ESORICS 2017, Part II. LNCS, vol. 10493, pp. 153–173. Springer, Cham (2017). https://doi.org/10.1007/978-3-319-66399-9_9
5. Liu, J.K., Wei, V.K., Wong, D.S.: Linkable spontaneous anonymous group signature for Ad Hoc groups. In: Wang, H., Pieprzyk, J., Varadharajan, V. (eds.) ACISP 2004. LNCS, vol. 3108, pp. 325–335. Springer, Heidelberg (2004). https://doi.org/10.1007/978-3-540-27800-9_28
6. Maxwell, G., Poelstra, A.: Borromean Ring Signatures (2015)
7. Moser, M.: Anonymity of Bitcoin Transactions (2013)
8. Möser, M., et al.: An empirical analysis of traceability in the monero blockchain. PoPETs **2018**(3), 143–163 (2018)
9. Nakamoto, S.: Bitcoin: A peer-to-peer electronic cash system (2008)
10. Noether, S., Mackenzie, A., et al.: Ring confidential transactions. Ledger **1**, 1–18 (2016)
11. Pedersen, T.P.: Non-interactive and information-theoretic secure verifiable secret sharing. In: Feigenbaum, J. (ed.) CRYPTO 1991. LNCS, vol. 576, pp. 129–140. Springer, Heidelberg (1992). https://doi.org/10.1007/3-540-46766-1_9
12. Ron, D., Shamir, A.: Quantitative analysis of the full Bitcoin transaction graph. In: Sadeghi, A.-R. (ed.) FC 2013. LNCS, vol. 7859, pp. 6–24. Springer, Heidelberg (2013). https://doi.org/10.1007/978-3-642-39884-1_2
13. Van Saberhagen, N.: Cryptonote v 2.0 (2013)

Goshawk: A Novel Efficient, Robust and Flexible Blockchain Protocol

Cencen Wan[1], Shuyang Tang[1], Yuncong Zhang[1], Chen Pan[1],
Zhiqiang Liu[1,2(✉)], Yu Long[1(✉)], Zhen Liu[1(✉)], and Yu Yu[1(✉)]

[1] Shanghai Jiao Tong University, Shanghai, China
{ilu_zq,longyu,liuzhen}@sjtu.edu.cn, yuyu@cs.sjtu.edu.cn
[2] Shanghai Viewsource Information Science and Technology Co., Ltd.,
Shanghai, China

Abstract. Proof of Work (PoW), a fundamental blockchain protocol, has been widely applied and thoroughly testified in various decentralized cryptocurrencies, due to its intriguing merits including trustworthy sustainability, robustness against Sybil attack, delicate incentive-compatibility, and openness to any participant. Meanwhile, PoW-powered blockchains still suffer from poor efficiency, potential selfish mining, to-be-optimized fairness and extreme inconvenience of protocol upgrading. Therefore, it is of great interest to design new PoW-driven blockchain protocol to address or relieve the above issues so as to make it more applicable and feasible. To do so, we present Goshawk, a novel hybrid consensus protocol, in which a two-layer chain structure with two-level PoW mining strategy and a ticket-voting mechanism are elaborately combined. We show that this newly-proposed protocol has the merits of high efficiency, strong robustness against "51%" attack of computation power, as well as good flexibility for future protocol updating. As far as we know, Goshawk is the first blockchain protocol with these three key properties. Last but not the least, this scheme has been implemented and deployed in the testnet of the public blockchain project Hcash(https://github.com/HcashOrg) for months, and has demonstrated its stability and high efficiency with such real-world test.

Keywords: Blockchain · Consensus protocol · Proof of work · Ticket-voting mechanism · Hybrid consensus

1 Introduction

To date, Bitcoin [27] and a variety of other cryptocurrencies have drawn much attention from researchers and fintech industry. Their attractive innovations show great promise of fundamental change in payments, economics and politics around the world [28,38]. Recently, cryptocurrencies' global market capitalizations have reached more than \$250 billions [5]. The blockchain technique, which is the underlying technique of various decentralized cryptocurrencies, is an ingenious combination of multiple technologies such as peer-to-peer network,

© Springer Nature Switzerland AG 2019
F. Guo et al. (Eds.): Inscrypt 2018, LNCS 11449, pp. 49–69, 2019.
https://doi.org/10.1007/978-3-030-14234-6_3

consensus protocol over a distributed network, cryptographic schemes, and so on. This technique provides a decentralized way to securely manage ledgers, which is fundamental for building trust in our social and economic activities.

Proof of Work (PoW), which relies on computational puzzles (a.k.a. moderately hard functions) introduced by Dwork and Naor [12], is a blockchain protocol used to maintain the consistency of distributed ledger in a decentralized setting so as to prevent fraud and double-spending attacks. So far it has been implemented in 250 cryptocurrencies or more such as Bitcoin, Ethereum, and so on, serving as the underlying blockchain protocol. PoW has amazing features including trustworthy sustainability, robustness against Sybil attack, delicate incentive-compatibility, and openness to any participant (i.e., participants could join and leave dynamically), though it still needs to be improved in the following aspects:

- *Efficiency.* The transaction throughput of PoW-driven blockchain does not scale well. For instance, Bitcoin supports very limited transaction throughput (say, up to 7 transactions per second [2]), while the demand from practical applications is much higher (MasterCard and VISA are reported to process 1200 to 56000 transactions per second).
- *Fairness.* PoW-based blockchains have been criticized for the potential of centralization of computation power [28]. Even a minor enhancement in fairness is welcome, since it provides fewer incentives for miners to join forces to enjoy the advantage of mining in a larger pool. This mitigates the centralization of the mining power, thus improving the security property of blockchains.
- *Robustness.* It is known that in PoW protocol, selfish mining attack [13,15,29] allows that adversaries deviating from the protocol may gain a disproportionate share of reward, much more than they deserve. Besides, PoW protocol is intrinsically subject to "51%" attack of computation power.
- *Flexibility.* In practice, it is extremely difficult to fulfill blockchain protocol evolution. For example, modification to scale up existing protocol is a raging debate in the Bitcoin community [6,17,18,31].

Till now, many attempts have been made to address or mitigate the issues related to PoW protocol so as to make it more powerful. One approach is to reduce the block interval to shorten latency. However, this approach compromises certain stability or security of the decentralized system, which has been proven by the practice of Ethereum [8]. Specifically, the short block interval (12s averagely) adopted in Ethereum brings instability to the system. To solve this issue, Ethereum implements the GHOST protocol [36] which maintains the main chain at a fork by choosing the side whose sub-tree contains more work (accumulated over all blocks in the sub-tree). GHOST improves the mining power utilization and fairness under high contention, but has the weakness that in some cases, no single node has enough information to determine which is the main chain. The second approach is to enlarge the block. It improves throughput, but aggravates communication burden to the network, which in turn increases the stale block rate, and finally damages the security of PoW-based blockchain [19]. The third approach is to use sharding mechanism to achieve a sweet spot between PoW and classical

Byzantine consensus protocol [25], which leads to throughput scaling. The key idea in this approach is to partition the network into smaller committees, each of which processes a disjoint set of transactions. Each committee has a reasonably small number of members so they can run a classical Byzantine consensus protocol to decide their agreed set of transactions in parallel. The fourth approach is to perform transactions off the chain, such as lightening network [32], raiden network [1], and so on [11, 21, 26]. These works allow for extensive payment networks where transactions can be performed efficiently and scalably without trusted middlemen, especially targeting on fast micropayments. Moreover, Eyal et al. proposed Bitcoin-NG [14], a scalable blockchain protocol, by introducing a two-layer chain structure which consists of keyblocks and microblocks. Bitcoin-NG boosts transaction throughput by decoupling PoW protocol into two planes: leader election and transaction serialization. Once a miner generates a keyblock by solving the computational puzzle, he is elected as a potential leader and entitled to serialize transactions into microblocks unilaterally until a new leader is chosen. Although the above approaches provide some interesting ideas for improving PoW protocol, they mainly focus on the efficiency issue related to PoW.

On the other hand, alternative blockchain protocols have been introduced to replace PoW. Among them the most promising ones may be the *Proof of Stake* (PoS) [23, 34] and its variants such as Snow White [7], Ouroboros [22], Ouroboros Praos [10] and Algorand [20]. PoS protocol grants the right of generating blocks to stakeholders instead of miners with computational power. Specifically, in PoS protocol, rather than miners investing computational resources in order to participate in the leader election (i.e., block generation) process, they instead run a process that randomly selects one of them proportionally to the stake that each possesses according to the current blockchain ledger. The rationale behind PoS is that stakeholders are motivated to maintain the consistency and security of blockchain, since the value of their stake will shrink when these properties are compromised. Although PoS protocol owns intriguing potential, its practicality, applicability and robustness still need to be examined extensively via a mass of public blockchains implementing PoS as their underlying protocol before it is widely admitted. Another interesting direction is to adopt DAG(Directed Acyclic Graph)-based framework instead of blockchain structure to acquire high throughput by exploiting the high concurrency nature of DAG structure [9, 24, 33]. However, to date, there has not been any rigorous security guarantee for DAG-based distributed ledger technology, thus the security of this technology needs to be investigated further.

As PoW protocol has already demonstrated its practicality – PoW-powered blockchains currently account for more than 90% of the total market capitalization of existing digital cryptocurrencies, and its importance in permission-less network was also stated by Pass and Shi in [30], it is of great interest to strength PoW further by addressing or mitigating the related issues mentioned above. Nevertheless, it can be seen that the current state of the art in improving PoW protocol is still far from satisfactory.

1.1   Our Contribution

In this work, we propose Goshawk, the first brand-new candidate of PoW-powered blockchain protocol with high efficiency, strong robustness, as well as good flexibility. Goshawk is actually a hybrid consensus protocol, in which a two-layer chain structure with two-level PoW mining strategy and a ticket-voting mechanism are combined delicately. More specifically, we adopt the two-layer chain structure (i.e., keyblocks/microblocks) given in Bitcoin-NG, and further improve it by introducing two-level PoW mining strategy (i.e., keyblocks and microblocks with two different mining difficulties, respectively). This guarantees the high throughput of our scheme, while obviating the vulnerability to the attack of microblock swamping in Bitcoin-NG. Furthermore, we borrow the idea of the ticket-voting approach presented in DASH [3] and Decred [4], and refine this idea by formalizing it into a more rigorous mechanism, then we combine this mechanism with the above chain structure elaborately to attain strong security and good flexibility. Security analysis of our scheme shows that it is incentive-compatibility, and robust against selfish mining and "51%" attack of computation power. Besides, we demonstrate that our scheme also allows good flexibility for future protocol updating effectively. At last, this scheme has been implemented and deployed in the testnet of the public blockchain project Hcash for months, and has demonstrated its good stability and promising scalability with such real-world test. This also suggests the interesting potential that our scheme could be employed in next-generation cryptocurrencies.

1.2   Paper Organization

The remainder of the paper is organized as follows. Sect.2 presents Goshawk, a novel hybrid consensus protocol. Then we analyze the security of this protocol in Sect.3. Further, we introduce a two-phase upgrade process to demonstrate the flexibility of Goshawk in Sect.4. The protocol evaluation and performance test of Goshawk in a real-world setting are shown in Sect.5. Finally, we conclude our work in Sect.6.

2   The Goshawk Protocol

The Goshawk protocol extends the Bitcoin-NG scheme, which significantly improves the scalability of Bitcoin by introducing a two-layer chain structure consisting of keyblocks and microblocks, while avoiding the microblock swamping attack in Bitcoin-NG[1]. Besides, Goshawk adopts ticket-voting mechanism

---

[1] Considering the cheap and quick generation of microblocks, a leader can swamp the system with microblocks. Specifically, in Bitcoin-NG, although a minimal interval between two sequential microblocks could be set to avoid massive microblocks in a single microblock chain, the malicious leader could generate tremendous amount of microblock branches. For other parties, since each branch is self-consistent, they have to relay all these branches. This eventually paralyzes the whole network, causing legal transactions and blocks fail to spread.

Table 1. Table of Notations

Notation	Description
D	The confirmations required for tickets maturity
E	The maximum number of tickets per keyblock
$\mathcal{F}$	The price adjustment function
L	System optimal size of ticket pool
N	The number of tickets selected by each keyblock
P	The Ticket price
$\mathcal{P}$	The function mapping keyblock to N tickets
R	The initial key height of the ticket-voting mechanism
S	Total amount of stakes
T	The average keyblock generation interval
TP	The ticket pool

elaborately to achieve strong security and good flexibility. Table 1 presents some of the notations used in this section.

2.1 Two-Level Mining Mechanism

Similar to the idea of subchains [35, 37], we propose a *two-level mining mechanism*, in which we set two levels of difficulty for computation puzzle, to address the microblock swamping attack on Bitcoin-NG. Solving the puzzle with low difficulty allows a miner to generate a *microblock*. While if the solution simultaneously meets the requirement of higher difficulty, the resulting block is a *keyblock*. The ratio of mining difficulty between keyblock and microblock is set to be m. If the average keyblock generation interval is T, then the average microblock generation interval is $t = T/m$.

A *fork* happens when multiple blocks follow the same parent. In that case, we say the blockchain has more than one *branch*es. We define *main chain* as the branch containing the most keyblocks. If there are more than one branches that satisfy the condition above, a miner will select one of them randomly as the main chain. This is called the *longest keyblock chain rule*. We define the *height* of a block (either keyblock or microblock) as the number of blocks preceding it and the *key height* of a block as the number of keyblocks preceding it, in the same branch.

Definition 1 presents the structure of the block in our scheme.

Definition 1 (Block Structure I). *We define a block, denoted by B, as the following tuple*

$$B = (H_{tip,B}, H_{tip,K}, h, k, \{tx\}, n)$$

where

- $H_{tip,B}$ *is the hash of previous block (either keyblock or microblock);*
- $H_{tip,K}$ *is the hash of previous keyblock;*
- *h is the block height;*
- *k is the key height;*
- *{tx} is the transaction set contained in the block;*
- *n is the nonce found by the miner.*

B *is a valid keyblock if* $\mathsf{Hash}(B) \leq T_K$, *where* T_K *is the threshold of computation puzzle for keyblock;* B *is a valid microblock if* $T_K < \mathsf{Hash}(B) \leq T_M$, *where* T_M *is the threshold for microblock.*

We denote the block being mined by miner P as B_{temp}. Let $H_{\text{temp}} = \mathsf{Hash}(B_{\text{temp}})$. Miner P increments n starting from 0, until $H_{\text{temp}} \leq T_M$. If $H_{\text{temp}} \leq T_K$, P broadcasts B_{temp} as a new keyblock K_{new}, otherwise P broadcast B_{temp} as a new microblock M_{new}. Other participants determine whether a received block is a keyblock or microblock depending on its hash value, and update their main chain according to the longest keyblock chain rule. It can be easily inferred that in our two-level mining mechanism, for miners mining both keyblocks and microblocks, no additional computation power needs to be consumed compared with miners only mining keyblocks.

Fork. Since mining microblock is relatively easy, microblock forks frequently. However, once a new keyblock is created, all honest nodes will follow the chain with the most keyblocks and such forks vanish. The new scheme will also experience keyblock forks, which happens rarer than microblocks. The duration of such a fork may be long and the fork finally dissolved in several keyblock confirmations. Though the works for microblocks contribute nothing to the selection of branches, it is hard enough for spaming. According to the *common prefix property* described in [16], we declare a block is *stable* if we prune all of the blocks after it in the main chain, the probability that the resulting pruned chain will not be mutual prefix of other honest miners' main chain is less than a security parameter $2^{-\lambda}$.

2.2 Ticket-Voting Mechanism

In our scheme, we refine the idea of ticket-voting approach given in DASH and Decred to make it more applicable by formalizing it into a more rigorous mechanism. The core idea is stakeholders purchase *ticket* by locking their stakes to proportionally obtain rights for a future *vote*. The ticket structure is presented in Definition 2 and vote structure is presented in Definition 3.

Definition 2 (Ticket Structure). *We define ticket a special transaction, denoted by tk, as the following tuple*

$$tk = (\langle \mathsf{Hash}(tx), i, sig \rangle, \langle P, pk \rangle)$$

where

- $\langle \mathsf{Hash}(tx), i, sig \rangle$ *is the input of ticket;*
- *tx is a transaction as the source of funding for ticket purchasing;*
- *i is the order of output in tx. The amount of stakes in this output must larger than P;*
- *sig is the signature used to verify input;*
- $\langle P, pk \rangle$ *is the output of the ticket which will lock P stakes for ticket purchasing;*
- *P is a certain amount (called* ticket *price) of stakes locked for purchasing ticket;*
- *pk is a public key.*

Only tickets contained in keyblocks are considered valid. The number of tickets contained in each keyblock is limited to E such that no one can spam tickets into blockchain.

Definition 3 (Vote Structure). *We define vote a special transaction, denoted by vt, as the following tuple*

$$vt = (\langle \mathsf{Hash}(tk), sig \rangle, \langle V, pk \rangle)$$

where

- $\langle \mathsf{Hash}(tk), sig \rangle$ *is the input of vote;*
- *tk is the ticket for voting;*
- $\langle V, pk \rangle$ *is the output of the vote which will refund the locked stakes;*
- *V is a specific amount of rewards.*

Ticket Pool. A ticket is considered *mature*, denoted by mtk, if the keyblock containing it gets at least D confirmations, i.e., it becomes stable. If a mature ticket was spent on voting, we denote it by stk. We call the set of all unspent mature tickets the *ticket pool*, denoted by TP, i.e, $\mathsf{TP} = \{mtk\} \setminus \{stk\}$. Since tickets in TP are stable, the sets of TP in different branches with the same key height are exactly the same.

Validation Rule. A keyblock is considered valid only if a majority (more than half) of its votes are collected by its successive keyblock. We stipulate that miners can only mine after a validated keyblock (or a microblock preceded by a validated keyblock) by collecting votes as a validation proof for this keyblock, which is called the *validation rule*. If a keyblock is not validated by majority votes, miners would ignore this keyblock.

The ticket-voting mechanism is divided into the following four steps.

- Participants purchase tickets which will be added to the ticket pool after D confirmations.
- Each latest keyblock is mapped into N random tickets from TP via a function $\mathcal{P}$ which is defined in Definition 4.

- Owners of selected tickets issue *votes*, if the corresponding keyblock is valid.
- Miners collect votes and select mining strategies according to the validation rule.

Definition 4 (Mapping Function). *We define a mapping function*

$$\mathcal{P}(\mathsf{TP}, \mathsf{Hash}(K)) = \{tk_j\}_{j \in [N]} = \underset{tk_1, \cdots, tk_N \in \mathsf{TP}}{\arg\max} \left\{ \sum_{i=1}^{N} \mathsf{Hash}(\mathsf{Hash}(tk_i) \oplus \mathsf{Hash}(K)) \right\}$$

where K is a keyblock.

Each ticket can only be chosen once and then be removed from ticket pool even if the owner missed the voting, in which case the ticket is considered *missed*. The owner of a selected ticket will be refunded with the stake locked by this ticket, and a voted (not missed) ticket additionally brings the owner a specific amount of rewards.

Ticket Price Adjustment Function. Ticket price is automatically adjusted by the function $\mathcal{F}(|\mathsf{TP}|, P, L)$ which takes as input the size of TP, current ticket price P and a parameter L. The initial ticket price is set as a system parameter. $\mathcal{F}$ returns a new price P' which increases exponentially compared to P if $|\mathsf{TP}| > L$, while decreases when $|\mathsf{TP}| < L$. Therefore, when $|\mathsf{TP}| > L$, users are reluctant to purchase tickets, while if $|\mathsf{TP}| < L$ users are more willing to. In this way, the size of TP fluctuates around L, thus on average each ticket waits time $(L/N + D) \times T$ before it is chosen.

A stakeholder with a p fraction of total stakes gains a disproportionate advantage by engaging in ticket purchasing if others do not devote all their stakes into tickets. To reduce such advantage, L should be large enough such that $L \times P \approx S/f$, where S is the total amount of stakes and f is a constant greater than 1. A stakeholder who holds β fraction of the tickets in TP has a probability of $M(N, \beta)$ to reach majority in the chosen tickets of a keyblock, where

$$M(N, \beta) = \sum_{i=\lfloor N/2 \rfloor + 1}^{N} \binom{N}{i} \beta^i (1 - \beta)^{N-i}.$$

On startup, PoW is the only consensus protocol because ticket pool is empty at the beginning of the chain. The ticket-voting mechanism begin at key height R which is selected such that $R = L/E + D$.

2.3   Goshawk: Hybrid Consensus Scheme

By delicately combining the improved two-layer blockchain structure with the ticket-voting mechanism mentioned above, we construct a novel hybrid consensus scheme, Goshawk. The new block structure is presented in Definition 5.

Definition 5 (Block Structure II). *We define a block, denoted by B, as the following tuple*

$$B = (H_{tip,B}, H_{tip,K}, h, k, \{tx\}, \{tk\}, \{vt\}, n)$$

where $H_{tip,B}$, $H_{tip,K}$, h, k, $\{tx\}$, n are as in Definition 1.

Compared to the mining process described in Sect. 2.1, in this combined scheme, the miner P needs to take the following additional steps.

- In addition to the transaction $\{tx\}$, B_{temp} also contains a set of ticket purchasing transactions $\{tk\}$, which were collected and stored locally by P similar to ordinary transactions.
- P collects at least $\lfloor N/2 \rfloor + 1$ votes for the previous keyblock (whose hash is $H_{\text{tip},K}$), and put this set of votes $\{vt\}$ into B_{temp}. If P fails to collect enough votes for $H_{\text{tip},K}$, it abandons this keyblock and continue to mine after the previous keyblock.
- The $\{tk\}$ and $\{vt\}$ will be ignored if B_{temp} turns out to be a microblock, since they are only valid in keyblocks.

When a newly generated keyblock K_{new} is broadcast, those stakeholders chosen by this keyblock check this keyblock, issuing and broadcasting votes if it is valid. Other miners collect these votes and switch to mine after K_{new} as soon as the votes satisfy the majority rule. The mining process is described in Algorithm 1. The structure of Goshawk is shown in Fig. 1.

Algorithm 1. Mining process in Goshawk

1: **procedure** MINING
2:    *loop*:
3:       $B_{\text{temp}} \leftarrow H_{\text{tip},B} \| H_{\text{tip},K} \| h \| k \| n \| \{tx\} \| \{tk\} \| \{vt\}$
4:       **if** $\mathsf{Hash}(B_{\text{temp}}) \leq T_K$ **then**
5:          $K_{\text{new}} \leftarrow B_{\text{temp}}$
6:          P broadcast K_{new}
7:       **else if** $\mathsf{Hash}(B_{\text{temp}}) \leq T_M$ **then**
8:          $M_{\text{new}} \leftarrow B_{\text{temp}}$
9:          P broadcast M_{new}
10:      **end if**
11:     **if** P recieved K_{new} **and** ReceiveMajorityVotesOf(K_{new})
12:          **and** IsTipOfMainChain(K_{new}) **then**
13:       $H_{\text{tip},B} \leftarrow \mathsf{Hash}(K_{\text{new}})$
14:       $H_{\text{tip},K} \leftarrow \mathsf{Hash}(K_{\text{new}})$
15:       $h \leftarrow \mathsf{GetHeightOf}(K_{\text{new}}) + 1$
16:       $k \leftarrow \mathsf{GetKeyHeightOf}(K_{\text{new}}) + 1$
17:     **else if** P recieved M_{new}
18:          **and** ReceiveMajorityVotesOf(GetPreviousKeyBlockOf(M_{new}))
19:          **and** IsTipOfMainChain(M_{new}) **then**
20:       $H_{\text{tip},B} \leftarrow \mathsf{Hash}(M_{\text{new}})$
21:       $H_{\text{tip},K} \leftarrow \mathsf{Hash}(\mathsf{GetPreviousKeyBlockOf}(M_{\text{new}}))$
22:       $h \leftarrow \mathsf{GetHeightOf}(M_{\text{new}}) + 1$
23:       $k \leftarrow \mathsf{GetKeyHeightOf}(M_{\text{new}})$
24:     **end if**
25:    $n \leftarrow n + 1$
26:    **goto** *loop.*
27: **end procedure**

Incentive Mechanism. Block reward is divided into two parts, a ratio w to keyblock miners, the rest to the voters, therefore each voter earns $(1-w)/N$ of the block reward. Block rewards are spendable only after the containing keyblock is followed by D keyblocks. To encourage keyblock miners to collect as many votes as they can, the actual block reward a miner earned is based on how many votes it collects. For example, if M votes are collected, $(1-w)M/N$ is the precise reward. If a voter misses to vote, it also misses the reward. Microblock miners share the transaction fees, which is split into three parts, where 60% is given to the miner whose block (either keyblock or microblock) contains the transaction, 30% to the next block and 10% to the next keyblock.

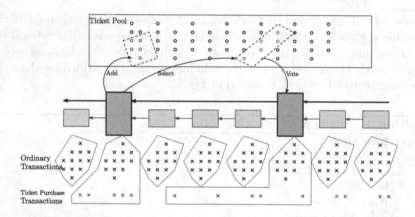

Fig. 1. The structure of Goshawk. The tickets are denoted by dots, the transactions are denoted by cross marks, the keyblocks are denoted by big rectangles, and the microblocks are denoted by small rectangles. A keyblock contains transactions and add tickets into ticket pool. Meanwhile, a keyblock pseudo-randomly selects tickets which will be removed from ticket pool. Chosen stakeholders vote for keyblock to validate it and votes will be contained by the next keyblock.

3   Security Analysis

Our protocol has two goals. One is the incentive compatibility. All rational participants would operate honestly since they benefit nothing deviating from the protocol. Another one is robustness against "51%" attack and selfish mining attack.

3.1   Incentive Compatibility

We show that our Goshawk scheme is incentive-compatible (i.e. each participant benefits nothing from deviating from the protocol) under the assumption that all participants are rational.

Table 2. Table of Notations

Notation	Description
a	The fraction of transaction fee included in one block for the current block owner
b	The fraction of transaction fee included in one block for the next block owner
B	The block reward for a keyblock
c	The fraction of transaction fee included in one block for the next keyblock owner
F	Total transaction fees included in one block
m	The difficulty ratio, i.e. the ratio of difficulties of mining a keyblock and mining a microblock
q	The probability for one miner to generate the next block, and this block is keyblock

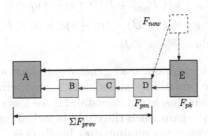

Fig. 2. Mining Strategy in Case 1.

Strategy of Rational Participants. In this part, we show that all rational participants obey the mining rule. That is, rational participants always mine on the latest validated block. In another word, any participant gains no marginal revenue by deviating from the rule above (i.e. the Nash equilibrium of Goshawk). The latest valid block can be a keyblock or a microblock, in the following, we will discuss the rational strategies for each case respectively. Table 2 presents some of the notations used subsequently.

Case 1. A Keyblock as the Latest Valid Block. As shown in Fig. 2, when the latest valid block is a keyblock, one participant may mine after the latest keyblock (block E), or after the previous microblock (block D) to reach a higher revenue. We compare the expected revenues with two strategies above and prove that following the longest keyblock rule (i.e. mining after block E) is the rational choice. In the following discussion, we use q to denote the probability of one participant's generating the next block and the block is keyblock, then its probability for her to generate the next block and the block is a microblock is $(m-1)q$. Also, we assume each keyblock contains block reward B, and each block (keyblock or microblock) contains the same amount of transaction fee F.

For distinction, we denote the transaction fee in a microblock by F_{pm}, the fee in a keyblock by F_{pk}, and the fee in the block currently being mined by F_{now}. Moreover, ΣF_{prev} (ideally $\Sigma F_{prev} \approx mF$) denotes the sum of all transaction fees included from the previous keyblock (block A in Fig. 2) to the previous microblock (block D) (Table 3).

Table 3. Revenues Following Block E or D.

	Mining a keyblock	Mining a microblock
Block E	$(a + c) \times F_{pk} + b \times F_{now} + B$	$a \times F_{pk} + b \times F_{now}$
Block D	$c \times \Sigma F_{prev} + a \times F_{pm} + b \times F_{now} + B$	$a \times F_{pk} + b \times F_{now}$

Hence, the expected revenue following the right block (block E) is

$$
\begin{aligned}
R &= q \times ((a + c) \times F_{pk} + b \times F_{now} + B) + (m - 1)q \times (a \times F_{pk} + b \times F_{now}) \\
&= q \times ((a + c) \times F + b \times F + B) + (m - 1)q \times (a \times F + b \times F) \\
&= ((1 - c) \times m + c)q \times F + q \times B.
\end{aligned}
$$

By deviating the rule, a miner may generate a block after block D. In this case, we regard that the probability of its block's conquering the existing block is smaller than $1/2$. This is simple to understand since less than half participants switches to an alternative chain when the chain is forked into two branches. Due to this, the expected revenue via mining after block D is

$$
\begin{aligned}
R' &< \frac{1}{2} \times q \times (c \times \Sigma F_{prev} + a \times F_{pm} + b \times F_{now} + B) \\
&\quad + \frac{1}{2} \times (m - 1)q \times (a \times F_{pk} + b \times F_{now}) \\
&= 0.5mq \times F \times (a + b) + 0.5q \times c \times \Sigma F_{prev} + 0.5q \times B.
\end{aligned}
$$

Obviously, ΣF_{prev} is related to the number of microblocks between two keyblocks. Let X be a random variable which denotes the number of microblocks between two keyblocks. Then, X follows a geometric distribution with parameter m. Thus, we have: $P(X = k) = \frac{1}{m}(1 - \frac{1}{m})^{k-1}$. For a given parameter θ, we can get:

$$
P_1 := \sum_{k=\theta}^{\infty} P(X = k) = \sum_{k=\theta}^{\infty} \frac{1}{m}(1 - \frac{1}{m})^{k-1} = (1 - \frac{1}{m})^{\theta \times m - 1}
$$

This probability P_1 increases in m, and we have $\lim_{m \to \infty} P_1 = e^{-\theta}$. Thus, we get $P_1 < e^{-\theta}$. If we set parameter $\theta = 5$, the probability that there are $5m$ microblocks between two keyblocks is under 0.62%, which is small. According to above analysis, $\Sigma F_{prev} \leq 5mF$, (ideally $\Sigma F_{prev} \approx mF$). Thus,

$$
\begin{aligned}
R' &< 0.5mq \times F \times (a + b) + 0.5q \times c \times \Sigma F_{prev} + 0.5q \times B \\
&< 0.5mq \times F \times (1 + 4c) + 0.5q \times B.
\end{aligned}
$$

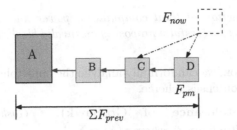

Fig. 3. Mining Strategy in Case 2.

Letting $R > R'$, we get $\frac{1}{2}(1+4c) < 1-c$ and hence $c < \frac{1}{6}$. In our implementation, we select $a = 0.3, b = 0.6, c = 0.1$. Then, the expected revenue following the right block (block E) is

$$R \approx ((1-c) \times m + c)q \times F + q \times B = (0.9m + 0.1)q \times F + q \times B.$$

And the expected revenue via mining after block D is

$$R' < 0.5mq \times F \times (1 + 4c) + 0.5q \times B \approx 0.7mq \times F + 0.5q \times B.$$

Obviously $R' < R$, which leads to the conclusion that the rational strategy is to follow the right block E.

Case 2. A Microblock as the Latest Valid Block. In the second case (as shown in Fig. 3), one miner may mine a block following C or D. However, all the revenues received by following C can also be received by following D. Moreover, the miner will lost transaction fees of block D, if it mines after block C and successfully finds a keyblock. For this reason, rational participants always mine after the latest block in this case.

3.2 Robustness

Fault-Tolerance Property. We assume a worst adversary who tries to undermine the system by proposing an invalid block without considering its own merits.

In this part, microblocks are not considered since they have nothing to do with the forks of the main chain. Therefore, we directly use "block" in place of "keyblock" when no ambiguity exists. In a purely PoW-based cryptocurrency like Bitcoin, the probability of one participant's undermining the system is roughly same as the fraction of its computation power among all participants. This is the fault-tolerance property of PoW. However, in a hybrid scenario, the description of the fault-tolerance property is more sophisticated. To begin with, we propose a definition.

Definition 6 (φ-fault-tolerance). *For a binary function $\varphi : [0,1] \times [0,1] \rightarrow [0,1]$, a cryptocurrency scheme achieves φ-fault-tolerance, if and only if for any* *adversary with α fraction of total computation power and β fraction of total stake, its probability of successfully proposing an invalid block should be no greater than $\varphi(\alpha, \beta)$.*

From this definition, we can formally analyze the fault-tolerance of our newly proposed Goshawk consensus scheme.

Theorem 1 (Fault-tolerance of Goshawk). *Goshawk achieve an $\frac{\alpha\gamma(\beta)}{1-\alpha-\gamma(\beta)+2\alpha\gamma(\beta)}$-fault-tolerance, where $\gamma(\beta) = \sum_{i=\lfloor N/2 \rfloor+1}^{N} \binom{N}{i}\beta^i(1-\beta)^{N-i}$, N is number of tickets each block selects.*

Proof. Since $\varphi(\alpha, \beta)$ is an upper-bound of adversary's advantage, we can assume that all malicious computation power and stakes are held by one single adversary. By the definition of fault-tolerance, the adversary with computation power of rate α and stake of rate β tries to mine an invalid block and proposes this block (i.e. the malicious block is voted by most corresponding ticket voters, since honest voters will not vote to invalid blocks, this equals to having at least half voters controlled by this adversary). Also, the adversary does not vote on all blocks generated by honest parties.

For simplicity, we define the following three events.

- E_A: A keyblock is found by the adversary, and more than half of its corresponding tickets are controlled by the adversary.
- E_B: A keyblock is found by the adversary, while more than half of its corresponding tickets are at hands of honest parties.
- E_C: A keyblock is found by an honest participant, while more than half of its corresponding tickets are controlled by the adversary.

From here, we can calculate the upper-bound of adversary's chance of proposing an invalid block. Obviously,

$$\varphi(\alpha, \beta) = \sum_{i=1}^{\infty} (\Pr[E_B \vee E_C])^{i-1} \Pr[E_A] = \sum_{i=1}^{\infty} (\alpha(1-\gamma) + (1-\alpha)\gamma)^{i-1} \alpha\gamma$$
$$= \frac{\alpha\gamma}{1-\alpha-\gamma+2\alpha\gamma}$$

where γ is the probability that most corresponding tickets regarding to one block is held by the adversary: $\gamma(\beta) = \sum_{i=\lfloor N/2 \rfloor+1}^{N} \binom{N}{i}\beta^i(1-\beta)^{N-i}$.

We can observe that when $\gamma = 1$, the adversary can successfully deny any blocks not proposed by herself, and hence $\varphi(\beta) = 1$. On the contrary, when $\gamma = 0$, any adversary block is denied by honest participants, and therefore $\varphi(\beta) = 0$. These are satisfied in case of $\varphi(\alpha, \beta) = \frac{\alpha\gamma(\beta)}{1-\alpha-\gamma(\beta)+2\alpha\gamma(\beta)}$.

For any adversary with α fraction of total computation power and β fraction of total stake, to perform a "51%" attack, it should at least attain $\varphi(\alpha, \beta) > \frac{1}{2}$. That is, $\frac{\alpha\gamma}{1-\alpha-\gamma+2\alpha\gamma} > \frac{1}{2} \iff \alpha > 1 - \gamma$. Assuming that $\beta = 20\%$, $N = 5$, then $\gamma \approx 6\%$, and the adversary must have over $1 - \gamma \approx 94\%$ total computation power to successfully launch a "51%" attack.

Selfish Mining Resistance. In a purely PoW-based cryptocurrency system, the selfish mining can be relatively easily performed by continuously mining in a separated environment, and is thereby hard to notice, and hard to prevent. For instance, an adversary with more than 1/3 total hash rate (instead of 1/2) can launch the selfish mining attack. However, in Goshawk, a block has to be validated by corresponding voters. That is to say, to secretly mining a continuous sequence of blocks, a block is only "useful" when its corresponding tickets are mostly held by itself. Formally, to prevent adversary's launching the selfish mining attack, instead of purely PoW-based cryptocurrencies' $\alpha < \frac{1}{3}$ (see explanation in [15]), we have an upper bound $\varphi(\alpha, \beta) < \frac{1}{3}$. That is,

$\frac{\alpha\gamma}{1-\alpha-\gamma+2\alpha\gamma} < \frac{1}{3} \iff \alpha < \frac{1-\gamma}{1+\gamma}$. Supposing $\beta = 20\%$, $N = 5$, then $\gamma \approx 6\%$, and

the adversary has to attain $\frac{1-\gamma}{1+\gamma} \approx 89\%$ overall computation power to launch the selfish mining attack.

4   Flexibility of Protocol Upgrade

A *hardfork change* is a change to the blockchain protocol that makes previously invalid rules valid, and therefore requires all participants to upgrade. Any alteration to blockchain which changes the blockchain structure (including block hash), difficulty algorithm, voting rules or enlarges the scope of valid transactions is a hardfork change. These hardforks are inevitable for the evolution of blockchain, however, it is extremely difficult to implement in a distributed network. For example, where to scale up existing protocol is a raging debate in the Bitcoin community and is not well settled yet. The reason why hardfork changes are difficult to implement is that stakeholders can not participate fairly in the protocol upgrade events which is usually determined by a small group of powerful parties such as core developers, wealthy participants and influential organizations. If some participants refuse to upgrade, a permanent fork will emerge.

Inspired by DASH and Decred, we introduce a two-phase upgrade process to grant decision-making power to each stakeholder via ticket-voting mechanism, activating the hardfork changes if the protocol upgrade wins the voting. We denote every W keyblock intervals by a Rule Change Interval (RCI). The two-phase upgrade process is described in Algorithm 2.

First Phase. The first phase is to meet the upgrade requirement over the network. After the hardfork code which initially disables new functions is released, a majority of participants need to upgrade firstly. The hardfork changes are divided into two categories: changes of mining and changes of voting. For the first one, At least x percent of the last W keyblocks must have the latest block version. For the second one, y percent of the votes in the last W keyblocks must have the latest vote version. Once upgrade threshold is met, the voting is scheduled to begin from the first keyblock of the next RCI.

Second Phase. The second phase is the actual voting. There are at most $W \times N$ votes cast during a single RCI. The final keyblock of the RCI tallies the votes within the RCI, and determines outcomes prior to the next keyblock being mined. Possible outcomes are as follows:

- If the number of votes fail to meet the Yes (or No) majority threshold (i.e., z percent of votes are Yes (or No)), the voting process keeps on for the next RCI.
- If the number of votes reach the Yes majority threshold, the voting process exits and the hardfork changes will activate after next RCI (the next RCI is set aside for unupgraded users to upgrade).
- If the number of votes reach the No majority threshold, the voting process exits and the hardfork changes will never activate.
- If the voting process never reaches the majority vote threshold in Z rounds of RCI, the voting process expires and the hardfork changes will never activate.

With the design of the two-phase upgrade process, stakeholders fairly participate in the protocol upgrade. Successful hardfork changes, which obtain the majority of votes, smoothly accomplish activation and implementation, while failed changes would naturally be buried. The upgrade for the benefit of the majority achieves healthy evolution of the blockchain ecology.

5 Protocol Evaluation and Performance Test

Implementation. This scheme has been implemented by Hcash. The source code of Hcash can be found in Github[2]. We deployed a global network (the *testnet*) to test our code of Hcash. The testnet was maintained for three months, during which we have simulated various possible attacks and a pressure test on this network. Results show that our scheme is practical and robust within all scenarios under our considerations.

The Testnet. The testnet was deployed and maintained from September 29th to December 21st of 2017. The block size was set to be 2MB and keyblocks were generated every 5 min. The difficulty of mining a microblock was $\frac{1}{32}$ that of key-block, i.e., $T_M/T_K = 32$ (except for the pressure test, where the block size and T_M/T_K were variables). The expected volume of the ticket pool was 40960 tickets. Each keyblock was voted by 5 randomly selected tickets, adding at most 20 new tickets into the ticket pool. Each ticket became mature after the generation of 128 new keyblocks.

We deployed 9 nodes as *DNSSeeds* via cloud services provided by *Alibaba* and *Amazon*[3], located in Beijing, San Francisco, Shanghai, Shenzhen, Sidney, Singapore, and Tokyo, respectively. In particular, 25 nodes were physically deployed in Shanghai to constitute the network. Moreover, during the test period of three

---

[2] https://github.com/HcashOrg/hcashd.
[3] https://aws.amazon.com/, https://www.alibabacloud.com/en.

Algorithm 2. two-phase upgrade process

```
 1: procedure UPGRADE
 2:     isVote ← 0
 3:     voteBegin ← 0
 4:     expire ← 3
 5: loop:
 6:     if keyHeight mod W = 0 and MeetUpgradeRequirement() then
 7:         voteBegin ← 1
 8:     end if
 9:     if voteBegin = 1 and isVote = 0 and TicketIsSelected() then
10:         VoteForUpgrade()
11:         isVote = 1
12:     end if
13:     if keyHeight mod W = 0 and voteBegin = 1 then
14:         if VoteFailed() then return false
15:         else if VotePassed() then
16:             ActiveUpgradeAfterNextRCI() return false
17:         else
18:             if expire > 0 then
19:                 expire ← expire − 1
20:                 isVote = 0
21:             else   return false
22:             end if
23:         end if
24:     end if
25:     goto loop.
26: end procedure
```

months, hundreds of nodes were detected to join and leave the network dynamically from over ten countries worldwide. In another word, the testnet had experienced complex conditions, hence its robustness has been thoroughly tested.

Malfunction of Voters. As described in our protocol, each keyblock is validated by certain voters, each corresponding to one randomly selected element of the ticket pool. In practice, a certain fraction of selected voters might be malfunction nodes, who fail to broadcast its vote due to either a breakdown or malicious purposes. In this case, some keyblock may not be validated by enough votes and hence the growth rate of the chain is reduced. To simulate this, we randomly had certain voters withhold their votes. As a result of our simulations, Fig. 4 shows the deceleration rate of chain growth (the resultant growth rate of keyblocks over the rate without malfunction) varying according to different percentages of malfunction voters. Obviously, such a malfunction affects the chain grow rate to only a minor extent even if 20% voters fall into a malfunction.

The Pressure Test. We launched a pressure test to measure the scalability of Goshawk. During our test, the expected keyblock interval was constantly 5 min

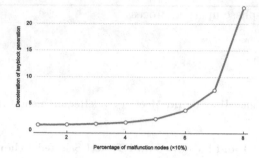

Fig. 4. Deceleration of Chain Growth under Different Percentage of Malfunction Voters

along with various block sizes and difficulty ratios. We deployed 28 nodes, of whom 4 took part in the PoS via ticket purchasing and voting, 20 took part in the PoW via mining and 4 kept producing an overloaded amount of transactions. This test proceeded for four days, and the results are compared with Bitcoin, Ethereum and Decred as shown in Table 4.

Table 4. Throughput Comparison where values marked by • stand for upper bounds, ○ for lower bounds, ⋆ for measurements.

Blockchain	Keyblock Interval	Block Size	Microblock Interval	Transaction Size	Throughtput (TPS)
Bitcoin	10 min	1 MB •	–	250 B ○	7 •
Ethereum	15 s	–	–	–	25 ⋆
Decred	5 min	0.384 MB •	–	250 B ○	5 •
Goshawk	5 min	2 MB •	18.75 s	250 B ○	270 ⋆
Goshawk	5 min	8 MB •	9.38 s	250 B ○	1550 ⋆

6   Conclusion

Past experience has proven that PoW fits for various permission-less blockchains very well as a powerful distributed agreement protocol, though it still needs to be improved in the aspects of efficiency, fairness, robustness and flexibility. Consequently, many attempts have been made to address or mitigate the issues related to PoW, while the current state of art focuses on the solutions to one or a few parts of the issues and is still far from satisfactory.

In this paper, we proposed Goshawk, the first novel PoW-driven blockchain protocol with high efficiency, strong robustness, as well as good flexibility. Goshawk is actually a hybrid consensus protocol, in which a two-layer chain structure with two-level PoW mining strategy and a ticket-voting mechanism are combined delicately. More specifically, we adopted the two-layer chain structure (i.e., keyblocks/microblocks) given in Bitcoin-NG, and further improved it by introducing two-level PoW mining strategy (i.e., keyblocks and microblocks with two different mining difficulties, respectively). This guarantees the high throughput of our scheme, while obviating the vulnerability to the attack of microblock swamping in Bitcoin-NG. Furthermore, we borrowed the idea of ticket-voting approach presented in DASH and Decred, and refined this idea by formalizing it into a more rigorous mechanism, then we combined this mechanism with the above chain structure elaborately to attain strong security and good flexibility. Security analysis of our scheme showed that it is incentive-compatibility, and robust against selfish mining and "51%" attack of computation power. Besides, a two-phase upgrade process was introduced to demonstrate good flexibility of our scheme in protocol upgrading. Finally, our scheme offered good stability and promising scalability in the real-world testnet of the public blockchain project Hcash and suggested strong usability in next-generation cryptocurrencies.

Acknowledgement. We would like to thank the anonymous reviewers for their helpful feedback. The authors are supported by the National Natural Science Foundation of China (Grant No. 61672347, 61572318, 61672339).

References

1. Raiden network. http://raiden.network/
2. Scalability. Bitcoin wiki (2015). https://en.bitcoin.it/wiki/Scalability
3. Dash official documentation. Dash Core Group Inc. (2017). https://docs.dash.org
4. Decred documentation. Decred Technology website (2017) https://docs.decred.org/
5. Cryptocurrency market capitalizations. https://coinmarketcap.com/. Accessed April 2018
6. Andresen, G.: Bitcoin improvement proposal, 101 (2015). https://github.com/bitcoin/bips/blob/master/bip-0101.mediawiki
7. Bentov, I., Pass, R., Shi, E.: Snow white: provably secure proofs of stake. IACR Cryptology ePrint Archive, 919 (2016)
8. Buerger, H.-H.: Ethereum White Paper (2016). https://github.com/ethereum/wiki/wiki/White-Paper
9. Churyumov, A.: Byteball: a decentralized system for storage and transfer of value (2016). https://byteball.org/Byteball.pdf
10. David, B., Peter, G., Kiayias, A., Russell, A.: Ouroboros Praos- an adaptively-secure, semi-synchronous proof-of-stake protocol. IOHK paper (2017)
11. Decker, C., Wattenhofer, R.: A fast and scalable payment network with bitcoin duplex micropayment channels. In: Pelc, A., Schwarzmann, A.A. (eds.) SSS 2015. LNCS, vol. 9212, pp. 3–18. Springer, Cham (2015). https://doi.org/10.1007/978-3-319-21741-3_1
12. Dwork, C., Naor, M.: Pricing via processing or combatting junk mail. In: Brickell, E.F. (ed.) CRYPTO 1992. LNCS, vol. 740, pp. 139–147. Springer, Heidelberg (1993). https://doi.org/10.1007/3-540-48071-4_10
13. Eyal, I.: The miner's dilemma. In: Proceedings of IEEE Symposium on Security and Privacy, volume, pp. 89–103 (2015)

14. Eyal, I., Gencer, A.E., Sirer, E.G., van Renesse, R.: Bitcoin-NG: a scalable Blockchain protocol. In: Usenix (2015)
15. Eyal, I., Sirer, E.G.: Majority is not enough: Bitcoin mining is vulnerable. In: Christin, N., Safavi-Naini, R. (eds.) FC 2014. LNCS, vol. 8437, pp. 436–454. Springer, Heidelberg (2014). https://doi.org/10.1007/978-3-662-45472-5_28
16. Garay, J., Kiayias, A., Leonardos, N.: The Bitcoin backbone protocol: analysis and applications. In: Oswald, E., Fischlin, M. (eds.) EUROCRYPT 2015, Part II. LNCS, vol. 9057, pp. 281–310. Springer, Heidelberg (2015). https://doi.org/10.1007/978-3-662-46803-6_10
17. Garzik, J.: Bitcoin improvement proposal, 102 (2015). https://github.com/bitcoin/bips/blob/master/bip-0102.mediawiki
18. Garzik, J.: Making decentralized economic policy (2015). http://gtf.org/garzik/bitcoin/BIP100-blocksizechangeproposal.pdf
19. Gervais, A., Karame, G.O., Wüst, K., Glykantzis, V., Ritzdorf, H., Capkun, S.: On the security and performance of proof of work Blockchains. In: Proceedings of the 2016 ACM SIGSAC Conference on Computer and Communications Security, CCS 2016, pp. 3–16 (2016)
20. Gilad, Y., Hemo, R., Micali, S., Vlachos, G., Zeldovich, N.: Algorand: scaling byzantine agreements for cryptocurrencies. In: Proceedings of the 26th Symposium on Operating Systems Principles, SOSP 2017, pp. 51–68. ACM, New York (2017)
21. Khalil, R., Gervais, A.: Revive: rebalancing off-blockchain payment networks. In: Proceedings of the 2017 ACM SIGSAC Conference on Computer and Communications Security, CCS 2017, pp. 439–453. ACM, New York (2017)
22. Kiayias, A., Russell, A., David, B., Oliynykov, R.: Ouroboros: a provably secure proof-of-stake Blockchain protocol. In: Katz, J., Shacham, H. (eds.) CRYPTO 2017, Part I. LNCS, vol. 10401, pp. 357–388. Springer, Cham (2017). https://doi.org/10.1007/978-3-319-63688-7_12
23. King, S., Nadal, S.: PPCoin: Peer-to-Peer Crypto-Currency with Proof-of-Stake (2012). ppcoin.org
24. Lerner, S.D.: Dagcoin: a cryptocurrency without blocks (2015). https://bitslog.files.wordpress.com/2015/09/dagcoin-v41.pdf
25. Luu, L., Narayanan, V., Zheng, C., Baweja, K., Gilbert, S., Saxena, P.: A secure sharding protocol for open blockchains. In: Proceedings of the 2016 ACM SIGSAC Conference on Computer and Communications Security, CCS 2016, pp. 17–30. ACM, New York (2016)
26. Miller, A., Bentov, I., Kumaresan, R., McCorry, P.: Sprites: payment channels that go faster than lightning. CoRR, abs/1702.05812 (2017)
27. Nakamoto, S.: Bitcoin: A Peer-to-Peer Electronic Cash System, p. 9 (2008). www.bitcoin.org
28. Narayanan, A., Bonneau, J., Felten, E., Miller, A., Goldfeder, S.: Bitcoin and Cryptocurrency Technologies Introduction to the book (2016)
29. Nayak, K., Kumar, S., Miller, A., Shi, E.: Stubborn mining: generalizing selfish mining and combining with an eclipse attack. In: Proceedings - 2016 IEEE European Symposium on Security and Privacy, EURO S and P 2016, pp. 305–320 (2016)
30. Pass, R., Shi, E.: Rethinking large-scale consensus. In: IEEE 30th Computer Security Foundations Symposium (CSF), pp. 115–129, August 2017
31. Peck, M.E.: Adam back says the Bitcoin fork is a coup (2015). http://spectrum.ieee.org/tech-talk/computing/networks/the-bitcoin-for-is-a-coup
32. Poon, J., Dryja, T.: The Bitcoin Lightning Network: Scalable Off-Chain Instant Payments. Technical Report (draft), p. 59 (2016). https://lightning.network/lightning-network-paper.pdf

33. Popov, S.: The Tangle (2016). https://www.iotatoken.com/IOTA_Whitepaper.pdf
34. QuantumMechanic: Proof of Stake Instead of Proof of Work. GitHub (2011)
35. Rizun, P.R.: Subchains: a technique to scale bitcoin and improve the user experience. Ledger **1**, 38–52 (2016)
36. Sompolinsky, Y., Zohar, A.: Accelerating Bitcoin's Transaction Processing. Fast Money Grows on Trees, Not Chains. IACR Cryptology ePrint Archive, 881:1–31 (2013)
37. TierNolan: Decoupling transactions and pow (2013). https://bitcointalk.org/index.php?topic=179598.0
38. Tschorsch, F., Scheuermann, B.: Bitcoin and beyond: a technical survey on decentralized digital currencies. IEEE Commun. Surv. Tutor. **18**(3), 2084–2123 (2016)

AFCoin: A Framework for Digital Fiat Currency of Central Banks Based on Account Model

Haibo Tian[1,2(✉)], Xiaofeng Chen[3], Yong Ding[2], Xiaoyan Zhu[3], and Fangguo Zhang[1]

[1] Guangdong Key Laboratory of Information Security, School of Data and Computer Science, Sun Yat-Sen University, Guangzhou 510275, Guangdong, People's Republic of China
tianhb@mail.sysu.edu.cn
[2] Guangxi Key Laboratory of Cryptography and Information Security, Guilin, China
[3] Xidian University, Xi'an 710071, Shanxi, People's Republic of China

Abstract. Currently, the technique choices of issuing digital fiat currencies include RSCoin, Corda and Quorum etc. RSCoin is specially designed for central banks based on Bitcoin. Corda and Quorum are permissioned distributed ledger techniques based on Bitcoin and Ethereum, respectively. There lacks a framework specially for central banks based on Ethereum. We here introduce AFCoin: a framework based on the account model and smart contract of Ethereum. AFCoin shows a possible way to issue and manage fiat currencies by central banks. It can be deployed in an evolutionary way and enjoys good efficiency, regulation and privacy properties.

Keywords: Digital fiat currency · Account mode · Efficiency · Privacy

1 Introduction

Digital fiat currency is a new concept. Bordo and Levin [6] define a digital currency as an asset stored in electronic form as physical currency. Bitcoin [8] and Ether [12] could be viewed as kinds of digital currency if they could be viewed as assets. Meaning et al. [5] define a central bank digital currency as an electronic, fiat liability of a central bank that can be used to settle payments or as a store of value. RSCoin [3] could be viewed as fiat coin since it relies on a central bank to issue coins. Yao [13] describes fiat currency as a credit and algorithm based smart currency supported by cryptographic techniques. So a main difference about fiat currency and non-fiat currency is the issuer of coins. Note that the fiat currency here is not similar to the traditional e-cash concept [15] since there are no digital coins to be really transferred between users.

As a new form of coin, digital fiat currency has attracted the attention of many central banks. The Bank of England has published a serial of staff working

© Springer Nature Switzerland AG 2019
F. Guo et al. (Eds.): Inscrypt 2018, LNCS 11449, pp. 70–85, 2019.
https://doi.org/10.1007/978-3-030-14234-6_4

papers to discuss topics about fiat currency [2]. The work of Meaning et al. [5] is just one of their achieved paper. The RSCoin system is also inspired by their research agenda [3]. The Bank of Canada [1] has also published a serial of staff working papers and a Jasper project is in progressing to settle interbank payments. The European Central Bank [14], the Sveriges Riksbank [11] and the People's Bank of China [13] also give research works and experimental projects to study the digital fiat currency.

Among the experimental projects, the RSCoin [3] system is distinguished. It uses the Bitcoin transaction formats so that the coins are embedded in unspent transaction outputs (UTXOs). The UTXOs are divided into shards by transaction identities and each shard is managed by a few mintettes. When some coins are to be spent, a user has to find endorsements from the mintettes managed the coins, and to register new coins to responsible mintettes, which is the essence of their two-phase commitment consensus. The changes of managed coins are recorded by mintettes locally and are submitted to a central bank to form a public ledger. New coins could be poured into the system by the central bank with a blank input. Han et al. [4] gave a user friendly RSCoin system to improve the efficiency of user's client.

Corda [7] system is also designed for financial services. It heavily developed the script abilities of Bitcoin. A transaction is used as a contract of involved participants. Notaries are trusted entities in the system to track the status of transaction outputs. There is no global ledger but notaries may run some consensus algorithm to maintain a permissioned ledger. Quorum [9] system also maintains a permissioned ledger. Smart contracts are used to ensure that only known parties can join the network. For private transactions, only hashes of the transactions are maintained in the permissioned ledger. The plain transaction is kept locally by related nodes.

It is well-known the distributed ledger technology (DLT) could be divided into three categories according to the write rights to the ledger. The Bitcoin and Ethereum ledgers are certainly public ledgers. Corda and Quorum could be classified as consortium ledger. The RSCoin is in fact a private ledger as there is only one trust point in the system. Scorer [10] explained that it may be unnecessary to use DLT for fiat currency. We believe the private ledger just reflects the minimal requirement of DLT in a central bank environment.

We here propose an Ethereum based RSCoin like framework. It is expected to remove the two phase commitment consensus algorithm since the coins are in an account and the account address is a natural delimiter to divide coins into shards. In each shard, smart contracts are used to manipulate account states by commercial banks. Commercial banks submit their transactions and state information to the central bank for regulatory and compliance process. The central bank publishes hashes of transactions in a private ledger with public read rights.

2   Common Definitions

We define shard, state, transaction, block and ledger in the system.

Shard. Each entity in the AFCoin system has an address account. As in the Ethereum, an entity X uses the ECDSA algorithm to produce (pk_X, sk_X). The address account of X is $addr_X = pk_X \bmod 2^{160}$.

For an address $addr_X$, we define a function *owner* to denote the responsible bank of the address. Simply, if the entity X is a commercial bank, the *owner* function returns the address of the central bank. If the entity X is a user of a commercial bank, the *owner* function returns the address of the commercial bank. The size of a shard is naturally defined by the number of users of a bank.

We assume the banks have the responsibility to build a reliable information system to manage their address accounts. For example, banks should have a hot backup system to improve the reliability of online services. And banks should build a server farm if the number of transactions per second is too much. Note that hot backup and server farm technologies are off-the-shelf.

State. Given an address account of an entity, there are related states of the address. They include the following data fields.

- Type: An address account may be a bank account (BA) or a user account (UA).
- Balance: It is the balance of an address account.
- Nonce: It is a counter of the account to prevent replay attacks.
- Deposit: It is the deposit amount of an address account. When some digital coins are deposited, the coins are transferred from the user's account to the bank's account.
- Code Hash: If the account is a BA account, this field includes a list of hashes referring to smart contracts in a code repository that implements the policies of banks, such as a smart contract to compute interest of a deposit. If the account is UA account, it is empty.
- Events: It records events useful for an entity.
- Storage: It records any byte sequence that is valuable to the system.

Initially, the Balance, Nonce, and Deposit fields are zero, and the Events and Storage fields are empty. If the Type field is UA, the Code Hash field is empty. If the Type field is BA, the Code Hash field is a key value pair list where the key is an operation code and the value is a hash value pointing to a smart contract in a code repository.

All address accounts managed by a bank and the address account of the bank compose the state of the bank. A modified MPT structure [12] and an auxiliary database are used to store states in a bank. The key in the MPT tree is the address itself. The value is the hash of the state information corresponding to the address. The hash of the state information and the information itself are stored as another key-value pair in the local database.

Transaction. A transaction includes operation data and a signature who issued the transaction.

- Operation Code: It denotes the operation that the transaction creator wants to execute.
- Operation Parameters: They are parameters required by the operation.
- Nonce: It is the current nonce in the account of the transaction creator.
- Time Stamp: It is the local time of the transaction creator.
- Public Key: It is the public key of the transaction creator.
- Signature: It is a signature that could be verified by the public key in the transaction

Block. The hashes of transactions and their responses are bundled to form a block by a bank. The head of a block has the following fields.

- Previous Block Hash: It is the hash value of the previous block head.
- State Root Hash: It is the root hash of an MPT containing the hashes of state information.
- Transaction Root Hash: It is the root hash of an MPT containing the hashes of transactions in the block.
- Response Root Hash: It is the root hash of an MPT containing the hashes of responses in the block.
- Time Stamp: It is the local time of block creator.
- Creator Public Key: It is the public key of the block creator.
- Creator Signature: It is a signature that could be verified by the public key of the block creator.
- Verification Proofs: It optionally includes public key and signature pairs of other verifiers of the block.

If a block is a genesis one, the three fields before the Time Stamp are used as a container to include any byte sequences. The Time Stamp, Creator Public Key and Creator Signature fields are computed as usual. The Previous Block Hash is totally zero, and the Verification Proofs is empty.

The body of a block simply includes the hashes of transactions that makes the state change, and the hashes of responses corresponding to the transactions.

Ledger. The ledger here is a simple distributed database managed by the central bank. Only the central bank could write to the database. The following data are expected to be included in the ledger.

- Blockchains: Commercial banks form their own blockchain locally and submit their blocks, transactions, responses and related key value pairs of state information to the central bank. After verification, a blockchain of a commercial bank is written to the ledger. The central bank also receives transactions from and gives responses to commercial banks. So the central bank also publishes its own blockchain to the ledger. The Blockchains could be read by any entity.

- Node List: The central bank publishes valid public keys of all commercial banks as key value pairs where the key is a domain name of the bank and the value is its registered public key. The Node List could be read by registered banks.
- Policy Repository: The central bank publishes valid polices in the repository that could be read by registered banks.
- Code Repository: The central bank publishes smart contracts as key value pairs where the key is the hash of the contract and the value is the contract code. A commercial bank may submit their special contracts to the central bank. The central bank checks the regulation of the contracts and publishes them in the repository. The Code Repository could be read by registered banks.

Each commercial bank could be a node of the distributed database so that the information in the database could be obtained locally and the commercial bank could provide query services of the ledger.

3   The AFCoin Framework

3.1   Overview

Our system includes a central bank CB, some commercial banks CMB and a lot of users U as in Fig. 1. Basically, CB issues fiat currency to CMB. CMB manages fiat currency for users. The three kinds of entities run protocols to fulfil their functions and we use double arrowhead solid line to denote their conversations. Each user could check the public ledger from interfaces mainly provided by the CB to confirm their address account in their bank is treated rightly and we use double arrowhead dashed line to denote their queries and responses.

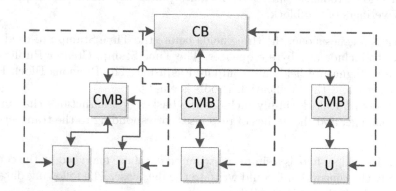

Fig. 1. The AFCoin framework

We assume there is a delay bounded communication network among these entities. Considering the practises of bank communication in China, we assume a client could establish a secure channel with a server. The client could authenticate the server and transfer messages to the server with integrity and confidentiality. Note that we do not require a mutual authentication channel since a transaction is qualified to authenticate the owner of an account. There is usually no need for a user with address account to transfer their username and password to a bank.

CMB takes care of accounts of users. They receive user's transactions and give responses. CMB includes the hashes of transactions and responses in a block. The block is signed by the CMB and double checked and signed by two other $CMBs$. A signed block is given to the CB with its related transactions, responses and related key value pairs of their local state. CB checks the blocks and publishes them in the public ledger. Note the related transactions are not included in the public ledger.

As in the real life, the CB is totally trusted by $CMBs$ and users. It is supposed that a CB faithfully executes its functions, including issuing currency, withdrawing currency, auditing transactions and so on. However, since the public ledger maintained by the CB is publicly readable, and the transactions and blocks are usually linked, it could be audited if the CB modifies or deletes hashes of some transactions. $CMBs$ are trusted by users and are audited by the CB. It is supposed that a CMB faithfully executes its functions, including depositing, withdrawing and transferring user coins and so on. If a CMB is corrupted, the CB or other two $CMBs$ could audit the transactions of the CMB. Since the two $CMBs$ are selected randomly by the CMB, if the honest $CMBs$ occupies $\frac{1}{2}$ of the total $CMBs$, the two $CMBs$ are both dishonest with a probability about $\frac{1}{4}$. With a probability about $\frac{3}{4}$, a dishonest CMB could be identified. Even a CMB finds two dishonest $CMBs$ for a block, the CB still has an opportunity to check their transactions when a user complains a CMB. Users in the system could only read the public ledger or issuing transactions. They are not trusted by the whole system so their transactions are checked carefully by the $CMBs$.

3.2   The Central Bank

In this paper, we assume that the CB only has three main functions: making monetary policy, issuing currency and withdrawing currency from circulation. Suppose the CB provides currency to $CMBs$ through loan operations. When a loan expires, the CMB pays the currency to the CB.

A CMB has a client program C_{CMB} as the wallet of CMB. It communicates with a program in the CB called as S_{CB}. The program S_{CB} manages a global state σ_{CB} including the address accounts of directly connected $CMBs$. The CB has a TLS certificate $Cert_E^{CB}$. C_{CMB} establishes a secure channel with the central bank CB by the TLS protocol. S_{CB} provides three functions: loan, repayment and policy update.

- Loan: C_{CMB} takes as input a loan credential description LCD and loan credentials LC.
  - C_{CMB} reads the local timestamp TS_{CMB}, forms a loan transaction T_L and sends it to S_{CB} where

$$T_L = (LA, (LCD, LC), Nonce_{CMB}, TS_{CMB}, pk_{CMB}, \delta_{CMB}).$$

- S_{CB} receives T_L and verifies the signature, timestamp and nonce. If the verifications passed, S_{CB} executes the LA smart contract, which matches the LCD with its current policies and checks the validity of LC and determines a value v according to the rules of the matched policy. If there are no matching policies, it stops the request and decreases a reputation value in the Storage field addressed by $addr_{CMB}$ in σ_{CB}. Otherwise, it adds $-v$ in the Balance field, new events in the Events field of $addr_{CB}$, and adds a positive balance v, updates an increased nonce, an increased reputation and events in the related fields addressed by $addr_{CMB}$ in δ_{CB}. S_{CB} then forms a R_L transaction as

$$R_L = (addr_{CMB}, h(T_L), (Balance_{CMB}, Storage_{CMB}), TS_{CB}, \delta_{CB})$$

  where the third field is the updated state information of the CMB.
- C_{CMB} receives R_L and verifies the timestamp, signature, $h(T_L)$ and $addr_{CMB}$. If the verifications passed, it updates its local state information.
- Repayment: C_{CMB} takes as input a loan transaction T_L.
- C_{CMB} reads the local timestamp TS_{CMB}, forms a repayment transaction T_{RP} and sends it to S_{CB} where

$$T_{RP} = (RP, (h(T_L), v), Nonce_{CMB}, TS_{CMB}, pk_{CMB}, \delta_{CMB}).$$

- S_{CB} receives T_{RP} and verifies the signature, nonce and timestamp. If the verifications passed, S_{CB} executes the RP smart contract, which finds the T_L transaction by $h(T_L)$ and checks the LCD and LC in the T_L with the current timestamp and policies to check v. If the value is suitable, S_{CB} reduces the balance field of $addr_{CMB}$ to $Balance - v$, increases the reputation in the storage field of $addr_{CMB}$, and adds v to the balance field of $addr_{CB}$. S_{CB} then gives a response transaction as

$$R_{RP} = (addr_{CMB}, h(T_{RP}), Storage_{CMB}, TS_{CB}, \delta_{CB}).$$

- C_{CMB} receives R_{RP} and verifies the timestamp, signature, $h(T_{RP})$ and $addr_{CMB}$. If the verifications passed, it updates its local state information.
- Policy Update: We assume each policy has a description PD and detailed items PD_i. When a new policy is to be announced or a policy is updated, the CB produces a T_P transaction:

$$T_P = (UP, (PD, PD_0, ..., PD_p), Nonce_{CB}, TS_{CB}, pk_{CB}, \delta_{CB})$$

where $p \in Z$ is the number of items of a policy. S_{CB} then executes the UP smart contract to modify the Nonce field of the state information of $addr_{CB}$, and publishes the policies in the transaction in the policy repository of the ledger.

Besides the main functions, the CB has some auxiliary functions to make the system smooth.

- Register: A CMB registers its public key pk_{CMB} to the CB through the register function. It may follow the registration routine in a certificate authority. The CB only communicates with registered CMBs. The CMB gets the public key of CB at the registration phase.
- Audit: A CMB submits its local block with auxiliary transactions, responses and states to the CB. If the number of signatures of the block is less than 3, the CB checks each transaction and response related to the block. If all checks passed or the number of signatures is enough, it accepts the block and publishes it to the ledger. If necessary, the central bank could reconstruct the state MPT of each commercial banks for regulatory and compliance process. It could audit all users and commercial banks in the framework.
- Publish: The CB has a counter and a timeout mechanism to trigger a publish procedure. If the number of transactions has exceeded a threshold b or the timeout counter has been reduced to 0, the CB packages the hashes of transactions and responses in a block, and publishes a new block to the ledger.
- Code Repository: A CMB should submit their smart contracts with referenced polices to the central bank. If the contracts are verified successfully by the central bank, they are published on the ledger. Contracts of a commercial bank could be updated by the central bank.

3.3   A Commercial Bank

Suppose a commercial bank CMB. Suppose two users of the CMB bank, Alice and Bob. Both have installed clients C_A and C_B provided by the CMB, respectively. A server program S_{CMB} in the CMB tackles the requests of clients. The CMB has a TLS Certificate $Cert_E^{CMB}$.

We assume there is a financial policy for a user to exchange their money in a bank account to their address account in the form of fiat coins. This assumption is important since it allows a gradual deployment of our framework. Any bank with a good information system could partially deploy our framework locally. Note that if a user has opened an address account, they need no password and bank account to manage their money in the bank. So a fishing website of a bank is useless. This merit of an address account may be a direct reason to attract users opening address accounts.

Next, we focus on the conversations between the client of Alice C_A and the server program S_{CMB}. Suppose C_A has been downloaded from the official website of the CMB. A qualified TLS certificate of the CMB is embedded in C_A. C_A establishes a secure channel with the CMB by the TLS protocol. Suppose Alice has a bank account in the CMB. There may be several different conversations between the bank and the user as follows.

- Open Account: If C_A finds no address account of Alice, it asks Alice to provide its normal account number NAN, her password PWD and an initial value IV to open an address account.
  - C_A reads the local timestamp TS_A, creates a T_O transaction, and sends it to S_{CMB} where

$$T_O = (OA, (NAN, PWD, IV), 0, TS_A, pk_A, \delta_A).$$

- S_{CMB} receives T_O, verifies the nonce, timestamp and signature. If the verifications passed, S_{CMB} authenticates the user with NAN and PWD. If the user is a normal user in the bank, S_{CMB} verifies that the balance of the NAN is not less than the value IV. S_{CMB} then reduces the balance in the NAN by subtracting IV. It returns R_O to the client C_A where

$$R_O = (addr_A, h(T_O), IV, TS_{CMB}, \delta_{CMB})$$

  S_{CMB} then runs OA smart contract with parameters (T_O, R_O) to update the state information addressed by $addr_A$ as

$$(UA, IV, 1, 0, \bot, \{(h(T_O), h(R_O))\}, 0)$$

- Deposit: Alice gives C_A the amount of value v and the deposit type t.
  - C_A reads local timestamp TS_A, creates a transaction T_D and sends it to S_{CMB} where

$$T_D = (DP, (v, t), Nonce_A, TS_A, pk_A, \delta_A).$$

  - S_{CMB} receives T_D and verifies the timestamp, nonce and signature. If the verifications passed, S_{CMB} checks that v is less than the Balance field of the state information addressed by $addr_A$. If it does, S_{CMB} returns R_D to C_A where

$$R_D = (addr_A, h(T_D), (Balance - v, Deposit + v), TS_{CMB}, \delta_{CMB}).$$

  It then runs the DP smart contract with parameters (T_D, R_D) to update the state information indexed by $addr_A$ to

$$(UA, Balance - v, Nonce + 1, Deposit + v, \bot, Events', 0),$$

  where $Events' = Events \bigcup \{(h(T_D), h(R_D))\}$. The smart contract also updates the state information addressed by $addr_{CMB}$ to

$$(BA, Balance + v, Nonce, Deposit, CodeHash, Events', Storage)$$

- Withdraw: Alice gives C_A the withdraw item identified by $h(R_D)$. C_A establishes a secure channel with the bank CMB by the TLS protocol.
  - C_A reads the local timestamp TS_A, creates a transaction T_W and sends it to S_{CMB} where

$$T_W = (WD, h(R_D), Nonce_A, TS_A, pk_A, \delta_A).$$

  - S_{CMB} receives T_W and verifies the timestamp, nonce and signature. If the verifications passed, S_{CMB} finds the deposit transaction T_D by $h(T_D)$ that is included in R_D indexed by $h(R_D)$ in its local database. If the transaction is found, S_{CMB} makes sure that the event including $h(T_D)$ appears only once in the Events field addressed by $addr_A$. If so, it runs the smart contract for WD with parameter (T_W, T_D). The code first calculates the interest in of the T_D according to the bank's polices, and updates the state information indexed by $addr_A$ to

$$(UA, Balance + v + in, Nonce + 1, Deposit - v, \bot, Events, 0).$$

The code also updates the state information indexed by $addr_{CMB}$ to

$$(BA, Balance - v - in, Nonce, Deposit, CodeHash, Events, Storage).$$

S_{CMB} then returns the response R_W to C_A where

$$R_W = (addr_A, h(T_W), Balance, Deposit, TS_{CMB}, \delta_{CMB}).$$

S_{CMB} finally runs the WD code again with inputs (T_W, T_D, R_W), which updates the Events field of the state information addressed by $addr_A$ and $addr_{CMB}$ as $Events \bigcup \{(h(T_W), h(T_D), h(R_W))\}$.

Remark 1. The above conversations happen between a user Alice and a bank CMB. Alice opens an address account, deposits money to the bank and withdraws the money with interest. It shows a great difference between a bank account and an address account. An employee in bank could modify the balance of user's normal account. However, only transactions with users' signatures could modify the balance of a user. If an employee in bank modifies the state information manually, the neighbored root hashes of the state and the transaction hash root could provide a full evidence chain to audit the modification. Besides, the bank could design a more elaborate account data structure to support more bank businesses.

To further explore our framework, we consider Alice transfers some money to Bob. Note that Bob is also a user of the same bank.

– Transfer: Alice gets Bob's account address $addr_B$, for example, by scanning a QR code. She also specifies the value v to be transferred to C_A. C_A establishes a secure channel with the bank CMB by the TLS protocol.
  • C_A reads local timestamp TS_A, creates a transaction T_T and sends it to S_{CMB} where

  $$T_T = (TR, (v, addr_B), Nonce_A, TS_A, pk_A, \delta_A).$$

  • S_{CMB} receives T_T and verifies the timestamp, nonce and signature. If the verifications passed, S_{CMB} checks that v is not greater than the Balance field of the state information addressed by $addr_A$, and that $addr_B$ is a valid account in its state tree. If they do, S_{CMB} returns R_{T_0} and R_{T_1} to C_A where

  $$R_{T_0} = (addr_A, h(T_T), Balance - v, TS_{CMB}, \delta_{CMB})$$

  and

  $$R_{T_1} = (addr_B, h(T_T), Balance + v, TS_{CMB}, \delta_{CMB}).$$

It then runs the TR smart contract with parameters (T_T, R_{T_0}, R_{T_1}). The code updates the state information indexed by $addr_A$ to

$$(UA, Balance - v, Nonce + 1, Deposit, \perp, Events', 0)$$

where $Events' = Events \bigcup \{(h(T_T), h(R_{T_0}))\}$. The code also updates the state information addressed by $addr_B$ to

$$(UA, Balance + v, Nonce, Deposit, \perp, Events'', 0)$$

where $Events'' = Events \bigcup \{(h(T_T), h(R_{T_1}))\}$.

- Alice may send $h(R_{T_1})$ to Bob for verification of the money transfer. Bob may also subscribe some notification service of the bank so that the balance change event could be pushed to Bob's client immediately.

Now we obtain a digital currency solution for a solo bank without the help of a central bank. Users in the bank could control their money by themselves and has a higher security guarantee. User experience is just similar to the AliPay or WeChat Pay for money transfer.

With the help of the central bank and the money deposited by a user, a CMB may carry out loan and credit businesses. It transfers coins to user's account similarly to a normal Transfer operation. A CMB must reports their accounts to the central bank for audit. Besides the main functions, a CMB has the following functions to make the system smooth.

- Block: A CMB has a counter for received transactions and a timeout for a block. If the timeout is reduced to 0, or the counter has exceeded a threshold b, a local block is created. The body of the block includes the hashes of transactions and responses. The CMB signs the block.
- Cross Verify: A CMB gets the current node list in the ledger. Suppose the size of the list is M. It uses the transaction root hash in the block head as a big number trh and calculates the reminder $h(trh, 0) \bmod M$ and $h(trh, 1) \bmod M$ to get two random CMBs to verify the block. Suppose the two CMBs are CMB_i and CMB_j. The CMB gives CMB_i and CMB_j the block, the transactions and responses of the block, the state MPT of the previous block, the key value pairs of the modified state. They check the public ledger for the previous block of the CMB and the code repository, check the state MPT and related key-value pairs. It then execute the code to verify the changes of the state and the responses in the block. If the final state is the same as that in the block, the verification successes. CMB_i and CMB_j returns their signatures for the block body.
- Block Submit: The CMB submits a fully verified block with three signatures or an immature block with at least its own signature. In both cases, the CMB submits the transactions, responses, changes of state MPT and related key value pairs to the central bank.

3.4   Inter-Bank Transfer

Now suppose there are two commercial banks CMB_A and CMB_B. Both developed their fiat currency businesses for their users. Now a user Alice is in CMB_A and another user Bob is in CMB_B. We consider the money transfer operation between them.

– Transfer: Alice get Bob's account address $addr_B$, for example, by scanning a QR code. She also specifies the value v to be transferred to C_A. C_A establishes a secure channel with the bank CMB_A by the TLS protocol.
  - C_A reads local timestamp TS_A, creates a transaction T_T and sends it to S_{CMB_A} where

$$T_T = (TR, (v, addr_B), Nonce_A, TS_A, pk_A, \delta_A).$$

  - S_{CMB_A} receives T_T and verifies the timestamp, nonce and signature. If the verifications passed, S_{CMB_A} checks that v is not greater than the Balance field in the state information addressed by $addr_A$, and $addr_B$ is not a valid account in its local state. If so, S_{CMB_A} finds the node CMB_B by $owner(addr_B)$, reads its local time TS_{CMB_A}, forms a remote transfer transaction T_{RT} and sends it to S_{CMB_B} where

$$T_{RT} = (RTR, REF, Nonce_{CMA_A}, TS_{CMB_A}, pk_{CMB_A}, \delta_{CMB_A})$$

  where $REF = (hash(T_T), v, addr_B)$. S_{CMB_A} then runs the RTR smart contract with parameters (T_T, T_{RT}). The code updates the state information addressed by $addr_A$ to

$$(UA, Balance - v, Nonce + 1, Deposit, \perp, Events', 0)$$

  and updates the state information addressed by $addr_{CMB_A}$ to

$$(UB, Balance, Nonce + 1, Deposit, CodeHash, Events', Storage),$$

  where $Events' = Events \bigcup \{(h(T_T), h(T_{RT}))\}$.
  - S_{CMB_B} receives T_{RT} and verifies the timestamp and signature. The $Nonce_{CMB_A}$ in the T_{RT} is for the central bank audit later. If the verifications passed, S_{CMB_B} makes sure that $addr_B$ is a valid address account in its state tree. If so, it forms a response message R_{TR} and sends it back to CMB_A where

$$R_{TR} = (addr_{CMB_A}, h(T_{RT}), (addr_B, v), TS_{CMB_B}, pk_{CMB_B}, \delta_{CMB_B}).$$

  S_{CMB_B} then runs the RTR smart contract with parameters (T_{RT}, R_{TR}). The code updates the state information indexed by $addr_B$ to

$$(UA, Balance + v, Nonce, Deposit, \perp, Events', 0)$$

  and updates the state information indexed by $addr_{CMB_B}$ to

$$(UB, Balance, Nonce, Deposit, CodeHash, Events', Storage),$$

  where $Events' = Events \bigcup \{(h(T_{RT}), h(R_{TR}))\}$.

- S_{CMB_A} receives R_{TR} and verifies the timestamp and signature. If the verifications passed, S_{CMB_A} creates a response message R_T, and sends it to C_A where

$$R_T = (addr_A, h(T_T), RES, TS_{CMB_A}, pk_{CMB_A}, \delta_{CMB_A})$$

where $RES = (h(T_{RT}), h(R_{TR}), Balance_A)$. S_{CMB_A} runs the RTR smart contract again to update the Events fields in the state information addressed by $addr_A$ and $addr_{CMB_A}$ as $Events \bigcup \{(R_{TR}, R_T)\}$.

- Alice sends $h(R_{RT})$ to Bob if she is required. Bob could then verify the transfer by the Events field of his state. Note that, Bob could also subscribe some service of the bank so that the balance change event could be pushed to Bob's client immediately.

4 Analysis

4.1 Efficiency

When a user wants to deposit, withdraw or transfer money, only one transaction is needed. A transaction includes a signature of the user.

A commercial bank needs to produce one response for deposit and withdraw transactions. If the operation is money transfer, the bank should produce one response or one response and one transaction. A commercial bank also has the requirement to loan coins from the central bank with one transaction. The routine work of a commercial bank include producing local blocks, verifying blocks of other banks and produce signatures for the verified blocks.

The central bank needs to give responses for loan and repayment transactions. It should produce a transaction to update the policy. The routine work of the central bank is to verify all immature blocks and accept qualified blocks. It may reconstruct the state of a special account with information collected from commercial banks.

We need no special technology to implement the public ledger. Since only the central bank has the write rights, all other entities could only read information from the ledger. A normal distributed database is qualified for the task. If we assume each commercial bank has a node to run the database, the information in the public ledger could be queried locally by the banks.

4.2 Regulation

The framework supports at least three approaches for the regulatory and compliant process.

- User regulation: Since the hashes of users' transactions are packaged into blocks by commercial banks and finally collected by the central bank to the public ledger, a user could make sure their transactions have been treated carefully if the hash of their transaction is included in the public ledger.

If not, a user could take the response of a commercial bank as an evidence to complain a commercial bank. For any complaint, the central bank should try to reconstruct the address account of the user for a clear judgement and punish the faulty party.

- Peer regulation: We have designed a cross verification mechanism so that a block could be verified by two other random commercial banks. If a commercial block has three signatures, the central bank may accept the block without further verification. However, if a block is submitted in an immature fashion, the block will be checked carefully and the block creator or the helpful commercial banks may be punished.
- Senior regulation: The central bank could make a blind sample policy for blocks with three signatures. It should open a complaint port for users to complain commercial banks and do a careful check for immature blocks.

In addition, we have defined a reputation value in the Storage field. The central bank could use this value to evaluate the regulation of a commercial bank. A commercial bank could similarly set a reputation value for a user to evaluate the regulation of a user.

4.3   Privacy

Generally, the public information of the system is in the public ledger. They are simply hash values. User's transactions and responses are available to their commercial bank, two verifying banks, and the central bank. If a bank is corrupted, the account information of the bank and the transactions verified by the bank could be disclosed. To alleviate this point, we require a local encryption mechanism to make sure that the history transactions, responses, and state key value pairs are encrypted.

The identity information of user's address account is stored in a bank. When some payment actions happen, the bank only knows that Alice has transferred some money to Bob if both are registered in the bank. When Alice in a bank transfers money to Bob in another bank, the bank endorses the money transfer and hides even the address account of Alice. Now the bank of Alice knows that Alice wants to transfer some money to an address and knows nothing about the identity of the address. The bank of Bob knows that Bob has new income and knows nothing who transfers that to him. Note that the central bank does not have the registration information. Although the central bank could verify each transaction, it could not link a transaction to its issuer's identity trivially. In contrast, the Alipay or WeChat certainly know both the identities of the sender and receiver of a money transfer operation. From this point, we believe the privacy of our system is stronger than the current payment methods and certainly weaker than paper cash.

4.4 Reliability

In the example framework, the reliability relies on the reliability of information system in each bank. If the information system of a bank stops, the users of the bank cannot pay. To alleviate this problem, we propose two possible methods.

- A hardware wallet could be used to support off-line payment. When the information system of a bank stops, there is another approach for payment.
- Some commercial banks could establish a simple consortium blockchain to manage their shared address accounts. For example, three branches of the same bank in different places could build a small consortium blockchain to provide enhanced reliability.

4.5 Deployment

A commercial bank could follow the protocols in Sect. 3.3 to carry out fiat currency businesses for their users. Two commercial banks could ally to run a distributed database as a public ledger for their users. The central bank could make policies and adopt the running distributed databases of allied commercial banks. When all commercial banks carry out their fiat currency businesses and submit their local blocks to the central bank, the whole system emerges.

5 Conclusion

We show a framework for central banks to issue and manage fiat currency. It is evidently has a better privacy than the AliPay and WeChat system. It is expected to have a better efficiency and is suitable for the current "central bank-commercial bank" binary model. It also has a good regulation property. More importantly, the framework may be deployed gradually by commercial banks and the central bank.

Further, we design new transfer operations to support fair digital assets exchange and more functions. A security model for the framework is also developing.

Acknowledgment. This work is supported by the National Key R&D Program of China (2017YFB0802503), Supported by Guangxi Key Laboratory of Cryptography and Information Security (No. GCIS201711), Natural Science Foundation of China (61672550), and Fundamental Research Funds for the Central Universities (No. 17lgjc45).

References

1. Bank of Canada, S.: Staff working papers (2018). https://www.bankofcanada.ca/research/browse/?content_type[]=31. Accessed 12 Aug 2018
2. Bank of England, S.: Staff working papers (2018). https://www.bankofengland.co.uk/news/publications. Accessed 12 Aug 2018

3. George, D., Sarah, M.: Centrally banked cryptocurrencies. In: Network and Distributed System Security Symposium, NDSS 2016, pp. 1–14. ACM (2016). http://dx.doi.org/10.14722/ndss.2016.23187

4. Han, X., Liu, Y., Xu, H.: A user-friendly centrally banked cryptocurrency. In: Liu, J.K., Samarati, P. (eds.) ISPEC 2017. LNCS, vol. 10701, pp. 25–42. Springer, Cham (2017). https://doi.org/10.1007/978-3-319-72359-4_2

5. Meaning, J., Dyson, B., Barker, J., Clayton, E.: Broadening narrow money: monetary policy with a central bank digital currency (2018). https://www.bankofengland.co.uk/working-paper/2018/. Accessed 12 Aug 2018

6. Bordo, M., Levin, A.: Central bank digital currency and the future of monetary policy (2017). https://www.hoover.org/sites/default/files/bordo-levin_bullets_for_hoover_may2017.pdf. Accessed 12 Aug 2018

7. Mike, H.: Corda: a distributed ledger (2016). https://docs.corda.net/_static/corda-technical-whitepaper.pdf. Accessed 12 Aug 2018

8. Nakamoto, S.: Bitcoin: a peer-to-peer electronic cash system (2008). https://bitcoin.org/bitcoin.pdf. Accessed 4 Aug 2017

9. Quorum: Welcome to the quorum wiki! (2016). https://github.com/jpmorganchase/quorum/wiki. Accessed 12 Aug 2018

10. Scorer, S.: Central bank digital currency: DLT, or not DLT? That is the question (2017). https://bankunderground.co.uk/2017/06/05/. Accessed 12 Aug 2018

11. Sveriges Riksbank, S.: The Riksbank's e-krona project (2018). https://www.riksbank.se/globalassets/media/rapporter/e-krona/2017/handlingsplan_ekrona_171221_eng.pdf. Accessed 12 Aug 2018

12. Wood, D.G.: Ethereum: a secure decentralised generalised transaction ledger homestead (2014). http://gavwood.com/paper.pdf. Accessed 4 Aug 2017

13. Yao, Q.: A systematic framework to understand central bank digital currency. Sci. China Inf. Sci. **61**(3), 033101 (2018). https://doi.org/10.1007/s11432-017-9294-5

14. Yves, M.: Digital base money: an assessment from the ECB's perspective (2017). http://www.ecb.europa.eu/press/key/date/2017/html/sp170116.en.html. Accessed 12 Aug 2018

15. Zhang, F., Zhang, F., Wang, Y.: Fair electronic cash systems with multiple banks. In: Qing, S., Eloff, J.H.P. (eds.) SEC 2000. ITIFIP, vol. 47, pp. 461–470. Springer, Boston, MA (2000). https://doi.org/10.1007/978-0-387-35515-3_47

Anonymity Reduction Attacks to Monero

Dimaz Ankaa Wijaya[1]([⊠]), Joseph Liu[1], Ron Steinfeld[1], Dongxi Liu[2],
and Tsz Hon Yuen[3]

[1] Faculty of Information Technology, Monash University, Melbourne, Australia
{dimaz.wijaya,joseph.liu,ron.steinfeld}@monash.edu
[2] Data61, CSIRO, Eveleigh, Australia
dongxi.liu@data61.csiro.au
[3] Huawei, Singapore, Singapore
yuen.tsz.hon@huawei.com

Abstract. Monero is one of the most valuable cryptocurrencies in the market, focusing on users' privacy. The built-in features in Monero help users to obfuscate the information of the senders and the receivers, hence achieve a better privacy compared to other cryptocurrencies such as Bitcoin. Previous studies discovered multiple problems within Monero systems, and based on these findings, Monero system has been improved.

Although improvements have been made, we discovered that new attacks targeting the anonymity reduction can still be conducted in Monero system. In this paper we propose two attacks. The first is an extension of a known attack called Monero Ring Attack. The second one exploits Payment ID to discover the real output of a mixin. We then propose countermeasures to these attacks.

Keywords: Monero · Anonymity · Attack · Traceability · Ring signature

1 Introduction

Bitcoin is the first cryptocurrency deployed in 2009 by Satoshi Nakamoto [1]. It allows every user to join or leave the payment system instantly. In accordance to the idea, Bitcoin relies on cryptographic methods such as public key cryptography to avoid user registration process and to provide the proof of ownership of the coins. This mechanism decouples the Bitcoin transactions with the users' real identities. Therefore, Bitcoin was supposed to be anonymous.

The term anonymity can be determined by 2 adjacent forms: **unlinkability** and **untraceability** [2]. Unlinkability is related to the privacy of the receiver, where different transactions cannot be identified to be sent to the same receiver. Untraceability, on the other hand, is related to the sender's privacy. A system is considered as untraceable when it is infeasible to determine the real sender of a transaction.

The anonymity assumption in Bitcoin environment was proven to be incorrect. Several studies have shown that information related to Bitcoin users can be revealed, either by using clustering methods [3] or extracting additional information from websites [4]. Quantitative analysis of Bitcoin transactions was able to determine malicious activities conducted by the Mt.Gox hacker(s) [5]. Consequently, Bitcoin is

F. Guo et al. (Eds.): Inscrypt 2018, LNCS 11449, pp. 86–100, 2019.
https://doi.org/10.1007/978-3-030-14234-6_5

now considered as pseudo-anonymous, since the users' identities can be revealed through some analyses.

Monero is a different type of cryptocurrency compared to Bitcoin. Monero is one of the most valuable cryptocurrencies in the world with a total market value of US $3.5billion[1]. The technology offered by Monero focuses on enhancing the anonymity of the users. The anonymity in Monero is implemented by obfuscating the information of the real senders and the real receivers, making it hard for observers to make a direct relationship of the senders and the receivers. The anonymity features of Monero are achieved by employing ring signature and stealth address in the system. The privacy-protection mechanism was further enhanced by implementing RingCT technology, which obfuscates the amount of coins transacted.

We define an anonymity reduction attack as an effort made by a malicious user (or an attacker) who tries to de-anonymise other users' transaction. This attack is done by creating transactions and breaking the attacker's own anonymity. An example of this attack is Monero Ring Attack [6]. The aforementioned attack works on both non-RingCT and RingCT environment, and does not rely on zero-mixin transactions as in [7, 8].

Contributions. We summarise our research contributions as follows.

1. We propose a mitigation strategy on a known Monero anonymity attack exploiting the users' freedom when creating mixins [9]. Our mitigation strategy uses a list of hash values of existing mixins. New transactions are not allowed to use any mixins that have existed in the system, in which their hash values are on the list. By employing the mitigation strategy, future attacks using the same method can be completely prevented.
2. We propose an extension of the attack in [6]. Our new scheme achieves the same goals of the previous attack in [6] but nullifies the mitigation strategy we designed. The new scheme provides an obfuscation method when choosing the mixins, hence identical mixins are no longer needed.
3. We propose a solution to avoid the new attack we propose. Monero developers have been working on a new blacklisting mechanism called "blackball" which will blacklist all known bad outputs to mitigate an attack over key reuse[2]. In our solution, we developed a new metric as a quantitative measurement towards the suspicious level of anonymity reduction attack. The metric is useful to complement the existing blacklisting method, either by implementing it in the Monero core software or as a separate service.
4. We propose a novel anonymity reduction attack by utilizing an extra information called Payment ID (PID) which is usually embedded in Monero transactions. The scheme enables the attacker to trace the real outputs spent in the transactions. We also suggest a possible countermeasure on the attack.

Organization. The rest of the paper is organized as follows. In Sect. 2 we present the basic knowledge about the field of the research. Section 3 describes previous studies

---

[1] Based on information provided by Coinmarketcap.com on 22 March 2018.
[2] https://github.com/monero-project/monero/pull/3322.

related to our research. In Sect. 4 we propose a mitigation strategy of a known attack, while in Sect. 5 we improve the known attack by removing the weaknesses and propose a stronger attack trait. Lastly, Sect. 6 presents a novel attack related to Payment ID usage.

2 Background

2.1 CryptoNote Protocol

The CryptoNote protocol was originally proposed in 2013 [2]. The purpose of the CryptoNote protocol is to create a privacy-preserving cryptocurrency with built-in features that will help users to keep anonymous, although it still preserves similarities with Bitcoin, such as transparent transaction data (inputs, outputs, and the amount of coins transacted). The main idea of the protocol is to employ a linkable ring signature [10, 11] to avoid the sender from being traced. The one-time public key (stealth address) is also implemented to make sure all users create a new address for every transaction.

By using a linkable ring signature, it is infeasible to distinguish the real output being spent by a transaction over a set of outputs. In the linkable ring signature, the user needs to construct a set of outputs as an input of the transaction, which are assumed to be picked randomly over a large set of outputs available on the network. The user needs to insert her own output to the set, which is the real output to be spent in the transaction. The other outputs are actually the decoys that help obfuscating the real output.

The linkable ring signature also protects the system from a double spending attack by allowing detection if such thing happens. Each public key is associated with a secret value; in order to spend a public key, the corresponding secret value needs to be exposed to the blockchain. If a secret key appears more than once, it means a double spending attempt occurs [11].

In the one-time public key mechanism, the receiver provides a set of master public keys to the sender, which will be used by the sender to create new public keys. Hence, the destination of the payment is created by the sender, not the receiver. When receiving payments, the receiver scans the blockchain and applies a method to determine which payments are destined to the receiver.

2.2 Monero

Monero is a CryptoNote-based cryptocurrency. As with any other cryptocurrency products, there are applications required to run the system, namely Monero daemon and Monero wallet. A Monero daemon is the node keeping a full record of all transactions happening in the network, while a Monero wallet does not need to store all transactions locally. Monero wallet can be used to create new transactions by connecting to a Monero daemon.

When creating a new transaction, the Monero wallet first sends a request to the Monero daemon. The purpose of the request is to get an information about potential public keys (outputs) to be used as decoys in the ring signature construction. Using a random sampling algorithm, the wallet selects a set of global indexes from the histogram provided by the daemon, then the daemon will need to provide the corresponding outputs. The index of the real output is also included in the request for two reasons: as a test whether the daemon sends the correct outputs and to obfuscate the final ring signature from a curious daemon.

Monero developers have adopted an additional protection on users's privacy. The Confidential Transaction (CT) is added into ring signature construction to create RingCT [12]. Confidential transaction is a Pedersen commitment to encrypt the amount of money sent from the sender to the receiver so that they cannot be visible to the world; only the respective participants can decrypt the amount [13]. RingCT was deployed in January 2017 and became mandatory since September 2017 [14].

RingCT has caused a major change on the way users create mixins. In a non-RingCT transaction, an output can only be mixed with other outputs with the same amount. Before RingCT is available, an output having a unique amount of coins cannot be mixed with other outputs, hence zero-mixin transaction occurs. Zero-mixin transaction is a transaction containing an input that does not have any mixin. By using RingCT, the amount of money will be hidden, thus an output can be mixed with any outputs.

2.3 Monero Transaction

In Monero, a transaction contains at least one input and zero or more outputs. An input contain at least one unspent output from an existing transaction confirmed in the blockchain and the input can also include several other outputs as decoys or "mixins". The transaction can also produce outputs which are the fund sent by the sender to one or more receivers. The structure of the transaction can be seen in Fig. 1.

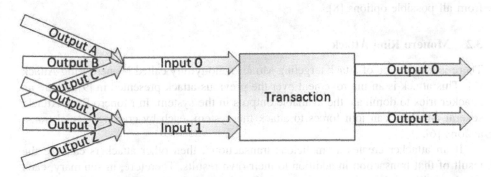

Fig. 1. In Monero, an input may contain several existing outputs. Only one output in an input to be spent, while the other outputs are decoys. [6]

2.4 Monero Payment ID

As with any other CryptoNote-based cryptocurrency, it is infeasible to distinguish a specific sender among a set of senders in Monero [2]. In the Bitcoin system, creating a new destination address for each user is practical by using a deterministic or hierarchical deterministic (HD) wallet as in [15]. In Monero, each wallet can only have one Monero address (we exclude subaddress [16] in the discussion). Therefore, a metadata called Payment ID is added into Monero transaction to help the receiver to determine the sender of the payment.

The unencrypted Payment ID is 32 bytes data inserted into the extra field on the transaction data, which is usually represented into 64 digits hexadecimal on the Monero blockchain explorer [17]. A new feature named integrated address encrypts the Payment ID into the destination address, where only the receiver can decrypt the Payment ID. The Payment ID for the integrated address is 8 bytes long or 16 digits hexadecimal [17]. In this paper, we will use the term UPID to refer the unencrypted Payment ID and EPID to refer the encrypted Payment ID.

3   Related Works

3.1   Monero Zero-Mixin Problems

In general, it is obvious that a receiver of a transaction can determine that her outputs are being used as decoys by other transactions. Therefore, it is possible that a user tries to attack the system by creating a large number of outputs in order to reduce the anonymity of other transactions [9]. In the attack, the attacker needs to pay a huge amount of transaction fees. The attacker also needs to keep creating new transactions if she wants to control a majority of the outputs available in the network [9].

Recent studies show that zero-mixin transactions have impacted the anonymity of other transactions. A research finds that at least 87% of the mixins up to a point were de-anonymised [7]. Another research proposes a change in the way the Monero wallet samples the mixins by prioritizing new outputs rather than randomly picks the mixins from all possible options [8].

3.2   Monero Ring Attack

There is a new type of attack targeting Monero anonymity called Monero Ring Attack [6]. This attack is an improvement over the previous attack presented in [9], where an attacker tries to dominate the available outputs in the system. In Monero Ring Attack, several attackers can join forces to attack the system, each by crafting special transactions [6].

If an attacker creates a "malicious transaction", then other attackers can use the result of that transaction in addition to their own results. Therefore, in summary, each attacker will pay less transaction fees, but with bigger impact. During the attack, the attackers do not need to trust each other or communicate with each other. All they need to do is scanning the blockchain data and determine the malicious transactions created by others.

The key point on this attack is using identical mixins on the malicious transactions. Let r as the minimum number of mixins in the system; an attacker needs to have at least r outputs or sets of r outputs. Then, the attacker constructs the inputs by using r outputs as the mixins. These constructions help any attackers to determine that all the outputs used in the mixins have been spent. It is impossible that other transactions that include the outputs are double spending the outputs, hence these outputs are just the decoys.

The Monero Ring Attack has 3 phases: preparation phase, setup phase, and attack phase. In the preparation phase, the attacker prepares r outputs. In the setup phase, the attacker constructs spending transactions using identical mixins, each mixin has r outputs as the ring members. Then, in the attack phase, the attacker expands the outputs (active attack) and analyse the result of the attack (passive attack).

The purpose of the attack is to trace the real outputs spent by mixins or at least reduce the k-anonymity of the transaction mixins. The goal is achieved by creating multiple malicious transactions such that the outputs of the attack are expected to be used as mixins by honest transactions.

4 Mitigating Monero Ring Attack

4.1 Overview

The setup phase in Monero Ring Attack as described in [6] has a unique characteristic where identical mixins are used multiple times. By determining this characteristic, the attack can simply be detected. The detection is done by hashing all mixins in the blockchain then search for any hash duplicates. If any duplicates are found, then it indicates that the attack has occured.

4.2 Detection Method

We propose a method to detect whether the attack has occurred in the blockchain. Scanning and blacklisting steps of detecting the attack can be summarized as follows.

1. For all mixins in the blockchain $M = \{m_0, m_1, m_2, ... m_n\}$, produce a set of hash values $H = \{h_0, h_1, h_2, ..., h_n\}$ by using hash function FH such that $h_0 = FH(m_0)$. A mixin m_0 is a list of outputs $mo_0 = \{o_v, o_w, o_x, o_y, o_z, ...\}$ where $v, w, x, y, z, ...$ are the output indexes.
2. For all mixins M, compute the corresponding ring size $R = \{r_0, r_1, r_2, ..., r_n\}$ such that r_0 is the ring size of mixin m_0.
3. For all hash values in H, compute the number of occurrence $U = \{u_0, u_1, u_2, ..., u_n\}$ such that u_0 is the number of occurrence of h_0.
4. For each mixin m_j where $0 \leq j \leq n$, if $r_j = u_j$ then the mixin m_j is considered as an attack. All outputs in mo_j needs to be included in a blacklist B.
5. For each mixin m_k where $0 \leq k \leq n$, check if mo_k contains any outputs from B. If yes, then add mo_k to the blacklist B.

The blacklist B, as the result of the detection method provided above, could then be published. All of the outputs in the blacklist B are discouraged to be used when sampling outputs for creating mixins.

4.3   Mitigation Strategy: Forbid Mixin Duplicates

The Monero Ring Attack has a characteristic of using mixin duplicates when launching the attack. In order to countermeasure this type of attack, Monero daemon can be equipped by a mechanism to reject new transactions having identical mixins. Furthermore, the daemon can maintain a list of mixin hash values that have been used in the system. New transactions need to prove that the hash values of their mixins have never existed in the blockchain. Considering that creating new mixins are easy, rejected transactions can be resubmitted after revising the duplicated mixins.

5   Extending the Monero Ring Attack

5.1   Overview

The idea of using sets of transactions and creating identical mixins in the setup phase as explained in Sect. 3.2 can simply be extended to obfuscate the attack. Instead of using identical mixins, combinations of outputs can be utilised. The result of this modification is identical as the Monero Ring Attack, but the method is harder to detect. The hashing method cannot be applied to the new attack. Below is the comparison between the Monero Ring Attack (MRA) and our proposed attack (Table 1).

Table 1. Comparison between the existing Monero Ring Attack and our proposed attack

Parameters	MRA	Ours
Attacking untraceability and anonymity	v	v
Cooperation between attackers without trust	v	v
Undetected using hash table	x	v

Both attacks are useful when launched against specific targets, such as coin exchange users, rather than targeting random Monero users. Targeting random users requires a massive amount of money to pay the transaction fee, while targeting a specific users will reduce the attack cost. The governments or regulators can enforce business entities under their jurisdictions to implement this scheme in order to secretly discover the users' activities in Monero system.

5.2   Security Model

The security model is similar to the one proposed in [6]. It is assumed that an attacker can access the public blockchain. The attacker might also have an access to wallet services or trading platforms in order to launch the attack without paying transaction fees (the transaction fees are paid by the customers). Although the attacker has an access to the public blockchain, but the attacker does not have the capability to modify any transactions that have been confirmed in the blockchain.

The goal of the attack is to define the real outputs spent by other transactions or reduce the anonymity of the transactions created by the users. The attack enables multiple attackers to analyse the work of other attackers and aggregate the result to maximize their efforts.

5.3 Attack Mode

Table 2 is an example how 6 outputs $O = \{O_1, O_2, O_3, O_4, O_5, O_6\}$ can be spent in six inputs $I = \{I_A, I_B, I_C, I_D, I_E, I_F\}$, with each input has a ring size of 5. We assume the system's mandatory ring size is 5 as in Monero fork version 6 (software version v0.11.0.0). The rasterized cells indicate the real outputs being spent in the input. The attack can be obfuscated further by employing a large set of outputs O which will be spent by a large set of inputs I. These inputs can be executed in one transaction or can also be spent in multiple transactions.

Table 2. Spending 6 outputs in 6 inputs. The rasterized cells are the ones being spent

Outputs	I_A	I_B	I_C	I_D	I_E	I_F
O_1	v		v	v	v	v
O_2	v	v		v	v	v
O_3	v	v	v		v	v
O_4	v	v	v	v		v
O_5	v	v	v	v	v	
O_6		v	v	v	v	v

We denote by $_nC_r$ the number of possible ways of choosing a ring of size r out of a total of n possible outputs. For example, a case where $n = 80$ and $r = 5$, we find $C = 24,040,016$ possible combinations to spend 80 outputs in 80 inputs. The calculation shows that it is infeasible to determine the attack by using a trivial mechanism.

5.4 Collaborating with Other Attackers

The proposed attack can be a collaborated attack among multiple attackers. The attackers do not need to trust each other to decide whether they have conducted the attack. Therefore, trust is not needed on the collaboration, since all of the information can always be validated by the attackers. The validation process is easy: if the number of outputs and inputs match, then the attack really occurs.

In order to make the validation process faster, the attackers still need to share a part of the information related to the attacks they conduct. The information to be shared includes:

- A list of all outputs used in the attack.
- A list of all inputs involved in the attack.

5.5   Detecting the Attack

The strategy described in Sect. 4 is not applicable to mitigate the new attack; therefore, we define a new method. It is assumed that the shared information mentioned in Sect. 5.4 is kept secret among the attackers. We simulated this attack and determined two important features that distinguish the malicious transactions and honest transactions:

- The malicious transactions repeatedly include a subset of outputs O as the mixins.
- A subset of the outputs O have a high usage value, which might be higher than the average usage value.

Precisely determining whether this type of attack has occurred in Monero and listing all related transactions might be infeasible due to the number of possible combinations. Consequently, we explore the features of this attack which will be identifiable within a set of transactions.

The diagrams in Fig. 2 shows several information regarding the average usage per output, number of transactions, and number of mixins aggregated for every 10,000 blocks. The information is useful to distinguish between regular output usages and suspected output usages. The sharp increase in the diagram A is suspected to be caused by the mandatory RingCT scheme implementation, which left the users to have limited options of outputs to be used as their mixins. At the same time, the minimum ring size was increased to five.

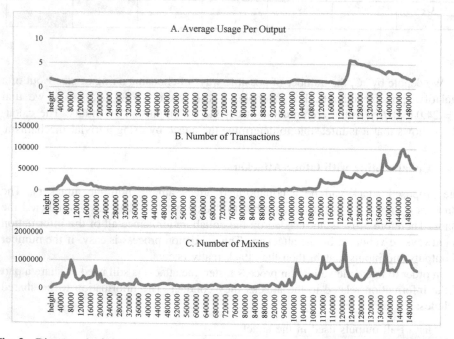

Fig. 2. Diagram A shows the average usage per output from the blocks. Diagram B shows the number of transactions on the blocks. Diagram C shows the number of mixins of the transactions on the blocks. The data is aggregated for every 10,000 blocks. The horizontal axis shows the block height, while the vertical axis shows the value.

We then evaluated the data from the Monero blockchain up to block 1,542,882 containing 24.8 million outputs, where 4.7 million outputs are from RingCT transactions. Based on the finding, we divide the transactions into non-RingCT and RingCT transactions due to their data characteristics. The diagrams are shown in Fig. 3. The average output usage for all non-RingCT transactions is 1.96, while the average output usage for all RingCT transactions is 3.68. Overall, the average output usage is 2.28.

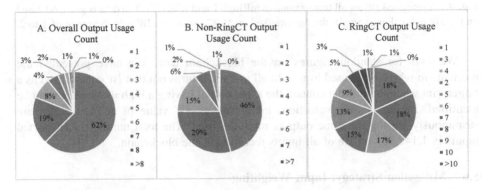

Fig. 3. The aggregate data of all output usages with the legends describe the number of output usage. Diagram A shows the aggregate output usage count on Non-RingCT and RingCT transactions. Diagram B shows the same data on Non-RingCT transactions. Diagram C shows the data on RingCT transactions. Data less than 1% is aggregated.

The difference between non-RingCT and RingCT transactions might also be affected by a change in mixin sampling method. Triangular distribution is used to replace uniform distribution to increase the data resemblance with users behaviors as suggested by [8]. The impact of the triangular distribution towards the evaluated data is ignored to simplify the case.

We define an output weight OW as the number of inputs where an output O is involved as one of the mixins. We also define an input weight IW as the average value of OW for all outputs in the input.

$$IW_s = \frac{\sum_{k=0}^{r} OW_k}{r} \qquad (1)$$

We scanned the blockchain and computed the value of IW for all inputs up to block 1,545,153 (timestamped on 5 April 2018). We found a total of 45,650,192 inputs on the blockchain. The data is then aggregated and presented on Fig. 4.

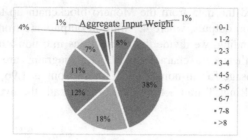

Fig. 4. Aggregated *IW* for all transactions (nonRingCT and RingCT). The data is grouped based on the *IW* range. For example, the data marked as "1-2" means the *IW* is in the range of 1 to 2.

We look for standout figures on the blockchain data. We have presented the mechanism where *IW* is used to weight all mixins. It turns out that *IW* can be used as a fingerprint where inputs that contain the same output having a high usage value can be identified. Based on our evaluation, inputs having *IW* value of at least seven are suspiciously reusing the same outputs multiple times. The total number of suspected inputs is 1,142,383 or 2% of all inputs recorded in the blockchain.

5.6 Mitigation Strategy: Input Weighting

The current triangular distribution sampling method does not guarantee that the users will use outputs that are not a part of anonymity reduction attack. Thus, there is an urgent need to improve the sampling protocol.

Our research shows that Monero outputs are not as fungible as claimed in [18]. Fungibility in Monero describes that all outputs have the same value regardless who creates the outputs. Our results show that a subset of the outputs are potentially harming the anonymity of the transactions than other outputs. Hence, the term fungibility can also be applied on the mixins, since they determine the level of anonymity gained by the users.

To increase the anonymity and mitigate the attack, we propose the use of *Input Weight* (*IW*) as one of the criterion when sampling the outputs during mixin creation. The higher the *IW* value of an output, the higher the chance of the output being a part of an attack.

Based on our evaluation, the current *IW* threshold to distinguish between "normal transactions" and "suspicious transactions" is seven. It is also possible that the threshold is changed due to changes in the system, specifically when the number of RingCT outputs increases or the mandatory ring size increases. The rule for determining the threshold is that the lower the threshold, the lower the risk would be.

6 Leveraging Monero UPID

6.1 Overview

The unencrypted Payment ID (UPID) poses an anonymity problem, where an observer can easily collect the information from the public blockchain and decode the message.

A user investigated Monero payments associated to TheShadowBroker, a hacking group that wanted to auction their secret information gained unlawfully. The investigation managed to collect email addresses of TheShadowBrokers' clients [19].

By using the similar technique, we evaluated the use of UPID in relation to the users' anonymity. The UPID is optional; hence, it is not commonly used if it is not mandatory. A user uses the same UPID to be included in multiple transactions when sending payments to the same merchant. Therefore, we assume that transactions using the same UPID are sent by the same sender to the same receiver.

Based on the above scenario, if a user uses a UPID in a transaction and creates a second transaction including same UPID which includes the outputs from the first transaction to the input mixins, then it is likely that these outputs are the outputs being spent by the latter transaction. The scheme might be possible, since the reused outputs are the change money. The change money is not transferred to the receiver and returned back to the sender's address. The scenario is described in Fig. 5.

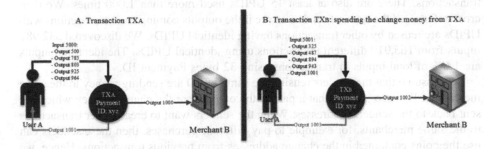

Fig. 5. User A reusing the change money from the previous transaction in a new transaction. Both transactions are sent to the same merchant. Note "Output 1001" of TX$_A$ from diagram A is included in "Input 5001" in TX$_B$.

6.2 Results

We collected the transaction data from Monero blockchain and extracted the information into a relational database. The number of transactions using Payment ID is significant, that more than half of the transactions ever recorded in the Monero blockchain are using Payment IDs, as shown in Fig. 6.

From the genesis block up to block 1,535,607 (timestamped on 22 March 2018), we found 2,584,535 non-coinbase transactions (containing 23,108,911 inputs). Within the result, there are 1,033,891 transactions (containing 12,383,714 inputs) using UPIDs and 420,153 transactions using EPIDs.

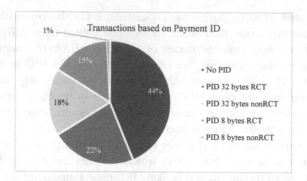

Fig. 6. The transaction percentages based on Payment ID

We further investigated the transactions using UPID and managed to cluster the data based on the UPID reuse. There are 338,318 unique UPIDs found within the 1,033,891 transactions. There are also at least 15 UPIDs used more than 1,000 times. We then cross-referenced the transaction data to see if the outputs coming from transactions with UPIDs are reused by other transactions having identical UPIDs. We discovered 332,987 inputs from 165,919 different transactions using identical UPIDs. The identified inputs are 1.6% of total inputs in transactions using 32 bytes Payment ID.

We assume that the senders reusing the same UPID are sending money to the same merchants. We also assume that a part of the outputs are the change money which are sent back to the senders' addresses. When the senders want to create other transactions to the same merchants, for example to pay different purchases, then these senders can use the coins contained in the change addresses from previous transactions. Hence, we conclude that these outputs are being spent by the new transactions.

We investigated a number of cryptocurrency exchanges supporting Monero as one of their tradeable assets, such as HitBTC, Binance, Bitfinex, Poloniex, and Kraken. Based on information in Coinmarketcap.com, these cryptocurrency exchanges hold significant Monero trading volumes among other trading platforms.

Table 3. A list of trading platforms and their Payment ID details

No.	Platform	Trading Volume[3]	Payment ID[4]	User can create a new deposit address or a new payment ID
1	HitBTC	37.68%	EPID	No
2	Binance	16.67%	UPID	No
3	Bitfinex	13.84%	UPID	Yes
4	Poloniex	6.56%	EPID	No
5	Kraken	6.23%	EPID	Yes
6	Livecoin	3.82%	UPID	No

Table 3 shows that there are three cryptocurrency exchanges using UPID, namely Binance, Bitfinex, and Poloniex. We can determine that Binance and Livecoin users will always have the same UPID for the same user, while Bitfinex is using the UPID but provides a feature where the users can regenerate the addresses and UPID by themselves.

Repeated transactions are likely to be created by the trading platforms or cryptocurrency exchange users, since the main function of cryptocurrencies such as Bitcoin nowadays are tradeable assets rather than as a payment method [20]. Repeated deposits to the trading platforms are also possible, for example sending mining rewards directly from a mining pool to the miners' accounts in cryptocurrency markets.

Cryptocurrency trading platforms rely on the Payment ID to identify the customers' deposit as it is infeasible to distinguish the correct Monero transactions belonging to different customers. As their platforms may receive thousands of Monero deposits per day, the Payment ID is useful to automate the identification process, which will credit the correct customers' accounts with the correct amount of coins they transferred.

6.3   Possible Countermeasure: Encrypted Payment ID

We have presented a case where using the same UPID can be harmful to the users' anonymity, where an attacker is able to determine the real outputs spent by the transactions. The UPID is still widely used by cryptocurrency trading platforms.

To mitigate the problem, the UPID should no longer be used, and the merchants are urged modify their system to support the EPID. By using the EPID, the users' deposits can still be determined, hence there is no change in the merchants' business process that the correct accounts can be credited based on the payments received.

7   Conclusion and Future Works

In this research, we propose a mitigation strategy of an existing attack in [6]. Then, we formulate an extension of the attack, where the improvement of the new attack makes the previous mitigation method obsolete. By using distinguishable features we found in the transactions, we propose a simple approach yet effective as one of the considerations during the mixin sampling protocols.

We also propose a second anonymity reduction attack by exploring the use of Payment ID. The Payment ID is a common method being used by Monero merchants to distinguish payments from different users. We found that transactions having the same UPID is closely linked, such that at least 1.6% of the inputs are traceable.

For future works, we plan to implement the proposed mitigation strategies in a working system. The hardened system contains all standard anonymity features such as traceable ring signature and one-time public key, including mitigation strategies as we have proposed in the paper. Then, we will analyse the impact of the newly created

---

[3] The information is taken from Coinmarketcap.com on 4 April 2018. The value of trading volume is calculated by summarizing all trading pair volumes.

[4] The information is taken from the platforms on 4 April 2018.

wallet into the anonymity of the users and to evaluate whether new attack methods can be developed.

References

1. Nakamoto, S.: Bitcoin: A Peer-To-Peer Electronic Cash System (2008)
2. van Saberhagen, N.: Cryptonote v 2.0 (2013)
3. Meiklejohn, S., et al.: A Fistful of Bitcoins: Characterizing Payments Among Men with No Names. USENIX; login (2013)
4. Reid, F., Harrigan, M.: An analysis of anonymity in the bitcoin system. In: Altshuler, Y., Elovici, Y., Cremers, A., Aharony, N., Pentland, A. (eds.) Security and Privacy in Social Networks. Springer, New York (2013). https://doi.org/10.1007/978-1-4614-4139-7_10
5. Ron, D., Shamir, A.: Quantitative analysis of the full bitcoin transaction graph. In: Sadeghi, A.-R. (ed.) FC 2013. LNCS, vol. 7859, pp. 6–24. Springer, Heidelberg (2013). https://doi.org/10.1007/978-3-642-39884-1_2
6. Wijaya, D.A., Liu, J., Steinfeld, R., Liu, D.: Monero Ring Attack: Recreating Zero Mixin Transaction Effect. Cryptology ePrint Archive (2018)
7. Kumar, A., Fischer, C., Tople, S., Saxena, P.: A traceability analysis of monero's blockchain. In: IACR Cryptology ePrint Archive 2017, p. 338 (2017)
8. Miller, A., Möser, M., Lee, K., Narayanan, A.: An Empirical Analysis of Linkability in the Monero Blockchain. arXiv preprint arXiv:1704.04299 (2017)
9. Noether, S., Noether, S., Mackenzie, A.: MRL-0001: A note on chain reactions in traceability in cryptonote 2.0. Technical report (2014)
10. Fujisaki, E., Suzuki, K.: Traceable ring signature. In: Okamoto, T., Wang, X. (eds.) PKC 2007. LNCS, vol. 4450, pp. 181–200. Springer, Heidelberg (2007). https://doi.org/10.1007/978-3-540-71677-8_13
11. Liu, J.K., Wei, V.K., Wong, D.S.: Linkable spontaneous anonymous group signature for ad hoc groups. In: Wang, H., Pieprzyk, J., Varadharajan, V. (eds.) ACISP 2004. LNCS, vol. 3108, pp. 325–335. Springer, Heidelberg (2004). https://doi.org/10.1007/978-3-540-27800-9_28
12. Noether, S., Mackenzie, A.: Ring confidential transactions. Ledger 1, 1–18 (2016)
13. Maxwell, G.: Confidential Transactions (2015)
14. Getmonero. https://getmonero.org/resources/moneropedia/ringCT.html
15. Bitcoin BIP. https://github.com/bitcoin/bips/blob/master/bip-0032.mediawiki
16. Noether, S., Goodell, B.: An Efficient Implementation of Monero Subaddresses (2017)
17. Getmonero. https://getmonero.org/resources/moneropedia/paymentid.html
18. Getmonero. https://getmonero.org/resources/moneropedia/fungibility.html
19. Steemit.   https://steemit.com/shadowbrokers/@wh1sks/theshadowbrokers-may-have-received-up-to-1500-monero-usd66-000-from-their-june-monthly-dump-service
20. Glaser, F., Zimmermann, K., Haferkorn, M., Weber, M.C., Siering, M.: Bitcoin - asset or currency? Revealing users' hidden intentions. In: Twenty Second European Conference on Information Systems (2014)

Analysis of Variance of Graph-Clique Mining for Scalable Proof of Work

Hiroaki Anada[1], Tomohiro Matsushima[2], Chunhua Su[3(✉)], Weizhi Meng[4], Junpei Kawamoto[2], Samiran Bag[5], and Kouichi Sakurai[2]

[1] Department of Information Security, University of Nagasaki, Nagasaki, Japan
anada@sun.ac.jp
[2] Department of Informatics, Graduate School and Faculty of Information Science and Electrical Engineering, Kyushu University, Fukuoka, Japan
sakurai@inf.kyushu-u.ac.jp
[3] Division of Computer Science, University of Aizu, Aizuwakamatsu, Japan
chsu@u-aizu.ac.jp
[4] Department of Applied Mathematics and Computer Science, Technical University of Denmark, Kongens Lyngby, Denmark
weme@dtu.dk
[5] School of Computing Science, Newcastle University, Newcastle upon Tyne, UK
samiran.bag@ncl.ac.uk

Abstract. Recently, Bitcoin is becoming one of the most popular decentralized cryptographic currency technologies, and Bitcoin mining is a process of adding transaction records to Bitcoin's public ledger of past transactions or blockchain. To obtain a bitcoin, the mining process involves compiling recent transactions into blocks and trying to solve a computationally difficult puzzle, e.g., proof of work puzzle. A proof of work allows miners the ability to quantify how much work a given proof contains. Basically, the required time for mining is decided in advance, but problems will occur if the value is large for dispersion. In this paper, we first accept that the required time between consecutive blocks follows the exponential distribution. That is, the variance is stable as long as the expected time is fixed. Then, we focus on the graph clique mining technique proposed by the literature, like Tromp (BITCOIN 2015) and Bag-Ruj-Sakurai (Inscrypt 2015), which is based on a computational difficulty problem of searching cliques of undirected graphs, where a clique is a subset of vertices. In particular, when the clique size is two, graph clique mining can be used to gain Bitcoins. The previous work also claimed that if the clique size is parameterized and increased, even if the expected time is fixed, the variance would not be stable. However, no qualitative or quantitative results were given to support their claim. Motivated by this issue, in this work, we propose a simple search algorithm for graph cliques mining, and perform a small scale evaluation on Bitcoin and Graph cliques's solo mining to investigate the variance issue.

Keywords: Blockchain · Proof of work · Graph-Clique Mining · Bitcoin · Mining competition

© Springer Nature Switzerland AG 2019
F. Guo et al. (Eds.): Inscrypt 2018, LNCS 11449, pp. 101–114, 2019.
https://doi.org/10.1007/978-3-030-14234-6_6

1   Introduction

Before the year of 2009, currency transactions were conducted through trusted third parties such as banks and credit card companies, but Bitcoin [11], one cryptographic currency released in 2009, allows a decentralized digital currency without a central bank or single administrator. Bitcoin system guarantees the legitimacy of a transaction without requiring a trusted agency. Transactions are verified by network nodes through cryptography and recorded in a public distributed ledger called a blockchain. It is regarded as an open ledger that epitomizes a general consensus among the online participants with respect to historicity of all validly executed transactions over the Bitcoin network. A newly constructed block gets appended to the already existing block chain after an approximately constant time interval (e.g., 10 min) [1,14].

A proof of work (PoW) in the context of blockchain is a piece of data that is difficult to generate due to the cost and time-consumption, but is easy for others to verify. To generate a proof of work can be a random process with a low probability, which means that many efforts should be made before a valid PoW is obtained. In particular, Bitcoin uses the Hashcash proof of work system. In order for a block to be accepted by network participants, miners must complete a proof of work that covers all of the data in the block. The difficulty of this work is adjusted so as to limit the rate at which new blocks can be generated by the network to one every 10 min. Due to the very low probability of successful generation, this makes it unpredictable which worker computer in the network will be able to generate the next block. In other words, under the incentive of getting a bitcoin reward, bitcoin miners have to repeat mining competition for each block. PoW's computational nature allows miners to quantify how much work a given proof contains.

In this paper, we consider the statistical time dispersion of mining competition in such PoW system. Regarding Bitcoin mining, the expected time required for mining is decided as 10 min in advance. However, an extremely lucky miner may finish the mining competition in a short time, i.e., much shorter than the expected time, or an extremely unlucky miner may take a longer time while cannot find any. The difficulty is expected to rise with the popularity of Bitcoin, but the following three problems would occur [9,12].

1. It is known that the utility of money is concave. Thus, the time variance in the supply of money would result in the difficulty of finance management (or plans) and the decrease of a person's utility.
2. Bitcoin blocks are not published at fixed time intervals, but are randomly found in a Poisson process. As payment is not made regularly, it is technically difficult to validate whether all systems are working properly.
3. The Bitcoin model differs from the mint model in a sense that it uses a finality confirmation structure via mining competition. That is, a high time dispersion may cause much stress among all mining participants.

Regard the convenience and security of a virtual currency network, it is desirable that the time variance required for mining is small enough according to the above three issues. However, in Bitcoin's PoW system, by given a hash value, we have to find the input of a hash function where the size of the problem space is constant irrespective of the number of trials. The time distribution required for mining can be regarded as an exponential distribution, so that the time dispersion depends only on the expected time required for mining. In the context of Bitcoin, this can be considered as one of the important tasks to make the time dispersion scalable, by properly setting it to a (desirable) small value that is as small as possible [9,12].

In the literature, the proof-of-work algorithms proposed by Bag et al. [2] and Tromp [15] are based on a computationally difficult problem of searching cliques in an undirected graph, where a clique is a subset of fully connected vertices. It is worth noting that the problem of searching for a clique of the specified number of vertices (size) is NP complete [6]. In the previous study [2], they utilized the problem of finding the largest clique in a big graph as a replacement for the existing Bitcoin PoW scheme. They handled a graph having $O(2^{30})$ vertices and $O(2^{48})$ edges, which is constructed deterministically using the set of transactions executed within a certain time slot. They then proposed an enhanced algorithm to solve this PoW puzzle by doing $O(2^{80})$ hash calculations. Their scheme forces both computing power and memory of a miner. Taking the advantage of the graph clique search problem, the time variance required for mining is scalable with the size of cliques.

1.1 Our Contributions

Motivated by this challenge, in this work, we propose a simple search algorithm for graph cliques mining, and perform a small scale evaluation on both Bitcoin and Graph cliques's solo mining to investigate the variance issue. Our contributions can be summarized as follows.

- Firstly, we conduct a theoretical evaluation of solo mining. Our interest is that the graph clique mining can become a Bitcoin mining scheme when the clique size is two. Our theoretical evaluation validates this observation.
- Secondly, we propose a easy-to-use search algorithm for mining graph cliques. Although our algorithm is not performed the fastest as compared with the existing search algorithms, it is much easier to implement.
- Further, we perform an evaluation to test the performance of our algorithm in the context of Bitcoin, i.e., exploring graph cliques via solo mining and investigating the variance issue.

1.2 The Organization of This Paper

In Sect. 2, we introduce the notation and primitives used in this paper, including hash function, Bitcoin mining technique [11], and various mining approaches, i.e., solo mining and pooled mining. In Sect. 3, we conduct a theoretical analysis on solo mining time in Bitcoin, based on the existing research [8,12]. In Sect. 4, we analyze the existing studies on graph clique mining like [2], discuss the mining time variance compared to Bitcoin, and perform an evaluation on Bitcoin solo mining and Graph cliques's solo mining.

Finally, we conclude this work with future directions in Sect. 5.

2   Preliminaries

In this section, we introduce the notations used in this paper, and summarize key requirements for cryptographic hash functions. Then, we make a brief introduction on Bitcoin mining [11], two mining ways of solo mining and pooled mining [12], as well as mining competition.

Bitcoin is a decentralized cash system that does not depend on a centralized server. The corresponding public key can be used to publicly verify the authenticity of the transaction. The process of Bitcoin mining involves compiling recent transactions into blocks and trying to solve a computationally difficult puzzle [11]. Bitcoin network maintains a publicly auditable ledger called Bitcoin block chain that is aimed at preventing double spending of Bitcoins. A Bitcoin block is constructed by users called miners and it requires one to execute a nontrivial amount of computation.

For an undirected graph with a finite number of vertices, a clique is a complete subgraph of a graph. Clique problem involves finding two types of cliques: maximal clique and maximum clique. The former is one that cannot be extended to form a clique of bigger size, while the latter is a clique that has the size equal to that of the largest clique in the same graph. Clique problem is defined as the problem of finding the largest clique in a graph or listing all maximal cliques in the graph. When the number of vertices is k, we say it is a clique of size k or a k-clique. When a finite number of vertices is given, the problem of searching for one clique of size k can be known as 'k-clique search problem'.

Solo mining refers to the process of calculating hashes individually, in order to find a valid block whose reward will be paid entirely to the person in ownership of the hashing computer. Pooled mining refers to a joint effort between several miners to work on finding blocks together, and split the rewards among the participants in proportion to their contribution.

2.1   Cryptographic Hash Function

The cryptographic hash function is a function H that takes an input of an arbitrary-length message and outputs a fixed length bit string, which is called 'hash value'. It has the following three major features:

1. *Pre-image resistance.* When the value h is given, finding the input m such that $h = H(m)$ is computationally difficult.
2. *Second pre-image resistance.* Given an input m_1, it should be difficult to find a different input m_2 such that $H(m_1) = H(m_2)$. Hash functions are vulnerable to second-preimage attacks without this property.

3. *Collision resistance.* It should be difficult to find two different messages m_1 and m_2 such that $H(m_1) = H(m_2)$. Such a pair is called a cryptographic hash collision. To defend against birthday attacks, strong collision resistance is desirable, which requires a hash value at least twice as long as that required for pre-image resistance.

At the analysis in Sect. 2.3, we assume that the hash function H is a random oracle.

2.2   Background on Bitcoin Mining

Bitcoin mining used in this paper refers to how to search for a hash value in relation to Bitcoin transactions described in the original paper [11].

In particular, Bitcoin's network has a timestamp server, which is responsible for hashing the data (e.g., transaction information) to be time-stamped using the SHA-256 algorithm and broadcasting the hash value throughout the network. Bitcoin mining is intentionally designed to be resource-intensive and difficult, so that the number of blocks found each day by miners remains steady. Individual blocks must contain a proof of work to be considered valid. The mining process requires miners to perform competitive computation in finding a solution for a puzzle, based on the broadcasted hash value. The primary purpose of mining is to allow Bitcoin nodes to reach a secure, tamper-resistant consensus. Bitcoin mining is difficult because the SHA-256 hash of a block's header must be lower than or equal to the target in order for the block to be accepted.

To obtain a Bitcoin, miners have to search for a *nonce* (described later) that satisfies a condition, and if they find the correct solution, then they have to broadcast that *nonce* and the solution to the whole network. Only by doing this, a miner can become the winner of the computational competition. In other words, miners perform some computation on the data, and then send the timing data to the time stamp server. This is required by the server to decide who found the solution *nonce* first. It should be noted that the time consumption of propagating *nonce* to the entire computer network is much shorter than the time consumption for completing a mining process. Due to this, the required time for propagation can be neglected.

In the mining process, we have two types of data: the data in a blockchain include all received transactions up to now; and the data of transaction information from the last time-stamp to the next received time-stamp. The use of timestamp is to prove that the existence of transaction at the time when the transaction is timestamped. To obtain a reward, a miner has to concatenate *nonce* to these two values, perform a hash calculation, and search for a *nonce* that can make the hash value less than or equal to a predetermined threshold. Assume that the hash value of an agreed blockchain is B, and the data of all the transaction histories are T. Let D denote the value determined from the adjustment of the mining difficulty. Then the goal of mining process is to search for a *nonce* (a string) that can satisfy the following conditional expression (the concatenation of the string a and b is written as $a \parallel b$).

$$H(B \parallel T \parallel nonce) < D. \tag{1}$$

2.3 Mining Ways and Competition

There are two major mining ways [12]: solo mining and pooled mining. Solo mining is a solo process where a miner completely does his task of mining operations without joining a pool. These blocks are mined and generated in a way to the task completed by the miner's credit. In contrast, pooled mining refers to a scenario that most miners do the mining in pools, which is the pooling of resources by miners, who share their processing power over a network, to split the reward equally, according to the amount of work they contributed to the probability of finding a valid block.

On the other hand, the mining process consists in repeatedly computing hashes of variants of a data structure called a block header, until one is found whose numerical value is low enough. When this happens, it allows releasing a valid block, for which the miner is rewarded with bitcoins in an amount (known as mining competition). To be a winner, miners have to solve the above computational problem (1), which allows them to chain together blocks of transactions.

A graph is a set of vertices V and set of edges $E(\subset V \times V)$, which can be determined by (V, E). In this paper, we denote the number of vertices $|V|$ as N. Thus, a subset C of V is a clique of size k if $|C| = k$ and for any $(v_1, v_2) \in C \times C$ s.t. $v_1 \neq v_2$, $(v_1, v_2) \in E$ holds.

In our paper, we use the random graphs proposed in [4]. If we set a constant number $0 \leq p \leq 1$, then the probability $\Pr[(v_1, v_2) \in E]$ is p, which determines the probability of $(v_1, v_2) \in V \times V$ being an edge. Note that the coin tossings are independent of each other in repeated trials (the probability of becoming "head" is p). A random graph determined by (N, p) is written as $\mathcal{G}_{N,p}$. For all cliques of $\mathcal{G}_{N,p}$, let $Z(\mathcal{G}_{N,p})$ be the maximum value of the clique size. According to the previous study [7], the asymptotic behavior of $Z(\mathcal{G}_{N,p})$ can be represented as follows.

$$Z(\mathcal{G}_{N,p}) = \frac{2 \log_e N}{\log_e (1/p)} + O(\log_e n).$$

Furthermore, according to the work [10], given a value of k, the probability $\Pr[Z(\mathcal{G}_{N,p}) \geq k]$ can be evaluated by combinatorics. For example, we have:

$$\Pr[Z(10^{10}, 0.25) = 30] > 0.9997.$$

As mentioned earlier, it is worth noting that the problem of searching for a clique of the specified number of vertices (size) is NP complete [6]. Based on these facts, Bag et al. [2] advised to use the maximum clique search problem for mining against the random graph $\mathcal{G}_{N,p}$, which can be determined from the transaction history decisively. However, in fact, we estimate the value k of $Z(\mathcal{G}_{N,p})$ in advance for the random graph $\mathcal{G}_{N,p}$, and prefix k-clique search problem. In particular, we adopt the following value for k in this work.

$$k := \frac{2 \log_e N}{\log_e(1/p)}.$$

Then, it is important to know how to determine the number of vertices and edges of the graph. In this work, we denote the number of vertices as $N := |V|$, where $N = 2^n$ (power of 2) for benefiting bit shift. For the purpose of replacing Bitcoin's proof of work $n = 30$, $N = 2^{30}$ is appropriate according to the work [2]. Another issue is how to define the sides, we assume that a set of transaction histories that a miner wishes to capture is $\{T_s; s = 0, \ldots, N_t - 1\}$, and denote the order number of the transaction history as $N_t = 2^\nu$ (the power of 2).

For the purpose of positioning it as generalization of Bitcoin mining using graph clique, we should slightly change the way of setting sides. First of all, for N vertices, adding an integer value v_l to each vertex as follows.

$$v_l \overset{\text{def}}{=} (T_{l/2^{n-\nu}} \cdot 2^{n-\nu}) \parallel (l \% 2^{n-\nu}),$$
$$l = 0, \ldots, N - 1.$$

As an example, if $n = 4$ and $\nu = 2$, the number of vertices is $N = 16$ and the number of transaction histories is $N_t = 4$. For $\{v_l; l = 0, \ldots, N - 1\}$, we determine the edges in the adjacency matrix $A = (A_{i,j})_{0 \leq i,j < N}$ as follows.

$$A_{i,j} \overset{\text{def}}{=} \begin{cases} 0 \text{ if } i = j, \\ 1 \text{ if } H(v_i \parallel v_j) = (0^m \parallel x), \\ 0 \text{ otherwise,} \end{cases} \quad 0 \leq i \leq j < N,$$

$$A_{i,j} \overset{\text{def}}{=} A_{j,i}, \qquad\qquad 0 \leq j < i < N.$$

Here, $0^m \parallel x$ represents the concatenation of m 'zero' strings and arbitrary string x, and m is a parameter. According to the work [2], we set $m = 12$ for $n = 30$. Viewing the hash function H to be a random oracle, the parameter p is estimated as follows.

$$p = 2^{-m}.$$

In the mining in $\mathcal{G}_{N,p}$, the miner has to find a solution for the clique search problem. The solution denotes a submatrix of the adjacency matrix A, at which all the components are 1. The miner sets the already agreed hash value as B, the transactions as $T := T_0 \parallel \cdots \parallel T_{N_t-1}$, and the solution as a string $clique$. Then we have the following value as the next agreed hash value that should be included in the blockchain.

$$H(B \parallel T \parallel clique). \tag{2}$$

As a result, the above graph clique mining process can be regarded as Bitcoin mining, if we assume that $n = 256$ (means the bit length of SHA-256's end region) and $k = 2$.

3   Our Analysis of Bitcoin Mining Time

In this section, we review the existing studies [3,8,12] regarding the probability distribution of time interval, which the winner of the mining competition follows during Bitcoin mining.

3.1   Bitcoin Solo Mining Time: Exponential Distribution

In Bitcoin solo mining, a miner's evaluation of each *nonce* (Expression (1)) does not use the evaluation results before the evaluation (i.e. memoryless trials [12]). Hence we stand on the following assumption.

– A miner samples *nonce* uniformly at random every time.

According to the general theory of probability distribution, memoryless continuous probability distribution is limited to the exponential distribution [5]. In the following discussion, we show this derivation briefly (for details, see [16], etc.). When Δx is sufficiently small, the probability of occurrence of an event between time x and $x + \Delta x$, which is denoted by $P(x \leq t \leq x + \Delta x)$, can be obtained by the definition of the probability density function $f(x)$:

$$P(x \leq t \leq x + \Delta x) = f(x)\Delta x. \tag{3}$$

On the other hand, the same probability is described in another way by the above assumption as

(the probability that the event does not occur until a time x) (4)

$\times$(the probability that the event occurs between x and $x + \Delta x$) (5)

That is,

$$P(x \leq t \leq x + \Delta x) = (1 - \int_0^x f(t)dt) \times \lambda\Delta x, \tag{6}$$

where λ denotes the average number of occurrence in the Bernoulli trials per a unit time, which is a constant. Note here that, due to the above assumption, the second factor $\lambda\Delta x$ does not depend on x.

Therefore, we obtain the following integral equation:

$$f(x) = \lambda - \lambda \int_0^x f(t)dt$$

We then differentiate these two sides and solve the differential equation. The solution is the following function.

$$f(x) = \lambda e^{-\lambda x}. \tag{7}$$

This is an exponential function. That is, the probability density function is limited to the probability density function of the exponential distribution (7).

In terms of the above ground-truth, from the point at which the winner appears in the i-th slot of Bitcoin mining competition, the time interval x_i until the next winner appears in the $i+1$-th slot of Bitcoin mining competition should follow the exponential distribution [12]. That is, if set the time interval $x_i, i = 1, 2, \ldots$, to be handled by the random variable X, then X follows the exponential distribution. Also, $(X_i)_{i=1,2,\ldots}$ becomes a Poisson process when we treat x_i as probabilistic variable X_i [8,12]. Some studies based on actual data like [3] indicate that the time for solo mining in Bitcoin follows the exponential distribution.

3.2   Bitcoin Mining Time Variance

In the exponential distribution (7) of X, the expected value is $E_f(X) = 1/\lambda$ and the variance is $V_f(X) = 1/\lambda^2$. Therefore, if we set the difficulty level D (Expression (1)), then the expected value is set as $1/\lambda$. By performing adjustment which is the case for Bitcoin, the expected value $1/\lambda = 10[\min]$, and therefore the variance must be $1/\lambda^2 = 100[\min^2]$ (standard deviation is therefore $1/\lambda = 10[\min]$) .

Hence, for Bitcoin mining, as long as the expected time is fixed, there might be a problem that the variance cannot be reduced, as we mentioned in Introduction.

3.3   Bitcoin Mining Time: Relationship with Geometric Distribution

The exponential distribution is a type of continuous probability distribution, and the geometric distribution is type of discrete probability distribution, while these two can become equivalent via conversion (see an example in [13]). In general, the probability mass function $f(i)$ of a geometric distribution can be determined by one parameter p, $0 \leq p \leq 1$, as below.

$$f(i) = (1 - p)^{i-1}p. \tag{8}$$

We denote the random variable that follows the geometric distribution as Y, and we denote the expected value as $E_f(Y) =: \mu$. Then, the variance is represented as $V_f(Y) = \sigma^2 = \mu^2 - \mu$.

4   Our Experimental Analysis of Graph Clique Mining Time

In this section, we try to analyze the probability distribution for the graph clique mining, where the time interval at which the winner of the mining competition should follow.

4.1   Graph Clique/ Solo Mining Time

In the case of graph clique solo mining, Expression (6) established by Bitcoin solo mining does not hold anymore. This is because the probability multiplication factor (5) would not be $\lambda \Delta x$ in Expression (6) anymore.

4.2 Time Variance of Graph Creek Mining

In the previous study [2], they set the number of vertices to be constant (under the parameter settings), and the graph's edges is subjected to the clique search and the transaction history. If an efficient algorithm is available for searching cliques, then the problem space can become smaller. This is because the vertex out of any clique becomes known in the process of searching the clique. Therefore, in the graph clique search problem, the time variance required for mining is expected to be smaller than that required for Bitcoin.

4.3 Experimental Evaluation

In this section, we begin by introducing experimental results on validating the theoretical analysis of the Bitcoin solo mining and then discuss experimental results regarding the graph clique solo mining.

Table 1 describes our experimental environment with a 64-bit Linux machine. Python version 3.5 was used as the programming language for algorithm implementation. Due to the availability, we used 12 cores of CPU, but we did not particularly leverage the parallel processing capability in the evaluation. The size of available memory was 62.9 GB.

Table 1. Experimental environment and settings.

Programming language	Python 3.5
CPU	Intel Core i7-3960X
	CPU3.30GHz×12
RAM	62.9GB
OS	64bit, Linux

4.4 Experiments on Bitcoin Solo Mining and Results

Algorithm for Bitcoin Solo Mining. The algorithm used to evaluate the expression (1) iteratively, that is, our iterative generation of *nonce*, was to use the random function provided by Python 3.5 with the time as a seed.

For Bitcoin solo mining, the hash value B is fixed, and the data T is set to the value of the random function (seeding time). In addition, we set the value D specified for mining difficulty adjustment to 2^{228} (SHA-256 hash value, leading 28 bits is 0). The number of trials to find *nonce* should satisfy the expression (1) (the number of trials is to find a solution for different T) was set to 800 times (or trials).

In particular, Table 2 shows that the theoretical standard deviation can be estimated from the average value as $\sqrt{\mu^2 - \mu} = \sqrt{(538.6)^2 - 538.6} = 538.1$. It is approximately equal to $\sigma = 535.3$ (root of unbiased variance), indicating that

Table 2. Experimental results of bitcoin solo mining

Experiment number	Expected value μ[sec]	Standard deviation σ[sec]
Number 0	538.6	535.3

it follows the geometric distribution, as well as the exponential distribution (as these two can be adjusted to be equal). In addition, Fig. 1 shows the approximate shape of the exponential distribution; that is, the time consumption required by Bitcoin solo mining.

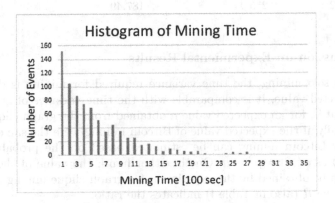

Fig. 1. Time consumption of bitcoin solo mining

4.5 Experiments on Graph Clique Solo Mining

Algorithm of graph clique solo mining. We used a naive algorithm to explore the clique search problem as below.

1. Compute the values attached to the vertex $v_l, l = 0, \ldots, N - 1$,
2. Initialize all the components $A_{i,j}$ in adjacency matrix $A = (A_{i,j})_{0 \leq i,j < N}$ with -1.
3. Search for cliques of size k; the hash value $H(v_i \parallel v_j)$ is evaluated only for $A_{i,j} = -1$.

Experimental Result. Table 3 indicates how we set parameters for the graph clique mining. The transaction history data $T_s, s = 0, \ldots, N_t - 1$ were generated by the random function (using seeding time).

In this work, we set the number of trials to find a solution (for different T_s) to 200 times. It is worth noting that the parameter value m^* (for Number 2 in Table 3) is not an integer value but a value slightly smaller than 7, calculated as $\frac{(0^6 \parallel x)_{10}}{2^{256}} < 3/2^7$. The component of the adjacency matrix is assumed to be 1 (the vertices i and j are connected by an edge). This is because if $m^* = 7$, then no solution was found in the experiment. Table 4 details our experimental results.

Table 3. Experimental parameters of graph clique solo mining

Experiment Number	n	N	ν	N_t	m	k
Number 1	14	16384	8	256	8	4
Number 2	14	16384	8	256	m^*	5

Table 4. Experimental results on graph clique solo mining

Experiment number	Expected value μ[sec]	Standard deviation σ[sec]	ratio R
Number 1	327.56	313.24	96%
Number 2	255.94	187.49	73%

4.6 Discussion on Experimental Results

For Bitcoin solo mining, the time variance required for mining is determined by the expected value. It is comparable with the time variance of graph clique mining. That is, for an expected value μ obtained from the graph clique mining experimentally, if the expected value of Bitcoin mining were the same, then the variance for Bitcoin mining can be estimated based on the probability mass function (8) as $\sigma_{\mathrm{BC}}^2 := \mu^2 - \mu$. On the other hand, the value of the unbiased variance can be obtained by the experiment for graph clique mining as σ^2. The following value R (also in Table 4) indicates the ratio.

$$R \overset{\text{def}}{=} \frac{\sigma}{\sqrt{\mu^2 - \mu}}. \tag{9}$$

In the experiment with Number 1, the ratio R_1 is computed as below.

$$R_1 = \sigma_1/\sqrt{\mu_1^2 - \mu_1}$$
$$= 313.24/\sqrt{(327.56)^2 - (327.56)}$$
$$= 0.95722 \approx 0.96.$$

For the same expected value μ_1, it is found that the difference between the standard deviation σ_1 of the graph clique mining and the standard deviation of Bitcoin mining ($\sqrt{\mu_1^2 - \mu_1}$) is $1 - 0.96 = 0.04$ (i.e. 4%).

In the experiment with Number 2, the ratio value of R_2 is computed as below.

$$R_2 = \sigma_2/\sqrt{\mu_2^2 - \mu_2}$$
$$= 187.49/\sqrt{(255.94)^2 - (255.94)}$$
$$= 0.73399 \approx 0.73.$$

Similarly, for the same expected value μ_2, the difference between the standard deviation σ_2 of the graph clique mining and the standard deviation of Bitcoin mining ($\sqrt{\mu_2^2 - \mu_2}$) is $0.73 = 0.27$ (i.e. 27%).

5   Conclusion and Future Work

In this work, we firstly conducted a theoretical analysis on Bitcoin solo mining and graph clique mining, and then proposed a simple search algorithm for graph cliques mining. We accepted that the required time between consecutive blocks follows the exponential distribution. In the evaluation, we perform a small scale evaluation on Bitcoin and graph clique solo minings to validate the correctness of our theoretical evaluation. We investigated the variance issue. It is found experimentally that the the standard deviation of unbiased variance of the graph clique mining is reduced compared with the standard deviation (dispersion) of Bitcoin mining.

In future, we plan to conduct a more complete theoretical evaluation on graph clique solo mining. We also plan to do experiments to study graph clique solo mining. In addition, we plan to compare the Bitcoin pooled mining and the graph clique-based pooled mining under various conditions.

Acknowledgement. In the first stage of this research, Hiroaki Anada, Junpei Kawamoto and Kouichi Sakurai were supported by JSPS Kiban(B) JP15H02711. Hiroaki Anada, Chunhua Su and Kouichi Sakurai are supported by JSPS Kiban(B) JP18H03240. Chunhua Su is also supported by JSPS Kiban(C) JP18K11298. Samiran Bag is supported by the ERC starting grant, no. 306994. The authors would like to thank all anonymous reviewers for their insightful comments and suggestions.

References

1. Antonopoulos, A.M.: Mastering Bitcoin: Unlocking Digital Crypto-Currencies, 1st edn. O'Reilly Media Inc., Sebastopol (2014)
2. Bag, S., Ruj, S., Sakurai, K.: On the application of clique problem for proof-of-work in cryptocurrencies. In: Lin, D., Wang, X.F., Yung, M. (eds.) Inscrypt 2015. LNCS, vol. 9589, pp. 260–279. Springer, Cham (2016). https://doi.org/10.1007/978-3-319-38898-4_16
3. Bitcoinwiki: Confirmation. https://en.bitcoin.it/wiki/Confirmation. Accessed 15 Dec 2016
4. Erdős, P., Renyi, A.: On the evolution of random graphs. In: Publication of the Mathematical Institute of the Hungarian Academy of Sciences, pp. 17–61 (1960)
5. Feller, W.: An Introduction to Probability Theory and Its Applications, vol. 1. Wiley, York (1968)
6. Garey, M.R., Johnson, D.S.: Computers and Intractability: A Guide to the Theory of NP-Completeness. W. H. Freeman & Co., New York (1979)
7. Grimmett, G.R., McDiarmid, C.J.H.: On colouring random graphs. Math. Proc. Cambridge Philos. Soc. **77**, 313–324 (1976)
8. Kraft, D.: Difficulty control for blockchain-based consensus systems. Peer Peer Netw. Appl. **9**(2), 397–413 (2016). https://doi.org/10.1007/s12083-015-0347-x
9. Matsushima, T., Anada, H., Kawamoto, J., Bag, S., Sakurai, K.: Evaluation of bitcoin-mining for search problem of graph cliques. In: Hinokuni Symposium on Information 2016, Miyazaki, Japan, 2–3 March 2016, p. 4B-2 (2016)
10. Matula, D.: On the complete subgraph of random graph. In: Combinatory Mathematics and Its Applications, pp. 356–369 (1970)

11. Nakamoto, S.: Bitcoin: A Peer-to-Peer Electronic Cash System (2008). http:// bitcoin.org/bitcoin.pdf
12. Rosenfeld, M.: Analysis of bitcoin pooled mining reward systems. CoRR abs/1112.4980 (2011). http://arxiv.org/abs/1112.4980
13. Saito, R.: Deriving exponential distribution from geometric distribution. http:// chianti.ucsd.edu/~rsaito/ENTRY1/WEB_RS3/PDF/JPN/Texts/half_life1_1.pdf. Accessed 15 Dec 2016
14. Swan, M.: Blockchain: Blueprint for a New Economy, 1st edn. O'Reilly Media Inc., Sebastopol (2015)
15. Tromp, J.: Cuckoo cycle: a memory bound graph-theoretic proof-of-work. In: Brenner, M., Christin, N., Johnson, B., Rohloff, K. (eds.) FC 2015. LNCS, vol. 8976, pp. 49–62. Springer, Heidelberg (2015). https://doi.org/10.1007/978-3-662-48051-9_4
16. WIKIPEDIA: Memorylessness. https://en.wikipedia.org/wiki/Memorylessness. Accessed 15 Dec 2016

Lattice-Based Cryptology

Preprocess-then-NTT Technique and Its Applications to KYBER and NEWHOPE

Shuai Zhou[1,2,3], Haiyang Xue[1,2,3], Daode Zhang[1,2,3(✉)], Kunpeng Wang[1,2,3],
Xianhui Lu[1,2,3], Bao Li[1,2,3], and Jingnan He[1,2,3]

[1] School of Cyber Security, University of Chinese Academy of Sciences,
Beijing, China
[2] Data Assurances and Communications Security, Institute of Information
Engineering, Chinese Academy of Sciences, Beijing, China
[3] State Key Laboratory of Information Security, Institute of Information
Engineering, Chinese Academy of Sciences, Beijing, China
{zhoushuai,zhangdaode}@iie.ac.cn

Abstract. The Number Theoretic Transform (NTT) provides efficient algorithm for multiplying large degree polynomials. It is commonly used in cryptographic schemes that are based on the hardness of the Ring Learning With Errors problem (RLWE), which is a popular basis for post-quantum key exchange, encryption and digital signature.

To apply NTT, modulus q should satisfy that $q \equiv 1 \mod 2n$, RLWE-based schemes have to choose an oversized modulus, which leads to excessive bandwidth. In this work, we present "Preprocess-then-NTT (PtNTT)" technique which weakens the limitation of modulus q, i.e., we only require $q \equiv 1 \mod n$ or $q \equiv 1 \mod n/2$. Based on this technique, we provide new parameter settings for KYBER and NEWHOPE (two NIST candidates). In these new schemes, we can reduce public key size and ciphertext size at a cost of very little efficiency loss.

Keywords: NTT · Preprocess-then-NTT · Kyber · NewHope ·
Ring Learning With Errors · Module Learning With Errors

1 Introduction

Fast Fourier Transform (FFT) algorithms can be applied to the efficient nega-cyclic convolution of two integer sequences of length n. When the coefficients of sequence (or polynomial) are specialized to come from a finite field, the FFT is called the Number Theoretic Transform (NTT) [11] and can be used to compute polynomial multiplication efficiently over this specific finite field. For example, when polynomials come from $\mathcal{R}_q = \mathbb{Z}_q[x]/x^n + 1$, the product corresponds to a nega-cyclic convolution of the coefficient sequences. Note that $\mathbb{Z}_q$ denotes the quotient ring $\mathbb{Z}/q\mathbb{Z}$ of the rational integers ring $\mathbb{Z}$, and $n = 2^{n'-1}$ such that $x^n + 1$ is the $2^{n'}$-th cyclotomic polynomial. In this setting, the NTT is usually computed with a special type of FFT algorithm that can be efficiently implemented when q is a prime satisfying that $q \equiv 1 \mod 2n$ [17], which in turn means that the underlying finite field contains $2n$-th roots of unity.

F. Guo et al. (Eds.): Inscrypt 2018, LNCS 11449, pp. 117–137, 2019.
https://doi.org/10.1007/978-3-030-14234-6_7

1.1   RLWE-Based Cryptography

Lattice-based cryptography has emerged as a promising candidate for public-key cryptography that is still secure after the likely advent of quantum computers. The first lattice-based encryption scheme was proposed by Ajtai and Dwork [1]. This scheme was later simplified and improved by Regev [19]. And a major achievement of Regev was the introduction of Learning With Errors problem (LWE), which was relatively simple to use in cryptographic constructions.

The LWE assumption is asymptotically at least as hard as some standard worst-case lattice problems [19]. Based on the LWE problem, Lyubashevsky et al. [18] proposed a variant of LWE over polynomial rings and showed that the variant enjoyed a worst-case hardness guarantee. The variant was defined as Ring-Learning With Errors problem (RLWE). The polynomial rings in RLWE assumption are usually defined as $\mathcal{R}_q = \mathbb{Z}_q[x]/x^n + 1$ as mentioned above. RLWE-based schemes have been proposed for public-key encryption [18], digital signatures [16] and key exchange [8]. In order to compute the multiplication of polynomials efficiently, most RLWE-based schemes invoke the NTT technique [17] which requires that q is a prime and satisfies $q \equiv 1 \mod 2n$. As a result, these schemes have higher efficiency than that without applying the NTT algorithm.

RLWE-based schemes also have some drawbacks. Stebila et al. [20] reported the performance of standalone post-quantum cryptographic operations of key exchange protocols (passively secure key encapsulation mechanisms, KEMs), as well as standard cryptographic operations for comparison. As is shown in Table 1 [20], the key exchange scheme based on RLWE assumption (NewHope) has a significant increase in running time, while its bandwidth is too large comparing with ECDH nistp256. Reducing the bandwidth (even if only a few tens of bytes) makes sense in RLWE-based post-quantum cryptographic schemes, especially in some special scenario. For example, in the wireless sensor nodes, power is very crucial factor and most of the power is due to the RF transceiver module. Thus, decreasing the bandwidth by reducing the sizes of keys and ciphertexts will be hugely beneficial in the scenario.

Table 1. Performance of standalone cryptographic operations, showing mean runtime in milliseconds of standalone cryptographic operations, communication sizes (public key messages) in bytes, and claimed security level in bits.

Scheme	Alice 0 (ms)	Bob (ms)	Alice1 (ms)	Communication (bytes)		Claimed security	
				$A \to B$	$B \to A$	Classical	Quantum
RSA 3072-bit	–	0.09	4.49	387/0*	384	128	–
ECDH nistp256	0.37	0.70	0.33	32	32	128	–
NewHope	0.11	0.16	0.03	1824	2048	229	206

1.2   Our Contribution

Because modulus q is required to satisfy that $2n|q-1$ in the NTT, RLWE-based schemes have to choose an oversized modulus, which leads to excessive bandwidth. To reduce the bandwidth of RLWE-based schemes in the case of using NTT, we present a method to preprocess the polynomials first by using a divide-and-conquer strategy, and then apply the NTT, which is called Preprocess-then-NTT (PtNTT). According to the times of preprocess, our PtNTT algorithm can be classified as 1-round PtNTT (1PtNTT) and 2-round PtNTT (2PtNTT).

Polynomial multiplication over a finite field is one of fundamental operations required in cryptographic schemes based on the RLWE problem, and NTT is commonly used in the RLWE-based schemes. So, our PtNTT can be applied to a large portion of RLWE-based schemes to reduce the value of modulus q, which will decrease the bandwidth.

1.2.1   1PtNTT and Its Application to KYBER

In 1PtNTT, we first divide the polynomial f with n coefficients into two new low-dimensional polynomials of degree $n/2$ according to the parity of index, and then apply the NTT to the two low-dimensional polynomials respectively. So, our 1PtNTT algorithm only requires that $q \equiv 1 \mod n$ instead of $q \equiv 1 \mod 2n$ in the NTT, i.e., weakens the limitation of modulus q. There exist some advantages and disadvantages of 1PtNTT compared with the NTT algorithm:

- **Advantages.** Our 1PtNTT algorithm weakens the limitation of modulus q, i.e., we require that $q \equiv 1 \mod n$ instead of $q \equiv 1 \mod 2n$ in the NTT.
- **Disadvantages.** Although our 1PtNTT algorithm is very efficient, it is still slightly less efficient than the NTT. The computational cost of 1PtNTT to compute the product of two polynomials of degree n is about 1.17 times that of the NTT algorithm.

Its Application to KYBER. According to the three parameter sets for KYBER[1] [6] which are called KYBER512-CCA-KEM, KYBER768-CCA-KEM, KYBER1024-CCA-KEM, we will give a series of new parameter settings. Because the modulus q in our schemes is smaller, we call our scheme small-KYBER, i.e., small-KYBER512-CCA-KEM, small-KYBER768-CCA-KEM, and small-KYBER1024-CCA-KEM. Comparing with the original KYBER schemes, there are some advantages and disadvantages of small-KYBER:

- **Advantages.** Because the mudulus q is smaller in small-KYBER, we can reduce both public key size and ciphertext size of schemes. More precisely,
  - In small-KYBER512-CCA-KEM, the public key size and the ciphertext size are 64 and 64 bytes respectively fewer than that of KYBER512-CCA-KEM;

---

[1] KYBER was constructed under the Module Learning With Errors (MLWE) assumption, which is a module version of the RLWE assumption.

- In small-KYBER768-CCA-KEM, the public key size and the ciphertext size are 96 and 32 bytes respectively fewer than that of KYBER768-CCA-KEM;
- In small-KYBER1024-CCA-KEM, the public key size and the ciphertext size are 128 and 128 bytes respectively fewer than that of KYBER1024-CCA-KEM.

Note that small-KYBER has a similar decryption error probability and a same security level compared with KYBER. Please see more details in Tables 4 and 5.

- **Disadvantages**. Although small-KYBER schemes have achieved high efficiency, they are slightly slower than the original KYBER schemes. For a worst case of three parameter sets, the cycle counts of "Key Generation", "Encapsulation" and "Decapsulation" in small-KYBER1024-CCA-KEM are 1.3296, 1.2856 and 1.4138 times that in KYBER1024-CCA-KEM. However, the purpose of decreasing the bandwidth is more meaningful than improving the efficiency of KYBER schemes. In small-KYBER1024-CCA-KEM, the running time of "Key Generation", "Encapsulation" and "Decapsulation" are 0.118 ms, 0.149 ms and 0.188 ms. While in KYBER1024-CCA-KEM, they are 0.089 ms, 0.116 ms and 0.133 ms. Note that, all results are obtained on a 3.3 GHz CPU. Please see more details in Table 6.

In short, we can use fewer bytes to store public keys and ciphertexts to reduce the bandwidth of schemes at a cost of very little loss of efficiency.

1.2.2 2PtNTT and Its Application to NEWHOPE

In the NEWHOPE [2], there are two parameter settings for n, i.e., $n = 512$ and $n = 1024$ respectively. Even though 1PtNTT technique can weaken the limitation of modulus q and requires that $q \equiv 1 \bmod n$, there is still no suitable prime modulus to satisfy the weakened requirement for two values of n, 512 and 1024, simultaneously. That's to say, we can not apply 1PtNTT technique to NEWHOPE schemes directly. So we propose 2PtNTT technique to address this problem.

In 2PtNTT, we first divide the polynomial f with n coefficients into two new low-dimensional polynomials of degree $n/2$ according to the parity of index, and then divide each polynomial of degree $n/2$ into two polynomials of degree $n/4$ according to the parity of index. After that, we apply the NTT to the four polynomials of degree $n/4$ respectively. So, our 2PtNTT algorithm only requires that $q \equiv 1 \bmod n/2$ instead of $q \equiv 1 \bmod 2n$ in the NTT, i.e., further weakens the limitation of modulus q. There exist some advantages and disadvantages of 2PtNTT compared with the NTT algorithm:

- **Advantages**. Our 2PtNTT algorithm weakens the limitation of modulus q, i.e., we require that $q \equiv 1 \bmod n/2$ instead of $q \equiv 1 \bmod 2n$ in the NTT.
- **Disadvantages**. Although our 2PtNTT algorithm is also efficient, it is still slightly less efficient than the NTT. The computational cost of 2PtNTT to compute the product of two polynomials of degree n is 1.25 times that of the NTT algorithm.

Its Application to NEWHOPE. According to the two parameter settings for NEWHOPE [2] which are called NEWHOPE512, NEWHOPE1024, we will give two new parameter settings. Because the modulus q in our schemes is smaller, we call our scheme small-NEWHOPE, i.e., small-NEWHOPE and small-NEWHOPE1024. Comparing with the original NEWHOPE schemes, there are some advantages and disadvantages of small-NEWHOPE:

- **Advantages.** Because the modulus q is smaller in small-NEWHOPE, we can reduce both public key size and ciphertext size of schemes. More precisely,
    - In small-NEWHOPE512-CPA-KEM, the public key size and the ciphertext size are64 and 64 bytes respectively fewer than that of NEWHOPE512-CPA-KEM;
    - In small-NEWHOPE512-CCA-KEM, the public key size and the ciphertext size are64 and 64 bytes respectively fewer than that of NEWHOPE512-CCA-KEM;
    - In small-NEWHOPE1024-CPA-KEM, the public key size and the ciphertext size are128 and 128 bytes respectively fewer than that of NEWHOPE-1024-CPA-KEM.
    - In small-NEWHOPE1024-CCA-KEM, the public key size and the ciphertext size are 128 and 128 bytes respectively fewer than that of NEWHOPE-1024-CCA-KEM.

    Note that small-NEWHOPE has a similar decryption error probability and a same security level compared with NEWHOPE. Please see more details in Tables 7 and 8.
- **Disadvantages.** Although our small-NEWHOPE schemes have achieved high efficiency, they are slightly slower than the original NEWHOPE schemes. For a worst case of two parameter settings, the cycle counts of "Key Generation", "Encapsulation" and "Decapsulation" in small-NEWHOPE1024-CCA-KEM are 1.4747, 1.6202 and 2.3130 times that in NEWHOPE1024-CCA-KEM. However, the purpose of decreasing the bandwidth is more meaningful than improving the efficiency of NEWHOPE schemes. In small-NEWHOPE1024-CCA-KEM, the running time of"Key Generation", "Encapsulation" and "Decapsulation" are 0.082 ms, 0.133 ms and 0.049 ms. While in NEWHOPE1024-CCA-KEM, they are 0.056 ms, 0.082 ms and 0.021 ms. Note that, all results are obtained on a 3.3 GHz CPU. Please see more details in Table 9.

In brief, we can use fewer bytes to store public keys and ciphertexts to reduce the bandwidth of schemes at a cost of very little loss of efficiency.

1.3 Our Technique

Because 2PtNTT is similar to 1PtNTT, in this subsection, we will only introduce one of our main techniques, 1PtNTT. Our 1PtNTT algorithm only requires that the modulus q satisfies that $q - 1$ can be divided by n, i.e., $n|(q-1)$. However, in this case, if $2n \nmid (q-1)$, we can not exploit the negative wrapped convolution [17] and this is why we need to preprocess the polynomials. Similar to the process of computing polynomial multiplication by using NTT, our 1PtNTT technique contains 2 phases: 1PtNTT and 1PtNTT^{-1}.

In 1PtNTT, we first divide the polynomial $f(x) \in \mathbb{Z}_q[x]/(x^n + 1)$ with n coefficients into two low-dimension polynomials of degree $n/2$ according to the parity of index, $f_{even}(y) \in \mathbb{Z}_q[y]/(y^{n/2} + 1)$ and $f_{odd}(y) \in \mathbb{Z}_q[y]/(y^{n/2} + 1)$, where f_{even} contains all the even-indexed coefficients of f and f_{odd} contains all the odd-indexed coefficients of f, and $y = x^2$. It is easy to see that $f(x) = f_{even}(x^2) + x \cdot f_{odd}(x^2)$. As a result, we can apply the NTT to the two low-degree polynomials. So we define $1\text{PtNTT}(f) = (\text{NTT}(f_{even}), \text{NTT}(f_{odd}))$. In order to recover f from its 1PtNTT transformed representation $\widehat{f} = (\widehat{f}_{even}, \widehat{f}_{odd})$, we define $1\text{PtNTT}^{-1}(\widehat{f}) = (\text{NTT}^{-1}(\widehat{f}_{even}), \text{NTT}^{-1}(\widehat{f}_{odd}))$. It is very obvious that the following equation $1\text{PtNTT}^{-1}(1\text{PtNTT}(f)) = (f_{even}, f_{odd}) = f$ holds.

As we all know, the NTT provides an efficient algorithm for multiplying large degree polynomials. Here comes a question how can we use 1PtNTT to compute the product of two polynomials f and g? Let y denote x^2 and let $p(x) \in \mathcal{R}_q$ denote the product of $f(x)$ and $g(x)$, then

$$p_{even}(y) = f_{even}(y) \cdot g_{even}(y) + f_{odd}(y) \cdot (y \cdot g_{odd}(y)) \in \mathbb{Z}_q[y]/(y^{n/2} + 1),$$

$$p_{odd}(y) = f_{odd}(y) \cdot g_{even}(y) + f_{even}(y) \cdot g_{odd}(y) \in \mathbb{Z}_q[y]/(y^{n/2} + 1).$$

And $p(x) = p_{even}(x^2) + x \cdot p_{odd}(x^2) \in \mathbb{Z}_q[x]/(x^n + 1)$.

If we define $\overrightarrow{g_{odd}}$ as $\left(-g_{odd}[\frac{n}{2} - 1], g_{odd}[0], g_{odd}[1], \ldots, g_{odd}[\frac{n}{2} - 2]\right)$, and a bow-tie multiplication as

$$1\text{PtNTT}(f) \bowtie 1\text{PtNTT}(g) = (\text{NTT}(f_{even}) \circ \text{NTT}(g_{even}) + \text{NTT}(f_{odd}) \circ \text{NTT}(\overrightarrow{g_{odd}}),$$
$$\text{NTT}(f_{odd}) \circ \text{NTT}(g_{even}) + \text{NTT}(f_{even}) \circ \text{NTT}(g_{odd})),$$

where $\circ$ denotes coefficient-wise multiplication. Then the following equation $p = 1\text{PtNTT}^{-1}(1\text{PtNTT}(f) \bowtie 1\text{PtNTT}(g))$ holds, which is very similar to $p = \text{NTT}^{-1}(\text{NTT}(f) \circ \text{NTT}(g))$ in the NTT algorithm.

1.4   Related Work

Inspired by KYBER [6], D'Anvers et al. [12,13] also proposed a family of cryptographic primitives, i.e., Saber which includes three IND-CCA secure KEMs LightSaber-KEM, Saber-KEM and FireSaber-KEM. Saber-KEMs have similar public key and ciphertext sizes respectively compared with our small-KYBER-KEMs. Moreover, Saber-KEMs have better efficiency than KYBER-KEMs, so it is easy to get a conclusion that Saber-KEMs are more efficient than our small-KYBER-KEMs. We emphasize that, there exist two main differences between Saber and our small-KYBER.

- In order to get rid of the constraint to modulus q caused by applying the NTT algorithm, D'Anvers et al. [12,13] invoked the Karatsuba polynomial multiplication method which does not require any special modulus. As a result, all moduli in Saber schemes are powers of 2, i.e., $q = 2^{13}$, while all moduli in our small-KYBER schemes are primes, i.e., $q = 3329$, which *might* increase confidence in security. It is more popular for constructions of schemes using prime modulus than non-prime modulus.

- Saber-KEMs rely on the hardness of the Module Learning With Rounding (MLWR) problem, while our small-KYBER-KEMs are constructed under the Module Learning With errors problem. As a result, Saber does not require sampling of error polynomials, thus saving in computation time.

1.5 Outline

The remainder of the paper is organized as follows. In Sect. 2 we review the necessary background. In Sect. 3 we present our Preprocess-then-NTT technique and describe its complexity. The applications of PtNTT to KYBER and NEWHOPE are given in Sect. 4, followed by the implementation and performance of new schemes. In Sect. 5, we give the conclusion.

2 Preliminaries

Polynomial Rings and Vectors. Let $\mathbb{Z}$ be the ring of rational integers. Let $\mathbb{Z}_q$ denote the quotient ring $\mathbb{Z}/q\mathbb{Z}$, for an integer $q \geq 1$. We denote by $\mathcal{R}$ the ring $\mathbb{Z}[x]/x^n + 1$ and by $\mathcal{R}_q$ the ring $\mathbb{Z}_q[x]/x^n + 1$, where $n = 2^{n'-1}$ such that $x^n + 1$ is the $2^{n'}$-th cyclotomic polynomial. Throughout this paper, the values of n, n' are $256, 9$, respectively. Regular font letters denote element in $\mathcal{R}_q$ and bold lower-case letters represent vectors with coefficients in $\mathcal{R}_q$. By default, all vectors will be column vectors. Bold upper-case letters are matrices.

For an element $a \in \mathcal{R}_q$, we write $a = \sum_{i=0}^{n-1} a_i x^i$, $a_i \in \mathbb{Z}_q$. We also use the same symbol a to denote the coefficient vector $a = (a_0, \ldots, a_{n-1})$. Let $a \circ b$ denote pointwise or coefficient-wise multiplication of $a, b \in \mathcal{R}_q$. For a vector $\mathbf{a}$ (or matrix $\mathbf{A}$), we denote by $\mathbf{a}^\top$ (or $\mathbf{A}^\top$) its transpose.

Sets and Distributions. For a set S, we write $s \overset{\$}{\leftarrow} S$ to denote s is chosen uniformly at random form S. In case S is a probability distribution over $\mathcal{R}$, then $x \overset{\$}{\leftarrow} S$ means the sampling of $x \in \mathcal{R}$ according to S. For a probabilistic algorithm $\mathcal{A}$ we denote by $y \leftarrow \mathcal{A}$ that the output of $\mathcal{A}$ is assigned to y and that $\mathcal{A}$ is running with randomly chosen coins. We define the centered binomial distribution ψ_η for some positive integer η as follows:

$$(a_1, \ldots, a_\eta, b_1, \ldots, b_\eta) \overset{\$}{\leftarrow} \{0, 1\}^{2\eta} \text{ and output } \Sigma_{i=1}^{\eta}(a_i - b_i).$$

The distribution ψ_η is centered (its mean is 0), has variance $\eta/2$ and gives a standard deviation of $\sqrt{\eta/2}$. The function Sam is an extendable function. If we would like Sam to take as input x and then produce a value y that is distributed according to distribution $\mathcal{S}$, we write $y \sim \mathcal{S} = \mathsf{Sam}(x)$.

Compression and Decompression. We define a function $\mathsf{Compress}_q(x,d)$ that takes an element $x \in \mathbb{Z}_q$ and outputs an integer in $\{0,1,\ldots,2^d-1\}$, where $d < \lceil \log q \rceil$. We furthermore define a function $\mathsf{Decompress}_q(x,d)$, such that $x' = \mathsf{Decompress}_q(\mathsf{Compress}_q(x,d),d)$ is an element close to x. The two functions are defined as:

$$\mathsf{Compress}_q(x,d) = \lceil (2^d/q) \cdot x \rfloor \mod 2^d;$$

$$\mathsf{Decompress}_q(x,d) = \lceil (q/2^d) \cdot x \rfloor.$$

2.1 Ring LWE and Module LWE Problems

The Learning with Errors (LWE) problem was popularized by Regev [19] who proved that, solving a random LWE instance is as hard as solving worst-case instances of certain lattice problems under a quantum reduction. Later on, Lyubashevsky, Peikert and Regev [18] proposed a variant of the LWE problem– the Ring-LWE problem which relies on module lattices, and its hardness can be related to the worst case hardness of finding short vectors in ideal lattices [18,21]. Recently, Langlois and Stehlé [15] proposed a module version of Ring-LWE, Module-LWE.

The Ring Learning with Errors Problem, Decisional Version. The decisional version of the Ring Learning with Errors problem, $\mathrm{DRLWE}_{m,q,\chi}$, with m unknowns, $m \geq 1$ samples, modulo q and error distribution χ, is defined as follows: for a uniform random secret $s \in \mathcal{R}_q$, and given m samples either all of the form $(a, b = a \cdot s + e \mod q)$ where the coefficients of e are independently sampled following the distribution χ (i.e., $e_i \xleftarrow{\$} \chi$), or from the uniform distribution $(a,b) \in \mathcal{R}_q \times \mathcal{R}_q$, decide whether the samples come from the former or the latter case.

In fact, we will use a variant of the above problem, where the secret $\mathbf{s}$ are chosen from the same distribution as the error e. This variant was proven to be equivalent to the original problem by Applebaum et al. in [5].

The Module Learning with Errors Problem, Decisional Version. The decisional version of the Module Learning with Errors problem, $\mathrm{DMLWE}_{m,q,\chi}$, consists in distinguishing m samples either all of the form $(\mathbf{a}, b = \mathbf{a}^\top \mathbf{s} + e)$ with $\mathbf{s} \xleftarrow{\$} \chi^k$ common to all samples and $e \xleftarrow{\$} \chi$ fresh for every sample, or from the uniform distribution $(\mathbf{a}, b) \in \mathcal{R}_q^k \times \mathcal{R}_q$, decide whether the samples come from the former or the latter case.

2.2 Number-Theoretic Transform

There exist many efficient algorithms in the literature to compute the multiplication of two polynomials and a survey which introduces fast multiplication algorithms can be found in [7]. In this subsection, we recall the Number Theoretic Transform (NTT) [11] which is a specialized version of the Fast Fourier Transform (FFT) where the roots of unity are taken from a finite ring instead of the complex number.

Let n be a power of 2 and q be a prime satisfying that $q \equiv 1 \mod 2n$. Let ω be an n-th primitive root of unity in $\mathbb{Z}_q$, i.e., $\omega^n \equiv 1 \mod q$. For an element $f \in \mathcal{R}_q$, the forward transformation $\hat{f} = \mathsf{NTT}(f)$ is given by $\hat{f}_i = \sum_{j=0}^{n-1} f_j \cdot \omega^{ij} \mod q$ and the inverse transformation $f = \mathsf{NTT}^{-1}(\hat{f})$ is defined by $f_i = n^{-1} \sum_{j=0}^{n-1} \hat{f}_j \cdot \omega^{-ij} \mod q$, where $i = 0, \dots, n-1$. The following equation $\mathsf{NTT}^{-1}(\mathsf{NTT}(f)) = f$ holds.

Because applying the above NTT transform provides a cyclic convolution, computing $p = f \cdot g \mod x^n + 1$ with two polynomials f, g would require applying the NTT of length $2n$ and thus should append n zeros to each input. This effectively doubles the length of the inputs and also requires the computation of an explicit reduction modulo $x^n + 1$. In order to avoid this issue, Lyubashevsky et al. [17] introduced the negative wrapped convolution: let γ be a $2n$-th primitive root of unity such that $\gamma = \sqrt{\omega} \mod q$. Define $\tilde{f} = (f_0, \gamma f_1, \dots, \gamma^{n-1} f_{n-1})$ and $\tilde{g} = (g_0, \gamma g_1, \dots, \gamma^{n-1} g_{n-1})$, then the negative wrapped convolution of f, g is given by $p = (1, \gamma, \dots, \gamma^{n-1}) \circ \mathsf{NTT}^{-1}(\mathsf{NTT}(\tilde{f}) \circ \mathsf{NTT}(\tilde{g}))$. This operation satisfies $p = f \cdot g$ in $\mathcal{R}_q$ and implicitly includes the reduction modulo $x^n + 1$ without increasing the length of the inputs. More precisely, for a polynomial $f \in \mathcal{R}_q$, we define its forward transformation $\hat{f} = \mathsf{NTT}(f)$ with $\hat{f}_i = \sum_{j=0}^{n-1} \gamma^j f_j \cdot \omega^{ij} \mod q$ and its inverse transformation $f = \mathsf{NTT}^{-1}(\hat{f})$ with $f_i = n^{-1} \gamma^{-i} \sum_{j=0}^{n-1} \hat{f}_j \cdot \omega^{-ij} \mod q$. Using NTT and NTT^{-1}, we can compute the product $f \cdot g$ very efficiently as $p = \mathsf{NTT}^{-1}(\mathsf{NTT}(f) \circ \mathsf{NTT}(g))$.

The computational cost of a forward NTT transformation NTT is determined by a function $T(n) = n \log n$ in [10]. By comparing the definitions of NTT and NTT^{-1}, we see that by modifying the NTT algorithm to switch the roles of f and $\hat{f}$, replace ω by ω^{-1}, and divide each element of the result by n, we can compute the inverse transformation NTT^{-1}. So the computational cost of an inverse NTT transformation NTT^{-1} is same as that of its forward NTT transformation NTT, i.e., $T(n) = n \log n$. If we use NTT to compute the multiplication of two polynomials, the total computation includes two forward NTT transformations, one point-wise multiplication of degree bounded by n and one inverse NTT transformation. Obviously, the computational cost of multiplication by using NTT is $T_1(n) = 3n \log n + n$.

3   1-Round Preprocess-then-NTT (1PtNTT)

In 1PtNTT algorithm, we only require that modulus q satisfies that $q - 1$ can be divided by n, i.e., $n \mid (q - 1)$. However, in this case, we can not exploit the negative wrapped convolution [17] if $2n \nmid (q - 1)$, because there does not exist any $2n$-th root of unity in $\mathbb{Z}_q$.

Our 1-round preprocess-then-NTT technique employs a divide-and-conquer strategy, using the even-indexed and odd-indexed coefficients of $f(x) \in \mathbb{Z}_q[x]/(x^n + 1)$ separately to define two new polynomials $f_{even}(y)$ and $f_{odd}(y)$

whose degrees are bounded by $\frac{n}{2}$:

$$f_{even}(y) = f_0 + f_2 \cdot y + f_4 \cdot y^2 + \cdots + f_{n-2} \cdot y^{n/2-1} \in \mathbb{Z}_q[y]/(y^{n/2} + 1),$$
$$f_{odd}(y) = f_1 + f_3 \cdot y + f_5 \cdot y^2 + \cdots + f_{n-1} \cdot y^{n/2-1} \in \mathbb{Z}_q[y]/(y^{n/2} + 1).$$

It follows that

$$f(x) = f_{even}(x^2) + x \cdot f_{odd}(x^2) \in \mathbb{Z}_q[x]/(x^n + 1). \tag{1}$$

It is easy to see that f_{even} contains all the even-indexed coefficients of f and f_{odd} contains all the odd-indexed coefficients of f.

If we denote x^2 by y, the two polynomials of degree $n/2$, $f_{even}(y)$ and $f_{odd}(y)$, are both in $\mathbb{Z}_q[y]/(y^{n/2}+1)$, then we can apply the NTT to get their transformed representations, i.e., $\mathsf{NTT}(f_{even})$ and $\mathsf{NTT}(f_{odd})$. Define

$$\mathsf{1PtNTT}(f) = \widehat{f} = (\mathsf{NTT}(f_{even}), \mathsf{NTT}(f_{odd})),$$
$$\mathsf{1PtNTT}^{-1}(\widehat{f}) = \left(\mathsf{NTT}^{-1}(\widehat{f}_{even}), \mathsf{NTT}^{-1}(\widehat{f}_{odd})\right).$$

Then the following equation $\mathsf{1PtNTT}^{-1}(\mathsf{1PtNTT}(f)) = (f_{even}, f_{odd}) = f$ holds.

As mentioned above, we first divide $f(x)$ to define two new polynomials of degree $n/2$ and then apply the NTT. We call our technique "1-round Preprocess-then-NTT" (1PtNTT, for short).

3.1 How to Compute the Product of Two Polynomials f and g?

As we all know, the NTT provides an efficient algorithm for multiplying large degree polynomials. It is commonly used in cryptographic schemes that are based on the hardness of the RLWE problem to efficiently implement modular polynomial multiplication. Here comes a question how can we use 1PtNTT to compute the product of two polynomials f and g?

As the same way in Eq. 1, for $g(x) \in \mathbb{Z}_q[x]/(x^n + 1)$, we can use the coefficients of $g(x)$ separately to define two new polynomials $g_{even}(y), g_{odd}(y) \in \mathbb{Z}_q[y]/(y^{n/2} + 1)$ satisfying the following equation

$$g(x) = g_{even}(x^2) + x \cdot g_{odd}(x^2) \in \mathbb{Z}_q[x]/(x^n + 1). \tag{2}$$

Let $p(x) \in \mathbb{Z}_q[x]/(x^n + 1)$ denote the product of $f(x)$ and $g(x)$ and let

$$p_{even}(y) = f_{even}(y) \cdot g_{even}(y) + f_{odd}(y) \cdot (y \cdot g_{odd}(y)) \in \mathbb{Z}_q[y]/(y^{n/2} + 1),$$
$$p_{odd}(y) = f_{odd}(y) \cdot g_{even}(y) + f_{even}(y) \cdot g_{odd}(y) \in \mathbb{Z}_q[y]/(y^{n/2} + 1).$$

Then, according to Eqs. 1 and 2, the following equation $p(x) = p_{even}(x^2) + x \cdot p_{odd}(x^2) \in \mathbb{Z}_q[x]/(x^n + 1)$ holds.

An anticirculant vector of g_{odd} is defined by the following Toeplitz vector:

$$\overrightarrow{g_{odd}} := \left(-g_{odd}[\frac{n}{2} - 1], g_{odd}[0], g_{odd}[1], \ldots, g_{odd}[\frac{n}{2} - 2]\right) \in \mathbb{Z}_q^{n/2},$$

which denotes $y \cdot g_{odd}(y) \in \mathbb{Z}_q[y]/(y^{n/2} + 1)$. Using 1PtNTT and 1PtNTT^{-1} we can compute the product p of two elements $f, g \in \mathcal{R}_q$ very efficiently through the following equation 1PtNTT^{-1} (1PtNTT$(f) \bowtie$ 1PtNTT(g)), where $\bowtie$ denotes bow-tie multiplication defined as following:

$$1\mathsf{PtNTT}(f) \bowtie 1\mathsf{PtNTT}(g)$$
$$= (\mathsf{NTT}(f_{even}), \mathsf{NTT}(f_{odd})) \bowtie (\mathsf{NTT}(g_{even}), \mathsf{NTT}(g_{odd}), \mathsf{NTT}(\overrightarrow{g_{odd}}))$$
$$= \left(\widehat{f}_{even}, \widehat{f}_{odd} \right) \bowtie \left(\widehat{g}_{even}, \widehat{g}_{odd}, \mathsf{NTT}(\overrightarrow{g_{odd}}) \right)$$
$$= \left(\widehat{f}_{even} \circ \widehat{g}_{even} + \widehat{f}_{odd} \circ \mathsf{NTT}(\overrightarrow{g_{odd}}), \widehat{f}_{odd} \circ \widehat{g}_{even} + \widehat{f}_{even} \circ \widehat{g}_{odd} \right).$$

3.2 Complexity of 1PtNTT and Its Comparison with NTT

In this subsection, we first analyse the theoretical complexity of 1PtNTT algorithm. Then we present some implementation results for different parameters to show the performance of 1PtNTT algorithm and its comparison with NTT.

The Complexity of 1PtNTT. As for 1PtNTT, its forward transformation 1PtNTT embeds two forward NTT transformations of two different polynomials of degree $n/2$. As a result, the computational complexity of a 1PtNTT is bounded by $T_2(n) = n \log(n/2)$. In a similar way, we can also get a conclusion that the complexity of an inverse transformation 1PtNTT^{-1} is $T_3(n) = n \log(n/2)$. In order to show the difference between these two algorithms, we present the ratios of the time cost of 1PtNTT to that of NTT as follows:

$$ratio_{1ptntt/ntt} = \frac{\log n - 1}{\log n} \quad \text{and} \quad ratio_{1ptntt^{-1}/ntt^{-1}} = \frac{\log n - 1}{\log n}.$$

Next, we analyse the complexity of computing two polynomials' product by using 1PtNTT algorithm. According to the computation rule of 1PtNTT, there exist two forward 1PtNTT transformations (one includes two forward NTT transformations, the other embeds three forward NTT transformations), four point-wise multiplications of two polynomials of degree bounded by $n/2$, and one inverse 1PtNTT transformation. As a result, the computational cost of computing product of two polynomials by using 1PtNTT is

$$T_4(n) = (2+3) \cdot \frac{n}{2} \log \frac{n}{2} + 2n + T_3(n) = \frac{7n}{2} \log \frac{n}{2} + 2n,$$

which is $ratio_1 = \dfrac{7 \log n - 3}{6 \log n + 2}$ times that using NTT.

Comparison of 1PtNTT and NTT. Although 1PtNTT can use some parameters that are not suitable for NTT, we analyse and compare the computational cost of 1PtNTT and NTT for the same parameters, so that we can make it easy to demonstrate the efficiency of 1PtNTT. In our implementation, we specify the details of the two methods for $(n, q) \in \{(256, 7681), (512, 12289), (1024, 12289)\}$ which are used in [2–4,6,9]. The results are reported in Table 2, and were

Table 2. Results of our C implementations of 1PtNTT on a 3.30 GHz Inter Core i5-6600 processor with Turbo Boost and Hyperthreading disabled. Results are compared with the implementation of the NTT.

Operation	n = 256, q = 7681	n = 512, q = 12289	n = 1024, q = 12289
1PtNTT	13161	21523	47436
NTT	14056	24057	52034
Experimental-ratio	0.9363	0.8947	0.9116
Theoretical-ratio	0.8750	0.8889	0.9000
1PtNTT^{-1}	10940	23038	50512
NTT^{-1}	11845	25091	55075
Experimental-ratio	0.9236	0.9182	0.9171
Theoretical-ratio	0.8750	0.8889	0.9000
Multiplication by using 1PtNTT	51213	90116	197427
Multiplication by using NTT	42959	81368	180347
Experimental-ratio	1.1921	1.1075	1.0947
Theoretical-ratio	1.0600	1.0714	1.0806

obtained by running the implementation on a 3.30GHZ Inter Core i5-6600 processor with Turbo Boost and Hyperthreading disabled. We compiled our C implementation with gcc-5.4.0 and flags **-O3 -fomit-frame-pointer -march=native**. For all other routines we report the average of 10000 runs. We denote the ratio of theoretical computational cost of PtNTT operations to that of NTT operations by "Theoretical-ratio". And "Experiment-ratio" represents the ratio of practical cycle counts of 1PtNTT to that of NTT.

4   2-Round Preprocess-then-NTT (2PtNTT)

In 2PtNTT algorithm, we only require that modulus q satisfies that $q - 1$ can be divided by $\frac{n}{2}$, i.e., $\frac{n}{2} \mid (q - 1)$. However, in this case, we can not exploit the negative wrapped convolution [17] if $2n \nmid (q - 1)$, because there does not exist any $2n$-th root of unity in $\mathbb{Z}_q$.

Based on the first round preprocess, we use the even-indexed and odd-indexed coefficients of $f(x) \in \mathbb{Z}_q[x]/(x^n + 1)$ separately to define two new polynomials $f_{even}(y)$ and $f_{odd}(y)$ whose degrees are bounded by $\frac{n}{2}$. Then, by using the same preprocess again to $f_{even}(y)$ and $f_{odd}(y)$, we can define four polynomials $f_{ee}(z)$, $f_{eo}(z)$, $f_{oe}(z)$ and $f_{oo}(z)$ of degree-bound $\frac{n}{4}$. In fact, $f_{ee}(z)$ and $f_{eo}(z)$ contains all the coefficients f_i of f satisfying that $i \equiv 0 \mod 4$ and $i \equiv 2 \mod 4$, respectively. $f_{oe}(z)$ and $f_{oo}(z)$ contains all the coefficients f_i of f satisfying that $i \equiv 1 \mod 4$ and $i \equiv 3 \mod 4$, respectively. It follows that

$$f(x) = f_{ee}(x^4) + x \cdot f_{oe}(x^4) + x^2 \cdot f_{eo}(x^4) + x^3 \cdot f_{oo}(x^4) \in \mathbb{Z}_q[x]/(x^n + 1). \quad (3)$$

Note that the four polynomials of degree $n/4$, $f_{ee}(z)$, $f_{eo}(z)$, $f_{oe}(z)$ and $f_{oo}(z)$, are all in $\mathbb{Z}_q[z]/(z^{n/4} + 1)$, then we can apply the NTT to get their transformed representations. Define

$$2\text{PtNTT}(f) = \widehat{f} = (\text{NTT}(f_{ee}), \text{NTT}(f_{oe}), \text{NTT}(f_{eo}), \text{NTT}(f_{oo})),$$

$$2\text{PtNTT}^{-1}(\widehat{f}) = \left(\text{NTT}^{-1}(\widehat{f}_{ee}), \text{NTT}^{-1}(\widehat{f}_{oe}), \text{NTT}^{-1}(\widehat{f}_{eo}), \text{NTT}^{-1}(\widehat{f}_{oo})\right).$$

Then the following equation $2\text{PtNTT}^{-1}(2\text{PtNTT}(f)) = (f_{ee}, f_{oe}, f_{eo}, f_{oo}) = f$ holds.

4.1 How to Compute the Product of Two Polynomials f and g?

2PtNTT is an extension of 1PtNTT. Therefore, the rule of 2PtNTT for polynomial multiplication is similar to 1PtNTT.

As the same way in Eq. 3, for $g(x) \in \mathbb{Z}_q[x]/(x^n+1)$, we can use the coefficients of $g(x)$ separately to define four new polynomials of degree $n/4$, i.e., $g_{ee}(z)$, $g_{eo}(z), g_{oe}(z), g_{oo}(z) \in \mathbb{Z}_q[z]/(z^{n/4}+1)$ satisfying the following equation

$$g(x) = g_{ee}(x^4) + x \cdot g_{oe}(x^4) + x^2 \cdot g_{eo}(x^4) + x^3 \cdot g_{oo}(x^4) \in \mathbb{Z}_q[x]/(x^n+1). \quad (4)$$

Let $p(x) \in \mathbb{Z}_q[x]/(x^n+1)$ denote the product of $f(x)$ and $g(x)$. An anticirculant vector of g_{ee} is defined by the following Toeplitz vector:

$$\overrightarrow{g_{ee}} := \left(-g_{odd}[\frac{n}{4}-1], g_{odd}[0], g_{odd}[1], \ldots, g_{odd}[\frac{n}{4}-2]\right) \in \mathbb{Z}_q^{n/4},$$

which denotes $z \cdot g_{odd}(z) \in \mathbb{Z}_q[z]/(z^{n/4}+1)$. Using 2PtNTT and 2PtNTT^{-1} we can compute the product p of two elements $f, g \in \mathcal{R}_q$ very efficiently through the following equation $2\text{PtNTT}^{-1}(2\text{PtNTT}(f) \bowtie 2\text{PtNTT}(g))$, where $\bowtie$ denotes bow-tie multiplication defined as following:

$$2\text{PtNTT}(f) \bowtie 2\text{PtNTT}(g)$$
$$= (\text{NTT}(f_{ee}), \text{NTT}(f_{oe}), \text{NTT}(f_{eo}), \text{NTT}(f_{oo})) \bowtie$$
$$(\text{NTT}(g_{ee}), \text{NTT}(g_{oe}), \text{NTT}(g_{eo}), \text{NTT}(g_{oo}), \text{NTT}(\overrightarrow{g_{oe}}), \text{NTT}(\overrightarrow{g_{eo}}), \text{NTT}(\overrightarrow{g_{oo}}))$$
$$= \left(\widehat{f}_{ee}, \widehat{f}_{oe}, \widehat{f}_{eo}, \widehat{f}_{oo}\right) \bowtie (\widehat{g}_{ee}, \widehat{g}_{oe}, \widehat{g}_{eo}, \widehat{g}_{oo}, \text{NTT}(\overrightarrow{g_{oe}}), \text{NTT}(\overrightarrow{g_{eo}}), \text{NTT}(\overrightarrow{g_{oo}}))$$
$$= (\widehat{f}_{ee} \circ \widehat{g}_{ee} + \widehat{f}_{oe} \circ \text{NTT}(\overrightarrow{g_{oo}}) + \widehat{f}_{eo} \circ \text{NTT}(\overrightarrow{g_{eo}}) + \widehat{f}_{oo} \circ \text{NTT}(\overrightarrow{g_{oe}}),$$
$$\widehat{f}_{ee} \circ \widehat{g}_{oe} + \widehat{f}_{oe} \circ \widehat{g}_{ee} + \widehat{f}_{eo} \circ \text{NTT}(\overrightarrow{g_{oo}}) + \widehat{f}_{oo} \circ \text{NTT}(\overrightarrow{g_{eo}}),$$
$$\widehat{f}_{ee} \circ \widehat{g}_{eo} + \widehat{f}_{oe} \circ \widehat{g}_{oe} + \widehat{f}_{eo} \circ \widehat{g}_{ee} + \widehat{f}_{oo} \circ \text{NTT}(\overrightarrow{g_{oo}}),$$
$$\widehat{f}_{ee} \circ \widehat{g}_{oo} + \widehat{f}_{oe} \circ \widehat{g}_{eo} + \widehat{f}_{eo} \circ \widehat{g}_{oe} + \widehat{f}_{oo} \circ \widehat{g}_{ee}).$$

4.2 Complexity of 2PtNTT and its Comparison with NTT

In this subsection, we first analyse the theoretical complexity of 2PtNTT algorithm. Then we present some implementation results for different parameters to show the performance of 2PtNTT algorithm and its comparison with NTT.

The Complexity of 2PtNTT. According to the analysis of complexity of 1PtNTT, it is simple to get a conclusion that the computational complexity of a 2PtNTT is bounded by $T_5(n) = n \log(n/4)$ and the complexity of an inverse transformation PtNTT^{-1} is $T_6(n) = n \log(n/4)$. In order to show the difference between these two algorithms, we present the ratios of the time cost of PtNTT to that of NTT as follows:

$$ratio_{2\text{ptntt/ntt}} = \frac{\log n - 2}{\log n} \quad \text{and} \quad ratio_{2\text{ptntt}^{-1}/\text{ntt}^{-1}} = \frac{\log n - 2}{\log n}.$$

According to the computation rule of 2PtNTT, there exist two forward 2PtNTT transformations (one includes 4 forward NTT transformations, the other embeds 7 forward NTT transformations), 16 point-wise multiplications of two polynomials of degree bounded by $n/4$, and one inverse 2PtNTT transformation. As a result, the time cost of computing the product of two polynomials by using 2PtNTT is

$$T_7(n) = (4 + 7) \cdot \frac{n}{4} \log \frac{n}{4} + 4n + T_6(n) = \frac{15n}{4} \log \frac{n}{4} + 4n,$$

which is $ratio_2 = \dfrac{15 \log n - 14}{12 \log n + 4}$ times that using NTT.

Table 3. Results of our C implementations of 2PtNTT on a 3.30 GHz Inter Core i5-6600 processor with Turbo Boost and Hyperthreading disabled. Results are compared with the implementation of the NTT.

Operation	n = 256, q = 7681	n = 512, q = 12289	n = 1024, q = 12289
2PtNTT	10072	17384	38092
NTT	13621	20294	45176
Experimental-ratio	0.7394	0.8566	0.8432
Theoretical-ratio	0.7500	0.7778	0.8000
2PtNTT^{-1}	8728	17374	38840
NTT^{-1}	10232	21858	47790
Experimental-ratio	0.8530	0.7949	0.8127
Theoretical-ratio	0.7500	0.7778	0.8000
Multiplication by using 2PtNTT	46356	83648	180252
Multiplication by using NTT	37046	69048	152722
Experimental-ratio	1.2513	1.2028	1.1803
Theoretical-ratio	1.0600	1.0804	1.0968

Comparison of 2PtNTT and NTT. Although 2PtNTT can use some parameters that are not suitable for NTT, we analyse and compare the computational cost of 2PtNTT and NTT for the same parameters, so that we can make it easy to demonstrate the efficiency of 2PtNTT. In our implementation, we specify the details of the two methods for $(n, q) \in \{(256, 7681), (512, 12289), (1024, 12289)\}$ which are used in [2–4,6,9]. The results are reported in Table 3, and were obtained in the same environment of experiments as 1PtNTT.

5 Application of 1PtNTT to KYBER

Recently, Avanzi et al. [6] submitted a suite of public-key encapsulation mechanisms denoted as KYBER to NIST as a candidate of the standard of post-quantum cryptography, based on the conjectured quantum hardness of the MLWE problem. The KYBER cryptosystem is based on a variant of their previously proposed Kyber [9] scheme which is a semantically secure public-key encryption (PKE) scheme with respect to adaptive chosen plaintext attacks (CPA).

5.1 Small-KYBER Parameter Sets

In [6], Avanzi et al. defined three parameter sets for KYBER, which they call these schemes KYBER512, KYBER768, KYBER1024. According to their three KYBER schemes, we will give new parameter setting. As shown in Table 4, the modulus q in our schemes is smaller, so we call our scheme small-KYBER, i.e., small-KYBER512, small-KYBER768, small-KYBER1024. Note that Table 4 also lists the derived parameter δ, which is the probability that the decryption of a valid KYBER-CPA-PKE ciphertext fails.

The parameters were obtained via the following approaching: (1) n is set to 256 because the goal is to encapsulate 256-bit symmetric keys. (2) q is set to the smallest prime satisfying $n|(q - 1)$, which is required to enable the 1PtNTT-based multiplication. (3) k is selected to fix the lattice dimension as a multiple of n. (4) The remaining parameters η, d_u, d_v, d_t were chosen to balance between security, public-key and ciphertext size and failure probability.

The failure probability δ is computed following the approach outlined above using the analysis script `small_Kyber.py` which is available online at https://github.com/ncepuzs/Preprocess_Then_NTT/tree/master/Small_Kyber. In addition, we also present the classical and quantum core-SVP hardness of the different proposed parameter sets of small-KYBER with the claimed security level in Table 4. The lower bounds of the cost of the primal and dual attack [20] were computed with the help of the Python script `small_Kyber.py`. Note that `small_Kyber.py` is same as the Python script `Kyber.py` [6] except that parameter sets are different.

5.2 Interconversion to KEM

Small-KYBER-CPA-PKE can be converted to an IND-CPA-secure key encapsulation mechanism small-KYBER-CPA-KEM by using the public key encryption scheme to convey a secret. Furthermore, we can apply the $\mathrm{QFO}_m^{\perp}$ transform in [14] to construct an IND-CCA-secure key encapsulation mechanism small-KYBER-CCA-KEM from small-KYBER-CPA-PKE and four hash functions same

Table 4. Parameters of small-KYBER-CPA-PKE and KYBER-CPA-PKE and derived high-level properties.

	n	k	q	η	(d_u, d_v, d_t)	δ	Security (classical,quantum)	Security level
KYBER512	256	2	7681	5	(11,3,11)	2^{-145}	(112,102)	1
KYBER768	256	3	7681	4	(11,3,11)	2^{-142}	(178,161)	3
KYBER1024	256	4	7681	3	(11,3,11)	2^{-169}	(242,219)	5
Our schemes								
small-KYBER512	256	2	3329	2	(10,3,10)	2^{-138}	(111,100)	1
small-KYBER768	256	3	3329	2	(10,5,10)	2^{-144}	(181,164)	3
small-KYBER1024	256	4	3329	1	(10,3,10)	2^{-192}	(232,210)	5

as that in [6]. Instantiating small-KYBER-CCA-KEM by the parameter sets in Table 4, we can provide public key, secret key, and ciphertext sizes in Table 8 for our three KEMs that support the transmission of a 256-bit message or key.

Performance of Reference. Here, we give all the remaining details of results of our implementations for small-KYBER-CCA-KEM in Table 6. Both implementations are fully protected against timing attack. All cycle counts are obtained by running the implementation on a 3.30 GHZ Inter Core i5-6600 processor with Turbo Boost and Hyperthreading disabled. They are median cycle counts over 100 measurements. We compiled our C implementation with gcc-5.4.0 and flags -**O3 -fomit-frame-pointer -march=native**. The implementation of our protocols is available at https://github.com/ncepuzs/Preprocess_Then_NTT/tree/master/Small_Kyber.

Table 5. Sizes of public keys, secret keys, and ciphertexts of small-KYBER and KYBER in bytes.

Scheme	$|pk|$ (Bytes)	$|sk|$ (Bytes)	$|ciphertext|$ (Bytes)
KYBER512-CCA-KEM	736	1632	800
small-KYBER512-CCA-KEM	672	1504	736
Difference value	64	128	64
KYBER768-CCA-KEM	1088	2400	1152
small-KYBER768-CCA-KEM	992	2208	1120
Difference value	96	192	32
KYBER1024-CCA-KEM	1440	3168	1504
small-KYBER1024-CCA-KEM	1312	2912	1376
Difference value	128	256	128

Table 6. Cycle counts of key generation, encapsulation, and decapsulation of small-KYBER and KYBER.

Scheme	Key generation	Encapsulation	Decapsulation
small-KYBER512-CCA-KEM	143628	203364	285379
KYBER512-CCA-KEM	122748	175528	209074
Ratio	1.1701	1.1586	1.3650
small-KYBER768-CCA-KEM	251538	332148	427738
KYBER768-CCA-KEM	203356	274274	321248
Ratio	1.2369	1.2110	1.3315
small-KYBER1024-CCA-KEM	390326	490956	620420
KYBER1024-CCA-KEM	293562	381882	438824
Ratio	1.3296	1.2856	1.4138

6 Application of 2PtNTT to NEWHOPE

Recently, Alkim et al. [2] submitted a suite of public-key encapsulation mechanisms denoted as NEWHOPE to NIST as a candidate of the standard of post-quantum cryptography, based on the conjectured quantum hardness of the RLWE problem. The NEWHOPE cryptosystem is based on a variant of their previously proposed NewHope-Simple [4] scheme which is a semantically secure public-key encryption scheme with respect to adaptive chosen plaintext attacks (CPA).

6.1 Small-NEWHOPE Parameter Sets

In [2], Alkim et al. defined two parameter sets for NEWHOPE, which they call these two schemes NEWHOPE512, NEWHOPE1024. According to their NEWHOPE schemes, we will give two new parameter settings. As shown in Table 7, the modulus q in our schemes is smaller, so we call our scheme small-NEWHOPE, i.e., NEWHOPE512, small-NEWHOPE1024. Note that the table also lists the derived parameter δ, which is the probability that the decryption of a valid small-NEWHOPE-CPA-PKE ciphertext fails.

The parameters were obtained via the following approaching: (1) n is set to 512 or 1024 because the goal is to encapsulate 256-bit symmetric keys. (2) q is set to the smallest prime satisfying $\frac{n}{2}|(q-1)$ for $n = 512, 1024$, which is required to enable the 2PtNTT-based multiplication. (4) The remaining parameter η was chosen to balance between security and failure probability.

The failure probability δ is computed following the approach outlined above using the analysis script `small_NewHope.py` which is available online at https://github.com/ncepuzs/Preprocess_Then_NTT/tree/master/Small_NewHope. In addition, we also present the classical and quantum core-SVP hardness of the different proposed parameter sets of small-KYBER with the claimed security level in Table 7. The lower bounds of the cost of the primal and dual attack [20] were computed with the help of the Python script `small_NewHope.py`. Note that `small_NewHope.py` is same as the Python script `scripts/PQsecurity.py` [2] except that parameter sets are different.

6.2 Interconversion to KEM

Small-NEWHOPE-CPA-PKE can be converted to an IND-CPA-secure key encapsulation mechanism small-NEWHOPE-CPA-KEM by using the public key encryption scheme to convey a secret. Furthermore, we can apply the $QFO_m^\perp$ transform in [14] to construct an IND-CCA-secure key encapsulation mechanism small-NEWHOPE-CCA-KEM from small-NEWHOPE-CPA-PKE and three hash functions same as that in [2]. Instantiating small-NEWHOPE-CPA-KEM and small-NEWHOPE-CCA-KEM by the parameter sets in Table 7, we can provide public

Table 7. Parameters of small-NewHope-CPA-PKE and NewHope-CPA-PKE and derived high-level properties.

	n	q	η	δ	Security (classical,quantum)	Security level
NEWHOPE512-CPA-PKE	512	12289	8	2^{-213}	(112,101)	1
NEWHOPE1024-CPA-PKE	1024	12289	8	2^{-216}	(257,233)	5
Our schemes						
small-NEWHOPE512-CPA-PKE	512	7681	5	2^{-261}	(112,101)	1
small-NEWHOPE1024-CPA-PKE	1024	7681	5	2^{-224}	(257,233)	5

Table 8. Sizes of public keys, secret keys, and ciphertexts of small-NEWHOPE and NEWHOPE in bytes.

Scheme	$|pk|$ (Bytes)	$|sk|$ (Bytes)	$|ciphertext|$ (Bytes)
NEWHOPE512-CPA-KEM	928	896	1088
small-NEWHOPE512-CPA-KEM	864	832	1024
Difference value	64	64	64
NEWHOPE512-CCA-KEM	928	1888	1120
small-NEWHOPE512-CCA-KEM	864	1760	1056
Difference value	64	128	64
NEWHOPE1024-CPA-KEM	1824	1792	2176
small-NEWHOPE1024-CPA-KEM	1696	1664	1048
Difference value	128	128	128
NEWHOPE1024-CCA-KEM	1824	3680	2208
small-NEWHOPE1024-CCA-KEM	1696	3424	2080
Difference value	128	256	128

key, secret key, and ciphertext sizes in Table 8 for our four KEMs that support the transmission of a 256-bit message or key.

Performance of Reference. Here, we give all the remaining details of results of our implementations for small-NEWHOPE KEMs in Table 9. Both implementations are fully protected against timing attack. All cycle counts are obtained on the same platform as the test of KYBER with the same instructions. They are median cycle counts over 100 measurements.The implementation of our protocols is available at https://github.com/ncepuzs/Preprocess_Then_NTT/tree/master/Small_NewHope.

Table 9. Cycle counts of key generation, encapsulation, and decapsulation of small-NEWHOPE and NEWHOPE.

Scheme	Key generation	Encapsulation	Decapsulation
small-NEWHOPE512-CPA-KEM	114033	167178	73210
NEWHOPE512-CPA-KEM	91292	133902	34534
Ratio	1.2491	1.2485	2.1199
small-NEWHOPE512-CCA-KEM	132886	200420	266202
NEWHOPE512-CCA-KEM	105178	155156	175661
Ratio	1.2634	1.2917	1.5154
small-NEWHOPE1024-CPA-KEM	272060	439358	161848
NEWHOPE1024-CPA-KEM	184488	271180	69974
Ratio	1.4747	1.6202	2.3130
small-NEWHOPE1024-CCA-KEM	289157	427598	538098
NEWHOPE1024-CCA-KEM	210072	314130	361852
Ratio	1.3765	1.3612	1.4870

7 Conclusion

We have presented Preprocess-then-NTT technique to weaken the limination for modulus q of the NTT. We further apply PtNTT to KYBER [6] and NEWHOPE [2], and provide new parameter settings. Because of the usage of PtNTT, our new schemes achieve smaller public key sizes, smaller ciphertext sizes and a similar failure probability at a same security level. Also, it is interesting to see that the order of savings in size of the public keys and ciphertexts are the same for both the NEWHOPE and KYBER schemes, which is due to the fact that only one bit is saved per coefficient due to the reduction in modulus. The PtNTT algorithm enables that the aforementioned improvemenzts can be also achieved in a large portion of existing RLWE-based schemes.

Acknowledgments. We thank the anonymous Inscrypt'2018 reviewers for their helpful comments. This work was supported by the National Basic Research Program of China (973 project, No.2014CB340603), the National Cryptography Development Fund MMJJ20170116 and the National Natural Science Foundation of China (No. 61572495, No.61602473, No.61772515, No.61672030, No.61272040).

References

1. Ajtai, M., Dwork, C.: A public-key cryptosystem with worst-case/average-case equivalence. In: Proceedings of the Twenty-Ninth Annual ACM Symposium on Theory of Computing, pp. 284–293. ACM (1997)
2. Alkim, E., et al.: Newhope-algorithm Specifications and Supporting Documentation. https://newhopecrypto.org/
3. Alkim, E., Ducas, L., Pöppelmann, T., Schwabe, P.: Post-quantum key exchange - a new hope. In: 25th USENIX Security Symposium, pp. 327–343 (2016)
4. Alkim, E., Ducas, L., Pöppelmann, T., Schwabe, P.: Newhope without reconciliation. IACR Cryptology ePrint Archive, 2016:1157 (2016). http://eprint.iacr.org/2016/1157
5. Applebaum, B., Cash, D., Peikert, C., Sahai, A.: Fast cryptographic primitives and circular-secure encryption based on hard learning problems. In: Halevi, S. (ed.) CRYPTO 2009. LNCS, vol. 5677, pp. 595–618. Springer, Heidelberg (2009). https://doi.org/10.1007/978-3-642-03356-8_35
6. Avanzi, R.: CRYSTALS - kyber: Algorithm Specifications and Supporting Documentation. https://pq-crystals.org/
7. Bernstein, D.J.: Fast multiplication and its applications. Algorithmic Number Theor. **44**, 325–384 (2008)
8. Bos, J.W., Costello, C., Naehrig, M., Stebila, D.: Post-quantum key exchange for the TLS protocol from the ring learning with errors problem. In: 2015 IEEE Symposium on Security and Privacy, SP 2015, pp. 553–570 (2015)
9. Bos, J.W., et al.: CRYSTALS - kyber: a CCA-secure module-lattice-based KEM. IACR Cryptology ePrint Archive 2017:634 (2017)
10. Chu, E., George, A.: Inside the FFT Black Box: Serial and Parallel Fast Fourier Transform Algorithms. CRC Press, Boca Raton (1999)
11. Cooley, J.W., Tukey, J.W.: An algorithm for the machine calculation of complex fourier series. Math. Comput. **19**(90), 297–301 (1965)
12. D'Anvers, J.-P., Karmakar, A., Sinha Roy, S., Vercauteren, F.: Saber: module-LWR based key exchange, CPA-secure encryption and CCA-secure KEM. In: Joux, A., Nitaj, A., Rachidi, T. (eds.) AFRICACRYPT 2018. LNCS, vol. 10831, pp. 282–305. Springer, Cham (2018). https://doi.org/10.1007/978-3-319-89339-6_16
13. D'Anvers, J., Karmakar, A., Roy, S.S., Vercauteren, F.: Saber: Module-LWR based KEM. https://csrc.nist.gov/Projects/Post-Quantum-Cryptography/Round-1-Submissions
14. Hofheinz, D., Hövelmanns, K., Kiltz, E.: A modular analysis of the Fujisaki-Okamoto transformation. In: Kalai, Y., Reyzin, L. (eds.) TCC 2017. LNCS, vol. 10677, pp. 341–371. Springer, Cham (2017). https://doi.org/10.1007/978-3-319-70500-2_12
15. Langlois, A., Stehlé, D.: Worst-case to average-case reductions for module lattices. Des. Codes Cryptogr. **75**(3), 565–599 (2015)

16. Lyubashevsky, V.: Lattice signatures without trapdoors. In: Pointcheval, D., Johansson, T. (eds.) EUROCRYPT 2012. LNCS, vol. 7237, pp. 738–755. Springer, Heidelberg (2012). https://doi.org/10.1007/978-3-642-29011-4_43
17. Lyubashevsky, V., Micciancio, D., Peikert, C., Rosen, A.: SWIFFT: a modest proposal for FFT hashing. In: Nyberg, K. (ed.) FSE 2008. LNCS, vol. 5086, pp. 54–72. Springer, Heidelberg (2008). https://doi.org/10.1007/978-3-540-71039-4_4
18. Lyubashevsky, V., Peikert, C., Regev, O.: On ideal lattices and learning with errors over rings. In: Gilbert, H. (ed.) EUROCRYPT 2010. LNCS, vol. 6110, pp. 1–23. Springer, Heidelberg (2010). https://doi.org/10.1007/978-3-642-13190-5_1
19. Regev, O.: On lattices, learning with errors, random linear codes, and cryptography. J. ACM **56**(6), 34:1–34:40 (2009)
20. Stebila, D., Mosca, M.: Post-quantum key exchange for the internet and the open quantum safe project. In: Avanzi, R., Heys, H. (eds.) SAC 2016. LNCS, vol. 10532, pp. 14–37. Springer, Cham (2017). https://doi.org/10.1007/978-3-319-69453-5_2
21. Stehlé, D., Steinfeld, R., Tanaka, K., Xagawa, K.: Efficient public key encryption based on ideal lattices. In: Matsui, M. (ed.) ASIACRYPT 2009. LNCS, vol. 5912, pp. 617–635. Springer, Heidelberg (2009). https://doi.org/10.1007/978-3-642-10366-7_36

Two-Round PAKE Protocol over Lattices Without NIZK

Zengpeng Li[1] and Ding Wang[2(✉)]

[1] College of Computer Science and Technology, Qingdao University, Qingdao, China
lizengpeng@hrbeu.edu.cn
[2] School of EECS, Peking University, Beijing 100871, China
wangdingg@pku.edu.cn

Abstract. Reducing the number of communication rounds of Password-based Authenticated Key Exchange (PAKE) protocols is of great practical significance. At PKC'15, Abdalla et al. relaxed the requirements of Gennaro-Lindell's framework for three-round PAKE protocols, and obtained a two-round PAKE protocol under the traditional DDH-based smooth projective hash function (SPHF). At ASIACRYPT'17, Zhang and Yu proposed a lattice-based two-round PAKE protocol via the approximate SPHF. However, the language of Zhang-Yu's SPHF depends on simulation-sound non-interactive zero-knowledge (NIZK) proofs, for which there is *no* concrete construction without random oracle under lattice-based assumptions. To our knowledge, how to design a lattice-based two-round PAKE protocol via an efficient SPHF scheme without NIZK remains a challenge. In this paper, we propose the first two-round PAKE protocol over lattices without NIZK. Our protocol is in accordance with the framework of Abdalla et al. (PKC'15) while attaining post-quantum security. We overcome the limitations of existing schemes by relaxing previous security assumptions (i.e., both the client and the sever need IND-CCA-secure encryption), and build two new lattice-based SPHFs, one for IND-CCA-secure Micciancio-Peikert ciphertext (at the client side) and the other for IND-CPA-secure Regev ciphertext (at the server side). Particularly, our protocol attains provable security.

Keywords: Password-based Authenticated Key Exchange ·
Smooth projective hash function · Lattice-based · Provable security

1 Introduction

Password-based Authenticated Key Exchange (PAKE) protocols are perhaps the most widely used cryptographic protocols, dating back to Bellovin and Merritt's PAKE protocol (named EKE) in 1992 [1]. They showed how two parties, each of which pre-shares a human-memorized password and communicate over a public network, can verify the authenticity of each other and establish a cryptographically robust session key to protect their ensuing data communications. Their EKE is successful in preventing low-entropy passwords from being offline guessed

© Springer Nature Switzerland AG 2019
F. Guo et al. (Eds.): Inscrypt 2018, LNCS 11449, pp. 138–159, 2019.
https://doi.org/10.1007/978-3-030-14234-6_8

by dictionary attacks, and therefore demonstrates the feasibility of employing password-only protocols to build secure communication channels over public networks, which is a key goal of cryptography. Owing to the practicality of PAKE, Bellovin-Merritt's seminal paper [1] has been followed by hundreds of PAKE proposals with varied security and complexity, such as KOY [2], J-PAKE [3] and OPAQUE [4].

In order to generalize the KOY scheme, Gennaro and Lindell [5] introduced the smooth projective hash function (or SPHF) to instantiate the KOY scheme in the Bellare, Pointcheval, and Rogaway (BPR) security model [6]. It is common to abbreviate the general KOY scheme to Gennaro-Lindell framework. Since then, considerable attention has been devoted to developing secure and efficient PAKE protocols via SPHFs, some notable ones include [7,8].

Most of these existing PAKE protocols under the Gennaro-Lindell framework are three-rounds and depend on an "IND-CCA2-secure" encryption scheme to establish a high-entropy session key. How to reduce the number of rounds and relax the security assumption(s) are two important concerns. At SAC'04, Jiang and Gong [9] relaxed the security of Gennaro-Lindell framework by using the combination of an IND-CPA scheme at the server side and an IND-CCA2 scheme at the client side, and did not require the IND-CCA2 scheme at the server side, but their protocol still needs three rounds. At PKC'15, Abdalla et al. [10] reduced the communication rounds by relaxing the Gennaro-Lindell framework and obtained a two-round PAKE under the traditional DDH-based SPHF. In their protocol, the client requires an indistinguishable against plaintext checkable attacks (or IND-PCA) scheme and the server requires an IND-CPA scheme.[1]

At ASIACRYPT'17, Zhang and Yu [11] proposed a lattice-based two-round PAKE protocol via approximate SPHF. However, the language of their SPHF relies on simulation-sound non-interactive zero-knowledge (NIZK) proofs, for which there is no concrete construction without the random oracle under lattice-based assumptions. In a nutshell, it still remains an open question as to:

Whether is it possible to construct a secure and efficient two-round PAKE protocol without NIZK via the LWE-based SPHFs?

1.1   Our Results and Techniques

In this work, we answer the above question in the affirmative. At PKC'15, Abdalla et al. [10] pointed out that, their IND-PCA-secure PKE scheme is also IND-CCA2-secure for small message space. Inspired by this observation, we first adopt the existing IND-CCA-secure LWE-based Micciancio and Peikert scheme [12] to meet the requirements of IND-PCA-secure PKE scheme, and then follow the SPHF design principles suggested by Katz and Vaikuntanathan [13] and propose one lattice-based MP−SPHF for IND-CCA-secure Micciancio-Peikert ciphertext (at the client side) and the other lattice-based Reg−SPHF for

---

[1] Note that every IND-CCA2-secure scheme is also an IND-PCA-secure scheme.

IND-CPA-secure Regev ciphertext [14] (at the server side). Finally, armed with Reg$-$SPHF and MP$-$SPHF, we construct a two-round PAKE in line with the principles of [10]. In all, we make the following contributions:

- **New two-round PAKE protocol.** Zhang and Yu [11] proposed the first lattice-based two-round PAKE protocol in the random oracle model which is built upon the splittable PKE scheme along with the non-adaptive approximate SPHF.[2] However, their construction depends on the IND-CCA1-secure Katz-Vaikuntanathan [13] scheme and simulation soundness NIZK from lattices in the random oracle model. The main drawbacks are that: the Katz-Vaikuntanathan scheme [13] needs to invoke the Invert($\cdot$) algorithm many times until the plaintext is recovered, and there is no concrete construction involving NIZK but without random oracle under lattice-based assumptions. To overcome both limitations, we introduce the Micciancio-Peikert scheme [12] and the Regev scheme [14] to design two lattice-based SPHFs (i.e., MP$-$SPHF for the client side and Reg$-$SPHF for the server side) as the building blocks of our lattice-based PAKE.
- **Weaker security assumptions.** Though some one-round PAKE protocols were proposed (e.g., [7,15]), these constructions require stronger (i.e., IND-CCA) assumptions for both client and server sides in the security model. Thus, relaxing the security assumptions is another important issue [8,9]. Abdalla et al. [10] constructed a DDH-based two-round PAKE protocol by introducing the new IND-PCA-secure cryptographic primitive to relax the security requirement of the server side from IND-CCA to IND-PCA. In our PAKE, IND-CCA-secure encryption is required at the client side, while IND-CPA-secure encryption is required at the server side.
- **New security formulation.** When formulating the attacker $\mathcal{A}$'s advantage **Adv**, existing PAKE literature (e.g., [7–9,11,16]) invariably assume that passwords come from a uniformly random distribution, and **Adv** is thus formulated as $Q(\lambda)/|\mathcal{D}| + \text{negl}(\lambda)$ for an attacker making at most $Q(\lambda)$ on-line guesses, where λ is the system security parameter and $\mathcal{D}$ is the password space. However, user-chosen passwords are *not* uniformly distributed, but follow the Zipf's law [17,18]. Thus, we use the formulation $C' \cdot Q(\lambda)^{s'} + \text{negl}(\lambda)$ to more accurately capture $\mathcal{A}$'s advantage **Adv**, where $s' \in [0.15, 0.30]$ and $C' \in [0.001, 0.1]$ [17,18] are constant CDF-Zipf regression parameters of $\mathcal{D}$.

1.2 Related Works

We now give a brief history of PAKE and SPHF.

PAKE. We first remark that we use *flow* to denote the unidirectional communication between the parties, and the *round* can be used to denote the bidirectional communication between the parties. If the messages are sent asynchronously, then the round and flow are the same notation. But if the messages are sent

---

[2] The non-adaptive approximate SPHF means the adversary can see the projective key ph before choosing the word W.

simultaneously, then each round contains two flows. Actually, if the PAKE protocols were divided according to the communication rounds, then there exist three types of PAKE protocols. **(1)** Three-round (or three-flow) PAKE as first introduced by Katz, Ostrovsky and Yung [2] was only achieved based on DDH assumption in the standard model. After that, a series of works [5,8,9,13] were proposed to improve the three-round PAKE protocols. **(2)** Two-round (or two-flow) PAKE as first introduced by Abdalla et al. [10] was achieved by introducing a new cryptographic primitive IND-PCA-secure PKE scheme, followed by Zhang and Yu who proposed the first two-round PAKE over lattices. **(3)** Katz and Vaikuntanathan [15] proposed the general one-round (but two-flow) PAKE framework which requires the client and the server to send messages to each other simultaneously. Alternatively, Groce and Katz [8] extended the Jiang-Gong scheme [9] in the universal composability (UC) framework [19,20] and proved it secure. Afterwards, a series of PAKE in UC-model were discussed [4,21,22].

SPHF. Cramer and Shoup [23] first proposed the concept of SPHF which is a special kind of hash proof system and defined on the NP language L over a domain X. Concretely, there are two basic keyed functions (i.e., Hash($\cdot$) and ProjHash($\cdot$)) in SPHFs. The participants can compute Hash($\cdot$) by taking as input the private hashing key hk and a word W. Similarly, the one can compute the function ProjHash($\cdot$) by taking the public projective hashing key ph, a witness w and a word W, where the word W contains the message msg and corresponding labeled IND-CCA ciphertext $\mathbf{c}$. Notably, the output distributions of the two functions are statistically indistinguishable for a word W over the language L.

2   Preliminaries

We denote vector $\mathbf{x}$ via bold lower-case letter and matrix $\mathbf{A}$ via bold upper-case letter, and λ the security parameter. An m-dimension lattice can be written as $\Lambda = \{\mathbf{Bs} \mid \mathbf{s} \in \mathbb{Z}^n\}$, where $\mathbf{B} \in \mathbb{Z}^{m \times n}$ is called basis of Λ for $m \geq n\lceil \log q \rceil$. Notably, the determinant of Λ is $det(\Lambda) = \sqrt{det(\mathbf{B}^T\mathbf{B})}$. Meanwhile, we adopt the typical deterministic rounding function of [13] to discard the noise elements.

Definition 1 (The Square-Signal Function, [13]). *The typical deterministic rounding function (a.k.a., the so-called square-signal) was defined as* $R(x) = \lfloor 2x/q \rceil \pmod 2$. *The value of $R(h)$ can be viewed as a number in* $[-\frac{(q-1)}{2}, \cdots, \frac{(q-1)}{2}]$ *and output $b \in \{0,1\}$.*

Definition 2 (Hamming Metric). *For any two strings of equal length $x, y \in \{0,1\}^v$, the Hamming distance is one of several string metrics for measuring the edit distance between two strings. We write it HD(x, y).*

2.1   Lattice Background and Learning with Errors

Definition 3 ([24]). *A distribution ensemble $\chi = \chi(\lambda)$ over the integers is called B-bounded (denoted $|\chi| \leq B$) if there exists:* $\Pr_{x \xleftarrow{\$} \chi} [|x| \geq B] \leq 2^{-\tilde{\Omega}(n)}$.

Definition 4 (Decision-LWE$_{n,q,\chi,m}$). *Assume given an independent sample* $(\mathbf{A}, \mathbf{b}) \in \mathbb{Z}_q^{m \times n} \times \mathbb{Z}_q^{m \times 1}$, *where the sample is distributed according to either:* *(1)* $\mathcal{A}_{\mathbf{s},\chi}$ *for a uniform random* $\mathbf{s} \in \mathbb{Z}_q^n$ *(i.e.,* $\{(\mathbf{A}, \mathbf{b}) : \mathbf{A} \leftarrow \mathbb{Z}_q^{m \times n}, \mathbf{s} \leftarrow \mathbb{Z}_q^{n \times 1}, \mathbf{e} \leftarrow \chi^{m \times 1}, \mathbf{b} = \mathbf{A} \cdot \mathbf{s} + \mathbf{e} \pmod{q})\}$*), or (2) the uniform distribution* *(i.e.,* $\{(\mathbf{A}, \mathbf{b}) : \mathbf{A} \leftarrow \mathbb{Z}_q^{m \times n}, \mathbf{b} \leftarrow \mathbb{Z}_q^{m \times 1}\}$*). Then, the above two distributions are computationally indistinguishable.*

Remark 1. Reductions between the LWE assumption and approximating the shortest vector problem in lattices (for appropriate parameters) were shown in [14, 25–27], here we omit the corollary of these schemes' results.

Lemma 1 (From [12]). *The* PPT *algorithm* Invert($\cdot$) *can be used to invert the injective trapdoor function* $g_{\mathbf{A}}(\mathbf{s}, \mathbf{e}) = \mathbf{s}^T \cdot \mathbf{A} + \mathbf{e} \pmod{q}$, *and satisfies the following requirements:*

- *The algorithm takes as input the following parameters:* **(1)**. *a parity-check matrix* $\mathbf{A} \in \mathbb{Z}_q^{n \times m}$ *along with* **(2)**. *a* **G**-*trapdoor* $\mathbf{R} \in \mathbb{Z}^{\bar{m} \times n\ell_q}$, *where* $\mathbf{A} \cdot \left(\frac{\mathbf{R}}{\mathbf{I}}\right) = \mathbf{H} \cdot \mathbf{G}$ *for the invertible tag* $\mathbf{H} \in \mathbb{Z}_q^{n \times n}$ *of* $\mathbf{R}$. **(3)**. *an* LWE *instance* $\mathbf{b}$ *satisfying* $\mathbf{b} = \mathbf{s}^T \cdot \mathbf{A} + \mathbf{e} \pmod{q}$.
- *The algorithm outputs the secret vector* $\mathbf{s}$ *(which depends on the value of* $\mathbf{b}^T \cdot \left(\frac{\mathbf{R}}{\mathbf{I}}\right)$*.) and the noise vector* $\mathbf{e} = \mathbf{b} - \mathbf{A}^T\mathbf{s}$.

2.2 Smooth Projective Hash Functions

Cramer and Shoup [23] first introduced the projective hash function families at EUROCRYPT'02. SPHF acts as an important type of the projective hash function which requires the existence of a domain X and an underlying NP language $L \subseteq X$ such that it is computationally hard to distinguish a random element in L from a random element in $X \setminus L$. More precisely, an SPHF contains four PPT algorithms over $L \subseteq X$

$$\mathsf{SPHF} = (\mathsf{HashKG}, \mathsf{ProjKG}, \mathsf{Hash}, \mathsf{ProjHash}),$$

which is defined as follows:

- HashKG(L) inputs an NP language L and outputs a hash key hk.
- ProjKG(hk, L, W) inputs an NP language L, a hk, and a word $W \in L$ and outputs a projective hash key ph.
- Hash(hk, L, W) inputs an NP language L, a hk, and a $W \in L$ and outputs a hash value h over $\{0, 1\}^v$ for some positive integer $v = \Omega(\lambda)$.
- ProjHash(ph, L, W, w) inputs an NP language L, a ph, a $W \in L$, and a witness w and outputs a projective hash value $p \in \{0, 1\}^v$.

Meanwhile, the SPHFs satisfy the notions of (approximate) correctness and smoothness:

- **Approximate Correctness:** We say the property of approximate correctness (i.e., ε-correct) holds, if the Hamming metric between $\mathsf{Hash}(hk, L, W)$ and $\mathsf{ProjHash}(hk, L, W)$ is larger than $\varepsilon \cdot v$, then the probability of Hamming distance is negligible, i.e.,

$$\Pr[\mathsf{HD}(\mathsf{Hash}(hk, L, W), \mathsf{ProjHash}(hk, L, W)) > \varepsilon \cdot v] = \mathsf{negl}(\lambda).$$

- **Smoothness:** We say the property of the smoothness holds, if the following two distributions are statistical indistinguishable:

  (1)$\{(ph, h) \mid hk \leftarrow \mathsf{HashKG}(L), ph = \mathsf{ProjKG}(hk, L, W), h \leftarrow \mathsf{Hash}(hk, L, W)\}$.
  (2)$\{(ph, h) \mid hk \leftarrow \mathsf{HashKG}(L), ph = \mathsf{ProjKG}(hk, L, W), h \leftarrow \{0, 1\}^v\}$.

Here, we stress that we call the approximate SPHF as SPHF if $\varepsilon = 0$, i.e., ε-correct. However, obtaining the 0-correct in lattice setting is not easy, thus our constructed $\mathsf{Reg-SPHF}$ and $\mathsf{MP-SPHF}$ are also approximated SPHFs.

2.3   The Bellare-Pointcheval-Rogaway Security Model

In this subsection, we follow the definition of Bellare, Pointcheval, and Rogaway [6] which is the follow-up work of [28–30].

Participants, Passwords, and Initialization. For any execution of the protocol, there is an initialization phase during which public parameters are established. We assume a fixed set U of protocol users. For every distinct U_1, $U_2 \in$ U, we assume that U_1 and U_2 share a password pw_{U_1,U_2}, (i.e., pw). Meanwhile, each pw_{U_1,U_2} is independently sampled from the password space $D(\lambda)$ according to the Zipf's law [17,18].

Execution of the Protocol. In reality, a protocol describes the behaviours of the user after receiving inputs from their environment. In the formal model, the adversary $\mathcal{A}$ will decide the inputs for the user, and each user is allowed to instantiate an unlimited number of instances and can run the protocol multiple times (possibly concurrently) with different partners. We denote instance i of user U as Π_U^i. Each instance may be used only once. The adversary is given oracle access to these different instances; furthermore, each instance maintains (local) state which is updated during the course of the experiment. In particular, each instance Π_U^i maintains local state that includes the following variables:

- sid_U^i, session id; pid_U^i, partner id; skey_U^i, session key id.
- acc_U^i, a boolean variable denoting acceptance at the end of the execution.
- term_U^i, a boolean variable denoting termination at the end of the execution.

Adversarial Model. The adversary $\mathcal{A}$ is allowed to fully control the external network, namely that he is able to do whatever one wants, such as he can (1) block, inject, modify, and delete messages; (2) request any session keys adaptively. Formally, we model how the adversary $\mathcal{A}$ interacts with various instances by the following oracles:

- $\mathsf{Send}(U_C, i, M)$. The oracle sends the message M to instance $\Pi^i_{U_C}$. Upon receiving the message from the oracle Send, the instance $\Pi^i_{U_C}$ then runs according to the protocol specification, updating state as the approach. We remark that, the output of $\Pi^i_{U_C}$ (i.e., the message sent by the instance) is given to $\mathcal{A}$.
- $\mathsf{Execute}(U_C, i, U_S, j)$. The oracle executes the protocol between instances $\Pi^i_{U_C}$ and instances $\Pi^j_{U_S}$. The outputs of the oracle is the protocol transcript, i.e., the ordered messages can be exchanged between the instances.
- $\mathsf{Reveal}(U_C, i)$. The oracle allows the adversary to learn session keys from previous and concurrent executions and outputs the session key skey^i_U. Meanwhile, erasures the improper session keys.
- $\mathsf{Test}(U_C, i)$. The oracle allows the adversary to query it only once and outputs a random bit b. If $b = 1$, then the adversary is obtained a session key skey^i_U. If $b = 0$, then the adversary is obtained a uniform session key. Lastly, the adversary guesses a random bit b'. If $b = b'$ then the adversary is successful.

Partnering. Let U_C, $U_S \in U$. Instances $\Pi^i_{U_C}$ and $\Pi^j_{U_S}$ are partnered if: (1) $\mathsf{sid}^i_U = \mathsf{sid}^i_{U_C} \neq \mathrm{NULL}$; and (2) $\mathsf{pid}^i_{U_C} = U_C$ and $\mathsf{pid}^j_{U_S} = U_S$.

Correctness. If the instance $\Pi^i_{U_C}$ and instance $\Pi^j_{U_S}$ are partnered then there exist $\mathsf{acc}^i_{U_C} = \mathsf{acc}^j_{U_S} = \mathrm{TRUE}$ and $\mathsf{skey}^i_{U_C} = \mathsf{skey}^j_{U_S}$ and they both obtained the common session key.

Definition 5. *For all* PPT *adversaries $\mathcal{A}$ making at most $Q(\lambda)$ on-line guessing attacks, if it holds that $\mathbf{Adv}_{\mathcal{A},\Pi}(\lambda) \leq C' \cdot Q^{s'}(\lambda) + \mathrm{negl}(\lambda)$, then the* PAKE *protocol Π is a secure protocol, where $s' \in [0.15, 0.30]$ and $C' \in [0.001, 0.1]$ are constant CDF-Zipf regression parameters depending on the password space $\mathcal{D}$ [17,18].*

Remark 2. In most existing PAKE studies (e.g., [7–9,11]) and other kinds of password-based protocols (e.g., two-factor authentication [31] and password authenticated keyword search [32]), passwords are assumed to follow a uniformly random distribution, and the real attacker's advantage **Adv** is thus formulated as $Q(\lambda)/|D| + \mathrm{negl}(\lambda)$, where $|D|$ is the size of the password dictionary D, and $Q(\lambda)$ is the number of $\mathcal{A}$'s active on-line password guessing attempts (which is analogous to Q_{send} in [9], q_{send} in [33], n_{se} in [16] and q_s in [7,31,32]). Instead, we prefer the CDF-Zipf model [17,33], and the attacker $\mathcal{A}$'s advantage **Adv** can be formulated as $C' \cdot Q^{s'}(\lambda) + \mathrm{negl}(\lambda)$ for the Zipf parameters C' and s'. Figure 1 shows that the traditional uniform-model based formulation $Q(\lambda)/|D| + \mathrm{negl}(\lambda)$ always significantly underestimates the real attacker $\mathcal{A}$'s **Adv** $(\forall Q(\lambda) \in [1, |D|])$. Fortunately, the CDF-Zipf based formulation $C' \cdot Q^{s'}(\lambda) + \mathrm{negl}(\lambda)$ well approximates $\mathcal{A}$'s advantage **Adv**: $\forall Q(\lambda) \in [1, |D|]$, *the largest deviation* between $C' \cdot Q^{s'}(\lambda) + \mathrm{negl}(\lambda)$ and

Adv is as low as 0.617%. This CDF-Zipf based formulation is also drastically more accurate than other occasionally used formulations like the Min-entropy model in [10] and Becerra et al.'s obscure one (see Eq. 1 in [34]) which undesirably defeats the advantage of the *quantitativeness* of provable security.

3   Reg−SPHF from the Regev Scheme

We now describe how to follow the Katz-Vaikuntanathan framework [13] to design a SPHF for the ciphertext of the Regev scheme [14].

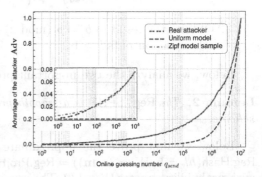

It is well known that the Regev scheme is one of the most classical IND-CPA-secure scheme under the decisional LWE assumption. The others are the Gentry-Peikert-Vaikuntanathan (a.k.a., dual-Regev) scheme [35] and the Lindell-Peikert scheme [36]. In line with the principles of the SPHF of Katz-Vaikuntanathan (KV) construction [13], we adopt Regev scheme as the building block to design the SPHF,

Fig. 1. Online guessing advantages **Adv** of the real attacker, the uniform-modeled attacker and our Zipf-modeled attacker (using 15.25 million 000Webhost passwords [17]).

for simplicity, we abbreviate it to Reg−SPHF. We remark that the other lattice-based PKE schemes also can be used to design the SPHF which follows the framework of Katz-Vaikuntanathan.

- $hk \leftarrow$ Reg.HashKG(params): inputs a random vector $\mathbf{h} \leftarrow \mathbb{Z}_q^{n \times 1}$ and outputs the hashing key $hk := \mathbf{h} \in \mathbb{Z}_q^{m \times 1}$.
- $ph \leftarrow$ Reg.ProjKG(params, $hk = \mathbf{h}, pk = \mathbf{A}$): inputs $\mathbf{h}$ and the public key of IND-CPA-secure scheme $\mathbf{A} \in \mathbb{Z}_q^{n \times m}$, then outputs the projective hashing key $ph := \mathbf{p}_{reg} = \mathbf{A} \cdot \mathbf{h} \in \mathbb{Z}_q^{n \times 1}$. We stress that, in Reg−SPHF setting, we only obtain the "approximate correctness".
- $h \leftarrow$ Reg.Hash($hk = \mathbf{h}, W := (c, \mathbf{m})$) :
  1. The algorithm inputs $\mathbf{h}$ and the word W, where the word W contains a ciphertext $c = \mathbf{c} \in \mathbb{Z}_q^{m \times 1}$ and the plaintext $\mathbf{m}$.
  2. The hash function works as follows:

$$h = \mathsf{Hash}(hk = \mathbf{h}, W := (c, \mathbf{m}))$$
$$= R\Big(\big[\mathbf{c} - (\lfloor \tfrac{q}{2} \rfloor \cdot \mathbf{m})\big]^T \cdot \mathbf{h}\Big) = R\Big(\big[\mathbf{r}^T \cdot \mathbf{A}\big] \cdot \mathbf{h}\Big)$$
$$= R\Big((\mathbf{r}^T \cdot \mathbf{A}) \cdot \mathbf{h} \pmod q) \in \mathbb{Z}_q\Big) \in \{0, 1\}.$$

  3. Obtains $b := h \pmod 2 \in \{0, 1\}$, where h is a number in $[-(q-1)/2, \cdots, (q-1)/2]$ and outputs $b = 0$ if $h < 0$, otherwise, outputs $b = 1$.

– $p = \mathsf{Reg.ProjHash}(ph = \mathbf{p}_{reg}, W := (c, \mathbf{m}); w = \mathbf{s})$ (Projection)

1. The algorithm inputs $ph = \mathbf{p}_{reg} \in \mathbb{Z}_q^{n \times 1}$, the word W, and the witness $\mathbf{s} \in \mathbb{Z}_q^{n \times 1}$.

2. The algorithm computes

$$p = \mathsf{Reg.ProjHash}(ph = \mathbf{p}_{reg}, W := (c, \mathbf{m}); w = \mathbf{r})$$
$$= R\left(\mathbf{r}^T \cdot \mathbf{p}_{reg}\right) = R\left(\mathbf{r}^T \cdot (\mathbf{A}h) \pmod q\right) \in \{0, 1\}.$$

3. Obtains the result of $b := p \pmod 2 \in \{0, 1\}$, and outputs $b = 0$ if $p < 0$, otherwise, outputs $b = 1$.

Below, we analyze the two important properties of $\mathsf{Reg{-}SPHF}$.

Lemma 2. *The* $\mathsf{Reg{-}SPHF}$ *is a smooth projective hash function for the Regev scheme.*

Below we first prove the approximate correctness. Our goal is to prove $\mathsf{Reg.Hash}(hk = \mathbf{h}, W := (c, \mathbf{m})) = \mathsf{Reg.ProjHash}(ph = \mathbf{p}_{reg}, W := (c, \mathbf{m}); w = \mathbf{s})$ with probability greater than $1/2$. The correctness of $\mathsf{Reg{-}SPHF}$ means that the relationship between the hash key hk and the word W from language L equals the relationship between the projective hash key ph and the witness w for any word in L. The smoothness of $\mathsf{Reg{-}SPHF}$ is that the hash value is independent of the projective hash key ph for any word in $X \setminus L$. Moreover, in order to discard the noise elements, we adopt the typical deterministic rounding function $R(x) = \lfloor 2x/q \rceil \pmod 2$ (a.k.a., the so-called square-signal) which was proposed by Katz and Vaikuntanathan [13].

– **Projective (or Correctness).** If the result of $\langle \mathbf{e}, \mathbf{h} \rangle$ is small for $n, m \geq n\sqrt{\log q}$, then the following equation holds

$$R\left(\mathsf{Reg.Hash}(hk = \mathbf{h}, W := (c, \mathbf{m}))\right)$$
$$= R\left(\mathsf{Reg.ProjHash}(ph = \mathbf{p}_{reg}, W := (c, \mathbf{m}); w = \mathbf{s})\right).$$

Proof. In this paper, we follow the methodology of [13] and adopt the typical deterministic rounding function $R(x) = \lfloor 2x/q \rceil \pmod 2$ to calculate $\mathsf{Hash}(\cdot)$ and $\mathsf{ProjHash}(\cdot)$ respectively. Regarding the following two equations Eqs. (3.1) and (3.2),

$$\left(\mathsf{Reg.Hash}(hk = \mathbf{h}, W := (c, \mathbf{m}))\right)$$
$$= \left([\mathbf{r}^T \cdot \mathbf{A}] \cdot \mathbf{k}\right) = \left((\mathbf{r}^T \cdot \mathbf{A}) \cdot \mathbf{k} \pmod q\right). \tag{3.1}$$

$$\left(\mathsf{Reg.Hash}(hk = \mathbf{h}, W := (c, \mathbf{m}))\right)$$
$$= \left(\mathbf{r}^T \cdot \mathbf{p}_{reg}\right) = \left(\mathbf{r}^T \cdot (\mathbf{A}k) \pmod q\right). \tag{3.2}$$

we can easily find that the above two equations Eqs. (3.1) and (3.2) are equal, then we can utilize the rounding function $R(\cdot)$ and find that the output of $R\Big(\mathsf{Reg.Hash}(hk = \mathbf{h}, W := (c, \mathbf{m}))\Big)$ and $R\Big(\mathsf{Reg.ProjHash}(ph = \mathbf{p}_{reg}, W :=$ $(c, \mathbf{m}); w = \mathbf{s})\Big)$ are equal. □

– **Smoothness.** Below we prove the smoothness property of Reg–SPHF.

Proof. Consider the word $W := (c, \mathbf{m}) \notin L$, that means c is not an encryption of $\mathbf{m}$, under the public key $pk = \mathbf{A}$. Hence the above implies that the following two distributions have negligible statistical distance in λ,

(1).$\{(ph, h) \mid \mathsf{HashKG}(L) \to \mathbf{h}, \mathsf{ProjKG}(hk, L, W) \to \mathbf{Ah}$,
$\underline{\mathsf{Hash}(hk, L, W) = (\mathbf{r}^T \mathbf{A})\mathbf{h}}\}$.

(2).$\{(ph, h) \mid \mathsf{HashKG}(L) \to \mathbf{h}, \mathsf{ProjKG}(hk, L, W) \to \mathbf{Ah}, h \leftarrow \{0, 1\}\}$.

We note that, $\mathsf{Hash}(hk, W) = (\mathbf{r}^T \mathbf{A})\mathbf{h}$ given $\mathsf{ProjKG}(hk, pk) = \mathbf{Ah}$. Due to $\mathbf{r}$ is witness vector, thus $\mathsf{ProjKG}(hk, pk)$ provides no information on $\mathsf{Hash}(hk, W)$ and $\mathsf{Hash}(hk, W)$ is uniformly distributed over $\{0, 1\}$, given $\mathsf{ProjKG}(hk, pk)$.

Hence, we conclude that the projective hash function is smooth. □

4   MP–SPHF from the Miccianio-Peikert Scheme

The MP construction is IND-CCA1-secure, but the Katz-Vaikuntanathan framework requires the IND-CCA2-secure scheme along with the corresponding SPHF. Hence, we can use either strongly unforgeable one-time signature [37], or a message authentication code (MAC) and weak form of commitment [38] to obtain the IND-CCA2 security. Below we first present the labeled IND-CCA1-secure scheme. For the sake of simplicity, we omit the generic transformation to IND-CCA2 at this stage which can be found in [37].

We first fix the label by $u \neq 0$ and obtain the labeled MP scheme, then we use it to develop an SPHF. Following the Katz-Vaikuntanathan (KV) construction, below we present an SPHF based on MP scheme, we call it MP–SPHF.

– $hk \leftarrow \mathsf{MP.HashKG}(\text{params})$: samples $\mathbf{k} \leftarrow \mathbb{Z}_q^{n \times 1}$ and sets it as the hashing key $hk := \mathbf{k} \in \mathbb{Z}_q^{m \times 1}$.
– $ph \leftarrow \mathsf{MP.ProjKG}(\text{params}, hk = \mathbf{k}, pk = \mathbf{A}_u)$: inputs the $\mathbf{k}$ and the public key of IND-CCA scheme $\mathbf{A}_u = [\bar{\mathbf{A}} \mid h(u)\mathbf{G} - \bar{\mathbf{A}}\mathbf{R}] \in \mathbb{Z}_q^{n \times m}$ with the fixed label u, then outputs the projective hashing key $ph := \mathbf{p} = \mathbf{A}_u \cdot \mathbf{k} \in \mathbb{Z}_q^{n \times 1}$.
– $h \leftarrow \mathsf{MP.Hash}(hk = \mathbf{k}, W := (c, \mathbf{m}))$:
  1. The algorithm inputs $\mathbf{k}$ and the word W, where W contains a ciphertext $c = (\text{label}, \mathbf{c} \in \mathbb{Z}_q^{m \times 1})$ and the plaintext $\mathbf{m}$.
  2. The hash function works as follows:

$$h = \mathsf{MP.Hash}(hk = \mathbf{k}, W := (c, \mathbf{m}))$$
$$= R\Big([\mathbf{c} - (\mathbf{0} \mid \mathsf{encode}(\mathbf{m}))]^T \cdot \mathbf{k}\Big) = R\Big([\mathbf{s}^T \cdot \mathbf{A}_u + \mathbf{e}^T] \cdot \mathbf{k}\Big)$$
$$= R\Big((\mathbf{s}^T \cdot \mathbf{A}_u) \cdot \mathbf{k} + \mathbf{e}^T \cdot \mathbf{k} \pmod{q}\Big) \in \mathbb{Z}_q\Big) \in \{0, 1\}.$$

We stress that $\mathbf{e}^T \cdot \mathbf{k}$ is the noise element $\mathbf{e}^T \cdot \mathbf{k}$ and bounded by $|\mathbf{e}^T\mathbf{k}| \leq \|\mathbf{e}^T\| \cdot \|\mathbf{k}\| \leq (r\sqrt{mn}) \cdot (\alpha q\sqrt{mn}) < \varepsilon/2 \cdot q/4$.

3. Outputs $b := h \pmod 2 \in \{0,1\}$, where h is a number in $[-(q-1)/2, \cdots, (q-1)/2]$ and the algorithm outputs $b = 0$ if $h < 0$, otherwise, outputs $b = 1$.

- $p = \mathsf{MP.ProjHash}(ph = \mathbf{p}, W := (c, \mathbf{m}); w = \mathbf{s})$
  1. It inputs $ph = \mathbf{p} \in \mathbb{Z}_q^{n \times 1}$, the word W, and the witness $\mathbf{s} \in \mathbb{Z}_q^{n \times 1}$.
  2. The algorithm computes and outputs

$$p = \mathsf{ProjHash}(ph = \mathbf{p}, W := (c, \mathbf{m}); w = \mathbf{s})$$
$$= R\Big(\mathbf{s}^T \cdot \mathbf{p}\Big) = R\Big(\mathbf{s}^T \cdot (\mathbf{A}_u \mathbf{k}) \pmod q\Big) \in \{0,1\}.$$

  3. Obtains $b := p \pmod 2 \in \{0,1\}$, and outputs $b = 0$ if $p < 0$, otherwise, outputs $b = 1$.

Lemma 3. *The MP–SPHF is a smooth projective hash function for the MP scheme.*

Below we first prove our scheme achieves approximate correctness. Similar to the projective property of Reg–SPHF, our goal is to prove $\mathsf{MP.Hash}(hk = \mathbf{k}, W := (c, \mathbf{m})) = \mathsf{MP.ProjHash}(ph = \mathbf{p}, W := (c, \mathbf{m}); w = \mathbf{s})$ with probability greater than $1/2$. Moreover, we still use the rounding function $R(x) = \lfloor 2x/q \rceil \pmod 2$ to discard the noise elements.

- **Projective (or Approximate Correctness).** If the result of $\langle \mathbf{e}, \mathbf{k} \rangle$ is small for n, $m \geq n\sqrt{\log q}$, then the following equation holds

$$R\Big(\mathsf{Hash}(hk = \mathbf{k}, W := (c, \mathbf{m}))\Big) = R\Big(\mathsf{ProjHash}(ph = \mathbf{p}, W := (c, \mathbf{m}); w = \mathbf{s})\Big).$$

Proof. In this paper, we adopt the typical deterministic rounding function $R(x) = \lfloor 2x/q \rceil \pmod 2$ and follow the methodology of [13] to round the outputs of $\mathsf{Hash}(\cdot)$ and $\mathsf{ProjHash}(\cdot)$ respectively. Regarding the following two equations,

$$\Big(\mathsf{Hash}(hk = \mathbf{k}, W := (c, \mathbf{m}))\Big) = \Big([\mathbf{s}^T \cdot \mathbf{A}_u + \mathbf{e}^T] \cdot \mathbf{k}\Big)$$
$$= \Big((\mathbf{s}^T \cdot \mathbf{A}_u) \cdot \mathbf{k} + \mathbf{e}^T \cdot \mathbf{k} \pmod q\Big) \quad (4.1)$$

$$\Big(\mathsf{ProjHash}(ph = \mathbf{p}, W := (c, \mathbf{m}); w = \mathbf{s})\Big) = \Big(\mathbf{s}^T \cdot \mathbf{p}\Big)$$
$$= \Big(\mathbf{s}^T \cdot (\mathbf{A}_u \mathbf{k}) \pmod q\Big) \quad (4.2)$$

We first consider the equation Eq. (4.1) and the Definition 1, the result of $R(h)$ can be viewed as a number in $[-\frac{(q-1)}{2}, \cdots, \frac{(q-1)}{2}]$, and we can obtain the result $b \in \{0, 1\}$. Moreover, the noise element $\mathbf{e}^T \cdot \mathbf{k}$ is bounded by $|\mathbf{e}^T \mathbf{k}| \leq \|\mathbf{e}^T\| \cdot \|\mathbf{k}\| \leq (r\sqrt{mn}) \cdot (\alpha q \sqrt{mn}) < \varepsilon/2 \cdot q/4$. Hence, the result of $R(\mathbf{e}^T \mathbf{k})$ is identical with 0. Thus, there exists

$$b = \begin{cases} 0, & \text{if } R(h) < 0; \\ 1, & \text{if } R(h) > 0. \end{cases}$$

Consider the equation Eq. (4.2) and the Definition 1, we have that

$$b = \begin{cases} 0, & \text{if } R\big(\mathbf{s}^T \cdot (\mathbf{A}_u \mathbf{k})\big) < 0; \\ 1, & \text{if } R\big(\mathbf{s}^T \cdot (\mathbf{A}_u \mathbf{k})\big) > 0. \end{cases}$$

Obliviously, the above two results are equal since the size of the noise $\|\mathbf{e}^T \mathbf{k}\|$ is bounded by $q\varepsilon/8 < q/4$. $\square$

– **Smoothness.** Below we prove the smoothness property of MP−SPHF.

Proof. Consider the word $W := (c, \mathbf{m}) \notin L$, that means c is not an encryption of $\mathbf{m}$, under the public key $pk = \mathbf{A}_u$. Hence the above implies that the following two distributions have negligible statistical distance in λ,

(1).$\{(ph, h) \mid \mathsf{HashKG}(L) \to \mathbf{k}, \mathsf{ProjKG}(hk, L, W) \to \mathbf{A}_u \mathbf{k},$
  $\underline{\mathsf{Hash}(hk, L, W) = (\mathbf{s}^T \mathbf{A}_u + \mathbf{e}^T)\mathbf{k}}\}.$

(2).$\{(ph, h) \mid \mathsf{HashKG}(L) \to \mathbf{k}, \mathsf{ProjKG}(hk, L, W) \to \mathbf{A}_u \mathbf{k},$
  $\underline{h \leftarrow \{0, 1\}}\}.$

We note that, $\mathsf{MP.Hash}(hk, W) = (\mathbf{s}^T \mathbf{A}_u + \mathbf{e}^T)\mathbf{k}$ given $\mathsf{MP.ProjKG}(hk, pk) = \mathbf{A}_u \mathbf{k}$. Due to $\mathbf{s}$ is witness vector, thus $\mathsf{MP.ProjKG}(hk, pk)$ provides no information on $\mathsf{MP.Hash}(hk, W)$ and $\mathsf{MP.Hash}(hk, W)$ is uniformly distributed over $\{0, 1\}$, given $\mathsf{MP.ProjKG}(hk, pk)$.

Hence, we conclude that the projective hash function is smooth. $\square$

5   Two-Round **PAKE** Protocol over Lattices

At ASIACRYPT'17, Zhang and Yu proposed a lattice-based two-round PAKE protocol [11] using simulation-sound NIZK in the random oracle model. At PKC'15, Abdalla et al. [10] proposed the new cryptographic primitive "IND-PCA-secure PKE" to design two-round PAKE protocols without NIZK.[3] However, this PAKE builds on the DDH assumption and cannot prevent quantum attacks. To our knowledge, it remains an open question to construct a two-round PAKE protocol under the LWE setting without NIZK in the random oracle model.

---

[3] They improved the Gennaro-Lindell framework to reduce the round number to two.

COMMON REFERENCE STRING(PUBLIC KEY):
$pk_{cca} \leftarrow$ MP.KeyGen($\cdot$) and $pk_{cpa} \leftarrow$ Reg.KeyGen($\cdot$).

Client C	Server S
with a low-entropy password π	with a low-entropy password π

1). Invokes $hk_C^{cca} \leftarrow$ MP.HashKG(params)
2). $ph_C^{cca} \leftarrow$ MP.ProjKG(params, hk_C^{CCA}, pk)
3). Sets label $\ell = C \parallel S \parallel ph_C^{cca}$
4). $\mathbf{c}_C^{cca} \leftarrow$ MP.Enc(params, $pk_{cca}, \pi; r \leftarrow \mathbb{Z}_p$)

$\xrightarrow{\mathbf{c}_C^{cca}, ph_C^{cca}}$ 5). Receives ph_C^{cca} and $\mathbf{c}_C^{cca}$.
6). Sets label $\ell = C \parallel S \parallel ph_C^{cca}$
7). $\mathbf{c}_S \leftarrow$ Reg.Enc(params, $pk_{cpa}, \pi; r \leftarrow \mathbb{Z}_p$)
8). Invokes $hk_S^{cpa} \leftarrow$ Reg.HashKG(params, ℓ)
9). $ph_S^{cpa} \leftarrow$ Reg.ProjKG(params, ℓ, hk_S^{cpa}, pk)

10). Receives ph_S^{cpa} and $\mathbf{c}_S^{cpa}$. $\xleftarrow{\mathbf{c}_S^{cpa}, ph_S^{cpa}}$
11). MP.ProjHash(ph_S^{cpa},   11). Reg.ProjHash(ph_C^{cca},
$\quad W_C^{cca} = (\mathbf{c}_C^{cca}, \pi); w_C = r$). $\quad W_S^{cpa} = (\mathbf{c}_S^{cpa}, \pi); w_S = \bar{r}$).
Obtains p_S Obtains p_C
12). MP.Hash($hk_C^{cca}, W_S^{cpa} := (\mathbf{c}_S^{cpa}, \pi)$)   12). Reg.Hash($hk_S^{cpa}, W_C^{cca} := (\mathbf{c}_C^{cca}, \pi)$)
Outputs h_C Outputs h_S
Outputs key $:= (p_S \cdot h_C)$ Outputs key $:= (p_C \cdot h_S)$
Erases everything except π and key   Erases everything except π and key

Fig. 2. A sketch of our two-round lattice-based PAKE protocol.

In this section, armed with the above MP−SPHF and Reg−SPHF, we follow the framework of Abdalla-Benhamouda-Pointcheval and design a new lattice-based two-round PAKE protocol. Here we provide a high view of our protocol:

- **First round.** The client runs the Miccianio-Peikert scheme with an associated MP−SPHF, then sends the first flow message (i.e., the ciphertext of Miccianio-Peikert scheme along with the corresponding signature and the projective hash key of MP−SPHF) to the server.
- **Second round.** Upon receiving the information from the client, the server first checks the legitimacy of the signature, then runs the Regev scheme with an associated Reg−SPHF. Subsequently, the server returns the second flow message (i.e., the ciphertext of the Regev scheme and the projective hash key of Reg−SPHF) to the client.
- **Local computation.** After receiving the messages from the other party, both parties perform the calculation locally on the received message and the local message. Concretely, the client generates the common session key $= (p_S \cdot h_C)$ and the server generates the common session key $= (p_C \cdot h_S)$.

Figure 2 illustrates the detailed description of the two-round PAKE protocol over lattices. Since every IND-CCA2-secure encryption is also IND-PCA-secure, we follow the road-map of [10] and achieve the expected two-round PAKE. Importantly, we do not depend on a simulation-sound NIZK [11] and the detailed explanation can be found in [39]. In this case, we can omit the issue of the gap between correctness and smoothness because the proof of the resulting two-round PAKE works exactly as in [10]. The details are provided in Appendix of [39].

Moreover, as far as we know, if the label of the label-IND-CCA2 encryption scheme is fixed in advance to some public constant, then the resulting scheme is IND-CPA. Hence, we can follow the generic transformation of [39] to convert a label-IND-CCA2 encryption scheme with message space $\{0,1\}$ and label space $\{0,1\}^\lambda$ into a IND-CCA2 encryption scheme with message space $\{0,1\}^v$ (for some v polynomial in λ) and label space $\{0,1\}^*$ according to [37]. In a concrete way, a strongly unforgeable one-time signature scheme (Gen, Sign, Ver) was introduced to achieve the above goal. The client invokes the algorithm Sign and takes as input the ciphertext c_C^{cca}. Subsequently, the server will verify the signature of the ciphertext using the algorithm Ver. For the sake of explanation, we omit this transformation step in the above protocol.

5.1 Correctness Analysis

In this subsection, we analyze the correctness of our PAKE protocol.

Lemma 4. *If the two communication parties obtained the same common session key, then the correctness holds.*

Proof. For the client side, the client C obtained the session key as follows

$$
\begin{aligned}
\mathsf{skey}_C &= p_S' \cdot (p_S \cdot h_C) \cdot h_C' \\
&= R\Big(s^T(\frac{A_u}{A})Ah\Big) \cdot R\Big(s^T Ah\Big) \cdot R\Big(r^T Ak\Big) \cdot R\Big(r^T A(\frac{A_u}{A}k)\Big) \\
&= R\Big(s^T A_u h\Big) \cdot R\Big(s^T Ah\Big) \cdot R\Big(r^T Ak\Big) \cdot R\Big(r^T A_u k\Big)
\end{aligned}
$$

Meanwhile, for the server side, the server S obtained the session key as follows

$$
\begin{aligned}
\mathsf{skey}_S &= p_C' \cdot (p_C \cdot h_S) \cdot h_S' \\
&= R\Big(r^T(\frac{A}{A_u})A_u k\Big) \cdot R\Big(r^T A_u k\Big) \\
&\quad \cdot R\Big((s^T A_u + e^T)h\Big) \cdot R\Big((s^T A_u + e^T)(\frac{A_u}{A})h\Big) \\
&= R\Big(r^T Ak\Big) \cdot R\Big(r^T A_u k\Big) \cdot R\Big((s^T A_u + e^T)h\Big) \cdot R\Big((s^T A + e^T(\frac{A_u}{A}))h\Big)
\end{aligned}
$$

In order to meet the requirements of the Lemma 3 and the typical deterministic rounding function $R(x) = \lfloor 2x/q \rfloor \pmod 2$ from [13], we consider $max\{\|e^T h\|, \|e^T(\frac{A_u}{A})h\|\} \leq q/4$ for the bound of $\|e^T h\| \leq mB$ and $\|e^T(\frac{A_u}{A})h\| \leq O(mB)$.[4] In this setting, the output of the typical deterministic rounding function $R\Big((s^T A_u + e^T)h\Big) = R\Big((s^T A_u)h\Big)$ and the output of $R\Big((s^T A + e^T(\frac{A_u}{A}))h\Big) = R\Big((s^T A))h\Big)$. Hence, we have that $\mathsf{skey}_C = \mathsf{skey}_S$. □

---

[4] We use big-O notation to asymptotically bound the growth of a running time to within constant factors.

5.2   Security Analysis

Theorem 1. *The two-round lattice-based PAKE protocol from Fig. 2 is secure in the BPR model, under the LWE assumption.*

Proof. Below we provide the sketched proof because of the space limitation. Roughly speaking, this proof follows the schemes given in Benhamuda et al. [5,7,40], we only check that our primitives (Reg−SPHF and MP−SPHF) fulfill the same properties in order to be able to modularly apply the proof given in [40].

Experiment Expt.0. This is the real attack game, the advantage was denoted by $\mathsf{Adv}_{\mathcal{A}}^{\mathsf{Expt.0}}(\lambda) = \varepsilon$. Then, we incrementally modify the simulate procession to make the trivial attacks possible. In this experiment, all of the private input values of the honest players can be used by the simulator. Following [7,15], there exist three types of Send queries:

- $\mathsf{Send}_0(C, i, S)$-query. In this setting, the adversary asks the instance $\varPi_C^i$ to initiate an execution with an instance of S. Then S answers the query by a flow and returns it to C.
- $\mathsf{Send}_1(S, j, \mathsf{msg})$-query. The adversary sends the first flow message msg to the instance $\varPi_S^j$. The oracle defines his own session key and returns second flow which answered back by the instance $\varPi_S^j$.
- $\mathsf{Send}_2(C, i, \mathsf{msg})$-query. The adversary sends the second flow message msg to the instance $\varPi_C^i$. The oracle gives no answer back, but defines his own session key, for possible later Reveal or Test queries.

We remark that, if there exists $\pi_C = \pi_{C,S}$, then the client C and the server S are compatible. Actually, the definition of "compatibility" was defined by Katz et al. [30,41] which means even if the password was changed during the execution of the protocol, the changed password does not have an effect on the execution.

Experiment Expt.1. We first modify the way how to deal with the Execute-queries. Concretely, in response to a query $\mathsf{Execute}(U_C, i, U_S, j)$, we use the encryption of dummy passwords π_C^0 and $\pi_{C,S}^0$ from Zipf distribution to replace the ciphertext $\mathbf{c}_C$ and $\mathbf{c}_S$. Apparently, the fake passwords π_C^0 and π_S^0 are not in language L and the random elements are not used in the generation of the fake ciphertext. This is indistinguishable from Expt.0 under the IND-CPA property of the encryption scheme. Moreover, due to the hash key and projective key are known by the players, hence they can compute the common session key

$$
\begin{aligned}
\mathsf{key} &= \mathsf{Hash}(hk_C, W_S := (\mathbf{c}_S, \pi)) \cdot \mathsf{ProjHash}(ph_S, W_C = (\mathbf{c}_C, \pi); w_C = r) \\
&= \mathsf{Hash}(hk_S, W_C := (\mathbf{c}_C, \pi)) \cdot \mathsf{ProjHash}(ph_C, W_S = (\mathbf{c}_S, \pi); w_S = \bar{r}) \\
&= \mathsf{key}
\end{aligned}
$$

Since we could have first modified the way to compute key, which has no impact at all from the soundness of the SPHF, the unique difference comes from the different ciphertexts. Actually, this is indistinguishable property of the probabilistic encryption scheme, for each Execute-query.

For future convenience, we define this experiment as Event Ev_0 whose probability is computed in Expt.8. Thus we can obtain $|\mathsf{Adv}_{\mathcal{A}}^{\mathsf{Expt}.1}(\lambda) - \mathsf{Adv}_{\mathcal{A}}^{\mathsf{Expt}.0}(\lambda)| \leq \mathsf{negl}(\lambda)$ by using a series of hybrid hops.

Experiment Expt.2. In this experiment, again, we modify the way of the Execute-queries response. We sample a random value from uniform distribution, then use it to replace the common session key. In this setting, the "password" is not satisfied, the indistinguishability property is guaranteed by the smoothness, i.e., $|\mathsf{Adv}_{\mathcal{A}}^{\mathsf{Expt}.2}(\lambda) - \mathsf{Adv}_{\mathcal{A}}^{\mathsf{Expt}.1}(\lambda)| \leq \mathsf{negl}(\lambda)$.

Experiment Expt.3. This experiment is identical to the Expt.2 except that we change the way how to deal with the Send_1-queries. Concretely, in this experiment, we use a Miccianio-Peikert decryption oracle (or alternatively knowing the decryption key of Miccianio-Peikert scheme) to decrypt the "unused" received message $\mathsf{msg} = (ph_C, \mathbf{c}_C)$, three cases can appear:

1. If the msg has been altered (even generated) by the simulator in the name of the client C, then one can obtain the word W by checking whether the ciphertext $\mathbf{c}_C$ contains the expected password $\pi_{S,C}$ or not, along with the label $\ell = C||S||ph_C$. Then, there exist two cases:
   (a) If they are correct $W \in L$ (or the expected password is encrypted) and consistent with the receiver's values, then one can assert that the adversary $\mathcal{A}$ succeeds (i.e., $b' = b$) and terminates the game.
   (b) If they are not both correct and consistent with the receiver's values, then one chooses key at random.
2. If the msg is used previously (or, it is a replay of a previous flow sent by the simulator which in the name of the client C), then, in particular, the simulator knows the hash key and obtains the projective key, then the simulator can compute the common session key by using the hash key and the projective key. Namely key $= \mathsf{Hash}(hk_C, W_S := (\mathbf{c}_S, \pi)) \cdot \mathsf{ProjHash}(ph_S, W_C = (\mathbf{c}_C, \pi); w_C = r)$, where we stress that $\mathbf{c}_S$ is not generated by using the randomness, which is similar to Expt.2.

For future convenience, we define the first case (1a) as Event Ev_1 whose probability is computed in Expt.6. We note that the change of the case (1a) can only increase the advantage of $\mathcal{A}$. Actually, the second change in the case (1b) only increases the advantage of the adversary by a negligible term due to it is indistinguishable under the adaptive-smoothness. Meanwhile, the third change in the case (2) does not affect the way the key is computed, so finally $|\mathsf{Adv}_{\mathcal{A}}^{\mathsf{Expt}.3}(\lambda) - \mathsf{Adv}_{\mathcal{A}}^{\mathsf{Expt}.2}(\lambda)| \leq \mathsf{negl}(\lambda)$.

Experiment Expt.4. This experiment is identical to the Expt.3 except that we change the way how to deal with the Send_2-queries. Concretely, in this experiment, the simulator can query a Regev decryption oracle (or alternatively knowing the decryption key of the Regev scheme), namely that the simulator in the name of the server instance $\Pi_{U_S}^j$ sends the second flow $\mathsf{msg} = (ph_S, \mathbf{c}_S)$ to the client instance $\Pi_{U_C}^i$. Three cases can appear:

1. If the msg has been altered (even generated) by the simulator in the name of the server S, in order to response to first flow message msg $= (ph_C, \mathbf{c}_C)$ that sent by the client instance $\Pi^i_{U_C}$, then one can obtain the word W by checking whether the ciphertext $\mathbf{c}_C$ contains the expected password $\pi_{S,C}$ or not, along with the label $\ell = C||S||ph_C$. Then, there exist two cases:
   (a) If they are correct $W \in L$ (or the expected password is encrypted) and consistent with the receiver's values, then one can assert that the adversary $\mathcal{A}$ succeeds (i.e., $b' = b$) and terminates the simulation.
   (b) If they are not both correct and consistent with the receiver's values, then one chooses key at random.
2. After receiving the first flow msg $= (ph_C, \mathbf{c}_C)$, if the msg is used previously (or, it is a replay of a previous flow sent by the simulator which in the name of the client $\Pi^j_{U_S}{}'$), then, $\Pi^i_{U_C}$ and $\Pi^j_{U_S}{}'$ are partners. In particular,
   (a) If S and C are compatible, then the simulator knows the hash key and obtains the projective key, then the simulator can compute the common session key by using the hash key and the projective key. Namely key $=$ Hash$(hk_C, W_S := (\mathbf{c}_S, \pi)) \cdot$ ProjHash$(ph_S, W_C = (\mathbf{c}_C, \pi); w_C = r)$, where we stress that $\mathbf{c}_S$ is not generated by using the randomness, which is similar to Expt.2.
   (b) Otherwise, we choose a random common session key.

For future convenience, we define the first case (1a) as Event Ev_2 whose probability is computed in Expt.8. We note that the change of the case (1a) can only increase the advantage of $\mathcal{A}$. Actually, the second change in the case (1b) only increases the advantage of the adversary by a negligible term due to it is indistinguishable under the adaptive-smoothness property. Meanwhile, the third change in the case (2a) does not affect the way the key is computed, so finally $|\mathsf{Adv}^{\mathsf{Expt.4}}_{\mathcal{A}}(\lambda) - \mathsf{Adv}^{\mathsf{Expt.3}}_{\mathcal{A}}(\lambda)| \leq \mathrm{negl}(\lambda)$.

Experiment Expt.5. We change the way of the Send$_1$-queries response. Now two cases will appear after a "used" message msg $= (ph_C, \mathbf{c}_C)$ is sent.

- If there exists an instance $\Pi^i_{U_C}$ of U_C partnered with an instance $\Pi^j_{U_S}$ of U_S, then set key $=$ skey$^i_C =$ skey^j_S.
- Otherwise, one chooses key at random.

Note that, in the first case, due to the "used" message is a reply of a previous flow, thus the common session key remains identical. In the second case, Due to the adaptive-smoothness [7,15], even if when hashing keys and ciphertexts are re-used, all the hash values are random looking. Hence, the indistinguishable holds and there exists $|\mathsf{Adv}^{\mathsf{Expt.5}}_{\mathcal{A}}(\lambda) - \mathsf{Adv}^{\mathsf{Expt.4}}_{\mathcal{A}}(\lambda)| \leq \mathrm{negl}(\lambda)$.

Experiment Expt.6. We change the way the Send$_1$-queries respond. Now two cases will appear after a "used" message msg $= (ph_S, \mathbf{c}_S)$ is send.

- If there exists an instance Π^j_S of U_S partnered with an instance Π^i_C of U_C, then set key $=$ skey$^i_C =$ skey^j_S.
- Otherwise, one chooses key at random.

Similar to the Expt.5, the indistinguishability holds and there exists $|\mathsf{Adv}_{\mathcal{A}}^{\mathsf{Expt}.6}(\lambda) - \mathsf{Adv}_{\mathcal{A}}^{\mathsf{Expt}.5}(\lambda)| \leq \mathrm{negl}(\lambda)$.

Experiment Expt.7. We now modify the way how to deal with the Send_0-queries. We remark that, in previous experiments, we don't need to know the random $\mathbf{r}_C$ (a.k.a., witness $w_C = \mathbf{r}_C$) which can be used to obtain the ciphertext $\mathbf{c}_C$. In this experiment, instead of encrypting the correct and real passwords, one encrypts the fake π_0 which does as in Expt.1 for Execute-queries to answer the query $\mathsf{Send}_0(C, i, S)$. Due to it is necessary to simulate the decryption of the Send_1-queries, then the indistinguishability holds for IND-CCA-secure Miccianio-Peikert PKE scheme. Therefore, we have $|\mathsf{Adv}_{\mathcal{A}}^{\mathsf{Expt}.7}(\lambda) - \mathsf{Adv}_{\mathcal{A}}^{\mathsf{Expt}.6}(\lambda)| \leq \mathrm{negl}(\lambda)$.

Experiment Expt.8. This experiment is identical to the Expt.5 except that we adopt the dummy private inputs for the hash key hk and the projective key ph. Concretely, hk and ph do not depend upon the word W, the distributions of these keys are independent of the auxiliary private inputs, hence there exists $|\mathsf{Adv}_{\mathcal{A}}^{\mathsf{Expt}.8}(\lambda) - \mathsf{Adv}_{\mathcal{A}}^{\mathsf{Expt}.7}(\lambda)| \leq \mathrm{negl}(\lambda)$. Putting them together, we can obtain

$$\mathsf{Adv}_{\mathcal{A}}^{\mathsf{Expt}.8}(\lambda) \geq \mathsf{Adv}_{\mathcal{A}}^{\mathsf{Expt}.0}(\lambda) - \mathrm{negl}(\lambda) = \varepsilon - \mathrm{negl}(\lambda).$$

Actually, the Expt.8 is only used for declaring whether $\mathcal{A}$ won the event Ev or not. So the advantage is exactly: $\mathsf{Adv}_{\mathcal{A}}^{\mathsf{Expt}.6}(\lambda) = \Pr[Ev]$. Therefore, we have

$$\varepsilon \leq \Pr[Ev_0] + \Pr[Ev_1] + \Pr[Ev_2] + \mathrm{negl}(\lambda).$$

As mentioned earlier, **(1)**. the event Ev_0 means that $\mathcal{A}$ wins the Expt.1 during the Execute($\cdot$) queries. $\Pr[Ev_0] = \Pr[\exists k_0 \in Q_e^{s'}(\lambda) : \pi_{C,S}(k_0) = \pi_C(k), W \in L]$, where $k_0 \in Q_e^{s'}(\lambda)$ is the index of the recepient of k_0-th Execute-query and $Q_e^{s'}(\lambda)$ is the number of the Execute-queries. **(2)**. The event Ev_1 means that the adversary has encrypted (π) that are correct $(W \in L)$ and consistent with the receiver's values $(\pi_{C,S} = \pi)$. Since the random values (or witness) for the honest players are never used during the simulation, we can assume we choose them at the very end only to check whether event Ev_1 happened:

$$\Pr[Ev_1] = \Pr[\exists k_1 \in Q_{s1}^{s'}(\lambda) : \pi_{C,S}(k_1) = \pi_C(k), W \in L],$$

where $k_1 \in Q_{s1}^{s'}(\lambda)$ is the index of the recepient of k_1-th Send_1-query and $Q_{s1}^{s'}(\lambda)$ is the number of the Send_1-queries. Similarly, **(3)**. the event Ev_3 means that the adversary has encrypted (π) that are correct $(W \in L)$ and consistent with the receiver's values $(\pi_{C,S} = \pi)$. Since the random values (or witness) for the honest players are never used during the simulation, we can assume we choose them at the very end only to check whether event Ev_2 happened:

$$\Pr[Ev_2] = \Pr[\exists k_2 \in Q_{s3}^{s'}(\lambda) : \pi_{C,S}(k_2) = \pi_C(k), W \in L],$$

where $k_2 \in Q_{s2}^{s'}(\lambda)$ is the index of the recepient of k_2-th Send_1-query and $Q_{s2}^{s'}(\lambda)$ is the number of the Send_2-queries.

In other words, it first has to guess the private values, and then once it has guessed them, it has to find a word in the language, hence, there exists

$$\Pr[Ev_1] + \Pr[Ev_2] + \Pr[Ev_3] \leq C' \cdot \left(Q_e^{s'}(\lambda) + Q_{s1}^{s'}(\lambda) + Q_{s2}^{s'}(\lambda) \right) \times Succ^L(\lambda),$$

where $Succ^L(\lambda)$ is the best success an adversary can get in finding a word in a language L. Then, by combining all the inequalities, one can get

$$\varepsilon \leq C' \cdot \left(Q_e^{s'}(\lambda) + Q_{s1}^{s'}(\lambda) + Q_{s2}^{s'}(\lambda) \right) \times Succ^L(t) + \mathrm{negl}(\lambda).$$

This completes the proof.   □

Table 1. A comparison of related PAKE protocols under LWE assumption.

Scheme	SPHF	Rounds	Client&Server	Framework	Building blocks
Katz-Vaikuntanathan[13]	KV[13]	3	CCA & CCA	KV[13]	Peikert Enc[25]
Zhang-Yu[11]	GL[5]	2	CCA & CCA	GL[5]	Peikert Enc[25]
Bonhamouda et al.[39]	KV[13]	1(2-flow)	CCA & CCA	KV[15]	Mic-Pei Enc[12]
Our scheme	KV[13]	2	CCA & CPA	ABP[10]	Mic-Pei Enc[12] & Regev enc[14]

KV−SPHF implies that adaptive smoothness and the ph dependents on W.
GL−SPHF implies that non-adaptive smoothness and the ph independent on W.

6   Conclusion

In this paper, we first design two types of new lattice-based SPHFs (i.e., the IND-CCA-secure MP−SPHF at client side and the IND-PCA-secure Reg−SPHF at server side) by following the KV−SPHF methodology. Then, we construct the first lattice-based two-round PAKE protocol via Reg−SPHF and MP−SPHF, avoiding using the simulation-sound NIZK in random oracle model as compared to the foremost two-round PAKE protocol by Zhang and Yu at ASIACRYPT'17 [11]. Besides, as shown in Table 1, our protocol builds on weaker security assumptions than those state-of-the-art PAKE protocols [11,13,39] from the LWE assumption.

Acknowledgments. The authors would like to thank the anonymous reviewers for their helpful advice and comments. This work was supported by the National Natural Science Foundation of China (No. 61802006 and No. 61802214).

References

1. Bellovin, S.M., Merritt, M.: Encrypted key exchange: password-based protocols secure against dictionary attacks. In: Proceedings of the IEEE S&P 1992, pp. 72–84 (1992)
2. Katz, J., Ostrovsky, R., Yung, M.: Efficient password-authenticated key exchange using human-memorable passwords. In: Pfitzmann, B. (ed.) EUROCRYPT 2001. LNCS, vol. 2045, pp. 475–494. Springer, Heidelberg (2001). https://doi.org/10.1007/3-540-44987-6_29
3. Hao, F., Ryan, P.: J-PAKE: authenticated key exchange without PKI. In: Gavrilova, M.L., Tan, C.J.K., Moreno, E.D. (eds.) Part II. LNCS, vol. 6480, pp. 192–206. Springer, Heidelberg (2010). https://doi.org/10.1007/978-3-642-17697-5_10
4. Jarecki, S., Krawczyk, H., Xu, J.: OPAQUE: an asymmetric PAKE protocol secure against pre-computation attacks. In: Nielsen, J.B., Rijmen, V. (eds.) EURO-CRYPT 2018, Part III. LNCS, vol. 10822, pp. 456–486. Springer, Cham (2018). https://doi.org/10.1007/978-3-319-78372-7_15
5. Gennaro, R., Lindell, Y.: A framework for password-based authenticated key exchange. In: Biham, E. (ed.) EUROCRYPT 2003. LNCS, vol. 2656, pp. 524–543. Springer, Heidelberg (2003). https://doi.org/10.1007/3-540-39200-9_33
6. Bellare, M., Pointcheval, D., Rogaway, P.: Authenticated key exchange secure against dictionary attacks. In: Preneel, B. (ed.) EUROCRYPT 2000. LNCS, vol. 1807, pp. 139–155. Springer, Heidelberg (2000). https://doi.org/10.1007/3-540-45539-6_11
7. Benhamouda, F., Blazy, O., Chevalier, C., Pointcheval, D., Vergnaud, D.: New techniques for SPHFs and efficient one-round PAKE protocols. In: Canetti, R., Garay, J.A. (eds.) CRYPTO 2013, Part I. LNCS, vol. 8042, pp. 449–475. Springer, Heidelberg (2013). https://doi.org/10.1007/978-3-642-40041-4_25
8. Groce, A., Katz, J.: A new framework for efficient password-based authenticated key exchange. In: Proceedings of the ACM CCS 2010, pp. 516–525 (2010)
9. Jiang, S., Gong, G.: Password based key exchange with mutual authentication. In: Handschuh, H., Hasan, M.A. (eds.) SAC 2004. LNCS, vol. 3357, pp. 267–279. Springer, Heidelberg (2004). https://doi.org/10.1007/978-3-540-30564-4_19
10. Abdalla, M., Benhamouda, F., Pointcheval, D.: Public-key encryption indistinguishable under plaintext-checkable attacks. In: Katz, J. (ed.) PKC 2015. LNCS, vol. 9020, pp. 332–352. Springer, Heidelberg (2015). https://doi.org/10.1007/978-3-662-46447-2_15
11. Zhang, J., Yu, Y.: Two-round PAKE from approximate SPH and instantiations from lattices. In: Takagi, T., Peyrin, T. (eds.) ASIACRYPT 2017, Part III. LNCS, vol. 10626, pp. 37–67. Springer, Cham (2017). https://doi.org/10.1007/978-3-319-70700-6_2
12. Micciancio, D., Peikert, C.: Trapdoors for lattices: simpler, tighter, faster, smaller. In: Pointcheval, D., Johansson, T. (eds.) EUROCRYPT 2012. LNCS, vol. 7237, pp. 700–718. Springer, Heidelberg (2012). https://doi.org/10.1007/978-3-642-29011-4_41
13. Katz, J., Vaikuntanathan, V.: Smooth projective hashing and password-based authenticated key exchange from lattices. In: Matsui, M. (ed.) ASIACRYPT 2009. LNCS, vol. 5912, pp. 636–652. Springer, Heidelberg (2009). https://doi.org/10.1007/978-3-642-10366-7_37
14. Regev, O.: On lattices, learning with errors, random linear codes, and cryptography. In: Proceedings of ACM STOC 2005, pp. 84–93 (2005)

15. Katz, J., Vaikuntanathan, V.: Round-optimal password-based authenticated key exchange. In: Ishai, Y. (ed.) TCC 2011. LNCS, vol. 6597, pp. 293–310. Springer, Heidelberg (2011). https://doi.org/10.1007/978-3-642-19571-6_18
16. Abdalla, M., Benhamouda, F., MacKenzie, P.: Security of the J-PAKE password-authenticated key exchange protocol. In: Proceedings of IEEE S&P 2015, pp. 571–587 (2015)
17. Wang, D., Wang, P.: On the implications of Zipf's law in passwords. In: Askoxylakis, I., Ioannidis, S., Katsikas, S., Meadows, C. (eds.) ESORICS 2016, Part I. LNCS, vol. 9878, pp. 111–131. Springer, Cham (2016). https://doi.org/10.1007/978-3-319-45744-4_6
18. Wang, D., Cheng, H., Wang, P., Huang, X., Jian, G.: Zipf's law in passwords. IEEE Trans. Inform. Foren. Secur. **12**(11), 2776–2791 (2017)
19. Canetti, R., Krawczyk, H.: Universally composable notions of key exchange and secure channels. In: Knudsen, L.R. (ed.) EUROCRYPT 2002. LNCS, vol. 2332, pp. 337–351. Springer, Heidelberg (2002). https://doi.org/10.1007/3-540-46035-7_22
20. Canetti, R., Halevi, S., Katz, J., Lindell, Y., MacKenzie, P.: Universally composable password-based key exchange. In: Cramer, R. (ed.) EUROCRYPT 2005. LNCS, vol. 3494, pp. 404–421. Springer, Heidelberg (2005). https://doi.org/10.1007/11426639_24
21. Gentry, C., MacKenzie, P., Ramzan, Z.: A method for making password-based key exchange resilient to server compromise. In: Dwork, C. (ed.) CRYPTO 2006. LNCS, vol. 4117, pp. 142–159. Springer, Heidelberg (2006). https://doi.org/10.1007/11818175_9
22. Dupont, P.-A., Hesse, J., Pointcheval, D., Reyzin, L., Yakoubov, S.: Fuzzy password-authenticated key exchange. In: Nielsen, J.B., Rijmen, V. (eds.) EUROCRYPT 2018, Part III. LNCS, vol. 10822, pp. 393–424. Springer, Cham (2018). https://doi.org/10.1007/978-3-319-78372-7_13
23. Cramer, R., Shoup, V.: Universal hash proofs and a paradigm for adaptive chosen ciphertext secure public-key encryption. In: Knudsen, L.R. (ed.) EUROCRYPT 2002. LNCS, vol. 2332, pp. 45–64. Springer, Heidelberg (2002). https://doi.org/10.1007/3-540-46035-7_4
24. Brakerski, Z.: Fully homomorphic encryption without modulus switching from classical GapSVP. In: Safavi-Naini, R., Canetti, R. (eds.) CRYPTO 2012. LNCS, vol. 7417, pp. 868–886. Springer, Heidelberg (2012). https://doi.org/10.1007/978-3-642-32009-5_50
25. Peikert, C.: Public-key cryptosystems from the worst-case shortest vector problem: extended abstract. In: Proceedings of ACM STOC 2009, pp. 333–342 (2009)
26. Peikert, C., Waters, B.: Lossy trapdoor functions and their applications. In: Proceedings of ACM STOC 2008, pp. 187–196 (2008)
27. Li, Z., Ma, C., Wang, D.: Leakage resilient leveled FHE on multiple bit message. IEEE Trans. Big Data. https://doi.org/10.1109/TBDATA.2017.2726554
28. Bellare, M., Rogaway, P.: Entity authentication and key distribution. In: Stinson, D.R. (ed.) CRYPTO 1993. LNCS, vol. 773, pp. 232–249. Springer, Heidelberg (1994). https://doi.org/10.1007/3-540-48329-2_21
29. Bellare, M., Rogaway, P.: Provably secure session key distribution: the three party case. In: Proceedings of ACM STOC 1995, pp. 57–66 (1995)
30. Katz, J., Ostrovsky, R., Yung, M.: Efficient and secure authenticated key exchange using weak passwords. J. ACM **57**(1), 3:1–3:39 (2009)

31. Jarecki, S., Krawczyk, H., Shirvanian, M., Saxena, N.: Two-factor authentication with end-to-end password security. In: Abdalla, M., Dahab, R. (eds.) PKC 2018, Part II. LNCS, vol. 10770, pp. 431–461. Springer, Cham (2018). https://doi.org/10.1007/978-3-319-76581-5_15

32. Huang, K., Manulis, M., Chen, L.: Password authenticated keyword search. In: Proceedings of PAC 2017, pp. 129–140 (2017)

33. Wang, D., Wang, P.: Two birds with one stone: two-factor authentication with security beyond conventional bound. IEEE Trans. Depend. Secure Comput. 15(4), 708–722 (2018)

34. Becerra, J., Iovino, V., Ostrev, D., Šala, P., Škrobot, M.: Tightly-secure PAK(E). In: Capkun, S., Chow, S.S.M. (eds.) CANS 2017. LNCS, vol. 11261, pp. 27–48. Springer, Cham (2018). https://doi.org/10.1007/978-3-030-02641-7_2

35. Gentry, C., Peikert, C., Vaikuntanathan, V.: Trapdoors for hard lattices and new cryptographic constructions. In: Proceedings of ACM STOC 2008, pp. 197–206 (2008)

36. Lindner, R., Peikert, C.: Better key sizes (and attacks) for LWE-based encryption. In: Kiayias, A. (ed.) CT-RSA 2011. LNCS, vol. 6558, pp. 319–339. Springer, Heidelberg (2011). https://doi.org/10.1007/978-3-642-19074-2_21

37. Dolev, D., Dwork, C., Naor, M.: Nonmalleable cryptography. SIAM J. Comput. 30(2), 391–437 (2000)

38. Boneh, D., Canetti, R., Halevi, S., Katz, J.: Chosen-ciphertext security from identity-based encryption. SIAM J. Comput. 36(5), 1301–1328 (2007)

39. Benhamouda, F., Blazy, O., Ducas, L., Quach, W.: Hash proof systems over lattices revisited. In: Abdalla, M., Dahab, R. (eds.) PKC 2018, Part II. LNCS, vol. 10770, pp. 644–674. Springer, Cham (2018). https://doi.org/10.1007/978-3-319-76581-5_22

40. Abdalla, M., Ben Hamouda, F., Pointcheval, D.: Tighter reductions for forward-secure signature schemes. In: Kurosawa, K., Hanaoka, G. (eds.) PKC 2013. LNCS, vol. 7778, pp. 292–311. Springer, Heidelberg (2013). https://doi.org/10.1007/978-3-642-36362-7_19

41. Katz, J., Ostrovsky, R., Yung, M.: Forward secrecy in password-only key exchange protocols. In: Cimato, S., Persiano, G., Galdi, C. (eds.) SCN 2002. LNCS, vol. 2576, pp. 29–44. Springer, Heidelberg (2003). https://doi.org/10.1007/3-540-36413-7_3

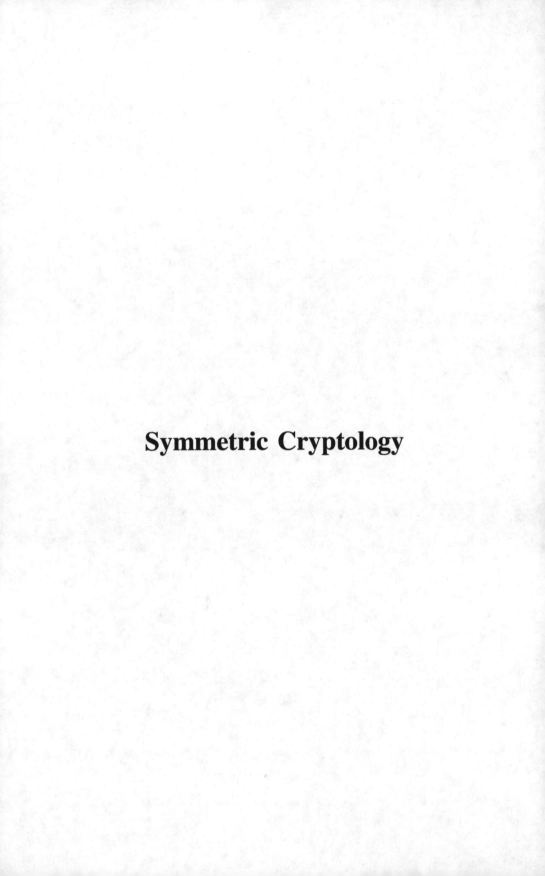

Symmetric Cryptology

Improved Integral Attacks
on PRESENT-80

Shi Wang, Zejun Xiang, Xiangyong Zeng[✉], and Shasha Zhang

Faculty of Mathematics and Statistics,
Hubei Key Laboratory of Applied Mathematics, Hubei University,
Wuhan 430062, China
wuhanwangs@163.com, xiangzejun@iie.ac.cn,
xiangyongzeng@aliyun.com, amushasha@163.com

Abstract. In this paper, we propose an improved integral attack against round-reduced PRESENT-80. First, we find a new 7-round integral distinguisher by analyzing the algebraic degree of PRESENT. Then, we propose an algebraic method to recover the master key by solving a system of linear equations which are extracted from the last three rounds of the cipher. Using this method, we can attack 10-round PRESENT-80 with time complexity $2^{27.6}$ and data complexity 2^{27}, and 12-round PRESENT-80 with time complexity 2^{66} and data complexity 2^{64}. Moreover, a key partition technique is proposed to gain one more round such that we could attack 11-round PRESENT-80 with time complexity 2^{58} and data complexity 2^{48}, and 13-round PRESENT-80 with time complexity 2^{74} and data complexity 2^{64}.

Keywords: PRESENT · Integral attack · Gaussian elimination

1 Introduction

Integral attack was firstly proposed by Daemen et al. to evaluate the security of block cipher Square [3] and then formalized by Knudsen and Wagner [4]. It mainly has two phases: integral distinguisher construction and key recovery. An attacker firstly constructs a set of 2^d plaintexts by traversing d bits and fixing other bits to a constant value. If some bits of the state after r-round encryption have a zero-sum property, a d-th order integral distinguisher of r rounds is thus obtained. In the key recovery phase, the attacker partially decrypts each ciphertext for several rounds by guessing involved subkeys and checks whether certain bits of the XOR of all intermediate values equal 0. If this is the case, the guessed subkey is a right candidate. Otherwise, the subkey is a wrong guess.

However, integral attack initially can only be applied to word-based block ciphers. Until 2008, Z'aba et al. proposed a new notion called bit-Pattern [12], which extended integral attack to bit-based block ciphers, such as Noekeon, Serpent and PRESENT. Although integral attack does not pose a serious threat to these block ciphers, it reveals that integral attacks may be not only suitable for

© Springer Nature Switzerland AG 2019
F. Guo et al. (Eds.): Inscrypt 2018, LNCS 11449, pp. 163–182, 2019.
https://doi.org/10.1007/978-3-030-14234-6_9

word-based block ciphers but also suitable for bit-based ones. In 2013, Wu and Wang [10] discovered that some properties of PRESENT's Sbox help to make a more accurate evaluation of the algebraic degree and they found a 7-round integral distinguisher. In 2015, Zhang et al. [15] attacked 10-round PRESENT-80 and 11-round PRESENT-128 by using the 7-round integral distinguisher and the Match-through-the-Sbox technique (MTTS).

At Eurocrypt 2015, Todo [7] proposed a generalized integral property named division property. It has been pointed out that the propagation characteristic of division property for a nonlinear function is related to its algebraic degree, and ciphers with low-degree functions are vulnerable to this analysis. After the proposal, new understandings of division property and new applications have been proposed [2,5,6,8,14]. In 2016, both [9] and [11] found a 9-round integral distinguisher by bit-based division property, and 12-round PRESENT-80 and 13-round PRESENT-128 were attacked in [9] by using this 9-round integral distinguisher.

Our Contribution. In this paper, we propose an improved integral attack against PRESENT-80. Firstly, we propose a technique for evaluating the algebraic degree of PRESENT, and thus find a new 7-round integral distinguisher. Secondly, inspired by [10], we try to decrypt the ciphertext three rounds, and get the algebraic normal form of each bit of the internal state in terms of the ciphertext and the master key. Then a linear equation can be constructed for a given integral distinguisher. Moreover, a system of linear equations can be constructed by repeating this procedure for multiple distinguisher which only differ in the constant part. Thus, the master key can be recovered by solving these equations. Using this technique, we can attack 10-round PRESENT-80 with time complexity $2^{27.6}$ and data complexity 2^{27}, and 12-round PRESENT-80 with time complexity 2^{66} and data complexity 2^{60}.

Moreover, we propose a key partition technique which divides the 4-bit Sbox subkey into four disjoint subsets by analyzing the differential property of Sbox, and this allows us to gain one more round such that 11-round PRESENT-80 can be attacked with time complexity 2^{58}, data complexity 2^{48}, and 13-round PRESENT-80 can be attacked with time complexity 2^{74}, data complexity 2^{64}. Table 1 summarizes the integral attacks on PRESENT-80.

Organization. Section 2 gives a brief review of PRESENT cipher and integral attack. The technique of obtaining the new integral distinguisher is elaborated in Sect. 3. In Sect. 4, we mainly describe integral attacks of 10- and 12-round PRESENT. In Sect. 5, the 11-round PRESENT is attacked by a new partition technique. In Sect. 6, the 13-round PRESENT is attacked by another partition. Finally, Sect. 7 concludes the paper.

2   Preliminaries

In this section, we briefly recall some background knowledge on PRESENT cipher and integral attack.

Table 1. The comparison of integral attacks of PRESENT-80

Round	Data	Time	Memory	Order	Ref
6	$2^{22.4}$	$2^{41.7}$	-	4	[12]
9	$2^{20.3}$	2^{60}	2^{20}	16	[10]
10	$2^{21.5}$	2^{35}	$2^{35.9}$	16	[15]
10	2^{27}	$2^{27.6}$	-	16	in Sect. 4.3
11	2^{48}	2^{58}	2^{51}	16	in Sect. 5.2
12	-	$2^{80-N}, N = 1, \cdots, 16$	-	60	[9]
12	2^{64}	2^{66}		60	in Sect. 4.4
13	2^{64}	2^{74}	2^{64}	60	in Sect. 6.2

2.1 Description of PRESENT

PRESENT is a 31-round lightweight block cipher with block size 64 bits, and two key lengths of 80 and 128 bits are supported [1]. PRESENT adopts SP-network and its round function consists of addRoundKey, sBoxLayer and pLayer.

In addRoundKey layer, the 64-bit round key is XORed to the state. Then, a 4-bit Sbox is applied 16 times in parallel in sBoxLayer. Finally, a fully wired permutation on 64 bits is employed in pLayer.

Since we focus on PRESENT with 80 bits key in the rest of our paper, we only briefly recall the 80-bit key schedule. Initially, the 80 bits are stored in a key register represented as $k_{79}k_{78} \cdots k_0$. In round i, the most significant 64-bit keys are extracted as the subkey $k^i = k_{79}k_{78} \cdots k_{16}$. Then, the key register is updated as follows.

1. $[k_{79}k_{78} \cdots k_1 k_0] = [k_{18}k_{17} \cdots k_0 k_{79} \cdots k_{20}k_{19}]$;
2. $[k_{79}k_{78}k_{77}k_{76}] = S[k_{79}k_{78}k_{77}k_{76}]$;
3. $[k_{19}k_{18}k_{17}k_{16}k_{15}] = [k_{19}k_{18}k_{17}k_{16}k_{15}] \oplus \text{round\_counter}$.

In the remainder of this paper, we denote X^i the internal state which is the input of round i before subkey XOR, and denote Y^i the output after subkey XOR, where $0 \le i \le 31$. Thus, $C = Y^n$ denotes the ciphertext for a reduced PRESENT of n rounds. Let $X^i = (x_{63}^i, x_{62}^i, \cdots, x_0^i)$, where x_j^i denotes the j-th bit of X^i with $0 \le j \le 63$, and $X_{[j_1, j_2, \cdots, j_k]}^i$ represents the set of bits $x_{j_1}^i, x_{j_2}^i, \cdots, x_{j_k}^i$. Let K represent the master key and k^i represent the round key used in round i. Moreover, we denote K^i the state of the key register before extracting k^i.

2.2 Integral Attack

Integral attack is composed of two phases: integral distinguisher construction and key recovery.

Let X^0 be a plaintext and $E = E^{n-r} \circ E^r$ represent the encryption function of n-round PRESENT, where E^r is the first r rounds of E and E^{n-r} is the last $n-r$ rounds of E. Then the ciphertext C can be computed by

$$C = E(X^0) = E^{n-r}(E^r(X^0)).$$

If there is a set Λ consisting of 2^d plaintexts such that

$$\bigoplus_{X \in \Lambda} E^r(X) = 0,$$

then we call the set Λ an r-round (d-th order) integral distinguisher. In the key recovery phase, suppose that the attacker chooses a set Λ of plaintexts and gets the corresponding ciphertexts. Then, the attacker decrypts each ciphertext $(n-r)$-round by guessing the involved subkeys. If the XOR of all decrypted texts equals 0, then the subkey is a right candidate, and the remaining key bits can be recovered by exhaustive search.

3   Integral Distinguishers of PRESENT

This section proposes a new 7-round (16-th order) integral distinguisher based on degree evaluation.

A Boolean function f from $\mathbb{F}_2^n$ to $\mathbb{F}_2$ can be expressed as a polynomial in $\mathbb{F}_2[x_1, \cdots, x_n]$, which is called the *algebraic normal form* (ANF) of f. The *algebraic degree* of f, denoted by $\deg(f)$, is the number of variables in the highest order terms with nonzero coefficients [10].

Let X^0, K be a plaintext and a master key, respectively. Then the algebraic degree of Y^i with respect to X^0 can be obtained by computing the ANF of Y^i. However, with the round number increasing, the ANF of Y^i contains a huge number of monomials, thus it is infeasible to evaluate the algebraic degree of Y^i in this way. To find an upper bound on the algebraic degree of Y^i with respect to X^0, we exploit a new method, in which each bit of Y^i is treated as a polynomial over the ring of integers and all bits in K are set to 1. In the iterations of round function, monomials which have nonzero coefficients in the ANF of Y^i cannot vanish in this new polynomial (over the integer ring). Therefore, the algebraic degree of each bit of Y^i cannot exceed the maximal number of different variables in all monomials of the new polynomial. Thus, an upper bound on the algebraic degree of Y^i can be obtained. This can be illustrated by the following example.

Example 1. Let S be the function of Sbox used in PRESENT, and $x = (x_3, x_2, x_1, x_0)$, $y = (y_3, y_2, y_1, y_0)$ be the input and output of S respectively. Then the ANF of S is listed as follows.

$$\begin{cases} y_3 = 1 + x_0 + x_1 + x_3 + x_1 x_2 + x_0 x_1 x_2 + x_0 x_1 x_3 + x_0 x_2 x_3, \\ y_2 = 1 + x_2 + x_3 + x_0 x_1 + x_0 x_3 + x_1 x_3 + x_0 x_1 x_3 + x_0 x_2 x_3, \\ y_1 = x_1 + x_3 + x_1 x_3 + x_2 x_3 + x_0 x_1 x_2 + x_0 x_1 x_3 + x_0 x_2 x_3, \\ y_0 = x_0 + x_2 + x_3 + x_1 x_2. \end{cases} \qquad (1)$$

Suppose $X = (x_3 + k_3, x_2 + k_2, x_1 + k_1, x_0 + k_0)$ is the input of PRESENT Sbox and $Z = (z_3, z_2, z_1, z_0) = S(S(x_3 + k_3, x_2 + k_2, x_1 + k_1, x_0 + k_0))$.

We regard z_0 as a polynomial over the ring of integers and let $k_0 = k_1 = k_2 = k_3 = 1$. Then the terms with the maximal number of different variables in this polynomial are

$$(4 + 8k_0k_3 + 6k_3 + 2k_1 + 4k_0k_1 + 4k_0 + 4k_0k_2)x_0x_1x_2x_3$$
$$+ (2k_2 + 2k_1 + 4k_3 + 2)x_0^2x_1x_2x_3 + (2k_0 + 1)x_0x_1^2x_2x_3 + 2k_0x_0x_1x_2^2x_3$$
$$+ (4k_0 + 3)x_0x_1x_2x_3^2 + x_0^2x_1^2x_2x_3 + x_0^2x_1x_2^2x_3 + 2x_0^2x_1x_2x_3^2.$$

Since $k_0 = k_1 = k_2 = k_3 = 1$, all coefficients of the above terms are nonzero integers obviously, thus the maximal number of different variables in all monomials is 4. However, the coefficient of the highest order term $x_0x_1x_2x_3$ in the ANF of z_0 is equal to 0 and the algebraic degrees of z_0 is small than 4. Thus, the algebraic degree of z_0 is less than 4 which is the maximal number of different variables in all monomials of the new polynomial over the ring of integers.

Let $X^0 = (0, 0, 0, x_{60}, 0, 0, 0, x_{56}, \cdots, 0, 0, 0, x_0)$ and $K = (1, \cdots, 1)$, where x_i ($i = 0, 4, 8, \cdots, 60$) are variables. Then the expression of each bit of Y^i ($i = 1, \cdots, 5$) as a polynomial over the ring of integers can be obtained. By this estimation, we have that the algebraic degree of y_j^5 is not exceeding 16 for $1 \leq j \leq 63$, and the algebraic degrees of y_0^5 and $y_{16}^5 + y_{48}^5 = y_0^4 + y_1^4y_2^4 + y_1^4y_3^4 + y_2^4y_3^4 + 1$ are not exceeding 15. Thus, $\bigoplus_{(x_0, \cdots, x_{16}) \in \mathbb{F}_2^{16}} y_0^5$ and $\bigoplus_{(x_0, \cdots, x_{16}) \in \mathbb{F}_2^{16}} (y_{16}^5 + y_{48}^5)$ equal 0. That is to say, y_0^5 and $y_{16}^5 + y_{48}^5$ are balanced bits.

For a fixed vector $(x_{63}, \cdots, x_{16})$, define

$$\Gamma_{(x_{63}, \cdots, x_{16})} = \{(x_{63}, \cdots, x_{16}, x_{15}, \cdots, x_0) \mid x_i \in \mathbb{F}_2 \text{ for } 0 \leq i \leq 15\}$$

and

$$\mathcal{A} = \{\Gamma_{(x_{63}, \cdots, x_{16})} \mid x_i \in \mathbb{F}_2 \text{ for } 16 \leq i \leq 63\}. \tag{2}$$

Then $\mathcal{A}$ contains 2^{48} elements and each element is a set consisting of 2^{16} vectors which traverse the 16 bits of $X^0_{[0,\cdots,15]}$ and fix other bits to constants.

If one constructs a set belonging to $\mathcal{A}$, all the intermediate values after two-round encryption traverse the 16 bits of $X^2_{[0,4,\cdots,60]}$, and take a constant value on other bits. Combining this with the above analysis, a 7-round integral distinguisher of PRESENT can be found [10]. This can be shown in Fig. 1 with bold lines, and it is summarized as the following proposition.

Proposition 1. *Choose a set of 2^{16} plaintexts, which traverses the 16 bits of $X^0_{[0,\cdots,15]}$ and fixes other bits to arbitrary constants. Then, both y_0^7 and $y_{16}^7 + y_{48}^7$ are balanced.*

Note that y_0^5 is a balanced bit corresponding to the integral distinguisher found in [10], and $y_{16}^5 + y_{48}^5$ is a new balanced bit found by our technique.

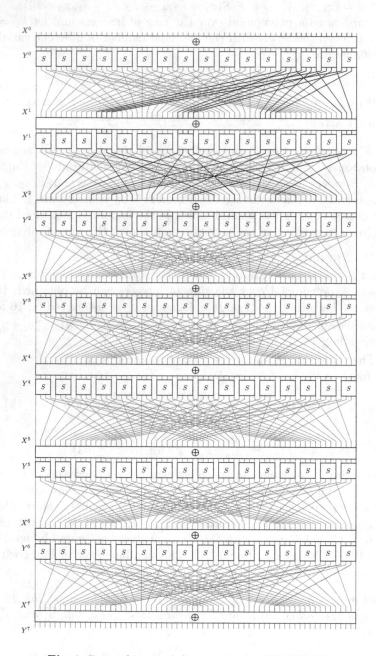

Fig. 1. 7-round integral distinguishers of PRESENT

4   Integral Attack on Reduced-Round PRESENT-80

Firstly, in Subsect. 4.1, we give a general model of attacking the block cipher PRESENT-80. The relation between the bits y_0^{n-3}, $y_{16}^{n-3} + y_{48}^{n-3}$ and the key register K^n is obtained in Subsect. 4.2. Next, we attack 10-round PRESENT-80 by using the 16-th order integral distinguisher in Subsect. 4.3. Finally, we attack 12-round PRESENT by using the 60-th order integral distinguisher in Subsect. 4.4.

4.1   General Model of Integral Attack

Let $C = Y^n = (y_{63}^n, \cdots, y_0^n)$ and $K^n = (k_{79}^n, \cdots, k_0^n)$ be the ciphertext and the state of the key register after n-round encryption, respectively.

Since the key schedule is invertible, Y^n can be decrypted by r rounds and then y_0^{n-r} can be expressed as $y_0^{n-r} = f^{-r}(Y^n, K^n)$, where f is the round function of PRESETN. In the following, we try to represent y_0^{n-r} as

$$y_0^{n-r} = \bigoplus_{i=1}^{m} y_i' k_i',$$

where y_i' ($i = 1, \cdots, m$) are polynomials in Y^n and k_i' ($i = 1, \cdots, m$) are polynomials in K^n.

Given the ANF of y_0^{n-r} as a polynomial in Y^n and K^n, by merging the terms which just involve the same variable $k_{j_1}^n \cdots k_{j_s}^n$ from K^n, we can represent y_0^{n-r} as $\bigoplus y_i' k_{j_1}^n \cdots k_{j_s}^n$, where y_i' is a polynomial in Y^n. Next, by merging the terms which involve the same variable y_i', we can express y_0^{n-r} as $\bigoplus_{i=1}^{m} y_i' k_i'$.

Then, the nonlinear relation between y_0^{n-r} and variables in K^n can be simplified to the following linear relation with respect to variables k_i':

$$y_0^{n-r} = \bigoplus_{i=1}^{m} y_i' k_i'.$$

Example 2. Denote S the Sbox used in PRESENT. Let $x = (x_3, x_2, x_1, x_0)$ and $y = (y_3, y_2, y_1, y_0)$ be the input and output of S respectively. Then the ANF of inverse S can be computed and listed as follows.

$$\begin{cases} x_3 = y_0 + y_1 + y_2 + y_3 + y_0 y_1 + y_0 y_1 y_2 + y_0 y_2 y_3, \\ x_2 = 1 + y_3 + y_0 y_1 + y_0 y_2 + y_0 y_3 + y_1 y_2 + y_1 y_3 + y_0 y_1 y_2 + \quad y_0 y_1 y_3 + \\ \qquad\qquad\qquad\qquad\qquad\qquad\qquad\qquad\qquad\qquad\qquad y_0 y_2 y_3, \qquad (3) \\ x_1 = y_0 + y_1 + y_3 + y_0 y_2 + y_1 y_3 + y_2 y_3 + y_0 y_1 y_2 + y_0 y_1 y_3 + y_0 y_2 y_3, \\ x_0 = 1 + y_0 + y_2 + y_1 y_3. \end{cases}$$

Let $Y^n = (y_{63}^n, \cdots, y_0^n)$ and $K^n = (k_{79}^n, \cdots, k_0^n)$. According to Eq. (3), we have

$$y_0^{n-1} = y_1' + y_2' k_2' + y_3' k_3' + k_4',$$

where $y_1' = y_0^n + y_{32}^n + y_{16}^n y_{48}^n$, $y_2' = y_{16}^n$, $y_3' = y_{48}^n$ and $k_2' = k_{48}^n, k_3' = k_{16}^n$, $k_4' = k_{16}^n k_{48}^n + k_0^n + k_{32}^n$.

Given an $(n - r)$-round integral distinguisher Λ, we have

$$\bigoplus_\Lambda Y_0^{n-r} = 0.$$

Since $y_0^{n-r} = \bigoplus_{i=1}^m y_i' k_i'$, the above equation can be rewritten as

$$\bigoplus_\Lambda \left(\bigoplus_{i=1}^m y_i' k_i' \right) = 0.$$

Therefore a linear equation in k_i''s can be obtained for a given distinguisher. Repeating the above steps for multiple copies of the distinguishers which only differ in the constant part, we try to find more than m linear equations in k_i''s. Thus, we can retrieve k_i''s by Gaussian elimination.

4.2 Expressions of Internal States

Next, the expressions of internal states with respect to the secret key K^n will be given, where the expression of bit y_0^{n-2} is illustrated in detail.

Let $C = Y^n = (y_{63}^n, \cdots, y_1^n, y_0^n)$, $K^n = (k_{79}^n, \cdots, k_1^n, k_0^n)$ be the ciphertext and the state of the key register after n-round encryption, where $y_i, k_j \in \mathbb{F}_2$, $0 \le i \le 63$, $0 \le j \le 80$. In order to derive the expression of y_0^{n-2}, we have to retrieve the expressions of y_0^{n-1}, y_{16}^{n-1}, y_{32}^{n-1} and y_{48}^{n-1}. According to Eq. (3), we have

$$y_0^{n-1} = 1 + y_0^n + y_{32}^n + y_{16}^n y_{48}^n + y_{48}^n k_{48}^n + y_{16}^n k_{64}^n + k_{32}^n k_{64}^n + k_{16}^n + k_{48}^n,$$
$$y_{16}^{n-1} = 1 + y_4^n + y_{36}^n + y_{20}^n y_{52}^n + y_{20}^n k_{68}^n + y_{52}^n k_{36}^n + k_{36}^n k_{68}^n + k_{20}^n + k_{52}^n,$$
$$y_{32}^{n-1} = 1 + y_8^n + y_{40}^n + y_{24}^n y_{56}^n + y_{24}^n k_{72}^n + y_{56}^n k_{40}^n + k_{40}^n k_{72}^n + k_{24}^n + k_{56}^n,$$
$$y_{48}^{n-1} = 1 + y_{12}^n + y_{44}^n + y_{28}^n y_{60}^n + y_{28}^n k_{76}^n + y_{60}^n k_{44}^n + k_{44}^n k_{76}^n + k_{28}^n + k_{60}^n,$$

and

$$y_0^{n-2} = y_0^{n-1} + y_{32}^{n-1} + y_{16}^{n-1} y_{48}^{n-1} + y_{48}^{n-1} k_{32}^{n-1} + y_{16}^{n-1} k_{64}^{n-1} + k_{32}^{n-1} k_{64}^{n-1} + 1 + k_{16}^{n-1} + k_{48}^{n-1}.$$

Therefore, we have

$$
\begin{aligned}
y_0^{n-2} = {} & (u_4 + u_2 + u_3 u_1) + y_{24}^n k_{72}^n + y_{56}^n k_{40}^n + y_{16}^n k_{64}^n + u_3 t_1 + y_{48}^n k_{32}^n + \\
& y_{52}^n u_1 k_{36}^n + u_1 t_3 + y_{20}^n u_1 k_{68}^n + u_3 y_{60}^n k_{44}^n + u_3 y_{28}^n k_{76}^n + y_{20}^n k_{68}^n t_1 + \\
& y_{60}^n t_3 k_{44}^n + y_{52}^n k_{36}^n t_1 + y_{28}^n t_3 k_{76}^n + y_{20}^n y_{28}^n k_{68}^n k_{76}^n + y_{20}^n y_{60}^n k_{68}^n k_{44}^n + \\
& y_{52}^n y_{60}^n k_{44}^n k_{36}^n + y_{28}^n y_{52}^n k_{36}^n k_{76}^n + (t_4 + t_2 + t_3 t_1),
\end{aligned}
\tag{4}
$$

where $t_i = k_{48-4i}^n k_{80-4i}^n + k_{32-4i}^n + k_{64-4i}^n + k_{16i}^{n-1}$, $u_i = y_{32-4i}^{n-1} y_{64-4i}^{n-1} + y_{16-4i}^{n-1} + y_{48-4i}^{n-1}$, $i = 1, 2, 3, 4$. Thus the expression of y_0^{n-2} contains 11 variables k_{72}^n, k_{40}^n, k_{64}^n, k_{32}^n, k_{36}^n, t_1, t_3, k_{68}^n, k_{44}^n, k_{76}^n, $t_4 + t_2 + t_3 t_1$. Then, we introduce new variables k_i' ($i = 1, \cdots, 20$) and y_i' ($i = 1, \cdots, 20$) to simplify the expression, where $k_1' = 1$, $k_2' = k_{72}^n$, $k_3' = k_{40}^n$, $k_4' = k_{64}^n$, $k_5' = k_{32}^n$, $k_6' = k_{36}^n$, $k_7' = t_1$, $k_8' = t_3$, $k_9' = k_{68}^n$, $k_{10}' = k_{44}^n$, $k_{11}' = k_{76}^n$, $k_{12}' = k_{68}^n t_1$, $k_{13}' = t_3 k_{44}^n$, $k_{14}' = k_{36}^n t_1$, $k_{15}' = t_3 k_{76}^n$, $k_{16}' = k_{68}^n k_{76}^n$, $k_{17}' = k_{68}^n k_{44}^n$, $k_{18}' = k_{44}^n k_{36}^n$, $k_{19}' = k_{76}^n k_{36}^n$, $k_{20}' = t_4 + t_2 + t_3 t_1$, $y_1' = u_4 + u_2 + u_3 u_1$, $y_2' = y_{24}^n$, $y_3' = y_{56}^n$, $y_4' = y_{16}^n$, $y_5' = u_3$, $y_6' = y_{48}^n$, $y_7' = y_{52}^n u_1$, $y_8' = u_1$, $y_9' = y_{20}^n u_1$, $y_{10}' = u_3 y_{60}^n$, $y_{11}' = u_3 y_{28}^n$, $y_{12}' = y_{20}^n$, $y_{13}' = y_{60}^n$, $y_{14}' = y_{52}^n$, $y_{15}' = y_{28}^n$, $y_{16}' = y_{20}^n y_{28}^n$, $y_{17}' = y_{20}^n y_{60}^n$, $y_{18}' = y_{52}^n y_{60}^n$, $y_{19}' = y_{28}^n y_{52}^n$, $y_{20}' = 1$. Thus (4) can be rewritten as the following form

$$y_0^{n-2} = \bigoplus_{i=1}^{20} y_i' k_i'.$$

Furthermore, by the same method we can derive the expressions of y_{16}^{n-2}, y_{32}^{n-2} and y_{48}^{n-2}, and thus y_0^{n-3} can be derived. Similar as the procedure to compute y_0^{n-3}, the expression of $y_{16}^{n-3} + y_{32}^{n-3}$ can also be retrieved. The details are omitted here and the expressions of $Y_{[0,16,32,48]}^{n-2}$ is presented in Appendix A.

Proposition 2. *Let* $C = Y^n = (y_{63}^n, \cdots, y_1^n, y_0^n)$, $K^n = (k_{79}^n, \cdots, k_1^n, k_0^n)$ *be the ciphertext and the state of the key register after n-round encryption, respectively.*

– y_0^{n-3} *can be expressed as*

$$y_0^{n-3} = \bigoplus_{i=1}^{436} y_i' k_i',$$

where $k_1' = 1$ *and* k_i' ($i = 2, \cdots, 436$) *are polynomials in 42 variables of* K^n. *In particular, among all* k_i''s, *32 of them are monomials with degree one, and each of these 32* k_i' *is equal to one bit in* $K_{[32,\cdots,47,64,\cdots,79]}^n$.

– *If* $K_{[32,\cdots,47,64,\cdots,79]}^n$ *are fixed and known bits, then*

$$y_{16}^{n-3} + y_{48}^{n-3} = \bigoplus_{i=1}^{1489} y_i' k_i',$$

where $k_1' = 1$ *and* k_i' ($i = 2, \cdots, 1489$) *are polynomials in* $K_{[0,\cdots,31,48,\cdots,63]}^n$. *In particular, among all* k_i''s, *32 of them are monomials with degree one, and each of these 32* k_i' *is equal to one bit in* $K_{[16,\cdots,31,48,\cdots,63]}^n$.

4.3   Integral Attack on 10-round PRESENT-80 Using the (16-th Order) Integral Distinguisher

In this subsection, we present an integral attack on 10-round PRESENT-80 using the 7-round distinguisher presented in Sect. 3. The key recovery process of the attack is composed of three steps: the first step recovers 32 bits of $K^n_{[32,\cdots,47,64,\cdots,79]}$ by utilizing the fact that y^7_0 is a balanced bit, the second step recovers $K^n_{[16,\cdots,31,48,\cdots,63]}$ by the balancedness of $y^7_{16}+y^7_{48}$ and the key information of $K^n_{[32,\cdots,47,64,\cdots,79]}$ recovered in the first step, and the last step recovers the remaining 16 bits by exhaustive search. The detailed attack procedure is presented as follows.

1. Prepare a set $\varLambda$ of 2^{16} plaintexts, whose rightmost 16 bits take all possible values of $\mathbb{F}^{16}_2$, while other bits are chosen to be arbitrary constants.
2. For each $X^0 \in \varLambda$, we acquire the corresponding ciphertext $C = Y^{10} = E^{10}(X^0)$ and denote the set of all ciphertexts by $\varLambda_c$.
3. According to Propositions 1 and 2, y^7_0 can be expressed as $y^7_0 = \bigoplus^{436}_{i=1} y'_i k'_i$, where y'_i are polynomials on Y^{10} and

$$\bigoplus_{y\in\varLambda_c} y^7_0 = \bigoplus_{y\in\varLambda_c} \left(\bigoplus^{436}_{i=1} y'_i k'_i \right) = \bigoplus^{436}_{i=1} \left(\bigoplus_{y\in\varLambda_c} y'_i \right) k'_i = 0$$

$$= \bigoplus^{435}_{i=1} \left(\bigoplus_{y\in\varLambda_c} y'_i \right) k'_i = 0.$$

The last equation is owing to $\bigoplus_{y\in\varLambda_c} y'_{436} = \bigoplus_{y\in\varLambda_c} 1 = 0$. Thus we can obtain a linear equation of k'_i, $i = 2, 3, \cdots, 435$ (k'_1 is a constant value which equals 1).
4. Choose another 499 different sets $\varLambda$ and repeat the Step 1–3. We can get 500 linear equations.
5. Solve the linear equations by Gaussian elimination to obtain k'_i, $i = 2, 3, \cdots, 435$, and then $K^n_{[32,\cdots,47,64,\cdots,79]}$ can be retrieved.
6. Choose 2000 different sets $\varLambda$ and repeat Step 1–5 for $\bigoplus_{y\in\varLambda_c} y^7_{16} + y^7_{48} = 0$. Then, we can establish a system of linear equations and $K^n_{[16,\cdots,31,48,\cdots,63]}$ can be recovered.
7. Recover the remaining 16 bits by exhaustive search.

Complexity: According to our attack method, we need 2000 different $\varLambda$ sets to mount the attack, thus $2^{16} \times 2000$ plaintexts should be encrypted. So the data complexity of our attack is 2^{27}. Note that we always construct a slightly more linear equations than the number of variables such that the rank of the linear equations is as large as possible. The memory complexity of this attack is negligible.

Next, we compute the time complexity. Here, "one" time complexity is the process that a plaintext is encrypted to a ciphertext by the encryption system, and in the following we will estimate the time complexity of one multiplication. In each round of PRESENT, 400 multiplications are preformed. That is to say, the time complexity of one multiplication is about $\frac{1}{4000}$ if the attacking system is 10-round PRESENT-80. In the attack procedure, we first choose 2^{27} plaintexts and get the corresponding ciphertexts. The time complexity is 2^{27} in Step 1–2. In order to obtain a linear equation by ciphertexts, we need to compute about 2^9 multiplications. So the time complexity is $500 \times 2^{16+9}/(4000) = 2^{22}$ in Step 4. Solving the system of linear equations needs about 434^3 multiplications, so the time complexity of this step is $434^3/4000 \approx 2^{15}$. Similarly, in Step 6, the time complexity is about $2^{434-N_1}(2^{16} \times 2^{11} \times 2^{11}/4000)$, where N_1 is the rank of the system of linear equations deduced in Step 4.

Then, we estimate the value of the rank N_1 by the following theorem.

Theorem 1. *[13] Let $A = (a(i,j)_{m \times n})$ be an $m \times n$ random binary matrix with entries satisfying independently from each other, the distribution $p(a(i,j) = 0) = \frac{1}{2}$. Then for any integer r, $0 < r \leqslant n$, the probability for A to have rank r is*

$$p(rank(A) = r) = C_n^r 2^{-m(n-r)} \prod_{i=m-r+1}^{m} (1 - \frac{1}{2^i}).$$

Therefore, the rank of deduced 500 linear equations takes a value of $N_1 = 434$ with probability 0.999, the overall time complexity of this attack is about $2^{26}2^{434-N_1} + 2^{27} \approx 2^{27.6}$. Since the complexity is practical, we can attack 10-round PRESENT experimentally and the details can be found in Appendix B.

Comparatively, [10] proposed a 10-round integral attack on PRESENT-80 with time complexity $2^{35.5}$.

4.4 Integral Attack on 12-round PRESENT-80 Using the 60-th Order Integral Distinguisher

A 9-round (60-th order) integral distinguisher consisting of 2^{60} plaintexts has been found in both [9] and [11], which fixes the rightmost 4 bits and traverses the leftmost 60 bits. In this section we will attack 12-round PRESENT-80 by using this 9-round integral distinguisher.

However, we can't get enough equations in attacking 12-round PRESENT-80 compared with the attack of 10-round PRESENT-80, since there are at most $2^4 = 16$ different 9-round distinguishers and these can be used to construct at most 16 linear equations. According to Proposition 2, the ANF of y_0^{n-3} is related to 42 bits of K^n. Thus, we need to guess 26 key bits involved in the ANF and then linearize this reduced ANF by introducing some new variables. And this leads to a linear equation with about 20 new variables. The overall attack procedure is presented as follows.

1. Prepare a set Λ of 2^{60} plaintexts, whose leftmost 60 bits take all possible values of $\mathbb{F}_2^{16}$, while other bits are chosen to be arbitrary constants.
2. For each $X^0 \in \Lambda$, encrypt X^0 by 12-round to get the corresponding ciphertext, and denote the set of all ciphertexts by Λ_c.
3. In order to obtain the polynomial of y_0^9, we guess the values of 26 key bits before linearization and this leads to a linear equation with 20 new variables. We illustrate in Appendix A the guessed variables and the resulting linear equation.
4. Since the system of deduced linear equations contains 16 equations with 20 variables, the values of 4 variables of these 20 variables need to be guessed. In this case, we get 16 linear equations with 16 variables. Denote N the rank

of the system of linear equations, then we can get 2^{16-N} solutions. Since these 16 variables and the guessed 4 variables are not independent, we check each of the 2^{16-N} solutions whether it corresponds to the values of guessed 4 variables, and we keep the solution as a candidate if there is no contradiction.
5. Repeat the above two processes 2^{26} times. We can find $T(N)$ candidate keys.
6. We guess 38 appropriately selected bits of K^{12}, and test whether the deduced K^{12} is correct. We need to verify the secret key K^{12} about $2^{38}T(N)$ times.

The time complexity is $\min\{16 \times (2^{60+9})/4400 + 2^{64} + 2^{38}T(N), 2^{80}\}$ and the data complexity is 2^{64}, $N = 1, \cdots, 16$, where N is the rank of the system of linear equations obtained by linearizing the previous 16 equations.

In the following, we estimate the rank of the equations by Theorem 1 and the value of $T(N)$. Assume that the considered linear equations are randomly chosen from the set of all possible linear equations, then the probability that $N = 16$ is

$$P_{(N=16)} = (1 - \frac{1}{2^{20}})(1 - \frac{1}{2^{19}})\cdots(1 - \frac{1}{2^5}) \approx 0.9388,$$

and the probability that $N \geq 15$ is

$$P_{(N\geq15)} \geq (1 - \frac{1}{2^{20}})(1 - \frac{1}{2^{19}})\cdots(1 - \frac{1}{2^7})(1 - \frac{1}{2^{14}}) \approx 0.9845.$$

Therefore, the expectation of N is larger than 15 and $T(N) = 2^{26} \times 2^{16-N} \approx 2^{27}$, which means that the time complexity is about 2^{66}.

5   Integral Attack on 11-round PRESENT-80 by Key Partition

In this section we propose a key partition technique which helps us to attack the 11-round PRESENT-80.

5.1   Differential Property of PRESENT's Sbox

By inspecting PRESENT's Sbox, we find that if the difference of two inputs p and p' of Sbox equals $0x7$ or $0xF$, the equation $S(p + v_k) + S(p' + v_k) = 0x1$ always has 4 solutions. Thus, we can carefully choose four pairs of inputs (p_i, p'_i) such that

$$\bigcup_{j=1}^{4} \{v_k \in \mathbb{F}_2^4 \mid S(p_i + v_k) + S(p'_i + v_k) = 0x1\} = \mathbb{F}_2^4.$$

By a thorough analysis, set $P_1 = \{p_1 = 0x0, p'_1 = 0x7\}$, $P_2 = \{p_2 = 0x0, p'_2 = 0xF\}$, $P_3 = \{p_3 = 0x1, p'_3 = 0xE\}$, $P_4 = \{p_4 = 0x1, p'_4 = 0x6\}$, and we have

$$\{v_k \in \mathbb{F}_2^4 \mid S(p_1 + v_k) + S(p'_1 + v_k) = 0x1\} = \{0x0, 0x7, 0x8, 0xF\} = I_1,$$

$$\{v_k \in \mathbb{F}_2^4 \mid S(p_2 + v_k) + S(p'_2 + v_k) = 0x1\} = \{0x2, 0x4, 0xB, 0xD\} = I_2,$$

$$\{v_k \in \mathbb{F}_2^4 \mid S(p_3 + v_k) + S(p_3' + v_k) = 0x1\} = \{0x3, 0x5, 0xA, 0xC\} = I_3,$$

$$\{v_k \in \mathbb{F}_2^4 \mid S(p_4 + v_k) + S(p_4' + v_k) = 0x1\} = \{0x1, 0x6, 0x9, 0xE\} = I_4.$$

Moreover, $\bigcup_{i=1}^4 I_i = \mathbb{F}_2^4$. Thus, all 16 keys are exactly divided into four disjoint sets I_1, I_2, I_3 and I_4. Table 2 lists the choices of the other four pairs I_j' and their corresponding v_k.

Table 2. A partition of the key space by P_j, P_j'

P_j	P_j'	v_k
$\{0x0, 0x7\}$	$\{0x8, 0xF\}$	$\{0x0, 0x7, 0x8, 0xF\}$
$\{0x0, 0xF\}$	$\{0x6, 0x9\}$	$\{0x2, 0x4, 0xB, 0xD\}$
$\{0x1, 0xE\}$	$\{0x7, 0x8\}$	$\{0x3, 0x5, 0xA, 0xC\}$
$\{0x1, 0x6\}$	$\{0x9, 0xE\}$	$\{0x1, 0x6, 0x9, 0xE\}$

Suppose that one chooses a pair of inputs $(0x0, 0x7)$ and checks whether the corresponding output difference is equal to $0x1$. If the output difference is equal to $0x1$, v_k must belong to I_1. Otherwise, the key v_k does not belong to I_1. By choosing different input pairs at most four times, we can determine which set of I_i's such that v_k belongs to.

Suppose the 64-bit round key is $(0x0, 0x0, \cdots, 0x0, 0x0)$ and a set consists of plaintexts

$$\{(v_{15}, v_{14}, \cdots, v_1, v_0) \mid v_j \in P_1, \text{for } 0 \le j \le 15\}. \tag{5}$$

Therefore, when X^0 runs through the set in (5), the corresponding output X^1 belongs to $\mathcal{A}$ (in (2)) after one round encryption. This together with Proposition 1 shows that the bits y_0^8 and $y_{16}^8 + y_{48}^8$ have a zero-sum property. This is illustrated in Fig. 2, where blue lines denote constant bits and bold lines denote active bits.

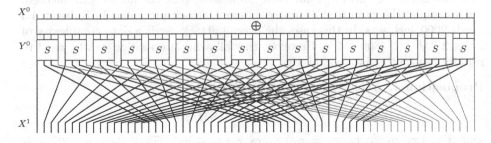

Fig. 2. One round propagation for 16-th order distinguisher (Color figure online)

Proposition 3. *An attack can always construct 2^{32} sets, and each of which consists of 2^{16} plaintexts. Moreover, there must exist a set such that all the values within the set traverse at the rightmost 16 bits and take a constant value on other bits after one round encryption, and thus, the bits y_0^8 and $y_{16}^8 + y_{48}^8$ have a zero-sum property.*

Proof. Let $\alpha = (\alpha_{15}, \cdots, \alpha_0)$ denote a 16-dimensional vector, and each coordinate of α ranges from 1 to 4. For a fixed vector α, we can construct a set

$$\Lambda_\alpha = \{(v_{15}, v_{14}, \cdots, v_1, v_0) \mid v_j \in P_{\alpha_j} \text{ for } 0 \le j \le 15\}.$$

Moreover, Λ_α contains 2^{16} elements and we can construct 2^{32} such sets for different α.

Denote the secret key $K = (v_{k_{15}}, \cdots, v_{k_0})$, where $v_{k_j} \in \mathbb{F}_2^4$ for $0 \le j \le 15$. Note that by Table 2, each subkey v_{k_j} of K belongs to a unique set I_{u_j} where u_j is determined by v_{k_j} and $1 \le u_j \le 4$. Let $\alpha' = (u_{15}, \cdots, u_0)$, then the set of elements after the first round encryption of $\Lambda_{\alpha'}$ belongs to $\mathcal{A}$. This together with Proposition 1 gives that the bits y_0^8 and $y_{16}^8 + y_{48}^8$ have a zero-sum property.

Remark 1. For $0 \le j \le 15$ and $i = 1, 2, 3, 4$, if we can determine which I_i's that v_{k_j} belongs to, 2^{16} Λ_s sets can be constructed such that y_0^8, $y_{16}^8 + y_{48}^8$ of each Λ_s have a zero-sum property. For example, let $v_{k_j} \in I_1$, $0 \le j \le 15$ and denote

$$\Lambda = \{(v_{15}, v_{14}, \cdots, v_1, v_0) \mid v_j \in P_1 \text{ for } 0 \le j \le 15\}.$$

Then y_0^8, $y_{16}^8 + y_{48}^8$ of Λ have a zero-sum property. According to Table 2, for each set

$$\Lambda' = \{(v_{15}, v_{14}, \cdots, v_1, v_0) \mid v_j \in G_j \text{ for } 0 \le j \le 15\},$$

y_0^8 and $y_{16}^8 + y_{48}^8$ of Λ' also have a zero-sum property, where $G_j = P_1$ or $G_j = P_1'$ for $0 \le j \le 15$. Note that it is always possible to construct 2^{16} such sets.

Thus, we first need to construct 2^{32} sets and each consists of 2^{16} plaintexts. According to Proposition 3, there must be one set such that y_0^8 and $y_{16}^8 + y_{48}^8$ have a zero-sum property. Then we need to guess which I_i's that each Sbox subkey belongs to, and this needs to guess for 2^{32} times. Moreover, we have to construct some extra sets for each guess such that the attack can succeed. For example, the Step 6 of 10-round integral attack presented in Subsect. 4.3 needs 2000 such sets. In this case, the overall attack needs a data complexity of $2^{32} \times 2^{16+11+11}/4800 = 2^{58}$. However, the following proposition can be used to rapidly reduce the data complexity.

Proposition 4. *Denote Λ_0 a set of 2^{48} plaintexts, where*

$$\Lambda_0 = \{(v_{15}, v_{14}, \cdots, v_1, v_0) \mid v_j \in A\},$$

and $A = \{x_3, x_2, x_1, x_0 \mid x_1 = x_2, \ x_3, x_2, x_1, x_0 \in \mathbb{F}_2\}$. Then there are 2^{16} subsets of Λ_0 such that all the intermediate values within each subset traverse at the rightmost 16 bits and take a constant value on other bits after one round encryption. Furthermore, the bits y_0^8 and $y_{16}^8 + y_{48}^8$ have a zero-sum property.

Proof. For any fixed key $K = (v_{k_{15}}, \cdots, v_{k_0})$, if k_j belongs to I_{u_j}, 2^{16} sets can be constructed as

$$\{(v_{15}, v_{14}, \cdots, v_1, v_0) \,|\, v_j \in G_{u_j}\},$$

where $G_{u_j} = P_{u_j}$ or $G_{u_j} = P'_{u_j}$. Then the bits y_0^8 and $y_{16}^8 + y_{48}^8$ have a zero-sum property. On the other hand, $P_i, P'_i \subseteq A$ for all $i = 1, \cdots, 4$. Therefore, the above constructed sets of plaintexts are subsets of Λ_0.

5.2 Integral Attack on 11-round PRESENT-80 Using the 16-th Order Integral Distinguisher

The 11-round integral attack can be obtained by appending one round before the 10-round integral attack. Denote the secret key $K = (v_{k_{15}}, \cdots, v_{k_0})$. According to Proposition 4, we need to construct a set Λ_0 of plaintexts where

$$\Lambda_0 = \{(v_{15}, v_{14}, \cdots, v_1, v_0) \,|\, v_j \in A\}.$$

Thus the data complexity is 2^{48}.

Since the internal state bit y_0^8 can be expressed as $y_0^8 = \bigoplus_{i=1}^{436} y'_i k'_i$, we can compute for a given plaintext all y'_i's by its corresponding ciphertext, and the time complexity of this step is 2^{48}. Storing values of y'_i's needs a memory complexity of $2^{48} \times (436/64) \approx 2^{51}$.

Next, we have to guess which I_i's that each Sbox subkey belongs to for the first round. For each guess, we can construct 2^9 integral distinguishers by carefully choosing $2^9 \times 2^{16} = 2^{25}$ elements from Λ_0 and the following steps are the same as those of 10-round integral attack. Since there are 2^{32} key set guesses, we have to repeat the above process 2^{32} times for each guess. Therefore the total computation time complexity is $2^{32} \times 2^{26} + 2^{48} \approx 2^{58}$.

6 Integral Attack on 13-round PRESENT-80 by Key Partition

6.1 Partition of the Secret Key Space

In order to attack the 13-round PRESENT-80, we give a new key partition which divides the key space into four disjoint subsets. Similar as that presented in Sect. 5.1, we can compute $\{y \,|\, y = S(v_k \bigoplus p_i), i = 1, \cdots, 8\}$ and check whether the rightmost bit of all y contained in this set is a fixed constant. If this is true, v_k is stored as a candidate key.

For example, given a set of inputs

$$P = \{0x0, 0x2, 0x5, 0x6, 0x9, 0xB, 0xC, 0xF\},$$

when $k = 0x0, 0x1, 0x8$, and $0x9$, it can be verified that

$$\begin{aligned}
\Lambda_{0x0} &= \{S(0x0 \oplus p_i) \,|\, p_i \in P, i = 1, \cdots, 8\} \\
&= \Lambda_{0x9} = \{S(0x9 \oplus p_i) \,|\, p_i \in P, i = 1, \cdots, 8\} \\
&= \{(y_3, y_2, y_1, 0) \,|\, y_1, y_2, y_3 \in \mathbb{F}_2\}
\end{aligned} \tag{6}$$

and

$$\Lambda_{0x1} = \{S\,(0x1 \oplus p_i)\,|\,p_i \in P, i = 1, \cdots, 8\}$$
$$= \Lambda_{0x8} = \{S\,(0x8 \oplus p_i)\,|\,p_i \in P, i = 1, \cdots, 8\} \qquad (7)$$
$$= \{(y_3, y_2, y_1, 1)\,|\,y_1, y_2, y_3 \in \mathbb{F}_2\}.$$

Thus, the keys $0x0$, $0x1$, $0x8$ and $0x9$ should be included in a same set. By repeating the above steps several times, four sets of plaintexts can be found whose corresponding key candidate sets form the whole space $\mathbb{F}_2^4$. These sets of the inputs and the corresponding keys v_k are listed in Table 3. In this case, all possible Sbox subkeys are divided into four disjoint sets and we denote them by

Table 3. A partition of the key space

Q_j	v_k
$\{0x0, 0x2, 0x5, 0x6, 0x9, 0xB, 0xC, 0xF\},$	$0x0, 0x1, 0x8, 0x9$
$\{0x0, 0x2, 0x4, 0x7, 0x9, 0xB, 0xD, 0xE\},$	$0x2, 0x3, 0xA, 0xB$
$\{0x0, 0x3, 0x5, 0x7, 0x9, 0xA, 0xC, 0xE\},$	$0x4, 0x5, 0xC, 0xD$
$\{0x0, 0x3, 0x4, 0x6, 0x9, 0xA, 0xD, 0xF\},$	$0x6, 0x7, 0xE, 0xF$

$I_1' = \{0x0, 0x1, 0x8, 0x9\}$, $I_2' = \{0x2, 0x3, 0xA, 0xB\}$, $I_3' = \{0x4, 0x5, 0xC, 0xD\}$ and $I_4' = \{0x6, 0x7, 0xE, 0xF\}$. Other alternatives are listed in Appendix C.

Moreover, denote

$$Q_1 = \{0x0, 0x2, 0x5, 0x6, 0x9, 0xB, 0xC, 0xF\},$$
$$Q_2 = \{0x0, 0x2, 0x4, 0x7, 0x9, 0xB, 0xD, 0xE\},$$
$$Q_3 = \{0x0, 0x3, 0x5, 0x7, 0x9, 0xA, 0xC, 0xE\},$$
$$Q_4 = \{0x0, 0x3, 0x4, 0x6, 0x9, 0xA, 0xD, 0xF\},$$

and $\alpha = (\alpha_3, \alpha_2, \alpha_1, \alpha_0)$ is a 4-dimensional vector whose coordinates range from 1 to 4. Thus, we can construct a set

$$\Lambda_\alpha = \{(v_{15}, \cdots, v_0)\,|\,v_i \in \mathbb{F}_2^4, 4 \le i \le 15, v_i \in Q_{\alpha_i}, 0 \le i \le 3\}.$$

When α varies, 2^8 such sets can be constructed. Moreover, there must exist an α' such that all intermediate values obtained by one round encryption of $\Lambda_{\alpha'}$ take a constant value on the rightmost four bits. This is illustrated in Fig. 3 where active bits, guessed bits and constant bits are denoted by black lines, yellow lines and blue lines, respectively.

Proposition 5. *An attacker can always construct 2^8 sets, and each consists of 2^{60} plaintexts. Moreover, there must exist a set such that the values of the rightmost four bits are constants and other bits are traversed after one round encryption, and thus, the rightmost bit of y_0^{10} has a zero-sum property.*

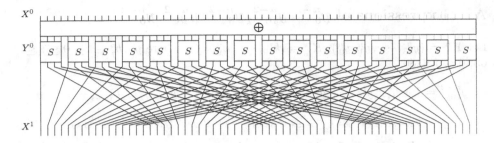

Fig. 3. One round propagation for 60-th order distinguisher (Color figure online)

6.2 Integral Attack on 13-round PRESENT Using the 60-th Order Integral Distinguisher

For the attack on the 13-round PRESENT-80, we denote the secret key $K = (v_{k_{15}}, \cdots, v_{k_0})$ and guess which I'_i ($i = 1, 2, 3, 4$) in Table 3 the subkey $k_j \in \mathbb{F}_2^4$ should belong to. The following steps of the attack procedure are the same as those in the 12-round attack. Since there are 2^8 key set guesses, we have to repeat the attack procedure 2^8 times for each guess. Thus the overall time complexity is 2^{74} and data complexity is 2^{64}.

7 Conclusions

In this paper, we propose a new approach to estimate the algebraic degree of PRESENT cipher, and we find a new 7-round integral distinguisher by this new method. Then, we express 3-round decryption as a Boolean polynomial and linearize this polynomial by introducing some new variables. Using this linearized polynomial we can attack 10- and 12-round PRESENT-80 by solving a system of linear equations with the aid of two 7-round integral distinguishers and one 9-round integral distinguisher. Further, we propose a key partition technique which divides the 4-bit Sbox subkeys into four disjoint subsets, and this technique helps us attack one more round based on the 10-and 12-round integral attacks on PRESENT-80. Therefore, the 11-and 13-round PRESENT-80 are attacked, and the attack against 13-round PRESENT-80 is the best result with respect to integral attack for PRESETN-80.

Note that division property is a newly proposed and widely used technique to search integral distinguishers for block ciphers, however, the new 7-round integral distinguisher found in our paper can not be retrieved by division property. Since division property outputs that Y_{16}^7 and Y_{48}^7 are undetermined bits, thus $Y_{16}^7 + Y_{48}^7$ will also be a undetermined bit according to division property.

Acknowledgements. We are very grateful to the anonymous reviewers. This work was supported by the National Natural Science Foundation of China (Grant No. 61802119).

A   Expressions of $y_0^{n-2}, y_{16}^{n-2}, y_{32}^{n-2}, y_{48}^{n-2}, y_0^{n-3}$

Let $Y^n = (y_{63}^n, \cdots, y_1^n, y_0^n)$, $K^n = (k_{79}^n, \cdots, k_1^n, k_0^n)$, where $y_i^n, b_j^n \in \mathbb{F}_2$, $0 \le i \le 63$, $0 \le j \le 80$.

$$y_{16s}^{n-2} = 1 + y_{4+s}' y_{12+s}' + y_s' + y_{8+s}' + y_{16+s}^n k_{64+s}^n + y_{4+s}' y_{28+s}^n k_{76+s}^n +$$

$$y_{20+s}^n y_{12+s}' k_{68+s}^n + y_{48+s}^n k_{32+s}^n + t_{4+s} y_{12+s}' + y_{52+s}^n y_{12+s}' k_{36+s}^n +$$

$$y_{4+s}' t_{12+s} + y_{56+s}^n k_{40+s}^n + y_{24+s}^n k_{72+s}^n + y_{60+s}^n y_{4+s}' k_{44+s}^n +$$

$$y_{52+s}^n y_{28+s}^n k_{36+s}^n k_{76+s}^n + y_{20+s}^n k_{68+s}^n t_{12+s} + y_{52+s}^n k_{36+s}^n t_{12+s} +$$

$$y_{20+s}^n y_{28+s}^n k_{68+s}^n k_{76+s}^n + y_{60+s}^n t_{4+s} k_{44+s}^n + y_{52+s}^n y_{60+s}^n k_{36+s}^n k_{44+s}^n +$$

$$y_{28+s}^n t_{4+s} k_{76+s}^n + y_{20+s}^n y_{60+s}^n k_{68+s}^n k_{44+s}^n + t_{8+s} + t_s + t_{4+s} t_{12+s},$$

where $s = 0, 1, 2, 3$, $y_d' = y_d^n + y_{d+32}^n + y_{d+16}^n y_{d+48}^n + 1$, $d = 0, \cdots, 15$, $l = 1, \cdots, 15$, and

$$t_l = k_{16+l}^n + k_{48+l}^n + k_{32+l}^n k_{64+l}^n,$$

$$t_0 = k_{16}^n + k_{48}^n + k_{32}^n k_{64}^n + k_{76}^n + k_{77}^n + k_{79}^n + k_{76}^n k_{78}^n + k_{77}^n k_{79}^n +$$

$$k_{78}^n k_{79}^n + k_{76}^n k_{77}^n k_{78}^n + k_{76}^n k_{77}^n k_{79}^n + k_{76}^n k_{78}^n k_{79}^n.$$

Denote

$$T = \{K_{[2i+1]}^n, K_{[36,38,68,70]}, B_{2j-1} \mid i = 16, \cdots, 23, 32, \cdots, 39, j = 1, \cdots, 8\}.$$

We guess the value of each element of the set T. Then

$$y_0^{n-3} = c_0 + c_1 k_{32}^n + c_2 k_{34}^n + c_3 k_{40}^n + c_4 k_{42}^n + c_5 k_{44}^n + c_6 k_{46}^n + c_7 k_{64}^n + c_8 k_{70}^n +$$

$$c_9 k_{72}^n + c_{10} k_{74}^n + c_{11} k_{76}^n + c_{12} k_{78}^n + c_{13} K_4 + c_{14} K_6 + c_{15} K_{12} + c_{16} K_{14} +$$

$$c_{17} K_6 k_{46}^n + c_{18} K_6 k_{78}^n + c_{19} K_4 k_{44}^n + c_{20} K_4 k_{76}^n,$$

where each c_i, $(i = 1, \cdots, 20)$ is expressed by variables in Y^n.

B   10-round Integral Attack on PRESETN-80

The experiment is conducted on the following platform: Intel Core i3-2350M @ 2.3 GHz, 4.00G RAM, 64-bit Windows 7 system.

The chosen random master key is $K = 0x93e41c6e20911b9b36bc$, then the state of the key register after 10 rounds encryption K^{10} equals to $0x2e74c0f2739072ad8205$. The first step of the attack procedure is to recover

32 bits $K^{10}_{[79,\cdots,64,47,\cdots,32]}$ of K^{10}. We chosen 500 different Λ sets such that we can get 500 linear equations, and the rank of these linear equations equals to 434, thus we can uniquely determine the value of $K^{10}_{[79,\cdots,64,47,\cdots,32]}$. The second step of the attack is to recover $K^{10}_{[63,\cdots,48,31,\cdots,16]}$ and we chosen 2000 different Λ sets to get 2000 linear equations. The rank of these 2000 linear equations equals to 1473 which is less than the number of variables 1489, however, we can also uniquely retrieve the value of $K^{10}_{[63,\cdots,48,31,\cdots,16]}$ since these variables are fixed in the solution space.

C Other Result of Partition of the Key Space

See Table 4.

Table 4. A partition of the key space with a set of inputs

Q'	key v_k
$\{0x1, 0x3, 0x4, 0x7, 0x8, 0xA, 0xD, 0xE\}$,	$0x0, 0x1, 0x8, 0x9$
$\{0x1, 0x3, 0x5, 0x6, 0x8, 0xA, 0xC, 0xF\}$,	$0x2, 0x3, 0xA, 0xB$
$\{0x1, 0x2, 0x4, 0x6, 0x8, 0xB, 0xD, 0xF\}$,	$0x4, 0x5, 0xC, 0xD$
$\{0x1, 0x2, 0x5, 0x7, 0x8, 0xB, 0xC, 0xE\}$,	$0x6, 0x7, 0xE, 0xF$

References

1. Bogdanov, A., et al.: PRESENT: an ultra-lightweight block cipher. In: Paillier, P., Verbauwhede, I. (eds.) CHES 2007. LNCS, vol. 4727, pp. 450–466. Springer, Heidelberg (2007). https://doi.org/10.1007/978-3-540-74735-2_31
2. Boura, C., Canteaut, A.: Another view of the division property. In: Robshaw, M., Katz, J. (eds.) CRYPTO 2016. LNCS, vol. 9814, pp. 654–682. Springer, Heidelberg (2016). https://doi.org/10.1007/978-3-662-53018-4_24
3. Daemen, J., Knudsen, L., Rijmen, V.: The block cipher square. In: Biham, E. (ed.) FSE 1997. LNCS, vol. 1267, pp. 149–165. Springer, Heidelberg (1997). https://doi.org/10.1007/BFb0052343
4. Knudsen, L., Wagner, D.: Integral cryptanalysis. In: Daemen, J., Rijmen, V. (eds.) FSE 2002. LNCS, vol. 2365, pp. 112–127. Springer, Heidelberg (2002). https://doi.org/10.1007/3-540-45661-9_9
5. Sun, B., Hai, X., Zhang, W., Cheng, L., Yang, Z.: New observation on division property. Sci. China Inf. Sci. **60**(9), 98102 (2017)
6. Todo, Y.: Integral cryptanalysis on full MISTY1. In: Gennaro, R., Robshaw, M. (eds.) CRYPTO 2015. LNCS, vol. 9215, pp. 413–432. Springer, Heidelberg (2015). https://doi.org/10.1007/978-3-662-47989-6_20
7. Todo, Y.: Structural evaluation by generalized integral property. In: Oswald, E., Fischlin, M. (eds.) EUROCRYPT 2015. LNCS, vol. 9056, pp. 287–314. Springer, Heidelberg (2015). https://doi.org/10.1007/978-3-662-46800-5_12

8. Todo, Y., Morii, M.: Bit-based division property and application to SIMON family. In: Peyrin, T. (ed.) FSE 2016. LNCS, vol. 9783, pp. 357–377. Springer, Heidelberg (2016). https://doi.org/10.1007/978-3-662-52993-5_18

9. Todo, Y., Morii, M.: Compact representation for division property. In: Foresti, S., Persiano, G. (eds.) CANS 2016. LNCS, vol. 10052, pp. 19–35. Springer, Cham (2016). https://doi.org/10.1007/978-3-319-48965-0_2

10. Wu, S., Wang, M.: Integral attacks on reduced-round PRESENT. In: Qing, S., Zhou, J., Liu, D. (eds.) ICICS 2013. LNCS, vol. 8233, pp. 331–345. Springer, Cham (2013). https://doi.org/10.1007/978-3-319-02726-5_24

11. Xiang, Z., Zhang, W., Bao, Z., Lin, D.: Applying MILP method to searching integral distinguishers based on division property for 6 lightweight block ciphers. In: Cheon, J.H., Takagi, T. (eds.) ASIACRYPT 2016. LNCS, vol. 10031, pp. 648–678. Springer, Heidelberg (2016). https://doi.org/10.1007/978-3-662-53887-6_24

12. Z'aba, M.R., Raddum, H., Henricksen, M., Dawson, E.: Bit-pattern based integral attack. In: Nyberg, K. (ed.) FSE 2008. LNCS, vol. 5086, pp. 363–381. Springer, Heidelberg (2008). https://doi.org/10.1007/978-3-540-71039-4_23

13. Zeng, K., Yang, C.H., Rao, T.R.N.: On the linear consistency test (LCT) in cryptanalysis with applications. In: Brassard, G. (ed.) CRYPTO 1989. LNCS, vol. 435, pp. 164–174. Springer, New York (1990). https://doi.org/10.1007/0-387-34805-0_16

14. Zhang, H., Wu, W.: Structural evaluation for generalized feistel structures and applications to LBlock and TWINE. In: Biryukov, A., Goyal, V. (eds.) INDOCRYPT 2015. LNCS, vol. 9462, pp. 218–237. Springer, Cham (2015). https://doi.org/10.1007/978-3-319-26617-6_12

15. Zhang, H., Wu, W., Wang, Y.: Integral attack against bit-oriented block ciphers. In: Kwon, S., Yun, A. (eds.) ICISC 2015. LNCS, vol. 9558, pp. 102–118. Springer, Cham (2016). https://doi.org/10.1007/978-3-319-30840-1_7

Improved Differential Fault Analysis on Authenticated Encryption of PAEQ-128

Ruyan Wang[1], Xiaohan Meng[1], Yang Li[2(✉)], and Jian Wang[1]

[1] College of Computer Science and Technology,
Nanjing University of Aeronautics and Astronautics, Nanjing, Jiangsu, China
[2] Department of Informatics, University of Electro-Communications,
1-5-1 Chofugaota, Chofu, Tokyo, Japan
liyang@uec.ac.jp

Abstract. PAEQ is an AES-based authenticated encryption proposed by Biryukov and Khovratovich in 2014, which stays in the CAESAR competition until the second round. In CHES 2016, Dhiman Saha and Dipanwita Roy Chowdhury first discussed the differential fault analysis to PAEQ. Their work shows that the nonce used in PAEQ that is usually considered as a natural DFA countermeasure can be overcome by carefully constructing the encryption message and injecting two faults. This work presents a fully optimized DFA attack on PAEQ-128 with regard to the key recovery process. We apply the information theoretical analysis and the DFA techniques for AES into the DFA key recovery on PAEQ-128. As a result, without changing the attack assumption, the key recovery complexity is reduced from 2^{50} to 2^{24} for PAEQ-128. The successful key recovery together with its computational complexity have been verified with the key recovery simulations.

1 Introduction

In 1997, Biham and Shamir introduced a new type of cryptanalytic attack in [2], as differential fault analysis (DFA). In DFA, attackers intentionally disturb the cryptographic calculations and collect pairs of fault-free output and faulty output under the same input. Then, the attackers construct a set of non-linear equations for a part of cryptographic calculation using the input difference known as the fault model and the known output difference. These sets of non-linear equations are used to restrict the key space until the key recovery.

DFA has been applied to almost every secret key cryptosystem. DFA is especially effective in attacking symmetric-key constructions. Only a few fault injections are enough to recover the secret key effectively. For example, the DFA attacks on AES [4,5,7] have been extensively studied for many years. For AES-128, a two stage algorithm could recover the AES key using only 1 fault injection [11].

This work focuses on the DFA attack on an Parallelizable Authenticated Encryption based on Quadrupled AES (PAEQ), which is an authenticated encryption (AE) primitive proposed by Biryukov and Khovratovich [3]. An ongoing

© Springer Nature Switzerland AG 2019
F. Guo et al. (Eds.): Inscrypt 2018, LNCS 11449, pp. 183–199, 2019.
https://doi.org/10.1007/978-3-030-14234-6_10

competition for AE named CAESAR (Competition for Authenticated Encryption: Security, Applicability and Robustness) [1] will identify a portfolio of authenticated cipher that offers advantages over AES-GCM. PAEQ is one of the candidates until the 2nd round competition.

Effectiveness of DFA on AE is an important research topic to be investigated as a part of the security evaluation. Saha and Chowdhury presented the DFA attack against PAEQ [8] in CHES 2016, which is generalized to relax the fault injection requirement in [9]. PAEQ is considered to be resistant to DFA attack since the nonce used in its calculation randomizes each execution. Generally, nonce is considered as a natural countermeasure against DFA attacks since attackers cannot repeat the same encryptions for multiple times. Saha and Chowdhury proposed a practical DFA technique in the presence of nonce. The proposed technique uses a multiple-block plaintext and a faulty ciphertext to execute the attack. Saha and Chowdhury proposed a practical DFA technique in the presence of nonce. They used the fact that all parallel branches are structured similarly in the parallel mode of operation. These parallel branches provide opportunities to apply the DFA attack bypassing the nonce countermeasure. In their work, two random faults are injected to the parallelizable authenticated encryption of PAEQ. The first fault is injected to create two branches whose inputs are exactly the same. The second fault is injected to obtain a pair of fault-free and faulty outputs.

With different key sizes, PAEQ has three versions as PAEQ-64, PAEQ-80 and PAEQ-128. According to [8] and [9], the DFA attacks on these three PAEQ variations have different key recovery complexities. For PAEQ-64 and PAEQ-80, the complexity i.e. the key space for exhaustive search is around 2^{16}, while for PAEQ-128, the complexity is estimated to be around 2^{50}.

This work reviews the DFA on PAEQ to analyze the relationship between the key size and DFA key recovery complexities. We result in an improved DFA key recovery on PAEQ-128 so that the complexity is reduced from 2^{50} to 2^{24}. We are able to run the key recovery simulations to verify the correctness of the proposed key recovery procedures. This paper explains the details to achieve this improvement.

- We first apply an information theoretical analysis inspired from [10] to analyze the existing attack. We find a possibility to improve DFA on PAEQ-128 since the existing attacks don't fully exploit the information from the injected fault.
- We propose to add an additional key recovery operation named 2ndInBound. In 2ndInBound operation, we apply a technique called group-and-combine to reduce its computational complexity. Theoretically, the time complexity of the entire DFA key recovery is reduced from 2^{50} to 2^{24} for PAEQ-128.
- We conduct the DFA attack simulations and successfully verify the theoretically estimated results.

The rest of this paper is organized as follows: In Sect. 2, we briefly explain the relations between AES and PAEQ. In Sect. 3, we describe the existing DFA attacks on AES and PAEQ. In Sect. 4, our improvement of DFA on PAEQ-128 is described in details. Section 5 shows the simulation results of our DFA attack. Section 6 concludes this paper.

2 AES and PAEQ

This section briefly reviews AES and PAEQ. Note that PAEQ uses AES round operations in the internal permutation.

2.1 AES

Advanced Encryption Standard (AES) [6] is structured as a substitution-permutation network. AES state is 128-bit that is usually presented as a 4×4 array of bytes. AES encryption consists of 4 operations as SubBytes (SB), ShiftRows (SR), MixColumns (MC) and AddRoundKey (AK). SB substitute each byte into a new value. SR shifts the byte positions. MC operates on the columns of the AES state and AK performs XOR operation between round key and AES state.

2.2 PAEQ

PAEQ was proposed by Biryukov and Khovratovich in ISC 2014 [3]. PAEQ is designed based on Quadrupled AES and follows a generic mode of operation named PPAE (Parallelizable Permutation-based Authentication Encryption).

The Structure of PPAE. The structure and internal permutation of PAEQ is summarized as follows. PAEQ in PPAE mode consists of the encryption part and the authentication part as shown in Fig. 1. The top half is the encryption part while the bottom half is the authentication process that generates a tag. The core part of the encryption is the internal permutation, which is called AESQ.

In the encryption process, the plaintext is divided into several blocks and encrypted independently. The plaintext blocks are XORed with the outputs of corresponding branches after AESQ. Thus, the ciphertext can be obtained in the form of several blocks. Since the output of AESQ is truncated for generating the tag, the DFA attackers have to deal with unknown bytes in the processed information.

AESQ. The internal permutation AESQ plays an important role in the encryption of PAEQ. Internal **state** of the PAEQ is defined as a 4-tuple of **substates**, each substate is same with an AES state. A state is denoted by s, while each substate is represented by s^m, where m denotes the substate index and $m \in \{1, 2, 3, 4\}$. The elements of s^m are denoted by $s^m_{i,j}$. A column of s^m is denoted as $s^m_{*,j}$ while a row is denoted as $s^m_{i,*}$.

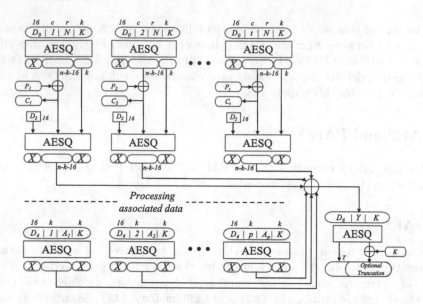

Fig. 1. PPAE mode of operation [8]

For the input of each substate, the first part is a 16-bit domain separator. The second part is the counter value, whose size differs for different key lengths and nonce lengths. The third part is the nonce and the last part is the master key. Different variants of PAEQ have different key length and nonce length, which are denoted as k and r, respectively.

AESQ is considered to be 20 AES round functions and 10 shuffle operations, which is shown in Fig. 2. After every two round functions, there is a shuffle operation that shifts different columns in four substates as shown in Table 1. In this paper, the rth round function is denoted as R_r. Each round function consists of four operations as SubBytes, ShiftRows, MixColumns and AddRoundConstants. Some bytes of the output of AESQ are truncated.

Table 1. Shuffle operation [8]

	s^1				s^2			
Before	$s^1_{*,0}$	$s^1_{*,1}$	$s^1_{*,2}$	$s^1_{*,3}$	$s^2_{*,0}$	$s^2_{*,1}$	$s^2_{*,2}$	$s^2_{*,3}$
After	$s^1_{*,3}$	$s^4_{*,3}$	$s^3_{*,2}$	$s^2_{*,2}$	$s^1_{*,1}$	$s^4_{*,1}$	$s^3_{*,0}$	$s^2_{*,0}$
	s^3				s^4			
Before	$s^3_{*,0}$	$s^3_{*,1}$	$s^3_{*,2}$	$s^3_{*,3}$	$s^4_{*,0}$	$s^4_{*,1}$	$s^4_{*,2}$	$s^4_{*,3}$
After	$s^1_{*,2}$	$s^4_{*,2}$	$s^3_{*,3}$	$s^2_{*,3}$	$s^1_{*,0}$	$s^4_{*,0}$	$s^3_{*,1}$	$s^2_{*,1}$

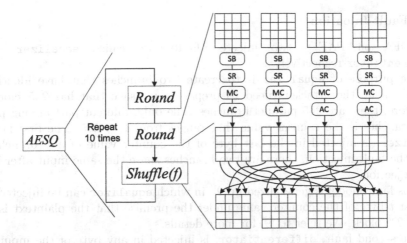

Fig. 2. The internal permutation of PAEQ

3   DFA on PAEQ

In this section, we review the DFA on PAEQ that was proposed in [8].

Usually, DFA attacks require a pair of faulty-free ciphertext and faulty ciphertext with repeated plaintext. When referring to nonce-based encryption such as PAEQ, since the nonce is different in every execution, it actually provides a built-in countermeasure against DFA. To overcome the nonce barrier for DFA attack, the proposal in [8] only requires 1 PAEQ encryption.

The idea is to take advantage of the similarities between different branches of PAEQ encryption. The attackers need to inject two faults. The first fault is to make sure that two branches share the same input. The second fault is to introduce a difference into the calculation, which is similar to the fault injected in the existing DFA attacks. This approach successfully overcomes the nonce barrier for DFA against PAEQ.

Specifically, the DFA attack procedure can be summarized as follows:

1. Inject two faults and find a branch pair (i, j) where their inputs to AESQ are the same.
2. Use the differential of fault-free and faulty outputs to restrict the space of intermediate values, in which all diagonal guesses of the second fault are used to restrict the state vector. The calculation can be further divided into the InBound phase and the OutBound phase.
3. Verify every candidate of the state vector and retrieve the master key. This step can be considered as an exhaustive search over all the remaining key candidates.

The following section explains the entire DFA attack by breaking it down into 4 phases as fault injection, InBound phase, OutBound phase and key recovery.

3.1 Fault Injection

For DFA on PAEQ, two injected faults are called `equalizer` and `differentiator` respectively.

The purpose of `equalizer` is to create two branches that have identical inputs. In [8], the attackers need to prepare a message that has 255 blocks. Therefore, there are 255 parallel branches. The only different part among parallel branches is the counter value that ranges from 1 to 255. The first fault, `equalizer`, is injected in the last byte of the counter value of any branch j. After the fault injection, there are two branches share the same input after the fault injection.

This fault model is generalized in [9], in which `equalizer` can be injected in the last t-byte of the counter value under the premise that the plaintext is in size of 2^{8t}-block. We refer to [9] for more details.

The second fault, `differentiator`, is injected in any byte of the input of R_{17} of AESQ in the same branch of `equalizer`. Differentiator enables the exploration of the difference of internal states and the characteristics of fault diffusion to restrict candidates of internal state.

After two fault injections, there are two branches that share the same inputs, one of which is faulty-free branch i and the other is faulty branch j. The faulty branch j can be determined with the information of fault-free branch i and the output of branch i. At this moment, a pair (i, j) can be uniquely identified.

When the second fault is injected at the input of R_{17}, the fault diffusion process is shown in Fig. 3. The single-byte fault is propagated to every bytes of AESQ state after 3 rounds of calculation. Different from DFA on AES, some bytes of the AESQ output are not available to the attackers. Hereafter, the attackers use `InBound` phase and `OutBound` phase to exploit the difference byte relations and restrict the number of candidates of internal state.

3.2 InBound Phase

In the InBound phase, the attackers first use a method named `FINDQ` to determine the branch pair (i, j) so that branches i and j have the same input. Then, the differential state between these two branches is calculated reversely to SB_{19}. The unknown bytes in the differential state will be solved with byte relations after R_{19}. After that, all the possible byte inter-relations of differential state before R_{19} are guessed. Noted that there are four possible byte inter-relations according to four different diagonal positions corresponding to different faulty byte position. Several differential equations are solved with the results from both directions.

The procedures of `InBound` phase is illustrated in Fig. 4. The `InBound` phase generates four column vectors. Each column vector corresponds to one substate.

3.3   OutBound Phase

The column vectors obtained from InBound phase and the output of fault-free branch are used as the input to this phase. Each time for OutBound phase, one substate of the output of fault-free branch and one column from the column vector corresponding to that substate are chosen as the input, for example, one substate candidate for s^1 and one column candidate corresponding to s^1. On one hand, the substate is inverted to R_{19} after MC_{19}. On the other hand, the column corresponding to that substate is restored to the substate to R_{19} after SR_{19}. Afterwards, linear equations need to be solved based on MixColumns operation for these two substates. One substate vector is obtained after OutBound phase for each time. Four substate vectors are obtained by repeating OutBound phase for four times.

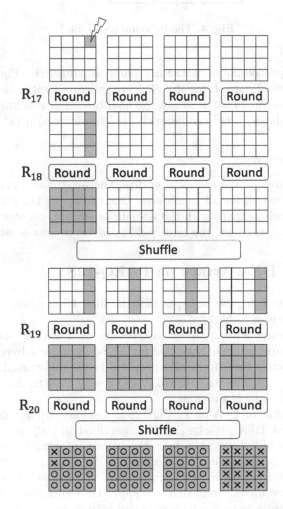

Fig. 3. Diffusion of an internal-difference in the first substate in 4 rounds of AESQ [8]

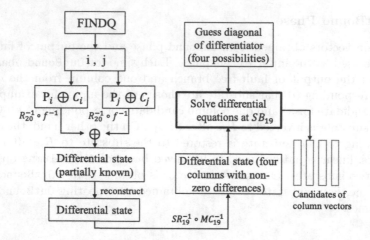

Fig. 4. The InBound phase [8]

The specific procedure of OutBound phase is shown in Fig. 5. After the OutBound phase, candidate states after R_{20} are generated with the cross product of four substate vectors. That is to say, the final candidates include all combinations of (s^1 candidates) || (s^2 candidates) || (s^3 candidates) || (s^4 candidates).

3.4 Key Recovery

With the candidates of the states after R_{20}, the master key can be retrieved by an exhaustive search for all candidates. One can invert the candidate to the input of AESQ and compare with the domain separator, counter and nonce. If the comparison is consistent, the retrieved key is the correct master key.

4 Improved DFA Attack on PAEQ-128

According to [8] and [9], the key space for the final key recovery for 3 variates of PAEQ are shown in Table 2.

The inconsistency among the attack results of 3 PAEQ variates already implies possible improvement. Note that for AES-128 under 1-byte random fault model, after exploiting the information provided by the differential, the key space can be restricted to 2^8. The structure of PAEQ is very close to that of AES, while the attack result is largely different.

The improvement of DFA on PAEQ-128 is inspired by the information theoretical analysis of DFA attacks [10]. As described in [10], the optimal DFA attacks should be able to exploit fully the leaked information to retrieve the secret key with a practical level of complexity. We'd like to analyze the limits of the DFA attack from an information theoretical approach to find the possible room of improvement. After that, we apply DFA techniques to achieve the improvement within a practical level of complexity.

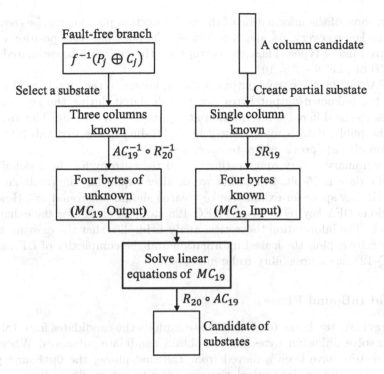

Fig. 5. The OutBound phase [8]

Table 2. The attack complexities for three PAEQ variates in [8] and [9]

PAEQ	PAEQ-64	PAEQ-80	PAEQ-128
Key space	$2^{16.14}$	$2^{16.14}$	2^{50}(estd.)

4.1 Information Theoretical Analysis

We take the information theoretical approach to check whether or not the DFA attack can be improved theoretically for PAEQ-128. In [10], the authors introduce a method to estimate the leaked information for the fault model. Then, the estimated leaked information can be used to evaluate whether an attack has taken advantage of all the information provided by the fault.

We apply their concept to roughly estimate the attack efficiency for DFA on PAEQ-128. Basically, we assume that the key space after fully exploiting the injected fault should similar to the entropy of injected fault and public data. For the described attack on PAEQ-128, the entropy of the fault is roughly 14-bit since the value (8-bit) and the position of the injected fault (6-bit) is unknown.

However, some of the information of the fault injection position can be recovered during the key recovery. As mentioned in [8], the fault injection position can be summarized into 4 types. Thus, the entropy for the fault can be estimated to be around 10-bit, i.e. $8 + 2 = 10$.

For PAEQ-128, the partial output is also unknown to the attackers. However, most of the unknown output bytes can be calculated during the key recovery according to the difference information at R_{20} input. Eventually, The unknown bits of the public data is mainly the 2 bytes (16-bit) in the first substate. This estimation also fits previous key recovery result.

As a summary, a very rough estimation of the entropy for the injected fault and public data is 26-bit. In another word, after exploiting the available information, the key space for exhaustive key search should be around 2^{26}. However, the previous DFA key recovery of PAEQ-128 stopped at 2^{50} for the exhaustive key search. The information theoretical analysis implies that the existing attack does not fully exploit the leaked information and the complexity of DFA attack of PAEQ-128 has a possibility to be improved.

4.2   2nd InBound Phase

In the previous attack, the OutBound phase exploits the candidates from InBound phase to solve unknown bytes and to obtain candidate substates. When four column vectors have been achieved from InBound phase, the OutBound phase takes these candidates into calculations in order to get specific substates of the fault-free branch. In other words, the OutBound phase exploits the candidates from InBound phase to solve those unknown bytes in a substate. After OutBound phase, we add a new key recovery phase named 2ndInBound phase to further restrict the key space after InBound and OutBound phases.

2ndInBound phase uses the proportion of the non-zero difference column to further restrict the candidate states. For four substate vectors, each candidate substate from them is inverted to the beginning of R_{18} and the difference relation is checked.

4.3   Group and Combine

In the previous DFA attack of PAEQ, it is suggested to generate state vectors with the cross-product of four substate vectors. For the 2ndInBound phase, if we follow this straightforward method and check every possible key candidate, the process takes 2^{50} calculations. In this section, we propose a technique called group-and-combine to reduce the key recovery complexity.

It can be observed that the combination of four candidate substates from four substate vectors does not always make sense. Due to the shuffle operation, there exists a connection between the candidates of s^1, s^2, s^3 and s^4. As a result, the candidate states generated in the way of cross-product include some invalid ones. The group-and-combine operation is to eliminate invalid candidate states, which further reduces the amount of candidate states.

In the 2ndInBound phase, we achieve four substate vectors and each substate corresponds to one non-zero difference byte retrieved. As for the group part, four substate vectors are divided into (256×4) groups, each substate vector has 256 groups. The non-zero byte value retrieved corresponds to the group index. For example, all the candidate substates for the difference byte $0x01$ belong to group-01 and all the candidate substates for the difference byte $0x05$ belong to group-05. The numbers of candidate substates of these groups differ from each other and some groups may be empty.

For the combine step, we utilize the correct proportion to combine (256×4) groups of candidate substates. In s^1 before R_{17}, there are four possible diagonals for the injected fault and each diagonal has four positions, each position corresponds to one kind of difference byte-relation after R_{17}. For example, if the fault position is the twelfth byte (the 1st row and the 4th column) of s^1, which belongs to diagonal 3 then the non-zero difference column of s^1 is the fourth column and the proportion is $\{2, 1, 1, 3\}$ after R_{17}. The difference relations of the other three positions of the same diagonal are $\{3, 2, 1, 1\}$ in the first column; $\{1, 3, 2, 1\}$ in the second column; $\{1, 1, 3, 2\}$ in the third column. We traverse each possible difference byte value from 0x01 to 0xff and select four candidates respectively from four substate vectors according to the proportion to combine the matched candidates. For difference value "$0x02$" and proportion $\{2, 1, 1, 3\}$, we choose one substate from group-06 of s^1 vector, one substate from group-04 of s^2 vector, one substate from group-02 of s^3 vector and one substate from group-02 of s^4 vector to combine. The operation for other three relations is similar to it. The operation guarantees that four substates of each candidate state after combination are matched, and the final candidate states do not include invalid ones.

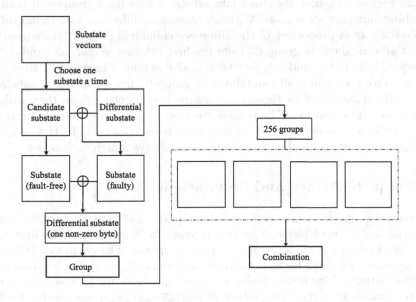

Fig. 6. The 2ndInBound phase

When the combination is performed, we multiply the numbers of candidate substates from four substate vectors. Then the complexity of exhaustive search can be calculated by accumulating the number of valid candidate substates.

The complete procedures of 2ndInBound phase is shown in Fig. 6.

Example of Improved Key Recovery. Here a detailed example is given for better understanding how our techniques work.

Assume that one single-byte fault is injected in the twelfth byte of s^1 before R_{17}. After the InBound phase, four column vectors are obtained, and each column vector corresponds to one substate. After the OutBound phase, four substate vectors are obtained that are independent of each other, the outputs from InBound phase are used in this phase.

Then, the 2ndInBound phase comes. First, for each candidate substate from the substate vector of s^1, it is inverted to the beginning of R_{20} to get the corresponding substate for faulty branch. Second, the substates for two branches are inverted to the beginning of R_{19}. Third, the candidate substate for fault-free branch and that for faulty branch are retrieved to the first column in s^1 and s'^1 after R_{18}. At last, two columns for two branches are retrieved respectively to the $0^{th}, 5^{th}, 10^{th}, 15^{th}$ byte in s^1 and s'^1 before R_{18}, and XOR operation is performed on the four bytes for both branches. In four difference bytes, only the difference of two 15th bytes is non-zero, so this candidate substate for fault-free branch is grouped relying on the value of the non-zero difference byte.

Here is where the group-and-combine operation works. Assume that the non-zero difference value is $0x03$, then this candidate substate belongs to group-03. The above process will be performed for all candidate substates from four substate vectors. When all the candidate substates have been grouped, it is time to combine four substate vectors. We start traversing difference value from value 1. Since the correct proportion of the difference column is $\{2, 1, 1, 3\}$, we need to pick out all candidates in group-03 from the first substate vector, all candidates in group-02 from the second substate vector, all candidates in group-01 from the third substate vector and all candidates in group-01 from the fourth substate vector. All combinations of these four groups are matched since they satisfy the difference byte relation. The combination operation is not finished until all possible difference values from 1 to 255 have been traversed. In the end, all candidate states are generated whose substates always match each other.

5   Complete Attack and Simulations

The complete attack mainly contains three parts: InBound phase, OutBound phase and 2ndInBound phase. The experiments in [8] consist of the first two parts, the third part is an additional step we proposed. The output of InBound phase are the candidates for four columns of four substates at the beginning of R_{18}. The output of OutBound phase are the candidates for four substates for fault-free branch after R_{20}. The output of 2ndInBound phase are candidates for states that are composed by four substates for fault-free branch after R_{20}.

Before the InBound phase, a process called FINDQ is used to find the pair (i, j) after two fault injections. Then, the diagonal position of differentiator fault is guessed and four diagonal positions are considered. For each guess of a diagonal, the InBound, OutBound and 2ndInBound phases are performed successively. Each phase needs the results from the previous phase. After guessing all possible positions, the final candidate states are obtained, which are combinations of four substates. Figure 7 shows the procedure of all phases in our attack and Algorithm 1 shows the complete attack.

Next the complexity analysis and simulation experiments are introduced.

5.1 Complexity Analysis

Attack in [8]. The complexity analysis of the attack proposed in [8] will be reviewed. As claimed in [8], the process of $AESQ^{-1}$ is the most expensive operation in their complete attack. Therefore the times of performing $AESQ^{-1}$, which equals to the size of state vector, is considered to be the complexity of the attack. Saha and Chowdhury provided the classification of substates for fault-free branch after R_{20} based on the number of unknown bytes, which is shown in Fig. 8 in [8]. In a Type-1 substate, there is no unknown byte. There are three completely known columns both in a Type-2 substate and a Type-3 substate. A Type-3 substate has one unknown column while a Type-2 substate only has two unknown bytes. A Type-4 substate has one completely unknown columns and two unknown bytes. The complexity analysis is related to these four types of substates. They focused on Type-3 substates and described other substates in terms of Type-3 substates, which can be seen in Table 2 in that paper. In that table, the size of Type-3 is denoted as q and their experiments prove that q is

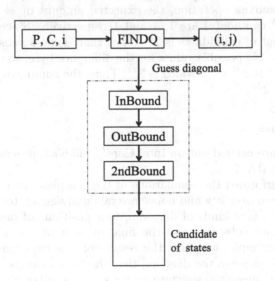

Fig. 7. The procedure of all phases

Algorithm 1. The complete attack

Input: P : one known plaintext with 255 complete blocks; C : one known ciphertext with 255 complete blocks; i : index of faulty-branch;

Output: K : the Master Key;

1: $(i,j) \leftarrow \text{FINDQ}(P,C,i)$;

2: **for** each $d \leftarrow$ diagonal **do**

3:     Four Column Vectors $\xleftarrow{\text{INBOUND}} (P_i \oplus C_i, P_j \oplus C_j, d)$;

4:     Four Substate Vectors $\xleftarrow{\text{OUTBOUND}} (P_j \oplus C_j, \text{Column Vectors})$;

5:     State Vector $\xleftarrow{\text{2ndInBound}}$ Four Substate Vectors;

6: **end for**

7: **for all** $e \in$ State Vector **do**

8:     $(D_x \| j_x \| N_x \| K) \leftarrow AESQ^{-1}(f(e))$;

9:     **if** $(D_x \| j_x \| N_x) = (D_0 \| j \| N)$ **then**

10:         return K

11:     **end if**

12: **end for**

around 2^8. The theoretical complexity for PAEQ-64, PAEQ-80 and PAEQ-128 in [8] are 2^{16}, 2^{16} and 2^{50}. The theoretical complexity for PAEQ-64 and PAEQ-80 were confirmed by the experimental results while that for PAEQ-128 was only estimated.

Our Attack. Considering our improvement, the process of $AESQ^{-1}$ is still the most expensive operation in the attack. Therefore, we also use the size of state vectors to estimate the complexity. According to their classification of substates, s^1, s^2 and s^3 are Type-3 substates while s^4 belongs to Type-4. After the `group-and-combine` operation, the expected amount of s^1 candidates, s^2 candidates and s^3 candidates are 1, 1 and 1 respectively. Since s^4 belongs to Type-4, the amount of candidates is 2^{16} times than Type-3 substates, which is 2^{16}. There are 255 (2^8) possible values for the difference byte, so the size of state vectors is $1 \times 1 \times 1 \times 2^{16} \times 2^8$, which is 2^{24}. Thus, the complexity of our attack is estimated to be 2^{24}.

5.2 Experiments

The experiments are carried out on Intel Core^{TM} i5-6500 processor running at 3.4 GHz with 4GB RAM.

In total, we performed the simulations of the complete attack for 30 times. The plaintext, the master key and nonce are randomly generated for each time. In the experiments, four kinds of diagonal, four positions of one diagonal, the amount of candidate substates and the final number of candidate states are recorded. As an example, we show the results of one experiment in Table 3. The first column represents the diagonal that the fault belongs to we assumed. The values below s^i mean the substate vector size of s^i after R_{20}. $|k|$ represents the key search space in the attack, which is the amount of final candidates.

Figure 8 shows the number of Type-3 substates obtained by experiments, Fig. 9 shows the number of Type-4 substates and the amount of final candidate states is given in Fig. 10. As shown in Fig. 8, the amount of Type-3 substates is confirmed to be around 2^8, which is consistent with that in the previous attack for the Type-3 substates. In Fig. 9, the experimental results show that the amount of Type-4 substates is around 2^{24}, which is also consistent with the value in [8]. By simulations, the experimental complexity of our attack is turned out to be around 2^{24}, which is greatly improved compared with 2^{50}. Figure 10 displays the distribution of all intervals in detail.

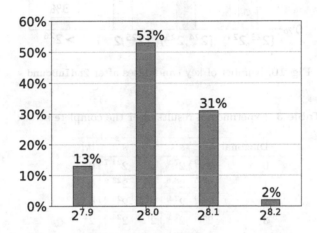

Fig. 8. Number of Type-3 substates after R_{20}

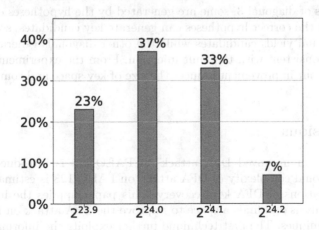

Fig. 9. Number of Type-4 substates after R_{20}

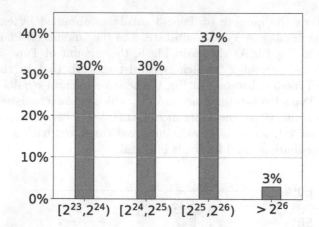

Fig. 10. Number of key candidates after 2ndInBound

Table 3. Experimental results after the complete attack

Diagonal	s^1	s^2	s^3	s^4	$|k|$
0	$2^{7.9}$	$2^{7.9}$	$2^{7.9}$	$2^{24.7}$	0
1	$2^{8.5}$	$2^{8.6}$	$2^{8.6}$	$2^{23.9}$	0
2	$2^{7.9}$	$2^{7.9}$	$2^{7.9}$	$2^{23.9}$	0
3	$2^{8.6}$	$2^{7.9}$	$2^{7.9}$	$2^{24.5}$	$2^{23.5}$

The positions of the fault injected in experiments are chosen randomly, thus it can be observed from the table that some candidate states are generated by the hypotheses of diagonal 3, some are generated by the hypotheses of diagonal 0, 1 or 2. Only the correct hypotheses can generate key candidates, so each time only one diagonal yields candidates while the other diagonals generate none as they are not consistent with the fault injection. From the experimental results, it is clear that our improvement reduces the size of key space and computational complexity.

6   Conclusions

In this paper, an improved DFA attack on PAEQ-128 is introduced. In [8], the computational complexity of DFA attack on PAEQ-128 is estimated as 2^{50} and the simulations of DFA key recovery. This paper applies the information theoretical analysis and finds a space to improve the DFA attack on PAEQ-128 using two techniques. The first technique further exploits the information from the fault induced by adding the 2ndInBound phase. The second replaces the cross-product of four substate vectors with the group-and-combine operation, which enables an efficient reduction of the size of key space. Using 30 simulations, we verified that the complexity of the DFA attack can be reduced from 2^{50} to around 2^{24}, in which the experimental results are consistent with the theoretical analysis.

Acknowledgement. This work was supported by National Natural Science Foundation of China 61602239, Jiangsu Province Natural Science Foundation BK20160808 and JSPS KAKENHI Grant Number JP18H06460.

References

1. Caesar: Competition for authenticated encryption: security, applicability, and robustness. http://competitions.cr.yp.to/caesar.html
2. Biham, E., Shamir, A.: Differential fault analysis of secret key cryptosystems. In: Kaliski, B.S. (ed.) CRYPTO 1997. LNCS, vol. 1294, pp. 513–525. Springer, Heidelberg (1997). https://doi.org/10.1007/BFb0052259
3. Biryukov, A., Khovratovich, D.: PAEQ: parallelizable permutation-based authenticated encryption. In: Chow, S.S.M., Camenisch, J., Hui, L.C.K., Yiu, S.M. (eds.) ISC 2014. LNCS, vol. 8783, pp. 72–89. Springer, Cham (2014). https://doi.org/10.1007/978-3-319-13257-0_5
4. Dusart, P., Letourneux, G., Vivolo, O.: Differential fault analysis on A.E.S. In: Zhou, J., Yung, M., Han, Y. (eds.) ACNS 2003. LNCS, vol. 2846, pp. 293–306. Springer, Heidelberg (2003). https://doi.org/10.1007/978-3-540-45203-4_23
5. Giraud, C.: DFA on AES. In: Dobbertin, H., Rijmen, V., Sowa, A. (eds.) AES 2004. LNCS, vol. 3373, pp. 27–41. Springer, Heidelberg (2005). https://doi.org/10.1007/11506447_4
6. National Institute of Standards and Technology: Advanced Encryption Standard. NIST FIPS PUB 197 (2001)
7. Piret, G., Quisquater, J.-J.: A differential fault attack technique against SPN structures, with application to the AES and Khazad. In: Walter, C.D., Koç, Ç.K., Paar, C. (eds.) CHES 2003. LNCS, vol. 2779, pp. 77–88. Springer, Heidelberg (2003). https://doi.org/10.1007/978-3-540-45238-6_7
8. Saha, D., Chowdhury, D.R.: EnCounter: on breaking the nonce barrier in differential fault analysis with a case-study on PAEQ. In: Gierlichs, B., Poschmann, A. (eds.) CHES 2016. LNCS, vol. 9813. Springer, Heidelberg (2016). https://doi.org/10.1007/978-3-662-53140-2_28
9. Saha, D., Chowdhury, D.R.: Internal differential fault analysis of parallelizable ciphers in the counter-mode. J. Crypt. Eng. 1–15 (2017)
10. Sakiyama, K., Li, Y., Iwamoto, M., Ohta, K.: Information-theoretic approach to optimal differential fault analysis. IEEE Trans. Inf. Forensics Secur. **7**(1), 109–120 (2012)
11. Tunstall, M., Mukhopadhyay, D., Ali, S.: Differential fault analysis of the advanced encryption standard using a single fault. Community Ment. Health J. **49**(6), 658–667 (2011)

Improved Indifferentiability Security Bound for the Prefix-Free Merkle-Damgård Hash Function

Kamel Ammour[1](✉) and Lei Wang[1,2]

[1] School of Electronic Information and Electrical Engineering,
Shanghai Jiao Tong University, Shanghai 200240, China
`kammour@sjtu.edu.cn`, `wanglei@cs.sjtu.edu.cn`
[2] Westone Cryptologic Research Center, Beijing 100070, China

Abstract. The indifferentiability framework has been tailored to evaluate the security of cryptographic hash functions such that an iterative hash function must be indifferentiable from a random oracle in order to behave as a random oracle in cryptosystems. It was found that popular (strengthened) Merkle-Damgård transformation cannot satisfy the notion of indifferentiability from a random oracle due to a length-extension attack. Thus, a series of Merkle-Damgård variants have been proposed. This paper mainly revisits one of them, Prefix-Free Merkle-Damgård (PF-MDHF), which is to use a prefix-free message padding. Our main contribution is to provide a tighter security bound for prefix-free Merkle-Damgård with respect to the indifferentiability from a random oracle. More precisely, our bound is $O((\ell^2 q + \ell q^2)/2^n)$, while in previous papers the bound is $O(\ell^2 q^2/2^n)$, where ℓ is the maximum block length of queries, and q is the maximum number of queries.

Keywords: Merkle-Damgård · Random Oracle · Indifferentiability · Prefix free

1 Introduction

Many practical cryptographic hash function such as SHA-2 [2] is based on the (strengthened) Merkle-Damgård hash mode [13,25]. This mode has been widely used in cryptography since 1990's. It consists of two parts: (a) a basic cryptographic primitive $\mathcal{F}$ that has a finite domain and range and (b) an iterative mode of operation $\mathcal{H}^{\mathcal{F}}$ that uses $\mathcal{F}$ in an iterative manner in order to handle messages string of arbitrary length. This hash mode preserves the collision resistance property of $\mathcal{F}$; i.e., if $\mathcal{F}$ is collision resistant then $\mathcal{H}^{\mathcal{F}}$ is also collision resistant too. However, the limitations of the Merkle-Damgård hash functions have been revealed by several attacks, such that Joux's multicollisions attack [18], Kelsey-Shneier second preimage attack [20], length extension attack [12] and the herding attack [19]. It is important to note that all these attacks focus on the iteration mode of the hash function and assume the cryptographic primitive is ideal.

© Springer Nature Switzerland AG 2019
F. Guo et al. (Eds.): Inscrypt 2018, LNCS 11449, pp. 200–219, 2019.
https://doi.org/10.1007/978-3-030-14234-6_11

Based on these observations, the cryptographic community has made several improvements to the aforementioned hash mode in order to strengthen it and to yield more secure variants. The first improvement proposed on the literature consists on adding a post processing to the Merkle-Damgård hash mode to avoid length extension attacks. Examples include Prefix-free encoding Merkle-Damgård hash function (PF-MDHF), Chop-MD hash function, NMAC and HMAC [12], HAIFA [8], MDP [17], EMD [5]. Afterwards, the output size of $\mathcal{F}$ was increased in order to avoid Joux's multicollisions attacks (Sponge [6], Grostl [16], Parazoa [3]). Another variants make a multiple call to $\mathcal{F}$ with the same message block [22].

Another line of research suggests to develop new security framework that may include, in addition to known attacks, attacks not yet known [27]. Indifferentiability, introduced by Maurer et al. [24] in 2004, was one among these security frameworks. In 2005, Coron et al. [12] applied indifferentiability framework on the hash mode of operation. Roughly speaking, indifferentiability measures the similarity degree between a hash function and a Random Oracle ($\mathcal{RO}$) under the assumption that the underlying compression function is ideal (like ideal cipher, ideal permutation or $\mathcal{RO}$). Indeed, the indifferentiability of a hash function from $\mathcal{RO}$ provides resistance to several attacks such that (Multi-) collision, (second) preimage and length extension attacks, etc., as long as the complexity does not exceed the indifferentiability bound. Accordingly, the indifferentiability notion has become a requirement to recognize a hash mode as a standard [26, 28]. However, it is worth noting that indifferentiability has certain limitations as shown in [15, 29], without the effect of diminishing the guarantee that offers against several generic attacks.

Relevant work. To enhance the security of Merkle-Damgård hash function against the length extension attack, Coron et al. [12] have proposed to process the message M by a prefix free padding before calling the Merkle-Damgård mode. Prefix free encoding Merkle-Damgård hash function (PF-MDHF) is the name of this construction. PF-MDHF is indifferentiable from $\mathcal{RO}$ when the underlying cryptographic primitive $\mathcal{F}$ is viewed as a Fix-Input-Length-Random Oracle (FIL-$\mathcal{RO}$). They provide an upper bound of indifferentiability which is $O(\frac{\ell^2 q^2}{2^n})$ where ℓ is the maximum length of the message M queried by the adversary, q is the number of queries made by the adversary and n is the hash output size. Following that, several works have investigated the indifferentiability of PF-MDHF. Chang et al. have presented a formal proof of indifferentiability for PF-MDHF [9] and improved its bound to $O(\frac{\ell^2 q^2}{2^{n-1}})$. However Luo et al. [23] pointed out that the given indifferentiability bound (of PF-MDHF) in [9] should be revised since a problem in the maximum advantage of the distinguisher has been highlighted.

In [11], Chang et al. proposed a new bound of indifferentiability which is $O(\frac{\sigma(\sigma + 1)}{2^{n+1}})$ where σ is the total block length of q queries and q is up to $2^{n/2}$.

So far in the literature, we observe all indifferentiability proofs is based on the assumption that all the internal values of Merkle-Damgård are distinct [12] in order to ensure that every call to the underlying primitive $\mathcal{F}$ is new. This strong assumption guarantees the adversary defeat.

Our Contribution. Our contributions are two folds. Firstly, we propose a fix to the problem raised by Luo et al. in [23] regarding the computation of the distinguisher's advantage in the indifferentiability of the PF-MDHF from $\mathcal{RO}$ proposed by Chang et al. in [9]. Indeed, Chang et al. [9] defined the distinguisher's advantage bounded by $2 \times \max(\Pr(BE_1, BE_2))$ where $\Pr(BE_1)$ (resp. $\Pr(BE_2)$) is the occurrence probability of bad events when the distinguisher interacts with the system $(\mathcal{RO}, \mathcal{S})$ (reps. (PF-MDHF, $\mathcal{F}$)). Along with mathematical simplifications, we arrive at an advantage of indifferentaibility bounded by $3 \times \max(\Pr(BE_1), \Pr(BE_2))$ (refer to Sect. 3 for more details).

Secondly, we improve the indifferentiability security bound of PF-MDHF to $O(\dfrac{\ell^2 q + \ell q^2}{2^n})$ which is the main contribution of our work. In addition, we argue that our novel proof technique can be of independent interest since it can potentially be used to improve the security analyses of HMAC, NMAC and Chop-MD [12]. We used a well known game-playing argument to show the indifferentiability of PF-MDHF and improve the indifferentiability security bound. Recall that the use of a random oracle in PF-MDHF allows the adversary to use only forward queries. The main problem in such type of analysis is to construct an efficient simulator able to withstand adversary.

The computation of the indifferentiability security bound in our approach is different from what has been done so far. In fact, we think that the assumption about distinction of all intermediate values of a hash function (which are no more than successive query-response to the FIL-$\mathcal{RO}$) is too generous and includes more cases than the adversary can effectively exploit to differentiate between the two system's $(\mathcal{RO}, \mathcal{S})$ and (PF-MDHF, FIL-$\mathcal{RO}$). A new set (i.e., three) of carefully chosen bad events is defined, which include all the cases that adversary can exploit to differentiate the two systems. This approach allowed us to clearly define the adversay's view which is restricted only to the answers provided by FIL-$\mathcal{RO}$ and the output values of PF-MDHF.

Our indifferentiability security bound guarantees the absence of generic attacks on PF-MDHF (using a n-bit FIL-$\mathcal{RO}$) with work less than $2^{n/2}$. When the digest-size is n bits, the hash mode is resistant to all generic attacks up to (approximately) $2^{n/2}$ computations of the underlying fixed input length Random Oracle (FIL-$\mathcal{RO}$). This bound is the best known for PF-MDHF.

Organization. The rest of the paper is organized as follows: In Sect. 2, we introduce some notations and definitions used in. In Sect. 3, we propose a correction to the adversary's advantage to differentiate PF-MDHF from $\mathcal{RO}$ as defined in [9] which allowed us to re-write the proposed theorem. Section 4 describes our main theorem and the improved indifferentiability bound of PF-MDHF. The security games for PF-MDHF and some observations on the indifferentiability bound is provided in Sect. 5. Finally, we conclude in Sect. 6.

2   Preliminaries

We let n denote the output bit length of the PF-MDHF. For concatenation of fixed length strings a and b, we use $a||b$, or just ab if the meaning is clear. We write $A^B \Rightarrow b$ to denote an algorithm A with oracle access to B outputting b. In pseudo-code descriptions, left arrow ($\leftarrow$) is used to denote the assignment operation.

Random Oracle. Define a Fixed-Input-Length Random Oracle (FIL-RO) f such that $f : \{0,1\}^m \mapsto \{0,1\}^n$ chooses the value of $f(x)$ randomly from $\{0,1\}^n$ for each $x \in \{0,1\}^m$. More precisely, suppose a subset of the input-output relations of f is known: $f(x_1) = y_1, f(x_2) = y_2, \ldots, f(x_t) = y_t$. Denote it by $f(X) = Y$ for the simplicity, where $X = x_1, x_2, \ldots, x_t$, and $Y = y_1, y_2, \ldots, _t$. For any $x \in \{0,1\}^m/X$, $\Pr[f(x) = y | f(X) = Y] = \dfrac{1}{2^n}$ for any $y \in \{0,1\}^n$. In this paper, a random oracle $\mathcal{RO}$ is referred to as the one with arbitrary-length inputs, whose domain is usually denoted as $\{0,1\}^*$. Let $\mathcal{F}$ is the set of all functions f with the same domain and range. The compression function $\mathcal{CF}$ can be equally regarded as a function f uniformly and randomly selected from $\mathcal{F}$.

Padding. a padding rule Pad is any injective function such that $\text{Pad}\{0,1\}^* \mapsto (\{0,1\}^b)^+$. Pad is said prefix free padding if for any $M_1 \neq M_2$, $\text{Pad}(M_1)$ is not prefix of $\text{Pad}(M_2)$.

Merkle-Damgård Hash Functions. Merkle-Damgård (MD) mode [13] used to be most popular domain extension algorithm for hash functions, e.g. SHA [1], RIPEMD [14], which use a padding function Pad in order to make the message be a multiple blocks long [21], then splits the padded messages into blocks $m_1||m_2||...||m_\ell$, and finally hashes one block by one block sequentially. $MD^{\mathcal{CF}}(M) = \mathcal{CF}(...\mathcal{CF}(\mathcal{CF}(IV, m_1), m_2)..., m_\ell)$ where IV is a public constant usually called Initial Value.

PF-MDHF. Define Prefix Free Merkle-Damgård hash function, PF-MDHF, as $PFMD^{\mathcal{CF}}_{\text{Pad}}(M) = MD^{\mathcal{CF}}(\text{Pad}(M))$ where Pad is a prefix free padding. For simplicity we will use PF-MDHF(M) instead of $PFMD^{\mathcal{CF}}_{\text{Pad}}(M)$. (See Fig. 1).

Algorithm 1. Function PF-MDHF(M)

---

let y_0 is a Fixed Initial Value IV.
$\text{Pad}(M) = (m_1, m_2, ...m_\ell)$
for i=1 to ℓ
$y_i \leftarrow \mathcal{CF}(y_{i-1}, m_i)$
return y_ℓ

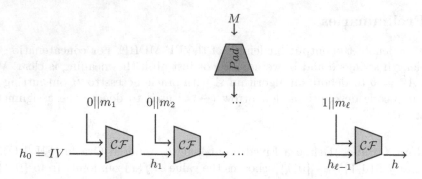

Fig. 1. Prefix free encoding Merkle-Damgård hash function.

Indifferentiability. As defined in [12,24], the indifferentiability is that an algorithm $\mathcal{H}$ with access to an ideal primitive $\mathcal{CF}$ is said to be $(t_{\mathcal{A}}, t_{\mathcal{S}}, q, \epsilon)$–indifferentiable from an ideal primitive $\mathcal{RO}$ if there is a simulator $\mathcal{S}$ such that for any distinguisher $\mathcal{A}$ it holds that:

$$\mathrm{Adv}(\mathcal{A}) = |\Pr[\mathcal{A}^{\mathcal{H},\mathcal{CF}} = 1] - \Pr[\mathcal{A}^{\mathcal{RO},\mathcal{S}} = 1]| \leq \epsilon,$$

where $\mathcal{A}$ runs in time at most $t_{\mathcal{A}}$ and makes at most q queries. $\mathcal{S}$ has oracle access to $\mathcal{RO}$ and runs in time at most $t_{\mathcal{S}}$. See Fig. 2.

Suppose that an algorithm $\mathcal{H}$ based on another ideal primitive $\mathcal{CF}$ (e.g. a FIL-$\mathcal{RO}$) is indifferentiable from an ideal primitive $\mathcal{RO}$. Then any cryptographic system C based on $\mathcal{RO}$ is as secure as C based on $\mathcal{H}^{\mathcal{CF}}$ (i.e., $\mathcal{RO}$ replaces $\mathcal{H}^{\mathcal{CF}}$ in C) [24]. Refer to [24] for more details.

In this paper, $\mathcal{CF}$ is defined as FIL-RO, $\mathcal{H}$ is the PF-MDHF. $\mathcal{RO}$ has the same domain and range with $\mathcal{H}$. The role of the simulator $\mathcal{S}$ is to simulate $\mathcal{CF}$. $\mathcal{A}$ interacts with $(\mathcal{O}_1, \mathcal{O}_2)$, where $\mathcal{O}1$ can be $\mathcal{H}$ or $\mathcal{RO}$ and $\mathcal{O}_2$ can be $\mathcal{CF}$ or $\mathcal{S}$. The goal of the distinguisher is to distinguish after queries to $(\mathcal{O}_1, \mathcal{O}_2)$ which scenario it is.

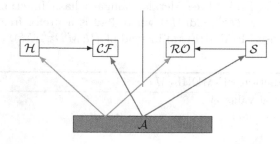

Fig. 2. Indifferentiability framework of MD hash function

View. Denote a distinguisher or an attacker as $\mathcal{A}$ who has an access to two oracles $\mathcal{O}_1$ and $\mathcal{O}_2$ and makes successive queries. We assume that all queries are distinct and it makes almost q_i queries to $\mathcal{O}_i$. Let r_j defines the jth query-response relation made by $\mathcal{A}$ to $\mathcal{O}_i$, that is, if the jth query made by $\mathcal{A}$ to $\mathcal{O}_1$ with a long message M_j, and got h_j as the response then $r_j = (IV, \mathtt{Pad}(M_j), h_j)$, else if the jth query made by $\mathcal{A}$ to $\mathcal{O}_2$ with a message block m_j and x_j, and got y_j as the response then $r_j = (x_j, m_j, y_j)$. From the first i query-response relations $r_1, r_2, ..., r_i$, $\mathcal{A}$ derives more relations using the following rules:

1. If $(x_1, M_1, x_2), (x_2, M_2, x_3) \in R_2$, $\mathcal{A}$ derives $(x_1, M_1 \| M_2, x_3)$;
2. If $(x_1, M_1 \| M_2, x_3), (x_1, M_1, x_2) \in R_2$ then $\mathcal{A}$ derives (x_2, M_2, x_3).

Denote all the relations that $\mathcal{A}$ knows, namely the knowledge or the view $\mathcal{V}$ of $\mathcal{A}$, after the first i queries-responses as R_i. Note R_i consists of both previous query-responses $r_1, r_2, ..., r_i$ and the derived relations. Denote IV and all the hash chaining values in R_i as $H_i := \{a : (a, b, c) \in R_i\} \cup \{c : (a, b, c) \in R_i\} \cup \{IV\}$. Following the folklore, we separate the queries into trivial and non-trivial queries.

For a query q_i made to $\mathcal{O}1$, where q_i is an arbitrary long message, it is called trivial if there is a relation $(a, b, c) \in R_{i-1}$ such that (a, b) is equal to $(IV, \mathtt{Pad}(q_i))$, and non-trivial otherwise. For a query q_i made to $\mathcal{O}2$, where q_i is a fixed-length pair (x, y), it is called trivial if there is a relation $(a, b, c) \in R_{i-1}$ such that (a, b) is equal to (x, y), and non-trivial otherwise.

PF-MDHF Indifferentiability. Coron et al. proved that PF-MDHF is $(t_{\mathcal{A}}, t_{\mathcal{S}}, q, \epsilon)$-indifferentiable from $\mathcal{RO}$, in the random oracle model for the compression function, for any $t_{\mathcal{A}}$, with $t_{\mathcal{S}} = \mathcal{O}(\ell q^2)$ and $\epsilon = \dfrac{\ell^2 q^2}{2^n}$ where ℓ is the maximum length of a query made by $\mathcal{A}$. In [9], Chang et al. improved indifferentiable security bound for PF-MDHF. More precisely, PF-MDHF is $(t_{\mathcal{A}}, t_{\mathcal{S}}, q, \epsilon)$-indifferentiable from $\mathcal{RO}$, for any $t_{\mathcal{A}}$, with $t_{\mathcal{S}} = \mathcal{O}(\ell q)$ and $\epsilon = \dfrac{\ell^2 q^2}{2^{n-1}}$ where ℓ is the maximum length of a query made by $\mathcal{A}$.

To study the indifferentiability security of the PF-MDHF, Coron et al. follow the usual game playing techniques [4,30]. It consists in the use of several games starting from $(\mathcal{H}, \mathcal{CF})$ (or $(\mathcal{RO}, \mathcal{S})$) in order to arrive to $(\mathcal{RO}, \mathcal{S})$ (or $(\mathcal{H}, \mathcal{CF})$ respectively) with as little as possible difference between games. There is two crucial steps in the game playing techniques: (a) construction of an efficient simulator $\mathcal{S}$ able to emulate the compression function $\mathcal{CF}$ on the one hand and to remain consistent with $\mathcal{RO}$'s answers on the other hand. In Sect. 5, we describe our simulator $\mathcal{S}$. (b) determining equivalences between successive pairs of games. We begin by providing a formal definition of this notion. A game is a probabilistic algorithm that takes an adversary-generated query as input and return an output after updating the current state.

Let (x_i, y_i) denote the i-th query and response pair from the game G. The view of the game G after j queries (with respect to the adversary $\mathcal{A}$), is the sequence $(x_1, y_1), ..., (x_j, y_j)$. Denote the views of the games G_1 and G_2 after

i queries by V_1^i and V_2^i. The games G_1 and G_2 are said to be equivalent (with respect to the adversary $\mathcal{A}$) if and only if $V_1^i \ {}^\sim V_2^i$ for all $i \geq 0$. Equivalence between the games G_1 and G_2 is denoted by $G1 \equiv G2$.

3   Revising Indifferentiability Security Bound of PF-MDHF Given in [9]

Following the problem highlighted by Luo et al. [23] on the $\mathcal{A}$'s advantage indifferentiability of PF-MDHF provided by Chang et al.'s [9], we revise the indifferentiability security bound.

Before starting, we need to define an event denoted BadEvent.

Definition of BadEvent. We say that a BadEvent (BE) occurs for the i-th query-response relation $r_i = (a, b, c)$, where a is IV in the case that q_i is made to $\mathcal{O}_1$, if q_i is non-trivial and $c \in R_{i-1} \cup \{a\} \cup \{IV\}$. Thus, there are BE1 and BE2 when $\mathcal{A}$ interacts with $(\mathcal{H}, \mathcal{CF})$ and $(\mathcal{RO}, \mathcal{S})$ respectively.

$$
\begin{aligned}
Adv^{\mathcal{A}} =&\mid \Pr[\mathcal{A}^{\mathcal{H},\mathcal{CF}} = 1] - \Pr[\mathcal{A}^{\mathcal{RO},\mathcal{S}} = 1] \mid \\
=&\mid \Pr[\mathcal{A}^{\mathcal{H},\mathcal{CF}} = 1|BE1] \times \Pr[BE1] + \Pr[\mathcal{A}^{\mathcal{H},\mathcal{CF}} = 1|\neg BE1] \times \Pr[\neg BE1] \\
&- \Pr[\mathcal{A}^{\mathcal{RO},\mathcal{S}} = 1|BE2] \times \Pr[BE2] - \Pr[\mathcal{A}^{\mathcal{RO},\mathcal{S}} = 1|\neg BE2] \times \Pr[\neg BE2] \mid
\end{aligned}
$$

$$
\begin{aligned}
=&\mid \Pr[\mathcal{A}^{\mathcal{H},\mathcal{CF}} = 1|BE1] \times \Pr[BE1] + \Pr[\mathcal{A}^{\mathcal{H},\mathcal{CF}} = 1|\neg BE1] \times \Pr[\neg BE1] \\
&- \Pr[\mathcal{A}^{\mathcal{RO},\mathcal{S}} = 1|BE2] \times \Pr[BE2] - \Pr[\mathcal{A}^{\mathcal{RO},\mathcal{S}} = 1|\neg BE2] \times \Pr[\neg BE2] \\
&+ \Pr[\mathcal{A}^{\mathcal{RO},\mathcal{S}} = 1|BE2] \times \Pr[BE1] - \Pr[\mathcal{A}^{\mathcal{RO},\mathcal{S}} = 1|BE2] \times \Pr[BE1] \mid
\end{aligned}
$$

$$
\begin{aligned}
\leq\ & \Pr[BE1] \times \mid \Pr[\mathcal{A}^{\mathcal{H},\mathcal{CF}} = 1|BE1] - \Pr[\mathcal{A}^{\mathcal{RO},\mathcal{S}} = 1|BE2] \mid \\
&+ \Pr[\mathcal{A}^{\mathcal{RO},\mathcal{S}} = 1|BE2] \times \mid \Pr[BE1] - \Pr[BE2] \mid \\
&+ \Pr[\mathcal{A}^{\mathcal{H},\mathcal{CF}} = 1|\neg BE1] \times \Pr[\neg BE1] - \Pr[\mathcal{A}^{\mathcal{RO},\mathcal{S}} = 1|\neg BE2] \times \Pr[\neg BE2].
\end{aligned}
$$

As BadEvent is defined carefully such that $(\mathcal{H}, \mathcal{CF})$ and $(\mathcal{RO}, \mathcal{S})$ are identically distributed conditioned on the past view of $\mathcal{A}$ and BE does not occur then

$$
\Pr[\mathcal{A}^{\mathcal{H},\mathcal{CF}} = 1|\neg BE1] = \Pr[\mathcal{A}^{\mathcal{RO},\mathcal{S}} = 1|\neg BE2]
$$

So,

$$
\begin{aligned}
Adv^{\mathcal{A}} \Longleftrightarrow\ & \Pr[BE1] \times \mid \Pr[\mathcal{A}^{\mathcal{H},\mathcal{CF}} = 1|BE1] - \Pr[\mathcal{A}^{\mathcal{RO},\mathcal{S}} = 1|BE2] \mid \\
&+ \Pr[\mathcal{A}^{\mathcal{RO},\mathcal{S}} = 1|BE2] \times \mid \Pr[BE1] - \Pr[BE2] \mid \\
&+ \Pr[\mathcal{A}^{\mathcal{H},\mathcal{CF}} = 1|\neg BE1] \times \mid \Pr[\neg BE1] - \Pr[\neg BE2] \mid
\end{aligned}
$$

As $\mid \Pr[BE1] - \Pr[BE2] \mid = \mid \Pr[\neg BE1] - \Pr[\neg BE2] \mid$
then

$$Adv^{\mathcal{A}} \iff \Pr[BE1] \times \mid \Pr[\mathcal{A}^{\mathcal{H},\mathcal{CF}} = 1|BE1] - \Pr[\mathcal{A}^{\mathcal{RO},\mathcal{S}} = 1|BE2] \mid$$
$$+ \mid \Pr[BE1] - \Pr[BE2] \mid \times \mid \Pr[\mathcal{A}^{\mathcal{RO},\mathcal{S}} = 1|BE2]$$
$$+ \Pr[\mathcal{A}^{\mathcal{H},\mathcal{CF}} = 1|\neg BE1]$$

If $\Pr[BE1]$, $\Pr[BE2] \leq \max\{Pr[BE1], Pr[BE2]\}$, where max is some negligible function then

$$Adv^{\mathcal{A}} \leq \max \times \mid \Pr[\mathcal{A}^{\mathcal{H},\mathcal{CF}} = 1|BE1] - \Pr[\mathcal{A}^{\mathcal{RO},\mathcal{S}} = 1|BE2] \mid$$
$$+ \max \times \mid \Pr[\mathcal{A}^{\mathcal{RO},\mathcal{S}} = 1|BE2] + \Pr[\mathcal{A}^{\mathcal{H},\mathcal{CF}} = 1|\neg BE1] \mid$$

As $\Pr[\mathcal{A}^{\mathcal{H},\mathcal{CF}} = 1|BE1] \leq 1$ and
$\mid \Pr[\mathcal{A}^{\mathcal{RO},\mathcal{S}} = 1|BE2] + \Pr[\mathcal{A}^{\mathcal{H},\mathcal{CF}} = 1|\neg BE1] \mid \leq 2$ then

$$Adv^{\mathcal{A}} \leq 3 \max\{BE1, BE2\}$$

Thus the advantage of $\mathcal{A}$ is bounded by the probability of the maximum BE holds.

From Lemma 2 of [9] where $\Pr[BE1] = O(\frac{\ell q^2}{2^n})$ and $\Pr[BE2] = O(\frac{q^2}{2^n})$, we propose this theorem.

Theorem 1. *In the random oracle model, PF-MDHF is $(t_{\mathcal{A}}, t_{\mathcal{S}}, q, \epsilon)$-indifferentiable from a random oracle, for any $t_{\mathcal{A}}$ with $t_{\mathcal{S}} = \ell O(q)$ and $\epsilon = O(\ell^2 q^2)/(2^n)$ where ℓ is the maximum length of queries.*

4   Main Theorem

All the indifferentiability analysis proof for PF-MDHF [7,9,10,12] was done under the assumption that all intermediate hash values $h_1^1, h_2^1, \ldots h_{l-1}^q, h_l^q$ are distinct except common prefix. Bad event (BE) is defined if any collision founded. Indeed, indifferentiability is measured by computing the advantage of $\mathcal{A}$ in distinguishing the two games $(\mathcal{RO}, \mathcal{S})$ and (PF-MDHF, $\mathcal{CF}$). Typically, it is based on the BE probability computation (collision of one output of $\mathcal{S}$ with any previous value in the $\mathcal{A}$'s view). This condition ensures randomness such that for every call of $\mathcal{CF}$ (respect. to $\mathcal{S}$) we have a new output. All the known proof use this condition to avoid any BE problem or collision and guarantee that $\mathcal{A}$ can never succeed in distinguishing between the system $(\mathcal{H}, \mathcal{CF})$ and $(\mathcal{RO}, \mathcal{S})$.

Nevertheless, this calculation method, leads us to ask whether the obtained bound is tight.

Indeed, we think that this condition is too large and does not reflect the reality. It permits to think that if we have a collision between the internal values, $\mathcal{A}$ can distinguish between $\mathcal{H}$ and $\mathcal{RO}$ which is not really true.

In fact, we studied the indistinguishability between (PF-MDHF, $\mathcal{CF}$) and $(\mathcal{RO}, \mathcal{S})$ and we observed two cases.

First case: a concrete distinguisher can be found if we have a collision $h_s^i = h_s^j$ in the internal values of $\mathcal{H}(M_i)$ with $\mathcal{H}(M_j)$ of two different messages M_i and M_j (of the same length ℓ). To illustrate our remark we give an example. Let $M_i = m_1^i m_2 m_3$, $M_j = m_1^j m_2 m_3$ two different messages of the same suffix $(m_2 m_3)$. Let $h_1^i = h_1^j$. As M_i and M_j share the same suffix $(m_2 m_3)$, it is obvious that $\mathcal{H}(M_i) = \mathcal{H}(M_j)$ while the $\mathcal{RO}(M_i) = \mathcal{RO}(M_j)$ with probability $1/2^n$. Then, $\mathcal{A}$ can distinguish between $\mathcal{H}$ and $\mathcal{RO}$ and wins the game.

Second case: we did not find any concrete distinguisher if the output of two messages M_i and M_j (of different length even if they share the same suffix) are different even if we have a collision $h_s^i = h_t^j$ in the internal values of $\mathcal{H}(M_i)$ with $\mathcal{H}(M_j)$ for some $s \neq t$.

On the basis of this observation, we propose to restrict the conditions that make the two systems $(\mathcal{RO}, \mathcal{S})$ and $(\mathcal{H}, \mathcal{CF})$ indistinguishable to:

- In the same message M^i, all the intermediate hash values $\{IV, h_1^i, h_2^i, \ldots, h_\ell^i\}$ are distinct.
- At the same position i from the end of all messages M^j where $1 \leq j \leq q$, all the intermediate hash values $h_i^1, h_i^2, \ldots, h_i^q$ of different messages are distinct.
- There is no collision between a $\mathcal{S}$'s response for an $\mathcal{A}$'s queries with an internal hash values of PF-MDHF.

Given these conditions and using game playing technique we propose the following theorem whose detailed proof is presented in the next section:

Theorem 2. *The PF-MDHF based on FIL-$\mathcal{RO}$ is indifferentiable from a random oracle $\mathcal{RO}$ for any $t_\mathcal{A}$ and $t_\mathcal{S} \leq \dfrac{q(q+1)}{2}$ with $\epsilon \leq \dfrac{\ell^2 q + \ell q^2}{2^n}$ where q is the $\mathcal{A}$'s total queries and ℓ is the maximum length of message queried to PF-MDHF or $\mathcal{RO}$.*

Execution Time of $\mathcal{S}$. As defined in $\mathcal{S}$ (see Table 8: Game $G_7(\mathcal{RO}, \mathcal{S})$), its answers for a new query with a random value until it found the possibility of combination of the current query with the previous entries in the table $T_\mathcal{A}$ in order to be consistent with the queries to $\mathcal{RO}$. Since the number of entries in $T_\mathcal{A}$ is at most q, the running time of the simulator is $t_s \leq \dfrac{q(q+1)}{2^n}$.

5   Proof of Theorem 2

In this section, we give a formal indifferentiability proof of PF-MDHF based on a hybrid argument starting with (PF-MDHF, $\mathcal{CF}$) going to $(\mathcal{RO}, \mathcal{S})$ through a sequence of mutually indifferentiable hybrid games. The pseudo-code for all the games are given in Appendix A.

PF-MDHF, $PFMD_1$, $PFMD_2$, $PFMD_3$ and $\mathcal{RO}$ are mapping from $\{0,1\}^* \mapsto \{0,1\}^n$. $\mathcal{CF}$ and $\mathcal{CF}_i$, for $1 \leq i \leq 5$, are FIL-$\mathcal{RO}$ from $\{0,1\}^n \rightarrow \{0,1\}^n$. $\mathcal{S}$ is mapping from $\{0,1\}^n \rightarrow \{0,1\}^n$.

Game(PF-MDHF, $\mathcal{CF}$). This game shows the communication of $\mathcal{A}$ with PF-MDHF and $\mathcal{CF}$.

$G_1(PFMD_1, \mathcal{CF}_1)$. We denote by IH a subroutine that emulates the iteration process of the PF-MDHF. This game exactly emulates PF-MDHF and $\mathcal{CF}$. It is identical to Game (PF-MDHF, $\mathcal{CF}$) except that FIL-RO $\mathcal{CF}$ is chosen in a "lazy" manner. Namely, it keeps the history of all queries to $\mathcal{CF}$ in table $T_{\mathcal{CF}}$. Initially, the table is empty. Upon receiving a query from $\mathcal{A}$ to $\mathcal{CF}_1$, this later first checks in its table $T_{\mathcal{CF}}$ for an entry corresponding to the query and if found, it returns that entry to $\mathcal{A}$ consistently. Otherwise it returns a random value for the query. In addition, $\mathcal{CF}_1$ is used by a subroutine, denoted IH, that emulates the iteration process of PF-MDHF to answer the queries of $\mathcal{A}$ to PF-MDHF. Now, we can see that G_1 is a syntactic representation of G(PF-MDHF, $\mathcal{CF}$). Thus, p1 = p0.

$G_2(PFMD_1, \mathcal{CF}_2)$. This game is identical to G_1 except we differentiate queries received by $\mathcal{CF}_2$ following the senders ($\mathcal{A}$ or IH). The $\mathcal{A}$ (resp. IH)'s queries and its response is saved in table $T_{\mathcal{A}}$ (resp. T_{IH}). However, it has no effect on the random selection of the values returned to $\mathcal{A}$. Thus, p2 = p1.

$G_3(PFMD_1, \mathcal{CF}_3)$. In this game, some restrictions are applied on the values returned to $\mathcal{A}$. For a query to $\mathcal{CF}_3$, the returned values should be restricted such that they never satisfy certain specific failure conditions. If the response of $\mathcal{CF}_3$ satisfies one of these conditions, then it fails explicitly instead of sending this response.

The failure conditions describe some dependencies that could arise among the $\mathcal{CF}_3$'s responses which could be exploited by the distinguisher. $\mathcal{CF}_3$ provides a response $y_i^j \in \{0,1\}^n$ similar to the original $\mathcal{CF}_2$, for a query (y_{i-1}^j, m_i^j), and it checks for the following conditions:

- Bad Event1 BE_1: There are a non trivial query-response $(y_{i-1}^j, m_i^j, y_i^j)$ such that y_i^j is an intermediate hash value of a valid padding message $\text{Pad}(M)$.
- Bad Event2 BE_2: In the same valid padding message $\text{Pad}(M)$, it exists two internal values y_i^j and $y_{i'}^j$ such that $y_i^j = y_{i'}^j$.
- Bad Event3 BE_3: For two valid padding messages $\text{Pad}(M_1)$ and $\text{Pad}(M_2)$ of length ℓ and ℓ' respectively, there exists a value i such that there is a collision between two internal values $y_{\ell-i}$ and $y'_{\ell'-i}$.

$\mathcal{CF}_3$ explicitly fails if the returned response y_i^j matches one of the previous BadEvent.

Let us briefly describe how $\mathcal{A}$ can exploit each of these conditions to its advantage. If BadEvent1 holds the distinguisher could possibly force a sequence query to $\mathcal{CF}_3$ of a valid padding $\text{Pad}(M)$ where it does not know the first message block (for example) to be different with $PFMD_1(M)$. Hence $\mathcal{CF}_3$ cannot be consistent with $PFMD_1$.

If BadEvent2 holds then the distinguisher could possibly force two different $PFMD_1$ query sequences to end in the same block, where one input is the suffix of the other one in the case of IV collision or the two inputs share a common suffix in the other cases. Hence the simulator can be consistent with at most one of these two $PFMD_1$ inputs.

If Bad Event3 holds, then the distinguisher can again force two query sequences to end in the same block. However, in this case the two $PFMD_1$ inputs have a common suffix and the simulator can be consistent with at most one of these inputs.

It is obvious that G_3 and G_2 are identical until a bad event is set to true in G_3. This is denoted by $BE_i \leftarrow true$ for i=1, 2 or 3. Hence, the maximum advantage of $\mathcal{A}$ in distinguishing G_3 from G_2 is at most the maximum probability of the occurrence of bad events. Thus:

$\Pr[\mathcal{A}^{G_3} \Rightarrow 1] - \Pr[\mathcal{A}^{G_2} \Rightarrow 1] \leq \Pr[\mathcal{A}^{G_3} \Rightarrow (BE_1 \leftarrow true \cup BE_2 \leftarrow true \cup BE_3 \leftarrow true)]$. The probability that the bad events (explained below) BE_1, BE_2 or BE_3 are set to true in G_3 is denoted as $\Pr_{G_3}^{BE_1}$, $\Pr_{G_3}^{BE_2}$ and $\Pr_{G_3}^{BE_3}$ respectively. Thus:

$\Pr[\mathcal{A}^{G_3} \Rightarrow (BE_1 \leftarrow true \cup BE_2 \leftarrow true \cup BE_3 \leftarrow true)] \leq \Pr_{G_3}^{BE_1} + \Pr_{G_3}^{BE_2} + \Pr_{G_3}^{BE_3}$.

Now we bound each of the bad events as follows:

$\Pr(BE_1^{G_3})$. In this case, if we take a query-response $(y_{i-1}^j, m_i^j, y_i^j)$ of $\mathcal{CF}_3$, we identify two possibilities where y_i^j is an intermediate hash value of a valid $\texttt{Pad}(M)$.

a. $(y_{i-1}^j, m_i^j, y_i^j)$ is not in a chained query.

By not a chained query, we mean a query where y_{i-1}^j is not in the view of $\mathcal{A}$ before this query. The probability of this query-response collide with the internal values of hash function $PFMD_1$ is equal to the probability of y_{i-1}^j or y_i^j is in the internal values H_1 of $PFMD_1$.

$\Pr[y_{i-1}^j \in H_1] = \dfrac{\ell q_{PFMD_1}}{2^n} q_{\mathcal{CF}}$. Where $q_{\mathcal{CF}}$ is the number of queries that a distinguisher $\mathcal{A}$ sent to $\mathcal{CF}_3$ and q_{PFMD_1} is the number of queries that a distinguisher $\mathcal{A}$ sent to $PFMD_1$ of length ℓ blocks.

It is same for the probability of y_i^j.

$\Pr[(y_{i-1}^j \in H \text{ or } y_i^j \in H] = 2\dfrac{\ell q_{\mathcal{CF}}}{2^n} q_{PFMD_1}$.

b. $(y_{i-1}^j, m_i^j, y_i^j)$ is a chained query.

By a chained query, we mean that $\mathcal{A}$ knows (IV, m_1^j, y_1^j), (y_1^j, m_2^j, y_2^j), ..., $(y_{i-2}^j, m_{i-1}^j, y_{i-1}^j)$.

The probability of y_i^j is in the internal values H_1 of PFMD$_1$ but $m_1^j \| m_2^j \| \dots \| m_{i-1}^j \| m_i^j$ is not prefix of any queried $\texttt{Pad}(M)$ to PFMD$_1$ is equal to

$\Pr[y_{i-1}^j \in H_1 \text{ or } y_i^j \in H_1] = 2\dfrac{\ell q_{\mathcal{CF}}}{2^n} q_{PFMD_1}$

Then, $\Pr[BE_1] = 4\dfrac{\ell q_{C\mathcal{F}}}{2^n}q_{PFMD_1}$

$$\Pr[BE_1] < 4\frac{\ell q^2}{2^n} \quad \text{with} \quad q = q_{C\mathcal{F}} + q_{PFMD_1}.$$

$\Pr(BE_2^{G_3})$. In this case, there are two intermediate hash values h_i and h_j in the same $\mathtt{Pad}(M)$ such that $h_i = h_j$.

$\Pr[BE_2^{G_3}] = 1 - \Pr[\neg BE_2^{G_3})]$ where $\Pr[\neg BE_2^{G_3})]$ is the probability where all the intermediate chaining values of a message $\mathtt{Pad}(M)$ in $PFMD_1$ are distinct. The probability to distinct each intermediate value inside a message M is $\dfrac{(2^n - (i-1))}{2^n}$. If M has length ℓ, so

$$\Pr(\neg BE_2) = \prod_{i=1}^{\ell} \frac{(2^n - (i-1))}{2^n}.$$

$$\Pr(BE_2) = 1 - \Pr(\neg BE_2) = 1 - \prod_{i=1}^{\ell} \frac{(2^n - (i-1))}{2^n}$$

$$\leq q \sum_{i=1}^{\ell} \frac{(i-1)}{2^n} = \frac{(\ell)(\ell)}{2^n}$$

In total, there are at most q_{PFMD_1} queries, so the $\Pr(BE_2) = \dfrac{\ell^2}{2^n}q_{PFMD_1}$.

Hence, $\Pr(BE_2) < O(\ell^2 q/2^n)$

$\Pr(BE_3^{G_3})$. We restrict ourselves to the fact that if we take two distinct messages M and M' of different length ℓ and ℓ' respectively (with $\ell' < \ell$), it should have distinct chaining value located at the same distance to their final outputs. If we make q_{PFMD_1} queries of messages to $PFMD_1$, so we have $q_{PFMD_1}^2$ possible pairs of messages of length (ℓ, ℓ'). The probability to have collision between the intermediate hash values in each couple of message M and M' is $\dfrac{\ell + \ell'}{2^n}$. As we have $q_{PFMD_1}^2$ possible pairs, the probability to have collision in the intermediate hash values of all the couples is $\dfrac{\ell + \ell'}{2^n}q_{PFMD_1}^2$.

$$\Pr[BE_3] = \frac{q_{PFMD_1}^2(\ell + \ell')}{2^n} < \frac{q_{PFMD_1}^2(\ell + \ell)}{2^n}$$

$$\Pr[BE_3] < 2\frac{q^2\ell}{2^n}$$

Thus

$$|\Pr[\mathcal{A}^{G_3} \Rightarrow 1] - \Pr[\mathcal{A}^{G_2} \Rightarrow 1]| \leq \Pr_{G_3}^{BE_1} + \Pr_{G_3}^{BE_2} + \Pr_{G_3}^{BE_3}$$

$$\leq O(\frac{q^2\ell + q\ell^2}{2^n})$$

In addition, $\mathcal{CF}_3$ uses two important subroutines to detect Bad Event in its interaction with $\mathcal{A}$ and IH.

Get_Int_Val. The function $\text{get\_Int\_Val}(y_{i-1}^j, m_i^j)$ for a query (y_{i-1}^j, m_i^j) returns all the intermediates hash values generated from IV to y_{i-1}^j using message blocks $m_1^j, m_2^j, \ldots m_{i-1}^j$. For example, the function $\text{get\_Int\_Val}(y_3, m_3)$ returns the set $\{IV, y_1, y_2, y_3 \}$ such that $\mathcal{CF}_3(IV, m_1) = y_1$, $\mathcal{CF}_3(y_1, m_2) = y_2$ and $\mathcal{CF}_3(y_2, m_3) = y_3$.

Get_Val_Same_Pos. The function $\text{Get\_Val\_Same\_Pos}(y_{i-1}^j)$ for an internal hash value (y_{i-1}^j) returns the set $\{y_{\ell-i+1}^k\}$ of all intermediates hash values of the other messages padding k such that $k \neq j$ which are at the same position from the end of the message padding $(\ell - i + 1)$.

$G_4(PFMD_2, \mathcal{CF}_4)$. In this Game, IH does not directly communicate with $\mathcal{CF}_3$ but we change IH such that the FIL-ROs $\mathcal{CF}_3$ is simulated in IH. It is clear that G_3 are identical to G_4 until a bad event BE_1 is set in G_3 or $\mathcal{CF}_4$ returns a value to $\mathcal{A}$ in G_4 such that it matches BE_1 of G_3. These two events are identical in terms of their probability of occurrence because the distribution of the responses of $\mathcal{CF}_3$ and $\mathcal{CF}_4$ is identical. Let G_4 denote the event that $\mathcal{A}$ outputs 1 in game G_4, so that $\Pr[G_4] = \Pr[\mathcal{A}^{PFMD_2, \mathcal{CF}_4} \Rightarrow 1]$. Then we can deduce that $|\Pr[G_4] - \Pr[G_3]| \leq \Pr[BE_1 \text{ in game } 3] + \Pr[BE_1 \text{ should have detected in game } 4]$

$$|\Pr[G_4] - \Pr[G_3]| \leq O(\frac{\ell^2 q}{2^n})$$

$G_5(PFMD_2, \mathcal{CF}_5)$. G_5 is similar to G_4 except for a new query to $\mathcal{CF}_5$ which searches for a message that connects IV to y_{i-1}^j of the current query $(y_{i-1}^j, m_i^j, y_i^j)$. If it finds such path, $\mathcal{CF}_5$ queries IH_1 with message blocks found in that path concatenated to the current message. The difference between G_4 and G_5 arises only when BE_2 or BE_3 is set to true in G_5 for a query from $\mathcal{CF}_5$ to IH_1. Let G_5 denote the event that $\mathcal{A}$ outputs 1 in game G_5, so that $\Pr[G_5] = \Pr[\mathcal{A}^{PFMD_2, \mathcal{CF}_5} \Rightarrow 1]$. Then we can deduce that
$|\Pr[G_5] - \Pr[G_4]| \leq \Pr[BE_2 + BE_3 \text{ in game } 5]$

$$|\Pr[G_5] - \Pr[G_4]| \leq O(\frac{\ell^2 q}{2^n})$$

In addition to the above functions used before, we define a new function (Get_Msg) used by $\mathcal{CF}_5$.

The function *Get-Msg(y_i^j)* for a chaining value $y_j^i \in \{0,1\}^n$ returns a sequence of message blocks that connects the chaining value y_i^j to IV. In the case of the non existence of a path the function returns false. If the function finds several paths (that can be tracked from IV to y_i^j which requires a collision in the output of $\mathcal{CF}_5$) Get-Msg(y_i^j) returns Error.

$G_6(PFMD_3, \mathcal{CF}_5)$. In game G_6, IH_2 replaces IH_1 and returns a random value for any new query. In G_5, $IH_1(IV, \text{Pad}(M))$ is the PF-MDHF iteration. The returned values from $PFMD$ in G_6 and G_5 are determined by the IH subroutine. For a new query $(IV,\texttt{Pad}(M))$ to PFMD, both games return random values. In G_5, PFMD answers such queries by invoking $\mathcal{CF}_3$ ℓ times (since $\texttt{Pad}(M)$ consists of ℓ message blocks m_i (for i $= 1, \dots, \ell$) and checking for BE_2 and BE_3 where as in G_6 the value is selected randomly from $\{0,1\}^n$. Hence, in G_6 we avoid BE_2 and BE_3.

Let G_6 denote the event that $\mathcal{A}$ outputs 1 in game G_6, so that $\Pr[G_6] = \Pr[\mathcal{A}^{PFMD_3, \mathcal{CF}_5} \Rightarrow 1]$. Then we can deduce that, $|\Pr[G_6] - \Pr[G_5]| \leq \Pr[BE_2 + BE_3$ in game $5]$

$$|\Pr[G_6] - \Pr[G_5]| \leq O(\frac{\ell^2 q}{2^n})$$

$G_7(\mathcal{RO}, \mathcal{S})$. G_7 is the 'ideal' game that simulates $\mathcal{RO}$ and $\mathcal{S}$. In this game, we modify $PFMD_3$ such that it does not send its query to IH_2 any more. $PFMD_4$ responds to any new query randomly. However, $\mathcal{A}$ does not observe any changes to the returned values. So the advantage of $\mathcal{A}$ in G_7 and G_6 is identical and p7 = p6. In this game, $PFMD_4$ is exactly the same as $\mathcal{RO}$, and $\mathcal{CF}_5$ is precisely equivalent to $\mathcal{S}$, our proposed simulator.

By combining Games 0 to 7 we complete the proof. Recall that G_0 emulates $(PFMD, \mathcal{CF})$ and G7 $(\mathcal{RO}, \mathcal{S})$. We conclude that:

$$Adv_{\mathcal{RO}, \mathcal{S}}^{indif}(\mathcal{A}) = |\Pr[\mathcal{A}^{PFMD, \mathcal{CF}}] - \Pr[\mathcal{A}^{\mathcal{RO}, \mathcal{S}}]|$$
$$\leq O(\frac{\ell^2 q + \ell q^2}{2^n}) \qquad \square$$

6 Conclusion

This paper revisits previous indifferentiability security bound of prefix free Merkle-Damgård hash function. All previous works have fixed the security bound to $\frac{\ell^2 q^2}{2^n}$ where ℓ is the maximum length of a query and q is the number of queries made by a distinguisher. Our indifferentiability security bound is $\frac{\ell^2 q + \ell q^2}{2^n}$. To our knowledge, this is the best bound known so far.

Acknowledgments. Kamel Ammour and Lei Wang are supported by National Natural Science Foundation of China (61602302, 61472250, 61672347), Natural Science Foundation of Shanghai (16ZR1416400), Shanghai Excellent Academic Leader Funds (16XD1401300), 13th five-year National Development Fund of Cryptography (MMJJ20170114).

A Formal description of the games

A formal description of the games used in the indifferentiability analysis in Sect. 5 is given in the following (Tables 1, 2, 3, 4, 5, 6, 7, 8).

Table 1. Game(PFMD,$\mathcal{CF}$)

On query (IV, M^j) to PFMD	On query (y_{i-1}^j, M_i^j) to $\mathcal{CF}$
1. $Pad(M^j) \leftarrow (m_1^j, m_2^j, \ldots, m_\ell^j)$ // Pad is a prefix free padding.	1. $y_i^j \leftarrow \mathcal{CF}(y_{i-1}^j, M_i^j)$
2. $y_0^j = IV$	2. Return (y_ℓ^j)
3. for i=1; $i \leq \ell$	
$\quad y_i^j \leftarrow \mathcal{CF}(y_{i-1}^j, m_i^j)$	
4. Return (y_ℓ^j)	

Table 2. Game G1($PFMD_1, \mathcal{CF}_1$)

On query (IV, M^j) to $PFMD_1$	On query (y_{i-1}^j, m_i^j) to $\mathcal{CF}_1$
1. $(m_1^j, m_2^j, \ldots, m_\ell^j) \leftarrow Pad(M^j)$ // Pad is a prefix free padding.	1. $y_i^j \leftarrow \{0,1\}^n$
2. Return IH(IV,$m_1^j \| m_2^j \| \ldots \| m_\ell^j$)	2.if $(y_{i-1}^j, m_i^j) \in T_{\mathcal{CF}}$
On query to IH(IV, $m_1^j \| m_2^j \| \ldots \| m_\ell^j$)	$\quad\quad y_i^j \leftarrow T_{\mathcal{CF}}$
1. $y_0^j = IV$	$\quad\quad$ Return (y_i^j)
2. for i=1; $i \leq \ell$	3. $\mathcal{CF}(y_{i-1}^j, m_i^j) \leftarrow y_i^j$
$\quad y_i^j \leftarrow \mathcal{CF}_1(y_{i-1}^j, m_i^j)$	4. $T_{\mathcal{CF}} = T_{\mathcal{CF}} \cup \{y_{i-1}, m_i, y_i\}$
3. Return (y_ℓ^j)	5. return(y_i^j)

Table 3. Game $G_2(PFMD_1, \mathcal{CF}_2)$

On query (IV, M^j) to $PFMD_1$	On query (y_{i-1}^j, m_i^j, k) to $\mathcal{CF}_2$
1.$(m_1^j, m_2^j, \ldots, m_\ell^j) \leftarrow Pad(M^j)$ // Pad is a prefix free padding.	//k =0 : $\mathcal{A}$ queries $\mathcal{CF}_2$ and k $\neq$ 0: IH queries CF_2 with a message of ℓ length.
2. Return IH(IV,$m_1^j \| m_2^j \| \ldots \| m_\ell^j$)	1. if (k=0) then
	$\quad\quad y_i^j \leftarrow \{0,1\}^n$
	$\quad\quad$ if $(y_{i-1}^j, m_i^j) \in T_A$
	$\quad\quad\quad\quad y_i^j \leftarrow T_A[y_{i-1}^j, m_i^j]$
	$\quad\quad\quad\quad$ Return (y_i^j).
	$\quad\quad\quad\quad T_A = T_A \cup \{y_{i-1}^j, m_i^j, y_i^j\}$
	$\quad\quad\quad\quad$ Return (y_i^j)
	2. if (k$\neq$ 0) then
	$\quad\quad y_i^j \leftarrow \{0,1\}^n$
On query to IH(IV, $m_1^j \| m_2^j \| \ldots \| m_\ell^j$)	$\quad\quad$ if $(y_{i-1}^j, m_i^j) \in T_{IH}$
1. $y_0^j = IV$	$\quad\quad\quad\quad y_i^j \leftarrow T_{IH}[y_{i-1}^j, m_i^j]$
2. for i=1; $i \leq \ell$	$\quad\quad\quad\quad$ Return (y_i^j).
$\quad y_i^j \leftarrow \mathcal{CF}_2(y_{i-1}^j, m_i^j)$	$\quad\quad\quad\quad T_{IH} = T_{IH} \cup \{y_{i-1}^j, m_i^j, y_i^j\}$
3. Return (y_ℓ^j)	$\quad\quad\quad\quad$ Return (y_i^j)

Table 4. Game $G_3(PFMD_1, \mathcal{CF}_3)$

On query (IV, M^j) to $PFMD_1$	On query (y_{i-1}^j, m_i^j, k) to $\mathcal{CF}_3$
1. $(m_1^j, m_2^j, \ldots, m_\ell^j) \leftarrow Pad(M^j)$ // Pad is a prefix free padding. 2. Return IH(IV,$m_1^j \| m_2^j \| \ldots \| m_\ell^j$)	//k =0 : A queries CF_2 and k $\neq$ 0: IH queries CF_3 with a message of ℓ length. 1. if (k=0) then $\quad$ a. $y_i^j \leftarrow \{0,1\}^n$ $\quad$ b. if $(y_{i-1}^j, m_i^j) \in T_A$ $\qquad y_i^j \leftarrow T_A[y_{i-1}^j, m_i^j]$ $\qquad$ Return (y_i^j). $\quad$ c. $T_A = T_A \cup \{y_{i-1}^j, m_i^j, y_i^j\}$ $\quad$ d. if $(y_{i-1}^j, m_i^j, y_i^j) \in T_{IH}$ $\qquad BE_1 \leftarrow True$ $\qquad y_i^j \leftarrow \{0,1\}^n \backslash T_{IH}$ $\qquad$ Return (y_i^j) 2. if (k$\neq$ 0) then $\quad$ a. $y_i^j \leftarrow \{0,1\}^n$ $\quad$ b. if $(y_{i-1}^j, m_i^j) \in T_{IH}$ $\qquad y_i^j \leftarrow T_{IH}[y_{i-1}^j, m_i^j]$ $\qquad$ Return (y_i^j). $\quad$ c. $T_{IH} = T_{IH} \cup \{y_{i-1}^j, m_i^j, y_i^j\}$ $\quad$ d. ligne= $getIntVal(y_{i-1}^j, m_i^j)$ $\quad$ e. col =$getValSamPos(y_{i-1}^j)$. $\quad$ f. if$(y_i^j) \in ligne \vee cologne$ $\qquad BE_2 \leftarrow true \vee BE_3 \leftarrow true$ $\qquad y_i^j \leftarrow \{0,1\}^n \backslash ligne \cup col$ $\qquad$ Return (y_i^j)
On query to IH(IV, $m_1^j \| m_2^j \| \ldots \| m_\ell^j$)	
1. $y_0^j = IV$ 2. for i=1; $i \leq \ell$ $\quad y_i^j \leftarrow \mathcal{CF}_3(y_{i-1}^j, m_i^j)$ 3. Return (y_ℓ^j)	

Table 5. Game $G_4(PFMD_2, \mathcal{CF}_4)$

On query (IV, M^j) to $PFMD_1$	On query (y_{i-1}^j, m_i^j) to $\mathcal{CF}_3$
1. $(m_1^j, m_2^j, \ldots, m_\ell^j) \leftarrow Pad(M^j)$ // Pad is a prefix free padding. 2. Return IH_1(IV,$m_1^j \| m_2^j \| \ldots \| m_\ell^j$)	//We have only $\mathcal{A}$ query to CF_4. 1. $y_i^j \leftarrow \{0,1\}^n$ 2. if $(y_{i-1}^j, m_i^j) \in T_A$ $\qquad y_i^j \leftarrow T_A[y_{i-1}^j, m_i^j]$ $\qquad$ Return (y_i^j). 3. $T_A = T_A \cup \{y_{i-1}^j, m_i^j, y_i^j\}$ 4. Return (y_i^j)
On query to IH_1(IV, $m_1^j \| m_2^j \| \ldots \| m_\ell^j$)	
1. $y_0^j = IV$ 2. for i=1; $i \leq \ell$ $\quad y_i^j \leftarrow \{0,1\}^n$ $\quad$ if $(y_{i-1}^j, m_i^j) \in T_{IH}$ $\qquad y_i^j \leftarrow T_{IH}[y_{i-1}^j, m_i^j]$ $\qquad$ Return (y_i^j). $\quad$ ligne= $getIntVal(y_{i-1}^j, m_i^j)$ $\quad$ col =$getValSamPos(y_{i-1}^j)$. $\quad$ if$(y_i^j) \in ligne \vee col$ $\qquad BE_2 \leftarrow true \vee BE_3 \leftarrow true$ $\qquad y_i^j \leftarrow \{0,1\}^n \backslash ligne \cup col$. $\quad T_{IH} = T_{IH} \cup \{y_{i-1}^j, m_i^j, y_i^j\}$ $\quad$ Return (y_i^j)	

Table 6. Game $G_5(PFMD_2, \mathcal{CF}_5)$

On query (IV, M^j) to $PFMD_2$	On query (y^j_{i-1}, m^j_i) to $\mathcal{CF}_5$
1.$(m^j_1, m^j_2, \ldots, m^j_\ell) \leftarrow Pad(M^j)$ // Pad is a prefix free padding.	//We have only $\mathcal{A}$ query to CF_5.
2. Return $IH_1(\text{IV}, m^j_1 \| m^j_2 \| \ldots \| m^j_\ell)$	1. $y^j_i \leftarrow \{0,1\}^n$
	2. if $(y^j_{i-1}, m^j_i) \in T_A$
	$\qquad\qquad\qquad y^j_i \leftarrow T_A[y^j_{i-1}, m^j_i]$
On query to $IH_1(\text{IV}, m^j_1 \| m^j_2 \| \ldots \| m^j_\ell)$	$\qquad\qquad\qquad$ Return (y^j_i).
1. $y^j_0 = IV$	3. $\mathcal{M} = \text{Get\_Msg}(y^j_{i-1})$
2. for i=1; $i \leq \ell$	if $|\mathcal{M}| = 1 \wedge M' \| m^j_i = Pad(M)$
$\quad y^j_i \leftarrow \{0,1\}^n$	$\qquad\qquad y^j_i \leftarrow IH_1(IV, Pad(M))$
$\quad$ if $(y^j_{i-1}, m^j_i) \in T_{IH}$	3. $T_A = T_A \cup \{y^j_{i-1}, m^j_i, y^j_i\}$
$\qquad\qquad y^j_i \leftarrow T_{IH}[y^j_{i-1}, m^j_i]$	4. Return (y^j_i)
$\qquad\qquad$ Return (y^j_i).	
$\quad$ ligne= $getIntVal(y^j_{i-1}, m^j_i)$	
$\quad$ col $= getValSamPos(y^j_{i-1})$.	
$\quad$ if$(y^j_i) \in ligne \vee col$	
$\qquad\qquad BE_2 \leftarrow true \vee BE_3 \leftarrow true$	
$\qquad\qquad y^j_i \leftarrow \{0,1\}^n \backslash ligne \cup col$.	
$\quad T_{IH} = T_{IH} \cup \{y^j_{i-1}, m^j_i, y^j_i\}$	
$\quad$ Return (y^j_i)	

Table 7. Game $G_6(PFMD_3, \mathcal{CF}_5)$

On query (IV, M^j) to $PFMD_3$	On query (y^j_{i-1}, m^j_i) to $\mathcal{CF}_5$
1.$(m^j_1, m^j_2, \ldots, m^j_\ell) \leftarrow Pad(M^j)$ // Pad is a prefix free padding.	//We have only $\mathcal{A}$ query to CF_5.
2. Return $IH_2(\text{IV}, m^j_1 \| m^j_2 \| \ldots \| m^j_\ell)$	1. $y^j_i \leftarrow \{0,1\}^n$
	2. if $(y^j_{i-1}, m^j_i) \in T_A$
	$\qquad\qquad\qquad y^j_i \leftarrow T_A[y^j_{i-1}, m^j_i]$
	$\qquad\qquad\qquad$ Return (y^j_i).
	3. $\mathcal{M} = \text{Get\_Msg}(y^j_{i-1})$
On query to $IH_2(\text{IV}, m^j_1 \| m^j_2 \| \ldots \| m^j_\ell)$	if $|\mathcal{M}| = 1 \wedge M' \| m^j_i = Pad(M)$
if $IH_2(IV, m^j_1 \| m^j_2 \| \ldots \| m^j_\ell) = \perp$	$\qquad\qquad y^j_i \leftarrow IH_2(IV, Pad(M))$
$\quad IH_2(IV, m^j_1 \| m^j_2 \| \ldots \| m^j_\ell) \leftarrow \{0,1\}^n$	3. $T_A = T_A \cup \{y^j_{i-1}, m^j_i, y^j_i\}$
Return $IH_2(IV, m^j_1 \| m^j_2 \| \ldots \| m^j_\ell)$	4. Return (y^j_i)

Table 8. Game $G_7(\mathcal{RO}, \mathcal{S})$

On query (IV, M^j) to $\mathcal{RO}$	On query (y_{i-1}^j, m_i^j) to $\mathcal{S}$
1. if $\mathcal{RO}(IV, m_1^j \| m_2^j \| \ldots \| m_\ell^j) = \perp$ $\quad \mathcal{RO}(IV, m_1^j \| m_2^j \| \ldots \| m_\ell^j) \leftarrow \{0,1\}^n$ Return $\mathcal{RO}(IV, m_1^j \| m_2^j \| \ldots \| m_\ell^j)$	1. $y_i^j \leftarrow \{0,1\}^n$ 2. if $(y_{i-1}^j, m_i^j) \in T_A$ $\qquad\qquad y_i^j \leftarrow T_A[y_{i-1}^j, m_i^j]$ $\qquad\qquad$ Return (y_i^j). 3. $\mathcal{M} = \text{Get\_Msg}(y_{i-1}^j)$ if $|\mathcal{M}| = 1 \wedge M' \| m_i^j = Pad(M)$ $\qquad\qquad y_i^j \leftarrow \mathcal{RO}(IV, Pad(M))$ 3. $T_A = T_A \cup \{y_{i-1}^j, m_i^j, y_i^j\}$ 4. Return (y_i^j)

References

1. FIPS PUB 180-2, secure hash standard (SHS). U.S.Department of Commerce/National Institute of Standards and Technology (2002)
2. FIPS PUB 180-3, secure hash standard (SHS). U.S.Department of Commerce/National Institute of Standards and Technology (2008)
3. Andreeva, E., Mennink, B., Preneel, B.: The parazoa family: generalizing the sponge hash functions. Int. J. Inf. Sec. **11**(3), 149–165 (2012)
4. Bagheri, N., Gauravaram, P., Knudsen, L.R., Zenner, E.: The suffix-free-prefix-free hash function construction and its indifferentiability security analysis. Int. J. Inf. Sec. **11**(6), 419–434 (2012)
5. Bellare, M., Ristenpart, T.: Multi-property-preserving hash domain extension and the EMD transform. In: Lai, X., Chen, K. (eds.) ASIACRYPT 2006. LNCS, vol. 4284, pp. 299–314. Springer, Heidelberg (2006). https://doi.org/10.1007/11935230_20
6. Bertoni, G., Daemen, J., Peeters, M., Van Assche, G.: On the indifferentiability of the sponge construction. In: Smart, N. (ed.) EUROCRYPT 2008. LNCS, vol. 4965, pp. 181–197. Springer, Heidelberg (2008). https://doi.org/10.1007/978-3-540-78967-3_11
7. Bhattacharyya, R., Mandal, A., Nandi, M.: Indifferentiability characterization of hash functions and optimal bounds of popular domain extensions. In: Roy, B., Sendrier, N. (eds.) INDOCRYPT 2009. LNCS, vol. 5922, pp. 199–218. Springer, Heidelberg (2009). https://doi.org/10.1007/978-3-642-10628-6_14
8. Biham, E., Dunkelman, O.: A framework for iterative hash functions - HAIFA. IACR Cryptology ePrint Archive 2007/278 (2007)
9. Chang, D., Lee, S., Nandi, M., Yung, M.: Indifferentiable security analysis of popular hash functions with prefix-free padding. In: Lai, X., Chen, K. (eds.) ASIACRYPT 2006. LNCS, vol. 4284, pp. 283–298. Springer, Heidelberg (2006). https://doi.org/10.1007/11935230_19
10. Chang, D., Nandi, M.: Improved indifferentiability security analysis of chopMD hash function. In: Nyberg, K. (ed.) FSE 2008. LNCS, vol. 5086, pp. 429–443. Springer, Heidelberg (2008). https://doi.org/10.1007/978-3-540-71039-4_27

11. Chang, D., Sung, J., Hong, S., Lee, S.: Indifferentiable security analysis of choppfMD, chopMD, a chopMDP, chopWPH, chopNI, chopEMD, chopCS, and chopESh hash domain extensions. IACR Cryptology ePrint Archive 2008/407 (2008)

12. Coron, J.-S., Dodis, Y., Malinaud, C., Puniya, P.: Merkle-Damgård revisited: how to construct a hash function. In: Shoup, V. (ed.) CRYPTO 2005. LNCS, vol. 3621, pp. 430–448. Springer, Heidelberg (2005). https://doi.org/10.1007/11535218_26

13. Damgård, I.B.: A design principle for hash functions. In: Brassard, G. (ed.) CRYPTO 1989. LNCS, vol. 435, pp. 416–427. Springer, New York (1990). https://doi.org/10.1007/0-387-34805-0_39

14. Dobbertin, H., Bosselaers, A., Preneel, B.: RIPEMD-160: a strengthened version of RIPEMD. In: Gollmann, D. (ed.) FSE 1996. LNCS, vol. 1039, pp. 71–82. Springer, Heidelberg (1996). https://doi.org/10.1007/3-540-60865-6_44

15. Fleischmann, E., Gorski, M., Lucks, S.: Some observations on indifferentiability. In: Steinfeld, R., Hawkes, P. (eds.) ACISP 2010. LNCS, vol. 6168, pp. 117–134. Springer, Heidelberg (2010). https://doi.org/10.1007/978-3-642-14081-5_8

16. Gauravaram, P., et al.: A sha-3 candidate. In: Handschuh, H., Lucks, S., Preneel, B., Rogaway, P. (eds.) Symmetric Cryptography, number 09031 in Dagstuhl Seminar Proceedings, Dagstuhl, Germany. Schloss Dagstuhl - Leibniz-Zentrum fuer Informatik, Germany (2009)

17. Hirose, S., Park, J.H., Yun, A.: A simple variant of the Merkle-Damgård scheme with a permutation. In: Kurosawa, K. (ed.) ASIACRYPT 2007. LNCS, vol. 4833, pp. 113–129. Springer, Heidelberg (2007). https://doi.org/10.1007/978-3-540-76900-2_7

18. Joux, A.: Multicollisions in iterated hash functions. Application to cascaded constructions. In: Franklin, M. (ed.) CRYPTO 2004. LNCS, vol. 3152, pp. 306–316. Springer, Heidelberg (2004). https://doi.org/10.1007/978-3-540-28628-8_19

19. Kelsey, J., Kohno, T.: Herding hash functions and the Nostradamus attack. In: Vaudenay, S. (ed.) EUROCRYPT 2006. LNCS, vol. 4004, pp. 183–200. Springer, Heidelberg (2006). https://doi.org/10.1007/11761679_12

20. Kelsey, J., Schneier, B.: Second preimages on n-bit hash functions for much less than 2^n work. In: Cramer, R. (ed.) EUROCRYPT 2005. LNCS, vol. 3494, pp. 474–490. Springer, Heidelberg (2005). https://doi.org/10.1007/11426639_28

21. Lai, X., Massey, J.L.: Hash functions based on block ciphers. In: Rueppel, R.A. (ed.) EUROCRYPT 1992. LNCS, vol. 658, pp. 55–70. Springer, Heidelberg (1993). https://doi.org/10.1007/3-540-47555-9_5

22. Lucks, S.: A failure-friendly design principle for hash functions. In: Roy, B. (ed.) ASIACRYPT 2005. LNCS, vol. 3788, pp. 474–494. Springer, Heidelberg (2005). https://doi.org/10.1007/11593447_26

23. Luo, Y., Lai, X., Gong, Z.: Indifferentiability of domain extension modes for hash functions. In: Chen, L., Yung, M., Zhu, L. (eds.) INTRUST 2011. LNCS, vol. 7222, pp. 138–155. Springer, Heidelberg (2012). https://doi.org/10.1007/978-3-642-32298-3_10

24. Maurer, U., Renner, R., Holenstein, C.: Indifferentiability, impossibility results on reductions, and applications to the random oracle methodology. In: Naor, M. (ed.) TCC 2004. LNCS, vol. 2951, pp. 21–39. Springer, Heidelberg (2004). https://doi.org/10.1007/978-3-540-24638-1_2

25. Merkle, R.C.: One way hash functions and DES. In: Brassard, G. (ed.) CRYPTO 1989. LNCS, vol. 435, pp. 428–446. Springer, New York (1990). https://doi.org/10.1007/0-387-34805-0_40

26. Moody, D., Paul, S., Smith-Tone, D.: Improved indifferentiability security bound for the JH mode. Des. Codes Crypt. **79**(2), 237–259 (2016)
27. Moody, D., Paul, S., Smith-Tone, D.: Indifferentiability security of the fast wide pipe hash: breaking the birthday barrier. J. Math. Cryptol. **10**(2), 101–133 (2016)
28. Naito, Y.: Indifferentiability of double-block-length hash function without feed-forward operations. In: Pieprzyk, J., Suriadi, S. (eds.) ACISP 2017. LNCS, vol. 10343, pp. 38–57. Springer, Cham (2017). https://doi.org/10.1007/978-3-319-59870-3_3
29. Ristenpart, T., Shacham, H., Shrimpton, T.: Careful with composition: limitations of the indifferentiability framework. In: Paterson, K.G. (ed.) EUROCRYPT 2011. LNCS, vol. 6632, pp. 487–506. Springer, Heidelberg (2011). https://doi.org/10.1007/978-3-642-20465-4_27
30. Smith-Tone, D., Tone, C.: A measure of dependence for cryptographic primitives relative to ideal functions. Rocky Mt. J. Math. **45**(4), 1283–1309 (2015)

Applied Cryptography

Privacy-Preserving Data Outsourcing with Integrity Auditing for Lightweight Devices in Cloud Computing

Dengzhi Liu[1], Jian Shen[1,2]([✉]), Yuling Chen[2], Chen Wang[1], Tianqi Zhou[1], and Anxi Wang[1]

[1] Jiangsu Engineering Center of Network Monitoring,
Nanjing University of Information Science and Technology, Nanjing, China
liudzdh@126.com, s_shenjian@126.com, wangchennuist@126.com,
tq_zhou@126.com, anxi_wang@126.com
[2] Guizhou Provincial Key Laboratory of Public Big Data, Guiyang, China
61997525@qq.com

Abstract. The cloud can provide unlimited storage space to users via the Internet. Unlike locally data storing, users will lose the direct control of the data after outsourcing it to the cloud. Moreover, the cloud is an untrusted entity. It is possible that the cloud may try to extract, discard and destroy users' data due to benefits. Hence, the data security in cloud computing needs to be well guaranteed. In this paper, we propose a privacy-preserving data outsourcing scheme with integrity auditing for lightweight devices in cloud computing. On the one hand, the blind signature is used in the proposed scheme to delegate the generation of users' data signatures to the TPA. On the other hand, based on the property of the BLS signature, the blinded signatures received from the TPA can be verified by the user and the data integrity stored in the cloud can be audited by the TPA. In addition, the proposed scheme supports batch operation. Security analysis shows that the proposed scheme achieves the properties of correctness, privacy-preserving and non-forgeability. Performance analysis indicates that the proposed scheme can be performed with high efficiency.

Keywords: Cloud computing · Data outsourcing · Integrity auditing · Batch operation

1 Introduction

In recent years, with the developments of the high-speed network construction and the emerging electronic communication technology, the technology of cloud computing has developed very rapidly [29]. As we all know, cloud computing is developed from distributed computing [15,16]. The distributed cloud servers are connected each other via the wired or wireless network. The cloud service provider (CSP) is responsible for managing and maintaining cloud servers,

© Springer Nature Switzerland AG 2019
F. Guo et al. (Eds.): Inscrypt 2018, LNCS 11449, pp. 223–239, 2019.
https://doi.org/10.1007/978-3-030-14234-6_12

and users need to pay for their cloud usage as a manner of pay-per-use [14,18]. Currently, there are many cloud service providers around the world, such as Amazon, Microsoft, IBM and China's Alibaba, Tencent and Baidu. The cloud can provide various services to users. For users, especially for resource-constrained users with mobile devices, they can access the cloud to enjoy the unlimited storage and computing resource via the Internet [5,7,21].

The cloud is curious-but-honest to users' data [31]. That is to say, the cloud may abide by security protocols, but will still try to obtain users' data for profit reasons [22]. Some researchers have proposed many schemes to enhance the data security in the cloud system. To avoid the leakage of the data to the cloud, the data must be encrypted before outsourcing. Due to the feature of cloud computing, some traditional security assurance methods cannot be directly used [12,25,35]. On the one hand, to improve the efficiency of the data usage in cloud computing, the cloud data search schemes are proposed by some researchers, which allows users to search the data in the cloud using keywords [2,23,27]. The searched data will be sorted according to the relevance of keywords. On the other hand, to enable the cloud to securely provide data services to users, some researchers proposed data sharing schemes based on the key agreement protocol and digital signatures [13,20]. In addition, to protect the data in the cloud, the cloud data access control schemes are proposed by researchers [24,33]. Note that the attribute-based encryption is widely used in the design of the cloud data access control schemes, which can satisfy the requirement of the cloud data access for mass users in cloud computing.

To save the storage space, it is a possible that the cloud may discard or modify the infrequently used data [11]. Hence, the cloud should allow users to check the integrity of the data at any time. In 2007, Ateniese et al. proposed a PDP (provable data possession) scheme that allows users to check whether the remote server possesses the data [1]. In the same year, Juels et al. proposed a POR (proof of retrievability) scheme that can let users check the possession and the retrievability of the data stored in the remote server [9]. However, PDP and POR are not suitable for cloud computing due to the high computational overhead at the user side. In 2010, Wang et al. first proposed a cloud storage auditing for cloud computing with the assist of a third party auditor (TPA) [28]. The auditing tasks in Wang et al.'s scheme are delegated to the TPA, which greatly improves the efficiency and the fairness of the auditing. Subsequently, many researchers have devoted themselves to the research of the cloud auditing and proposed many outstanding cloud auditing protocols with the assist of the TPA [19,26,30,32].

1.1 Related Works

The cloud data auditing is developed from the studies of PDP [1,17] and POR [8,9]. PDP allows the local user to check whether the remote server stores the data without retrieving all the data from the server. In PDP, if the user wants to check the stored data, he/she needs to send a request to the remote server. Then, the server can compute a storage proof for the user according to the checking request. In 2007, Juels *et al.* proposed a POR that can not only supports data possession checking, but also verify whether the stored data can be retrieved to the local side.

In PDP and POR, the data storage is checked by the user, which brings much computational burden to the user side. In order to reduce the user side's computational overhead and improve the fairness of the data integrity checking, some researchers resorted to the TPA to design the data integrity checking. Wang *et al.* in [26] proposed a privacy-preserving public auditing protocol based on the technologies of homomorphic authenticator and random masking. The TPA is used to audit the stored data in the cloud on behalf of users in Wang *et al.*'s protocol. Moreover, the TPA cannot learn any information of users' data in the process of data auditing. In 2011, Wang *et al.* proposed a public auditing protocol that supports data dynamics for cloud computing. The Merkle Hash Tree is used to design the auditing protocol with data dynamics in [30]. Note that the auditing protocols in studies [26,30] can support the multiple users' data auditing. In [32], Yang *et al.* extend the data auditing protocol to support multiple cloud servers auditing and multiple users auditing.

However, in the previous auditing schemes, the user side needs to generate the signature for the data, which is not suitable for the resource-constrained lightweight device.

1.2   Contributions

In this paper, we propose a privacy-preserving data outsourcing scheme with integrity auditing for lightweight devices in cloud computing. The contributions of the proposed scheme are listed as follows:

- We resort to the property of the blind signature to delegate the computation tasks of the signature generation to the TPA. Moreover, the proposed scheme can prevent the TPA from learning the original data block during the signature generation.
- The BLS signature is utilized in this scheme for verification. On the one hand, the user can verify the correctness of the received blinded signature from the TPA. On the other hand, the TPA can audit the stored data in the cloud on behalf of the user.
- The proposed scheme supports batch verification for the user's multiple blinded signatures and batch auditing for multiple users' stored data. In addition, the proposed scheme supports public verification and public auditing. That is to say, the public key can be used to verify the blinded signature and audit the stored data without using the secret key.

1.3 Organization

The rest of this paper is organized as follows. Section 2 presents the preliminaries of the proposed scheme. Section 3 describes the system model and the design goals. Section 4 introduces the proposed scheme in detail. Section 5 analyzes the security and the performance of the proposed scheme. Finally, this paper is concluded in Sect. 6.

2 Preliminaries

In this section, the preliminaries of this paper are introduced. First, the bilinear pairing is presented. Then, the technologies of the blind signature and the BLS signature are briefly described.

2.1 Bilinear Pairing

Let $\mathbb{G}_1$, $\mathbb{G}_2$ and $\mathbb{G}_T$ be multiplicative groups of large prime order q. The bilinear pairing can be denoted as $\hat{e}$: $\mathbb{G}_1 \times \mathbb{G}_2 \rightarrow \mathbb{G}_T$. Suppose that $\mathcal{A} \in \mathbb{G}_1$, $\mathcal{B} \in \mathbb{G}_2$, x, $y \in \mathbb{Z}_q^*$. $\mathcal{G}_1$ and $\mathcal{G}_2$ are the generator of $\mathbb{G}_1$ and $\mathbb{G}_2$, respectively. For any $\mathcal{A}_1$, $\mathcal{A}_2 \in \mathbb{G}_1$, we have $\hat{e}(\mathcal{A}_1 \cdot \mathcal{A}_2, \mathcal{B}) = \hat{e}(\mathcal{A}_1, \mathcal{B}) \cdot \hat{e}(\mathcal{A}_2, \mathcal{B})$. The properties of the bilinear pairing are listed as follows:

- Bilinear: $\hat{e}(\mathcal{A}^x, \mathcal{B}^y) = \hat{e}(\mathcal{A}, \mathcal{B})^{xy}$.
- Non-degenerate: $\hat{e}(\mathcal{G}_1, \mathcal{G}_2) \neq 1$.
- Computable: $\hat{e}(\mathcal{A}, \mathcal{B})$ can be efficiently computed by an algorithm.

2.2 Blind Signature

The blind signature was firstly proposed by Chaum in 1982 [3]. In the blind signature, the signer can sign the user's data without knowing the original content of the data. Moreover, the signer cannot match the content with the result of the signature.

- Data Blinding: The data owner blinds the data using his/her public key. Then, the data owner sends the blinded data to the signer.
- Blinded Signature Generation: The signer computes a signature on the blinded data based on his/her secret key. Then, the blinded signature is returned to the data owner.
- Verification: Upon receiving the blinded signature from the signer, the data owner can verify the correctness of the blinded signature using the public key.
- Recovery: If the blinded signature cannot pass the above verification, the protocol outputs 'Fails'; otherwise, the data owner may recover the original signature from the blinded signature using his/her secret key.

2.3 BLS Signature

The BLS signature was proposed by Boneh, Lynn and Shacham in 2001 [6]. The BLS signature can verify the signature using the public key. The process of the BLS signature is shown as follows:

(1) KeyGen: We define $\mathbb{G}$ and $\mathbb{G}_T$ are groups with prime order q and $\mathbb{G}_1 \times \mathbb{G}_1 \to \mathbb{G}_T$. Suppose that $\mathcal{P}$ is the generator of $\mathbb{G}$. $\mathcal{H}$ is a hash function, and $\mathcal{H}:\{0, 1\}^* \to \mathbb{G}$. Randomly choose r from $\mathbb{Z}_q^*$ as the secret key. Then, the public key can be computed as $pk = \mathcal{P}^r$.

(2) Sign: Suppose that a message is $m \in \{0, 1\}^*$. The signer computes the hash value of the message as $h = \mathcal{H}(m)$. Then, the signer computes the signature of the hash value as $\delta = h^r$.

(3) Verify: The verifier can use the public key pk to verify the correctness of the signature δ via checking equation $\hat{e}(\mathcal{P}, \delta) \overset{?}{=} \hat{e}(pk, h)$. If the equation can hold, the verifier can determine that the signature of the message is correct.

3   Problem Statement

In this section, the system model and the design goals of the proposed scheme are introduced.

3.1   The System Model

The system of the proposed scheme consists of three entities: Users, TPA and Cloud. The system model is shown as Fig. 1. The detailed introduction of the entities is shown as follows:

- Users: In the proposed scheme, users are the lightweight devices. For ease of description, in this paper, we use 'users' and 'user' to denote multiple lightweight devices and single lightweight device, respectively. Compared to the TPA and the cloud, the user has lower computation capability and storage resource. The user can enjoy cloud services via the Internet, such as unlimited storage, entertainment services and data sharing. Of course, the cloud usage is not free. The user needs to pay for the cloud usage as a manner of pay-per-use.
- TPA: The TPA is a fully-trusted third party auditor, which can audit the stored data in the cloud on behalf of users. In this paper, the TPA can also generate signatures for users according to the blinded data from users.
- Cloud: The cloud consists of many distributed servers. The cloud is untrusted and is managed by the CSP. Moreover, the cloud may discard the infrequently used data to save cloud storage space. In the proposed scheme, the cloud can generate storage proofs for the TPA according to the auditing challenges.

3.2 Design Goals

The following design goals should be achieved in the proposed scheme.

- Signatures Generation Delegation: The signature generation of the user's data blocks can be delegated to the TPA.
- Signatures Public Verification: The received blinded signatures can be verified by the user using the public key.
- Public Auditing: The integrity of user's data stored in the cloud can be audited by the TPA using the public key.
- Batch Operation: The proposed scheme can support batch operation. On the one hand, one user's multiple blinded signatures can be verified by the user simultaneously. On the other hand, multiple users' stored data in the cloud can be audited by the TPA at the same time.

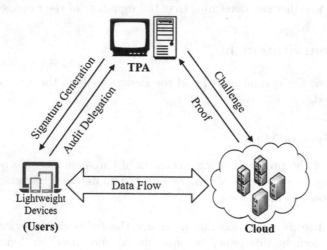

Fig. 1. The system model

4   The Proposed Scheme

In this section, the proposed scheme is presented. The main process of the proposed scheme can be seen in Fig. 2. The detailed description of the proposed scheme is shown in the following:

(1) Security Parameters Generation
   One security parameter λ is used as the input of the system. The outputs are $\{\mathbb{G}_1, \mathbb{G}_2, \mathbb{G}_T, \hat{e}, q, H, \mathcal{P}\}$, which are used for the construction of proposed scheme execution. Note that $\mathbb{G}_1$, $\mathbb{G}_2$ and $\mathbb{G}_T$ are multiplicative groups of large prime order q and the bilinear map $\hat{e}$ is $\mathbb{G}_1 \times \mathbb{G}_2 \to \mathbb{G}_T$. H is a one-way hash function, which can map a string to a point on $\mathbb{G}_1$. $\mathcal{P}$ is the generator of group $\mathbb{G}_2$. Assume that the data file of the user is $F = \{b_i\}_{1 \leq i \leq n}$.

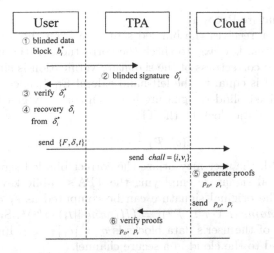

Fig. 2. The process of the proposed scheme

The corresponding data indexes are $\{I_i, \cdots, I_n\}$. The user chooses a random signing key pair (spk, ssk) and computes $t = name \parallel SSig_{ssk}(name)$, where $name$ is the data file's identifier and $SSig_{ssk}(name)$ is the signature of $name$. The TPA randomly chooses x from $\mathbb{Z}_q^*$ as the secret key. The public key of the TPA can be computed as $pk_T = \mathcal{P}^x$. The user randomly selects r from $\mathbb{G}_1$ and y from $\mathbb{Z}_q^*$, where r is to blind the original data block and y is the secret key of the user. Then, the user computes his/her public key as $pk_U = \mathcal{P}^y$.

(2) **Blinded Signature Generation**

To reduce the computational overhead of the signature generation at the user side, the TPA is utilized to generate signatures for users. The correctness of signatures in the cloud system is important to users and the CSP, which affects users' judgement of data integrity in the cloud. Hence, the data blocks of users should be signed by the TPA without leaking the original content. In the proposed scheme, the blind signature is resorted to generate the signatures for the user. Suppose that the user wants to sign his/her data block b_i. First, the user utilizes his/her public key to blind the data block as $b_i^* = pk_U \cdot (H(name\|I_i) \cdot r^{b_i}) = H(name\|I_i) \cdot r^{b_i} \cdot \mathcal{P}^y$. Then, the blinded data block of b_i^* is sent to the TPA for the blind signature generation. Upon receiving the blinded data block from the user, the TPA uses its secret key x to compute the blinded signature as $\delta_i^* = (b_i^*)^x = (H(name\|I_i) \cdot r^{b_i} \cdot \mathcal{P}^y)^x$. Finally, the blinded signature of δ_i^* is sent to the user. Note that the transmission channel between the user and the TPA is secure.

(3) Original Signature Recovery

When the user receives the blinded signature from the TPA, he/she uses the TPA's public key pk_U to check the correctness of the received blinded signature. The correctness of the signature verification is shown as Eq. 1. If the right-hand is equal to the left-hand side of Eq. 1, it can be determined that the received blinded signature has been correctly generated according to the blinded data block by the TPA.

$$\widehat{e}(\delta_i^*, \mathcal{P}) \stackrel{?}{=} \widehat{e}(b_i^*, pk_T) \tag{1}$$

If Eq. 1 is hold, the user may utilize the correct blinded signature to recovery the original signature employing the TPA's public key and the user's secret key. The original signature can be computed as $\delta_i = pk_T^{-y} \cdot \delta_i^* = (\mathcal{P}^x)^{-y} \cdot (H(name||I_i) \cdot r^{b_i} \cdot \mathcal{P}^y)^x = (H(name||I_i) \cdot r^{b_i})^x$. Suppose that the signature set of the user's data blocks is $\sigma = \{\delta_i\}_{1 \leq i \leq n}$. Finally, $\{F, \sigma, t\}$ are outsourced to the cloud in a secure channel.

(4) Data Integrity Auditing

In this phase, the user can delegate the TPA to audit the integrity of the stored data in the cloud. First, the TPA needs to retrieve the data file tag t and use spk to verify the correctness of t. If t cannot pass the verification, the data integrity auditing cannot be executed and the TPA outputs $\perp$. Otherwise, the TPA extracts data file identifier $name$ from t. When the TPA receives the data integrity auditing request from the user, it chooses a random subset $S = \{s_i\}_{1 \leq i \leq p}$ with p elements for the auditing. Moreover, the TPA randomly chooses value v_i for each element s_i. The auditing challenge can be generated as $Chall = \{i, v_i\}$. Then, $Chall$ is sent to the cloud for the auditing proofs generation. Upon receiving $chall$ from the TPA, the corresponding data blocks storage proof and the tag proof can be computed as $p_D = \sum_{i=1}^{s_p} (v_i \cdot b_i)$ and $p_t = \prod_{i=1}^{s_p} \delta_i^{v_i}$, respectively. Then, proofs p_D and p_t are sent to the TPA for the integrity auditing. The TPA can determine whether the corresponding data blocks are stored completely in the cloud by checking the correctness of Eq. 2.

$$\widehat{e}(\prod_{i=1}^{s_p} (H(name||I_i)^{v_i}, pk_T) \cdot \widehat{e}(r^{p_D}, pk_T) \stackrel{?}{=} \widehat{e}(p_t, \mathcal{P}) \tag{2}$$

(5) Batch Operation

- Batch Signatures Verification. Suppose that one user delegate the TPA to sign k data blocks, where $1 \leq k \leq n$. The aggregated signature of k data blocks can be computed as $\delta_{agg} = \prod_{i=1}^{k} \delta_i^*$. The user can check whether Eq. 3 can hold. If the left-hand side of Eq. 3 equals to the right-hand side, it can be determined that the user's k blinded signatures are correct.

$$\widehat{e}(\prod_{i=1}^{k} \delta_i^*, \mathcal{P}) \stackrel{?}{=} \prod_{i=1}^{k} \widehat{e}(b_i^*, pk_T) \tag{3}$$

- Batch Integrity Auditing. Suppose that m users enjoy the cloud storage services and every user j's data file consists of n data blocks, where $1 \leq j \leq m$. The detailed description of security keys generation and parameters generation is omitted here. Upon receiving the audit challenge from the TPA, the corresponding data blocks' storage proof and the tag proof of user j can be computed as $p_{j,D} = \sum_{i=1}^{s_p} (v_i \cdot b_{j,i})$ and $p_{j,t} = \prod_{i=1}^{s_p} \delta_{j,i}^{v_i}$ by the cloud. If Eq. 4 is hold, it can be determined that the request users' data blocks in the cloud are stored completely.

$$\prod_{j=1}^{m} (\widehat{e}(\prod_{i=1}^{s_p} H(name\|I_{j,i})^{v_i}, pk_\mathrm{T}) \cdot \widehat{e}(r_j^{p_{j,D}}, pk_\mathrm{T})) \stackrel{?}{=} \prod_{j=1}^{m} \widehat{e}(p_{j,t}, \mathcal{P}) \quad (4)$$

5   Evaluation

The security analysis and the performance analysis are introduced in this section. In the security analysis, the properties of correctness, privacy-preserving, non-forgeability, public signatures verification and public integrity auditing of the proposed scheme are proved. In the performance analysis, the comparison and the simulation of our scheme and previous schemes are presented.

5.1   Security Analysis

Theorem 1. *The proposed scheme can be proved to be correct.*

Proof. Suppose that all security parameters are generated and computed correctly. The transmission channel in the system is secure. If Eqs. 1–4 can be proved to be correct, it can be determined that the proposed scheme is correct. Equation 1 demonstrates the correctness of the blinded signature verification. The detailed elaboration of Eq. 1 is shown as follows:

$$\begin{aligned}
&\widehat{e}(\delta_i^*, \mathcal{P}) \\
&= \widehat{e}((H(name\|I_i) \cdot r^{b_i} \cdot P^y)^x, \mathcal{P}) \\
&= \widehat{e}((H(name\|I_i) \cdot r^{b_i} \cdot P^y), \mathcal{P}^x) \\
&= \widehat{e}(b_i^*, pk_T)
\end{aligned}$$

Equation 2 can determine the correctness of the integrity auditing, which is demonstrated as follows:

$$\widehat{e}(\prod_{i=1}^{s_p} (H(name||I_i))^{v_i}, pk_T) \cdot \widehat{e}(r^{p_D}, pk_T)$$

$$= \widehat{e}(\prod_{i=1}^{s_p} (H(name||I_i))^{v_i}, pk_T) \cdot \widehat{e}(r^{\sum_{i=1}^{s_p} v_i \cdot b_i}, pk_T)$$

$$= \widehat{e}(\prod_{i=1}^{s_p} (H(name||I_i))^{v_i}, pk_T) \cdot \widehat{e}(\prod_{i=1}^{s_p} (r^{b_i})^{v_i}, pk_T)$$

$$= \widehat{e}(\prod_{i=1}^{s_p} (H(name||I_i) \cdot r^{b_i})^{v_i}, \mathcal{P}^x)$$

$$= \widehat{e}(\prod_{i=1}^{s_p} ((H(name||I_i) \cdot r^{b_i})^x)^{v_i}, \mathcal{P})$$

$$= \widehat{e}(\prod_{i=1}^{s_p} \delta_i^{v_i}, \mathcal{P}c)$$

$$= \widehat{e}(p_t, \mathcal{P})$$

Equations 3 and 4 can verify the correctness of batch operation of this scheme. Equation 3 proves the correctness of the batch signatures verification. The elaboration of Eq. 3 is shown as follows:

$$\widehat{e}(\prod_{i=1}^{k} \delta_i^*, \mathcal{P})$$

$$= \widehat{e}(\prod_{i=1}^{k} (H(name||I_i) \cdot r^{b_i} \cdot \mathcal{P}^y)^x, \mathcal{P})$$

$$= \widehat{e}(\prod_{i=1}^{k} (H(name||I_i) \cdot r^{b_i} \cdot \mathcal{P}^y), \mathcal{P}^x)$$

$$= \prod_{i=1}^{k} \widehat{e}(b_i^*, pk_T)$$

Equation 4 reveals the correctness of the batch auditing, which can be proved as follows:

$$\prod_{j=1}^{m} (\widehat{e}(\prod_{i=1}^{s_p} (H(name||I_{j,i}))^{v_i}, pk_T) \cdot \widehat{e}(r_j^{p_{j,D}}, pk_T))$$

$$= \prod_{j=1}^{m} (\widehat{e}(\prod_{i=1}^{s_p} (H(name||I_{j,i}))^{v_i}, pk_T) \cdot \widehat{e}(r_j^{\sum_{i=1}^{s_p} v_i \cdot b_{j,i}}, pk_T))$$

$$= \prod_{j=1}^{m} (\widehat{e}(\prod_{i=1}^{s_p} (H(name||I_{j,i}))^{v_i}, pk_T) \cdot \widehat{e}(\prod_{i=1}^{s_p} r_j^{v_i \cdot b_{j,i}}, pk_T))$$

$$= \prod_{j=1}^{m} \widehat{e}(\prod_{i=1}^{s_p} (H(name||I_{j,i}) \cdot r_j^{b_{j,i}})^{v_i}, \mathcal{P}^x)$$

$$= \prod_{j=1}^{m} \widehat{e}(\prod_{i=1}^{s_p} (((H(name||I_{j,i}) \cdot r_j^{b_{j,i}})^x)^{v_i}, \mathcal{P}))$$

$$= \prod_{j=1}^{m} \widehat{e}(\prod_{i=1}^{s_p} \delta_{j,i}^{v_i}, \mathcal{P})$$

$$= \prod_{j=1}^{m} \widehat{e}(p_{j,t}, \mathcal{P})$$

$\square$

Theorem 2. *The proposed scheme can provide properties of privacy-preserving and non-forgeability.*

Proof. (a) *Privacy-preserving*: Privacy-preserving requires that the user's identity information and the data content should be well protected [10]. In the proposed scheme, the data file's identifier *name* and identity I_i of the user are concealed by the hash function as $H(name||I_i)$. The original data of the user is blinded by the secret value r. Moreover, the blinded data and identity information are encrypted by the user's public key pk_U in the signature. That is to say, the TPA and the cloud cannot learn any information about the original data content and user's identity. Hence, the proposed scheme can provide the property of privacy-preserving. (b) *Non-forgeability*: The signature of the data block is generated by the TPA referring to the property of the blind signature. As the description in [34], the blind signature can be proven to be unforgeable under the hardness assumption of CDHP. The proof of the non-forgeability is omitted here.   □

Theorem 3. *The proposed scheme supports public verification for the blinded signature and public auditing for the data integrity.*

Proof. In the signature recovery phase, the user can verify the correctness of the received blinded signature using the TPA's public key pk_T. Note that the original data content and privacy information in the blinded data block b_i^* and the corresponding blinded signature δ_i^* are concealed. That is to say, the signature verification can be executed by anyone else who possesses b_i^* and δ_i^* in the system. In the data integrity auditing, the data can be audited by the third party TPA using the public key pk_T. As the definitions of the public verification [4] and the public auditing [26,30], it can be determined that the proposed scheme supports public verification for the blinded signature and public auditing for the data integrity.   □

5.2 Performance Analysis

(1) Comparison Analysis
The computational cost of the proposed scheme is compared with that of the similar schemes [26,30]. For ease of expression, we use PPA and EPA to denote references [26] and [30], respectively. In order to reveal the difference in the efficiency, the computational cost at the user side and the server side are compared respectively. Compared to PPA and EPA, our scheme has a blinded signature verification. To make the comparison more fair, the cost of the blinded signature verification is ignored in the comparison. The comparison result can be seen in Table 1. Note that the symbols of T_H, T_E, T_{Mul}, T_P, T_{Add} and T_C are used to denote the time required to perform the operations of hash function, exponentiation, multiplication, pairing, addition and concatenation. Because the user needs to generate blinded data blocks, our scheme has much computational cost at the user side compared to that of PPA. Compared to EPA, our scheme has additional cost of multiplication, but the cost of hash function, exponentiation

and concatenation in our scheme is less than that of EPA. From the comparison result at the server side, we can find that the computational cost of PPA, EPA and our scheme is $(n+1)T_H. + (2n+4)T_E. + (2n+3)T_{Mul.} + 1T_{Add.} + 3T_P.$, $(n+2)T_H. + (2n+4)T_E. + (3n+1)T_{Mul.} + nT_{Add.} + 2T_P.$ and $nT_H. + (2n+1)T_E. + 2nT_{Mul.} + nT_{Add.} + 3T_P.$, respectively. Although the $T_{Add.}$ parameter is larger than that of PPA and the $T_P.$ parameter in our scheme is 1 more than that of EPA, PPA and EPA has higher computational cost of hash function, exponentiation and concatenation. That is to say, the server side of our scheme has less computational cost compared to that of PPA and EPA.

(2) Simulation Analysis

The similar schemes [26,30] and our scheme are simulated on a computer configured with 8 GB RAM and Intel Xeon E5-2650 v2 at 2.60 GHZ. The computer is installed with the Linux system and constructed based on GMP (GNU Multiple Precision Arithmetic) and PBC (Pairing Based Cryptography).

Table 1. Computational cost comparison

Scheme	User side	Server side
PPA [26]	$1T_H.+2T_E.+2T_C.+1T_{Mul.}$	$(n+1)T_H.+(2n+4)T_E.+(2n+3)T_{Mul.}+1T_{Add.}+3T_P.$
EPA [30]	$2T_H.+4T_E.+5T_C.+1T_{Mul.}$	$(n+2)T_H.+(2n+4)T_E.+(3n+1)T_{Mul.}+nT_{Add.}+2T_P.$
Our Scheme	$1T_H.+3T_E.+1T_C.+3T_{Mul.}$	$nT_H.+(2n+1)T_E.+2nT_{Mul.}+nT_{Add.}+3T_P.$

$*n$: The number of the data blocks.
$*T_H.$: The time required to perform the hash function.
$*T_E.$: The time required to perform the exponentiation.
$*T_C.$: The time required to perform the concatenation.
$*T_{Mul.}$: The time required to perform the multiplication.
$*T_{Add.}$: The time required to perform the addition.
$*T_P.$: The time required to perform the pairing map.

We simulate the time cost of the signature generation at the user side. In the proposed scheme, the signature generation tasks are delegated to the TPA. The operation of the data blocks blinding can be seen as the offline data pre-process, which can be finished before the data signing. That is to say, the data blocks can be blinded by other trusted devices or data source devices with high computing capability. Hence, it can be considered that the signature generation cost of our scheme only consists of public key computational cost and original signature recovery cost. The signature generation of our scheme and the two similar schemes are simulated 20 times. The simulation result can be seen in Fig. 3. The x-axis and the y-axis denote the number of the trail and the computational time, respectively. From the simulation result, we can find that the computational time of signature generation in our scheme is about 0.06 s. The signature generation needs to take about 0.15 s and 0.18 s in PPA and EPA, respectively. Hence, it can be determined that the signature generation of our scheme is more efficient than that of PPA and EPA.

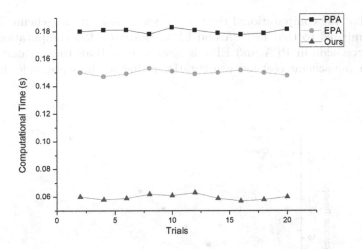

Fig. 3. Simulation of the signature generation at the user side

Figures 4 and 5 show the simulation of the computation at the user side and the server side. Note that the x-axis and the y-axis in Figs. 4 and 5 denote computing counts and computational time. From Fig. 4, we find that the growth rate of our scheme is lower than that of EPA but is higher than that of PPA. The main reason is described above in the comparison analysis. Although our scheme has much time at the user side compared to that of PPA, the computational time of our scheme is still within an acceptable level. Figure 5 shows the simulation result of the computation at the server side. From the simulation result in Fig. 5,

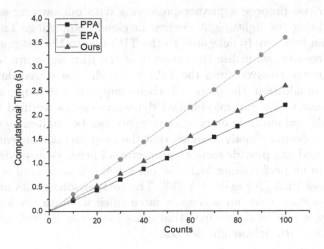

Fig. 4. Simulation of the computation at the user side

we find that the computational time of the server side in our scheme increases slowly compared to that in PPA and EPA. Moreover, the computational time of the server side in PPA and EPA is always more than that in our scheme. Therefore, our scheme cost less computational time at the server side than PPA and EPA.

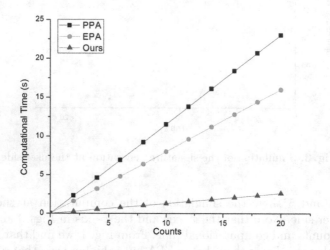

Fig. 5. Simulation of the computation at the server side

6   Conclusion

In this paper, we propose a privacy-preserving data outsourcing scheme with integrity auditing for lightweight devices in cloud computing. The signature generation can be securely delegated to the TPA due to the usage of the blind signature. Moreover, we utilize the property of the BLS signature to verify the blinded signatures received from the TPA and audit the stored data integrity in the cloud. In addition, the proposed scheme supports batch operation, which implies that one user's multiple blinded signatures can be verified by the user simultaneously and multiple users' data integrity can be audited by the TPA at the same time. Security analysis shows that the proposed scheme can be proved to be correct and can provide security properties of privacy-preserving and non-forgeability. In he performance analysis, our scheme is compared with the two similar schemes PPA [26] and EPA [30]. The comparison results and the simulation results show that our scheme is more efficient. With the ideal security and efficiency, it can be determined that our scheme can be well used in cloud storage services with lightweight devices.

Acknowledgments. This work is supported by the National Natural Science Foundation of China under Grant No. U1836115, No. 61672295, and No. 61672290, the Natural Science Foundation of Jiangsu Province under Grant No. BK20181408, the Foundation of Guizhou Provincial Key Laboratory of Public Big Data under Grant No. 2018BDKFJJ003, Guangxi Key Laboratory of Cryptography and Information Security under Grant No. GCIS201715, the State Key Laboratory of Information Security under Grant No. 2017-MS-10, the CICAEET fund, and the PAPD fund.

References

1. Ateniese, G., et al.: Provable data possession at untrusted stores. In: ACM Conference on Computer and Communications Security, pp. 598–609 (2007)
2. Cao, N., Wang, C., Li, M., Ren, K., Lou, W.: Privacy-preserving multi-keyword ranked search over encrypted cloud data. IEEE Trans. Parallel Distributed Syst. **25**(1), 222–233 (2013)
3. Chaum, D.: Blind signatures for untraceable payments. In: Chaum, D., Rivest, R.L., Sherman, A.T. (eds.) Advances in Cryptology, pp. 199–203. Springer, Boston (1983). https://doi.org/10.1007/978-1-4757-0602-4_18
4. Chen, X., Li, J., Huang, X., Ma, J., Lou, W.: New publicly verifiable databases with efficient updates. IEEE Trans. Dependable Secure Comput. **12**(5), 546–556 (2015)
5. Chen, X., Li, J., Weng, J., Ma, J., Lou, W.: Verifiable computation over large database with incremental updates. IEEE Trans. Comput. **65**(10), 3184–3195 (2016)
6. Boneh, D., Lynn, B., Shacham, H.: Short signatures from the Weil pairing. In: Boyd, C. (ed.) ASIACRYPT 2001. LNCS, vol. 2248, pp. 514–532. Springer, Heidelberg (2001). https://doi.org/10.1007/3-540-45682-1_30
7. Dikaiakos, M.D., Katsaros, D., Mehra, P., Pallis, G., Vakali, A.: Cloud computing: distributed internet computing for it and scientific research. IEEE Internet Comput. **13**(5), 10–13 (2009)
8. Dodis, Y., Vadhan, S., Wichs, D.: Proofs of retrievability via hardness amplification. In: Reingold, O. (ed.) TCC 2009. LNCS, vol. 5444, pp. 109–127. Springer, Heidelberg (2009). https://doi.org/10.1007/978-3-642-00457-5_8
9. Juels, A., Kaliski, B.S.: PORs: proofs of retrievability for large files. In: ACM Conference on Computer and Communications Security, pp. 584–597 (2007)
10. Lins, S., Schneider, S., Sunyaev, A.: Trust is good, control is better: creating secure clouds by continuous auditing. IEEE Trans. Cloud Comput. **6**, 890–903 (2016)
11. Lins, S., Grochol, P., Schneider, S., Sunyaev, A.: Dynamic certification of cloud services: trust, but verify!. IEEE Secur. Priv. Mag. **14**(2), 66–71 (2016)
12. Liu, D., Shen, J., Wang, A., Wang, C.: Lightweight and practical node clustering authentication protocol for hierarchical wireless sensor networks. Int. J. Sens. Netw. **27**(2), 95–102 (2018)
13. Liu, X., Zhang, Y., Wang, B., Yan, J.: Mona: secure multi-owner data sharing for dynamic groups in the cloud. IEEE Trans. Parallel Distributed Syst. **24**(6), 1182–1191 (2013)
14. Marston, S., Li, Z., Bandyopadhyay, S., Zhang, J., Ghalsasi, A.: Cloud computing-the business perspective. Decis. Support Syst. **51**(1), 176–189 (2011)
15. Mell, P., Grance, T.: The NIST definition of cloud computing. Commun. ACM **53**(6), 50 (2011)

16. Moritoh, Y., Imai, Y., Inomo, H., Shiraki, W.: A cloud service on distributed multiple servers for cooperative learning and emergency communication. Commun. Comput. Inf. Sci. **188**, 377–390 (2011)
17. Sebe, F., Domingo-ferrer, J., Martnez-ballest, A., Deswarte, Y., Quisquater, J.J.: Efficient remote data possession checking in critical information infrastructures. IEEE Trans. Knowl. Data Eng. **20**(8), 1034–1038 (2008)
18. Shen, J., Liu, D., Bhuiyan, M.Z.A., Shen, J., Sun, X., Castiglione, A.: Secure verifiable database supporting efficient dynamic operations in cloud computing. IEEE Trans. Emerg. Top. Comput. (2017). https://doi.org/10.1109/TETC.2017. 2776402
19. Shen, J., Liu, D., Lai, C.F., Ren, Y., Wang, J., Sun, X.: A secure identity-based dynamic group data sharing scheme for cloud computing. J. Internet Technol. **18**(4), 833–842 (2017)
20. Shen, J., Wang, C., Wang, A., Ji, S., Zhang, Y.: A searchable and verifiable data protection scheme for scholarly big data. IEEE Trans. Emerg. Top. Comput. (2018). https://doi.org/10.1109/TETC.2018.2830368
21. Shen, J., Zhou, T., He, D., Zhang, Y., Sun, X., Xiang, Y.: Block design-based key agreement for group data sharing in cloud computing. IEEE Trans. Dependable Secure Comput. **1**, 1 (2017)
22. Shi, J., Li, H., Zhou, L.: The technical security issues in cloud computing. Int. J. Inf. Commun. Technol. **5**(3–4), 109–116 (2013)
23. Sun, W., et al.: Verifiable privacy-preserving multi-keyword text search in the cloud supporting similarity-based ranking. IEEE Trans. Parallel Distributed Syst. **25**(11), 3025–3035 (2014)
24. Wan, Z., Liu, J., Deng, R.H.: HASBE: a hierarchical attribute-based solution for flexible and scalable access control in cloud computing. IEEE Trans. Inf. Forensics Secur. **7**(2), 743–754 (2012)
25. Wang, C., Shen, J., Lai, C.F., Huang, R., Wei, F.: Neighborhood trustworthiness based vehicle-to-vehicle authentication scheme for vehicular ad hoc networks. In: Practice and Experience, Concurrency and Computation (2018)
26. Wang, C., Chow, S.S.M., Wang, Q., Ren, K., Lou, W.: Privacy-preserving public auditing for secure cloud storage. IEEE Trans. Comput. **62**(2), 362–375 (2013)
27. Wang, C., Ren, K., Yu, S., Urs, K.M.R.: Achieving usable and privacy-assured similarity search over outsourced cloud data. In: Proceedings of International Conference on Computer Communication, pp. 451–459 (2012)
28. Wang, C., Wang, Q., Ren, K., Lou, W.: Privacy-preserving public auditing for storage security in cloud computing. In: Proceedings of International Conference on Computer Communications, pp. 1–9 (2010)
29. Wang, L., et al.: Cloud computing: a perspective study. New Gener. Comput. **28**(2), 137–146 (2010)
30. Wang, Q., Wang, C., Ren, K., Lou, W., Li, J.: Enabling public auditability and data dynamics for storage security in cloud computing. IEEE Trans. Parallel Distributed Syst. **22**(5), 847–859 (2011)
31. Yang, J., Chen, Z.: Cloud computing research and security issues. In: Proceedings of the International Conference on Computational Intelligence and Software Engineering, pp. 1–3 (2010)
32. Yang, K., Jia, X.: An efficient and secure dynamic auditing protocol for data storage in cloud computing. IEEE Trans. Parallel Distributed Syst. **24**(9), 1717–1726 (2013)

33. Yu, S., Wang, C., Ren, K., Lou, W.: Achieving secure, scalable, and fine-grained data access control in cloud computing. In: Proceedings of International Conference on Computer Communication, pp. 1–9 (2010)

34. Zhang, F., Kim, K.: Efficient ID-based blind signature and proxy signature from bilinear pairings. In: Safavi-Naini, R., Seberry, J. (eds.) ACISP 2003. LNCS, vol. 2727, pp. 312–323. Springer, Heidelberg (2003). https://doi.org/10.1007/3-540-45067-X_27

35. Zhou, T., Shen, J., Li, X., Wang, C., Shen, J.: Quantum cryptography for the future internet and the security analysis. Secur. Commun. Netw. (2018). https://doi.org/10.1155/2018/8214619

Cloud-Based Data-Sharing Scheme Using Verifiable and CCA-Secure Re-encryption from Indistinguishability Obfuscation

Mingwu Zhang[1,2]($\boxtimes$), Yan Jiang[3], Hua Shen[1], Bingbing Li[1], and Willy Susilo[4]

[1] School of Computers, Hubei University of Technology, Wuhan, China
csmwzhang@gmail.com
[2] Hubei Key Laboratory of Intelligent Geo-Information Processing,
China University of Geosciences, Wuhan, China
[3] College of Computer Science and Technology,
Nanjing University of Aeronautics and Astronautics, Nanjing, China
[4] Institute of Cybersecurity and Cryptology,
School of Computing and Information Technology, University of Wollongong,
Wollongong, Australia

Abstract. A cloud-based re-encryption scheme allows a semi-trusted cloud proxy to convert a ciphertext under delegator's public-key into a ciphertext of delegatee's. However, for an untrusted cloud proxy, as the *re-encryption program was outsourced on the cloud, the cloud can debug the program and might have illegal activities in practice, such as monitoring the program executing, returning an incorrect re-encryption ciphertext, or colluding with the participants to obtain the sensitive information.* In this work, we propose a construction of cloud-based verifiable re-encryption by incorporating new cryptographic primitives of *indistinguishability obfuscation* and *puncturable pseudorandom functions*, which can achieve the *master-secret security* even if the proxy colludes with the delegatee. Furthermore, our scheme can provide the white-box security in re-encryption procedure to *implement the sensitive-data protection in the presence of white-box access*, and it resists on chosen-ciphertext attacks in both the first-level encryption and the second-level encryption. The decryption is very efficient since it only requires several symmetric PRF operations, which can be deployed and applied in the light-weight security device such as Mobile Phones (MPs), Wireless Body Area Networks (WBANs) and nodes in Internet-of-Things (IoTs).

Keywords: Data sharing · E-mail forwarding · White-box access ·
Re-encryption · Indistinguishability obfuscation · Puncturable PRF

This work is supported by the National Natural Science Foundation of China (61672010, 61702168), the open research project of The Hubei Key Laboratory of Intelligent Geo-Information Processing (KLIGIP-2017A11), and the fund of Hubei Key Laboratory of Transportation Internet of Things (WHUTIOT-2017B001).

F. Guo et al. (Eds.): Inscrypt 2018, LNCS 11449, pp. 240–259, 2019.
https://doi.org/10.1007/978-3-030-14234-6_13

1   Introduction

Proxy re-encryption (PRE), initially introduced by Blaze et al. [4], allows a semi-trusted proxy to convert a ciphertext under the delegator's public-key into a ciphertext of the delegatee, without observing the underlying plaintext and the secret key of either delegator or delegatee. In traditional PRE schemes, a proxy is modeled as a *semi-trusted server*, who should execute the functionality of re-encryption honestly. However, it may not be suitable for some applications, e.g., secure cloud-based data sharing.

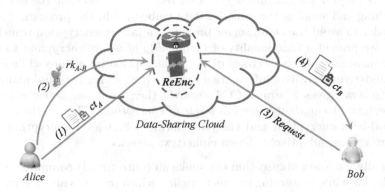

Fig. 1. Scenario of data-sharing

Consider encrypted data sharing as an example which is depicted in Fig. 1. User Alice's data is encrypted and uploaded onto cloud server. If Alice's friend, Bob, requests Alice's data from cloud server, the data cannot be read by Bob correctly since it was indeed encrypted by Alice's public key. In order to allow Bob to decrypt and read the encrypted data, a salutary approach is to specify a re-encryption key $rk_{A \rightarrow B}$, which is generated by Alice and sent onto cloud server. Then, cloud server can convert Alice's encrypted data into re-encrypted data of Bob using $rk_{A \rightarrow B}$. However, since cloud server might be *conscious and malicious*, it may return fake data, or produce re-encrypted data but not what user Bob needs. Hence, it is mandatory to check and verify the correctness of a re-encrypted ciphertext. Besides the attempt to obtain users' sensitive information. cloud server may also execute the data-sharing program in a white-box access model such that it can debug the program, set the breakpoints, and monitor the memories or variables during the executing.

OUR CONTRIBUTION AND TECHNIQUES. In this work, we explore a verifiable cloud-based proxy re-encryption that employs the primitives of indistinguishability obfuscation $i\mathcal{O}$ and puncturable pseudorandom functions. Our scheme can be used in the secure and sensitive data-sharing in cloud system while keeping the confidentiality of the sensitive information. Besides the security of general proxy re-encryption, our contribution is benefit as follows:

- The scheme reinforces the *master secret-key security* so that the adversary (i.e., a dishonest cloud server) cannot obtain the master secret-key of the sender even if the cloud proxy colludes with the delegatee.
- The proposed scheme obtains the *white-box access security for the cloud proxy*. As the re-encryption program was executed in the cloud, to obtain more sensitive data in the program, the cloud can debug the re-encryption program step-by-step, trace into the program, and monitor the memory and register. We employ the*program obfuscation technique* to prevent the cloud from watching and stealing the sensitive data embedded in the program.
- In order to avoid the cloud server providing a fake re-encryption transformation, we present a functionality of *verifiability of the re-encryption* to ensure the consistency and correctness of the re-encryption procedure while keeping the underlying sensitive information security (i.e., secret keys and plaintexts).
- Our scheme gives a *strong CCA security* (i.e., resist on active attacks on ciphertexts) to guarantee *for two levels of encryptions*. That is, the (original) second-level encryption and the (transformed) first-level encryption are all secure against adaptively chosen-ciphertext attacks.

Actually, program obfuscation can make an (outsourced) computer program unintelligible while preserving its functionality, which provides an effective mechanism to securely and perfectly hide the sensitive data in outsourced program even the program executer has access the program in a white-box manner, such as debugging the program, tracing into the variables or setting the breakpoints.

We are now ready to describe our construction that employs the indistinguishability obfuscation. The setup algorithm at firsts picks up the puncturable keys (k_1, k_2). Next, it creates the public key as an obfuscation version of a program to perfectly hide the keys (k_1, k_2). Then the encryption algorithm can call this obfuscated program to encrypt a cleartext as follows: Compute $u = F_1(k_1, (m, r))$ where r was a randomness, run the obfuscated program on input r and u, and output the ciphertext ct as $(\alpha = H(m, r, u), \beta = F_2(k_2, \alpha) \oplus (m, r))$, where F_1 and F_2 are puncturable pseudorandom functions.

To avoid the cloud obtaining the clear re-encryption key $rk_{r \to j}$, the re-encryption key $rk_{i \to j}$ will be created as an obfuscated program, which will take as input a second-level ciphertext $ct_i = (\alpha, \beta)$ and outputs a transformed first-level ciphertext ct_j. The program first computes $(m, r) = \beta \oplus F_2(k_2, \alpha)$, $u = F_1(k_1, (m, r))$ and then checks whether $\alpha = H(m, r, u)$.

To invalidate the re-encryption key query from the adversary, we hardwire the punctured PRF key to generate a randomness r' for the re-encryption ciphertext and then puncture the key using the challenge ciphertext. Due to the security of puncturable PRF, we can invalidate the re-encryption key from the challenge user to another. In order to verify the original ciphertext and the re-encryption ciphertext that holds the same message m, we compute $u' = F_1(k_1, (m, r'))$ and run the obfuscated encryption circuit on r' and u', and output the re-encryption ciphertext $\widehat{ct}$ as $(\alpha' = H(m, r', u'), \beta' = F_j(k_{j,2}, \alpha'), u')$.

The security proof of our scheme is proceeded by a sequence of indistinguishable games. At first, we use puncturable PRF keys (k_1, k_2) to create the obfuscated program $\mathcal{P}^{\mathsf{Enc}}$ and $\mathcal{Q}^{\mathsf{REnc}}$. Next, we employ the punctured programming techniques to replace those normal evaluations of programs with hardwired and randomly sampled value. In the final game, any $p.p.t$ adversary $\mathcal{A}$ has negligible advantage in guessing the underlying cleartext.

RELATED WORKS. Blaze et al. [4] proposed the first bi-directional PRE scheme based on ElGamal PKE scheme. Subsequently, Ateniese et al. [2], Canetti and Hohenberger [7], Libert and Vergnud [24], and Chow et al. [9] proposed different PRE schemes with various properties. Avoid employing the pairings, Shao and Cao proposed a PRE scheme without pairing. However, Zhang et al. [8] pointed out that it is not secure in the Libert and Vergnaud security model.

Hohenberger et al. [19] introduced a mechanism in how to securely obfuscate the re-encryption functionality. Hanaoka et al. [18] and Isshiki et al. [21] presented the construction of chosen-ciphertext secure uni-directional PRE scheme, respectively. Kirshanova [22] proposed a lattice-based PRE scheme. However, none of those schemes consider the verifiability of re-encryption procedure.

Verifiable PRE proposed by Ohata et al. [26] is constructed by employing re-encryption verification. Using this approach, the delegator splits his secret key into tsk_1 and tsk_2 by a re-splittable threshold public key encryption [18]. Next, it computes $\psi = \mathsf{Enc}(pk_j, tsk_1)$, and sends ψ to user j. Then, the proxy re-encrypts the original ciphertext c_i by using the re-encryption key $rk_{i \rightarrow j}$ (imply tsk_2). That is, it computes $u_2 = \mathsf{Dec}(tsk_2, c_i)$ and sets the re-encrypted ciphertext as $\widehat{c}_j = \mathsf{Enc}(\widehat{pk}_j, u_2 \| c_i)$. The delegatee computes $u_2 \| c_i = \mathsf{Dec}(\widehat{dk}_j, \widehat{c}_j)$ and $u_1 = \mathsf{Dec}(dk_j, \psi)$, and outputs $m \leftarrow TCom(c, u_1, u_2)$. To achieve the re-encryption verifiability, by augmenting the dedicated re-encryption algorithm. On input $(pk_i, sk_j, c, \widehat{c})$, it executes the first-level decryption algorithm to recover the "*embedded*" second-level ciphetext c', and checks whether $c = c'$.

Liu et al. [25] indicated that the Ohata et al.'s scheme can not resist against collusion attack and they also proposed a new scheme to achieve CPA security based on $i\mathcal{O}$. More precisely, their approach is built on the key encapsulated mechanism. That is, an encryption of a message m using symmetric key k_{SE} and an encryption of k_{SE} using the public key pk_1, where k_{SE} is the output of a key extractor. Zhang et al. [28] presented a flexible and controllable obfuscated multi-hop re-encryption in (somewhat inefficient) multilinear groups.

PAPER ORGANIZATION. The rest of this paper is organized as follows. Section 2 reviews some preliminaries including mathematical notations, indistinguishability obfuscation and puncturable pseudo random functions. In Sect. 3, we propose the model and security definition for verifiable PRE. In Sect. 4, we present our concrete construction and give the security analysis. We provide the practical deployment of secure data-sharing in Sect. 5 and draw the conclusion in Sect. 6.

2 Preliminaries

Throughout of this paper, we use λ to denote the security parameter, and let *p.p.t* denote a probabilistic polynomial-time algorithm (Turing Machine). For an integer n, we write $[n]$ to denote the set $\{1, 2, \cdots, n\}$.

A negligible function $\mu(n)$ is a function that for all positive polynomial p there exists a positive integer $\mathbf{N}$ s.t. for all $n > \mathbf{N}$, $\mu(n) < 1/p(n)$. Let $\mathcal{A}$ be an algorithm, and x be the input of $\mathcal{A}$, the evaluation of the Turing machine running the algorithm $\mathcal{A}$ on the input tape with the encodings of x is denoted by $y \leftarrow \mathcal{A}(x)$ where the result y is the output of $\mathcal{A}$. An algorithm $\mathcal{A}$ is said to have oracle access to machine $\mathcal{O}$ if $\mathcal{A}$ can write an input for $\mathcal{O}$ on a special tape, and tell the oracle to execute on that input and then write its output to the tape, which is denoted by $\mathcal{A}^{\mathcal{O}}$.

For any polynomial-size distinguisher $\mathcal{D}$, the advantage $\delta = |\Pr[\mathcal{D}(\mathbf{Expt}(1^\lambda, 0)) = 1] - \Pr[\mathcal{D}(\mathbf{Expt}(1^\lambda, 1))]|$ is bounded by δ, we write as $\mathbf{Expt}(1^\lambda, 0) \approx_\delta \mathbf{Expt}(1^\lambda, 1)$. If δ is negligible in parameter λ, we call two distributions (experiments) indistinguishable.

We now recall the notion of indistinguishability obfuscation ($i\mathcal{O}$) and puncturable pseudorandom function and their security requirements.

Definition 1 (Indistinguishability Obfuscation ($i\mathcal{O}$)). *A uniform p.p.t algorithm $i\mathcal{O}$ is called an indistinguishability obfuscator for a circuit class $\{\mathcal{C}_\lambda\}_{\lambda \in N}$ if the following conditions are satisfied:*

- **Correctness:** *For all security parameters $\lambda \in N$, for all $C \in \{\mathcal{C}_\lambda\}$ and all inputs $x \in \{0,1\}^{poly(\lambda)}$, it holds that,*

$$\Pr[C'(x) = C(x) : C' \leftarrow i\mathcal{O}(\lambda, C)] = 1 \qquad (1)$$

- **Indistinguishability:** *For any p.p.t algorithm Samp and distinguisher $\mathcal{D}$, there exists a negligible function $\mu(\cdot)$ such that the following holds, i.e., if*

$$\Pr[\forall x, C_0(x) = C_1(x) : (C_0, C_1, aux) \leftarrow \mathrm{Samp}(1^\lambda)] > 1 - \mu(\cdot) \qquad (2)$$

we have,

$$\left| \Pr\left[\mathcal{D}(aux, i\mathcal{O}(\lambda, C_0)) = 1 : (C_0, C_1, aux) \leftarrow \mathrm{Samp}(1^\lambda)\right] \right.$$
$$\left. - \Pr\left[\mathcal{D}(aux, i\mathcal{O}(\lambda, C_1)) = 1 : (C_0, C_1, aux) \leftarrow \mathrm{Samp}(1^\lambda)\right] \right| \leq \mu(\lambda) \qquad (3)$$

where aux is the auxiliary information output by the algorithms in the system.

Definition 2 (Puncturable Pseudorandom Function). *A puncturable family of PRFs F consisting of three Turing Machines $(\mathrm{Key}_F, \mathrm{Punc}_F, \mathrm{Eval}_F)$, and a pairs of computing functions $n(\cdot)$ and $m(\cdot)$, satisfies the following properties:*

- **Functionality preserved under puncturing point:** *For every p.p.t algorithm $\mathcal{A}$ that takes as input 1^λ and outputs a set $S \subseteq \{0,1\}^{n(\lambda)}$, for all $x \notin S$, we have,*

$$\Pr\left[\mathrm{Eval}(k, x) = \mathrm{Eval}(k_S, x) : k \leftarrow \mathrm{Key}_F(1^\lambda), k_S = \mathrm{Punc}_F(k, S)\right] = 1 \qquad (4)$$

- **Pseudorandom at punctured points**: *For every p.p.t adversary* $(\mathcal{A}_1, \mathcal{A}_2)$ *such that* $\mathcal{A}_1$ *takes as input* 1^λ *and outputs a set* $S \subseteq \{0,1\}^{n(\lambda)}$. *For all* $k \leftarrow \text{Key}_F(1^\lambda)$, $k_S = \text{Punc}_F(k, S)$, *and* $x \in S$, *we have,*

$$\left| \Pr\left[\mathcal{A}_2(k_S, x, \text{Eval}(k, x)) \right] = 1 - \Pr\left[\mathcal{A}_2(k_S, x, U_{m(\lambda)}) = 1 \right] \right| \leq \mu(\lambda) \quad (5)$$

where $U_{m(\lambda)}$ *denotes the uniform distribution over* $m(\lambda)$ *bits.*

Remark 1. In order to simplify notation, in this paper, we write $F(k, S)$ to stand for $Eval_F(k, x)$ and $k(S)$ for $Punc_F(k, S)$, respectively.

Puncturable PRFs can easily be constructed from GGM's PRFs [12] which are based on one-way functions. The following lemma states that the statistical injective PPRF can be constructed.

Lemma 1 *[27]. If one-way functions exist, then for all efficiently computable functions* $\ell(\lambda)$, $m(\lambda)$ *and* $e(\lambda)$ *such that* $\ell(\lambda) \geq 2m(\lambda) + e(\lambda)$, *there exists a statistically injective puncturable PRF family with failure probability* $1/2^{e(\lambda)}$ *that maps* $\ell(\lambda)$ *bits to* $m(\lambda)$ *bits.*

3 Models and Definitions

3.1 Algorithms and Definitions of VPRE

Our syntax for verifiable proxy re-encryption (VPRE) roughly follows in the line of [26] except that we generate an additional verifiable key in the encryption process for the verifiability of re-encryption ciphertext. A single-hop unidirectional VPRE comprises of the following six algorithms whose flowchart is described in Fig. 2:

- $\text{KGen}(1^\lambda) \rightarrow (pk, sk)$: Key generation algorithm is a polynomial algorithm that takes the security parameter λ, and outputs public keys pk and secret keys sk.
- $\text{Enc}(pk_i, m) \rightarrow (ct, vk)$: Original encryption algorithm takes the public key pk_i, a message m and a randomness r and outputs an original second-level ciphertext ct_i, and a verifiable key vk.
- $\text{RKey}(sk_i, pk_j) \rightarrow rk_{i \rightarrow j}$: Re-key generation algorithm takes the secret key of user i, i.e., sk_i, and the public key pk_j of user j, and outputs a re-key $rk_{i \rightarrow j}$.
- $\text{REnc}(rk_{i \rightarrow j}, ct_i) \rightarrow \widehat{ct_j}$: Re-encryption algorithm takes the re-key $rk_{i \rightarrow j}$ and a second-level ciphertext ct_i, and outputs a first-level ciphertext $\widehat{ct_j}$.
- $\text{Dec}_2(sk_i, ct_i) \rightarrow m|\bot$: Second-level decryption algorithm takes a secret key sk_i, and an original second-level ciphertext ct_i, and outputs a message m or the special symbol $\bot$.
- $\text{Dec}_1(sk_j, \widehat{ct_j}) \rightarrow m|\bot$: First-level decryption algorithm takes a secret key sk_j and a first-level ciphertext $\widehat{ct_j}$, and outputs a message m or $\bot$, which indicates that the ct_i is invalid.

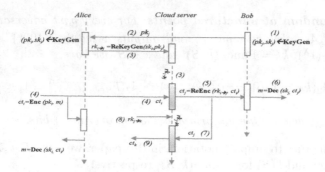

Fig. 2. Workflow of cloud-based verifiable proxy re-encryption

Let $\mathcal{M}$ be the message space. A VPRE scheme is consistent and correct if for all messages $m \in \mathcal{M}$ and any key pairs $(pk_i, sk_i), (pk_j, sk_j) \leftarrow \mathsf{KGen}(1^\lambda)$, the following conditions hold:

1. The second-level decryption correctness:

$$\Pr\left[\mathsf{Dec}_2(sk_i, \mathsf{Enc}(pk_i, m)) \neq m\right] \leq \mu(\lambda) \tag{6}$$

2. The first-level decryption consistency:

$$\Pr\left[\mathsf{Dec}_1\big(sk_j, \mathsf{REnc}(\mathsf{RKey}(sk_i, pk_j), \mathsf{Enc}(pk_i, m))\big) \neq m\right] \leq \mu(\lambda)$$

3.2 CCA Security

We adopt the chosen-ciphertext attack (CCA) security of VPRE scheme that is defined as follows.

Definition 3 (CCA Security for Second-level Ciphertext). *A uni-directional VPRE scheme is said to be CCA secure at second level if the probability is negligibly close to 1/2 for any p.p.t adversary $\mathcal{A}$ which is shown as follows*

$$\Pr\left[b' = b : \begin{array}{l} (pk^*, sk^*) \leftarrow \mathsf{KGen}(1^\lambda), \ \{(pk_c, sk_c) \leftarrow \mathsf{KGen}(1^\lambda)\}, \\ \{(pk_h, sk_h) \leftarrow \mathsf{KGen}(1^\lambda)\}, \ \{rk_{c \to *} \leftarrow \mathsf{RKey}(sk_c, pk^*)\}, \\ \{rk_{* \to h} \leftarrow \mathsf{RKey}(sk^*, pk_h)\}, \ \{rk_{h \to *} \leftarrow \mathsf{RKey}(sk_h, pk^*)\}, \\ \{rk_{h \to c} \leftarrow \mathsf{RKey}(sk_h, pk_c)\}, \ \{rk_{c \to h} \leftarrow \mathsf{RKey}(sk_c, pk_h)\}, \\ \{rk_{h \to h'} \leftarrow \mathsf{RKey}(sk_h, pk_{h'})\}, \ \{rk_{c \to c'} \leftarrow \mathsf{RKey}(sk_c, pk_{c'})\}, \\ (m_0, m_1, aux) \leftarrow \mathcal{A}^{\mathcal{O}_{\mathsf{Dec}_1}, \mathcal{O}_{\mathsf{Dec}_2}, \mathcal{O}_{\mathsf{REnc}}}\Big(pk^*, \{pk_c, sk_c\}, \\ \qquad\qquad \{pk_h\}, \{rk_{c \to *}\}, \{rk_{h \to *}\}, \{rk_{* \to h}\}, \\ \qquad\qquad \{rk_{c \to h}\}, \{rk_{h \to c}\}, \{rk_{h \to h'}\}, \{rk_{c \to c'}\}\Big), \\ b \xleftarrow{R} \{0,1\}, \ \ ct^* = \mathsf{Enc}(pk^*, m_b), \\ b' \leftarrow \mathcal{A}^{\mathcal{O}_{\mathsf{Dec}_1}, \mathcal{O}_{\mathsf{Dec}_2}, \mathcal{O}_{\mathsf{REnc}}}\big(ct^*, aux\big) \end{array} \right] \leq \mu(\lambda)$$

In this case, aux is a state information held by $\mathcal{A}$ and (pk^*, sk^*) is the challenge user's key pair generated by the challenger. For honest users, keys are indicated by h or h' and we indicate corrupt users by c or c'. The adversary is given all re-encryption keys except for those that could re-encrypt the ciphertext from the challenge one to the corrupt one. In the security experiment, $\mathcal{A}$ is said to have advantage ε if this probability is at least $1/2 + \varepsilon$.

In the above CCA security experiments, Oracles $\mathcal{O}_{\mathsf{Dec}_1}, \mathcal{O}_{\mathsf{Dec}_2}, \mathcal{O}_{\mathsf{REnc}}$ work as follows:

- **Re-encryption Oracle** $\mathcal{O}_{\mathsf{REnc}}$: for a re-encryption query (pk_i, pk_j, ct_i), the oracle responds follows: If $(pk_i, ct_i) = (pk^*, ct_i^*)$ and $pk_j \notin pk_h$, then the oracle returns the special symbol $\perp$ to $\mathcal{A}$. Otherwise, the oracle answers with $\mathsf{REnc}(\mathsf{RKey}(sk_i, pk_j), ct_i)$.
- **First-level Decryption Oracle** $\mathcal{O}_{\mathsf{Dec}_1}$: For a first-level decryption query $(pk_i, \widehat{ct_i})$, the oracle responds as follows: If $\mathcal{A}$ has required a re-encryption query (pk^*, pk_i, ct_i^*) and obtained $\widehat{ct_i}$ before, then the oracle searches the tuple in the record table and returns the tuple to $\mathcal{A}$. If the adversary $\mathcal{A}$ has requested a re-encryption key query (pk^*, pk_i) previously and $\mathsf{Dec}_1(sk_i, \widehat{ct_i}) \in \{m_0, m_1\}$, then the oracle ansers with "$test$" to $\mathcal{A}$. Otherwise, the oracle answers with $\mathsf{Dec}_1(sk_i, \widehat{ct_i})$.
- **Second-level Decryption Oracle** $\mathcal{O}_{\mathsf{Dec}_2}$: For a second-level decryption query (pk_i, ct_i), the oracle responds with $\mathsf{Dec}_2(sk_i, ct_i)$, except for the challenge ciphertext. i.e., if $(pk_i, ct_i) = (pk^*, ct_i^*)$, then the oracle answers with a symbol $\perp$.

In the security of first-level ciphertexts for uni-directional VPRE schemes, $\mathcal{A}$ is allowed to have access to all the re-encryption keys in the definition. Since all first-level ciphertexts cannot be re-encrypted, there is indeed no reason to keep adversary from obtaining all honest to corrupt re-encryption keys. The re-encryption oracle becomes futile because of all the re-encryption keys are available to adversary $\mathcal{A}$.

Definition 4 (CCA Security for First-level Ciphertext). *A single-hop unidirectional VPRE scheme is said to be CCA secure at first-level if the probability is negligible for any p.p.t adversary $\mathcal{A}$, where the challenge user's key pair (sk^*, pk^*) and the challenge ciphertext $\widehat{ct^*}$ are generated by the challenger, which is shown as follows*

$$
\Pr \left[b' = b :
\begin{array}{l}
(pk^*, sk^*) \leftarrow \mathsf{KGen}(1^\lambda), \ \{(pk_c, sk_c) \leftarrow \mathsf{KGen}(1^\lambda)\}, \\
\{(pk_h, sk_h) \leftarrow \mathsf{KGen}(1^\lambda)\}, \ \{rk_{c \to *} \leftarrow \mathsf{RKey}(sk_c, pk^*)\}, \\
\{rk_{* \to h} \leftarrow \mathsf{RKey}(sk^*, pk_h)\}, \ \{rk_{h \to *} \leftarrow \mathsf{RKey}(sk_h, pk^*)\}, \\
\{rk_{h \to c} \leftarrow \mathsf{RKey}(sk_h, pk_c)\}, \ \{rk_{c \to h} \leftarrow \mathsf{RKey}(sk_c, pk_h)\}, \\
\{rk_{h \to h'} \leftarrow \mathsf{RKey}(sk_h, pk_{h'})\}, \ \{rk_{c \to c'} \leftarrow \mathsf{RKey}(sk_c, pk_{c'})\}, \\
(m_0, m_1, sk_\mathcal{A}, pk_\mathcal{A}) \leftarrow \mathcal{A}^{\mathcal{O}_{\mathsf{Dec}_1}, \mathcal{O}_{\mathsf{Dec}_2}} \big(pk^*, \{pk_c, sk_c\}, \{pk_h, sk_h\}, \\
\{rk_{c \to *}\}, \{rk_{h \to *}\}, \{rk_{* \to h}\}, \{rk_{c \to h}\}, \{rk_{h \to c}\}, \{rk_{h \to h'}\}, \{rk_{c \to c'}\} \big), \\
b \xleftarrow{R} \{0, 1\}, \\
ct = \mathsf{Enc}(pk_\mathcal{A}, m_b), \ \widehat{ct^*} = \mathsf{REnc}(\mathsf{RKey}(sk_\mathcal{A}, pk^*), ct), \\
b' \leftarrow \mathcal{A}^{\mathcal{O}_{\mathsf{Dec}_1}, \mathcal{O}_{\mathsf{Dec}_2}}(\widehat{ct^*})
\end{array}
\right] \leq \mu(\lambda)
$$

Ohata et al. [26] introduces a new functionality for proxy re-encryption with verifiability of re-encryption procedure. Ateniese et al. [2] defines the property for unidirectional PRE schemes, i.e., master secret key security. We give the security requirements of verifiable PRE with master-key security as follows:

Definition 5 *(CCA-VPRE Security). A VPRE scheme is said to be CCA-secure verifiable VPRE against master-key exposure if both the first-level encryption and the-second level encryption are CCA secure.*

1. **Master secret security.** *Master secret security captures the inability to obtain the master secret key even if the cloud proxy and the delegatee collude. More formally, the following probability should be negligible in security parameter λ,*

$$\Pr\left[\chi = sk^* : \begin{array}{l} (pk^*, sk^*) \leftarrow KGen(1^\lambda), \\ \{(pk_c, sk_c) \leftarrow KGen(1^\lambda)\}, \\ \{rk_{c\rightarrow *} \leftarrow RKey(sk_c, pk^*)\}, \\ \{rk_{*\rightarrow c} \leftarrow RKey(sk^*, pk_c)\}, \\ \chi \leftarrow \mathcal{A}(\{pk_c, sk_c\}, \{rk_{c\rightarrow *}\}, \{rk_{*\rightarrow c}\}) \end{array}\right] \leq \mu(\lambda)$$

2. **Re-encryption verifiability.** *Re-encryption verifiability ensues that,*
   (a) *If the adversary who obtains a re-encryption key $rk_{i\rightarrow j}$ and is given an original (second-level) ciphertext ct_i, it can produce only a re-encrypted ciphertext $\widehat{ct_j}$ that can decrypt the same message as the decryption result of ct_i.*
   (b) *If the adversary does not have the re-encryption key $rk_{i\rightarrow j}$, then it cannot create a valid re-encryption ciphertext $\widehat{ct_j}$ at all.*
   Concretely, for any p.p.t adversary $\mathcal{A}$, the following probability is negligible.

$$\Pr\left[m' \neq m^* \wedge m' \neq \bot : \begin{array}{l} (pk^*, sk^*) \leftarrow KGen(1^\lambda), \ \{(pk_c, sk_c) \leftarrow KGen(1^\lambda)\}, \\ \{(pk_h, sk_h) \leftarrow KGen(1^\lambda)\}, \ \{rk_{c\rightarrow *} \leftarrow RKey(sk_c, pk^*)\}, \\ \{rk_{*\rightarrow h} \leftarrow RKey(sk^*, pk_h)\}, \ \{rk_{h\rightarrow *} \leftarrow RKey(sk_h, pk^*)\}, \\ \{rk_{h\rightarrow c} \leftarrow RKey(sk_h, pk_c)\}, \ \{rk_{c\rightarrow h} \leftarrow RKey(sk_c, pk_h)\}, \\ \{rk_{h\rightarrow h'} \leftarrow RKey(sk_h, pk_{h'})\}, \ \{rk_{c\rightarrow c'} \leftarrow RKey(sk_c, pk_{c'})\}, \\ m \leftarrow \mathcal{A}^{\mathcal{O}_{\text{Dec}_1}, \mathcal{O}_{\text{REnc}}}\big(pk^*, \{pk_c, sk_c\}, \{pk_h\}, \{rk_{c\rightarrow *}\}, \{rk_{h\rightarrow *}\}, \\ \quad \{rk_{*\rightarrow h}\}, \{rk_{c\rightarrow h}\}, \{rk_{h\rightarrow c}\}, \ \{rk_{h\rightarrow h'}\}, \{rk_{c\rightarrow c'}\}\big), \\ ct^* = \text{Enc}(pk^*, m^*), \\ m' \leftarrow \mathcal{A}^{\mathcal{O}_{\text{Dec}_1}, \mathcal{O}_{\text{Dec}_2}}(\widehat{ct^*}, pk_{R_j}) \end{array}\right]$$

$$\leq \mu(\lambda)$$

4   Proposed Construction

4.1   Main Idea

We now describe the main idea of our scheme. The functionality of re-encryption is easily realized that if it is allowed to decrypt the ciphertext and to re-encrypt the underlying cleartext by the cloud proxy. However, we should guarantee that the cloud proxy cannot gain any sensitive data during performing the transformation. That is, *"decrypt-then-encrypt"* procedure guarantees that be not able to expose the secret key of the delegator, or the embedded cleartext.

Let the length of a message be ℓ. Let F_1 be a puncturable PRF that takes input of $(\ell + \lambda)$-bit and outputs ℓ_δ-bit, and F_2 be a puncturable PRF that takes input of ℓ_α-bit and outputs $(\ell + \lambda)$-bit. Let H be a collision-resistant cryptographic hash function that takes input of $(\ell + \lambda + \ell_\delta)$-bit and outputs the size of ℓ_α-bit.

In our scheme, to protect the secret key of delegator from exposing from the re-encryption key, we set the re-encryption key as the obfuscated program by the use of indistinguishability obfuscation $i\mathcal{O}$. To achieve the re-encryption verifiability, we design the VPRE scheme by employing Sahai and Waters' short signature scheme [27]. Before executing the obfuscated circuit $\mathcal{P}^{\mathsf{Enc}}$, it at first evaluates the signature $u = F_1(k_1, (m, r))$ on message m and randomness r.

In the re-encryption circuit, we need to re-randomize the signature and randomness for user j. To complete the security proof, we add the puncturable PRF key k_3 in the re-encryption circuit and generate the updated randomness for re-encryption by using k_3.

Encrypt-Circuit

CONSTANT: puncturable PRF keys k_2.

INPUT: message $m \in \{0,1\}^\ell$,
       randomness $r \in \{0,1\}^\lambda$,
       signature $u \in \{0,1\}^{\ell_\delta}$.

PROCEDURE:

1. Compute $\alpha = H(u, m, r)$.
2. Compute $\beta = F_2(k_2, \alpha) \oplus (m, r)$.
3. Output $ct = (\alpha, \beta)$.

Fig. 3. Program of Encrypt-Circuit

Verify-key

CONSTANTS: puncturable PRF key k_1.

INPUT: message $m \in \{0,1\}^\ell$,
       randomness $r \in \{0,1\}^\lambda$,
       signature $u \in \{0,1\}^{\ell_\delta}$.

PROCEDURE:

Check $f(u) = f(F_1(k_1, (m, r)))$. Output *"accept"* if true, *"reject"* otherwise.

Fig. 4. Program of Verify-key

```
                          ReEnc-Circuit
CONSTANTS: puncturable PRF keys k_{i,1}, k_{i,2}: second-level secret key of user i,
           k_3: puncturable PRF key,
           iO(P_j^Enc): public key of user j.
INPUT: ct_i = (α_i, β_i): second-level ciphertext
PROCEDURE:
  1. Compute (m, r) = F_2(k_{i,2}, α_i) ⊕ β_i.
  2. Compute u = F_1(k_{i,1}, (m, r)).
  3. If α_i ≠ H(u, m, r), outputs ⊥ and aborts. Otherwise, continue to the next
     steps.
  4. Compute r' = F_3(k_3, ct_i).
  5. Compute u' = F_1(k_{i,1}, (m, r')).
  6. Evaluate iO(P_j^Enc, λ)(m, r', u').
  7. Output ct_j = (α', β', u')
```

Fig. 5. Program of Re-encryption Circuit

4.2 Our Construction

The concrete construction of VPRE = (KGen, Enc, RKey, REnc, Dec$_1$, Dec$_2$) is described as follows:

- KGen($1^λ$): The key generation algorithm at first chooses a puncturable key $k_1 \leftarrow Key_{F_1}(1^λ)$ and $k_2 \leftarrow Key_{F_2}(1^λ)$. Next, it creates an obfuscation of program **Encrypt-Circuit** as

$$\mathcal{P}^{Enc} \leftarrow iO(1^λ, \text{Encrypt-Circuit} : [k_2]) \tag{7}$$

The circuit **Encrypt-Circuit** is formally defined in Fig. 3. This obfuscated program, $\mathcal{P}^{Enc}$, servers as the public key, $pk = \mathcal{P}^{Enc}$, and the corresponding secret key is $sk = (k_1, k_2)$.

- Enc($pk = \mathcal{P}^{Enc}, m \in \{0,1\}^ℓ, r \in \{0,1\}^λ$): The encryption algorithm at first computes $u = F_1(k_1, (m, r))$. Next it produces an obfuscated program $Γ^{vk}$, which is defined in Fig. 4. It at random chooses $r \in \{0,1\}^λ$, and then runs the obfuscated program $\mathcal{P}^{Enc}$ on inputs r, m and u to obtain: $(α, β) \leftarrow \mathcal{P}^{Enc}(m, r, u)$. The output of second-level ciphertext is $ct = (α, β)$.

- RKey($sk_i = (k_{i,1}, k_{i,2}), pk_j = \mathcal{P}_j^{Enc}$): Let $sk_i = (k_{i,1}, k_{i,2})$ be the delegator's secret key, and $pk_j = \mathcal{P}_j^{Enc}$ be the public key of delegatee j. The re-key generation algorithm at random chooses a puncturable PRF key $k_3 \leftarrow Key_{F_3}(1^λ)$, and then produces an obfuscated program $\mathcal{Q}^{REnc}$ by obfuscating

$$\mathcal{Q}^{REnc} \leftarrow iO(1^λ, \text{ReEnc-Circuit} : [k_1, k_2, k_3, iO(\mathcal{P}_j^{Enc})]) \tag{8}$$

which is described in Fig. 5. The re-encryption key is set as $rk_{i \to j} = \mathcal{Q}^{REnc}$.

- REnc($rk_{i \to j} = \mathcal{Q}^{REnc}, ct_i = (α_i, β_i)$): The re-encryption algorithm takes as inputs ct_i of a second-level ciphertext of user i and a re-encryption key $rk_{i \to j}$ which is an obfuscated program $\mathcal{Q}_{i \to j}^{REnc}$. It then runs the circuit $\mathcal{Q}_{i \to j}^{REnc}(ct_i)$ and outputs a first-level ciphertext $ct_j = (α', β', u')$.

- $\mathsf{Dec}_2(sk_i = (k_{i,1}, k_{i,2}), ct_i = (\alpha_i, \beta_i))$: The second-level decryption algorithm takes as inputs a secret key sk and a ciphertext ct_i. At first it computes $(m, r) = F_2(k_{i,2}, \alpha_i) \oplus \beta_i$. Next, it computes $u = F_1(k_{i,1}, (m, r))$ and then checks the equation $\alpha_i = H(u, m, r)$. If the equation does not hold, it outputs $\bot$ and stops. Otherwise, it outputs m.
- $\mathsf{Dec}_1(sk_j, \widehat{ct_j})$: The first-level decryption algorithm takes as inputs a secret key sk_j and a first-level ciphertext $\widehat{ct_j}$. At first it computes $(m, r) = F_2(k_{j,2}, \alpha') \oplus \beta'$, and checks if $vk(m, r, u') = 1$ and $\alpha = H(m, r, u') = 1$. Finally, it outputs a message m if the equations hold or symbol $\bot$ otherwise.

Correctness. At first, we ensure the correctness of decryption of the original (second level) ciphertext. Actually, the second-level ciphertext has the form: $ct = (\alpha, \beta) = (H(m, r, u), F_2(k_2, \alpha) \oplus (m, r))$, and the secret key is (k_1, k_2). When we decrypt the ciphertext, we calculate $(m, r) = F_2(k_2, \alpha) \oplus \beta$ and $u = F_1(k_1, (m, r))$. If the check $\alpha = H(m, r, u)$ holds, the result of decryption is valid.

Furthermore, we ensure the consistency of decryption of the (transformed) first-level ciphertext. The transformed (first-level) re-encrypted ciphertext has the form: $\widehat{ct} = (\alpha', \beta', u') = (H(m, r', u'), F_2(k_{j,2}, \alpha' \oplus (m, r')), F_{i,1}(k_{i,1}, (m, r')))$, and the secret key has the form: $sk_j = (k_{j,1}, k_{j,2})$. When decrypting a re-encrypted first-level ciphertext, we will compute $(m, r') = F_2(k_{j,2}, \alpha') \oplus \beta'$. If the check $vk(m, r', u') = 1$ and $\alpha = H(m, r', u')$ hold, the result of this decryption outputs the message m which satisfies the consistency of the second-level ciphertext.

4.3   Proof of Security

We use a series of games to prove the security of our scheme. In the sequence of games, the first game is defined as the original experiment of second-level CCA security. Then we show that any $p.p.t$ adversary's advantage in each game must be negligibly close to the previous game and the adversary has negligible advantage in the final game. We have the following theorem.

Theorem 1. *Suppose that the indistinguishability obfuscation scheme is a secure iO, F_1 and F_2 are secure puncturable PRFs, $f(\cdot)$ is a cryptographically secure one-way function and H is modeled as a collision-resistant hash function, the proposed VPRE scheme is CCA secure for the second-level encryption.*

Proof. We give the proof that is based on a series of games as follows.

Expt$_0$: The first game Expt$_0$ is set as the original second-level CCA security game instantiated in our construction, which works as follows.

1. The adversary $\mathcal{A}$ selectively gives the challenger the messages m^*.
2. The challenger $\mathcal{C}$ at random selects keys $k_1 \leftarrow Key_{F_1}(1^\lambda), k_2 \leftarrow Key_{F_2}(1^\lambda), k_3 \leftarrow Key_{F_3}(1^\lambda)$ and also picks a random coin $b \in \{0, 1\}$.
3. $\mathcal{C}$ computes $u^* = F_1(k_1, (m^*, r^*))$.
4. The challenger $\mathcal{C}$ creates $\mathcal{P}^{\mathsf{Enc}} \leftarrow i\mathcal{O}(1^\lambda, \texttt{Encrypt-Circuit} : [k_1])$ and sends $\mathcal{P}^{\mathsf{Enc}}$ to the adversary $\mathcal{A}$.

5. Phase-1 queries and response as follows in an adaptive manner:
   (a) The challenger $\mathcal{C}$ generates the re-encryption key $rk_{i \to j}$ by calling $\mathcal{Q}^{\mathsf{REnc}} \leftarrow iO(1^\lambda, \mathtt{ReEnc\text{-}Circuit} : [k_1, k_2, k_3, iO(\mathcal{P}_j^{\mathsf{Enc}})])$ and returns $\mathcal{Q}^{\mathsf{REnc}}$ to $\mathcal{A}$.
   (b) $\mathcal{A}$ asks the query for ciphertext ct to oracle $\mathcal{O}_{\mathsf{REnc}}$.
   (c) $\mathcal{A}$ requests the query for ciphertext $\widehat{ct}$ to oracle $\mathcal{O}_{\mathsf{Dec}_2}$ and re-encryption ciphertext ct to oracle $\mathcal{O}_{\mathsf{Dec}_1}$.
6. The challenger $\mathcal{C}$ runs $ct^* \leftarrow iO(1^\lambda, \mathtt{Encrypt\text{-}Circuit}: [k_1])(m^*, r^*, u^*)$, and returns ct^* to the adversary.
7. Phase-2 queries are the same as in Phase-1, except that, for the adversary $\mathcal{A}$, the following additional restrictions are satisfied:
   (a) Cannot request a re-encryption query to tuple (pk_{i^*}, pk_j, ct^*) s.t. $pk_j \in pk_c$.
   (b) Cannot request a decryption query to (pk_k, ct_k) so that ct_k is the result of a re-encryption query (pk_{i^*}, pk_k, ct^*).
   (c) Cannot request the decryption query to tuple (pk_{i^*}, ct^*)
8. The adversary $\mathcal{A}$ outputs a bit b' and wins the game if $b' = b$.

Expt$_1$: The challenger $\mathcal{C}$ sets $\alpha^* = H(m^*, r^*, u^*)$ and $\widetilde{ct^*} = F_2(k_2, \alpha^*) \oplus (m^*, r^*)$. It creates the obfuscated program of $\mathcal{P}^{\mathsf{Enc}^*}$ as the obfuscation version of $\mathtt{Encrypt\text{-}circuit}^*$ defined in Fig. 6. By the iO security, no adversary can distinguish **Expt$_1$** and **Expt$_0$**.

Encrypt-Circuit**

CONSTANTS: puncturable PRF keys $k_2\{\alpha^*\}$, α^* and $\widetilde{ct^*}$.
INPUT: message $m \in \{0,1\}^\ell$,
       randomness $r \in \{0,1\}^\lambda$,
       signature $u \in \{0,1\}^{\ell_\delta}$.
PROCEDURE:

1. If $\alpha^* = H(m, r, u)$, output $\widetilde{ct^*}$.
2. Else compute $\alpha = H(u, m, r)$.
3. Compute $\beta = F_2(k_2, \alpha) \oplus (m, r)$.
4. Output $ct = (\alpha, \beta)$.

Fig. 6. Program of Encrypt-Circuit*

Expt$_2$: $\mathcal{C}$ computes $z^* = f(F_1(k_1, (m^*, r^*)))$ and sets vk as the obfuscation of program $\mathtt{Verify\text{-}key}^*$ defined in Fig. 7. It is easily to see that no adversary can distinguish **Expt$_2$** and **Expt$_1$** by the security of indistinguishability obfuscation.

Expt$_3$: The challenger sets $z^* = f(y)$ for randomly selected y from $\{0,1\}^{\ell_\delta}$. By the security of puncturable PRF, no adversary can distinguish **Expt$_3$** and **Expt$_2$**.

Verify-key*

CONSTANTS: puncturable PRF key $k_1\{m^*, r^*\}$,
$\qquad\qquad m^* \in \{0,1\}^\ell$,
$\qquad\qquad r^* \in \{0,1\}^\lambda$,
$\qquad\qquad z^*$.

INPUT: message $m \in \{0,1\}^\ell$,
$\qquad$ randomness $r \in \{0,1\}^\lambda$,
$\qquad$ signature $u \in \{0,1\}^{\ell_\delta}$.

PROCEDURE:

1. If $(m,r) = (m^*, r^*)$,
   Then, check whether $f(u) = z^*$.
   Output "*accept*" if the equation holds,
   and output "*reject*" otherwise.
2. Else, check if $f(u) = f(F_1(k_1, (m,r)))$.
   Output "*accept*" if the equation holds, and output "*reject*" otherwise.

Fig. 7. Program of Verify-key*

Expt$_4$: The challenger $\mathcal{C}$ at first computes the output when ct^* are input to the re-encryption circuit $\mathcal{Q}_{*\rightarrow j}^{\mathsf{REnc}^*}$ defined in Fig. 8. Here, it hardwires the output $\widehat{ct^*}$ (i.e., re-encrypted ciphertext) to $\mathcal{Q}^{\mathsf{REnc}^*}$. Next, it computes punctured keys $k_{i,1}^*\{m^*, r^*\}$, $k_{i,2}^*\{\alpha^*\}$ and $k_3\{ct^*\}$. By the security of indistinguishability obfuscation $i\mathcal{O}$ and the collision-resistance of hash function, it is easily to show that no adversary can distinguish **Expt$_4$** and **Expt$_3$**.

Expt$_5$: The challenger replaces the second component of the hardwired ciphertext to a random one. By the pseudorandom security in punctured points of puncturable PRF, no adversary can distinguish **Expt$_5$** and **Expt$_4$**.

Expt$_6$: The challenger answers the re-encryption query (pk_i, pk_j, ct_i) such that $pk_i = pk^*$. It does as follows:

1. If the input ciphertext is ct^*, then output $\widehat{ct^*}$.
2. Compute $(m,r) = F_2(k_{i,2}^*\{\alpha^*\}, \alpha_i) \oplus \beta_i$.
3. Compute $u = F_1(k_{i,1}^*\{m^*, r^*\}, (m,r))$.
4. Check whether $\alpha_i \neq H(u, m, r)$. If not, output $\perp$ and abort.
5. Compute $r' = F_3(k_3\{ct^*\}, ct_i)$ and $u' = F_1(k_{i,1}^*\{m^*, r^*\}, (m, r'))$
6. Compute $i\mathcal{O}(\mathcal{P}_j^{\mathsf{Enc}}, \lambda)(m, r', u')$ and send the result to the adversary.

By the collision-resistant security of hash function, there does not exist any adversary in distinguishing **Expt$_6$** and **Expt$_5$**.

Expt$_7$: The challenger $\mathcal{C}$ answers the first-level decryption query $(pk_i, \widehat{ct_i})$ as follows.

1. Compute $(m, r') = F_2(k_{i,2}, \alpha_i) \oplus \beta_i$.
2. Check whether $vk(m, r', u')$ and $\alpha_i \neq H(m, r', u')$. Output $\perp$ if fail.
3. Output m as the answer.

ReEnc-Circuit*

CONSTANTS: punctuable PRF keys $k_{i,1}^*\{m^*, r^*\}$, $k_{i,2}^*\{\alpha^*\}$(secret key of user i),
$k_3\{ct^*\}$ (puncturable PRF key),
$i\mathcal{O}(P_j^{\mathsf{Enc}})$(public key of user j),
ciphertext $\widehat{ct^*}$.

INPUT: ct_i.
PROCEDURE:

1. If the input ciphertext is ct^*, then it outputs $\widehat{ct^*}$.
2. Compute $(m, r) = F_2(k_{i,2}^*\{\alpha^*\}, \alpha_i) \oplus \beta_i$.
3. Compute $u = F_1(k_{i,1}^*\{m^*, r^*\}, (m, r))$.
4. Check whether $\alpha_i \neq H(u, m, r)$ holds. If not, output $\perp$ and abort.
5. Compute $r' = F_3(k_3\{ct^*\}, ct_i)$ and $u' = F_1(k_{i,1}^*\{m^*, r^*\}, (m, r'))$
6. Compute $i\mathcal{O}(\mathcal{P}_j^{\mathsf{Enc}}, \lambda)(m, r', u')$.
7. Output $ct_j = (\alpha', \beta', u')$

Fig. 8. Program of REnc-Circuit*

By the security of one-way function and collision-resistance of hash function, there does not exist any adversary in distinguishing **Expt$_7$** and **Expt$_6$**.

Expt$_8$: The challenger $\mathcal{C}$ answers the second-level decryption query (pk_i, ct) such that $pk_i = pk^*$ as follows:

1. Compute $(m, r) = F_2(k_{i,2}, \alpha_i) \oplus \beta_i$.
2. Compute $u = F_1(k_{i,1}, (m, r))$.
3. Check whether $\alpha_i \neq H(u, m, r)$ holds. If not, outputs $\perp$.
4. Return m as the answer.

By the collision-resistance of hash function, it is easily to show that no adversary can distinguish **Expt$_8$** and **Expt$_7$**.

Expt$_9$: Replace $F_1(k_1, (m^*, r^*))$ with a randomly and uniformly selected value. By the security of puncturable PRF, no adversary can distinguish **Expt$_9$** from **Expt$_8$**.

Expt$_{10}$: The challenger $\mathcal{C}$ sets $\alpha^* = t^*$ for randomly selected $t^* \leftarrow \{0, 1\}^{\ell_\alpha}$. By the security of puncturable PRF, no adversary can distinguish **Expt$_{10}$** and **Expt$_9$**.

Expt$_{11}$: The challenger $\mathcal{C}$ at random chooses $x^* \leftarrow \{0, 1\}^{\ell+\lambda}$ and sets (t^*, x^*) as the challenge ciphertext.

Notice that, in **Expt$_{11}$**, the challenge ciphertext $ct^* = (t^*, x^*)$ where t^* and x^* are distributed uniformly, and thus, the adversary $\mathcal{A}$ has a negligible advantage in the second-level CCA-VPRE game. Therefore, the advantage of the adversary in **Expt$_0$** is negligible in actual attack experiment. This completes the proof of Theorem 1.

Theorem 2. *If the obfuscation scheme is a secure indistinguishably obfuscator, F_1 and F_2 are secure punctured PRFs, $f(\cdot)$ is a cryptographically secure one-way function and H is a collision-resistant hash function, the proposed* VPRE *scheme is CCA secure for the first-level encryption.*

Proof. We also use a series of games that are proved to be indistinguishable as follows.

$\mathbf{Expt_0}$: $\mathbf{Expt_0}$ is described as the first-level CCA experiment of VPRE scheme.

$\mathbf{Expt_1}$: This game is the same as $\mathbf{Expt_0}$, except that the re-encrypted ciphertext is set as $(\alpha', \beta', u' = W)$ for randomly selected $W \in \{0, 1\}^{\ell_\delta}$. By the security of puncturable PRF, it is easily to see that no adversary can distinguish $\mathbf{Expt_1}$ and $\mathbf{Expt_0}$.

$\mathbf{Expt_2}$: This game is the same as $\mathbf{Expt_1}$, except that the re-encrypted ciphertext is set as $(\alpha' = U, \beta', W)$ for randomly selected $U \in \{0, 1\}^{\ell_\alpha}$. By the security of puncturable PRF and collision-resistance of hash function, no adversary can distinguish $\mathbf{Expt_2}$ and $\mathbf{Expt_1}$.

$\mathbf{Expt_3}$: This game is the same as $\mathbf{Expt_1}$, except that the re-encrypted ciphertext is set as $(U, \beta' = V, W)$ for randomly chosen $V \in \{0, 1\}^{\ell+\lambda}$. By the security of puncturable PRF, it is easily to show that no adversary is able to distinguish $\mathbf{Expt_3}$ and $\mathbf{Expt_2}$.

By a series of hybrid arguments, it declares that a *p.p.t* adversary's advantage in the original security $\mathbf{Expt_0}$ can be at most negligibly greater than its advantage in $\mathbf{Expt_3}$. We note that the advantage of the adversary in $\mathbf{Expt_3}$ is negligible in security parameter λ, since it provides no information on the coin b and thus completes the proof of Theorem 2.

Theorem 3. *Suppose that $i\mathcal{O}$ is a secure indistinguishability obfuscator in Definition 1, then the proposed scheme is master secret-key secure.*

Proof. Suppose that, in the VPRE scheme, the master secret-key sk_i is revealed when the malicious cloud colludes with the delegatee j, then we can construct an $i\mathcal{O}$ distinguisher $\mathcal{B} = (\mathcal{B}_1, \mathcal{B}_2)$ to distinguish the obfuscated circuits in the circuit family. The deployment of $\mathcal{B}$ works as follows:

At first, $\mathcal{B}_1$ constructs a re-encryption key $\mathcal{Q}^{\mathsf{REnc}}$ as in Fig. 5. We denote this circuit as C_0. Next, $\mathcal{B}_1$ constructs a re-encryption key $\mathcal{Q}^{\mathsf{REnc}^*}$ as in Fig. 8. We denote this circuit as C_1. Note that the functionality of these two circuits C_0 and C_1 are completely the same. $\mathcal{B}_1$ outputs (C_0, C_1) and aborts.

$\mathcal{B}_2$ is given $i\mathcal{O}(1^\lambda, C^*)$ from the challenger $\mathcal{C}$. That is, this $i\mathcal{O}(1^\lambda, C^*)$ is either $i\mathcal{O}(1^\lambda, C_0)$ or $i\mathcal{O}(1^\lambda, C_1)$. When the re-encryption key queried from the challenge user to j by the adversary $\mathcal{A}$, $\mathcal{B}_2$ returns the $i\mathcal{O}(1^\lambda, C^*)$ to $\mathcal{A}$ and receives a secret key sk. If $sk = sk^*$, $\mathcal{B}_2$ decides that $i\mathcal{O}(1^\lambda, C^*)$ is C_0. Otherwise, $\mathcal{B}_2$ decicdes that $i\mathcal{O}(1^\lambda, C^*)$ is C_1. Obviously, a *p.p.t* adversary can distinguish between C_0 and C_1 which will lead the constructed algorithm $\mathcal{B}$ to break the indistinguishability security of $i\mathcal{O}$. As we employ the secure $i\mathcal{O}$, we conclude that the propose VPRE scheme satisfies the master secret-key security.

Theorem 4. *Suppose that* $f(\cdot)$ *is a secure one-way function and* $i\mathcal{O}$ *is a secure indistinguishability obfuscator, then the proposed VPRE scheme is verifiably secure of re-encryption.*

Proof. If there exists an adversary $\mathcal{A}$ who can against the verifiable security of re-encryption, we can construct an algorithm $\mathcal{B}$ to break the security of one-way function f.

At first, algorithm $\mathcal{B}$ sets a verify key circuit defined in Fig. 4. Next, $\mathcal{B}$ runs $\mathcal{P}^{\mathsf{Enc}}$ to obtain a challenge ciphertext $ct^* = (\alpha^*, \beta^*)$, and sends the tuple (ct^*, vk) to adversary $\mathcal{A}$. Later, $\mathcal{A}$ outputs $\widehat{ct} = (\alpha', \beta', \sigma)$. By the definition of $\mathcal{B}$ that has computed σ such that $f(\sigma) = y$. We say that $\mathcal{A}$ will win if and only if (1) $m' \neq m$, (2) $m' \neq \bot$ and, (3) $vk(m, r', \sigma) = 1$. If the one-way function f is cryptographically secure, it is easily to show that no $p.p.t$ adversary $\mathcal{A}$ in the above equations with non-negligible advantage.

5   Deployment in Secure Data-Sharing in Cloud

In this section, we present a practical deployment of secure data-sharing that empolys our scheme as the basic primitive.

Assume that user A wants to share his sensitive sports data or holiday photos in his smart watch to his friend circle shown in Fig. 9. In order to keep the privacy of the data, user A needs to encrypt the sensitive data with his own public-key pk_A and then stores ct_A on the clouds [29]. When he is going to share the encrypted data, he can generate a re-encryption key for the friend group, e.g., $rk_{A \to G_1}$, and requests the cloud server to perform the re-encryption program to create the re-encrypted ciphertext so that all the members in the group can obtain the clear sport data or photos by decrypting the re-encrypted ciphertexts.

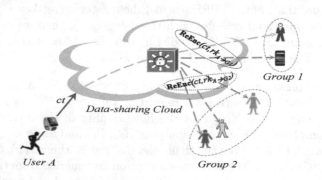

Fig. 9. Scenario of secure data-sharing in clouds

It is easy to see that, using our proposed VPRE as primitive in cloud-based data-sharing environments, it has the following benefits:

1. *Data sharing and storing security.* The sensitive data are encrypted and shared in a secure manner in which the cloud server can perform the sharing program without obtaining any shared clear-data. Actually, the original data are encrypted by the sharer, i.e., using the public key of user A in Fig. 9, and the encrypted data are stored on the cloud.
2. *Sensitive-data protection in the transformation in the presence of white-box access.* If A wants to share his data, he can creates a re-encryption key to the cloud and allows the cloud to perform the data-sharing transformation (i.e., re-encryption program) on inputs the re-encryption key and the encrypted data. We ensure that, even the cloud executes the re-encryption program in white-box manner (i.e., debug the program, monitor the memory and register and set the breakpoints etc.), the cloud server cannot gain any embedded sensitive information such as cleartext data and secret key.
3. *Sharer privacy preservation.* Even the cloud colludes with terminal users, i.e., user in Group 1 and Group 2 in Fig. 9, it cannot obtain the sharer's secret key, which is guaranteed by the master secret-key security of our scheme.
4. *Data-sharing for group users.* We can facilitate a group of users and set a group key, and use this group public-key to create the re-encryption key. Any user in the group can decrypt the re-encrypted ciphertext and it will improve the data-sharing efficiency.
5. *Reasonable allocate the operation.* In our deployment, the time-consuming operations are computed by the cloud, and the operations of terminal user in Group 1 or Group 2 is very fast as it only needs several symmetric PRF operations. We can effectively deploy the data-sharing to light-weight nodes such as Wireless Sensor Networks, Wireless Body Area Network and Internet-of-Things etc.

6   Conclusion

In this paper, we presented a cloud-based data-sharing scheme that is based on a cloud-based re-encryption scheme by using the cryptographic primitives of indistinguishability obfuscation and puncturable pseudorandom functions. Our scheme provides several helpful properties such as white-box security in the secure data-sharing (re-encryption), CCA security of both first-level cipertext and second-ciphertext, re-encryption verifiability of master secret-key security, and reasonable allocation of the operations. Moreover, the proposed scheme is efficient in decryption since it only needs several symmetric PRF operations, which is fruitful to deploy the scheme in light-weight nodes such as WSNs, WBANs and IoTs.

References

1. Asharov, G., Segev, G.: Limits on the power of indistinguishability obfuscation and functional encryption. In: 56th FOCS 2015, pp. 191–209 (2015)
2. Ateniese, G., Fu, K., Green, M., Hohenberger, S.: Improved proxy re-encryption schemes with applications to secure distributed storage. ACM Trans. Inf. Syst. Secur. **9**(1), 1–30 (2006)
3. Bishop, A., Kowalczyk, L., Malkin, T., Pastro, V., Raykova, M., Shi, K.: A simple obfuscation scheme for pattern-matching with wildcards. In: Shacham, H., Boldyreva, A. (eds.) CRYPTO 2018. LNCS, vol. 10993, pp. 731–752. Springer, Cham (2018). https://doi.org/10.1007/978-3-319-96878-0_25
4. Blaze, M., Bleumer, G., Strauss, M.: Divertible protocols and atomic proxy cryptography. In: Nyberg, K. (ed.) EUROCRYPT 1998. LNCS, vol. 1403, pp. 127–144. Springer, Heidelberg (1998). https://doi.org/10.1007/BFb0054122
5. Boneh, D., Gupta, D., Mironov, I., Sahai, A.: Hosting services on an untrusted cloud. In: Oswald, E., Fischlin, M. (eds.) EUROCRYPT 2015. LNCS, vol. 9057, pp. 404–436. Springer, Heidelberg (2015). https://doi.org/10.1007/978-3-662-46803-6_14
6. Boneh, D., Waters, B.: Constrained pseudorandom functions and their applications. In: Sako, K., Sarkar, P. (eds.) ASIACRYPT 2013. LNCS, vol. 8270, pp. 280–300. Springer, Heidelberg (2013). https://doi.org/10.1007/978-3-642-42045-0_15
7. Canetti, R., Hohenberger, S.: Chosen-ciphertext secure proxy re-encryption. In: Proceedings of the 14th ACM Conference on Computer and Communications Security, pp. 185–194. ACM (2007)
8. Chen, M.R., Zhang, X., Li, X.: Comments on Shao-Cao's unidirectional proxy re-encryption scheme from PKC 2009. J. Inf. ci. Eng. **27**(3), 1153–1158 (2011)
9. Chow, S.S.M., Weng, J., Yang, Y., Deng, R.H.: Efficient unidirectional proxy re-encryption. In: Bernstein, D.J., Lange, T. (eds.) AFRICACRYPT 2010. LNCS, vol. 6055, pp. 316–332. Springer, Heidelberg (2010). https://doi.org/10.1007/978-3-642-12678-9_19
10. Cohen, A., Holmgren, J., Nishimaki, R., Vaikuntanathan, V., Wichs, D.: Watermarking cryptographic capabilities. In: 48th ACM STOC 2016, pp. 1115–1127 (2016)
11. Gentry, C., Lewko, A.B., Sahai, A., Waters, B.: Indistinguishability obfuscation from the multilinear subgroup elimination assumption. In: FOCS 2015, pp. 151–170 (2015)
12. Goldreich, O., Goldwasser, S., Micali, S.: How to construct random functions. J. ACM **33**(4), 792–807 (1986)
13. Garg, S., Gentry, C., Halevi, S., Raykova, M., Sahai, A., Waters, B.: Candidate indistinguishability obfuscation and functional encrytion for all circuits. In: FOCS 2013, pp. 40–49. IEEE (2013)
14. Gaurav, P., Purushothama, B.R.: Proxy visible re-encryption scheme with application to e-mail forwarding. In: Proceedings of the 10th International Conference on Security of Information and Networks (SIN 2017), pp. 212–217 (2017)
15. Gaurav, P., Purushothama, B.R.: On efficient access control mechanisms in hierarchy using unidirectional and transitive proxy re-encryption schemes. In: Proceedings of the 14th International Joint Conference on e-Business and Telecommunications (ICETE 2017), pp. 519–524 (2017)

16. Komargodski, I., Yogev, E.: Another step towards realizing random oracles: non-malleable point obfuscation. In: Nielsen, J.B., Rijmen, V. (eds.) EUROCRYPT 2018. LNCS, vol. 10820, pp. 259–279. Springer, Cham (2018). https://doi.org/10.1007/978-3-319-78381-9_10

17. Kitagawa, F., Nishimaki, R., Tanaka, K.: Obfustopia built on secret-key functional encryption. In: Nielsen, J.B., Rijmen, V. (eds.) EUROCRYPT 2018. LNCS, vol. 10821, pp. 603–648. Springer, Cham (2018). https://doi.org/10.1007/978-3-319-78375-8_20

18. Hanaoka, G., et al.: Generic construction of chosen ciphertext secure proxy re-encryption. In: Dunkelman, O. (ed.) CT-RSA 2012. LNCS, vol. 7178, pp. 349–364. Springer, Heidelberg (2012). https://doi.org/10.1007/978-3-642-27954-6_22

19. Hohenberger, S., Rothblum, G.N., Shelat, Vaikuntanathan, V.: Securely obfuscating re-encryption. In: Vadhan, S.P. (ed.) TCC 2007. LNCS, vol. 4392, pp. 233–252. Springer, Heidelberg (2007). https://doi.org/10.1007/978-3-540-70936-7_13

20. Hohenberger, S., Koppula, V., Waters, B.: Adaptively secure puncturable pseudo-random functions in the standard model. In: Iwata, T., Cheon, J.H. (eds.) ASIACRYPT 2015. LNCS, vol. 9452, pp. 79–102. Springer, Heidelberg (2015). https://doi.org/10.1007/978-3-662-48797-6_4

21. Isshiki, T., Nguyen, M.H., Tanaka, K.: Proxy re-encryption in a stronger security model extended from CT-RSA2012. In: Dawson, E. (ed.) CT-RSA 2013. LNCS, vol. 7779, pp. 277–292. Springer, Heidelberg (2013). https://doi.org/10.1007/978-3-642-36095-4_18

22. Kirshanova, E.: Proxy re-encryption from lattices. In: Krawczyk, H. (ed.) PKC 2014. LNCS, vol. 8383, pp. 77–94. Springer, Heidelberg (2014). https://doi.org/10.1007/978-3-642-54631-0_5

23. Lai, J., Huang, Z., Au, M.H., Mao, X.: Constant-size CCA-secure multi-hop uni-directional proxy re-encryption from indistinguishability obfuscation. In: Susilo, W., Yang, G. (eds.) ACISP 2018. LNCS, vol. 10946, pp. 805–812. Springer, Cham (2018). https://doi.org/10.1007/978-3-319-93638-3_49

24. Libert, B., Vergnaud, D.: Unidirectional chosen-ciphertext secure proxy re-encryption. In: Cramer, R. (ed.) PKC 2008. LNCS, vol. 4939, pp. 360–379. Springer, Heidelberg (2008). https://doi.org/10.1007/978-3-540-78440-1_21

25. Liu, M., Wu, Y., Chang, J., Xue, R., Guo, W.: Verifiable proxy re-encryption from indistinguishability obfuscation. In: Qing, S., Okamoto, E., Kim, K., Liu, D. (eds.) ICICS 2015. LNCS, vol. 9543, pp. 363–378. Springer, Cham (2016). https://doi.org/10.1007/978-3-319-29814-6_31

26. Ohata, S., Kawai, Y., Matsuda, T., Hanaoka, G., Matsuura, K.: Re-encryption verifiability: how to detect malicious activities of a proxy in proxy re-encryption. In: Nyberg, K. (ed.) CT-RSA 2015. LNCS, vol. 9048, pp. 410–428. Springer, Cham (2015). https://doi.org/10.1007/978-3-319-16715-2_22

27. Sahai, A., Waters, B.: How to use indistinguishability obfuscation: deniable encryption, and more. In: STOC 2014, pp. 475–484. ACM (2014)

28. Zhang, M., Jiang, Y., Mu, Y., Susilo, W.: Obfuscating re-encryption algorithm with flexible and controllable multi-hop on untrusted outsourcing server. IEEE Access 5(1), 26419–26434 (2017)

29. Zhang, M., Yao, Y., Li, B., Tang, C.: Accountable mobile e-commerce scheme in intelligent cloud system transactions. J. Ambient Intell. Humaniz. Comput. 9(6), 1889–1899 (2018)

An Encrypted Database with Enforced Access Control and Blockchain Validation

Zhimei Sui[1,2(✉)], Shangqi Lai[2(✉)], Cong Zuo[2(✉)], Xingliang Yuan[2(✉)],
Joseph K. Liu[2(✉)], and Haifeng Qian[1(✉)]

[1] East China Normal University, Shanghai, China
zhimeisui@gmail.com, hfqian@cs.ecnu.edu.cn
[2] Monash University, Clayton, Melbourne, Australia
{shangqi.lai,cong.zuo1,xingliang.yuan,joseph.liu}@monash.edu

Abstract. Data privacy and integrity is top of mind for modern data applications. To tackle with the above issue, we propose an encrypted database system with access control capabilities and blockchain validation in this paper. Compared to the existing encrypted database system, our design proposes a proxy-free architecture, which avoids the need for a trusted proxy for access control. In order to protect the integrity of user data, our system leverages the blockchain technology to realize a tampering protection mechanism. The mechanism ensures that modification logging is compulsory and public-available but hardened. Users can validate and easily detect the tampered data. Finally, we implement a prototype system and conduct evaluations on each component of the proposed system.

Keywords: Encrypted database · Data privacy · Blockchain · Access control

1 Introduction

Outsourced data storage provides a convenient way to help its users manage and access their data. However, with weekly data security scandals [10], individuals are becoming more and more aware and concerned about the privacy and integrity of their data.

This illustrates the needs to

- Encrypt data in an outsourced database because compromises can still occur in this database with standard security mechanisms such as data access control and database trace logging.
- Provide a data validation mechanism to avoid the tampering on the outsourced data because the cloud provider can fully control the outsourced data and intentionally modify it for some malicious purposes.

In this work, we propose a decentralized and encrypted database with enforced access control and blockchain validation to protect both the privacy and integrity of data in outsourced database.

© Springer Nature Switzerland AG 2019
F. Guo et al. (Eds.): Inscrypt 2018, LNCS 11449, pp. 260–273, 2019.
https://doi.org/10.1007/978-3-030-14234-6_14

To protect the data privacy, our system follows the paradigm of encrypted database [11,21,24] to encrypt the data in database before outsourcing it. We then design a search algorithm to support SQL-like queries over the encrypted database. In addition, our system implements fine-grained access control over columns by Attribute-based Encryption (ABE). Each user is associated with specific attributes and the user can only access the column if its attributes match with the access policy. Compared to the existing SQL-enabled encrypted database system like CryptDB [21], our system leverages a proxy-free architecture: the users in our system can communicate with the remote database directly. The proxy-free architecture eliminates the intermediate server to avoid the possible service interruption in the event of proxy failure. Also, it makes the system more suitable for cloud-based scenarios as it allows geologically distributed users to access the cloud database without connecting to a fixed proxy in advance.

In order to resolve the integrity concerns on the encrypted database, we combine our encrypted database system with the blockchain technology. More specifically, all modifications and the corresponding logs are recorded in the blockchain. Due to the public-availability and unchangeable properties of the blockchain, our system ensures that all authorized modifications are trackable to the users. Besides, any unauthorized change leads to record inconsistency between database and blockchain which helps the users to detect the tampering behavior on their data.

Our Contributions. In this paper, we focus on the encrypted database and the confidentiality of its data. Our contributions are listed as follows:

- We propose a distributed encrypted database with Advanced Encryption Standard (AES). It ensures the confidentiality of data while being efficient in encryption.
- Our system implements the access control by Attribute-based Encryption (ABE). Specifically, we employ CP-ABE [26] where a given ciphertext can only be decrypted by a user with corresponding attributes.
- Our system provides a method to validate data via the blockchain technology, such that it is easy for users to validate the results from queries made to the database. Noted that most of the blockchain protocols are compatible with our system. In our implementation, we employ BigchainDB [16] as the underlying blockchain protocol.
- We construct an attack model and use it to analyse the security of our system. We have also identified potential threats to our system from the analysis.
- We implement our system on MySQL [19] and evaluate its performance and we compare the results with a plaintext implementation.

1.1   Related Work

Encrypted Database and Search Methods. Database encryption [4,5,22] schemes are used to transform data stored in a database into "ciphertext" that is incomprehensible without being decrypted firstly. The purpose of database encryption is to protect the data stored in a database from being accessed by individuals with "malicious" intentions. There are multiple techniques and technologies available for the encrypted database. For example, CryptDB [21] is an encrypted database with encrypted query processing. It protects the confidentiality of data from the remote database management system. Searchable encryption [12,23,25,27] is a search protocol for ciphertext, which is proposed to improve the availability of encrypted database. The latest searchable encryption scheme is able to support conjunctive queries [12,25] and range queries [27]. In addition, the dynamic update on searchable encryption database [23,27] and search result verification [25] are also being studied in prior work. Note that the above schemes require keys to be generated by a centralized source.

Blockchain. Blockchain, is well-known as Bitcoin [20], has influence in almost every aspect of our society from the economy, health care to industries and transportation [7,14,17,20]. The blockchain part of our system is related to some existing works [1,2,15,28]. These works use the blockchain with various methods to achieve privacy in database. IBM's blockchain Everledger [15] locates each device with a specific SSL certificate, which is used in the blockchain to protect against tampering. However, a centralized organization is still needed in the above system. Damiano et al. propose a database system which implements the access control with attributes on the blockchain [28], but their work only focuses on how to realise a decentralized access control in the system. Another works [1,2] solve the search problem in the blockchain. In specific, private keyword search is devised by a blockchain-based secure data storage in [2], and it is further extended to support private search in distributed network via the blockchain technology [1].

1.2 Organization

We start by introducing some standard notations in Sect. 2. Then, we formalise the system framework and the corresponding attack model in Sect. 3. In Sect. 4, we give a brief overview of our proposed system and its security analysis. Next, we present our implementation in Sect. 5 . Finally, we give the conclusion and discuss our future work in Sect. 6.

2 Preliminaries

In this paper, λ is the security parameter and $[n]$ denotes a set of integers $\{1, \cdots, n\}$. To store the encrypted data of a table TB which has r rows and c columns as illustrated in Table 1, we need a dictionary DX and a new table ETB, which is the same size as TB's. Dictionary DX is used to store the column identifier ID_j ($j \in [c]$) of TB and the ABE ciphertext CT_j pairs, where CT_j is the encryption of the private key key_j used in symmetric key encryption (SKE). For a data value $data_{i,j}$ (the i-th row and j-th column, $i \in [r]$ and $j \in [c]$) in TB, we use a SKE with key_j[1] to encrypt it and store the SKE ciphertext $C_{i,j}$ in the i-th row and j-th column of ETB.

---

[1] For every column, we use a new private key key_j to encrypt the data.

Table 1. An example of TB

Student ID	Name	Age	Sex	Grade	⋯
00001	Alice	18	Female	80	⋯
00002	Bob	17	Male	78	⋯
00003	Charlie	18	Male	88	⋯
00004	Dave	19	Male	79	⋯

2.1 Ciphertext-Policy Attribute Based Encryption (CP-ABE)

Ciphertext-Policy Attributed-based encryption (CP-ABE) [26] consists the following algorithms:

- $(pp, msk) \leftarrow$ ASetup$(1^\lambda, \mathbf{U})$: This algorithm takes as input the security parameter λ and attribute universe $\mathbf{U}$. It outputs the public parameter pp and a master secret key msk.
- $usk_{\mathbf{S}} \leftarrow$ AKGen$(pp, msk, \mathbf{S})$: This algorithm takes as input the public parameter pp, the master secret key msk and a user attribute set $\mathbf{S}$, where $\mathbf{S} \subseteq \mathbf{U}$. It outputs a user secret key $usk_{\mathbf{S}}$.
- CT $\leftarrow$ AEnc$(pp, m, policy)$: This algorithm takes as input the public parameter pp, the message m and a policy $policy$. It outputs a ciphertext CT.
- $(m$ or $\perp) \leftarrow$ ADec$(pp, usk_{\mathbf{S}}, \text{CT})$: This algorithm takes as input the public parameter pp, the user secret key $usk_{\mathbf{S}}$ and the ciphertext CT. It outputs the message m if $\mathbf{S}$ satisfy the underlying policy $policy$. Otherwise, it outputs $\perp$.

2.2 Symmetric Key Encryption (SKE)

Symmetric Key Encryption (SKE) [6,18] consists the following algorithms:

- $key \leftarrow$ SSetup(1^λ): This algorithm takes as input the security parameter λ. It outputs a private key key.
- C $\leftarrow$ SEnc$(key, data)$: This algorithm takes as input the private key key and the data $data$. It outputs the ciphertext C.
- $data \leftarrow$ SDec(key, C): This algorithm takes as input the private key key and the ciphertext C. It outputs the data $data$.

In this paper, we use the deterministic SKE (e.g. AES [18] in CBC mode with same IV). The client can send an encrypted data to the server, the server can search the ciphertext where the underlying data and private key are the same by comparing every ciphertext in ETB.

2.3 Notations

The list of notations used is given in Table 2.

Table 2. Notations (used in our constructions)

TB	A table (e.g. Table 1)
ETB	An encrypted form of TB
DX	A dictionary
r	The number of rows of TB
c	The number of columns of TB
ID_i	i-th row identifier
ID_j	j-th column identifier
K	The private keys of SKE which are used to encrypt the columns of TB
Policy	A set of policies
Row	All satisfied rows of a user query
H	A hash function
row_i	The i-th row of ETB

3 Framework and Attack Model

In this section, we formalize the system model and attack model considered in this paper.

3.1 Our Framework

Figure 1 shows the architecture of our encrypted database supporting enforced access control and blockchain validation. There are four main entities in our framework: Data Owners (DOs), Cloud, Blockchain and Users.

- Data Owner (DO): DO is responsible for encrypting his/her data (TB) and sending the encrypted data to the cloud. In addition, he also needs to generate the user secret keys which enable users to search for certain encrypted data. Specifically, DO firstly generates c SKE private keys and uses them to encrypt every column of TB separately. Furthermore, DO publishes the hash values of rows to the blockchain. Then, DO generates the public parameter pp and master secret key msk of CP-ABE. After that, DO uses the pp and a specify *policy* to encrypt the private keys. Finally, DO stores the column identifier and CP-ABE ciphertext pairs in the dictionary.

- Cloud: Cloud stores the database cluster for DO. Upon receiving a search query from a user, Cloud retrieves the satisfied rows of ETB by comparing the SKE ciphertext in the search query with the one in ETB[2]. Then, Cloud validates the hash values of these rows with the hash values in the blockchain. Finally, Cloud returns the rows which has the same hash values in the blockchain to the user.
- Blockchain: Blockchain is used to store the hash values of the rows and database operations which can prevent data from tampering. In addition, each DO is supposed to commit the hash values of all updated data and operation log to Blockchain. After a user get the results from Cloud, these blockchain records provide a validation mechanism: if there is a value on the blockchain, which is the same as the hash values of search results, the user will accept the search results.
- User: If a user wants to issue search queries, he firstly needs to get his user secret key from the DO which corresponds to his/her attribute set. Then, he can use this key to get the SKE private keys from the dictionary entries where the attribute set satisfies the policy of the corresponding CP-ABE ciphertexts. After that, he can use SKE and these private keys to encrypt data and send the SKE ciphertext to the server.

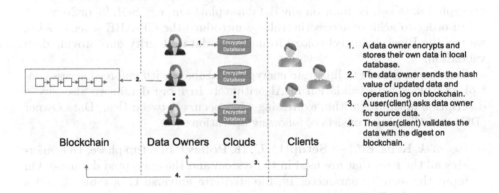

Fig. 1. Architecture of our framework

3.2   Attack Model

In this paper, we consider the following attack models:

- Access Control: The adversary cannot search the columns which he/she is not authorized to search. In other words, a user cannot decrypt a ciphertext without permission in our model, as the access control protocol asks for the correct attributes.

---

[2] Since SKE is deterministic, the SKE ciphertexts are the same if the underlying data is identical.

- Tamper Protection: A malicious node cannot modify the history of blockchain without being known. It is possible for a node to change a blockchain history locally, however, these tampered records will not be accepted by the majority of this system.
- SPOF Protection: Single point of failure (SPOF) cannot bring an obvious problem to the blockchain network. When a malicious or innocent node failed in the network, users still can get the response from the other active nodes.

4 Construction

4.1 Overview

Blockchain technology allows decentralization which can ease the reliance on traditional centralized system. In this section, we propose a scheme that realizes a decentralized encrypted database. Furthermore, it also supports decentralized access control and blockchain validation. This enables data owners to encrypt their data locally and share the encrypted data with a specific group of users.

Our construction contains the following properties: (1) a decentralized encrypted database, (2) the access control over the encrypted database and (3) the validation of the encrypted data. In particular, our construction encrypts the database with SKE and uploads the ciphertext to Cloud. The storage of the encrypted data can be built on any database platform, e.g. SQL [3] or NoSQL[3].

In order to achieve access control, we introduce the CP-ABE scheme. Also, we use the Blockchain technology to maintain data integrity and provide data validation.

Now we are ready to illustrate encrypted database with enforced access control and blockchain validation in Algorithm 1. In more detail, we also give a description of this algorithm expressing what occurs between User, Data Owner (DO) and Cloud. It consists of following operations:

- $(pp, msk, \mathbf{K}, \text{DX}, \text{ETB}) \leftarrow \mathbf{Setup}(1^\lambda, \mathbf{U}, \text{TB}, \mathbf{Policy})$: In setup phase, DO generates all the keys that are used in the system and the encrypted database. On input the security parameter 1^λ, the attribute universe $\mathbf{U}$, a table TB and a set of policies $\mathbf{Policy}$, DO generates $(pp, msk, \mathbf{K}, \text{DX}, \text{ETB})$, where pp and msk are the public parameter and master secret key of a CP-ABE, respectively. $\mathbf{K}$ are private keys of SKE. DX is a dictionary which stores the column identifier and the encrypted private key pairs. ETB is the encryption of table TB which stores the encrypted data and is sent to Cloud. Note that, for each DO, this algorithm is only executed once.
- $usk_\mathbf{S} \leftarrow \mathbf{UKGen}(pp, msk, \mathbf{S})$: In user secret key generation phase, the user sends a request with his attribute set $\mathbf{S}$ to DO. Then, DO takes the input as the public parameter pp, master secret key $mask$ and the user attribute set $\mathbf{S}$ and outputs the user secret key $usk_\mathbf{S}$ and sends it to the user. Once the user receives his/her user secret key, he/she then has the permission to decrypt the specific ciphertext owned by the DO.

---

[3] The NoSQL database has a wide variety of data models, including key-value, document, columnar and graph formats.

- **Row** ← **Search**(usk_S, ID_j, $data$, DX, ETB): In the search phrase, this protocol is executed between a user and Cloud. Cloud is used to store the encrypted database for DO. The user uses his/her user secret key to get the column key key_j. Then, he/she uses key_j to encrypt the data value $data'$ and issues a search query with the encrypted data to Cloud. If the data value $data'$ is equal to the data value $data$ stored on Cloud, then the corresponding ciphertexts C are equal. Because they are encrypted by using deterministic SKE. After that, Cloud retrieves the satisfied rows and sends them to the user. Finally, the user can validate the rows in validation phase.
- $state$ ← **Val**(ID_i, row_i): In the validation phrase, the user connects with several nodes who store the records of blockchain. This algorithm is used to validate whether the retrieved data is valid or not. On input the row identifier ID_i and the row row_i, it compares the input hash values and the hash values that stored on the blockchain and outputs "true" if the row_i has a corresponding hash value on the blockchain or "false" otherwise. If the algorithm outputs "true", the data is accepted by the user. Otherwise, the data is tampered by Cloud.

4.2 Security Discussion

Theorem 1. *Our encrypted database with enforced access control and blockchain validation can achieve* Access Control.

Under the CP-ABE scheme, DO only allows a user to decrypt a ciphertext with the specified user secret keys. If the attribute set of a user secret key does not satisfy the policy that is embedded in the ciphertext, the user cannot decrypt the ciphertext. Thus, the user cannot get the private key of SKE to issue search queries. Hence, Access Control of the encrypted database is achieved.

Theorem 2. *Our encrypted database with enforced access control and blockchain validation can achieve* Tamper Protection.

Blockchain provides the data integrity and unchangeable protocol to support the tamper protection. DO needs to commit all hash values of the database operation log to the blockchain, and each user achieves the validation by trusting the record on blockchain, which is assumed to be proven safe. Therefore, anyone in this system is not able to change the blockchain records that have been accepted by the majority.

Theorem 3. *Our encrypted database with enforced access control and blockchain validation can achieve* SPOF Protection.

Blockchain network is a peer-to-peer network, where nodes in the network are equal peer nodes acting as both a "client" and a "server". User usually sends the request to several nodes in the meantime, and the availability of the system is not affected by the failure of a single node or a minority of nodes.

Algorithm 1. Blockchain Access Control

Setup$(1^\lambda, \mathbf{U}, \text{TB}, \mathbf{Policy})$
Input Security parameter 1^λ, attribute universe $\mathbf{U}$, a Table TB and a set of policies **Policy**
Output $(pp, msk, \mathbf{K}, \text{DX}, \text{ETB})$
1: $(pp, msk) \leftarrow \text{ASetup}(1^\lambda, \mathbf{U})$
2: DX $\leftarrow$ empty dictionary
3: $\mathbf{K} \leftarrow$ empty array
4: **for** $j \in [c]$ **do**
5:     $key_j \leftarrow \text{SSetup}(1^\lambda)$
6:     $\mathbf{K}[j] \leftarrow key_j$
7:     $\text{CT}_j \leftarrow \text{AEnc}(pp, key_j, policy)$ ▷ $policy \in \mathbf{Policy}$
8:     $\text{DX}[\text{ID}_j] \leftarrow \text{CT}_j$
9: **end for**
10: ETB $\leftarrow$ empty table
11: **for** $i \in [r], j \in [c]$ **do**
12:     $\text{C}_{i,j} \leftarrow \text{SEnc}(\mathbf{K}[j], data_{i,j})$
13:     $\text{ETB}_{i,j} \leftarrow \text{C}_{i,j}$
14: **end for**
15: **for** $i \in [r]$ **do**
16:     $h_{row_i} \leftarrow H(row_i)$ ▷ row_i is i-th row of ETB and H is a hash function.
17:     Put h_{row_i} with row identifier ID_i to the blockchain.
18: **end for**
19: **return** $(pp, msk, \mathbf{K}, \text{DX}, \text{ETB})$

UKGen$(pp, msk, \mathbf{S})$
Input Public parameter pp, master secret key msk, and attribute set $\mathbf{S}$
Output User secret key $usk_\mathbf{S}$
1: $usk_\mathbf{S} \leftarrow \text{AKGen}(pp, msk, S)$

2: **return** $usk_\mathbf{S}$

Val(ID_i, row_i)
Input Row identifier ID_i, row_i
Output A state $state$
1: $state \leftarrow False$
2: $h_{row_i} \leftarrow H(row_i)$
3: Get h_{row} with the row identifier ID_i from the blockchain
4: **if** $h_{row_i} == h_{row}$ **then**
5:     $state = True$
6: **end if**
7: **return** $state$

Search$(usk_\mathbf{S}, \text{ID}_j, data, \text{DX}, \text{ETB})$
Client:
Input $usk_\mathbf{S}$, ID_j, $data$, DX
Output The encrypted data C
1: $\text{CT}_j \leftarrow \text{DX}[\text{ID}_j]$
2: $key_j \leftarrow \text{ADec}(pp, usk_\mathbf{S}, \text{CT}_j)$
3: $\text{C} \leftarrow \text{SEnc}(key_j, data)$
4: Send C to the server.
Server:
Input C, ETB
Output Satisfied rows **Row**
5: **Row** $\leftarrow$ empty set
6: **for** $i \in c$ **do**
7:     Get $\text{C}_{i,j}$ from ETB
8:     **if** $\text{C} == \text{C}_{i,j}$ **then**
9:         Get (ID_i, row_i) from ETB
10:         **Row** $\leftarrow$ **Row** $\cup (\text{ID}_i, row_i)$
11:     **end if**
12: **end for**
13: Send **Row** to the user.

---

5   Experimentation

In this section, we evaluate the performance of three building blocks of our proposed system: the latency when inserting data and querying on MySQL, the transaction latency of blockchain and the performance of ABE. In Blockchain tests, we build a blockchain platform based on BigchainDB, which inherits its throughput, high capacity, low latency, and a full featured efficient NoSQL query [8,9] language. Our system runs on a MacBook Pro with 3.1 GHz Intel Core i5 processor, 8 GB 2133 MHz LPDDR3 memory, macintosh HD of Disk, where MySQL 8.0.11 server and BigchainDB 1.3.0 proxy and clients are installed, using Java as the main programming language.

Performance of MySQL. We used two datasets of different sizes, containing 1,000 and 100,000 rows respectively. Firstly, the smaller dataset is input to the system to run 1 epoch, which means 1,000 times for each insert and query operation test with plaintext and SKE ciphertext on MySQL separately. The results are shown in Figs. 2 and 3. To get rid of the influence of data preprocessing, the top 10 results of each text type are dropped. In Fig. 2, the lines represent latency per insert on MySQL for ciphertext and plaintext, respectively, where the solid line represents plaintext and the dashed line represents ciphertext. We can see that more than 90% of the ciphertext insert operations finished within 0.002 s, while almost 100% of the plaintext insert operations cost less than 0.002 s. Figure 3 shows the query latency on MySQL of AES-based ciphertext and plaintext. It is easy to see that all query operations of plaintext complete within 0.01 s and ciphertext query operation need more than 0.02 s. The extra latency of ciphertext operations compared with the operations in plaintext in both charts are caused by the encryption/decryption time. Furthermore, we run 100,000 insert and query operations on another dataset with 100,000 rows in the same manner as the former one. Figures 4 and 5 show the latency of insert and query operations, respectively. It can be seen that most latency of insert operation in Fig. 4 is 0.001 s, and it is about a 50% decrease compared to the results of the smaller dataset. In Fig. 5, as we can see, the results show that most latency timings are similar to the small dataset for both the plaintext and ciphertext.

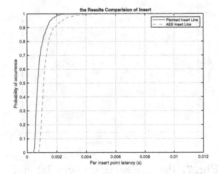

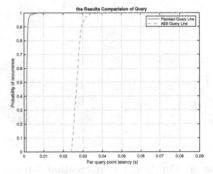

Fig. 2. Insert comparison test with 1,000 datasets

Fig. 3. Query comparison test with 1,000 datasets

The Latency of BigchainDB. Figures 6 and 7 show the transaction creation and query latency on BigchainDB. Similar to the tests above, we run transaction creation and query operations for 100 times and choose the 80 middle results for each operation to for out graphs. The latency of each transaction creation operation is shown in Fig. 6. We can see that 90% of the operations could be performed within 0.02 s. It shows that our system achieves higher efficiency compared to the most of the Blockchain-based projects. Figure 7 show the latency for query operations. We can see a completed query operation always costs more

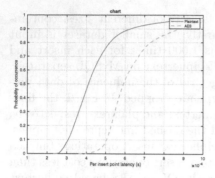

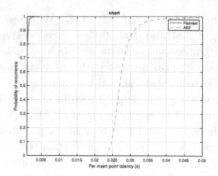

Fig. 4. Insert comparison test with 100,000 datasets

Fig. 5. Query comparison test with 100,000 datasets

than 8 s, which is due to the fact that the entire chain will be scanned for each query request. BigchainDB has low latency in transaction creation and query compared to the majority of the current Blockchain projects [13,20]. Furthermore, BigchainDB has no PoW consensus, and we build the server and client locally. So there is no network latency.

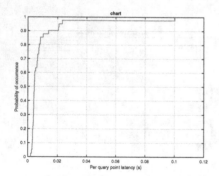

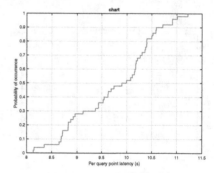

Fig. 6. Per transaction creation latency on BigchainDB

Fig. 7. Per transaction query latency on BigchainDB

The Performance of CP-ABE. We use the JPBC with the Type A elliptic curve. Table 3 shows the performance of CP-ABE algorithm [26] for attributes of different sizes. In this table, the notations U stands for the attribute numbers. We set U to 4, 8, 16, 32, 64 and run the algorithm 10 times and get the average running time for each phase.

Table 3. The running time of CP-ABE algorithm (ms)

Attributes number	Setup time	KeyGen time	Encrypt time	Decrypt time
U = 4	34.9	63.4	133.0	52.5
U = 8	38.9	103.6	255.8	102.2
U = 16	52.3	189.1	502.2	192.9
U = 32	76.2	350.6	1012.3	379.8
U = 64	124.4	685.1	2036.9	782.4

6 Conclusion

In this paper, we review the encrypted database, blockchain technology, symmetric encryption and attribute-based encryption. Then, we propose a distributed database with enforced access control and blockchain validation. Finally, we implement a prototype system and evaluate the performance of our system in each part.

Our scheme shows that the personal data can be stored and protected by their data owner, which means a person can deal with their data without involving third parties in the trend of data collecting and analyzing. Finally, we discuss several possible threats from different attacks which are proven secure. Furthermore, we want to implement this scheme with smart contracts to make it possible for dynamic data access control, which means the data owner can share the old data with a new member without the need to update their database.

Acknowledgments. The authors are grateful to the Inscrypt 2018 anonymous reviewers for their helpful comments. This work is supported by the National Natural Science Foundation of China (No. 61571191), the "Dawn" Program of Shanghai Municipal Education Commission (No. 16SG21) and the Monash-HKPU-Collinstar Blockchain Research Lab.

References

1. Cai, C., Yuan, X., Wang, C.: Hardening distributed and encrypted keyword search via Blockchain. In: IEEE PAC 2017, pp. 119–128 (2017)
2. Cai, C., Yuan, X., Wang, C.: Towards trustworthy and private keyword search in encrypted decentralized storage. In: IEEE ICC 2017, pp. 1–7 (2017)
3. Date, C.J., Darwen, H.: A guide to the SQL Standard: A User's Guide to The Standard Relational Language SQL. Addison-Wesley, Boston (1989)
4. Davida, G.I., Wells, D.L., Kam, J.B.: A database encryption system with subkeys. ACM Trans. Database Syst. **6**(2), 312–328 (1981)
5. Davida, G.I., Wells, D.L., Kam, J.B.: Database Encryption and Decryption Circuit and Method Using Subkeys. U.S. Patent 4,375,579 (1983)
6. Delfs, H., Knebl, H.: Symmetric-key encryption. Introduction to Cryptography, pp. 11–31 (2007)

7. Friedlmaier, M., Tumasjan, A., Welpe, I.: Disrupting industries With Blockchain: the industry. Venture Capital Funding, and Regional Distribution of Blockchain Ventures (2016). Accessed 16 Jan 2017
8. Han, J., Haihong, E., Le, G., Du, J.: Survey on NoSQL Database. In: IEEE ICPCA 2011, pp. 363–366 (2011)
9. Hecht, R., Jablonski, S.: NoSQL evaluation: a use case oriented survey. In: IEEE ICCSC 2011, pp. 336–341 (2011)
10. Information is Beautiful: World's Biggest Data Breaches (2018). http://www. informationisbeautiful.net/visualizations/worlds-biggest-data-breaches-hacks/
11. Kamara, S., Lauter, K.: Cryptographic cloud storage. In: Sion, R., Curtmola, R., Dietrich, S., Kiayias, A., Miret, J.M., Sako, K., Sebé, F. (eds.) FC 2010. LNCS, vol. 6054, pp. 136–149. Springer, Heidelberg (2010). https://doi.org/10.1007/978-3-642-14992-4_13
12. Lai, S., et al.: Result pattern hiding searchable encryption for conjunctive queries. In: ACM CCS 2018, pp. 745–762 (2018)
13. Lee, C.: Litecoin (2011). https://litecoin.org
14. Lei, A., Cruickshank, H., Cao, Y., Asuquo, P., Ogah, C.P.A., Sun, Z.: Blockchain-based dynamic key management for heterogeneous intelligent transportation systems. IEEE Internet Things J. 4(6), 1832–1843 (2017)
15. Lomas, N.: Everledger is Using Blockchain to Combat Fraud, Starting with Diamonds (2015). https://techcrunch.com/2015/06/29/everledger
16. McConaghy, T., et al.: BigchainDB: A Scalable Blockchain Database (2016). https://mycourses.aalto.fi/pluginfile.php/378362/mod_resource/content/1/bigchaindb-whitepaper.pdf
17. Mettler, M.: Blockchain technology in healthcare: the revolution starts here. In: IEEE HealthCom 2016, pp. 1–3 (2016)
18. Miller, F.P., Vandome, A.F., McBrewster, J.: Advanced Encryption Standard. Alpha Press, Orlando (2009)
19. MySQL, A.: MySQL Database Server (2004). http://www.mysql.com
20. Nakamoto, S.: Bitcoin: A Peer-to-Peer Electronic Cash System (2008). https://bitcoin.org/bitcoin.pdf
21. Popa, R.A., Redfield, C., Zeldovich, N., Balakrishnan, H.: CryptDB: protecting confidentiality with encrypted query processing. In: ACM SOSP 2011, pp. 85–100 (2011)
22. Shmueli, E., Vaisenberg, R., Elovici, Y., Glezer, C.: Database encryption: an overview of contemporary challenges and design considerations. ACM SIGMOD Record 38(3), 29–34 (2010)
23. Sun, S.F., et al.: Practical backward-secure searchable encryption from symmetric puncturable encryption. In: ACM CCS 2018, pp. 763–780 (2018)
24. Wang, C., Chow, S.S., Wang, Q., Ren, K., Lou, W.: Privacy-preserving public auditing for secure cloud storage. IEEE Trans. Comput. 62(2), 362–375 (2013)
25. Wang, J., Chen, X., Sun, S.-F., Liu, J.K., Au, M.H., Zhan, Z.-H.: Towards efficient verifiable conjunctive keyword search for large encrypted database. In: Lopez, J., Zhou, J., Soriano, M. (eds.) ESORICS 2018, Part II. LNCS, vol. 11099, pp. 83–100. Springer, Cham (2018). https://doi.org/10.1007/978-3-319-98989-1_5
26. Waters, B.: Ciphertext-policy attribute-based encryption: an expressive, efficient, and provably secure realization. In: Catalano, D., Fazio, N., Gennaro, R., Nicolosi, A. (eds.) PKC 2011. LNCS, vol. 6571, pp. 53–70. Springer, Heidelberg (2011). https://doi.org/10.1007/978-3-642-19379-8_4

27. Zuo, C., Sun, S.-F., Liu, J.K., Shao, J., Pieprzyk, J.: Dynamic searchable symmetric encryption schemes supporting range queries with forward (and backward) security. In: Lopez, J., Zhou, J., Soriano, M. (eds.) ESORICS 2018, Part II. LNCS, vol. 11099, pp. 228–246. Springer, Cham (2018). https://doi.org/10.1007/978-3-319-98989-1_12

28. Zyskind, G., Nathan, O., et al.: Decentralizing privacy: using Blockchain to Protect Personal Data. In: IEEE SPW 2015, pp. 180–184 (2015)

Using Blockchain to Control Access to Cloud Data

Jiale Guo[1], Wenzhuo Yang[1], Kwok-Yan Lam[1(✉)], and Xun Yi[2]

[1] Nanyang Technological University, Singapore, Singapore
kwokyan.lam@ntu.edu.sg
[2] RMIT University, Melbourne, Australia
xun.yi@rmit.edu.au

Abstract. As cloud storage becomes more common, data security is an increasing concern. In this paper, we propose a new approach to control access to the user's data stored in the cloud with the state-of-the-arts decentralized blockchain technology. In general, an access control solution for cloud data involves three components: authentication, authorization and auditing. It is expensive for the cloud server to ensure authentication, authorization and auditing for access control of the user's data in cloud computing environment. In addition, it is hard to prevent the malicious cloud server from access to the user's data and disclose the user's privacy. Our approach distributes the access control tasks for authentication, authorization and auditing to a network of nodes like bitcoin. In particular, we keep the auditing records in the transparent blockchain. In addition, we employ the Shamir secret sharing scheme to manage the encryption key for cloud users.

Keywords: Access control · Blockchain · Cloud computing · Shamir secret sharing

1 Introduction

Companies have been increasing their use of services like Google Drive for some time, and lots of individual users also store files on Dropbox, Box, Amazon Drive, Microsoft OneDrive and the like. They are no doubt concerned about keeping their information private. Millions more users might store data online if they were more certain of its security.

A complete access control solution for cloud data involves three components [9]: authentication, authorization and auditing. Authentication refers to unique identifying information from each data user, generally in the form of a user-name and password. System administrators monitor and add or delete authorized users from the system. Authorization refers to the process of adding or denying individual user access to a computer network and its resources. Users may be given different authorization levels that limit their access to the cloud data. Authorization determination may be based on geographical location restrictions,

© Springer Nature Switzerland AG 2019
F. Guo et al. (Eds.): Inscrypt 2018, LNCS 11449, pp. 274–288, 2019.
https://doi.org/10.1007/978-3-030-14234-6_15

date or time-of-day restrictions, frequency of logins or multiple logins by single individuals or entities. Other associated types of authorization service include route assignments, IP address filtering, bandwidth traffic management and encryption. Auditing refers to the record-keeping and tracking of user activities on a computer network. For a given time period this may include, but is not limited to, real-time auditing of time spent accessing the cloud data, the network services employed or accessed, capacity and trend analysis, network cost allocations, billing data, login data for user authentication and authorization, and the data or data amount accessed or transferred.

Data stored in the cloud is usually in an encrypted form that would need to be decrypted before anyone could read the information. Commercial cloud storage systems encrypt each user's data with a specific encryption key. The decryption key can be stored either by the service itself, or by individual users. Most services keep the key themselves, letting their systems see and process user data, such as indexing data for future searches. These services also access the key when a user logs in with a password, unlocking the data so the person can use it. However, it is not secure enough. Just like regular keys, if someone else has them, they might be stolen or misused without the data owner knowing. And some services might have flaws in their security practices that leave users' data vulnerable.

A few less popular cloud services, including Mega [5] and SpiderOak [11], require users to upload and download files through service-specific client applications that include encryption functions. That extra step lets users keep the encryption keys themselves. These services are not perfect - there is still a possibility that their own apps might be compromised or hacked, allowing an intruder to read your files either before they are encrypted for uploading or after being downloaded and decrypted. An encrypted cloud service provider could even embed functions in its specific app that could leave data vulnerable.

To maximize cloud storage security, it is best to combine the features of these various approaches. Before uploading data to the cloud, first encrypt it using your own encryption software. Then upload the encrypted file to the cloud. To get access to the file again, log in to the service, download it and decrypt it yourself. However, this prevents users from taking advantage of many cloud services, like sharing documents with other cloud users.

For people who do not want to learn how to program their own tools, there are two basic choices: Find a cloud storage service with trustworthy upload and download software that is open-source and has been validated by independent security researchers. Or use trusted open-source encryption software to encrypt your data before uploading it to the cloud.

In current cloud data storage systems, there are the following common data security and performance issues:

- A single point failure: Cloud data storage is a centralized solution. Authentication, authorization and auditing are managed by the cloud server. If the cloud server is compromised by an attacker, the privacy of user data will be disclosed.

- Data ownership: Data users do not own their data once uploading it to the cloud. The cloud server has full access to the data of users. Malicious cloud server may even disclose the user data to the third party.
- Data transparency and auditability: Data users do not have transparency over what data is being collected about him and how they are accessed.
- Cost: It is expensive for the cloud server to comply with all data security requirements and keep all security audit.

To address these issues, in recent years, some efforts [6,7,14] started using a disruptive technology for the access control, namely blockchain. The blockchain is a public, decentralized, Byzantine fault-tolerant and immutable ledger, where registers are appended in a chronological order [12]. It was already employed in a plenty of areas [13], like cryptocurrencies, transportation systems, management of medical records, decentralization of the Web, predictions and applications platforms. The main advantages of the blockchain are no downtime, no censorship, no fraud and no third-party interference.

FairAccess [6,7] is an access control framework based on blockchain. In this framework, the blockchain is used to distribute access tokens using smart contracts. However, their proposal has some issues, like the support to token-based authorizations only, necessity of contact with the owner of the resource for each new access or each token expiration, the high time cost involved in getting an access permission and the lack of integration of the access control with a proper relationship network that has a big importance in a collaborative and integrated IoT.

Zyskind et al. [14] proposed a protocol that turns a blockchain into an automated access-control manager that does not require trust in a third party. Unlike Bitcoin, transactions in their system are not strictly financial - they are used to carry instructions, such as storing, querying and sharing data. Their framework focuses on ensuring that users own and control their personal data. As such, the system recognizes the users as the owners of the data and the services as guests with delegated permissions. Each user has complete transparency over what data is being collected about her and how they are accessed. One major concern with mobile applications is that users are required to grant a set of permissions upon sign-up. These permissions are granted indefinitely and the only way to alter the agreement is by opting-out. Instead, in their framework, at any given time the user may alter the set of permissions and revoke access to previously collected data.

Our Contributions

In this paper, we propose a new approach to control access to the user's data stored in the cloud with the state-of-the-arts decentralized blockchain technology. Our approach distributes the access control tasks for authentication, authorization and auditing to a network of nodes like Bitcoin. In particular, we keep the auditing records in the transparent blockchain.

Our work is mainly motivated by [14]. Like [14], our access control approach is also built on blockchain. Unlike [14], we have different algorithms for policy and access transaction generation and verification. In addition, we employ the Shamir secret sharing scheme [10] to manage the encryption keys for cloud users.

The rest of the paper is arranged as follows. We introduce our models in Sects. 2 and 3, describe our protocols in Sect. 4 and cloud data access control in Sect. 5. The security and performance analysis is carried out in Sect. 6. Conclusions are drawn in the last section.

2 System Model

2.1 Overview

Our system can be modeled with four main parts as shown in Fig. 1. Cloud data storage server - an encrypted database storing the data from the users; Cloud security servers (SS) - multiple servers keeping the encryption key pieces in a distributed way; User group - including data owner (O) and data user (U), data owner sends the encrypted data and encryption key pieces to the cloud data storage and security severs, respectively. Data user can download the data from the cloud, but only when they get the permission to have encryption key, the corresponding data can be decrypted. Blockchain - recording data usage transactions, verifying the data access control policy and maintaining the audit information of the system. In the following sections, we introduce the function of each part in details.

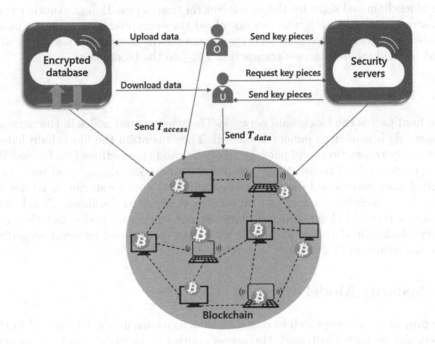

Fig. 1. Overview of our system model

2.2 Cloud Data Storage Server

The cloud data storage server is an encrypted database storing the data from the users. Every data owner can store their data into the cloud. Because the cloud itself can not be trusted and everyone in the system can download the data from the cloud, data will be encrypted before uploading to the cloud.

2.3 Cloud Security Servers

Besides the cloud data storage server, our system has multiple servers, called Security Servers (SS). The key for the encrypted data is distributed and kept in the multiple security servers. Each cloud security server checks the blockchain to judge whether the user satisfies the access control policy to get the key when the user requests for the key. If the user are verified successfully, each cloud security server will send a key piece to the user.

2.4 User Group

As we have introduced, there are two kinds of users in our system. One type of users is data owner (O), who can upload and update his data in the cloud data storage server. Data owner sends access control policies (ACP) for his data to the blockchain and signs for the access control transaction T_{access}. Another type of users is data user (U), who can download the encrypted data from the cloud and send request to the cloud security servers for the decryption key. They also need to send the data access transaction T_{data} to the blockchain.

2.5 Blockchain

The final part is the blockchain network. There are several nodes in the network whose role is similar to miners in bitcoin. They maintain the blockchain ledger that verify transactions and package all of the valid transactions into blocks. We design two kinds of transactions: the access transaction T_{access} used for access control management and the data transaction T_{data} used for storing or retrieving data. The blockchain ledger can be seen as distributed database. Cloud data storage server and cloud security server are not blockchain nodes, but they can query blockchain database and assist with data storage and retrieval according to transactions in blockchain.

3 Security Model

We propose a new approach to control access to secure user's data stored in the cloud. As we have illustrated, the access control tasks mainly include authentication, authorization and auditing. Accordingly, our security model mainly considers how to prevent three following potential attacks.

The first potential attack to our system is the impersonation attack. The impersonation attack is that an adversary pretends to be one of the legitimate parties in the system with the goal of obtaining information or access to some cloud data. In our system, the impersonation attack may refer that an adversary pretends to be the legal user and wants to get identity authenticated, then he can have an access to the data owner's data. According to our system model, only when the user meets three conditions, including identity verified, encrypted data downloaded, decryption key obtained, the user can really get the data he wants.

The second potential attack is the collusion attack. The collusion attack is that a cooperation or conspiracy of two or more malicious parties deceive others to obtain an objective forbidden by the system. In our system model, no matter whether the user or the cloud data storage server wants to get the data, he need to get the decryption key from the multiple cloud security servers, each of them is required to check the access control policies and the identity of the user. We assume that some cloud security servers are trusted not to collude with malicious servers.

The third potential attack is the modification attack where the attacker who wants to get authentication and authorization may want to modify the identity information and access control policies in the system. Because all these information are coded in the blocks of a blockchain, the attacker needs to change the information in the blocks or replace blocks. The blocks are linked by hash pointers. We assume that hash function used in the blockchain has two properties: one way and collision resistant, which means that it is computationally infeasible to find either a data object that maps to a pre-specified hash result (the one-way property) or two data objects that map to the same hash result (the collision-resistant property).

The security requirement for our system is that our system must be secure against all the above three potential attacks.

4   Protocols for Using Blockchain to Control Access to Cloud Data

In this section, we follow our model to design some protocols for using blockchain to control access to cloud data. Basically, there are three protocols as follows: blockchain identity initialization protocol, access control transaction or data transaction generation protocol and the protocol for miners dealing with transactions. To simplify the model, we assume a single data owner (o) provides access to m guests ($u_1, u_2, \cdots, u_m$) respectively. Besides, suppose there are n security servers in the system that each server maintains a piece of encryption key for providers.

To be compatible with the existing blockchain for Bitcoin, we use *Elliptic Curve Digital Signature Algorithm* (ECDSA) with *secp256k1* curve [3]. We denote the generator, signature and verification functions as 3-tuple $(\mathcal{G}_{sig}, \mathcal{S}_{sig}, \mathcal{V}_{sig})$. And function $\mathcal{H}$ represents the cryptographic hash function -*SHA-256* [8].

4.1   Protocol for Pseudo-identity Generation

Due to the nature of discentralization, a pseudo-identity mechanism is utilized in permissionless blockchain. For example, a bitcoin address comprising a hashed public key represents user's identity. Similarly, for each access control group, both data owners and users should initialize a public key as their access control identity at first. Protocol 1 illustrates the identity generation procedure for data owner (o) and users $(U_i, i \in 1, 2, \cdots, m)$.

Algorithm 1. Pseudo-Identity Generation

Require: $seed_i (i = o, 1, 2, \cdots, m)$
Ensure: $pk_{sig}^o, sk_{sig}^o, pk_{sig}^i, sk_{sig}^i (i = 1, 2, \cdots, m)$
  1: $(pk_{sig}^o, sk_{sig}^o) \leftarrow \mathcal{G}_{sig}(seed_o)$
  2: **for** $i = 1$ to m **do**
  3:    $(pk_{sig}^i, sk_{sig}^i) \leftarrow \mathcal{G}_{sig}(seed_i)$
  4: **end for**
  5: **return** $pk_{sig}^o, sk_{sig}^o, pk_{sig}^i, sk_{sig}^i, (i = o, 1, 2, \cdots, m)$

Meanwhile, the owner needs to generate an encryption key sk_{enc}^o before granting access to other users, as the requirement of data protection. Then t out n Shamir secret sharing scheme is employed here, data owner divide his/her encryption key into n parts, and shares each server s_i with one part. A user can reconstruct the secret key only if he/she has any t of the parts.

4.2   Protocols for Access Control Transaction

Access Control Transaction Format. To realize the access control for cloud data, the data owner should first register legal user identities along with the access control policies and the number of data accesses into blockchain ledger through access control transaction T_{access} shown in Fig. 2. The information is recorded as transaction outputs of T_{access}. The generation of access transaction is restricted to the data owner.

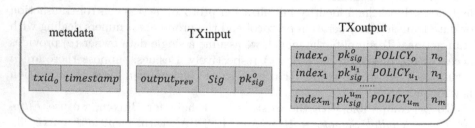

Fig. 2. The access transaction format

The $txid$ is computed by double hashing of the transaction. It can be seen as a hash pointer used to uniquely identify a particular transaction. Besides, the $timestamp$ is also applied to avoid the replay attack. In bitcoin transaction format, there are some other information such as version and lock time. To simplify our protocol, we ignore those fields.

Before setting data access policies, the data owner should pay for this specific service to the blockchain. It can be a bitcoin transaction. Therefore, a $output_{prev}$ is included in this $TXinput$ for this payment. The $output^i_{prev}$ consists of two fields: a hash pointer and an index (the hash pointer points to the previous transaction and the index refers to the specific output for this payment. Moreover, the data owner also should attach his $scriptSig$ including his signature on the whole transaction and the corresponding public key. It can also prove the authentication and integrity of the transaction.

In transaction output, access control policy $POLICY_{u_i}$ states specific approved documents and levels of access rights to a data user u_i. For example, $POLICY_{u_i} = \{\text{read}\}$ means that user i could read the cloud data. Then $POLICY_{u_i}$ will be linked to user i's address in blockchain when miners include this transaction into a block. The first output address should be the owner's address stating the ownership and privilege of the data. In one access control transaction, data owner can grant several permissions to different authorized users, as shown in Fig. 2. In addition, n_i stands for the number of times that the user u_i can get access to the data owner's data.

Access Control Transaction Generation. The generation of access control transaction is restricted to the data owner and can be described as Algorithm 2.

Algorithm 2. Access Control Transaction Generation

Require: $pk^o_{sig}, sk^o_{sig}, \{pk^{u_i}_{sig}, POLICY_{u_i}, n_i\}(i = 1, 2, \cdots,$
  $m), timestamp$
Ensure: T_{access}
 1: Let $TXoutput = \{pk^o_{sig}, POLICY_o, n_o\}$
 2: **for** $i = 1$ to m **do**
 3:    $TXoutput = TXoutput \parallel \{pk^{u_i}_{sig}, POLICY_{u_i}, n_i\}$
 4: **end for**
 5: Let $M = \{timestamp, output_{prev}, TXoutput\}$
 6: Let $Sigature = \mathcal{S}_{sig}(sk^o_{sig}, M)$
 7: Let $TXinput = \{output_{prev}, Signature, pk^o_{sig}\}$
 8: Let $TXcontent = \{timestamp, TXinput, TXoutput\}$
 9: Compute the transaction ID $txid = \mathcal{H}\big(\mathcal{H}(TXcontent)\big)$
10: Let $T_{access} = txid \parallel TXcontent$
11: **return** T_{access}

Access Control Transaction Verification. When blockchain nodes receive an access transaction, they should firstly verify the signature of the massage to authenticate the data owner's identity and make sure that the message is not tampered as described in Algorithm 2.

Afterwards, the miners would organize it into a blockchain block followed by involving it into the blockchain. Later, users can use data access transaction T_{data} to get access to the cloud data permitted by access control policies.

Algorithm 3. Access Control Transaction Verification

Require: T_{access}
Ensure: s
1: $s \leftarrow 0$
2: $\{txid, timestamp, TXinput, TXoutput\} = T_{access}$
3: $\{Sig, pk_o\} = TXinput,$
4: **if** $\mathcal{V}_{sig}(pk_{sig}^o, Sig, TXinput \parallel TXoutput) = 1$ **then**
5: $\quad s \leftarrow 1$
6: **end if**
7: **return** s

4.3   Protocol for Data Access Transaction

After the access control transaction is included in the blockchain, data user who meets the access control policies can get access to the cloud data by submitting a data access transaction to the blockchain network.

Data Access Transaction Format. A data access transaction T_{data} is submitted to the blockchain network when the data owner or a data user wants to upload or download data in the cloud. Figure 3 shows its format. The transaction input refers to the previous transaction output, and includes the signature on the whole transaction to provide authentication and integrity.

metadata		TXinput			TXoutput			
$txid$	$timestamp$	$output_{prev}$	Sig	$pk_{sig}^{u_k}$	$index_0$	pk_{sig}^o	$POLICY_{u_k}$	1
					$index_1$	$pk_{sig}^{u_k}$	$POLICY_{u_k}$	$l-1$

Fig. 3. The data transaction format

Like the access control transaction, the data access transaction contains the identifier and timestamp. The most important thing is that the user should refer to the related previous transaction output as a part of the transaction input, which could be an output of the access control transaction setting access control policies or the last data access transaction he generated. $TXinput$ contains the signature on the whole transaction as well to provide authentication and integrity.

The transaction output represents the access identity, policy and the rest times user can access for the user's next access. The access identity and policy must remain the same to the user's input which corresponding to what the owner granted. Unless the user is permitted to share access times with others, he can provide other identities as output addresses. Assume that the data user is currently allowed to get access the cloud data for ℓ times. $TXinput$ contains two fields: One field is to return 1 access back to the data owner, and another field is to reduce the number of his data access by 1. The data user must input correct ℓ according to the number in his/her last unspent data transaction output. Otherwise, this transaction will be denied by blockchain miners to avoid double-spending access numbers.

As all the historical accesses are recorded into the blockchain, the data owner has a transparent and comprehensive picture of his data access history.

Data Access Transaction Generation. Data access transaction is generated by a data user u_k. The generation of a data access transaction can be described in Algorithm 4.

Algorithm 4. Data Access Transaction Generation

Require: $pk_{sig}^o, pk_{sig}^k, sk_{sig}^k, POLICY_k, \ell, timestamp$
Ensure: T_{data}
1: Let $TXoutput = \{pk_{sig}^o, POLICY_k, l\}$
2: Let $TXoutput = TXoutput \| \{pk_{sig}^k, POLICY_k, \ell - 1\}$
3: Let $M = \{timestamp, output_{prev}, TXoutput\}$
4: Let $Sigalure = \mathcal{S}_{sig}(sk_{sig}^k, M)$
5: Let $TXinput = \{output_{prev}, Signature, pk_{sig}^k\}$
6: Let $TXcontent = \{timestamp, TXinput, TXoutput\}$
7: Compute the transaction ID $txid = \mathcal{H}\Big(\mathcal{H}(TXcontent)\Big)$
8: Let $T_{data} = txid \| TXcontent$
9: **return** T_{data}

Data Access Transaction Verification. Like access control transaction verification, the miners need to check the signature of data transaction. Apart from identity authentication, they should make sure that the operations $POLICY_k$ originator proposed is indeed allowed in the access policy and the information in transaction output like rest access time are correct before recording it into blockchain. The verification can be described in Algorithm 5.

Algorithm 5. Data Access Transaction Verification

Require: T_{data}
Ensure: s
1: $s \leftarrow 0$
2: $\{txid, timestamp, TXinput, TXoutput\} = T_{data}$
3: $\{txid_{previous}, Sig, pk_{sig}^k\} = TXinput$
4: $\{pk_{sig}^0, POLICY_k, 1\} \| \{pk_{sig}^k, POLICY_k, l-1\} = TXoutput$
5: $\{pk_{sig}^{k'}, POLICY_{k'}, \ell'\} \leftarrow Parse(BC[txid_{previous}])$
6: **if** $pk_{sig}^{k'} = pk_{sig}^k$ and $\mathcal{V}_{sig}(pk_{sig}^k, Sig, TXinput \| TXoutput) = 1$ **then**
7:     **if** $POLICY_k = POLICY_{k'}$ and $l' = l+1$ **then**
8:         $s \leftarrow 1$
9:     **end if**
10: **end if**
11: **return** s

Meanwhile, the cloud storage server and security servers, should follow the blockchain to perform the data access control. Once data transactions are submitted into blockchain, they should prepare to address upload or download requests from different users. It means the cloud storage server manages the encrypted data from the owner, and have responsibility to send the required parts to authenticated users. Besides, each of the cloud security servers should send their piece of decryption key to the authenticated users. These messages could be off-chain network messages in reality.

5 Cloud Data Access Control

Data upload and download are two important processes for the cloud data access control in our system. Now we describe how the data owner uploads the data to cloud and how the data user downloads the data from the cloud in details.

5.1 Data Upload

Before data upload, the data owner randomly chooses a 128-bit encryption key sk_{enc}^o, and then uses the Advanced Encryption Standard (AES) algorithm [2] to encrypt the data. After being encrypted by AES-128, the encrypted data is sent to the cloud data storage server along with $txid$ of the access control transaction T_{access} and his signature on the encrypted data.

Based on $txid$, the cloud data storage server searches for the T_{access} in the blockchain and extract the public key pk_{sig}^o of the data owner and verify the signature of the data owner. If the signature is valid, the cloud data storage server saves the encrypted data together with $txid_o$ in the cloud.

In addition, the data owner splits the decryption key sk_{enc}^o (the encryption key is the same as the decryption key) into n pieces according to the (t, n) Shamir's secret sharing scheme [10] as follows.

The data owner randomly chooses a polynomial

$$f(x) = a_0 + a_1 x + a_2 x^2 + a_3 x^3 + \cdots + a_{t-1} x^{t-1} \tag{1}$$

over a finite fields $GF(p)$ where $p > 2^{128}$, $a_{t-1} \neq 0$, and a_0 denotes the decryption key, i.e., $a_0 = sk_{enc}^o$. Next, the data owner constructs n different points on $f(x)$ by setting $x = 1, \ldots, n$ and computing $y = f(x)$. Then, the data owner sends the point $(i, f(i))$ along with $txid_o, p$ to the the i-th security server with the Secure Socket Layer (SSL) protocol [4]. The security server keeps $txid_o, p, (i, f(i))$ in its database.

5.2 Data Download

When a data user wants to get the access to the encrypted data, he must submit a data access transaction T_{data} to blockchain network for identity and access control policy verification at first. Once the transaction is recorded in blockchain ledger, the data user can request the encrypted data and decryption key pieces as follows.

The data user sends $txid_o$ of the access control transaction T_{access} and $txid$ of the data access transaction T_{data} with his signature on $txid_o \| txid$ to the cloud data storage server. The server searches for T_{data} from the blockchain according to $txid$ to extract the public key $pk_{sig}^{u_i}$ of the data user from the transaction T_{data}, and verifies the signature of the data user. If it is authenticated, the server searches for the encrypted data according to $txid_o$ in its database and sends the encrypted data to the data user.

Next, the data user sends $txid_o$ and $txid$ with his signature on $txid_o \| txid$ to any t out of the n security servers. Without loss of generalization, we assume that the t security servers are the first t security servers, where each server searches for T_{data} from the blockchain according to $txid$ to extract the public key $pk_{sig}^{u_i}$ of the data user from the transaction T_{data}, and verifies the signature of the data user. If it is authenticated, the i-th security server searches for $(txid_o, p, (i, f(i)))$ according to $txid_o$ in its database and sends $p, (i, f(i))$ to the data user through a secure channel established between the data user and the server according to $pk_{sig}^{u_i}$.

After receiving $p, (x_i, f(x_i))$ $(i = 1, 2, \cdots, t)$ from t security servers, the data user computes the decryption key

$$sk_{enc}^o = f(0) = \sum_{j=1}^{t} f(x_j) \prod_{\substack{i=1 \\ i \neq j}}^{t} \frac{x_i}{x_i - x_j} (mod\ p) \tag{2}$$

Finally the data user decrypts the encrypted cloud data with the decryption key sk_{enc}^o to obtain the cloud data.

6 Security and Performance Analysis

In this section, we analyze the security and performance of our approach for using blockchain to control access to cloud data.

6.1 Security Analysis

In our security model described in Sect. 3, we have listed three potential attacks - the impersonation attack, the collusion attack and the modification attack - to our system. Now we describe how our system is secure against the three attacks, respectively, as follows:

At first, let us consider the impersonation attack to our system. The attacker attempts to impersonate a legal user to get access to the data owner's data. To access to the data owner's data, the attacker must meet the access control policies for the legal user specified by the data owner. He has to generate a signature of the legal user on an data access transaction and the signature must be verified with the public key corresponding to the access control policies by the network of nodes in the blockchain. The attacker does not have the corresponding private key of the legal user to generate the signature. Therefore, the attacker cannot generate a data access transaction accepted by the network of nodes and thus he cannot impersonate any legal user to get access to the data owner's data in cloud.

Next, let us consider the collusion attack to our system. The attack attempts to collude with some cloud security servers to obtain the decryption key of the data owner. Our system makes use of the t out of n Shamir secret sharing scheme to distribute the decryption key of the data owner to n cloud security servers. If the attack colludes with less than t cloud security servers, he cannot obtain the decryption key of the data owner. Therefore, the data owner's data in the cloud is secure if there are less than t security server collude.

At last, let us consider the modification attack. The attacker who wants to spoof identity, modify access control policies or change other information in the system must change the content coded in the blocks of the blockchain. As we assume that the hash function used in the blockchain has the one-way and collision-resistant properties. This makes it impossible to modify the blocks in the blockchain. Once the input of the hush function has been changed, even a little, the output must be completely different from the original one. The data owner specifies the data access control policies to the blockchain. The nodes in the blockchain verify the identity of the users by their signatures and check the data access operations. All the transactions are unchangeable in blockchain history. Therefore, our system is secure against the modification attack.

Besides, our blockchain can resist double-spending attack. The data owner define the access policies and number of access times for data users in blockchain. The data user is not allowed to use ta single access time twice. Because in the new transaction input, the generator must provide legal public key and corresponding signature to unlock the last unspent data transaction output in blockchain ledger which indicates the access policy and the rest number of access times. Like the way bitcoin miners verify a UTXO in bitcoin blockchain, in our system the miners will maintain an unspent data access transaction output set that can be redeemed by new transactions. Before committing a transaction into blockchain, miners will verify the signature, access policy, the number of access times and output information to ensure the correctness and validity of this transaction. Therefore, our system is secure against the double-spending attack.

6.2 Performance Analysis

For our system, we have proposed protocols for pseudo-identity generation, access control transaction generation and verification, data access transaction generation and verification. Now we analyze their performance as follows.

In the pseudo-identity generation protocol, each user needs to generate a pair of public and private keys for ECDSA signature generation and verification. It requires to compute one point multiplication over elliptic curve.

In the access control transaction generation protocol, the data owner needs to generate an ECDSA signature on access control policies. It also requires to compute a point multiplication over elliptic curve.

In the access control transaction verification protocol, the node of blockchain network needs to verify the ECDSA signature on access control policies. It requires to compute two point multiplication over elliptic curve.

Like the access control transaction generation and verification protocols, the data access transaction generation and verification protocols require the data user to compute one point multiplication and the node of blockchain network to compute two point multiplications.

According to [1], the generation of ECDSA signature over $GF(p)$ (where $p \approx 2^{256}$) takes about 0.56 ms and the verification of ECDSA signature takes about 2.02 ms.

7   Conclusion

In this paper, we propose a new approach to control the access to the cloud data with blockchain. Our approach distributes the access control tasks for authentication, authorization and auditing to a network of nodes like bitcoin. In particular, we keep the auditing records in the transparent blockchain. In addition, we employ the Shamir secret sharing scheme to manage the encryption key for cloud users.

The security analysis has shown that our solution is able to prevent the impersonation attack, the collusion attack and the modification attack. The performance analysis also shown that our solution is efficient because the generation and verification of a transaction need to compute a couple of point multiplication over elliptic curve only.

References

1. Crypto++ 6.0.0 Benchmarks. https://www.cryptopp.com/benchmarks.html
2. Daemen, J., Rijmen, V.: Rijndael, the advanced encryption standard. Dr. Dobb's J. **26**(3), 137–139 (2001)
3. Johnson, D., Menezes, A., Vanstone, S.: The elliptic curve digital signature algorithm (ECDSA). Int. J. Inf. Secur. **1**(1), 36–63 (2001)
4. Freier, A., Karlton, P., Kocher, P.: The secure sockets layer (SSL) protocol version 3.0, No. RFC 6101 (2011). https://tools.ietf.org/html/rfc6101
5. Mega Homepage. https://mega.nz
6. Ouaddah, A., Abou Elkalam, A., Ait Ouahman, A.: FairAccess: a new Blockchain-based access control framework for the Internet of Things. Secur. Commun. Netw. **9**(18), 5943–5964 (2016)
7. Ouaddah, A., Elkalam, A.A., Ouahman, A.A.: Towards a novel privacy-preserving access control model based on blockchain technology in IoT. In: Rocha, Á., Serrhini, M., Felgueiras, C. (eds.) Europe and MENA Cooperation Advances in Information and Communication Technologies. Advances in Intelligent Systems and Computing, vol. 520, pp. 523–533. Springer, Cham (2017). https://doi.org/10.1007/978-3-319-46568-5_53
8. National Institute of Standards and Technology (NIST). FIPS 180–2: Secure Hash Standard (SHS), Current version of the Secure Hash Standard (SHA-1, SHA-224, SHA-256, SHA-384, and SHA-512) (2004)
9. Sandhu, R.S., Samarati, P.: Access control: principle and practice. IEEE Commun. Mag. **32**(9), 40–48 (1994)
10. Shamir, A.: How to share a secret. Commun. ACM **22**(11), 612–613 (1979)
11. Spideroak Homepage. https://spideroak.com
12. Swan, M.: Blockchain: Blueprint for a New Economy. O'Reilly Media Inc., Sebastopol (2015)
13. Zheng, Z., Xie, S., Dai, H.N., Wang, H.: Blockchain challenges and opportunities: A survey. Work Pap. (2016). http://inpluslab.sysu.edu.cn/?les/blockchain/blockchain.pdf
14. Zyskind, G., Nathan, O.: Decentralizing privacy: using blockchain to protect personal data. In: Security and Privacy Workshops (SPW), 2015 IEEE, pp. 180–184. IEEE (2015)

A Multi-client DSSE Scheme Supporting Range Queries

Randolph Loh[1](✉), Cong Zuo[1,2](✉), Joseph K. Liu[1](✉),
and Shi-Feng Sun[1,2](✉)

[1] Faculty of Information Technology, Monash University, Clayton 3168,
Australia
rglohl@student.monash.edu, {cong.zuol,joseph.liu,
shifeng.sun}@monash.edu
[2] Data61, CSIRO, Melbourne/Sydney, Australia

Abstract. We consider the need for security while providing services that are comparable to that of traditional applications to fully exploit cloud services to its fullest potential. While Dynamic Searchable Symmetric Encryption (DSSE) supports such needs, we want to be able to protect against file-injection attacks. Hence, we require forward privacy and a scheme which allows for a wide range of searching capabilities. We propose an extension, based on the RSA problem, to a DSSE scheme that supports range queries allowing the scheme to also support multiple clients. Furthermore, we describe how we can further manage clients using Attribute-Based Encryption (ABE) such that clients cannot decrypt ciphertexts that fall outside of their access rights.

Keywords: Multi-client · Range queries · RSA ·
Dynamic Searchable Symmetric Encryption

1 Introduction

Cloud services aid various types of users for their various needs at a much cheaper cost. This compared to that of conventional systems where users must manually set-up and maintain such systems. The cost and convenience of being able to access these services when and wherever contributed to the large reliance on cloud services. This is especially true for data storage facilities where users opt to save what may be private information in the cloud because of its perks. This led to the need for additional security features s.t only authorized parties are allowed access to the stored information. Namely to encrypt the data before storing it on the cloud. This requires an efficient method to retrieve information when needed. Hence the introduction of Searchable Encryption (SE) where a user can efficiently retrieve a specific piece of information from the encryption data.

As defined by Kamara and Lauter [1], SE schemes hide search indices which are only retrieved by a legitimate user who can produce a token through a proposed query or keyword. Although this can result in information such as search patterns given a query and its results being accessible by a potential adversary, that is the extent of it. We can classify SE schemes into two main types, used for different purposes.

© Springer Nature Switzerland AG 2019
F. Guo et al. (Eds.): Inscrypt 2018, LNCS 11449, pp. 289–307, 2019.
https://doi.org/10.1007/978-3-030-14234-6_16

Searchable Symmetric Encryption (SSE) which assumes a single data owner/client, uses the same key to encrypt and decrypt data. Asymmetric Searchable Encryption (ASE) which assumes a data owner and a separate client, uses a pair of keys to encrypt and decrypt data.

In this paper we assume the case of a single data owner with multiple clients or users, hence the need for the ability to allow other clients or users to perform searches over the encrypted data. This was introduced as an extension of SSE by Curtmola et al. [2], the multi-user searchable encryption scheme (MSSE) which makes use of broadcast encryption schemes. Moving forward with the advancements of SSE schemes, support for conjunctive searches and other querying capabilities have been implemented on top of past schemes which were mainly single-keyword search schemes. Just as multi-user or multi-client schemes such as the Multi-Client SSE scheme (MC-SSE), as referred to by Jarecki et al. [3], that extends an SSE scheme capable of Boolean queries, the Oblivious Cross-Tags protocol (OXT) by Cash et al. [4], to support multiple clients.

Our Contributions. We contribute by further extending the DSSE scheme by Zuo et al. [5] to a scheme that supports multiple clients by leveraging on the RSA problem. Thus, creating a multi-client forward secure DSSE scheme that supports range queries. Our extension only requires the data owner to generate a client key during the initial setup phase like the non-interactive multi-client SSE scheme of Sun et al. [6]. Meaning clients will not need to the probe the data owner for search token every time they wish to perform a query.

We also note the use of Attribute-Based Encryption (ABE) can further control a user's access rights. A user may be able to perform queries for a file and retrieve its encrypted ciphertext. However, if the user does not satisfy a predetermined policy, the user will not be able to decrypt the ciphertext to retrieve the file.

1.1   Related Works

The first SSE scheme introduced by Song et al. [7] was a scheme that supported searches over encrypted data using a single keyword. As previously mentioned the scheme assumes a single data owner who also acts as the client. Revisiting the topic, there have been numerous improvements made to SSE schemes. Such as multi-user capabilities of a scheme and adaptive and non-adaptive security the which was formally defined by Curtmola et al. in [2].

The OXT protocol of Cash et al. [4] was a base for many schemes [3, 6, 8–14] which seek to leverage some of its properties, the support for Boolean queries and its scalability in supporting large databases. These include additions for dynamic capabilities [8, 13] and extending searches to include range and sub-string queries [10]. As well as applying the protocol in a multi-client setting [3, 6, 9, 11–13].

A desirable strong property of DSSE schemes is forward privacy, which seeks to limit information leaked from update operations as stated by Stefanov et al. [15]. Bost's Σοφος scheme is a forward private SSE scheme which seeks performance efficiency [16]. Zuo et al. further extended Σοφος, which originally performs single keyword searches, to support range queries [5]. Bost et al. also proved forward security against malicious servers [17].

MSSE or MC-SSE schemes can be split into interactive and not interactive schemes. Interactive schemes require the data-owner to take part in the generation of search tokens, as in the scheme proposed by Jarecki et al. where the data-owner is required to check if the queries performed by a client complies with a predetermined policy [3]. Non-interactive schemes only require the data-owner to perform a function of sorts one time initially, this can be the distribution of search keys between a group of clients through key sharing like the scheme proposed by Kasra K. et al. [12] or the distribution of keys based on a client's given permission as by Sun et al. [6].

1.2 Organization

The remaining sections of this paper are organized as follows. Section 2 forms a base through limited information and definitions. We present our construction in Sect. 3 with details for the base of our construction explaining the scheme in [5]. We provide our security analysis in Sect. 4. We propose a possible improvement to our construction in Sect. 5. Finally concluding in Sect. 6.

2 Preliminaries

This section provides information on the notations used in our construction. It also includes a brief description of the assumption to the problems and definitions which our construction is based on.

2.1 Notation

We present here the notations used in this paper as described in the following Table 1.

Table 1. Notations.

Notation	Description
1^λ	A security parameter
ind_i	File index of the ith file
W_i	A set of keywords corresponding to the ith file
$DB = (ind_i, W_i)_{i=1}^d$	A database of file indices and keyword-set pairs
ABT	An assigned binary tree
BT	A binary tree
CBT	A complete binary tree
d	Depth of a binary tree
e	Encrypted file index
F	A pseudorandom function (PRF)
K	A key randomly sample from the security parameter and used in PRF F
K_n	Result of PRF F for a node n
m	Maximum range of values starting from 0 to $m - 1$.
$\mathcal{M}$	A set of values of co-domain to a set of value in group D

(continued)

Table 1. (*continued*)

Notation	Description
n_{org}, n_{new}	An original node n_{org} and a new node n_{new}
N	A map which is used to store a search token and counter value pair of a node
NSet	A set of nodes, containing all nodes from the root node to the specified leaf node
PBT	A perfect binary tree
R	A set of value in a group for trapdoor permutation operations
RSet	A minimum set of nodes needed to conduct a search
ST_c	Current search token for a node
T	A map which is used to store the encrypted database EDB
(TPK, TSK)	Trapdoor permutation keypair where TPK is the public key and TSK is the secret key.
UT_c	Current update token for a node
v	A value s.t $0 \leq v < m$
VBT	A virtual binary tree
σ	Current state of the EDB
$A \leftarrow B$	Set value of B to A
$a \xleftarrow{\$} A$	Uniformly sample a random element a from A
$A[a]$	Retrieve value at a from A
$[a, b]$	Defining a range of values starting from a to b

2.2 Hardness Assumption

Our construction relies on the hardness of the Decisional Diffie-Hellman (DDH) problem and the RSA problem for its security. We follow the definitions in [6] as follows.

Definition 1 (DDH Problem). For a cyclic group of prime order p, $\mathbb{G}$, the DDH problem can differentiate, for a group of elements g in the cycle group $\mathbb{G}$ ($g \in \mathbb{G}$), a set of values $\{(g, g^a, g^b, g^{ab})\}$ from $\{(g, g^a, g^b, g^z)\}$ where a, b, z belong to $\mathbb{Z}_p (a, b, z \in \mathbb{Z}_p)$. The advantage for any probabilistic polynomial time (PPT) distinguisher D is defined as

$$Adv_{D,G}^{DDH}(\lambda) = \left| \Pr\left[D(g, g^a, g^b, g^{ab}) = 1\right] - \Pr\left[D(g, g^a, g^b, g^z) = 1\right] \right|$$

s.t the DDH assumption holds for any PPT distinguisher D of advantage $Adv_{D,G}^{DDH}(\lambda)$ to be negligible in λ.

Definition 2 (Strong RSA Problem). For large primes numbers p and q of λ-bits, $p = 2\bar{q} + 1$ and $q = 2\bar{p} + 1$ for some primes $\bar{p}, \bar{q}$. Let N be the product of p and q ($N = p * q$). Of a random element in $\mathbb{Z}_n^*$, g, when values (N, g) are entered into an algorithm as inputs the resulting outputs are (z, e) s.t $z^e = g \mod N$, the RSA problem is resolved.

2.3 Pseudorandom Functions

We follow the definition in [6] for a pseudorandom function (PRF), PRF F maps inputs (K, X) to an output Y s.t $F : \{0, 1\}^{\lambda} \cdot X \to Y$. Of all adversaries $\mathcal{A}$ with advantage defined as

$$Adv_{F, \mathcal{A}}^{PRF}(\lambda) = \left| \Pr\left[\mathcal{A}^{F(K, \cdot)}(1^{\lambda})\right] - \Pr\left[\mathcal{A}^{f(\cdot)}(1^{\lambda})\right] \right|$$

where the advantage $Adv_{F, \mathcal{A}}^{PRF}(\lambda)$ is negligible in λ where K is randomly sampled from $\{0, 1\}^{\lambda}$ $\left(K \xleftarrow{\$} \{0, 1\}^{\lambda}\right)$ and f a random function from X to Y.

2.4 Trapdoor Permutation

We follow the trapdoor permutation (TDP) Π as defined in [5] that for a set group R a permutation occurs s.t (1) for any value in the set group $\mathbb{R}$, computing Π is relatively easy with the public key, and (2) for any value belonging to the co-domain $\mathcal{M}$, performing inverse Π^{-1} is relatively easy only if a matching secret key is known. The set of algorithms are as follows.

- (TPK, TSK) $\leftarrow$ TKeyGen(1^{λ}): For a security parameter 1^{λ} as input, output a pair of cryptographic keys, public key TPK and secret key TSK.
- $y \leftarrow \Pi(\text{TPK}, x)$: For public key TPK and value x as input, output y. Where x is a value that belongs to $\mathbb{R}$ and y a value that belongs to ($x \in \mathbb{R}; y \in \mathcal{M}$).
- $x \leftarrow \Pi^{-1}(\text{TSK}, y)$: For secret key TSK and value y as input, output x. Where x is a value that belongs to $\mathbb{R}$ and y a value that belongs to ($x \in \mathbb{R}; y \in \mathcal{M}$).

2.5 Searchable Symmetric Encryption

We define a database (DB) to be made of index/keyword pairs s.t (DB $= (ind_i, W_i)_{i=1}^{d}$), where ind_i is the index of a file while W_i is the keyword of ind_i at i. We also note W as the set of unique keywords s.t ($W = \cup_{i=1}^{d} W_i$) and $|W|$ the total number of said keywords. For D as the number of documents in DB, N to be the number of document/keyword pairs s.t $\left(N = \sum_{i=1}^{D} |W_i|\right)$. Additionally, we also note DB(w) to be a set of documents that corresponds to the keyword w where w is from set $W(w \in W)$.

We follow the definition of a dynamic searchable symmetric encryption (DSSE) scheme as in [16] where for a DSSE scheme Δ consists of three algorithms: Setup, Search, Update; ($\Delta = $ Setup, Search, Update) defined as follows.

- (EDB, K, σ) $\leftarrow$ Setup(DB, 1^{λ}): For a database DB and security parameter 1^{λ} as input, output a corresponding encrypted database EDB, a key K and a client state σ.
- (E) $\leftarrow$ Search(EDB, K, σ, q): For an encrypted database EDB, key K, client state σ and query q as input, output E s.t E is the set of encrypted indices of DB(w) and e to be the encrypted index of each document in E ($e \in E$).

- $(EDB', \sigma') \leftarrow$ Update(EDB, K, σ, op, in): For an encrypted database EDB, key K, client state σ, operation op and input in as input, output an updated encrypted database EDB' and updated client state σ'. Where op can be an addition or deletion of an index $(op = add|del)$ and in which is parsed index/keywords pair (ind, w) s.t w is a set of keywords that corresponds to the specified ind.

2.6 Security Definition

We follow the definition as provided by Bost in [16]. Where forward privacy (a strong property of the SSE leakage function of DSSE schemes) is concern with hiding the relationship between changes made to a document and keywords that were previously queried. Bost gave a formal definition as follows.

Definition 3 (Forward Privacy). *A $\mathcal{L}$-adaptively-secure DSSE scheme Δ supports forward privacy if the update leakage function $\mathcal{L}^{\text{Updt}}$ reflects the below equation*

$$\mathcal{L}^{\text{Updt}}(op, in) = \mathcal{L}'(op, \{(ind_i, \mu_i)\})$$

where the set of modified documents $\{(ind_i, \mu_i)\}$ accompanies μ_i number of modified keywords for the updated document ind_i.

Following from which the definition by Zuo et al. in [5] extends Definition 3 through the use of games $\text{DSSEReal}_{\mathcal{A}}^{\Delta}(1^\lambda)$ and $\text{DSSEIdeal}_{\mathcal{A},S}^{\Delta}(1^\lambda)$. Where $\text{DSSEReal}_{\mathcal{A}}^{\Delta}(1^\lambda)$ is equal to the DSSE scheme Δ and $\text{DSSEIdeal}_{\mathcal{A},S}^{\Delta}(1^\lambda)$ simulated using information leaked from Δ. We denote the leakage function as $\mathcal{L} = (\mathcal{L}^{\text{Stp}}, \mathcal{L}^{\text{Srch}}, \mathcal{L}^{\text{Updt}})$, describing information leaked to adversary $\mathcal{A}$. For a pair of games that are indistinguishable, we say that $\mathcal{A}$ will not gain other information except that which can be deduced from $\mathcal{L}$. We describe the games as follows.

- $\text{DSSEReal}_{\mathcal{A}}^{\Delta}(1^\lambda)$: For a DB chosen by $\mathcal{A}$, generate a corresponding EDB through the real setup algorithm Setup$(DB, 1^\lambda)$. $\mathcal{A}$ can then perform searches or update operations repeatedly. The game returns operation results to $\mathcal{A}$. $\mathcal{A}$ will eventually output a bit.
- $\text{DSSEIdeal}_{\mathcal{A},S}^{\Delta}(1^\lambda)$: For a DB chosen by $\mathcal{A}$, generate a corresponding EDB through a simulated setup algorithm $S(\mathcal{L}^{\text{Stp}}(DB, 1^\lambda))$. Then using $\mathcal{L}$, simulate search results $S(\mathcal{L}^{\text{Srch}}(q))$ and update results $S(\mathcal{L}^{\text{Updt}}(op, in))$ can then perform searches or update operations repeatedly. The game returns operation results to $\mathcal{A}$. $\mathcal{A}$ will eventually output a bit.

Definition 4 ($\mathcal{L}$-adaptively-secure). *A DSSE scheme Δ is $\mathcal{L}$-adaptively-secure if, for every PPT adversary $\mathcal{A}$, there exists an efficient simulator S s.t*

$$\left| \Pr\left[\text{DSSEReal}_{\mathcal{A}}^{\Delta}(1^\lambda)\right] - \Pr\left[\text{DSSEIdeal}_{\mathcal{A},S}^{\Delta}(1^\lambda) = 1\right] \right| \leq negl(1^\lambda)$$

is negligible for the security parameter 1^λ.

2.7 Binary Tree

We describe the construction of a binary tree (BT) in [5], a BT may consist of a number of nodes and every node can have at most 2 child nodes and may or may not have a parent node. Each child node is connected to its parent via an edge. The root node, the highest node in a BT, does not have a parent. In this paper, we denote nodes in a BT as follows. The highest node as *root*, its children as *root.left* and *root.right*. The parent of these nodes is the node *root* can also be written as *root.left.parent* and *root.right.parent* respectively (s.t *root* = *root.left.parent* = *root.right.parent*). Finally, we call nodes at the lowest depth of the BT as leaf nodes.

We call a BT with a depth of d (must not be less than 0), which has the maximum possible number of children nodes from the root node of depth 0 to $d - 1$ but may not have the maximum possible number of leaf nodes at depth d in the BT filled, a complete binary tree (CBT). Whereas a BT with a depth of d, which has the maximum possible number of children nodes from the root node of depth 0 to $d - 1$ and has the maximum possible number of leaf nodes at depth d in the BT filled, is a special CBT we call a perfect binary tree (PBT). We call a CBT that has been assigned values an assigned binary tree (ABT) and a copy of a CBT that has not been assigned values a virtual binary tree (VBT). Note that values are assigned to from the left most leaf node to the right most leaf node.

2.8 Binary Database

We describe the construction of a binary database (BDB) as in [5]. In a BT, every node in the BT can be represented as a keyword/file indices pair. For BT with a depth of d, each node that does not belong to d will also be associated to file indices of its children. As such, for a range query [0, 3] that consists the following values (0, 1, 2, 3) only a node at depth $d - 2$ is required to return all file indices that falls within that range. Additionally, for a range query [0, 2] that consists of the following values (0, 1, 2) two nodes are needed to satisfy this query (Fig. 1 and Table 2).

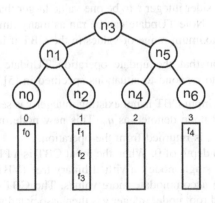

Fig. 1. Binary Tree architecture. (Binary tree of depth 3)

Table 2. Binary database distribution of values.

Nodes	Values	File indices
n_0	0	f_0
n_1	0, 1	f_0, f_1, f_2, f_3
n_2	1	f_1, f_2, f_3
n_3	0, 1, 2, 3	f_0, f_1, f_2, f_3, f_4
n_4	2	
n_5	2, 3	f_4
n_6	3	f_4

2.9   Binary Tree Construction

The construction method of a BT in [5], we call T, is made of five algorithms which are used to support the BDB. These are: TCon, TAssign, TAssignSub, TGetNodes, TUpdate; (T = TCon, TAssign, TAssignSub, TGetNodes, TUpdate) defined as follows.

- CBT $\leftarrow$ TCon(m): For an integer m as input, output a complete binary tree CBT s.t CBT has a depth of $\lceil \log m \rceil$ and all leaf nodes are associated with m consecutive integers.
- ABT $\leftarrow$ TAssign(CBT): For a complete binary tree CBT as input, output an assigned binary tree ABT s.t nodes within the ABT are labelled appropriately with an integer value and are then assigned keywords.
- ABT $\leftarrow$ TAssignSub(CBT, c): For a complete binary tree CBT and counter c as input, output an assigned binary tree ABT s.t the operates as a recursive function, assigning integer values to nodes incrementally, starting from 0.
- NSet $\leftarrow$ TGetNodes(ABT, n): For an assigned binary tree ABT and an integer m as input, output a set of nodes NSet s.t all nodes from node n to the root node is identified and placed in the set.
- CBT$'$ $\leftarrow$ TUpdate(add, v, CBT): For an operation add, an integer v and a complete binary tree CBT as input, output an updated complete binary tree CBT$'$. To simplify the operation, we consider integer v to be one value larger than the maximum range of values in the CBT. Note TUpdate can be ran as many times as the difference in the value of v and maximum range of values in the CBT if it is many times larger.

We wish to mention that the update operation TUpdate changes its behavior depending on integer v to respond to situations specified in [5] as follows.

- CBT $= \perp$: When the input CBT is not existing, integer v is set to 0 and is associated with a newly created node denoted as n_n. This new node, now the updated completed database CBT$'$, is returned from the operation.
- CBT $=$ PBT or has a depth of 0: When the input CBT is a PBT or has a depth of 0 (only consisting of a single node), a virtual binary tree (VBT) needs to be created expanding the BT to accommodate more values. The CBT and VBT are merged under a newly created root node. Integer v is then associated with the left most node of the VBT and its parent nodes are set to real. Where in Fig. 2 (a) for $v = 4$, a VBT

with nodes n_{8-14} is created and merged under the new root node n_7, node n_8 has been assigned the value 4 and its parents are set to real, denoted with solid lines.

- Otherwise, the integer v is then associated with the left most virtual node of the existing CBT and its parent nodes are set as real. Where in Fig. 2 (b) for $v = 5$, the left most node of the existing CBT node n_9 has been assigned the value 5 and its parents are set to real, denoted with solid lines.

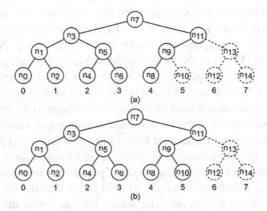

Fig. 2. Update operation example [5]. The binary tree updates (a) for $v = 4$ and (b) for $v = 5$.

3   Multi-client DSSE with Range Queries

In general, for a DB defined in Sect. 2.5, when a user searches for a file using a keyword will return all file indices corresponding to that keyword. In range queries, it is noted that a given file can only be associated with a single keyword. Additionally, a set of values can be used to represent keywords where for m as the maximum number of values in the set, a query can be of range 1 to m written as $[0, m - 1]$. This results in the query returning all file indices for each value of the specified range, which is not efficient. Hence the solution proposed by Zuo et al. in [5], employed a binary tree (BT) and binary database (BDB), Sects. 2.7 and 2.8 respectively.

We provide a short description of the basic construction in the following section, please refer to the original work for more details [5]. We present our construction in Sect. 3.2. Our construction makes use of the RSA problem to extend the original scheme while preserving the base scheme's original capabilities into a multi-client DSSE scheme.

3.1   Basic Construction

We look into the DSSE for range queries as in [5] which is an enhancement based on the combination of the schemes in [10, 16]. The Σοφος scheme proposed by Bost in [16] is a forward secure searchable encryption scheme while Faber et al. in [10] describe a method to conduct range queries.

The DSSE scheme, construction A, proposed by Zuo et al. applies the BT described in Sect. 3.1 to the Σοφος scheme. It resulted in a DSSE scheme that is forward-secure and supports range queries. The scheme, we call Γ_A, consists of three main algorithms/protocols: Setup, Search, Update; ($\Gamma_A = $ Setup, Search, Update) defined as follows.

- $(TPK, TSK, \mathbf{T}, \mathbf{N}, m, K) \leftarrow$ Setup(1^λ): For a security parameter 1^λ as input, output a pair of TDP keys (TPK, TSK), maps $(\mathbf{T}, \mathbf{N})$, integer m and a key K. Where the TDP keys, the public key (TPK) is given to the server and the secret key (TSK) is held by the client. Map $\mathbf{T}$, which is the EDB, maps the encrypted file indices denoted as e to a corresponding update token (UT). Map $\mathbf{N}$ maps a search token/counter pair (ST, c) to its corresponding node n. The integer m is maximum number of values in the range. Key K is the key for a PRF function denoted as F.
- $IND \leftarrow$ Search$([a, b], \sigma, \mathbf{T}, m, K)$: For a set of values $[a, b]$, state σ, map $\mathbf{T}$, integer m and key K as input, output a set of indices IND. Where $[a, b]$ defines the range of file indices to be retrieved and m defines the maximum value in the range s.t $0 \le a \le b \le m$. We denote the current state of the EDB as σ and MinNodes() as an operation to find the minimum set of nodes (RSet) needed for a given range. For each node n in RSet a corresponding tuple of parameters comprising of the output of PRF F as K_n, search token of the current node denoted as ST_c and counter $c(K_n, ST_c c)$ is sent to the server. The server then searches map $\mathbf{T}$ to retrieve a corresponding file index ind and returns it to the client for each tuple of parameters it received s.t IND is a collection of ind (ind returned individually).
- $\mathbf{T}' \leftarrow$ Update$(add, v, ind, \sigma, \mathbf{T}, m, K)$: For an operation add, an integer v, a file index ind, current EDB state σ, map $\mathbf{T}$, integer m and key K as input, output map $\mathbf{T}'$ s.t $\mathbf{T}'$ is an updated version of map $\mathbf{T}$. Where the operation add signifies an addition of file index ind to a node associated to the value of integer v for a range of values with a maximum of m values.

We wish to mention that the update operation Update changes its behavior depending on integer v to respond to situations specified in [5] as follows.

- $v = m$: When v is equal to m, the client needs to perform a transformation of sorts to the BT to accommodate a new node for the operation. Where (1) the new node which can be a virtual node and all nodes in the path from the root node to the virtual node to be assigned is now set to real (we denote this set of nodes as the NSet) or (2) a VBT is created to merge with the existing BT thereby expanding it, as described in Sect. 2.9 followed by (1). If a new root node $(root_N)$ is created when expanding a BT the contents of the previous BT, the original root $(root_O)$, needs to be added to the new expanded BT.
- $v < m$: When v is smaller than m, the client simply performs the operation on an existing node in the BT. The operation affects all nodes from the root node to the node associated with the value of v.

- $v > m$: When v is larger than m, the update operation is repeated for as many times as the difference in the value of v and m as described in Sect. 2.9. For simplicity, integer v is assumed to be one value larger than m.

3.2 Multi-client DSSE with Range Queries

Here we extend the Γ_A scheme to support multiple clients. We call this extension, MC-Γ_A, Algorithm 1. We present the MC-Γ_A scheme as a collection of the algorithms/ protocols: Setup, Search, Update, ClientKeyGen; (MC-Γ_A = Setup, Search, Update, ClientKeyGen). Where changes have been made to the Γ_A scheme to support multiple clients with an additional ClientKeyGen algorithm which generates a key for a potential client reader. These changes are shown as red text in Algorithm 1. The algorithms are described as follows.

Original Algorithms

- $(\text{TPK}, \text{TSK}, \mathbf{T}, \mathbf{N}, m, K) \leftarrow \text{Setup}(1^\lambda)$: For a security parameter 1^λ as input, output a pair of trapdoor permutation (TDP) keys (TPK, TSK), maps $(\mathbf{T}, \mathbf{N})$, integer m and a key K. This algorithm remains unchanged from the Γ_A scheme.
- $IND \leftarrow \text{Search}([a, b], \sigma, \mathbf{T}, m, K, K_c)$: For a set of values $[a, b]$, state σ, map $\mathbf{T}$, integer m, keys K and K_c as input, output a set of indices IND. Where for each node n in the RSet, the corresponding parameter K_n which is the result of PRF F is computed differently with the addition of key K_c, discussed later in this section. The remainder of the algorithm remains unchanged from the Γ_A scheme.
- $\mathbf{T}' \leftarrow \text{Update}(add, v, ind, \sigma, \mathbf{T}, m, K)$: For an operation add, an integer v, a file index ind, current EDB state σ, map $\mathbf{T}$, integer m and key K as input, output map $\mathbf{T}'$ s.t $\mathbf{T}'$ is an updated version of map $\mathbf{T}$. Where for each node n in the NSet, the corresponding parameter K_n which is the result of PRF F is computed differently, discussed later in this section. The remainder of the algorithm remains unchanged from the Γ_A scheme.

New Algorithm

- ClientKeyGen(σ, m, K): For a state σ, integer m and key K as input, results in the state σ, integer m, keys K and K_c being sent to the client. Where the current state of the EDB is denoted as σ, m, defines the maximum value in the range, key K and K_c input parameters for PRF F. Key K_c is computed as

$$K_c = g^{\frac{1}{\prod_{i=1}^{j} n_i}} \bmod N$$

for a set of nodes, we call KSet s.t KSet $= (n_1, n_2, \ldots, n_j)$, contains the nodes that a client is permitted to perform queries over. Its product is applied in the above equation. The data owner sends to the client (σ, m, K, K_c) as parameters needed to perform searches.

Algorithm 1. Multi-client Extension MC-Γ_A

<u>**Setup** (1^λ)</u>

Data Owner:

Inputs: Security parameter 1^λ

Outputs: (TPK, TSK, **T**, **N**, m, K)

1: $K \xleftarrow{\$} \{0,1\}^\lambda$

2: (TPK, TSK) $\leftarrow$ TKeyGen(1^λ)

3: Initialize **T** as an empty map indexed by update token UT_c and **N** as an empty map indexed by n

4: $m \leftarrow 0$

5: **Return** (TPK, TSK, **T**, **N**, m, K)

<u>**ClientKeyGen** (σ, m, K)</u>

Data owner:

Inputs: σ, m, K

1: $K_c \leftarrow g^{\frac{1}{\prod_{i=1}^{n_i}}} \bmod N$

2: Send to client (σ, m, K, K_c)

<u>**Search** $([a,b], \sigma, \mathbf{T}, m, K, K_c)$</u>

Client:

Inputs: $[a, b], \sigma, m, K, K_c$

Outputs: (K_n, ST_c, c)

1: CBT $\leftarrow$ TCon(m)

2: ABT $\leftarrow$ TAssign(CBT)

3: RSet $\leftarrow$ MinNodes($[a, b]$)

4: For each node n in RSet do

5:    $K_n \leftarrow F(K, K_c^{\prod_{n \in A_n \setminus \{\bar{n}\}} n} \bmod N)$

6:    $(ST_c, c) \leftarrow \mathbf{N}[n]$

7:    If $(ST_c, c) \neq \bot$ then

8:        Sent to server (K_n, ST_c, c)

9:    End if

10: End for

Server:

Inputs: (K_n, ST_c, c), **T**

Outputs: ind

1: For $i = c$ to 0 do

2:    $UT_i \leftarrow H_1(K_n, ST_i)$

3:    $e \leftarrow \mathbf{T}[UT_i]$

4:    $ind \leftarrow e \oplus H_2(K_n, ST_i)$

5:    Return to client ind

6:    $ST_{i-1} \leftarrow \Pi(\text{TPK}, ST_i)$

7: End for

<u>**Update** $(add, v, ind, \sigma, \mathbf{T}, m, K)$</u>

Data Owner:

Inputs: $add, v, ind, \sigma, m, K$

Outputs: (UT_{c+1}, e)

1: CBT $\leftarrow$ TCon(m)

2: If $v = m$ then

3:    CBT $\leftarrow$ TUpdate(add, v, m)

4:    $m \leftarrow m + 1$

5:    If CBT added a new root node then

6:        $(ST_c, c) \leftarrow \mathbf{N}[root_{org}]$

7:        $\mathbf{N}[root_{new}] \leftarrow (ST_c, c)$

8:    End if

9:    Get the leaf node n_v of value v

10:    ABT $\leftarrow$ TAssign(CBT)

11:    NSet $\leftarrow$ TGetNodes(n_v, ABT)

12:    For every node n in NSet

13:        $K_n \leftarrow F\left(K, g^{\frac{1}{n}} \bmod N\right)$

14:        $(ST_c, c) \leftarrow \mathbf{N}[n]$

15:        If $(ST_c, c) = \bot$ then

16:            $ST_0 \leftarrow \mathcal{M}$

17:            $c \leftarrow -1$

18:        Else

19:            $ST_{c+1} \leftarrow \Pi^{-1}(\text{TSK}, ST_c)$

20:        End if

21:        $\mathbf{N}[n] \leftarrow (ST_{c+1}, c+1)$

22:        $UT_{c+1} \leftarrow H_1(K_n, ST_{c+1})$

23:        $e \leftarrow ind \oplus H_2(K_n, ST_{c+1})$

24:        Send to the Server (UT_{c+1}, e)

25:    End for

26: Else if $v < m$ then

27:    Repeat steps 9 - 25

28: End if

Server:

Inputs: (UT_{c+1}, e), **T**

Outputs: **T**$'$

1: $\mathbf{T}[UT_{c+1}] \leftarrow e$

We bring to your attention the changes made in the generation of the PRF F output parameter K_n. Where for a given node n we define K_n as

$$K_n = F\left(K, g^{\frac{1}{n}} mod\, N\right)$$

s.t through modular exponentiation, K_c will return the $g^{\frac{1}{n}} mod\, N$ as follows

$$g^{\frac{1}{n}} mod\, N = K_c^{\Pi_{n \in A_n \setminus \{\bar{n}\}} n} mod\, N = \left(g^{\frac{1}{\Pi_{i=1}^j n_i}}\right)^{\Pi_{n \in A_n \setminus \{\bar{n}\}} n} mod\, N$$

where $\Pi_{n \in A_n \setminus \{\bar{n}\}} n$ is the product of all nodes which are not included in the query of the client. For a client passing K_c to the PRF F results in producing the same K_n for a give node n. We note that we require the values of n to be a prime number as in [6].

4 Security Analysis

In this section, we present the security analysis of our scheme. We consider the information leakage of a basic SSE scheme (common leakage) and the security of a DSSE scheme (adaptive security). We also examine if a client can solve the RSA problem efficiently s.t solving the RSA problem results a client capable of forging search requests.

4.1 Common Leakage

We consider information leakage to be between the server and a separate entity (data owner or client). The base algorithm reflects the information leakage to the server, as in [5] which are derived from [16], as follows.

- Search pattern sp(w), several searches have been performed using keyword w.
- History Hist(w), the history of operations performed on keyword w, including all updates made to the database based on keyword w DB(w).
- Contain pattern cp(w), the relationship between search queries prior to keyword w.
- Time Time(w), the number of updates made to the database based on keyword w DB(w) and when it occurred.

Where range queries are of concern, because of how the BDB is constructed as explained in Sect. 2.8, information can be leaked while inheriting leakage of other keywords. This means a query for keyword w' that falls in the range of keyword w will results in file indices of w' to be a subset of the file indices of w s.t cp(w) contains cp(w').

4.2 Adaptive Security

Appropriately the security of our scheme can be derived from [5]. Proving its security in the Random Oracle Model (ROM), while we allow slight modifications in the proof. We describe the sketch here, please refer to the appendix for the full proof.

Theorem 1 (Adaptive security of MC - Γ_A).

$$For, \mathcal{L}_{\text{MC-}\Gamma_A} = \left(\mathcal{L}_{\text{MC-}\Gamma_A}^{\text{Srch}}, \mathcal{L}_{\text{MC-}\Gamma_A}^{\text{Updt}} \right)$$
$$s.t \, \mathcal{L}_{\text{MC-}\Gamma_A}^{\text{Srch}}(n) = (\text{sp}(n), \text{Hist}(n), \text{cp}(n)),$$
$$\mathcal{L}_{\text{MC-}\Gamma_A}^{\text{Updt}}(add, n, ind) = \bot$$

Then MC-Γ_A is $\mathcal{L}_{\text{MC-}\Gamma_A}$-adaptively-secure.

Proof (sketch). Where information leakage is the same as in [5]. The server is unable to gain information about a keyword/file index pair that corresponds to the keyword a client previously queried without knowledge of the secret key used in the TDP function. Even though the server performs single keyword searches and updates a keyword/file index pair individually.

4.3 Malicious Clients

We describe here the security of MC-Γ_A against malicious clients. Where no client can forge a search request for a given query that was previously made to the server.

Theorem 2 (Security against malicious clients). We say MC-Γ_A is secure against malicious clients, that is a search request is unforgeable against adaptive attacks, assuming the Strong RSA Problem holds.

Proof. For some non-authorized keyword n, no client can generate a valid search request s.t $g^{1/n} \, mod \, N$ can only be computed with knowledge of values g and N. For an adversary $\mathcal{A}$ who generates a valid search request for some non-authorized keyword n, indicates $\mathcal{A}$ can find for $g^{1/n} mod \, N$ the values of g and N. We can then construct an efficient algorithm β to solve the Strong RSA Problem with a non-negligible probability as in [6].

Choose at random a strong RSA instance (N, h_j) where $h_j \leftarrow \mathbb{Z}_n^*$. Algorithm β runs the Setup algorithm and extracts key K for $\mathcal{A}$. Following which $\mathcal{A}$ creates a list of nodes $\boldsymbol{n} = (n_1, \ldots, n_j)$ where each n is a keyword for a query and sends them to β requesting to generate K_c. β computes g s.t $g = h_j^{\Pi_{i=1}^j n_i} \, mod \, N$ and $h_j = g^{1/\Pi_{i=1}^j n_i} \, mod \, N$, sets $K_c = h_j$ and returns K_c to $\mathcal{A}$. $\mathcal{A}$ then forms guess s for some non-authorized keyword $n' \notin \boldsymbol{n}$ for β to verify its correctness s.t $s = g^{1/n'} \, mod \, N$ and $s^{n'} = g \, mod \, N$. If it is correct, β then solves the strong RSA instance.

For each keyword mapped to a unique prime number, the greatest common divider (gcd) of a given pair of keywords will result as $\gcd(\Pi_{i=1}^j n_i, n') = 1$. Using the extended Euclidean algorithm, for the following equation $a(\Pi_{i=1}^j n_i) + b(n') = 1$, we can calculate integers a, b. Resulting in the value of $h_j^{1/n'}$ s.t $h_j^{1/n'} = (g^{1/n'})^a \cdot h_j^b = \left(h_j^{\Pi_{i=1}^j n_i/n'} \right)^a \cdot h_j^b \, mod \, N$. Solving the strong RSA instance $\left(n', h_j^{1/n'} \right)$.

Concluding that a client is only able to create a valid search request at best with negligible probability.

5 Fine-Grained Access Control

We present a possible addition to the MC-Γ_A scheme. In [6], Sun et al. further implemented fine-grain access control through the use of ABE. This was introduced by Sahai and Waters [18], ABE uses a set of descriptive attributes to allow a secondary party to be able to decrypt a given ciphertext that was encrypted by a primary party that holds a close to similar identity, or as defined by a given policy.

The variant which was employed was Ciphertext-Policy Attribute-Based Encryption (CP-ABE) [19, 20], where by predefining a set of rules governing the access to the data, a decryption key can be generated in such a way that it complies with said rules. That is a ciphertext can be decrypted when the key used for decryption satisfy the access policies.

We can simply apply CP-ABE during the phase when file indices are stored and retrieved from the map s.t the data owner encrypts the file indices with reference to a predefined policy and clients can decrypt the encrypted file indices if they satisfy the requirements.

6 Conclusion

In this paper, we provided an extension to a scheme in [5] which was based on the RSA problem as did Sun et al. in [6]. Allowing the scheme to support multiple clients while keeping its forward privacy property with support for range queries. This extension does not need to generate search tokens for clients at every request, while most multi-client schemes do, reducing communication overhead. We also note that in our construction we can limit the search confining a client's query to a specific range (search space). Our extension, however, does not cater to the scenario where we want to revoke the authorization of a currently authorized client. Examples of revocation may include limiting the number of searches a client may be allowing to perform, imposing a rule s.t the client's key is only valid for a defined period of time. These are areas to venture further into in the future.

Appendix

Proof of Theorem 1. For a one-way trapdoor permutation Π, a PRF F, random oracle hash functions H_1 and H_2 that outputs μ and λ bits respectively.

$$For, \mathcal{L}_{\text{MC-}\Gamma_A} = \left(\mathcal{L}_{\text{MC-}\Gamma_A}^{\text{Srch}}, \mathcal{L}_{\text{MC-}\Gamma_A}^{\text{Updt}} \right)$$
$$s.t\, \mathcal{L}_{\text{MC-}\Gamma_A}^{\text{Srch}}(\mathbf{n}) = (\text{sp}(\mathbf{n}), \text{Hist}(n), \text{cp}(n)),$$
$$\mathcal{L}_{\text{MC-}\Gamma_A}^{\text{Updt}}(add, n, ind) = \bot$$

where **n** *is a set of queried keywords s.t* $n \in$ **n**. *Then* MC-Γ_A *is* $\mathcal{L}_{\text{MC-}\Gamma_A}$-*adaptively-secure.*

Proof. Inherited from [5], we create a set of games, DSSEReal$_A^{\text{MC-}\Gamma_A}(1^\lambda)$ and DSSEIdeal$_{A,S}^{\text{MC-}\Gamma_A}(1^\lambda)$.

Game G_0. G_0 is precisely portrays the real-world game DSSEReal$_A^{\text{MC-}\Gamma_A}(1^\lambda)$.

$$\Pr\left[DSSEReal_A^{\text{MC-}\Gamma_A}(1^\lambda) = 1\right] = \Pr[G_0 = 1]$$

Game G_1. In G_1, a random key is select for an input of new keyword n, instead of generating K_n through F, removing the need to generate a client key, as such in Algorithm 2. The key is then stored in a table for later use. If an adversary $\mathcal{A}$ can differentiate games G_0 and G_1, we can then make a reduction table to distinguish between F and a true random function. More formally, an efficient adversary B_1 is made present s.t

$$\Pr[G_0 = 1] - \Pr[G_1 = 1] \leq Adv_{F,B_1}^{PRF}(1^\lambda)$$

Game G_2, G_3. We replace hash functions H_1 and H_2 with random strings in G_2 and G_3 respectively. These games are as described in more detail in [5]. Where differentiating these games is depends on the hardness of the Π, we conclude present an efficient adversary B_2 s.t

$$\Pr[G_1 = 1] - \Pr[G_3 = 1] \leq 2N \cdot Adv_{\Pi,B_2}^{OneWay}(1^\lambda)$$

where N is the number of times H_1 and H_2 ran.

Game G_4. In G_4, for the random generated encrypted strings of H_1 and H_2 that are stored, later reused in the search protocol for H_1 and H_2. Results in G_4 to behave exactly like games G_2 and G_3 s.t

$$\Pr[G_4 = 1] = \Pr\left[G_{2,3} = 1\right]$$

Simulator S. With respect to information leakage "contain pattern" (cp), an update token UT can be specifically reused to determine inclusive relationships between keywords. Consequently, the same can be done with "search pattern" (sp) "history" (Hist) to simulate the Search and Update operations. In Algorithm 3, we map range queries to a set of specified keywords **n** s.t

$$\Pr[G_4 = 1] = \Pr\left[DSSEIdeal_{A,S}^{\text{MC-}\Gamma_A}(1^\lambda) = 1\right]$$

Finally,

$$\Pr\left[\text{DSSEReal}_A^{\text{MC-}\Gamma_A}(1^\lambda)\right] - \Pr\left[\text{DSSEIdeal}_{A,S}^{\text{MC-}\Gamma_A}(1^\lambda) = 1\right]$$
$$\leq Adv_{F,B_1}^{PRF}(1^\lambda) + 2N \cdot Adv_{\Pi,B_2}^{OneWay}(1^\lambda)$$

completing the proof.

Algorithm 2. Game G_1, G_2 outlined with $\boxed{H_1}$ and G_3 outlined with $\boxed{H_2}$

Setup (1^λ)
1: (TPK, TSK) $\leftarrow$ TKeyGen(1^λ)
2: Initialize **T** as an empty map indexed by update token UT_c and **N** as an empty map indexed by n
3: $m \leftarrow 0$
4: **Return** (TPK, TSK, **T**, **N**, m, K)

Search $([a, b], \sigma, \mathbf{T}, m)$
Client:
1: CBT $\leftarrow$ TCon(m)
2: ABT $\leftarrow$ TAssign(CBT)
3: RSet $\leftarrow$ TGetCover$([a, b],$ ABT$)$
4: For each node n in RSet do
5:     $K_n \leftarrow Key(n)$
6:     $(ST_c, c) \leftarrow \mathbf{N}[n]$
7:     If $(ST_c, c) \neq \perp$ then
8:         Sent to server (K_n, ST_c, c)
9:     End if
10: End for
Server:
1: For $i = c$ to 0 do
2:     $\boxed{UT_i \leftarrow H_1(K_n, ST_i)}$
3:     $e \leftarrow \mathbf{T}[UT_i]$
4:     $\boxed{ind \leftarrow e \oplus H_2(K_n, ST_i)}$
5:     Return to client ind
6:     $ST_{i-1} \leftarrow \Pi(\text{TPK}, ST_i)$
7: End for

Update $(add, v, ind, \sigma, \mathbf{T}, m)$
Data Owner:

1: CBT $\leftarrow$ TCon(m)
2: If $v = m$ then
3:     CBT $\leftarrow$ TUpdate(add, v, m)
4:     $m \leftarrow m + 1$
5:     If CBT added a new root node then
6:         $(ST_c, c) \leftarrow \mathbf{N}[root_{org}]$
7:         $\mathbf{N}[root_{new}] \leftarrow (ST_c, c)$
8:     End if
9:     Get the leaf node n_v of value v
10:     ABT $\leftarrow$ TAssign(CBT)
11:     NSet $\leftarrow$ TGetNodes$(n_v,$ ABT$)$
12:     For every node n in NSet do
13:         $K_n \leftarrow Key(n)$
14:         $(ST_c, c) \leftarrow \mathbf{N}[n]$
15:         If $(ST_c, c) = \perp$ then
16:             $ST_0 \leftarrow \mathcal{M}$
17:             $c \leftarrow -1$
18:         Else
19:             $ST_{c+1} \leftarrow \Pi^{-1}(\text{TSK}, ST_c)$
20:         End if
21:         $\mathbf{N}[n] \leftarrow (ST_{c+1}, c + 1)$
22:         $\boxed{UT_{c+1} \leftarrow H_1(K_n, ST_{c+1})}$
23:         $\boxed{e \leftarrow ind \oplus H_2(K_n, ST_{c+1})}$
24:         Send to the Server (UT_{c+1}, e)
25:     End for
26: Else if $v < m$ then
27:     Repeat steps 9 - 25
28: End if
Server:
1: $\mathbf{T}[UT_{c+1}] \leftarrow e$

Algorithm 3. Simulator S	

S. Setup (1^λ)
1: (TPK, TSK) ← TKeyGen(1^λ)
2: **T** and **N** as empty maps
3: $u \leftarrow 0$
4: **Return** (TPK, TSK, T, N)

S. Update ()
Client:
1: $UT[u] \xleftarrow{\$} \{0,1\}^\mu$
2: $e[u] \xleftarrow{\$} \{0,1\}^\lambda$
3: Send to the Server ($UT[u], e[u]$)
4: $u \leftarrow u + 1$

S. Search (sp(n), Hist(n), cp(n))
Client:
1: $n \leftarrow$ sp(**n**)
2: $K_n \leftarrow Key[n]$
3: Parse Hist(n) as (add, u_0, ind_0, ...,
add, u_c, ind_c)
4: Parse cp(n) as (c', n')
5: If $c' < c$ then
  ▸ Keyword n contains previously queried keyword n'

6: If $c' = -1$ then
  ▸ Keyword n does not contain previously queried keywords
7:    $c' \leftarrow 0$
8:    $ST_0 \leftarrow$ **N**$[n]$
9: Else
10:   $ST_{c'} \leftarrow$ **N**$[n']$
11: End if
12: For $i = c'$ to c do
13:   Result of $H_1(K_n, ST_i) \leftarrow UT[u_i]$
14:   Result of $H_2(K_n, ST_i) \leftarrow e[u_i] \oplus ind_i$
15:   $ST_{i+1} \leftarrow \Pi^{-1}(TSK, ST_i)$
16: End for
17: Send to the Server (K_n, ST_c)
18: Else if $c' \geq c$ then
  ▸ Keyword n' contains previous queried keyword n
19: Get c^{th} search token ST_c of previous queries keyword n'
20: Send to the Server (K_n, ST_c)
21: End if

References

1. Kamara, S., Lauter, K.: Cryptographic cloud storage. In: Sion, R., Curtmola, R., Dietrich, S., Kiayias, A., Miret, Josep M., Sako, K., Sebé, F. (eds.) FC 2010. LNCS, vol. 6054, pp. 136–149. Springer, Heidelberg (2010). https://doi.org/10.1007/978-3-642-14992-4_13
2. Curtmola, R., Garay, J., Kamara, S., Ostrovsky, R.: Searchable symmetric encryption: improved definitions and efficient constructions. J. Comput. Secur. **19**(5), 895–934 (2011)
3. Jarecki, S., Jutla, C., Krawczyk, H., Rosu, M., Steiner, M.: Outsourced symmetric private information retrieval. In: Proceedings of the 2013 ACM SIGSAC Conference on Computer & Communications Security 2013, pp. 875–888. ACM (2013)
4. Cash, D., Jarecki, S., Jutla, C., Krawczyk, H., Roşu, M.-C., Steiner, M.: Highly-scalable searchable symmetric encryption with support for boolean queries. In: Canetti, R., Garay, Juan A. (eds.) CRYPTO 2013. LNCS, vol. 8042, pp. 353–373. Springer, Heidelberg (2013). https://doi.org/10.1007/978-3-642-40041-4_20

5. Zuo, C., Sun, S., Liu, J.K., Shao, J., Pieprzyk, J.: Dynamic searchable symmetric encryption schemes supporting range queries with forward (and backward) security. IACR Cryptology ePrint Archive, vol. 2018, p. 628 (2018)

6. Sun, S.-F., Liu, Joseph K., Sakzad, A., Steinfeld, R., Yuen, T.H.: An efficient non-interactive multi-client searchable encryption with support for boolean queries. In: Askoxylakis, I., Ioannidis, S., Katsikas, S., Meadows, C. (eds.) ESORICS 2016. LNCS, vol. 9878, pp. 154–172. Springer, Cham (2016). https://doi.org/10.1007/978-3-319-45744-4_8

7. Dawn Xiaoding, S., Wagner, D., Perrig, A.: Practical techniques for searches on encrypted data. In: Proceedings of 2000 IEEE Symposium on Security and Privacy. S&P 2000, pp. 44–55 (2000)

8. Cash, D., et al.: Dynamic Searchable Encryption in Very-Large Databases: Data Structures and Implementation. Citeseer (2014)

9. Deng, Z., Li, K., Li, K., Zhou, J.: A multi-user searchable encryption scheme with keyword authorization in a cloud storage. Future Gener. Comput. Syst. **72**, 208–218 (2017)

10. Faber, S., Jarecki, S., Krawczyk, H., Nguyen, Q., Rosu, M.-C., Steiner, M.: Rich queries on encrypted data: beyond exact matches. IACR Cryptology ePrint Archive, vol. 2015, p. 927 (2015)

11. Jiang, H., Li, X., Xu, Q.: An improvement to a multi-client searchable encryption scheme for boolean queries (in English). J. Med. Syst. **40**(12), 1–11 (2016)

12. Kasra Kermanshahi, S., Liu, Joseph K., Steinfeld, R.: Multi-user cloud-based secure keyword search. In: Pieprzyk, J., Suriadi, S. (eds.) ACISP 2017. LNCS, vol. 10342, pp. 227–247. Springer, Cham (2017). https://doi.org/10.1007/978-3-319-60055-0_12

13. Sun, L., Xu, C., Zhang, Y.: A dynamic and non-interactive boolean searchable symmetric encryption in multi-client setting. J. Inf. Secur. Appl. **40**, 145–155 (2018)

14. Zuo, C., Macindoe, J., Yang, S., Steinfeld, R., Liu, J.K.: Trusted boolean search on cloud using searchable symmetric encryption. In: 2016 IEEE Trustcom/BigDataSE/ISPA, pp. 113–120 (2016)

15. Stefanov, E., Papamanthou, C., Shi, E.: Practical dynamic searchable encryption with small leakage. In: NDSS, vol. 71, pp. 72–75 (2014)

16. Bost, R.: $\sum o\varphi o\varsigma$: forward secure searchable encryption. In: Proceedings of the 2016 ACM SIGSAC Conference on Computer and Communications Security, pp. 1143–1154. ACM (2016)

17. Bost, R., Fouque, P.-A., Pointcheval, D.: Verifiable dynamic symmetric searchable encryption: optimality and forward security. IACR Cryptology ePrint Archive, vol. 2016, p. 62 (2016)

18. Sahai, A., Waters, B.: Fuzzy identity-based encryption. In: Cramer, R. (ed.) EUROCRYPT 2005. LNCS, vol. 3494, pp. 457–473. Springer, Heidelberg (2005). https://doi.org/10.1007/11426639_27

19. Bethencourt, J., Sahai, A., Waters, B.: Ciphertext-policy attribute-based encryption. In: 2007 IEEE Symposium on Security and Privacy (SP 2007), pp. 321–334 (2007)

20. Waters, B.: Ciphertext-policy attribute-based encryption: an expressive, efficient, and provably secure realization. In: Catalano, D., Fazio, N., Gennaro, R., Nicolosi, A. (eds.) PKC 2011. LNCS, vol. 6571, pp. 53–70. Springer, Heidelberg (2011). https://doi.org/10.1007/978-3-642-19379-8_4

Image Authentication for Permissible Cropping

Haixia Chen[1,2], Shangpeng Wang[2,3], Hongyan Zhang[1,2], and Wei Wu[2,3](✉)

[1] Concord University College Fujian Normal University, Fuzhou, China
[2] Fujian Provincial Key Lab of Network Security and Cryptology, Fuzhou, China
weiwu@fjnu.edu.cn
[3] College of Mathematics and Informatics, Fujian Normal University, Fuzhou, China

Abstract. In a digital society, it is not easy to achieve a balance between privacy and authentication. Privacy requires some modifications of the original image and signed data, but image authentication needs to ensure its integrity as much as possible. The most common method of privacy protecting is deleting some sensitive data in the original data. In this paper, we propose a practical scheme of image authentication for permissible cropping operation, using a textbook RSA signature scheme and a message commitment scheme. The security of our scheme is implied by the security of underlying cryptographic primitives. Experimental results show that the proposed scheme is practical and can be embedded in some on-line systems.

Keywords: Image authentication · Textbook RSA signature ·
Commitment · Image cropping

1 Introduction

Nowadays, computers and network are the most two necessary components of a digital society. Being integrated with mobile phones and portable computers, digital camera is so ubiquitous that images have become prevalent medias. For example, when a traffic incident happens, the videos captured by a surveillance system are important evidence for the police. Other digital images, such as scanning copies of certificates, screen capture for chatting records in social networks and electronic bills for E-bank transactions, also contain significant information and play important roles in our everyday life.

With the rapid development of the Internet, people have been used to sharing their personal data with others by E-mails or on-line systems. However, the opening network also increases the possibility of tampering with original messages. It is crucial to verify the integrity of images which are sent from thousands of miles away.

Supported by Fujian Provincial Department of Education Project (JA15635), National Natural Science Foundation of China (61822202, 61872089).

F. Guo et al. (Eds.): Inscrypt 2018, LNCS 11449, pp. 308–325, 2019.
https://doi.org/10.1007/978-3-030-14234-6_17

The most two useful security technologies for image authentication are watermarking [1,7,8,12,15,17–19] and digital signatures [2–6,9–11,13,14,16]. The former embeds a piece of information called watermarks, which are often invisible, to the original image by transforming the image, and the extraction of the watermarks is an inverse transformation. The advantages of watermarking are invisibility and robustness. When an image is embedded with a watermark, invisibility ensures that it looks almost the same as the original one and the utility of the image would not be affected. With the property of robustness, watermarks can also been extracted correctly even the loaded image suffers from some attacks such as noising and geometric transformation. But it is difficult for watermarks to provide non-reputation and unforgeablity, since watermarks can be embedded again to other unauthorized images.

Compared with watermarks, digital signatures take more computation cost but provide a higher level of protection, such as unforgeability and non-repudiation. An ordinary signature scheme uses a private key to sign the image and a matching public key to verify the image-signature pair. An ordinary signature scheme must be existentially unforgeable against adaptive chosen message attacks [4]. Without the private key, it is computationally difficult to forge a valid signature of a new message. Therefore, digital signatures are becoming more and more popular in image authentication with the rapid development of computers hardware. But image authentication using an ordinary signature scheme has a disadvantage: slight modifications on the image will invalidate the original image. But in image processing, modification such as geometric transformation and compress are often needed and sometime necessary (e.g., for privacy protection).

Privacy and authenticity are often contradictory. The image recipient would like to verify the integrity and the source of the image. When this image is used again, deletion and masking are the two often operations to hide sensitive parts. These modifications would cause significant difficulties to image authentication. A promising method to alleviate the conflict of these two requirements is redactable signature [13]. In a redactable signature scheme, the signer define a redact policy which includes a subset of the indices that should be retained or removed, and a legitimate redactor revises the message by deleting or masking some sensitive information and outputs a revised signature without the private key. Anyone with the public key can verify the image-signature pair. In this paper, we will present an authenticated image cropping scheme from redactable signatures.

1.1   Our Contributions

It is a common method to protect privacy by deleting some sensitive information in signed messages. To protect the privacy of images, we need to remove some sensitive pixels from the original image by cropping. Authenticated image cropping must take into account two security issues. First, image consists of pixels and each pixel has its position. Identical pixels at different positions would lead to different images. As a result, image cropping should not affect the remained data. Second, to preserve the content of images, deletions can not be defined too meticulously, and an area is more practical than a subset of pixels. In fact, our intention is to provide user with the maximum flexibility when cropping image, as long as the integrity of the remained image is guaranteed.

In this paper, we give a formal definition of permissible image cropping based on rectangular areas in images. After that, we use a redactable signature scheme to design an image authentication scheme, called Image Signature for Permissible Cropping (ISPC). ISPC is particularly suitable for image authentication when the signed image can only be partly disclosed after having been signed. In an ISPC scheme (Fig. 1), instead of sending a full image and its signature to Cindy (receiver and verifier), Alice (the signer of an image) allows Bob (the owner of the image or a legitimate user) to crop the image and outputs a revised signature to Cindy who has a public key to verify the signature. A revised image is valid if it is cut by Bob with permissible cropping operation defined by Alice.

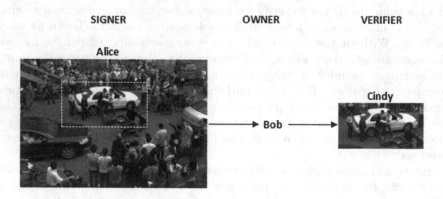

Fig. 1. The framework of authenticated image cropping

The rest of the paper is organized as follows. We describe some related works in Sect. 2. In Sect. 3, we present the preliminaries required by this paper. Section 4 presents formal definitions of ISPC and its security models. In Sect. 5 we describe our ISPC scheme and give its security analysis. Some experiment data is given in Sect. 6 and we conclude this paper in Sect. 7.

2 Related Works

2.1 Image Authentication

As we have mentioned in Sect. 1, watermarking and digital signatures are the most two popular image authentication methods. Watermarking embeds invisible information in the image to copyright protection and image content authentication. Fragile watermarks [7,8,15,17] are used to detect tampering due to its sensitive response to manipulation in images. The scheme proposed in [8] is a novel multipurpose watermarking scheme, in which both robust and fragile watermarks are embedded for the purpose for copyright protection and content authentication. Another scheme is proposed in [17] to detect any modification on image and indicate the specific locations that have been modified. Fragile watermarking is useful to detect tampering, but it is so sensitive that any transformation including denoising, compression and other rational manipulations would hamper the extraction of watermarks.

Semi-fragile watermarking is introduced to tolerate rational manipulation in image authentication [1,12,18,19]. The method in [18] proposed a modification-detect method by measuring the errors between the watermarked image and the manipulated image, to distinguish tampering and rational manipulation. The method in [1] is based on a modified DWT quantization-based algorithm, which embeds a random watermark bit sequence into the DWT domain. This method employs an expanded-bit multiscale quantization-based technique to adjust watermarked location. Zhuvikin et al. [19] use image finite differences, such as the Haar wavelet transform coefficients, to embed watermarks and resist compress transformation.

Recent years have seen increasing attention on image authentication from cryptographic tools, such as digital signatures. An effective technique for image authentication was proposed to prevent malicious manipulations and allow JPEG lossy compression [5]. The scheme is based on the invariance of the relationships among discrete cosine transform (DCT) coefficients at the same position in separate blocks of an image.

Another method in [7] uses a content based digital signature for image authentication scheme and signs the feathers extracted from images. A threshold value is defined to allow modifications on the signed image, and the verification would succeed if the difference between the modified image and its original one is less than the pre-defined threshold. This scheme can partly reduce the conflicts between image processing and authentication, but cannot provide a strong security protection. Given a valid signature σ of an image I, an adversary can create a new valid image-signature pair (I', σ) as long as the difference between I and I' satisfies the threshold.

In 2016, Naveh and Tromer [9] proposed a common model by taking into account the security and manipulation of images. After permissible transformations with a certified image, cryptographic proofs are added to the image, with which a subsequent verifier can verify image integrity. In their approach, additional data which they called "photoproofs" is attached to the signed image and the subsequent verifier with these proofs can verify the signature successfully. It is not easy to instantiate the model because "photoproofs" are difficult to construct without the private key, and new proofs must be attached to the image even if the same kind of transformation is executed again. In addition, without defining constraint conditions in the initial stage, the original signer is hard to control the subsequent editions of the original image effectively. This would cause serious security issues in many applications.

All aforementioned schemes are sensitive to image cropping. Kim et al. [6] proposed a privacy-aware and secure signature scheme by utilizing a chameleon hash to reconstruct the image after deleting some objects in a signed image. This scheme can be used to delete objects from a signed image, but its effectiveness is questionable since it needs to compute hash value for each data block and sign separately. Furthermore, the scheme in [6] is not flexible since the image must be divided into several blocks and sign separately.

Another disadvantage in existing schemes is that images are treated as discrete data. In fact, an image consists of pixels which are related with each other and these continuous elements together compose a meaningful image. The positions of pixels are useful for image processing. It is more meaningful to process a block than a pixel, especially for image cropping due to privacy protection. In the remainder of this paper, we will give some useful definition of block cropping in image processing.

3   Preliminaries

In this section, we will present some preliminaries required by this paper, including formal definition of permissible image cropping and the cryptographic tools used in our scheme.

3.1   Image and Rectangular Areas

A digital image consists of pixels. We denote an image by a unique integer matrix $M \in \{0, 1, ..., 255\}^{m \times n}$, where m and n are integers and $m \times n$ is the size of the image. Each matrix element m_{ij} represents the value of a pixel, where i is the column number and j is the row number. In order to define a pixel more clearly, we will denote a pixel m_{ij} by an integer pair (i, j) in this paper.

In order to describe more areas of an image, we denote a rectangular area in an image by an ordered pair (x_1, y_1, x_2, y_2). Here (x_1, y_1) is the top left pixel and (x_2, y_2) is the low right pixel of the area, which are called *corner pixels*. Given the *corner pixels* a rectangular area in an image can be uniquely located. Therefore, we will use an integer pair with four integers to denote a rectangular area R_i, i.e., $R_i = (x_{1i}, y_{1i}, x_{2i}, y_{2i})$ and i is the index of the area. We also define some additional notations about rectangular areas in an image as follows (Fig. 2).

Fig. 2. A rectangular area in an image

Definition 1 *(A Pixel in a Rectangular Area $\in_R$). Given a pixel $p = (x, y)$ and a rectangular area $R_i = (x_{1i}, y_{1i}, x_{2i}, y_{2i})$, we say $p \in_R R_i$ if*

$$x_{1i} \leq x \leq x_{2i} \text{ and } y_{1i} \leq y \leq y_{2i}.$$

Here, we call that the pixel p is included in a rectangular area R_i.

Definition 2 *(Rectangular Area Relation $\subseteq_R$). For any pair of rectangular areas in an image $R_i = (x_{1i}, y_{1i}, x_{2i}, y_{2i})$ and $R_j = (x_{1j}, y_{1j}, x_{2j}, y_{2j})$, we say $R_i \subseteq_R R_j$ if*

$$x_{1j} \leq x_{1i} \leq x_{2i} \leq x_{2j} \text{ and } y_{1j} \leq y_{1i} \leq y_{2i} \leq y_{2j}.$$

The above two definitions help us clarify the relationship between pixels and rectangular areas. We will assume that a digital image is divided into several overlapping rectangular areas, and we denote by R_i the ith rectangular area. According to the above definition, a rectangular areas R_i can be defined as $R_i = (x_{1i}, y_{1i}, x_{2i}, y_{2i})$. Therefore, an image is represented in a form which encodes an ordering of the rectangular areas. We use $[n]$ to denote the set of integers $1, 2, ..., n$, num to denote the number of rectangular areas, and $< R_i >_i \in [num]$ to denote an image (Fig. 3).

There are scenarios that the owner of an image would like someone else to modify the image. For example, when transmitted in the network, it would be necessary to remove insignificant areas (for bandwidth saving) or sensitive areas (for privacy protection). But the image owner wants to ensure that certain areas of the image are unchanged. This calls for the need of an image authentication method with permissible cropping. We will define a detect method for a permissible cropping in an image as follows:

Definition 3 *(Permissible Cropping Detect PCrop). Input a $m \times n$ image M, a subset R which includes all the rectangular areas retained in an image, and a rectangular area M_C, we denote a detect function for permissible cropping by $\mathsf{PCrop}(M, R, M_C)$ as follows:*

$$\begin{aligned} &if \quad for \; all \; i \quad R_i \subseteq_R M_C \\ &\qquad \mathsf{PCrop}(M, R, M_C) = true \\ &else \\ &\qquad \mathsf{PCrop}(M, R, M_C) = false \end{aligned}$$

Here, R_i is the ith area defined in a retained subset R, and R is usually defined by the owner or signer of the image to produce a cropping policy, which is also an additional input of the signing algorithm. M_C is the area retained after cropping operation. If PCrop returns true, we say that the area M_C is cut by a permissible cropping.

Fig. 3. An example of permissible cropping

3.2 Cryptographic tools

"RSA Signatures": We describe the textbook RSA signature scheme here. Although the scheme is insecure, it is still useful when combined with other schemes in many applications. The textbook RSA signature scheme [4] consists of three algorithms: RSA = (KeyGen, Sign, Vrfy):

- Gen: on input 1^n to obtain (N, e, d), satisfying $ed = 1 \mod \phi(N)$. The public key is (N, e), the private key is (N, d).
- Sign: on input a private key $sk = (N, d)$ and a message $m \in Z_N^*$, compute the signature $\sigma = m^d \pmod{N}$.
- Vrfy: on input a public key $pk = (N, e)$, a signature $\sigma \in Z_N^*$ and a message $m \in Z_N^*$, output 1 if and only if $m = \sigma^e \pmod{N}$.

Commitment Schemes. In modern cryptography, a commitment scheme allows one party to 'commit' to a message m by sending a commitment value *com*, while obtaining the following seemingly contradictory properties [4,14]:

- Hiding: the commitment reveals nothing about m.
- Binding: it is infeasible for the committer to output a commitment *com* that it can later "open" as two different messages m, m'.

Formally, a commitment scheme is defined by a randomized algorithm Gen that outputs public parameters *params* and an algorithm Com that takes *params* and a message $m \in \{1, n\}^n$ and outputs a commitment *com*; we will make the randomness used by Com explicit, and denote it by r. A sender commits to m by choosing uniform r, computing $com := \mathsf{Com}(params, m; r)$, and sending it to a receiver. The Sender can later decommit *com* and reveal m by sending m, r to the receiver; the receiver verifies this by checking that $\mathsf{Com}(params, m; r) \overset{?}{=} com$.

4 Image Signature Schemes for Permissible Cropping (ISPC)

As discussed in Sect. 2, we will design a signature scheme for image authentication. Our scheme allows permissible cropping defined by the signer. We shall define the syntax of image signature for permissible cropping and its security requirements.

4.1 Definition of an Image Signature for Permissible Cropping

A digital image signature scheme for permissible cropping ISPC consists of the following four algorithms: ISPC = (KeyGen, CropSign, CropExt, CropVrfy).

- KeyGen: The Key Generation Algorithm KeyGen that takes a security parameter λ as a input, returns a key pair (pk, sk) as the public key and private key. That is: $(pk, sk) \leftarrow$ KeyGen(1^λ).
- CropSign: The Signing Algorithm CropSign that takes as input the private key sk, an image M and a subset R of rectangular areas which should be retained in the image, and outputs a permissible cropping signature σ_F. That is: $\sigma_F \leftarrow$ CropSign(sk, M, R).
- CropExt: The Signature Cropping Algorithm CropExt that takes a public key pk, an image M, a permissible cropping signature σ_F, and a remained rectangular area R_C when cropping the image, outputs a cropped signature σ_C. That is: $\sigma_C \leftarrow$ CropExt(pk, M, σ_F, R_C).
- CropVrfy: The Signature Verification Algorithm CropVrfy that takes the public key pk, a cropped signature σ_C, and cropped subimage M', outputs a bit $b \in \{0, 1\}$. That is $b \leftarrow$ Vrfy(pk, σ_C, M') (Fig. 4).

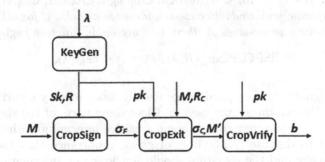

Fig. 4. An overview of ISPC

4.2 Security Properties of ISPC

This section defines the security properties of an ISPC scheme must possess, including unforgeability and privacy.

Unforgeability: The unforgeability of our ISPC is analogous to the "existential unforgeability" in [3,14], with an additional requirement of reaction control [2, 16]. In our scheme, the signer has a full control of image areas should be retained. Any removal of these areas is considered as 'unauthentic cropping', and it must be infeasible to produce a valid signature after unauthentic cropping. This explains why we include a subset R as an additional input to the signing algorithm.

IAPC – Unforgeability Requirement: It is infeasible for an attacker, having access to an ISPC signing oracle $CropSign(sk, ., .)$, with a fixed public key pk generated by a signer, to produce an image M^* with a valid signature σ, where M^* is not the image which have been signed by signer or M^* is obtained by 'unauthentic' cropping operation.

Let ISPC = (KeyGen, CropSign, CropExt, CropVrfy) be an image signature scheme for permissible cropping. The unforgeability of ISPC is defined by the following experiment:

$$
\begin{array}{l}
\text{Experiment ISPCUPExp}_{\mathcal{A}}(R, \lambda, M) \\
(pk, sk) \leftarrow \text{KeyGen}(1^\lambda) \\
\sigma_F^* \leftarrow \mathcal{A}(pk | \text{CropSign}(sk, ., .) \\
\sigma_C^* \leftarrow \mathcal{A}(pk | \text{CropExt}(pk, \sigma_F, ., .)) \\
b \leftarrow \text{CropVrfy}(pk, M^*, \sigma_C^*) \\
\quad \text{if } b{=}1, M^* \notin \Omega \text{ and } \text{PCrop}(M, R, M^*) = false \\
\quad \text{then return } 1 \\
\quad \text{else return } 0
\end{array}
$$

Here Ω is the set of all queries that $\mathcal{A}$ asked its oracle, and M^* is the subimage which has been cut from the original image.

Definition 4. *A scheme* ISPC = (KeyGen, CropSign, CropExt, CropVrfy) *is existentially unforgeable under adaptive chosen-message attacks, if for all probabilistic polynomial-time adversaries $\mathcal{A}$, there is a negligible function* negl *such that:*

$$
\Pr[\text{ISPCUPExp}_{\mathcal{A}}(R, \lambda, M) = 1] \leq \text{negl}(\lambda).
$$

Privacy: A signature for cropped image usually has a privacy security requirement. Indeed, the reason for the user to delete some parts of the signed image just because these parts may contain some sensitive information which the user does not want to disclose [3,14]. It is of great importance that the reserved parts of the image and the signature should not leak any information of those been removed. Our definition of **ISPC – Privacy-Requirement** is based on an undistinguishable experiment defined as follows.

ISPC – PrivacyRequirement. It is infeasible for an attacker to obtain any information about the removed areas in the original image from the signature σ of a cropped image M'.

Firstly, the attacker $\mathcal{A}$ executes the Choose algorithm and obtains a pair of images M_0 and M_1, which are identical in the rectangular area R but differ in other areas. Then, the attacker chooses a random bit $b \in \{0, 1\}$. Let $M^* = M_b$ be the input of the sign oracle and σ_C^* be the cropped signature given to the attacker. At last, the attacker executes the guess algorithm Guess to decide which image has been signed and outputs a bit b^*. If $b^* = b$, the attacker succeeds.

Let ISPC = (KeyGen, CropSign, CropExt, CropVrfy) be an image signature scheme for permissible cropping, and Choose and Guess be two algorithms of attacker $\mathcal{A}$:

Experiment $\mathsf{ISPCPRExp}_{\mathcal{A}}(R, \lambda, M)$
  $(pk, sk) \leftarrow \mathsf{KeyGen}(1^{\lambda})$
  $(M_0, M_1) \leftarrow \mathcal{A}(pk|\mathsf{Choose}(R));$
  $b \xleftarrow{\$} \{0, 1\}$
  $\sigma_F^* \leftarrow \mathcal{A}(pk|\mathsf{CropSig}(sk, M_b, R))$
  $(M_C^*, \sigma_C^*) \leftarrow \mathcal{A}(pk|\mathsf{CropExt}(pk, \sigma_F^*, ., M_b))$
  $b^* \leftarrow \mathcal{A}(pk|\mathsf{Guess}(\sigma_C^*, M_0, M_1, R)$
  if $b = b^*$
      then return 1
  else return 0

Definition 5. *For a scheme* ISPC = (KeyGen, CropSign, CropExt, CropVrfy), *we define its privacy requirement as an attacker* $\mathcal{A}$*'s success in experiment* ISPCPRExp *with negligible advantage. There is a negligible function* negl *such that:*

$$\Pr[\mathsf{ISPCPRExp}_{\mathcal{A}}(R, \lambda, M) = 1] - \frac{1}{2} \le \mathsf{negl}(\lambda).$$

5 Construction

5.1 Algorithm

Our design is motivated by the content extraction signature scheme in [14], taking into account the features of image.

Let ISPC = (KeyGen, CropSign, CropExt, CropVrfy) be a image signature scheme for permissible cropping. We build our scheme as follows:

– KeyGen: On input λ, compute $(pk, sk) \leftarrow \mathsf{Gen}(1^{\lambda})$, the private key (N, d) for the signer and the public key (N, e) for the verifier.

Algorithm $\mathsf{Gen}(1^{\lambda})$
  $(p, q) \leftarrow \mathsf{GetPrime}(1^{\lambda})$
  $N \leftarrow p \times q$
  $\phi(N) \leftarrow (p - 1) \times (q - 1)$
  $e \leftarrow Z_N^*$ and $\gcd(e, \phi(N)) = 1$
  $d \leftarrow e^{-1} \bmod \phi(N)$
  $pk \leftarrow (N, e)$
  $sk \leftarrow (N, d)$

- CropSign: Given an image M, we denote a subset R of rectangular areas which should be retained in M. On input R and the private key (N, d), output a signature σ_F.

Algorithm CropSign($(N, d), M, R$)
for i=1 to m and $j = 1$ to n
$\quad c_{ij} \leftarrow \mathsf{Com}(m_{ij}, r_{ij})$
$h \leftarrow \mathsf{H}(c_{00}||c_{01}||...||c_{ij}||...||c_{mn}, R)$
$\sigma_R \leftarrow h^d \mod N$
$\sigma_F \leftarrow (R, \sigma_R, < r_{ij} >_{(m_{ij}) \in_R M})$
return σ_F

Here r_{ij} is the randomness value for m_{ij}, Com is a committing function, c_{ij} is the commitment of pixel m_{ij} and R is the subset of rectangular areas defined by signer, implying the contents that should not be modified by users. H is a hash function with inputs of the concatenation of all commitments, and R and σ_R is a RSA signature. σ_F is a collection of the RSA signature σ_R, subset R and commitments of all pixels.

- CropExt: On input an image M, a rectangular area R_C to be removed, a public key (N, e) and an image signature σ_F, output a cropped signature σ_E and a cropped image M' denoted by m'_{ij}.

Algorithm CropExt(pk, M, σ_F, R_C)
Parse $\sigma_F \leftarrow (R, \sigma_C, < c_{ij} >_{m_{ij} \in M})$
for all $m_{ij} \notin_R R_C$
$\quad c_{ij} \leftarrow \mathsf{Com}(m_{ij}, r_{ij})$
$\sigma_E \leftarrow (\sigma_C, < c_{ij} >_{m_{ij} \in_R M \backslash R_C}, < r_{ij} >_{m_{ij} \in_R R_C})$
return σ_E

Here, R_c is a rectangular area, and also is a subimage which has been cut from the original according to subset R. σ_E is a collection of original signature σ_C, a subset of commitments $< c_{ij} >$ of pixels located in R and a subset of randomness $< r_{ij} >$ of pixels not in R (Fig. 5).

- CropVrfy: On input a cropped image M', a public key pk and a cropped signature σ_E, output a bit $b \in \{0, 1\}$.

Algorithm CropVrfy(pk, M', σ_E)
Parse $\sigma_E \leftarrow (\sigma_C, < c_{ij} >_{m_{ij} \in_R M \backslash R_C}, < r_{ij} >_{m_{ij} \in_R R_C})$
for all $m_{ij} \in_R M'$
    $c_{ij} \leftarrow \mathsf{Com}(m_{ij}, r_{ij})$
$h \leftarrow \mathsf{H}(c_{00}||c_{01}||...||c_{ij}||...||c_{mn}, R)$
if $\sigma_C^e = h \bmod N$ and $\mathsf{PCrop}(M, R, M') = true$
    $b \leftarrow 1$
else
    $b \leftarrow 0$

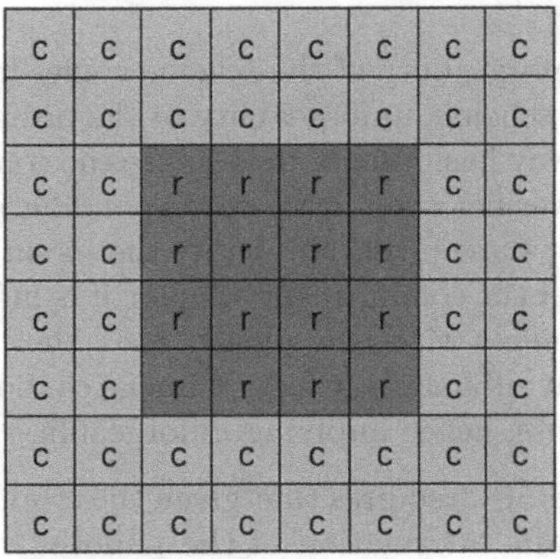

Fig. 5. The randomness for a rectangular area

5.2 Algorithm Analysis

Correctness: The correctness of ISPC is due to the correctness of an RSA signature for concatenation of all commitments. If the original image is cropped under the permissible policy, every pixel of R is included in the retained subimage M'. and no pixel which without commitment is deleted, so all the pixels' commitments can be collected to reconstruct the concatenation of all commitments, the hash value h can be computed correctly as an input of a RSA signature, because of the correctness of RSA signatures, we take it for grant that an ISPC scheme is correct.

Computation: In our scheme, the computation cost consists of two major operations: commitment generation and signature production. As we all know, it is efficient to compute commitments using collision-resistant hash function. On the other side, our scheme takes only one signing operation on the whole image, instead of signing every image pixel. As a result, our scheme is efficient for practical use.

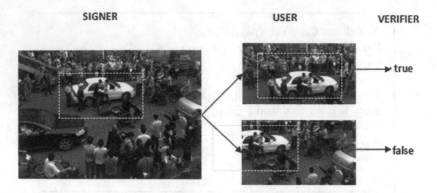

Fig. 6. Test for image 'traffic.jpg'

Unforgeablity: The unforgeablity of the scheme comes from the binding property of the commitment scheme, unforgeablity of the ordinary signature scheme and security of the one-way hash function. Because the commitments in retained areas are removed, the verifier should use corresponding randomness to recompute the commitments of these pixels and verify the signature correctly. Because of the binding property of the commitment scheme, it is infeasible for an attacker to 'open' these commitments with new pixels. Also, the hiding property of the commitment ensures that subimages in signed image cannot be modified without affecting the commitments, hence implying unforgeablity.

Privacy: The privacy of ISPC requires that given the cropping signature, it must be infeasible to obtain any information of the removed sub-image. Because of hiding property of a commitment scheme, it is infeasible for an attacker to get any information of the message m if r is not given. The hiding property of the commitment scheme ensures that without the randomness r, no attacker can obtain any information of the removed message.

6   Experiments

We use OpenCV and Crypto++ libraries to evaluate of CropSign. In our experiments, firstly we use SHA-3 algorithm to create digests of test images and compute commitments. After that, we use a textbook RSA to sign the digests of images. The hash function MD5 can compress a message with arbitrary length to a much shorter message with fixed length.

Firstly, we use a 700 × 405 image to simulate the signature application. In this image, the original number of pixels is 283500, so we compute a 128-bit commitment of each pixel. We also define a rectangular area R, and the concatenation of all commitments and R are inputs of MD5. The size of original message is 2268000 bits, we use MD5 compress the original image to 128-bit. The key size for a RSA signature is 2048 bits. We test two kinds of cropping and got two verification results (Fig. 6).

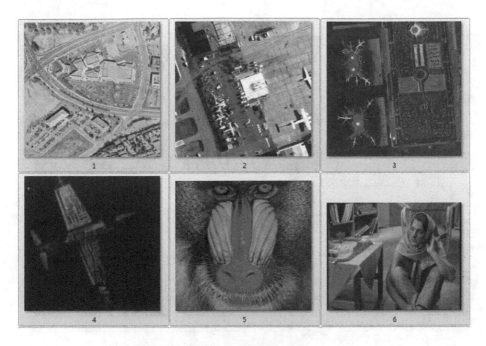

Fig. 7. Test images (1)

Fig. 8. Test images (2)

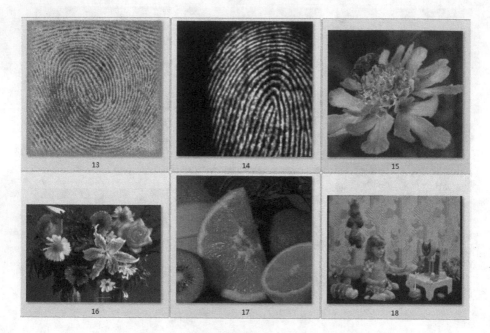

Fig. 9. Test images (3)

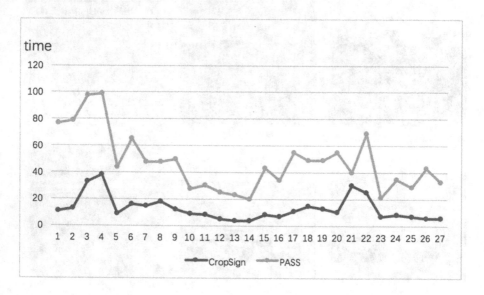

Fig. 10. Time-consuming compared with PASS

Table 1. Test Images

No.	Image name	Resolution	Size (byte)
1	aerial	512 × 512	258K
2	airfield	512 × 512	258K
3	airfild2	1024 × 1024	1026K
4	airplaneU2	1024 × 1024	258K
5	baboon	500 × 480	703K
6	barbara	720 × 576	1216K
7	boats	720 × 576	407K
8	BoatsColor	787 × 576	1330K
9	bridge	512 × 512	258K
10	cablecar	512 × 480	721K
11	cornfield	512 × 548	721K
12	dollar	512 × 512	258K
13	finger	256 × 256	66K
14	fingerprint	256 × 256	66K
15	flower	512 × 480	721K
16	flowers	500 × 362	531K
17	fruits	512 × 480	721K
18	girl	720 × 576	1216K
19	goldhill	720 × 576	1216K
20	lenna	512 × 512	769K
21	man	1024 × 1024	1026K
22	monarch	768 × 512	1153K
23	pens	512 × 480	721K
24	pepper	512 × 512	769K
25	sailboat	512 × 512	769K
26	soccer	512 × 480	721K
27	yacht	512 × 480	721K

Our experiment shows that the proposed scheme is practical for on-line systems. To further evaluate the efficiency of our scheme, we also choose 27 standard sample pictures (Figs. 7, 8 and 9) to carry our experiments in a PC (CPU: Intel Core I5 5200U; Memory: 8 GB (1333 MHz)). Table 1 summarizes the information of these pictures. The simulation results are given in Table 2. We also compare our scheme with [6] it terms of time-consuming and results are shown in Fig. 10.

Table 2. Time-consuming of some test Images

No.	Size of R	Length of input	Signing time in a PC
1	100×100	6291456 bits	11 ms
2	75×43	6291456 bits	13 ms
3	55×47	25165824 bits	17 ms
4	100×100	25165824 bits	8 ms
5	88×75	19405824 bits	6 ms
6	49×49	475693056 bits	5 ms
7	155×125	475693056 bits	33 ms
8	77×49	10879488 bits	20 ms
9	125×49	6291456 bits	17 ms
10	40×55	5898240 bits	8 ms

7   Conclusions

In this paper, we proposed a scheme of image authentication for permissible cropping operation, using the textbook digital signature scheme combined with a message commitment scheme. The security of the scheme is implied by the security of RSA signatures and commitment schemes. This is a practical scheme and can be used in on-line systems for image authentication. Compared with other schemes, our scheme allows legitimate users, following specified cropping rules, to remove sensitive data from a signed image but the integrity of the remained image can be verified. Experimental results show that the proposed scheme is efficient. A disadvantage of our scheme is that the number of commitments is large and adds significant cost to computation and transmission. Another disadvantage is that our scheme can only support cropping operation of images. Our future work is to design more practical schemes to support more kinds of permissible transformations in image authentication.

Acknowledgement. The authors would like to thank anonymous reviewers for their helpful comments.

References

1. Al-Otum, H.M.: Semi-fragile watermarking for grayscale image authentication and tamper detection based on an adjusted expanded-bit multiscale quantization-based technique. J. Vis. Commun. Image Represent. **25**(5), 1064–1081 (2014)
2. Chabanne, H., Hugel, R., Keuffer, J.: Verifiable document redacting. In: Foley, S.N., Gollmann, D., Snekkenes, E. (eds.) ESORICS 2017, Part I. LNCS, vol. 10492, pp. 334–351. Springer, Cham (2017). https://doi.org/10.1007/978-3-319-66402-6_20
3. Chang, E., Lim, C.L., Xu, J.: Short redactable signatures using random trees. IACR Cryptology ePrint Archive 2009, vol. 25 (2009)

4. Katz, J., Lindell, Y.: Introduction to Modern Cryptography, 2nd edn. CRC Press, Boca Raton (2014)
5. Kee, E., Johnson, M.K., Farid, H.: Digital image authentication from JPEG headers. IEEE Trans. Inf. Forensics Secur. **6**(3–2), 1066–1075 (2011)
6. Kim, J., Lee, S., Yoon, J., Ko, H., Kim, S., Oh, H.: PASS: privacy aware secure signature scheme for surveillance systems. In: 14th IEEE International Conference on Advanced Video and Signal Based Surveillance, AVSS 2017, Lecce, Italy, 29 August–1 September 2017, pp. 1–6 (2017)
7. Liu, X., Lin, C., Yuan, S.: Blind dual watermarking for color images' authentication and copyright protection. IEEE Trans. Circuits Syst. Video Technol. **28**(5), 1047–1055 (2018)
8. Lu, C., Liao, H.M.: Multipurpose watermarking for image authentication and protection. IEEE Trans. Image Process. **10**(10), 1579–1592 (2001)
9. Naveh, A., Tromer, E.: Photoproof: cryptographic image authentication for any set of permissible transformations. In: IEEE Symposium on Security and Privacy, SP 2016, San Jose, CA, USA, 22–26 May 2016, pp. 255–271 (2016)
10. Okawa, M.: Offline signature verification with VLAD using fused KAZE features from foreground and background signature images. In: 14th IAPR International Conference on Document Analysis and Recognition, ICDAR 2017, Kyoto, Japan, 9–15 November 2017, pp. 1198–1203 (2017)
11. Ozdil, O., Esin, Y.E., Demirel, B.: Forming representative signature for vegetation detection in hyperspectral images. In: 25th Signal Processing and Communications Applications Conference, SIU 2017, Antalya, Turkey, 15–18 May 2017, pp. 1–4 (2017)
12. Rehman, O., Zivic, N.: A robust watermarking technique for image content authentication. In: Communication Papers of the 2017 Federated Conference on Computer Science and Information Systems, FedCSIS 2017, Prague, Czech Republic, 3–6 September 2017, pp. 223–226 (2017)
13. Schneider, M., Chang, S.: A robust content based digital signature for image authentication. In: Proceedings 1996 International Conference on Image Processing, Lausanne, Switzerland, 16–19 September 1996, pp. 227–230 (1996)
14. Steinfeld, R., Bull, L., Zheng, Y.: Content extraction signatures. IACR Cryptology ePrint Archive 2002, vol. 16 (2002)
15. Wang, C., Zhang, H., Zhou, X.: Review on self-embedding fragile watermarking for image authentication and self-recovery. JIPS **14**(2), 510–522 (2018)
16. Wang, H., Ma, J.: A classification method of multispectral images which is based on fuzzy SVM. In: International Conference on Computer Science and Software Engineering, CSSE 2008, Volume 1: Artificial Intelligence, Wuhan, China, 12–14 December 2008, pp. 815–818 (2008)
17. Wong, P.W., Memon, N.D.: Secret and public key image watermarking schemes for image authentication and ownership verification. IEEE Trans. Image Process. **10**(10), 1593–1601 (2001)
18. Yu, X., Wang, C., Zhou, X.: Review on semi-fragile watermarking algorithms for content authentication of digital images. Future Internet **9**(4), 56 (2017)
19. Zhuvikin, A., Korzhik, V.I., Morales-Luna, G.: Semi-fragile image authentication based on CFD and 3-bit quantization. CoRR abs/1608.02291 (2016)

Information Security

Chord: Thwarting Relay Attacks Among Near Field Communications

Yafei Ji[1,2], Luning Xia[1,2(✉)], Jingqiang Lin[1,2], Qiongxiao Wang[1,2], Lingguang Lei[1,2], and Li Song[1,2]

[1] State Key Laboratory of Information Security, Institute of Information Engineering of Chinese Academy of Sciences, Beijing, China
{jiyafei,xialuning,linjingqiang,wangqiongxiao, leilingguang,songli}@iie.ac.cn
[2] Data Assurance and Communication Security Research Center, Chinese Academy of Sciences, Beijing, China

Abstract. Near field communication (NFC) is an emerging and promising technology envisioned to support a large gamut of applications such as payment and ticketing applications. Unfortunately, there emerges a variety of vulnerabilities that could leave an unwitting user vulnerable to attacks along with the increase of NFC applications. One such potential devastating attack is relay attack, in which adversaries establish a transparently transferring channel between two distant NFC-enabled devices, thus break the assumption that NFC can only work within a rather near distance. In this paper, we propose Chord, an effective method for detecting relay attack. Via measuring the strength of received signal, i.e, the Received Signal Strength Indication (RSSI) during a time span, the two devices are expected to get the same "trace" of RSSI's variation because of physical proximity. Therefore, the relay attack can be revealed if the peers get a different "trace" from each other, which implies that they do not communicate directly via NFC link. The results of our implementation show that our proposal works as intended, and exhibits an improvement of security with reasonable performance impact.

Keywords: Near field communication · Relay attack · RSSI

1 Introduction

Near field communication (NFC) [1] is a contactless radio communication technology to establish short-range ad-hoc connections between devices. It is built upon its predecessor Radio Frequency Identification (RFID) [3] and standardized by ISO/IEC 18092 [2]. The radio interface operates at 13.56 MHz with a communication range up to 10 cm, depending on the physical implementation of the two communicating devices. One of the advantages of NFC over other wireless technologies is simplicity: transactions are initialized automatically after touching a reader, another NFC device or an NFC compliant transponder. Due to its simplicity, companies are exploring novel ways to leverage the technology in

© Springer Nature Switzerland AG 2019
F. Guo et al. (Eds.): Inscrypt 2018, LNCS 11449, pp. 329–348, 2019.
https://doi.org/10.1007/978-3-030-14234-6_18

new and enhanced services such as e-ticketing, mobile payments and access control system [19]. In addition, the integration of NFC technology into smartphones offers many reliable applications. For example, Android 4.4 released in Oct. 2013, Google introduced a new platform, Google Wallet, for NFC-based transactions and it is supported on most NFC-equipped mobile devices powered by Android 4.4. In Sept. 2014, Apple also announced to support NFC-powered transactions as part of its Apple Pay program. For another example, NFC-enabled handsets can be deployed to transfer information between NFC-devices by tapping, device discovery [21] for other wireless technologies (e.g., Bluetooth and Wi-Fi), smart posters (e.g., for acquiring coupons), e-identity (e.g., car or home key), among others.

With increasing application comes increasing concern on privacy and security. Although the distance limit of communication confers security advantages, NFC systems are susceptible to attacks and security remains an open issue [4–6]. In particular, NFC is vulnerable to relay attack [7] (which RFID is also vulnerable to), where an adversary directly relays communications between two distant victim NFC devices, an NFC reader and an NFC token, to maliciously force an NFC link. During the relay attack, the adversary uses a proxy-token and proxy-reader to relay the communication between the victim reader and the victim token over a greater distance than intended. Therefore, the victim reader is tricked to believe that the real token is in close proximity although it is not. A plain scenario of relay attack is to compromise the door access control system. An employee leaves his office for lunch with his NFC-enabled badge still around his neck and stands in line for his order. Unfortunately, the one standing right before him in the queue is a sophisticated attacker who has put a proxy-reader inside his backpack. At the same time, a conspiring attacker taps the proxy-token over the door reader at the entrance of the employees' office and relays the challenge message from the door reader to the proxy-reader, which activates the employees' badge to receive the right response and then relays the response message back to the proxy-token. The door reader will naturally accept the proxy-token as a legitimate token, and thus the conspiring attacker can circumvent the entrance guard system.

To the best of our knowledge, almost none of the extant cryptographic authentication protocols are immune to such kind of attacks. The reason is obvious: all data can be relayed, although it is encrypted. The adversary needs to know neither any clue about the secret key nor the details about the protocol. He can commit the attack successfully just by relaying the messages transparently. Therefore, countermeasures in application layer like cryptographic approaches are invalid to defend against relay attack. Towards thwarting relay attack, several attempts have been made by researchers to reduce the occurrence probability of such attacks in recent years. The main approaches to resist relay attacks include enforcing timing constrains [8], distance-bounding protocol [9, 22–25], GPS [26], and noise [10]. Nevertheless, effective counteracting relay attack is still a challenging task due to various technical and marketing reasons. In this paper we present Chord, a method for detecting and thwarting relay attack. The conception of Chord is to employ an unrelayable factor in the authentication process between the two NFC-enabled devices. We make use of Received Signal Strength Indication (RSSI), which is a physical quantity derived directly from the radio frequency signal between the communication peers. Prior to transmitting messages the two communicating devices measure the strength of their received signals respectively while the relative position from one device to another is varied continuously. In terms of the electromagnetic field theory, varied relative position in non-uniform magnetic field corresponds to varied strength of received signal. Thus the two devices can figure out their own variation traces of RSSI respectively. When the peers communicate directly via a NFC link, i.e. there is no relay attack; the two variation traces should be identical or highly similar with each other. Otherwise, the two are completely irrelevant. By comparing the variation traces measured during the authenticating process, the victim devices of relay attack are expected to be conscious of the existence of the malicious relay channel. Given that the variation trace of RSSI is subject to both sides of NFC link, the adversary can hardly fabricate a trace that can be accepted by both victim peers. Therefore, communication is likely to be aborted due to the failed authentication.

The rest of this paper is organized as follows. In Sect. 2, we first review the related background and preliminaries. On the basis of this knowledge, we describe the full details of Chord in Sect. 3. Evaluation and discussions are presented in Sect. 4. The related works about relay attack against NFC are discussed in Sect. 5. Finally, we give the concluding remarks in Sect. 6.

2   Background and Preliminaries

In this section, we present a brief overview of NFC and relay attack. Also, the Received Signal Strength Indicator (RSSI) and spatial distribution of magnetic field are discussed in detail.

2.1   Near Field Communication

Near field communication (NFC) is a relatively new and increasingly popular communication technology, first standardized as ISO/IEC 18092 [2], and later earned a further international accredited standard ISO/IEC 21481 [27]. It operates at 13.56 MHz at transfer rate from 106 kilobits per second up to 424 kilobits per second [2]. NFC is designed to be a short range communications link, up to approximately 10 cm for normal operation. A NFC-enabled device can act as "contactless reader", "contactless card", or just be one peer in a peer-to-peer communication. NFC-enabled devices are compatible with existing contactless systems adhering to ISO 14443 [31], ISO 15693 [32] and FeliCa [33].

The NFC standards define two communication modes: passive mode and active mode. The characteristics of the two communication modes are compared in Table 1. The difference between two modes is reflected in the generation of RF field. In active mode, both devices generate their own RF field when they want to transmit message to the other peer, while in passive mode only one

Table 1. Characteristics of the two communication modes in NFC

Mode	Communication range	Transfer speed	RF generator
Passive	Up to 10 cm	106,212,424 kbps	Only initiator
Active	Up to 10 cm	106,212,424 kbps	Alternative (initiator or target)

device generates the RF field to power the other device and support a half-duplex communication between them. In an NFC link, the two NFC devices are referred as the initiator and the target respectively. The device who starts the data exchange is called Initiator while the other device is called Target. In active mode, the Initiator and the Target use their own generated RF field to communicate with each other. First the Initiator generates an RF carrier, which is used to send data to the target subsequently. The Initiator switches the carrier off when acknowledgment from the target is received. The Target then switches on its own carrier and transmits a response to the Initiator. In passive mode, the Initiator is the only device that generates RF signal, the target device responds by modulating the existing field which the initiator devices listens out for, and then processes therefore transferring data.

There has three basic operation modes for NFC devices: reader/writer mode, peer-to-peer mode, and card emulation mode. Table 2 shows the basic function corresponding to every operation mode.

Table 2. Basic function corresponding to operation mode

Operation mode	Function
Reader/write	Read/write tags
Peer-to-Peer	Exchange small chunks of data
Car emulation	Act as passive contactless card

In reader/writer mode NFC-enabled device is able to read or write NFC tags specified by the NFC Forum, e.g., smart posters or tags with embedded text, URLs or signatures. Peer-to-peer mode, with respect to RF technology, is an operating mode specific to NFC and allows two NFC devices to exchange small chunks of data with each other. For example, you can use peer-to-peer mode to set parameters for Bluetooth connections, Wi-Fi connections or virtual business cards. For the last mode, the card emulation mode, the NFC device acts as a normal passive contactless card which can be accessed via a typical ISO14443A RFID reader. This allows NFC devices to integrate with existing RFID infrastructure without making any modification to the legacy system.

2.2   Relay Attack

Relay attack is not a novel concept in the field of information security. The attack was first described by Conway [28]. He explained how a player who didn't know the rules of Chess could simultaneously play against two grand masters by challenging both of them to a postal game. The player forwards the move originating from one grand to the other, and therefore each grand master thinks that they are playing against each other. The attack employed to security protocol was first discussed in [29], and it has subsequently been referred to as a 'wormhole attack' [30] or a 'relay attack' [23]. Some practical implementations of relay attacks against contactless system have been published in recent years. Though some of them depend on custom-built hardware [34,35], more recent implementations only require NFC-enabled mobile phones, which makes the attack working far more easily [26][38].

Someone would consider relay attack as a kind of man-in-the-middle (MITM) attack, but they are completely different. MITM attacks occur when an attacker attempts to intercept communications between two parties without their knowledge. In MITM attacks two parties are tricked into thinking they are communicating securely with each other, while the attacker actually sits in between them, communicating with both. The attacker catches messages sent by one party and then sets up a new communication with the other party. Then he catches the response of the second party and sends his own response to the first device. By doing this, the attacker becomes "the man in the middle." Both parties are unaware of the attacker's presence. Acting as a proxy, the attacker can both review and manipulate the contents of the messages he is relaying between the two parties. However, the attackers in relay attack just works as proxies. Any information transmitted by one legitimate party is just be relayed to another legitimate party without any changes. The attackers care about neither the semantic of the data nor the secret key. As long as a relay channel is established successfully, the attack works.

In order to execute a successful relay attack, an adversary needs two proxy devices which act as a proxy initiator and a proxy target, respectively. The two proxy devices are connected via a suitable communication channel (Internet, Bluetooth, etc.) to relay information over a far greater distance than 10 cm. The basic diagram for relay attack is shown in Fig. 1. The device A and B are legitimate while the device C and D are employed by the adversary as the proxy devices.

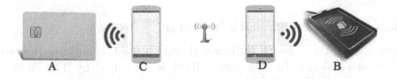

Fig. 1. Schematic diagram of basic relay attack setup

According to the expected situation, device A and B will be put close enough (not more than 10 cm) and messages are transmitted via wireless radio between them. While in a situation of relay attack, device A and device B are located faraway from each other. It seems impossible to establish a NFC link between them, but the adversary makes it possible by deploying proxy device C and proxy device D, and the channel between C and D, to relay the messages between A and B. From the perspective of B, it sends the challenge successfully to A and receives the correct response from A. From the perspective of A, it believes that it has received a challenge from B and then sends the response back. Both A and B can't be aware of the existence of the proxy devices and the relay channel. Each of them is deceived to believe that the opposite side is just around itself. Thus the legitimate devices will do as the adversary want, e.g., open the door.

The above reveals that almost all the authentication protocols of the application layer of NFC are lack of the ability of resisting relay attack. The reason is rather clear: all the proofs about the identity of another peer, e.g., digital signatures, are received via the communication channel between them, which is subject to be relayed. To defense against relay attack, the legitimate device has to apply a kind of information that it can figure out itself instead of receiving from the other peer. Thus the primary task is to explore the NFC communication and try to find such kind of information. An obvious fact is that, we may only find such kind of information in physical layer because all data in other layers has to be transmitted through the communication channel. According to the electromagnetic theory, the radio signal strength received by a receiver varies with position and orientation towards radio source. This variation is influenced by the sender and receiver simultaneously, which implies that it cannot be determined only by one peer. In a relay attack, the adversary will establish two NFC links, i.e. two radio links on both sides of the relay channel, coupling the legitimate tag with the proxy reader and the legitimate reader with the proxy tag respectively. The two NFC links have their own RF characteristics that are independent with each other. The main idea of our method is that one legitimate device measures radio signal strength and transmit it to the opposite side with source authenticity and integrity guarantee. The other legitimate device measures the radio strength also and compares it with the received one to determine whether they match. Mismatch will be detected if relay attack exists because the two values are actually come from two independent radio links and irrelevant with each other. The adversary is unable to modify the value because of the authenticity and integrity guarantee. Following this way, the relay attack can be detected and resisted effectively.

2.3   Received Signal Strength Indicator

The Received Signal Strength Indicator (RSSI) is used to indicate the strength level of received signal. In this paper, RSSI is measured by TRF7970A from Texas Instruments. The RSSI blocks of measuring system are connected to RF input pins, and the peak value of induced voltage is latched after the end of each received packet. The RSSI values are reset with every transmission by the reader. This guarantees an updated RSSI measurement for each new response. The nominal relationship between input RF voltage and RSSI value is shown in Fig. 2.

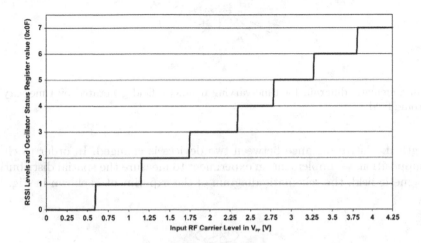

Fig. 2. Schematic diagram of basic relay attack setup

The RSSI has 7 steps with a typical increment of about 4 dB. The operating range is between 600 mVpp and 4.2 Vpp with a typical step size of about 600 mV. The level of the RF signal received at the antenna is measured and stored in register.

2.4 Spatial Distribution of Magnetic Field

Because our proposed protocol is based on the strength of received signal and the signal is transmitted via inductive electromagnetic coupling, we first describe the space distribution of magnetic field. On the basis of magnetic field we present our protocol in detail.

Spatial Distribution of Magnetic Field. In terms of electromagnetic field theory, a loop wire carrying electric current produces magnetic field with closed field lines surrounding the wire which is shown in Fig. 3. A conventional way to depict the pattern of the magnetic is to draw magnetic lines such that each line is parallel to the magnetic field $\overrightarrow{B}$. The direction of magnetic field at the center of the loop is perpendicular to the plane which can be determined by the "right hand rule". The strength of magnetic field is indicated by the density of magnetic lines and calculated from Biot-Savart Law. As shown in Fig. 3 the spatial distribution of magnetic field is not uniform and magnetic strength is varied at different point. From the above analysis towards magnetic field, it is supposed that during the communication of two NFC enabled devices, each device can receive varied signal

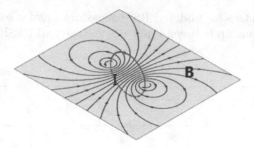

Fig. 3. Schematic diagram for time-varying magnetic field generated by time-varying electronic field.

strength if relative distance between two devices is changed. In order to check the supposition, we implement an experiment to measure the spatial distribution of magnetic field, the schematic diagram of the experiment is shown in Fig. 4.

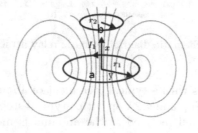

Fig. 4. Schematic diagram of the experiment for measuring RSSI. Device b is moved along x and y directions, respectively

Device a and b are both NFC enabled devices. In the experiment device a is hold still while the device b is moved along x and y direction, respectively. Device b continuously transmit messages to device a while moving, and measures the strength of received signal by Received Signal Strength Indication (RSSI). Figure 4 shows the results of the spatial distribution of RSSI along the two directions.

In the experiment we use relative RSSI strength by normalizing the measured RSSI to facilitate comparison of the RSSI variation in two directions. The two NFC devices is first placed face to face while device b is moved along x continuously. It can be found from Fig. 5(a) that RSSI in general decreases gradually along x direction while remaining stable in a small range. To measure the variation in y direction, we set the distance on x to a fixed value (10 mm). Figure 5(b) shows the variation of RSSI along y direction. The results of Fig. 5(a) and (b) indicates that the relative distance between the two communicating devices can impose a vital effect on signal strength.

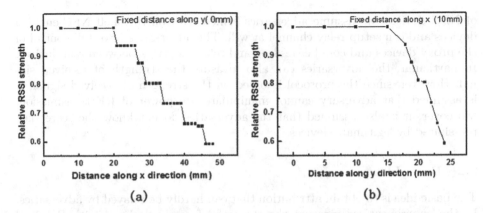

Fig. 5. Spatial distribution of RSSI within different relative distance from radio source device a. (a) Two NFC devices are placed face to face while device b is moved along x continuously; (b) Moved along y direction continuously while distance on x direction is set to a fixed value 10 mm.

3   Chord

The idea of Chord is to add a RSSI Test procedure into the process of a NFC link. The RSSI is locally measured by both peers respectively. One peer transmits the RSSI value it measured to the other during the communication. Once the other peer calculates a mismatch result, the link will be terminated. If we imagine the radio signal as a chord that links the two peers, we expect the two peers to experience a same or similar rhythm when the chord is vibrating. This is the origin of the name "Chord". The detail of Chord is described in the following four parts: threat model and security assumption, basic idea, Chord method and security analysis.

3.1   Threat Model and Security Assumptions

The main security goal of Chord is to detect whether the NFC communication is under relay attack. Designed for resource-constrained NFC devices, Chord involves no computationally-expensive or time-consuming processing (e.g., public-key cryptographic computations). In Chord, the two legitimate devices are assumed to pre-share a secret session key. For the purpose of confidentiality, all of the transmitted messages including the protocol should be encrypted by pre-shared secret key. Only when both of the devices pass the authentication can messages be transmitted via NFC.

In Chord, the two legitimate devices are picked up by the owner. However, he cannot determine the device he intends to communicate is a legitimate one. We do not consider physical attacks, exploits of software vulnerabilities on both NFC devices, as well as attacks on the underlying cryptography. The detail steps of Chord are publicly known. As the commonly available customer hardware of NFC devices, we assume adversaries armed with off-the-shelf NFC-enabled devices and can setup relay channel at will. The adversaries have full control of the proxy devices and could eavesdrop and relay messages between real devices. In particular, the adversaries can also measure the strength of received signal. However, since the protocol is based on the strength of received signal, it is assumed that adversary cannot manipulate the power of RF transmission. Moreover, it is also assumed that the adversaries do not know the secret key pre-shared by legitimate devices.

3.2 Basic Idea

The basic idea is to obtain attribution that can hardly be relayed by adversaries. In the experiment we measure the strength of received signal with Received Signal Strength Indication (RSSI) to work as major parameter for the protocol. The two legitimate devices record a variation "trace" of RSSI, respectively. When there is no relay attack, the two variation tracks should be identical or highly similar with each other. Otherwise, the two tracks are completely irrelevant. Since the variation "trace" is subject to both sides of NFC link, the adversary can hardly fabricate a track that can be accepted by both victim peers. By comparing the variation track, the victim devices are expected to aware of the existence of relay attack.

3.3 Chord Method

Signal strength measured by device can be affected by many factors such as transmit power, environment disturbance, relative distance and so on. However, transmit power of an off-the-shelf device is basically constant and can hardly be modulated by users at will. On the other hand, the communication range of NFC devices is 10 cm and therefore environment disturbance is presumed trivial. In this work, we only consider the influence of relative distance on signal strength. In the experiment, we use received signal strength indicator (RSSI) to roughly determine the relative movement. Figure 6 shows the diagram of the proposed method.

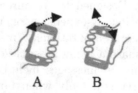

A   B

Fig. 6. The two devices are waved randomly by users.

Relative distance between the device A and B is varied randomly while the two devices communicate continuously. In the communication, device A first sends command "SENSE-REQ" and waits response from device B. After receiving the response "SENSE-RES", device A record one RSSI of device B.

In the same way, the device B then record one RSSI of device A. Both of the two devices repeat the procedure for several times and therefore a set of RSSI are recorded by the two devices respectively. Given that the two devices may have different precision on measuring RSSI, we cannot compare the RSSI measured by the two devices directly. However, since the rule revealed by a set of RSSI represents movements between two devices, so the two sets of RSSI should identical or highly similar. Based on the above analysis, we calculate cross correlation between the two sets of RSSI measured. The authentication method using cross correlation between measured RSSI is detailed in Fig. 7.

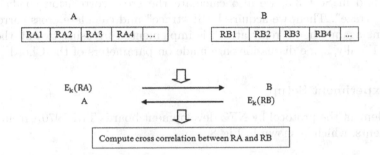

Fig. 7. Detail of proposed authentication protocol.

The RSSI measured by legitimate device A and B can be represented by RA (e.g., RA1, RA2, RA3) and RB (e.g., RB1, RB2, RB3) respectively. The two legitimate devices exchange the measured RSSI which should be encrypted by pre-shared secret key with their counterpart. AES can be chosen as encryption algorithm to encrypt all messages. After receiving the encrypted RSSI from another part, the two legitimate devices first decrypt ciphertext and then compute cross correlation between RA and RB. Cross correlation is a standard method of estimating the degree to which two series are correlated. Cross correlation coefficient is defined as follow:

$$correl(x,y) = \frac{\Sigma(x - \bar{x})(y - \bar{y})}{\sqrt{\Sigma(x - \bar{x})^2 \Sigma(y - \bar{y})^2}} \tag{1}$$

Where $\bar{x}$ and $\bar{y}$ are the average of x and y. If the correlation between RA and RB is poor, the two legitimate devices can confirm that the communication is under attack, otherwise, the two parties in communication are recognized as legitimate devices.

3.4 Security Analysis

The main characteristic of the protocol is that the two legitimate devices measure the strength of received signal successively whereby detecting whether the communication is under attack. The two legitimate devices compute cross correlation between measured RSSI to determine whether the communication is under attack. Since the adversary can hardly fabricate tracks that have good correlation with both victim peers, therefore, communication is likely to be aborted due to the failed authentication.

4   Evaluation and Discussion

Data acquisition and comparison of RSSI "trace" have significant influence on the practicability of Chord. In this section, we first establish a NFC link by using two NFC development board and acquire two RSSI "trace" by employing the method in Sect. 3.3, we also calculate the cross correlation coefficient of the two "trace". Then, we acquire RSSI "trace" and calculate cross correlation coefficient again when a relay attack is implemented by using two off-the-shelf phones. Finally, some discussions are made on parameters of the Chord.

4.1   Experiment Setup

We implement the protocol by NFC development boards TRF7970A from Texas Instruments, which is shown in Fig. 8.

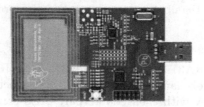

Fig. 8. TRF7970A development board from Texas Instruments.

The TRF7970A is an integrated analog front end and data-framing device for a 13.56-MHz RFID/Near Field Communication system. Built-in programming options make it suitable for a wide range of applications for proximity and vicinity identification systems. It can perform in one of three modes: RFID/NFC Reader, NFC Peer, or in Card Emulation mode. Built-in user-configurable programming options make it suitable for a wide range of applications.

The microcontroller of the development board is MSP430F2370. The Texas Instruments MSP430 family of ultralow-power microcontrollers consists of several devices featuring different sets of peripherals targeted for various applications. The architecture, combined with five low-power modes is optimized to achieve extended battery life in portable measurement applications. The devices feature a powerful 16-bit RISC CPU, 16-bit registers, clock module with internal frequencies up to 16 MHz, and constant generators that contribute to maximum code efficiency.

In the communication, device A first sends command "SENSE-REQ" and waiting response from device B. After receiving the response "SENSE-RES", device A record one RSSI of device B. In the same way, the device B then record one RSSI of device A. Both of the two devices repeat the procedure for several times and therefore a set of RSSI are recorded by the two devices respectively.

4.2 Experiment Results

According to the Chord, device A should first sends command "SENSE-REQ" and waits for response "SENSE-RES" from device B and record the RSSI; then device B sends command "SENSE-REQ" and record RSSI of response from device A. It can be found that there is a time slot t1 between the measurement of RSSI by the two devices. The time slot t1 begins when the device B sends command "SENSE-REQ" and ends when it receives response from device A. Since the two device are moved continuously while device B waiting for response, relative distance between the two devices is varied constantly. The shorter the time slot t1, the more similarity between the two RSSI measured by both devices. In the experiment, we try our best to optimize code and finally the time slot is set as 11.9 ms. On the other hand, Chord also needs both of the two devices to measure RSSI for several rounds in the same way. In each round, both of the two devices measure one "point" of the RSSI "trace". The shorter the time interval t2 between each round, the more "points" can be measured in the same time. In the experiment, we set the t2 as zero millisecond in order to measure more points. Finally, we should determine the number of points N in the "trace". The more are the points, more reliable are the results. However, more time is needed if we measured more points.

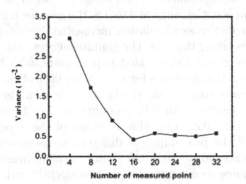

Fig. 9. Relationship between variance and the number of measured points.

To determine an appropriate number of points, we measure 4 points, 8 points, 12 points, 16 points, 20 points, 24 points, 28 points, 32 points one by one. We repeat the experiment for one hundred times on each point (e.g., measure 4 point for 100 times). After acquiring the points, we calculate cross correlation and compare variance of the cross coefficient of every point. Figure 9 shows the relationship between variance and the number of measured points. It can be found from Fig. 9 that the variance decreases dramatically from 4 to 16 which means the data becomes more and more reliable. However, the variance floats in a small range after 16, which indicates that the data is in steady state and is highly reliable. Thus, considering the data reliability and the time for measuring RSSI, we determine 16 as the optimum point.

In the following, we will test the performance of the chord with 16 point on thwarting relay attack. First we use the chord in normal communication without attack, and then it is implemented in communication with relay attack.

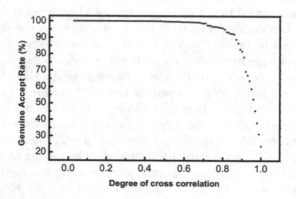

Fig. 10. Genuine accept rate in communication without relay attack.

Figure 10 shows the experiment results without relay attacks. When the cross correlation coefficient is in the range of 0 to 0.8, the genuine accept ratio decreases slowly with the degree of cross correlation increasing. However, when the degree of cross correlation is larger than 0.8, the genuine accept ratio decreases sharply. From the above results, one can see that experiments, with the degree of cross correlation larger than 0.8, accounts for more than 90% of the total experiments results are highly cross correlation. It also can be seen that with the degree of cross correlation smaller than 0.8, accounts for less than 10% of the total experiment results, indicating that the accuracy of the experiment results are highly accurate, and the probability of different measurement results between the two instruments is smaller. Figure 11 shows the experiment results with relay attacks, and the genuine accept ratio decreases straightly with the degree of cross correlation increasing.

Figure 12 shows the false accept ratio and false reject ratio as a function of degree of cross correlation with red dot line and black dot line respectively. In this experiment, the false accept ratio can indicate the probability that instruments cannot detect the attack when under attack in the communication process, and the false reject ratio can indicate the probability that instruments detect the attack without attack in the communication process. One can see that with

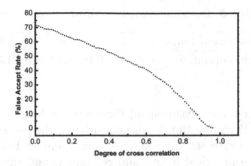

Fig. 11. False accept rate in communication with relay attack.

degree of cross correlation increasing, the false accept ratio decreases while the false reject ratio increases, and they cross at the degree of cross correlation 0.85. This cross point is called equal false ratio, and the corresponding degree of cross correlation is 0.85, and the false ratio is 14%. At this point, the false accept ratio and false reject ratio achieve a balance. If the threshold value of the degree of cross correlation is set at 0.85 to judge the concurrency of the attack, the probability to detect the attack under this protocol is 86% and the probability of false result is 14%.

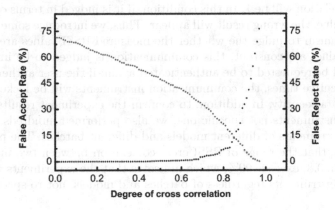

Fig. 12. Relationship between false accept rate and false reject rate. (Color figure online)

To evaluate the efficiency of the proposed protocol, we record the duration for measuring RSSI. Table 3 shows the time and number of times to measurement the RSSI value.

One can see that the measurement time positively linearly depends on the number of times to measurement the RSSI value. When the number of measurement times is less than 64, the duration is less than 1 s. And when measurement

Table 3. Duration needed for RSSI measurement

Measurement times	2	4	8	16	32	64
Duration (unit: s)	0.05	0.1	0.19	0.38	0.76	1.53

times is larger than 64, the measurement time is more than 1 s. In this condition, if the encoding and decoding time is also considered, the measurement time will be further prolonged. We set the reference measurement times of RSSI at 16 considering both the practical utility and reliability, and the user can also set their own number of measurement times based on the specific conditions.

4.3 Analysis

In this part, we further analyze and discuss the experiment results. From the protocol, it is known that whether the communication between the legal instruments is attacked by relay can be judged in terms of the range of cross correlation between the two measured RSSI values. If the range of cross correlation is larger than the fixed threshold value, the communication is considered to be not attacked, and vice versa. However, when two attack instruments attack the communication, and these two attack instruments are motionless relative to the two legal ones, the RSSI value will be measured to constant, and then the range of cross correlation will be 1. In this condition, if it is judged in terms of the fixed threshold value, the wrong result will appear. Thus, we introduce some more new judge mechanism to judge the whether the measured RSSI values are varied. If the RSSI values are constant, this communication is judged to be invalid, and the user will be requested to be authenticated again; if the user authenticate for many consecutive times, the communication instruments will be locked to guarantee the data security. In addition, to confirm the experiment results are valid to general instruments not specific one, we also performed hundreds of experiments on instruments of different models and different batches. The probability of condition, that the range of RSSI cross correlation between two instruments is larger than 0.8, exceeds 90%, which indicates that the experiments results are valid to all instruments regardless of batches and models, not to specific ones.

5 Related Work

Relay attack may cause serious security threat, however, it is not always considered to be a major risk (like eavesdropping). According to [7], some comprehensive industrial and government guidelines as well as academic survey publications [3,5] do not take relay attack into consideration. One reason may be that security experts tend to treat this attack as a mixture of conventional man-in-the-middle and skimming attacks. Unfortunately, relay attack is not easy to defend against since it can effectively circumvent any application layer security.

With the popularity of smart phone, NFC-enabled devices are used as platform for relay attack. For example, it has been proposed that NFC-enabled mobile phones could be used as a generic relay attack platform without any additional hardware, but this has not been successfully demonstrated in practice. Lishoy Francis et al. present a practice implementation of a NFC-enabled relay attack, requiring only suitable mobile software applications [14]. The implementation reduces the complexity for relay attacks and therefore has potential security implications for current contactless system. They also discuss several potential countermeasures capable of mitigating relay attack in a mobile environment such as timing, distance bounding, application restriction and location verification. With the emergency of the Google Wallet, an existing mobile contactless payment system, a software-based relay attack is successfully mounted on it [15]. Thomas Korak et al. [16] use smart phones and custom-made proxy device to implement relay attack. During the "three phone in the middle" attack one NFC phone is used to act as access point for two other phones, and therefore the communication distance is successfully extended to more than 110 m. Furthermore, a custom-made proxy device is used to perform active relay attack, and it can overcome many relay attack restrictions compared to NFC-enabled devices, such as cloning of the victim's ID, direct request for Waiting Time Extensions or modifications in the low-level RFID protocols. The custom-made proxy is highly flexible and more sophisticated attacks than using NFC-enabled smart phones.

Recent years, many researchers have made various efforts to detect and prevent relay attacks. The main approach against relay attack is the distance-bounding protocol [8,9][39,40] that determine an upper bound for the physical between two communicating parties based on the Round-Trip-Time (RTT). This method is based on an accurate time measurement towards challenge-response pairs. However, to achieve accurate distance bound the protocol needs to be run over a special communication channel since conventional channels introduce timing uncertainty that can obscure the delay introduced by relay attack. There are also some studies that focus on using additional verification procedures. For example, Reid [10] proposed a general paradigm based on multichannel protocols and discusses several instantiations (e.g., accelerometers and polarized photons); Drimer [11] used an appropriately piece of paper from verifier to exchange secret message; Brands [12] employed a simple interface with a button for relay attack prevention; Hancke [13] presented the first solution based on the chaos suppression theory and exploits the chaotic characteristics of a dynamic Lorenz controller to distinguish a legitimate RFID reader from a proxy reader; Stajano [17] addressed relay attack through ambient condition measurements and proposes an elliptic curve-based mutual authentication protocol that refer to the surface temperature of the prover measured by prover and verifier. Nevertheless, all of these countermeasures complicate the transaction process for the user which in certain applications is not feasible.

Countermeasures mentioned above require special equipment (e.g., distance-bounding protocol), complicate transaction process (e.g., require interaction with user), or need sophisticated computation (e.g., implement ECC). These observations motivate us to propose a solution that easy to implement and doesn't require large amount computation.

6 Conclusion

In this work, we investigate the relay attack and propose Chord, an authentication protocol based on RSSI for detecting relay attack. The original idea of Chord is to employ an unrelayable factor in the authentication process between the two NFC-enabled devices. The principle of this protocol is that prior to the start of the authenticating process, the two communicating devices measure the strength of their received signals respectively while the relative position from one device to another is varied continuously. According to the measured RSSI, the two devices can deduce a moving "trace" respectively. By comparing the variation traces during authentication process, the victim devices of relay attack are expected to be conscious of the existence of the malicious relay channel. Our experiment indicates that this protocol is easy to implement and exhibits an improvement of security with reasonable performance impact.

Acknowledgement. This work was supported by the National Key Research and Development Program of China (No. 2017YFB0802100).

References

1. Coskun, V., Ozdenizci, B., Ok, K.: A survey on near field communication (NFC) technology. Wirel. Pers. Commun. **71**, 2259–2294 (2013)
2. Roberts, C.M.: Radio frequency identification (RFID). Comput. Secur. **25**, 18–26 (2006)
3. ISO/IEC 18092:2013, Near Field Communication Interface and Protocol (NFCIP-1), March 2013
4. Madlmayr, G., Langer, J., Kantner, C., Scharinger, J.: NFC devices: security and privacy. In: Proceedings of the 3rd International Conference on Availability, Reliability and Security (ARES 2008), pp. 642–647 (2008)
5. Still not a wallet, NFC has a second life as a safe, simple pairing tool. http://gigaom.com/2013/08/08/still-nota-wallet-nfc-has-a-second-life-as-a-safe-simplepairing-tool/
6. Mulliner, C.: Vulnerability analysis and attacks on NFC-enabled mobile phones. In: International Conference on Availability, Reliability and Security (2009)
7. Ernst Haselsteiner, K.B.: Security in near field communication (NFC) strengths and weaknesses. In: Workshop on RFID Security (RFIDSec 2006), July 2006
8. Nelson, D., Qiao, M., Carpenter, A.: Security of the near field communication protocol: an overview. J. Comput. Sci. Coll. **29**, 94–104 (2013)
9. Hancke, G.P., Mayes, K.E., Markantonakis, K.: Confidence in smart token proximity: relay attacks revisited. Comput. Secur. **28**, 615–627 (2009)

10. Reid, J., Nieto, J.M.G., Tang, T., Senadji, B.: Detecting relay attacks with timing-based protocols. In: Proceedings of the 2nd ACM Symposium on Information, Computer and Communication Security (ASIACCS 2007), pp, 204–213, March 2007

11. Drimer, S., Murdoch, S.J.: Keep your enemies close: distance bounding against smartcard relay attacks. In: Proceedings of the 16th USENIX Security Symposium (USENIX Sec2007), pp. 87–1C102, August 2007

12. Brands, S., Chaum, D.: Distance-bounding protocols. In: Helleseth, T. (ed.) EURO-CRYPT 1993. LNCS, vol. 765, pp. 344–359. Springer, Heidelberg (1994). https://doi.org/10.1007/3-540-48285-7_30

13. Hancke, G.P., Kuhn, M.G.: An RFID distance bounding protocol. In: Proceedings of the International Conference of Security and Privacy for Emerging Areas in Communication Networks(SecureComm), Athens, Greece, pp. 67–73 (2005)

14. Munilla, J., Peinado, A.: Distance bounding protocols for RFID enhanced by using void-challenges and analysis in noisy channels. Wirel. Commun. Mob. Comput. 8(9), 1227–1232 (2008)

15. Kim, C.H., Avoine, G.: RFID distance bounding protocol with mixed challenges to prevent relay attacks. In: Garay, J.A., Miyaji, A., Otsuka, A. (eds.) CANS 2009. LNCS, vol. 5888, pp. 119–133. Springer, Heidelberg (2009). https://doi.org/10.1007/978-3-642-10433-6_9

16. Francis, L., Hancke, G., Mayes, K., Markantonakis, K.: Practical NFC peer-to-peer relay attack using mobile phones. In: Ors Yalcin, S.B. (ed.) RFIDSec 2010. LNCS, vol. 6370, pp. 35–49. Springer, Heidelberg (2010). https://doi.org/10.1007/978-3-642-16822-2_4

17. Stajano, F., Wong, F.-L., Christianson, B.: Multichannel protocols to prevent relay attacks. In: Sion, R. (ed.) FC 2010. LNCS, vol. 6052, pp. 4–19. Springer, Heidelberg (2010). https://doi.org/10.1007/978-3-642-14577-3_4

18. ISO: Near Field Communication Interface and Protocol-2 (NFCIP-2), ISO/EIC 21481:2012 (2013)

19. ISO/IEC 14443: Identification cards Contactless integrated circuit cards Proximity cards. http://www.iso.org/. Accessed 31 Mar 2010

20. ISO/IEC 15693: Identification cards - Contactless integrated circuit cards - Vicinity cards. http://www.iso.org/. Accessed 31 Mar 2010

21. FeliCa: http://www.sony.net/Products/felica/. Accessed 31 Mar 2010

22. Conway, J.H.: On Numbers and Games. Academic Press, London (1976)

23. Desmedt, Y., Goutier, C., Bengio, S.: Special uses and abuses of the fiat-shamir passport protocol (extended abstract). In: Pomerance, C. (ed.) CRYPTO 1987. LNCS, vol. 293, pp. 21–39. Springer, Heidelberg (1988). https://doi.org/10.1007/3-540-48184-2_3

24. Hu, Y.C., Perrig, A., Johnson, D.B.: Wormhole attacks in wireless networks. IEEE J. Sel. Areas Commun. (JSAC) pp. 370–380 (2006)

25. Hancke, G.P.: Practical attacks on proximity identification systems (short paper). In: Proceedings of IEEE Symposium on Security and Privacy, pp. 328–333, May 2006

26. Francillon, A., Danev, B., Capkun, S.: Relay attacks on passive keyless entry and start systems in modern cars. In: Proceedings of Network and Distributed System Security Symposium (NDSS) (2011)

27. Libnfc: Public Platform Independent Near Field Communication (NFC) Library. http://nfc-tools.org/index.php?title=Libnfc:nfc-relay

28. RFID IO Tools: http://www.rfidiot.org/

29. Weiss, M.: Performing Relay Attacks on ISO 14443 Contactless Smart Cards using NFC Mobile Equipment. Master Thesis, Technischen Universitat Munchen, Munich, Germany (2010)
30. Francis, L., Hancke, G., Mayesc, K.: A practical generic relay attack on contactless transactions by using NFC mobile phones. Int. J. RFID Secur. Crypt. (IJRFIDSC) **2**(1–4), 92–106 (2013)
31. Roland, M., Langer, J., Scharinger, J.: Applying relay attacks to Google Wallet. In: Proceedings of the 5th International Workshop on Near Field Communication (NFC 2013), 6 p., February 2013
32. Korak, T., Hutter, M.: On the power of active relay attacks using custom-made proxies. In: Proceedings of the 8th Annual IEEE International Conference on RFID (IEEE RFID 2014), pp. 126–133, April 2014
33. Cagalj, M., Perkovic, T., Bugaric, M., Li, S.: Fortune cookies and smartphones: weakly unrelayable channels to counter relay attacks. Pervasive Mob. Comput. **20**, 64–81 (2015)
34. Kang, S., Kim, J., Hong, M.: Button-based method for the prevention of nearfield communication relay attacks. Int. J. Commun. Syst. **28**, 1628–1638 (2014)
35. Malek, B., Miri, A.: Chaotic masking for securing RFID systems against relay attacks. Secur. Commun. Netw. **6**, 1496–1508 (2013)
36. Urien, P., Piamuthu, S.: Elliptic curve-based RFID/NFC authentication with temperature sensor input for relay attacks. Decis. Support Syst. **59**, 28–36 (2014)

Analyzing Use of High Privileges on Android: An Empirical Case Study of Screenshot and Screen Recording Applications

Mark H. Meng[1]([✉]), Guangdong Bai[2], Joseph K. Liu[3], Xiapu Luo[4], and Yu Wang[5]

[1] Institute for Infocomm Research, Agency for Science, Technology and Research (A*STAR), Singapore, Singapore
menghs@i2r.a-star.edu.sg
[2] Griffith University, Brisbane, Australia
g.bai@griffith.edu.au
[3] Monash University, Melbourne, Australia
joseph.liu@monash.edu
[4] Hong Kong Polytechnic University, Hong Kong, Hong Kong S.A.R.
csxluo@comp.polyu.edu.hk
[5] Guangzhou University, Guangzhou, China
yuwang@gzhu.edu.cn

Abstract. The number of Android smartphone and tablet users has experienced a rapid growth in the past few years and it raises users' awareness on privacy and security issues of their mobile devices. There are lots of users rooting their Android devices for some useful functions, which are not originally provided to developers and users, such as taking screenshot and screen recording. However, after observing the danger of rooting devices, the developers begin to look for non-root alternatives to implement those functions. Android Debug Bridge (ADB) workaround is one of the best known non-root alternatives to help app gain a higher privilege on Android. It used to be considered as a secure practice until some cases of ADB privilege leakage have been found. In this paper, we propose an approach to identify the potential privilege leakage in Android apps that using ADB workaround. We apply our approach to analyze three real-world apps that are downloaded from Google Play Store. We then present a general methodology to conduct exploitation on those apps using ADB workaround. Based on our study, we suggest some mitigation techniques to help developers create their apps that not only satisfy users' needs but also protect users' privacy from similar attacks in future.

Keywords: Android security · Application analysis · Privilege escalation · ADB workaround · Exploit

This work was supported by NSFC Project 61802080.

© Springer Nature Switzerland AG 2019
F. Guo et al. (Eds.): Inscrypt 2018, LNCS 11449, pp. 349–369, 2019.
https://doi.org/10.1007/978-3-030-14234-6_19

1   Introduction

The rise of mobile devices has greatly enriched people's lives in this digital era. As the dominator of current mobile device market, Android has reserved over 77.3% of the global smartphone market share by July of 2018 [20].

At the moment of this paper being drafted, the global number of monthly active Android devices has exceeded 2 billion [16]. The over-reliance on mobile devices makes people save all the data regardless of personal or business purpose onto their smartphones or tablets, which may lead their privacy under exposure if no proper protection has been enforced.

Android is well-known by its rich functionality and customization, but there are still some features that could not be implemented merely using the official application programming interfaces (APIs). Google creates a collection of permission labels to define the privilege of apps running on Android operating system (OS). Some actions like reading the content displaying on the screen, in another word taking screenshot and screen recording, are marked as *signature* level permissions, hence are not allowed to be realized by common third party apps. However, as long as the requirement of users exists, the developers would never stop to push the boundary. For that reason, developers are all motivated and successfully come up with two approaches to solve the permission dilemma, namely "rooting the phone" and "ADB workaround".

Rooting the devices could enable users to gain the administration privileges to do anything they want such as removing pre-installed apps, unlocking more functionalities, or changing the theme of UI. According to a statistic done by Lucic [14], there are over 27.44% users indicating that they have rooted their smartphones to remove redundant and useless pre-installed applications. There are several security issues behind the "rooting" because it circumvents the permission mechanism on Android system. The good news says there is an increasing number of people who have realized the risk of rooting their devices, and have started seeking non-root approaches. Gaining a higher privilege through *Android Debug Bridge (ADB)* is one of the best known and widely used workarounds. Users can connect their devices to a PC via either USB or wireless network, launch the ADB and then invoke a service with system level privilege running in the background. After that, an application could communicate with that service, send command to it, and thereby trigger it to work for the application with system privilege. In this manner, that app can do the job even without APIs provided by Android. There are plenty of apps on Google Play Store adopting this ADB workaround to satisfy users' specific needs, including, but not be limited to, performing backup and restoration, taking screenshot, recording screen, etc. Those apps that use ADB workaround to achieve high privilege are very popular in recent years while Google has not yet granted corresponding permissions to developers.

The security concern of ADB workaround has been raised up after some exploitation being successfully conducted. In this work, we design an approach to discover the vulnerabilities of ADB workaround. We apply this approach to three real-world apps downloaded from Google Play Store, analyze them and eventually identify the potential privilege leakage on each of three apps. In addition, we conduct an exploitation on one of these three apps named "No Root Screenshot It" and successfully prove the existence of vulnerabilities that we have recently found. Based on the outcome of our exploitation, we find that all the apps found by us that uses ADB workaround to achieve privilege escalation are vulnerable to the attack through the socket channel. Once the attacker finds a way to install the malicious application on the target device, the user privacy stored on the device will be in great risk of being stolen or leaked. Last but not the least, we provide some advices to the developers to mitigate security risk and thereby achieve users' requirement and meanwhile protect users' data and privacy.

Therefore, this paper marks the following contributions:

- We discuss the potential vulnerability of ADB workaround usage on Android devices by conducting our empirical case study.
- We propose a general approach to perform exploitation to any application using ADB workaround to achieve privilege escalation.
- We carry out our exploitation on a real application downloaded from Google Play Store and we prove that the ADB workaround brings with a significant security loophole.
- We emphasize that the security consideration during the application design and implementation is crucial to the preservation of users' privacy and hence we provide our mitigating suggestions to the developer community.

This paper is organized as follows. In the next section, we briefly introduce the security mechanism of Android, the concept of ADB workaround and related works. In Sect. 3, we present the dataset we have collected and then we explain our approach to conduct case study. We also summarize a methodology to perform exploitation and we test our exploit app on actual Android devices in that section. Section 4 is made up of our investigation based on 3 experiments of Android applications. We also present our corresponding observation in each experiment. Moreover, we provide our suggested mitigation in Sect. 5. Finally, we wrap up this paper in Sect. 6 with our concluding remarks.

2   Background

2.1   Privilege and Permission on Android

Privilege is a security attribute required for certain operations. In Unix-like OS, the process privileges are assigned in the principle of file system ownership. Its privilege mechanism is organized in shape of a flat tree where users' privilege is presented as the leaves and the superuser is described as the *root* [17]. Android, as a mobile operating system built based on Unix, takes advantages of the user-based privilege mechanism to identify, isolate and protect the resources used by applications. Every app is assigned with a unique user identification (UID), runs within the application sandbox where it only has limited permissions to access resources from the OS or other apps [4].

From the perspective of application, Android adopts the concept of ownership-based permission system from the underlying Linux kernel and develops its own access control mechanism, which is also known as the discretionary access control (DAC) [5]. On Android platform, permissions are classified into several protection levels. Most of the Android developers are made available to the *normal* level permissions and the *dangerous* level permissions in their development. The *normal* level permissions, such as Internet, vibration, NFC or setting alarm, are considered as having no great risk to the user's privacy or security. It will not prompt users for consent if the usage of those permissions is properly declared in manifest during the development. The *dangerous* level permissions indicate that the application needs access to private data or control over the device that may potentially have a negative impact to user. Unlike the *normal* level, all the operations classified in *dangerous* level will not be executed until obtaining user consent. In addition to aforementioned two permission levels, there are two more protection levels namely *signature* level and *signature or system* level defining risky permissions. The former is only granted to the application signed by the same encryption key with the one it declared the permission in advance. Furthermore, some *signature* level permissions are not made available for third party developers and they can only be granted to a trusted party like Android development group, as Table 1 shows. The latter could only be granted to the apps that are embedded in Android system image or signed by vendors of the system image [8]. The grant of these two permission levels is not to be approved by users, instead, it is conducted by signature validation mechanism of Android system during installation [19]. Many functions that users require but not provided as public APIs by Android OS, like backing up, taking screenshot and screen recording, belong to the *signature* level permission.

It is noteworthy that the DAC is only effective with the premise that all the apps are executed by an unprivileged user. Similar to other Unix-like operating systems, Android also has a number of privileged users defined in its Linux kernel, such as root, system, and radio. The root, for instance, is the most supreme user in Android and has full access to all apps' data. The Android OS does not prevent the root user or any app executed with root privilege from accessing and even modifying the resources of system or other apps [9].

2.2 Privilege Escalation

In order to implement the functions like backup, taking screenshot or screen recording, developers have to find a way to escalate the privilege of their apps till the *signature* level or even higher. There are two privilege escalation approaches on Android, namely rooting and non-root workarounds.

Rooting

Rooting is the process of allowing users of Android devices to attain privileged control. Once an Android device is rooted, users can take advantage of the root privilege and arbitrarily access the system resource. Furthermore, users can assign specific privilege to any app installed on the rooted devices, and thereby enjoy massive personalized functionality to maximize the usage of their Android devices [3]. Due to those benefits, there are plenty of users rooting their Android devices even Google officially discourage to do so [6,12].

Android rooting is described as a double-edged sword in the paper of [22]. It offers users with more permission and freedom to use their devices, and meanwhile, it also exposes all the data and program to the adversary and bring severe security vulnerabilities [15,18].

Table 1. Some examples of *signature* level permissions that are not granted to the third party developers by API level 19

Permission API	Level	Description
BROADCAST_SMS	2	Broadcast an SMS receipt notification
CALL_PRIVILEGED	1	Initiate a call without user confirmation
CAPTURE_AUDIO_OUTPUT	19	Capture audio output stream
CAPTURE_VIDEO_OUTPUT	19	Capture video output stream
DELETE_PACKAGE	1	Uninstall package
DIAGNOSTIC	1	Read and write the diagnostic resources
DUMP	1	Retrieve state dump from system services
INSTALL_PACKAGES	1	Install packages
MODIFY_PHONE_STATE	1	Modify phone state (e.g. power on, mmi, etc)
MOUNT_UNMOUNT_FILESYSTEMS	1	Mount/unmount file systems or removable storage
READ_FRAME_BUFFER	1	Access to the frame buffer data (e.g. screenshot)
READ_LOGS	1	Read system log files
REBOOT	1	Reboot the system
SET_TIME	8	Set system time
WRITE_APN_SETTINGS	1	Overwrite APN setting

Non-root Alternative

Rooting an Android device is a risky practice because it may void the warranty, brick the device and bring with numerous security vulnerabilities. Not all Android users are willing to root their device for the exchange of additional freedom and customization. Therefore, developers start to seek non-root alternatives to escalate privilege. There is an alternative approach called ADB workaround to attain high level privilege without rooting the device, and it becomes popular whilst the growth of users' concern to their device security.

Take the programmatic screenshot as an example. An app needs to have a *signature* level permission from the system to take screenshot, which is impossible for normal developers to obtain through *normal* level permission request in user interface. However, there are still two workarounds even without the permission given from Android development team: (1) taking screenshot on rooted devices; or (2) making use of a process with higher privilege to indirectly escalate the privilege of the app. The latter approach does not require the holistic change to the Android devices like "rooting". In another word, it has better security and reliability [13].

ADB is a development tool provided by Google to allow developers to debug their apps through *shell* commands from their PCs. A process requiring *signature* level permissions, such as taking screenshot, is not allowed to be implemented in app by third party developers, but could be started from an ADB shell window. That is the reason why ADB workaround could achieve a higher privilege. By using ADB workaround, developers could implement all methods requiring *signature* level permissions, pack all of them into an executive binary that could be started on ADB and run them in the background of Android OS as a service. As long as the service is not killed (e.g. power-off, restart), the unprivileged app could communicate with the privileged proxy to achieve the functionality which are not able to be done solely by itself.

2.3   Access the Screen Display on Android Devices

It is a very common demand for users to take a screenshot to save and share what is happening on her mobile device. Android only officially provides screenshot function to users and developers since its version 4.0. The most common way for user to capture the screen content is pressing a key combination of power key and volume down key. However, in those earlier versions before 4.0, Android OS neither offers users a function to take screenshot, nor provides public APIs to developer to produce third party apps to do so [10]. For those reasons, there is only one way to enable user taking screenshot on their Android device, which is privilege escalating.

Android system uses Linux OS as its kernel, and therefore it shares same approach to take screenshot with traditional Linux OS. In Linux system, the display output stream is managed by a software library named *"framebuffer"*. By accessing the *framebuffer* library, an application or a process can obtain the display data of whole screen. In early history of Android system until 3.0, reading data from the *framebuffer* is the only approach to take screenshot. The framebuffer approach is concise and traditional but faces some challenges. First of all, the Linux applies very strict access control to the *framebuffer* library, which is borrowed by Android OS as well. There are only 2 user groups, *root* and *graphic*, being able to access data from the *framebuffer* on Android platform. Moreover, nowadays Android apps become complex and sometimes using multiple *framebuffers* to form an overlaid display. Reading *framebuffer* is very likely no longer capable to obtain the entire screen display.

Starting from version 4.0. Google introduces an interface specially for taking screenshot called *SurfaceFliger*, together with a permission called READ_FRAME_BUFFER to invoke that interface. Nonetheless, Android remains its strict access control policy to the new API. Only the apps running with *system* or *graphics* user group are eligible to use such API to take screenshot – which is impossible for normal third party apps to achieve.

The developer community can always find a solution although there are number of restrictions to achieve screenshot. *"ddms"* is the most popular approach which adopts the idea of ADB workaround to eliminate the privilege restriction of screenshot taking within a third party app. *ddms* refers to the *Dalvik Debug Monitor Server*, which is a debugging tool brought with Android SDK and is also integrated into the official Android development software called Android

Studio. By accessing the *ddms*, user can make use of a third party process to send commands to the *framebuffer* service through the ADB channel. Unlike the third party app itself, an ADB session is given the shell user permission, at which all processes launched in an active ADB session are eligible to be assigned with privileges of *graphic* user group. Hence the *ddms* approach could achieve the screenshot functionality without needs to gain a higher privilege [7].

2.4   Related Work

There are some previous studies unveiling the security risk of ADB workaround despite it is considered much safer than device rooting. Security concern of ADB workaround mainly comes from the difference between roles of proxy and application on Android OS. In this project, these risks could be summarized into two types:

(1) whether other apps could obtain control to the opening proxy by sending commands; and
(2) whether the communication between app and proxy is properly protected if the scenario of (1) is possible to happen.

The description of the first kind of security concern could be found in the paper written by Lin et al. [13]. The communication channel between the application and its ADB proxy relies on network sockets without any protection enforced. For that reason, once an ADB proxy has been activated, any application has the privilege to communicate with it and even request service from it at any time without restrictions. This vulnerability gives attackers a chance to analyze the protocol of such communication and build a malicious application to request service from ADB proxy exactly as same as what genuine application does.

Some developers have realized the fact that the communication channel between the application and ADB proxy may be risky, and therefore implemented some authentication routines to strengthen security. However in the paper of Bai et al., it was proved that such authentication was ineffective as long as the reverse engineering and analysis being feasible on given application. What developer can do to secure the communication is only applying some basic authentication since there is no way to enforce strong protection onto the socket network. That authentication is usually very weak in front of analysis [1]. Some application like *"Helium"*, a backup/restore application mentioned in the paper written by Bai, et al., has been found using protection during the communication between application and ADB proxy. ADB proxy requests a password that sent out from a specific process to provide service. Unfortunately, vulnerability was found in the protocol of password distribution. The password generated each time when ADB proxy being activated, and it is independent of app's life cycle. In this way, the proxy has to find a place that readable by apps executed with user group privilege, save the password into a file and waiting for app to read from it. This life cycle inconsistency makes adversary possible to find the current using password and thereby exploit the Android device by carrying out a replay attack to the ADB proxy.

3   Approach

The Android app using ADB workaround is usually a combination of a normal application with restricted permissions, and a proxy started by ADB which has *signature* level permissions. In Android, most of apps communicate with proxies through the socket channel, which has no strong protection and generic access control. A malicious app could easily obtain the control of proxy if it knows the protocol of communication between app and itself. The security concern arises if the proxy interface is not well protected against the third party access. Some apps implement password authentication into the protocol to strengthen protection to the proxy. However, due to the inconsistency of app and proxy's life cycles, there usually be a mechanism to temporarily save the password. By this means, a malicious app could still have chance to obtain the password if proper analysis has been done. Therefore, an ineffective or insecure mechanism of password authentication constitutes another potential security concern.

In this work, we raise our hypothesis that all the apps using ADB workaround to attain a higher privilege are vulnerable to the attack. To prove that hypothesis, we collect a number of Android apps from Google Play Store. By filtering out those apps that do not adopt ADB workaround, we conduct a series of analysis in Sect. 3.2 to find out their mechanisms to achieve privilege escalation. *Static analysis* is the first step of application assessment, which will be conducted on both the proxy activation program running on the PC and the app itself. Static analysis helps us locate the involved classes for the proxy communication and thereby gain the knowledge of the overall procedure. *Dynamic analysis*, on the other hand, is capable of elaborating the runtime behavior of the target app and exposing the potential error and vulnerability. Dynamic analysis, such as hooking, is a good complement of the static analysis for our app assessment especially in case of strong obfuscation has been enforced. The protocol between the proxy and the app is supposed to be completely discovered after the static analysis and dynamic analysis. For the purpose to conduct exploitation and thereby prove our hypothesis, we may also need to conduct authentication analysis to bypass the limited security mechanism applied in the target app. With all the key information gathered, we shall proceed to exploitation design, which will be introduced in Sect. 3.3.

3.1   Data Set

We collect a batch of 13 screenshot apps and 2 screen recording apps from Google Play Store, with the criteria that the app must be compatible with earlier Android versions that do not have official support of screenshot functions. We install those apps on a Nexus 7 device installed with Android 4.4, followed by reading their official user instructions and observing the functionality of each of them. Those 15 apps, as shown in Table 2, covers all well-known approaches to take screenshots or screen recording on Android devices. There are 4 apps using ADB workaround approach to enable users to take screenshots or recording without needs to root their devices in advance. 6 other screenshot apps achieve screenshot by asking user to press key combination (e.g. power key and volume down key). Those apps essentially do not contain screenshot implementation, instead they detect the device configuration and then display the screenshot instruction if either the corresponding manufacture has official built-in function, or the Android system version installed is 4.0 or later [11], to help users to achieve screenshot functionality – in another word, those 6 apps are more like an assistant to guide users to take and manage screenshot pictures. Moreover, there are 5 more apps explicitly declaring that they are not working on devices without being rooted. In this paper, we only focus our study on those apps that using ADB workaround.

Table 2. List of screenshot and screen recording apps found on Google Play Store

#	App name and identity package name	Root required	App type[a]	Unrooted approach	Size
1	Screen capture - Sigourney com.mobilescreen.capture	No	S	Hardkey	5.2 M
2	Screenshot easy com.icecoldapps.screenshoteasy	No	S	Hardkey	5.2 M
3	Screenshot ultimate com.icecoldapps.screenshotultimate	No	S	ADB	3.2 M
4	Screenshot capture com.tools.screenshot	No	S	Hardkey	3.1 M
5	NoRoot screenshot lite com.mobikasa.screenshot.lite	Yes	S	N.A.[b]	545 k
6	Screenshot and draw com.conditiondelta.screenshotanddraw.trial	Yes	S	N.A.	1.1 M
7	Screenshot com.enlightment.screenshot	No	S	Hardkey	2.4 M
8	Screenshot com.geekslab.screenshot	No	S	Hardkey	1.2 M
9	Screenshot com.icondice.screenshot	No	S	Hardkey[c]	4.86 M
10	Screenshot com.geeksoft.screenshot	Yes	S	N.A.	2.3 M
11	Screenshot ER demo fahrbot.apps.screen.demo	Yes	S	N.A.	3.2 M
12	No root screenshot It com.edwardkim.android.screenshotitfullnoroot	No	S	ADB	838 k
13	Screenshot It com.edwardkim.android.screenshotitfull	Yes	S	N.A.	840 k
14	FREE screen recorder NO ROOT uk.org.invisibility.recordablefree	No	R	ADB	7.5 M
15	Mobizen screen recorder – record, capture, Edit 3.1.0 com.rsupport.mvagent	No	R	ADB	19.9 M

[a]'S' stands for screenshot app and 'R' stands for screen recording apps.
[b]N.A. indicates that application only work on rooted devices.
[c]Only compatible with devices made by some fixed manufactures

3.2 Application Assessment

Executing the application on an Android device by following the user instruction is obviously not sufficient for the purpose of application assessment. A complete application assessment is composed of static analysis and dynamic analysis. Figure 1 illustrates some common approaches to conduct application assessment on Android platform. The static analysis is to find a rough picture of the functionality of an Android application by analyzing source code, binary or other supporting materials such as the manifest file. While the dynamic analysis makes use of the findings from static analysis, and consequently unveils the runtime behavior of the target application [2]. In this work, our approach to analyze the app and find the vulnerabilities of ADB workaround is initiated based on two potential concerns that we have mentioned above. We summarized our approach into four step:

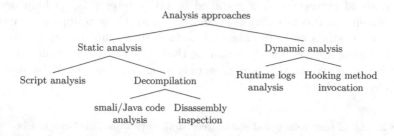

Fig. 1. Approach of app analysis

(1) **Analysis on the proxy activation.** This analysis could be done on reading proxy activation script if exists. The script is usually a batch file or bash script, which depends on the OS environment, i.e. the Windows or Linux, to be run with. Some apps do not provide script file to the user for Windows OS, for instead, a desktop application with graphic user interface (GUI) is provided to achieve better user experience. In this circumstance, the Linux version of activation package is recommended to be download because the script file is more widely used on Linux OS. A script file could disclose some details of the protocol of communication between app and proxy, such as the name of service proxy, the native executive file of proxy if any, and how the service being activated. Besides the analysis onto the script file, the name, process ID and permission group of service proxy running in the background could also be found by typing command "`adb shell ps`" in ADB through USB to the device. Moreover, the port opened for the communication between service proxy and app could be found in similar way by typing ADB command "`adb shell netstat`" to retrieve all active network usage on the device. However, in this step, the pairing of process and specific port listening may not be able to be observed if multiple proxies had been activated.

(2) **Analysis on the apk file.** Reverse engineering, such as apk decompilation, is involved in this step. Once the service proxy and port number have been identified, the next step is to discover the implementation of the communication between proxy and app in apk file. The apk file could be unpackaged and then decompiled into smali/Java source code by using tools like *Apktool* or *dex2jar*. The smali/Java code has supreme readability which may help us to look through different classes to locate the code of protocol's implementation. In fact, the decompilation analysis may not always to be proved as a smooth and easy process because a large amount of developers obfuscate their code before releasing the apk files to the app store [21]. There are a number of Android obfuscation tools available on the Internet that facilitate developers to obfuscate their apps to preserve copyright and intellectual property [23]. In this situation, the

disassembly will be helpful and a supplement to the smali/Java code reading. Reading assembly code could help us recognize the constant strings and numbers defined within same class.

(3) **Dynamic analysis.** Only reading the script and source code may not be sufficient to sketch out the entire protocol between proxy and app. The objective of dynamic analysis is to find both control flow and data flow occurred when the app interacts with service proxy. Reading logs through `logcat` is a simple but effective way to gain a brief understanding to the protocol. However, hooking by *Xposed* framework will be one of the best solutions to complete the analysis when the source code has been enforced with strict obfuscation or an authentication has been applied onto the socket channel between app and proxy server. Hooking method could be enforced onto the key methods in the class that takes responsibility to the communication between app and proxy, then sniff and extract the arguments passed in and return value through the system logs. According to the case studies in this work, the methods to be hooked are mostly used to handle the action trigger (e.g. `takeScreenshot`) and socket channel I/O (e.g. `write`). Hooking on the prior method(s) by printing logs could show us the control flow of the protocol, and hooking on the latter method(s) by extracting arguments' value could help us understand the data flow between service proxy and app itself. By now with both control flow and data flow confirmed, the communication protocol has been unveiled.

(4) **Authentication analysis.** There is very likely an authentication process if any series of numbers or a random string to be found in the data flow of the protocol. In that case, it is encouraged to clarify if the password is a constant string or dynamically generated. For the dynamically generated password, the password issuing should be solely performed by either the proxy or the app itself. The password is generally stored at somewhere that both the app and proxy have permission to read.

Once these four steps listed above have been fully understood and conducted, attackers are theoretically able to exploit an app that uses ADB workaround in a programmatic manner. We will perform an empirical case study of 3 apps that uses ADB workaround and we will present our findings in next section.

3.3   Exploitation

Theoretically, the user privacy displayed on device could be unperceivably compromised at arbitrary time if there is a malicious app installed on that device where the proxy of original app running in the background. In this subsection, we present our methodology to conduct the exploitation. Furthermore, we also select one of those 3 apps that are mentioned in the case study as the target to carry out a real exploitation, and we depict the implementation details as well as the exploitation outcome.

Based on our analysis on the apps collected for this work, we find all the apps that uses ADB workaround are vulnerable by attacking through socket channel and thereby obtain screenshot or screen recording of victim's device. Moreover, we find there is a large group of Android apps using socket channel

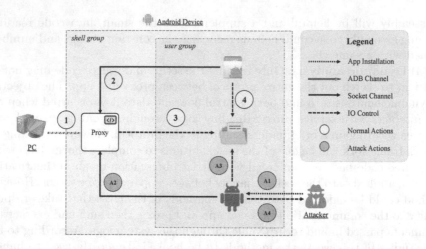

Fig. 2. Process to conduct ADB workaround exploitation

communication aided by ADB workaround to achieve privilege escalation. For those reasons, we summarize the exploitation methodology into a set of technical processes and we extend our focus scope to all apps that use ADB workaround to achieve privileged functionality.

As shown in Fig. 2, the exploitation is achieved by replay attack initiated by a malicious app, which follows the same protocol as the original app but without compliance with users' control over their devices. It could carry out theft of user's privacy at any time as long as the proxy is running in the background. Generally a successful exploitation is constituted by 4 key steps, which are:

($A1$) the attacker finds a way to install the exploitation app on the victim's device, where the benign app has also been installed on.

($A2$) the malicious app identifies the proxy and then conduct a replay attack;

($A3$) the malicious app gains access to the specific file directory where the output media files locate; and

($A4$) the malicious app finds a way to transmit the stolen data to the attacker.

In this paper, we introduce our exploitation conducted to the app II and then we present the outcome of exploitation.

We implemented an app named "*exploitNoRootScreenshotIt*" simulating the malicious exploitation of the app named "*No Root Screenshot It*" (app II in following case study) for the demonstration purpose.[1] In that exploitation app, there are in total 4 messages being organized into 2 batches and sent out to the `localhost` on port 6003 through the socket channel. The first 2 messages are used for the configuration purpose. Once the acknowledgment of first batch messages has been received from the proxy, which is "`screenshotService`" running in the background, the last 2 messages are sent out as screenshot taking commands.

---

[1] The source code of our exploitation could be downloaded from http://mark-h-meng. github.io/attachments/analysing-use-of-high-privileges/source_code_folder.zip.

The screenshot obtained is converted to a *bmp* file under the sub-directory named "`temp`"[2]. The access permission of that folder was set as read-only to the user group. Therefore, once the screenshot has been taken by the proxy, the exploitation app could access to the newly captured screenshot located in the "`temp`" folder and make a copy to the target location such as folder under external storage "**/sdcard/hack_screenshots/**". The screenshot image is renamed according to the capture time to avoid being overwritten and facilitate maintenance at the same time. As the result, our exploit app has been successfully tested on 2 devices in our lab (a *Nexus 7* with Android 4.4 installed, and a *Xiaomi Rednote 3G* with Android 4.2 installed). This exploitation could even been further designed and programmed to take screenshot automatically with specific frequency without any notice of user, hence the user's privacy could be consequently exposed to the attacker.

4   Empirical Case Study

In this section, we perform our case studies on 3 apps that use ADB workaround to achieve screenshot function. Firstly, we analysis the app titled as *Screenshot Ultimate* developed by "icecoldapps" and we note it as app I. Then we study the app named *No Root Screenshot It* developed by "edwardkim", which is represented by app II. After that, we conduct our analysis on the third app called *FREE screen recorder NO ROOT*, which is produced by "Invisibility Ltd" and noted as app III.

4.1   App I – Screenshot Ultimate

"*Screenshot Ultimate*" is a typical screenshot app that does not require a rooted device. It supports screenshot taking through ADB workaround. However, that usage is veiled since too obvious instruction may lead to a ban from Google. The ADB workaround is mentioned in a paragraph of "Help" instruction, and the URL to download the script and other necessary files are given in another place and could only be found on the screen display within the app. The developer has provided detailed step-by-step instruction and troubleshooting notes.

Analysis on the Proxy Activation
The native executable file, named "`screenshotultimatenative1`", and scripts for both Linux and Windows OS could be downloaded as a zipped file from the URL given in the help instruction. After reading through the script file, we found the execution of script pushed that native executable to the file directory of the application in the device, then configured another native executable named `absel` located in the application file directory to user executable mode, and finally launched both native execution files to make them run in the background. We summarize the flow of service activation and show it in Fig. 3. With the

---

[2] The full directory path is /data/data/com.edwardkim.android.screenshotitfullnoro ot/temp.

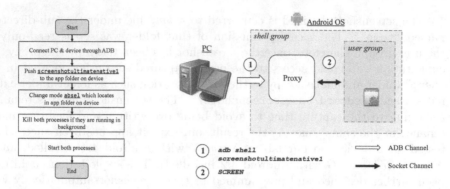

Fig. 3. Proxy activation of app I   **Fig. 4.** Process of taking screenshot on app I

process name of service running in the background, we can analyze the apk file and unveil the protocol of screenshot taking process between app and that service.

Analysis on the apk File

The reverse engineering tool "dex2jar" is used to decompile the apk file to the jar format. Then further Java decompilation has been done by "JD-GUI". Unfortunately, the class organization of the source code obtained from the decompilation of "Screenshot Ultimate" is not quite readable because the obfuscation is believed to be applied. Some core methods which control the logic flow of screenshot taking are missing. Clues could only be found by analyzing package structure, libraries imported and source code from the remaining classes.

Obfuscation cannot perfectly hide everything in the decompiled source code. After carefully reading through the source code of *"Screenshot Ultimate"*, we find some clues to shape the mechanism of screenshot taking. For example, there is an address in Android OS partition, which is in form of a string variable with the value as "/system/bin/fbread", appearing more than once in the obfuscated classes. Its occurrence suggests that this app is very likely taking screenshot by reading image data from *framebuffer*, which is commonly expressed as short writing "fb" in Android development. Reading framebuffer to take screenshot is usually achieved by a library called *Android screenshot library* (known as "ASL")[3]. We downloaded the ASL from Android open source repository and compared the checksum value with the native executive that we downloaded from the URL given by the app developer. The comparison result reveals that 2 executive files are exactly equivalent, which proves our hypothesis that the app I makes use of ASL to read framebuffer and thereby capture the screen display.

The ASL enables Android developer to write screenshot app without root requirement. Once the user follows the instruction and executed the native executive file by running the given scripts, proxy with shell permission could help user

---

[3] Android screenshot library is available at https://code.google.com/archive/p/android-screenshot-library/downloads.

take screenshot which the application has no privilege to do so. Take "Screenshot Ultimate" as example, user could just click the "Screenshot" button at the moment that user wants to take screenshot of his/her device, then the app send the screenshot command to the proxy running in background via socket channel, following by the proxy as a process named "`screenshotultimatenative1`" reading the current hardware framebuffer, converting to the image format and saving to the specific location. Furthermore, we find the command that the app I sends to the background service through socket channel. The message is a constant string with a value as "`SCREEN`". The communication is carried out by a plaintext messaging mechanism through a fixed port number, which is obviously not secure at all. In the end, we sketch out the protocol of communication between app and proxy and place it into a bigger scale of the entire life cycle of the app I. We present the process diagram of app I in Fig. 4.

4.2   App II – "No Root Screentshot It"

Unlike the *"Screenshot Ultimate"*, the app II *"No Root Screenshot It"* has additional security feature and protection enforcement being implemented during the development. The obfuscation has been conducted onto both service activator and apk file. Meanwhile, the communication channel between app and proxy has also been protected by using some identification trick like a password.

Analysis on the Proxy Activation

Instead of simply running a batch script, the service activation of app II is performed by executing a *.Net* application named "Screenshot It Enabler". Therefore the decompilation of *.Net* application is involved in the static analysis of app II. Moreover, the script file was not found in the enabler's package, which means it has been packaged into the apk and the purpose of the enabler is just to run the "shell" command to execute it. A *.Net* decompilation tool named "JetBrains dotPeek"[4] has been used to conduct the reverse engineering of the activation tool. Even though the enabler application has been obfuscated, some variables and C# code logics could still be recovered after the decompilation. The scripts to enable the proxy has been unveiled by observing the C# code from the decompilation result. We noticed there is a string "screenshot" that occurs in the decompiled C# code as one of the argument while launching ADB service. For that reason, we believe that there is a script file named "screenshot" being executed during the service activation. Then the script file's location could be easily found by browsing the file manager on a rooted phone, or by decompiling the apk file and searching the file name (Fig. 5).

Analysis on the apk File

After clarifying the ADB communication to activate the proxy, the following step focuses on discovering the communication between app and the proxy, thereby obtain the commands to control proxy to take screenshot at any occasion. On the apk side, the obfuscation has been applied very strongly onto both class

---

[4] DotPeek is available on https://www.jetbrains.com/decompiler/.

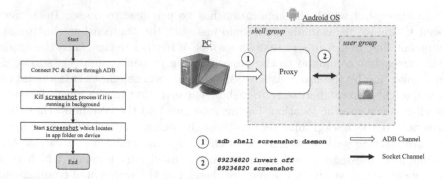

Fig. 5. Proxy activation of app II   **Fig. 6.** Process of taking screenshot on app II

names and variable names, which makes it difficult to observe the entire protocol by just reading the decompiled Java code. It is cleared that the class named **ScreenshotService** is in charge of the communication with the proxy but the code is not as readable as the app I. What worse is that there is magic number, 89234820, being found and referenced multiple times by reading through the assembly code of **ScreenshotService** class. There is a great possibility that the app has (1) multiple communication session with proxy to take a screenshot; and/or (2) an authentication trick to indicate the app's identity, which might be the reason of the existence of the magic number 89234820.

Dynamic Analysis

Unlike what we have done in case study of app I, only static analysis is not adequate to find the protocol that used for communication between the app II "*No Root Screentshot It*" and its proxy. In order to unveil what kind of command that the app sends to the proxy to take screenshot and how they interact with each other, a dynamic analysis technique called "hooking" is adopted in this project. Hooking system APIs on Android could be enabled by using a framework known as *Xposed* on a rooted device. By reading the decompiled code during the static analysis, the communication between the proxy and app has been found carry out through the socket channel. Therefore, the monitoring of the socket channel during the communication between the proxy and app could be done by writing a module based on Xposed framework which hooks all the socket channel related packet data IO functions in specific source codes.

After implementing and deploying our Xposed module named "*hookNoRoot-ScreenshotIt*", all the necessary data has been logged and printed out during the IO operation of the socket channel. The control flow of the app and proxy communication is finally unveiled and shown in Fig. 6.

4.3   App III – "FREE Screen Recorder NO ROOT"

In addition to those 2 screenshot apps, a screen recording app *"FREE screen recorder NO ROOT"* has also been investigated in this paper. According to the description on Google Play Store, this app could enable users to record their screen regardless of which app or activity is on the top of stack, and then export the recorded video in MP4 format. The entire process doesn't request users to root their devices.

Analysis on the Proxy Activation
Similar with those two screenshot apps we have analyzed previously, this app also needs user to complete the proxy activation before the app unlocking the record function. The activation process is launched by an *exe* file on Windows OS, and an executable *jar* file on Linux OS. Missing of activation script doesn't mean the identification of proxy is impossible. Actually, with the help of ADB, we could still find the details proxy(s) activated, including the process name, PID and the port(s) listening. Here, two ADB commands, "ps" and "netstat", have been used to retrieve the list of running processes and active ports on the Android device. By this means the proxy and the ports number could be found. There are two services namely "videoserv" and "inputserv" running on the background to enable users to record their screen. One of them uses port 7938, and the other one uses port 7940 to communicate with app. However, we are still yet to completely discover the protocol without knowing the identification of the process which actively engages with those two ports. For that reason, the decompilation is needed for the further analysis.

Analysis on the apk File
Firstly, the apk file has been extracted out of the device, and then been decompiled into smali code. The clues that recently found, two port numbers 7938 and 7940, could be searched within the source code to locate the key classes we will analyze on. As the searching result of keyword 7938 shown below, we found the variable name which bearing that port number, namely "video_port". Similarly, the port 7940 has been found in variable name "input_port" recorded in same *xml* file. Next, we continued searching the occurrence of two variables "video_port" and "audio_port". After filtering from the search result, we preliminarily confirmed that the code reflecting the control flow and data flow was located in class "RecordService" and "Projection" separately. Take the communication between video server and app as example, the core function in charge of the communication flow is supposed to be "videoWrite", which located in line 1038 in the smali code of RecordService. This videoWrite method has been called many time once after the occurrence of the constant string with all letter being capitalized, which is suspected to be the command sending to the server. Moreover, by browsing through the smali code, a method named "openSocket" has been called within the class RecordService, which helps us to confirm that the protocol we are going to discover is performed through the socket channel.

Dynamic Analysis and Authentication Analysis

Similar with the analysis of app II, we used hooking to sketch out the complete control flow and data flow of the protocol. The target function to be hooked has been confirmed during the previous analysis, which is "videoWrite" located in class named "RecordService". In order to find as many details about the protocol as possible, some other methods located in the same class of "videoWrite" have also been hooked. With the information obtained from the output logs of methods' hooking, the protocol of the communication between video server and app to start screen recording has been found. A sixteen-digit-long string ce2757a06d455af2 grabbed our attentions because it was presumed to be the authentication code, or password for short, according to the location of its occurrence. Nevertheless, it has not yet been confirmed to be a string constant or a dynamic changing string so far. In order to clarify the nature of that password, a series of experiments has been conducted (Fig. 7).

Firstly, we closed the app after taking a screen recording video clips, then re-opened it and took another screen recording. Hooking logs shown in logcat console showed that the password didn't change. In that means, the password is independent of the app's life-cycle. We have repeated the above steps for many times and all the results proved that our assumption is correct. Next, we killed all proxies related to this app and launch the service activation again. As a result, we noticed that the password has changed. Thus the password could be confirmed to be dynamically generated after each time that the proxy being re-activated. Since the password is proved to be generated by proxy, there must be a place that the proxy stored the code at somewhere that the app with user privilege could access and read. After searching, we finally located the password in a *log* file named videoserv.log under the directory data/local/tmp, and

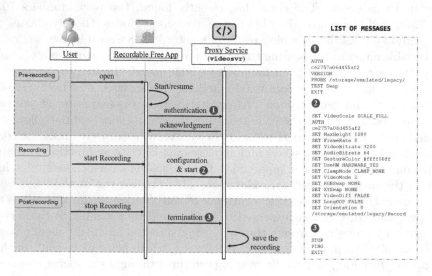

Fig. 7. The sequence diagram of screen video recording on app III

luckily find the first occurrence of the current password was always after the word "AUTH" in the log file. With those information, An attacker could all along hold the current password by writing a simple program on the target device to read the log file and then extract the string at given location.

5 Mitigation

In order to find a solution to the concerns we raised in Sect. 2.4, we summarize some suggestions for the Android development throughout the study and research in this project. The Android developers are strongly advised to raise security awareness and take some security practices into account when implementing the functionality based on ADB workaround, including:

1. **Identity verification for the application.** One possible solution for this issue may be writing a *handshake* process in the proxy implementation, to make both the app and the proxy exchange their authentication. And the ADB proxy will execute the command only after a successful validation. Thus the proxy service can only accept the command sent from the exactly same app. Once the app is removed and re-installed, regardless of genuine app or malicious app, another handshake validation should be required thereby to ensure the ADB proxy would not be misused.
2. **Password protection for socket channel communication.** Another possible solution is to implement a stronger password mechanism. For the purpose to prevent from the replay attack, the password could be dynamically generated at first and then updated after a specific time period. Besides that, an *out-of-bounds* password mechanism could be another option as the password is randomly generated and issued by the activation program. To synchronize the password between the proxy and the app, the activation program can display its password on the PC screen and ask user to manually type in the benign app. Thus no other application could attain the password and thereby leaves no chance to attackers to carry out exploitation.

6 Conclusion

In this paper, we analyze the approach to find privacy loophole and security vulnerabilities of ADB workaround on Android platform. By conducting investigation on 3 different apps, we find that most of apps using ADB workaround have risk of being exploited. We propose a methodology to conduct exploitation to all similar apps that use ADB workaround through the socket channel. We also implement an exploit application on Android, which successfully proves our findings and verifies our proposed methodology. In the end, we provide our recommendation to app developers to mitigate security risks and produce their apps with higher privacy-preserving capability.

References

1. Bai, G., et al.: All your sessions are belong to us: investigating authenticator leakage through backup channels on android. In: Proceedings of the 20th International Conference on Engineering of Complex Computer Systems (ICECCS) (2015)
2. Batyuk, L., Herpich, M., Camtepe, S.A., Raddatz, K., Schmidt, A., Albayrak, S.: Using static analysis for automatic assessment and mitigation of unwanted and malicious activities within android applications. In: 2011 6th International Conference on Malicious and Unwanted Software, pp. 66–72, October 2011
3. Bishop, M.: Unix security: threats and solutions (1996)
4. Bugiel, S., Davi, L., Dmitrienko, A., Fischer, T., Sadeghi, A.R., Shastry, B.: Towards taming privilege-escalation attacks on android. In: NDSS. vol. 17, p. 19. Citeseer (2012)
5. Chen, H., Li, N., Enck, W., Aafer, Y., Zhang, X.: Analysis of seandroid policies: combining MAC and DAC in android. In: Proceedings of the 33rd Annual Computer Security Applications Conference, pp. 553–565. ACM (2017)
6. Chris, H.: The case against root: why android devices don't come rooted (2012). https://www.howtogeek.com/132115/the-case-against-root-why-android-devices-dont-come-rooted/
7. Ferrill, P.: Navigating the android SDK. In: Pro Android Python with SL4A, pp. 57–82. Apress (2011)
8. Google: <permission>, Android Developers (2018). http://developer.android.com/guide/topics/manifest/permission-element.html. Accessed 18 Mar 2016
9. Google: System and kernel security (2018). https://source.android.com/security/overview/kernel-security.html. Accessed 18 Mar 2016
10. Gordon, W.: How to take a screenshot on android, April 2013. https://www.lifehacker.com.au/2013/04/how-to-take-a-screenshot-on-android/. Accessed 12 July 2018
11. Hoffman, C.: How-to geek: how to take screenshots on android devices since 4.0, June 2012. http://www.howtogeek.com/121133/how-to-take-screenshots-on-android-devices-since-4.0. Accessed 20 Mar 2016
12. Kristijan, L.: Over 27.44% users root their phone(s) in order to remove built-in apps, are you one of them? (2014). https://www.androidheadlines.com/2014/11/50-users-root-phones-order-remove-built-apps-one.html
13. Lin, C.C., Li, H., Zhou, X.Y., Wang, X.: Screenmilker: how to milk your android screen for secrets. In: NDSS (2014)
14. Lucic, K.: Over 27.44% users root their phone(s) in order to remove built-in apps, are you one of them? November 2014. https://www.androidheadlines.com/2014/11/50-users-root-phones-order-remove-built-apps-one.html. Accessed 14 Mar 2016
15. Meng, H., Thing, V.L.L., Cheng, Y., Dai, Z., Zhang, L.: A survey of android exploits in the wild. Comput. Secur. **76**, 71–91 (2018)
16. Popper, B.: Google announces over 2 billion monthly active devices on Android (2017). https://www.theverge.com/2017/5/17/15654454/android-reaches-2-billion-monthly-active-users. Accessed 01 July 2018
17. Provos, N., Friedl, M., Honeyman, P.: Preventing privilege escalation. In: USENIX Security, vol. 3 (2003)
18. Ravenscraft, E.: Rooted vs. unrooted android: your best arguments, July 2014. http://lifehacker.com/rooted-vs-unrooted-android-your-best-arguments-1599101019. Accessed 18 Mar 2016

19. Shabtai, A., Fledel, Y., Kanonov, U., Elovici, Y., Dolev, S., Glezer, C.: Google android: a comprehensive security assessment. IEEE Secur. Priv. 8(2), 35–44 (2010)
20. StatCounter: Mobile operating system market share worldwide (2018). http://gs.statcounter.com/os-market-share/mobile/worldwide. Accessed 14 Aug 2018
21. Wang, Y., Rountev, A.: Who changed you?: obfuscator identification for android. In: Proceedings of the 4th International Conference on Mobile Software Engineering and Systems, pp. 154–164. IEEE Press (2017)
22. Zhang, H., She, D., Qian, Z.: Android root and its providers: a double-edged sword. In: Proceedings of the 22nd ACM SIGSAC Conference on Computer and Communications Security, pp. 1093–1104. ACM (2015)
23. Zhang, L., Meng, H., Thing, V.L.L.: Progressive control flow obfuscation for android applications. Region 10 Conference, TENCON 2018 IEEE (2018)

Blockchain-Based Privacy Preserving Deep Learning

Xudong Zhu[1(✉)], Hui Li[2], and Yang Yu[1]

[1] Xi'an University of Architecture Technology, Xi'an 710055, Shaanxi, China
zhudongxu@vip.sina.com
[2] Xidian University, Xi'an 710126, Shaanxi, China

Abstract. Smart mobile devices have access to huge amounts of data appropriate to deep learning models, which in turn can significantly improve the end-user experience on mobile devices. But massive data collection required for machine learning introduce obvious privacy issues. To this end, the notion of federated learning (FL) was proposed, which leaves the training data distributed on the mobile devices, and learns a shared model by aggregating locally-computed updates. However, in many applications one or more Byzantine devices may suffice to let current coordination learning mechanisms fail with unpredictable or disastrous outcomes. In this paper, we provide a proof-of-concept for managing security issues in federated learning systems via blockchain technology. Our approach uses decentralized programs executed via blockchain technology to establish secure learning coordination mechanisms and to identify and exclude Byzantine members. We studied the performance of our blockchain-based approach in a collective deep-learning scenario both in the presence and absence of Byzantine devices and compared our results to those obtained with an existing collective decision approach. The results show a clear advantage of the blockchain approach when Byzantine devices are part of the members.

Keywords: Smart mobile device · Federated learning · Byzantine devices · Blockchain technology

1 Introduction

More and more smart mobile devices, such as mobile phones and tablet computers, have become the main computing equipment for most people [1]. The powerful sensors (such as cameras, accelerometers, and GPS) on these mobile devices which are frequently carried produce and have access to an unprecedented amount of data, much of it private in nature. Models learned on such data can greatly improve usability by powering more smart applications, but the private nature of the data means there are risks and responsibilities to storing it in a centralized location.

Supported by Natural Science Fund of Shaanxi Province #K05074.

ⓒ Springer Nature Switzerland AG 2019
F. Guo et al. (Eds.): Inscrypt 2018, LNCS 11449, pp. 370–383, 2019.
https://doi.org/10.1007/978-3-030-14234-6_20

To address the challenges of the private data inclusion in deep learning, McMahan et al. [2] proposed federated learning, a learning technique that allows users to collectively reap the benefits of shared models trained from this rich data, without the need to centrally store it. Each participating device has a local training dataset which is never uploaded to the server. And each participating device computes an update to the current global model maintained by the server, and only this update is communicated. A principal advantage of this approach is the decoupling of model training from the need for direct access to the raw training data. FL can significantly reduce privacy and security risks by limiting the attack surface to only the device, rather than the device and the cloud.

But federated learning network is often claimed to be highly fault-tolerant, in some cases one or more Byzantine devices – devices that show arbitrarily faulty or malicious behavior – may suffice to let current coordination learning mechanisms fail. In real-world, devices in federated learning network will face situations in which some of the devices become Byzantine devices. Robustness to Byzantine devices will therefore become of paramount importance. Until now federated learning research has left unaddressed the problem of how to manage the security issues generated by the presence of Byzantine devices: (i) *tampered devices or failing sensors:* the messages sent from these devices can contain wrong or deceptive information; (ii) *attacked or noisy communication channels*: messages can be manipulated or destroyed while propagating through the peer-to-peer network; (iii) *loss of availability*: information stored on a device's hard drive might be deleted; the device might be captured or destroyed.

In this paper, we argue that blockchain technology might be used to provide solutions to the aforementioned security issues. In particular, we show that it allows a federated learning network to achieve consensus in a collective learning problem even in the presence of Byzantine devices. While blockchain technology was originally developed as a peer-to-peer financial system in the context of the cryptocurrency Bitcoin [3], recently there have been proposals for using blockchain technology as a distributed computing platform where arbitrary programs (blockchain-based smart contracts) can be run. The best known example of such a platform is Ethereum [4,5]. Blockchain-based smart contracts allow decentralized systems with mutually distrusting nodes to agree on the outcome of the programs. We provide the first proof-of-concept for using blockchain technology in federated learning applications. We do so by laying the foundation of a secure general framework for addressing collective learning problems.

Our approach is based on the federated learning scenario of McMahan et al. [2]. Via blockchain technology, we add a security layer on top of the classical approach that allows for taking care of the presence of Byzantine devices. Our blockchain approach also allows for logging events in a tamper-proof way: these logs can then be used, if necessary, to analyze the behavior of the devices in the network without incurring the risk that some malicious device has modified them. In addition, it provides a new way to understand how we debug and how we can approach data forensics in decentralized systems such as federated learning network. We use the simulator to vary the number of Byzantine devices and compare the performance – in terms of consensus time and probability of a correct outcome – of McMahan et al.'s [2] strategies and our blockchain-based variants both in the presence and in the absence of Byzantine devices.

The remainder of this paper is structured as follows. Section 2 reviews related work. Section 3 presents our proposed blockchain-based privacy-preserving deep learning framework. Section 4 evaluates the performance of the approaches through experiments in simulation. Section 4.5 discusses advantages and disadvantages of our blockchain approaches. Section 5 presents our conclusions and provides directions for future work.

2   Related Work

2.1   Privacy in Deep Learning

Deep learning aims to extract complex features from high-dimensional data and use them to build a model that relates inputs to outputs (e.g., classes). Deep learning architectures are usually constructed as multi-layer networks so that more abstract features are computed as nonlinear functions of lower-level features. Deep learning has been shown to outperform traditional techniques for speech recognition [8,9], image recognition [10,11] and face detection [12].

The existing literature on privacy protection in machine learning mostly targets conventional machine learning algorithms, as opposed to deep learning, and addresses **three objectives**: *(i) privacy of the data used for learning a model or as input to an existing model, (ii) privacy of the model, and (iii) privacy of the model's output.*

(1) Techniques based on **Secure Multi-party Computation (SMC)** can help protect intermediate steps of the computation, such as decision trees [13], linear regression functions [14], association rules [15], Naive Bayes classifiers [16], and k-means clustering [17], when multiple parties perform collaborative machine learning on their proprietary inputs. But SMC techniques impose non-trivial performance overheads and their application to privacy-preserving deep learning remains an open problem.

(2) Techniques based on **differential privacy** have been proposed to guarantee the confidentiality of personal data while training a differentially-private model [18–25]. Most of these techniques for differentially-private machine learning are usually based on adding noise during the training, which leads to a challenging trade-off between accuracy and privacy.

(3) Techniques based on **privacy-preserving distributed learning** have been proposed to learn information from data owned by different entities without disclosing either the data or the entities in the data. Shokri and Shmatikov [26] and McMahan et al. [2] propose solutions where multiple parties jointly learn a neural-network model for a given objective by sharing their learning parameters, but without sharing their input datasets. A different approach

is proposed by Hamm et al. [27] and Papernot et al. [28], where privacy-preserving models are learned locally from disjoint datasets, and then combined on a privacy-preserving fashion. However, the privacy guarantees of some of these solutions have recently been called into question [29].

Unlike previously proposed techniques, our system achieves all three privacy objectives in the context of collaborative neural-network training: it protects privacy of the training data, enables participants to control the learning objective and how much to reveal about their individual models, and lets them apply the jointly learned model to their own inputs without revealing the inputs or the outputs. This solution brings most of the data processing to where the data resides and not the other way around, exactly as the edge computing paradigm calls for [30]. Recent work have demonstrated the feasibility of running complex deep learning inferences on local devices such as smartphones [31]. While in these works models are previously trained in an offline manner, our experiments proved that both the inference and the local retraining can be performed locally on a low-power device in a timely manner.

2.2 Blockchain

Blockchain is a peer-to-peer distributed ledger technology that was initially used in the financial industry [3]. The blockchain, a chronological ledger of transactions that ensures the integrity of the information included, can be used to capture and log both queries and its correspondent answers. Blockchain 2.0 introduces the concept of smart contracts [32], which is no longer limited to transactions between currencies, and there will be more extensive instruction embedded in the blockchain. The smart contract does not need mutual trust, as it is not only defined by the code, but executed by the code. Besides, it's completely automatic and cannot be intervened.

(1) Blockchain storage model, with non-tampering feature and traceability, ensures the privacy and credibility of the data.
(2) The smart contract that automatically execute the default instruction and the complete de-centric model guarantee the security of data sharing.
(3) Establish a reliable big data distribution system without trusting third parties.

The properties of blockchain make it a promising tool in many privacy informatics applications [33]: from building decentralized backbones for data exchange and interoperability, protocols enforced by immutable ledgers that keep track of data usage [35], and data provenance [36,37], to maintain user's privacy and security through the persistence of consent statements in blockchain [38]. Moreover, the blockchain technology offers practical means to safely and securely store and track the use of personal data as well as the parameters of the deep learning models. This increases the users' trust in the system and provides a rich source of information that can be used to better design future services. Our proposed framework deploys blockchain technology where anyone can read and validate transaction entries, but only authorized entities are able to create or write transaction to the blockchain.

3   Proposed Architecture

As shown in Fig. 1, our system design three major parts, namely, mobile devices (i.e. participants), hub, and blockchain network. The data producers collect the massive data through the smart contract to store in the blockchain, for the use of data sharing. The smart contract code runs on the contract layer of blockchain, which provides the authority to control the system.

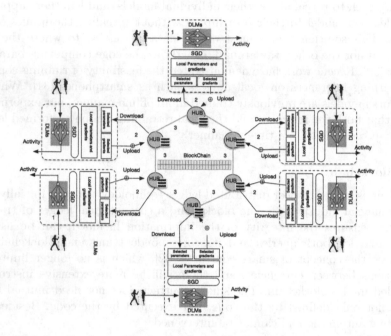

Fig. 1. High-level architecture of our deep learning system for activity recognition.

3.1   Participants

① **Inference.** We assume that each participant (R_i) relies on the deep learning models (DLMs), M_i, when conducting a inference. Specifically, R_i checkouts M_i from its local hub and uses it to conduct the inference. During this, R_i stores the information captured by its sensors, producing the inference data ($\mathbf{ID}_i$). $\mathbf{ID}_i$ allow R_i to update/improve the existing M_i. Specifically, a supervised machine learning approach is adopted: $\mathbf{ID}_i$ are used as input to M_i, while the class scores $\mathbf{O}_i$ (e.g. human activities) as the target output. Then, the fine-tunning of the DLM parameters $\mathbf{W}_i$ to the newly acquired data $\mathbf{ID}_i$ is accomplished using the standard back-propagation technique and by selecting an optimizer. With these new parameters, the participant is expected to increase its competences and adaptability to target inference.

Algorithm 1. Inference (based on CNN forward and backward propagation.)

Require: M-dimensional data, $\mathbf{ID_i} = [I_1, \cdots, I_n]^T$
Ensure: The class scores, $\mathbf{O_i} = [O_1, \cdots, O_c]$
 1: _Download_ $\theta \times |\mathbf{w}^{(i)}|$ parameters from local hub.
 2: **for** $l := 1 \rightarrow \#HiddenLayers$ **do**
 3:     **for** $i := 1 \rightarrow \#RowunitinLayerl$ **do**
 4:         **for** $j := 1 \rightarrow \#ColumnunitinLayerl$ **do**
 5:             **Find** the layer activations by,
 6:             $O^l_{ij} = \varphi(a^l_{ij} w^l_{ij}) + b^l_{ij}$
 7:             **Compute** next layer inputs
 8:         **end for**
 9:     **end for**
10: **end for**
11: **Keep** the final output as O^l
12: **Calculate** error at the output layer.
13: **for** $l := 1 \rightarrow \#HiddenLayers$ **do**
14:     **Find** error partial derivation.
15:     **Find** error at the previous layer.
16: **end for**
17: **Calculate** the gradient of the error.

3.2 Hubs

② **Re-training.** After the inference, the data (ID) and class score (**O**) are used together to improve the inference by re-training their DLMs (Ms). This can be done on the data-processing servers of the local hub. To this end, different learning strategies can be adopted. For instance, the participants (Rs) can create, store, and update Ms after each inference, or after a sufficient amount of ID has been collected. The design of specific learning strategies depends on the inference type. Then, these new Ms are committed and stored in the local repository, similar to the version control systems, of the local hub. Once created and stored, it is assumed that these new Ms cannot be used to recreate the raw ID of R. Therefore, all personal data remain safe as they do not leave the hub. Furthermore, they are deleted after all Ms are updated.

The stored Ms are further deployed locally and assigned a cumulative score S based on the **O** derived by validation of this model within new local inferences. As a result, a new candidate model (M_C) along with its performance score (S) is then created and locked on the local hub. To allow knowledge sharing – one of the key ingredients of the framework – this new M_C is then evaluated by the participant peers operating at other sites, i.e., different hubs within a network. To this end, the local hub publishes the changes (e.g., the difference between the previous version of M_j and M_C). Finally, the hub announces the update to the entire network. The goal of this is to assure a fair validation of the M_C before it can be adopted as the new version of the Ms for target inference.

Algorithm 2. Re-training (based on Distributed selective SGD)

Require: Choose initial parameters $\mathbf{w}^{(i)}$ and learning rate α.
1: **repeat**
2:     *Get* $\theta \times |\mathbf{w}^{(i)}|$ parameters from the blockchain and replace the corresponding local parameters.
3:     *Run* stochastic gradient descent (SGD) on the local dataset and update the local parameters $\mathbf{w}^{(i)}$.
4:     *Compute* gradient vector $\triangle \mathbf{w}^{(i)}$ which is the vector of changes in all local parameters due to SGD.
5:     *Store* $\triangle \mathbf{w}^{(i)}$ to the blockchain, where S is the set of indices of at most $\theta_u \times |\mathbf{w}^{(i)}|$ gradients
6: **until** an approximate minimum is obtained

3.3 Parameter Blockchain

③ **Updates. I. Publish.** First, the source participant $(R_{(s)})$ 'advertises' the new candidate model (M_C^s) by announcing the DLM updates to the entire network. Then, the destination participants $(R_{(d,i)})$, where $i = 1 \cdots N$ denotes the target hubs, are notified by their local hub that there is an update available in the network. This can be achieved by the subscription pipeline they have with their local hub. In case the updates are available, the participants can retrieve and apply them to their working directory. Once $M_{(C)}^s$ is adopted from the source hub, $R_{(d,i)}$ starts its evaluation, quantified in terms of the scores $(S_{(R_{(d,i)}, M_{(C)}^s)})$. Additionally, in order to leverage the new local data, the destination hubs can also return the model updates to the source hub (obtained in a similar fashion as when creating the M_C). These, in turn can be used to construct the new model at the source hub (Fig. 2).

II. Validate. During the next stage, $R_{(s)}$ is to consolidate the feedback information from the destination hubs. This can be achieved using time-constraints (i.e., waiting for a pre-defined period of time to receive the feedback), and/or when a target consensus is achieved. If the score for the M_C is higher than for the currently accepted model (M_s), i.e., $\overline{S_{(i,M_C^s)}} > \overline{S_{(i,M_s)}}$, R_s creates a new model $M_{(s+1)}$, which is then published to all connected hubs, and committed to their participants' local repositories. In this way, the new baseline model for future inferences is endorsed by the network. This process can be implemented via modern control version systems in order to store and share the resulting model configurations (e.g., the DLM topology, hyper-parameters, etc.) obtained after new inferences. This is an important feature of our framework since it allows the participants to rollback to the last consensual version of M_{s+1}, in case a consensus did not take place within the network. Moreover, since the participants keep the list of all changes in their local repository, there is a promising research approach in analyzing the metadata available in the updates applied to the repository.

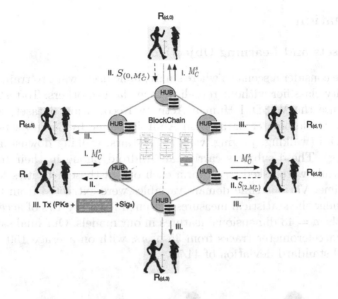

Fig. 2. A BlockChain-based deep learning network.

III. Consensus. In order to notarize and log the creation of the new models and their consensus processes within the network, $R_{(s)}$ is required to send a transaction to a blockchain including information such as the timestamp of the global update broadcast, a hash string that encapsulates the information about the model update (e.g., differences in the weights, hyper-parameters, etc.), and an encrypted data field signed by $R_{(s)}$ containing information such as the public IDs of the participants that took part in the consensus process and their correspondent feedback scores. This transaction on the blockchain is necessary to allow participants within the network to prove/validate how models were created, who participated in their consensus process, and when did those transaction take place. It is also important to highlight that the hash string included in this transaction is useful to check and confirm that the models acquired by participants are indeed the version agreed upon by the network, and not a corrupted version from a third-party agent. In addition, the encrypted data field signed by $R_{(s)}$ contain sufficient information to allow the users to confirm their participation in the consensus process and check that $R_{(s)}$ was not biased at the moment of promoting $M_{(j)}$. This information is readable by any participant in the network, since they know the public identifier (i.e., public key) of $R_{(s)}$. By contrast, the peers connected to the blockchain but not members of the private clinical network do not have the means to decrypt this information or identify the nodes involved in the consensus process. This is because all required public/private keys remain within the boundaries of the clinical private network. Finally, note that the whole consensus reaching process could have been implemented directly on the blockchain via 'smart contracts' in order to prevent intruders from 'attacking' the network; yet, we assume here that the network access is protected.

4   Evaluation

4.1   Datasets and Learning Objectives

As Fig. 3, we consider a scenario where smartphone users want to train a motion-based activity classifier without revealing their data to others. To test the algorithms, we use the WISDM Human Activity Recognition dataset, which is a collection of accelerometer data on an Android phone by 35 subjects performing 6 activities (walking, jogging, walking upstairs, walking downstairs, sitting and standing). These subjects carried an Android phone in their front pants leg pocket while were asked to perform each one of these activities for specific periods of time. Various time domain variables were extracted from the signal, and we consider the statistical measures obtained for every 10 s of accelerometer samples as the $d = 43$ dimensional features in our models. Our final sample contains 5,418 accelerometer traces from 35 users, with on average 150.504 traces per user and standard deviation of 44.73.

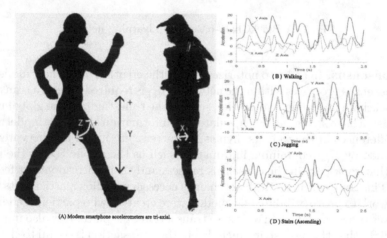

Fig. 3. (A) Modern smartphone accelerometers are tri-axial. (B–D) Accelerometer graphs for three dynamic activities.

4.2   Computing Framework

We use Torch7 and Torch7 *nn* packages. This popular deep-learning library has been used and extended by major Internet companies such as Facebook.

4.3   Neural Network Architectures

We used a Multi-Layer Perceptron as the supervised learning algorithm for recognising activity using accelerometer traces. A Multi-Layer Perceptron or MLP is a type of feed-forward Artificial Neural Network that consists of two layers, input and output, and one or more hidden layers between these two layers.

The input layer is passive and merely receives the data, while both hidden and output layers actively process the data. The output layer also produces the results. Figure 4 shows a graphical representation of a MLP with a single hidden layer. Each node in a layer is connected to all the nodes in the previous layer. Training this structure is equivalent to finding proper weights and bias for all the connections between consecutive layers such that a desired output is generated for a corresponding input.

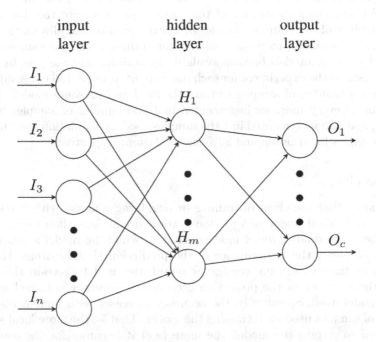

Fig. 4. The architecture of the two-layer feed-forward network.

4.4 Experimental Setup

We set up a Multilayer Perceptron with 2 layers for activity recognition, including 1 hidden layer with 128 nodes and 1 logistic regression layer, resulting in 6, 406 parameters to be determined during training. We construct the input layer using the statistical measures of users' accelerometer traces. Because of the sensitivity learning stages to feature scaling we normalise all statistical measures to have zero mean and unit standard deviation. In the output layer each unit corresponds to an activity inference class, such that unit states can be interpreted as posterior probabilities.

All training procedures were implemented in python using the *Theano* deep learning library. The training and testing were performed with 5-fold cross validation, using early stopping as well as l2-regularisation to prevent overfitting. Each neuron's weight in the *shared* and *local* models was initialised randomly from $N(0,1)/\sqrt{2.0/n}$, where n is the number of its inputs, and biases were all initialised to zero. Parameters in the *personal* model were initialised to the values obtained in the *shared* model. Finally, we used grid search to determine the optimal values of the hyper-parameters, setting the learning rate to 0.05 for the shared model and to 0.001 for the local and personal models, and the l_2-regularisation strength to $1e^{-5}$ for all the models. The training epochs were set to 1000 in all models, while the batch size was set equal to the size of the training sets in the *shared* model, and to 1 (online learning) in the *local* and *personal* ones. The reasons behind this are the small size of the dataset, and the availability of the training samples in a real scenario (samples for the shared model can be assumed to be all available for training, whereas samples in the *local* and *personal* models become available for training as time goes by).

We repeated the experiment for each participant, using 5-fold cross-validation and different number of samples to train the *local* and *personal* models. In each simulation of every user, we incremented in 1 the number of samples used for training, and also incremented in 1 the samples used for validation until reaching 60% of samples for training and 20% for validation, respectively.

4.5   Results

Results show that the effect of training or retraining a model with few samples from the individual under test produces worse predictions than using samples from other individuals (*shared* model). That is, while the model is adapting to the new *scenario*, the performance of the prediction slightly drops. However, when more samples (20 on average or more) are used to retrain this *shared* model, the accuracy of the prediction exceeds the accuracy obtained with the *shared* model itself. Specifically, the accuracy increases with increments in the number of samples used for retraining the model. That is, the more local samples considered to retrain the model, the more *local* it becomes for the considered individual. However, although the improvement on the accuracy with the increment of the number of samples is also shared with the *local* model, more samples per individual are required for training a model from scratch (local model) in order to obtain the same accuracy than when starting from a shared model. We also observe that, after on average 163 samples, the *local* model performs better than the personal model. This means that the user would need to perform and label, on average, 163 activities in order to get a local model that outperforms her personal one. However, this is not significant, since there is one unique user in the dataset with that number of samples or higher available for training. In summary,

(i) retraining a shared model locally using 20 or more samples from the user increases the accuracy with respect to that obtained with the shared model, and

(ii) to obtain the same accuracy when training a model from scratch using only local samples, more than 150 training samples are required on average.

5 Conclusions and Future Work

Creating and training of deep learning models have been a computationally-hungry process. So the adoption of these models in embedded devices has been a challenging task, especially for low-cost mobile devices. Federated learning, one decentralized approach, learns a shared model by aggregating locally-computed updates, and leaves the training data distributed on the mobile devices. The federated learning network interconnecting the participants' devices is not public. Thus, it requires a permission of one or several parties to join and start contributing to the deep learning process. We understand that some form of trust is required in the institutions that deal with a sensitive task.

In this paper we proposed the first deep learning approach for tackling the privacy issues in the use of personal data by mobile devices. We illustrated this framework using activity recognition as an example which is conducted simultaneously in multiple mobile devices. While the approach proposed here offers the main principles for secure data and models sharing between multiple mobile devices. To this end, we aim to collect the data from several parties in order to test the framework in a data-exchange scenario. Then, we aim to run in real time on private network to enable efficient and real-time learning of models. For this, existing deep learning approaches will need to be adapted so that they can efficiently be integrated with the blockchain technologies. Also, These are topics of our ongoing research.

References

1. Poushter, J.: Smartphone ownership and internet usage continues to climb in emerging economies. Pew Research Center Report (2016)
2. McMahan, H.B., Moore, E., Ramage, D., Hampson, S., et al.: Communication-efficient learning of deep networks from decentralized data (2016). arXiv preprint: arXiv:1602.05629
3. Nakamoto, S.: Bitcoin: a peer-to-peer electronic cash system (2008). https://bitcoin.org/bitcoin.pdf
4. Buterin, V.: A next-generation smart contract and decentralized application platform. Ethereum project white paper (2014). https://github.com/ethereum/wiki/wiki/White-Paper
5. Wood, G.: Ethereum: a secure decentralised generalised transaction ledger. Ethereum project yellow paper (2014). http://gavwood.com/paper.pdf
6. Hannun, A., Case, C., Casper, J., et al.: DeepSpeech: scaling up end-to-end speech recognition (2014). arXiv:1412.5567
7. He, K., Zhang, X., Ren, S., Sun, J.: Delving deep into rectifiers: surpassing human-level performance on ImageNet classification (2015). arXiv:1502.01852
8. Graves, A., Mohamed, A.R., Hinton, G.: Speech recognition with deep recurrent neural networks. In: ICASSP (2013)
9. Hinton, G., Deng, L., Yu, D., Dahl, G., et al.: Deep neural networks for acoustic modeling in speech recognition: the shared views of four research groups. IEEE Signal Process. Mag. **29**(6), 82–97 (2012)
10. Krizhevsky, A., Sutskever, I., Hinton, G.: ImageNet classification with deep convolutional neural networks. In: NIPS (2012)

11. Simard, P., Steinkraus, D., Platt, J.: Best practices for convolutional neural networks applied to visual document analysis. In: Document Analysis and Recognition (2013)
12. Taigman, Y., Yang, M., Ranzato, M., Wolf, L.: DeepFace: closing the gap to human-level performance in face verification. In: CVPR (2014)
13. Lindell, Y., Pinkas, B.: Privacy preserving data mining. In: Bellare, M. (ed.) CRYPTO 2000. LNCS, vol. 1880, pp. 36–54. Springer, Heidelberg (2000). https://doi.org/10.1007/3-540-44598-6_3
14. Du, W., Han, Y., Chen, S.: Privacy-preserving multivariate statistical analysis: linear regression and classification. In: SDM, vol. 4, pp. 222–233 (2004)
15. Vaidya, J., Clifton, C.: Privacy preserving association rule mining in vertically partitioned data. In: KDD (2002)
16. Vaidya, J., Kantarcoğlu, M., Clifton, C.: Privacy-preserving Naive Bayes classification. VLDB **17**(4), 879–898 (2008)
17. Jagannathan, G., Wright, R.: Privacy-preserving distributed k-means clustering over arbitrarily partitioned data. In: KDD (2005)
18. Dwork, C., Rothblum, G., Vadhan, S.: Boosting and differential privacy. In: FOCS (2010)
19. Chaudhuri, K., Sarwate, A., Sinha, K.: A near-optimal algorithm for differentially-private principal components. JMLR **14**(1), 2905–2943 (2013)
20. Chaudhuri, K., Monteleoni, C.: Privacy-preserving logistic regression. In: NIPS (2009)
21. Zhang, J., Zhang, Z., Xiao, X., Yang, Y., Winslett, M.: Functional mechanism: regression analysis under differential privacy. VLDB **5**(11), 1364–1375 (2012)
22. Rubinstein, B., Bartlett, P., Huang, L., Taft, N.: Learning in a large function space: privacy-preserving mechanisms for SVM learning. J. Priv. Confidentiality **4**(1), 4 (2012)
23. Sarwate, A., Chaudhuri, K.: Signal processing and machine learning with differential privacy: algorithms and challenges for continuous data. IEEE Signal Process. Mag. **30**(5), 86–94 (2013)
24. Chaudhuri, K., Monteleoni, C., Sarwate, A.: Differentially private empirical risk minimization. JMLR **12**, 1069–1109 (2011)
25. Wainwright, M., Jordan, M., Duchi, J.: Privacy aware learning. In: NIPS (2012)
26. Shokri, R., Shmatikov, V.: Privacy-preserving deep learning. In: Proceedings of the 22nd ACM SIGSAC Conference on Computer and Communications Security, pp. 1310–1321. ACM (2015)
27. Hamm, J., Cao, P., Belkin, M.: Learning privately from multiparty data. In: Proceedings of the 33rd International Conference on Machine Learning, pp. 555–563 (2016)
28. Papernot, N., Abadi, M., Erlingsson, U., Goodfellow, I., Talwar, K.: Semi-supervised knowledge transfer for deep learning from private training data. In: Proceedings of the 5th International Conference on Learning Representations (2017)
29. Hitaj, B., Ateniese, G., Pérez-Cruz, F.: Deep models under the GAN: information leakage from collaborative deep learning. CoRR, vol. abs/1702.07464 (2017)
30. Shi, W., Cao, J., Zhang, Q., Li, Y., Xu, L.: Edge computing: vision and challenges. IEEE Internet Things J. **3**(5), 637–646 (2016)
31. Georgiev, P., Lane, N.D., Rachuri, K.K., Mascolo, C.: DSP.Ear: leveraging co-processor support for continuous audio sensing on smartphones. In: Proceedings of the 12th ACM Conference on Embedded Network Sensor Systems, pp. 295–309. ACM (2014)

32. Peters, G.W., Panayi, E.: Understanding modern banking ledgers through blockchain technologies: future of transaction processing and smart contracts on the internet of money. In: Tasca, P., Aste, T., Pelizzon, L., Perony, N. (eds.) Banking Beyond Banks and Money. NEW, pp. 239–278. Springer, Cham (2016). https://doi.org/10.1007/978-3-319-42448-4_13

33. Kuo, T.T., Kim, H.-E., Ohno-Machado, L.: Blockchain distributed ledger technologies for biomedical and health care applications. J. Am. Med. Inform. Assoc. **24**(6), 1211–1220 (2017)

34. Kuo, T.T., Ohno-Machado, L.: ModelChain: decentralized privacy-preserving healthcare predictive modeling framework on private blockchain networks (2018). arXiv preprint: arXiv:1802.01746

35. Topol, E.J.: Money back guarantees for non-reproducible results? BMJ **353**, i2770 (2016)

36. Baxendale, G.: Can blockchain revolutionise EPRs? ITNOW **58**(1), 38–39 (2016)

37. Taylor, P.: Applying blockchain technology to medicine traceability (2016)

38. Brodersen, C., Kalis, B., Leong, C., et al.: Applying blockchain technology to medicine traceability (2016)

SpamTracer: Manual Fake Review Detection for O2O Commercial Platforms by Using Geolocation Features

Ruoyu Deng[1], Na Ruan[1(✉)], Ruidong Jin[1], Yu Lu[1], Weijia Jia[1], Chunhua Su[2], and Dandan Xu[3]

[1] Department of CSE, Shanghai Jiao Tong University, Shanghai, China
{dengruoyu,naruan,tracyking,luyu97,jiawj}@sjtu.edu.cn
[2] Division of CS, University of Aizu, Aizuwakamatsu, Japan
suchunhua@gmail.com
[3] China Unicom Research Institute, Beijing, China
xudd18@chinaunicom.cn

Abstract. Nowadays, O2O commercial platforms are playing a crucial role in our daily purchases. However, some people are trying to manipulate the online market maliciously by opinion spamming, a kind of web fraud behavior like writing fake reviews, due to fame and profits, which will harm online purchasing environment and should be detected and eliminated. Moreover, manual fake reviewers are more deceptive compared with old web spambots. Although several efficient methods were proposed in the fake review detection field, the manual fake reviewers are also evolving rapidly. They imitate to be benign users to control the velocity of review fraud actions, and deceive the detection system. Our investigation presented that geolocation factor is potential and can well reflect the distinctions between fake reviewers and benign users. In this research, we analyzed the geolocations of shops in reviews, found the distinct distribution features of those in fake reviewers and benign users, and proposed a *SpamTracer* model that can identify fake reviewers and benign users by exploiting an improved HMM (Hidden Markov Model). Our experiment demonstrated that SpamTracer could achieve 71% accuracy and 76% recall in the unbalanced dataset, outperforming some excellent classical approaches in the aspect of stability. Furthermore, SpamTracer can help to analyze the regularities of review fraud actions. Those regularities reflect the time and location in which online shops are likely to hire fake reviewers to increase their turnover. We also found that a small group of fake reviewers tend to work with plural shops located in a small business zone.

Keywords: O2O commercial platform ·
Manual fake review detection · Geolocation · Hidden Markov Model

© Springer Nature Switzerland AG 2019
F. Guo et al. (Eds.): Inscrypt 2018, LNCS 11449, pp. 384–403, 2019.
https://doi.org/10.1007/978-3-030-14234-6_21

1   Introduction

With the explosive growth of electronic commerce and social media, O2O (Online To Offline) commerce has become a heated topic in public. O2O refers to the use of online enticement to drive offline sales, and feedbacks from offline consumption can promote the online dissemination of products [18]. As the feedback part in O2O, reviews of experienced users can provide significant reference values for consumers and help them to make decisions. Opinions in reviews are essential to the evaluation and business volume of a target product in current O2O platforms such as Amazon[1], Booking[2], and Yelp[3]. Positive reviews can bring profits and fame, while negative ones are harmful to products. Due to the pursuit of interest, deceptive reviews and fake reviewers appeared. Moreover, the continuous and rapid evolution of social media makes fake reviewers themselves evolve rapidly and pose a significant challenge to the community [3]. It has been a common practice that shops tend to hire fake reviewers to promote themselves secretly. Those kinds of activities are called opinion spam [9].

Prior researchers have been working on manual fake review detection for several years [21]. At the early stage, methods of opinion spam were elementary and easy to identify. Researchers proposed many approaches based on text analysis [20]. Besides, simple machine learning methods could also be used to classify the suspect reviews by analyzing features of reviews and reviewers [15]. Meanwhile, commercial platforms realized the hazard of opinion spam and built their own filtering systems to find deceptive and inferior quality reviews. Those systems helped purify the disordered review environment, but they also prompted fake reviewers to enrich their poor review contents. Even some skilled fake reviewers were able to deceive the detecting system [24]. As the elapse of time, fake reviewers were becoming more and more cautious and tended to disguise as normal users, and those laggard traditional approaches wouldn't work efficiently anymore. The spotlight on manual fake review detection was gradually shifting from text contents to features and patterns. Some features were proved useful in manual fake review detection like time [10], ranking pattern [5], topics [16] and activity volume [6]. These new approaches did provide several new ideas in opinion spam detection.

We exploit a creative *SpamTracer* method to do manual fake review detection by exploiting the geolocation features. Geolocation is potential in manual fake review detection task. Fake reviewers and benign users may have similar geolocation records. However, fake reviewers don't pay much attention to the position order during review fraud actions. Their strange actions appear to be inconsistent with general behaviors of benign users. The different action concepts between fake reviewers and benign users will cause distinctions in the statistics and the frequency distribution of geolocation features. After computing on a partly labeled reviews and reviewers dataset, we found that both reviewers and benign users have double peak distributions regarding the geolocation features. Our method can fit the geolocation features well. Some prior works have

---

[1] www.amazon.com.

[2] www.booking.com.

[3] www.yelp.com.

discussed the practice of geolocation features in manual fake review detection tasks. Zhang et al. [25] used geolocation features in OSNs (Online Social Networks) to detect fake reviewers, and Gong et al. [7] used LSTM model and check-in information in LBSNs (Location-Based Social Networks) for malicious account detection. Their works enlighten us that location information can reflect some review fraud features.

Apart from detecting fake reviewers, we also discussed the feasibility of discovering the time and location regularities of hiring fake reviewers. There exist some rules in online shop's tendency of hiring fake reviewers regarding time and location. For example, online shops tend to hire fake reviewers in the beginning period to accumulate popularities and obtain a higher rank in searching results, etc. We can draw some conclusions that explain some important regularities based on a large scale dataset expanded by SpamTracer.

In summary, our work makes the following special contributions:

1. We exploit geolocation features to do manual fake review detection in O2O commercial platforms. We extracted the geolocation features of shops, and arrange those from the reviews written by the same person in time order.
2. We built a special SpamTracer model to describe the distribution of geolocation features of fake reviewers and benign users. It's creative that SpamTracer receives geolocation features sequences and gives prediction results.
3. We proposed three significant propositions regarding time and location of review fraud regularities. Our experiment confirmed those propositions and gave reasonable explanations.

The remainder of this paper is organized as follows. In Sect. 2, we introduce the preliminary works. In Sect. 3, we present the detailed design and construction of SpamTracer model. The dataset, experiment, and evaluation are demonstrated in Sect. 4. Finally, we conclude our research in Sect. 5.

2   Preliminaries

2.1   Terminology

To describe our work precisely, we first introduce some definitions as following.

Definition 1. *Shop: A shop is an officially registered online shop and holds a unique webpage usually. A shop's webpage contains the detailed description of the shop and a large number of reviews of this particular shop.*

Definition 2. *User: A user is an officially registered account and holds a personal webpage. A user's webpage contains detailed personal profile and reviews that the user has posted.*

Remark 1. In this paper, we categorize all users into two types: **benign users** and **fake reviewers**. **Benign users** are those who post honest reviews, and **fake reviewers** are those who post fake reviews to promote the target shops.

Definition 3. *Fake review: Fake reviews are reviews posted by fake reviewers. They post fake reviews without offline experiences. Fake reviews contain fabricated text and imaginary stories, are crafted to mislead normal consumers.*

2.2   Classification Algorithms in Manual Fake Review Detection

Spamming behaviors are categorized into several different types like web spam [21], e-mail spam [2], telecommunication spam [23], and opinion spam [9], etc. Manual fake review detection problem belongs to opinion spam. It can be regarded as a binary classification problem. The critical problem is the selection of approaches and models. According to prior researches, there are several main approaches to detect manual fake reviews.

Texture-Based Approaches. In 2008, when opinion spamming was firstly proposed by Jindal [9], researchers were focusing on the classification and summarization of opinions by using Natural Language Processing (NLP) approaches and data mining techniques. From 2011, researchers tried to improve the methods of text analysis. Ott et al. [17] built an Support Vector Machine (SVM) classifier using text features including unigrams and bigrams. Shojaee et al. [20] focused on the lexical and syntactic features to identify fake reviews, and Chen et al. [4] proposed a semantic analysis approach that calculates the similarity between two texts by finding their common content words. Traditional texture-based approaches are simple, and they can not reach a high efficiency when manual fake reviewers began to enrich their fake review contents.

Feature-Based Approaches. From 2014, with the rapid development of machine learning, more and more machine learning algorithms are applied on the fake review detection field. Li et al. [12] proposed a PU-Learning (Positive Unlabeled Learning) model that can improve the performance of Dianping[4]'s filtering system by cooperating with Dianping. Kumar et al. [11] proposed an improved SVM model named DMMH-SVM (Dual-Margin Multi-Class Hypersphere Support Vector Machine) to solve web spamming problem. Chino et al. [6] trained a log-logistic distribution model consisting of time interval and activity volume of one's each review to fit users' behavior, and calculated the dispersion of reviews written by different users to identify those who are isolated from the majority. Li et al. [13] proposed an LHMM (Labeled Hidden Markov Model) combined with time interval features to do fake review detection in a sizeable Dianping dataset and gave an excellent result. Feature-based approach is a powerful weapon in fake review detection, but the features need to continually evolve since the fake reviewers are also evolving themselves simultaneously.

Graph-Based Approaches. From 2016, some researchers chose graph models to find the relations among the products, users, and reviews. A detailed graph model can even capture the deceptive reviewer clusters. Agrawal et al. [1] showed an unsupervised author-reporter model for fake review detection based on Hyper-Induced Topic Search (HITS) algorithm. Hooi et al. [8] proposed a camouflage-resistant algorithm FRAUDAR to detect fake reviews in bipartite

---

[4] www.dianping.com.

graph of users and products they review. Chen et al. [5] proposed a novel approach to identify attackers of collusive promotion groups in the app store by exploiting the unusual ranking changes of apps to identify promoted apps. They measured the pairwise similarity of app's ranking changing patterns to cluster targeted app and finally identified the collusive group members. Zheng et al. [26] proposed an ELSIEDET system to detect elite sybil attacks and sybil campaigns. Feature-based approaches mainly focus on feature selection, while graph-based approaches attach more importance to patterns and links.

2.3 Hidden Markov Model

HMM (Hidden Markov Model) is a classic probabilistic graphical model that uses the graph to represent relations among variables. HMM has two states: observation state and hidden state. Hidden states form a sequence, and every hidden state emits one observation state. In the beginning, HMM has an initial state probability to determine which hidden state will be the first. Every time a new state comes after, hidden states may transform to other states by following a certain transition probability, and the hidden state has a certain emission probability of emitting different kinds of observation states. HMM obeys two significant assumptions. One is that each hidden state only relies on the former one. It guarantees the rationality of transition probability. Another is that each observation state exclusively relies on the corresponding hidden state. It ensures the rationality of emission probability. The two assumptions have been widely acknowledged in practice. In conclusion, an HMM can be represented by three parameters: initial state probability, transition probability, and emission probability under the guarantee of two reasonable assumptions above.

There exist some prior works that apply HMM to manual fake review detection task. Malmgren et al. [14] proposed a basic double-chain HMM and used an efficient inference algorithm to estimate the model parameters from observed data. Washha et al. [22] also proved the qualification of using HMM in manual fake review detection work. Li et al. [13] proposed an LHMM (Labeled Hidden Markov Model) combined with time interval features to detect fake reviews in a sizeable Dianping dataset and gave an excellent result.

3   Manual Fake Review Detection Model

3.1   Symbols and Definitions

Table 1 gives a complete list of the symbols used throughout this chapter.

3.2   Structure Overview

In this section, we are going to introduce SpamTracer model used for detecting manual fake reviews. Our detection process is shown in Fig. 1. First, extracting the geolocation features from the dataset. Then, arranging the feature sequence

Table 1. Symbols and definitions

Symbol	Interpretation
x_i	ith location in review sequence of a reviewer
C	Center point
$Distance(A, B)$	The interval distance between two locations A and B
γ_{x_i}	Distance between x_i and C
$f(x; \mu, \sigma)$	Gaussian distribution function with parameters μ, σ
$N(\mu, \sigma^2)$	Gaussian distribution with parameters μ, σ
L	Label variable
$\lambda = \{\mathbf{A}, \mathbf{B}, \pi\}$	Hidden Markov Model
$\mathbf{A}$	Transition probability of HMM
$\mathbf{B}$	Emission probability of HMM
π	Initial state probability of HMM
X_i	The ith observation state
$X_{1:T}$	The observation states from X_i to X_T
P	Probability
Y_i	The ith hidden state
$Y_{1:T}$	The hidden states from Y_i to Y_T
$a_{j,k}$	The element in the matrix of transition probability $\mathbf{A}$
$b_j()$	The distribution of emission probability

in time series. Next, inputing the feature sequence into SpamTracer. Finally, we get prediction results from SpamTracer. SpamTracer makes predictions based on the calculation of possibilities. The prediction results given by SpamTracer are responsible for classifying data samples into fake reviewers or benign users.

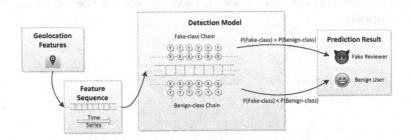

Fig. 1. The structure of manual fake review detection process.

All the symbols and definitions in this chapter are listed in Sect. 3.1. Then the rationality of the selection of geolocation features will be discussed in Sect. 3.3. The methods of modeling geolocation features will be detailedly introduced in Sect. 3.4. Finally, a discovery of review fraud action regularities will be discussed in Sect. 3.5.

3.3 Selecting Geolocation Features

Posting reviews is a random process. It means that the posting events are continuously and independently occurring at a constant average rate. Under such process, the related features will follow a particular distribution. As for the feature selection, there were several mature feature distributions discovered by prior work like time intervals and activity volume, etc. However, geolocation features were seldom used in manual fake review detection. The related statistics and the frequency distribution of the location-related feature in fake reviewers and benign users can be calculated and analyzed respectively, and the manual fake review detection problem can be solved by finding the distinctions between them. We use a useful location-related feature, Radius, to measure the disorder degree of users' movement tracks. First, we introduce the definitions of review location, center point and radius:

Definition 4. *Review location:* *Review locations are geolocation points of shops that appear in users' reviews. It notes the location where the user purchased offline.*

Definition 5. *Center point:* *A center point is the geometric center of the shops in a user' reviews. Determine a user's center contains two steps:*

(1) Find the city that the user lives in by the number of reviews.
(2) Find the geometric center of shops that the user has posted reviews in the city he lives in.

Definition 6. *Radius:* *Radius is the distance between each review location and the center point.*

Figure 2 shows an example of the definition of radius feature. Most of the review locations are located in New York, so the center point is also located in New York. The lines connecting the center point and each review location represent the interval distances between them, which are the radius for these review locations.

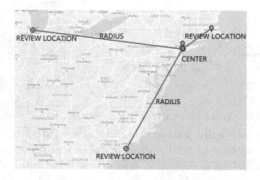

Fig. 2. Definition of radius feature on Google Map.

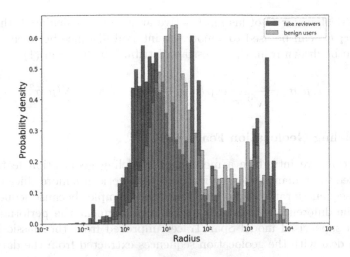

Fig. 3. Frequency distributions of radius.

Table 2. Statistics of radius

	Average value	Standard deviation
Fake reviewers	310.0604	678.4959
Benign users	568.5133	999.4281

The statistics and the histograms of the radius calculated on a labeled dataset are shown in Table 2 and Fig. 3. The average value and standard deviation show the differences between two reviewer types. The histograms demonstrate that the peaks and slopes are much distinct between fake reviewers and benign users. The frequency distributions can be regarded as the overlap of several Gaussian distributions with different parameters under the log scale x-axis. The double peak distribution pattern is quite reasonable. In general, the range of human activity can be divided into two modes: home range and far range. Benign users tend to purchase near home, and sometimes go far places. It leads to the result that their radius features have the characteristic of double peaks. Although fake reviewers also have two active ranges, they usually take a detour during review fraud action since fake reviewers don't pay much attention to the location order of fake reviews. The location order of fake reviews written by the same fake reviewer is inconsistent with general behaviors of those belonging to benign users. This is the reason why both fake reviewers and benign users have identical double peak patterns and different peak points and slopes.

The problem can be solved by building a model that can handle with radius sequences. As mentioned above, the distributions of the radius can be seen as the overlap of Gaussian distributions with different parameters. Supposing that $x_i, i = 1, \ldots, T$ is the location in one's review sequence arranged in time order, the geometrical center C of his most active area can be calculated, then $\gamma_{x_i} = Distance(x_i, C)$ can be used to denote the interval distance between x_i and C, and γ_{x_i} can be drawn from the Gaussian distribution shown in (1).

$$f(x; \mu, \sigma) = \frac{1}{\sqrt{2\pi}\sigma} \exp\left(-\frac{(x-\mu)^2}{2\sigma^2}\right) \qquad \gamma_x \sim N(\mu, \sigma^2) \tag{1}$$

3.4   Modeling Geolocation Features

In this section, we introduce a method of modeling geolocation features and features used to do manual fake review detection work. It's more efficient to deal with data sequences rather than individual data samples because sequences can optimize the differences of action patterns and augment the performance. We proposed a supervised model SpamTracer improved from the classic HMM so that it can deal with the geolocation sequences extracted from the dataset.

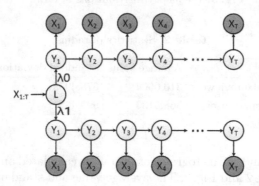

Fig. 4. Representation of SpamTracer.

As illustrated in Fig. 4, SpamTracer contains two HMM subchains and a label variable connecting two chains. Label variable is denoted by $L \in \{0, 1\}$, where 0 stands for benign users and 1 stands for fake reviewers. Two subchains $\lambda_0 = \{\mathbf{A}_0, \mathbf{B}_0, \pi_0\}$ and $\lambda_1 = \{\mathbf{A}_1, \mathbf{B}_1, \pi_1\}$ represent benign class and fake class, and are trained by two kinds of data samples respectively. When a feature sequence comes, two subchains will calculate the possibility that generates this sequence. The value of the possibility is a score that measures the fitness between the feature sequence and the class of subchain.

Supposing there is a feature sequence $X_{1:T}$ with unknown label L, the model will calculate its scores under λ_0 and λ_1 respectively, then choose the label by the model that gives a higher score. $X_{1:T}$ also serves as the observation sequences of the subchains. It's rational that the more probable label L takes is the one that generates the observation sequence better.

Our target is comparing the possibility of different label $L \in \{0, 1\}$ under a certain $X_{1:T}$, as expression (2). According to Bayesian theorem, the calculation of

$P(L = l | X_{1:T})$ can be converted to the calculation of $P(X_{1:T} | \lambda_l)$ under different λ. First, denominator $P(X_{1:T})$ is independent of L. Thus it is a constant value and won't affect the comparison result, and then it can be dropped. Next, it's easy to get the value of $P(L = l)$ by counting the number of each kind of samples in the dataset. Therefore the problem is the calculation of $P(X_{1:T} | \lambda_l)$. It's equal to the calculation of $P(X_{1:T})$ under different subchains. The detailed calculation process will be introduced next.

$$
\begin{aligned}
\widehat{L} &= \max_l P(L = l | X_{1:T}) \\
&= \max_l \frac{P(X_{1:T} | \lambda_l) \cdot P(L = l)}{P(X_{1:T})}, l \in \{0, 1\}
\end{aligned}
\tag{2}
$$

Supposing that $x_i, i = 1, ..., T$ is the location in one's review sequence arranged in time order, then γ_{x_i} represents the radius feature of each review x_i. In the subchains of SpamTracer, $X_i = \gamma_{x_i}$ serves as the continuous observation variables, and it follows different Gaussian distributions depending on the hidden state. Considering that a hidden state variable Y_i has two possible values $\{0, 1\}$. Hidden variable Y_i denotes the mode of the point x_i, and the set of $\{0, 1\}$ represents home range mode and far range mode respectively.

The initial state probability π is given as $\pi = \{\pi_j\} = \{P(Y_i = j)\}, j \in \{0, 1\}$. According to the first significant assumption that Y_i only depends on Y_{i-1} and is independent of previous hidden states, the transition probability $\mathbf{A}$ is given as $\mathbf{A} = \{a_{jk}\}$, where $a_{j,k} = P(Y_i = k | Y_{i-1} = j), j, k \in \{0, 1\}$. The observation value X_i is available directly from the dataset. It is emitted by one of the two Gaussian distributions corresponding to the hidden state $Y_i \in \{0, 1\}$. X_i can be demonstrated by (3), where μ and σ are parameters of the Gaussian distribution.

$$
X_i = \gamma_{x_i} \sim
\begin{cases}
N(\mu_0, \sigma_0^2) & Y_i = 0 \\
N(\mu_1, \sigma_1^2) & Y_i = 1
\end{cases}
\tag{3}
$$

Combined with expression (1), the emission probability $\mathbf{B} = \{b_j(X_i)\}$ can be calculated as expression (4).

$$
b_j(X_i) = b_j(\gamma_{x_i}) = P(\gamma_{x_i} | Y_i = j) = f(\gamma_{x_i}; \mu_j, \sigma_j) \quad j \in \{0, 1\}
\tag{4}
$$

Now the calculation of $\lambda = \{\mathbf{A}, \mathbf{B}, \pi\}$ in the subchains has been stated, as well as how they fit the distribution of radius γ_{x_i}. Supposing $X_{1:T}$ denotes the observation variable sequence from x_1 to x_T, and $Y_{1:T}$ denotes the hidden variable sequence from x_1 to x_T. Expression (5) formulate the joint probability of $X_{1:T}$ and $Y_{1:T}$. The calculation of $P(X_{1:T}, Y_{1:T})$ means the calculation of the probability that both $X_{1:T}$ and $Y_{1:T}$ appear at the $1 \sim T$ places in order. The time complexity is $O(T)$.

$$P(X_{1:T}, Y_{1:T})$$
$$=P(Y_1, X_1, Y_2, X_2, ..., Y_T, X_T)$$
$$=P(Y_1) \prod_{i=1}^{T} P(X_i|Y_i) \prod_{i=2}^{T} P(Y_i|Y_{i-1}) \tag{5}$$
$$=\pi_{Y_1} \prod_{i=1}^{T} b_i(X_i) \prod_{i=2}^{T} a_{Y_i Y_{i-1}}$$

However, the corresponding $Y_{1:T}$ is unknown when given a certain $X_{1:T}$ in SpamTracer. Therefore, all the possible hidden states need to be taken into consideration. SpamTracer needs to calculate 2^T different possibilities of the sequence $Y_{1:T}$. In this situation, the probability $P(X_{1:T})$ can be calculated as expression (6):

$$P(X_{1:T})$$
$$= \sum_{Y_{1:T}} P(X_{1:T}, Y_{1:T})$$
$$= \sum_{Y_{1:T}} P(Y_1) \prod_{i=1}^{T} P(X_i|Y_i) \prod_{i=2}^{T} P(Y_i|Y_{i-1}) \tag{6}$$

If directly calculating $P(X_{1:T})$ by following the approach above, the time complexity will be $O(T \cdot 2^T)$. Such high complexity is almost uncomputable. In this case, a dynamic algorithm named Forward-backward algorithm [19] was proposed to solve the estimating problem by reducing the time complexity to linear time.

As a result, the calculation of $P(X_{1:T})$ under different subchains is proved practicable. SpamTracer is theoretically qualified as a supervised model and can make predictions. The prediction result given by SpamTracer can be regarded as a score measuring the fitness of data samples and different classes.

3.5 Application of Fake Review Detection Model

In this section, we discuss the review fraud regularities exploration from the dataset with the assistance of SpamTracer. Several empirical conclusions are spreading in public about how to identify fake reviewers. For example, fake reviews hold a large part in the beginning period of most online shops, and there are some periods when fake reviews regularly burst, etc. Besides, fake reviewers tend to look for restaurants competing with others in the same business zone to persuade them to use their review fraud services. As an owner of a restaurant in a hot business zone, it's easy for him to be forced to hire fake reviewers when he finds that rivals around here are all working with fake reviewers. Fake reviews can be recognized better if their action regularities are revealed. Contraposing to those hypotheses, SpamTracer, and the dataset can tell whether those empirical rules are rumors or truths.

The expansion of labeled data is essential in the review fraud regularities exploration. A more substantial amount of labeled data can lead to much more reliable results. After dataset expansion, all the reviews are labeled, and all the fake reviews are clearly exposed to us. Our research mainly concerns three relations among fake reviewers, time and geolocation:

Date Period and Fake Reviewers. We consider the relation between the number of daily fake reviews and the date period, and the regular period of fake review burst. First, SpamTracer identifies the unlabeled reviews in the dataset. Then SpamTracer collects all the fake reviews and their posting time. Fake reviews are categorized by weekdays and months, and a line chart is drawn to explore the regular burst periods.

Shop Opening Days and Fake Reviewers. We mainly consider the relation between the number of daily fake reviews and shop opening days, and try to validate the proposition that there are more fake reviewers and reviews in the beginning period of shops. Maybe new shops tend to hire some fake reviewers in the beginning days to help them obtain more population and rise rapidly in the rank. The expansion dataset can show us precisely in which stage restaurants are likely to hire fake reviewers. First, the SpamTracer model identifies the unlabeled reviews in the dataset. Then the fake reviews are assembled by the shops they belong to. Since the dataset contains the shops information, the opening date of shops is available, and the interval days between the shop opening day and review posting day can be calculated. Finally, a histogram chart is drawn to find the distribution of fake reviews posting day.

Shared Fake Reviewers and Interval Distances. First, we introduce the definition of shared fake reviewers:

Definition 7. *Shared fake reviewers: shared fake reviewers are the fake reviewers who simultaneously work with plural shops in a small business zone.*

The existence of shared fake reviewers accelerates the competition in small business zones. Fake reviewers try to force shop owners to use their service by cooperating with their competitors. We plan to count the number of shared fake reviewers and the interval distance between two shops where shared fake reviewers appear. The relation between them can be discovered by drawing a distribution chart.

A simple Algorithm 1 is proposed to calculate the shared fake reviewers of each pair of shops. A review number threshold is set to simplify the computation cost. Only those shops hold a certain degree of review numbers can be included in our calculation. First, the algorithm filters shops with fewer reviews, assembling reviewers by shops, and runs the classification model to get their labels (line 1–6). After all the useful shops are prepared, the algorithm travels all the shop pairs and calculates the interval distance and the number of shared fake reviewers

---

Algorithm 1. Calculate the interval distance and amount of shared fake reviewers between two shops

---

Input: Set of shops M, set of reviewers R, Threshold of shop review number δ;
Output: Pairs of distances and amount of shared fake reviewers $H(d, n)$

1 for $\forall m \in M$ do
2   if $m.numberOfReviews < \delta$ then continue;
3      $R_m = \{r \in R | m.reviewer = r\}$;
4   Run SpamTracer on R_m to get the class of every reviewer stored as $r.status$;
5   Add m into set M', M' is a set stores all the useful shops;
6 end
7 for $i = 1, ..., length(M')$ do
8   for $j = 1, ..., i$ do
9          $d = Distance(M'[i].reviewer, M'[j].reviewer)$;
10          $n = 0$;
11          $List = M'[i].reviewer + M'[j].reviewer$;
12   Sort List by the name of reviewers;
13   for $k = 1, ..., length(List) - 1$ do
14   if $List[k].name = List[k+1].name$ && $List[k].status = fake$ && $List[k].shop != List[k+1].shop$ then $n = n + 1$;
15   end
16   Add (d, n) into set H;
17   end
18 end

(line 7–18). The time complexity is $O(klog(k)n^2)$ where k is the average number of reviews in every shop, and n is the number of useful shops. k can be regarded as a constant value, so the time complexity is $O(n^2)$.

In conclusion, the three propositions are validated with the assistant of dataset expanded by SpamTracer. Some charts demonstrating the links among fake reviewers, time and space will be displayed in the experiment chapter.

4 Experiments

4.1 Dataset Description

Our experiment is based on a Yelp dataset used by KC et al. [10]. It is a partly labeled dataset, contains location information, and its reviews are arranged on each reviewer rather than shops. For the labeled part, each review is labeled as fake or benign by Yelp's filtering system. The dataset information is shown in Table 3. It contains 3,142 labeled users, all of whose reviews are labeled, out of total 16,941 users and 107,264 labeled reviews out of total 760,212 reviews. As for the label reviews, there are 20,267 fake reviews out of 107,624 labeled reviews. A clear boundary is necessary to classify two kinds of users. We referred to Nilizadeh's work [16], calculated the filter rate (i.e., the percentage of filtered reviews out of one's all reviews) of each user, and set a boundary filter rate to cluster two kinds of users. The dataset holds a special characteristic that the filter rate of each user is distributed either in the range of 0–20% or the range of 90%-100%. To separate fake reviewers and benign users, we set a filtering standard that we regard users whose filter rates are higher than 90% as a fake reviewer and lower than 20% as a benign user. Under this standard, there are 1,299 fake reviewers out of 3,124 labeled users. Also, users holding few reviews need to be excluded from the dataset to decrease the unexpected errors. There are 1,796 labeled users and total 11,917 users left if we set the review number threshold as 5.

Table 3. Dataset information

	Labeled	Total
Reviews	107624	760212
Users	3142	16941
Fake reviews	20267	N/A
Fake reviewers	1299	N/A
Users after filtering	1796	11917

We rely on the Yelp filtering system for the label work. Yelp filtering system creates the ground-truth dataset and can automatically filter some typical inferior quality and fake reviews. These officially labeled reviews are qualified as the ground-truth dataset. Some prior works used manually labeled data for fake review detection task. However, manual work is not only tedious but also much too subjective. Manual labels are difficult to lead to excellent results.

4.2   Model Evaluation

In this section, the experiment implementation and evaluation of SpamTracer will be presented. The geolocation features are calculated by latitudes and longitudes of every review shop. They are translated from *Arcgis* Map addresses by a python package named *geocoder*. Parameters of SpamTracer are trained from the training dataset, and the evaluation is based on the testing dataset. Training dataset and testing dataset are disjointed parts in labeled data. The ratio of fake reviewers and benign users in labeled data is unbalanced, which is about 1:3. The number of fake reviewers in real O2O platforms is also a minority. And classifiers are required to hold the resistance to the interference from the unbalanced dataset. Many traditional classification algorithms can't perform well in such situation while SpamTracer can tolerate the impact of large misleading data and recognize the minority fake reviewers exactly.

SpamTracer needs to be compared with other existing excellent approaches to show its advantages in performance. Impartially, some traditional supervised classifiers are selected as the comparison group since SpamTracer is supervised.

The comparison group contains four typical classification algorithms: NB (Naive Bayes), AdaBoost Classifier, SVM (Support Vector Machine) and MLP (Multi-layer Perceptron). Those comparison models receive several account character-istics (i.e., friends number, reviews number, etc.) from dataset and output the prediction of fake reviewers or benign user. Besides, our experiment uses a 10-fold CV (Cross Validation) to guarantee the evaluation result. All involved models and their results are presented below:

(1) **SpamTracer**: SpamTracer that receives radius sequences and outputs the prediction.
(2) **NB**: A Naive Bayes Classifier.
(3) **AdaBoost**: An AdaBoost Classifier.
(4) **SVM-rbf**: A Support Vector Machine with Radial Basis Function serving as the kernel function.
(5) **MLP-relu**: A Multi-layer Perceptron with Rectified Linear Unit serving as the activation function.

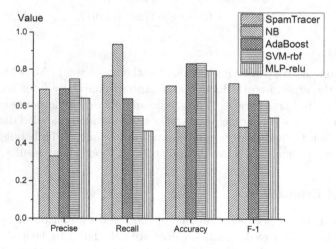

Fig. 5. Precise, Recall, Accuracy, and F1-score of models. SpamTracer performs most stable in all four measures, while other methods fluctuate severely in all four measures.

The evaluation of models is based on four standard performance measures: Accuracy, Precision, Recall, and F1-score. Figure 5 illustrates the four perfor-mance measures of all the five models, and shows that SpamTracer performs most stable in all four measures. NB holds the highest Recall but performs poorest in other three measures. AdaBoost and SVM-rbf perform almost the same as SpamTracer, but they still fluctuate much, and they fall much behind SpamTracer in Recall. MLP-relu holds an excellent Precise and Accuracy while it also holds the worst Recall and F1-score. In summary, SpamTracer is the most stable one in our experiment. Table 4 presents the numerical values of Fig. 5.

Table 4. Precise, Recall, Accuracy, and F1-score data of models

	Precise	Recall	Accuracy	F1-score
SpamTracer	0.6917	0.7657	0.7122	0.7268
NB	0.3332	0.9365	0.4962	0.4916
AdaBoost	0.6945	0.6430	0.8336	0.6677
SVM-rbf	0.7484	0.5482	0.8346	0.6328
MLP-relu	0.6443	0.4694	0.7946	0.5431

As for the restriction of the performance of SpamTracer, we have some ideas. First, the length of sequences is vital to the performance. The chain structure of SpamTracer determines that the longer data sequences are, the better performance will be. Besides, the scale of dataset also puts a limitation on their performance.

In conclusion, SpamTracer holds excellent stability and performs above the average in all four measures under an unbalanced dataset. Interfered by the unbalanced dataset environment, those classical approaches can't find a compromise among those measures. If we need a stable and precise review filter in O2O platforms, they will not be a good choice since they are likely to miscalculate many normal users or let off many fake reviewers. It's undeniable that SpamTracer will be a better choice for manual fake review detection task.

4.3 Regularities of Review Fraud Action

In this section, we are going to state some regularities of review fraud action obtained by applying SpamTracer to the expanded dataset mentioned in Sect. 3.5. After expanding, there are 694,020 reviews, 228,859 shops and 4,269 fake reviewers out of 11,058 reviewers. All the data samples are labeled. Those reviews mainly covered the period from 2008 to 2011. We mainly concentrate on three relations: fake reviewers and date period, fake reviewers and shop opening days, as well as shared fake reviewers and the interval distance between two shops. Next, we will expound our discoveries and present some figures that can support them.

Date Period. Fake reviewers tend to burst in summer days of a year and on weekends of a week. The dataset collected the posting date of each fake review and group them by months and weekdays. Figure 6(a) and (b) illustrate the month and weekday distribution of fake reviewer bursts from 2008 to 2011. Figure 6(a) illustrates that as the elapse of time, fake reviewers tend to make a burst during summer days. According to the data offered by NTTO (National Travel & Tourism Office)[5], most of the overseas tourists visiting the USA came in the 3rd quarter (July, August, and September) from 2008 to 2011. The tourism

---

[5] https://travel.trade.gov/research/monthly/arrivals/index.asp.

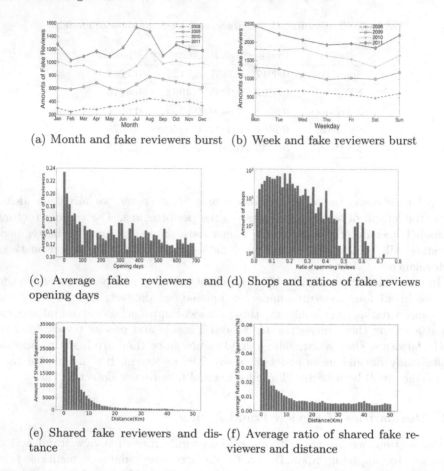

(a) Month and fake reviewers burst (b) Week and fake reviewers burst

(c) Average fake reviewers and (d) Shops and ratios of fake reviews
opening days

(e) Shared fake reviewers and dis- (f) Average ratio of shared fake re-
tance   viewers and distance

Fig. 6. Regularities of review fraud action. Figure (a)(b) reflect the date period and fake reviewers, figure (c)(d) reflect the shop opening days and fake reviewers, and figure (e)(f) reflect the interval distance and shared fake reviewers.

data reflects a phenomenon that summer is a busy season for traveling. Excessive tourist flows stimulate shop owners to hire more fake reviewers to gain popularity and income. Besides, Fig. 6(b) illustrates that fake reviewers tend to write fake reviews on Sunday and Monday. Moreover, both two graphs state a common practice that the amount of fake reviewers is increasing year by year. There were 67,705 fake reviews in 2008 while those grew to 140,722 in 2011. It also reflects that review fraud action is gradually developing in recent years.

Shop Opening Days. Fake reviewers most appear in the early stage of shop opening days. Since shops possessing few reviews and shop opening days will interfere final result, we set a filter threshold that only those who have been opening for more than one year and holding more than five reviews are taken into consideration. There are 21,000 shops left after filtering. Figure 6(c) illustrates the final results offered by the dataset and describes the review fraud tendency. X-axis stands for shop opening days, and y-axis stands for the average number of daily fake reviewers in each shop. It shows that more fake reviewers appear in the early shop opening days, and gradually decrease as the elapse of opening days. Besides, we also draw a Fig. 6(d) illustrating the number of online shops categorized by the ratio of fake reviews they hold. Figure 6(d) demonstrates that fake reviewers appear in large part of shops. Even there exist some shops whose half of reviews are posted by fake reviewers. It validates a common practice: shops tend to hire fake reviewers to promote themselves secretly.

Interval Distance. We discovered a regularity that the amount of shared fake reviewers is inversely proportional to the interval distance between two shops. However, shared fake reviewers only hold a limited percentage of review fraud actions. We set the threshold of shop review number as 2 in our algorithm, and the number of remaining shops after filtering is 102,478. The amount and average ratio of shared fake reviewers are demonstrated in Fig. 6(e) and (f) respectively. Figure 6(e) shows that there does exist share fake reviewers. However, Fig. 6(f) tells that the average ratio of shared fake reviewer is extraordinarily low. It starts from almost 0.06% when the interval distance is nearly 0 and is stabilized at 0.006% with the increase of distance. Two graphs lead to a conclusion that there does exist a phenomenon that some fake reviewers are working with plural shops located in a small business zone, but it's not the main trend of review fraud actions.

5 Conclusion

In this paper, we conducted a research about exploiting geolocation to detect fake reviewers in O2O commercial platforms. We improved a novel detection model, SpamTracer, based on Hidden Markov Model to detect fake reviewers by exploiting the unique distinctions of location features between fake reviewers and benign users. Our evaluation is based on a large scale Yelp dataset and demonstrates that our approach can take manual fake review detection task with excellent accuracy and stability. Also, we discovered some significant regularities in review fraud actions regarding time and location. Fake reviewers tend to launch review fraud actions in the summer season of a year, on weekends of a week, and in the beginning stage of shop opening days. We also found that there existed a negative correlation between the number of shared fake reviewers and the interval distance between two shops.

Acknowledgments. This work is supported by: Chinese National Research Fund (NSFC) No. 61702330, Chinese National Research Fund (NSFC) Key Project No. 61532013, National China 973 Project No. 2015CB352401, JSPS Kiban(C) JP18K11298 and JSPS Kiban(B) JP18H0324.

References

1. Agrawal, M., Leela Velusamy, R.: Unsupervised spam detection in hyves using SALSA. In: Das, S., Pal, T., Kar, S., Satapathy, S.C., Mandal, J.K. (eds.) Proceedings of the 4th International Conference on Frontiers in Intelligent Computing: Theory and Applications (FICTA) 2015. AISC, vol. 404, pp. 517–526. Springer, New Delhi (2016). https://doi.org/10.1007/978-81-322-2695-6_43

2. Castillo, C., Donato, D., Gionis, A., Murdock, V., Silvestri, F.: Know your neighbors: web spam detection using the web topology. In: Proceedings of the 30th Annual International ACM SIGIR Conference on Research and Development in Information Retrieval, Amsterdam, The Netherlands, pp. 423–430 (2007)

3. Chakraborty, M., Pal, S., Pramanik, R., Chowdary, C.R.: Recent developments in social spam detection and combating techniques: a survey. Inf. Process. Manage. **52**, 1053–1073 (2016)

4. Chen, C., Wu, K., Srinivasan, V., Zhang, X.: Battling the internet water army: detection of hidden paid posters. In: 2013 IEEE/ACM International Conference on Advances in Social Networks Analysis and Mining, Niagara Falls, Canada, pp. 116–120 (2013)

5. Chen, H., He, D., Zhu, S., Yang, J.: Toward detecting collusive ranking manipulation attackers in mobile app markets. In: Proceedings of the 2017 ACM on Asia Conference on Computer and Communications Security, Abu Dhabi, UAE, pp. 58–70 (2017)

6. Chino, D.Y.T., Costa, A.F., Traina, A.J.M., Faloutsos, C.: VolTime: unsupervised anomaly detection on users' online activity volume. In: Proceedings of the 2017 SIAM International Conference on Data Mining, Houston, USA, pp. 108–116 (2017)

7. Gong, Q., et al.: Deepscan: exploiting deep learning for malicious account detection in location-based social networks. In: IEEE Communications Magazine, Feature Topic on Mobile Big Data for Urban Analytics, vol. 56 (2018)

8. Hooi, B., Song, H.A., Beutel, A., Shah, N., Shin, K., Faloutsos, C.: Fraudar: bounding graph fraud in the face of camouflage. In: Proceedings of the 22nd ACM SIGKDD International Conference on Knowledge Discovery and Data Mining, San Francisco, USA, pp. 895–904 (2016)

9. Jindal, N., Liu, B.: Opinion spam and analysis. In: Proceedings of the 2008 International Conference on Web Search and Data Mining, New York, USA, pp. 219–230 (2008)

10. KC, S., Mukherjee, A.: On the temporal dynamics of opinion spamming: case studies on yelp. In: Proceedings of the 25th International Conference on World Wide Web, pp. 369–379. Republic and Canton of Geneva, Switzerland (2016)

11. Kumar, S., Gao, X., Welch, I., Mansoori, M.: A machine learning based web spam filtering approach. In: IEEE 30th International Conference on Advanced Information Networking and Applications, Crans-Montana, Switzerland, pp. 973–980 (2016)

12. Li, H., Chen, Z., Liu, B., Wei, X., Shao, J.: Spotting fake reviews via collective positive-unlabeled learning. In: 2014 IEEE International Conference on Data Mining, Shenzhen, China, pp. 899–904 (2014)

13. Li, H., et al.: Bimodal distribution and co-bursting in review spam detection. In: Proceedings of the 26th International Conference on World Wide Web, pp. 1063–1072. Republic and Canton of Geneva, Switzerland (2017)

14. Malmgren, R.D., Hofman, J.M., Amaral, L.A., Watts, D.J.: Characterizing individual communication patterns. In: Proceedings of the 15th ACM SIGKDD International Conference on Knowledge Discovery and Data Mining, KDD 2009, New York, USA, pp. 607–616 (2009)
15. Mukherjee, A., Liu, B., Glance, N.: Spotting fake reviewer groups in consumer reviews. In: Proceedings of the 21st International Conference on World Wide Web, Lyon, France, pp. 191–200 (2012)
16. Nilizadeh, S., et al.: Poised: spotting twitter spam off the beaten paths. In: Proceedings of the 2017 ACM SIGSAC Conference on Computer and Communications Security, Dallas, USA, pp. 1159–1174 (2017)
17. Ott, M., Choi, Y., Cardie, C., Hancock, J.T.: Finding deceptive opinion spam by any stretch of the imagination. In: Proceedings of the 49th Annual Meeting of the Association for Computational Linguistics: Human Language Technologies, Stroudsburg, USA, vol. 1, pp. 309–319 (2011)
18. Phang, C.W., Tan, C.H., Sutanto, J., Magagna, F., Lu, X.: Leveraging O2O commerce for product promotion: an empirical investigation in mainland China. IEEE Trans. Eng. Manage. **61**, 623–632 (2014)
19. Rabiner, L.R.: A tutorial on hidden markov models and selected applications in speech recognition. Proc. IEEE **77**, 257–286 (1989)
20. Shojaee, S., Murad, M.A.A., Azman, A.B., Sharef, N.M., Nadali, S.: Detecting deceptive reviews using lexical and syntactic features. In: 13th International Conference on Intellient Systems Design and Applications, Malaysia, pp. 53–58 (2013)
21. Spirin, N., Han, J.: Survey on web spam detection: principles and algorithms. SIGKDD Explor. Newslett. **13**, 50–64 (2012)
22. Washha, M., Qaroush, A., Mezghani, M., Sedes, F.: A topic-based hidden markov model for real-time spam tweets filtering. Procedia Comput. Sci. **112**, 833–843 (2017)
23. Yao, W., Ruan, N., Yu, F., Jia, W., Zhu, H.: Privacy-preserving fraud detection via cooperative mobile carriers with improved accuracy. In: 2017 14th Annual IEEE International Conference on Sensing. Communication, and Networking, San Diego, USA, pp. 1–9 (2017)
24. Yao, Y., Viswanath, B., Cryan, J., Zheng, H., Zhao, B.Y.: Automated crowdturfing attacks and defenses in online review systems. In: Proceedings of the 2017 ACM SIGSAC Conference on Computer and Communications Security, Dallas, USA, pp. 1143–1158 (2017)
25. Zhang, X., Zheng, H., Li, X., Du, S., Zhu, H.: You are where you have been: sybil detection via geo-location analysis in OSNs. In: 2014 IEEE Global Communications Conference, Austin, USA, pp. 698–703 (2014)
26. Zheng, H., et al.: Smoke screener or straight shooter: detecting elite sybil attacks in user-review social networks. In: The 2018 Network and Distributed System Security Symposium, San Diego, USA (2018)

A Light-Weight and Accurate Method of Static Integer-Overflow-to-Buffer-Overflow Vulnerability Detection

Mingjie Xu[1,2], Shengnan Li[3], Lili Xu[1(✉)], Feng Li[1], Wei Huo[1,2], Jing Ma[4], Xinhua Li[1], and Qingjia Huang[1]

[1] Institute of Information Engineering, Chinese Academy of Sciences, Beijing, China
{xumingjie, xulili, lifeng, huowei, lixinhua, huangqingjia}@iie.ac.cn
[2] School of Cyber Security, University of Chinese Academy of Sciences, Beijing, China
[3] National Computer Network Emergency Response Technical Team/Coordination Center of China, Beijing, China
lisn@cert.org.cn
[4] Science and Technology on Information Assurance Laboratory, Beijing, China
xxbzsys@163.com

Abstract. The Integer-Overflow-to-Buffer-Overflow (IO2BO) vulnerability is an underrated source of security threats. Despite many works have been done to mitigate integer overflow, existing tools either report large number of false positives or introduce unacceptable time consumption. To address this problem, in this paper we present a new static analysis framework. It first utilizes inter-procedural dataflow analysis and taint analysis to accurately identify potential IO2BO vulnerabilities. Then it uses a light-weight method to further filter out false positives. Specifically, it generates constraints representing the conditions under which a potential IO2BO vulnerability can be triggered, and feeds the constraints to SMT solver to decide their satisfiability. We have implemented a prototype system LAID based on LLVM, and evaluated it on 228 programs of the NIST's SAMATE Juliet test suite and 6 known IO2BO vulnerabilities in real world. The experiment results show that our system can effectively and efficiently detect all known IO2BO vulnerabilities.

Keywords: Integer-Overflow-to-Buffer-Overflow (IO2BO) vulnerability · Inter-procedural dataflow analysis · Taint analysis · Path satisfiability

1 Introduction

Integer overflow is one of the most common types of software vulnerabilities. According to the Common Vulnerability and Exploit (CVE) [1], integer overflow has become the second most critical type of coding errors, second only to buffer overflows [2]. If the malformed value generated by integer overflow is used for determining how much memory to allocate, it will cause a buffer overflow, which is known as the Integer

F. Guo et al. (Eds.): Inscrypt 2018, LNCS 11449, pp. 404–423, 2019.
https://doi.org/10.1007/978-3-030-14234-6_22

Overflow to Buffer Overflow vulnerability (IO2BO [3]). According to [4], it is difficult to distinguish integer overflow vulnerabilities from benign overflows, but in the context of IO2BO, the involved integer overflow cannot be benign and it must be a real vulnerability.

In recent years, IO2BO is being widely exploited by attackers to cause severe damages to computer systems, such as [5, 6, 22]. According to statistics, from February 2016 to February 2017, the National Vulnerability Database (NVD [7]) has recorded 53 IO2BO vulnerabilities, which makes up nearly one third of integer overflow vulnerabilities (165 in total) and heap overflow vulnerabilities (182 in total) recorded by NVD in the same period.

As IO2BO vulnerabilities have become a dominant kind of integer overflow vulnerabilities in practice, a variety of solutions have been proposed for IO2BO detection. The solutions can be categorized into approaches based on static analysis (e.g. [17, 21]) and those depended on dynamic testing (e.g. [4, 18, 29, 30]). Dynamic testing approaches are commonly used during software deployment, but their efficiency highly relies on the completeness of the test inputs. Static analysis approaches do not require the availability of test inputs and usually take all possible paths of the programs into consideration, which makes them more populate in practice. However, the key limitation of static analysis approaches is that the reported integer overflow vulnerabilities contain too many false positives due to the lack of execution information. To solve this problem, tools such as PREfix + Z3 [23] and IntScope [21] employ symbolic execution [24] to generate path constraints and prune infeasible paths in order to alleviate false positives. However, these tools may suffer from path explosion when applied to large programs. Another state-of-the-art tool, KINT [17], also collects path constraints to prune false positive but it only generates intra-procedural path constraints for each reported integer overflow program point. It also ignores implicit data dependencies imported by memory operations or complex data structures. Our experiments in Sect. 5 shows that the false negatives reported by KINT remain high when detecting IO2BO vulnerabilities.

In this paper, we present a static analysis framework utilizing an improved taint analysis (compared with KINT) and a lightweight approach for path constraint generation and solving to detect IO2BO vulnerabilities. Specifically, first, we use taint analysis to identify potential IO2BO vulnerabilities. We add the support for implicit data flow and complex data structures, which improves the accuracy of detection. Then we apply an inter-procedural path-satisfiability analysis to filter out false positives. The analysis generates conditions under which an IO2BO vulnerability can be triggered in practice and then performs constraints solving by feeding the generated conditions into a solver. If the conditions of a potential IO2BO vulnerability cannot be satisfied, the potential IO2BO vulnerability will be filtered out as a false positive. Compared with symbolic execution that needs to model the runtime environment, this approach has less space and time consumption.

We implement our framework, LAID (short for a Light-weight and Accurate method of static IO2BO vulnerability Detection), based on LLVM [8, 9] and evaluate its effectiveness and efficiency on 228 programs of the NIST's SAMATE Juliet test suite [27] and 6 real-world open-source applications each of which involves known IO2BO vulnerabilities. Our experimental results show that LAID is capable of detecting IO2BO vulnerabilities in the real-world applications with low false positives and false negative rates.

In summary, this paper makes the following contributions:

- We propose an accurate method to identify IO2BO vulnerabilities, which combines inter-procedural dataflow analysis and taint analysis. This method supports implicit data flow introduced by memory operations (load and store) and dataflow propagation on complex data structures, which improves the accuracy of program analysis.
- We propose a light-weight method for constraints generation and solving, which is used to verify if potential IO2BO vulnerabilities can be triggered in the program's execution. This method reduces high false positive rates that static analysis solutions typically suffer from.
- We implement the prototype of the framework and apply it to 228 programs of the NIST's SAMATE Juliet test suite and 6 real-world applications with known IO2BO vulnerabilities. The experiment result shows that our framework can catch all harmful IO2BOs in the SAMATE suite with no false positive, and for real-world applications, it can significantly reduce the number of false positives and detect more known vulnerabilities than KINT.

The rest of this paper is organized as follows. Our system overview is shown in Sect. 2. In Sect. 3, we describe how to use taint analysis to identify potential IO2BO vulnerabilities. In Sect. 4, we describe how to use constraint solving to filter out potential IO2BO vulnerabilities that cannot be triggered. Section 5 shows the experiment results. Related work and conclusion are discussed in Sects. 6 and 7, respectively.

2   System Overview

In this section, we describe the architecture of our system as illustrated in Fig. 1. It takes LLVM intermediate representation (IR) as input, which is obtained by compiling C source code using Clang, and performs a two-stage analysis to detect IO2BO vulnerabilities in these IRs. At the end of analysis, it outputs the detected IO2BOs along with their locations. The first stage performs taint analysis with sensitive taint sources and sinks given by our built-in annotations as well as user annotations, and identifies potentially vulnerable integer operations by comparing them to the pattern of IO2BO vulnerabilities; the second stage performs constraint generation and solving for each potential IO2BO vulnerability, if the constraint of a potential IO2BO vulnerability cannot be satisfied, the vulnerability will be filtered out, which helps reduce false positives.

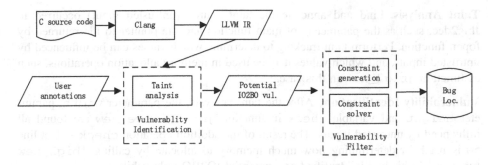

Fig. 1. The structure of our framework

Next we use a real IO2BO vulnerability existed in Jbig2dec (a JBIG2 decoder library) showed in Fig. 2 as an example to explain how our system works. The IO2BO vulnerability (CVE-2016-9601) occurs in function `jbig2_image_new` at line 56 (highlighted in the red color) of jbig_image.c. The addition operation at line 56 overflows and results in a memory allocation less than expected.

```
//jbig_image.c
34. Jbig2Image *
35. jbig2_image_new(Jbig2Ctx *ctx, int width, int height)
36. {    /*width and height are from user space*/
37.      Jbig2Image *image;
38.      int stride;
39.      int64_t check;
41.      image = jbig2_new(ctx, Jbig2Image, 1);
...
47.      stride = ((width - 1) >> 3) + 1;
49.      check = ((int64_t) stride) * ((int64_t) height);
50.      if (check != (int)check) {
...
54.      }
56.      image->data = jbig2_new(ctx, uint8_t, (int)check + 1);
         /* integer addition overflow */
...
69. }
```

```
//jbig2_halftone.c
119. static Jbig2PatternDict *
120. jbig2_decode_pattern_dict(Jbig2Ctx *ctx, Jbig2Segment *segment,
121.     const Jbig2PatternDictParams *params, const byte *data, const
         size_t size, Jbig2ArithCx *GB_stats)
122. {
123.     Jbig2Image *image = NULL;
...
129.     image = jbig2_image_new(ctx, params->HDPW * (params->GRAYMAX +
             1), params->HDPH);
...
175. }
```

Fig. 2. A real-world IO2BO vulnerability in Jbig2dec

Taint Analysis. Find and annotate the taint source (untrusted input) occurred in Jbig2dec, such as the parameters of main function and the pointer to file returned by fopen function. Perform taint tracking to determine which values can be influenced by untrusted inputs, and which values may be used in memory allocation operations, such as function jbig2_new in this case.

Vulnerability Identification. After the taint analysis, the parameter width, parameter height and variable check in function jbig2_image_new are found all influenced by untrusted inputs. The result of the addition operation check + 1 at line 56 is used for determining how much memory to allocate by calling jbig2_new function, so this line is identified as a potential IO2BO vulnerability.

Vulnerability Filter. We perform constraint generation and solving for this potential IO2BO vulnerability to verify whether it can be triggered in program's execution. The constraint can be divided into overflow condition and path constraint:

Overflow Condition. If the involved integer operation overflows, the condition *(int) check + 1 > INT_MAX* should be satisfied.

Path Constraint. We generate the path constraints from the caller of jbig2_image_new to the integer overflow point. Usually one function has more than one caller. As long as the path from one caller is satisfiable, we consider the IO2BO vulnerability as feasible. We take one of jbig2_image_new's callers: function jbig2_decode_pattern_dict as an example, which is shown in the lower part of Fig. 2. The control flow condition from its function entry to the callsite of jbig2_image_new (highlighted in the blue color) is always *true*. Furthermore, in jbig2_image_new, if the program executes to overflow point, it should satisfy the branch condition at line 50, i.e., *check == (int)check*.

So the complete constraint is

$$((int)check + 1 > INT\_MAX) \bigwedge true \bigwedge (check == (int)check)$$

The SMT solver is invoked to decide whether or not the above constraint can be satisfied, if not, we treat the potential vulnerability as a false positive and hence filter it out, otherwise we report it as an IO2BO vulnerability.

3   Identify Potential IO2BO Vulnerabilities

The input of this module is the LLVM intermediate representation (IR) translated using clang from source code. First we annotate taint source and taint sink on LLVM IR. Second, we do taint propagation in a manner similar to classic dataflow analysis. We add the support for implicit dataflow caused by the load or store operation on the same memory address, and implement field-sensitive taint propagation for complex data structures, that is, the taint information can be propagated on specific fields of a Struct data type, which improves the accuracy of taint analysis.

If any operand of an arithmetic operation is tainted (thus untrusted) and the result is used in a memory allocation function, there exists a potential IO2BO vulnerability.

After the taint propagation, some candidate IO2BO vulnerabilities are generated and we collect them for further filtering.

3.1   Taint Source Initialization

Taint source represents the untrusted input of the program, which can be files, network data, input messages of mouse and keyboard. Generally, it is necessary to provide untrusted input source information according to the specific program under analysis. In the experiments, we annotate the parameters of the main function, the file pointer returned by the fopen function, the pointer to the buffer used in fread function, etc. as the taint source.

3.2   Taint Propagation

Given the information of taint source, taint propagation is performed according to the algorithm shown in Fig. 3. Since our implementation is based on LLVM IR, the algorithm mainly describes the strategies of taint propagation for several typical instructions in IR. Given the LLVM bytecode of program P, the algorithm starts with the provided taint source, propagates the tainted data and records the instructions influenced by dirty data. Finally it annotates all tainted instructions by adding metadata information on LLVM IR for corresponding instructions and outputs the modified LLVM bytecode as P'.

Algorithm 1 TaintPropagation (Program P, Program P')
```
 1: Compute a call graph CG of P, mapping a callsite to all potential callees;
 2: Let Δ be the set of tainted instructions in P;
 3: Δ = annotateTaintSource();
 4: bool changed = true;
 5: while (changed) do
 6:     changed = false;
 7:     for each instruction in each function of each module in P:
 8:         if it is a memory instruction:
 9:             changed | = memory_propapgation(Δ);
10:         else if it is a function call instruction:
11:             Obtain the callee according to the constructed CG;
12:             changed | =call_propapgation(Δ);
13:         else:
14:             changed | = other_propapgation(Δ);
15:         end if
16:     end for
17: end while
18: P' = P by adding to each instruction in Δ a new metadata indicating that this instruction is
    tainted;
```

Fig. 3. Taint propagation algorithm.

In Algorithm 1, we first generate a system-wide call graph for program P. To increase the precision of the analysis, we use the method of function type analysis to resolve the called functions that a function pointer may point to. We use the symbol Δ to denote the set of instructions tainted by untrusty input, which is initialized to the taint source annotated by users. The main algorithm consists of a while loop, taint propagation rule is applied to each instruction in P iteratively and newly tainted instructions are added to Δ. Once there is no newly tainted instruction in an iteration, i.e., the flag variable *changed* is false, the process will terminate.

For different kinds of instructions, different taint propagation rules are applied. We divide the instructions into three categories: memory related instructions, function call instructions and other instructions, corresponding to the *memory_propapgation*, *call_propapgation* and *other_propapgation* sub-processes respectively in Algorithm 1.

The taint propagation strategies for these three categories of instructions are described in Table 1 below, specifying the taint status for data derived from tainted or untainted operands. Since taint can be represented with a bit, propositional logic is usually used to express the propagation policy, $T1 \bigvee T2$ indicates that the result is tainted if T1 or T2 is tainted.

Table 1. The strategies of taint propagation for different kinds of instructions

Instruction type	Intermediate representation	Strategy T
Memory instructions	**store** *val, ptr*	$T(ptr) = T(val)$
	val = **load** *ptr*	$T(val) = T(ptr)$
	resptr = **getelementptr** [*struct*].[*ptr*]. [*idx*]	(1) $T(resptr) = T(ptr) \bigvee T(ptr + idx)$ (2) $T(ptr + idx) = T(resptr)$
Function Call Instructions	*retval* = **call** fun(*arg*) //Definition of fun function: **define** fun(*arg_fun*) {... **ret** *retval_fun*}	(1) $T(arg\_fun) = T(arg)$ (2) $T(retval) = T(retval\_fun)$
	//special library function call, e.g.: *retval* = **call** fopen(*pathname, mode*)	$T(retval) = T(pathname)$
Other instructions	*res* = **OP** *op1, op2, ..., opn*	$T(res) = T(op1) \bigvee T(op2) \vee \cdots \vee T(opn)$

The meaning of the taint propagation strategies in Table 1 are described in detail below:

Memory Instructions. The memory instructions include **store, load** instruction and the closely related **getelementptr** instruction which computes positions in a Struct data type.

Store and Load Operation. For store instruction: **store** *val, ptr*, the *val* operand is the value to be stored and the *ptr* operand specifies the address at which to store *val*. The rule $T(ptr) = T(val)$ says that if the *val* operand is tainted, the *ptr* operand is set to be tainted. For load instruction: val = **load** ptr, the rule $T(val) = T(ptr)$ means that if the ptr operand that specifies the memory address from which to load is tainted, the val operand is set to be tainted.

Getelementptr Operation. Getelementptr instruction: $resptr$ = **getelementptr** [$struct$]. [ptr].[idx], is used to get the address of the idx-th sub-element of the $struct$ type pointer variable ptr. The first rule $T(resptr) = T(ptr) \bigvee T(ptr + idx)$ means that if the ptr operand is tainted or the address of the idx-th sub-element is tainted, the $resptr$ is set to be tainted.

In fact, the getelementptr instruction performs address calculation only and does not access memory. Notice that the result of getelementptr instruction is usually used in load and store instructions. In order to realize a field-sensitive taint propagation for complex data structures, namely, to propagate taint data on specific fields of a Struct type, we need to record the taint status of the specific sub-element obtained through the getelementptr instruction. Essentially, the second rule $T(ptr + idx) = T(resptr)$ implies that if the address $resptr$ obtained by the getelementptr instruction has been used to store dirty data, the corresponding sub-element's address $ptr + idx$ is also set to be tainted.

We illustrate intuitively how the taint propagation strategy for memory-related instructions works using the toy sample code below.

Example 1. The following code is a snippet of LLVM IR omitting type information for the sake of readability. It first uses getelementptr instruction to get the address of variable bar of struct TEST pointer x, namely, $a1$. Tainted data is then stored into $a1$. The address of variable bar in Struct TEST pointer x is calculated again as $a2$. The value $b1$ is read from address $a2$ and used in malloc for determining how much memory to allocate (Fig. 4).

```
1: a1 = getelementptr [TEST].[x].[2]
2: store taint_data, a1
3: a2 = getelementptr [TEST].[x].[2]
4: b1 = load a2
5: call = call malloc(b1)
//variable x is a pointer to Struct TEST, the definition of TEST is as follow.
struct TEST
{
    unsigned int   foo1;
    unsigned int   foo2;
    unsigned long  bar;
}
```

Fig. 4. Sample code for memory operation

The variable *taint_data* is initialized to be tainted, by applying the aforementioned taint propagation strategy, the taint propagation process is as follows (Table 2):

Table 2. An example of detailed taint propagation process

Step	Line No. in IR	Taint propagation	Applied rule
Initialization	–	T(*taint_data*) = true	Initialization
The first loop	2	T(*a1*) = T(*taint_data*)	Store rule
The second loop	1	T(*x- > bar*) = T(*a1*)	Getelementptr rule 2
	3	T(*a2*) = T(*x-> bar*)	Getelementptr rule 1
	4	T(*b1*) = T(*a2*)	Load rule

The result of the taint propagation shows that the operand *b1* is tainted. Since the tainted *b1* is used in memory allocation function malloc, we conclude that there exists a security risk.

Function Call Instructions. Call instruction represents a simple function call. We divided the function calls into programmer-defined function calls and special library function calls.

Programmer-defined Function. The form is *retval* = **call** fun(*arg*), where the definition of fun is: **define** fun(*arg_fun*) {... **ret** *retval_fun*}. The first rule T(*arg_fun*) = T (*arg*) implies that if the actual parameter of called function is tainted, the formal parameter of called function is set to be tainted. Similarly, the second rule T(*retval*) = T (*retval_fun*) indicates that if the return value of called funtion is tainted, the result of function call instruction is tainted.

Special Library Function. Thanks to the special effects of some library functions, we can directly determine the taint status of their return values or certain actual parameters. Take function fopen as an example, *retval* = **call** fopen(*pathname*, *mode*), parameter *pathname* indicates the file to be opened, parameter *mode* indicates the file access mode and *retval* is a pointer to the opened file. If *pathname* is tainted, *retval* is set to be tainted.

Other Instructions. The form is *res* = **OP** *op1, op2, ..., opn*, such as **add**, **sub** and **mul** instructions in LLVM IR. The rule T(*res*) = T(*op1*) $\bigvee$ T(*op2*) $\vee \cdots \vee$ T(*opn*) says that if any operand of the instruction is tainted, the return value is set to be tainted.

3.3 Vulnerability Identification

After annotating taint source and taint propagation, all values influenced by taint source will be marked as tainted. We identify the instructions that satisfy the following 3 conditions as potential IO2BO vulnerabilities:

1. The instruction is an integer arithmetic operation;
2. The instruction is influenced by taint source;
3. The result of the instruction is used in memory allocation function such as malloc for determining how much memory to allocate.

Example 2. Figure 5 shows a snippet of code of LLVM IR omitting type information and type conversion for the sake of readability. It first uses alloca to allocate 16 bytes memory for variable *buf*. A file *f0* is opened and the first 16 bytes of the file is stored into the memory pointed by *buf*. Lastly, the content of the second byte in *buf* is multiplied by 4 and the result is used in malloc for determining how much memory to allocate.

Assuming that the opened file is provided by user, the return value *f0* is thus tainted, and the argument *buf* used in fread function is also set to be tainted. The variable *conv* obtains the contents pointed by the second byte of the *buf*, so *conv* is set to be tainted. All tainted variables are denoted in blue in Fig. 5.

The variable *mul* is the result of multiplying *conv* by 4, and it is used in malloc, i.e., the variable *mul* is affected by taint source and is eventually used in memory allocation.

According to the above identification principles, the instruction *mul* = **mul** *conv*, 4 at line 6 (highlighted in red) will be marked as a potential IO2BO vulnerability and used for further filtering.

```
1:  buf = alloca [16 x i8]
2:  f0 = call fopen(filename, mode)
3:  call0 = call fread(buf, 1, 16, f0)
4:  arrayidx  = getelementptr [16 x i8].[buf].[1]
5:  conv = load arrayidx
6:  mul = mul conv, 4        # This line is marked as a candidate IO2BO vulnerability
7:  call = call malloc(mul)
```

Fig. 5. Sample code for illustrating potential IO2BO vulnerabilities identification (Color figure online)

4   Vulnerability Filter

After the taint analysis, the candidate IO2BO vulnerabilities are generated. However the taint analysis is path-insensitive, thus there may be many infeasible paths which bring false positives.

To eliminate the false positives, we examine whether the overflow conditions under which an integer overflow may occur, and the path constraints that associated with the paths from caller functions' entry points, going through overflow points and reaching the corresponding sinks could both be satisfied. Given a candidate IO2BO vulnerability, the tactic validates if it is genuine as follows:

1. The overflow condition is calculated for the overflow point according to Table 3.
2. The path constraint encodes the conditions on both the paths from caller functions' entry points to the overflow point, and the paths from the overflow point to the corresponding sinks, also known as *forward vulnerable paths*.
3. A whole constraint formula, denoted by Π, is obtained by integrating the overflow condition and the path constraint with a logical conjunction.
4. The SMT solver is invoked to solve whether or not Π can be satisfied. If not, then the vulnerability is a false positive and hence filtered out.

4.1 Overflow Condition

An N-bit signed integer is in the bounds -2^{N-1} to $2^{N-1} - 1$ and an N-bit unsigned integer is in the bounds 0 to $2^N - 1$. Table 3 lists the requirements of producing an out-of-bounds result for each integer operation. The second column indicates the operands are unsigned or signed and the third column indicates the bit-width of the operands. Taking division operation as an example, the divisor should be non-zero and the signed division $-2^{N-1}/-1$ is not in bounds, because the expected mathematical result $2^N - 1$ is out of the bounds of N-bit signed integers.

Table 3. Overflow condition for integer operations

Integer operation	Sign	Width	Overflow condition
$x+y$	<S, S>	<N, N>	$x+y \notin [-2^{N-1}, -2^{N-1}]$
	<U, U>	<N, N>	$x+y \notin [0, 2^N - 1]$
$x-y$	<S, S>	<N, N>	$x-y \notin [-2^{N-1}, -2^{N-1}]$
	<U, U>	<N, N>	$x-y \notin [0, 2^N - 1]$
$x \times y$	<S, S>	<N, N>	$x \times y \notin [-2^{N-1}, -2^{N-1}]$
	<U, U>	<N, N>	$x \times y \notin [0, 2^N - 1]$
x / y	<S, S>	<N, N>	$(y = 0) \vee (x = -2^{N-1} \wedge y = -1)$
	<U, U>	<N, N>	$y = 0$
$x \ll y, x \gg y$	<S, S>	<N, N>	$y \notin [0, N - 1]$
	<U, U>	<N, N>	

4.2 Path Constraint

We refer to the function where the integer overflow locates as the defective function and refer to the function that calls the defective function as the caller function. When generating path constraint, we collect the conditions on paths starting from the entry point of the caller function, passing through the overflow point and reaching the memory allocation operation in the defective function where the overflowed integer is used.

We do not consider the conditions on paths originating from the entry point of the whole program under test. In Sect. 5 we will illustrate by experiments that, when considering the whole path constraints for real-world programs, the time consumption of constraints solving increases but the effectiveness of false positives filter is not improved significantly. This basically shows the fact that for heavy-weight programs, the conditions really affecting the existence of an integer overflow are usually imposed within the defective function and its caller function. We believe that for light-weight programs, considering whole path constraints can impact more on the filter. We leave it as future work to design a strategy to strike a balance between performance and low false positive rate.

The path constraint is divided into two parts for construction, intra-procedural path constraint and one-level inter-procedural path constraint.

1. First, we generate the conditions on paths within the defective function, namely, the paths starting from the defective function's entry point, passing through the risky integer operation and reaching the corresponding sinks. We denote this constraint by *IntraPC*.
2. Then we generate the conditions on paths within the caller function, namely, the paths starting from the caller's entry point to the callsite of the defective function. We denote this constraint by *InterPC*.
3. We denote by *ParamPassing* the equality relations between the actual parameters in the caller function and the formal parameters in the defective function.
4. Thus, the complete path constraint is composed of:

$$IntraPC \bigwedge InterPC \bigwedge ParamPassing.$$

These constraints *IntraPC* and *InterPC* arise from two sources: assignments to variables involved in the integer operation and conditional branches along the execution path. We denote by $PC(start, end)$ the constraint on paths from basic block(BB) *start* to BB *end*, which is calculated as follows:

$$PC(start, end) = \begin{cases} True; \ if \ start = end \\ \bigvee_{p \in Pred(end)}(PC(start, p) \wedge br \wedge as); otherwise \end{cases}$$

where p is a predecessor BB of *end*, br is the branch condition from p to BB *end*, and as are the assignments to variables along the path from p to *end*. We denote by *dEntry* the entry BB of the defective function, by *io* the BB where the integer overflow point locates and by *mem* the BB where the risky memory operation locates, then $IntraPC = PC(dEntry, io) \bigwedge PC(io, mem)$. Analogously, we denote by *cEntry* the entry BB of the caller function and by *cs* the BB where the callsite of the defective function locates, then $InterPC = PC(cEntry, cs)$.

```
Struct test
{
    unsigned long x;
    char ch;
};
int foo(Struct *t)
{
    unsigned long n = t->x;
    if (n > 1<<30)
        return ERROR;
    void *p = malloc(n * 8);
    /* integer multiplication overflow */
    ...
}
void bar()
{
    Struct test *s = /* from user space */;
    If (s->x >= 0 && s->x <=100)
        foo(s);
}
```

Fig. 6. Sample code for illustrating how filter module works

Next we use the code snippet shown in Fig. 6 to explain how the vulnerability filter module works.

Example 3. According to the principles presented in Sect. 3, the variable n in function *foo* is influenced by user input, and the result of $n * 8$ is used in malloc, so the line highlighted in red is identified as a potential IO2BO vulnerability.

In this example, the function *foo* is the defective function and the function *bar* is the caller function. The overflow condition for the argument used in malloc is $n > MAX/8$. In *foo*, the malloc operation will be executed under the condition (intra-procedural path constraint) that $(n <= 1 < <30 \land n = t\text{->} x)$. In *bar*, the callsite to *foo* will be executed under the condition (the one-level inter-procedural path constraint) $(s\text{->} x >= 0 \land s\text{->} x <= 100)$. The actual parameter s passed to *foo* function is equal to the formal parameter t in *foo* function prototype. Thus, the parameter passing condition is $s\text{->} x = t\text{->} x$. The complete path constraint is a conjunction of the previous three parts.

The whole constraint Π is a conjunction of the complete path constraint and the overflow condition. Lastly, Π is fed into the solver to see if it is satisfiable. In this case, it is impossible to satisfy $n > MAX/8$ and $n <= 100$ at the same time, so the candidate vulnerability is a false positive and hence filtered out (Table 4).

Table 4. The condition of the code snippet in Fig. 6

Condition		Content of Condition
Overflow condition		n > MAX/8
Path constraint	Intra-procedural path constraint (*IntraPC*)	n <= 1 < <30 ∧ n = t-> x
	One-level inter-procedural path constraint (*InterPC*)	s-> x > = 0 ∧ s-> x <=100
	Parameter passing condition (*ParamPassing*)	s-> x = t-> x
The whole constraint Π		(n > MAX/8) ∧ (n <= 1 < <30 ∧ n = t-> x) ∧ (s-> x > = 0 ∧ s-> x <=100) ∧ (s-> x = t-> x)

5   Evaluation

We implement our framework as a prototype tool LAID based on LLVM passes. The vulnerability identification module consists of three passes: *annotation* pass, *taint* pass and *check* pass. The *annotation* pass is used to recognize the taint source occurred in the program to be tested. After the *taint* pass performing taint tracking to determine which values can be influenced by untrusted sources, the *check* pass will identify the potential vulnerabilities according to the IO2BO pattern. The vulnerability filter module consists of two passes: *intrasat* pass and *intersat* pass. The *intrasat* pass generates the overflow condition and the *intersat* pass generates the path constraint. A conjunction of the overflow condition and the path constraint is fed into the SMT solver Boolector, which provides APIs for conveniently constructing efficient overflow detection conditions.

We have tested LAID on 228 programs in the NIST's SAMATE Juliet test suite version 1.2 and 6 real-world open-source applications. The evaluation was performed on Ubuntu14.04 virtual machine with 1 GB memory and 1 process of an Intel Core i5 3.0 GHz host machine.

5.1   Experiments on Juliet Test Suite

SAMATE [27] has a suite of test bench programs in C, C++ and Java to demonstrate common security problems and presents security errors in design, source code, binaries, etc. For C/C++ code, the SAMATE's Juliet test suite version 1.2 provides 61,387 test programs for 118 different CWEs. Specially, CWE 680 describes the integer overflow to buffer overflow vulnerabilities. We choose all C programs (228 programs) in CWE 680 as our experimental subjects. Each program has a good function and a bad function. The good function demonstrates normal behavior and the bad function demonstrates a vulnerability.

We applied LAID on all these 228 programs and had detected vulnerabilities in 152 programs. For the remaining 76 programs, the values involved in the overflowed integer expressions are either constants or those generated by random functions, and therefore are beyond the scope of IO2BO conditions mentioned in Sect. 3.3. In other words, LAID had successfully reported all harmful IO2BOs in the 228 programs with no false positive.

5.2   Experiments on Real IO2BOs

In order to evaluate LAID in real IO2BOs, 6 real-world open-source applications are chosen, each of which contains a known IO2BO CVE. Their information is listed in Table 5. Columns 1–4 describe the CVE number, the vulnerable software, version and LOC(lines of code), respectively. Columns **IO_op** and **MEM** show the type of the overflowed integer operation and the name of the risky sink, respectively.

Table 5. Information of applications used in evaluation

CVE Number	Programs	Version	LOC	IO_op	MEM
CVE-2005-1141 [11]	gocr	0.40	21608	$*_s$	malloc
CVE-2011-4517 [12]	jasper	1.900.1	28279	$*_u$	jas_malloc
CVE-2014-9112 [13]	cpio	2.9	30309	$+_u$	xmalloc
CVE-2016-6328 [15]	libexif	0.6.21	10828	$*_u$	exif_mem_alloc
CVE-2016-9601 [14]	jbig2dec	0.13	10750	$+_s$	jbig2_new
CVE-2017-16868 [16]	swftools	0.9.2	211618	$*_s$	malloc

Effectiveness of Vulnerability Identification. We first evaluate the effect of vulnerability identification. Usually in large software, developers will encapsulate memory allocation operations. Therefore, we do not only annotate malloc, calloc, realloc, etc. as the sinks of taint analysis, but also annotate corresponding wrapped memory allocation functions in the testcases as sinks, such as "jas_malloc", "exif_mem_alloc" and "jbig2_new".

Table 6. Performance of Vulnerability Identification

Application	#Total-int-ops	#IO2BO-sites	Ratio
gocr	4583	23	0.5%
jasper	2482	84	3.4%
cpio	655	17	2.6%
libexif	597	19	3.18%
jbig2dec	778	10	1.29%
swftools	8253	233	2.70%
Average	–	–	**2.28%**

Table 6 shows, for each benchmark program, the number of total integer arithmetic operations in the program (column 2) and the number of integer arithmetic operations identified as potential IO2BO sites (column3). Column 4 shows the checking ratio, i.e., (the number of integer arithmetic operations identified as potential IO2BO sites)/(the total number of integer arithmetic operations). Results show that, the percentage of integer operations that need to be checked is reduced to very small, on average 2.28%, by vulnerability identification module.

Effectiveness of Vulnerability Filter. In this section, we evaluate the effect of filter module. The experimental results are given in Table 7. Column 1 lists the names of the benchmarks. Column 2 shows the number of potential IO2BO vulnerabilities obtained after performing vulnerability identification. Columns 3 to 5 show the number of remaining potential IO2BO sites after doing vulnerability filter of one-level inter-procedural path constraints, the filter ratio and its time usage in seconds. The filter module successfully filters out a significant portion of potential IO2BO vulnerabilities that cannot be triggered, on average, 49.2% of integer operations are filtered out. Particularly, for swftools, more than two-thirds of the suspicious points are filtered out.

As mentioned in Sect. 4.2, we compare the performance of filter strategies between one-level inter-procedural path constraints and whole program path constraints. Columns 6 to 8 in Table 7 show the number of remaining potential IO2BO sites after doing vulnerability filter of whole program path constraints, the filter ratio and its time usage in seconds. The last two columns of Table 7 show the performance comparison in terms of the reduction ratio in the number of filtered sites, as well as the ratio of the increased time overhead. As shown in the table, the filter module considering whole program path constraints improves the filter effect by 8.8% on average, however, it costs on average 4.1X more time on path constraints generation and solving than the filter module considering one-level inter-procedural path constraints. Particularly, in the cases of libexif, jbig2dec and swftools, no suspicious point is further filtered out. Thus, LAID decides to generate one-level inter-procedural path constraints only.

Table 7. Performance of Vulnerability Filter

Application	Vuln. Identif.	Vuln.Filter with one-level inter-procedural path constraint			Vuln.Filter with whole program path constraint			Performance Comparison	
		Number of remaining IO2BO sites	Filter ratio	Time (sec)	Number of remaining IO2BO sites	Filter ratio	Time (sec)	Filter improvement	Overhead in time
gocr	23	10	56.5%	11.8	7	69.6%	23.3	13.1%	2X
jasper	84	51	39.3%	8.4	37	56.0%	25.3	16.7%	3X
cpio	17	13	23.5%	1.1	9	47.1%	1.7	23.6%	1.5X
libexif	19	8	57.9%	2.2	8	57.9%	9.8	0	4.5X
jbig2dec	10	5	50.0%	1428	5	50.0%	1725.2	0	1.2X
swftools	233	75	67.8%	1466	75	67.8%	18369.2	0	12.5X
Average	–	–	**49.2%**	–	–	**58.0%**	–	**8.8%**	**4.1X**

Comparison with KINT. KINT is a well-known static tool that utilizes taint analysis and constraint solving to locate and filter integer overflow. Contrary to our work, KINT attempts to denote all integer errors in a program and does not make a clear distinction between classic errors and IO2BO errors that constitute vulnerabilities.

To compare with KINT fairly, we annotate the same taint source and taint sink for KINT and set the same time threshold for SMT solver. Among the integer overflows reported by KINT, only those involving data from an untrusted input (source) and being used in a sensitive context (sink) are counted.

Table 8 summarizes the results of comparison. Column "Detected" shows whether a tool reports the IO2BO vulnerabilities, notation "√" means the corresponding vulnerability is detected while notation "×" means not. Column "Time1" and "Time2" in LAID are the time usages in seconds for taint analysis and for constraint generation and solving, respectively. Column "Whole time" in KINT is the time usage of the whole process.

Table 8. Statistics of comparison experiment

Application	LAID			KINT	
	Detected?	Time1(sec) (Vuln.Identif.)	Time2(sec) (Vuln.Filter)	Detected?	Whole time(sec)
Gocr	√	2.1	11.8	×	3012.2
Jasper	√	2.9	8.4	×	768.8
Cpio	√	1.1	1.1	×	18.5
Libexif	√	0.6	2.2	×	6.3
jbig2dec	√	0.5	1428	×	190.3
Swftools	√	11.4	1466	×	25823.9

The comparison experiment shows that LAID successfully detected all the 6 IO2BO vulnerabilities under examination while KINT detected none. The reason lies in that KINT's support for implicit data streams (such as memory-related operations load/store) and complex data structures during the process of taint propagation is not accurate enough. In this way, although some of these 6 real vulnerabilities are reported by KINT, none of them are marked as simultaneously influenced by taint source and used in taint sink. The result also shows that our system is generally faster than KINT.

6 Related Work

Source Code Analysis. There has been a number of tools proposed to detect integer overflow at the source code level. These approaches can be classified into two broad groups: instrumenting the source code with runtime integer overflow check (e.g. [4, 18, 25]) and using static analysis to detect integer overflow (e.g. [17]).

RICH [25] is a compiler-based tool that instruments programs to capture runtime overflows. It protects against many kinds of integer errors, including signedness error, integer overflow/underflow or truncation error. However, benign and unexpected overflows are not distinguished.

IOC [18] performs a compiler-time transformation operating on the Abstract Syntax Tree (AST) to add integer overflow check. Then a runtime library is linked into the compiler's output and handles integer overflows as they occur.

IntPatch [4] is built on top of LLVM and detects vulnerabilities utilizing the type inference on LLVM IR. If a variable involved in an arithmetic operation has an untrusted source and the respective sink may overflow, IntPatch will insert a check statement after that vulnerable arithmetic operation to catch vulnerability at runtime. However, IntPatch would produce false positives if sanitization routines are added by developers. Similar to IntPatch, IntTracker [28] instruments integer arithmetic operations to monitor overflows at runtime while integrates an efficient overflow tracking technique to bypass the false positives caused by sanitization routines troubling IntPatch.

Using tools that instrument the source code with runtime overflow check to find integer overflows requires carefully chosen inputs to trigger them. Because integer errors typically involve corner cases, these tools tend to have low coverage.

KINT [17] performs three different analyses including function-level analysis, range analysis and taint analysis on LLVM IR to detect all integer errors in a program. To avoid path explosion, KINT performs constraint solving at the level of individual functions and statically generates a single path constraint for each integer operation. Despite substantial effort, KINT reports a large number of false positives. Compared with our system, KINT attempts to find all integer errors in a program not just IO2BO vulnerabilities. KINT only considers if the overflow point can be triggered within a function and its analysis for implicit data flow and complex data structures is not accurate enough.

Binary Analysis. Many tools have been proposed to detect overflow in binaries. Followings are some representative works.

IntFinder [20] recovers type information from binaries and creates the suspect integer bug set, then uses its implemented dynamic detection tool that combined with taint analysis to rule out false positives. IntScope [21] performs a path sensitive data flow analysis on its own IR by leveraging symbolic execution and taint analysis to identify the vulnerable point of integer overflow. To deal with false positives, it relies on a dynamic vulnerability test case generation tool to generate test cases which are likely to cause integer overflows. Both IntFinder and IntScope use static analysis to find suspicious integer overflow vulnerabilities, then dynamically check each suspicious vulnerability. However, this mechanism suffer from low efficiency because of high positives of static analysis and large time consumption of dynamically checking.

INDIO [26] is a static analysis based framework to detect and validate integer overflow vulnerabilities in Windows binaries. INDIO integrates the techniques of pattern-matching, vulnerability ranking, and selective symbolic execution to detect integer overflow in x86 binaries. At the end of its analysis, INDIO outputs the detected integer overflow vulnerabilities, as well as example inputs to the binaries that expose these vulnerabilities.

[30] chooses suitable instructions to generate constraint dynamically with taint analysis and loop analysis by launching target program. If the constraint expression is satisfiable, an overflow vulnerability is reported. RICB [29] decompiles binaries to assembly language, locates the overflow points and checks run-time integer overflow via buffer overflow. Since RICB and [30] are dynamic analysis tools with runtime check, the effectiveness depends on the set of inputs used to execute the program.

IO2BO can be considered as a special kind of heap overflow, HOTracer [31] proposes a new offline dynamic analysis solution to discover heap vulnerabilities. It selects useful testcases for programs to generate execution traces. Then it reasons about the path conditions and vulnerability conditions built by tracking heap objects' spatial and taint attributes during execution traces to generate a PoC to find heap vulnerabilities.

7 Conclusions

In this paper, we present a framework that utilizes static analysis techniques to detect IO2BO vulnerabilities in source code, while significantly reduces the number of false positives being reported. It applies taint analysis to accurately and quickly identify potential IO2BO vulnerabilities and uses light-weight constraint generation and solving to verify if an IO2BO vulnerability can be triggered in the program's execution.

A prototype tool named LAID is implemented based on LLVM. The results of our evaluation demonstrate that our tool can work on real-world IO2BO vulnerabilities and achieve a better performance compared with the state-of-the-art tool KINT.

In this paper we focus on IO2BO vulnerabilities, as integer overflows in the context of IO2BO can not be bengin [4] and tend to be more exploitable. Note that our framework can be generalized to detect other types of vulnerabilities, by accordingly modifying the vulnerability condition. For example, for buffer overflow vulnerabilities, the original data's possible length must be bigger than the targeted buffer's real capacity, which constructs the buffer overflow condition.

As of future work, with the analysis results of LAID, we plan to combine symbolic execution and fuzzing to verify the authenticity of the suspicious IO2BO vulnerabilities and construct a PoC (Proof of Concept) that can trigger the corresponding IO2BO vulnerability. This would improve the practicality of our tool and form a complete tool chain that integrates identification, filtering and verification for finding vulnerabilities.

Acknowledgments. We are grateful to the anonymous reviewers for their insightful comments and suggestions. This research was supported in part by the National Natural Science Foundation of China (Grant No. 61802394, Grant NO. 61602470), Foundation of Science and Technology on Information Assurance Laboratory (No. KJ-17-110), Key Research and Development Program of Beijing Municipal Science & Technology Commission, Research on intelligent vulnerability analysis and penetration testing technology (Grant No. D181100000618004), Strategic Priority Research Program of the CAS (XDC02000000), Program of Key Laboratory of Network Assessment Technology, the Chinese Academy of Sciences and Program of Beijing Key Laboratory of Network Security and Protection Technology.

References

1. Common vulnerabilities and exposures (CVE). http://cve.mitre.org/
2. Christey, S., Martin, R.A.: Vulnerability Type Distributions in CVE, May 2007. http://cve.mitre.org/docs/vuln-trends/vuln-trends.pdf
3. CWE-680: IO2BO vulnerabilities. http://cwe.mitre.org/data/definitions/680.html
4. Zhang, C., Wang, T., Wei, T., Chen, Y., Zou, W.: IntPatch: automatically fix integer-overflow-to-buffer-overflow vulnerability at compile-time. In: Gritzalis, D., Preneel, B., Theoharidou, M. (eds.) ESORICS 2010. LNCS, vol. 6345, pp. 71–86. Springer, Heidelberg (2010). https://doi.org/10.1007/978-3-642-15497-3_5
5. Chen, S., Xu, J., Sezer, E.C., Gauriar, P., Iyer, R.K.: Non-control-data attacks are realistic threats. In: Proceedings of the 14th Conference on USENIX Security Symposium, p. 12 (2005)
6. Sotirov, A.: Heap feng shui in javascript. In: Proceedings of Blackhat Europe (2007)
7. National vulnerability database. http://nvd.nist.gov/
8. Lattner, C.: LLVM: An Infrastructure for Multi-Stage Optimization. Master's thesis, Computer Science Dept., University of Illinois at Urbana-Champaign, Urbana, IL, December 2002
9. Lattner, C., Adve, V.: LLVM: a compilation framework for lifelong program analysis & transformation. In: Proceedings of the 2004 International Symposium on Code Generation and Optimization (CGO 2004), Palo Alto, California, March 2004
10. Clang C language family frontend for LLVM. http://clang.llvm.org/
11. CVE-2005-1141. https://cve.mitre.org/cgi-bin/cvename.cgi?name=CVE-2005-1141
12. CVE-2011-4517. https://cve.mitre.org/cgi-bin/cvename.cgi?name=CVE-2011-4517
13. CVE-2014-9112. https://cve.mitre.org/cgi-bin/cvename.cgi?name=CVE-2014-9112
14. CVE-2016-9601. https://cve.mitre.org/cgi-bin/cvename.cgi?name=CVE-2016-9601
15. CVE-2016-6328. https://cve.mitre.org/cgi-bin/cvename.cgi?name=CVE-2016-6328
16. CVE-2017-16868. http://cve.mitre.org/cgi-bin/cvename.cgi?name=CVE-2017-16868
17. Wang, X., Chen, H., Jia, Z., Zeldovich, N., Kaashoek, M.F.: Improving integer security for systems with KINT. In: Proceedings of the 10th USENIX Conference on Operating Systems Design and Implementation, pp. 163–177 (2012)
18. Dietz, W., Li, P., Regehr, J., Adve, V.: Understanding integer overflow in C/C ++. In: Proceedings of the 34th International Conference on Software Engineering, ICSE 2012, pp. 760–770. IEEE Press, Zurich (2012)

19. Pomonis, M., Petsios, T., Jee, K., Polychronakis, M., Keromytis, A.D.: IntFlow: improving the accuracy of arithmetic error detection using information flow tracking. In: Proceedings of the 30th Annual Computer Security Applications Conference, ACSAC 2014, pp. 416–425. ACM, New Orleans (2014)

20. Chen, P., et al.: IntFinder: automatically detecting integer bugs in x86 binary program. In: Qing, S., Mitchell, C.J., Wang, G. (eds.) ICICS 2009. LNCS, vol. 5927, pp. 336–345. Springer, Heidelberg (2009). https://doi.org/10.1007/978-3-642-11145-7_26

21. Wang, T., Wei, T., Lin, Z., Zou, W.: IntScope: automatically detecting integer overflow vulnerability in x86 binary using symbolic execution. In: Proceedings of the Network and Distributed System Security Symposium (2009)

22. Vreugdenhil, P.: Pwn2Own 2010 Windows 7 Internet Explorer 8 exploit (2010). http://vreugdenhilresearch.nl/Pwn2Own-2010-Windows7-InternetExplorer8.pdf

23. Moy, Y., Bjørner, N., Sielaff, D.: Modular bug-finding for integer overflows in the large: sound, efficient, bit-precise static analysis. Technical report MSR-TR-2009-57, Microsoft Research (2009)

24. Brummayer, R.: Efficient SMT Solving for Bit-Vectors and the Extensional Theory of Arrays. Ph.D thesis, Johannes Kepler University, Linz, Austria, November 2009

25. Brumley, D., Chiueh, T.c, Johnson, R., Lin, H., Song, D.: Rich: automatically protecting against integer-based vulnerabilities. In: Proceedings of the 14th Annual Network and Distributed System Security Symposium, NDSS 2007 (2007)

26. Zhang, Y., et al.: Improving accuracy of static integer overflow detection in binary. In: Bos, H., Monrose, F., Blanc, G. (eds.) RAID 2015. LNCS, vol. 9404, pp. 247–269. Springer, Cham (2015). https://doi.org/10.1007/978-3-319-26362-5_12

27. National Institute of Standard and Technology (NIST). SAMATE-software assurance metrics and tool evaluation. http://samate.nist.gov/SARD/testsuite.php

28. Sun, H., Zhang, X., Su, C., Zeng, Q.: Efficient dynamic tracking technique for detecting integer-overflow-to-buffer-overflow vulnerability. In Proceedings of the 10th ACM Symposium on Information, Computer and Communications Security, pp. 483–494. ACM (2015)

29. Wang, Y., Gu, D., Xu, J., Wen, M., Deng, L.: RICB: integer overflow vulnerability dynamic analysis via buffer overflow. In: Lai, X., Gu, D., Jin, B., Wang, Y., Li, H. (eds.) e-Forensics 2010. LNICST, vol. 56, pp. 99–109. Springer, Heidelberg (2011). https://doi.org/10.1007/978-3-642-23602-0_9

30. Chen, K., Feng, D., Su, P.: Dynamic overflow vulnerability detection method based on finite CSP. Chin. J. Comput. 35(5), 898–909 (2012). (in Chinese)

31. Jia, X., Zhang, C., Su, P., Yang, Y., Huang, H., Feng, D.: Towards efficient heap overflow discovery. In: Proceedings of the 26th USENIX Conference on Security Symposium (2017)

Asymmetric Encryption

Fully Secure Decentralized Ciphertext-Policy Attribute-Based Encryption in Standard Model

Chuangui Ma[1], Aijun Ge[2,3]($\boxtimes$), and Jie Zhang[3]

[1] Army Aviation Institute, Beijing, China
[2] Key Laboratory of Cryptologic Technology and Information Security, Ministry of Education, Shandong University, Jinan, China
geaijun@163.com
[3] State Key Laboratory of Mathematical Engineering and Advanced Computing, Zhengzhou, China

Abstract. In this paper, we introduce a new multi-authority ciphertext policy attribute-based encryption (MA-CP-ABE) system. In our system, there are multiple central authorities (CAs) and attribute authorities (AAs). The CAs will not need to coordinate or even be aware of each other, and so do the AAs. In particular, we present two constructions that will be proved secure in the standard model. Our first scheme is fully secure under static assumptions in composite-order bilinear group, and can work for any monotone access structure. The second one achieves constant size ciphertexts for AND-gate policy in prime-order group. The security can be proved under the decisional linear (DLIN) assumption.

Keywords: Attribute based encryption · Ciphertext-policy · Multi-authority · Standard model

1 Introduction

Attribute-based encryption (ABE), which was introduced by Sahai and Waters [19], is a powerful encryption technique used in cloud computing, internet of things (IoT), and social networks. In an ABE system, sender can encrypt a message for multiple receivers by their attributes, rather designating recipient in advance like traditional cryptosystems. Goyal et al. [9] divided ABE system into two categories: key policy attribute-based encryption (KP-ABE) and ciphertext policy attribute-based encryption (CP-ABE). Take CP-ABE as an example, user's private key is associated with his attributes and ciphertext specifies an access policy defined over attributes. A user can decrypt if and only if his attributes satisfy the access policy.

Supported by the National Natural Science Foundation of China (No. 61379150, No. 61502529 and No. 61502533).

F. Guo et al. (Eds.): Inscrypt 2018, LNCS 11449, pp. 427–447, 2019.
https://doi.org/10.1007/978-3-030-14234-6_23

Due to its great power of expression and flexibility, ABE is poured attention into and researched widely in recent years. A considerable amount of research [1,5–8,11,17,21] has been done during the last decade. However, most of the ABE systems have only a single authority to manage attributes, which have some limitations on flexibility and scalability for practical use. It mainly displays in the following aspects.

– *Flexibility:* All attributes are managed by the single authority. This may not be desirable in some applications that someone wants to share information in light of a policy over attributes managed by different organizations.
– *Scalability:* Key generation relied on a single authority becomes a bottleneck in the system, especially when a host of users exist in the system. At worst, the entire system cannot work when the authority goes down.

Aiming at the above problems, a multi-authority ABE (MA-ABE) system with one central authority (CA) and multiple attribute authorities (AAs) was given in [3] by Chase. Subsequently, Chase and Chow [4] remove the CA by using a distributes pseudo random function. Both of [3,4] can only support AND-gates policy. A MA-ABE that supports threshold policy was provided by Lin et al. [14]. CA is not required for their system. However, the authorities are fixed and they must interact during setup. The MA-ABE proposed in [3,4,14] look only at the KP-ABE setting. Müler, Katzenbeisser and Eckert [16] proposed the first multi-authority CP-ABE (MA-CP-ABE) supports policies written in disjunctive normal form (DNF) with one CA and multiple AAs. The system can be only proven secure in generic group model. In addition, all these above systems can only defend selective attacks, i.e., the attacker must commit to a target access structure before setup phase. Lewko and Waters [13] first obtained a fully secure MA-CP-ABE by using dual system encryption technique [12,20]. Their system can support any monotone access structures and no need for CA. They proved security under static assumptions in the random oracle model. Liu et al. [15] proposed a MA-CP-ABE where there are multiple CAs and AAs. In their system, they used a (n, n) threshold policy to distribute the master secret to prevent the authority decrypts ciphertexts independently. The system can be proven fully secure in the standard model. Scheme [13,15] are built on the composite order group, which resulted in low efficiency of the systems [10]. An improvement design was carried out in prime order bilinear group in [18].

Although a lot of effort is being spent on MA-ABE, most of these works only concerned on improving flexibility but ignored scalability. The system in [15] has multiple CAs, nevertheless, all of the CAs must work together to issue an identity-related key to the user and key generation is still a bottleneck in the system. The scheme presented in [13] is decentralized, i.e. the authorities in system are equal and need not even be aware of each other. They used a hash function to tie keys in different authorities together. The hash function, which is modeled as a random oracle, is crucial in security proof. However, the provable secure scheme in the random oracle machine can only be seen as a heuristic argument, will not guarantee the security in realization. It is worth to construct a fully secure MA-CP-ABE has the advantages of flexibility and scalability combined in the standard model. The challenge to design MA-ABE is to counteract collusion attacks. Prior ABE systems with a single authority achieved collusion resistance by binding a common random number to different components of a user's secret key. Unfortunately, we cannot use this technique in MA-ABE since the key components may come from different authorities. To cross this barrier, we introduce a MA-ABE system with multiple CAs and AAs. Different from prior ABE systems, the master keys of CAs in our system do not participate in the encryption. CAs are only responsible for providing eligible users with a random value. The random number is tied to the user's global identifier and attribute set by using a existentially unforgeable signature scheme. The collusion between any users is bound to fail since they share different random values. A user can register and get his identity-related key at any CA. AA manages a different domain of attributes and generates keys related to the attributes for users. Different authorities can work independently or even needs not to know each other.

Our Contribution. In this paper, we introduce decentralized MA-CP-ABE systems with multiple CAs and AAs. Specifically, we propose two kinds of decentralized MA-CP-ABE schemes. Our first scheme is built on the composite-order bilinear group. It can support any monotone access structure and achieve full security under static assumptions. Our second scheme achieves short ciphertexts for an AND-gate policy in the prime-order bilinear group. It is fully secure under the standard DLIN assumption and decryption algorithm only needs constant number of pairing operations. In order to compress the size of ciphertexts, we utilize the compression technique in [5]. By pooling all the attributes in an AND-gate policy together, we can encrypt the message with the "aggregated" attribute. Hence, the size of ciphertexts achieves a constant value, regardless of the number of underlying attributes. Both of our schemes are proven secure in the standard model. Our systems realize the load balancing among CAs and improves the performance to a certain extent. A comparison in terms of efficiency and security between current MA-CP-ABE systems and our work is given in Table 1.

Organization. The definition of MA-CP-ABE and its security model are presented in Sect. 2. In the next section, we put forward our first scheme, and proof its security in Sect. A. We give our second scheme in Sect. 4 and proof its security in Sect. B. Finally, we conclude the paper in Sect. 5.

Table 1. Comparing among existing MA-CP-ABE schemes. l is the number of attributes in the access policy, LSSS denotes linear secret sharing scheme. We note that any monotone access structure can be realized by a linear secret sharing scheme

	Size of ciphertext	Pairing of decryption	Access structure	Assumption	Fully secure	Decentralized CA	Standard model
[16]	$\mathcal{O}(l)$	$\mathcal{O}(1)$	DNF	-	✗	✗	✗
[13]	$\mathcal{O}(l)$	$\mathcal{O}(l)$	LSSS	Static	✓	✓	✗
[15]	$\mathcal{O}(l)$	$\mathcal{O}(l)$	LSSS	Static	✓	✗	✓
[18]	$\mathcal{O}(l)$	$\mathcal{O}(l)$	LSSS	DLIN	✓	✓	✗
[5]	$\mathcal{O}(1)$	$\mathcal{O}(1)$	AND	n-BDHE	✓	✓	✗
Ours	$\mathcal{O}(1)$	$\mathcal{O}(1)$	AND	DLIN	✓	✓	✓
	$\mathcal{O}(l)$	$\mathcal{O}(l)$	LSSS	Static	✓	✓	✓

2 Definition and Security Model

2.1 Definition

An MA-CP-ABE consists of three types entities: the central authorities (CAs), attribute authorities (AAs) and users. We let U_i denote the attribute set managed by AA_i, $U = \bigcup U_i$ denote the universe of attributes. For $i \neq j$, we assume that $U_i \bigcap U_j = \Phi$. An MA-CP-ABE system consists of the following seven algorithms:

GlobalSetup(1^λ) $\to$ GPK. This algorithm takes as input a security parameter λ and outputs the global public parameters GPK.

CASetup(GPK) $\to$ CPK$_j$, CSK$_j$. This algorithm is run by CA_j. It takes as input global parameters GPK and outputs public parameters CPK$_j$ and master key CSK$_j$.

AASetup(GPK, U_j) $\to$ APK$_j$, ASK$_j$. This algorithm is run by AA_j. It takes as input global parameters GPK and its attribute domain U_j, outputs public parameters APK$_j$ and master key ASK$_j$.

CKeyGen(GPK, CSK$_j$, GID, S) $\to$ SK$_{GID,S}$. This algorithm is run by CA_j. It takes as input global parameters GPK, CA_j's master key CSK$_j$, user's global identifier GID and a attribute set S, and returns an identity key SK$_{GID,S}$.

AKeyGen(GPK, CPK$_j$, ASK$_k$, SK$_{GID,S}$, att_i) $\to$ SK$_{GID,i}$. This algorithm is run by AA_k. It takes as input GPK, CPK$_j$, ASK$_k$, SK$_{GID,S}$ and an attribute att_i belonging to AA_k, and returns an attribute key SK$_{GID,i}$.

Enc(GPK, $\{$APK$_j\}$, Y, m) $\to$ CT$_Y$. This algorithm takes as input GPK, $\{$APK$_j\}$, an access policy Y and a message $m \in \mathcal{M}$, and outputs a ciphertext CT$_Y$.

Dec(CT$_Y$, SK$_{GID,S}$, $\{$SK$_{GID,i}\}_{att_i \in S}$) $\to$ m. This algorithm takes as input SK$_{GID,S}$, $\{$SK$_{GID,i}\}_{att_i \in S}$ and CT$_Y$. If S satisfies the access policy Y, it outputs a message m; otherwise, it outputs $\bot$.

2.2   Security Model

We define security for MA-CP-ABE by the following game run between a challenger $\mathcal{B}$ and an adversary $\mathcal{A}$. $\mathcal{A}$ can only corrupt AAs statically, but can make key queries adaptively. Without loss of generality, we assume that $\mathcal{A}$ corrupts all AAs but AA_1.

Setup: The challenger $\mathcal{B}$ executes GlobalSetup, CASetup, AASetup algorithm. It gives the GPK, $\{CPK_j\}$ and $\{APK_j\}$ to the adversary $\mathcal{A}$. For corrupt authorities, $\mathcal{B}$ also gives the corresponding $\{ASK_j\}$ to $\mathcal{A}$.

Key Query Phase 1: In this phase, $\mathcal{A}$ can make two kinds of queries.
  - CKeyGen Query: $\mathcal{A}$ makes identity key query by submitting (GID, S) to $\mathcal{B}$. $\mathcal{B}$ returns $SK_{GID,S}$ to $\mathcal{A}$.
  - AKeyGen Query: $\mathcal{A}$ makes attribute key query by submitting $(SK_{GID,S}, att_i)$ to $\mathcal{B}$, where att_i belonging to $AA_1 \cap S$. $\mathcal{B}$ returns $SK_{GID,i}$ or $\perp$ to $\mathcal{A}$ depend on $SK_{GID,S}$.

Challenge: $\mathcal{A}$ submits two equal-length messages m_0, m_1, and an access policy Y with the following constraint. We let V denote the the subset of attributes controlled by corrupt AAs. For each identity GID, V_{GID} denotes the subset of attributes att_i for which $\mathcal{A}$ has queried. For each GID, we require that $V \cup V_{GID}$ cannot satisfy Y. $\mathcal{B}$ randomly chooses $\beta \in \{0,1\}$ and encrypts m_β under Y. It sends the ciphertext to $\mathcal{A}$.

Key Query Phase 2: $\mathcal{A}$ continually queries $\mathcal{B}$ as in phase 1 in the same constraint.

Guess: $\mathcal{A}$ outputs a guess β' for β.

The adversary's advantage is defined to be $|Pr[\beta' = \beta] - 1/2|$.

Definition 1. *An MA-CP-ABE scheme is secure if for all probabilistic polynomial-time (PPT) adversaries, the advantage is negligible in the above security game.*

3   Scheme I: MA-CP-ABE in Composite-Order Bilinear Group

3.1   Composite-Order Bilinear Group

Composite-Order Bilinear Group. The composite-order group was first introduced in [2]. Group generator $\mathcal{G}$ takes a security parameter λ as input and outputs $(N = p_1 p_2 p_3, G, G_T, e)$, where G and G_T are cyclic groups of order N, p_1, p_2, p_3 are distinct primes, $e : G \times G \to G_T$ is an admissible bilinear map.

We let G_{p_1}, G_{p_2} and G_{p_3} denote the subgroups of order p_1, p_2 and p_3 in G respectively. An important point to realize here is that the map e holds the orthogonality property of $G_{p_1}, G_{p_2}, G_{p_3}$. That is to say, let $g_i \in G_i$ $(i = 1, 2, 3)$, then $e(g_i, g_j)$ is the identity element in G_T when $i \neq j$.

Cryptographic Assumptions. Our construction relies on the following assumptions which are given in [13].

$-\mathsf{Adv}_{\mathcal{A}}^{Assu1}(\lambda) = |\Pr[\mathcal{A}(D, T_1) = 1] - \Pr[\mathcal{A}(D, T_2) = 1]|$

  where $D = (N, G, G_T, e; g_1), T_1 \leftarrow G, T_2 \leftarrow G_{p_1}, g_1 \leftarrow G_{p_1}$.

$-\mathsf{Adv}_{\mathcal{A}}^{Assu2}(\lambda) = |\Pr[\mathcal{A}(D, T_1) = 1] - \Pr[\mathcal{A}(D, T_2) = 1]|$

  where $D = (N, G, G_T, e; g_1, g_3, X_1 X_2), T_1 \leftarrow G_{p_1}, T_2 \leftarrow G_{p_1 p_2}$,

  and $g_1, X_1 \leftarrow G_{p_1}, X_2 \leftarrow G_{p_2}, g_3 \leftarrow G_{p_3}$.

$-\mathsf{Adv}_{\mathcal{A}}^{Assu3}(\lambda) = |\Pr[\mathcal{A}(D, T_1) = 1] - \Pr[\mathcal{A}(D, T_2) = 1]|$

  where $D = (N, G, G_T, e; g_1, X_1 X_3, Y_2 Y_3), T_1 \leftarrow G_{p_1 p_2}, T_2 \leftarrow G_{p_1 p_3}$,

  and $g_1, X_1 \leftarrow G_{p_1}, Y_2 \leftarrow G_{p_2}, X_3, Y_3 \leftarrow G_{p_3}$.

$-\mathsf{Adv}_{\mathcal{A}}^{Assu4}(\lambda) = |\Pr[\mathcal{A}(D, T_1) = 1] - \Pr[\mathcal{A}(D, T_2) = 1]|$

  where $D = (N, G, G_T, e; g_1^a, g_1^b g_3^b, g_1^c, g_1^{ac} g_3^d), T_1 = e(g_1, g_1)^{abc}, T_2 \leftarrow G_T$,

  and $g_1 \leftarrow G_{p_1}, g_2 \leftarrow G_{p_2}, g_3 \leftarrow G_{p_3}, a, b, c, d \leftarrow \mathbb{Z}_N$.

Assumption 1 (resp. 2, 3, 4) asserts that for any PPT adversary $\mathcal{A}$, the advantage $\mathsf{Adv}_{\mathcal{A}}^{Assu1}(\lambda)$ (resp. 2, 3, 4) is negligible in λ.

3.2   Construction

GlobalSetup(1^λ) : A bilinear group G of order $N = p_1 p_2 p_3$ and a existentially unforgeable signature scheme $\Sigma_{sign} = (\mathsf{KeyGen}, \mathsf{Sign}, \mathsf{Verify})$ are chosen. Output global public parameters.

$$GPK := \{N, G, G_T, e, g_1, \Sigma_{sign}\}$$

CASetup(*GPK*): The j'th central authority gets a pair of keys ($\mathsf{Signkey}_j, \mathsf{Verifykey}_j$) by running KeyGen in Σ_{sign}. It outputs

$$CSK_j = \mathsf{Signkey}_j \text{ and } CPK_j = \mathsf{Verifykey}_j.$$

AASetup(GPK, U_j) : For each attribute $att_i \in U_j$, the attribute authority samples $\alpha_i, t_i \in \mathbb{Z}_N$, and outputs

$$ASK_k = \{\alpha_i, t_i\}_{att_i \in U_j}$$
$$APK_k = \{e(g_1, g_1)^{\alpha_i}, g_1^{t_i}\}_{att_i \in U_j}.$$

CKeyGen(GPK, CSK_j, GID, S) : The user submits his global identity GID and attribute set S to CA_j. CA_j randomly chooses $r \leftarrow \mathbb{Z}_N$ and computes

$$SK_{GID,S} = \{GID, S, g_1^r, j, \mathsf{Sign}(Signkey_j, GID||S||g_1^r||j)\}$$

AKeyGen($GPK, CPK, ASK_j, SK_{GID,S}, att_i$): The user submits $SK_{GID,S}$ and attribute att_i to AA_j. AA_j checks the signature under the corresponding verify key. If the signature is valid and att_i belongs to S, then AA_k computes

$$SK_{GID,i} = g_1^{\alpha_i}(g_1^r)^{t_i}$$

Enc($GPK, \{APK_j\}, m, (\mathbf{M}, \rho)$): The encryption algorithm takes as input GPK, $\{APK_j\}$, a message m, an $n \times l$ access matrix $\mathbf{M}$ with ρ maps each row of $\mathbf{M}$ to an attribute. We restrict that ρ is an injection in this paper. It chooses random vectors $\boldsymbol{v} = (s, v_2, \ldots, v_l)$ and $\boldsymbol{w} = (0, w_2, \ldots, w_l)$. We let $\lambda_x = \mathbf{M}_x \cdot \boldsymbol{v}$ and $w_x = \mathbf{M}_x \cdot \boldsymbol{w}$. For each row $\mathbf{M}_x$ of $\mathbf{M}$, it chooses random number $s_x \in \mathbb{Z}_N$, then sets

$$C_0 = m \cdot e(g_1, g_1)^s, C_{1,x} = e(g_1, g_1)^{\lambda_x} e(g_1, g_1)^{\alpha_{\rho(x)} s_x},$$
$$C_{2,x} = g_1^{s_x}, C_{3,x} = g_1^{s_x t_{\rho(x)}} g_1^{w_x}.$$

Dec($CT, SK_{GID,S}, \{SK_{GID,i}\}_{att_i \in S}$): If S satisfies the access policy, then finds ω_x such that $\sum_{\rho(x) \in S} \omega_x \mathbf{M}_x = (1, 0, \ldots, 0)$. The decryptor computes

$$\frac{e(g_1, g_1)^{\lambda_x} \cdot e(g_1, g_1)^{\alpha_{\rho(x)} s_x} \cdot e(g_1^{s_x t_{\rho(x)}} g_1^{w_x}, g_1^r)}{e(g_1^{\alpha_{\rho(x)}} g_1^{r t_{\rho(x)}}, g_1^{s_x})} = e(g_1, g_1)^{\lambda_x} e(g_1, g_1)^{r w_x}.$$

$$\prod_{\rho(x) \in S} (e(g_1, g_1)^{\lambda_x} e(g_1, g_1)^{r w_x})^{\omega_x} = e(g_1, g_1)^s.$$

Then the message can be recovered:

$$m = C_0 / e(g_1, g_1)^s.$$

Theorem 1. *Our MA-CP-ABE scheme is fully secure based on assumptions 1, 2, 3 and 4 if the signature scheme Σ_{sign} is existentially unforgeable under adaptive chosen message attacks.*

4   Scheme II: MA-CP-ABE in Prime-Order Bilinear Group

4.1   Revisiting Dual System Groups

Prime-Order Bilinear Group. The prime-order group generator $\mathcal{G}$ takes a security parameter λ as input and outputs $(p, G_1, G_2, G_T, g_1, g_2, e)$, where G_1, G_2 and G_T are cyclic groups of prime order p, g_1, g_2, g_T are generators of G_1, G_2, G_T respectively, $e : G_1 \times G_2 \to G_T$ is an admissible bilinear map.

$\mathcal{D}_k$ is a matrix distribution that outputs matrices $(\mathbf{A}, \boldsymbol{a}^\top) \in \mathbb{Z}_p^{(k+1)\times k} \times \mathbb{Z}_p^{k+1}$. Moreover, $\mathbf{A}^\top \boldsymbol{a}^\perp = \mathbf{0}$ and $\boldsymbol{a}^\perp \neq \mathbf{0}$, $e(g_1^\mathbf{A}, g_2^\mathbf{B}) := e(g_1, g_2)^{\mathbf{A}^\top \mathbf{B}}$, $\mathbf{A}, \mathbf{B}$ are either vectors or matrices. In particular, we focus on the following distribution:

$$\mathbf{A} := \begin{pmatrix} a_1 & & & \\ & a_2 & & \\ & & \ddots & \\ & & & a_k \\ 1 & 1 & \ldots & 1 \end{pmatrix} \in \mathbb{Z}_p^{(k+1)\times k} \quad \text{and} \quad \boldsymbol{a}^\perp := \begin{pmatrix} a_1^{-1} \\ a_2^{-1} \\ \vdots \\ a_k^{-1} \\ -1 \end{pmatrix} \in \mathbb{Z}_p^{k+1}.$$

Dual System Groups [6]. The dual system groups consists of six randomized algorithms defined as follows:
SampP$(1^\lambda, 1^n)$:

- run $(p, G_1, G_2, G_T, g_1, g_2, e) \leftarrow \mathcal{G}(1^\lambda)$, where $\mathcal{G}(1^\lambda)$ is an asymmetric prime order group generator;
- define $(\mathbb{G}, \mathbb{H}, \mathbb{G}_T, e) := (G_1^{k+1}, G_2^{k+1}, G_T, e)$;
- sample $(\mathbf{A}, \boldsymbol{a}^\perp), (\mathbf{B}, \boldsymbol{b}^\perp) \leftarrow \mathcal{D}_k$, $\mathbf{W}_1, \ldots, \mathbf{W}_n \leftarrow_R \mathbb{Z}_p^{(k+1)\times(k+1)}$;
- set $h^* := g_2^{\boldsymbol{a}^\perp}$.

Output

$$\mathsf{pp} := \left((p, \mathbb{G}, \mathbb{H}, \mathbb{G}_T, e), \begin{matrix} g_1^\mathbf{A}, g_1^{\mathbf{W}_1^\top \mathbf{A}}, \ldots, g_1^{\mathbf{W}_n^\top \mathbf{A}} \\ g_2^\mathbf{B}, g_2^{\mathbf{W}_1 \mathbf{B}}, \ldots, g_2^{\mathbf{W}_n \mathbf{B}} \end{matrix} \right)$$

SampGT$([\boldsymbol{p}]_T)$: Pick $\boldsymbol{s} \leftarrow \mathbb{Z}_p^k$ and output $g_T^{\boldsymbol{s}^\top \boldsymbol{p}} \in G_T$.

SampG(pp): Pick $\boldsymbol{s} \leftarrow \mathbb{Z}_p^k$ and output $\left(g_1^{\mathbf{A}\boldsymbol{s}}, g_1^{\mathbf{W}_1^\top \mathbf{A}\boldsymbol{s}}, \ldots, g_1^{\mathbf{W}_n^\top \mathbf{A}\boldsymbol{s}} \right) \in (G_1^{k+1})^{n+1}$.

SampH(pp): Pick $\boldsymbol{r} \leftarrow \mathbb{Z}_p^k$ and output $\left(g_2^{\mathbf{B}\boldsymbol{r}}, g_2^{\mathbf{W}_1 \mathbf{B}\boldsymbol{r}}, \ldots, g_2^{\mathbf{W}_n \mathbf{B}\boldsymbol{r}} \right) \in (G_2^{k+1})^{n+1}$.

$\widehat{\mathsf{SampG}}(\mathsf{pp},\mathsf{sp})$: Pick $\hat{s} \leftarrow \mathbb{Z}_p^*$ and output $\left(g_1^{\boldsymbol{b}^\perp \hat{s}}, g_1^{\mathbf{W}_1^\top \boldsymbol{b}^\perp \hat{s}}, \ldots, g_1^{\mathbf{W}_n^\top \boldsymbol{b}^\perp \hat{s}} \right) \in (G_1^{k+1})^{n+1}$.

$\widehat{\mathsf{SampH}}(\mathsf{pp},\mathsf{sp})$: Pick $\hat{r} \leftarrow \mathbb{Z}_p^*$ and output $\left(g_2^{\boldsymbol{a}^\perp \hat{r}}, g_2^{\mathbf{W}_1 \boldsymbol{a}^\perp \hat{r}}, \ldots, g_2^{\mathbf{W}_n \boldsymbol{a}^\perp \hat{r}} \right) \in (G_2^{k+1})^{n+1}$.

The first four algorithms are used in the real system, and the remaining two algorithms are only used in the proof of security.

Assumption 1 (k-**Lin**[1]: *the k-linear assumption in G_1*). *For any PPT adversary $\mathcal{A}$, the advantage of $\mathcal{A}$ is negligible in λ:*

$$\mathsf{Adv}_\mathcal{A}^{k-Lin} := |\Pr[\mathcal{A}((p, G_1, G_2, G_T, g_1, g_2, e); [\mathbf{A}]_1, [\mathbf{A}\boldsymbol{s}]_1) = 1]$$
$$-\Pr[\mathcal{A}((p, G_1, G_2, G_T, g_1, g_2, e); [\mathbf{A}]_1, [\boldsymbol{z}]_1) = 1]|$$

where $(p, G_1, G_2, G_T, g_1, g_2, e) \leftarrow \mathcal{G}(1^\lambda); (\mathbf{A}, \boldsymbol{a}^\perp) \leftarrow \mathcal{D}_k; \boldsymbol{s} \leftarrow_R \mathbb{Z}_p^k; \boldsymbol{z} \leftarrow_R \mathbb{Z}_p^{k+1}$.

---

[1] We note that 1-Lin is DDH, and 2-Lin is DLIN.

We will use the following lemma from [6] in the security analysis of our scheme.

Lemma 1 (*left subgroup indistinguishability from k-Lin*). *For any* PPT *adversary* $\mathcal{A}$, *there exists an adversary* $\mathcal{B}$ *such that:*

$$\mathsf{Adv}_{\mathcal{A}}^{LS}(\lambda) \leq \mathsf{Adv}_{\mathcal{B}}^{k-Lin} + 2/p$$

where $\mathsf{Adv}_{\mathcal{A}}^{LS}(\lambda) := \left| \Pr[\mathcal{A}(\mathsf{pp}, \boxed{g}) = 1] - \Pr[\mathcal{A}(\mathsf{pp}, \boxed{g \cdot \hat{g}}) = 1] \right|$

$(\mathsf{pp}, \mathsf{sp}) \leftarrow \mathsf{SampP}(1^\lambda, 1^n); g \leftarrow \mathsf{SampP}(\mathsf{pp}); \hat{g} \leftarrow \widehat{\mathsf{SampG}}(\mathsf{pp}, \mathsf{sp}).$

Lemma 2 (*right subgroup indistinguishability from k-Lin*). *For any* PPT *adversary* $\mathcal{A}$, *there exists an adversary* $\mathcal{B}$ *such that:*

$$\mathsf{Adv}_{\mathcal{A}}^{RS}(\lambda) \leq \mathsf{Adv}_{\mathcal{B}}^{k-Lin} + 2/p$$

where $\mathsf{Adv}_{\mathcal{A}}^{RS}(\lambda) := \left| \Pr[\mathcal{A}(\mathsf{pp}, h^*, g \cdot \hat{g}, \boxed{h}) = 1] - \Pr[\mathcal{A}(\mathsf{pp}, h^*, g \cdot \hat{g}, \boxed{h \cdot \hat{h}}) = 1] \right|$

$(\mathsf{pp}, \mathsf{sp}) \leftarrow \mathsf{SampP}(1^\lambda, 1^n); g \leftarrow \mathsf{SampP}(\mathsf{pp}); \hat{g} \leftarrow \widehat{\mathsf{SampG}}(\mathsf{pp}, \mathsf{sp});$

$h^* = g_2^{a^\perp}, h \leftarrow \mathsf{SampH}(\mathsf{pp}); \hat{h} \leftarrow \widehat{\mathsf{SampH}}(\mathsf{pp}, \mathsf{sp}).$

Lemma 3 (*parameter hiding*). *The following two distributions are identical:*

$$\{\mathsf{pp}, h^*, \boxed{\hat{g}, \hat{h}}\} \text{ and } \{\mathsf{pp}, h^*, \boxed{\hat{g} \cdot \hat{g}', \hat{h} \cdot \hat{h}'}\}$$

where $(\mathsf{pp}, \mathsf{sp}) \leftarrow \mathsf{SampP}(1^\lambda, 1^n), h^* = g_2^{a^\perp};$

$\hat{g} = (\hat{g}_0, \ldots) \leftarrow \widehat{\mathsf{SampG}}(\mathsf{pp}, \mathsf{sp}); \hat{h} = (\hat{h}_0, \ldots) \leftarrow \widehat{\mathsf{SampH}}(\mathsf{pp}, \mathsf{sp});$

$\hat{g}' = (1, \hat{g}_0^{\hat{u}_1}, \ldots, \hat{g}_0^{\hat{u}_n}); \hat{h}' = (1, \hat{h}_0^{\hat{u}_1}, \ldots, \hat{h}_0^{\hat{u}_n}); \hat{u}_1, \ldots, \hat{u}_n \leftarrow \mathbb{Z}_p.$

4.2 Construction

$\mathsf{GlobalSetup}(1^\lambda)$: Sample $(\mathbf{A}, a^\perp), (\mathbf{B}, b^\perp) \leftarrow \mathcal{D}_k$, where $k = 2$. An existentially unforgeable signature scheme $\Sigma_{sign} = (\mathsf{KeyGen}, \mathsf{Sign}, \mathsf{Verify})$ is chosen. Output global public parameters

$$GPK := \{p, G_1^{k+1}, G_2^{k+1}, G_T, e; g_1^{\mathbf{A}}, g_2^{\mathbf{B}}, \Sigma_{sign}\}$$

$\mathsf{CASetup}(GPK)$: The j'th central authority gets a pair of keys (Signkey$_j$, Verifykey$_j$) by running KeyGen in Σ_{sign}. It outputs

$$CSK_j = \mathsf{Signkey}_j \text{ and } CPK_j = \mathsf{Verifykey}_j$$

$$ASK_k = \{k_i, \mathbf{W}_i\}_{att_i \in U_j}$$

$$APK_k = \{e(g_1, g_2)^{k_i^\top \mathbf{A}}, g_1^{\mathbf{W}_i \mathbf{A}}\}_{att_i \in U_j}.$$

CKeyGen(GPK, CSK_j, GID, S): The user submits his global identity GID and attribute set S to CA_j. CA_j randomly chooses $r \leftarrow \mathbb{Z}_p^k$ and computes

$$SK_{GID,S} = \{GID, S, g_2^{\mathbf{B}r}, j, \mathsf{Sign}(Signkey, GID||S||g_2^{\mathbf{B}r}||j)\}$$

AKeyGen($GPK, CPK, ASK_j, SK_{GID,S}, att_i$): The user submits $SK_{GID,S}$ and attribute att_i to AA_j. AA_j checks the signature under the corresponding verify key. If the signature is valid and att_i belongs to S, then AA_j computes

$$SK_{GID,i} = g_2^{k_i + \mathbf{W}_i \mathbf{B}r}$$

Enc($GPK, \{APK_j\}, m, Y$): The encryption algorithm takes $GPK, \{APK_j\}$, a message m, an AND-gates on multi-valued attributes $Y = \bigwedge_{att_i \in \Omega} att_i$ as input. It samples $s \leftarrow \mathbb{Z}_p^k$ and sets

$$C_0 = m \cdot \prod_{att_i \in \Omega} e(g_1, g_2)^{k_i^\top \mathbf{A}s}, C_1 = \prod_{att_i \in \Omega} g_1^{\mathbf{W}_i^\top \mathbf{A}s}, C_2 = g_1^{\mathbf{A}s}.$$

Output $CT_Y = \{C_0, C_1, C_2\}$.
Dec($CT_Y, SK_{GID,S}, \{SK_{GID,i}\}_{att_i \in S}$): Given $CT_Y = \{C_0, C_1, C_2\}$, if $\Omega \subseteq S$, then compute

$$M = C_0 \cdot \frac{e(C_1, g_2^{\mathbf{B}r})}{e(C_2, \prod_{att_i \in \Omega} SK_{GID,i})}.$$

Theorem 2. *Our MA-CP-ABE scheme is fully secure based on the left and right subgroup indistinguishability if the signature scheme Σ_{sign} is existentially unforgeable under adaptive chosen message attacks.*

5   Conclusion

In this paper, we present two decentralized MA-CP-ABE systems. The first scheme is expressive, can support any monotone access structures. Then, we construct the second scheme in prime-order groups, which achieves short ciphertexts and constant pairing costs for an AND-gate policy, to further increase efficiency. Both schemes can lighten the pressure of CA and can be proved fully secure in the standard model. In future, it would be desirable to design fully secure decentralized MA-CP-ABE systems in the standard model with flexible access structures in prime-order groups.

A   Proof of Security for Scheme I

We first define the semi-functional ciphertexts and semi-functional keys as follows.

Semi-functional Ciphertexts. We let $C_0', C_{1,x}', C_{2,x}', C_{3,x}'$ denote the normal ciphertexts. We define $V_G = \{\mathbf{M}_x | \rho(x)$ belongs to good authorities$\}$, $V_C = \{\mathbf{M}_x | \rho(x)$ belongs to corrupted authorities$\}$. We choose random values $y_i, z_i \in \mathbb{Z}_N$

for each attribute att_i, two random vectors $\boldsymbol{u}_2, \boldsymbol{u}_3 \in \mathbb{Z}_N^l$, and set $\delta_x = \mathbf{M}_x \cdot \boldsymbol{u}_2, \sigma_x = \mathbf{M}_x \cdot \boldsymbol{u}_3$. For each row $\mathbf{M}_x \in V_G$, we choose $\gamma_x, \psi_x \in \mathbb{Z}_N$ randomly. We define the semi-functional ciphertexts as follows: $C_0 = C_0'$,

$$C_{1,x} = C_{1,x}', C_{2,x} = C_{2,x}' g_2^{\gamma_x} g_3^{\psi_x}, C_{3,x} = C_{3,x}' g_2^{\delta_x + \gamma_x y_{\rho(x)}} g_3^{\sigma_x + \psi_x z_{\rho(x)}}, \mathbf{M}_x \in V_G$$

$$C_{1,x} = C_{1,x}', C_{2,x} = C_{2,x}', C_{3,x} = C_{3,x}' g_2^{\delta_x} g_3^{\sigma_x}, \mathbf{M}_x \in V_C$$

Semi-functional Keys. There are two types of semi-functional keys. They are defined as follows. Pick random value $c \in \mathbb{Z}_N$, then set

$$\text{Type } 1 : SK_{GID,S} = \{GID, S, g_1^r g_2^c, j, \mathsf{Sign}(Signkey, GID\|S\|g_1^r g_2^c\|j)\}$$

$$SK_{GID,i} = g_1^{\alpha_i} g_1^{rt_i} g_2^{cy_i}$$

$$\text{Type } 2 : SK_{GID,S} = \{GID, S, g_1^r g_3^c, j, \mathsf{Sign}(Signkey, GID\|S\|g_1^r g_3^c\|j)\}$$

$$SK_{GID,i} = g_1^{\alpha_i} g_1^{rt_i} g_3^{cz_i}$$

Game Sequence. We let $\mathsf{Adv}_{\mathcal{A}}^{\mathsf{Game}_X}$ denote the advantage of $\mathcal{A}$ in Game_X.

- Game_0: the real security game.
- Game_1: the challenge ciphertext becomes semi-functional.
- $\mathsf{Game}_{2,\eta,1}$ for $\eta = 1,\ldots,q$: the first η-1 queried identities, the received keys become semi-functional of type 2, and the received key for the η'th queried identity becomes semi-functional of type 1.
- $\mathsf{Game}_{2,\eta,2}$ for $\eta = 0,\ldots,q$: the first η queried identities, the received keys become semi-functional of type 2. We let $\mathsf{Game}_{2,0,2}$ denote Game_1.
- Game_3: generate a semi-functional ciphertext of a random message $m' \in \mathbb{G}_T$ as the challenge ciphertext.

Theorem 1 is accomplished in the following lemmas.

Lemma 4 (from Game_0 to Game_1). *For any PPT adversary $\mathcal{A}$, there exists an adversary $\mathcal{B}$ such that* $\left|\mathsf{Adv}_{\mathcal{A}}^{\mathsf{Game}_0}(\lambda) - \mathsf{Adv}_{\mathcal{A}}^{\mathsf{Game}_1}(\lambda)\right| \leq \mathsf{Adv}_{\mathcal{B}}^{Assu1}(\lambda)$.

Proof. The adversary $\mathcal{B}$ gets input (N, g_1, T), where T is from G_{p_1} or G, $\mathcal{B}$ proceeds as follows.

Setup: Pick $\alpha_i, t_i \in \mathbb{Z}_N$, a UF-CMA secure signature scheme $\Sigma_{sign} = (\mathsf{KeyGen}, \mathsf{Sign}, \mathsf{Verify})$. Output $GPK = \{N, G, G_T, e, g_1, \Sigma_{sign}\}, CPK_j = \mathsf{Verifykey}_j, APK_j = \{e(g_1, g_1)^{\alpha_i}, g_1^{t_i}\}_{att_i \in U_j}$. In addition, $\{\alpha_i, t_i | att_i \in U \backslash U_1\}$ are given to the adversary $\mathcal{A}$.

KeyQueries: $\mathcal{B}$ answers $\mathcal{A}$ by executing CKeyGen, AKeyGen algorithm for CKeyGen Query and AKeyGen Query, respectively.

Challenge: Upon receiving challenge m_0, m_1 and $(\mathbf{M}, \rho)$, $\mathcal{B}$ picks a random bit $\beta \in \{0, 1\}$. $\mathcal{B}$ chooses two random vectors $\boldsymbol{v} = (s, v_2, \ldots, v_l)$ and $\boldsymbol{w}' = (0, w_2, \ldots, w_l)$. We let $\lambda_x = \mathbf{M}_x \cdot \boldsymbol{v}$ and $w'_x = \mathbf{M}_x \cdot \boldsymbol{w}'$. For $\mathbf{M}_x \in V_G$, $\mathcal{B}$ chooses random number $s'_x \in \mathbb{Z}_N$. For $\mathbf{M}_x \in V_C$, $\mathcal{B}$ chooses random number $s_x \in \mathbb{Z}_N$. Then set $C_0 = m_\beta \cdot e(g_1, g_1)^s$. For $\mathbf{M}_x \in V_C, C_{1,x} = e(g_1, g_1)^{\lambda_x} e(g_1, g_1)^{\alpha_{\rho(x)} s_x}, C_{2,x} = g_1^{s_x}, C_{3,x} = g_1^{s_x t_{\rho(x)}} T^{w'_x}$; For $\mathbf{M}_x \in V_G, C_{1,x} = e(g_1, g_1)^{\lambda_x} e(g_1, T)^{\alpha_{\rho(x)} s'_x}, C_{2,x} = T^{s_x}, C_{3,x} = T^{s'_x t_{\rho(x)}} T^{w'_x}$.

If $T \in G_{p_1}$, suppose that $T = g_1^a$ where a is a random value. We have a well distributed normal ciphertext with $s_x = as'_x$ (for rows in V_G), $w_x = aw'_x = \mathbf{M}_x \cdot a\boldsymbol{w}$.

If $T \in G$, suppose that $T = g_1^a g_2^b g_3^c$ where a, b, c are random values. We have $w_x = aw'_x = \mathbf{M}_x \cdot a\boldsymbol{w} \mod p_1$, $\delta_x = bw'_x = \mathbf{M}_x \cdot b\boldsymbol{w}' \mod p_2$, $\sigma_x = cw'_x = \mathbf{M}_x \cdot c\boldsymbol{w}' \mod p_3$. For rows in V_G, $s_x = as'_x \mod p_1$, $\gamma_x = bs'_x \mod p_2$, $\psi_x = cs'_x \mod p_3$, $y_{\rho(x)} = t_{\rho(x)} \mod p_2$, $z_{\rho(x)} = t_{\rho(x)} \mod p_3$.

Since $s'_x, t_{\rho(x)}$ are chosen randomly in $\mathbb{Z}_N$, by Chinese Remainder Theorem, $\gamma_x, \psi_x, y_{\rho(x)}, z_{\rho(x)}$ are randomly distributed. In addition, δ_x and σ_x are also well distributed except that the shares of them are 0. We now argue that this looks no difference with shares of a random value to the adversary.

We let R denote the space spanned by rows in V_C. We note that the vector $(1, 0, \ldots, 0)$ does not belong to R. Then there is some vector $\boldsymbol{u}$ meet the condition that $\boldsymbol{u}$ is orthogonal to R but not orthogonal to $(1, 0, \ldots, 0)$. We fix a basis including the vector $\boldsymbol{u}$, and write $b\boldsymbol{w}' = \boldsymbol{w}'' + f\boldsymbol{u} \mod p_2$, where $f \in \mathbb{Z}_{p_2}$ and $\boldsymbol{w}''$ is in the span of the basis elements exclude vector $\boldsymbol{u}$. Since $\boldsymbol{u}$ is not orthogonal to $(1, 0, \ldots, 0)$, the first entry of $b\boldsymbol{w}' \mod p_2$ has a relationship with f. As $\boldsymbol{u}$ is orthogonal to R, the only places $f\boldsymbol{u}$ appears are in equations of the form: $\delta_x + \gamma_x z_{\rho(x)}$. Recall that ρ is injective, each of these equations increase a new unknown $z_{\rho(x)}$ that appears nowhere else as long as $\gamma_x \neq 0 \mod p_2$, and so no information about f is leaked to $\mathcal{A}$. Thus the shares δ_x are properly distributed in $\mathcal{A}$'s view. Similarly, we can prove that σ_x are also properly distributed in $\mathcal{A}$'s view. Observe that, $\mathcal{B}$ perfectly simulates Game_0 when $T \in G_{p_1}$, and Game_1 when $T \in G$. Hence, $\mathcal{B}$ can determine the distribution of T by using $\mathcal{A}$.

Lemma 5 (from $\mathsf{Game}_{2,\eta-1,2}$ to $\mathsf{Game}_{2,\eta,1}$). *For any PPT adversary $\mathcal{A}$, there exists an adversary $\mathcal{B}$ such that* $\left| \mathsf{Adv}_{\mathcal{A}}^{\mathsf{Game}_{2,\eta-1,2}}(\lambda) - \mathsf{Adv}_{\mathcal{A}}^{\mathsf{Game}_{2,\eta,1}}(\lambda) \right| \leq \mathsf{Adv}_{\mathcal{B}}^{Assu2}(\lambda)$.

Proof. The adversary $\mathcal{B}$ gets input $(N, g_1, g_3, X_1 X_2, T)$, where T is from G_{p_1} or $G_{p_1 p_2}$, $\mathcal{B}$ proceeds as follows.

Setup: Pick $\alpha_i, t_i \in \mathbb{Z}_N$, a UF-CMA secure signature scheme $\Sigma_{sign} = $ (KeyGen, Sign, Verify). Output $GPK = \{N, G, G_T, e, g_1, \Sigma_{sign}\}, CPK_j = $ Verifykey$_j$, $APK_j = \{e(g_1, g_1)^{\alpha_i}, g_1^{t_i}\}_{att_i \in U_j}$ In addition, $\{\alpha_i, t_i | att_i \in U \backslash U_1\}$ are given to the adversary $\mathcal{A}$.

Key Queries : We let GID_θ denote the θ'th identity queried by $\mathcal{A}$.

- CKeyGen Query: When $\mathcal{A}$ queries an identity key of GID_θ along with attribute set S_θ, $\mathcal{B}$ chooses random values $r_\theta, c_\theta \in \mathbb{Z}_N$ and outputs

$$SK_{GID_\theta, S_\theta} = \begin{cases} \{GID_\theta, S_\theta, g_1^{r_\theta} g_3^{c_\theta}, k, \mathsf{Sign}(Signkey, *)\} & \theta < \eta \\ \{GID_\theta, S_\theta, T^{r_\theta}, k, \mathsf{Sign}(Signkey, *)\} & \theta = \eta \\ \{GID_\theta, S_\theta, g_1^{r_\theta}, k, \mathsf{Sign}(Signkey, *)\} & \theta > \eta \end{cases}$$

- AKeyGen Query: When $\mathcal{A}$ queries an attribute key of att_i of GID_θ, $\mathcal{B}$ first verifies the signature. If true, then outputs

$$SK_{GID_\theta, i} = \begin{cases} g_1^{\alpha_i} g_1^{r_\theta t_i} g_3^{c_\theta t_i} & \theta < \eta \\ g_1^{\alpha_i} T^{r_\theta t_i} & \theta = \eta \\ g_1^{\alpha_i} g_1^{r_\theta t_i} & \theta > \eta \end{cases}$$

Challenge: Upon receiving challenge m_0, m_1 and $(\mathbf{M}, \rho)$, $\mathcal{B}$ picks a random bit $\beta \in \{0, 1\}$. $\mathcal{B}$ chooses three random vectors $\boldsymbol{v} = (s, v_2, \ldots, v_l)$, $\boldsymbol{w}' = (0, w_2, \ldots, w_l)$ and $\boldsymbol{u}_3$. We let $\lambda_x = \mathbf{M}_x \cdot \boldsymbol{v}$, $w'_x = \mathbf{M}_x \cdot \boldsymbol{w}'$ and $\sigma_x = \mathbf{M}_x \cdot \boldsymbol{u}_3$. For $\mathbf{M}_x \in V_G$, $\mathcal{B}$ chooses random number $s'_x, \psi_x \in \mathbb{Z}_N$. For $\mathbf{M}_x \in V_C$, $\mathcal{B}$ chooses random number $s_x \in \mathbb{Z}_N$. Then set $C_0 = m_\beta \cdot e(g_1, g_1)^s$. For $\mathbf{M}_x \in V_C$, $C_{1,x} = e(g_1, g_1)^{\lambda_x} e(g_1, g_1)^{\alpha_{\rho(x)} s_x}$, $C_{2,x} = g_1^{s_x}$, $C_{3,x} = g_1^{s_x t_{\rho(x)}} (X_1 X_2)^{w'_x} g_3^{\sigma_x}$. For $\mathbf{M}_x \in V_G$, $C_{1,x} = e(g_1, g_1)^{\lambda_x} e(g_1, X_1 X_2)^{\alpha_{\rho(x)} s'_x}$, $C_{2,x} = (X_1 X_2)^{s'_x} g_3^{\psi_x}$, $C_{3,x} = (X_1 X_2)^{s'_x t_{\rho(x)}} (X_1 X_2)^{w'_x} g_3^{\psi_x t_{\rho(x)} + \sigma_x}$.

Suppose that $X_1 X_2 = g_1^a g_2^b$ where a, b are random values. We have $w_x = a w'_x = \mathbf{M}_x \cdot a\boldsymbol{w} \bmod p_1$, $\delta_x = b w'_x = \mathbf{M}_x \cdot b\boldsymbol{w}' \bmod p_2$. For rows in V_G, $s_x = a s'_x \bmod p_1$, $\gamma_x = b s'_x \bmod p_2$, $y_{\rho(x)} = t_{\rho(x)} \bmod p_2$, $z_{\rho(x)} = t_{\rho(x)} \bmod p_3$.

Since $s'_x, t_{\rho(x)}, \psi_x$ are chosen randomly in $\mathbb{Z}_N$, by Chinese Remainder Theorem, $\gamma_x, \psi_x, y_{\rho(x)}, z_{\rho(x)}$ are randomly distributed. σ_x is properly distributed since $\boldsymbol{u}_3$ is a random vector. However, δ_x's are shares of 0. We now argue that this looks no difference with shares of a random value to the adversary.

We let R denote the space spanned by rows in V_C and the rows whose attributes $\rho(x)$ are queried by $\mathcal{A}$ with identity GID_j. We note that the vector $(1, 0, \ldots, 0)$ does not belong to R. Then there is some vector $\boldsymbol{u}$ meet the condition that $\boldsymbol{u}$ is orthogonal to R but not orthogonal to $(1, 0, \ldots, 0)$. We fix a basis including the vector $\boldsymbol{u}$, and write $b\boldsymbol{w}' = \boldsymbol{w}'' + f\boldsymbol{u} \bmod p_2$, where $f \in \mathbb{Z}_{p_2}$ and $\boldsymbol{w}''$ is in the span of the basis elements exclude vector $\boldsymbol{u}$. Since $\boldsymbol{u}$ is not orthogonal to $(1, 0, \ldots, 0)$, the first entry of $b\boldsymbol{w}' \bmod p_2$ has a relationship with f. As $\boldsymbol{u}$ is orthogonal to R, the only places $f\boldsymbol{u}$ appears are in equations of the form: $\delta_x + \gamma_x z_{\rho(x)}$. Recall that ρ is injective, each of these equations increase a new unknown $z_{\rho(x)}$ that appears nowhere else as long as $\gamma_x \neq 0 \bmod p_2$, and so no information about f is leaked to $\mathcal{A}$. Thus the shares δ_x are properly distributed in $\mathcal{A}$'s view. Observe that, $\mathcal{B}$ perfectly simulates $\mathsf{Game}_{2,\eta-1,2}$ when $T \in G_{p_1}$, and $\mathsf{Game}_{2,\eta,1}$ when $T \in G_{p_1 p_2}$. Hence, $\mathcal{B}$ can determine the distribution of T by using adversary $\mathcal{A}$.

Lemma 6 (from $\mathsf{Game}_{2,\eta,1}$ to $\mathsf{Game}_{2,\eta,2}$). *For any PPT adversary $\mathcal{A}$, there exists an adversary $\mathcal{B}$ such that* $\left| \mathsf{Adv}_{\mathcal{A}}^{\mathsf{Game}_{2,\eta,1}}(\lambda) - \mathsf{Adv}_{\mathcal{A}}^{\mathsf{Game}_{2,\eta,2}}(\lambda) \right| \leq \mathsf{Adv}_{\mathcal{B}}^{Assu3}(\lambda)$.

Proof. The adversary $\mathcal{B}$ gets input $(N, g_1, X_1X_3, Y_2Y_3, T)$, where T is from $G_{p_1p_2}$ or $G_{p_1p_3}$, $\mathcal{B}$ proceeds as follows.

Setup: Pick $\alpha_i, t_i \in \mathbb{Z}_N$, a UF-CMA secure signature scheme $\Sigma_{sign} = $ (KeyGen, Sign, Verify). Output $GPK = \{N, G, G_T, e, g_1, \Sigma_{sign}\}, CPK_k = $ Verifykey$_k$, $APK_k = \{e(g_1, g_1)^{\alpha_i}, g_1^{t_i}\}_{att_i \in U_k}$ In addition, $\{\alpha_i, t_i | att_i \in U \backslash U_1\}$ are given to the adversary $\mathcal{A}$.

Key Queries : We let GID_θ denote the θ'th identity queried by $\mathcal{A}$.

- CKeyGen Query: When $\mathcal{A}$ queries an identity key of GID_θ along with attribute set S_θ, $\mathcal{B}$ chooses a random value $r_\theta \in \mathbb{Z}_N$ and outputs

$$SK_{GID_\theta, S_\theta} = \begin{cases} \{GID_\theta, S_\theta, (X_1X_3)^{r_\theta}, k, \mathsf{Sign}(Signkey, *)\} & \theta < \eta \\ \{GID_\theta, S_\theta, T^{r_\theta}, k, \mathsf{Sign}(Signkey, *)\} & \theta = \eta \\ \{GID_\theta, S_\theta, g_1^{r_\theta}, k, \mathsf{Sign}(Signkey, *)\} & \theta > \eta \end{cases}$$

- AKeyGen Query: When $\mathcal{A}$ queries an attribute key of att_i of GID_θ, $\mathcal{B}$ first verifies the signature. If true, then outputs

$$SK_{GID_\theta, i} = \begin{cases} g_1^{\alpha_i}(X_1X_3)^{r_\theta t_i} & \theta < \eta \\ g_1^{\alpha_i}T^{r_\theta t_i} & \theta = \eta \\ g_1^{\alpha_i}g_1^{r_\theta t_i} & \theta > \eta \end{cases}$$

Challenge: Upon receiving challenge m_0, m_1 and $(\mathbf{M}, \rho)$, $\mathcal{B}$ picks a random bit $\beta \in \{0, 1\}$. $\mathcal{B}$ chooses three random vectors $\boldsymbol{v} = (s, v_2, \ldots, v_l)$, $\boldsymbol{w} = (0, w_2, \ldots, w_l)$ and $\boldsymbol{u} = (u_1, \ldots, u_l)$. We let $\lambda_x = \mathbf{M}_x \cdot \boldsymbol{v}$, $w_x = \mathbf{M}_x \cdot \boldsymbol{w}$ and $\delta'_x = \mathbf{M}_x \cdot \boldsymbol{u}$. For each row $\mathbf{M}_x$, $\mathcal{B}$ chooses random number $s_x \in \mathbb{Z}_N$. Then set $C_0 = m_\beta \cdot e(g_1, g_1)^s$. For $\mathbf{M}_x \in V_C$, $C_{1,x} = e(g_1, g_1)^{\lambda_x}e(g_1, g_1)^{\alpha_{\rho(x)}s_x}$, $C_{2,x} = g_1^{s_x}$, $C_{3,x} = g_1^{s_x t_{\rho(x)}}g_1^{w_x}(Y_2Y_3)^{\delta'_x}$. For $\mathbf{M}_x \in V_G$, $C_{1,x} = e(g_1, g_1)^{\lambda_x}e(g_1, g_1)^{\alpha_{\rho(x)}s_x}$, $C_{2,x} = g_1^{s_x}(Y_2Y_3)^{s_x}$, $C_{3,x} = g_1^{s_x t_{\rho(x)}}g_1^{w_x}(Y_2Y_3)^{s_x t_{\rho(x)}+\delta'_x}$.

Suppose that $Y_2Y_3 = g_2^b g_3^c$ where b, c are random values. We have $\delta_x = b\delta'_x = \mathbf{M}_x \cdot b\boldsymbol{u} \bmod p_2$, $\sigma_x = c\delta'_x = \mathbf{M}_x \cdot c\boldsymbol{u} \bmod p_3$, $\gamma_x = bs_x \bmod p_2$, $\psi_x = cs_x \bmod p_3$, $y_{\rho(x)} = t_{\rho(x)} \bmod p_2$, $z_{\rho(x)} = t_{\rho(x)} \bmod p_3$.

Since $s_x, t_{\rho(x)}, \psi_x$ are chosen randomly in $\mathbb{Z}_N$, $\gamma_x, \psi_x, y_{\rho(x)}, z_{\rho(x)}$ are randomly distributed. We note that δ_x, σ_x are also properly distributed since $\boldsymbol{u}$ is a random vector. Observe that, $\mathcal{B}$ perfectly simulates Game$_{2,\eta,1}$ when $T \in G_{p_1p_2}$, and Game$_{2,\eta,2}$ when $T \in G_{p_1p_3}$. Hence, $\mathcal{B}$ can determine the distribution of T by using adversary $\mathcal{A}$.

Lemma 7 (from Game$_{2,q,2}$ to Game$_3$). *For any PPT adversary $\mathcal{A}$, there exists an adversary $\mathcal{B}$ such that* $\left| \mathsf{Adv}_{\mathcal{A}}^{\mathsf{Game}_{2,q,3}}(\lambda) - \mathsf{Adv}_{\mathcal{A}}^{\mathsf{Game}_3}(\lambda) \right| \leq \mathsf{Adv}_{\mathcal{B}}^{Assu4}(\lambda).$

Proof. The adversary $\mathcal{B}$ gets input $(N, g_1, g_2, g_3, g_1^a, g_1^b g_3^b, g_1^c, g_1^{ac}g_3^d, T)$, where $T = e(g, g)^{abc}$ or T is a random element in G_T, $\mathcal{B}$ proceeds as follows.

Setup: We assume that $\mathcal{A}$ corrupts all AAs but AA_1, for each attribute att_i belonging AA_1, $\mathcal{B}$ picks $\alpha'_i, t'_i \in \mathbb{Z}_N$, and implicitly sets $\alpha_i = \alpha'_i + ab, t_i = t'_i + a$. For each attribute att_i belonging to a corrupted authority, $\mathcal{B}$ picks $\alpha_i, t_i \in \mathbb{Z}_N$. $\mathcal{B}$ also chooses a UF-CMA secure signature scheme $\Sigma_{sign} = $ (KeyGen, Sign, Verify) and outputs $GPK = \{N, G, G_T, e, g_1, \Sigma_{sign}\}, CPK_j = \mathsf{Verifykey}_j$,

$$APK_j = \begin{cases} \{e(g_1^a, g_1^b g_3^b)e(g_1, g_1)^{\alpha_i'}, g_1^a g_1^{t_i'}\}_{att_i \in U_j}, & j = 1 \\ \{e(g_1, g_1)^{\alpha_i}, g_1^{t_i}\}_{att_i \in U_j} & j \neq 1 \end{cases}$$

In addition, $\{\alpha_i, t_i | att_i \in U \backslash U_1\}$ are given to the adversary $\mathcal{A}$.

CKeyGen Query : When $\mathcal{A}$ queries an identity key of GID along with attribute set S, $\mathcal{B}$ chooses random values $f, h \in \mathbb{Z}_N$ and outputs
$SK_{GID,S} = \{GID, S, (g_1^b g_3^b)^{-1} g_1^f g_3^h, k, \mathsf{Sign}(Signkey, *)\}$

AKeyGen Query : When $\mathcal{A}$ queries an attribute key of att_i of GID, $\mathcal{B}$ first verifies the signature. If true, then outputs

$$SK_{GID,i} = g_1^{\alpha_i' + ft_i'}(g_1^a)^f (g_1^b g_3^b)^{-t_i'} g_3^{ht_i'} = g_1^\alpha g_1^{(f-b)t_i} g_3^{(h-b)t_i'}$$

Challenge: Upon receiving challenge m_0, m_1 and $(\mathbf{M}, \rho)$, $\mathcal{B}$ picks a random bit $\beta \in \{0,1\}$. $\mathcal{B}$ chooses random vectors $\boldsymbol{v}_1 = (1, v_{1,2}, \ldots, v_{1,l})$ satisfies the condition that $\boldsymbol{v}_1$ is orthogonal to the rows in V_C, $\boldsymbol{v}_2 = (0, v_{2,2}, \ldots, v_{2,l})$, $\boldsymbol{w} = (0, w_2, \ldots, w_l)$ and $\boldsymbol{u} = (u_1, \ldots, u_l)$. We let $\boldsymbol{v} = abc\boldsymbol{v}_1 + \boldsymbol{v}_2$, $\lambda_x = \mathbf{M}_x \cdot \boldsymbol{v}$, $w_x = \mathbf{M}_x \cdot \boldsymbol{w}$ and $\delta_x = \mathbf{M}_x \cdot \boldsymbol{u}$. Then set $C_0 = m_\beta \cdot T$.
For $\mathbf{M}_x \in V_C$, $\mathcal{B}$ chooses random values $s_x \in \mathbb{Z}_N$ and sets
$C_{1,x} = e(g_1, g_1)^{\mathbf{M}_x \cdot \boldsymbol{v}_2} e(g_1, g_1)^{\alpha_{\rho(x)} s_x}$, $C_{2,x} = g_1^{s_x}$, $C_{3,x} = g_1^{s_x t_{\rho(x)}} g_1^{w_x}(g_2 g_3)^{\delta_x}$.
For $\mathbf{M}_x \in V_G$, $\mathcal{B}$ chooses random values $s_x', \gamma_x \in \mathbb{Z}_N$ and implicitly sets
$s_x = -c\mathbf{M}_x \cdot \boldsymbol{v}_1 + s_x'$, then outputs
$C_{1,x} = e(g_1, g_1^c)^{-\alpha_{\rho(x)}' \mathbf{M}_x \cdot \boldsymbol{v}_1} e(g_1^a, g_1^b g_3^b)^{s_x'} e(g_1, g_1)^{\mathbf{M}_x \cdot \boldsymbol{v}_2 + \alpha_{\rho(x)}' s_x'}$,
$C_{2,x} = (g_1^c)^{-\mathbf{M}_x \cdot \boldsymbol{v}_1 + s_x'}(g_2 g_3)^{\gamma_x}$,
$C_{3,x} = g_1^{w_x}(g_1^c)^{-t_{\rho(x)}' \mathbf{M}_x \cdot \boldsymbol{v}_1}(g_1^a)^{s_x'} g_1^{t_{\rho(x)}' s_x'}(g_1^{ac} g_3^d)^{-\mathbf{M}_x \cdot \boldsymbol{v}_1}(g_2 g_3)^{\gamma_x t_{\rho(x)}' + \delta_x}$.

If $T = e(g_1, g_1)^{abc}$, then this is a well distributed semi-functional ciphertext of m_β with $s = abc$. If T is a random element in G_T, then this is a semi-functional ciphertext of a random message. Observe that, $\mathcal{B}$ perfectly simulates $\mathsf{Game}_{2,q,2}$ when $T = e(g_1, g_1)^{abc}$, and Game_3 when T is a random element in G_T. Hence, $\mathcal{B}$ can determine the distribution of T by using adversary $\mathcal{A}$.

B   Proof of Security for Scheme II

We first define two auxiliary algorithms and then the semi-functional distributions via these auxiliary algorithms.

Auxiliary algorithms
$\widehat{\mathsf{Enc}}(pp, m, Y; g_2^{k_i}, \boldsymbol{t})$: On input $\boldsymbol{t} := (T_0, T_1, \ldots, T_n) \in \mathbb{G}^{n+1}$, output

$$C_0 = m \cdot \prod_{att_i \in \Omega} e(T_0, g_2^{k_i}), C_1 = \prod_{att_i \in \Omega} T_i, C_2 = T_0$$

$\widehat{\mathsf{CKeyGen}}(pp, CSK, GID, S; \boldsymbol{t})$: On input $\boldsymbol{t} := (T_0, \ldots, T_n) \in \mathbb{H}^{n+1}$, output

$$SK_{GID,S} = \{GID, S, T_0, \mathsf{Sign}(Signkey, GID\|S\|T_0)\}$$

$\mathsf{AKeyGen}(\mathrm{pp}, CPK, g_2^{k_i}, SK_{GID,S}, att_i; \boldsymbol{t})$: On input $\boldsymbol{t} := (T_0, \dots, T_n) \in \mathbb{H}^{n+1}$, output $SK_{GID,i} = g_2^{k_i} \cdot T_i$

Auxiliary distributions

Normal ciphertext: $\widehat{\mathsf{Enc}}(\mathrm{pp}, m, Y; g_2^{k_i}, \boldsymbol{g})$, where $\boldsymbol{g} \leftarrow \mathsf{SampG}(\mathrm{pp})$.

Semi-functional ciphertext: $\widehat{\mathsf{Enc}}(\mathrm{pp}, m, Y; g_2^{k_i}, \boxed{\boldsymbol{g} \cdot \hat{\boldsymbol{g}}})$, where $\boldsymbol{g} \leftarrow \mathsf{SampG}(\mathrm{pp})$, $\hat{\boldsymbol{g}} \leftarrow \widehat{\mathsf{SampG}}(\mathrm{pp}, \mathrm{sp})$.

Normal secret key:

$$SK_{GID,S} = \widehat{\mathsf{CKeyGen}}(\mathrm{pp}, CSK, GID, S; \boldsymbol{h}),$$

$$SK_{GID,i} = \widehat{\mathsf{AKeyGen}}(\mathrm{pp}, CPK, g_2^{k_i}, SK_{GID,S}, att_i; \boldsymbol{h}),$$

where $\boldsymbol{h} \leftarrow \mathsf{SampH}(\mathrm{pp})$.

Pseudo-normal secret key:

$$SK_{GID,S} = \widehat{\mathsf{CKeyGen}}(\mathrm{pp}, CSK, GID, S; \boxed{\boldsymbol{h} \cdot \hat{\boldsymbol{h}}}),$$

$$SK_{GID,i} = \widehat{\mathsf{AKeyGen}}(\mathrm{pp}, CPK, g_2^{k_i}, SK_{GID,S}, att_i; \boxed{\boldsymbol{h} \cdot \hat{\boldsymbol{h}}}),$$

where $\boldsymbol{h} \leftarrow \mathsf{SampH}(\mathrm{pp}), \hat{\boldsymbol{h}} \leftarrow \widehat{\mathsf{SampH}}(\mathrm{pp}, \mathrm{sp})$.

Pseudo-semi-functional secret key:

$$SK_{GID,S} = \widehat{\mathsf{CKeyGen}}(\mathrm{pp}, CSK, GID, S; \boldsymbol{h} \cdot \hat{\boldsymbol{h}}),$$

$$SK_{GID,i} = \widehat{\mathsf{AKeyGen}}(\mathrm{pp}, CPK, \boxed{g_2^{k_i} \cdot (h^*)^{\alpha_i}}, SK_{GID,S}, att_i; \boldsymbol{h} \cdot \hat{\boldsymbol{h}}),$$

where $\boldsymbol{h} \leftarrow \mathsf{SampH}(\mathrm{pp}), \hat{\boldsymbol{h}} \leftarrow \widehat{\mathsf{SampH}}(\mathrm{pp}, \mathrm{sp}), \alpha_i \leftarrow \mathbb{Z}_p$.

Semi-functional secret key:

$$SK_{GID,S} = \widehat{\mathsf{CKeyGen}}(\mathrm{pp}, CSK, GID, S; \boxed{\boldsymbol{h}}),$$

$$SK_{GID,i} = \widehat{\mathsf{AKeyGen}}(\mathrm{pp}, CPK, g_2^{k_i} \cdot (h^*)^{\alpha_i}, SK_{GID,S}, att_i; \boxed{\boldsymbol{h}}),$$

where $\boldsymbol{h} \leftarrow \mathsf{SampH}(\mathrm{pp}), \alpha_i \leftarrow \mathbb{Z}_p$.

Game Sequence. We let $\mathsf{Adv}_{\mathcal{A}}^{\mathsf{Game}_X}$ denote the advantage of $\mathcal{A}$ in Game_X.

- Game_0: the real security game.
- Game_1: the challenge ciphertext becomes semi-functional.
- $\mathsf{Game}_{2,\eta,1}$ for $\eta = 1, \dots, q$: the first η-1 queried identities, the received keys become semi-functional, and the received key for the η'th queried identity becomes pseudo-normal.
- $\mathsf{Game}_{2,\eta,2}$ for $\eta = 1, \dots, q$: the first η-1 queried identities, the received keys become semi-functional, and the received key for the η'th queried identity becomes pseudo-semi-functional.
- $\mathsf{Game}_{2,\eta,3}$ for $\eta = 0, \dots, q$: the first η queried identities, the received keys become semi-functional. We let $\mathsf{Game}_{2,0,3}$ denote Game_1.

– Game$_3$: generate a semi-functional ciphertext of a random message $m' \in \mathbb{G}_T$ as the challenge ciphertext.

Theorem 2 is accomplished in the following lemmas.

Lemma 8 (from Game$_0$ to Game$_1$). *For any* PPT *adversary* $\mathcal{A}$, *there exists an adversary* $\mathcal{B}$ *such that* $\left| \mathsf{Adv}_{\mathcal{A}}^{\mathsf{Game}_0}(\lambda) - \mathsf{Adv}_{\mathcal{A}}^{\mathsf{Game}_1}(\lambda) \right| \leq \mathsf{Adv}_{\mathcal{B}}^{LS}(\lambda)$.

Proof. The adversary $\mathcal{B}$ gets input (pp, t), where t is g or $g \cdot \hat{g}$ with $g \leftarrow \mathsf{SampG}(\mathsf{pp})$ and $\hat{g} \leftarrow \widehat{\mathsf{SampG}}(\mathsf{pp}, \mathsf{sp})$, $\mathcal{B}$ proceeds as follows:
Setup: Pick $\boldsymbol{k}_i \leftarrow \mathbb{H}$, a UF-CMA secure signature scheme $\Sigma_{sign} = (\mathsf{KeyGen}, \mathsf{Sign}, \mathsf{Verify})$, and for those attributes belong to corrupted authorities, pick $\mathbf{W}_i \leftarrow \mathbb{Z}_p^{(k+1)\times(k+1)}$. Output $GPK = \{p, G_1^{k+1}, G_2^{k+1}, G_T, e; g_1^{\mathbf{A}}, g_2^{\mathbf{B}}, \Sigma_{sign}\}$, $CPK_j = Verifykey_j$, $APK_j = \{e(g_1, g_2)^{\boldsymbol{k}_i^{\top}\mathbf{A}}, g_1^{\mathbf{W}_i\mathbf{A}}\}_{att_i \in U_j}$ In addition, $\{\boldsymbol{k}_i, \mathbf{W}_i | att_i \in U \backslash U_1\}$ are given to the adversary $\mathcal{A}$.
Key Queries : In this phase, $\mathcal{A}$ queries on two occasions

– CKeyGen Query : When $\mathcal{A}$ queries an identity key of GID along with attribute set S, $\mathcal{B}$ sample $\boldsymbol{h} \leftarrow \mathsf{SampH}(\mathsf{pp})$ and stores $(GID, S, \boldsymbol{h})$ so that it can respond consistently. Then, $\mathcal{B}$ outputs $SK_{GID,S} = \widehat{\mathsf{CKeyGen}}(\mathsf{pp}, CSK, GID, S; \boldsymbol{h})$
– AKeyGen Query : When $\mathcal{A}$ queries an attribute key of att_i of GID, $\mathcal{B}$ first verifies the signature. Then outputs $SK_{GID,i} = \widehat{\mathsf{AKeyGen}}(\mathsf{pp}, CPK, g_2^{\boldsymbol{k}_i}, SK_{GID,S}, att_i; \boldsymbol{h})$

Challenge: Upon receiving challenge (Y^*, M_0, M_1), pick a random bit $\beta \in \{0, 1\}$ and output $CT_{Y^*} = \widehat{\mathsf{Enc}}(\mathsf{pp}, M_\beta, Y^*; g_2^{\boldsymbol{k}_i}, t)$.
Observe that, $\mathcal{B}$ perfectly simulates Game$_0$ when $t = g$, and Game$_1$ when $t = g \cdot \hat{g}$. Hence, $\mathcal{B}$ can determine the distribution of t by using adversary $\mathcal{A}$.

Lemma 9 (from Game$_{2,\eta-1,3}$ to Game$_{2,\eta,1}$). *For any* PPT *adversary* $\mathcal{A}$, *there exists an adversary* $\mathcal{B}$ *such that* $\left| \mathsf{Adv}_{\mathcal{A}}^{\mathsf{Game}_{2,\eta-1,3}}(\lambda) - \mathsf{Adv}_{\mathcal{A}}^{\mathsf{Game}_{2,\eta,1}}(\lambda) \right| \leq \mathsf{Adv}_{\mathcal{B}}^{RS}(\lambda)$.

Proof. Given $(\mathsf{pp}, h^*, g \cdot \hat{g}, t)$, where t is either $\boldsymbol{h}$ or $\boldsymbol{h} \cdot \hat{\boldsymbol{h}}$ with $\boldsymbol{h} \leftarrow \mathsf{SampH}(\mathsf{pp})$ and $\hat{\boldsymbol{h}} \leftarrow \widehat{\mathsf{SampH}}(\mathsf{pp}, \mathsf{sp})$, $\mathcal{B}$ proceeds as follows.
Setup: Pick $\boldsymbol{k}_i \leftarrow \mathbb{H}$, a UF-CMA secure signature scheme $\Sigma_{sign} = (\mathsf{KeyGen}, \mathsf{Sign}, \mathsf{Verify})$, and for those attributes belong to corrupted authorities, pick $\mathbf{W}_i \leftarrow \mathbb{Z}_p^{(k+1)\times(k+1)}$. Output $GPK = \{p, G_1^{k+1}, G_2^{k+1}, G_T, e; g_1^{\mathbf{A}}, g_2^{\mathbf{B}}, \Sigma_{sign}\}$, $CPK_j = Verifykey_j$, $APK_j = \{e(g_1, g_2)^{\boldsymbol{k}_i^{\top}\mathbf{A}}, g_1^{\mathbf{W}_i\mathbf{A}}\}_{att_i \in U_j}$. In addition, $\{\boldsymbol{k}_i, \mathbf{W}_i | att_i \in U/U_1\}$ are given to the adversary $\mathcal{A}$.
Key Queries : We let GID_θ denote the θ'th identity queried by $\mathcal{A}$.

– CKeyGen Query : When $\mathcal{A}$ queries an identity key of GID_θ along with attribute set S_θ, $\mathcal{B}$ samples $\boldsymbol{h}_\theta \leftarrow \mathsf{SampH}(\mathsf{pp})$ and outputs

$$SK_{GID_\theta, S_\theta} = \begin{cases} \widehat{\mathsf{CKeyGen}}(\mathsf{pp}, CSK, GID_\theta, S_\theta; \boldsymbol{h}_\theta) & \theta \neq \eta \\ \widehat{\mathsf{CKeyGen}}(\mathsf{pp}, CSK, GID_\theta, S_\theta; t) & \theta = \eta \end{cases}$$

- AKeyGen Query : When $\mathcal{A}$ queries an attribute key of att_i of GID_θ, $\mathcal{B}$ first verifies the signature. If true, then outputs

$$SK_{GID_j,i} = \begin{cases} \widehat{\mathsf{AKeyGen}}(\mathsf{pp}, CPK, g_2^{k_i} \cdot (h^*)^{\alpha_i}, SK_{GID_\theta,S_\theta}, att_i; \boldsymbol{h_\theta}) & \theta < \eta \\ \widehat{\mathsf{AKeyGen}}(\mathsf{pp}, CPK, g_2^{k_i}, SK_{GID_\theta,S_\theta}, att_i; \boldsymbol{t}) & \theta = \eta \\ \widehat{\mathsf{AKeyGen}}(\mathsf{pp}, CPK, g_2^{k_i}, SK_{GID_\theta,S_\theta}, att_i; \boldsymbol{h_\theta}) & \theta > \eta \end{cases}$$

Challenge : Upon receiving challenge (Y^*, m_0, m_1), pick a random bit $\beta \in \{0,1\}$ and output $CT_{Y^*} = \widehat{\mathsf{Enc}}(\mathsf{pp}, m_\beta, Y^*; \boldsymbol{k_i}, \boldsymbol{g} \cdot \hat{\boldsymbol{g}})$.

Observe that, $\mathcal{B}$ perfectly simulates $\mathsf{Game}_{2,\eta,3}$ when $\boldsymbol{t} = \boldsymbol{h}$, and $\mathsf{Game}_{2,\eta,1}$ when $\boldsymbol{t} = \boldsymbol{h} \cdot \hat{\boldsymbol{h}}$. Hence, $\mathcal{B}$ can determine the distribution of $\boldsymbol{t}$ by using adversary $\mathcal{A}$.

Lemma 10 (from $\mathsf{Game}_{2,\eta,1}$ to $\mathsf{Game}_{2,\eta,2}$). *For $\eta = 1, \ldots, q$, we have*

$$\left| \mathsf{Adv}_{\mathcal{A}}^{\mathsf{Game}_{2,\eta,1}}(\lambda) - \mathsf{Adv}_{\mathcal{A}}^{\mathsf{Game}_{2,\eta,2}}(\lambda) \right| = 0.$$

Proof. Setup : $\mathcal{A}$ specifies a set of corrupt authorities. For each attribute att_i belongs to a corrupted authority, $\mathcal{B}$ picks $\mathbf{W}_i \leftarrow \mathbb{Z}_p^{(k+1)\times(k+1)}$. Given $(\mathsf{pp}, \boldsymbol{k_i}, (h^*)^{\alpha_i})$, and a UF-CMA secure signature scheme $\Sigma_{sign} = (\mathsf{KeyGen}, \mathsf{Sign}, \mathsf{Verify})$, we can output $GPK = \{p, G_1^{k+1}, G_2^{k+1}, G_T, e; g_1^{\mathbf{A}}, g_2^{\mathbf{B}}, \Sigma_{sign}\}, CPK_j = Verifykey_j, APK_j = \{e(g_1, g_2)^{k_i^\top \mathbf{A}}, g_1^{\mathbf{W}_i \mathbf{A}}\}_{att_i \in U_j}, \{\boldsymbol{k_i}, \mathbf{W}_i | att_i \in U/U_1\}$ are given to $\mathcal{A}$.

Key Queries : We let GID_θ denote the θ'th identity queried by $\mathcal{A}$. When $\mathcal{A}$ queries an identity key of GID_θ along with attribute set S_θ, $\mathcal{B}$ samples $\boldsymbol{h_\theta} \leftarrow \mathsf{SampH}(\mathsf{pp})$. For $\theta < \eta$, $\mathcal{B}$ answers the queries $SK_{GID_\theta,S_\theta} = \widehat{\mathsf{CKeyGen}}(\mathsf{pp}, CSK, GID_\theta, S_\theta; \boldsymbol{h_\theta})$, $SK_{GID_\theta,i} = \widehat{\mathsf{AKeyGen}}(\mathsf{pp}, CPK, g_2^{k_i} \cdot (h^*)^{\alpha_i}, SK_{GID_\theta,S_\theta}, att_i; \boldsymbol{h_\theta})$. For $\theta > \eta$, $\mathcal{B}$ answers the queries $SK_{GID_\theta,S_\theta} = \widehat{\mathsf{CKeyGen}}(\mathsf{pp}, CSK, GID_\theta, S_\theta; \boldsymbol{h_\theta})$,
$SK_{GID_\theta,i} = \widehat{\mathsf{AKeyGen}}(\mathsf{pp}, CPK, g_2^{k_i}, SK_{GID_\theta,S_\theta}, att_i; \boldsymbol{h_\theta})$.
For $\theta = \eta$, $\mathcal{B}$ answers the key queries by using

$$SK_{GID_\theta,S_\theta} = \widehat{\mathsf{CKeyGen}}(\mathsf{pp}, CSK, GID_\theta, S_\theta; \boldsymbol{h} \cdot \hat{\boldsymbol{h}})$$

$$SK_{GID_\theta,i} = \widehat{\mathsf{AKeyGen}}(\mathsf{pp}, CPK, g_2^{k_i}, SK_{GID_\theta,S_\theta}, att_i; \boldsymbol{h} \cdot \hat{\boldsymbol{h}})$$

$$\text{or } SK_{GID_\theta,i} = \widehat{\mathsf{AKeyGen}}(\mathsf{pp}, CPK, g_2^{k_i} \cdot (h^*)^{\alpha_i}, SK_{GID_\theta,S_\theta}, att_i; \boldsymbol{h} \cdot \hat{\boldsymbol{h}})$$

Challenge : Upon receiving challenge (Y^*, m_0, m_1), pick a random bit $\beta \in \{0,1\}$ and output

$$CT_{Y^*} = \widehat{\mathsf{Enc}}(\mathsf{pp}, m_\beta, Y^*; g_2^{k_i}, \boldsymbol{g} \cdot \hat{\boldsymbol{g}})$$

By linearity, we rewrite the η'th key and the challenge ciphertext as follows:

$$\widehat{\mathsf{Enc}}(\mathsf{pp}, m_\beta, Y^*; g_2^{\boldsymbol{k}_i}, \boldsymbol{g} \cdot \hat{\boldsymbol{g}}) = \widehat{\mathsf{Enc}}(\mathsf{pp}, m_\beta, Y^*; g_2^{\boldsymbol{k}_i}, g) \cdot \widehat{\mathsf{Enc}}(\mathsf{pp}, 1, Y^*; g_2^{\boldsymbol{k}_i}, \hat{\boldsymbol{g}})$$

$$\widehat{\mathsf{AKeyGen}}(\mathsf{pp}, CPK, g_2^{\boldsymbol{k}_i}, SK_{GID_\eta, S_\eta}, att_i; \boldsymbol{h} \cdot \hat{\boldsymbol{h}})$$

$$= \widehat{\mathsf{AKeyGen}}(\mathsf{pp}, CPK, g_2^{\boldsymbol{k}_i}, SK_{GID_\eta S_\eta}, att_i; h) \cdot \widehat{\mathsf{AKeyGen}}(\mathsf{pp}, CPK, 1, SK_{GID_\eta, S_\eta}, att_i; \hat{h})$$

$$\widehat{\mathsf{AKeyGen}}(\mathsf{pp}, CPK, g_2^{\boldsymbol{k}_i} \cdot (h^*)^{\alpha_i}, SK_{GID_\eta, S_\eta}, att_i; \boldsymbol{h})$$

$$= \widehat{\mathsf{AKeyGen}}(\mathsf{pp}, CPK, g_2^{\boldsymbol{k}_i}, SK_{GID_\eta S_\eta}, att_i; h) \cdot \widehat{\mathsf{AKeyGen}}(\mathsf{pp}, CPK, (h^*)^{\alpha_i}, SK_{GID_\eta, S_\eta}, att_i; \hat{h})$$

By parameter-hiding, we may replace $(\mathsf{pp}, h^*, \hat{\boldsymbol{g}}, \hat{\boldsymbol{h}})$ with $(\mathsf{pp}, h^*, \hat{\boldsymbol{g}} \cdot \hat{\boldsymbol{g}}', \hat{\boldsymbol{h}} \cdot \hat{\boldsymbol{h}}')$. We expand $\widehat{\mathsf{Enc}}$ and $\widehat{\mathsf{AKeyGen}}$ as follows:

$$\widehat{\mathsf{Enc}}(\mathsf{pp}, 1, Y^*; g_2^{\boldsymbol{k}_i}, \hat{\boldsymbol{g}} \cdot \hat{\boldsymbol{g}}') = \{C_0 = \prod_{att_i \in \Omega} e(\hat{g}_0, g_2^{\boldsymbol{k}_i}), C_1 = \hat{g}_0^{\sum_{att_i \in \Omega} \hat{u}_i} \cdot \prod_{att_i \in \Omega} \hat{g}_i, C_2 = \hat{g}_0\}$$

$$\widehat{\mathsf{AKeyGen}}(\mathsf{pp}, CPK, 1, SK_{GID_\eta, S_\eta}, att_i; \hat{\boldsymbol{h}} \cdot \hat{\boldsymbol{h}}') = \hat{h}_i \cdot \hat{h}_0^{\hat{u}_i}$$

$$\widehat{\mathsf{AKeyGen}}(\mathsf{pp}, CPK, (h^*)^{\alpha_i}, SK_{GID_\eta, S_\eta}, att_i; \hat{\boldsymbol{h}} \cdot \hat{\boldsymbol{h}}') = (h^*)^{\alpha_i} \hat{h}_i \cdot \hat{h}_0^{\hat{u}_i} = \hat{h}_i \cdot \hat{h}_0^{\alpha_i' + \hat{u}_i}$$

As the attribute in $S_\eta \cup V$ cannot satisfies Y^*, there must exists some other attributes appeared in C_1 except the attribute appeared in S_η. That is to say, $\{\hat{u}_i | att_i \in U_1\}$ are hidden from $\mathcal{A}$, and α_i' are perfectly hided by $\hat{u}_i$. The lemma then follows readily.

Lemma 11 (from $\mathsf{Game}_{2,\eta,2}$ to $\mathsf{Game}_{2,\eta,3}$). *For any PPT adversary $\mathcal{A}$, there exists an adversary $\mathcal{B}$ such that* $\left| \mathsf{Adv}_{\mathcal{A}}^{\mathsf{Game}_{2,\eta,2}}(\lambda) - \mathsf{Adv}_{\mathcal{A}}^{\mathsf{Game}_{2,\eta,3}}(\lambda) \right| \leq \mathsf{Adv}_{\mathcal{B}}^{RS}(\lambda).$

Proof. The proof is analogous to Lemma 9.

Lemma 12 (from $\mathsf{Game}_{2,q,3}$ to Game_3). *For any PPT adversary $\mathcal{A}$, there exists an adversary $\mathcal{B}$ such that* $\left| \mathsf{Adv}_{\mathcal{A}}^{\mathsf{Game}_{2,q,3}}(\lambda) - \mathsf{Adv}_{\mathcal{A}}^{\mathsf{Game}_3}(\lambda) \right| = 0.$

Proof. Setup: For each $att_i \in U_1$, $\mathcal{B}$ picks $\hat{\boldsymbol{k}}_i \leftarrow_R \mathbb{H}, \alpha_i \leftarrow_R \mathbb{Z}_p$, and set $g_2^{\boldsymbol{k}_i} = g_2^{\hat{\boldsymbol{k}}_i} \cdot (h^*)^{-\alpha_i}$. For other attributes, $\mathcal{B}$ picks $\boldsymbol{k}_i \leftarrow_R \mathbb{H}$. A UF-CMA secure signature scheme $\Sigma_{sign} = (\mathsf{KeyGen}, \mathsf{Sign}, \mathsf{Verify})$ is chosen. Output $GPK = \{p, G_1^{k+1}, G_2^{k+1}, G_T, e; g_1^{\mathbf{A}}, g_2^{\mathbf{B}}, \Sigma_{sign}\}, CPK_j = Verifykey_j, APK_j = \{e(g_1, g_2)^{\boldsymbol{k}_i^{\top}\mathbf{A}}, g_1^{\mathbf{W}_i \mathbf{A}}\}_{att_i \in U_j}$. In addition, $\{\boldsymbol{k}_i, \mathbf{W}_i | att_i \in U/U_1\}$ are given to the adversary $\mathcal{A}$.

Key Queries : For the j'th query, output $SK_{GID,S} = \widehat{\mathsf{CKeyGen}}(CSK, GID, S; h)$. When $\mathcal{A}$ queries an attribute key of att_i of GID, $\mathcal{B}$ first verifies the signature. If true, then outputs $SK_{GID,i} = \widehat{\mathsf{AKeyGen}}(\mathsf{pp}, CPK, g_2^{\hat{\boldsymbol{k}}_i}, SK_{GID,S}, att_i; h)$.

Challenge : Upon receiving challenge (Y^*, m_0, m_1), pick a random bit $\beta \in \{0,1\}$ and output $C_0 = m_\beta \cdot \prod\limits_{att_i \in \Omega} e(g_1^{\mathbf{A}s+b^\perp \hat{s}}, g_2^{k_i}), C_1 = \prod\limits_{att_i \in \Omega} g_1^{\mathbf{W}_i^\top (\mathbf{A}s+b^\perp \hat{s})}$, $C_2 = g_1^{\mathbf{A}s+b^\perp \hat{s}}$ We note that $U_1 \cap \Omega \neq \Phi$, there must exist at least one attribute in U_1. Then we have

$$C_0 = m_\beta \cdot \prod_{att_i \in \Omega/U_1} e(g_1^{\mathbf{A}s+b^\perp \hat{s}}, g_2^{k_i}) \cdot \prod_{att_i \in U_1} e(g_1^{\mathbf{A}s+b^\perp \hat{s}}, g_2^{k_i})$$

$$= m_\beta \cdot \prod_{att_i \in \Omega/U_1} e(g_1^{\mathbf{A}s+b^\perp \hat{s}}, g_2^{k_i}) \cdot \prod_{att_i \in U_1} e(g_1^{\mathbf{A}s+b^\perp \hat{s}}, g_2^{\hat{k}_i}) \cdot \prod_{att_i \in U_1} e(g_1^{b^\perp \hat{s}}, g_2^{a^\perp})^{-\alpha_i}.$$

Recall that $(\mathsf{pp}, \hat{k}_i, \boldsymbol{g} \cdot \hat{\boldsymbol{g}})$ are all statistically independent of $\alpha_i \leftarrow \mathbb{Z}_p$, then $\prod\limits_{att_i \in U_1} e(g_1^{b^\perp \hat{s}}, g_2^{a^\perp})^{-\alpha_i}$ distributes uniformly in $\mathbb{G}_T$. This means that the distribution of challenge ciphertext and a semi-functional encryption of a random message are identical. Hence, $\left| \mathsf{Adv}_{\mathcal{A}}^{\mathsf{Game}_{2,q,3}}(\lambda) - \mathsf{Adv}_{\mathcal{A}}^{\mathsf{Game}_3}(\lambda) \right| = 0.$

References

1. Bethencourt, J., Sahai, A., Waters, B.: Ciphertext-policy attribute-based encryption. In: 2007 IEEE Symposium on Security and Privacy (SP 2007), pp. 321–334. IEEE Press, Oakland (2007)
2. Boneh, D., Goh, E.-J., Nissim, K.: Evaluating 2-DNF formulas on ciphertexts. In: Kilian, J. (ed.) TCC 2005. LNCS, vol. 3378, pp. 325–341. Springer, Heidelberg (2005). https://doi.org/10.1007/978-3-540-30576-7_18
3. Chase, M.: Multi-authority attribute based encryption. In: Vadhan, S.P. (ed.) TCC 2007. LNCS, vol. 4392, pp. 515–534. Springer, Heidelberg (2007). https://doi.org/10.1007/978-3-540-70936-7_28
4. Chase, M., Chow, S.S.: Improving privacy and security in multi-authority attribute-based encryption. In: Proceedings of the 16th ACM Conference on Computer and Communications Security, CCS 2009, pp. 121–130. ACM, New York (2009)
5. Chen, C., Zhang, Z., Feng, D.: Efficient ciphertext policy attribute-based encryption with constant-size ciphertext and constant computation-cost. In: Boyen, X., Chen, X. (eds.) ProvSec 2011. LNCS, vol. 6980, pp. 84–101. Springer, Heidelberg (2011). https://doi.org/10.1007/978-3-642-24316-5_8
6. Chen, J., Gay, R., Wee, H.: Improved dual system ABE in prime-order groups via predicate encodings. In: Oswald, E., Fischlin, M. (eds.) EUROCRYPT 2015. LNCS, vol. 9057, pp. 595–624. Springer, Heidelberg (2015). https://doi.org/10.1007/978-3-662-46803-6_20
7. Cheung, L., Newport, C.: Provably secure ciphertext policy ABE. In: Proceedings of the 14th ACM Conference on Computer and Communications Security, CCS 2007, pp. 456–465. ACM, New York (2007)
8. Goyal, V., Jain, A., Pandey, O., Sahai, A.: Bounded ciphertext policy attribute based encryption. In: Aceto, L., Damgård, I., Goldberg, L.A., Halldórsson, M.M., Ingólfsdóttir, A., Walukiewicz, I. (eds.) ICALP 2008, Part II. LNCS, vol. 5126, pp. 579–591. Springer, Heidelberg (2008). https://doi.org/10.1007/978-3-540-70583-3_47

9. Goyal, V., Pandey, O., Sahai, A., Waters, B.: Attribute-based encryption for fine-grained access control of encrypted data. In: Proceedings of the 13th ACM Conference on Computer and Communications Security, CCS 2006, pp. 89–98. ACM, New York (2006)

10. Guillevic, A.: Comparing the pairing efficiency over composite-order and prime-order elliptic curves. In: Jacobson, M., Locasto, M., Mohassel, P., Safavi-Naini, R. (eds.) ACNS 2013. LNCS, vol. 7954, pp. 357–372. Springer, Heidelberg (2013). https://doi.org/10.1007/978-3-642-38980-1_22

11. Lewko, A., Okamoto, T., Sahai, A., Takashima, K., Waters, B.: Fully secure functional encryption: attribute-based encryption and (hierarchical) inner product encryption. In: Gilbert, H. (ed.) EUROCRYPT 2010. LNCS, vol. 6110, pp. 62–91. Springer, Heidelberg (2010). https://doi.org/10.1007/978-3-642-13190-5_4

12. Lewko, A., Waters, B.: New techniques for dual system encryption and fully secure HIBE with short ciphertexts. In: Micciancio, D. (ed.) TCC 2010. LNCS, vol. 5978, pp. 455–479. Springer, Heidelberg (2010). https://doi.org/10.1007/978-3-642-11799-2_27

13. Lewko, A., Waters, B.: Decentralizing attribute-based encryption. In: Paterson, K.G. (ed.) EUROCRYPT 2011. LNCS, vol. 6632, pp. 568–588. Springer, Heidelberg (2011). https://doi.org/10.1007/978-3-642-20465-4_31

14. Lin, H., Cao, Z., Liang, X., Shao, J.: Secure threshold multi authority attribute based encryption without a central authority. In: Chowdhury, D.R., Rijmen, V., Das, A. (eds.) INDOCRYPT 2008. LNCS, vol. 5365, pp. 426–436. Springer, Heidelberg (2008). https://doi.org/10.1007/978-3-540-89754-5_33

15. Liu, Z., Cao, Z., Huang, Q., Wong, D.S., Yuen, T.H.: Fully secure multi-authority ciphertext-policy attribute-based encryption without random oracles. In: Atluri, V., Diaz, C. (eds.) ESORICS 2011. LNCS, vol. 6879, pp. 278–297. Springer, Heidelberg (2011). https://doi.org/10.1007/978-3-642-23822-2_16

16. Müller, S., Katzenbeisser, S., Eckert, C.: Distributed attribute-based encryption. In: Lee, P.J., Cheon, J.H. (eds.) ICISC 2008. LNCS, vol. 5461, pp. 20–36. Springer, Heidelberg (2009). https://doi.org/10.1007/978-3-642-00730-9_2

17. Okamoto, T., Takashima, K.: Fully secure functional encryption with general relations from the decisional linear assumption. In: Rabin, T. (ed.) CRYPTO 2010. LNCS, vol. 6223, pp. 191–208. Springer, Heidelberg (2010). https://doi.org/10.1007/978-3-642-14623-7_11

18. Okamoto, T., Takashima, K.: Decentralized attribute-based signatures. In: Kurosawa, K., Hanaoka, G. (eds.) PKC 2013. LNCS, vol. 7778, pp. 125–142. Springer, Heidelberg (2013). https://doi.org/10.1007/978-3-642-36362-7_9

19. Sahai, A., Waters, B.: Fuzzy identity-based encryption. In: Cramer, R. (ed.) EUROCRYPT 2005. LNCS, vol. 3494, pp. 457–473. Springer, Heidelberg (2005). https://doi.org/10.1007/11426639_27

20. Waters, B.: Dual system encryption: realizing fully secure IBE and HIBE under simple assumptions. In: Halevi, S. (ed.) CRYPTO 2009. LNCS, vol. 5677, pp. 619–636. Springer, Heidelberg (2009). https://doi.org/10.1007/978-3-642-03356-8_36

21. Waters, B.: Ciphertext-policy attribute-based encryption: an expressive, efficient, and provably secure realization. In: Catalano, D., Fazio, N., Gennaro, R., Nicolosi, A. (eds.) PKC 2011. LNCS, vol. 6571, pp. 53–70. Springer, Heidelberg (2011). https://doi.org/10.1007/978-3-642-19379-8_4

Outsourced Ciphertext-Policy Attribute-Based Encryption with Equality Test

Yuzhao Cui[1], Qiong Huang[1(✉)], Jianye Huang[1], Hongbo Li[1], and Guomin Yang[2]

[1] College of Mathematics and Informatics, South China Agricultural University, Guangzhou 510642, China
qhuang@scau.edu.cn
[2] School of Computing and Information Technology, University of Wollongong, Wollongong, NSW 2522, Australia

Abstract. In the cloud era people get used to store their data to the cloud server, and would use encryption technique to protect their sensitive data from leakage. However, encrypted data management is a challenging problem, for example, encrypted data classification. Besides, how to effectively control the access to the encrypted data is also an important problem. Ciphertext-policy attribute-based encryption with equality test (CP-ABEET) is an efficient solution to the aforementioned problems, which enjoys the advantage of attribute-based encryption, and in the meanwhile supports the test of whether two different ciphertexts contain the same message without the need of decryption. However, the existing CP-ABEET schemes suffer from high computation costs. In this paper, we study how to outsource the heavy computation in CP-ABEET scheme to a third-party server. We introduce the notion of CP-ABEET supporting outsourced decryption (OCP-ABEET), which saves a lot of local computation loads of CP-ABEET. We propose a concrete construction of OCP-ABEET, and prove its security based on a reasonable number-theoretic assumption in the random oracle model. Compared with the existing CP-ABEET schemes, our scheme is more computationally efficient.

Keywords: Attribute-based encryption · Authorization · Classification · Equality test · Outsourced decryption

This work was supported by Guangdong Natural Science Funds for Distinguished Young Scholar (No. 2014A030306021), Pearl River Nova Program of Guangzhou (No. 201610010037), the National Natural Science Foundation of China (Nos. 61872152, 61472146), and Guangdong Program for Special Support of Top-notch Young Professionals (No. 2015TQ01X796).

F. Guo et al. (Eds.): Inscrypt 2018, LNCS 11449, pp. 448–467, 2019.
https://doi.org/10.1007/978-3-030-14234-6_24

1   Introduction

Along with the rapid development of cloud computing, cloud storage has become a main way for company or individual to store large amounts of data. However, while bringing convenience, cloud storage has caused data privacy threat at the same time because of the openness of public clouds. In order to protect data security and user privacy in cloud storage, people are used to store their privacy data in encrypted form. But people's various need on their data could not be satisfied due to the fact encryption hides information. For example, people cannot directly search on their data in cloud using a traditional search method. A naive method is to download all the encrypted files from the cloud, decrypt them and then use traditional methods to search over the plaintext files. Although in this way the data can be searched, but it is cumbersome and requires a large computation and storage cost, as well as a high requirement on the bandwidth, which is impractical. In this situation, *searchable encryption* [4,22] rises to solve this problem.

As a variant of public key encryption with keyword search, Yang et al. [23] introduced the notion of *public key encryption with equality test* (PKEET), which allows users to efficiently check whether two ciphertexts encrypted under (possibly) different public keys contain the same plaintext. This special property makes it suitable for implementing label classification. Attribute-based encryption (ABE), originally introduced by Sahai et al. [16], is a good technique for access control. Ciphertext-policy ABE (CP-ABE) is a variant of ABE, in which each ciphertext is associated with an access policy, and each user is associated with a set of attributes. A user can decrypt ciphertexts whose access policy can be satisfied by the attributes of the user. *Ciphertext-policy attribute-based encryption with equality test* (CP-ABEET), introduced by Wang et al. [18], is a combination of PKEET and CP-ABE, which can be used to solve the problem of encrypted data classification, and in the meanwhile, implement flexible access control policy for the encrypted data stored in the cloud server. Recently, Cui et al. [5] formally defined the notion of *Controlled Classification of Encrypted Data* and proposed a more secure and concise CP-ABEET scheme.

When a company outsources the storage of a large amount of encrypted data to the cloud, data management becomes a complex problem. It is necessary to label the data and classify them into different categories. There is a need for a mechanism to efficiently divide the encrypted data into groups according to data labels. On the other hand, access control of (encrypted) data in a company is also a key issue. Each employee in the company has different attributes. Different employees are provided different privileges to access different part of these data. User privileges are usually authorized according to their attributes. CP-ABEET can effectively handle these problems.

However, CP-ABEET has a drawback inherited from ABE, i.e. the computation cost is heavy. We consider a new scenario described as follows. *Controlled classification of encrypted data* has a high computation cost in terms of decryption and equality test. When a small-scale company or organization has the same need for controlled classification of encrypted data, the high computation cost may influence their work efficiency. In this case, a third-party server who has a large computation power can help them deal with this problem. Before the equality test and decryption, the data manager(s) can send the ciphertexts to the third-party server with a specific transformation key associated with the corresponding attribute set. The third-party server will partially decrypt the ciphertexts via a transformation process and send back the partially decrypted ciphertexts to the data manager(s). Then the data manager(s) can decrypt the ciphertexts using its secret key or send it to the data classifier for equality test. By using the outsourcing technique, the local computation cost can be reduced significantly without revealing any information about the plaintexts to the third-party server.

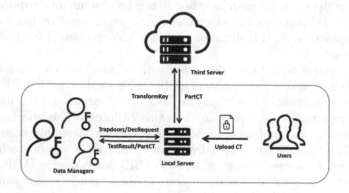

Fig. 1. System architecture of OCP-ABEET

We propose to outsource the decryption process to improve the efficiency of CP-ABEET. Outsourced Decryption of ABE was firstly introduced by Green et al. [8] and it can reduce the computation overhead of ABE to a great extent. In this paper, we propose a concrete CP-ABEET scheme with equality test and outsourced decryption, which is based on the CP-ABEET scheme in [5].

Figure 1 shows the system architecture of OCP-ABEET. The local server undertakes data storage and a small amount of calculations while the third-party server has a powerful computation capability. Meanwhile, the local server also plays the role of data classifier. First of all, attribute distribution is under control of the regulatory agency of the company. There are some data managers in the company, and each of them is in charge of the management and maintenance of different part of the company's data. Authorization privileges for data classification are represented by attribute sets. Employees of the company, including the data managers, receive their attribute related secret keys from the regulatory agency. Data users upload their encrypted files to the local server and each of them has a label encrypted by OCP-ABEET. Only the manager whose attribute set can satisfy the access policy embedded in the encrypted label has rights to operate on its ciphertext. The data classifier server obtains trapdoors from different data managers before classifying the data. The way in which data managers obtain the trapdoors is similar with that in secret key generation phase. Given the trapdoors, the local server could ask the third-party server for transforming the ciphertexts to partially decrypted ciphertexts. Then it can operate the equality test function of OCP-ABEET on them quickly. If two pieces of data are attached with the same label, they will be put into the same category. On the other hand, data managers are able to decrypt the encrypted label under the control of access policy. Upon receiving the partially decrypted ciphertexts from the third-party server, the data manager can recover the original data using their attribute related secret key. In our scheme, different users have different transformation keys generated according to their attribute sets, and these keys are sent to the third-party server for transforming different ciphertexts. The majority of computational cost of decryption is then transferred to the third-party server due to the transformation. The third-party server sends back partially decrypted ciphertexts to the local server. After that, the receiver can quickly finish the final step of decryption and the local server can perform the equality test for classification efficiently. It is ensured that the transform keys do not help the third-party server to learn information about the messages.

(Our Contributions). Although concrete CP-ABEET schemes have already been proposed by Wang et al. [18] and Huang et al. [5], they all require a large computation cost on the server, which makes it not quite suitable for small-scale company or organization with low computation capacity.

In this paper, we formally define the notion of outsourced ciphertext-policy attribute-based encryption with equality test (OCP-ABEET), propose an efficient construction of OCP-ABEET supporting outsourced decryption, and prove in the random oracle model that our scheme achieves one-wayness if the adversary is given test trapdoors, and achieves indistinguishability if the adversary is not given the corresponding trapdoors. Compared with previous CP-ABE-ET schemes, our scheme is more computationally efficient in terms of **Extract**, **Decrypt** and **Test** algorithms. Besides, our scheme is CCA-type secure, while Wang et al.'s scheme [18] is only CPA-type secure. The price of our scheme is that we need a stronger number-theoretic assumption. Readers can refer to Table 1 (p. 18) for a detailed comparison between our scheme and some related schemes, e.g. [13,18,24].

Paper Organization. In Sect. 2 we review some related works. Then in Sect. 3 we introduce the preliminaries which are necessary for our construction. In Sect. 4 we give the definition of OCP-ABEET and its security models in this paper. The security analysis of our scheme is provided in Sect. 6. We give the comparison of our scheme with some related schemes in Sect. 7. Finally, the paper is concluded in Sect. 8.

2   Related Works

The notion of public key encryption with equality test (PKEET) was firstly introduced by Yang et al. [23] as a new kind of searchable encryption. In PKEET, users are allowed to check whether two ciphertexts contain the same message without decryption. In Yang et al.'s scheme, any entity can perform the equality test on the ciphertexts. There may exists an authorization requirement to accurately control who can perform the equality test on their ciphertexts. Based on this observation, Tang et al. [17] proposed the fine-grained authorization policy PKEET (FG-PKEET) to realize the accurate authorization where only two authorized users can perform the equality test. Besides, Ma et al. [15] presented a public key encryption with delegated equality test (PKE-DET) where only the delegated party can do the test. To make the authorization more flexible, Ma et al. [14] proposed a flexible PKEET which can support four types of authorization.

Considering the advantage of identity-based encryption (IBE), Ma et al. [13] firstly presented the notion of identity-based encryption with outsourced equality test in cloud computing (IBEET) which simplifies the certificate management of PKEET and supports a single type of authorization. A user in IBEET can compute a trapdoor using the identity-related secret key and sends it to cloud server for equality test, and the user's trapdoor delegates out the capability of equality test on its ciphertexts. Equality test can be well used in encrypted database systems, where the server hosts the encrypted database and users can do the equality test between a target ciphertext in the database and a queried ciphertext. If there is an *honest-but-curious*' database server, it may illegally benefit from the brute force attacks because that the ciphertexts can be generated publicly. To solve this problem, Wu et al. [21] presented an IBEET scheme secure against insider attacks. In 2018, Wu et al. [20] proposed an efficient IBEET scheme by reducing the use of time-consuming HashToPoint functions. In their scheme, they restrict that only the particular keyword can be tested to improve the security level.

Generally, IBEET is a combination of PKEET and IBE. As an extension from IBE, attribute based encryption (ABE) has the advantage of more flexible authorization, which can be applied on PKEET. The notion of Attribute-Based Encryption was first proposed by Sahai and Water et al. [16] in 2005. In 2006, Goyal et al. [7] first presented a Key-Policy ABE scheme. In KP-ABE schemes [1,7,9], access structures are embedded in private keys while attribute sets are embedded in ciphertexts. In 2007, Bethencourt and Sahai et al. [3] first presented the Ciphertext-Policy ABE scheme. In CP-ABE scheme [3,6,19], private keys are embedded with attribute sets while ciphertexts are embedded with access structures. A user can decrypt the ciphertext only if its attribute set can satisfy the access structure within the ciphrtext. Waters et al. [19] proposed a new methodology for realizing CP-ABE under concrete and non-interactive cryptographic assumptions in the standard model.

To the best of our knowledge, there are not many works focusing on attribute based encryption with equality test (ABEET). The first attribute-base encryption with equality test (ABEET) was proposed by Zhu et al. [24]. Their key-policy attribute based encryption with equality test (KP-ABEwET) which combines the key-policy ABE with PKEET, provides a more flexible authorization than previous work. Then, Wang et al. [18] proposed a ciphertext-policy attribute based encryption with delegated equality test that combines the ciphertext-policy ABE with PKEET. There exists some deficiencies in both of their schemes that the schemes have high computation complexity. Furthermore, security of their schemes are of CPA type. In [5], Cui et al. proposed a more efficient ciphertext-policy attribute based encryption with equality test (CP-ABEET) which has a more concise construction. And their CP-ABEET schemes achieves the OW-SAS-CCA and IND-SAS-CCA security in random oracle model.

Outsourced Decryption. ABE shows its power in access control, however, it suffers from the problem of low efficiency, i.e. ciphertext size and decryption cost grow with the complexity of access policy. Green et al. [8] gave a new method of efficiently and securely outsourcing the decryption of ABE ciphertexts to a third-party server, which reduces the overhead of local users significantly. Since Green et al.'s work, researchers have done a lot to improve the security and efficiency of ABE. For example, Li et al. [11] proposed an outsourced ABE scheme not only supporting outsourced decryption but also enabling delegating key generation. It reduces the local computation by outsourcing the task of generating partial private keys to a key generation service provider. Besides, their scheme realizes the checkability on outsourced results against a selfish third-party server. There are also some related work to realize the verifiability of outsourcing decryption [10,12]. To further improve the computation performance and reduce communication overhead, Li et al. [12] proposed a new verifiable outsourcing scheme with constant-size ciphertexts. However, as far as we know, there is a lack of an efficient ABEET scheme which supports outsourced decryption. How to achieve a secure ABEET scheme supporting outsourced decryption is still an open problem.

3 Preliminaries

3.1 Access Structure

Definition 1 (Access Structure). *Let $\{P_1, P_2, \cdots, P_n\}$ be a set of parties. A collection $\mathbb{A} \subseteq 2^{\{P_1, P_2, \dots, P_n\}}$ is monotone if $\forall B, C$, it holds that if $B \in \mathbb{A}$ and $B \subseteq C$ then $C \in \mathbb{A}$. An access structure (respectively, monotone access structure) is a collection (respectively, monotone collection) $\mathbb{A}$ of non-empty subsets of $\{P_1, P_2, \cdots, P_n\}$, i.e., $\mathbb{A} \in 2^{\{P_1, P_2, \cdots, P_n\}} \setminus \{\emptyset\}$. The sets in $\mathbb{A}$ are called the* authorized sets, *and the sets not in $\mathbb{A}$ are called the* unauthorized sets.

In our context, the role of the parties is taken by the attributes. Thus, the access structure $\mathbb{A}$ will contain the authorized sets of attributes. We restrict our attention to monotone access structures.

Definition 2 (Linear Secret Sharing Scheme, LSSS [2]). *A secret sharing scheme Π over a set of parties $\mathcal{P}$ is called linear (over $\mathbb{Z}_p$) if*

1. *the shares for each party form a vector over $\mathbb{Z}_p$; and*
2. *there exists a matrix M with ℓ rows and n columns called the share generating matrix for Π. For all $i = 1, \cdots, \ell$, the i-th row of M, we let the function ρ defined the party labeling row i as $\rho(i)$. When we consider the column vector $v = (s, r_2, \cdots, r_n)$, where $s \in \mathbb{Z}_p$ is the secret to be shared and $r_2, \cdots, r_n \in \mathbb{Z}_p$ are randomly chosen, then Mv is the vector of ℓ shares of the secret s according to Π. The share $(Mv)_i$ belongs to party $\rho(i)$.*

Beimel [2] showed that every linear secret sharing scheme according to the above definition enjoys the linear reconstruction property, defined as follows: Suppose that Π is an LSSS for the access structure $\mathbb{A}$. Let $S \in \mathbb{A}$ be any authorized set, and let $I \subset \{1, \cdots, \ell\}$ be defined as $I = \{i : \rho(i) \in S\}$. Then, there exist constants $\{\omega_i \in \mathbb{Z}_p\}_{i \in I}$ such that, if λ_i's are valid shares of a secret s according to Π, then $\sum_{i \in I} \omega_i \lambda_i = s$. Furthermore, it is shown in [2] that these constants $\{\omega_i\}$ can be found in time polynomial in the size of the share generating matrix M.

By convention, the vector $(1, 0, \cdots, 0)$ is the target vector in LSSS, which is in the span of any satisfying set of rows I of M. For any unauthorized set of rows I, the target vector would not be in its span. Besides, there will exist a vector w which satisfies $w \cdot (1, 0, \cdots, 0) = -1$ and $w \cdot M_i = 0$ for all $i \in I$.

3.2   Bilinear Pairing

Let $\mathbb{G}$ and $\mathbb{G}_T$ be two multiplicative cyclic groups of prime order p. Let g be a generator of $\mathbb{G}$ and e be a bilinear map, $e : \mathbb{G} \times \mathbb{G} \to \mathbb{G}_T$. The bilinear pairing $\hat{e}$ has the following properties:

- **Bilinearity**: for all $u, v \in \mathbb{G}$ and $a, b \in \mathbb{Z}_p$, we have $\hat{e}(u^a, v^b) = \hat{e}(u, v)^{ab}$.
- **Non-degeneracy**: $\hat{e}(g, g)$ is not the identity of group $\mathbb{G}_T$.
- **Computability**: There exists a polynomial time algorithm which computes $\hat{e}(u, v)$ for any $u, v \in \mathbb{G}$.

3.3   Decisional Parallel Bilinear Diffie-Hellman Exponent Assumption

Decisional q-parallel Bilinear Diffie-Hellman Exponent problem (BDHE) is defined as follows. Choose a group $\mathbb{G}$ of prime order p according to the security parameter. Randomly choose the elements $a, s, b_1, \cdots, b_q \in \mathbb{Z}_p$ and let g be a generator of $\mathbb{G}$. Given

$$
\begin{aligned}
y := & \left(g, g^s, g^a, \cdots, g^{(a^q)}, , g^{(a^{q+2})}, \cdots, g^{(a^{2q})}, \right. \\
& \forall_{1 \le j \le q} \; g^{s \cdot b_j}, g^{a/b_j}, \cdots, g^{(a^q/b_j)}, g^{(a^{q+2}/b_j)}, \cdots, g^{(a^{2q}/b_j)}, \\
& \left. \forall_{1 \le j, k \le q, k \ne j} \; g^{(a \cdot s \cdot b_k / b_j)}, \cdots, g^{(a^q \cdot s \cdot b_k / b_j)} \right),
\end{aligned}
$$

it is hard for the adversary to distinguish $T = \hat{e}(g,g)^{a^{q+1}s} \in \mathbb{G}_T$ from a random element of $\mathbb{G}_T$. An algorithm $\mathcal{B}$ that outputs $z \in \{0,1\}$ has advantage ϵ in solving the decisional q-parallel BDHE problem if

$$|\Pr[\mathcal{B}(\mathbf{y}, T = \hat{e}(g,g)^{a^{q+1}s}) = 0] - \Pr[\mathcal{B}(\mathbf{y}, T = R) = 0]| \geq \varepsilon.$$

Definition 3 (Decisional q-parallel BDHE Assumption). *The decisional q-parallel BDHE assumption holds if there is no PPT algorithm that can solve the decisional q-parallel BDHE problem with a non-negligible advantage.*

4 Outsourced Ciphertext-Policy Attribute-Based Encryption with Equality Test

4.1 Definition

Definition 4 (OCP-ABEET). *An outsourced ciphertext-policy attribute-based encryption with equality test (OCP-ABEET) scheme is defined by the following six (probabilistic) polynomial-time (PPT) algorithms:*

- **Setup** *takes as input the security parameter 1^k and maximal number U of attributes in the system, and returns a system public key* Mpk *and a master secret key* Msk. *Denote it by* (Mpk, Msk) $\leftarrow$ **Setup**$(1^k, U)$.
- **Encrypt** *takes as input the master public key* Mpk, *an access structure (M, ρ) and a message m, and returns a ciphertext* Ct. *Denote it by* Ct $\leftarrow$ **Encrypt**(Mpk, $(M, \rho), m$).[1]
- **KeyGen** *takes as input the master secret key* Msk *and a set S of attributes, and returns the secret key* Sk$_S$ *which contains a transformation key* Tk$_S$ *and a decryption key* Dk$_S$ *w.r.t. S. Denote it by* Sk$_S$:= (Tk$_S$, Dk$_S$) $\leftarrow$ **KeyGen**(Msk, S).
- **Trapdoor** *takes as input the master secret key* Msk *and a set S of attributes, and returns a trapdoor* Td$_S$ *w.r.t. S. Denote it by* Td$_S$ $\leftarrow$ **Trapdoor**(Msk, S).
- **Transform** *takes as input a ciphertext* Ct *and the transformation key* Tk$_S$, *and returns the partially decrypted ciphertext* PCt. *Denote it by* PCt $\leftarrow$ **Transform**(Ct, Tk$_S$).
- **Test** *takes as input a ciphertext* Ct$_A$ *and a trapdoor* Td$_A$ *of user A, and a ciphertext* Ct$_B$ *and a trapdoor* Td$_B$ *of user B, and returns 1 if* Ct$_A$ *and* Ct$_B$ *contain the same plaintext, and 0 otherwise. Denote it by* 1/0 $\leftarrow$ **Test**(Ct$_A$, Td$_A$, Ct$_B$, Td$_B$).
- **Decrypt** *takes as input the master public key* Mpk, *a ciphertext* Ct *and a secret key* Sk$_S$, *and returns a plaintext m or a special symbol $\perp$ indicating decryption failure. If the ciphertext has not been partially decrypted, it will firstly run the algorithm* **Transform**(Ct, Tk$_S$) *to transform and then use decryption key* dk$_S$ *to decrypt the partially decrypted ciphertext. Otherwise, it*

---

[1] Here we do not consider to hide the access structure used in encryption. Therefore, we assume that the access structure is included as part of the ciphertext.

will directly decrypt the ciphertext. Denote it by $m/\perp \leftarrow$ **Decrypt**$(\mathsf{Mpk}, \mathsf{Ct},$ $\mathsf{Sk}_S)$. *The decryption would return $\perp$ if the attributes associated with Sk_S do not satisfy the access structure contained in* Ct.

Correctness could be defined naturally. Here we omit it for simplicity. Below we introduce the security models of OCP-ABEET.

4.2   Security Models

We consider two security properties of OCP-ABEET. We require that the adversary could not recover the message if it is not given the trapdoor, and that the adversary cannot distinguish a given ciphertext is the encryption of which message if it does not have the trapdoor. Formally, we define the two security properties via the following games, in which $\mathcal{C}$ is the challenger and $\mathcal{A}$ is the adversary.

One-wayness Game:

- **Init**. The adversary $\mathcal{A}$ submits a challenge access structure (M^*, ρ^*).
- **Setup**. The challenger $\mathcal{C}$ generates a master key pair $(\mathsf{Mpk}, \mathsf{Msk})$, and gives Mpk to $\mathcal{A}$.
- **Query Phase 1**. $\mathcal{A}$ is allowed to issue queries to the following oracles for polynomially many times.
  - *OExtract*: Given an attribute set S, it returns the corresponding secret key Sk_S.
  - *OTrapdoor*: Given an attribute set S, it returns the corresponding trapdoor Td_S.
  - *ODecrypt*: Given an attribute set S and a ciphertext Ct, it returns the corresponding decryption output.
- **Challenge Phase**. The challenger randomly chooses a message m, computes the challenge ciphertext $\mathsf{Ct}^* \leftarrow$ **Encrypt**$(\mathsf{Mpk}, (M^*, \rho^*), m)$, and returns Ct^* to the adversary.
- **Query Phase 2**. $\mathcal{A}$ continues to issues queries as in **Query Phase 1**.
- **Guess**. Finally, $\mathcal{A}$ outputs a message m', and wins the game if $m' = m^*$ and the following conditions hold:
  1. $\mathcal{A}$ did not query the *OExtract* oracle for the secret key of an attribute set satisfying (M^*, ρ^*);
  2. $\mathcal{A}$ did not query the *ODecrypt* oracle on input (S, Ct^*) for any attribute set S satisfying (M^*, ρ^*).

The advantage of $\mathcal{A}$ in the game above, $\mathrm{Adv}_{\mathcal{A}}^{\mathsf{OW\text{-}SAS\text{-}CCA}}(k)$, is defined to be the probability that it wins the game.

Definition 5 (OW-SAS-CCA Security). *An OCP-ABEET scheme is said to be one-way against selective access structure and chosen ciphertext attacks (OW-SAS-CCA secure) if for any PPT adversary $\mathcal{A}$, its advantage $\mathrm{Adv}_{\mathcal{A}}^{\mathsf{OW\text{-}SAS\text{-}CCA}}(k)$ is negligible.*

Indistinguishability Game:

- **Init.** The adversary $\mathcal{A}$ submits a challenge access structure (M^*, ρ^*).
- **Setup.** The challenger $\mathcal{C}$ generates a master key pair $(\mathsf{Mpk}, \mathsf{Msk})$, and gives Mpk to the adversary $\mathcal{A}$.
- **Query Phase 1.** Same as **Query Phase 1** of **One-wayness Game**.
- **Challenge Phase.** $\mathcal{A}$ submits two equal-length messages m_0, m_1. $\mathcal{C}$ flips a random coin $\beta \in \{0,1\}$, computes the challenge ciphertext $\mathsf{Ct}^* \leftarrow \mathbf{Encrypt}$ $(\mathsf{Mpk}, (M^*, \rho^*), m_\beta)$ and returns Ct^* to $\mathcal{A}$.
- **Query Phase 2.** Same as **Query Phase 1**.
- **Guess.** $\mathcal{A}$ outputs a bit $\beta' \in \{0,1\}$, and wins the game if $\beta' = \beta$, and
  1. $\mathcal{A}$ did not query the $OExtract$ oracle on input an attribute set S satisfying (M^*, ρ^*);
  2. $\mathcal{A}$ did not query the $OTrapdoor$ oracle on input S nor query $ODecrypt$ on input (S, Ct^*) such that S satisfies (M^*, ρ^*).

The advantage of $\mathcal{A}$ in the game above, $\mathrm{Adv}_{\mathcal{A}}^{\mathsf{IND\text{-}SAS\text{-}CCA}}(k)$, is defined to the gap between $\Pr[\beta' = \beta]$ and $1/2$.

Definition 6 (IND-SAS-CCA Security). *An OCP-ABEET scheme is said to be* indistinguishable against selective access structure and chosen ciphertext attacks *(IND-SAS-CCA secure) if for any PPT adversary $\mathcal{A}$, its advantage $\mathrm{Adv}_{\mathcal{A}}^{\mathsf{IND\text{-}SAS\text{-}CCA}}(k)$ is negligible.*

5 Our OCP-ABEET Scheme

In this section, we propose the concrete construction of our OCP-ABEET scheme.

- **Setup**$(1^k, U)$. Given the security parameter and the maximal number U of attributes in the system, the algorithm generates a bilinear pairing parameters $(\mathbb{G}, \mathbb{G}_T, e, g, p)$ as described in Sect. 3. It also chooses U random group elements $h_1, \cdots, h_U \in \mathbb{G}$ that are associated with the U attributes in the system, chooses random exponents $\alpha, \alpha', a \in \mathbb{Z}_p$, and chooses two cryptographic hash functions: $H_1 : \mathbb{G}_T \rightarrow \mathbb{G}_1$ and $H_2 : \{0,1\}^* \rightarrow \{0,1\}^{l_1+l_2}$ where l_1 and l_2 are security parameters specifying representation length of a $\mathbb{G}_1$ element and that of a $\mathbb{Z}_p$ element, respectively. The master public key is defined to be

$$\mathsf{Mpk} = (g, \hat{e}(g,g)^\alpha, \hat{e}(g,g)^{\alpha'}, g^a, h_1, \cdots, h_U),$$

  and the master private key is $\mathsf{Msk} = (g^\alpha, g^{\alpha'})$.
- **Encrypt**$(\mathsf{Mpk}, (M, \rho), m)$. Given Mpk, an access structure (M, ρ) and a message m, where M is an $\ell \times n$ matrix and ρ associates rows of M to attributes, the algorithm chooses a random vector $v = (s, y_2, \cdots, y_n) \in \mathbb{Z}_p^n$, and calculates $\lambda_i = v \cdot M_i$ for $i = 1$ to ℓ, where M_i is the vector corresponding to the i-th row of M. It also chooses at random $u, r_1, \cdots, r_\ell \in \mathbb{Z}_p$, and computes

$$C = m^u \cdot H_1(\hat{e}(g,g)^{\alpha s}), \quad C' = g^s, \quad C'' = g^u,$$

$$\forall 1 \le i \le \ell, \ C_i = g^{a\lambda_i} \cdot h_{\rho(i)}^{-r_i}, \quad D_i = g^{r_i},$$

$$C^* = (m\|u) \oplus H_2((\hat{e}(g,g)^{\alpha' s}, C, C', C'', \boldsymbol{E}),$$

where $E = (C_1, D_1, \cdots, C_\ell, D_\ell)$. The algorithm returns $\mathsf{Ct} = (C, C', C'', C_1, D_1, \cdots, C_\ell, D_\ell, C^*)$.

- **KeyGen**(Msk, S). Given Msk and a set S of attributes, the algorithm chooses at random $z, z' \in \mathbb{Z}_p$, and sets the decryption key $\mathsf{Dk}_S = (z, z')$. It then chooses at random $t, t' \in \mathbb{Z}_p$, and sets $\hat{t} = t/z$ and $\hat{t}' = t'/z'$, and calculates the transformation key $\mathsf{Tk}_S = (\widehat{\mathsf{Tk}}_S, \widehat{\mathsf{Tk}}'_S)$ where

$$\widehat{\mathsf{Tk}}_S : \hat{K} = g^{\alpha/z} g^{a\hat{t}}, \quad \hat{L} = g^{\hat{t}}, \quad \{\hat{K}_x = h_x^{\hat{t}}\}_{x \in S},$$
$$\widehat{\mathsf{Tk}}'_S : \hat{K}' = g^{\alpha'/z'} g^{a\hat{t}'}, \quad \hat{L}' = g^{\hat{t}'}, \quad \{\hat{K}'_x = h_x^{\hat{t}'}\}_{x \in S}.$$

It returns the secret key $\mathsf{Sk}_S = (\mathsf{Tk}_S, \mathsf{Dk}_S) = ((\widehat{\mathsf{Tk}}_S, \widehat{\mathsf{Tk}}'_S), (z, z'))$.

- **Trapdoor**(Msk, S). Given Msk and a set S of attributes, the algorithm chooses at random $z, \hat{t} \in \mathbb{Z}_p$, computes and returns the trapdoor

$$\mathsf{Td}_S = \left(z, \hat{K} = g^{\alpha/z} \cdot g^{a\hat{t}}, \quad \hat{L} = g^{\hat{t}}, \quad \{\hat{K}_x = h_x^{\hat{t}}\}_{x \in S} \right).$$

Notice that Td_S is actually part of the secret key w.r.t. the attribute set S, i.e. $\mathsf{Td}_S = (z, \widehat{\mathsf{Tk}}_S)$. However, there is no requirement that the random elements z, t used in the trapdoor generation should be the same as those in the key generation.

Both the attribute authority who holds the master secret key and the data manager who holds a secret key w.r.t its attributes can generate trapdoors. The former runs the **Trapdoor** algorithm to generate a trapdoor using fresh randomness, while the latter simply outputs $(z, \widehat{\mathsf{Tk}}_S)$ as the trapdoor, which are parts of its secret key.

- **Transform**$(\mathsf{Ct}, \mathsf{Tk}_S)$. Given a ciphertext Ct and the transformation key Tk_S, the algorithm works as follows. Suppose that S satisfies the access structure (M, ρ) in Ct. Let I be the set $I = \{i : \rho(i) \in S\}$. Define the set $\{w_i \in \mathbb{Z}_p\}_{i \in I}$ such that if $\{\lambda_i\}$ are valid shares of the secret value s according to M, it holds that $\sum_{i \in I} w_i \cdot \lambda_i = s$. The algorithm computes

$$X_{sub} = \hat{e}(C', \hat{K})/(\prod_{i \in I} (\hat{e}(C_i, \hat{L})\hat{e}(D_i, \hat{K}_{\rho(i)}))^{w_i})$$
$$= \hat{e}(g, g)^{\alpha s/z} \hat{e}(g, g)^{as\hat{t}}/(\prod_{i \in I} \hat{e}(g, g)^{\hat{t} a \lambda_i w_i})$$
$$= \hat{e}(g, g)^{\alpha s/z},$$
$$X'_{sub} = \hat{e}(C', \hat{K}')/(\prod_{i \in I} (\hat{e}(C_i, \hat{L}')\hat{e}(D_i, \hat{K}'_{\rho(i)}))^{w_i})$$
$$= \hat{e}(g, g)^{\alpha' s/z'} \hat{e}(g, g)^{as\hat{t}'}/(\prod_{i \in I} \hat{e}(g, g)^{\hat{t}' a \lambda_i w_i})$$
$$= \hat{e}(g, g)^{\alpha' s/z'},$$

and returns $\mathsf{PCt} = (X_{sub}, X'_{sub})$.

– **Test**$(\mathsf{Ct}_A, \mathsf{Td}_{S_A}, \mathsf{Ct}_B, \mathsf{Td}_{S_B})$. Given ciphertexts Ct_A, Ct_B and trapdoors Td_{S_A}, Td_{S_B}, the algorithm works as follows. Suppose that S_A and S_B satisfy the access structures (M_A, ρ_A) of Ct_A and (M_B, ρ_B) of Ct_B, respectively. Let I_A be the set $I_A = \{i : \rho_A(i) \in S_A\}$. Define the set $\{w_{A,i} \in \mathbb{Z}_p\}_{i \in I_A}$ such that if $\{\lambda_{A,i}\}$ are valid shares of secret s_A according to M_A, we have $\sum_{i \in I_A} w_{A,i} \cdot \lambda_{A,i} = s_A$. Define I_B and $\{w_{B,i} \in \mathbb{Z}_p\}_{i \in I_B}$ similarly. Parse Ct_A as $\mathsf{Ct}_A = (C_A, C'_A, C''_A, C_{A,1}, D_{A,1}, \cdots, C_{A,\ell}, D_{A,\ell}, C^*_A)$ and Ct_B as $\mathsf{Ct}_B = (C_B, C'_B, C''_B, C_{B,1}, D_{B,1}, \cdots, C_{B,\ell}, D_{B,\ell}, C^*_B)$. The algorithm runs **Transform** $(\mathsf{Ct}_A, \mathsf{Tk}_{s_A})$ and **Transform**$(\mathsf{Ct}_B, \mathsf{Tk}_{s_B})$ to get the partially decrypted ciphertexts (X_{sub_A}, X'_{sub_A}) and (X_{sub_B}, X'_{sub_B}). It computes

$$X_A = \frac{C_A}{H_1((X_{sub_A})^{z_A})} \text{ and } X_B = \frac{C_B}{H_1((X_{sub_B})^{z_B})},$$

and outputs 1 if the following equation

$$\hat{e}(C''_A, X_B) = \hat{e}(C''_B, X_A)$$

holds, and 0 otherwise.

Remark. Notice that the major computation of **Test** algorithm could also be outsourced to the third-party server. Namely, the data classifier could ask the third-party server to transform Ct to $\mathsf{PCt} = (X_{sub}, X'_{sub})$. Then it could do the test quickly by conducting some simple computation.

– **Decrypt**$(\mathsf{Sk}_S, \mathsf{Ct})$. Given a ciphertext Ct and a secret key Sk_S, the algorithm parses Ct as $\mathsf{Ct} = (C, C', C'', C_1, D_1, \cdots, C_\ell, D_\ell, C^*)$, runs **Transform**$(\mathsf{Ct}, \mathsf{Tk}_S)$ to get its partially decrypted ciphertext (X_{sub}, X'_{sub}), and computes

$$m\|u \leftarrow C^* \oplus H_2\big((X'_{sub})^{z'}, C, C', C'', E\big)$$

where $E = (C_1, D_1, \cdots, C_\ell, D_\ell)$. It outputs m if

$$C'' = g^u \text{ and } C = m^u \cdot H_1((X_{sub})^z)$$

hold, and 0 otherwise.

The correctness of our scheme could be verified in a straight-forward way. Here we omit it for the sake of page limit.

6   Security Analysis

Below we analyze the security of our OCP-ABEET scheme under the security models given in Sect. 4.2.

Theorem 1. *Our OCP-ABEET scheme is OW-SAS-CCA secure if the decisional q-parallel BDHE assumption holds.*

Proof. Suppose that there exists an adversary $\mathcal{A}$ that has non-negligible advantage ϵ in the one-wayness game against our CP-ABEET scheme, we use it to build an algorithm $\mathcal{B}$ to solve the decisional q-parallel BDHE problem. $\mathcal{B}$ is given a q-parallel BDHE challenge $(\mathbf{y}, T)$ (see Definition 3 for the definition of $\mathbf{y}$). Define a bit b, which is 0 if $T = \hat{e}(g, g)^{a^{q+1}s}$, and is 1 if T is a random element of $\mathbb{G}_T$. $\mathcal{B}$ tries to guess the bit b, and works as below.

1. **Init.** $\mathcal{A}$ chooses a challenge access structure (M^*, ρ^*) and sends it to $\mathcal{B}$.
2. **Setup.** $\mathcal{B}$ randomly chooses $\alpha_1, \alpha_2 \in \mathbb{Z}_p$, and implicitly sets $\alpha = \alpha_1 + a^q$ by letting $\hat{e}(g, g)^\alpha = \hat{e}(g, g)^{\alpha_1} \cdot \hat{e}(g, g^{a^q})$ and $\alpha' = \alpha_2 + a^{q+1}$ by letting $\hat{e}(g, g)^{\alpha'} = \hat{e}(g, g)^{\alpha_2} \cdot \hat{e}(g^a, g^{a^q})$. It then chooses a random value z_x for each attribute $x \in \{1, \cdots, U\}$. Denote by X the set $\{i : \rho(i) = x\}$. $\mathcal{B}$ programs group elements h_x as

$$h_x = g^{z_x} \prod_{i \in X} g^{aM^*_{i,1}/b_i} \cdot g^{a^2 M^*_{i,2}/b_i} \cdots g^{a^n M^*_{i,n}/b_i}.$$

It gives $\mathsf{Mpk} = (g, \hat{e}(g, g)^\alpha, \hat{e}(g, g)^{\alpha'}, g^a, h_1, \cdots, h_U)$ to the adversary.
3. **Query Phase 1.** $\mathcal{B}$ maintains two hash tables HT_1, HT_2 which are initially empty, and simulates the oracles as below. If not specified, we assume that the attribute sets submitted by $\mathcal{A}$ to the oracles do not satisfy the challenge access structure, and that $\mathcal{A}$ does not repeat its queries to the same oracle.
   - H_1 *Oracle.* Given an element $Q \in \mathbb{G}_T$, $\mathcal{B}$ randomly chooses a value $h_1 \in \mathbb{G}_1$, stores (Q, h_1) into HT_1, and returns h_1 to $\mathcal{A}$.
   - H_2 *Oracle.* Given $\mathbf{Q} = (Q, C, C', C'', C_1, D_1, \cdots, C_\ell, D_\ell)$ as input, $\mathcal{B}$ chooses a random $h_2 \in \{0, 1\}^{l_1 + l_2}$, and stores $(\mathbf{Q}, h_2)$ into HT_2. $\mathcal{B}$ returns h_2 to $\mathcal{A}$.
   - *OExtract.* Given an attribute set S, $\mathcal{B}$ firstly computes $\widehat{\mathsf{Tk}}'_S$. $\mathcal{B}$ selects at random $r, z' \in \mathbb{Z}_p$ and finds a vector $\mathbf{w} = (w_1 = -1, w_2, \cdots, w_n) \in \mathbb{Z}_p^n$ such that $\mathbf{w} \cdot M^*_i = 0$ for all $i \in I = \{i : \rho(i) \in S\}$. It implicitly sets the value $\hat{t}'$ as

$$\hat{t}' = r/z' + w_1 a^q/z' + w_2 a^{q-1}/z' + \cdots + w_n a^{q-n+1}/z'$$

by computing

$$\hat{L}' = g^{r/z'} \prod_{i=1, \cdots, n} (g^{a^{q+1-i}})^{w_i/z'} = g^{\hat{t}'}.$$

Then it calculates the value of $\hat{K}'$ as

$$\hat{K}' = g^{\alpha'/z'} g^{a\hat{t}'} = g^{(\alpha_2 + a^{q+1})/z'} g^{a\hat{t}'} = g^{\alpha_2/z'} \cdot g^{ar/z'} \prod_{i=2, \cdots, n} (g^{a^{q+2-i}})^{w_i/z'}.$$

Notice that the term $g^{-a^{q+1}/z'}$ of component $g^{a\hat{t}'}$ which cannot be simulated, will cancel out with the term $g^{a^{q+1}/z'}$ of $g^{\alpha'/z'}$.

For any $x \in S$, if there is no i such that $\rho(i) = x$, $\mathcal{B}$ computes $\hat{K}'_x = h_x^{\hat{t}} = (g^{z_x})^{\hat{t}} = (g^{\hat{t}})^{z_x} = \hat{L}'^{z_x}$. Otherwise, $\mathcal{B}$ computes $\hat{K}'_x$ as

$$\hat{K}'_x = \hat{L}'^{z_x} \prod_{i \in X} \prod_{j=1,\cdots,n} \left(g^{(a^j/b_i)r} \cdot \prod_{\substack{k=1,\cdots,n \\ k \neq j}} (g^{a^{q+1+j-k}/b_i})^{w_k} \right)^{M^*_{i,j}/z'},$$

where $X = \{i : \rho(i) = x\}$. Note that the terms g^{a^{q+1}/b_i} will all cancel out due to that $\boldsymbol{w} \cdot M^*_i = 0$.

So far $\mathcal{B}$ has computed $\widehat{\mathsf{Tk}}'_S = (\hat{K}', \hat{L}', \{\hat{K}'_x\}_{x \in S})$. It then computes $\widehat{\mathsf{Tk}}_S$ as follows. $\mathcal{B}$ randomly chooses new elements $\hat{t}, z \in \mathbb{Z}_p$. $\mathcal{B}$ computes the component $\hat{K}$ as

$$\hat{K} = g^{\alpha/z} \cdot g^{\hat{t}} = g^{(\alpha_1 + a^q)/z} \cdot g^{\hat{t}} = g^{\alpha_1/z} g^{a^q} \cdot g^{\hat{t}}.$$

$\mathcal{B}$ then computes $\hat{L} = g^{\hat{t}}$ and $\{\hat{K}_x = h_x^{\hat{t}}\}_{x \in S}$. It returns the secret key $\mathsf{Sk}_S = ((\widehat{\mathsf{Tk}}_S, \widehat{\mathsf{Tk}}'_S), (z, z'))$.

- *OTrapdoor.* Given an attribute set S, $\mathcal{B}$ computes $\mathsf{Td}_S = (z, \widehat{\mathsf{Tk}}_S)$ in the same way as above if S does not satisfy (M^*, ρ^*). Otherwise, $\mathcal{B}$ randomly chooses $z, \hat{t}$ and computes $\mathsf{Td}_S = (z, \widehat{\mathsf{Tk}}_S)$ as the trapdoor using the method described in the simulation of *OExtract* oracle.
- *ODecrypt.* Given an attribute set S and a ciphertext $\mathsf{Ct} = (C, C', C'', C_1, D_1, \cdots, C_\ell, D_\ell, C^*)$, $\mathcal{B}$ distinguishes the following two cases.
- (a) Case 1: S does not satisfy (M^*, ρ^*). $\mathcal{B}$ computes the corresponding secret key Sk_S as in dealing with an Extract query, uses Sk_S to decrypt Ct by following the decryption algorithm, and returns the decryption result.
- (b) Case 2: S satisfies (M^*, ρ^*). $\mathcal{B}$ firstly computes the trapdoor $\mathsf{Td}_S = (z, \widehat{\mathsf{Tk}}_S)$ as above, and calls the **Transform** algorithm to compute

$$X_{sub} = \frac{\hat{e}(C', \hat{K})}{\prod_{i \in I}(\hat{e}(C_i, \hat{L}) \cdot \hat{e}(D_i, \hat{K}_{\rho(i)}))^{w_i}}.$$

It searches table HT_1 for a tuple $((X_{sub})^z, h_1)$, and outputs $\perp$ if not found; otherwise, it searches table HT_2 to see if there exits a tuple $(((X'_{sub})^{z'}, C, C', C'', C_1, D_1, \cdots, C_\ell, D_\ell), h_2)$. If not found, $\mathcal{B}$ outputs $\perp$; otherwise, for each tuple found in HT_2, $\mathcal{B}$ computes $m\|u = C^* \oplus h_2$, and outputs m if the following equations hold:

$$C'' = g^u, \quad C = m^u \cdot H_1((X_{sub})^z).$$

If no tuple satisfies the equations above, $\mathcal{B}$ outputs $\perp$.

4. **Challenge.** $\mathcal{B}$ selects at random a message m^* and $u \in \mathbb{Z}_p$, and computes

$$\hat{C} = (m^*)^u \cdot H_1(\hat{e}(g^s, g^\alpha)), \quad \hat{C}' = g^s, \quad \hat{C}'' = g^u.$$

It then chooses at random $y'_2, \cdots, y'_n \in \mathbb{Z}_p$ and shares the secret s using the vector $v = (s, sa + y'_2, sa^2 + y'_3, \cdots, sa^{n-1} + y'_n)$. Denote by A_i the set of all k's such that $k \neq i$ and $\rho(k) = \rho(i)$. $\mathcal{B}$ chooses at random $r'_1, \cdots, r'_\ell$, and computes

$$\hat{C}_i = h_{\rho(i)}^{r'_i} \Big(\prod_{j=2,\cdots,n} (g^a)^{M^*_{i,j}y'_j} \Big) \cdot (g^{b_i \cdot s})^{-z_{\rho(i)}} \cdot \Big(\prod_{k \in A_i} \prod_{j=1,\cdots,n} (g^{a^j \cdot s \cdot (b_i/b_k)})^{M^*_{k,j}} \Big),$$

$$\hat{D}_i = g^{-r'_i} g^{-sb_i}, \text{ and}$$

$$\hat{C}^* = (m^* \| u) \oplus H_2 \big(T \cdot \hat{e}(g^s, g^{\alpha_2}), \hat{C}, \hat{C}', \hat{C}'', \hat{C}_1, \hat{D}_1, \cdots, \hat{C}_\ell, \hat{D}_\ell \big).$$

$\mathcal{B}$ returns the challenge ciphertext $\mathsf{Ct}^* = (\hat{C}, \hat{C}', \hat{C}'', \hat{C}_1, \hat{D}_1, \cdots, \hat{C}_\ell, \hat{D}_\ell, \hat{C}^*)$ to the adversary.

5. **Query Phase 2.** $\mathcal{B}$ simulates the oracles in the same way as in **Query Phase 1**, with the additional restriction that the adversary is not allowed to issue a decryption query on input (S, Ct^*) for any S satisfying (M^*, ρ^*).
6. **Guess.** $\mathcal{A}$ outputs a message m'. $\mathcal{B}$ then outputs $b' = 0$ if $m' = m^*$, meaning that $T = \hat{e}(g, g)^{a^{q+1}s}$, and $b' = 1$ otherwise, meaning that T is randomly selected from $\mathbb{G}_T$.

Now we analyze the probability that $\mathcal{B}$ successfully guess the value of b. If $T = \hat{e}(g, g)^{a^{q+1}s}$, the simulation provided by $\mathcal{B}$ is perfect, and the view of $\mathcal{A}$ is the same as that in a real attack. We have that $\Pr[b' = 0 | b = 0] = \mathrm{Adv}_{\mathcal{A}}^{\mathsf{OW\text{-}SAS\text{-}CCA}}(k)$. On the other hand, if T is randomly selected from $\mathbb{G}_T$, Ct^* hides the message perfectly, and the probability that $\mathcal{A}$ outputs $m' = m^*$ is thus negligible, e.g. $\Pr[b' = 0 | b = 1] = \mathrm{negl}(k)$. Therefore, we have

$$\Pr[b' = b] = \Pr[b' = 0 \wedge b = 0] + \Pr[b' = 1 \wedge b = 1]$$

$$= \frac{1}{2} (\Pr[b' = 0 | b = 0] + \Pr[b' = 1 | b = 1])$$

$$= \frac{1}{2} (\Pr[b' = 0 | b = 0] + 1 - \Pr[b' = 0 | b = 1])$$

$$= \frac{1}{2} (\mathrm{Adv}_{\mathcal{A}}^{\mathsf{OW\text{-}SAS\text{-}CCA}}(k) + (1 - \mathrm{negl}(k)))$$

$$= \frac{1}{2} + \frac{1}{2} \mathrm{Adv}_{\mathcal{A}}^{\mathsf{OW\text{-}SAS\text{-}CCA}}(k) - \frac{1}{2} \mathrm{negl}(k).$$

If $\mathcal{A}$ breaks the OW-SAS-CCA security of our OCP-ABEET scheme with non-negligible advantage, $\mathcal{B}$ solves the decisional q-parallel BDHE problem with probability non-negligibly larger than $\frac{1}{2}$, contradicting the decisional q-parallel BDHE assumption.   □

Theorem 2. *Our OCP-ABEET scheme is IND-SAS-CCA secure if the decisional q-parallel BDHE assumption holds.*

Proof. Let $\mathcal{A}$ be an adversary which breaks IND-SAS-CCA security of our scheme with advantage $\mathrm{Adv}_{\mathcal{A}}^{\mathsf{IND\text{-}SAS\text{-}CCA}}(k)$. We use it to build an algorithm $\mathcal{B}$ to solve the decisional q-parallel BDHE problem. $\mathcal{B}$ takes a problem challenge $(\mathbf{y}, T)$ as input. Again, let $b = 0$ denote that $T = \hat{e}(g, g)^{a^{q+1}s}$, and $b = 1$ denote that T is randomly selected from $\mathbb{G}_T$. $\mathcal{B}$ works as follows.

1. **Init.** $\mathcal{A}$ chooses a challenge access structure (M^*, ρ^*) and sends it to $\mathcal{B}$.
2. **Setup.** $\mathcal{B}$ randomly chooses $\alpha_1, \alpha_2 \in \mathbb{Z}_p$, and implicitly sets $\alpha = \alpha_1 + a^{q+1}$ by letting $\hat{e}(g,g)^\alpha = \hat{e}(g,g)^{\alpha_1} \cdot \hat{e}(g^a, g^{a^q})$ and $\alpha' = \alpha_2 + a^{q+1}$ by letting $\hat{e}(g,g)^{\alpha'} = \hat{e}(g,g)^{\alpha_2} \cdot \hat{e}(g^a, g^{a^q})$. For each attribute $x \in \{1, \cdots, U\}$ it chooses a random value z_x, and computes h_x as

$$h_x = g^{z_x} \prod_{i \in X} g^{aM^*_{i,1}/b_i} \cdot g^{a^2 M^*_{i,2}/b_i} \cdots g^{a^n M^*_{i,n}/b_i},$$

where $X = \{i : \rho(i) = x\}$. It then gives $\mathsf{Mpk} = (g, \hat{e}(g,g)^\alpha, g^a, h_1, \cdots, h_U)$ to the adversary.
3. **Query Phase 1.** $\mathcal{B}$ simulates H_1, H_2 and $OTrapdoor$ oracles in the same way as in the proof of Theorem 1, with an additional restriction that the attribute sets submitted by $\mathcal{A}$ to $OTrapdoor$ should not satisfy the challenge access structure. The $OExtract$, $ODecrypt$ oracle are simulated by $\mathcal{B}$ as follows.

   - _OExtract._ Given an attribute set S, $\mathcal{B}$ computes $\widehat{\mathsf{Tk}}'_S$ as the same with that in the proof of Theorem 1. And it computes $\widehat{\mathsf{Tk}}_S$ as follows. $\mathcal{B}$ selects at random $r, z \in \mathbb{Z}_p$ and finds a vector $\boldsymbol{w} = (w_1 = -1, w_2, \cdots, w_n) \in \mathbb{Z}_p^n$ such that $\boldsymbol{w} \cdot M^*_i = 0$ for all $i \in I = \{i : \rho(i) \in S\}$. It implicitly sets the value $\hat{t}$ as

   $$\hat{t} = r/z + w_1 a^q/z + w_2 a^{q-1}/z + \cdots + w_n a^{q-n+1}/z$$

   by computing

   $$\hat{L} = g^{r/z} \prod_{i=1,\cdots,n} (g^{a^{q+1-i}})^{w_i/z} = g^{\hat{t}}.$$

   Then it calculates the value of $\hat{K}$ as

   $$\hat{K} = g^{\alpha/z} g^{a\hat{t}} = g^{(\alpha_1 + a^{q+1})/z} g^{a\hat{t}} = g^{\alpha_1/z} \cdot g^{ar/z} \prod_{i=2,\cdots,n} (g^{a^{q+2-i}})^{w_i/z}.$$

   Notice that the term $g^{-a^{q+1}/z}$ of component $g^{a\hat{t}}$ which cannot be simulated, will cancel out with the term $g^{a^{q+1}/z}$ of $g^{\alpha/z}$.
   It returns the secret key $\mathsf{Sk}_S = ((\widehat{\mathsf{Tk}}_S, \widehat{\mathsf{Tk}}'_S), (z, z'))$.
   - _ODecrypt._ Given an attribute set S and a ciphertext $\mathsf{Ct} = (C, C', C'', C_1, D_1, \cdots, C_\ell, D_\ell, C^*)$, $\mathcal{B}$ distinguishes the following two cases.
   - (a) Case 1: S does not satisfy (M^*, ρ^*). $\mathcal{B}$ acts in the same way as in the proof of Theorem 1.
   - (b) Case 2: S satisfies (M^*, ρ^*). $\mathcal{B}$ traverses table HT_2 to check if there is a tuple $(((X'_{sub})^{z'}, C, C', C'', C_1, D_1, \cdots, C_\ell, D_\ell), h_2)$. If not found, $\mathcal{B}$ returns $\perp$; otherwise, for each tuple found in HT_2, $\mathcal{B}$ computes

   $$m\|u = C^* \oplus h_2.$$

   If $C'' = g^u$ holds, $\mathcal{B}$ calculates $h_1 = C/m^u$, and searches table HT_1 for a tuple $((X_{sub})^z, h_1)$. If found, $\mathcal{B}$ returns m. Finally, if for all tuples found in HT_2, $\mathcal{B}$ did not return a message to $\mathcal{A}$, it returns $\bot$. Notice that there is a case in which $(X_{sub})^z$ is not the correct one used in the generation of the queried ciphertext. However, due to the randomness of the oracle H_1, the probability that the adversary does not query H_1 with a correct $(X_{sub})^z$ value in the generation of a well-formed ciphertext, is negligible.

4. **Challenge.** $\mathcal{A}$ submits two equal-length messages m_0^*, m_1^*. $\mathcal{B}$ selects random a bit $\beta \in \{0, 1\}$ and $u \in \mathbb{Z}_p$, and computes

$$\hat{C} = (m^*)^u \cdot H_1(T \cdot \hat{e}(g^s, g^{\alpha_1})), \ \hat{C}' = g^s, \ \hat{C}'' = g^u.$$

It then randomly selects $y_2', \cdots, y_n'$ and shares the secret s using the vector $v = (s, sa + y_2', sa^2 + y_3', \cdots, sa^{n-1} + y_n')$. Let A_i be the set of all k's with $k \neq i$ and $\rho(k) = \rho(i)$. $\mathcal{B}$ selects at random $r_1', \cdots, r_\ell' \in \mathbb{Z}_p$, and computes

$$\hat{C}_i = h_{\rho(i)}^{r_i'} \Big(\prod_{j=2,\cdots,n} (g^a)^{M_{i,j}^* y_j'} \Big) \cdot (g^{b_i \cdot s})^{-z_{\rho(i)}} \cdot \Big(\prod_{k \in A_i} \prod_{j=1,\cdots,n} (g^{a^j \cdot s \cdot (b_i/b_k)})^{M_{k,j}^*} \Big),$$

$$\hat{D}_i = g^{-r_i'} g^{-s b_i}, \text{ and}$$

$$\hat{C}^* = (m^* \| u) \oplus H_2(T \cdot \hat{e}(g^s, g^{\alpha_2}), \hat{C}, \hat{C}', \hat{C}'', \hat{C}_1, \hat{D}_1, \cdots, \hat{C}_\ell, \hat{D}_\ell).$$

$\mathcal{B}$ returns $\mathsf{Ct}^* = (\hat{C}, \hat{C}', \hat{C}'', \hat{C}_1, \hat{D}_1, \cdots, \hat{C}_\ell, \hat{D}_\ell, \hat{C}^*)$ to the adversary.

5. **Query Phase 2.** $\mathcal{B}$ simulates the oracles in the same way as that in the proof of Theorem 1, with an additional restriction that $\mathcal{A}$ should not submit an attribute set satisfying (M^*, ρ^*) to the $OTrapdoor$ oracle.

6. **Guess.** $\mathcal{A}$ outputs a bit $\beta' \in \{0, 1\}$. $\mathcal{B}$ then outputs $b' = 0$ if $\beta' = \beta$, meaning $T = \hat{e}(g, g)^{a^{q+1}s}$; otherwise, it outputs $b' = 1$, meaning T is randomly selected from $\mathbb{G}_T$.

If $T = \hat{e}(g, g)^{a^{q+1}s}$, the simulation provided by $\mathcal{B}$ is perfect, and the view of $\mathcal{A}$ is the same as that of a real attack. We have that $\Pr[b' = 0 | b = 0] = \frac{1}{2} + \mathrm{Adv}_{\mathcal{A}}^{\mathsf{IND\text{-}SAS\text{-}CCA}}(k)$. If T is randomly selected from $\mathbb{G}_T$, Ct^* hides the message perfectly, and the probability that $\mathcal{A}$ correctly guesses the bit β is only $\frac{1}{2}$. Thus, $\mathcal{B}$ correctly guesses the bit b with probability $\frac{1}{2}$ as well, e.g. $\Pr[b' = 0 | b = 1] = \frac{1}{2}$. Therefore, we have:

$$\Pr[b' = b] = \Pr[b' = 0 \wedge b = 0] + \Pr[b' = 1 \wedge b = 1]$$

$$= \frac{1}{2}(\Pr[b' = 0 | b = 0] + \Pr[b' = 1 | b = 1])$$

$$= \frac{1}{2}(\Pr[b' = 0 | b = 0] + 1 - \Pr[b' = 0 | b = 1])$$

$$= \frac{1}{2}\left(\frac{1}{2} + \mathrm{Adv}_{\mathcal{A}}^{\mathsf{IND\text{-}SAS\text{-}CCA}}(k) + \frac{1}{2}\right)$$

$$= \frac{1}{2} + \frac{1}{2}\mathrm{Adv}_{\mathcal{A}}^{\mathsf{IND\text{-}SAS\text{-}CCA}}(k).$$

If $\mathcal{A}$ breaks the IND-SAS-CCA security with non-negligible advantage, $\mathcal{B}$ solves the decisional q-parallel BDHE problem with probability non-negligibly larger than $\frac{1}{2}$ as well, contradicting the decisional q-parallel BDHE assumption. $\square$

7 Comparison

To demonstrate the advantage of our OCP-ABEET scheme, we compare it with some related schemes [5,18,24] in Table 1, in terms of computational complexity, functional properties, assumptions, security level and etc. In the comparison we consider the dominant computation in **Extract, Encrypt, Decrypt** and **Test** algorithms, e.g. bilinear pairing evaluation, exponentiation operation and etc. The second to the fifth rows of Table 1 show the computational costs of **Extract, Encrypt, Decrypt** and **Test** algorithms. The ciphertext size and secret key size are compared in the sixth and seventh rows. The eighth and ninth rows indicate whether the scheme is attribute based and whether it supports outsourced decryption. The tenth row shows the authorization type the scheme supports. The last two rows give the underlying assumptions and security levels.

Table 1. Performance comparison with related schemes

	KP-ABEwET [24]	CP-ABE-ET [18]	CP-ABEET [5]	OCP-ABEET
Extract	$2A_u E$	$(4 + 6A_u + 12A_u^2)E$	$(4 + 2A_u)E$	$(6 + 2A_u)E$
Encrypt	$(2A_u + 3)E$	$(2N_U + 11)E$	$(3\ell + 5)E + 2P$	$(3\ell + 5)E + 2P$
Decrypt	$(2A_u + 2)E$ $+ 2A_u P$	$(8A_u + 6)E$ $+ 12P$	$(2A_u + 2)E$ $+ (4A_u + 2)P$	$4E$
Test	$2A_u E + 2A_u P$	$(8A_u + 4)E + 14P$	$A_u E + (2A_u + 3)P$	$2E + 2P$
Ct_{size}	$(4 + 2A_u)|G| + 2|\mathbb{Z}_p|$	$8|G| + |\mathbb{Z}_p|$	$(4 + 2\ell)|G| + |\mathbb{Z}_p|$	$(4 + 2\ell)|G| + |\mathbb{Z}_p|$
Sk_{size}	$2A_u|G|$	$(4 + 6A_u)|G|$	$(4 + 2A_u)|G|$	$(4 + 2A_u)|G| + 2|\mathbb{Z}_p|$
Attribute-based	Yes	Yes	Yes	Yes
Outsourced-decryption	No	No	No	Yes
Authorization	Flexible	Flexible	Flexible	Flexible
Assumption	tDBDH	DLIN	q-parallel BDHE	q-parallel BDHE
Security	OW-CCA & T-CCA	IND-ID-CPA	OW-SAS-CCA & IND-SAS-CCA	OW-SAS-CCA & IND-SAS-CCA

1. T-CCA [24]: testability against chosen-ciphertext attack of authorization under the chosen sets of attributes.
2. N_U is the amount of attributes in Wang et al.'s system [18].
3. We use A_u to denote the number of attributes used in **Extract, Encrypt, Decrypt** and **Test** algorithms, and use $|G|$ and $|\mathbb{Z}_p|$ to denote the element size of G and $\mathbb{Z}_p$, respectively. In CP-ABEET and OCP-ABEET schemes, ℓ is the number of rows of the access matrix M.
4. Both the IND-ID-CPA model in [18] and OW-SAS-CCA and IND-SAS-CCA models in CP-ABEET and OCP-ABEET schemes consider the selective access structure security, in which the adversary submits its challenge access structure before seeing the public parameters.

Table 1 shows that our OCP-ABEET scheme provides almost the best security guarantee and efficiency among all the ABE schemes supporting equality test. As our OCP-ABEET scheme is based on the CP-ABEET scheme [5], it has almost the same computation and communication efficiency with [5], as well as the security level. However, as our OCP-ABEET supports outsourced decryption, the local decryption efficiency is much higher than that in [5].

8   Conclusion

We introduced the notion of outsourced ciphertext-policy attribute-based encryption supporting equality test, which aims to improve the computational efficiency in local decryption, with the aid of a third-party server to process most of the decryption computation. We proposed a construction of OCP-ABEET based on Huang et al.'s CP-ABEET scheme, and proved it to be secure based on a decisional q-parallel BDHE assumption. The scheme enjoys a pretty high efficiency in local decryption.

Security of our scheme resorts to the random oracle model, which is only heuristic. In the future, we consider to construct a concrete OCP-ABEET scheme with provable security in the standard model.

References

1. Attrapadung, N., Libert, B., de Panafieu, E.: Expressive key-policy attribute-based encryption with constant-size ciphertexts. In: Catalano, D., Fazio, N., Gennaro, R., Nicolosi, A. (eds.) PKC 2011. LNCS, vol. 6571, pp. 90–108. Springer, Heidelberg (2011). https://doi.org/10.1007/978-3-642-19379-8_6
2. Beimel, A.: Secure schemes for secret sharing and key distribution. Ph.D. thesis, Israel Institute of Technology, June 1996
3. Bethencourt, J., Sahai, A., Waters, B.: Ciphertext-policy attribute-based encryption. In: IEEE Symposium on Security and Privacy, Oakland, pp. 321–334. IEEE Computer Society, May 2007
4. Boneh, D., Di Crescenzo, G., Ostrovsky, R., Persiano, G.: Public key encryption with keyword search. In: Cachin, C., Camenisch, J.L. (eds.) EUROCRYPT 2004. LNCS, vol. 3027, pp. 506–522. Springer, Heidelberg (2004). https://doi.org/10.1007/978-3-540-24676-3_30
5. Cui, Y., Huang, Q., Huang, J., Li, H., Yang, G.: Ciphertext-policy attribute-based encrypted data equality test and classification. Cryptology ePrint Archive, Report 2018/1058 (2018). https://eprint.iacr.org/2018/1058
6. Goyal, V., Jain, A., Pandey, O., Sahai, A.: Bounded ciphertext policy attribute based encryption. In: Aceto, L., Damgård, I., Goldberg, L.A., Halldórsson, M.M., Ingólfsdóttir, A., Walukiewicz, I. (eds.) ICALP 2008. LNCS, vol. 5126, pp. 579–591. Springer, Heidelberg (2008). https://doi.org/10.1007/978-3-540-70583-3_47
7. Goyal, V., Pandey, O., Sahai, A., Waters, B.: Attribute-based encryption for fine-grained access control of encrypted data. In: ACM Conference on Computer and Communications Security, Alexandria, pp. 89–98. ACM, October 2006
8. Green, M., Hohenberger, S., Waters, B., et al.: Outsourcing the decryption of ABE ciphertexts. In: Proceedings of USENIX Security Symposium, San Francisco, pp. 34–34. USENIX Association, August 2011
9. Han, J., Susilo, W., Mu, Y., Yan, J.: Privacy-preserving decentralized key-policy attribute-based encryption. IEEE Trans. Parallel Distrib. Syst. 23(11), 2150–2162 (2012)
10. Lai, J., Deng, R.H., Guan, C., Weng, J.: Attribute-based encryption with verifiable outsourced decryption. IEEE Trans. Inf. Forensics Secur. 8(8), 1343–1354 (2013)
11. Li, J., Huang, X., Li, J., Chen, X., Xiang, Y.: Securely outsourcing attribute-based encryption with checkability. IEEE Trans. Parallel Distrib. Syst. 25(8), 2201–2210 (2014)

12. Li, J., Sha, F., Zhang, Y., Huang, X., Shen, J.: Verifiable outsourced decryption of attribute-based encryption with constant ciphertext length. In: Security and Communication Networks 2017 (2017)
13. Ma, S.: Identity-based encryption with outsourced equality test in cloud computing. Inf. Sci. **328**(C), 389–402 (2016)
14. Ma, S., Huang, Q., Zhang, M., Yang, B.: Efficient public key encryption with equality test supporting flexible authorization. IEEE Trans. Inf. Forensics Secur. **10**(3), 458–470 (2015)
15. Ma, S., Zhang, M., Huang, Q., Yang, B.: Public key encryption with delegated equality test in a multi-user setting. Comput. J. **58**(4), 986–1002 (2015)
16. Sahai, A., Waters, B.: Fuzzy identity-based encryption. In: Cramer, R. (ed.) EUROCRYPT 2005. LNCS, vol. 3494, pp. 457–473. Springer, Heidelberg (2005). https://doi.org/10.1007/11426639_27
17. Tang, Q.: Towards public key encryption scheme supporting equality test with fine-grained authorization. In: Parampalli, U., Hawkes, P. (eds.) ACISP 2011. LNCS, vol. 6812, pp. 389–406. Springer, Heidelberg (2011). https://doi.org/10.1007/978-3-642-22497-3_25
18. Wang, Q., Peng, L., Xiong, H., Sun, J., Qin, Z.: Ciphertext-policy attribute-based encryption with delegated equality test in cloud computing. IEEE Access **6**, 760–771 (2018)
19. Waters, B.: Ciphertext-policy attribute-based encryption: an expressive, efficient, and provably secure realization. In: Catalano, D., Fazio, N., Gennaro, R., Nicolosi, A. (eds.) PKC 2011. LNCS, vol. 6571, pp. 53–70. Springer, Heidelberg (2011). https://doi.org/10.1007/978-3-642-19379-8_4
20. Wu, L., Zhang, Y., Choo, K.K.R., He, D.: Efficient identity-based encryption scheme with equality test in smart city. IEEE Trans. Sustain. Comput. **3**(1), 44–55 (2018)
21. Wu, T., Ma, S., Mu, Y., Zeng, S.: ID-based encryption with equality test against insider attack. In: Pieprzyk, J., Suriadi, S. (eds.) ACISP 2017. LNCS, vol. 10342, pp. 168–183. Springer, Cham (2017). https://doi.org/10.1007/978-3-319-60055-0_9
22. Song, D.X., Wagner, D., Perrig, A.: Practical techniques for searches on encrypted data. In: Proceedings of IEEE Symposium on Security and Privacy, pp. 44–55. IEEE (2000)
23. Yang, G., Tan, C.H., Huang, Q., Wong, D.S.: Probabilistic public key encryption with equality test. In: Pieprzyk, J. (ed.) CT-RSA 2010. LNCS, vol. 5985, pp. 119–131. Springer, Heidelberg (2010). https://doi.org/10.1007/978-3-642-11925-5_9
24. Zhu, H., Wang, L., Ahmad, H., Niu, X.: Key-policy attribute-based encryption with equality test in cloud computing. IEEE Access **5**, 20428–20439 (2017)

Efficient Adaptively Secure Public-Key Trace and Revoke from Subset Cover Using Déjà Q Framework

Mriganka Mandal[✉] and Ratna Dutta

Department of Mathematics, Indian Institute of Technology Kharagpur,
Kharagpur 721302, India
{mriganka_mandal,ratna}@maths.iitkgp.ac.in

Abstract. We provide an efficient and secure construction for the *trace and revoke from subset cover* (TRSC) systems in the public-key setting, having ciphertext size proportional to the number of revoked users and public parameter of constant size. The system is obtained by tweaking the identity based encryption scheme of Wee (TCC 2016) under the subset cover framework. Existing TRSC constructions are inefficient with respect to the size of the parameters and derive their security from the q-type assumptions in the random oracle model. Our construction is the *first* adaptively secure TRSC system to achieve such parameters without using any random oracles. In addition, we are able to eliminate the q-type assumptions by integrating the Déjà Q framework of Chase and Meiklejohn (EUROCRYPT 2014) and its extension by Wee (TCC 2016) in our construction and analyze its security under the hardness of static subgroup decision problems over bilinear group setting. Moreover, this is the first proposal to feature optimally short private keys, even in the standard security model without any security breach.

Keywords: Broadcast encryption · Déjà Q framework ·
Subset cover framework · Information hiding and watermarking ·
Intrusion detection and revocation

1 Introduction

Broadcast Encryption. With the rapid development of the broad applications of e-commerce such as digital distribution, streaming media, electronic data interchange, automated data collection systems etc., the use of the Internet gathered momentum to each aspect of humans' life and has gradually become an indispensable part of it. Accordingly, the issues regarding unauthorized distributions and use of digital content have become a greater concern in recent years. *Broadcast encryption*, introduced by Fiat and Naor [7], is one of the major cryptographic primitive that provides enhanced confidentiality to mitigate these issues. Generally, a broadcast encryption scheme requires a broadcaster to efficiently broadcast an encrypted message to a set of receivers through a public

F. Guo et al. (Eds.): Inscrypt 2018, LNCS 11449, pp. 468–489, 2019.
https://doi.org/10.1007/978-3-030-14234-6_25

channel. A group manager assigns a private key in an off-line setup phase to each user in the system through a secure communication channel. The encrypted message along with the users pre-assigned private keys enable legitimate users to recover the original message. In contrast, the illegitimate users are unable to decrypt the encrypted content even if they collude.

Trace and Revoke System. *Trace and revoke* systems [3,12,14] are devised to aid a tracer to find traitors using a tracing algorithm and revoke them. Traitor tracing, introduced by Chor et al. [5], empowers a content broadcaster to identify conspiracy of defrauders who collude to create a *pirate decoder*. A pirate decoder contains an arbitrarily complex obfuscated malicious program capable of decrypting the encrypted digital content. The traitors might alter their private keys in such a way that the altered keys cannot be linked with their original private keys. They can resell or publish their altered private keys on the Internet. The tracing algorithm interacts with the pirate decoder as a *black-box* oracle and outputs with overwhelming probability identity of at least one traitor in the coalition forming the malicious program. Trace and revoke systems fall into two categories: *public-key traceable* systems [3,12] and *secret-key traceable* systems [2,5,11]. Public-key tracing require only the public parameter utilizing which anyone can run the tracing algorithm. On the other hand, in secret-key tracing only the group manager is able to execute the tracing algorithm and uses a secret tracing key to identify rogue users. Trace and revoke systems are useful ingredients in constructing collusion resistant broadcast encryption with intrusion detection and revocation. It is a powerful cryptographic primitive and can be designed by exploiting the *collusion resistance* property of the traditional broadcast encryption system and integrating the *watermarking* functionality of a trace and revoke system.

A public-key trace and revoke system may be constructed by employing a public-key broadcast encryption and a public-key tracing scheme. However, the resulting scheme may not provide security against *collusion attack* [3] and may not exhibit the revocation capability. Besides, the size of private keys and public keys are critical issue for resource constrained devices with low computational power and internal storage. There are many secret-key traceable schemes that are suitable for such devices. However, to the best of our knowledge, there is no efficient public-key traceable scheme as far that can be used for such devices. Designing a public-key trace and revoke system for resource constrained devices while achieving security in the standard model under standard cryptographic assumptions is a challenging task.

Related Work. In 2001, Naor et al. [14] introduced the concept of subset cover framework and proposed two trace and revoke schemes in symmetric-key setting which are secure in the *random oracle model* (ROM). One of these designs uses *complete subtree* (CS) method while the other employs *subset difference* (SubDif) technique. The first public-key trace and revoke scheme was constructed by Dodis et al. [6] integrating SubDif mechanism in the hierarchical identity based encryption scheme of Boneh et al. [1]. The construction is secure in the ROM under the *q-Simplified Multi-Exponent Bilinear Diffie-Hellman* (SMEBDH) assumption which is a non-standard q-type security assumption. Kiayias et al. [11] proposed t-collusion resistant tracing scheme where a collusion of at most t-users can construct a pirate decoder. The scheme has ciphertext size linear to t. The first fully collusion resistant broadcast encryption with tracing functionality was proposed by Boneh et al. [2,3] using *composite* order bilinear group with sublinear size parameters. Later, Garg et al. [8] developed a similar variant in *prime* order bilinear group setting.

The trace and revoke systems can be classified into two categories – trace and revoke from private linear broadcast encryption (PLBE) [2,3,8,13] and trace and revoke from subset cover (TRSC) [6,12,14]. In PLBE system, the size of ciphertext, users private keys and public parameter depend on the total number of users. Consequently, these systems support small number of users having large storage capacity. On the contrary, the ciphertext size in the TRSC system is linear to the size of the revoked users and are suitable where a small number of users get revoked. All the existing trace and revoke schemes based on PLBE follows the tracing approach of Kiyias et al. [11] whereas the TRSC systems adopt the tracing technique of Naor et al. [14]. Recently, Lee et al. [12] designed a trace and revoke scheme in *public-key* setting from the identity based encryption scheme of Boneh et al. [1] using the SubDif technique. The scheme is secure under the q-SMEBDH assumption in the ROM. In contrast to complete subtree technique based construction of [14], Lee et al. [12] reduced the number of ciphertext components from $O(r \log{(N/r)})$ to $O(r)$, and also the size of users' private key from $O(\log^2 N)$ to $O(\log^{1.5} N)$, where N the total number of users in the system and r is the number of revoked users.

Our Contribution. Our primary focus in this work is to build a secure and efficient TRSC system suitable for resource constrained devices. Designing an efficient *fully collusion resistance* and *public-key* TRSC system with *optimal* parameter size while achieving security in the standard model is a challenging task. We explore the applicability of Déjà Q framework, introduced by Chase et al. [4], in the trace and revoke setting and design a public-key TRSC system without non-standard q-type assumptions. The Déjà Q framework was introduced to eliminate various q-type complexity assumptions and their generalizations over *composite order* bilinear groups and achieve security under standard assumptions. The technique was further developed by Wee [15] to design identity based encryption schemes as well as the broadcast encryption schemes with *optimal* parameter sizes without relying on q-type assumptions. Utilizing this technique for more advanced cryptographic primitives with security under standard assumptions while achieving compact parameter sizes is an interesting research problem. We integrate the subset difference technique of [14] to the identity based encryption scheme of Wee [15] and design a *fully collusion resistant* and *publicly traceable* TRSC system secure under standard assumption without using the random oracle model. More precisely, our TRSC construction achieves the following interesting features.

- As exhibited in Table 1, our TRSC scheme significantly reduces the communication bandwidth ($|\mathsf{CT}|$) compared to the TRSC systems [6,14] as well as the

Table 1. Comparison summary of communication, storage and computation cost

Tracing via.	Scheme	Communication	Storage			Computation cost
		$|CT|$	$|SK|$	$|PP|$		DT
PLBE	[2]	$O(\sqrt{N})$	$O(1)$	$O(\sqrt{N})$		3PR + 3PD + 2EX
	[3]	$O(\sqrt{N})$	$O(\sqrt{N})$	$O(\sqrt{N})$		4PR + 4PD + 2EX
	[8]	$O(\sqrt{N})$	$O(\sqrt{N})$	$O(\sqrt{N})$		4PR + 4PD + 3EX
	[13]	2 in $\mathbb{G}_\varrho$, 3η, $\log(N)$	1 in $\mathbb{G}_\varrho$	$\mathrm{poly}(\log N, \eta)$		2PR + (N)PD + $(N+1)$EX
TRSC	[14]-I	$O(r \log \frac{N}{r})$	$O(\log^2 N)$	$O(\eta)$		$(\log \log N)$IN + 1PR
	[14]-II	$O(r)$	$O(\log^2 N)$	$O(\eta)$		$(\log \log N)$IN + 1PR
	[6]	$O(r)$	$O(\log^{2.5} N)$	$O(\log N)$		2PR
	[12]	$O(r)$	$O(\log^{1.5} N)$	$O(\eta)$		3PR + 3PD + 2EX
	Ours	$O(r)$	$O(\log^{1.5} N)$	$O(1)$		3PR + 2PD + 1EX

PR = pairing operation, PD = product, EX = exponentiation, IN = inversion, PLBE = private linear broadcast encryption, TRSC = trace and revoke from subset cover framework, CS = complete subtree, SubDif = subset difference, $|PP|$ = public parameter size, $|SK|$ = user secret key size, $|CT|$ = ciphertext size, DT = decryption time, $\mathbb{G}_\varrho$ = multilinear intermediate group, poly = polynomial, N = total number of users in the system and, r = size of revoked set, η = security parameter.

PLBE systems [2, 3, 8, 13] based on PLBE. We achieve similar ciphertext size, secret-key size, public parameter size and decryption cost as that of the TRSC construction of [12]. However, the construction in [12] is secure under the q-SMEBDH assumption in ROM. Although the decryption cost in our scheme is more than those in [6, 14], the constructions in [14] are in secret-key setting while that in [6] is in public-key setting, but is secure under non-standard q-type assumptions in the ROM. More interestingly, our TRSC scheme significantly reduces the size of the public parameter and the users' secret key over the TRSC of [6, 14]. Our scheme outperforms the existing PLBE systems [2, 3, 8, 13] in terms of communication bandwidth ($|CT|$) and public parameter size ($|PP|$) (where $r << N$) as well as decryption time. Even though the secret key size ($|SK|$) of [2] is constant while that in our TRSC is $O(\log^{1.5}(N))$, the PLBE of [2] is in secret-key setting. Note that the currently known PLBE construction [13] is based on multilinear maps and indistinguishability obfuscation whose practicality or even ability to instantiate with existing primitives is questionable. Besides, the construction is secure under the non-standard multilinear q-Decisional Hybrid Diffie-Hellman Exponent assumption.

- As shown in Table 2, the security of the TRSC systems [6, 12, 14] are in ROM where all the parties are given a *black-box access* to a truly random function. From the practical point of view, there does not exist such random looking functions and consequently, the proofs in ROM can be treated as *heuristic arguments*. At a technical level, hash functions are considered as random oracle which is a theoretical black-box that responds random reply to every query. However, there is a debate on the acceptance of a security proof in ROM as many security model which are secure in ROM may not be secure in standard security model. To circumvent the ROM, we utilize the identity based Déjà Q framework of [15] along with the *single revocation encryption*

Table 2. Comparative summary of traceability, security and other functionality

| Tracing via. | Scheme | Traceability | Security | | ROM | CovTech |
			SM	SA		
PLBE	[2]	Secret	Selective CPA	D3DH, DHSD, BSD	No	–
	[3]	Public	Adaptive CPA	D3DH, DHSD, BSD	No	–
	[8]	Public	Adaptive CPA	D3DH, XDH	No	–
	[13]	Public	Adaptive CCA	q-DHDHE	No	–
TRSC	[14]-I	Secret	Selective CPA	BDH	Yes	CS
	[14]-II	Secret	Selective CPA	BDH	Yes	SubDif
	[6]	Public	Adaptive CCA	q-SMEBDH	Yes	SubDif
	[12]	Public	Adaptive CPA	q-SMEBDH	Yes	SubDif
	Ours	Public	Adaptive CPA	SD	No	SubDif

SM = security model, SA = security assumption, ROM = random oracle model, CovTech = covering technique, CPA = chosen plaintext attack, CCA = chosen ciphertext attack, CS = complete subtree, SubDif = subset difference, D3DH = Decision 3-party Diffie-Hellman, DHSD = Diffie-Hellman Subgroup Decision, BSD = Bilinear Subgroup Decision, XDH = External Diffie-Hellman, q-SMEBDH = Simplified Multi-Exponent Bilinear Diffie-Hellman, BDH = Bilinear Diffie-Hellman, q-DHDHE = Decisional Hybrid Diffie-Hellman Exponent, SD = Subgroup Decision.

technique of [12] and utilizing the left-over hash lemma, achieving the first fully collusion resistant and public-key TRSC scheme adaptively secure under the subgroup decision (SD) assumption in standard security model without using any random oracle.

- Note that the PLBE tracing schemes [2, 3, 8] are secure under standard security assumptions. Consequently, there is no need to employ Déjà Q framework. On the other hand, the PLBE construction [13] is secure under the non-standard q-DHDHE assumption over prime order multilinear group setting and the currently known public-key TRSC schemes [6, 12] are secure under the hardness of the non-standard q-SMEBDH assumption. To exploit the Déjà Q framework over [6, 12, 13], we need to impose random elements of another prime order group to each component of the ciphertext, public parameter and the user secret key. In that case, the construction will be shifted to composite order group setting and the size of the parameters will become very large. However, converting a general q-type security assumption into a standard security assumption without increasing the parameter size is a difficult task even if the underlying group is in composite order. In our public-key TRSC construction, we skilfully merge the single revocation encryption technique of [12] and the identity based encryption scheme of [15] over composite order bilinear group setting and then utilize *left-over hash lemma* so that the q-type complexity assumption can be removed using the Déjà Q framework of [4] without sacrificing the parameter sizes.

2 Preliminaries

Notation. For an algorithm RandA, $y \leftarrow$ RandA(z) represents output by RandA on input z. The concatenation of two strings $s, t \in \{0,1\}^*$ is denoted by $s\|t$.

2.1 Full Binary Tree and Related Surveillance [14]

Full Binary Tree. A full binary tree (FBT) is a tree data structure where each node except the leaf nodes has exactly two children. We consider a FBT with $N = 2^\kappa$ leaf nodes. Note that the total number of nodes in FBT is $2N - 1$ and v_i denotes the i-th node in FBT for $1 \leq i \leq 2N - 1$. We assume that the root (RT) of FBT at level-0 with depth 0, all the N leaves at level-κ with depth κ and any other internal node v_i at level-d_i with depth d_i which is the length of the unique path from RT to v_i. For any node $v_i \in$ FBT, we define $\mathcal{S}_i$ as the set of all leaf nodes in the subtree rooted at v_i. Further, for any two nodes $v_i, v_j \in$ FBT with v_j is the descendant of v_i, we denote $\mathcal{S}_{i,j}$ as the set of all leaf nodes which are descendant of v_i but not v_j, that is, $\mathcal{S}_{i,j} = \mathcal{S}_i \setminus \mathcal{S}_j$. In FBT, $x_i = 0$ corresponds to left branch and $x_i = 1$ corresponds to right branch of any node $v_i \in$ FBT except the leaf nodes. Then any node v_i with depth d_i can be assigned by a fixed and unique identity bit string $\mathsf{str}_i = x_0 x_1 \ldots x_i$ obtained by reading all the labels of branches in the path from RT to v_i. For any two nodes $v_i, v_j \in$ FBT, we denote the *least common ancestor* $v \in$ FBT of v_i and v_j by $v = \mathsf{LCA}(v_i, v_j)$.

Identifier Function. We define the *identifier function* f^{ID} as follows.

- $f^{\mathsf{ID}}(v_i) = \mathsf{str}_i$ for a node $v_i \in$ FBT.
- $f^{\mathsf{ID}}(\mathcal{S}_i) = f^{\mathsf{ID}}(v_i) = \mathsf{str}_i$, where $\mathcal{S}_i$ and str_i are defined above.
- $f^{\mathsf{ID}}(\mathcal{S}_{i,j}) = \left(f^{\mathsf{ID}}(\mathcal{S}_i), f^{\mathsf{ID}}(\mathcal{S}_j)\right) = \left(f^{\mathsf{ID}}(v_i), f^{\mathsf{ID}}(v_j)\right) = (\mathsf{str}_i, \mathsf{str}_j)$, where $\mathcal{S}_{i,j}$ is the set of all leaf nodes which are descendant of v_i but not v_j.

Steiner Tree. Let $\mathcal{R}$ be a subset of leaf nodes belonging to the FBT. Then, the minimal subtree of the FBT that connects nodes in $\mathcal{R}$ and the root (RT) is called a Steiner tree $\mathcal{ST}(\mathcal{R})$ introduced by $\mathcal{R}$ and RT.

Inputs: $\mathcal{S}_{i,j}$, FBT
Output: Disjoint subsets $\mathcal{S}_{i_1,j_1}$ and $\mathcal{S}_{i_2,j_2}$ such that $\mathcal{S}_{i,j} = (\mathcal{S}_{i_1,j_1} \cup \mathcal{S}_{i_2,j_2})$.

1. From $\mathcal{S}_{i,j}$, extract the node v_i and find the location of v_i in the FBT.
2. Assume v_L be the left child and v_R be the right child of the node v_i such that v_j is the descendant of v_L.
3. Construct the subsets $\mathcal{S}_{L,j}$ and $\mathcal{S}_{i,L}$.
4. Return $\mathcal{S}_{i_1,j_1} = \mathcal{S}_{L,j}$ and $\mathcal{S}_{i_2,j_2} = \mathcal{S}_{i,L}$.

Fig. 1. The bifurcation algorithm SD$_{\mathsf{Bifur}}$

Bifurcation Property. Bifurcation property [14] under the context of subset cover framework is a deterministic algorithm $\mathsf{SD}_{\mathsf{Bifur}}$ that takes as input any subset $\mathcal{S}_{i,j}$ of leaf nodes of a FBT and outputs two roughly equal and disjoint subsets $\mathcal{S}_{i_1,j_1}$ and $\mathcal{S}_{i_2,j_2}$ as shown in Fig. 1 such that $\mathcal{S}_{i,j} = (\mathcal{S}_{i_1,j_1} \cup \mathcal{S}_{i_2,j_2})$.

2.2 Bilinear Groups and Complexity Assumptions

On input the security parameter η of the system, a group generator $\mathcal{G}$ outputs a description $\mathsf{bilgr} = (G, G_T, n, e)$ with G and G_T two multiplicative cyclic groups of same composite order $n = p_1 p_2 p_3$ where p_1, p_2, p_3 are the distinct primes with each $p_i > 2^\eta$. We denote g_i and g as the random generators for G_{p_i} and G respectively. The *bilinear map* $e : G \times G \to G_T$ amuses the following properties.

- *Bilinearity*: $\forall u, v \in G$ and $\forall a, b \in \mathbb{Z}_n$, $e(u^a, v^b) = e(u, v)^{ab}$.
- *Nondegeneracy*: $\exists\, g$ such that $e(g, g)$ has order n, that is, $e(g, g)$ is a generator of G_T.

  Further, we say that G, G_T are bilinear groups if the bilinear map e as well as the group operations in G and G_T are computable in deterministic polynomial time. In addition, we denote $G_{p_i}^*$ as $G_{p_i} \smallsetminus \{1\}$.

Subgroup Decision 1 (SD1) Problem [15]. The SD1 problem is to guess $\mu \in \{0, 1\}$ given $\chi_\mu = (\mathsf{bilgr}, g_1, g_3, T_\mu)$ generated by the generator $\mathcal{G}_\mu^{\mathsf{SD1}}$, which is shown in Fig. 2.

- Run the group generator $\mathcal{G}(\eta)$ to generate description $\mathsf{bilgr} = (G, G_T, n, e)$, where $n = p_1 p_2 p_3$, G and G_T be two multiplicative cyclic groups of same composite order n with $G = G_{p_1} G_{p_2} G_{p_3}$ and $e : G \times G \to G_T$.
- Pick randomly g_1 and g_3 from $G_{p_1}^*$ and $G_{p_3}^*$ respectively.
- Selects $B_1 \in_R G_{p_1}$, $B_1 B_2 \in_R G_{p_1} G_{p_2}$ and set $T_0 = B_1 \in_R G_{p_1}$, $T_1 = B_1 B_2 \in_R G_{p_1} G_{p_2}$.
- Return $\chi_\mu = (\mathsf{bilgr}, g_1, g_3, T_\mu)$.

Fig. 2. SD1 problem instance generator $\mathcal{G}_\mu^{\mathsf{SD1}}$

The advantage of a probabilistic polynomial time (PPT) algorithm $\mathcal{A}_1$ in solving the SD1 problem is defined as

$$\mathsf{Adv}_{\mathcal{A}_1}^{\mathsf{SD1}}(\eta) = |Pr[\mathcal{A}_1(\eta, \chi_0) \to 1] - Pr[\mathcal{A}_1(\eta, \chi_1) \to 1]|.$$

Definition 1 (SD1 Assumption). *The* SD1 *assumption is that* $\mathsf{Adv}_{\mathcal{A}_1}^{\mathsf{SD1}}(\eta)$ *is at most negligible for all* PPT *algorithms* $\mathcal{A}_1$.

Subgroup Decision 2 (SD2) Problem [15]. The SD2 problem is to guess $\mu \in \{0, 1\}$ given $\chi_\mu = (\mathsf{bilgr}, g_1, g_3, g_{1,2}, g_{2,3}, T_\mu)$ generated by the generator $\mathcal{G}_\mu^{\mathsf{SD2}}$, which is shown in Fig. 3.

- Run the group generator $\mathcal{G}(\eta)$ to generate description $\mathsf{bilgr} = (G, G_T, n, e)$, where $n = p_1 p_2 p_3$, G and G_T be two multiplicative cyclic groups of same composite order n with $G = G_{p_1} G_{p_2} G_{p_3}$ and $e : G \times G \to G_T$.
- Pick randomly g_1 and g_3 from $G_{p_1}^*$ and $G_{p_3}^*$ respectively, and randomly select $g_{1,2}$ and $g_{2,3}$ from $G_{p_1} G_{p_2}$ and $G_{p_2} G_{p_3}$ respectively.
- Select $R_1 R_3 \in_R G_{p_1} G_{p_3}$, $R_1 R_2 R_3 \in_R G_{p_1} G_{p_2} G_{p_3}$ and set $T_0 = R_1 R_3 \in_R G_{p_1} G_{p_3}$, $T_1 = R_1 R_2 R_3 \in_R G_{p_1} G_{p_2} G_{p_3}$.
- Return $\chi_\mu = (\mathsf{bilgr}, g_1, g_3, g_{1,2}, g_{2,3}, T_\mu)$.

Fig. 3. SD2 problem instance generator $\mathcal{G}_\mu^{\mathsf{SD2}}$

The advantage of a PPT algorithm $\mathcal{A}_2$ in solving the SD2 problem is defined as

$$\mathsf{Adv}_{\mathcal{A}_2}^{\mathsf{SD2}}(\eta) = |Pr[\mathcal{A}_2(\eta, \chi_0) \to 1] - Pr[\mathcal{A}_2(\eta, \chi_1) \to 1]|.$$

Definition 2 (SD2 Assumption). *The SD2 assumption is that* $\mathsf{Adv}_{\mathcal{A}_2}^{\mathsf{SD2}}(\eta)$ *is at most negligible for all PPT algorithms* $\mathcal{A}_2$.

2.3 Left-Over Hash Lemma

Definition 3 (Min-Entropy). *Let* X *be a random variable over some finite set* F. *The min-entropy* H_∞ *of the random variable* X *is defined as* $\mathsf{H}_\infty(X) = -\log(max_{x \in F} Pr[X = x])$.

Definition 4 (Pairwise Independent Hash Families). *Let* $F_1, F_2 \subset \{0,1\}^*$ *be finite sets. A family* $\mathbb{H}$ *of hash functions* $H : F_1 \to F_2$ *is called pairwise independent if for any* $s_1, s_2 \in F_1$ *with* $s_1 \neq s_2$, *there exists* $z_1, z_2 \in F_2$ *such that*

$$\Pr_{H \in_R \mathbb{H}}[(H(s_1) = z_1) \wedge (H(s_2) = z_2)] = \frac{1}{(|F_2|)^2}$$

where $|F_2|$ *denotes the cardinality of the set* F_2.

Lemma 1 (Left-Over Hash Lemma [10]). *Let* X *be a random variable over some finite set* F *and let* $\varkappa \in \mathbb{N}$. *Let* $H : F \to \{0,1\}^\varkappa$ *be sampled from a pairwise independent hash family* $\mathbb{H}$ *uniformly and independently of* X. *If* $\varkappa = \mathsf{H}_\infty(X) - 2\log\frac{1}{\epsilon} - O(1)$, *then* $\Delta((H(X), H), (U_\varkappa, H)) \leq \frac{\epsilon}{2}$, *where* $U_\varkappa$ *is the uniform random variable over* $\{0,1\}^\varkappa$ *and* $\Delta(V, W) = \frac{1}{2} \sum_{\partial \in \mathbb{D}} |Pr[V = \partial] - Pr[W = \partial]|$ *is a statistical distance between any two random variables* V *and* W *over some set* $\mathbb{D}$.

2.4 Overview of the Déjà Q Framework

The Déjà Q framework, introduced by Chase et al. [4], is an extension of the dual system technique that eliminates various q-type complexity assumption for deriving security of bilinear-map-based cryptographic constructions. Recently, Wee [15] has mitigated several shortcomings of [4] to make the framework competent for governing the advanced encryption systems such as broadcast encryption, where certain secret exponents shared in between ciphertext and user's decryption keys, i.e., on both arguments of the pairing.

Lemma 2 (Core Lemma of the Déjà Q Framework [4,15]). *Fix a prime p and define* $\mathsf{F}^q_{r_1,\ldots,r_q,x_1,\ldots,x_q} : \mathbb{Z}_p \to \mathbb{Z}_p$ *to be*

$$\mathsf{F}^q_{r_1,\ldots,r_q,x_1,\ldots,x_q}(\mathsf{Lev}_1) = \sum_{i=1}^{q} \frac{r_i}{x_i + \mathsf{Lev}_1}$$

Then, for any (possibly unbounded) adversary $\mathcal{A}$ that makes at most q queries, we have

$$\left| \Pr_{r_1,\ldots,r_q,x_1,\ldots,x_q \in_R \mathbb{Z}_p} \left[\mathcal{A}^{\mathsf{F}^q_{r_1,\ldots,r_q,x_1,\ldots,x_q}(\cdot)}(1^q) = 1 \right] - \Pr\left[\mathcal{A}^{\mathsf{RF}(\cdot)}(1^q) = 1 \right] \right| \leq O\left(\frac{q^2}{p}\right)$$

where $\mathsf{RF} : \mathbb{Z}_p \to \mathbb{Z}_p$ *is a truly random function.*

3   Our TRSC Construction

To maintain the page restriction, the generic description of our TRSC construction, which will be presented in the full version of the paper, has been omitted. However, following the works of [12], the communication model of our TRSC construction involves a group manager (GM), a broadcaster, several users and a tracer. Our scheme TRSC = (TRSC.Setup, TRSC.KeyGen, TRSC.Encrypt, TRSC.Decrypt, TRSC.Trace$^{\mathcal{D}}$) is described as follows.

- (trscmpk, trscmsk) ← TRSC.Setup(η, κ): The group manager (GM) on input the length κ of the user identities along with the security parameter η proceeds as follows.

Inputs: $\mathsf{path}_u = (\mathsf{RT} = v_0, v_1, \ldots, v_\kappa = v_u)$, u
Output: Unique private set prvt_u for the user u

    $\mathsf{prvt}_u \leftarrow \emptyset$;
    for ($i' = 0$ to $\kappa - 1$) do
        for ($j' = i' + 1$ to κ) do
            $\mathsf{prvt}_u \leftarrow \mathsf{prvt}_u \cup \mathcal{S}_{i',j'}$; // Description of $\mathcal{S}_{i',j'}$ is given in section 2.1.
        end do
    end do
    return prvt_u;

Fig. 4. Unique private set generation algorithm SD$_{\mathsf{KGen}}$

(i) It first constructs a full binary tree (FBT) of depth κ with $N = 2^\kappa$ users assigned in the leaf nodes. Consequently, the total number of nodes in FBT is $2N - 1$. For each node $v_i \in$ FBT, a fixed and unique identity bit string $\mathsf{str}_i = x_1 \ldots x_i$ is obtained by reading all the labels of branches in the path $\mathsf{path}_{v_i} = (v_0, v_1, \ldots, v_i)$ from the root (RT) $= v_0$ to the node v_i. It sets up an *identifier function* f^{ID} as described in Sect. 2.1.

(ii) It executes the bilinear group generator $\mathcal{G}(\eta)$ to generate the description of a bilinear group $\mathsf{bilgr} = (G, G_T, n, e)$ as shown in Sect. 2.2. Let g_i be a random generator of G_{p_i} for $i = 1, 2, 3$.

(iii) It also chooses an exponent $x \in_R \mathbb{Z}_n$, three group elements $\tau, \beta, \varrho \in_R G_{p_1}$ and a cryptographically secure hash function $H : G_T \to \{0,1\}^\eta$. It sets the master public key as $\mathsf{trscmpk} = (\mathsf{FBT}, \mathsf{bilgr} = (G, G_T, n, e), f^{\mathsf{ID}}, g_1, g_1^x, \beta, \varrho, H, \Delta = e(g_1, \tau))$ and the master secret key as $\mathsf{trscmsk} = (x, \tau, g_3)$.

Finally, it publishes $\mathsf{trscmpk}$ and keeps $\mathsf{trscmsk}$ secret to itself.

- $\mathsf{trpk}_u \leftarrow \mathsf{TRSC.KeyGen}(u, \mathsf{trscmpk}, \mathsf{trscmsk})$: On input any user index $u \in [N]$, the master public key $\mathsf{trscmpk} = (\mathsf{FBT}, \mathsf{bilgr} = (G, G_T, n, e), f^{\mathsf{ID}}, g_1, g_1^x, \beta, \varrho, H, \Delta = e(g_1, \tau))$ and the master secret key $\mathsf{trscmsk} = (x, \tau, g_3)$, the GM accomplishes following steps.

(i) It identifies the unique path $\mathsf{path}_u = (\mathsf{RT} = v_0, v_1, \ldots, v_\kappa = v_u)$ from root RT to leaf v_κ where user $u \in [N]$ is designated. The GM assigns a unique private set prvt_u to the user u by running the program $\mathsf{SD}_{\mathsf{KGen}}$ shown in Fig. 4.

(ii) It chooses a random exponent $r \in \mathbb{Z}_n$ and generates three random elements $\Gamma_1, \Gamma_2, \Gamma_3 \in G_{p_3}$ using generator g_3 of G_{p_3} extracted from $\mathsf{trscmsk}$.

Inputs: $\mathcal{S}_{i',j'} \in \mathsf{prvt}_u$, $r \in_R \mathbb{Z}_n$, Γ_1, Γ_2, $\Gamma_3 \in_R G_{p_3}$, $\mathsf{trscmpk} = (\mathsf{FBT}, \mathsf{bilgr}, f^{\mathsf{ID}}, g_1, g_1^x, \beta, \varrho, H, \Delta = e(g_1, \tau))$, $\mathsf{trscmsk} = (x, \tau, g_3)$
Output: Private key $\mathcal{K}_{\mathcal{S}_{i',j'}}$ corresponding to the subset $\mathcal{S}_{i',j'}$

1. Let, in the full binary tree FBT, $d_{j'}$ be the depth of the node $v_{j'} \in \mathsf{path}_u = (\mathsf{RT} = v_0, v_1, \ldots, v_\kappa = v_u)$ with the binary representation $\mathsf{bin}(d_{j'})$;

2. Compute: $(\mathsf{str}_{i'}, \mathsf{str}_{j'}) \leftarrow f^{\mathsf{ID}}(\mathcal{S}_{i',j'})$, where $\mathsf{str}_{i'}, \mathsf{str}_{j'} \in \{0,1\}^*$ and the function f^{ID} is extracted from $\mathsf{trscmpk}$;

3. Let, $\mathsf{Lev}_1^{(i')} \in \mathbb{Z}_n^*$ be the integer representation of the string $(\mathsf{str}_{i'} \| \mathsf{bin}(d_{j'})) \in \{0,1\}^*$ and $\mathsf{Lev}_2^{(j')} \in \mathbb{Z}_n^*$ be the integer representation of the string $\mathsf{str}_{j'} \in \{0,1\}^*$;

4. Compute:
$$K_0^{(i',j')} = (\tau)^{\frac{1}{x+\mathsf{Lev}_1^{(i')}}}(\beta)^{\frac{r}{x+\mathsf{Lev}_1^{(i')}}}\Gamma_1, \quad K_1^{(i',j')} = (\beta^{\mathsf{Lev}_2^{(j')}}\varrho)^r \Gamma_2, \quad K_2^{(i',j')} = g_1^{-r}\Gamma_3;$$

5. Return: $\mathcal{K}_{\mathcal{S}_{i',j'}} = (K_0^{(i',j')}, K_1^{(i',j')}, K_2^{(i',j')})$;

Fig. 5. The tracing private key generation program $\mathsf{TRSC}_{\mathsf{KGen}}$

For each subset $\mathcal{S}_{i',j'} \in \mathsf{prvt}_u$, it runs the program $\mathsf{TRSC}_{\mathsf{KGen}}$ of Fig. 5 and generates a private key $\mathcal{K}_{\mathcal{S}_{i',j'}}$ for the subset $\mathcal{S}_{i',j'}$.

Finally, the GM sends $\mathsf{trpk}_u = (\mathsf{prvt}_u, \{\mathcal{K}_{\mathcal{S}_{i',j'}} : \mathcal{S}_{i',j'} \in \mathsf{prvt}_u\})$ as the tracing private key to user u through a secure communication channel between the GM and the user u.

- $(\mathsf{CT}_{\mathcal{R}}) \leftarrow \mathsf{TRSC.Encrypt}(\mathcal{R}, M, \mathsf{trscmpk})$: On input a revoked set of users $\mathcal{R} \subseteq [N]$, a message $M \in \{0,1\}^\eta$ and the master public key $\mathsf{trscmpk} = (\mathsf{FBT}, \mathsf{bilgr}, f^{\mathsf{ID}}, g_1, g_1^x, \beta, \varrho, H, \Delta = e(g_1, \tau))$, the encryptor executes the following steps.

(i) Using the root RT of the FBT and the revoked user nodes in $\mathcal{R}$, it assembles the Steiner tree $\mathcal{ST}(\mathcal{R})$ which is the minimal subtree of the FBT that connects all the nodes in $\mathcal{R}$ and the root RT of the FBT. It runs the disjoint cover finding algorithm $\mathsf{SD}_{\mathsf{Cover}}$ of Fig. 6 to construct a disjoint cover (disjoint partition) $\mathsf{dcvr}_{\mathcal{R}}$ of the non-revoked users belonging to $[N] \setminus \mathcal{R}$.

Inputs: $\mathcal{ST}(\mathcal{R})$, FBT
Output: Disjoint cover $\mathsf{dcvr}_{\mathcal{R}} = \{\mathcal{S}_{i,j}\}$ of the non-revoked users in $[N] \setminus \mathcal{R}$

$\mathsf{dcvr}_{\mathcal{R}} \leftarrow \emptyset$;
while $(|\mathcal{ST}(\mathcal{R})| \neq 1)$ do
(i)   if $(\mathcal{ST}(\mathcal{R})$ has more than one leaf nodes) then
            Extract two leaf nodes v_i and v_j in $\mathcal{ST}(\mathcal{R})$ such that the subtree
            rooted at the least common ancestor $v = \mathsf{LCA}(v_i, v_j)$ does not contain
            any leaf node of $\mathcal{ST}(\mathcal{R})$ other than v_i and v_j. Let, the left child v_L of
            v is the ancestor of v_i, and the right child v_R of v is the ancestor of
            v_j. As $v = \mathsf{LCA}(v_i, v_j)$, v_L is not an ancestor of v_j and v_R is not an
            ancestor of v_i;
        end if
        else if $(\mathcal{ST}(\mathcal{R})$ has exactly one leaf node v_k) then
            Set: $v_i = v_j = v_k$, $\mathsf{LCA}(v_i, v_j) = v = \mathsf{RT}$ root of $\mathcal{ST}(\mathcal{R})$ and $v_L = v_R = v$;
        end else if
(ii) if $(v_L \neq v_i)$ then
        $\mathsf{dcvr}_{\mathcal{R}} = \mathsf{dcvr}_{\mathcal{R}} \cup \{\mathcal{S}_{L,i}\}$;
     end if
(iii) if $(v_R \neq v_j)$ then
        $\mathsf{dcvr}_{\mathcal{R}} = \mathsf{dcvr}_{\mathcal{R}} \cup \{\mathcal{S}_{R,j}\}$;
      end if
(iv) Remove the subtree rooted at v from $\mathcal{ST}(\mathcal{R})$ and make v a leaf node of $\mathcal{ST}(\mathcal{R})$;
end do
return $\mathsf{dcvr}_{\mathcal{R}} = \{\mathcal{S}_{i,j} : \forall (i \neq i') \wedge (j \neq j'), \mathcal{S}_{i,j} \cap \mathcal{S}_{i',j'} = \emptyset$ and $[N] \setminus \mathcal{R} = \bigcup_{\forall i,j} \mathcal{S}_{i,j}\}$;

Fig. 6. Disjoint cover finding algorithm $\mathsf{SD}_{\mathsf{Cover}}$

(ii) The encryptor chooses a random exponent $s \in \mathbb{Z}_n$. For each subset $\mathcal{S}_{i,j} \in$ dcvr$_\mathcal{R}$, it runs the ciphertext generation program TRSC$_{\mathsf{CTGen}}$ of Fig. 7 and generates the ciphertext ciphr$_{\mathcal{S}_{i,j}}$ corresponding to the subset $\mathcal{S}_{i,j}$.

Inputs: $\mathcal{S}_{i,j} \in$ dcvr$_\mathcal{R}$, $s \in_R \mathbb{Z}_n$, $M \in \{0,1\}^\eta$, trscmpk $= (\mathsf{FBT}, \mathsf{bilgr}, f^{\mathsf{ID}}, g_1, g_1^x, \beta, \varrho,$
$H, \Delta = e(g_1, \tau))$
Output: The ciphertext ciphr$_{\mathcal{S}_{i,j}}$ corresponding to the set $\mathcal{S}_{i,j}$

1. Let, d_j be the depth of the node v_j with the binary representation bin(d_j) in the full binary tree **FBT**;
2. Compute: $(\mathsf{str}_i, \mathsf{str}_j) \leftarrow f^{\mathsf{ID}}(\mathcal{S}_{i,j})$, where $\mathsf{str}_i, \mathsf{str}_j \in \{0,1\}^*$ and the function f^{ID} is extracted from trscmpk;
3. Let, $\mathsf{Lev}_1^{(i)} \in \mathbb{Z}_n^*$ be the integer representation of the string $(\mathsf{str}_i \| \mathrm{bin}(d_j)) \in \{0,1\}^*$ and $\mathsf{Lev}_2^{(j)} \in \mathbb{Z}_n^*$ be the binary representation of the string $\mathsf{str}_j \in \{0,1\}^*$;
4. Compute:
   $C_0^{(i,j)} = g_1^{\,s\left(x + \mathsf{Lev}_1^{(i)}\right)}$, $C_1^{(i,j)} = g_1^{\,s}$, $C_2^{(i,j)} = \left(\beta^{\mathsf{Lev}_2^{(j)}} \varrho\right)^s$, and $C_3^{(i,j)} = M \oplus H\left(\Delta^s\right)$;
5. Return: ciphr$_{\mathcal{S}_{i,j}} = \left(C_0^{(i,j)}, C_1^{(i,j)}, C_2^{(i,j)}, C_3^{(i,j)}\right)$;

Fig. 7. The ciphertext generation program TRSC$_{\mathsf{CTGen}}$

Finally, the encryptor publishes $\mathsf{CT}_\mathcal{R} = (\mathsf{dcvr}_\mathcal{R}, \{\mathsf{ciphr}_{\mathcal{S}_{i,j}} : \mathcal{S}_{i,j} \in \mathsf{dcvr}_\mathcal{R}\})$ as the ciphertext corresponding to the revoked set $\mathcal{R}$ of users and the message $M \in \{0,1\}^\eta$.

- $(M \vee \bot) \leftarrow$ TRSC.Decrypt($\mathsf{CT}_\mathcal{R}, \mathsf{trpk}_u, \mathsf{trscmpk}$): A user $u \in [N]$ uses its tracing private key trpk_u to recover the correct message $M \in \{0,1\}^\eta$ from the ciphertext $\mathsf{CT}_\mathcal{R}$, corresponding to the revoked set of users $\mathcal{R}$, utilizing the master public key trscmpk. It runs the decryption program TRSC$_{\mathsf{Dec}}$ of Fig. 8 and outputs either the correct message M or a designated symbol $\bot$ indicating decryption failure.

To be more specific, we require to ensure that if the decryptor u does not belong to the revoked set of users $\mathcal{R}$, then the condition 2.(b) of the program TRSC$_{\mathsf{Dec}}$ of Fig. 8 satisfies. As dcvr$_\mathcal{R}$ is the disjoint cover of the non-revoked users and $u \notin \mathcal{R}$, accordingly there exists exactly one subset $\mathcal{S}_{i,j} \in$ dcvr$_\mathcal{R}$ such that the leaf node v_u corresponding to the user u belongs to $\mathcal{S}_{i,j}$. However, the subset $\mathcal{S}_{i,j}$ can be represented utilizing only two nodes v_i and v_j, where the node v_u is descendant of v_i and v_j is not an ancestor of v_u. On the other hand, any subset $\mathcal{S}_{i',j'} \in$ prvt$_u$ can be represented utilizing two nodes $v_{i'}$ and $v_{j'}$, where both the nodes lie on the path from the root RT of the FBT to the leaf node v_u. Consequently, $v_{i'}$ and $v_{j'}$ of any subset $\mathcal{S}_{i',j'} \in$ prvt$_u$ are the ancestor of v_u. Therefore, in step 2.(a) of Fig. 8, the program will detect two subsets $\mathcal{S}_{i,j} \in$ dcvr$_\mathcal{R}$ and $\mathcal{S}_{i',j'} \in$ prvt$_u$ such that $v_i = v_{i'}$, $d_j = d_{j'}$ and $v_j \neq v_{j'}$, where d_j and $d_{j'}$ are the depth of v_j and $v_{j'}$ respectively.

Inputs: $CT_\mathcal{R}$, $u \in [N]$, $trpk_u$, $trscmpk = (FBT, bilgr, f^{ID}, g_1, g_1^x, \beta, \varrho, H, \Delta = e(g_1, \tau))$
Output: Either M or $\perp$

1. If $u \in \mathcal{R}$, return $\perp$ and stop;
2. Otherwise, execute the following steps;
   (a) Extract $dcvr_\mathcal{R}$ from $CT_\mathcal{R}$ and $prvt_u$ from $trpk_u$;
   (b) Find two subsets $\mathcal{S}_{i,j} \in dcvr_\mathcal{R}$ and $\mathcal{S}_{i',j'} \in prvt_u$ such that $i = i'$, $d_j = d_{j'}$ and $j \neq j'$, where d_j and $d_{j'}$ are the depth of v_j and $v_{j'}$ respectively;
   (c) Compute $str_j \leftarrow f^{ID}(v_j)$, $str_{j'} \leftarrow f^{ID}(v_{j'})$ and set $Lev_2^{(j)} = str_j$, $Lev_2^{(j')} = str_{j'}$;
   (d) Extract the ciphertext $ciphr_{\mathcal{S}_{i,j}} = \left(C_0^{(i,j)}, C_1^{(i,j)}, C_2^{(i,j)}, C_3^{(i,j)}\right)$ from $CT_\mathcal{R}$ corresponding to the subset $\mathcal{S}_{i,j}$;
   (e) Extract the key $\mathcal{K}_{\mathcal{S}_{i',j'}} = \left(K_0^{(i',j')}, K_1^{(i',j')}, K_2^{(i',j')}\right)$ from $prvt_u$ corresponding to the subset $\mathcal{S}_{i',j'}$;
   (f) Compute:
   $$A = \frac{e(C_0^{(i,j)}, K_0^{(i',j')})}{\left[e(C_1^{(i,j)}, K_1^{(i',j')}) \cdot e(C_2^{(i,j)}, K_2^{(i',j')})\right]^{\frac{1}{Lev_2^{(j')} - Lev_2^{(j)}}}} \quad \text{and} \quad M = C_3^{(i,j)} \oplus H(A);$$
   (g) Return: M;

Fig. 8. The decryption program $TRSC_{Dec}$

- $\mathbb{T}^{TTS} \leftarrow TRSC.Trace^\mathcal{D}(\mathcal{R}, \epsilon, trscmpk)$: Taking as input a revoked set $\mathcal{R}$ of users, a parameter ϵ and the master public key $trscmpk$, the tracer interacts polynomially many times with a pirate decoder box $\mathcal{D}$ by running the publicly executable algorithm $TRSC.Trace^\mathcal{D}$. The pirate decoder $\mathcal{D}$ is viewed as a probabilistic circuit that consists of some rogue users' secret keys. The tracer considers *black-box* tracing where $\mathcal{D}$ cannot be reversed engineered and the rogue users' secret key inside $\mathcal{D}$ cannot be revealed directly. With the knowledge from these interactions, the tracer finally outputs a set of users $\mathbb{T}^{TTS} \subseteq [N]$. Following Naor et al. [14], the overall tracing procedure of our TRSC scheme works as follows.

(i) At the beginning of the interactions, the tracer initializes the traitor set $\mathbb{T}^{TTS}$ to the empty set.
(ii) The tracer constructs the Steiner tree $ST(\mathcal{R} \cup \mathbb{T}^{TTS})$ by utilizing the current collection $\mathbb{T}^{TTS}$ and obtains a disjoint partition of the non-revoked users set $[N] \setminus (\mathcal{R} \cup \mathbb{T}^{TTS})$ by running the disjoint cover finding algorithm as in Fig. 6 to generate $\mathcal{P} = \{\mathcal{S}_{i_k, j_k}\}_{k=1}^t \leftarrow SD_{Cover}(\mathcal{R} \cup \mathbb{T}^{TTS}, FBT)$.
(iii) To identity at least one traitor from the subset belonging to the disjoint partition $\mathcal{P} = \{\mathcal{S}_{i_k, j_k}\}_{k=1}^t$, the tracer iteratively performs the following steps.

Inputs: $k \in [0, t]$, $\mathcal{P} = \{\mathcal{S}_{i_k, j_k}\}_{k=1}^{t}$
Output: flag_k

1. The tracer chooses a random message $R \in \{0,1\}^\eta$, a random exponent $s \in \mathbb{Z}_n$, computes

$$\text{ciphr}_{\mathcal{S}_{i_l, j_l}} = \begin{cases} \text{TRSC}_{\text{CTGen}}(\mathcal{S}_{i_l, j_l}, s, R) & \text{for } 0 \le l \le k \\ \text{TRSC}_{\text{CTGen}}(\mathcal{S}_{i_l, j_l}, s, M) & \text{for } k+1 \le l \le t \end{cases}$$

and sets

$$\text{CT}_{\mathcal{RUT}^{\text{TTS}}}^{(k)} = \mathcal{P} \cup \{\text{ciphr}_{\mathcal{S}_{i_l, j_l}} \mid 0 \le l \le t\};$$

2. The tracer submits $\text{CT}_{\mathcal{RUT}^{\text{TTS}}}^{(k)}$ to the pirate decoder $\mathcal{D}$ which in turn outputs $M' \in \{0,1\}^\eta$ to the tracer;

3. Then, tracer sets

$$\text{flag}_k = \begin{cases} \text{success} & \text{if } M = M' \\ \text{failure} & \text{otherwise} \end{cases}$$

Fig. 9. Tracing experiment TrExp_k for $k = 0, 1, \ldots, t$.

- The tracer runs the experiment TrExp_k of Fig. 9 for $k = 0, 1, \ldots, t$. Let $p_k = \Pr[\text{flag}_k = \text{success}]$ be the success probability in the above experiment TrExp_k for $k = 0, \ldots, t$. Clearly, TrExp_0 has the success probability $p_0 = p$ which is greater than the threshold value 0.5 (say), whereas in the experiment TrExp_t the success probability is $p_t = 0$ and hence the difference between the success probability in the experiment TrExp_t and in the experiment TrExp_0 is $|p_t - p_0| = p$. Using the triangular inequality, we can assume that there must exists at least one $m \in \{0, \ldots, t\}$ such that $|p_m - p_{m-1}| \ge \frac{p}{t}$. Let the advantage of breaking the security of indistinguishability of our TRSC scheme is $\epsilon = \text{Adv}_\mathcal{A}^{\text{Ind} - \text{TRSC}}(\eta) = |Pr[b' = b] - \frac{1}{2}|$, which is negligible. If $|p_m - p_{m-1}| \ge \frac{p}{t} \ge \epsilon$, then the collection $\mathcal{S}_{i_m, j_m}$ must contain at least one traitor user as explained below.

From the $\mathcal{D}$'s point of view $\text{CT}_{\mathcal{RUT}^{\text{TTS}}}^{(m-1)} = \mathcal{P} \cup \{\text{ciphr}_{\mathcal{S}_{i_l, j_l}} \mid 0 \le l \le t\}$ where

$$\text{ciphr}_{\mathcal{S}_{i_l, j_l}} = \begin{cases} \text{TRSC}_{\text{CTGen}}(\mathcal{S}_{i_l, j_l}, s, R) & \text{for } 0 \le l \le m-1 \\ \text{TRSC}_{\text{CTGen}}(\mathcal{S}_{i_l, j_l}, s, M) & \text{for } m \le l \le t \end{cases}$$

that contains $m - 1$ noisy encryption of the random message R is different from $\text{CT}_{\mathcal{RUT}^{\text{TTS}}}^{(m)} = \mathcal{P} \cup \{\text{ciphr}_{\mathcal{S}_{i_l, j_l}} \mid 0 \le l \le t\}$ where

$$\text{ciphr}_{\mathcal{S}_{i_l, j_l}} = \begin{cases} \text{TRSC}_{\text{CTGen}}(\mathcal{S}_{i_l, j_l}, s, R) & \text{for } 0 \le l \le m \\ \text{TRSC}_{\text{CTGen}}(\mathcal{S}_{i_l, j_l}, s, M) & \text{for } m+1 \le l \le t \end{cases}$$

that contains m noisy encryption of the random message R only if the decoder $\mathcal{D}$ is able to distinguish between $\text{ciphr}_{\mathcal{S}_{i_m, j_m}} = \text{TRSC}_{\text{CTGen}}(\mathcal{S}_{i_m, j_m}, s, M)$ and

$\mathsf{ciphr}_{\mathcal{S}_{i_m,j_m}} = \mathsf{TRSC}_{\mathsf{CTGen}}(\mathcal{S}_{i_m,j_m}, s, R)$. This is infeasible under the security of indistinguishability of TRSC scheme. As $|p_m - p_{m-1}| \geq \epsilon$, it must be the case that $\mathcal{D}$ contains the secret key $\mathcal{K}_{\mathcal{S}_{i_m,j_m}} = \left(K_0^{(i_m,j_m)}, K_1^{(i_m,j_m)}, K_2^{(i_m,j_m)}\right)$ corresponding to the collection $\mathcal{S}_{i_m,j_m}$.

- If the aforementioned procedure cannot find such subset $\mathcal{S}_{i_m,j_m}$ that contains at least one traitor users' identity, then the tracer stops all the iterations and outputs the set $\mathbb{T}^{\mathsf{TTS}}$ as the set of all traitors.
- If the collection $\mathcal{S}_{i_m,j_m}$ contains more than two users, then employ the bifurcation algorithm $\left(\mathcal{S}_{i_{m_1},j_{m_1}} \cup \mathcal{S}_{i_{m_2},j_{m_2}}\right) \leftarrow \mathsf{SD}_{\mathsf{Bifur}}(\mathcal{S}_{i_m,j_m})$ as explained in Fig. 1. It removes $\mathcal{S}_{i_m,j_m}$ from the disjoint partition $\mathcal{P}$ and adds $\mathcal{S}_{i_{m_1},j_{m_1}}, \mathcal{S}_{i_{m_2},j_{m_2}}$ to $\mathcal{P}$. Then, go to step (iii).
- If the collection $\mathcal{S}_{i_m,j_m}$ contains only one user u_f, then the tracer stops the current iteration and sets $\mathbb{T}^{\mathsf{TTS}} = \mathbb{T}^{\mathsf{TTS}} \cup \{u_f\}$. Then, go to step (ii).

(iv) Finally, the tracer outputs the set $\mathbb{T}^{\mathsf{TTS}}$ as the set of all traitor user.

Correctness. The correctness of our TRSC scheme requires to verify the two condition 2.(f) of the decryption program $\mathsf{TRSC}_{\mathsf{Dec}}$ of Fig. 8. Observe that in condition 2.(b) of the program $\mathsf{TRSC}_{\mathsf{Dec}}$ of Fig. 8, the decryptor u encounters $v_i = v_{i'}, d_j = d_{j'}$ and $v_j \neq v_{j'}$. Accordingly, it can derive $(\mathsf{str}_i, \mathsf{str}_j) \leftarrow f^{\mathsf{ID}}(v_i, v_j)$ and $(\mathsf{str}_{i'}, \mathsf{str}_{j'}) \leftarrow f^{\mathsf{ID}}(v_{i'}, v_{j'})$. Then, u can set $\mathsf{Lev}_1^{(i)} \in \mathbb{Z}_n^*$ as the integer representation of the string $(\mathsf{str}_i \| \mathsf{bin}(d_j)) \in \{0,1\}^*$, $\mathsf{Lev}_2^{(j)} = \mathsf{str}_j$, $\mathsf{Lev}_1^{(i')} \in \mathbb{Z}_n^*$ as the integer representation of the string $(\mathsf{str}_{i'} \| \mathsf{bin}(d_{j'})) \in \{0,1\}^*$ and $\mathsf{Lev}_2^{(j')} = \mathsf{str}_{j'}$. Since $v_i = v_{i'}$ and $d_j = d_{j'}$, thus $\mathsf{Lev}_1^{(i)} = \mathsf{Lev}_1^{(i')}$. However, $\mathsf{Lev}_2^{(j)} \neq \mathsf{Lev}_2^{(j')}$ as $v_j \neq v_{j'}$. Finally, the correctness of the condition 2.(f) of the program $\mathsf{TRSC}_{\mathsf{Dec}}$ of Fig. 8 can be verified as follows.

$$C_3^{(i,j)} \oplus H(e(C_0^{(i,j)}, K_0^{(i',j')})) \Big/ \left[e(C_1^{(i,j)}, K_1^{(i',j')}) \cdot e(C_2^{(i,j)}, K_2^{(i',j')})\right]^{\frac{1}{\mathsf{Lev}_2^{(j')} - \mathsf{Lev}_2^{(j)}}}$$

$$= M \oplus H\big(e(g_1,\tau)^s\big) \oplus H\left(\frac{e(g_1,\tau)^s \cdot e(g_1,\beta)^{rs}}{\left[e(g_1,\beta)^{rs\left(\mathsf{Lev}_2^{(j')} - \mathsf{Lev}_2^{(j)}\right)}\right]^{\frac{1}{\mathsf{Lev}_2^{(j')} - \mathsf{Lev}_2^{(j)}}}}\right) = M$$

Remark 1. The covering algorithm $\mathsf{SD}_{\mathsf{Cover}}$ of Fig. 6 is only defined for $r \geq 1$. One simple way to handle the case $r = 0$ is to use a dummy user that is always revoked. One important observation regarding the unique private set generation and the disjoint covering algorithm is formally stated by the following lemma.

Lemma 3 ([14]). *Let N be the number of leaf nodes in a full binary tree and r be the size of a revoked set of users. Then the algorithm $\mathsf{SD}_{\mathsf{KGen}}$ of Fig. 4 outputs a unique private set of size $O(\log^2 N)$ and the algorithm $\mathsf{SD}_{\mathsf{Cover}}$ of Fig. 6 outputs a disjoint partition of size at most $2r - 1$.*

Note that the $\mathsf{SD}_{\mathsf{KGen}}$ algorithm in a cryptosystem generally can be replaced by the LSubDif based key generation algorithm of Halevy and Shamir [9] since the LSubDif scheme is a special case of subset difference (SubDif) scheme.

Lemma 4 ([9]). *Let N be the number of leaf nodes in a full binary tree and r be the size of a revoked set. In the LSubDif scheme, the size of a private set is $O(\log^{1.5} N)$ and the size of a covering set is at most $4r - 2$.*

4   Security

Theorem 1 (Security of Indistinguishability). *Adopting the SubDif technique, our TRSC scheme, presented in Sect. 3, achieves adaptive CPA-security under the subgroup decision (SD) assumptions mentioned in Sect. 2.2.*

Proof. We assume that there exists a PPT adversary $\mathcal{A}$ that makes at most polynomial number of queries (say q) against our TRSC. In order to prove the theorem, we proceed via. a series of hybrid games. The first hybrid corresponds to the real indistinguishability security game of our TRSC, while the final hybrid corresponds to one in which the adversary has no advantage. To accomplish the aforementioned goal, we transform the challenge ciphertext from an encryption on a message M_0^* to an encryption on a message M_1^* in such a way that each hybrid game indistinguishable from the previous hybrid game. We use Adv_d to denote the advantage of $\mathcal{A}$ in Game d.

Sequence of Hybrid Games

Game 0. This game corresponds to the real indistinguishability security game of our TRSC. Due to the page restriction, the original security game will be presented in the full version of the paper.

Game 1. This game is identical to Game 0 with the only exception that we change the challenge ciphertext $\mathsf{CT}_{\mathcal{R}^*}^{(b)} = (\mathsf{dcvr}_{\mathcal{R}^*}, \{\mathsf{ciphr}_{S_{i,j}} : S_{i,j} \subset \mathsf{dcvr}_{\mathcal{R}^*}\})$ $\leftarrow$ TRSC.Encrypt $(\mathcal{R}^*, M_b^*, \text{trscmpk})$. For each $\mathsf{ciphr}_{S_{i,j}} = (C_0^{(i,j)}, C_1^{(i,j)}, C_2^{(i,j)}, C_3^{(i,j)})$, we change the distribution of $C_0^{(i,j)}, C_1^{(i,j)}, C_2^{(i,j)}, C_3^{(i,j)}$ from $C_0^{(i,j)}, C_1^{(i,j)}, C_2^{(i,j)}, C_3^{(i,j)} \in G_{p_1}$ to $C_0^{(i,j)}, C_1^{(i,j)}, C_2^{(i,j)}, C_3^{(i,j)} \in G_{p_1} G_{p_2}$. We choose four random exponents $\theta_1, z_1, z_2, l \in \mathbb{Z}_n$ and change each component of $\mathsf{ciphr}_{S_{i,j}}$ as follows.

$$\widetilde{C}_0^{(i,j)} = C_0^{(i,j)} \cdot g_2^{l\left(\theta_1 + \mathsf{Lev}_1^{(i)}\right)}, \qquad \widetilde{C}_1^{(i,j)} = C_1^{(i,j)} \cdot g_2^l,$$

$$\widetilde{C}_2^{(i,j)} = C_2^{(i,j)} \cdot g_2^{l\left(z_1 \mathsf{Lev}_2^{(j)} + z_2\right)}, \qquad \widetilde{C}_3^{(i,j)} = C_3^{(i,j)}$$

Note that θ_1, z_1, z_2, l are randomly chosen once and fixed to be used in other types of private keys. We now construct a PPT adversary $\mathcal{A}_1$ for which $\mathsf{Adv}_0 - \mathsf{Adv}_1 \leq \mathsf{Adv}_{\mathcal{A}_1}^{\mathsf{SD1}}(\eta)$. The adversary $\mathcal{A}_1$ that solves the SD1 problem using $\mathcal{A}$ is given $\chi_\mu = (\text{bilgr}, g_1, g_3, T_\mu)$, where either $T_0 = B_1 \in G_{p_1}$ or $T_1 = B_1 B_2 \in G_{p_1} G_{p_2}$. Then, $\mathcal{A}_1$ simulates the entire Game 1 with the TRSC adversary $\mathcal{A}$ as follows.

- Runs TRSC.Setup(η, κ) algorithm honestly by choosing random exponents $\widehat{x}, \widehat{u}, \widehat{h}, \widehat{w} \in \mathbb{Z}_n$ and setting $\text{trscmsk} = (\widehat{x}, \tau = g_1^{\widehat{w}}, g_3)$ and $\text{trscmpk} = (\text{FBT}, \text{bilgr}, f^{\mathsf{ID}}, g_1, g_1^{\widehat{x}}, \beta = g_1^{\widehat{u}}, \varrho = g_1^{\widehat{h}}, H, \Delta = e(g_1, T_\mu))$.

- To response private key queries in the KeyQuery phase, $\mathcal{A}_1$ perfectly answers all the secret key queries since it knows $\mathsf{trscmsk} = (\widehat{x}, \tau = g_1^{\widehat{w}}, g_3)$.
- The adversary $\mathcal{A}$ submits a challenge revoked set of users $\mathcal{R}^*$ and two equal size messages $M_0^*, M_1^* \in_R \mathcal{M}$. For each subset $\mathcal{S}_{i,j} \in \mathsf{dcvr}_{\mathcal{R}^*}$, sets $\mathsf{ciphr}_{\mathcal{S}_{i,j}}$ components by implicitly setting g_1^s to be the G_{p_1} part of T_μ as follows.

$$\widetilde{C}_0^{(i,j)} = T_\mu^{\left(\widehat{x}+\mathsf{Lev}_1^{(i)}\right)}, \ \widetilde{C}_1^{(i,j)} = T_\mu, \ \widetilde{C}_2^{(i,j)} = T_\mu^{\left(\widehat{u}\mathsf{Lev}_2^{(j)}+\widehat{h}\right)}, \ \widetilde{C}_3^{(i,j)} = H(\Delta^{\widehat{w}})\oplus M_\mu^*$$

Observe that if $T_\mu = B_1$, this is the original ciphertext of Game 0. If $T_\mu = B_1 B_2$, this is the modified ciphertext created at Game 1.

- Finally, $\mathcal{A}$ outputs a guess μ'. If $\mu = \mu'$, then $\mathcal{A}_1$ outputs 1. Otherwise, it outputs 0.

$\boxed{\text{Game 2.}}$ This game is identical to Game 1 with the only exception that we change the distribution of trpk_u for a user secret key query of $u \in [N]$ in the KeyQuery phase. For each subset $\mathcal{S}_{i',j'} \in \mathsf{prvt}_u$, we change the distribution of $\mathcal{K}_{\mathcal{S}_{i',j'}}$. Let us assume that $\widehat{K}_0^{(i',j')} = \tau^{\frac{1}{x+\mathsf{Lev}_1(i')}} \beta^{\frac{r}{x+\mathsf{Lev}_1(i')}}$. Following the Déjà Q framework of [4,15], we impose a random G_{p_2}- component in the secret key component $K_0^{(i',j')} = \widehat{K}_0^{(i',j')}\Gamma_1$ as follows.

$$\widehat{K}_0^{(i',j')}\Gamma_1 \xrightarrow{\mathsf{SD1}} \widehat{K}_0^{(i',j')} g_2^{\frac{r_1}{x+\mathsf{Lev}_1(i')}}\Gamma_1 \xrightarrow{\mathsf{CRT}} \widehat{K}_0^{(i',j')} g_2^{\frac{r_1}{x_1+\mathsf{Lev}_1(i')}}\Gamma_1$$

$$\xrightarrow{\mathsf{SD1}} \widehat{K}_0^{(i',j')} g_2^{\frac{r_2}{x+\mathsf{Lev}_1(i')}} g_2^{\frac{r_1}{x_1+\mathsf{Lev}_1(i')}}\Gamma_1 \xrightarrow{\mathsf{CRT}} \widehat{K}_0^{(i',j')} g_2^{\sum_{i=1}^{2}\frac{r_i}{x_i+\mathsf{Lev}_1(i')}}\Gamma_1$$

$$\xrightarrow{\quad} \quad \cdots \quad \xrightarrow{\mathsf{CRT}} \widehat{K}_0^{(i',j')} g_2^{\sum_{i=1}^{q+1}\frac{r_i}{x_i+\mathsf{Lev}_1(i')}}\Gamma_1$$

where $r_1,\ldots,r_{q+1}, x_1,\ldots,x_{q+1} \in_R \mathbb{Z}_n$, and q is the maximum number of key queries made by the adversary $\mathcal{A}$ in the KeyQuery phase. Observe that in the first transition, we employ the Subgroup Decision (SD) 1 assumption, which asserts that random elements of G_{p_1} and those of $G_{p_1}G_{p_2}$ are computationally indistinguishable, and indistinguishably switched to the second transition. In the second transition, we employ the Chinese Reminder Theorem (CRT), it follows that if $x \bmod p_1$ and $x \bmod p_2$ are independently random values, then we can replace $x \bmod p_2$ with $x_1 \bmod p_2$ for a randomly chosen $x_1 \in \mathbb{Z}_n$, as long as the public parameter, challenge ciphertext and the master secret key reveal no information about $x \bmod p_2$. Performing this two-step transition q times, the framework modifies the secret key component to $\widetilde{K}_0^{(i',j')} = \tau^{\frac{1}{x+\mathsf{Lev}_1(i')}} \beta^{\frac{r}{x+\mathsf{Lev}_1(i')}} g_2^{\sum_{i=1}^{q+1}\frac{r_i}{x_i+\mathsf{Lev}_1(i')}}\Gamma_1$.

Sequence of SubGames of Game 2

[SubGame $2 - d - 0$] and [SubGame $2 - d - 1$], $(d = 1,\ldots,q+1)$: For $d = 1, 2,\ldots, q+1$, we construct a sequence of sub-games $\overline{\text{SubGame } 2 - d - 0}$ and

SubGame $2 - d - 1$ as follows.

- In SubGame $2 - d - 0$, $\widetilde{K}_0^{(i',j')}$ is given by

$$\widetilde{K}_0^{(i',j')} = \tau^{\frac{1}{x+\mathsf{Lev}_1{(i')}}} \beta^{\frac{r}{x+\mathsf{Lev}_1{(i')}}} g_2^{\left\{\frac{r_d}{x+\mathsf{Lev}_1{(i')}}+\sum_{i=1}^{d-1}\frac{r_i}{x_i+\mathsf{Lev}_1{(i')}}\right\}} \Gamma_1$$

- In SubGame $2 - d - 1$, $\widetilde{K}_0^{(i',j')}$ is given by

$$\widetilde{K}_0^{(i',j')} = \tau^{\frac{1}{x+\mathsf{Lev}_1{(i')}}} \beta^{\frac{r}{x+\mathsf{Lev}_1{(i')}}} g_2^{\sum_{i=1}^{d}\frac{r_i}{x_i+\mathsf{Lev}_1{(i')}}} \Gamma_1$$

Observe that Game 1 is equivalent to SubGame $2 - 0 - 1$ and consequently, $\mathsf{Adv}_1 = \mathsf{Adv}_{2-0-1}$. Similarly, it readily follows that Game 2 is equivalent to SubGame $2 - (q+1) - 1$ and consequently, $\mathsf{Adv}_2 = \mathsf{Adv}_{2-(q+1)-1}$. Moreover, SubGame $2-d-0$ and SubGame $2-d-1$ are indistinguishable which is follows from the fact that $x \bmod p_2$ is completely hidden given master secret key and the challenge ciphertext, and hence we may replace $x \bmod p_2$ with $x_d \bmod p_2$. Consequently, $\mathsf{Adv}_{2-d-0} = \mathsf{Adv}_{2-d-1}$. We choose a random exponents $\gamma_1 \in \mathbb{Z}_n$ and change the distribution of $K_1^{(i',j')}$ and $K_2^{(i',j')}$ as follow.

$$\widetilde{K}_1^{(i',j')} = K_1^{(i',j')} \cdot g_2^{\gamma_1(z_1\mathsf{Lev}_2^{(j')}+z_2)}, \quad \widetilde{K}_2^{(i',j')} = K_2^{(i',j')} \cdot g_2^{-\gamma_1}$$

We now construct another PPT adversary $\mathcal{A}_2$ for which $\mathsf{Adv}_{2-(d-1)-1} - \mathsf{Adv}_{2-d-0} \leq \mathsf{Adv}_{\mathcal{A}_2}^{\mathsf{SD2}}(\eta)$. The adversary $\mathcal{A}_2$ that solves the SD2 assumption using the TRSC adversary $\mathcal{A}$ is given a challenge tuple $\chi_\mu = (\mathsf{bilgr}, g_1, g_3, g_{1,2}, g_{2,3}, T_\mu)$, where either $T_0 = R_1 R_3 \in_R G_{p_1} G_{p_2}$ or $T_1 = R_1 R_2 R_3 \in G_{p_1} G_{p_2} G_{p_3}$. Then, $\mathcal{A}_2$ simulates the entire experiment of Game 2 with the adversary $\mathcal{A}$ as follows.

- Runs TRSC.Setup(η, κ) algorithm honestly by choosing random exponents $x', u', h', w', t_1 \in \mathbb{Z}_n$ and setting $B_1 B_2 = g_{1,2}^{t_1}$, trscmsk $= (x', \tau = g_1^{w'}, g_3)$ and trscmpk $= (\mathsf{FBT}, \mathsf{bilgr}, f^{\mathsf{ID}}, g_1, g_1^{x'}, \beta = g_1^{u'}, \varrho = g_1^{h'}, H, \Delta = e(g_1, B_1 B_2))$.
- To response private key queries in the KeyQuery phase, $\mathcal{A}_1$ chooses $l_1 \in_R \mathbb{Z}_n$, $Y_0, Y_1, Y_2 \in_R G_{p_3}$ and sets

$$\widetilde{K}_0^{(i',j')} = T_\mu^{\frac{1}{x'+\mathsf{Lev}_1{(i')}}} \beta^{\frac{l_1}{x'+\mathsf{Lev}_1{(i')}}} g_{2,3}^{\sum_{i=1}^{d-1}\frac{r_i}{x_i'+\mathsf{Lev}_1{(i')}}} \cdot Y_0,$$

$$\widetilde{K}_1^{(i',j')} = T_\mu^{\left(u'\mathsf{Lev}_2^{(j')}+h'\right)l_1} \cdot Y_1, \quad \widetilde{K}_2^{(i',j')} = T_\mu^{-l_1} \cdot Y_2$$

- The adversary $\mathcal{A}$ submits a challenge revoked set of users $\mathcal{R}^*$ and two equal size message $M_0^*, M_1^* \in_R \mathcal{M}$. For each subset $\mathcal{S}_{i,j} \in \mathsf{dcvr}_{\mathcal{R}^*}$, sets ciphr$_{\mathcal{S}_{i,j}}$ components as $\widetilde{C}_0^{(i,j)} = (B_1 B_2)^{(x'+\mathsf{Lev}_1^{(i)})}$, $\widetilde{C}_1^{(i,j)} = B_1 B_2$, $\widetilde{C}_2^{(i,j)} = (B_1 B_2)^{(u'\mathsf{Lev}_2^{(j)}+h')}$ and $\widetilde{C}_3^{(i,j)} = H(\Delta^{w'}) \oplus M_\mu^*$.

– Finally, $\mathcal{A}$ outputs a guess μ'. If $\mu = \mu'$, then $\mathcal{A}_2$ outputs 1. Otherwise, it outputs 0.

Observe that if $T_0 = R_1 R_3 \in_R G_{p_1} G_{p_3}$, then this is exactly SubGame $2 - (d - 1) - 1$, and if $T_1 = R_1 R_2 R_3 \in G_{p_1} G_{p_2} G_{p_3}$, then this is exactly SubGame $2 - d - 0$. It follows readily that $\mathsf{Adv}_1 - \mathsf{Adv}_2 \leq (q+1) \cdot \mathsf{Adv}_{\mathcal{A}_2}^{\mathsf{SD2}}(\eta)$.

$\boxed{\text{Game 3.}}$ This game is identical to the previous game with the only exception that we replace $\sum_{i=1}^{q+1} \frac{r_i}{x_i + \mathsf{Lev}_1^{(i')}}$ in $\widetilde{K}_0^{(i',j')}$ with $\mathsf{RF}(\mathsf{Lev}_1^{(i')})$ where $\mathsf{RF} : \mathbb{Z}_n^* \to \mathbb{Z}_{p_2}$ is a truly random function. Indeed, $\widetilde{K}_0^{(i',j')}$ can now be written as $\widetilde{K}_0^{(i',j')} = \tau^{\frac{1}{x+\mathsf{Lev}_1^{(i')}}} \beta^{\frac{r}{x+\mathsf{Lev}_1^{(i')}}} g_2^{\mathsf{RF}(\mathsf{Lev}_1^{(i')})} \Gamma_1$, which have independently random G_{p_2} components. It follows from the core lemma of Déjà Q framework (Lemma 2) stated in Sect. 2.4 that $\mathsf{Adv}_2 - \mathsf{Adv}_3 \leq O\left(\frac{q^2}{p_2}\right)$.

$\boxed{\text{Game 4.}}$ This game is exactly same as the previous game except that we replace $H(\Delta^s) = H\left(e(g_1, \tau)^s\right)$ in $\widetilde{C}_3^{(i,j)}$ with a random element $\Phi \in \{0,1\}^\eta$. Observe the following quantity from which $H(\Delta^s)$ is derived.

$$\mathfrak{R} = e(\widetilde{C}_0^{(i,j)}, \widetilde{K}_0^{(i',j')}) \left/ \left[e(\widetilde{C}_1^{(i,j)}, \widetilde{K}_1^{(i',j')}) \cdot e(\widetilde{C}_2^{(i,j)}, \widetilde{K}_2^{(i',j')}) \right]^{\frac{1}{\mathsf{Lev}_2^{(j')} - \mathsf{Lev}_2^{(j)}}} \right.$$

$$= H(\Delta^s) \cdot \frac{e\left(g_2^{l\left(\theta_1 + \mathsf{Lev}_1^{(i)}\right)}, g_2^{\mathsf{RF}(\mathsf{Lev}_1^{(i')})}\right)}{\left[e(g_2^l, g_2^{\gamma_1(z_1 \mathsf{Lev}_2^{(j')} + z_2)}) \cdot e(g_2^{l\left(z_1 \mathsf{Lev}_2^{(j)} + z_2\right)}, g_2^{-\gamma_1}) \right]^{\frac{1}{\mathsf{Lev}_2^{(j')} - \mathsf{Lev}_2^{(j)}}}}$$

$$= H(\Delta^s) \cdot \mathsf{RV}$$

Clearly, the above quantity has $\mathsf{H}_\infty(\mathfrak{R}) = \log p_2 = \Theta(\eta)$ bits of min-entropy coming from $\mathsf{RF}(\mathsf{Lev}_1^{(i')})$ since $\mathsf{Lev}_2^{(j')} \neq \mathsf{Lev}_2^{(j)}$. This holds as long as the G_{p_2} components of RV are not the identity elements of the group, which happens with probability $1 - \frac{1}{p_2}$. Hence, with overwhelming probability the relation $\eta = \mathsf{H}_\infty(\mathfrak{R}) - 2 \log \frac{1}{\epsilon} - O(1)$ is satisfied by $\epsilon = 2^{-\Omega(\eta)}$. Further, note that $H : G_T \to \{0,1\}^\eta$ is sampled from a pairwise independent hash family $\mathbb{H}$ uniformly and independently of $\mathfrak{R}$. Thus, by the left-over hash lemma (Lemma 1) stated in the Sect. 2.3, it follows that the statistical distance $\Delta((H(\mathfrak{R}), H), (U_\eta, H)) \leq \frac{\epsilon}{2}$, U_η is the uniform random variable over $\{0,1\}^\eta$. Thus, in other words, $H(\Delta^s)$ generated in Game 4 is nearly uniformly distributed over $\{0,1\}^\eta$.

Therefore, the view of the adversary $\mathcal{A}$ is statistically independent of the challenge bit $b \in \{0,1\}$ since the distribution of the challenge ciphertext is uniformly random over $G_{p_1} G_{p_2}$, as well as, the users' secret keys are also uniformly random over $G_{p_1} G_{p_2} G_{p_3}$. Hence, the challenger $\mathcal{C}$ can change each components of the challenge ciphertext from an encryption on M_0^* to an encryption on M_1^*.

Moreover, $\mathcal{A}$ cannot distinguish the changes with more than a non-negligible probability since the number of hybrid game is just polynomial. Hence, the advantage in Game 4 is given by $\mathsf{Adv}_4 = 0$.

Theorem 2 (Security of Traceability). *Suppose that our* TRSC, *presented in Sect. 3, is indistinguishable under a chosen plaintext attack. Then, our publicly traceable* TRSC.Trace$^{\mathcal{D}}$ *algorithm outputs identity of all the traitors, i.e., fully collusion resistant.*

Proof. In the beginning, $\mathcal{C}$ provides $\mathcal{A}$ the total number of users N, security parameter η of the system and another parameter ϵ. We proceed via. following steps.

Setup. Taking as input the security parameter η and the length of each user identity κ, $\mathcal{C}$ executes the TRSC.Setup(η, κ) algorithm honestly to get the master public key trscmpk and the master secret key trscmsk. Afterward, $\mathcal{C}$ publishes trscmpk and keeps trscmsk secret to itself.

KeyQuery. The adversary $\mathcal{A}$ is allowed to submit polynomially many secret key queries for users $u_1, \ldots, u_q \in [N]$ to the challenger $\mathcal{C}$. For each user u_i with $1 \leq i \leq q$, $\mathcal{C}$ executes the key generation algorithm TRSC.KeyGen $(u_i,$ trscmpk, trscmsk) to generate the private key trpk$_{u_i}$. The challenger $\mathcal{C}$ first runs the program SD$_{\mathsf{KGen}}$ of Fig. 4 to determine a unique private set prvt$_{u_i}$ for the user u_i. Afterward, $\mathcal{C}$ runs the tracing private key generation program TRSC$_{\mathsf{KGen}}$ of Fig. 5 and outputs the private key trpk$_{u_i}$. Let $\mathcal{E}$ be the total set of users whose private keys were obtained by $\mathcal{A}$, i.e., $\mathcal{E} = \{u_1, u_2, \ldots, u_q\} \subseteq [N]$.

Challenge. Towards the end, $\mathcal{A}$ outputs a revoked set $\mathcal{R}_{\mathcal{D}}$ of users and a pirate decoder box $\mathcal{D}$ formed by a set of traitor users.

Trace$^{\mathcal{D}}$. Taking as input the revoked set of users $\mathcal{R}_{\mathcal{D}}$ from $\mathcal{A}$, the challenger $\mathcal{C}$ executes the tracing algorithm TRSC.Trace$^{\mathcal{D}}(\mathcal{R}_{\mathcal{D}}, \epsilon,$ trscmpk) to get a rogue user's set $\mathbb{T}^{\mathsf{TTS}}$. Let us assume that $\mathcal{D}$ can decrypt the ciphertext CT$_{\mathcal{R}_{\mathcal{D}}}$, corresponding to the revoked set of users $\mathcal{R}_{\mathcal{D}}$ and a random message $M \in \mathcal{M}$, with more than ϵ probability. So that $\mathcal{D}$ is a ϵ-useful decoder. According to the following Lemmas 5 and 6, we can prove that the traitor set $\mathbb{T}^{\mathsf{TTS}}$ outputted by our tracing algorithm TRSC.Trace$^{\mathcal{D}}$ is non-empty and also $\mathbb{T}^{\mathsf{TTS}} \subseteq \mathcal{E} \setminus \mathcal{R}_{\mathcal{D}}$. This completes our proof.

Lemma 5. *Assuming the indistinguishability security of our* TRSC *scheme, presented in Theorem 1, our tracing algorithm* TRSC.Trace$^{\mathcal{D}}$ *outputs the identity of at least one traitor, i.e.,* $\mathbb{T}^{\mathsf{TTS}}$ *is non-empty.*

Lemma 6. *Assume that the output of our tracing algorithm* TRSC.Trace$^{\mathcal{D}}$, *presented in Sect. 3, is non-empty, i.e.,* $\mathbb{T}^{\mathsf{TTS}} \neq \emptyset$. *Then,* $\mathbb{T}^{\mathsf{TTS}} \subseteq \mathcal{E} \setminus \mathcal{R}_{\mathcal{D}}$.

Due to the page limit, the proof of the Lemmas 5 and 6 will be given in the full version of the paper.

5 Conclusion

In this work, we have designed an *adaptively* secure *public-key* TRSC scheme from SubDif technique without ROM. Integrating the Déjà Q framework, we eliminate q-type assumptions and analyze the security in the *standard-security* model under the hardness of *subgroup decision* problem. Moreover, our construction outperforms the existing similar works by reducing the parameter sizes.

References

1. Boneh, D., Boyen, X., Goh, E.-J.: Hierarchical identity based encryption with constant size ciphertext. In: Cramer, R. (ed.) EUROCRYPT 2005. LNCS, vol. 3494, pp. 440–456. Springer, Heidelberg (2005). https://doi.org/10.1007/11426639_26
2. Boneh, D., Sahai, A., Waters, B.: Fully collusion resistant traitor tracing with short ciphertexts and private keys. In: Vaudenay, S. (ed.) EUROCRYPT 2006. LNCS, vol. 4004, pp. 573–592. Springer, Heidelberg (2006). https://doi.org/10.1007/11761679_34
3. Boneh, D., Waters, B.: A fully collusion resistant broadcast, trace, and revoke system. In: ACM-CCS 2006, pp. 211–220. ACM (2006)
4. Chase, M., Meiklejohn, S.: Déjà Q: using dual systems to revisit q-type assumptions. In: Nguyen, P.Q., Oswald, E. (eds.) EUROCRYPT 2014. LNCS, vol. 8441, pp. 622–639. Springer, Heidelberg (2014). https://doi.org/10.1007/978-3-642-55220-5_34
5. Chor, B., Fiat, A., Naor, M.: Tracing traitors. In: Desmedt, Y.G. (ed.) CRYPTO 1994. LNCS, vol. 839, pp. 257–270. Springer, Heidelberg (1994). https://doi.org/10.1007/3-540-48658-5_25
6. Dodis, Y., Fazio, N.: Public key broadcast encryption for stateless receivers. In: Feigenbaum, J. (ed.) DRM 2002. LNCS, vol. 2696, pp. 61–80. Springer, Heidelberg (2003). https://doi.org/10.1007/978-3-540-44993-5_5
7. Fiat, A., Naor, M.: Broadcast encryption. In: Stinson, D.R. (ed.) CRYPTO 1993. LNCS, vol. 773, pp. 480–491. Springer, Heidelberg (1994). https://doi.org/10.1007/3-540-48329-2_40
8. Garg, S., Kumarasubramanian, A., Sahai, A., Waters, B.: Building efficient fully collusion-resilient traitor tracing and revocation schemes. In: ACM-CCS 2010, pp. 121–130. ACM (2010)
9. Halevy, D., Shamir, A.: The LSD broadcast encryption scheme. In: Yung, M. (ed.) CRYPTO 2002. LNCS, vol. 2442, pp. 47–60. Springer, Heidelberg (2002). https://doi.org/10.1007/3-540-45708-9_4
10. Impagliazzo, R., Levin, L.A., Luby, M.: Pseudo-random generation from one-way functions. In: Proceedings of the Twenty-First Annual ACM Symposium on Theory of Computing, pp. 12–24. ACM (1989)
11. Kiayias, A., Yung, M.: On crafty pirates and foxy tracers. In: Sander, T. (ed.) DRM 2001. LNCS, vol. 2320, pp. 22–39. Springer, Heidelberg (2002). https://doi.org/10.1007/3-540-47870-1_3
12. Lee, K., Koo, W.K., Lee, D.H., Park, J.H.: Public-key revocation and tracing schemes with subset difference methods revisited. In: Kutyłowski, M., Vaidya, J. (eds.) ESORICS 2014, Part II. LNCS, vol. 8713, pp. 1–18. Springer, Cham (2014). https://doi.org/10.1007/978-3-319-11212-1_1

13. Mandal, M., Dutta, R.: Cost-effective private linear key agreement with adaptive CCA security from prime order multilinear maps and tracing traitors. In: SECRYPT 2018, pp. 356–363. SciTePress (2018)
14. Naor, D., Naor, M., Lotspiech, J.: Revocation and tracing schemes for stateless receivers. In: Kilian, J. (ed.) CRYPTO 2001. LNCS, vol. 2139, pp. 41–62. Springer, Heidelberg (2001). https://doi.org/10.1007/3-540-44647-8_3
15. Wee, H.: Déjà Q: Encore! un petit IBE. In: Kushilevitz, E., Malkin, T. (eds.) TCC 2016, Part II. LNCS, vol. 9563, pp. 237–258. Springer, Heidelberg (2016). https://doi.org/10.1007/978-3-662-49099-0_9

Attribute-Based Encryption with Efficient Keyword Search and User Revocation

Jingwei Wang[1], Xinchun Yin[1,2(✉)], Jianting Ning[3], and Geong Sen Poh[3]

[1] School of Information Engineering, Yangzhou University, Yangzhou 225100, China
M160437@yzu.edu.cn
[2] Yangzhou University Guangling College, Yangzhou 225100, China
xcyin@yzu.edu.cn
[3] Department of Computer Science,
National University of Singapore, Singapore, Singapore
{ningjt,pohgs}@comp.nus.edu.sg

Abstract. Ciphertext policy attribute-based encryption (CP-ABE) is a promising cryptographic technology and a key component that enable secure data sharing in a cloud environment through fine-grained access control. Since it was introduced, many interesting schemes have been proposed. However, in addition to managing data sharing through access control, a comprehensive scheme should also cater for user revocation and ciphertext queries. This is because in a cloud environment new users may join while existing users may leave the system. At the same time, given the potentially large amount of data stored in a cloud storage, user should be able to retrieve the required files efficiently in a privacy-preserving manner. To address the above issue, in this paper, we propose a practical searchable CP-ABE scheme supporting user revocation. In contrast to existing schemes that provide only single keyword query, our efficient search function provides conjunctive search, which allows user to locate a ciphertext related to a set of keywords. The computation overhead of our user revocation is at least on par with existing schemes. Besides, the security analysis indicates that the proposed scheme is secure under the decisional Bilinear Diffie-Hellman assumption. We also provide extensive experimental results to confirm the efficiency and feasibility of our proposed construction.

Keywords: Attribute-based encryption · Keyword search · User revocation · Access control · Cloud storage

1 Introduction

Data sharing has been regarded as one of the most promising applications of cloud computing in current research community as well as for commercial usage. A great number of companies and individuals nowadays prefer to outsource or upload their data to the cloud to enjoy the benefits provided by cloud server [29]. However, there still exist potential risks that threaten users' security. The key

© Springer Nature Switzerland AG 2019
F. Guo et al. (Eds.): Inscrypt 2018, LNCS 11449, pp. 490–509, 2019.
https://doi.org/10.1007/978-3-030-14234-6_26

concern is data privacy when sensitive data outsourced to the third-party cloud server provider [4, 21]. This is because once the data is stored in the cloud storage, generally the user loses control of the data if no security measure prepared. The data may be leaked due to unintentional human error or the cloud storage being compromised. As a result numerous mechanisms, including proposals based on attribute-based encryption, have been proposed by researchers to prevent data leakage and make sure only legitimate users can access these data [10, 14, 18, 31].

Attribute-based encryption (ABE), which was first proposed by Sahai and Water in [23], can be considered as a promising solution to the problem described above. ABE mainly consists of ciphertext-policy ABE (CP-ABE) [2] and key-policy ABE (KP-ABE) [6]. In CP-ABE, ciphertext is associated with an access structure and user's secret key is associated with an attribute set. Only when the attribute set related to user's secret key satisfies the access structure hidden in the ciphertext can the user perform decryption. This is in contrast to KP-ABE, where the secret key is associated with an access structure. As a reliable method to preserve privacy of data stored in the cloud, the access structure of CP-ABE is defined by data owner (DO), which makes CP-ABE more suitable in the context of cloud data sharing [16].

1.1 Our Motivation

Although CP-ABE fits the cloud environment well in addressing the issue of data privacy, there still exist some challenges that prevent its wide adoption in commercial applications. Consider a company that creates a project consisting of a group of employees, where the related file, encrypted under an access policy, are stored in the cloud server. Employees responsible for this project are assigned with several attributes (e.g., "group G", "project P"). Only employees with these attributes can access the data of the project. However, when one of the employees resign from the company or he moves to another group, how can we revoke his access ability? Besides, a company may have lots of projects in the cloud server. How can the staff retrieve files efficiently and safely?

One of the main solutions is to construct a user revocation mechanism for the system [33]. After revocation, the revoked users will not be able to decrypt the ciphertext anymore even if his attribute set satisfies the access structure. Collusion resistance mechanism should also be provided to prevent collusion attack launched by revoked users at the same time [9]. Besides, searching for the exact ciphertext in the cloud is not easy, especially when the number of ciphertext in the cloud server is large. Most of the existing ABE scheme assumed that the system is able to locate the correct ciphertext for data user (DU) automatically. We design and construct an efficient ciphertext search function to help data users search quickly with some keywords in the cloud server. In fact, it only needs twice bilinear pairing computation.

1.2   Our Contributions

Inspired by [25], we propose a practical ciphertext-policy attribute based encryption system, which focus on the problem of user revocation and ciphertext search. The contributions of our work are as follows:

1. **Effective ciphertext search.** We propose ciphertext (encrypted) search that cost only twice bilinear pairing computation. Specifically, when data owner (DO) upload the ciphertext to the cloud server, a set of related encrypted keywords will be attached to the ciphertext. If a data user wishes to access some of the encrypted data in the system, he should generate and send a trapdoor of the related keywords to cloud server provider (CSP). On receiving the trapdoor, CSP first checks whether this data user is authorized to access the ciphertext. Only if the data user has sufficient attributes can he access the data. Then CSP compares the trapdoor with the encrypted keywords in the ciphertext by a short bilinear pairing computation.
2. **User revocation.** We propose a new mechanism, in which the notion of version control is used to realize the function of user revocation. In our system, ciphertext and secret key are managed by a parameter called "ver". When a data user is removed from the system, trusted authority will randomly select a new "ver" so that cloud server provider and the remaining data users can update ciphertext alone with secret key by themselves. As a result, cloud server provider do not have to manage the revocation list. If the "ver" in the access request is not the same with the one in the system, then the request will not be performed.
3. **Collusion resistance.** The proposed system is resistant to collusion attack launched by revoked data users and the remaining data users in the system. Specifically, the secret key of each data user in the system is generated according to "ver" and the identity information both, so that the secret keys will be different even if the attribute set of two users are the same.

We further prove security of our system under the decisional Bilinear Diffie-Hellman assumption. Besides, we simulate the experiment and compare the performance of our system with existing works.

1.3   Related Work

ABE provides fine-grained access control to ciphertext stored in the cloud. This means data owners only need to outsource their data to third-party cloud server providers without worrying about data management. By doing so, the cloud server providers can assist the data owner to communicate with data users. However, the separation of data and the data owner brings new problems. When the information to be shared is sensitive, data owner may have concern on data leakage. To protect their data, many schemes have been proposed to secure data against unauthorized access [11,20]. For example, Ning et al. [17] proposed a solution to trace the malicious users who leaks their decryption keys to keep their data from leakage. On the other hand, cloud providers' resource is not infinite, they need to make full use of their platform to provide reliable server with minimal cost. Schemes focus on outsourcing computing such as [13,15] can greatly relief the expense of data user in the system.

The conventional solution to search over encrypted data is to download all the ciphertext in the cloud and retrieve the required data, which is inefficient and infeasible [12]. Practical schemes were then proposed. Since first introduced by Song et al. in [24], searchable encryption schemes [26,32] have been adopted by many researchers. Xiong et al. [30] provided a searchable CP-ABE in the cloud. In their scheme, homomorphic encryption is used to realize the search function. They encrypt the message under homomorphic encryption and the key of homomorphic encryption is encrypted by CP-ABE. But the computing expense is relatively high, which brings no benefit to its application. Su et al. [25] proposed a practical searchable CP-ABE scheme, which minimized computation of search phrase. However, their scheme only focuses on the problem of keyword search. We rich our scheme with the function of user revocation. Padhya et al. [22] proposed a searchable CP-ABE, which hides ciphertext policy. Wang et al. [27] proposed a method to achieve fast keyword search on ciphertext. However, both of their computation costs in the search algorithm require at least three times of bilinear pairing operation, which is more than that of ours. [5] proposed a scheme supporting fuzzy keyword search, so that data users can get all the related ciphertext with his keywords, but it cost a lot more in search phase than our's scheme.

User revocation is another concern for data sharing in the cloud. It is a common phenomenon to revoke a user from accessing sensitive data when he is no longer a member of the system. This means the ciphertext should be updated so that the revoked user cannot use his old secret key to decrypt the updated ciphertext anymore. In recent years, many CP-ABE scheme supporting user revocation have been proposed in the literature. Cui et al. [4] addressed this problem through disabling the search capability of revoked user. When a user should be revoked, the administrator in the system only has to update a secret value stored on the cloud server. Their scheme is efficient, but it is not clear how they classify the revoked users and non-revoked users. Padhya et al. [22] realized user revocation by adding a user revocation list to the ciphertext in the phase of encryption. But it only fits the situation when the number of system user is small. It will be complex to manage a revocation list in the cloud environment. Besides, employ an accountable authority to audit malicious operation in the system is also a smart solution to prevent the malicious attacks [19].

1.4 Organization

In Sect. 2, we state the preliminaries, including bilinear pairings, linear secret-sharing schemes, access structure, access tree and the computational assumption. Section 3 outlines the system model, definition and security model. In Sect. 4, an attribute-based encryption with efficient keyword search and user revocation is proposed. In Sect. 5, a security analysis about our scheme is given. We test the proposed scheme with an experiment in Sect. 6. Finally, Sect. 7 concludes this paper.

2 Preliminary

2.1 Bilinear Pairings

Let $\mathbb{G}$ and $\mathbb{G}_T$ be cyclic groups with prime order p and g is the generator of $\mathbb{G}$. A bilinear map e [8] has the following properties:

1. **Bilinearity:** For any $u, v \in \mathbb{G}$ and $a, b \in \mathbb{Z}_p$, $e(u^a, v^b) = e(u, v)^{ab}$.
2. **Non-degeneracy:** There exists $u, v \in \mathbb{G}$ such that $e(u, v) \neq 1$.
3. **Computability:** For all $u, v \in \mathbb{G}$, there is an efficient computation $e(u, v)$.

2.2 Linear Secret-Sharing Schemes (LSSS)

Let p be a prime and $\mathbb{U}$ be the attribute universe. A secret-sharing scheme $\prod$ with domain of secrets $\mathbb{Z}_p$ realizing access structures on $\mathbb{U}$ is linear over $\mathbb{Z}_p$ if:

1. The shares of a secret $p \in \mathbb{Z}_p$ for each attribute form a vector over $\mathbb{Z}_p$.
2. For each access structure $\mathbb{A}$ on $\mathbb{U}$, there exists a matrix $\mathbb{M} \in \mathbb{Z}_p^{l \times n}$, called the share-generating matrix, and a function ρ, that labels the rows of $\mathbb{M}$ with attributes from $\mathbb{U}$ (details can be found in [1]), which satisfy the following rules:

   During the generation of the shares, we consider the column vector $v = (s, r_2, r_3, \ldots, r_n)^\perp$, where $s \in \mathbb{Z}_p$ is the secret to be shared and $r_2, \ldots, r_n \in \mathbb{Z}_p$ are randomly chosen. Then the vector of l shares of the secret s according to $\prod$ is equal to $\mathbb{M}v \in \mathbb{Z}_p^{l \times 1}$. The share $(\mathbb{M}v)_j$ where j "belongs" to attribute $\rho(j)$.

   Generally speaking, access structure $\mathbb{A}$ will be represented by the pair $(\mathbb{M}, \rho)$.

2.3 Access Structure

Let $\{A_1, A_2, \ldots, A_n\}$ be a group of attributes. For $\forall B, C$, if $B \in A$ and $B \subseteq C$, then $C \in A$, we say that $A \subseteq 2^{\{A_1, A_2, \ldots, A_n\}}$ is monotone. An access structure contains a set A of non-empty subsets of $\{A_1, A_2, \ldots, A_n\}$. Elements in A are named the authorized elements, and the other elements are referred to as unauthorized elements.

2.4 Access Tree

Let $\mathcal{T}$ represents an access tree and x be a node of $\mathcal{T}$. Every non-leaf node x of $\mathcal{T}$ denotes a threshold gate, which is stated by the number of its children num_x and its threshold l_x, where $l_x \in [1, num_x]$. The threshold gate means an OR gate when $l_x = 1$. It means an AND gate when $l_x = num_x$. Each leaf node x of T is stated by an attribute and a threshold $l_x = 1$.

In the access tree, some functions are defined to facilitate working with $\mathcal{T}$. We depict the parent for the node x of the tree by $parent(x)$. The attribute associate with the leaf node x of the tree is represented by function $att(x)$. We use 1 to num_x to define the order of every node in the access tree $\mathcal{T}$. The function $index(x)$ denotes a number associated with the node x, where the index values are uniquely assigned to nodes of the access policy for a given ciphertext in an arbitrary manner.

Satisfying an Access Tree: Let $\mathcal{T}$ be an access tree with root R, and $\mathcal{T}_x$ represents the subtree rooted at the node x in $\mathcal{T}$. Namely, $\mathcal{T}$ can be replaced by $\mathcal{T}_R$. $\mathcal{T}_x(S) = 1$ is used to denote the situation that attribute set S satisfies $\mathcal{T}_x$. $\mathcal{T}_x(S)$ is evaluated recursively as follows: if x is a non-leaf node, we compute $\mathcal{T}_{x'}(S)$ for all children x' in node x. $\mathcal{T}_x(S)$ outputs 1 if and only if at least l_x children return 1. If x is a leaf node, then $\mathcal{T}_x(S)$ outputs 1 if and only if $att(x) \in S$.

2.5 The Decisional Bilinear Diffie-Hellman Assumption

A challenger selects a group G with prime order p according to the security parameter. Let g be a generator of G and $a, b, s \in Z_p$ be selected at random. If the challenger gives an adversary (g, g^a, g^b, g^s), it must be difficult for the adversary to distinguish a valid tuple $e(g, g)^{abs} \in G_T$ from a random element $R \in G_T$. An algorithm $\mathcal{B}$ that outputs $\vartheta \in \{0, 1\}$ has advantage ε in solving DBDH in G if:

$$|Pr[\mathcal{B}(g, g^a, g^b, g^s, Z = e(g, g)^{abs}) = 0] - Pr[\mathcal{B}(g, g^a, g^b, g^s, Z = R) = 0]| \geqslant \varepsilon.$$

Definition 1. *The DBDH assumption holds if all poly-time algorithms have at most a negligible advantage in solving DHDH problem.*

3   An Attribute-Based Encryption System with Efficient Keyword Search

3.1 System Model

As illustrated in Fig. 1, in the proposed scheme, there exists four types of entities: a trusted authority (TA), a cloud server provider (CSP), data user (DU) and data owner (DO).

TA: It is the only trusted entity in the system. It is responsible for not just generating system parameters, but also attribute authorizing and secret key issuing for the new enrolled users.

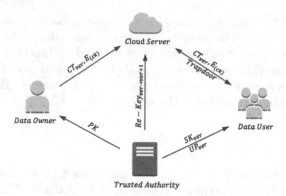

Fig. 1. System model of attribute-based encryption with efficient keyword search and user revocation

CSP: t is the manager of cloud server in the system. It provides the service of data storage, keyword search and ciphertext update. It is also a semi-trusted entity in the system, which means it will collect users' information as much as possible.

DU: Data user is a kind of user in the system. They would like to access the encrypted data in the cloud server. According to attribute-based encryption scheme, a data user is able to access the encrypted data, if and only if his attribute set satisfies the access tree defined by data owner.

DO: Data owner is another kind of user in the system. They would like to share their data in the cloud to some qualified people. Before they upload their data to the cloud server provider, data owners usually encrypt their data with an access policy defined by themselves. Besides, some encrypted keywords related to the data will also be attached to the ciphertext for the easement of searching.

3.2   Definition

Attribute-based encryption with efficient keyword search and user revocation is defined as follow:

- **Setup**$(1^\lambda, L) \to (PK, MSK)$: This is an initialization algorithm. On input a security parameter λ and an attribute universe $L = \{a_1, a_2, \ldots, a_m\}$, the algorithm outputs the public key PK and the master key MSK.
- **KeyGen**$(MSK, UID, S) \to SK_0$: This is a secret key generation algorithm. On input MSK, user identity UID and an attribute set S that depicts the key, the algorithm outputs a secret key SK.

- The encryption phrase consists of two parts. Firstly, data owner randomly selects a symmetric key ck to encrypt the data by employing a symmetric encryption algorithm, the encrypted data is denoted by $E_{ck}(M)$. Secondly, data owner encrypts ck with the following algorithms:
  Encryption$(PK, ck, T) \rightarrow CT$: This is a encryption algorithm. On input the PK, symmetric key ck and an access tree T, the algorithm outputs ciphertext CT which will be delivered to cloud server provider.
- **Update**$(PK, v_{ver}) \rightarrow (v_{ver+1}, Re - Key_{ver \rightarrow ver+1})$: This is an update algorithm. On input PK, and current version number v_{ver}, the algorithm outputs v_{ver+1} and re-encryption key $Re - Key_{ver \rightarrow ver+1}$. Moreover, CSP sends a UP_{ver} to users who still in the system so that they can update their secret key.
- **User_update**$(SK_{ver}, UP_{ver}) \rightarrow SK_{ver+1}$: This is an user update algorithm. Once DU receives the UP_{ver} from TA then he can update his secret key. The algorithm takes the old secret key SK_{ver} and update parameters UP_{ver} as input, and outputs new secret key SK_{ver+1}.
- **Re-Encryption**$(CT_{ver}, Re - Key_{ver \rightarrow ver+1}) \rightarrow CT_{ver+1}$: This is a re-encryption algorithm. On input the old version ciphertext CT_{ver} and $Re - Key_{ver \rightarrow ver+1}$, the algorithm outputs the updated ciphertext CT_{ver+1}. Besides, in order to facilitate the ciphertext search, DO encrypts several keywords and attaches them to the ciphertext.
- **KW_Encryption**$(PK, KW) \rightarrow CT_W$: This is a keyword encryption algorithm. On input PK and a set of keywords selected by data owner, the algorithm outputs the encrypted keywords CT_W.
- **Trapdoor**$(SK_{ver}, SKW) \rightarrow trapdoor$: This is a trapdoor generation algorithm. On input data user's secret key SK_{ver} and the keywords SKW that need to be search, the algorithm (run by data user) outputs the encrypted keywords $trapdoor$.
- **Search**$(CT_W, trapdoor) \rightarrow CT_{ver}$: This is a search algorithm. On input the CT_W and $trapdoor$, the algorithm outputs the matched ciphertext CT_{ver}.
- **Decryption**$(CT_{ver}, SK_{ver}, PK) \rightarrow ck$: This is a decryption algorithm. On input CT_{ver}, SK_{ver} and PK, the algorithm outputs the symmetric key ck. Then data owner can further decrypt the $E_{ck}(m)$ by ck.

3.3   Chosen Plaintext Attack (CPA) Security

The proposed attribute-based encryption with efficient keyword search and user revocation is chosen-plaintext attack secure, which can be defined by the security game below.

- **Init:** A probabilistic polynomial time (PPT) adversary $\mathcal{A}$ submits the challenge access policy T^* and version number ver^* to the challenger $\mathcal{B}$.
- **Setup:** $\mathcal{B}$ runs the $Setup()$ algorithm to generate public key PK. $\mathcal{B}$ randomly selects v_0 as version secret key. Then $\mathcal{B}$ runs the $Update()$ algorithm to update the version secret key from 0 to ver^* and generate the corresponding $UP_{ver+1}, ver \in [0, ver - 1]$. Finally, $\mathcal{B}$ sends the PK and $\{UP_{ver+1}\}_{0 \leqslant ver \leqslant ver^*-1}$ to $\mathcal{A}$.

- **Phrase 1:** Adversary $\mathcal{A}$ selects a UID and adaptively submits the attribute set S to $\mathcal{B}$ to query the secret key SK_0 about S. The restriction is that all queried attribute sets should not satisfy T^*. Then, the adversary $\mathcal{A}$ can update SK_0 to SK_{ver^*} according to the $\{UP_{ver+1}\}_{0 \leqslant ver \leqslant ver^*-1}$.
- **Challenge:** The adversary $\mathcal{A}$ submits the equal length message M_0 and M_1 to challenger $\mathcal{B}$. After receiving the message, $\mathcal{B}$ randomly chooses c from $\{0,1\}$ and runs $Encryption()$ to generate the ciphertext CT_b. Certainly, $\mathcal{B}$ should run the $Re-Encryption()$ algorithm to get the version of ver^* of the challenger ciphertext CT_c.
- **Phrase 2:** $\mathcal{A}$ launches queries as phrase 1 and $\mathcal{B}$ answers as phrase 1.
- **Guess:** When the query phrase is over, $\mathcal{A}$ outputs its guess $c' \in \{0,1\}$. $\mathcal{A}$ wins the game if $c' = c$ with the advantage of $Adv^{\mathcal{A}} = |Pr[c = c'] - 1/2|$.

Definition 2. *An attribute-based encryption with effective keyword search and user revocation scheme is CPA-secure if there exist no polynomial time adversaries can win this security game with a non-negligible advantage.*

3.4 Chosen-Keyword Attack (CKA) Security

The proposed attribute-based encryption with efficient keyword search and user revocation is chosen-keyword attack secure, which can be defined by the security game below.

- **Init:** A probabilistic polynomial time adversary $\mathcal{A}$ submits t keywords $\{W_1, W_2, \ldots, W_t\}$ and to the challenger $\mathcal{B}$.
- **Setup:** $\mathcal{B}$ runs the $Setup()$ algorithm to generate public key PK. $\mathcal{B}$ randomly selects v_0 as version secret key. Then $\mathcal{B}$ sends the PK to $\mathcal{A}$.
- **Phrase 1:** Adversary $\mathcal{A}$ selects a set of keywords SKW and submits it to $\mathcal{B}$ to query the $Trapdoor$ about SKW. The restriction is that all queried keywords should not contain W_1.
- **Challenge:** $\mathcal{B}$ randomly selects c from $\{0,1\}$ and runs $KW\_Encryption()$ algorithm to generate the encrypted keywords CT_c.
- **Phrase 2:** $\mathcal{A}$ launches queries as phrase 1 and $\mathcal{B}$ answers as phrase 1.
- **Guess:** When the query phrase is over, $\mathcal{A}$ outputs its guess $c' \in \{0,1\}$. And $\mathcal{A}$ wins the game if $c' = c$ with the advantage of $Adv^{\mathcal{A}} = |Pr[c = c'] - 1/2|$.

Definition 3. *An attribute-based encryption with effective keyword search and user revocation scheme is CKA-secure if there exist no polynomial time adversaries can win this security game with a non-negligible advantage.*

4 Attribute-Based Encryption with Efficient Keyword Search and User Revocation

For simplicity, we suppose that there are m attributes denoted by $L = \{a_0, a_1, \ldots, a_m\}$ in the system. Let $e : G \times G \to G_T$ be a bilinear map, and G be a bilinear group with prime order p and generator g. Let $H : (0,1)^* \to G$

be a security hash function, which maps any attribute to a random member of G. For any $i \in Z_p$, the Lagrange coefficient is $\Delta_{i,L}(x) = \Pi_{l \in L, l \neq i} \frac{x-l}{i-l}$. The detailed construction are as follows:

– **Setup**$(1^\lambda, L) \rightarrow (PK, MSK)$: The algorithm runs by TA. Its inputs are a security parameter λ and the universe attribute set L. This algorithm randomly selects a generator $g \in G$ and $\alpha, \beta, \gamma \in Z_p^*$. Then, TA calculates $g^\alpha, e(g,g)^\beta$ and g^γ. For each attribute $j \in L$, TA chooses a random $v_j \in Z_p^*$ and calculates $A_j = H(j)^{v_j}$. TA publishes the public key as $PK = \{G, g, g^\alpha, e(g,g)^\beta, g^\gamma, A_j\}$ and keeps the master key as $MSK = \{\alpha, \beta, v_j\}$ to its own.

– **KeyGen**$(MSK, UID, S) \rightarrow SK_0$: When a new user wants to join in the system, he should submit his attribute set $S = \{a_1, a_2, \ldots, a_n\}$ to TA so that he can get the secret key to decrypt and search. In our scheme, we use ver to present the currently version number. When user revocation occurs, the secret key will be updated to a new version. Specifically, TA randomly selects $v_0, t, r_1 \in Z_p^*$. Then TA computes $D = (g \times H(UID)^\alpha)^{v_{ver}t}$, for $\forall j \in S : D_j = H(UID)^{v_{ver}t} \times H(j)^{v_j t}$, and $D_j' = H(j)^{\alpha t}$, so that $SK = D, \forall j \in S : D_j, D_j'$. Then it sends the secret key as t, SK to DU secretly. After that, TA computes $\widehat{S_a} = g^{r_1}$ and $\widehat{S_b} = (g^\gamma H(j)^{\sum_{j \in S} v_j})^{r_1}$ as the key to search for DU. Finally, TA computes $\{UID, H(UID)^r\}$ in case that DU need to update his secret key.

– **The encryption algorithm consists of two steps.**
Symmetric encryption: As symmetric encryption is more efficient than asymmetric encryption, we decide to encrypt the data M by a symmetric algorithm first. Let the symmetric key be ck, and the symmetric ciphertext be $E_{ck}(M)$.
Encryption$(PK, ck, \mathcal{T}) \rightarrow CT$: DO defines an access tree $\mathcal{T}$ and encrypts ck by running the encryption algorithm to output the CT'. Specifically, for each node x in the access tree $\mathcal{T}$, the DO first selects a random polynomial q_x with degree $d_x = k_x - 1$, where k_x is the threshold value in the node x. Beginning from the root node R, these polynomials are selected in a top-down manner. The DO randomly chooses d_R other points of q_R to completely define them after selecting a random number $s \in Z_p^*$, and setting $q_R(0) = s$. For any other node x, it sets $q_x(0) = q_{parent(x)}(index(x))$ and selects d_x other points to completely define them. Let the set of leaf nodes in the access tree $\mathcal{T}$ be Y and the ciphertext CT' is as follows:

$$CT' = \left\{ \begin{array}{c} \mathcal{T}, \widetilde{C} - ck \cdot e(g,g)^{s(\beta + v_{ver})}, C = g^s, C' = g^{\alpha s}, \\ \forall y \in Y : C_y = g^{\alpha q_y(0)}, C_y' = g^{q_y(0) v_{att(y)}} \end{array} \right\}$$

– **Update**$(PK, v_{ver}) \rightarrow \{v_{ver+1}, Re - Key_{ver \rightarrow ver+1}\}$: Considering the situation of user revocation, TA performs the update algorithm to generate the new version secret key v_{ver+1}, and the re-encryption key $Re - Key_{ver \rightarrow ver+1}$ so that the updated ciphertext would not be accessed by revoked user. Besides, for every DU in the system, TA produces a secret key update component according their identity. So that they can update their secret key after the re-encryption. TA selects a v_{ver+1} as the new version secret key. Then TA computes $Re-Key_{ver\to ver+1} = g^{(v_{ver+1}-v_{ver})/\alpha}$. For each user in the system, TA generates a secret key update component by computing $H(UID)^{v_{ver+1}-v_{ver}}$ and $(g \times H(UID)^\alpha)^{v_{ver+1}-v_{ver}}$. TA sends the $Re-Key_{ver\to ver+1}$ to CSP to perform the re-encryption algorithm, and distributes the $UP_{ver+1} = \{UID, H(UID)^{v_{ver+1}-v_{ver}}, (g \times H(UID)^\alpha)^{v_{ver+1}-v_{ver}}\}$ to corresponding DU to update their secret key.

- **User_update**$(SK_{ver}, UP_{ver}) \to SK_{ver+1}$: Upon receiving the UP_{ver} from TA, DU computes $D = D \times (g \times H(UID)^\alpha)^{t(v_{ver+1}-v_{ver})} = (g \times H(UID)^\alpha)^{tv_{ver+1}}$. $\forall j \in S : D_j = D_j \times H(UID)^{t(v_{ver+1}-v_{ver})} = H(UID)^{v_{ver+1}t} \times H(j)^{v_j t}$. Then the updated secret key is as follow:

$$SK = \{(f \times H(UID)^\alpha)^{v_{ver+1}t}, \forall j \in S : H(UID)^{v_{ver+1}t}, H(j)^{\alpha t}\}$$

- **Re-Encryption**$(CT_{ver}, Re-Key_{ver\to ver+1}) \to CT_{ver+1}$: CSP is responsible for not only keeping the encrypted data, but also updating them when user revocation happens. The computing process is as follow:

$$\widetilde{C} = \widetilde{C} \times Re-Key_{ver\to ver+1}$$
$$= ck \cdot e(g,g)^{s(\beta+v_{ver+1})}$$

So that the revoked user will not be able to access again.
- **KW_Encryption**$(PK, KW) \to CT_W$: Let $KW = \{kw_1, kw_2, \ldots, kw_k\}$ denote the keywords related to the data. DO have to attach the encrypted keywords to the ciphertext formed in Encryption algorithm. Then DO randomly chooses a $u \in Z_p^*$ and prepares an attribute set S' that contains all the attributes in the access tree. DO computes $\widehat{C_a} = g^{\frac{u}{H(kw_1||kw_2||...||kw_k)}}$, $\widehat{C_b} = (g^\gamma \prod_{j\in S'} A_j)^u$ and $CT_{kw} = \{\widehat{C_a}, \widehat{C_b}\}$. Finally, DO sends the complete ciphertext $CT = \{E_{ck}(M), CT', CT_{kw}\}$ to the CSP.
- **Trapdoor**$(SK_{ver}, SKW) \to trapdoor$: When DU wants to search the data in the CSP, he first generates a trapdoor about the keywords he wants to search. Let $SKW = \{skw_1, skw_2, \ldots, skw_k\}$ denotes the keywords DU chooses. DU randomly selects $x \in Z_p^*$. Then DU computes $T_b = \widehat{S_b}^x$, $T_a = \widehat{S_a}^{\frac{x}{H(skw_1||skw_2||...||skw_k)}}$. Finally, DU sends the $trapdoor = \{T_a, T_b\}$ to CSP to search the data he needs.
- **Search**: Once the trapdoor is received, CSP conducts the search algorithm to check if the authorization of the user's keywords satisfies the keywords in the ciphertext. By computing $e(\widehat{C_a}, T_b)$ and $e(\widehat{C_b}, T_a)$, the ciphertext wanted will be send to DU later if the equation holds.
- **Decryption**$(CT_{ver}, SK_{ver}, PK) \to ck$: When DU gets the wanted ciphertext, he can decryption the data by the symmetric key ck encrypted in the CT'. The detailed process is as follow: The decryption procedure is defined as a recursive algorithm $DecryptNode(CT', SK, x)$, where x is a node in the access tree T. If x is a leaf node. Let $j = att(x)$. If $j \notin S$, then

$DecryptNode(CT', SK, x) = null$. But if $j \in S$, then:

$$DecryptNode(ct', SK, x) = \frac{e(D_j, C_y)}{e(D'_j, C'_y)}$$

$$= \frac{e(H(UID)^{v_{ver}t} \times H(j)^{v_j t}, g^{\alpha q_x(0)})}{e(H(j)^{\alpha t}, g^{q_x(0)v_{att(x)}})}$$

$$= \frac{e(H(UID), g)^{\alpha t v_{ver} q_x(0)} e(H(j), g)^{\alpha t v_j q_x(0)}}{e(H(j), g)^{\alpha t v_j q_x(0)}}$$

$$= e(H(UID), g)^{\alpha t v_{ver} q_x(0)}$$

If x is a non-leaf node, the recursive algorithm $DecryptNode(CT', SK, x)$ is defined as: for all nodes z that are children of x, it performs $F_z = DecryptNode(CT', Sk, z)$. Let S_x be an arbitrary K_x sized child nodes set $\{z\}$, then $F_z \neq null$. If not, F_z is calculated as:

$$F_z = \prod_{Z \in S_x} F_Z^{\Delta_{j, S'_x}(0)}$$

$$= \prod_{Z \in S_x} (e(H(UID), g)^{\alpha t v_{ver} q_z(0)})^{\Delta_{j, S'_x}(0)}$$

$$= \prod_{Z \in S_x} (e(H(UID), g)^{\alpha t v_{ver} q_{parent(z)}(index(z))})^{\Delta_{j, S'_x}(0)}$$

$$= \prod_{Z \in S_x} (e(H(UID), g)^{\alpha t v_{ver} q_x(j)})^{\Delta_{j, S'_x}(0)}$$

$$= e(H(UID), g)^{\alpha t v_{ver} q_x(0)}$$

where $j = index(z)$ and $S'_x = \{index(x) : z \in S_x\}$
If DU's attribute set S satisfies the access tree $\mathcal{T}$, the decryption algorithm can be called from the root node R of $\mathcal{T}$. And the result is as follow:

$$F_R = DecryptNoode(CT', SK, R)$$

$$= e(H(UID), g)^{\alpha t v_{ver} q_R(0)}$$

$$= e(H(UID), g)^{\alpha t v_{ver} s}$$

Compute $D' = D^{1/t} g^\beta = g^\beta g^{v_{ver}} H(UID)^{\alpha v_{ver}}$,
$F'_R = F_R^{1/t} = e(H(UID), g)^{\alpha v_{ver} s}$. Then Compute:

$$\frac{\tilde{C} \cdot F'_R}{e(D', C)} = \frac{ck \cdot e(g, g)^{s(\beta + v_{ver})} e(H(UID), g)^{\alpha v_{ver} s}}{e(g^\beta g^{v_{ver}} H(UID)^{\alpha v_{ver}}, g^s)}$$

$$= \frac{ck \cdot e(g, g)^{s(\beta + v_{ver})} e(H(UID), g)^{\alpha v_{ver} s}}{e(g, g)^{s(\beta + v_{ver})} e(H(UID), g)^{\alpha v_{ver} s}}$$

$$= ck$$

$E_{ck}(M)$ can be decrypted with ck by applying the symmetric decryption algorithm.

5 Security Analysis

5.1 Chosen Plaintext Attack Security

Theorem 1. *If there is a PPT adversary $\mathcal{A}$ that can break the scheme with non-negligible advantage $\varepsilon > 0$, then there exists a PPT algorithm $\mathcal{B}$ that can distinguish a DBDH tuple from a random tuple with the advantage of $\varepsilon/2$.*

Proof. We can construct an algorithm $\mathcal{B}$ that breaks DBDH assumption with the advantage $\varepsilon/2$. Namely, $\mathcal{B}$ can decide if $Z = e(g,g)^\theta$ according the tuple $\langle g, g^a, g^b, g^c, Z = e(g,g)^\theta \rangle$. Let G, G_T be bilinear groups of prime order p with generator g and $e : G \times G \to G_T$. $\mathcal{B}$ randomly select $a, b, s \in Z_p^*$ and an random element $E \in G_T$.

- **Init**: $\mathcal{A}$ submits a challenge access tree $\mathcal{T}^*$ and version number ver^* to the challenger $\mathcal{B}$.
- **Setup**: $\mathcal{B}$ randomly selects $\alpha, \beta, \gamma, v_0$ where $\beta = \beta' + ab$, then $\mathcal{B}$ calculates g^α, g^γ and $e(g,g)^\beta = e(g,g)^{\beta' + ab}$. For each attribute $j \in L$, TA chooses a random $v_j \in Z_p^*$ and calculates $A_j = H(j)^{v_j}$. Finally, $\mathcal{B}$ sends the public key $PK = \{G_0, g, g^\alpha, e(g,g)^\beta, g^\gamma, A_j\}$ to $\mathcal{A}$.
- **Phase 1**: In this phrase, $\mathcal{A}$ can launch two types of query: secret key query and update query. In secret key query, $\mathcal{A}$ submits an UID and an attribute set $S \in L$ which do not satisfy the access tree to get the secret key SK from $\mathcal{B}$. When $\mathcal{B}$ receives the query, it randomly selects $t, r_1 \in Z_p^*$ and computes $D = (g \times H(UID)^\alpha)^{v_0 t}, D_j = H(UID)^{v_0 t} \times H(j)^{v_j t}, D_j' = H(j)^{\alpha t}$ for $\forall j \in S$. $\mathcal{B}$ sends the secret key $SK = \{D, \forall j \in S : D_j, D_j'\}$ to $\mathcal{A}$. In order to update SK to the version of ver^*, $\mathcal{A}$ needs to perform the update query. Then $\mathcal{B}$ sends the $\{UP_{ver+1}\}_{0 \leq ver \leq ver^*-1}$ to $\mathcal{A}$, so that $\mathcal{A}$ can compute $D = D \times (g \times H(UID)^\alpha)^{t(v_{ver+1}-v_{ver})}$ and $\forall j \in S : D_j \times H(UID)^{t(v_{ver+1}-v_{ver})} = H(UID)^{v_{ver+1}t} \times H(j)^{v_j t}$. And the final $SK = \{(g \times H(UID)^\alpha)^{v_{ver^*}t}, \forall j \in S : H(UID)^{v_{ver^*}t} \times H(j)^{v_j t}, H(j)^{\alpha t}\}$.
- **Challenge**: $\mathcal{A}$ submits two equal length message M_0 and M_1 to challenger $\mathcal{B}$. After receiving the message, $\mathcal{B}$ randomly chooses c from $\{0,1\}$ and runs $Encryption()$ to generate the ciphertext CT_c. If $c = 0$, then $Z = E$. Otherwise, $\mathcal{B}$ computes $\widetilde{C} = M_c \cdot e(g,g)^{s(\beta + v_{ver})} = M_c \cdot e(g,g)^{s(\beta' + v_{ver})}, C = g^s, C' = g^{\alpha s}$ then $\mathcal{B}$ performs as follow. For each node x in the access tree $\mathcal{T}^*$, $\mathcal{B}$ first selects a random polynomial q_x with degree $d_x = k_x - 1$, where k_x is the threshold value in the node x. Beginning from the root node R, these polynomials are select in a top-down manner. $\mathcal{B}$ randomly chooses d_R other points of q_R to completely define them, and then set $q_R(0) = s$. For any other node x, it sets $q_x(0) = q_{parent(x)}index(x)$, then selects d_x other points to completely define them. Let the set of leaf nodes in the access tree $\mathcal{T}^*$ be Y.
- **Phase 2**: $\mathcal{A}$ launches queries as phrase 1 and $\mathcal{B}$ answers as phrase 1 too.
- **Guess**: $\mathcal{A}$ outputs its guess $c' \in \{0,1\}$. If $c' = c$, then $\mathcal{B}$ outputs 0, which means that $Z = e(g,g)^{abs}$; otherwise $\mathcal{B}$ outputs 1 means that $Z = E$. If $Z = e(g,g)^{abs}$, CT^* is a legal ciphertext and $\mathcal{A}$'s advantage is ε. Thus:

$$Pr[\mathcal{B}(g, g^a, g^b, Z = e(g,g)^{abs}) = 0] = 1/2 + \varepsilon.$$

If $Z = E$, then the CT' is invalid and:

$$Pr[\mathcal{B}(g, g^a, g^b, Z = E = 0] = 1/2.$$

At last, the advantage of $\mathcal{A}$ is:

$$\frac{1}{2} Pr\left[\mathcal{B}\left(g, g^a, g^b, Z = e(g, g)^{abs}\right) = 0\right] + \frac{1}{2} Pr\left[\mathcal{B}\left(g, g^a, g^b, Z = E\right) = 0\right] - \frac{1}{2} = \frac{\varepsilon}{2}.$$

5.2 Chosen-Keyword Attack Security

Theorem 2. *If there is a PPT adversary $\mathcal{A}$ that can break the scheme with non-negligible advantage $\varepsilon > 0$, then there exists a PPT algorithm $\mathcal{B}$ that can distinguish a DBDH tuple from a random tuple with the advantage of $\varepsilon/2$.*

Proof. We can construct an algorithm $\mathcal{B}$ that breaks DBDH assumption with the advantage $\varepsilon/2$. Namely, $\mathcal{B}$ can decide if $Z = e(g, g)^\theta$ according the tuple $\langle g, g^a, g^b, g^c, Z = e(g, g)^\theta \rangle$. Let G, G_T be bilinear groups of prime order p with generator g and $e : G \times G \to G_T$. $\mathcal{B}$ randomly selects $u, v \in Z_p^*$ and two random element $h_1, h_2 \in G$.

- **Init**: A probabilistic polynomial time adversary $\mathcal{A}$ submits t keywords $\{W_1, W_2, \ldots, W_t\}$ to the challenger $\mathcal{B}$.
- **Setup**: $\mathcal{B}$ randomly selects α, β, γ, then $\mathcal{B}$ calculates g^α, g^γ and $e(g, g)^\beta$. For each attribute $j \in L$, TA chooses a random $v_j \in Z_p^*$ and calculates $A_j = H(j)^{v_j}$. Finally, $\mathcal{B}$ sends the public key $PK = \{G_0, g, g^\alpha, e(g, g)^\beta, g^\gamma, A_j\}$ to $\mathcal{A}$.
- **Phrase 1**: Adversary $\mathcal{A}$ submits a set of keywords SKW, where $\{W_1, W_2\} \notin SKW$, to $\mathcal{B}$ to get the *Trapdoor*. On receiving the query, $\mathcal{B}$ computes $T_a = g^{\frac{v}{H(skw_1 \| skw_2 \| \ldots \| skw_k)}}$, $T_b = (g^\gamma H(j)^{\sum_{j \in S} v_j})^v$. Finally, $\mathcal{B}$ sends the *trapdoor* $= \{T_a, T_b\}$ to Adversary $\mathcal{A}$.
- **Challenge**: $\mathcal{B}$ randomly selects c from $\{0, 1\}$ and runs $KW\_Encryption()$ algorithm to generate the encrypted keywords CT_c. If $c = 0$, $\mathcal{B}$ randomly selects $h_1, h_2 \in G$ and let $\widehat{C_a} = h_1, \widehat{C_b} = h_2$. Otherwise, it prepares an attribute set S' that contains all the attributes in the access tree. $\mathcal{B}$ computes $\widehat{C_a} = g^{\frac{u}{H(kw_1 \| kw_2 \| \ldots \| kw_k)}}, \widehat{C_b} = (g^\gamma \prod_{j \in S'} A_j)^u$. Finally, $\mathcal{B}$ sends the encryption keywords $CT_c = \{\widehat{C_a}, \widehat{C_b}\}$ to the $\mathcal{A}$.
- **Phrase 2**: $\mathcal{A}$ launches queries as phrase 1 and $\mathcal{B}$ answers as phrase 1.
- **Guess**: $\mathcal{A}$ outputs its guess $c' \in \{0, 1\}$. If $c' = c$, then $\mathcal{B}$ outputs 1, which means that $\widehat{C_a} = g^{\frac{u}{H(kw_1 \| kw_2 \| \ldots \| kw_k)}}, \widehat{C_b} = (g^\gamma \prod_{j \in S'} A_j)^u$. Let $v = bc$, $\frac{u}{H(kw_1 \| kw_2 \| \ldots \| kw_k)} = a$ and $Z = e(\widehat{C_a}, T_b)$. Otherwise, $\mathcal{B}$ outputs 0 means that $\widehat{C_a} = h_1, \widehat{C_b} = h_2$, $Z = e(h_1, T_b)$.
  If $\widehat{C_a} = g^{\frac{u}{H(kw_1 \| kw_2 \| \ldots \| kw_k)}}, \widehat{C_b} = (g^\gamma \prod_{j \in S'} A_j)^u$, CT_c is a legal encrypted keyword and $\mathcal{A}'s$ advantage is ε. Thus:

$$Pr[\mathcal{B}(g, \widehat{C_b}, T_a, Z) = 0] = 1/2 + \varepsilon.$$

If $\widehat{C_a} = h_1, \widehat{C_b} = h_2$, then the CT_b is invalid and:

$$Pr[\mathcal{B}(g, \widehat{C_b}, T_a, Z) = 0] = 1/2.$$

At last, the advantage of $\mathcal{A}$ is:

$$\frac{1}{2} Pr \left[\mathcal{B} \left(g, \widehat{C_b}, T_a, Z \right) = 0 \right] + \frac{1}{2} Pr \left[\mathcal{B} \left(g, \widehat{C_b}, T_a, Z \right) = 0 \right] - \frac{1}{2} = \frac{\varepsilon}{2}.$$

And $\mathcal{A}$ wins the game if $c' = c$ with the advantage of $Adv^{\mathcal{A}} = |Pr[b = b'] - 1/2|$.

5.3 Collusion Resistance

In the phase of secret key generation, trusted authority generates the secret key with the parament of user's identity UID. So that the secret key of two user will not be the same even if their attributes are the same, which means data user in the system cannot use the secret key belong to others. Besides, the "ver" is used to manage the user revocation. When user revocation occurs, the "ver" will be update to "ver+1", which means the ciphertext alone with the secret keys will all be update. So that the revoked user's secret key won't be able to be used again.

5.4 Trapdoor Unlinkability

As the CSP is a semi-trusted entity in the system, it will be always curious about DU's information. If a DU wants to conceal the nature of his search, the trapdoor must be encrypted. When DU needs to generate the trapdoor in our scheme, a random number x will be chose to obfuscate the keywords. As a result, CSP will not be able to distinguish the keywords in the trapdoor, even the keywords in the trapdoor are the same with the other one. Thus, the trapdoor in our scheme is unlinkability.

6 Performance Evaluation

6.1 Theoretical Analysis

We analyze the efficiency of the proposed scheme, and compare it with [4,25,28]. We note that there exist some novel schemes which addressed the problem of user revocation and ciphertext search like [7,28]. In [7], the authors achieve the revocation with the help of a revocation list. Besides, their scheme is designed based on the multi-authority, which differ from the scheme in this paper. We assume that the hash computation is not included in the calculation.

The storage cost analysis is shown in Table 1. As we can see, the size of public key, secret key and ciphertext in our scheme is less than that in scheme [4]. In Table 2, the efficiency of encryption and search in our scheme is more superior compare to that in scheme [4]. Compare to the scheme in [25], the size

Table 1. Storage cost analysis.

	Our scheme	Scheme in [25]	Scheme in [4]	Scheme in [28]
PK size	$(l+3)L_G + L_{G_T}$	$(l+6)L_G + L_{G_T}$	$(3+2l)L_G$	$(n+4)L_G + Z_p^*$
MSK size	$(l+2)L_{Z_p^*}$	$lL_{Z_p^*} + L_G$	$(l+1)L_{Z_p^*}$	$4lL_G + 3Z_p^*$
SK size	$(2k+1)L_G$	$2L_G$	$(k+1)L_G$	$(7k+n+1)L_G$
CT size	$(2t+2)L_G + L_{G_T}$	$2L_G + L_{G_T}$	$(2t+3)L_G + L_{G_T}$	$(2t+2)L_G + L_{G_T}$

l stands for the number of all attributes in the scheme. n stands for the number of maximum number of revoked user set in the revocation list. k stands for the number of attributes in user's secret key. t stands for the number of attributes in ciphertext. L_G, L_{G_i} stands for the length of an element in G and G_i. $L_{Z_p^*}$ stands for the length of an element in Z_p^*.

of secret key and ciphertext is larger in our scheme. The reason is that the access structure in [25] is AND gate, and we use the tree structure. But we implement the function of user revocation which was not provided in [25]. In [28], the size of master secret key and secret key is much larger than that in our scheme. In the search phrase, the computing cost grows linearly with the size of keywords in the trapdoor, which will incur poor performance in efficient. Considering both the functions of revocation and ciphertext search are achieved, we believe our's scheme is more efficient and practical.

Table 2. Computing cost analysis.

	Our scheme	Scheme in [25]	Scheme in [4]	Scheme in [28]
Encryption	$(2t+2)G + G_T$	$(t+2)G + G_T$	$(2t+6)G + G_T$	$(2t+n+1)G + G_T$
Decryption	$2G + (2k+2)C_e$	$G_T + 2C_e$	×	$2kC_e + kG_T$
Re-Encryption	$2G + G_T + C_e$	×	×	×
Search	$2C_e$	$2C_e$	$3C_e$	$(2w+3)C_e + 2wG$

t stands for the number of attributes in ciphertext. w stands for the number of keywords in the trapdoor. k stands for the number of attributes in user's secret key. G, G_T stands for the exponentiation operation in G and G_i. C_e stands for the bilinear pairing operation.

6.2 Experiment Analysis

In this section, we evaluate the performance of the proposed scheme presented in Sect. 4. The experiment is performed on the Windows 7 system with an intel core i5-3210M CPU 2.50 GHz and 12 GB memory. We use JDK1.8 and java pairing-based cryptography 2.0.0 (JPBC) [3] to implement our scheme.

We analyze the performance of our scheme by comparing it with Cui's scheme [4] for the reason that this is the closest work to compare in terms of keyword encryption algorithm, trapdoor generation algorithm and search algorithm. As the cost of computing is closely related to the complexity of the access policy, we generate all the access policy in the form of n of $(\mathcal{S}_1, \mathcal{S}_2, \ldots, \mathcal{S}_n)$, where $\mathcal{S}_i$ is an attribute and n denotes the number of attributes in the policy. As depicted in Fig. 2(a) and (b), we examine the time cost of keyword encryption and trapdoor generation. In the process of keywords encryption, instead of dealing with every one of the keyword, we sum all the keywords together. As a result, the encrypted keyword is constant in size and the expense is small. To relief the time cost of trapdoor generation, we generate parts of the trapdoor in the secret key generation algorithm, so that we only need to do a little exponential operation. In addition, as we said before, the search operation is efficient in our scheme. We can see the time cost in Fig. 2(c) is very small, we only need twice bilinear pairing operation to finish the search operation while scheme [4] need three times. The time cost of the system initialization algorithm, secret key generation algorithm, encryption algorithm and decryption algorithm are depicted in Fig. 2(d), (e), (f) and (g). As the number of attributes grows, the time cost grows linearly.

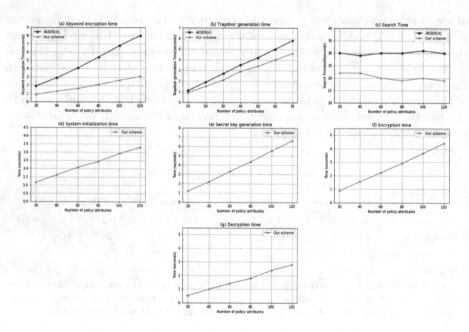

Fig. 2. Experimental results

7   Conclusion

In this paper, an attribute-based encryption with efficient keyword search and user revocation is proposed. Our scheme is practical and comprehensive. In addition to fine-grained access control through ABE scheme, our scheme also provides the function of user revocation and efficient keyword search. Specifically, it only takes twice bilinear mapping operation to get the search result in the search phrase. Our security analysis implied that the proposed scheme is secure under DBDH assumption. The efficiency analysis and experience demonstrate that the overhead of our scheme is acceptable.

Acknowledgements. We are grateful to the anonymous reviewers for their invaluable suggestions. This work was supported in part by the National Natural Science Foundation of China (61472343,61702237), the Natural Science Foundation of Jiangsu Province, China (BK20150241), National Research Foundation, Prime Minister's Office, Singapore, under its Corporate Laboratory@University Scheme, National University of Singapore, and Singapore Telecommunications Ltd.

References

1. Beimel, A.: Secure schemes for secret sharing and key distribution. Int. J. Pure Appl. Math. (1996)
2. Bethencourt, J., Sahai, A., Waters, B.: Ciphertext-policy attribute-based encryption. In: IEEE Symposium on Security and Privacy, SP 2007, pp. 321–334. IEEE (2007)
3. De Caro, A., Iovino, V.: JPBC: Java pairing based cryptography. In: Computers and Communications, pp. 850–855 (2011)
4. Cui, J., Zhou, H., Zhong, H., Yan, X.: Akser: attribute-based keyword search with efficient revocation in cloud computing. Inf. Sci. **423**, 343–352 (2018)
5. Ge, X., Jia, Y., Chengyu, H., Zhang, H., Hao, R.: Enabling efficient verifiable fuzzy keyword search over encrypted data in cloud computing. IEEE Access **6**, 45725–45739 (2018)
6. Goyal, V., Pandey, O., Sahai, A., Waters, B.: Attribute-based encryption for fine-grained access control of encrypted data. In: Proceedings of the 13th ACM Conference on Computer and Communications Security, pp. 89–98. ACM (2006)
7. Imine, Y., Lounis, A., Bouabdallah, A.: Revocable attribute-based access control in mutli-autority systems. J. Netw. Comput. Appl. **122**, 61–76 (2018)
8. Lewko, A., Waters, B.: New proof methods for attribute-based encryption: achieving full security through selective techniques. In: Safavi-Naini, R., Canetti, R. (eds.) CRYPTO 2012. LNCS, vol. 7417, pp. 180–198. Springer, Heidelberg (2012). https://doi.org/10.1007/978-3-642-32009-5_12
9. Li, J., Yao, W., Zhang, Y., Qian, H., Han, J.: Flexible and fine-grained attribute-based data storage in cloud computing. IEEE Trans. Serv. Comput. **10**(5), 785–796 (2017)
10. Li, J., Huang, Q., Chen, X., Chow, S.S.M., Wong, D.S., Xie, D.: Multi-authority ciphertext-policy attribute-based encryption with accountability. In: ACM Symposium on Information, Computer and Communications Security, ASIACCS 2011, Hong Kong, China, March, pp. 386–390 (2011)
11. Li, W., Xue, K., Xue, Y., Hong, J.: Tmacs: a robust and verifiable threshold multi-authority access control system in public cloud storage. IEEE Trans. Parallel Distrib. Syst. **27**(5), 1484–1496 (2016)
12. Liang, K., Susilo, W.: Searchable attribute-based mechanism with efficient data sharing for secure cloud storage. IEEE Trans. Inf. Forensics Secur. **10**(9), 1981–1992 (2017)
13. Lin, S., Zhang, R., Ma, H., Wang, M.: Revisiting attribute-based encryption with verifiable outsourced decryption. IEEE Trans. Inf. Forensics Secur. **10**(10), 2119–2130 (2017)

14. Ning, J., Cao, Z., Dong, X., Gong, J., Chen, J.: Traceable CP-ABE with short ciphertexts: how to catch people selling decryption devices on eBay efficiently. In: Askoxylakis, I., Ioannidis, S., Katsikas, S., Meadows, C. (eds.) ESORICS 2016, Part II. LNCS, vol. 9879, pp. 551–569. Springer, Cham (2016). https://doi.org/10. 1007/978-3-319-45741-3_28

15. Ning, J., Cao, Z., Dong, X., Liang, K., Ma, H., Wei, L.: Auditable σ -time outsourced attribute-based encryption for access control in cloud computing. IEEE Trans. Inf. Forensics Secur. **13**(1), 94–105 (2017)

16. Ning, J., Cao, Z., Dong, X., Liang, K., Wei, L., Choo, K.-K.R.: Cryptcloud+: secure and expressive data access control for cloud storage. IEEE Trans. Serv. Comput. (2018)

17. Ning, J., Cao, Z., Dong, X., Wei, L.: White-box traceable CP-ABE for cloud storage service: how to catch people leaking their access credentials effectively. IEEE Trans. Dependable Secur. Comput. **15**(5), 883–897 (2016)

18. Ning, J., Cao, Z., Dong, X., Wei, L., Lin, X.: Large universe ciphertext-policy attribute-based encryption with white-box traceability. In: Kutyłowski, M., Vaidya, J. (eds.) ESORICS 2014, Part II. LNCS, vol. 8713, pp. 55–72. Springer, Cham (2014). https://doi.org/10.1007/978-3-319-11212-1_4

19. Ning, J., Dong, X., Cao, Z., Wei, L.: Accountable authority ciphertext-policy attribute-based encryption with white-box traceability and public auditing in the cloud. In: Pernul, G., Ryan, P.Y.A., Weippl, E. (eds.) ESORICS 2015, Part II. LNCS, vol. 9327, pp. 270–289. Springer, Cham (2015). https://doi.org/10.1007/ 978-3-319-24177-7_14

20. Ning, J., Dong, X., Cao, Z., Wei, L., Lin, X.: White-box traceable ciphertext-policy attribute-based encryption supporting flexible attributes. IEEE Trans. Inf. Forensics Secur. **10**(6), 1274–1288 (2015)

21. Ning, J., Jia, X., Liang, K., Zhang, F., Chang, E.-C.: Passive attacks against searchable encryption. IEEE Trans. Inf. Forensics Secur. **14**(3), 789–802 (2019)

22. Padhya, M., Jinwala, D.: A novel approach for searchable CP-ABE with hidden ciphertext-policy. In: Prakash, A., Shyamasundar, R. (eds.) ICISS 2014. LNCS, vol. 8880, pp. 167–184. Springer, Cham (2014). https://doi.org/10.1007/978-3-319-13841-1_10

23. Sahai, A., Waters, B.: Fuzzy identity-based encryption. In: Cramer, R. (ed.) EUROCRYPT 2005. LNCS, vol. 3494, pp. 457–473. Springer, Heidelberg (2005). https:// doi.org/10.1007/11426639_27

24. Song, D.X., Wagner, D., Perrig, A.: Practical techniques for searches on encrypted data. In: IEEE Symposium on Security and Privacy, S&P 2000, Proceedings, pp. 44–55. IEEE (2000)

25. Su, H., Zhu, Z., Sun, L., Pan, N.: Practical searchable CP-ABE in cloud storage. In: 2nd IEEE International Conference on Computer and Communications (ICCC), pp. 180–185. IEEE (2016)

26. Sun, W., Yu, S., Lou, W., Hou, Y.T., Li, H.: Protecting your right: attribute-based keyword search with fine-grained owner-enforced search authorization in the cloud. In: IEEE Proceedings on INFOCOM 2014, pp. 226–234. IEEE (2014)

27. Wang, H., Dong, X., Cao, Z.: Multi-value-independent ciphertext-policy attribute based encryption with fast keyword search. IEEE Trans. Serv. Comput. (2017)

28. Wang, S., Zhang, X., Zhang, Y.: Efficiently multi-user searchable encryption scheme with attribute revocation and grant for cloud storage. Plos One **11**(11), e0167157 (2016)

29. Wang, S., Zhou, J., Liu, J.K., Yu, J., Chen, J., Xie, W.: An efficient file hierarchy attribute-based encryption scheme in cloud computing. IEEE Trans. Inf. Forensics Secur. **11**(6), 1265–1277 (2016)
30. Xiong, A.-P., Gan, Q.-X., He, X.-X., Zhao, Q.: A searchable encryption of CP-ABE scheme in cloud storage. In: 10th International Computer Conference on Wavelet Active Media Technology and Information Processing (ICCWAMTIP 2013), pp. 345–349. IEEE (2013)
31. Yang, Y., Liu, J.K., Liang, K., Choo, K.-K.R., Zhou, J.: Extended proxy-assisted approach: achieving revocable fine-grained encryption of cloud data. In: Pernul, G., Ryan, P.Y.A., Weippl, E. (eds.) ESORICS 2015, Part II. LNCS, vol. 9327, pp. 146–166. Springer, Cham (2015). https://doi.org/10.1007/978-3-319-24177-7_8
32. Yang, Y., Li, H., Liu, W., Yao, H., Wen, M.: Secure dynamic searchable symmetric encryption with constant document update cost. In: Global Communications Conference (GLOBECOM), IEEE 2014 , pp. 775–780. IEEE (2014)
33. Zhang, P., Chen, Z., Liang, K., Wang, S., Wang, T.: A cloud-based access control scheme with user revocation and attribute update. In: Liu, J.K.K., Steinfeld, R. (eds.) ACISP 2016, Part I. LNCS, vol. 9722, pp. 525–540. Springer, Cham (2016). https://doi.org/10.1007/978-3-319-40253-6_32

Public-Key Encryption with Selective Opening Security from General Assumptions

Dali Zhu[1,2], Renjun Zhang[1,2(✉)], Shuang Hu[3,4], and Gongliang Chen[3]

[1] Institute of Information Engineering, Chinese Academy of Sciences, Beijing, China
{zhudali,zhangrenjun}@iie.ac.cn
[2] School of Cyber Security, University of Chinese Academy of Sciences,
Beijing, China
[3] SKLIATIS, Shanghai Jiao Tong University, Shanghai, China
{hushuang,chengl}@sjtu.edu.cn
[4] Virginia Commonwealth University, Richmond, VA, USA

Abstract. In a selective opening (SO) attack, the attacker can corrupt a subset of senders (or receivers) to open some of the ciphertexts and try to learn information on the plaintexts of unopened ciphertexts. It is important and practical to consider SO attack in encryption scheme. In this paper we study public key encryption (PKE) schemes with SO security. Specifically:

- First, we define a new cryptographic primitive called tweaked lossy encryption, and we prove that it has simulation-based security against sender selective opening chosen plaintext attacks (denoted by SIM-SSO-CPA).
- Second, we provide a general construction of tweaked lossy encryption scheme from extractable Σ-protocol; and we propose two instantiations of tweaked lossy encryption, based on dual-mode commitments and Twin-Cramer-Shoup scheme respectively.
- Finally, we propose a general scheme satisfying indistinguishability-based security against receiver selective opening chosen plaintext attacks (denoted by IND-RSO-CPA), and we give a construction of the scheme from explainable hash proof systems (denoted by EHPS), and we provide the security analysis.

Our results provide a new insight about the relations among PKE schemes with SO security, extractable Σ-protocol and explainable hash proof systems.

Keywords: Selective opening security · Lossy encryption ·
Extractable Σ-protocol · Explainable hash proof systems

This work was supported in by the National Key Research and Development Program of China-the Key Technologies for High Security Mobile Terminals (Grant No. 2017YFB0801903).

© Springer Nature Switzerland AG 2019
F. Guo et al. (Eds.): Inscrypt 2018, LNCS 11449, pp. 510–530, 2019.
https://doi.org/10.1007/978-3-030-14234-6_27

1   Introduction

Sender Selective Opening Security. Sender selective opening (SSO) attacks are considered in public key encryption (PKE) schemes where an adversary may corrupt some of the senders to selectively open some of the ciphertexts. Specifically, an adversary may get a collection of some arbitrary challenge ciphertexts $c = (c_1, \ldots, c_N)$ of size N, and each ciphertext $c_i = \text{Enc}_{pk}(m_i; r_i)$ is obtained by encrypting the message m_i with a fresh randomness r_i under a public key pk. The adversary may adaptively chooses a subset $I \subseteq [N]$ of ciphertexts to open, thus learning the messages $\{m_i\}_{i \in I}$ and the corresponding randomness $\{r_i\}_{i \in I}$, and then the adversary tries to break into the unopened ciphertexts $\{c_i\}_{i \in [N] \setminus I}$ and obtain additional information on the corresponding plaintexts. The SSO security of PKE schemes requires that the privacy of the unopened ciphertexts is perserved.

Several formal analysis [2,4,6,15,26,27] indicated that SSO security definition is essentially stronger than traditional security definitions due to two added features. One is to enable partial revelation of the randomness, which allows the adversary to check the relation between ciphertexts and the corresponding messages. The other is that the adversary is allowed to open a selected subset of ciphertexts, which gives it more power to learn information on the plaintexts of unopened ciphertexts.

Bellare *et al.* [3] proposed two types of SSO security: indistinguishability-based selective opening (IND-SSO) security and simulation-based selective opening (SIM-SSO) security. IND-SSO security means that no adversary can distinguish between opened messages and unopened messages. It requires the distribution on the messages to be efficiently conditionally resamplable. SIM-SSO security is a stronger notion than IND-SSO security. In particular, SIM-SSO security requires that, a simulator that sees only the opened messages can simulate the output of any real adversary; and it has no restrictions on the message distribution. Unfortunately, SIM-SSO security is much harder to achieve than IND-SSO security [2], since for many natural encryption schemes, there exist no such simulator satisfying the definitions given in [3,13].

Relations among IND-SSO, SIM-SSO and standard security definitions have been discussed in many literatures such as in [2,4,15,19,26,27]. Encryption schemes with IND-SSO security against chosen plaintext attack (IND-SSO-CPA) and SIM-SSO security against chosen plaintext attack (SIM-SSO-CPA) were first given in [3], based on lossy encryption [37,38]. In particular, Bellare *et al.* proved that lossy encryption implies IND-SSO-CPA security, and lossy encryption with efficient opening implies SIM-SSO-CPA security [3]. Later, Hemenway *et al.* [20] proposed a general construction of lossy encryption from hash proof system (HPS). Following this research, Hofheinz *et al.* [25] showed that lossy encryption with efficient weak opening algorithm implies SIM-SSO-CPA security. Note that most of those constructions are based on non-interactive cryptographic primitives; however, the all-but-many encryption (ABME) scheme [16] is built on interactive cryptographic primitives - extractable Σ-protocol, which provides a new and meaningful insight to design SSO secure encryption and related schemes.

Selective Opening Security for the Receiver. Selective opening security for the receiver (RSO) is less studied than SSO security. In the RSO setting, one sender and n receivers hold public and secret keys that are generated independently. The attacker is allowed to learn the messages together with secret keys of a subset of the receivers by corrupting them. Security is requires that the privacy of the uncorrupted receivers is perserved.

There are also indistinguishability-based selective opening for receiver (IND-RSO) security and simulation-based selective opening for receiver (SIM-RSO) security [19]. Some formal arguments show that RSO secure scheme can be constructed from non-committing encryption (NCER) schemes [7,11,36], while there are a few constructions from standard assumptions. In [19], Hazay *et al.* introduced a tweaked variant of NCER which implies IND-RSO security against chosen plaintext attack (IND-RSO-CPA), and shows that tweaked NCER can be constructed from some standard primitives.

Related Work. Deniable encryption [6] and NCER [7] can also be used to construct SSO secure encryption scheme [14,34]. In the indistinguishability-based chosen-ciphertext (IND-SSO-CCA) and simulation-based chosen ciphertext (SIM-SSO-CCA) scenarios, handling additional decryption queries makes it even more difficult to construct schemes with IND-SSO and SIM-SSO security. Several IND-SO-CCA secure schemes have been constructed by lossy trapdoor functions [38], such as all-but-N lossy trapdoor functions [20], and all-but-many lossy trapdoor functions [5,24,32]. And existing SIM-SSO-CCA secure constructions follow dedicated approaches [14,24,29,34]. Heuer *et al.* [23] showed that if a PKE scheme consists of a key encapsulation mechanism (KEM) and a blockcipher-based data encapsulation mechanism (DEM), and the DEM is simulatable, then the PKE scheme is SIM-SO-CCA secure. For sender security, Heuer *et al.* [21,22] showed that some practical schemes, such as RSA-OAEP and DHIES, are SIM-SSO-CCA secure in the random oracle model. For receiver security, IND-RSO-CCA and SIM-RSO-CCA secure constructions were proposed in [18,28,30,31].

1.1 Our Contribution

First, we define a new cryptographic primitive called tweaked lossy encryption, and we show that it is SIM-SSO-CPA secure. We remark that our construction is inspired by that of ABME given by Fujisaki [16], and by that of dual-mode commitments in [33], and by that of simulatable DEMs in [23], and by that of instance-dependent cryptographic primitives in [12,35].

Second, we provide a general construction of tweaked lossy encryption based on extractable Σ-protocol. Furthermore, we give two instantiations of the scheme based on two ways of constructing extractable Σ-protocol, namely dual-mode commitments and Twin-Cramer-Shoup scheme. These instantiations are non-trivial, specifically, the property of efficient weak opening in lossy encryption is usually restricted to specific algebraic structures that are hard to obtain, so we need to limit the length of the plaintext to logarithmic length. While in a setting where extractable Σ-protocols are executed in parallel, there may be multiple random challenges; and each of them can be associated with a plaintext, therefore it is possible to encrypt longer plaintexts by dividing them into multiple short plaintexts and encrypting each short plaintext in parallel.

Third, we provide an IND-RSO-CPA secure scheme from explainable hash proof systems (denoted by EHPS). In [19], Hazay *et al.* proved that secure tweaked NCER implies IND-RSO-CPA secure PKE, and HPS implies tweaked NCER. Compared with the construction in [19], our tweaked NCER scheme changes the opening algorithm in several ways: for the opening algorithm in [19], an unbounded algorithm can find an appropriate secret key by searching exhaustively without a trapdoor. In our opening algorithm, EHPS provide the trapdoor information, thus the secret key can be obtained in probabilistic polynomial time. Abdalla *et al.* [1] have shown that such EHPS can be constructed.

Organization. The rest of our paper is organized as follows: In Sect. 2 we present some basic notions and tools used; In Sect. 3 we define a new cryptographic primitive called tweaked lossy encryption and show that it is SIM-SSO-CPA secure; In Sect. 4 we describe a generic construction of tweaked lossy encryption scheme from extractable Σ-protocol; In Sect. 5, we give two instantiations of tweaked lossy encryption; In Sect. 6, we give a construction of tweaked NCER from EHPS, and prove that it is IND-RSO-CPA secure.

2 Preliminaries

Notation. We use $\mathbb{N}$ to denote the set of natural numbers, and $\mathbb{Z}$ the set of integers. For $n \in \mathbb{N}$, $[n]$ denotes the set $\{1, \ldots, n\}$. The length of a string x is denoted by $|x|$. We abbreviate probabilistic polynomial-time and deterministic polynomial-time as PPT and DPT respectively. Let $x \leftarrow S$ denote the process of picking up x uniformly at random from a finite set S, or the process of sampling x according to a distribution S. Given a security parameter λ, a function $\text{negl}(\lambda)$ is negligible for a sufficiently large λ.

Public Key Encryption. A PKE scheme consists of three PPT algorithms. The key generation algorithm $\text{Gen}(1^\lambda)$ takes a security parameter λ as input, and outputs a public/secret key pair (pk, sk) where pk is a public key and sk is the secret key. The encryption algorithm $\text{Enc}(pk, m; r)$ takes the public key pk, a message $m \in \mathcal{M}$ and randomness $r \in \mathcal{R}$ as inputs, and outputs a ciphertext c, denoted as $c = \text{Enc}(pk, m; r)$. The decryption algorithm $\text{Dec}(sk, c)$ takes the secret key sk, a ciphertext c as inputs, and outputs either a message m denoted as $m = \text{Dec}(sk, c)$ or a special "$\perp$" indicating invalid ciphertext c. We say that a PKE scheme satisfies correctness, if $\text{Dec}(sk, c) = m$ with all but negligible probability for all (pk, sk) produced by $\text{Gen}(1^\lambda)$ and all c produced by $\text{Enc}(pk, m; r)$.

Selective Opening Security. There are several different ways of formalizing SSO security. Following the approach of [4], we consider the definition of
SIM-SSO-CPA security, which requires that the output of the adversary can be
simulated by an efficient simulator without seeing neither the ciphertext nor the
public key. To model adaptive corruptions, the definition provides an opening
oracle $\mathcal{O}$ for the adversary and the simulator.

Definition 1 (SIM-SSO-CPA Security [3,4]). *A PKE scheme* PKE =
(Gen, Enc, Dec) *is SIM-SSO-CPA secure iff for every polynomially bounded*
$n = n(1^\lambda) > 0$, *and every stateful PPT adversary* $\mathcal{A}$, *there exists a stateful*
PPT simulator $\mathcal{S}$ *such that*

$$\mathbf{Adv}^{\text{sim}-\text{sso}-\text{cpa}}_{\text{PKE},\mathcal{A},\mathcal{S}}(1^\lambda) = |\Pr[\text{Exp}^{\text{real}}_{\text{PKE},\mathcal{A}}(1^\lambda) = 1] - \Pr[\text{Exp}^{\text{ideal}}_{\mathcal{S}}(1^\lambda) = 1]|$$

is negligible. The experiments $\text{Exp}^{\text{real}}_{\text{PKE},\mathcal{A},Rel}$ *and* $\text{Exp}^{\text{ideal}}_{\mathcal{S},Rel}$ *are defined as follow-*
ing (Fig. 1):

Experiment. $\text{Exp}^{\text{real}}_{\text{PKE},\mathcal{A}}(1^\lambda)$:

$(pk, sk) \leftarrow \text{Gen}(1^\lambda)$
dist $\leftarrow \mathcal{A}(pk)$
$(M_i)_{i \in [n]} \leftarrow$ dist
$(R_i)_{i \in [n]} \leftarrow (\mathcal{R}_{\text{Enc}})^n$
$(C_i)_{i \in [n]} = \text{Enc}(pk, M_i; R_i)_{i \in [n]}$
$\mathbf{O} = (M_i, R_i)_{i \in [n]}$
$out_\mathcal{A} \leftarrow \mathcal{A}^{\mathcal{O}(\cdot)}(\text{select}, (C_i)_{i \in [n]})$
$I = \mathcal{O}(\text{get queries})$
return $((M_i)_{i \in [n]}, \text{dist}, I, out_\mathcal{A})$

Experiment. $\text{Exp}^{\text{ideal}}_{\mathcal{S}}(1^\lambda)$:

dist $\leftarrow \mathcal{S}(1^\lambda)$
$(M_i)_{i \in [n]} \leftarrow$ dist
$out_\mathcal{S} \leftarrow \mathcal{S}^{\mathcal{O}(\cdot)}(\text{select})$
$I = \mathcal{O}(\text{get queries})$
return $((M_i)_{i \in [n]}, \text{dist}, I, out_\mathcal{S})$

Fig. 1. The REAL-SIM-SSO-CPA and IDEAL-SIM-SSO-CPA experiments

Interactive Proof System. Let L be a NP language and R a binary relation.
An interactive proof system [17] (P, V) for L is a pair of interactive machines,
where the prover P is able to convince the verifier V of true statements $x \in L$,
which is defined by a binary relation R such that $(x, w) \in R$; while nobody
can fool V into believing false statements $x \notin L$. An interactive proof system is
zero knowledge [17] if for every interactive machine V^*, there exists an expected
probabilistic polynomial-time simulator M^* that can simulate the entire interaction transcript between P and V without accessing P's certificate information.
Σ-protocols are special cases of three-round honest verifier zero-knowledge
proofs.

Definition 2 (Σ-protocol [10]). *A three-round public-coin protocol $\Sigma = (P_1, P_2, V)$ is a Σ-protocol for a relation R, if it satisfies the following properties:*

- *Completeness: if honest P and V are given common input x and private input w for P, where $(x, w) \in R$, then V will always accept the transcripts.*
- *Special soundness: there exists a PPT algorithm that takes x and a pair of accepting transcripts (a, e, z) and (a, e', z') for x as input, where $e \neq e'$, then it can efficiently compute w such that $(x, w) \in R$.*
- *Special honest verifier zero knowledge: there exists a PPT simulator upon input $x \in L$ and the challenge $e \in \{0,1\}^n$, then outputs an accepting transcript of the form (a, e, z). Moreover, the distribution of the simulator's output is computationally indistinguishable from that of a real execution between P and V on input x.*

Extractable Σ-protocol. The notion of extractable Σ-protocol was proposed in [16]. The following definition essentially repeats the definition of extractable Σ-protocol from [16], expect minor changes to fit our requirement. Let $L = \{L_{pk}\}_{pk}$ be a NP language composed of a series of sets L_{pk} indexed by $pk \in \mathcal{PK}$, where $\mathcal{PK}$ is the space of pk. Let $R_{pk} = \{(x, w)\}$ be a polynomial-time binary relation related to L_{pk}. An extractable Σ-protocol $\Sigma^{\text{ext}} = (\mathrm{P}_\Sigma^{\text{com}}, \mathrm{P}_\Sigma^{\text{ans}}, \mathrm{V}_\Sigma^{\text{vrfy}}, \mathrm{simP}_\Sigma^{\text{com}}, \mathrm{Ext})$ is defined as follows: PPT algorithm $\mathrm{P}_\Sigma^{\text{com}}$ on input $(x, w) \in R_{pk}$ and a random coins r_a, then outputs a commitment $a = \mathrm{P}_\Sigma^{\text{com}}(x, w; r_a)$. DPT algorithm $\mathrm{P}_\Sigma^{\text{ans}}$ takes as input (x, w, r_a, e) and outputs $z = \mathrm{P}_\Sigma^{\text{ans}}(x, w, r_a, e)$, where e is a challenge. DPT algorithm $\mathrm{V}_\Sigma^{\text{vrfy}}$ verifies (x, a, e, z) and decide whether to accept or reject it. PPT algorithm $\mathrm{simP}_\Sigma^{\text{com}}$ takes as input (x, e) and outputs $(a, e, z) = \mathrm{simP}_\Sigma^{\text{com}}(x, e; r_z)$. Similarly, r_z is the random coins, and we additionally require that $r_z = z$, and this property can be satisfied by many sigma protocols. DPT algorithm Ext takes as input (sk, x, a) and outputs e or a special symbol $\perp$ indicating failure, where sk is a secret key corresponding to pk. A protocol Σ^{Ext} is said to be an extractable Σ-protocol on $L = \{L_{pk}\}_{pk}$ for relation R_{pk}, if for all pk, there is a set L_{pk}^{co} such that $L_{pk} \cap L_{pk}^{co} = \emptyset$, and the following properties hold:

- Completeness: if P and V follow the protocol for common input x and private input w for P, then for every $(x, w) \in R_{pk}$ and every r_a and e, the equation $\mathrm{V}_\Sigma^{\text{vrfy}}(x, \mathrm{P}_\Sigma^{\text{com}}(x, w; r_a), e, \mathrm{P}_\Sigma^{\text{ans}}(x, w, r_a, e)) = 1$ is always true.
- Special soundness: for every $x \notin L$ and every a, there exists *exactly one* e such that $\mathrm{V}_\Sigma^{\text{vrfy}}(x, a, e, z) = 1$.
- Extractability: we say that $(pk, sk^{\text{ext}}) \subset R^{\text{ext}}$ if there is $e' = \mathrm{Ext}(sk^{\text{ext}}, x, a)$ which satisfies $\mathrm{V}_\Sigma^{\text{vrfy}}(x, a, e', z) = 1$ for all $x \in L_{pk}^{co}$ and all a, so that the equation $\mathrm{V}_\Sigma^{\text{vrfy}}(x, a, e, z) = 1$ holds for an existing pair (e, z). If for all $pk \in \mathcal{PK}$, there is a sk^{ext} that satisfies the relation $(pk, sk^{\text{ext}}) \in R^{\text{ext}}$, we say that Σ^{ext} has the property of extractability on $\{L_{pk}^{co}\}_{pk}$. Combined with special soundness, for all $x \in L_{pk}^{co}$, all e and all z, we can get $e = \mathrm{Ext}(sk, x, \mathrm{simP}_\Sigma^{\text{com}}(x, e; z)_1)$, where $\mathrm{simP}_\Sigma^{\text{com}}(x, e; z)_1$ is the first output of $\mathrm{simP}_\Sigma^{\text{com}}(x, e; z)$.

- Enhanced Honest-Verifier Statistical Zero-Knowledge (eHVSZK): for every $(pk, sk^{\text{ext}}) \in R^{\text{ext}}$, every $(x, w) \in R_{pk}$, and every challenge e, the following two ensembles are statistically indistinguishable:

$$\{\text{simP}_{\Sigma}^{\text{com}}(x, e; r_z)\} \approx_s \{(\text{P}_{\Sigma}^{\text{com}}(x, w; r_a), e, \text{P}_{\Sigma}^{\text{ans}}(x, w, r_a, e))\}$$

3   Selective Opening Security from Tweaked Lossy Encryption

In this section, we define a new cryptographic primitive called tweaked lossy encryption (tLPKE), then we show that tLPKE is SIM-SSO-CPA secure. We can think of tLPKE as a lightweight ABME [16].

Definition 3 (Tweaked Lossy Encryption). *A tweaked lossy encryption scheme with message space $\mathcal{M}$ is a tuple of PPT algorithms such that:*

$\text{Gen}(1^\lambda)$: *take the security parameter λ as input and output (pk, sk) where pk is the real public key and sk is the corresponding secret key.*

$\text{LGen}(1^\lambda)$: *take the security parameter λ as input and output a key pair (pk, sk) where pk is the lossy public key and sk is the lossy secret key.*

$\text{Enc}(pk, m; r)$: *take a real or lossy public key pk, a message $m \in \mathcal{M}$, and a random coin $r \in R_{\text{Enc}}$ as inputs, output a ciphertext c.*

$\text{Dec}(sk, c)$: *take a ciphertext c and a secret key sk as inputs, output either a message $m \in \mathcal{M}$ or a special symbol "$\perp$" indicating decryption failure.*

$\text{Sim} = (\text{Fake}, \text{Open})$: *is a pair of PPT and DPT algorithms such that*
  - *$\text{Fake}(pk, r')$: take a lossy public key pk and a random coin $r' \leftarrow R_{\text{Enc}}$ as inputs, output a fake ciphertext e^* and an auxiliary parameter ε.*
  - *$\text{Open}(\varepsilon, m)$: take an auxiliary parameter ε and a message $m \in \mathcal{M}$ as inputs, output a random coin $r \in R_{\text{Enc}}$.*

Furthermore, tLPKE satisfies the following properties:

- Correctness: for all $(pk, sk) \leftarrow \text{Gen}(1^\lambda)$, message $m \in \mathcal{M}$, $c \leftarrow \text{Enc}(pk, m; r)$, it must satisfy $\text{Dec}(sk, c) = m$.
- Key indistinguishability: for any PPT distinguisher D, there exists a negligible function $\mu(\cdot)$ such that

$$\text{Adv}_{\text{tLPKE},D}^{\text{ind-lossy-key}} = \left| \begin{array}{l} \Pr[D(pk, 1^\lambda) = 1 | (pk, sk) \leftarrow \text{Gen}(1^\lambda)] - \\ \Pr[D(pk, 1^\lambda) = 1 | (pk, sk) \leftarrow \text{LGen}(1^\lambda)] \end{array} \right| \leq \mu(\lambda)$$

- Simulatability: define the following variables:
  - $\text{dist}^{\text{Enc}}(pk, m)$ denotes the random variable (c, r), where $r \leftarrow R_{\text{Enc}}$, $c = \text{Enc}(pk, m; r)$ and pk is the lossy public key.
  - $\text{dist}^{\text{Sim}}(pk, m)$ denotes the random variable (e^*, r), where $(e^*, \varepsilon) \leftarrow \text{Fake}(pk, r')$ and pk is the lossy public key; $r' \leftarrow R_{\text{Enc}}$; $r \leftarrow \text{Open}(\varepsilon, m)$.

Therefore the following ensembles are statistically indistinguishable:

$$\{\text{dist}^{\text{Enc}}(pk, m)\} \approx_s \{\text{dist}^{\text{Sim}}(pk, m)\}$$

Remarks. The recent work of Heuer *et al.* [23] defined a simulatability property that holds for DEM. Intuitively, the encapsulation algorithm could generate a ciphertext without seeing the corresponding message. Formally, they divided the encapsulation process into two parts in sequential order, *Fake* and *Make*. Firstly, Fake algorithm outputs a ciphertext c before seeing the message m; Then, Make algorithm takes as input the message m and tries to find a possible permutation instance, under which m would be encapsulated to the ciphertext c. Our ideas are similar to those of Heuer *et al.*, the main difference is that we use Open algorithm to replace the Make algorithm. Their Make algorithm exhaustively searches for the appropriate permutation, and may be inefficient. Our Open algorithm introduces auxiliary parameters, including the lossy secret key and some random coins, which makes the Open algorithm running in probabilistic polynomial time.

Theorem 1. *The tweaked lossy encryption scheme is SIM-SSO-CPA secure.*

Proof (Sketch). The proof of Theorem 1 is similar to the proof of lossy encryption with efficient opening implies SIM-SSO-CPA security in [3], so we will only sketch it here. Consider the following sequence of games:

$Game_0$: the REAL-SIM-SSO-CPA game.

$Game_1$: the same as $Game_0$ except that the adversary is given a lossy public key and lossy ciphertexts. $Game_1$ and $Game_0$ are indistinguishable by the property of key indistinguishability.

$Game_{2,0}$: the same as $Game_1$ except that for the first ciphertext we replace $\text{Enc}(pk, m_1; r_1)$ with $\text{Fake}(pk, r_1')$. In the corrupt procedure, instead of opening the first ciphertext by revealing the actual coins if $1 \in [I]$, $Game_{2,0}$ runs $\text{Open}(\varepsilon, \mathbf{M}[1])$ algorithm on the actual message and returns r_1, which is the random coins used to generate the first ciphertext. If $1 \notin [I]$, $Game_{2,0}$ reveals the actual coins and returns the output. The view of adversary in this game is statistically close to that in the $Game_0$, since the variables $\{\text{dist}^{\text{Enc}}(pk, m)\}$ and $\{\text{dist}^{\text{Sim}}(pk, m)\}$ are statistically indistinguishable.

$Game_{2,j}$: in the j-th hybrid game, we use $\text{Fake}(\cdot)$ algorithm instead of $\text{Enc}(\cdot)$ algorithm to generate the first j ciphertexts. In the corrupt procedure, $Game_{2,j}$ runs the $\text{Open}(\varepsilon, \mathbf{M}[k])$ algorithm on the actual messages and returns r_k if $k \in [I]$ and $k \le j$; Otherwise, $Game_{2,j}$ reveals the actual coins and returns the output.

$Game_{2,n}$: in the last hybrid, all ciphertexts are generated using the $\text{Fake}(\cdot)$ algorithm. In the corrupt procedure, $Game_{2,n}$ runs the $\text{Open}(\varepsilon, \mathbf{M})$ algorithm on the actual messages and returns the output.

$Game_3$: the same as $Game_{2,n}$ except that the sampling of $\mathbf{M}$ is moved before the $\text{Open}(\varepsilon, \mathbf{M})$ algorithm and after the $\text{Fake}(\cdot)$ algorithm. The $\text{Fake}(\cdot)$ algorithm no longer requires a message vector, therefore it does not change the view of the adversary.

Now we can construct a simulator $\mathcal{S}$ that runs the adversary $\mathcal{A}$ as its subroutine, just as $\mathcal{A}$ behaves in $Game_3$. Specially, $\mathcal{S}$ chooses a lossy key pair and gives $\mathcal{A}$

the lossy public key and n fake ciphertexts under lossy public key. In case of corruption, when $\mathcal{A}$ makes a query with a set I, $\mathcal{S}$ forwards the same set I to its own challenge oracle. After receiving the messages $\mathbf{M}_I$, $\mathcal{S}$ then uses the efficient algorithm $\text{Open}(\varepsilon, \mathbf{M})$ to open the fake ciphertexts to the messages $\mathbf{M}_I$. Finally, after $\mathcal{A}$ outputs a string out, the simulator $\mathcal{S}$ will output the same value. Since both $\mathcal{A}$ and $\text{Open}(\varepsilon, \mathbf{M})$ are efficient, the simulator $\mathcal{S}$ is also efficient. Because the neighboring games are either statistically indistinguishable or computationally indistinguishable, the theorem holds.

4   Tweaked Lossy Encryption Scheme from Extractable Σ-protocol

In this section, we build a tweaked lossy encryption scheme from extractable Σ-protocol that is defined on a membership-hard language L with efficient sampling [33].

4.1   Membership-Hard Languages with Efficient Sampling

Let L be a language. Let S_L be a sampling algorithm that takes a bit b as input. If $b = 0$, S_L outputs an instance in the language L together with a corresponding witness w. If $b = 1$, S_L outputs an instance not in the language L. It is required that no PPT distinguisher can tell which bit S_L received. Let S_L^x denote the instance of the output of the sampling algorithm S_L, we now recall the formal definition of the membership-hard languages with efficient sampling.

Definition 4 ([33]). *We say that a language L satisfies membership-hard with efficient sampling, if there exists a PPT sampling algorithm S_L such for any PPT distinguisher D, the advantage $\text{Adv}_D^x(n)$ defined below is negligible:*

$$\text{Adv}_D^x(n) = |\Pr[D(S_L^x(0, 1^n), 1^n) = 1] - \Pr[D(S_L(1, 1^n), 1^n) = 1]|$$

4.2   Our Scheme

Our scheme is inspired by the general framework for constructing ABME in [16], and is also inspired by the general construction of dual-mode commitment in [33]. The detailed construction of scheme (Gen, LGen, Enc, Dec, Sim.Fake, Sim.Open) as in Definition 3 is as following (denote by **Construction 1**):

Gen(1^λ): run the sampling algorithm $S_L(1, 1^\lambda)$ to get x, while $x \notin L$, where L is a membership-hard language. Let $\Sigma^{\text{ext}} = (\text{P}_\Sigma^{\text{com}}, \text{P}_\Sigma^{\text{ans}}, \text{V}_\Sigma^{\text{vrfy}}, \text{simP}_\Sigma^{\text{com}}, \text{Ext})$ be an extractable Σ-protocol defined on L, where Ext is a deterministic extraction algorithm, and let sk^{ext} be the secret key of Ext. The real public key is $pk = x$ and the real secret key is $sk = sk^{\text{ext}}$.

LGen(1^λ): run the sampling algorithm $S_L(0, 1^\lambda)$ to obtain (x, w), with w being the witness for $x \in L$. The lossy public key is $pk = x$ and the lossy secret key is $sk = w$.

$\text{Enc}(pk, m; r)$: to encrypt a message $m \in \{0, 1\}^n$, run $\text{simP}_{\Sigma}^{\text{com}}(x, m; r)$ algorithm and output (a, m, r), denoted as $(a, m, r) = \text{simP}_{\Sigma}^{\text{com}}(x, m; r)$. The ciphertext is $c = a$.

$\text{Dec}(sk^{\text{ext}}, x, c)$: take the secret key sk^{ext}, the public key x and the ciphertext c as inputs, output $m = \text{Ext}(sk^{\text{ext}}, x, c)$.

$\text{Sim.Fake}(pk, w; r_a)$: take the lossy public key pk, witness w and a random coins r_a as inputs, output (e^*, ε) such that $e^* = P_{\Sigma}^{\text{com}}(x, w; r_a)$ and $\varepsilon = (pk, w, r_a)$.

$\text{Sim.Open}(\varepsilon, m)$: take ε and m as inputs, and output $r = P_{\Sigma}^{\text{ans}}(x, w, r_a, m)$.

4.3 Security Analysis

We then prove that the scheme in **Construction 1** is a tweaked lossy encryption scheme.

Theorem 2. *The scheme in* **Construction 1** *is a tweaked lossy encryption scheme if L is a membership-hard language with efficient opening, and $\Sigma^{\text{ext}} = (\Sigma, \text{Ext})$ is an extractable Σ-protocol for L.*

Proof. **Correctness.** If $x \notin L$, according to the special soundness property of Σ-protocol, for every a, there exists a unique m such that (a, m, r) is an accepting transcription on x, therefore m can be decrypted correctly using secret key sk^{ext}.

Key indistinguishability. The real public key is an instance not in language L, while the lossy public key is an instance in language L. Since L is a membership-hard language, the real public key and the lossy public key are computationally indistinguishable.

Simulatability. While $x \in L$, Sim holds the witness for $x \in L$ and can run the real Σ-protocol: First, the prover runs the Sim.Fake algorithm $P_{\Sigma}^{\text{com}}(x, w; r_a)$ where $r_a \leftarrow R_{\text{Enc}}$ and outputs a commitment $a = P_{\Sigma}^{\text{com}}(x, w; r_a)$, then sends the commitment a to the verifier; Second, the verifier sends a challenge m after receiving the commitment a; Finally, the prover runs the Sim.Open $P_{\Sigma}^{\text{ans}}(x, w, r_a, m)$ algorithm and outputs $r = P_{\Sigma}^{\text{ans}}(x, w, r_a, m)$, where r is the random coins used in the encryption algorithm, then sends r to the verifier. Since $x \in L$, according to the eHVSZK property of extractable Σ-protocol, the following two distributions are statistically indistinguishable:

$$\{\text{simP}_{\Sigma}^{\text{com}}(x, m; r)\} \approx_s \{(P_{\Sigma}^{\text{com}}(x, w; r_a), m, P_{\Sigma}^{\text{ans}}(x, w, r_a, m))\}$$

where $(a, m, r) = \text{simP}_{\Sigma}^{\text{com}}(x, m; r)$, thus the simulatability property follows readily.

5 Instantiations

In this section, we present two instantiations of tLPKE scheme from extractable Σ-protocol, based on dual-mode commitments [33] and Twin-Cramer-Shoup scheme [8,9] respectively.

5.1   Instantiation of tLPKE from Dual-Mode Commitments

Let g be a generator of a group G of prime order q, and we assume that G is efficiently samplable. Let $u = g^x$ and $v = h^x$ with $h = g^r$ where $x, r \leftarrow \mathbb{Z}_q^*$. We define the language L as:

$$L = \{(u, v) | \exists\, x : u = g^x, v = h^x\}.$$

We then construct an instantiation of the tLPKE as follows, and we denote it as **Instantiation 1**.

- Gen(1^λ): given a security parameter λ, run $\mathcal{G}(1^\lambda)$ to obtain a tuple $(\mathbb{G}, q, g)$. Choose $r, x_1, x_2 \leftarrow \mathbb{Z}_q^*$, and compute $h = g^r$, $u = g^{x_1}$, $v = h^{x_2}$. Output the public key $pk = (\mathbb{G}, q, g, h, u, v)$ and the secret key $sk = r$.
- LGen(1^λ): given a security parameter λ, run $\mathcal{G}(1^\lambda)$ to obtain a tuple $(\mathbb{G}, q, g)$. Choose $r, x \leftarrow \mathbb{Z}_q^*$, and compute $h = g^r$, $u = g^x$, $v = h^x$. Output the lossy public key $pk = (\mathbb{G}, q, g, h, u, v)$ and the lossy secret key $sk = x$.
- Enc($pk, m; z$): to encrypt a message $m \in \{0, 1\}^k$ where $k = O(\log \lambda)$, choose $z \leftarrow \mathbb{Z}_q^*$, and compute $a = g^z \cdot u^m$, $b = h^z \cdot v^m$. Output the ciphertext as $c = (a, b)$.
- Dec(sk, c): take as input the real secret key $sk = r$ and the ciphertext $c = (a, b)$, search for $m \in \{0, 1\}^k$ such that

$$\frac{a^r}{b} = \left(\frac{u^r}{v}\right)^m$$

and output m.
- Sim.Fake(pk, w): choose $w \in \mathbb{Z}_q^*$ uniformly at random, and compute $a = g^w$, $b = h^w$. Output the fake ciphertext $e^* = (a, b)$ and the auxiliary parameter $\varepsilon = (x, w)$.
- Sim.Open: take as input the auxiliary parameter $\varepsilon = (x, w)$, the message m and the ciphertext (a, b), and output the random coins $z = w - mx$.

We can see that when using the real public key, the Enc algorithm runs a simulation algorithm of the extractable Σ-protocol on L; however, when using the lossy public key, the Enc runs a real extractable Σ-protocol on L with witness x. We now give a detailed analysis.

Theorem 3. *The **Instantiation 1** is a tweaked lossy encryption scheme if DDH assumption holds.*

Proof. **Correctness.** In the decryption mode, where $(u, v) \notin L$. Since $a = g^{z+x_1 m}$ and $b = g^{rz+rx_2 m}$, implying that:

$$\begin{pmatrix} \log a \\ \log b \end{pmatrix} = \begin{pmatrix} 1 & x_1 \\ r & rx_2 \end{pmatrix} \begin{pmatrix} z \\ m \end{pmatrix}$$

Since $x_1 \neq x_2$, the determinant of $\begin{pmatrix} 1 & x_1 \\ r & rx_2 \end{pmatrix}$ is nonzero, and $\begin{pmatrix} z \\ m \end{pmatrix}$ is uniquely determined, such that

$$\frac{a^r}{b} = \left(\frac{u^r}{v}\right)^m$$

Therefore the decryption algorithm can search $m \in \{0,1\}^k$ within $O(2^k)$ steps where $k = O(\log \lambda)$.

Key Indistinguishability. The real public keys and the lossy public keys are computationally indistinguishable under the DDH assumption.

Simulatability. Consider an extractable Σ-protocol scenario, where the prover knows x such that $u = g^x$, $v = h^x$ and $(u,v) \in L$. The messages of the protocol include (a,b), the challenge m and the random coins z which is the response to the challenge m. And $((a,b),m,z)$ forms an accepting transcript of the protocol's execution for challenge m, where $m \in \{0,1\}^\lambda$, $a = g^{z+mx}$ and $b = g^{rz+rmx} = a^r$. Since r,z,x are random elements of $\mathbb{Z}_q^*$, a and b are also random elements of $\mathbb{G}$, and the ciphertext (a,b) contains no information of the plaintext. Now consider the algorithm Sim.Fake and Sim.Open. Sim.Fake picks $w \in \mathbb{Z}_q^*$ uniformly at random, and let $a = g^w$, $b = h^w$. Sim.Open takes as input the auxiliary parameter $\varepsilon = (x,w)$, the message m and the ciphertext (a,b), and it outputs $z = w - mx$. Because z,w,x are in linear relations, the distribution of z is identical to that of w and x, therefore z is a random element in $\mathbb{Z}_q^*$. According to the above analysis, we have

$$\{(g^{z+mx}, g^{rz+rmx}), m, z\} \approx_s \{(g^w, h^w), m, z\}.$$

Thus, the simulatability property holds.

5.2   Instantiation of tLPKE from Twin-Cramer-Shoup Scheme

The instantiation in Sect. 5.2 is inspired by the similar instantiation of ABME from Twin-Cramer-Shoup in [16]. Let g be a generator of a group G of prime order q, and assume G is efficiently samplable and the DDH assumption holds on G. Choose $x \leftarrow \mathbb{Z}_q^*$ uniformly at random, and set $X = g^x$. Choose $\xi \leftarrow G$, $v_0 \leftarrow \mathbb{Z}_q^*$ uniformly at random, then compute $d_0 = g^{v_0}$, $e_0 = \xi^{-1}X^{v_0}$. Compute $d = g^v$, $e = \xi X^v$, where $v \leftarrow \mathbb{Z}_q^*$. Set $\lambda = O(\log k)$. Then we define the language L_{cs} under $pk = (g, X, d_0, d_0 d, e_0 e)$:

$$L_{cs} = \{(d,e) | \exists (\tilde{v}, v) : d_0 d = g^{\tilde{v}}, e_0 e = X^{\tilde{v}}, \text{where } \tilde{v} = v_0 + v\}.$$

We then build another instantiation of the tLPKE scheme as follows (denote by **Instantiation 2**):

- $\text{Gen}(1^\lambda)$: choose $x \leftarrow \mathbb{Z}_q^*$ uniformly at random, and set $X = g^x$. Choose $\xi \leftarrow G$, $v_1 \leftarrow \mathbb{Z}_q^*$ and $v_2 \leftarrow \mathbb{Z}_q^*$ uniformly at random, then compute $d_0 = g^{v_1}$ and $e_0 = \xi^{-1}X^{v_2}$. Let $d = g^v$, $e = \xi X^v$, where $v \leftarrow \mathbb{Z}_q^*$, let $\lambda = O(\log k)$, and finally output a pair of real keys (pk, sk), where $pk = (g, X, d_0, d_0 d, e_0 e)$ and $sk = x$.
- $\text{LGen}(1^\lambda)$: choose $x \leftarrow \mathbb{Z}_q^*, \xi \leftarrow G, v_0 \leftarrow \mathbb{Z}_q^*$ and $v \leftarrow \mathbb{Z}_q^*$ uniformly at random, and set $X = g^x$, $d_0 = g^{v_0}$, $e_0 = \xi^{-1}X^{v_0}$ and $d = g^v$, $e = \xi X^v$ respectively. Let $\lambda = O(\log k)$, and finally output a pair of lossy keys (pk, sk), where $pk = (g, X, d_0, d_0 d, e_0 e)$ and $sk = (v_0, v)$.

- Enc($pk, m; \boldsymbol{z}$): to encrypt a message $m \in \{0,1\}^n$, divide m into $(m_1, \ldots, m_l)$, where $l = n/\lambda$; and for all $1 \leq i \leq l$, $m_i \in \{0,1\}^\lambda$, choose $\boldsymbol{z} \leftarrow \mathbb{Z}_q^*$ uniformly at random, where $\boldsymbol{z} = (z_1, \ldots, z_l)$, then compute:

$$A = \begin{pmatrix} g & d_0 d \\ X & e_0 e \end{pmatrix} \begin{pmatrix} z_1 & \ldots & z_l \\ m_1 & \ldots & m_l \end{pmatrix}$$

And finally output the ciphertext $c = A$.
- Dec(sk, c): let $A = (\boldsymbol{a}_1, \ldots, \boldsymbol{a}_l)$, where $\boldsymbol{a}_i = (a_{1,i}, a_{2,i})^T$. For every $i \in [l]$, search for appropriate $m_i \in \{0,1\}^\lambda$ such that:

$$\frac{(a_{1,i})^x}{a_{2,i}} = \left(\frac{(d_0 d)^x}{e_0 e} \right)^{m_i}, \text{ if } e_0 e \neq (d_0 d)^x.$$

If such m_i can not be found, then output the decryption failure symbol "$\perp$"; Otherwise output $m = (m_1, \ldots, m_l) \in \{0,1\}^n$.
- Sim.Fake($pk; \boldsymbol{w}$): first divide m into $(m_1, \ldots, m_i)$, where $i \in [l]$, then pick up $w_i \in \mathbb{Z}_q^*$ uniformly at random, and compute $a_{1,i} = g^{w_i}$, $a_{2,i} = X^{w_i}$. Output the fake ciphertext $c = (a_{1,i}, a_{2,i})$ and $\varepsilon = (v_0, v, \boldsymbol{w})$ for $i \in [l]$.
- Sim.Open(ε, m): take as input the auxiliary parameter $\varepsilon = (x, w)$, the message $(m_1, \ldots, m_i)$ and the ciphertext $c = (a_{1,i}, a_{2,i})$ where $i \in [l]$, output $\boldsymbol{z}$ where $z_i = w_i - m_i \cdot \tilde{v}$ and $\tilde{v} = v_0 + v$.

We then prove that the **Instantiation 2** is a tweaked lossy encryption scheme.

Proof. **Correctness.** When $(d, e) \notin L_{cs}$, the encryption algorithm uses the real public key pk to encrypt message and the resulting ciphertext is

$$A = \begin{pmatrix} g^{z_1}(d_0 d)^{m_1} & \ldots & g^{z_i}(d_0 d)^{m_i} & \ldots & g^{z_l}(d_0 d)^{m_l} \\ X^{z_1}(e_0 e)^{m_1} & \ldots & X^{z_i}(e_0 e)^{m_i} & \ldots & X^{z_l}(e_0 e)^{m_l} \end{pmatrix}$$

Note that rank(A) = 2. Let $\boldsymbol{a}_i = (a_{1,i}, a_{2,i})^T$ denotes the i-th column of the matrix A, then $a_{1,i} = g^{z_i + (v_1 + v)m_i}$, and $a_{2,i} = X^{z_i + (v_2 + v)m_i} = (g^x)^{z_i + (v_2 + v)m_i}$. We can see that $e_0 e \neq (d_0 d)^x$, and therefore m_i can be recovered through the following equation:

$$\frac{(a_{1,i})^x}{a_{2,i}} = \left(\frac{(d_0 d)^x}{e_0 e} \right)^{m_i}$$

Therefore the decryption algorithm can output $m = (m_1, \ldots, m_l) \in \{0,1\}^n$ correctly.

Key indistinguishability. The lossy public key is $pk = (g, g^x, g^{v_0 + v}, g^{x(v_0 + v)})$, and the real public key is $pk = (g, g^x, g^{v_0 + v_1}, g^{x(v_0 + v_2)})$. Therefore, the lossy public key and the real public key are computationally indistinguishable under the DDH assumption.

Simulatability. When $(d, e) \in L_{cs}$, the encryption algorithm runs a real extractable Σ-protocol, where the common input is $(d_0 d, e_0 e)$ and the prover wants to prove that $\log_g d_0 d = \log_X e_0 e$. The vector $\boldsymbol{a}_i = (a_{1,i}, a_{2,i})^T$ is the first message of the protocol, $(m_1, \ldots, m_l)$ is the parallel challenge, and z_i corresponds to the response to each challenge m_i. Therefore $(A, \boldsymbol{m}, \boldsymbol{z})$ is an accepting proof of the parallel execution of the extractable Σ-protocols, where $\boldsymbol{m} = (m_1, \ldots, m_l)$ is the challenge, and $m_i \in \{0,1\}^\lambda$, and $i \in [l]$. Specifically, $(a_{1,i}, a_{2,i})^T = (g^{z_i + m_i \tilde{v}}, X^{z_i + m_i \tilde{v}})^T$, where $X = g^x$, $\tilde{v} = v_0 + v$, and $z_i, v_0, v \leftarrow \mathbb{Z}_q^*$. Since $\text{rank}(A) = 1$, the ciphertexts will be uniformly distributed over $\mathbb{G}$. Now, the Sim.Fake algorithm first divides m into $(m_1, \ldots, m_i)$, where $i \in [l]$, then it chooses $w_i \in \mathbb{Z}_q^*$ uniformly at random and sets $a_{1,i} = g^{w_i}$, $a_{2,i} = X^{w_i}$. The Sim.Open algorithm takes as input $\varepsilon = (v_0, v, \boldsymbol{w})$, and finally outputs $z_i = w_i - m_i \cdot \tilde{v}$, where $\tilde{v} = v_0 + v$. We can see that z_i is a random element of $\mathbb{Z}_q^*$. According to the above analysis, we have:

$$\{(g^{z_i + m_i \tilde{v}}, X^{z_i + m_i \tilde{v}})^T, m_i, z_i\}_{i \in [l]} \approx_s \{(g^{w_i}, X^{w_i})^T, m_i, z_i\}_{i \in [l]}$$

Thus, the variables $\text{dist}^{\text{Enc}}(pk, m)$ and $\text{dist}^{\text{Sim}}(pk, m)$ are statistically indistinguishable and the simulatability property holds.

6   Selective Opening Security for the Receiver

Following the work in [3,4,19], we recall the definition of IND-RSO-CPA, which is restricted to efficiently conditionally resamplable distributions.

Definition 5 (Efficiently Conditionally Resamplable [3,4]). *Let* dist *be a joint distribution over* $\mathcal{M}^n$*, where* $\mathcal{M}$ *is the message space. We say that* dist *is efficiently conditionally resamplable if there is a PPT algorithm* $\text{ReSamp}_{\text{dist}}$*, such that for any* $I \subset [n]$ *and any* $\boldsymbol{m}_I := (m_i)_{i \in I}$*,* $\text{ReSamp}_{\text{dist}}(\boldsymbol{m}_I)$ *outputs* $\boldsymbol{m}'_I$*, and* $\boldsymbol{m}'_I$ *is sampled from the distribution* dist*, conditioned on* $m'_i = m_i$ *for all* $i \in I$*.*

Experiment. $\text{Exp}_{\text{PKE}, \mathcal{A}}^{\text{IND-RSO-CPA}}(1^\lambda)$:

$b \leftarrow \{0,1\}$
$(\boldsymbol{pk}, \boldsymbol{sk}) := (pk_i, sk_i)_{i \in n} \leftarrow \text{Gen}(1^\lambda)$
$(\text{dist}, \text{ReSamp}_{\text{dist}}) \leftarrow \mathcal{A}(\boldsymbol{pk})$
$M_0 \leftarrow \text{dist}$
$C^* \leftarrow \text{Enc}(\boldsymbol{pk}, M_0)$
$I \leftarrow \mathcal{A}(C^*)$
$M_1 \leftarrow \text{ReSamp}_{\text{dist}}(M_{0I})$
$b' \leftarrow \mathcal{A}(\boldsymbol{sk}_I, M_b)$
Return 1 if $b' = b$ and 0 otherwise.

Fig. 2. The IND-RSO-CPA experiment

Definition 6 (IND-RSO-CPA Security [19]**).** *A PKE scheme* PKE = (Gen, Enc, Dec) *is IND-RSO-CPA secure if for any polynomially bounded* $n = n(1^\lambda) > 0$, *and any stateful PPT adversary* $\mathcal{A}$, *such that*

$$\mathbf{Adv}_{\text{PKE},\mathcal{A}}^{\text{IND-RSO-CPA}}(1^\lambda) = \Pr[\text{Exp}_{\text{PKE},\mathcal{A}}^{\text{IND-RSO-CPA}}(1^\lambda) = 1] - \frac{1}{2}$$

is negligible. The experiment $\text{Exp}_{\text{PKE},\mathcal{A}}^{\text{IND-RSO-CPA}}(1^\lambda)$ *is defined as in Fig. 2.*

6.1 Tweaked NCER for Receivers

In [19], Hazay *et al.* proved that secure tweaked NCER implies IND-RSO-CPA secure PKE. The following definition essentially repeats the definition of tweaked NCER from [19] with small changes: the tGen algorithm outputs a trapdoor for solving hard problem instances, and the tOpen algorithm may receive the trapdoor as an additional input.

A tweaked NCER scheme tPKE is a tuple of algorithms (tGen, tEnc, tEnc*, tDec, tOpen), where (tGen, tEnc, tDec) form a PKE. The fake encryption algorithm tEnc* takes the secret key sk, the public key pk and a message m as inputs, and it outputs a ciphertext $c^* \leftarrow \text{tEnc}^*(pk, sk, m)$. The opening algorithm tOpen takes as input the secret key sk, the trapdoor τ, the public key pk, fake ciphertext c^* where $c^* \leftarrow \text{tEnc}^*(pk, sk, m')$ for some $m' \in \mathcal{M}$ and a message m, and it outputs sk^* such that $m = \text{tDec}(sk^*, c^*)$. For correctness, we want $m = \text{tDec}(sk, c)$ hold for all $m \in \mathcal{M}$, all $(pk, sk) \leftarrow \text{tGen}(1^\lambda)$ and all $c \leftarrow \text{tEnc}(pk, m)$. For security, we require that real ciphertexts and fake ciphertexts are indistinguishable, and a fake ciphertext can be decrypted to a concrete predetermined plaintext (Fig. 3).

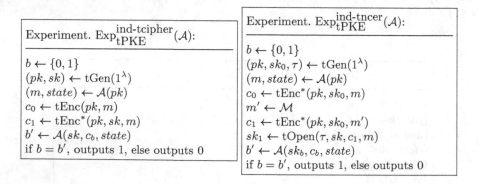

Fig. 3. Tweaked NCER

Definition 7 (Tweaked NCER [19]**).** *We say that a tweaked NCER scheme tPKE is secure if it satisfies the following two conditions:*

- *for any PPT adversary* $\mathcal{A}$, $\mathrm{Adv}_{tPKE,\mathcal{A}}^{ind\text{-}tcipher} := |\Pr[\mathrm{Exp}_{tPKE}^{ind\text{-}tcipher}(\mathcal{A}) = 1] - \frac{1}{2}|$ *is negligible.*
- *for any unbounded adversary* $\mathcal{A}$, $\mathrm{Adv}_{tPKE,\mathcal{A}}^{ind\text{-}tncer} := |\Pr[\mathrm{Exp}_{tPKE}^{ind\text{-}tncer}(\mathcal{A}) = 1] - \frac{1}{2}|$ *is negligible.*

Despite the fact that we use the trapdoor to help the tOpen algorithm output the secret key, the following lemma still follows from the corresponding proof in [19] with respect to the definition of tweaked NCER.

Lemma 1 ([19]**).** *If there exists an* {*ind-tcipher, ind-tncer*} *secure tweaked NCER, then there exists a PKE that is IND-RSO-CPA secure.*

6.2 Explainable Hash Proof Systems

Hash Proof Systems (HPS) or Smooth Projective Hash Functions (SPHFs) refer to a family of hash functions (Hash, ProjHash) defined on a language $L \subseteq X$, and are indexed by a pair of associated keys (hk, hp), where hk is the hashing key and the secret key, and hp is the projection key and the public key. The projective property of SPHFs stipulates that, for a word $x \in L$, the hash value can be computed using either a hashing key hk or a projection key hp with a witness w for $x \in L$. In contrast, the smoothness property of SPHFs stipulates that for a word $x \notin L$, the hash value should be completely undetermined.

Explainable Hash Proof Systems (EHPS) proposed by Abdalla *et al.* [1] are SPHFs with an additional property that: given the trapdoor, we can first generate a random-looking projection key hp, and finally output a valid hashing key hk corresponding to the projection key hp and any hash value H. The following definition of EHPS essentially repeats the definition from [1], except minor changes to fit our requirement. Formally, EHPS are a tuple of algorithms defined as follows:

- Setup(1^λ): take the security parameter λ as input and output a common reference string (CRS) crs together with a trapdoor τ.
- HashKG(crs): take the CRS crs as input and output a hashing key hk.
- ProjKG(hk, crs): take the hashing key hk and the CRS crs as inputs, generate the projection key hp.
- Hash(hk, crs, x): take the hashing key hk, the CRS crs and any word $x \in X$ as inputs, output the hash value H.
- ProjHash(hp, crs, x, w): take a word $x \in L$, the projection key hp, and the witness w as inputs, output the hash value H.
- SimKG(crs, τ, x): take as input crs, τ and a word $x \notin L$, output a projection key hp and an explainability key $expk$. For our purpose, we additionally require the hashing key hk to be part of the explainability key $expk$. We note that the first construction in [1] satisfy this property.

- Explain($hp, crs, x, H, expk$): take as input the projection key hp, the CRS crs, the word $x \notin L$, the hash value H and the explainability key $expk$, output the corresponding hashing key hk.

For any $(crs, \tau) \leftarrow \text{Setup}(1^\lambda)$, EHPS should satisfy the following properties:

- Explainability correctness: we require that $hp = \text{ProjKG}(hk, crs)$ and $H = \text{Hash}(hk, crs, x)$ hold for any hash value H and any $x \notin L$, if $(hp, expk) \leftarrow \text{SimKG}(crs, \tau, x)$ and $hk \leftarrow \text{Explain}(hp, crs, x, H, expk)$.
- Indistinguishability: for any $x \notin L$, the following two distributions are statistically indistinguishable:

$$\{(hk, hp)|H \leftarrow \Pi; (hp, expk) \leftarrow \text{SimKG}(crs, \tau, x); hk \leftarrow \text{Explain}(hp, crs, x, H, expk)\}$$
$$\approx_s \{(hk, hp)|hk \leftarrow \text{HashKG}(crs); hp \leftarrow \text{ProjKG}(hk, crs)\}.$$

6.3   IND-RSO-CPA Secure PKE from EHPS

Hazay *et al.* [19] demonstrated that HPS implies tweaked NCER, and we show that tweaked NCER can also be constructed from EHPS and it has multiple advantages. The tweaked NCER scheme we constructed is a tuple of five algorithms (tGen, tEnc, tEnc*, tDec, tOpen) as follows:

- tGen: take the security parameter λ as input, output the global parameter crs and the trapdoor τ. Invoke HashKG and ProjKG algorithms to obtain $hk \leftarrow \text{HashKG}(crs)$ and $hp \leftarrow \text{ProjKG}(hk, crs)$ respectively, finally output the public key hp and secret key hk.
- tEnc: take the public key hp and the plaintext m as inputs, choose a random $x \in L$ together with the witness w; compute $e = \text{ProjHash}(hp, x, w) \oplus m$, and output the ciphertext (x, e).
- tDec: take the secret key hk and the ciphertext (x, e) as inputs, output the plaintext $m = e \oplus \text{Hash}(hk, x)$.
- tEnc*: take the secret key hk and the plaintext m as inputs, choose a random $x^* \in X \setminus L$; compute $e^* = \text{Hash}(hk, x^*) \oplus m$, and output the fake ciphertext (x^*, e^*).
- tOpen: take as input the trapdoor τ, the secret key hk and the public key hp, fake ciphertext (x^*, e^*) and plaintext m; let $expk = (\tau, hk)$ and let $H = e^* \oplus m$, then invoke the Explain($hp, crs, x^*, H, expk$) algorithm, and finally output a secret key hk^*.

The ciphertexts generated by tEnc algorithm are real ciphertexts, while those generated by tEnc* algorithm are fake ciphertexts. Furthermore, the decryption of a fake ciphertext e^* is the plaintext m. Our scheme also satisfies the following properties:

- Completeness: it can be guaranteed by the projective property of EHPS.
- Security: according to the indistinguishability property of EHPS, the real and the fake ciphertexts are indistinguishable. In addition, the smoothness property of EHPS guarantees that $\text{Hash}(hk, x^*)$ is randomly distributed, for $x^* \in X \setminus L$. Hence, according to the explainability property, for a given m, there exists a hk^* corresponding to hp such that $\text{Hash}(hk^*, x^*) = e^* \oplus m$.

Compared with the construction of Hazay *et al.* [19], our construction mainly change the tOpen algorithm. Specifically, the tOpen algorithm in Hazay *et al.*'s [19] scheme allows an unbounded algorithm to find the right hk^* by searching exhaustively, while our tOpen algorithm is more likely to obtain hk^* efficiently by referring to the work in [1]. Abdalla *et al.* [1] proposed two schemes for constructing Explain($\cdot$) in the tOpen algorithm. The first one is running in $O(2^v)$ time, where v is the bit length of the hash value. If v is a polynomial in logarithmic space, then the Explain($\cdot$) algorithm is running in polynomial time. The second one is more efficient, where the Explain($\cdot$) algorithm runs in constant time but can only be constructed in a specific framework. We note that if we can construct a Explain($\cdot$) algorithm that runs in probabilistic polynomial time, then it is possible to construct a NCER scheme and thereby a SIM-RSO-CPA secure PKE scheme.

Remarks. The SimKG algorithm of EHPS is implicitly used in the construction of our tweaked NCER scheme. According to the explainability correctness of EHPS, the SimKG algorithm will generate the same public key hp as the output of ProjKG algorithm, and the explainability key $expk$ is consisted of a trapdoor τ and a secret key hk corresponding to the public key hp.

7 Conclusion

In this paper, we study PKE of security against SO attacks, which is an important topic in PKE schemes. In particular, first, we define a new cryptographic primitive called tweaked lossy encryption, mainly inspired by ABME, dual-mode commitments, simulatable DEMs, and instance-dependent cryptographic primitives; and we further show that tweaked lossy encryption satisfies the SIM-SSO-CPA security. Second, we provide a generic construction of tweaked lossy encryption from extractable Σ-protocol; in addition, we propose two instantiations of the scheme based on dual-mode commitments and Twin-Cramer-Shoup scheme respectively; and we offer solid proofs of the two instantiations satisfying our definition of tweaked lossy encryption. Finally, we further propose a generic scheme with IND-RSO-CPA security based on EHPS. Our work in this paper provides an insightful view about designing PKE schemes with SO security using cryptographic primitives, such as extractable Σ-protocol and EHPS.

Acknowledgments. The authors thank China Scholarship Council for supporting Shuang Hu's (CSC Student No. 201706230130) work, and she is a visiting student at Virginia Commonwealth University from 2017 to 2019. The authors would like to also thank Dingding Jia for helpful discussions and advice, as well as the anonymous reviewers for their invaluable comments and suggestions.

References

1. Abdalla, M., Benhamouda, F., Pointcheval, D.: Removing erasures with explainable hash proof systems. In: Fehr, S. (ed.) PKC 2017. LNCS, vol. 10174, pp. 151–174. Springer, Heidelberg (2017). https://doi.org/10.1007/978-3-662-54365-8_7
2. Bellare, M., Dowsley, R., Waters, B., Yilek, S.: Standard security does not imply security against selective-opening. In: Pointcheval, D., Johansson, T. (eds.) EUROCRYPT 2012. LNCS, vol. 7237, pp. 645–662. Springer, Heidelberg (2012). https://doi.org/10.1007/978-3-642-29011-4_38
3. Bellare, M., Hofheinz, D., Yilek, S.: Possibility and impossibility results for encryption and commitment secure under selective opening. In: Joux, A. (ed.) EUROCRYPT 2009. LNCS, vol. 5479, pp. 1–35. Springer, Heidelberg (2009). https://doi.org/10.1007/978-3-642-01001-9_1
4. Böhl, F., Hofheinz, D., Kraschewski, D.: On definitions of selective opening security. In: Fischlin, M., Buchmann, J., Manulis, M. (eds.) PKC 2012. LNCS, vol. 7293, pp. 522–539. Springer, Heidelberg (2012). https://doi.org/10.1007/978-3-642-30057-8_31
5. Boyen, X., Li, Q.: All-but-many lossy trapdoor functions from lattices and applications. In: Katz, J., Shacham, H. (eds.) CRYPTO 2017. LNCS, vol. 10403, pp. 298–331. Springer, Cham (2017). https://doi.org/10.1007/978-3-319-63697-9_11
6. Canetti, R., Dwork, C., Naor, M., Ostrovsky, R.: Deniable encryption. In: Kaliski, B.S. (ed.) CRYPTO 1997. LNCS, vol. 1294, pp. 90–104. Springer, Heidelberg (1997). https://doi.org/10.1007/BFb0052229
7. Canetti, R., Feige, U., Goldreich, O., Naor, M.: Adaptively secure multi-party computation. In: Miller, G.L. (ed.) Twenty-Eighth Annual ACM Symposium on the Theory of Computing. STOC 1996, pp. 639–648. ACM (1996)
8. Cash, D., Kiltz, E., Shoup, V.: The twin diffie-hellman problem and applications. In: Smart, N. (ed.) EUROCRYPT 2008. LNCS, vol. 4965, pp. 127–145. Springer, Heidelberg (2008). https://doi.org/10.1007/978-3-540-78967-3_8
9. Cramer, R., Shoup, V.: Design and analysis of practical public-key encryption schemes secure against adaptive chosen ciphertext attack. SIAM J. Comput. $33(1)$, 167–226 (2003)
10. Damgård, I., Groth, J.: Non-interactive and reusable non-malleable commitment schemes. In: Larmore, L.L., Goemans, M.X. (eds.) Proceedings of the 35th Annual ACM Symposium on Theory of Computing 2003, pp. 426–437. ACM (2003)
11. Damgård, I., Nielsen, J.B.: Improved non-committing encryption schemes based on a general complexity assumption. In: Bellare, M. (ed.) CRYPTO 2000. LNCS, vol. 1880, pp. 432–450. Springer, Heidelberg (2000). https://doi.org/10.1007/3-540-44598-6_27
12. Deng, Y., Lin, D.: Instance-dependent verifiable random functions and their application to simultaneous resettability. In: Naor, M. (ed.) EUROCRYPT 2007. LNCS, vol. 4515, pp. 148–168. Springer, Heidelberg (2007). https://doi.org/10.1007/978-3-540-72540-4_9
13. Dwork, C., Naor, M., Reingold, O., Stockmeyer, L.J.: Magic functions. In: 40th Annual Symposium on Foundations of Computer Science. FOCS 1999, pp. 523–534 (1999)
14. Fehr, S., Hofheinz, D., Kiltz, E., Wee, H.: Encryption schemes secure against chosen-ciphertext selective opening attacks. In: Gilbert, H. (ed.) EUROCRYPT 2010. LNCS, vol. 6110, pp. 381–402. Springer, Heidelberg (2010). https://doi.org/10.1007/978-3-642-13190-5_20

15. Fuchsbauer, G., Heuer, F., Kiltz, E., Pietrzak, K.: Standard security does imply security against selective opening for markov distributions. In: Kushilevitz, E., Malkin, T. (eds.) TCC 2016. LNCS, vol. 9562, pp. 282–305. Springer, Heidelberg (2016). https://doi.org/10.1007/978-3-662-49096-9_12

16. Fujisaki, E.: All-but-many encryption. A new framework for fully-equipped UC commitments. In: Sarkar, P., Iwata, T. (eds.) ASIACRYPT 2014. LNCS, vol. 8874, pp. 426–447. Springer, Heidelberg (2014). https://doi.org/10.1007/978-3-662-45608-8_23

17. Goldwasser, S., Micali, S., Rackoff, C.: The knowledge complexity of interactive proof-systems. In: Proceedings of the Seventeenth Annual ACM Symposium on Theory of Computing. STOC 1985, pp. 291–304. ACM, New York (1985)

18. Hara, K., Kitagawa, F., Matsuda, T., Hanaoka, G., Tanaka, K.: Simulation-based receiver selective opening CCA secure PKE from standard computational assumptions. In: Catalano, D., De Prisco, R. (eds.) SCN 2018. LNCS, vol. 11035, pp. 140–159. Springer, Cham (2018). https://doi.org/10.1007/978-3-319-98113-0_8

19. Hazay, C., Patra, A., Warinschi, B.: Selective opening security for receivers. In: Iwata, T., Cheon, J.H. (eds.) ASIACRYPT 2015. LNCS, vol. 9452, pp. 443–469. Springer, Heidelberg (2015). https://doi.org/10.1007/978-3-662-48797-6_19

20. Hemenway, B., Libert, B., Ostrovsky, R., Vergnaud, D.: Lossy encryption: constructions from general assumptions and efficient selective opening chosen ciphertext security. In: Lee, D.H., Wang, X. (eds.) ASIACRYPT 2011. LNCS, vol. 7073, pp. 70–88. Springer, Heidelberg (2011). https://doi.org/10.1007/978-3-642-25385-0_4

21. Heuer, F., Jager, T., Kiltz, E., Schäge, S.: On the selective opening security of practical public-key encryption schemes. In: Katz, J. (ed.) PKC 2015. LNCS, vol. 9020, pp. 27–51. Springer, Heidelberg (2015). https://doi.org/10.1007/978-3-662-46447-2_2

22. Heuer, F., Jager, T., Schäge, S., Kiltz, E.: Selective opening security of practical public-key encryption schemes. IET Inf. Secur. 10(6), 304–318 (2016)

23. Heuer, F., Poettering, B.: Selective opening security from simulatable data encapsulation. In: Cheon, J.H., Takagi, T. (eds.) ASIACRYPT 2016. LNCS, vol. 10032, pp. 248–277. Springer, Heidelberg (2016). https://doi.org/10.1007/978-3-662-53890-6_9

24. Hofheinz, D.: All-but-many lossy trapdoor functions. In: Pointcheval, D., Johansson, T. (eds.) EUROCRYPT 2012. LNCS, vol. 7237, pp. 209–227. Springer, Heidelberg (2012). https://doi.org/10.1007/978-3-642-29011-4_14

25. Hofheinz, D., Jager, T., Rupp, A.: Public-key encryption with simulation-based selective-opening security and compact ciphertexts. In: Hirt, M., Smith, A. (eds.) TCC 2016. LNCS, vol. 9986, pp. 146–168. Springer, Heidelberg (2016). https://doi.org/10.1007/978-3-662-53644-5_6

26. Hofheinz, D., Rao, V., Wichs, D.: Standard security does not imply indistinguishability under selective opening. In: Hirt, M., Smith, A. (eds.) TCC 2016. LNCS, vol. 9986, pp. 121–145. Springer, Heidelberg (2016). https://doi.org/10.1007/978-3-662-53644-5_5

27. Hofheinz, D., Rupp, A.: Standard versus selective opening security: separation and equivalence results. In: Lindell, Y. (ed.) TCC 2014. LNCS, vol. 8349, pp. 591–615. Springer, Heidelberg (2014). https://doi.org/10.1007/978-3-642-54242-8_25

28. Huang, Z., Lai, J., Chen, W., Au, M.H., Peng, Z., Li, J.: Simulation-based selective opening security for receivers under chosen-ciphertext attacks. Des. Codes Cryptogr. 1–27 (2018)

29. Huang, Z., Liu, S., Qin, B.: Sender-equivocable encryption schemes secure against chosen-ciphertext attacks revisited. In: Kurosawa, K., Hanaoka, G. (eds.) PKC 2013. LNCS, vol. 7778, pp. 369–385. Springer, Heidelberg (2013). https://doi.org/10.1007/978-3-642-36362-7_23

30. Jia, D., Lu, X., Li, B.: Receiver selective opening security from indistinguishability obfuscation. In: Dunkelman, O., Sanadhya, S.K. (eds.) INDOCRYPT 2016. LNCS, vol. 10095, pp. 393–410. Springer, Cham (2016). https://doi.org/10.1007/978-3-319-49890-4_22

31. Jia, D., Lu, X., Li, B.: Constructions secure against receiver selective opening and chosen ciphertext attacks. In: Handschuh, H. (ed.) CT-RSA 2017. LNCS, vol. 10159, pp. 417–431. Springer, Cham (2017). https://doi.org/10.1007/978-3-319-52153-4_24

32. Libert, B., Sakzad, A., Stehlé, D., Steinfeld, R.: All-but-many lossy trapdoor functions and selective opening chosen-ciphertext security from LWE. In: Katz, J., Shacham, H. (eds.) CRYPTO 2017. LNCS, vol. 10403, pp. 332–364. Springer, Cham (2017). https://doi.org/10.1007/978-3-319-63697-9_12

33. Lindell, Y.: An efficient transform from sigma protocols to NIZK with a CRS and non-programmable random oracle. In: Dodis, Y., Nielsen, J.B. (eds.) TCC 2015. LNCS, vol. 9014, pp. 93–109. Springer, Heidelberg (2015). https://doi.org/10.1007/978-3-662-46494-6_5

34. Liu, S., Paterson, K.G.: Simulation-based selective opening CCA security for PKE from key encapsulation mechanisms. In: Katz, J. (ed.) PKC 2015. LNCS, vol. 9020, pp. 3–26. Springer, Heidelberg (2015). https://doi.org/10.1007/978-3-662-46447-2_1

35. Micciancio, D., Ong, S.J., Sahai, A., Vadhan, S.: Concurrent zero knowledge without complexity assumptions. In: Halevi, S., Rabin, T. (eds.) TCC 2006. LNCS, vol. 3876, pp. 1–20. Springer, Heidelberg (2006). https://doi.org/10.1007/11681878_1

36. Nielsen, J.B.: Separating random oracle proofs from complexity theoretic proofs: the non-committing encryption case. In: Yung, M. (ed.) CRYPTO 2002. LNCS, vol. 2442, pp. 111–126. Springer, Heidelberg (2002). https://doi.org/10.1007/3-540-45708-9_8

37. Peikert, C., Vaikuntanathan, V., Waters, B.: A framework for efficient and composable oblivious transfer. In: Wagner, D. (ed.) CRYPTO 2008. LNCS, vol. 5157, pp. 554–571. Springer, Heidelberg (2008). https://doi.org/10.1007/978-3-540-85174-5_31

38. Peikert, C., Waters, B.: Lossy trapdoor functions and their applications. In: Proceedings of the 40th Annual ACM Symposium on Theory of Computing, pp. 187–196 (2008)

Foundations

Confused yet Successful:
Theoretical Comparison of Distinguishers for Monobit Leakages in Terms of Confusion Coefficient and SNR

Eloi de Chérisey[1]([✉]), Sylvain Guilley[1,2], and Olivier Rioul[1]

[1] Télécom ParisTech, Paris, France
{eloi.decherisey,sylvain.guilley,olivier.rioul}@telecom-paristech.fr
[2] Secure-IC S.A.S., Rennes, France

Abstract. Many side-channel distinguishers (such as DPA/DoM, CPA, Euclidean Distance, KSA, MIA, etc.) have been devised and studied to extract keys from cryptographic devices. Each has pros and cons and find applications in various contexts. These distinguishers have been described theoretically in order to determine which distinguisher is best for a given context, enabling an unambiguous characterization in terms of success rate or number of traces required to extract the secret key.

In this paper, we show that in the case of monobit leakages, the theoretical expression of all distinguishers depend only on two parameters: the confusion coefficient and the signal-to-noise ratio. We provide closed-form expressions and leverage them to compare the distinguishers in terms of convergence speed for distinguishing between key candidates. This study contrasts with previous works where only the asymptotic behavior was determined—when the number of traces tends to infinity, or when the signal-to-noise ratio tends to zero.

Keywords: Side-channel distinguisher ·
Differential Power Analysis (DPA) · Difference of Means (DoM) ·
Correlation Power Analysis (CPA) ·
Mutual Information Analysis (MIA) ·
Kolmogorov-Smirnov Analysis (KSA) · Confusion coefficient ·
Signal-to-noise ratio · Success rate · Success exponent

1 Introduction

Today's ciphering algorithms such as AES are considered resistant to cryptanalysis. This means that the best possible way to extract a 128-bit key is about as complex as an exhaustive search over the 2^{128} possibilities. With our current computational power, this is not achievable within a reasonable amount of time.

However, it is possible to use plaintexts, ciphertexts, along with additional side information in order to recover the secret key of a device. Indeed, the secret key may leak via *side-channels*, such as the time to compute the algorithm, the power consumption of the device during the computation of the algorithm, or the electro-magnetic radiations of the chip.

© Springer Nature Switzerland AG 2019
F. Guo et al. (Eds.): Inscrypt 2018, LNCS 11449, pp. 533–553, 2019.
https://doi.org/10.1007/978-3-030-14234-6_28

In order to secure chips from side-channel attacks, designers have to understand how these work and what could be the future security breaches in the cryptographic algorithm as well as in the hardware implementation. A preliminary step is to identify how the secret keys leak and deduce leakage models. Then, mathematical functions—called *distinguishers*—take the leakage as argument and return an estimation of the secret key. Such distinguishers come in many flavours[1] and have different figures of merit in different contexts. A given context not only involves the cryptographic algorithm and the device through the leakage model, but also the side-channel acquisition setup through the measurement characterized by its signal-to-noise ratio (SNR). This is illustrated in Fig. 1 borrowed from Heuser *et al.* [12] (with our annotations in red).

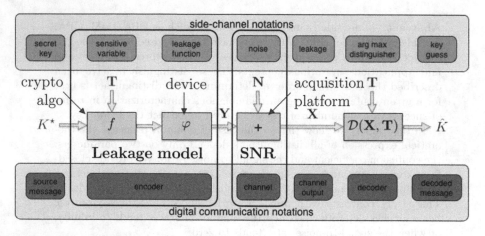

Fig. 1. Illustration of the two parts of the side-channel analysis context (in red). (Color figure online)

In practice one may encounter *monobit* leakages. This means that the output of the leakage model can only take two values. In this case, as we shall see, the mathematical computations turn to be simpler and information theoretic tools can be used to precisely describe the link between the leakage model and the real-world leaking traces. From another perspective, considering monobit leakages can also be seen as an "abstraction" trick meant to intentionally ignore the complex effect of the way the device leaks, thereby keeping only the contribution from the cryptographic algorithm in the leakage model.

A related question is how the choice of the substitution box in the cryptographic algorithm may "help" the attacker. The standard AES substitution box was designed to be very secure against linear and differential cryptanalysis [6]. On the contrary, under side-channel analysis, the substitution box may be helpful for the attacker, especially for monobit leakages as shown below.

---

[1] We cover in this paper the following distinguishers: Difference of Means (DoM) [13], Correlation Power Analysis (CPA) [3], Euclidean distance [12, §3], Kolmogorov-Smirnov Analysis (KSA) [22], and Mutual Information Analysis (MIA) [9].

Related Work. Distinguishers were often studied empirically, yet such an approach does not allow for generalizations to other contexts and measurement campaigns. A theoretical approach consists in analyzing the formal expressions of the distinguishers as mathematical functions. Fei et al. [8] have shown that distinguishers such as DoM and CPA can be expressed in terms of a *confusion coefficient*. They gave the impetus to extend this formal analysis to other types of distinguishers. In 2014, Heuser *et al.* [11] relate KSA to the confusion coefficient, and also noticed that the confusion coefficient can be related to the resistance of a substitution box against differential cryptanalysis.

Whitnall and Oswald [21] have proposed the *relative distinguishing margin* metric to compare distinguishers. However, it has been shown [18] that this metric may not be relevant in all contexts. Another way to compare distinguishers is to contrast how their success rate (SR) in key recovery depends on the number q of side-channel traces. Works such as [8,14] provide mathematically models for the SR. But the comparison between different distinguishers has never been actually carried out based on such frameworks. Instead, we shall leverage on the so-called *success exponent* (SE) [10] which allows to compare the SR of various distinguishers based on only one exponent parameter.

Our Contributions. In this paper, we consolidate the knowledge about side-channel attacks exploiting monobit leakages. We provide a rigorous proof that any distinguisher acting on monobit leakages depends only on two parameters: the *confusion coefficient* and the *noise variance*. Some distinguishers, namely DoM, CPA and KSA, have already been expressed as a function of those two parameters [8,11]. In this article, we derive this expression for MIA and we obtain a simple analytic function when the non zero values of the confusion coefficient are near $1/2$, which is the case of leakages occurring at cryptographically strong substitution boxes [4].

We derive the success exponent of these distinguishers in terms of the confusion coefficient and the standard deviation of the noise. Success exponents allow to characterize the efficiency (in terms of number of traces) of distinguishers to recover the key. Our closed-form expressions of the success exponent enable the comparison of distinguishers based only on these two parameters. The flow chart of Fig. 2 situates our contributions in relation to the current state of the art.

Organization. The remainder of this paper is organized as follows. In Sect. 2, we recall the main definitions. In Sect. 3, we consider all distinguishers in one mathematical framework and we show that they are only functions of two parameters. In Sect. 4, we compare the distinguishers in terms of the success exponent. Section 5 concludes. Appendices provide proofs for technical lemmas.

Notations. Throughout this paper, we use calligraphic letters to denote sets and lower-case letters for elements in this set (e.g. $x \in \mathcal{X}$). Capital letters denote random variables. For example, X is a random variable taking values in $\mathcal{X}$ and $x \in \mathcal{X}$ is a realization of X. The probability that X is x is noted $\mathbb{P}(X = x)$ or simply $\mathbb{P}(x)$ when there is no ambiguity. The expectation of a random variable is

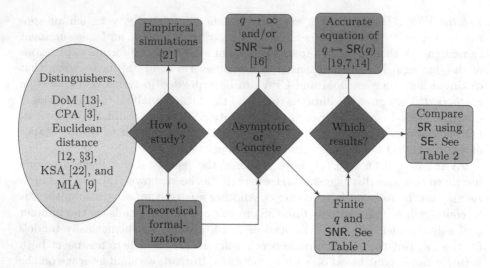

Fig. 2. The state of the art in relation to our contributions (in yellow boxes—see also Tables 1 and 2 below). (Color figure online)

noted $\mathbb{E}[X]$ and its variance $\text{Var}(X)$. The differential entropy $h(X)$ of a random variable X following distribution $p(x)$ is defined as

$$h(X) = - \int_{\mathbb{R}} p(x) \log_2 p(x) \, dx. \tag{1}$$

The mutual information between two random variables X and Y is defined as

$$I(X;Y) = h(X) - h(X|Y) = \mathbb{E}\left[\log_2 \frac{\mathbb{P}(X,Y)}{\mathbb{P}(X)\mathbb{P}(Y)}\right]. \tag{2}$$

2 Modelization and Definitions

2.1 The Leakage Model

In order to compare the different distinguishers for monobit leakages, we need a leakage model upon which our computations will be based. A plaintext t meets the secret key k^* through a leakage function $f(t, k^*)$. The resulting variable $y(k^*)$ is called the *sensitive* variable. The dependence in the plaintext t will be omitted to make equations easier to read when there is no ambiguity.

The attacker measures a noisy version of $y(k^*)$ called *trace* and denoted by x. When the key is unknown, the attacker computes a sensitive variable with a key hypothesis k, that is, $y(k) = f(t, k)$. Thus our model takes the form

$$\begin{cases} y(k) = f(t, k) \\ \quad x = y(k^*) + n \end{cases} \tag{3}$$

where n is an independent measurement noise.

As we consider monobit leakages, we suppose that $y(k)$ can take only two values. In practice, t (resp. k) are subsets of the full plaintext (resp. key). Typically, in the case of AES where attacks can be conducted using a divide-and-conquer approach on a per substitution box basis, t and k are 8-bit works (i.e., bytes).

The above leakage model can also be written using random variables. Let T the random variable for the plaintext, $Y(k)$ for the sensitive variable, X for the measurement, and N for the Gaussian noise. We have:

$$\begin{cases} Y(k) = f(T, k) \\ \quad X = Y(k^*) + N. \end{cases} \tag{4}$$

In a view to simplify further mathematical computations, we suppose that the leakage random variable is reduced, that is, centered ($\mathbb{E}[Y(k)] = 0$ for all k) and of unit variance ($\mathbb{E}[Y(k)^2] = 1$ for all k). The noise is also assumed Gaussian of zero mean and its standard deviation is noted $\sigma > 0$. Moreover, we assume that for any key hypothesis the sensitive variable is *balanced*, that is, $\mathbb{P}(y(k)) = \frac{1}{2}$. Since $Y(k)$ is a binary random variable, we necessarily have that $Y(k) \in \{\pm 1\}$ in our model, and consequently the signal-to-noise ratio equals $\mathsf{SNR} = 1/\sigma^2$.

Last, we suppose that the attacker has at his disposal a number of q traces $x_1, \dots, x_q$ obtained from leaking sensitive variables $y_1(k^*), \dots, y_q(k^*)$ under additive noise $n_1, \dots, n_q$.

2.2   The Confusion Coefficient

In the side-channel context, the confusion coefficient was defined by Fei et al. as the probability that two sensitive variables arising from two different key hypotheses are different [8, Section 3.1]. Mathematically, the confusion coefficient is written as

$$\kappa(k, k^*) = \mathbb{P}(Y(k) \neq Y(k^*)). \tag{5}$$

As the secret key k^* is constant and understood from the context, we can write $\kappa(k, k^*) = \kappa(k)$. Notice that in practical situations, the EIS (Equal Images under different Subkeys [20, Def. 2]) assumption holds, therefore κ is actually a function of the key bitwise XOR difference $k \oplus k^*$.

Figure 3 illustrates the confusion coefficient for a monobit leakage $Y(k) = \mathsf{SubBytes}(T \oplus k) \bmod 2$, where $\mathsf{SubBytes}$ is the AES substitution box (application $\mathbb{F}_2^8 \to \mathbb{F}_2^8$) and $\oplus$ is the bitwise exclusive or. We notice that except for $k = k^*$ (here taken $= 178 = \mathtt{0xb2}$), the confusion coefficient for the AES $\mathsf{SubBytes}$ is close to $1/2$. This results from the fact the AES $\mathsf{SubBytes}$ has been designed to be resistant against differential cryptanalysis. Specifically, Heuser et al. [11, Proposition 6] noticed that a "good" substitution box leads to confusion coefficients near $1/2$.

The original definition of the confusion coefficient [8] considers only monobit leakages. An extension for any type of leakage was proposed in [10] where $\kappa(k)$ is defined by

$$\kappa(k) = \mathbb{E}\left[\left(\frac{Y(k^*) - Y(k)}{2}\right)^2\right]. \tag{6}$$

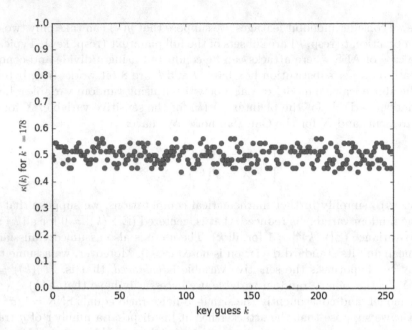

Fig. 3. Confusion coefficient for the AES SubBytes Least Significant Bit (LSB)

Equation (5) can be easily recovered from this more general expression by noting that when $Y(k)$ and $Y(k^*) \in \{\pm 1\}$, $\left(\frac{Y(k^*)-Y(k)}{2}\right)^2$ is 0 or 1 according to whether $Y(k) = Y(k^*)$ or $Y(k) \neq Y(k^*)$.

2.3 Distinguishers

Distinguishers aim at recovering the secret key k^* from the traces and the model. For every key k, the attacker computes the associated distinguisher. The key hypothesis that gives the highest value of the distinguisher is the estimated key. The attack is successful if the estimated key is equal to the secret key.

For every key hypothesis k, a distinguisher is noted $\widehat{\mathcal{D}}(k)$ and the estimated key is $\widehat{k} = \arg\max_k \widehat{\mathcal{D}}(k)$. Five classical distinguishers are:

– Difference of Means (DoM) [8], also known as the Differential Power Analysis (DPA) [13] where the attacker computes

$$\widehat{\mathcal{D}}(k) = \frac{\sum_{i|y_i(k)=+1} x_i}{\sum_{i|y_i(k)=+1}} - \frac{\sum_{i|y_i(k)=-1} x_i}{\sum_{i|y_i(k)=-1}}. \tag{7}$$

– Correlation Power Analysis (CPA) [3] where the attacker computes the absolute value of the Pearson coefficient

$$\widehat{\mathcal{D}}(k) = \left| \frac{\frac{1}{q}\sum_{i=1}^{q} x_i y_i(k) - \frac{1}{q}\sum_{i=1}^{q} x_i \cdot \frac{1}{q}\sum_{i=1}^{q} y_i(k)}{\sqrt{\mathrm{Var}(X)\mathrm{Var}(Y_i(k))}} \right|. \tag{8}$$

Notice that $\text{Var}(Y_i(k))$ do not depend on the index i, since repeated measurements are i.i.d.

- Euclidean distance, which corresponds to the Maximum Likelihood (ML) attack under the Gaussian noise hypothesis, where the attacker actually computes the negative Euclidean distance between the model and the trace

$$\widehat{\mathcal{D}}(k) = -\frac{1}{q} \sum_{i=1}^{q} (x_i - y_i(k))^2. \tag{9}$$

Maximizing the value of the distinguisher amounts to minimizing the Euclidean distance. According to [12], as the noise is Gaussian and additive, the Euclidean distance is the optimal distinguishing rule (ML rule) that maximizes the success probability.

- Kolmogorov-Smirnov Analysis (KSA) [22] where the traces are used to build an estimation of the cumulative density function $\widehat{F}(x)$, and the distinguisher is

$$\widehat{\mathcal{D}}(k) = -\mathbb{E}_{Y(k)} \left[\|\widehat{F}(x|Y(k)) - \widehat{F}(x)\|_\infty \right] \tag{10}$$

where the infinite norm is defined as $\|\widehat{F}(x)\|_\infty = \sup_x |\widehat{F}(x)|$. Maximizing the value of the distinguisher amounts to minimizing the expected infinite norm.

- Mutual Information Analysis (MIA) [9] where the attacker computes the mutual information between the traces and each model. The traces are used to build an estimation of the joint distribution of X and $Y(k)$, denoted by $\widehat{p}(X, Y(k))$, and with this estimation, we calculate the mutual information

$$\widehat{\mathcal{D}}(k) = \sum_{x,y(k)} \widehat{p}(x, y(k)) \log_2 \frac{\widehat{p}(x, y(k))}{\widehat{p}(x) \cdot \widehat{p}(y(k))}. \tag{11}$$

Given the available data, the attacker computes the distinguisher as a function of $x_1, \ldots, x_q$ and $y_1(k), \ldots, y_q(k)$. To emphasize the dependence on the data, we may write $\widehat{\mathcal{D}}(k) = \widehat{\mathcal{D}}(X_1, \ldots, X_q, Y_1(k), \ldots, Y_q(k))$. As these traces are realizations of random variables, we may also consider $\widehat{\mathcal{D}}(k)$ as a random variable which is a function of $X_1, \ldots, X_q$ and $Y_1(k), \ldots, Y_q(k)$, with expectation $\mathbb{E}[\widehat{\mathcal{D}}(k)]$ and a variance $\text{Var}(\widehat{\mathcal{D}}(k))$.

When the number of queries q tends to infinity, we assume that the distinguisher converges in the mean-squared sense:

Definition 1 (Theoretical Distinguisher [10]). *The theoretical value of the distinguisher is defined as the limit in the mean square sense when $q \to \infty$ of the distinguisher. The notation for the theoretical distinguisher is $\mathcal{D}(k)$, which is therefore implicitly defined as:*

$$\mathbb{E}[(\widehat{\mathcal{D}}(k) - \mathcal{D}(k))^2] \longrightarrow 0 \ as \ q \to \infty. \tag{12}$$

Put differently, $\widehat{\mathcal{D}}(k)$ can be seen as an estimator of $\mathcal{D}(k)$. It is easily seen that as $q \to +\infty$ the distinguishers presented previously have the following theoretical distinguishers:

– For DoM, the theoretical distinguisher is

$$\mathcal{D}(k) = \mathbb{E}[XY(k)]. \tag{13}$$

– For CPA, the theoretical distinguisher is

$$\mathcal{D}(k) = \frac{\left|\mathbb{E}[XY(k)] - \mathbb{E}[X]\mathbb{E}[Y(k)]\right|}{1 + \sigma^2}. \tag{14}$$

– For Euclidean distance (ML) distinguisher, we have:

$$\mathcal{D}(k) = -\mathbb{E}\left[(X - Y(k))^2\right]. \tag{15}$$

– For KSA, we have:

$$\mathcal{D}(k) = \mathbb{E}_{Y(k)}\left[\|F(x|Y(k)) - F(x)\|_\infty\right]. \tag{16}$$

– For MIA, it is the mutual information

$$\mathcal{D}(k) = I(X; Y(k)). \tag{17}$$

3   Theoretical Expressions for Distinguishers

In this section, we show that all distinguishers for monobit leakages are functions of only two parameters: the confusion coefficient $\kappa(k)$ and the SNR $= 1/\sigma^2$. This is confirmed by the closed-form expressions for classical distinguishers. In particular we derive the one corresponding to MIA.

3.1   A Communication Channel Between $Y(k)$ and $Y(k^*)$

To understand the link between any sensitive variable $Y(k)$ and the leaking sensitive variable $Y(k^*)$, consider the following information-theoretic communication channel between these two variables described in Fig. 4. This communication channel is simply a theoretical construction that helps explain the link between $Y(k)$ and $Y(k^*)$, which are both binary and equiprobable random variables taking their values in $\{\pm 1\}$. The parameters p and p' are the transition probabilities defined as $p = \mathbb{P}(Y(k^*) = +1|Y(k) = -1)$ and $p' = \mathbb{P}(Y(k^*) = -1|Y(k) = +1)$.

Lemma 1. *The communication channel defined in Fig. 4 is a binary symmetric channel (BSC) with transition probability equal to the confusion coefficient $\kappa(k)$.*

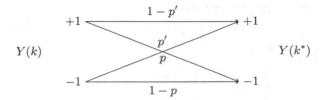

Fig. 4. Abstract communication channel between $Y(k)$ and $Y(k^*)$

Proof. To prove that the channel is symmetric, we show that both transition probabilities coincide: $p = p'$. In fact, from Fig. 4, $\frac{1}{2} = \mathbb{P}(Y(k^*) = 1) = p\mathbb{P}(Y(k) = -1) + (1 - p')\mathbb{P}(Y(k) = 1) = \frac{1}{2}(p + 1 - p')$ hence $p = p'$. Now the confusion coefficient $\kappa(k) = \mathbb{P}(Y(k) \neq Y(k^*))$ can be expanded as

$$\kappa(k) = \tfrac{1}{2}\big(\mathbb{P}(Y(k) \neq Y(k^*)|Y(k) = 1) + \mathbb{P}(Y(k) \neq Y(k^*)|Y(k) = -1)\big) \quad (18)$$

$$= \tfrac{1}{2}\big(\mathbb{P}(Y(k^*) = -1|Y(k) = 1) + \mathbb{P}(Y(k^*) = 1|Y(k) = -1)\big) \quad (19)$$

$$= \tfrac{1}{2}(p + p') = p = p'. \quad (20)$$

This proves that the BSC has transition probability equal to $\kappa(k)$. $\qquad\square$

According to a well-known information theoretic result [5, p. 187], the Shannon's *capacity* in bits per bit of this channel is

$$C = 1 - H_2(\kappa(k)), \quad (21)$$

where $H_2(x)$ is the binary entropy function defined by

$$H_2(x) = x \log_2\Big(\frac{1}{x}\Big) + (1 - x) \log_2\Big(\frac{1}{1 - x}\Big). \quad (22)$$

This is represented in Fig. 5 as a function of $\kappa(k)$. Interestingly, the value $\kappa(k) = 1/2$ corresponds to null capacity while the capacity is evidently 1 bit per bit for $\kappa(k^*) = 0$, since in this case the above communication channel reduces to the identity.

3.2 A General Result

We can now explain why all distinguishers for monobit leakages depend only on the two parameters $\kappa(k)$ and $\mathsf{SNR} = \sigma^{-2}$.

Theorem 1. *Any theoretical distinguisher $\mathcal{D}(k)$ for a binary leakage y can be expressed as a function of $\kappa(k)$ and σ.*

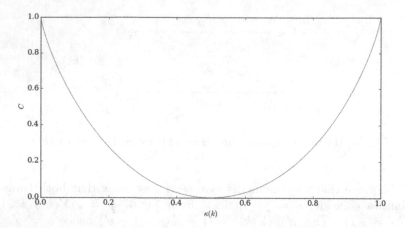

Fig. 5. Representation of the channel capacity according to $\kappa(k)$

Proof. Any theoretical distinguisher is defined in terms of the joint probability distribution of X and $Y(k)$, noted $p(x, y(k))$. Now for any $x \in \mathbb{R}$ and $y(k) = \pm 1$,

$$p(x, y(k)) = \mathbb{P}(y(k))\, p(x \mid y(k)) \tag{23}$$

$$= \frac{1}{2} p(y(k^*) + n \mid y(k)) \tag{24}$$

$$= \frac{1}{2} \sum_{y(k^*)} p(y(k^*) + n \mid y(k), y(k^*))\, \mathbb{P}(y(k^*) \mid y(k)) \tag{25}$$

where $\mathbb{P}(y(k^*) \mid y(k))$ is the transition probability of the channel defined in Fig. 4. There are two possibilities. Either $y(k) = y(k^*)$, and in this case $\mathbb{P}(y(k^*)|y(k)) = 1 - \kappa(k)$, or $y(k) \neq y(k^*)$ and in this case $\mathbb{P}(y(k^*)|y(k)) = \kappa(k)$. The sum over $y(k^*)$ has two terms and both cases are represented. Moreover, the Gaussian noise is independent from every other random variable. Therefore, we have two possibilities for the joint probability:

$$p(x, y(k)) = \begin{cases} \frac{1}{2}\left(\phi(\frac{1+n}{\sigma})\kappa(k) + \phi(\frac{-1+n}{\sigma})(1 - \kappa(k)) \right) \\ \frac{1}{2}\left(\phi(\frac{-1+n}{\sigma})\kappa(k) + \phi(\frac{1+n}{\sigma})(1 - \kappa(k)) \right) \end{cases} \tag{26}$$

where $\phi(x)$ is the probability density function of a standard normal random variable. As the noise is centered and Gaussian, the only parameter that characterizes ϕ is its standard deviation σ. Therefore, a joint distribution of a monobit leakage is fully characterized by σ and $\kappa(k)$.   □

This proves that the knowledge of the confusion coefficient and the noise power are essential to predict the performances of the side-channel attacks for monobit leakages.

3.3   Classical Distinguishers as Functions of $\kappa(k)$ and σ^2

To highlight the result of Sect. 3.2, we compute the classical distinguishers according to the confusion coefficient and the noise power. As we mentioned in the introduction, some of them have already been expressed according to these variables: we recall these results in Table 1 with references to the articles where the expression of the distinguisher in terms of $\kappa(k)$ is proven.

Table 1. Summary of classical distinguishers. Among all the classical theoretical distinguishers, we notice that the expression of the theoretical value of DoM with $\kappa(k)$ does not depend on σ.

Distinguisher	Original paper	Theoretical expression with $\kappa(k)$	Reference
DoM	[13]	$\mathcal{D}(k) = 2(1/2 - \kappa(k))$	[15]
CPA	[3]	$\mathcal{D}(k) = 2\frac{|1/2-\kappa(k)|}{\sqrt{1+\sigma^2}}$	[15]
Euclidean distance	[12, §3]	Lemma 2	This paper
KSA	[22]	$\mathcal{D}(k) = \mathrm{erf}\left(\frac{1}{2\sigma^2}\right)|1/2 - \kappa(k)|$	[11]
MIA	[9]	Lemma 3	This paper

The new results are given by the following lemmas.

Lemma 2. *For monobit leakages, the Euclidean distance distinguisher can be expressed as:*

$$\mathcal{D}(k) = 4(1/2 - \kappa(k)) - (\sigma^2 + 2). \tag{27}$$

Proof. We have $\mathcal{D}(k) = -\mathbb{E}\big[(X - Y(k))^2\big] = -\mathbb{E}\big[(Y(k^*) - Y(k) + N)^2\big] = -\mathbb{E}\big[(Y(k^*) - Y(k))^2\big] - \sigma^2$ since the noise is independent from $Y(k^*) - Y(k)$. Then by (6), $\mathcal{D}(k) = -4\kappa(k) - \sigma^2 = 4(1/2 - \kappa(k)) - 2 - \sigma^2$ where we have stressed the dependence in $1/2 - \kappa(k)$ as in Table 1. □

Lemma 3. *For monobit leakages, when $\kappa(k) \approx 1/2$ for $k \neq k^*$, the MIA distinguisher can be expressed at first order as:*

$$\mathcal{D}(k) = 2\log_2(e)(\kappa(k) - 1/2)^2 g(\sigma) \tag{28}$$

where

$$g(\sigma) = \frac{1}{2}\mathbb{E}\left[\tanh^2\left(\frac{Z}{\sigma} + \frac{1}{\sigma^2}\right) + \tanh^2\left(\frac{Z}{\sigma} - \frac{1}{\sigma^2}\right)\right] \tag{29}$$

and $Z \sim \mathcal{N}(0, 1)$. The function g satisfies

$$\lim_{\sigma \to 0} g(\sigma) = 1 \quad \text{and} \quad \lim_{\sigma \to \infty} \sigma^2 \times g(\sigma) = 1. \tag{30}$$

Proof. See Appendix A. □

Figure 6 plots the shape of $g(\sigma)$ which tends to 1 when $\sigma \to 0$ and is equivalent to $\frac{1}{\sigma^2}$ when $\sigma \to \infty$.

When $k = k^*$ the MIA distinguisher also has a simple expression since it reduces to the known expression of the channel capacity for channels with binary input and additive Gaussian noise [2, p. 274]:

$$\mathcal{D}(k^*) = \frac{1}{\sigma^2} - \int_{\mathbb{R}} \frac{e^{-\frac{1}{2}y^2}}{2\pi} \log_2 \cosh(\frac{1}{\sigma^2} - \frac{y}{\sigma^2}) dy. \qquad (31)$$

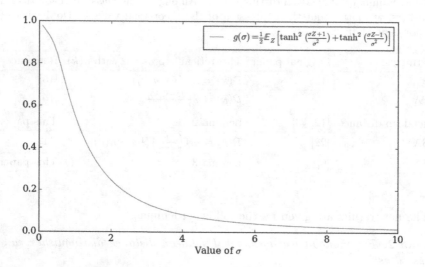

Fig. 6. Representation of $g(\sigma)$

Remark 1. With respect to their theoretical distinguishers, DoM is in bijection with the Euclidean distance, and CPA is in bijection with KSA. Indeed, the Euclidean distance is $\mathcal{D}(k) = 4(1/2 - \kappa(k)) - 2 - \sigma^2$ and σ is independent from the choice of the key. Therefore, there is a bijection between $4(1/2 - \kappa(k)) - 2 - \sigma^2$ and $2(1/2 - \kappa(k))$ which is the theoretical value of DoM. Regarding CPA and KSA, both distinguishers are functions of $|1/2 - \kappa(k)|$.

We also notice that MIA is in bijection with CPA (and therefore KSA). Indeed, according to the value of MIA with $\kappa(k)$, the distinguisher is a function of $(1/2 - \kappa(k))^2$ which is in bijection with $|1/2 - \kappa(k)| = \sqrt{(1/2 - \kappa(k))^2}$. This means that for monobit leakages, any attack that works with one of these distinguishers will also work with another, and *vice versa*.

4   Comparing Distinguishers with the Success Exponent

In the previous section, we have computed the theoretical values of the classical distinguishers in terms of $\kappa(k)$ and σ. Now, we wish to compare their success rate. As we mentioned Sect. 2.3, the attacker computes the estimated distinguisher

$\widehat{\mathcal{D}}(k)$ to recover the secret key. This is the main reason why all distinguishers do not perform equally in key recovery; indeed, they do not converge at the same speed towards their theoretical value.

In order to compare them, we have computed their *success exponent*, a metric proposed by Guilley *et al.* in [10] that evaluates how fast the success rate of a distinguisher converges to 100%. With a Gaussian assumption, they prove that the success rate can be modeled as

$$SR = 1 - \exp(-q \times SE), \tag{32}$$

where q is the number of traces and $SE \in \mathbb{R}^+$ is the so-called success exponent. Therefore, the greater the success exponent is, the faster the convergence of the success rate.

Table 2. Success exponents for the classical distinguishers. The numerical values of SE are obtained for AES SubBytes least significant bit leakage model and noise of standard deviation $\sigma = 4$. Notice that in the monobit case, Euclidean distance and DoM have strictly the same success rate because $-(X - Y(k))^2 = -X^2 + 2XY(k) - 1$, and X^2 is independent of the choice of the key.

Distinguisher	Closed form SE with $\kappa(k)$ and σ	Reference	Numerical value for AES SubBytes
DoM	$\dfrac{1}{2} \min\limits_{k \neq k^*} \dfrac{\kappa(k)}{1 + \sigma^2 - \kappa(k)}$	[10, Proposition 4]	3.39×10^{-3}
CPA	Lemma 4	This paper	3.39×10^{-3}
Euclidean distance	$\dfrac{1}{2} \min\limits_{k \neq k^*} \dfrac{\kappa(k)}{1 + \sigma^2 - \kappa(k)}$	[10, Proposition 5]	3.39×10^{-3}
KSA	Lemma 5	This paper	1.08×10^{-3}
MIA	Lemma 6	[10, Proposition 6]	8.52×10^{-5}

We present the theoretical values of the success exponent for the different distinguishers in Table 2. As a direct consequence of Theorem 1, all of these success exponents are function of $\kappa(k)$ and σ. Therefore, if the attacker only knows the type of substitution box that is used and the SNR of the leakage, he can predict how fast he recovers the secret key.

Lemma 4 (Success exponent of CPA). *The success exponent of* CPA^2 *is:*

$$SE = \frac{1}{2} \min_{k \neq k^*} \frac{1 - 2|{}^1\!/2 - \kappa(k)|}{1 + 2\sigma^2 + 2|{}^1\!/2 - \kappa(k)|}. \tag{33}$$

Proof. See Appendix B. □

---

[2] In [10], CPA is treated as a distinguisher, but without the absolute values. Those remove false positives which occur in monobit leakages when there are anti-correlations. Our value of the success exponent is, therefore, different from theirs.

Lemma 5 (Success exponent of KSA). *Assuming that the distributions are estimated with the kernel method using Heaviside step function, the success exponent of KSA is*

$$SE = \frac{1}{2} \min_{k \neq k^*} \frac{\text{erf}\left(\frac{1}{\sqrt{2}\sigma}\right)^2 (1/2 - |1/2 - \kappa(k)|)}{2 - \text{erf}\left(\frac{1}{\sqrt{2}\sigma}\right)^2 (1/2 - |1/2 - \kappa(k)|)}. \tag{34}$$

Proof. See Appendix C. □

Lemma 6 (Success exponent of MIA). *When $\sigma \gg 1$, the success exponent for an MIA computed with histograms is*

$$SE = \frac{4 \log_2(e)^2}{\sigma^4} \min_{k \neq k^*} \kappa(k)^2 (1 - \kappa(k))^2. \tag{35}$$

Proof. See Appendix D. □

In order to validate our theoretical results, we have simulated attacks within the monobit model presented in Sect. 2. The success rates of these attacks are presented in Fig. 7. In this figure, we notice that, as expected, the Euclidean distance (ML) is the best distinguisher, closely followed by CPA. Both have similar same success rate. The small difference is due to the use the the absolute values in the distinguishing function of CPA (see discussion in Remark 9 of [12]). The KSA is requiring a bit less than the double of traces, compared to Euclidean distance, DoM and CPA. The MIA performs really bad compared to the other distinguishers. Error bars represent the inaccuracy while estimating the SR (here, we ran 100 simulations).

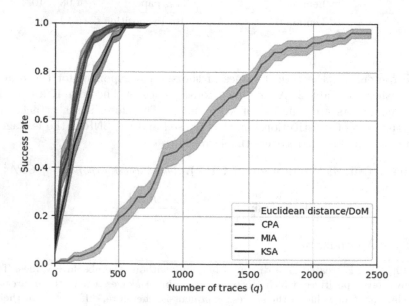

Fig. 7. Success rate for classical distinguishers ($\sigma = 4$)

These simulations are therefore in complete coherence with the theoretical results of Table 2. Indeed, the order of the distinguishers is the same w.r.t. the success rate and w.r.t. the success exponent. In addition, according to the definition of the success exponent SE in (32), the number of traces q to reach a given success rate (e.g., SR = 80%) is proportional to the inverse of SE. This quantitative law is satisfied in the simulation of Fig. 7.

5   Conclusion

In this paper, we have mathematically proven that only two parameters, the confusion coefficient and the SNR, determine the side-channel distinguishing efficiency for monobit leakages. Both of them are easy to compute because the confusion coefficient can be calculated with the knowledge of the operating substitution box and the SNR can be measured offline.

Our work is useful to predict how fast a distinguisher will succeed to recover the secret key. Long and painful simulations can be advantageously replaced by the computation of the success exponent using closed-form expressions.

This paper also consolidates the state of the art about the classical distinguishers, especially for MIA and KSA. We have derived the success exponent for these two distinguishers as a function of the confusion coefficient and the standard deviation of the noise.

A   Proof of Lemma 3

The MIA distinguisher is expressed as

$$\mathcal{D}(k) = I(Y(k^*) + N; Y(k)) = h(Y(k^*) + N) - h(Y(k^*) + N \mid Y(k)). \quad (36)$$

From Sect. 3.1, $Y(k^*)$ knowing $Y(k)$ is a binary random variable with probability $\kappa(k)$. As N is Gaussian independent from $Y(k)$, the pdf of $Y(k^*) + N$ knowing $Y(k)$ is a Gaussian mixture that can take two forms:

$$p_{\kappa(k)}(x) = \begin{cases} \frac{1}{\sqrt{2\pi}\sigma}[\kappa(k)e^{-\frac{(x-1)^2}{2\sigma^2}} + (1 - \kappa(k))e^{-\frac{(x+1)^2}{2\sigma^2}}] \\ \frac{1}{\sqrt{2\pi}\sigma}[\kappa(k)e^{-\frac{(x+1)^2}{2\sigma^2}} + (1 - \kappa(k))e^{-\frac{(x-1)^2}{2\sigma^2}}] \end{cases} , \quad (37)$$

By symmetry, their entropy $h(Y(k^*) + N \mid Y(k))$ will be the same and we can take any of these pdfs. Letting ϕ be the standard normal density, we can write

$$p_{\kappa(k)}(x) = p_{1/2}(x) - 2(1/2 - \kappa(k))\phi(x)e^{-\frac{1}{\sigma^2}}\sinh(\frac{x}{\sigma^2}) \quad (38)$$

$$= p_{1/2}(x)(1 - 2(1/2 - \kappa(k))\tanh(\frac{x}{2\sigma^2})). \quad (39)$$

where

$$p_{1/2}(x) = \frac{1}{2\sqrt{2\pi}\sigma}[e^{-\frac{(x-1)^2}{2\sigma^2}} + e^{-\frac{(x+1)^2}{2\sigma^2}}] = \frac{1}{\sigma}e^{-\frac{1}{2\sigma^2}}\phi(\frac{x}{\sigma})\cosh(\frac{x}{\sigma^2}). \quad (40)$$

For notational convenience define $\epsilon = 2(1/2 - \kappa(k))$, $p = p_{1/2}(x)$, and $t = \tanh(x)$. Then

$$I(X;Y(k)) = h(Y(k^*) + N) - h(Y(k^*) + N \mid Y(k)) \tag{41}$$

$$= -\int p \log_2 p + \int (p(1 - \epsilon t)) \log_2(p(1 - \epsilon t)) \tag{42}$$

$$= -\int \epsilon p t \log_2 p + \int p \log_2(1 - \epsilon t) - \int p \epsilon t \log_2(1 - \epsilon t). \tag{43}$$

The first term vanishes since p is even and t odd. We apply a Taylor expansion:

$$I(X;Y(k)) = \int p[-\epsilon t - \frac{\epsilon^2 t^2}{2} - \frac{\epsilon^3 t^3}{3} + O(\epsilon^4)] - \int \epsilon p t[-\epsilon t - \frac{\epsilon^2 t^2}{2} - \frac{\epsilon^3 t^3}{3} + O(\epsilon^4)]. \tag{44}$$

The odd terms of the expansion are null as t is odd and p even. We therefore obtain:

$$I(X;Y(k)) = \int p[-\frac{\epsilon^2 t^2}{2} + O(\epsilon^4)] - \int [-\epsilon^2 p t^2 + O(\epsilon^4)] = \int \frac{\epsilon^2 p t^2}{2} + O(\epsilon^4). \tag{45}$$

Thus, finally,

$$\mathcal{D}(k) = 2 \log_2(e)(1/2 - \kappa(k))^2 g(\sigma), \tag{46}$$

where

$$g(\sigma) = \frac{1}{\sigma} e^{-\frac{1}{2\sigma^2}} \int_{\mathbb{R}} \phi(\frac{x}{\sigma}) \cosh(\frac{x}{\sigma^2}) \tanh^2(\frac{x}{\sigma^2}) \mathrm{d}x. \tag{47}$$

There are several ways to express $g(\sigma)$. For example, we have:

$$g(\sigma) = e^{-\frac{1}{2\sigma^2}} \int_{\mathbb{R}} \phi(x) \cosh(\frac{x}{\sigma}) \tanh^2(\frac{x}{\sigma}) \mathrm{d}x. \tag{48}$$

This expression can be reduced to:

$$g(\sigma) = \frac{1}{2} \mathbb{E}_X \left[\tanh^2(\frac{X}{\sigma} + \frac{1}{\sigma^2}) + \tanh^2(\frac{X}{\sigma} - \frac{1}{\sigma^2}) \right], \tag{49}$$

where $X \sim \mathcal{N}(0,1)$. By the dominated convergence theorem ($\tanh^2(\frac{X}{\sigma} + \frac{1}{\sigma^2})$ is always smaller than 1) when $\sigma \to 0$, we obtain $g(0) = 1$ and when $\sigma \to \infty$ we obtain the equivalent $\frac{1}{\sigma^2}$.

B   Proof of Lemma 4

The success exponent is defined by

$$\mathrm{SE} = \frac{\mathbb{E}[\widehat{\mathcal{D}}(k^*) - \widehat{\mathcal{D}}(k)]^2}{2\mathrm{Var}(\widehat{\mathcal{D}}(k^*) - \widehat{\mathcal{D}}(k))}. \tag{50}$$

where in our case

$$\widehat{\mathcal{D}}(k) = \frac{1}{q\sqrt{1+\sigma^2}}\left|\sum_{i=1}^{q} X_i Y_i(k)\right|. \tag{51}$$

First for large q we can consider that $\mathbb{E}[|\sum_i X_i Y_i(k)|] = |\mathbb{E}[\sum_i X_i Y_i(k)]|$.

$$\mathbb{E}[\widehat{\mathcal{D}}(k)] = |\mathbb{E}[XY(k)]| = \frac{2 \times |1/2 - \kappa(k)|}{\sqrt{1+\sigma^2}} \tag{52}$$

hence

$$\mathbb{E}[\widehat{\mathcal{D}}(k^*) - \widehat{\mathcal{D}}(k)] = \frac{1 - 2 \times |1/2 - \kappa(k)|}{\sqrt{1+\sigma^2}}. \tag{53}$$

Secondly we have

$$\mathrm{Var}(\widehat{\mathcal{D}}(k^*) - \widehat{\mathcal{D}}(k)) = \frac{1}{q^2(1+\sigma^2)}\mathrm{Var}\left(\left|\sum_{i=1}^{q} X_i Y_i(k^*)\right| - \left|\sum_{i=1}^{q} X_i Y_i(k)\right|\right). \tag{54}$$

To remove the absolute values, we distinguish two cases whether the sum is positive or negative. We consider that q is large enough to have strictly positive or negative values.

$$\mathrm{Var}(\widehat{\mathcal{D}}(k^*) - \widehat{\mathcal{D}}(k)) = \frac{1}{q^2(1+\sigma^2)}\mathrm{Var}\left(\sum_{i=1}^{q} X_i Y_i(k^*) \mp \sum_{i=1}^{q} X_i Y_i(k)\right) \tag{55}$$

$$= \frac{1}{q^2(1+\sigma^2)}\mathrm{Var}\left(\sum_{i=1}^{q} X_i\bigl(Y_i(k^*) \mp Y_i(k)\bigr)\right) \tag{56}$$

$$= \frac{1}{q(1+\sigma^2)}\mathrm{Var}\bigl(X\bigl(Y(k^*) \mp Y(k)\bigr)\bigr) \tag{57}$$

$$= \frac{1}{q(1+\sigma^2)}\mathrm{Var}\bigl((Y(k^*) + N)\bigl(Y(k^*) \mp Y(k)\bigr)\bigr) \tag{58}$$

$$= \frac{1}{q(1+\sigma^2)}\mathrm{Var}\bigl(\mp Y(k^*)Y(k) + N(Y(k^*) \mp Y(k))\bigr). \tag{59}$$

The variance term is the difference of the two following quantities

$$\mathbb{E}\left[\bigl(\mp Y(k^*)Y(k) + N(Y(k^*) \mp Y(k))\bigr)^2\right] = 1 + 2\sigma^2(1 - 2|1/2 - \kappa(k)|) \tag{60}$$

$$\mathbb{E}\left[\mp Y(k^*)Y(k) + N(Y(k^*) \mp Y(k))\right]^2 = \bigl(2(1/2 - \kappa(k))\bigr)^2. \tag{61}$$

Combining all the above expressions we obtain (33).

C Proof of Lemma 5

To prove the success rate of KSA, we first need an estimator for the cumulative density function. We take as kernel a function Φ as simple as possible i.e. the Heaviside function $\Phi(x) = 0$ if $x < 0$ and $\Phi(x) = 1$ if $x \geq 0$.

With this function and for $x \in \mathbb{R}$, we can estimate $F(x|Y(k) = 1) - F(x)$ by the following estimator:

$$\tilde{F}(x|Y(k) = 1) - \tilde{F}(x) = \frac{\sum_{i|Y_i(k)=1} \Phi(x - X_i)}{\sum_{i|Y_i(k)=1} 1} - \frac{\sum_i \Phi(x - X_i)}{q}. \quad (62)$$

We suppose that q is large enough to consider that $\sum_{i|Y_i(k)=1} 1 = \frac{q}{2}$ (by the law of large numbers). Therefore we have:

$$\tilde{F}(x|Y(k) = 1) - \tilde{F}(x) = \frac{\sum_{i|Y_i(k)=1} \Phi(x - X_i)}{q} - 2\frac{\sum_i \Phi(x - X_i)}{q}. \quad (63)$$

We notice that $\sum_{i|Y_i(k)=1} \Phi(x - X_i) = \frac{1}{2}\sum_i(Y_i(k) + 1)\Phi(x - X_i)$. Therefore

$$\tilde{F}(x|Y(k) = 1) - \tilde{F}(x) = \frac{1}{q}\sum_{i=1}^{q} Y_i(k)\Phi(x - X_i). \quad (64)$$

This estimator is a sum of i.i.d. random variables. We can therefore apply the central limit theorem.

$$\mathbb{E}[\tilde{F}(x|Y(k) = 1) - \tilde{F}(x)] = \mathbb{E}[Y(k)\Phi(x - X_i)] \quad (65)$$

$$= \mathbb{E}[Y(k)\Phi(x - Y(k^*) - N)] \quad (66)$$

$$= \frac{1}{2}(\kappa(k) - 0.5)\left(\text{erf}\left(\frac{1-x}{\sigma\sqrt{2}}\right) + \text{erf}\left(\frac{1+x}{\sigma\sqrt{2}}\right)\right). \quad (67)$$

The maximum of the absolute value is for $x = 0$ and we obtain:

$$\|\mathbb{E}[\tilde{F}(x|Y(k) = 1) - \tilde{F}(x)]\|_\infty = |0.5 - \kappa(k)|\text{erf}\left(\frac{1}{\sigma\sqrt{2}}\right). \quad (68)$$

We notice that $\|\mathbb{E}[\tilde{F}(x|Y(k) = 1) - \tilde{F}(x)]\|_\infty = \|\mathbb{E}[\tilde{F}(x|Y(k) = -1) - \tilde{F}(x)]\|_\infty$. To calculate the variance, we consider that $x = 0$ as it is the value that maximizes the expectation of the distinguisher.

$$\text{Var}(\hat{\mathcal{D}}(k^*) - \hat{\mathcal{D}}(k)) = \text{Var}\left(\frac{1}{q}\left(\sum_{i=1}^{q} \Phi(x - X_i)(Y_i(k^*) - Y_i(k))\right)\right) \quad (69)$$

The computation of this variance gives:

$$\text{Var}(\hat{\mathcal{D}}(k^*) - \hat{\mathcal{D}}(k)) = 2(0.5 - |0.5 - \kappa(k)|) - \text{erf}\left(\frac{1}{\sigma\sqrt{2}}\right)^2(0.5 - |0.5 - \kappa(k)|)^2. \quad (70)$$

Overall, the success exponent is:

$$\text{SE} = \frac{1}{2}\min_{k \neq k^*} \frac{\text{erf}\left(\frac{1}{\sqrt{2}\sigma}\right)^2(1/2 - |1/2 - \kappa(k)|)}{2 - \text{erf}\left(\frac{1}{\sqrt{2}\sigma}\right)^2(1/2 - |1/2 - \kappa(k)|)}. \quad (71)$$

D   Proof of Lemma 6

For MIA, we refer to [10, Section 5.3] for the theoretical justifications. In order to obtain a simple closed-form expression of the success exponent, we suppose that $\sigma \gg 1$ and that the probability density functions are all Gaussian. This means that $X|Y(k)$ is a Gaussian random variable of standard deviation $\sqrt{4\kappa(k)(1 - \kappa(k)) + \sigma^2}$. Moreover, we will keep only the first order approximation in $\mathsf{SNR} = \sigma^{-2}$ of the SE.

$$h(X|Y(k)) - h(X|Y(k^*)) = \frac{1}{2} \log_2(2\pi e \cdot (4\kappa(k)(1 - \kappa(k)) + \sigma^2) - \frac{1}{2} \log_2(2\pi e \cdot \sigma^2) \quad (72)$$

$$= \frac{1}{2} \log_2 \frac{4\kappa(k)(1 - \kappa(k)) + \sigma^2}{\sigma^2} \quad (73)$$

$$\approx \frac{\log_2(e)4\kappa(k)(1 - \kappa(k))}{2\sigma^2} \quad (74)$$

The Fisher information of a Gaussian random variable of standard deviation ζ is equal to $\frac{1}{\zeta^2}$. Therefore the Fisher information of X knowing $Y = y(k)$ is:

$$F(X|Y(k) = y(k)) = \frac{1}{4\kappa(k)(1 - \kappa(k)) + \sigma^2}. \quad (75)$$

As this value does not depend on the value of $Y(k)$, we have:

$$F(X|Y(k)) = \frac{1}{4\kappa(k)(1 - \kappa(k)) + \sigma^2} \quad (76)$$

$$J(X|Y(k)) - J(X|Y(k^*)) = \frac{1}{4\kappa(k)(1 - \kappa(k)) + \sigma^2} - \frac{1}{\sigma^2} \quad (77)$$

$$\approx -\frac{\kappa(k)(1 - \kappa(k))}{\sigma^4}. \quad (78)$$

Last, we have to calculate $\mathrm{Var}(-\log_2 p(X|Y(k) = y(k)))$. Let $\zeta^2 = \sigma^2 + 4\kappa(k)(1 - \kappa(k))$ and C the normalization constant. We have:

$$\mathrm{Var}(-\log_2 p(X|Y(k) = y(k))) = \mathrm{Var}\left(-\log_2\left(C \exp\left(-\frac{1}{2}\frac{(X - \mu)^2}{\zeta^2}\right)\right)\right) \quad (79)$$

$$= \mathrm{Var}\left(-\log_2(C) + \frac{1}{2}\frac{(X - \mu)^2}{\zeta^2}\right) \quad (80)$$

$$= \frac{1}{4}\mathrm{Var}\left(\frac{(X - \mu)^2}{\zeta^2}\right) = \frac{1}{4\zeta^4}\mathrm{Var}(X^2) \quad (81)$$

$$= \frac{1}{4(\sigma^2 + 4\kappa(k)(1 - \kappa(k)))^2}2(1 + \sigma^2)^2 \approx \frac{1}{2}. \quad (82)$$

Overall, the success exponent defined in [10, Proposition 6] can be simplified in the case of monobit leakage as:

$$\mathsf{SE} \approx \min_{k \neq k^*} 4\frac{\log_2(e)^2\kappa(k)^2(1 - \kappa(k))^2}{\sigma^4}. \quad (83)$$

References

1. Batina, L., Robshaw, M. (eds.): CHES 2014. LNCS, vol. 8731. Springer, Heidelberg (2014). https://doi.org/10.1007/978-3-662-44709-3
2. Blahut, R.E.: Principles and Practice of Information Theory. Addison-Wesley Longman Publishing Co. Inc., Boston (1987)
3. Brier, É., Clavier, C., Olivier, F.: Correlation power analysis with a leakage model. In: Joye, M., Quisquater, J.-J. (eds.) CHES 2004. LNCS, vol. 3156, pp. 16–29. Springer, Heidelberg (2004). https://doi.org/10.1007/978-3-540-28632-5_2
4. Carlet, C., Heuser, A., Picek, S.: Trade-offs for S-boxes: cryptographic properties and side-channel resilience. In: Gollmann, D., Miyaji, A., Kikuchi, H. (eds.) ACNS 2017. LNCS, vol. 10355, pp. 393–414. Springer, Cham (2017). https://doi.org/10.1007/978-3-319-61204-1_20
5. Cover, T.M., Thomas, J.A.: Elements of Information Theory, 2nd edn. Wiley-Interscience, New York (2006). ISBN-10: 0471241954, ISBN-13: 978-0471241959
6. Daemen, J., Rijmen, V.: Rijndael for AES. In: AES Candidate Conference, pp. 343–348 (2000)
7. Fei, Y., Ding, A.A., Lao, J., Zhang, L.: A statistics-based success rate model for DPA and CPA. J. Cryptographic Eng. 5(4), 227–243 (2015). https://doi.org/10.1007/s13389-015-0107-0
8. Fei, Y., Luo, Q., Ding, A.A.: A statistical model for DPA with novel algorithmic confusion analysis. In: Prouff, E., Schaumont, P. (eds.) CHES 2012. LNCS, vol. 7428, pp. 233–250. Springer, Heidelberg (2012). https://doi.org/10.1007/978-3-642-33027-8_14
9. Gierlichs, B., Batina, L., Tuyls, P., Preneel, B.: Mutual information analysis. In: Oswald, E., Rohatgi, P. (eds.) CHES 2008. LNCS, vol. 5154, pp. 426–442. Springer, Heidelberg (2008). https://doi.org/10.1007/978-3-540-85053-3_27
10. Guilley, S., Heuser, A., Rioul, O.: A key to success. In: Biryukov, A., Goyal, V. (eds.) INDOCRYPT 2015. LNCS, vol. 9462, pp. 270–290. Springer, Cham (2015). https://doi.org/10.1007/978-3-319-26617-6_15
11. Heuser, A., Rioul, O., Guilley, S.: A theoretical study of Kolmogorov-Smirnov distinguishers – side-channel analysis vs. differential cryptanalysis. In: Prouff [17], pp. 9–28. https://doi.org/10.1007/978-3-319-10175-0_2
12. Heuser, A., Rioul, O., Guilley, S.: Good is not good enough - deriving optimal distinguishers from communication theory. In: Batina and Robshaw [1], pp. 55–74. https://doi.org/10.1007/978-3-662-44709-3_4
13. Kocher, P., Jaffe, J., Jun, B.: Differential power analysis. In: Wiener, M. (ed.) CRYPTO 1999. LNCS, vol. 1666, pp. 388–397. Springer, Heidelberg (1999). https://doi.org/10.1007/3-540-48405-1_25
14. Lomné, V., Prouff, E., Rivain, M., Roche, T., Thillard, A.: How to estimate the success rate of higher-order side-channel attacks. In: Batina and Robshaw [1], pp. 35–54. https://doi.org/10.1007/978-3-662-44709-3_3
15. Mangard, S., Oswald, E., Popp, T.: Power Analysis Attacks. Revealing the Secrets of Smart Cards. Springer, Boston (2007). https://doi.org/10.1007/978-0-387-38162-6
16. Mangard, S., Oswald, E., Standaert, F.: One for all - all for one: unifying standard differential power analysis attacks. IET Inf. Secur. 5(2), 100–110 (2011). https://doi.org/10.1049/iet-ifs.2010.0096
17. Prouff, E. (ed.): COSADE 2014. LNCS, vol. 8622. Springer, Cham (2014). https://doi.org/10.1007/978-3-319-10175-0

18. Reparaz, O., Gierlichs, B., Verbauwhede, I.: A note on the use of margins to compare distinguishers. In: Prouff [17], pp. 1–8. https://doi.org/10.1007/978-3-319-10175-0_1
19. Rivain, M.: On the exact success rate of side channel analysis in the Gaussian model. In: Avanzi, R.M., Keliher, L., Sica, F. (eds.) SAC 2008. LNCS, vol. 5381, pp. 165–183. Springer, Heidelberg (2009). https://doi.org/10.1007/978-3-642-04159-4_11
20. Schindler, W., Lemke, K., Paar, C.: A stochastic model for differential side channel cryptanalysis. In: Rao, J.R., Sunar, B. (eds.) CHES 2005. LNCS, vol. 3659, pp. 30–46. Springer, Heidelberg (2005). https://doi.org/10.1007/11545262_3
21. Whitnall, C., Oswald, E.: A fair evaluation framework for comparing side-channel distinguishers. J. Cryptographic Eng. 1(2), 145–160 (2011)
22. Whitnall, C., Oswald, E., Mather, L.: An exploration of the Kolmogorov-Smirnov test as a competitor to mutual information analysis. In: Prouff, E. (ed.) CARDIS 2011. LNCS, vol. 7079, pp. 234–251. Springer, Heidelberg (2011). https://doi.org/10.1007/978-3-642-27257-8_15

Searching BN Curves for SM9

Guiwen Luo[1,2]($\boxtimes$) and Xiao Chen[1,2]

[1] State Key Laboratory of Information Security, Institute of Information Engineering,
Chinese Academy of Sciences, Beijing 100093, China
{luoguiwen,chenxiao}@iie.ac.cn
[2] School of Cyber Security, University of Chinese Academy of Sciences,
Beijing 100049, China

Abstract. In 2016, State Cryptography Administration of China published Identity-based cryptographic algorithm SM9. A 256-bit BN curve recommended to construct system parameters in SM9 documents once was convinced to provide 128-bit security level. With the development of number field sieve, the complexity of discrete logarithm problem (DLP) in a finite field reduces, so does the security level of SM9 whose security is based on the difficulty of solving the DLPs. It's urgent to construct SM9 system parameters with higher security level. In this paper, we analyze the requirements of secure elliptic curves, search BN curves at length of 384-bit and 380–382-bit that show the best computation efficiency. Then we choose a 384-bit BN curve to construct the system parameters, making preparation for upgrading the original 256-bit SM9.

Keywords: SM9 · Identity-based cryptographic algorithm ·
System parameters · BN curve · R-ate pairing

1 Introduction

SM9 is an identity-based cryptosystem [1–5] based on bilinear pairing which makes connections between the cyclic subgroups of elliptic curves and the cyclic multiplication subgroup of finite field. SM9 chooses a BN curve to construct its system parameters and R-ate Pairing to implement all the cryptographic algorithms.

From the perspective of mathematics, SM9 is also a pairing-based cryptosystem whose security is based on the difficulty of DLPs on elliptic curves and finite field. Original SM9 has recommended 256-bit system parameters in order to provide 128-bit security level at the time. In 2016, there was a big improvement on number field sieve (NFS) algorithm [18], bringing down the difficulty of DLP in finite field. A variant of ordinary NFS named special ExTNFS is suitable for extension field $\mathbb{F}_{q^n}$ with prime q given by a polynomial of parameter t, such as the cases of BN curves. This leads to a result that the 256-bit BN curve in original SM9 could theoretically just provide the security level of around 100-bit [6]. It's urgent to construct system parameters of SM9 with higher security level to make preparation for upgrade.

© Springer Nature Switzerland AG 2019
F. Guo et al. (Eds.): Inscrypt 2018, LNCS 11449, pp. 554–567, 2019.
https://doi.org/10.1007/978-3-030-14234-6_29

Several recent works have been done to revise the key size of corresponding security level. Menezes et al. [20], Barbulescu et al. [6], and Scott et al. [28] proposed new key size estimations for pairing-based cryptography. Pairing-friendly elliptic curves, among which the most popular ones are BN curves [9], are commonly utilized to construct system parameters for pairing-based cryptosystem. A general survey about different families of pairing-friendly elliptic curves and their constructions is introduced in [14].

In this article, conditions that secure curves need to satisfy are analyzed and why those conditions are necessary is explained. An exhaustive search over Hamming weight of curve parameter is made, obtaining the best secure BN curves at length of 384-bit and 382-bit respectively. Then we compare and combine state-of-the-art algorithms to evaluate the R-ate pairing computation efficiency, which is the core part of SM9. Finally, the 384-bit BN curve is chosen to construct SM9 system parameters. In a word, we've done all the essential work to upgrade 256-bit SM9 to a higher security level.

2 Preliminaries

2.1 BN Curves

BN curves are a very important family of pairing-friendly elliptic curves broadly used in pairing-based cryptography. A BN curve is represented by integer triplet (t, q, n) with the relationship

$$q = q(t) = 36t^4 + 36t^3 + 24t^2 + 6t + 1,$$
$$n = n(t) = 36t^4 + 36t^3 + 18t^2 + 6t + 1, \tag{1}$$

where both q and n are prime integers. A 256-bit BN curve means the binary length of q and n is 256-bit. The curve equation can be written as

$$E : y^2 = x^3 + b, \ b \in \mathbb{F}_q. \tag{2}$$

The embedding degree of BN curve is $k = 12$, making it appropriate for pairing-based cryptography. Another important property of BN curves is that a twisted curve with degree 6 exists [24]. The twist is represented by the equation

$$E' : y^2 = x^3 + b/\beta, \tag{3}$$

where $\beta \in \mathbb{F}_{q^2} \setminus ((\mathbb{F}_{q^2})^2 \cup (\mathbb{F}_{q^2})^3)$. It helps us to represent the second R-ate pairing argument point in a quadratic extension field to achieve higher pairing computation efficiency. The corresponding isomorphism $\psi \in \hom(E', E)$ is

$$\psi : E' \to E, (x', y') \mapsto (\beta^{1/3}x', \beta^{1/2}y'). \tag{4}$$

2.2 Bilinear Pairing

Let $(G_1, +), (G_2, +)$ and $(G_T, \cdot)$ be three cyclic groups with the same order of prime integer n. Let P_1 and P_2 be the generators of G_1 and G_2 respectively. Suppose there exists a homomorphism ψ such that $\psi(P_2) = P_1$.

A bilinear pairing is a map

$$e : G_1 \times G_2 \to G_T$$

with bilinearity, non-degeneracy and computability.

Different kinds of bilinear pairings, including Weil Pairing, Tate Pairing, Ate Pairing and R-ate Pairing, are suitable for SM9. Original 256-bit SM9 [5] chooses R-ate Pairing as the recommended one.

Define $G_1 = \ker(\phi_q - [1]) = E(\mathbb{F}_q)$ and $G_2 = E[n] \cap \ker(\phi_q - [q]) \subseteq E(\mathbb{F}_{p^{12}})[n]$, where ϕ_q is the Frobenius endomorphism and G_T is a subgroup of $\mathbb{F}_{q^{12}}$ with a prime order n. Suppose the straight line acrossing points U and V on a BN curve is $\lambda x + \delta y + \tau = 0$, let function $g_{U,V}(Q)$ be

$$g_{U,V}(Q) = \lambda x_Q + \delta y_Q + \tau, \; where \; Q = (x_Q, y_Q).$$

If $U = V$, let $g_{U,V}$ be the tangent line acrossing U; if one of U and V is infinity O, let $g_{U,V}$ be the vertical line acrossing the other point. Then R-ate pairing on a BN curve can be computed as Algorithm 1 [1], which contains three key steps—the Miller loop (Line 1–10), adjustment step (Line 11–16) and final exponentiation (Line 17).

2.3 Algorithm Attacks on SM9

The security of SM9 is determined by the difficulty of discrete logarithm problem (DLP) in G_1, G_2, G_T. There are two different kinds of DLPs, one is the DLP in elliptic curves, the other is the DLP in finite field, i.e. G_T. The cost of DLPs is required to be big enough to meet the corresponding security level. This subsection introduces the most effective algorithm attacks on SM9. Those attacks are suitable for pairing-based cryptography, too.

The effective attack algorithm in curve side G_1, G_2 is Pollard's rho algorithm [14,25]. Since we employ BN curves in SM9, $q(t)$ and $n(t)$ have the same bit length, that we denote as l_1. Security evaluation on G_1 and G_2 is simple, $l_1 \geq 2l_2$ is sufficient for the requirement of l_2-bit security level.

Algorithm 1. Computing R-ate pairing on BN Curves

Input:$P \in G_1, Q \in G_2, a = |6t + 2|$.

Output:R-ate pairing f.

1:   Let $a = \sum_{i=0}^{L-1} a_i 2^i, a_{L-1} = 1, a_i \in \{-1, 0, 1\}$.

2:   $T \leftarrow Q, f \leftarrow 1$.

3:   **for** $i = L - 2$ *to* 0 **do**

4:     $f \leftarrow f^2 \cdot g_{T,T}(P), T \leftarrow [2]T$;

5:     **if** $a_i = 1$ **then**

6:       $f \leftarrow f \cdot g_{T,Q}(P), T \leftarrow T + Q$.

7:     **elseif** $a_i = -1$ **then**

8:       $f \leftarrow f \cdot g_{T,-Q}(P), T \leftarrow T - Q$.

9:     **endif**

10:   **endfor**

11:   **if** $t < 0$ **then**

12:   $T \leftarrow -T, f \leftarrow f^{q^6}$.

13:   **endif**

14:   $Q_1 \leftarrow \phi_q(Q), Q_2 \leftarrow \phi_{q^2}(Q)$.

15:   $f \leftarrow f \cdot g_{T,Q_1}(P), T \leftarrow T + Q_1$.

16:   $f \leftarrow f \cdot g_{T,-Q_2}(P)$.

17:   $f \leftarrow f^{(q^{12}-1)/n}$.

18:   **return** f.

Another attack in curve side is advised by Cheon [11,12]. Cheon shows that the strong Diffie-Hellman (SDH) problem with auxiliary inputs can be solved faster than ordinary DLP. Suppose attacker can repeat signatures for k times and collect the corresponding public keys, if $n - 1$ contains a divisor $d \leq \min\{k + 1, n^{1/2}\}$, or $n + 1$ contains a divisor $d \leq \min\{(k + 1)/2, n^{1/3}\}$, then the secret key can be found in $O(\sqrt{n/d})$, in other words security level could be reduced by $O(\sqrt{d})$. This implies that the security level of SDH problem could be lower than we expect if system parameters are randomly chosen. It is recommended to select a secure curve with a prime order n such that both $n + 1$ and $n - 1$ have no small divisor.

The best attack algorithm in finite field side is the number field sieve (NFS) algorithm. A variant of NFS, named special extended tower-NFS [7,18] (Special ExTNFS), is dedicated to extension field $\mathbb{F}_{q^n}$ with prime q given by a polynomial of parameter t, such as the case of BN curves. Since this area is developing, we can't give a clear and precise security evaluation in finite field side. Theoretical improvements on special ExTNFS have been done but real-life implementations are not available. In particular the relation collection step is a tough work and is not implemented at present. But we should still take those theoretical improvements seriously when evaluating the security level.

3   Conditions of SM9 Secure Curves

System parameters are carefully selected to ensure that SM9 system runs securely. They includes the elliptic curve parameters, the curve identifier, the order of cyclic group and it's cofactor, etc. The most important one is the elliptic curve which meets all the security requirements of SM9. Such elliptic curves are called secure curves. Since the supersingular curves are proved to be insecure, we focus on ordinary curves. Part 1 of SM9 documents states three conditions that a secure curve needs to meet:

Condition 1. Ordinary curve whose base field is $\mathbb{F}_q$, where q is a prime number greater than 2^{191}. The embedding degree $k = 2^i \cdot 3^j$, where $i > 0, j >= 0$.

Condition 2. $n - 1$ contains a prime factor greater than 2^{190}.

Condition 3. $n + 1$ contains a prime factor greater than 2^{120}.

The **Condition 2** and **Condition 3** are specified to reduce the impact caused by Cheon Attack. It's more appropriate to modify those two conditions as containing small prime factors as few as possible.

The 256-bit BN curve, presented in the SM9 documents, once was considered that the G_T provided security level higher than 128-bit, and that the weakness of the system was G_1 and G_2, whose security levels are no more than 128-bit by Pollard's rho algorithm. It was necessary to reduce the impact on G_1 and G_2 caused by Cheon Attack at the time. With the development of special ExTNFS, it's now commonly accepted that curve side is stronger than finite field side, so the urgency of those two conditions has gone, they can be the last to be considered. Furthermore, $n - 1$ and $n + 1$ always contain small prime factor such as 2, and in real life Cheon Attack is limited by the amount of public keys the attacker can collect and by the total number of system identities.

Other conditions that need to be considered are

Condition 4. $2q - n$ is a prime number.

This condition guarantees subgroup security [8]. The 256-bit BN in SM9 doesn't take it into consideration, so membership test is required every time. For a BN curve, the order of $E(\mathbb{F}_q)$ is a prime number, it naturally protects against the subgroup attacks that exploit small prime divisors of the cofactor. However, this is not the case of $E'(\mathbb{F}_{q^2})$ since its order equals $n(2q - n)$. The subgroup attack under this circumstance can be prevented by using membership tests, which may be expensive. If we want to avoid these tests, the curve parameter t should be chosen such that both n and $2q - n$ are prime numbers.

Condition 5. the Hamming weight of BN curve parameter t should be as small as possible.

It obviously helps Miller loop for R-ate pairing computation, and it's also beneficial to final exponentiation.

Condition 6. $t = 2$ or 10 modulo 12.

This condition guarantees the tower extension of $\mathbb{F}_q$ to be the same as SM9-Part5, which means the reduction modulo polynomials of field extension are irreducible polynomials $x^i + 2$, $i = 2, 4, 6, 12 \in \mathbb{F}_q[x]$. Under such a condition we can partly reutilize software implementation of $\mathbb{F}_{q^{12}}$ in the original 256-bit SM9 to reduce the expenditure of updating SM9. Actually we've also considered another tower extension case with irreducible polynomials $x^2 + 1 \in \mathbb{F}_q[x]$ and

$x^6 - (1 + \sqrt{-1}) \in \mathbb{F}_{q^2}[x]$. This extension case is a little faster than the former one if the Hamming weight of their curve parameter ts are equal, but no t with Hamming weight no more than 6 meets the case.

4   Searching BN Curves for SM9

The curve parameter t completely decides a BN curve. We represent t in non-adjacent form (NAF), restrict $q(t)$ and $n(t)$ in Eq. (1) as 384-bit prime numbers, then exhaustively search on t with increase of Hamming weight. When Hamming weight is no more than 5, there is no such t that meets all the conditions listed in Sect. 3. When Hamming weight is 6, there are 5 ts (listed in Table 1) meet all the conditions.

Table 1. ts that make $(t, q(t), n(t))$ satisfy all the conditions listed in Sect. 3. p_{n+1} denotes the biggest prime factor of $n + 1$. p_{n-1} denotes the biggest prime factor of $n - 1$.

NAF t	Length of q and n	$W_H(6t + 2)$	$Len(p_{n+1})$	$Len(p_{n-1})$
$-2^{95} + 2^{93} + 2^{61} + 2^{57} - 2^{31} + 2$	384	10	173	283
$-2^{95} + 2^{93} - 2^{63} - 2^{35} - 2^{32} - 2$	384	9	167	287
$-2^{95} + 2^{93} + 2^{80} - 2^{71} - 2^{58} - 2$	384	10	158	250
$2^{95} - 2^{93} + 2^{85} + 2^{31} - 2^3 + 2$	384	8	127	234
$-2^{95} + 2^{93} - 2^{91} - 2^{67} - 2^{65} + 2$	384	7	144	195

Although we aim to search 384-bit BN curves, but in practice the case when BN curves are 380–382-bit is also attractive. The binary length of such parameters aren't precisely the multiple of word size. It shows unique advantages when computing R-ate pairing on processors of 32-bit or 64-bit. We can employ residue number systems (RNS) [19] and lazy reduction techniques to improve the computation efficiency. Lazy reduction is well suited for expressions like $AB \pm CD \in \mathbb{F}_q$. According to normal steps, 2 module reductions are required, while lazy reduction performs only 1 module reduction. RNS and lazy reduction can be employed effectively only when the size of q is chosen to be a little bit smaller than an exact multiple of the word size of the processor architecture. When Hamming weight is no more than 4, no such t meets all the conditions listed in Sect. 3. When t's Hamming weight is 5, there are 2 ts (listed in Table 2) meet all the conditions.

Since the R-ate pairing computation efficiency is determined by the length of q, the Hamming weight of t and $6t + 2$, we can make further selection among those security curves. We denote the most efficient 384-bit BN security curve as t_{384}, and the 382-bit one as t_{382}, then

$$t_{384} = -2^{95} + 2^{93} - 2^{91} - 2^{67} - 2^{65} + 2,$$
$$t_{382} = -2^{94} - 2^{81} - 2^{11} - 2^3 + 2. \tag{5}$$

Table 2. ts that make $(t, q(t), n(t))$ satisfy all the conditions listed in Sect. 3. p_{n+1} denotes the biggest prime factor of $n + 1$. p_{n-1} denotes the biggest prime factor of $n - 1$.

NAF t	Length of q and n	$W_H(6t + 2)$	$Len(p_{n+1})$	$Len(p_{n-1})$
$-2^{94} - 2^{81} - 2^{11} - 2^3 + 2$	382	8	180	203
$-2^{94} - 2^{89} - 2^{62} - 2^5 - 2$	382	10	172	215

5   R-ate Pairing Computation

In this section, we suppose the basic arithmetic operations (addition, subtraction, multiplication and inversion) in $\mathbb{F}_q$ have been implemented, which means our analysis is independent of the underlying hardware architecture. Those basic arithmetics usually employ schoolbook method or Karatsuba method [19] and the Montgomery reduction [21] or the Barrett reduction [10]. Another way to implement $\mathbb{F}_q$ is to use residue number system [19] and lazy reduction [26]. Whatever the algorithms are employed in $\mathbb{F}_q$, it doesn't influence our efficiency comparison when computing R-ate pairings using different curve parameter t. We set the notations for $\mathbb{F}_{q^i}$ ($i = 1, 2, 4, 6, 12$) arithmetics as follows: A_i denotes an addition and A'_i denotes a doubling, M_i denotes a multiplication, sM_i denote a sparse multiplication (which is employed in Miller loop), S_i denotes a squaring and I_i denotes an inversion. We take the pairing computation down to the basic arithmetics in $\mathbb{F}_q$ to show the efficiency of pairing computation based on curve parameter t_{384} and t_{382} in Eq. (5).

5.1   Complexities of Arithmetics in Tower Extension Field

The well-known strategy to improve performance in $\mathbb{F}_{q^{12}}$ is to represent $\mathbb{F}_{q^{12}}$ using tower extension trick, it's faster than directly represent $\mathbb{F}_{q^{12}}$ as

$$\mathbb{F}_{q^{12}} = \mathbb{F}_q[w]/(w^{12} + 2).$$

The most efficient tower extension from $\mathbb{F}_q$ to $\mathbb{F}_{q^{12}}$ is 2-3-2 extension [13]. We assume that additions are not negligible and $A_1 \leq 0.33M_1$, under this assumption multiplications in all extension level (i.e. in $\mathbb{F}_{q^k}$, $k = 2, 6, 12$) are implemented by Karatsuba arithmetic, and the squaring in the degree 3 extension ($\mathbb{F}_{q^6}/\mathbb{F}_{q^2}$) is implemented by Chung-Hasan method.

Since our curve parameter $t = 2$ or 10 modulo 12, we can use the same tower extension as the original 256-bit SM9. The tower extension of $\mathbb{F}_q$ is as below:

$$\mathbb{F}_{q^2} = \mathbb{F}_q[u]/(u^2 - \alpha), \alpha = -2,$$
$$\mathbb{F}_{q^6} = \mathbb{F}_{q^2}[v]/(v^3 - u), u^2 = \alpha,$$
$$\mathbb{F}_{q^{12}} = \mathbb{F}_{q^6}[w]/(w^2 - v), v^3 = u.$$

Table 3. Complexities of arithmetics in tower extension fields

Operation	Number of operations
I_2	$I_1 + 2M_1 + 2S_1 + A_1 + A_1'$
M_2	$3M_1 + 5A_1 + A_1'$
S_2 (Complex method)	$2M_1 + 3A_1 + 2A_1'$
I_6	$I_1 + 35M_1 + 2S_1 + 65A_1 + 20A_1'$
M_6	$18M_1 + 60A_1 + 8A_1'$
S_6	$12M_1 + 35A_1 + 12A_1'$
I_{12}	$I_1 + 95M_1 + 2S_1 + 261A_1 + 61A_1'$
M_{12}	$54M_1 + 210A_1 + 25A_1'$
sM_{12}	$39M_1 + 115A_1 + 16A_1'$
S_{12}	$36M_1 + 129A_1 + 37A_1'$
S_{12} (Karabina's squaring)	$12M_1 + 50A_1 + 23A_1'$
S_{12} (Simult. decompression of k elt.)	$I_1 + (21k - 7)M_1 + 2S_1 + (47k - 14)A_1$ $+(21k - 2)A_1'$
S_{12} (Granger and Scott's method)	$18M_1 + 75A_1 + 34A_1'$

We count the operations of tower extensions based on $\mathbb{F}_q$ in Table 3. Note that the cyclotomic squaring in $\mathbb{F}_{q^{12}}$, which is utilized in the final exponentiation, is assumed to be implemented by Karabina's compress method [17] and Montgomery's simultaneous inversion trick [22]. Another cyclotomic squaring algorithm is Granger and Scott's method [16], which in most case is slower than Karabina's method unless the $\mathbb{F}_{q^2}$ inversion is very time consuming.

5.2   Complexities of R-ate Pairing Computation

R-ate pairing computation efficiency is determined by the length of q, the Hamming weight of t and $6t+2$. We utilize projective coordinates for adding and doubling points along with line computation in Miller loop. Scott et al.'s method [27] is taken to implement the final exponentiation step. Although Fuentes-Castaneda et al. [15] provide another method which can save $3M_{12}+1S_{12}$, but their method demands the redefinition of R-ate pairing to its fixed power. We count the number of operations for R-ate pairing corresponding to t_{384} and t_{382}, the result is presented in Table 4. It seems that pairing computation corresponding to t_{382} is just slightly faster than that corresponding to t_{384}, but in practice when utilizing RNS and lazy reduction, the advantage could be greater.

6   Matching Security Level

The security of SM9 is determined by the difficulty of discrete logarithm problem in G_1, G_2 (curve side) and G_T (finite field side).

Table 4. Complexities of R-ate pairing computation corresponding to t_{384} and t_{382}.

Operation	t_{384}	t_{382}
Doubling+LineEval.	$24M_1 + 59A_1 + 16A_1'$	$24M_1 + 59A_1 + 16A_1'$
Addition+LineEval.	$44M_1 + 80A_1 + 16A_1'$	$44M_1 + 80A_1 + 16A_1'$
Miller loop	$10101M_1 + 30561A_1 + 6885A_1'$	$10184M_1 + 30756A_1 + 6917A_1'$
Adjustment steps	$170M_1 + 390A_1 + 64A_1'$	$170M_1 + 390A_1 + 64A_1'$
Final exponentiation	$4I_1 + 5644M_1 + 8S_1$ $+ 21915A_1 + 7874A_1'$	$4I_1 + 5383M_1 + 8S_1$ $+ 20994A_1 + 7667A_1'$
R-ate pairing	$4I_1 + 15915M_1 + 8S_1$ $+ 52866A_1 + 14823A_1'$	$4I_1 + 15737M_1 + 8S_1$ $+ 52140A_1 + 14648A_1'$

We analyze the BN curve corresponding to t_{384} first. The curve order n is a 384-bit prime number, so its security level is no more than 192-bit by Pollard's rho algorithm. Then we consider Cheon attack, since

$$n + 1 = 2 \cdot 5 \cdot 7 \cdot 11 \cdot 131 \cdot 42992652371 \cdot 28839188139379$$
$$46545034377697 \cdot 4311174394100684103433361991367 \cdot d_1,$$

where d_1 is a 144-bit prime number,

$$n - 1 = 2^2 \cdot 3 \cdot 61 \cdot 547271 \cdot 29406309859180669069321 \cdot$$
$$93832952987412088626031291 \cdot d_2,$$

where d_2 is a 195-bit prime number. We take $d = \max\{2 \cdot 5 \cdot 7 \cdot 11 \cdot 131 \cdot 42992652371,\ 2^2 \cdot 3 \cdot 61 \cdot 547271\}$, according to Cheon attack, the security level can be reduced by 26-bit (the length of $\sqrt{d}$). Note that this reduction is just theoretical since in real life the attacker can't collect so enormous amount of public keys to conduct such an attack. Combine all together, the curve side can provide around 166-bit security level.

As for the finite field side, Freeman et al. [14] has made a well-known speculation about the exact sizes of q and q^k (where k denotes the embedding degree of the curve) required to match corresponding security level in 2010. They believed that one could achieve 128-bit security level by choosing a 256-bit prime number q and a proper embedding degree k such that the binary length of q^k was fell in the range 3000–5000, that was what the original SM9 had done. With the size of q^k 3072, it was convinced to provide 128-bit security level at the time.

But with the development of the special ExTNFS, security on the finite field side decreases, thus the security evaluation of pairing-based cryptography need to be reconsidered. The problem is complicated by the fact that the Special ExTNFS is developing, although theoretical improvements have been done but real-life implementations are missing. Barbulescu et al. proposed a new key size estimation for pairing-based cryptography [6], and Michael Scott followed their analysis to give his estimation on the security requirement for key size [28]. Although those estimation are rough and theoretical, it provide the new trend of security reduction in finite field side. According to [6,23,28], since we choose the BN curve corresponding to t_{384} whose embedding degree $k = 12$, special ExTNFS makes the security level be $(130 - \delta)$-bit, where δ is not precisely known. δ is usually about a dozen, so the 384-bit BN curve can theoretically provide around 118-bit security level. Note that a 384-bit BN curve might not be able to meet the 128-bit security level [23].

As the analysis shows, at present the weakness is on the finite field side. There are more than 62-bit security level margin for Cheon attack in the curve side, thus it's unnecessary to consider Cheon attack.

To sum up, BN curve corresponding to t_{384} theoretically provides around 118-bit security level. Follow the same analysis, BN curve corresponding to t_{382} provides security level which is 1-bit lower than that of t_{384} (Table 5).

Table 5. Security level provided by BN curves corresponding to t_{384} and t_{382}.

Curve parameter	Pollard rho	Cheon	G_1, G_2 security level	G_T security level	Security level
t_{384}	192-bit	26-bit	166-bit	$(130 - \delta)$-bit	$(130 - \delta)$-bit
t_{382}	191-bit	51-bit	140-bit	$(129 - \delta)$-bit	$(129 - \delta)$-bit

7 Constructing SM9 System Parameters with the 384-Bit BN Curve

When updating SM9 to a higher security level, two curves with different length are available—one is the 384-bit BN curve corresponding to t_{384}, another is the 382-bit BN curve corresponding to t_{382}. The 382-bit BN curve corresponding to t_{382} shows better R-ate pairing computation efficiency by taking advantages of RNS and lazy reduction in the context of sacrificing 1-bit security level. The issue of which one should be adopted when updating SM9 needs further discussion. We prefer to select the 384-bit one, here are our general opinions. As a specialized standard, it is more appropriate for SM9 to choose system parameters with the length of the multiple of word length. Furthermore, R-ate pairing computation is fast enough to achieve good performance when implementing SM9 with the 384-bit BN curve on software level. In addition to that, RNS and lazy reduction can also apply to the 384-bit BN curve by employing an extra word or by utilizing word length longer than the standard (for example, 36-bit) when implementing SM9 on hardware level, narrowing the efficiency gap to the 382-bit curve.

We choose the BN curve corresponding to t_{384} to construct SM9 system parameters, detailed definitions are contained in **Appendix A**.

8 Conclusion

In this paper, we analyze the conditions that the secure curves in SM9 system parameters need to meet, search 384-bit and 380–382-bit BN curves that satisfy all the conditions and study state-of-the-art algorithms to compute R-ate pairing. Then we select two BN curves, corresponding to curve parameters t_{384} and t_{382} in Eq. (5), to analyze their R-ate pairing computation complexity and security level. Those two BN curves show best computation efficiency at the length of 384-bit and 382-bit respectively among security curves. Finally, we construct SM9 parameters with the 384-bit BN curve corresponding to t_{384}, finishing the core work of updating SM9. While the original 256-bit system parameters presented in SM9-Part5 provide around 100-bit security level, new system parameters proposed by this paper provide around 118-bit security level. Our methods are also suitable for constructing and analyzing BN curves at other binary length for SM9.

Acknowledgment. We'd like to thank Ning Ma, Baofeng Wu and Yalan Ma for discussions and proofreading. We also thank the anonymous reviewers for their helpful comments. This work is supported by the National Defense Science and Technology Innovation Foundation (No. Y7H0041102).

A   Definitions of 384-bit SM9 System Parameters

We choose the BN curve with

$$t = -2^{95} + 2^{93} - 2^{91} - 2^{67} - 2^{65} + 2,$$

to construct 384-bit SM9 system, in this case

$$n + 1 = 2 \cdot 5 \cdot 7 \cdot 11 \cdot 131 \cdot 42992652371 \cdot 28839188139379$$
$$46545034377697 \cdot 431117439410068410343361991367 \cdot d_1,$$

where d_1 is a 144-bit prime number,

$$n - 1 = 2^2 \cdot 3 \cdot 61 \cdot 547271 \cdot 29406309859180669069321 \cdot$$
$$9383295298741208862603129 1 \cdot d_2,$$

where d_2 is a 195-bit prime number.

Parameters are represented in hexadecimal. We use column vector to express element in extension field, with higher dimension above and lower dimension below. The tower extension is the same as Subsect. 5.1.

Elliptic Curve Equation: $y^2 = x^3 + b$.
Parameter of Curve t: -68000009FFFFFFFFFFFFFFFE
Trace $tr(t) = 6t^2 + 1$:

FD800030C0000257FFFFFFF63FFFFF100000000000000019

Characteristic of Ground Field $q(t) = 36t^4 + 36t^3 + 24t^2 + 6t + 1$:

FB0640608C400DECD800E46E46DD77FBD1FF65C07FFB0F16
3400230A0001AF3FFFFFFD530FFFBE2400000000000003CD

Equation Parameter $b : 02$
Order of BN Curve $E(\mathbb{F}_q)$ $n(t) = 36t^4 + 36t^3 + 18t^2 + 6t + 1$:

```
FB0640608C400DECD800E46E46DD77FBD1FF65C07FFB0F15
368022D94001ACE7FFFFFD5CCFFFBF1400000000000003B5
```

Cofactor cf : 1
Embedding Degree k : 12
Twisted Curve $(E'/\mathbb{F}_{q^2} : y^2 = x^3 + b/\beta)$ Parameter $\beta : \sqrt{-2}$
Curve ID cid : 0x12
Generator of Group G_1 $P_1 = (x_{P_1}, y_{P_1})$:
Coordinate x_{P_1} :

```
5DE44C2E23720EBADC3046A8579979ACCF7C98875AE0EE84
76408737A19B77F54C6DC206EF3D4466B71500FEE1E4E456
```

Coordinate y_{P_1} :

```
6AD86724D049835A067B8AC1AD42EF44FCBAD8FF9CA0EACC
2FCABB12B666492A69BAE4F0E6A87C650FBEAE0C0B579BF7
```

Generator of Group G_2 $P_2 = (x_{P_2}, y_{P_2})$:
Coordinate x_{P_2} :

```
(B7CCB40627A621E2B9989403EA065CE58442FC3B14845D1A
 370A8CB90980D3A6F379173E5E73249BE25AE7EDD15B39DB,
 6CB21309922169AE2BD22EC4D5FC10FEB7470CDA26750225
 57CDA6F9D611A0257C3E2867D0342D75C46F22BCB0856010)
```

Coordinate y_{P_2} :

```
(3F8F3F72E49333C779890EDE7B9EADC4DCCF21D516A65CAD
 AAAE1209906C9D43B5E8DC93D11435A3C1C3A161A3A386D1,
 F4AB6C1084256BCF6C5CFBD13393F2859F83221CA28F8F9
 4004089F28C607D4B7B09172BB9625589035B90E1F0BDB13)
```

Example for R-ate Pairing Computation,
Computing element in G_T $g = e(P_1, P_2)$:

```
(7E1ACC6B5FE0ACD125BDA145891B2B2A8AAB29A307442AC1
 630B2FFC2120441ABBA17DDC90EC63A901095F1F1287D9BD,
 49565100D9EF20B734E8863D312F70BED296F243DA1004FB
 9BF3918B55DC0088954BABDD13A9ECEB574FB3B197B81B0E,
 D5D15ECF0A2ED474AA71979EB7FCF37EDE3EC9FEEE162197
 AECF428BBACC708FAC790B5A2297AEE0F9463623AF578247,
 1E73503EC80E80F69A439D8035D494A978DC589A4A86D969
 E0E34BA0B154659A4F060A454BB5FE9E236900F467E00D3F,
 D7C08D9EA24D7001C9EFD9B15B37B435328A65BC2B42C5F3
 3E37176BB6492176E845226676E6C51AF461B9249248AC0D,
 C0EB0A339CF12C0797FFFE43A04089CFD07B64DA9453D4B4
 E4BE9EADAC5B00B69C88745CFF5C2279A4C0EE58B9F9E694,
```

53FDD05837CEC5FB2DEB7E07D922F37E932D44D7B3ECE754
0A131EBA0A2B6353107C39F18311EF0AACC069A97D4BCBAB ,
6625857CF616CE14187D3D60B6222CE5784C2C962E166CE4
B81BED44403371ED92EDCE13772EA9595CE18DE1D20C23FF ,
 D2FF77AC1C4B0F4E97DE64986F80C4C19DBBBD3A2476561
773A522634E5A829260D8CF61FA6C85FF23742307710BD04 ,
993C7C074833ADC865D7F9240032148062E59BADB267D16A
3A6BC5B861B80608CB32EAF0F9B83908358A6983CB0A20E2 ,
EA2CA95D06C5DC9253842FC913F2FFD63CD7EFF5413181A6
B5283799CDCA461CD56192A13AA3D8BF2D31366490B99796 ,
4F6819DF53B329E0A4897EB5D11D2EC302492E7A4B55F395
14AF0C0A3CBE4B8103BF59C137999AB5AB555B1C69FF7985)

References

1. GM/T 0044.1-2016 Identity-based cryptographic algorithms SM9-Part 1: General
2. GM/T 0044.2-2016 Identity-based cryptographic algorithms SM9-Part 2: Digital signature algorithm
3. GM/T 0044.3-2016 Identity-based cryptographic algorithms SM9-Part 3: Key exchange protocol
4. GM/T 0044.4-2016 Identity-based cryptographic algorithms SM9-Part 4: Key encapsulation mechanism and public key encryption algorithm
5. GM/T 0044.5-2016 Identity-based cryptographic algorithms SM9-Part 5: Parameter definition
6. Barbulescu, R., Duquesne, S.: Updating key size estimations for pairings. J. Cryptol. **1**, 1–39 (2017)
7. Barbulescu, R., Gaudry, P., Kleinjung, T.: The tower number field sieve. In: Iwata, T., Cheon, J.H. (eds.) ASIACRYPT 2015. LNCS, vol. 9453, pp. 31–55. Springer, Heidelberg (2015). https://doi.org/10.1007/978-3-662-48800-3_2
8. Barreto, P.S.L.M., Costello, C., Misoczki, R., Naehrig, M., Pereira, G.C.C.F., Zanon, G.: Subgroup security in pairing-based cryptography. In: Lauter, K., Rodríguez-Henríquez, F. (eds.) LATINCRYPT 2015. LNCS, vol. 9230, pp. 245–265. Springer, Cham (2015). https://doi.org/10.1007/978-3-319-22174-8_14
9. Barreto, P.S.L.M., Naehrig, M.: Pairing-friendly elliptic curves of prime order. In: Preneel, B., Tavares, S. (eds.) SAC 2005. LNCS, vol. 3897, pp. 319–331. Springer, Heidelberg (2006). https://doi.org/10.1007/11693383_22
10. Barrett, P.: Implementing the Rivest Shamir and Adleman public key encryption algorithm on a standard digital signal processor. In: Odlyzko, A.M. (ed.) CRYPTO 1986. LNCS, vol. 263, pp. 311–323. Springer, Heidelberg (1987). https://doi.org/10.1007/3-540-47721-7_24
11. Cheon, J.H.: Security analysis of the strong Diffie-Hellman problem. In: Vaudenay, S. (ed.) EUROCRYPT 2006. LNCS, vol. 4004, pp. 1–11. Springer, Heidelberg (2006). https://doi.org/10.1007/11761679_1
12. Cheon, J.H.: Discrete logarithm problems with auxiliary inputs. J. Cryptol. **23**(3), 457–476 (2009)
13. Duquesne, S., Mrabet, N.E., Haloui, S., Rondepierre, F.: Choosing and generating parameters for pairing implementation on bn curves. Appl. Algebra Eng. Commun. Comput. **1**, 1–35 (2017)

14. Freeman, D., Scott, M., Teske, E.: A taxonomy of pairing-friendly elliptic curves. J. Cryptol. **23**(2), 224–280 (2010)
15. Fuentes-Castañeda, L., Knapp, E., Rodríguez-Henríquez, F.: Faster hashing to $\mathbb{G}_2$. In: Miri, A., Vaudenay, S. (eds.) SAC 2011. LNCS, vol. 7118, pp. 412–430. Springer, Heidelberg (2012). https://doi.org/10.1007/978-3-642-28496-0_25
16. Granger, R., Scott, M.: Faster squaring in the cyclotomic subgroup of sixth degree extensions. In: Nguyen, P.Q., Pointcheval, D. (eds.) PKC 2010. LNCS, vol. 6056, pp. 209–223. Springer, Heidelberg (2010). https://doi.org/10.1007/978-3-642-13013-7_13
17. Karabina, K.: Squaring in cyclotomic subgroups. Math. Comput. **82**(281), 542 (2013)
18. Kim, T., Barbulescu, R.: Extended tower number field sieve: a new complexity for the medium prime case. In: Robshaw, M., Katz, J. (eds.) CRYPTO 2016. LNCS, vol. 9814, pp. 543–571. Springer, Heidelberg (2016). https://doi.org/10.1007/978-3-662-53018-4_20
19. Knuth, D.E.: The Art of Computer Programming, Volume 2: Seminumerical Algorithms, 3rd edn. Addison-Wesley Longman Publishing Co., Inc., Boston (1997)
20. Menezes, A., Sarkar, P., Singh, S.: Challenges with assessing the impact of NFS advances on the security of pairing-based cryptography. In: Phan, R.C.-W., Yung, M. (eds.) Mycrypt 2016. LNCS, vol. 10311, pp. 83–108. Springer, Cham (2017). https://doi.org/10.1007/978-3-319-61273-7_5
21. Montgomery, P.L.: Modular multiplication without trial division. Math. Comput. **44**(170), 519–521 (1985)
22. Montgomery, P.L.: Speeding the pollard and elliptic curve methods of factorization. Math. Comput. **48**(177), 243–264 (1987)
23. Mrabet, N.E., Joye, M.: Guide to Pairing Based Cryptography. Taylor and Francis Group, LLC (2017)
24. Naehrig, M.: Constructive and computational aspects of cryptographic pairings. Dissertation for the Doctoral Degree. Duitsland, Technische Universiteit Eindhoven (2009)
25. Pollard, J.M.: Monte Carlo methods for index computation (mod p). Math. Comput. **32**(143), 918–924 (1978)
26. Scott, M.: Implementing cryptographic pairings. In: Proceedings of the First International Conference on Pairing-Based Cryptography, Pairing 2007, pp. 177–196. Springer, Heidelberg (2007)
27. Scott, M., Benger, N., Charlemagne, M., Dominguez Perez, L.J., Kachisa, E.J.: On the final exponentiation for calculating pairings on ordinary elliptic curves. In: Shacham, H., Waters, B. (eds.) Pairing 2009. LNCS, vol. 5671, pp. 78–88. Springer, Heidelberg (2009). https://doi.org/10.1007/978-3-642-03298-1_6
28. Scott, M., Guillevic, A.: A new family of pairing-friendly elliptic curves. Cryptology ePrint Archive, Report 2018/193 (2018). https://eprint.iacr.org/2018/193

Distribution Properties of Binary Sequences Derived from Primitive Sequences Modulo Square-free Odd Integers

Qun-Xiong Zheng[1,2,3]($\boxtimes$), Dongdai Lin[1], and Wen-Feng Qi[2,3]

[1] State Key Laboratory of Information Security, Institute of Information Engineering, Chinese Academy of Sciences, Beijing 100093, China
qunxiong_zheng@163.com, ddlin@iie.ac.cn
[2] State Key Laboratory of Cryptology, P.O. Box 5159, Beijing 100878, China
wenfeng.qi@263.net
[3] National Digital Switching System Engineering and Technological Research Center, Zhengzhou 450001, China

Abstract. Recently, a class of nonlinear sequences, modular reductions of primitive sequences over integer residue rings, was proposed and has attracted much attention. In particular, modulo 2 reductions of primitive sequences over $\mathbf{Z}/(2^{31}-1)$ were used in the ZUC algorithm. In this paper, we study the distribution properties of modulo 2 reductions of primitive sequences over $\mathbf{Z}/(M)$, where M is a square-free odd integer. Let $\underline{a}$ be a primitive sequence of order n over $\mathbf{Z}/(M)$ with period T and $[\underline{a}]_{\mathrm{mod}\,2}$ the modulo 2 reduction of $\underline{a}$. With the estimate of exponential sums over $\mathbf{Z}/(M)$, the proportion f_s of occurrences of s within a segment of $[\underline{a}]_{\mathrm{mod}\,2}$ of length μT is estimated, where $s \in \{0,1\}$ and $0 < \mu \leq 1$. Based on this estimate, it is further shown that for given M and μ, f_s tends to $\frac{M+1-2s}{2M}$ as $n \to \infty$. This result implies that there exists a small imbalance between 0 and 1 in $[\underline{a}]_{\mathrm{mod}\,2}$, which should be taken into full consideration in the design of stream ciphers based on $[\underline{a}]_{\mathrm{mod}\,2}$.

Keywords: Integer residue ring · Primitive sequence ·
Modular reduction · 0, 1 distribution · ZUC algorithm

1 Introduction

For an integer $m \geq 2$, let $\mathbf{Z}/(m)$ denote the integer residue ring modulo m. The set $\{0, 1, \ldots, m-1\}$ is always chosen as the complete set of representatives for

This work was supported by NSF of China (Nos. 61872383, 61402524, 61872359 and 61602510). The work of Qun-Xiong Zheng was also supported by Young Elite Scientists Sponsorship Program by CAST (2016QNRC001) and by National Postdoctoral Program for Innovative Talents (BX201600188) and by China Postdoctoral Science Foundation funded project (2017M611035).

© Springer Nature Switzerland AG 2019
F. Guo et al. (Eds.): Inscrypt 2018, LNCS 11449, pp. 568–585, 2019.
https://doi.org/10.1007/978-3-030-14234-6_30

the elements of the ring $\mathbf{Z}/(m)$. Thus a sequence $\underline{a}$ over $\mathbf{Z}/(m)$ is usually seen as an integer sequence over $\{0, 1, \ldots, m-1\}$. Moreover, for an integer a and a positive integer $b \geq 2$, let us denote the least nonnegative residue of a modulo b by $[a]_{\mathrm{mod}\,b}$, and similarly, for a sequence $\underline{a} = (a(t))_{t \geq 0}$ over $\mathbf{Z}/(m)$, denote $[\underline{a}]_{\mathrm{mod}\,b} = ([a(t)]_{\mathrm{mod}\,b})_{t \geq 0}$.

Let p be a prime number and e a positive integer. During the past two decades, the maximal period linear recurring sequences over $\mathbf{Z}/(p^e)$, called primitive sequences over $\mathbf{Z}/(p^e)$, have been paid much attention. An enormous amount of effort is directed toward the study of finding useful mappings to derive good pseudorandom sequences from primitive sequences over $\mathbf{Z}/(p^e)$, which are called compression mappings in literature, and proving that they are injective. Generally there are two kinds of compression mappings: one is based on e-variable functions over $\mathbf{Z}/(p)$ [10, 15–17, 20, 21]; the other is based on the modular arithmetic [13, 22]. Besides, the pseudorandom properties of these compression sequences are also extensively studied, such as periodicity [7, 13], linear complexity [3, 6, 15] and distribution properties [2, 8, 12, 23].

Recently research interests on primitive sequences over $\mathbf{Z}/(p^e)$ are further extended to primitive sequences over $\mathbf{Z}/(M)$ [4, 9, 24–27], where M is a square-free odd integer. One of important reasons for this is that the period of a primitive sequence $\underline{a}$ of order n over $\mathbf{Z}/(p^e)$ is undesirable if $e \geq 2$. Recall that the period $per(\underline{a})$ of a primitive sequence $\underline{a}$ of order n over $\mathbf{Z}/(p^e)$ is equal to $p^{e-1} \cdot (p^n - 1) \approx p^{e+n-1}$ [18]. It can be seen that for a fixed prime power p^e with $e \geq 2$, the period $per(\underline{a})$ increases slowly and far less than $p^{e \cdot n}$ as n increases. Therefore, to meet the requirement of long period in practical applications, n should be chosen large enough, which will be high resource consumption in hardware and software implementation. For example, to generate a sequence with period not less than 2^{64} over $\mathbf{Z}/(2^8)$, $\mathbf{Z}/(2^{16})$ and $\mathbf{Z}/(2^{32})$, the number of bit-registers required must be larger than 456, 784 and 1056, respectively. However for many choices of M, primitive sequences over $\mathbf{Z}/(M)$ have no such periodic weakness. For cryptographic applications, the moduli of the form $2^e - 1$ have attracted much attention since the operation "$\mathrm{mod}\,2^e - 1$" can be efficiently implemented both in hardware and software, and this offers new possibilities for advancement in the solution of applying linear recurring sequences over integer residue rings. For instance, primitive sequences over $\mathbf{Z}/(2^{31} - 1)$ are used to design the ZUC algorithm, a stream cipher that is the core of the standardised 3GPP confidentiality algorithm 128-EEA3 and the 3GPP integrity algorithm 128-EIA3, see [28].

By applying the operation $\mathrm{mod}\,2$ to primitive sequences over $\mathbf{Z}/(M)$, one can easily obtain a class of binary sequences, called modulo 2 reductions of primitive sequences over $\mathbf{Z}/(M)$. It is thought that the operation $\mathrm{mod}\,2$ destroys the original linear recurrence relation of primitive sequences over $\mathbf{Z}/(M)$ and the obtained binary sequences should have many desirable cryptographic properties if the modulus M and the order n are carefully chosen. One of the most interesting properties is the so-called "modulo 2 distinctness". Some progress has been made on the modulo 2 distinctness, see, for example, [9, 26]. From the viewpoint of cryptographic applications, it is naturally interested in the pseudorandom properties of modulo 2 reductions of primitive sequences over $\mathbf{Z}/(M)$. However, so far few result was obtained. In [25], to study the modulo 2 distinctness of primitive sequences over $\mathbf{Z}/(M)$, two distribution properties of primitive sequences over $\mathbf{Z}/(M)$ are investigated. One is to determine whether there is an integer $t \geq 0$ such that $a(t) = s$ for a given element $s \in \mathbf{Z}/(M)$ and a given primitive sequence $\underline{a}$ of order n over $\mathbf{Z}/(M)$. The other is to determine whether there is an integer $t \geq 0$ such that $a(t)$ is an even number for a given primitive sequence $\underline{a}$ of order 1 over $\mathbf{Z}/(M)$. In [9], Hu and Wang studied whether there is an integer $t \geq 0$ such that $a(t) = a$ and $b(t) = b$, for two given elements $a, b \in \mathbf{Z}/(M)$ and two given primitive sequences $\underline{a}, \underline{b}$ generated by a same primitive polynomial over $\mathbf{Z}/(M)$.

In this paper, we study the distribution properties of the binary sequence $[\underline{a}]_{\bmod 2}$, where $\underline{a}$ is a primitive sequence of order n over $\mathbf{Z}/(M)$ with period T. With the estimate of exponential sums over $\mathbf{Z}/(M)$, the proportion f_s of occurrences of s within a segment of $[\underline{a}]_{\bmod 2}$ of length μT is estimated, where $s \in \{0, 1\}$ and $0 < \mu \leq 1$. Based on this estimate, it is further shown that for given M and μ, f_s tends to $(M + 1 - 2s)/2M$ as $n \to \infty$. Generally speaking, if n is not too small (for example, $n \geq 3$ for $M = 2^{32} - 1$), then the value of f_s is very close to that of $(M + 1 - 2s)/2M$. This implies that there always exists a small imbalance (about $1/M$) between 0 and 1 in $[\underline{a}]_{\bmod 2}$. In order to provide a good resistance against the distinguishing attacks, such imbalance should be taken into full consideration in the design of stream ciphers based on $[\underline{a}]_{\bmod 2}$. Fortunately, by introducing a moderate amount of exclusive or operations, the imbalance of 0, 1 will be reduced to a small enough extent.

The rest of this paper is organized as follows. Section 2 presents some necessary preliminaries. Section 3 gives the main results of this paper. Finally, conclusions are drawn in Sect. 4.

2   Preliminaries

2.1   Primitive Polynomials and Primitive Sequences over Integer Residue Rings

Let m be an integer greater than 1. If a sequence $\underline{a} = (a(t))_{t \geq 0}$ over $\mathbf{Z}/(m)$ satisfies

$$a(t) = [c_{n-1}a(t-1) + \cdots + c_1 a(t-n+1) + c_0 a(t-n)]_{\bmod m} \qquad (1)$$

for all integers $t \geq n$, where n is a positive integer and $c_0, c_1, \ldots, c_{n-1} \in \mathbf{Z}/(m)$ are constant coefficients, then $\underline{a}$ is called a *linear recurring sequence* of order n over $\mathbf{Z}/(m)$ generated by $f(x) = x^n - c_{n-1}x^{n-1} - \cdots - c_0$ (or $\underline{a}$ is a sequence of order n over $\mathbf{Z}/(m)$ in short). For convenience, the set of sequences generated by $f(x)$ over $\mathbf{Z}/(m)$ is generally denoted by $G(f(x), m)$. Particular interests for cryptography are the maximal period linear recurring sequences also called primitive sequences over $\mathbf{Z}/(m)$, which are generated by primitive polynomials over $\mathbf{Z}/(m)$. Next we introduce the definitions of primitive polynomials and primitive sequences over $\mathbf{Z}/(m)$.

Let $f(x)$ be a monic polynomial of degree n over $\mathbf{Z}/(m)$. If $\gcd(f(0), m) = 1$, then there exists a positive integer T such that $x^T - 1$ is divisible by $f(x)$ in $\mathbf{Z}/(m)[x]$. The minimum of such T is called the period of $f(x)$ over $\mathbf{Z}/(m)$ and denoted by $per(f(x), m)$. For the case that m is a prime power, say $m = p^e$, it is known that $per(f(x), p^e) \leq p^{e-1}(p^n - 1)$, see [18]. If $per(f(x), p^e) = p^{e-1}(p^n - 1)$, then $f(x)$ is called a *primitive polynomial* of degree n over $\mathbf{Z}/(p^e)$. A sequence $\underline{a}$ over $\mathbf{Z}/(p^e)$ is called a *primitive sequence* of order n if $\underline{a}$ is generated by a primitive polynomial of degree n over $\mathbf{Z}/(p^e)$ and $[\underline{a}]_{\bmod p}$ is not an all-zero sequence. A primitive sequence $\underline{a}$ of order n over $\mathbf{Z}/(p^e)$ is (strictly) periodic and the period $per(\underline{a})$ is equal to $p^{e-1}(p^n - 1)$, see [18]. For the case of a general integer m, assume $m = p_1^{e_1} p_2^{e_2} \cdots p_r^{e_r}$ is the canonical factorization of m. A monic polynomial $f(x)$ of degree n over $\mathbf{Z}/(m)$ is called a *primitive polynomial* if for every $k \in \{1, 2, \ldots, r\}$, $f(x)$ is a primitive polynomial of degree n over $\mathbf{Z}/(p_k^{e_k})$. A sequence $\underline{a}$ over $\mathbf{Z}/(m)$ is called a *primitive sequence* of order n if $\underline{a}$ is generated by a primitive polynomial of degree n over $\mathbf{Z}/(m)$ and $[\underline{a}]_{\bmod p_k}$ is not an all-zero sequence for every $k \in \{1, 2, \ldots, r\}$, that is, $[\underline{a}]_{\bmod p_k^{e_k}}$ is a primitive sequence of order n over $\mathbf{Z}/(p_k^{e_k})$. It can be seen that the period of a primitive polynomial of degree n over $\mathbf{Z}/(m)$ and that of a primitive sequence of order n over $\mathbf{Z}/(m)$ are both equal to

$$\mathrm{lcm}\left(p_1^{e_1-1}(p_1^n - 1), p_2^{e_2-1}(p_2^n - 1), \ldots, p_r^{e_r-1}(p_r^n - 1)\right).$$

For convenience, the set of primitive sequences generated by a primitive polynomial $f(x)$ over $\mathbf{Z}/(m)$ is generally denoted by $G'(f(x), m)$.

2.2 Exponential Sums over Integer Residue Rings

Let m be a positive integer greater than 1, and let $e_m(\cdot)$ be the canonical additive character over $\mathbf{Z}/(m)$ given by $e_m(a) = e^{2\pi i a/m}$, where a is an integer. For an integer c, it is well-known that

$$\sum_{a=0}^{m-1} e_m(ca) = \begin{cases} m, & \text{if } m \mid c; \\ 0, & \text{otherwise.} \end{cases}$$

The following Lemma 1 is cited from [5, Theorem 1].

Lemma 1. *([5, Theorem 1]) Let $D \geq 1$, $m \geq 2$ and $g = \gcd(m, D)$. Then we have*

$$\sum_{a=1}^{m-1} \left| \frac{\sin \pi a D/m}{\sin \pi a/m} \right| < \frac{4}{\pi^2} m \ln m + 0.38m + 0.608 + 0.116 \frac{g^2}{m},$$

where $\ln(m)$ is the natural logarithm of m.

The following Lemma 2 is an improvement of a well-known result of Korobov [14, Theorem 13].

Lemma 2. *Let $\underline{a}$ be a primitive sequence of order n over $\mathbf{Z}/(m)$ with period T. Then for any integer h we have*

$$\left| \sum_{t=0}^{T-1} e_m\left(a\left(t\right)\right) e_T\left(ht\right) \right| \leq m^{\frac{n}{2}}. \tag{2}$$

In particular,

$$\left| \sum_{t=0}^{T-1} e_m\left(a\left(t\right)\right) \right| \leq m^{\frac{n}{2}}.$$

Moreover, we have

$$\left| \sum_{t=k}^{k+L-1} e_m\left(a\left(t\right)\right) \right| \leq m^{\frac{n}{2}} \left(\frac{4 \ln T}{\pi^2} + 0.409 + \frac{L+1}{T} \right) \tag{3}$$

for any integer $k \geq 0$ and $0 < L < T$.

Proof. Since the inequality (2) has been proved in [14, Theorem 13], we only prove the inequality (3). We start from the identity

$$\sum_{t=k}^{k+L-1} e_m\left(a\left(t\right)\right) = \sum_{t=k}^{k+T-1} e_m\left(a\left(t\right)\right) \sum_{j=0}^{L-1} \frac{1}{T} \sum_{h=0}^{T-1} e_T\left(h\left(t-k-j\right)\right) \text{ for } k \geq 0 \text{ and } 0 < L < T,$$

which is valid since the sum over j is 1 for $k \leq t \leq k + L - 1$ and 0 for $k + L \leq t \leq k + T - 1$. Rearranging terms, we get

$$\sum_{t=k}^{k+L-1} e_m\left(a\left(t\right)\right) = \frac{1}{T} \sum_{h=0}^{T-1} \left(\sum_{t=k}^{k+T-1} e_m\left(a\left(t\right)\right) e_T\left(ht\right) \right) \left(\sum_{j=0}^{L-1} e_T\left(-h\left(k+j\right)\right) \right),$$

and so we obtain

$$\left| \sum_{t=k}^{k+L-1} e_m\left(a\left(t\right)\right) \right| \leq \frac{1}{T} \sum_{h=0}^{T-1} \left| \sum_{t=k}^{k+T-1} e_m\left(a\left(t\right)\right) e_T\left(ht\right) \right| \left| \sum_{j=0}^{L-1} e_T\left(-h\left(k+j\right)\right) \right|$$

$$= \frac{1}{T} \sum_{h=0}^{T-1} \left| \sum_{t=0}^{T-1} e_m\left(a\left(t\right)\right) e_T\left(ht\right) \right| \left| \sum_{j=0}^{L-1} e_T\left(-hj\right) \right|.$$

Then by the inequality (2) we get

$$\left| \sum_{t=k}^{k+L-1} e_m\left(a\left(t\right)\right) \right| \leq \frac{m^{\frac{n}{2}}}{T} \sum_{h=0}^{T-1} \left| \sum_{j=0}^{L-1} e_T\left(-hj\right) \right|$$

$$= \frac{m^{\frac{n}{2}}}{T} \sum_{h=0}^{T-1} \left| \sum_{j=0}^{L-1} e_T\left(hj\right) \right|$$

$$\leq \frac{m^{\frac{n}{2}}}{T} \sum_{h=1}^{T-1} \left| \sum_{j=0}^{L-1} e_T\left(hj\right) \right| + \frac{L \cdot m^{\frac{n}{2}}}{T}. \tag{4}$$

We note that

$$\sum_{h=1}^{T-1}\left|\sum_{j=0}^{L-1} e_T\,(hj)\right| = \sum_{h=1}^{T-1}\left|\frac{e_T(hL) - 1}{e_T(h) - 1}\right|$$

$$= \sum_{h=1}^{T-1}\left|\frac{\cos(2\pi hL/T) + i\sin(2\pi hL/T) - 1}{\cos(2\pi h/T) + i\sin(2\pi h/T) - 1}\right|$$

$$= \sum_{h=1}^{T-1}\left|\frac{-2\sin^2(\pi hL/T) + 2i\sin(\pi hL/T)\cos(\pi hL/T)}{-2\sin^2(\pi h/T) + 2i\sin(\pi h/T)\cos(\pi h/T)}\right|$$

$$= \sum_{h=1}^{T-1}\left|\frac{\sin(\pi hL/T)}{\sin(\pi h/T)}\right|,$$

and so an application of Lemma 3 yields

$$\sum_{h=1}^{T-1}\left|\sum_{j=0}^{L-1} e_T\,(hj)\right| < \frac{4}{\pi^2}T\ln T + 0.38T + 0.608 + 0.116\frac{g^2}{T}$$

$$< \frac{4}{\pi^2}T\ln T + 0.409T + 1, \tag{5}$$

where the last inequality follows from the fact that $g = \gcd(L,T) < T/2$. Combining the inequalities (4) and (5), we get the desired result.

3   Main Results

Throughout the rest of this paper, we always assume that $M > 1$ is a given square-free odd integer and $M = p_1 p_2 \cdots p_r$ is the canonical factorization of M. Let $d > 1$ be a divisor of M. Suppose $d = p_{i_1} \cdots p_{i_k}$ with $1 \leq i_1 < \cdots < i_k \leq r$. Let us denote by $\lambda_n(d)$ the period of primitive sequences of order n over $\mathbf{Z}/(d)$, that is,

$$\lambda_n(d) = \mathrm{lcm}(p_{i_1}^n - 1, \ldots, p_{i_k}^n - 1).$$

The main results of this paper are stated in the following Theorems 1 and 2.

Theorem 1. *Let $\underline{a}$ be a primitive sequence of order n over $\mathbf{Z}/(M)$ with period $T = \lambda_n(M)$, and let $\underline{b} = [\underline{a}]_{\mathrm{mod}\,2}$. For $s \in \{0,1\}$, denote by $N\left(\underline{b}^T, s\right)$ the number of t, $0 \leq t \leq T - 1$, with $b(t) = s$. Then we have*

$$\frac{N\left(\underline{b}^T, s\right)}{T} - \frac{1}{2} + (-1)^s \cdot \frac{M^{n-1} - 1}{2M^n - 2} \tag{6}$$

if M is an odd prime number; and

$$\left|\frac{N\left(\underline{b}^T, s\right)}{T} - \frac{M + 1 - 2s}{2M}\right| < \frac{1}{M}\sum_{\substack{d \mid M \\ d > 1}}\frac{d^{n/2}}{\lambda_n\,(d)} \cdot \left(\frac{d\ln d}{\pi} + 0.538d\right) \tag{7}$$

if M has at least two different prime divisors.

Theorem 2. *Let $\underline{a}$ be a primitive sequence of order n over $\mathbf{Z}/(M)$ with period $T = \lambda_n(M)$. Let $\underline{b} = [\underline{a}]_{\bmod 2}$ and $\underline{b}^L = (b(k), b(k+1), \ldots, b(k+L-1))$ a segment of $\underline{b}$ with length $L = \mu T$, where $0 \leq k \leq T-1$ and $0 < \mu < 1$. For $s \in \{0, 1\}$, denote by $N\left(\underline{b}^L, s\right)$ the number of t, $0 \leq t \leq L-1$, with $b(k+t) = s$. Then we have*

$$\left| \frac{N\left(\underline{b}^L, s\right)}{L} - \frac{M+1-2s}{2M} \right| < \frac{1}{M} \sum_{\substack{d \mid M \\ d > 1}} \frac{d^{\frac{n}{2}}}{\lambda_n(d)} C(d, L),$$

where

$$C(d, L) = \left(\frac{\lambda_n(d)}{L} \left(\frac{4}{\pi^2} \ln \lambda_n(d) + 0.409 \right) + \frac{L+1}{L} \right) \left(\frac{d \ln d}{\pi} + 0.538d \right).$$

The rest of this section is divided into three subsections. Subsects. 3.1 and 3.2 are mainly devoted to the proof of Theorem 1 and the proof of Theorem 2, respectively. Finally, as an example, an application of Theorems 1 and 2 to the modulo 2 reductions of primitive sequences over $\mathbf{Z}/(2^{32} - 1)$ is given in Subsect. 3.3.

3.1   The Proof of Theorem 1

We first collect two well-known results on trigonometric functions in Lemma 3. The first result can be found in [19] and the second result can be found in [11, p. 447].

Lemma 3. *Let $\tan x = \sin x / \cos x$, $\sec x = 1 / \cos x$ and $\csc x = 1 / \sin x$ be the tangent function, the secant function and the cosecant function, respectively. Then we have:*
  (1) *$\int \sec x \, dx = \ln |\sec x + \tan x| + C$, where C is the constant of integration;*
  (2) *$\csc(\pi/m) \leq m/3$ if $m \geq 6$.*

Lemma 4. *For an odd integer $m > 1$, we have*

$$\sum_{h=1}^{m-1} \left| \sec \frac{h\pi}{m} \right| < \frac{2}{\pi} m \ln m + 1.076m.$$

Proof. It can be directly verified that the lemma holds for $m = 3$ or 5. Therefore, we assume that $m \geq 7$. Since it is clear that

$$\sec \frac{h\pi}{m} = -\sec \frac{(m-h) \cdot \pi}{m} > 0 \text{ for } 1 \leq h \leq \frac{m-1}{2},$$

we obtain

$$\sum_{h=1}^{m-1} \left| \sec \frac{h\pi}{m} \right| = 2 \sum_{h=1}^{\frac{m-1}{2}} \sec \frac{h\pi}{m}. \tag{8}$$

Note that the convexity of the function $\sec x$ implies that

$$\int_{u-\frac{\theta}{2}}^{u+\frac{\theta}{2}} \sec x\, dx > \theta \cdot \sec u \text{ for } \frac{\theta}{2} < u < \frac{\pi}{2} - \frac{\theta}{2}.$$

Thus by taking $\theta = \frac{\pi}{m}$ we get

$$\sum_{h=1}^{\frac{m-3}{2}} \sec \frac{h\pi}{m} < \frac{m}{\pi} \sum_{h=1}^{\frac{m-3}{2}} \int_{\frac{h\pi}{m}-\frac{\pi}{2m}}^{\frac{h\pi}{m}+\frac{\pi}{2m}} \sec x\, dx$$

$$= \frac{m}{\pi} \int_{\frac{\pi}{2m}}^{\frac{(m-2)\cdot\pi}{2m}} \sec x\, dx$$

$$< \frac{m}{\pi} \int_{0}^{\frac{(m-2)\cdot\pi}{2m}} \sec x\, dx$$

$$= \frac{m}{\pi} \cdot \ln\left(\sec \frac{(m-2)\cdot\pi}{2m} + \tan \frac{(m-2)\cdot\pi}{2m}\right)$$

$$= \frac{m}{\pi} \cdot \left(\ln\left(\sec \frac{(m-2)\cdot\pi}{2m}\right) + \ln\left(1 + \sin \frac{(m-2)\cdot\pi}{2m}\right)\right)$$

$$< \frac{m}{\pi} \cdot \left(\ln\left(\csc \frac{\pi}{m}\right) + \ln 2\right). \tag{9}$$

By combining (8) and (9), we obtain

$$\sum_{h=1}^{m-1} \left|\sec \frac{h\pi}{m}\right| < \frac{2m}{\pi} \cdot \left(\ln\left(\csc \frac{\pi}{m}\right) + \ln 2\right) + 2 \sec \frac{(m-1)\pi}{2m}$$

$$= \frac{2m}{\pi} \cdot \left(\ln\left(\csc \frac{\pi}{m}\right) + \ln 2\right) + 2 \csc \frac{\pi}{2m}. \tag{10}$$

By applying $\csc(\pi/m) \leq m/3$ to the right-hand side of (10) we get

$$\sum_{h=1}^{m-1} \left|\sec \frac{h\pi}{m}\right| < \frac{2}{\pi} m \ln m + \frac{2m}{\pi} (\ln 2 - \ln 3) + \frac{4}{3} m < \frac{2}{\pi} m \ln m + 1.076m.$$

This completes the proof.

Now we start to prove Theorem 1.

Proof (Proof of Theorem 1). If M is an odd prime number, then (6) immediately follows from the theory of m-sequences over finite fields (see, for example, [11]). Next we will prove the equality (7). Note that

$$\left|\frac{N\left(\underline{b}^T, 0\right)}{T} - \frac{M+1}{2M}\right| = \left|1 - \frac{N\left(\underline{b}^T, 1\right)}{T} - \frac{M+1}{2M}\right| = \left|\frac{N\left(\underline{b}^T, 1\right)}{T} - \frac{M-1}{2M}\right|,$$

and so it suffices to show (7) holds for the case that $s = 0$, that is,

$$\left| \frac{N\left(\underline{b}^T, 0\right)}{T} - \frac{M+1}{2M} \right| < \frac{1}{M} \sum_{\substack{d|M \\ d>1}} \frac{d^{n/2}}{\lambda_n(d)} \cdot \left(\frac{d \ln d}{\pi} + 0.538d \right). \tag{11}$$

Since

$$N\left(\underline{b}^T, 0\right) = \sum_{t=0}^{T-1} \sum_{x=0}^{\frac{M-1}{2}} \left(\frac{1}{M} \sum_{h=0}^{M-1} e_M\left(h\left(a\left(t\right) - 2x\right)\right) \right)$$

$$= \frac{1}{M} \sum_{h=0}^{M-1} \left(\sum_{t=0}^{T-1} e_M\left(ha\left(t\right)\right) \cdot \sum_{x=0}^{\frac{M-1}{2}} e_M\left(-2hx\right) \right)$$

$$= \frac{T \cdot (M+1)}{2M} + \frac{1}{M} \sum_{h=1}^{M-1} \left(\sum_{t=0}^{T-1} e_M\left(ha\left(t\right)\right) \cdot \sum_{x=0}^{\frac{M-1}{2}} e_M\left(-2hx\right) \right),$$

we get

$$\left| \frac{N\left(\underline{b}^T, 0\right)}{T} - \frac{M+1}{2M} \right| \leq \frac{1}{MT} \sum_{h=1}^{M-1} \left| \sum_{t=0}^{T-1} e_M\left(ha\left(t\right)\right) \right| \cdot \left| \sum_{x=0}^{\frac{M-1}{2}} e_M\left(-2hx\right) \right|. \tag{12}$$

We note that

$$\sum_{x=0}^{\frac{M-1}{2}} e_M\left(-2hx\right) = \frac{\left(e^{-\frac{4h\pi i}{M}}\right)^{\frac{M+1}{2}} - 1}{e^{-\frac{4h\pi i}{M}} - 1}$$

$$= \frac{e^{-\frac{2h\pi i}{M}} - 1}{e^{-\frac{4h\pi i}{M}} - 1}$$

$$= \frac{1}{e^{-\frac{2h\pi i}{M}} + 1}$$

$$= \frac{1}{\cos\frac{2h\pi}{M} - i \sin\frac{2h\pi}{M} + 1}$$

$$= \frac{1}{2\cos^2\frac{h\pi}{M} - 2i \sin\frac{h\pi}{M} \cos\frac{h\pi}{M}}$$

$$= \frac{1}{2} \cdot \frac{\sec\frac{h\pi}{M}}{e^{-\frac{h\pi i}{M}}}. \tag{13}$$

Applying (13) to (12) we obtain

$$\left| \frac{N\left(\underline{b}^T,0\right)}{T} - \frac{M+1}{2M} \right| \le \frac{1}{2MT} \sum_{h=1}^{M-1} \left| \sum_{t=0}^{T-1} e_M\left(ha\left(t\right)\right) \right| \cdot \left| \sec\frac{h\pi}{M} \right|$$

$$= \frac{1}{2MT} \sum_{\substack{d|M \\ d>1}} \sum_{\substack{1\le h\le M-1 \\ \gcd(h,M)=M/d}} \left| \sum_{t=0}^{T-1} e_M\left(ha\left(t\right)\right) \right| \cdot \left| \sec\frac{h\pi}{M} \right|$$

$$= \frac{1}{2MT} \sum_{\substack{d|M \\ d>1}} \sum_{\substack{1\le h\le d-1 \\ \gcd(h,d)=1}} \left| \sum_{t=0}^{T-1} e_d\left(ha\left(t\right)\right) \right| \cdot \left| \sec\frac{h\pi}{d} \right|. \quad (14)$$

Note that given a divisor $d > 1$ of M, $[h\underline{a}]_{\bmod d}$ is a primitive sequence over $\mathbf{Z}/(d)$ with period $\lambda_n\left(d\right)$ for every integer h coprime with d, and so it follows from Lemma 2 that

$$\left| \sum_{t=0}^{T-1} e_d\left(ha\left(t\right)\right) \right| = \left| \frac{T}{\lambda_n\left(d\right)} \cdot \sum_{t=0}^{\lambda_n(d)-1} e_d\left(ha\left(t\right)\right) \right| \le \frac{T\cdot d^{n/2}}{\lambda_n\left(d\right)}. \quad (15)$$

Combining (14) and (15) yields

$$\left| \frac{N\left(\underline{b}^T,0\right)}{T} - \frac{M+1}{2M} \right| \le \frac{1}{2MT} \sum_{\substack{d|M \\ d>1}} \sum_{\substack{1\le h\le d-1 \\ \gcd(h,d)=1}} \frac{T\cdot d^{n/2}}{\lambda_n\left(d\right)} \cdot \left| \sec\frac{h\pi}{d} \right|$$

$$= \frac{1}{2M} \sum_{\substack{d|M \\ d>1}} \frac{d^{n/2}}{\lambda_n\left(d\right)} \cdot \sum_{\substack{1\le h\le d-1 \\ \gcd(h,d)=1}} \left| \sec\frac{h\pi}{d} \right|$$

$$\le \frac{1}{2M} \sum_{\substack{d|M \\ d>1}} \frac{d^{n/2}}{\lambda_n\left(d\right)} \cdot \sum_{h=1}^{d-1} \left| \sec\frac{h\pi}{d} \right|, \quad (16)$$

and so (11) follows from (16) and Lemma 4.

Generally speaking, if n is sufficiently large, then the right-hand side of (6) is sufficiently small, and so the value of $N\left(\underline{b}^T,s\right)/T$ is very close to that of $(M+1-2s)/2M$ (for more details, see Table 1). In fact, we can give a more theoretical result on the asymptotic property of $N\left(\underline{b}^T,s\right)/T$ as $n \to \infty$.

Corollary 1. *Let $\underline{a}$ be a primitive sequence of order n over $\mathbf{Z}/(M)$ with period $T = \lambda_n\left(M\right)$, and let $\underline{b} = [\underline{a}]_{\bmod 2}$. Then for $s \in \{0,1\}$ we have*

$$\lim_{n\to\infty} \frac{N\left(\underline{b}^T,s\right)}{T} = \frac{M+1-2s}{2M}.$$

To prove Corollary 1, we first introduce a result of Bugeaud, Corvaja and Zannier [1].

Lemma 5. *([1, Theorem 1]) If $a < b$ are two integers greater than 1 which are multiplicatively independent (that is, the only integer solution (x, y) of the equation $a^x b^y = 1$ is $(x, y) = (0, 0)$), then for any given real number $\varepsilon > 0$, there exists an integer N_ε such that*

$$\gcd(a^n - 1, b^n - 1) < a^{n\varepsilon} \text{ for all integers } n > N_\varepsilon.$$

Remark 1. Note that a and b are multiplicatively independent if $\gcd(a, b) = 1$.

Proof (Proof of Corollary 1). Since Corollary 1 is obvious true for the case that M is an odd prime number, we assume that $M = p_1 p_2 \cdots p_r$ is the canonical factorization of M with $r \geq 2$ and $3 \leq p_1 < p_2 < \cdots < p_r$. Note that the inequality

$$\frac{d \ln d}{\pi} + 0.538 d \leq \frac{M \ln M}{\pi} + 0.538 M$$

holds for any divisor d of M, and so by Theorem 1 we get

$$\left| \frac{N\left(\underline{v}^T, s\right)}{T} - \frac{M + 1 - 2s}{2M} \right| < \left(\frac{M \ln M}{\pi} + 0.538 M \right) \cdot \sum_{\substack{d \mid M \\ d > 1}} \frac{d^{n/2}}{\lambda_n(d)}.$$

Therefore to prove Corollary 1, it suffices to show that

$$\lim_{n \to \infty} \sum_{\substack{d \mid M \\ d > 1}} \frac{d^{n/2}}{\lambda_n(d)} = 0,$$

that is

$$\lim_{n \to \infty} \sum_{k=1}^{r} \sum_{1 \leq i_1 < \cdots < i_k \leq r} \frac{\prod_{j=1}^{k} p_{i_j}^{n/2}}{\operatorname{lcm}\left(p_{i_1}^n - 1, p_{i_2}^n - 1, \ldots, p_{i_k}^n - 1\right)} = 0. \tag{17}$$

Given a real number $\varepsilon > 0$. For any $1 \leq u < v \leq r$, it follows from Lemma 5 and Remark 1 that there exists an integer $N_\varepsilon^{(u,v)}$ such that

$$\gcd(p_u^n - 1, p_v^n - 1) < p_u^{n\varepsilon} \text{ for all integers } n > N_\varepsilon^{(u,v)}.$$

Set

$$N_\varepsilon = \max\left\{ \left\lceil \frac{\ln p_u}{\ln p_1} \cdot N_\varepsilon^{(u,v)} \right\rceil \mid 1 \leq u < v \leq r \right\},$$

where $\lceil a \rceil$ denotes the smallest integer greater than or equal to a. Then it is clear that

$$\gcd(p_u^n - 1, p_v^n - 1) < p_1^{n\varepsilon}, \ 1 \leq u < v \leq r \text{ and } n > N_\varepsilon. \tag{18}$$

Let $2 \leq k \leq r$ and $1 \leq i_1 < \cdots < i_k \leq r$. It follows from (18) that if $n > N_\varepsilon$, then

$$\mathrm{lcm}\left(p_{i_1}^n - 1, p_{i_2}^n - 1, \ldots, p_{i_k}^n - 1\right) \geq \frac{\prod_{j=1}^k (p_{i_j}^n - 1)}{\prod_{1 \leq j < l \leq k} \gcd(p_{i_j}^n - 1, p_{i_l}^n - 1)}$$

$$> p_1^{-k^2 n\varepsilon/2} \cdot \prod_{j=1}^k (p_{i_j}^n - 1)$$

$$\geq p_1^{-r^2 n\varepsilon/2} \cdot \prod_{j=1}^k (p_{i_j}^n - 1).$$

Consequently, we have

$$\frac{\prod_{j=1}^k p_{i_j}^{n/2}}{\mathrm{lcm}\left(p_{i_1}^n - 1, p_{i_2}^n - 1, \ldots, p_{i_k}^n - 1\right)} \leq p_1^{r^2 n\varepsilon/2} \cdot \prod_{j=1}^k \frac{p_{i_j}^{n/2}}{p_{i_j}^n - 1}$$

$$< p_1^{r^2 n\varepsilon/2} \cdot \prod_{j=1}^k p_{i_j}^{1-n/2}$$

$$\leq p_1^{r^2 n\varepsilon/2} \cdot M \cdot \prod_{j=1}^k p_{i_j}^{-n/2}. \qquad (19)$$

Note that $k \geq 2$ and $p_{i_j} \geq p_1$ for $1 \leq j \leq k$, and so (19) yields

$$\frac{\prod_{j=1}^k p_{i_j}^{n/2}}{\mathrm{lcm}\left(p_{i_1}^n - 1, p_{i_2}^n - 1, \ldots, p_{i_k}^n - 1\right)} < p_1^{r^2 n\varepsilon/2} \cdot M \cdot p_1^{-nk/2}$$

$$\leq p_1^{r^2 n\varepsilon/2} \cdot M \cdot p_1^{-n}$$

$$= M \cdot p_1^{-\frac{n}{2} \cdot (2 - r^2 \varepsilon)}.$$

Hence it can be seen that

$$\sum_{k=1}^r \sum_{1 \leq i_1 < \cdots < i_k \leq r} \frac{\prod_{j=1}^k p_{i_j}^{n/2}}{\mathrm{lcm}\left(p_{i_1}^n - 1, p_{i_2}^n - 1, \ldots, p_{i_k}^n - 1\right)}$$

$$= \sum_{i=1}^r \frac{p_i^{n/2}}{p_i^n - 1} + \sum_{k=2}^r \sum_{1 \leq i_1 < \cdots < i_k \leq r} \frac{\prod_{j=1}^k p_{i_j}^{n/2}}{\mathrm{lcm}\left(p_{i_1}^n - 1, p_{i_2}^n - 1, \ldots, p_{i_k}^n - 1\right)}$$

$$< \frac{r}{p_1^{n/2} - 1} + 2^r \cdot M \cdot p_1^{-\frac{n}{2} \cdot (2 - r^2 \varepsilon)}.$$

Then choosing $\varepsilon < r^{-2}$, we get

$$0 \leq \sum_{k=1}^r \sum_{1 \leq i_1 < \cdots < i_k \leq r} \frac{\prod_{j=1}^k p_{i_j}^{n/2}}{\mathrm{lcm}\left(p_{i_1}^n - 1, p_{i_2}^n - 1, \ldots, p_{i_k}^n - 1\right)} < \frac{r}{p_1^{n/2} - 1} + 2^r \cdot M \cdot p_1^{-n/2}. \qquad (20)$$

Since r, M and p_1 are all fixed integers with $p_1 \geq 3$, we get

$$\lim_{n \to \infty} \frac{r}{p_1^{n/2} - 1} + 2^r \cdot M \cdot p_1^{-n/2} = 0,$$

and so (17) follows from (20).

3.2   The Proof of Theorem 2

Proof (Proof of Theorem 2). Since

$$\left| \frac{N\left(\underline{b}^L, 0\right)}{L} - \frac{M+1}{2M} \right| = \left| \frac{N\left(\underline{b}^L, 1\right)}{L} - \frac{M-1}{2M} \right|,$$

it suffices to show that

$$\left| \frac{N\left(\underline{b}^L, 0\right)}{L} - \frac{M+1}{2M} \right| < \frac{1}{M} \sum_{\substack{d|M \\ d>1}} \frac{d^{\frac{n}{2}}}{\lambda_n(d)} C(d, L). \tag{21}$$

First, it is clear that

$$N\left(\underline{b}^L, 0\right) = \sum_{t=k}^{k+L-1} \sum_{x=0}^{\frac{M-1}{2}} \left(\frac{1}{M} \sum_{h=0}^{M-1} e_M\left(h\left(a\left(t\right) - 2x\right)\right) \right)$$

$$= \frac{1}{M} \sum_{h=0}^{M-1} \left(\sum_{t=k}^{k+L-1} e_M\left(ha\left(t\right)\right) \cdot \sum_{x=0}^{\frac{M-1}{2}} e_M\left(-2hx\right) \right)$$

$$= \frac{L \cdot (M+1)}{2M} + \frac{1}{M} \sum_{h=1}^{M-1} \left(\sum_{t=k}^{k+L-1} e_M\left(ha\left(t\right)\right) \cdot \sum_{x=0}^{\frac{M-1}{2}} e_M\left(-2hx\right) \right).$$

Then proceed as in the proof of Theorem 1, we can get

$$\left| \frac{N\left(\underline{b}^T, 0\right)}{L} - \frac{M+1}{2M} \right| \leq \frac{1}{2ML} \sum_{\substack{d|M \\ d>1}} \sum_{\substack{1 \leq h \leq d-1 \\ \gcd(h,d)=1}} \left| \sum_{t=k}^{k+L-1} e_d\left(ha\left(t\right)\right) \right| \cdot \left| \sec\frac{h\pi}{d} \right|. \tag{22}$$

Note that given a divisor $d > 1$ of M, $[h\underline{a}]_{\bmod d}$ is a primitive sequence over $\mathbf{Z}/(d)$ with period $\lambda_n(d)$ for every integer h coprime with d, and so by Lemma 2 we have

$$\left| \sum_{t=k}^{k+L-1} e_d\left(ha\left(t\right)\right) \right| = \left| \sum_{t=k}^{k+[L]_{\bmod \lambda_n(d)}-1} e_d\left(ha\left(t\right)\right) + \left\lfloor \frac{L}{\lambda_n(d)} \right\rfloor \cdot \sum_{t=0}^{\lambda_n(d)-1} e_d\left(ha\left(t\right)\right) \right|$$

$$\leq \left| \sum_{t=k}^{k+[L]_{\bmod \lambda_n(d)}-1} e_d\left(ha\left(t\right)\right) \right| + \left\lfloor \frac{L}{\lambda_n(d)} \right\rfloor \cdot \left| \sum_{t=0}^{\lambda_n(d)-1} e_d\left(ha\left(t\right)\right) \right|$$

$$\leq d^{\frac{n}{2}} \left(\frac{4\ln \lambda_n(d)}{\pi^2} + 0.409 + \frac{[L]_{\bmod \lambda_n(d)}+1}{\lambda_n(d)} \right) + \left\lfloor \frac{L}{\lambda_n(d)} \right\rfloor \cdot d^{\frac{n}{2}}$$

$$= d^{\frac{n}{2}} \left(\frac{4\ln \lambda_n(d)}{\pi^2} + 0.409 + \frac{L+1}{\lambda_n(d)} \right), \tag{23}$$

where $\lfloor a \rfloor$ denotes the largest integer smaller than or equal to a. Combining (22) and (23) we get

$$
\left| \frac{N\left(\underline{b}^T, 0\right)}{L} - \frac{M+1}{2M} \right|
$$

$$
\leq \frac{1}{2M} \sum_{\substack{d|M \\ d>1}} \sum_{\substack{1 \leq h \leq d-1 \\ \gcd(h,d)=1}} \frac{d^{\frac{n}{2}}}{\lambda_n(d)} \left(\frac{\lambda_n(d)}{L} \left(\frac{4}{\pi^2} \ln \lambda_n(d) + 0.409 \right) + \frac{L+1}{L} \right) \cdot \left| \sec \frac{h\pi}{d} \right|
$$

$$
\leq \frac{1}{2M} \sum_{\substack{d|M \\ d>1}} \frac{d^{\frac{n}{2}}}{\lambda_n(d)} \left(\frac{\lambda_n(d)}{L} \left(\frac{4}{\pi^2} \ln \lambda_n(d) + 0.409 \right) + \frac{L+1}{L} \right) \cdot \sum_{h=1}^{d-1} \left| \sec \frac{h\pi}{d} \right|. \quad (24)
$$

and so (21) follows from (24) and Lemma 4.

Similar to Corollary 1, we can give the asymptotic property of $\frac{N(\underline{b}^L, s)}{L}$ as $n \to \infty$.

Corollary 2. *Let* $\underline{a}$ *be a primitive sequence of order* n *over* $\mathbf{Z}/(M)$ *with period* $T = \lambda_n(M)$. *Let* $\underline{b} = [\underline{a}]_{\mod 2}$ *and* $\underline{b}^L = (b(k), b(k+1), \ldots, b(k+L-1))$ *a segment of* $\underline{b}$ *with length* $L = \mu T$, *where* $0 \leq k \leq T-1$ *and* $0 < \mu < 1$. *Then for* $s \in \{0, 1\}$ *we have*

$$
\lim_{n \to \infty} \frac{N\left(\underline{b}^L, s\right)}{L} = \frac{M+1-2s}{2M}.
$$

Proof. Since

$$
\frac{\lambda_n(d)}{L} \left(\frac{4}{\pi^2} \ln \lambda_n(d) + 0.409 \right) + \frac{L+1}{L} < \frac{\lambda_n(M)}{L} \left(\frac{4}{\pi^2} \ln M^n + 0.409 \right) + 2
$$

$$
= \frac{1}{\mu} \left(\frac{4}{\pi^2} n \ln M + 0.409 \right) + 2
$$

$$
< \left(\frac{4 \ln M}{\mu \pi^2} + \frac{3}{\mu} \right) \cdot n
$$

and

$$
\frac{d \ln d}{\pi} + 0.538d \leq \frac{M \ln M}{\pi} + 0.538M
$$

hold for any divisor d of M with $d > 1$, it follows from Theorem 2 that

$$
\left| \frac{N\left(\underline{b}^L, s\right)}{L} - \frac{M+1-2s}{2M} \right| < D_\mu(M) \sum_{\substack{d|M \\ d>1}} \frac{n d^{\frac{n}{2}}}{\lambda_n(d)},
$$

where

$$
D_\mu(M) = \left(\frac{4 \ln M}{\mu \pi^2} + \frac{3}{\mu} \right) \cdot \left(\frac{M \ln M}{\pi} + 0.538M \right)
$$

is a constant only depended on M and μ. Therefore to prove Corollary 2, it suffices to show that

$$\lim_{n\to\infty} \sum_{\substack{d|M\\d>1}} \frac{nd^{\frac{n}{2}}}{\lambda_n(d)} = 0,$$

that is

$$\lim_{n\to\infty} \sum_{k=1}^{r} \sum_{1\leq i_1<\cdots<i_k\leq r} \frac{n\prod_{j=1}^{k} p_{i_j}^{n/2}}{\mathrm{lcm}\left(p_{i_1}^n-1, p_{i_2}^n-1, \ldots, p_{i_k}^n-1\right)} = 0. \tag{25}$$

Proceed as in the proof of Corollary 1 (but substitute $\prod_{j=1}^{k} p_{i_j}^{n/2}$ by $n\prod_{j=1}^{k} p_{i_j}^{n/2}$), finally we can get

$$0 \leq \sum_{k=1}^{r} \sum_{1\leq i_1<\cdots<i_k\leq r} \frac{n\prod_{j=1}^{k} p_{i_j}^{n/2}}{\mathrm{lcm}\left(p_{i_1}^n-1, p_{i_2}^n-1, \ldots, p_{i_k}^n-1\right)} < \frac{rn}{p_1^{n/2}-1} + 2^r M \cdot np_1^{-n/2}. \tag{26}$$

Since r, M and p_1 are all fixed integers with $p_1 \geq 3$, we get

$$\lim_{n\to\infty} \frac{rn}{p_1^{n/2}-1} + 2^r M \cdot np_1^{-n/2} = 0,$$

and so (25) follows from (26).

3.3   An Example: Element Distribution of Modulo 2 Reductions of Primitive Sequences over $\mathbf{Z}/(2^{32}-1)$

Let $\underline{a}$ be a primitive sequence of order n over $\mathbf{Z}/(2^{32}-1)$ with period $T = \lambda_n(2^{32}-1)$. Let $\underline{b} = [\underline{a}]_{\mathrm{mod}\,2}$ and $\underline{b}^L = (b(k), b(k+1), \ldots, b(k+L-1))$ a segment of $\underline{b}$ with length $L = \mu T$, where $0 \leq k < T$ and $0 < \mu \leq 1$. Then it follows from Theorems 1 and 2 that

$$\left| \frac{N\left(\underline{b}^L, s\right)}{L} - \frac{2^{31}-s}{2^{32}-1} \right| < \Lambda_n(\mu), \tag{27}$$

where

$$\Lambda_n(\mu) = \begin{cases} \dfrac{1}{2^{32}-1} \displaystyle\sum_{\substack{d|2^{32}-1\\d>1}} \dfrac{d^{n/2}}{\lambda_n(d)} B(d), & \text{if } \mu = 1; \\[4mm] \dfrac{1}{2^{32}-1} \displaystyle\sum_{\substack{d|2^{32}-1\\d>1}} \dfrac{d^{n/2}}{\lambda_n(d)} C(d, \mu T), & \text{if } 0 < \mu < 1, \end{cases}$$

with

$$B(d) = \frac{d\ln d}{\pi} + 0.538d$$

and

$$C(d, \mu T) = \left(\frac{\lambda_n(d)}{L} \left(\frac{4}{\pi^2}\ln\lambda_n(d) + 0.409 \right) \right) \cdot B(d).$$

The values of $\Lambda_n(\mu)$ are calculated and listed in Table 1 for $1 \le n \le 10$ and $\mu \in \{1, 1/2, 1/4, 1/8\}$. It can be seen from Table 1 that the estimate of (27) is nontrivial if (1) $\mu = 1$ and $n \ge 2$; or (2) $0 < \mu < 1$ and $n \ge 3$. Moreover for any $\mu \in \{1, 1/2, 1/4, 1/8\}$, the value of $\Lambda_n(\mu)$ is very close to 0 if $n \ge 3$, which is consistent with the results of Corollarys 1 and 2.

Table 1. The values of $\Lambda_n(\mu)$ for $1 \le n \le 10$ and $\mu \in \{1, 1/2, 1/4, 1/8\}$

n	$\Lambda_n(1)$	$\Lambda_n(1/2)$	$\Lambda_n(1/4)$	$\Lambda_n(1/8)$
1	9.867	5.580×10^2	1.106×10^3	2.202×10^3
2	2.035×10^{-1}	2.640×10	5.260×10	1.050×10^2
3	5.877×10^{-9}	2.825×10^{-7}	5.591×10^{-7}	1.112×10^{-6}
4	1.534×10^{-7}	2.317×10^{-5}	4.618×10^{-5}	9.220×10^{-5}
5	2.125×10^{-10}	2.125×10^{-10}	2.125×10^{-10}	2.125×10^{-10}
6	5.850×10^{-9}	1.326×10^{-7}	2.600×10^{-7}	5.140×10^{-7}
7	1.875×10^{-11}	1.875×10^{-11}	1.875×10^{-11}	1.875×10^{-11}
8	1.384×10^{-11}	1.384×10^{-11}	1.384×10^{-11}	1.384×10^{-11}
9	5.368×10^{-12}	5.368×10^{-12}	5.368×10^{-12}	5.368×10^{-12}
10	3.891×10^{-12}	3.891×10^{-12}	3.891×10^{-12}	3.891×10^{-12}

4   Conclusions

In this paper, the distribution properties of modulo 2 reductions of primitive sequences modulo square-free odd integers are studied. Let M be a square-free odd integer, n a positive integer, and $\underline{a}$ a primitive sequence of order n over $\mathbf{Z}/(M)$ with period T. For $s \in \{0, 1\}$ and $0 < \mu \le 1$, denote by f_s the proportion of occurrences of s within a segment of the binary sequence $[\underline{a}]_{\bmod 2}$, the modulo 2 reduction of $\underline{a}$, of length μT. Then it is shown that the difference of f_s from the average value $\frac{M+1-2s}{2M}$ tends to 0 as $n \to \infty$. Note that $\frac{M+1}{2M}$ differs from $\frac{M-1}{2M}$ by $\frac{1}{M}$. This implies that there exists a small imbalance between 0 and 1 occurring in the binary sequence $[\underline{a}]_{\bmod 2}$, and the bias of f_0 and f_1 is about $\frac{1}{M}$. To provide a good resistance against the distinguishing attacks, such imbalance should be taken into full consideration in the design of stream ciphers based on $[\underline{a}]_{\bmod 2}$. A simple method is to introduce the exclusive or operation. A bitwise exclusive or of several phase-shifts of $[\underline{a}]_{\bmod 2}$ will has smaller bias than $[\underline{a}]_{\bmod 2}$. Therefore, by introducing a moderate amount of exclusive or operations, the imbalance of 0, 1 will be reduced to a small enough extent. In the future we will be interested in other pseudorandom properties of $[\underline{a}]_{\bmod 2}$, such as the linear complexity of $[\underline{a}]_{\bmod 2}$.

References

1. Bugeaud, Y., Corvaja, P., Zannier, U.: An upper bound for the G.C.D. of $a^n - 1$ and $b^n - 1$. Math. Z. **243**, 79–84 (2003)
2. Bylkov, D.N., Kamlovskii, O.V.: Occurrence indices of elements in linear recurrence sequences over primary residue rings. Probl. Inf. Transm. **44**, 161–168 (2008)
3. Chan, A.H., Games, R.A.: On the linear span of binary sequences obtained from finite geometries. In: Odlyzko, A.M. (ed.) CRYPTO 1986. LNCS, vol. 263, pp. 405–417. Springer, Heidelberg (1987). https://doi.org/10.1007/3-540-47721-7_29
4. Chen, H.J., Qi, W.F.: On the distinctness of maximal length sequences over $\mathbf{Z}/(pq)$ modulo 2. Finite Fields Appl. **15**(1), 23–39 (2009)
5. Cochrane, T.: On a trigonometric inequality of Vinogradov. J. Number Theory **27**(1), 9–16 (1987)
6. Dai, Z.D., Beth, T., Gollmann, D.: Lower bounds for the linear complexity of sequences over residue rings. In: Damgård, I.B. (ed.) EUROCRYPT 1990. LNCS, vol. 473, pp. 189–195. Springer, Heidelberg (1991). https://doi.org/10.1007/3-540-46877-3_16
7. Dai, Z.D.: Binary sequences derived from ML-sequences over rings I: periods and minimal polynomials. J. Cryptol. **5**(3), 193–207 (1992)
8. Fan, S.Q., Han, W.B.: Random properties of the highest level sequences of primitive sequences over $\mathbf{Z}/(2^e)$. IEEE Trans. Inf. Theory **49**(6), 1553–1557 (2003)
9. Hu, Z., Wang, L.: Injectivity of compressing maps on the set of primitive sequences modulo square-free odd integers. Cryptogr. Commun. **7**(4), 347–361 (2015)
10. Huang, M.Q., Dai, Z.D.: Projective maps of linear recurring sequences with maximal p-adic periods. Fibonacci Q. **30**(2), 139–143 (1992)
11. Lidl, R., Niederreiter, H.: Finite Fields. Encyclopedia of Mathematics and Its Applications, vol. 20. Cambridge University Press, Cambridge (1997)
12. Kamlovskii, O.V.: Frequency characteristics of linear recurrences over Galois rings. Matematicheskii Sbornik **200**, 31–52 (2009)
13. Klapper, A., Goresky, M.: Feedback shift registers, 2-adic span, and combiners with memory. J. Crypt. **10**(2), 111–147 (1997)
14. Korobov, N.M.: Exponential Sums and Their Applications. Kluwer, Dordrecht (1992)
15. Kuzmin, A.S., Nechaev, A.A.: Linear recurring sequences over Galois ring. Russ. Math. Surv. **48**(1), 171–172 (1993)
16. Qi, W.F., Yang, J.H., Zhou, J.J.: ML-sequences over rings Z/(2^e): I. Constructions of nondegenerative ML-sequences II. Injectivness of compression mappings of new classes. In: Ohta, K., Pei, D. (eds.) ASIACRYPT 1998. LNCS, vol. 1514, pp. 315–326. Springer, Heidelberg (1998). https://doi.org/10.1007/3-540-49649-1_25
17. Tian, T., Qi, W.F.: Injectivity of compressing maps on primitive sequences over $\mathbf{Z}/(p^e)$. IEEE Trans. Inf. Theory **53**(8), 2966–2970 (2007)
18. Ward, M.: The arithmetical theory of linear recurring series. Trans. Am. Math. Soc. **35**(3), 600–628 (1933)
19. Wikipedia, Trigonometric functions, Wikipedia website (2018). https://en.wikipedia.org/wiki/Trigonometric_functions#Calculus
20. Zhu, X.Y., Qi, W.F.: Compression mappings on primitive sequences over $\mathbf{Z}/(p^e)$. IEEE Trans. Inf. Theory **50**(10), 2442–2448 (2004)
21. Zhu, X.Y., Qi, W.F.: Further result of compressing maps on primitive sequences modulo odd prime powers. IEEE Trans. Inf. Theory **53**(8), 2985–2990 (2007)

22. Zhu, X.Y., Qi, W.F.: On the distinctness of modular reduction of maximal length modulo odd prime numbers. Math. Comput. **77**(263), 1623–1637 (2008)
23. Zheng, Q.X., Qi, W.F.: Distribution properties of compressing sequences derived from primitive sequences over $\mathbf{Z}/(p^e)$. IEEE Trans. Inf. Theory **56**(1), 555–563 (2010)
24. Zheng, Q.X., Qi, W.F.: A new result on the distinctness of primitive sequences over $\mathbf{Z}/(pq)$ modulo 2. Finite Fields Appl. **17**(3), 254–274 (2011)
25. Zheng, Q.X., Qi, W.F., Tian, T.: On the distinctness of binary sequences derived from primitive sequences modulo square-free odd integers. IEEE Trans. Inf. Theory **59**(1), 680–690 (2013)
26. Zheng, Q.X., Qi, W.F.: Further results on the distinctness of binary sequences derived from primitive sequences modulo square-free odd integers. IEEE Trans. Inf. Theory **59**(6), 4013–4019 (2013)
27. Zheng, Q.X., Qi, W.F., Tian, T.: On the distinctness of modular reduction of primitive sequences over $\mathbf{Z}/(2^{32} - 1)$. Des. Codes Crypt. **70**(3), 359–368 (2014)
28. ETSI/SAGE Specification: Specification of the 3GPP Confidentiality and Integrity Algorithms 128-EEA3 & 128-EIA3. Document 4: Design and Evaluation Report; Version: 2.0; Date: 9th Sep. 2011. Tech. rep., ETSI 2011. http://www.gsmworld. com/our-work/programmes-and-initiatives/fraud-and-security/gsm_security_ algorithms.htm

Towards Malicious Security of Private Coin Honest Verifier Zero Knowledge for NP via Witness Encryption

Jingyue Yu[1,2,3(✉)]

[1] State Key Laboratory of Information Security, Institute of Information Engineering, Chinese Academy of Sciences, Beijing 100093, China
[2] State Key Laboratory of Cryptology, P.O. Box 5159, Beijing 100878, China
[3] School of Cyber Security, University of Chinese Academy of Sciences, Beijing 100093, China
yujingyue@iie.ac.cn

Abstract. We develop a new method for transforming private coin HVZK protocols into witness indistinguishable, and zero knowledge protocols, via witness encryption. This causes at most one additional round. Previously, the general way of transforming a private coin HVZK protocol into zero knowledge is to employ a standard commitment technique, which causes two more rounds. Following this method, we present two-round witness indistinguishable proofs for specific languages, such as OR-DDH, OR-QR, OR-LWE, based on the associated lossy encryption and witness encryption. We apply this witness encryption idea to the HVZK protocol in [Jawurek et al. CCS13] and present a three-round zero knowledge protocol with super-polynomial simulation (or zero knowledge in $\mathcal{F}_{OT}$-hybrid model) for NP, assuming the existence of Yao's garble circuit and two-message oblivious transfer protocol (or ideal oblivious transfer). In addition, our three-round zero knowledge protocol works for generic languages, avoiding expensive Karp reductions.

Keywords: Zero knowledge · Witness indistinguishability · Honest verifier zero knowledge · Witness encryption

1 Introduction

The notion of zero knowledge was introduced by [18] to guarantee the privacy of the prover. Zero knowledge (ZK) requires that the proof reveals nothing but the validity of the statement even to a malicious verifier, and it has been widely used in the designing of numerous cryptographic protocols.

For many practical applications of zero knowledge, such as coin-tossing and non-malleable protocols, they actually don't have to satisfy the simulation-based security but only require a weaker indistinguishable security. However, the round complexity of those protocols is determined by the round complexity of zero knowledge.

© Springer Nature Switzerland AG 2019
F. Guo et al. (Eds.): Inscrypt 2018, LNCS 11449, pp. 586–606, 2019.
https://doi.org/10.1007/978-3-030-14234-6_31

Witness indistinguishability (WI) and witness hiding (WH) [12] are two different relaxed notions of zero knowledge. Roughly, we say a protocol is witness indistinguishable if the statement has two independent witnesses, then the malicious verifier cannot distinguish which witness the prover is using. Witness hiding proofs guarantee that a malicious verifier cannot obtain any witness of the statement being proved from interacting with an honest prover.

Goldreich and Krawcyzk [16] showed that three-round zero knowledge arguments with black-box simulation do not exist for non-trivial languages. Bitansky and Paneth [6] used Yao's garbled circuit and two-message OT protocol [25] to construct a three-round witness hiding protocol and a three-round weak zero knowledge protocol, while their constructions also rely on point obfuscation.

Recently, Jain et al. [21] constructed a three-round distributional weak zero knowledge for NP, based on Σ-protocol, assuming the existence of two-message OT protocols with security against malicious receiver and semi-honest receiver [19,25]. They used a distinguisher-dependent (black-box) simulation to bypass lower bounds on black-box simulation [16]. This is a big break. Unfortunately, their constructions of three-round weak zero knowledge are not closed under sequential repetition.

Jawurek et al. [22] constructed a five-round efficient zero knowledge protocol using garbled circuits. To reduce the round-complexity of zero knowledge protocols using garbled circuits, Ganesh et al. [13] used a conditional verification to obtain a three-round zero knowledge protocol in the random oracle model (ROM).

Dwork and Naor [11] introduced zaps, which are two-round public coin witness indistinguishable protocols, and they gave a construction based on non-interactive zero knowledge proofs. Later, Bitansky and Paneth [7] realized zaps and non-interactive witness indistinguishability from indistinguishable obfuscation, which also use non-interactive zero knowledge as a tool. Recently, several works [3,21] follow the approach of [1,23] to reduce rounds in interactive protocols, expect that they used oblivious transfer (OT) protocols, instead of PIR schemes. In particular, they compressed a Σ-protocol into a two-round witness indistinguishable argument, using *sub-exponential* OT protocols.

Honest verifier zero knowledge (HVZK) is another relaxed notation of zero knowledge, in which the verifier follows the protocol honestly but tries to learn something about the prover's privacy from interaction with an honest prover. HVZK is a clear weaker notion of zero knowledge. For public coin HVZK protocols, such as the classic Blum protocol [8], Σ-protocol [9], they are three-round witness indistinguishable/witness hiding protocols w.r.t. hard distribution with two (or more) witnesses [12], and witness hiding w.r.t. hard distribution with unique witness which are indistinguishable from hard distributions with two (or more) witnesses [10]. Additionally, they can be transformed into zero knowledge by letting the verifier commit to his challenge bits (in the HVZK protocol) ahead of time. The resulting protocol is a four-round zero knowledge protocol.

Compared to public coin HVZK protocols, private coin HVZK protocols (with constant soundness error) can be achieved within two rounds, such as HVZK protocols for graph non-isomorphism (GNI), HVZK protocols from lossy encryption [5]. Note that the private coin HVZK protocols for NP might be not secure against a malicious verifier. The general way of transforming a private coin HVZK protocol into zero knowledge is to employ a standard commitment technique[1]: Rather than directly sending the prover message to the verifier, the prover makes a commitment to the prover message. Then the verifier reveals his randomness, demonstrating to the prover that he follows the protocol correctly, and only then the prover opens his commitment to the verifier. This causes two additional rounds.

1.1   Our Results

In this work, we start with a two-round private coin HVZK protocol for NP with constant soundness error from witness encryption. We show this HVZK protocol is not witness indistinguishable but witness hiding. Observe that witness hiding might not be closure under sequential/parallel repetitions of this protocol. For HVZK protocols with negligible soundness error from witness encryption, the prover's privacy against a malicious verifier is not clear.

Rather than using a commitment technique, we construct 3-round witness indistinguishable protocols for NP using a "witness encryption" technique. Furthermore, using this kind of "witness encryption" idea, we present the following two constructions:

- Two-round witness indistinguishable proof for OR-Composition of specific languages possessed of lossy encryption, such as OR-DDH, OR-QR, OR-LWE, from witness encryption.
- Three-round zero knowledge with super-polynomial simulation (or zero knowledge in $\mathcal{F}_{OT}$ model) for generic languages, based on the existence of Yao's garbled circuit and two-message oblivious transfer protocol (or ideal oblivious transfer).

Next, we give an overview of our main results.

HVZK from Witness Encryption. Recall that a witness encryption scheme [15] is defined for an NP language L with corresponding witness relation R_L. It consists of two algorithms (Enc, Dec): The encryption algorithm Enc takes a statement $x \in L$ and a message m as inputs and outputs a ciphertext ct. A user who owns $w \in R_L(x)$ can decrypt ct using the decryption algorithm Dec. Additionally, the two efficient algorithms need to satisfy the following two properties: Correctness requires that if $(x, w) \in R_L$, then $\mathsf{Dec}_w(\mathsf{Enc}_x(m; r)) = m$; Security requires that for any $x \notin L$, $\mathsf{Enc}_x(m; r)$ is semantic secure.

Now consider a two-round honest verifier zero knowledge protocol for an NP language L. The prover convinces the verifier of that $x \in L$ by using witness encryption. In the first round, the verifier encrypts a random bit under the

---

[1] For a private coin HVZK protocols for coNP, such as two-round HVZK protocols for graph non-isomorphism (GNI), the general way of transforming them into zero knowledge is through cut and choose protocols.

statement x, and sends the corresponding ciphertext ct to the prover. In the second round, the prover uses its witness $w \in R_L(x)$ to decrypt the ciphertext and sends the decryption bit to the verifier. The verifier accepts iff the received bit is equal to the bit chosen by itself.

It's not hard to see that the above two-round protocol is an honest verifier zero knowledge/witness hiding argument with constant soundness error. We observe that this protocol is not witness indistinguishability, since for a malformed ciphertext, the decryption results using different witnesses may be not the same.

To illustrate this consider a witness encryption scheme for an OR-composition of PRG language $L_{or} = L \vee L$. For an instance $x := x_0 \| x_1 \in L_{or}$ with two independent witnesses $w_0, w_1 \in R_{L_{or}}(x)$, where $w_0 \in R_L(x_0)$ and $w_1 \in R_L(x_1)$, a malicious verifier can efficiently find some $x' \in L$ such that $w_0 \in R_{L_{or}}(x')$ and $w_1 \notin R_{L_{or}}(x')$, by setting $x' = x_0 \| x_1'$, where $x_0 \in L$ but $x_1' \xleftarrow{\text{R}} \{0,1\}^n$. Then ciphertexts $ct = \text{Enc}_{x'}(m; r)$ under x' uses w_0 and w_1 as secret key to decrypt and the decryption results might be not the same. This WI attack follows the input-distribution-switching technique [10].

Fixing It Using a Witness Encryption Scheme. Note that in the above protocol, the cheating prover can fool the verifier with constant probability. For the rest discussion, we consider the protocol that the verifier sends a ciphertext $ct = \text{Enc}_x(m; r)$ for a random string $m \in \{0,1\}^n$, to achieve a negligible soundness error. In turn the prover responds with $m' = \text{Dec}_w(ct)$. The above witness indistinguishable attack still works.

Previously, this problem can be resolved by empolying a standard commitment technique $(\text{Com}, \text{Open})$: After receiving a ciphertext ct, the prover sends a commitment $com = \text{Com}(m')$, rather than sending $m' = \text{Dec}_w(ct)$; and it expects to receive back m, r such that $ct = \text{Enc}_x(m; r)$. Then the prover sends the opening of com to the verifier. The resulting protocol is a four-round zero knowledge argument.

In this work, we use a witness encryption scheme to ensure that a malicious verifier obtains the corresponding decryption only when the ciphertext ct is honestly generated. We first consider the following candidate two-round protocol: After receiving ct from the verifier, the prover sends $\tilde{ct} = \text{Enc}_{(x,ct)}(m')$ to the verifier, where $m' = 0^n$ if $\text{Dec}_w(ct) = \perp$, otherwise $m' = \text{Dec}_w(ct)$; and $(x, ct) \in \tilde{L}$. Let $\tilde{L} = \{(x, ct) : \exists m, r \text{ s.t. } ct = \text{Enc}_x(m; r)\}$ be an NP language consisting of all instance and legal witness encryption ciphertext pairs.

For witness indistinguishability, we consider the following two cases. In case $(x, ct) \in \tilde{L}$, we have for all ciphertext ct under x, $\text{Dec}_{w_0}(ct) = \text{Dec}_{w_1}(ct)$, by the correctness of witness encryption. In case $(x, ct) \notin \tilde{L}$, by the security of witness encryption, we have that $\{\text{Enc}_{(x,ct)}(m; \tilde{r})\} \stackrel{c}{\approx} \{\text{Enc}_{(x,ct)}(0^n; \tilde{r})\}$. Thus, no matter which is the case here, the distributions $\{\langle P(w_0), V^* \rangle (x)\}$ and $\{\langle P(w_1), V^* \rangle (x)\}$ are indistinguishable.

At first, it seems the resulting two-round protocol is sound, since for $x \notin L$, a cheating prover cannot recover m from ct. Thus the soundness would follow by the security of witness encryption. However, this is flawed. After receiving the challenged ciphertext ct, the reduction algorithm R passes ct to P^* and receives back $\tilde{ct}$. It expects to decrypt $\tilde{ct}$ and then breaks the security of $ct = \mathsf{Enc}_{x \notin L}(m; r)$, while a PPT reduction algorithm cannot decrypt $\tilde{ct}$ without m, r.

Three-Round WI Arguments for NP from Witness Encryption. To achieve soundness, we rely on the Feige-Shamir trapdoor paradigm, the prover adds some "trapdoor" to ensure that the reduction algorithm can decrypt $\tilde{ct}$ using this trapdoor. Inspired by [6], we let the prover first send $f(k)$ where $k \xleftarrow{\mathsf{R}} \{0,1\}^n$ and f is an injective one way function. Then the verifier computes a ciphertext $ct = \mathsf{Enc}_x(m)$ for a random string $m \xleftarrow{\mathsf{R}} \{0,1\}^n$ under the statement x. The prover decrypts ct using witness and obtains m', then it sends $ct' = \mathsf{enc}_k(m')$ and $\tilde{ct} = \mathsf{Enc}_{(x,ct)}(k)$ to the verifier, where enc is a private key encryption algorithm. The verifier uses (m, r) as witness to decrypt $\tilde{ct}$ and obtains k, then decrypts ct' and checks whether the decryption result is equal to m or not. For more details see Sect. 3.2.

Two-Round WI Proofs for Specific Languages from Lossy Encryption and Witness Encryption. If we require the witness encryption scheme for L is statistically secure (i.e. for any $x \notin L$, $\mathsf{Enc}_x(m; r)$ is statistically hiding m), then the candidate two-round WI protocol is sound. If there exists an (unbounded) cheating prover can fool the verifier with non-negligible probability, then there exists an (unbounded) reduction algorithm breaking the statistically secure of witness encryption. In particular, lossy encryption [4,20] can be seen as a statistical witness encryption for specific languages known as in SZK [5,15], such as DDH, Quadratic Residuosity (QR), LWE. Since WI is only meaningful for languages with two (or more) witnesses, we present a general two-round WI proof for OR-composition of languages possessed of lossy encryption in Sect. 4.

Three-Round Zero Knowledge Protocols for NP from Two-Message Secure Function Evaluation. Jawurek et al. [22] proposed an efficient zero knowledge protocols for generic languages based on Yao's garbled circuits and two-message OT protocols [24,26]. In a nutshell, P and V first execute a 2PC [17] to jointly compute a function $f_x^L(w, y)$, which on input (w, y) outputs $\hat{y} = y$ if $w \in R_L(x)$, otherwise $\hat{y} = \bot$: The prover sends $\mathsf{OT}_1(w)$ to V, and V plays the role of garbled circuit constructor to construct garbled circuit $\hat{C}$ for realizing $f_{x,y}^L(w) = f_x^L(w, y)$ and computes $\mathsf{OT}_2(lab_{i,0}, lab_{i,1})$. The prover can evaluate the circuit and retrieve $\hat{y}$. For privacy of the prover, the prover don't directly reveal $\hat{y}$ to V. They used a commitment technique to achieve zero knowledge: P sends a commitment of $\hat{y}$ to V, and until V sending a valid opening (all input labels) of the garbled circuit, he reveals $\hat{y}$ to V.

We use the witness encryption idea to ensure the prover's privacy. At a high level, P and V jointly run another 2PC to ensure that V learns $\hat{y}$ only if it honestly constructs the garbled circuit $\hat{C}$ for f_x^L. In this sub-protocol, P plays the role of garbled circuit constructor to construct a garbled circuit $\hat{D}$ for functionality $f_{\hat{C}}^{\hat{L}}$ which on input a legal opening of $\hat{C}$ outputs $\hat{y}$, otherwise $\bot$, where $\hat{L}$ is defined for all legal garbled circuits for f_x^L. This protocol is also flawed and it can be fix to be sound using the Feige-Shamir trapdoor paradigm as before. In Sect. 5, we present a three-round zero knowledge from two-message secure function evaluation, which in turn relies on the existence of Yao's garbled circuit and two-message OT protocol.

Ganesh et al. [13] used a conditional verification technique to obtain a three-round zero knowledge protocol in the random oracle model (ROM). Although the efficiency of our construction is slightly less than theirs, our protocol is under standard assumptions instead of random oracle. In the table below, we compared our protocol with the existing zero knowledge protocols using garbled circuits. Note that our three-round protocol can be adaptively secure, when plugged in with RE-OTs (Table 1).

Table 1. Comparison with other ZKGC protocols

Protocols	Rounds	Assumptions	Proof size
[JKO13]	5	OT + GC	$O(n \cdot |C|)$
[GKPS18]	3	OT + ROM	$O(n \cdot |C|)$
This paper	3	OT + GC	$O(n \cdot |C|) + O(n \cdot |D|)$

Furthermore, our constructions of zero knowledge can also avoid expensive Karp reductions to NP-COMPLETE languages for proving generic statements, such as "I know w s.t. $x = $ SHA-256(w)". Note that if the underlying two-message OT protocol is instantiated by weak OT [3], then the resulting three-round protocol is zero knowledge with super-polynomial simulation. If the underlying two-message OT protocol is instantiated by an ideal OT protocol like [22], then the resulting protocol is zero knowledge in $\mathcal{F}_{OT}$-hybrid model.

1.2   Related Work

Bitansky and Paneth [7] used the terminology of witness encryption to construct a non-interactive witness indistinguishable protocol, however in their construction, the witness encryption scheme can be only implemented by indistinguishable obfuscation. For our purpose, all potential constructions of witness encryption schemes [14,15] are fit in our protocols.

Our constructions of two-round WI proofs for specific languages are based on lossy encryption and witness encryption without using non-interactive zero knowledge. Zaps, two-round public coin WI protocols for NP are constructed using NIZK as a tool [7,11]. Recent works [3,21] transform Σ-protocol into two-round WI argument by using OT protocol against quasi-polynomial time receivers.

2 Preliminaries

2.1 Basic Notations

Throughout the paper, n denotes the security parameter. A function $\mathsf{negl}(n)$ is said to be negligible if for any polynomial $\mathsf{poly}(n)$ there exists an N such that for all $n \geq N$, $\mathsf{negl}(n) \leq \frac{1}{\mathsf{poly}(n)}$. We will abbreviate probabilistic polynomial-time with PPT.

For a positive integer κ, $[\kappa]$ denotes $\{1, 2, \ldots, \kappa\}$. For a set S, we write $x \xleftarrow{\text{R}} S$ to denote that x is chosen uniformly at random from S. For a distribution D over a finite set $S \subseteq \{0,1\}^*$, we denote by $x \leftarrow D$ the process that the sample $x \in S$ is drawn according to the distribution D.

2.2 Interactive Protocols

An interactive proof system $\langle P, V \rangle$ for an NP language L with its associated relation R_L consists of a pair of interactive Turing machines P and V. The prover P wants to convince the verifier V of some statement $x \in L$. We denote by $\langle P(w), V(z) \rangle(x)$ the transcript of an execution of $\langle P, V \rangle$ on common input x, P's private input w and V's auxiliary input z.

Definition 1 (Proof System). *An interactive argument $\langle P, V \rangle$ is an argument system with soundness error s for an NP language L, if it satisfies:*

- **Completeness.** *For any $(x, w) \in R_L$,*

$$\Pr[\langle P(w), V \rangle(x) = 1] \geq 1 - \mathsf{negl}(n)$$

- **Soundness.** *For any (unbounded) malicious P^*, any $x \notin L$,*

$$\Pr[\langle P^*, V \rangle(x) = 1] \leq s(n)$$

where s is called soundness error.

An *interactive argument* is defined similarly to an interactive proof except that soundness is only required to be hold for PPT cheating provers.

Definition 2 (Witness Indistinguishability). *Let L be an NP language defined by R_L. An interactive protocol $\langle P, V \rangle$ is said to be witness indistinguishable for relation R_L if for every PPT V^*, every auxiliary input $z \in \{0,1\}^*$ and every sequence $\{(x, w, w')\}_{x \in L}$, where $(x, w), (x, w') \in R_L$, the following two distribution ensembles are computationally indistinguishable:*

$$\{\langle P(w), V^*(z) \rangle(x)\}_{x \in L, z \in \{0,1\}^*} \overset{c}{\approx} \{\langle P(w'), V^*(z) \rangle(x)\}_{x \in L, z \in \{0,1\}^*}$$

Definition 3 (Hard Distribution). *Let L be an NP language defined by R_L. Let $\mathcal{D} = \{D_n = (X_n, W_n)\}_{n \in \mathbb{N}}$ be an efficiently samplable distribution ensemble on R_L. We say $\mathcal{D}$ is hard for R_L if for any PPT machine M*

$$\Pr[M(X_n) \in R_L(X_n)] \leq \mathsf{negl}(n)$$

Definition 4 (Witness Hiding). *Let L be an NP language defined by R_L. We say $\langle P, V \rangle$ is witness hiding for a hard distribution $\mathcal{D}$, if for any PPT machine V^**

$$\Pr[\langle P(W_n), V^* \rangle (X_n) \in R_L(X_n)] \leq \mathsf{negl}(n)$$

Definition 5 (Honest Verifier Zero Knowledge). *An interactive protocol $\langle P, V \rangle$ is said to be honest verifier zero knowledge for an NP language L, if there exists a PPT simulator Sim for any honest verifier V, when given any $x \in L$ simulates the transcript $\langle P(w), V(z) \rangle (x)$. That is, for any $(x, w) \in R_L$,*

$$\langle P(w), V(z) \rangle (x) \overset{c}{\approx} Sim(x)$$

Definition 6 (Zero Knowledge). *An interactive protocol $\langle P, V \rangle$ is said to be zero knowledge for an NP language L, if for any $x \in L$, there exists a PPT simulator Sim, for any PPT malicious verifier V^*,*

$$\langle P(w), V^* \rangle (x) \overset{c}{\approx} Sim^{V^*}(x)$$

2.3 Witness Encryption

Recall the definition of witness encryption from [15].

Definition 7 (Witness Encryption). *A witness encryption scheme for an NP language L (with corresponding witness relation R_L) consists of the following two algorithms:*

- *$ct \leftarrow \mathsf{Enc}_x(m; r)$: The encryption algorithm Enc takes as input a string $x \in X$ and a message $\{0, 1\}^n$, and outputs a ciphertext ct. For notational simplicity, we sometimes write $\mathsf{Enc}_x(m)$ for $\mathsf{Enc}_x(m; r)$.*
- *$m/\bot \leftarrow \mathsf{Dec}_w(ct)$: On inputs w and the ciphertext ct, the decryption algorithm Dec outputs m or $\bot$.*

The two algorithms $(\mathsf{Enc}, \mathsf{Dec})$ satisfy the following properties:

- **Correctness.** *For any message $m \in \{0, 1\}^n$, for any $x \in L$, and $w \in R_L(x)$, we have*
$$\Pr[\mathsf{Dec}_w(\mathsf{Enc}_x(m; r)) = m] = 1$$

- **Security.** *For any $x \notin L$, for any PPT adversary $\mathcal{A}$, we have*

$$|\Pr[\mathcal{A}(\mathsf{Enc}_x(m; r))] - \Pr[\mathcal{A}(\mathsf{Enc}_x(m'; r'))] = 1| = \mathsf{negl}(n)$$

where $(m, m') \leftarrow \mathcal{A}(x)$.

There have been several constructions of witness encryption (WE) for NP languages over the past few years. Garg et al. [15] gave us the first candidate construction of witness encryption, based on the NP-complete EXACT COVER problem and approximate multilinear maps (MLMs). Garg et al. [14] showed that indistinguishability obfuscation implies witness encryption.

2.4 Lossy Encryption

Lossy encryption can be seen as statistical witness encryption schemes for specific languages known to be in SZK [5,15]. Review the definition of lossy encryption from [4,20].

Definition 8 (Lossy Encryption). *A lossy encryption scheme is a tuple efficient algorithm* (LE.Gen, LE.Enc, LE.Dec) *such that*

- LE.Gen$(1^n, \text{inj})$ *outputs injective keys* (pk, sk).
- LE.Gen$(1^n, \text{loss})$ *outputs lossy keys* (pk, sk).

Additionally, the algorithms satisfy the followings:

1. **Correctness on injective keys.** *For all* $m \in \{0,1\}^n$,

$$\Pr[(pk, sk) \leftarrow \text{LE.Gen}(1^n, \text{inj}); r \xleftarrow{R} \{0,1\}^{\text{poly}(n)} : \text{LE.Dec}(sk, \text{LE.Enc}(pk, m; r)) = m] = 1$$

2. **Indistinguishability of keys.** *In lossy mode, public keys are computationally indistinguishable from those in the injective mode. Specifically, if* proj $: (pk, sk) \to pk$ *is the projection map, then*

$$\{\text{proj}(\text{LE.Gen}(1^n, \text{inj}))\} \approx_c \{\text{proj}(\text{LE.Gen}(1^n, \text{loss}))\}$$

3. **Lossiness of lossy keys.** *For* $(pk, sk) \leftarrow \text{LE.Gen}(1^n, \text{loss})$, *for all* $m_0, m_1 \in \{0,1\}^n$,

$$\{\text{LE.Enc}(pk, m_0; R)\} \overset{s}{\approx} \{\text{LE.Enc}(pk, m_1; R)\}$$

4. **Openability.** *If* $(pk, sk) \leftarrow \text{LE.Gen}(1^n, \text{loss})$ *and* $r \xleftarrow{R} \{0,1\}^{\text{poly}(n)}$, *then for all* $m_0, m_1 \in \{0,1\}^n$, *there exists* $r' \in \{0,1\}^{\text{poly}(n)}$ *such that* LE.Enc$(pk, m_0; r) = $ LE.Enc$(pk, m_1; r')$ *with overwhelming probability. That is, there is an (unbounded) algorithm* LE.open *that can open a lossy ciphertext to any plaintext with overwhelming probability.*

2.5 Two-Message Secure Function Evaluation

We consider a two-message secure function evaluation protocol (SFE) $(P_1(x_1), P_2(x_2))$: P_1 with private input x_1 and P_2 with private input x_2 jointly compute function $f(x_1, x_2)$ and only P_1 receives the output. We require malicious (indistinguishable) security against P_1^* and P_2^*.

- **Indistinguishable Security for Function Evaluator P_1.** For any $x_1^0, x_1^1 \in \{0,1\}^{\text{poly}(n)}$, the distributions of the first messages (sent to P_2) generated using x_1^0 and x_1^1 respectively are computationally indistinguishable.
- **Indistinguishable Security for Function Constructor P_2.** For any PPT malicious P_1^*, there exists an extractor Ext (not necessarily efficient) such that:

$$\Pr[\text{Exp}_0 \to 1] - \Pr[\text{Exp}_1 \to 1] \le \text{negl}(n)$$

where Exp_b is defined as follows, for $b \in \{0,1\}$.

1. P_1^* outputs the first message msg_1.
2. The extractor Ext takes msg_1 as input and outputs x_1^*.
3. Let x_2^0 and x_2^1 be two inputs such that $f(x_1^*, x_2^0) = f(x_1^*, x_2^1)$. On inputs x_2^b and msg_1, P_2 obtains msg_2 and sends it to P_1^*.
4. Based on msg_2, P_1^* outputs a bit b'.

Garbled Circuits. Recall the definition of garbling scheme for circuits [22, 27]. A garbling scheme for circuits consists of three PPT algorithms (Garble, Eval, Ver).

- $(\hat{C}, \overline{K} = \{lab_{\omega,b}\}_{\omega \in \mathsf{inp}(C), b \in \{0,1\}}) \leftarrow \mathsf{Garble}(1^n, C)$.
  The circuit garbling algorithm Garble takes as input a security parameter 1^n, a circuit C, and outputs a garbled circuit $\tilde{C}$ with labels $\overline{K} = \{lab_{\omega,b}\}_{\omega \in \mathsf{inp}(C), b \in \{0,1\}}$ for the input wires of C.

- $y \leftarrow \mathsf{Eval}(\hat{C}, \{lab_{\omega,x_\omega}\}_{\omega \in \mathsf{inp}(C)})$.
  Given a garbled circuit $\hat{C}$ and a sequence of input labels $\{lab_{\omega,x_\omega}\}_{\omega \in \mathsf{inp}(C)}$, the evaluation algorithm outputs a string y.

- $0/1 \leftarrow \mathsf{Ver}(f, \hat{C}, \{lab_{\omega,b}\}_{\omega \in \mathsf{inp}(C), b \in \{0,1\}})$.
  Given a garbled circuit $\hat{C}$ and both input labels of input wires $\{lab_{\omega,b}\}_{\omega \in \mathsf{inp}(C), b \in \{0,1\}}$, there exists a deterministic algorithm Ver that can recover the underlying circuit C' of garbled circuit $\hat{C}$ and compares it with the original functionality f. If $\hat{C}$ realize the functionality of f, the verification algorithm Ver outputs 1; otherwise, it outputs 0.

The three algorithms (Garble, Eval, Ver) satisfy correctness, soundness and verifiability. The details refer to the corresponding definitions in [22]. We give the definitions in the full version.

Oblivious Transfer. Oblivious transfer is a protocol between two parties— a sender S with a pair of inputs (m_0, m_1) and a receiver R with a choice bit $b \in \{0,1\}$. At the end of this protocol, the receiver R obtains m_b and nothing about m_{1-b}, while the sender S learns nothing about b. Formally, let $\pi = \langle S, R \rangle$ denote the protocol that computes the oblivious transfer functionality, $f_{OT}((m_0, m_1), b) = (\perp, m_b)$.

We recall the notion of two-message oblivious transfer [2,19] below. **A two-message OT protocol** $\pi = \langle S, R \rangle$ is defined by the following three algorithms $(\mathsf{OT}_1, \mathsf{OT}_2, \mathsf{OT}_3)$, and the three algorithms satisfy correctness, game-based receiver security and sender security [2,19].

- $(ot_1, st) \leftarrow \mathsf{OT}_1(1^n, b)$: The receiver R runs the algorithm OT_1 on inputs 1^n and the receiver's choice bit $b \in \{0,1\}$ and obtains ot_1 and the corresponding state st. We write $\mathsf{OT}_1(b)$ for simplifying notation.
- $ot_2 \leftarrow \mathsf{OT}_2(ot_1, m_0, m_1)$: After receiving ot_1 from R, the sender S runs $\mathsf{OT}_2(ot_1, m_0, m_1)$ to obtain ot_2, where m_0, m_1 are the inputs of the sender.
- $m_b \leftarrow \mathsf{OT}_3(ot_2, st)$: The receiver R can obtain m_b by evaluating $\mathsf{OT}_3(ot_2, st)$.

Instantiating the Two-Message Secure Function Evaluation. We can implement 2-message secure function evaluation $(P_1(x_1), P_2(x_2))$ that achieves security against malicious PPT P_1^* and malicious PPT P_2^* [2], using Yao's garbled circuit and 2-message OT [19,24–26]. Informally, in the first round, P_1 plays the role of OT receiver with choice bits x_1 and sends the corresponding ot_1 to P_2. In the second round, P_2 constructs a garbled circuit $\hat{F}$ for the circuit F (that realizes $f(x_1, x_2)$) and transfers the corresponding input labels to P_1 by acting as the OT sender. At the end of this protocol, P_1 obtains $\hat{F}$ and $\ell = |x_1|$ labels corresponding to the input wires to F; then P_1 computes the circuit as the function evaluator, obtaining $\hat{y}$. Formally, two-message secure funtion evaluation $(P_1(x_1), P_2(x_2))$ is defined as follows.

– **Inputs:** P_1 has x_1 and P_2 has x_2.
– **The Protocol** $(P_1(x_1), P_2(x_2))$:
  1. P_1 runs the OT-receiver program $\mathsf{OT}_1(x_{1,i}) \to (ot_{1,i}, st_i)$, for $i \in [\ell]$, and sends $\{ot_{1,i}\}_{i \in [\ell]}$ to P_2.
  2. P_2 constructs a circuit F with x_2 hardwired in it, and computes $f(x_1, x_2)$ on input x_1. P_2 generates the garbled circuit for F with x_2 hardwired in it: $(\hat{F}, \{lab_i^0, lab_i^1\}_{i \in [\ell]}) \leftarrow \mathsf{Garble}(F)$, where $\ell = |x_1|$; Then P_2 executes OT protocol using the input labels (lab_i^0, lab_i^1) as sender messages: for $i \in [\ell]$, $ot_{2,i} \leftarrow \mathsf{OT}_2(ot_{1,i}, lab_i^0, lab_i^1)$; P_2 sends $\hat{F}$ and $ot_2 = \{ot_{2,i}\}_{i \in [\ell]}$ to P_1.
  3. Following the above, P_1 can recover $\{lab_i^{x_{1,i}}\}_{i \in [\ell]}$ by running $\mathsf{OT}_3(st_i, ot_{2,i})$, for $i \in [\ell]$. P_1 then computes the circuit $\mathsf{Eval}(\hat{F}, \{lab_i^{x_{1,i}}\}_{i \in [\ell]})$ to obtain $f(x_1, x_2)$.

The details of the security proof against malicious PPT P_1^* and P_2^* refer to [2].

3   A Conditional Verification Technique via Witness Encryption

3.1   Warm-Up: Honest Verifier Zero Knowledge from Witness Encryption

In this subsection, we start by presenting an honest verifier zero knowledge from witness encryption, with constant soundness error. Inspired by honest verifier zero knowledge using lossy encryption [5], we consider the following protocol (see Fig. 1 for details) for an NP language L: given a statement x, the verifier V sends to the prover P an encryption of a random bit b under x as public key. P uses the corresponding witness w of x to decrypt the ciphertext and sends the decryption result to V.

Theorem 1. *Let* $(\mathsf{Enc}, \mathsf{Dec})$ *be a witness encryption scheme for all NP languages. The protocol in Fig. 1 is an honest verifier zero knowledge with* $\frac{1}{2}$ *soundness error.*

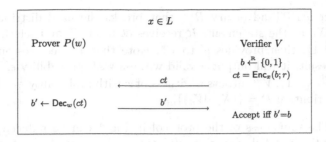

Fig. 1. Two-round HVZK for NP from witness encryption

Proof (sketch). The completeness/soundness of this protocol follow the correctness/security of witness encryption respectively. We prove that the above protocol is honest verifier zero knowledge by presenting a PPT simulator which can successfully guess the encrypted bit b with probability $\frac{1}{2}$.   □

Remark 1. Note that this protocol in Fig. 1 is only honest-verifier zero knowledge, since a cheating verifier can obtain extra knowledge by sending a random chosen ciphertext. This can be fixed to a 4-round zero knowledge argument by a standard commitment technique (Com, Open): Instead of sending b' directly, the prover sends $com = \mathsf{Com}(b'; r_p)$ to the verifier, and expects to receive back b, r such that $ct = \mathsf{Enc}_x(b; r)$. Then the prover opens the commitment com by sending b', r_p.

Claim. This protocol in Fig. 1 is not witness indistinguishable.

Proof. Here we show the protocol in Fig. 1 is not witness indistinguishable by presenting an attack. It's possible that there exists a PPT V^* that can distinguish $\{\langle P(w_0), V^*(z)\rangle(x)\}$ from $\{\langle P(w_1), V^*(z)\rangle(x)\}$, for some sequence $\{(x, w_0, w_1)\}$, where $(x, w_0) \in R_L$ and $(x, w_1) \in R_L$. Specifically, we define $\{X_n^1, W_n^1\}$ to be a distribution ensemble over $R_{L'}$ with unique witnesses and $\{X_n^2, W_n^2\}$ to be a distribution ensemble over R_L with multiple witnesses. We require that $\{X_n^1, W_n^1\} \stackrel{c}{\approx} \{X_n^2, W_n^2\}$. More details refer to [10].

Consider L be some OR-NP Language $L = T \vee T'$, where $T \subset X_T$ and $T' \subset X_{T'}$ are arbitrary NP languages. For $x \in L$, $x := x_0 \| x_1$, where $x_0 \in T$ and $x_1 \in T'$. In this sense, we consider $w_0 \in R_T(x_0)$, and $w_1 \in R_{T'}(x_1)$ as the two corresponding witnesses of $x \in L$. The malicious V^* could efficiently find some $x' \in L'$ such that $x' \in X_n^1$ with the corresponding witness $w_0 \in R_{L'}(x')$, but $w_1 \notin R_{L'}(x')$, by setting $x' := x_0 \| x_1'$, where $x_0 \in T$ and x_1' is sampled from $X_{T'}/T'$ instead of T'. Thus we have the desired ciphertext $ct = \mathsf{Enc}_{x'}(m; r)$ such that $\mathsf{Dec}_{w_0}(ct) \neq \mathsf{Dec}_{w_1}(ct)$.   □

Claim. This protocol in Fig. 1 is witness hiding.

Proof. Assume towards contradiction, there exists a PPT adversary V^* and a hard distribution $\mathcal{D} = \{(X_n, W_n)\}_{n \in \mathbb{N}}$ on R_L, such that

$$\Pr_{(x,w) \leftarrow (X_n, W_n)}[(P(w), V^*)(x) \in R_L(x)] \geq \epsilon = \frac{1}{\mathsf{poly}(n)}$$

We construct a PPT adversary R^{V^*} that breaks the hard distribution of $\mathcal{D}$. Given $x \leftarrow X_n$ as the statement, R receives ct from V^* and selects a random bit $b' \xleftarrow{\text{R}} \{0,1\}$, then provides b' to V^*. Note that V^* receives an accepting decryption result, it will output a valid witness with probability ϵ. Thus, after receiving $b' \xleftarrow{\text{R}} \{0,1\}$, V^* outputs a witness of x with probability $\frac{1}{2}\epsilon$. This breaks the hard distribution $\mathcal{D} = \{(X_n, W_n)\}_{n \in \mathbb{N}}$. $\qquad\square$

Remark 2. The soundness of the protocol in Fig. 1 can be reduced to negligible by sequential/parallel execution $\omega(n)$ times. However, the protocol in Fig. 1 may be not witness hiding under sequential/parallel execution. Consider a witness encryption scheme [7] implemented using indistinguishable obfuscation [14]: $\mathsf{Enc}_x(b)$ consists of an obfuscation $\tilde{E} \leftarrow io(E_x^b)$, where the circuit E_x^b with $b \in \{0,1\}$ and x hardwired in it, takes $w \in R_L(x)$ as input, and outputs b, otherwise $\perp$. The malicious verifier can generate a ciphertext $\tilde{E} \leftarrow io(E_x^{f_i})$ where $E_x^{f_i}$ is a circuit which on input w and outputs the i-th bit of w. Then the malicious verifier can recover the entire witness w bit by bit from the decryption results.

3.2   Three-Round Witness Indistinguishable Arguments from Witness Encryption

To prevent the above attacks, we require that the verifier can obtain the decryption results, only when the sending ciphertexts are honestly encrypted m under the statement x. For those malformed ciphertexts, the verifier cannot obtain the decryption.

In this subsection, we present a new construction of the witness indistinguishable protocol using witness encryption. In particular, we use an additional witness encryption to ensure that V^* gets the corresponding decryption only when the ciphertext is honestly generated by V^*.

Protocol 3.2. Three-Round WI Arguments from Witness Encryption

- **Ingredients:** Let $(\mathsf{Enc}, \mathsf{Dec})$ be a witness encryption scheme. $f : \{0,1\}^n \to \{0,1\}^n$ is an injective one way function. $(\mathsf{enc}, \mathsf{dec})$ is a private key encryption scheme for any uniform key.
- **Common input:** x.
- **Private input of the prover** P: $w \in R_L(x)$.
- **Interaction:**
  1. P chooses $k \xleftarrow{\text{R}} \{0,1\}^n$ and then sends $c = f(k)$ to the verifier.
  2. V selects $y \xleftarrow{\text{R}} \{0,1\}^n$ as the plaintext, and sends $ct = \mathsf{Enc}_x(y; r)$ to the prover.
  3. After receiving ct, P uses its private input w to decrypt ct and obtains $\tilde{y}$. If the decryption result is $\perp$, then we set $\tilde{y} = 0^n$. Then it computes $ct' = \mathsf{enc}_k(\tilde{y})$ and sends ct' to V. Furthermore, it uses $\tilde{x} = (x, ct)$ as a statement of $\tilde{L} = \{(x, ct) : \exists\, (m, r) \text{ s.t. } ct = \mathsf{Enc}_x(m; r)\}$ to encrypt k and sends the corresponding ciphertext $\tilde{ct} = \mathsf{Enc}_{\tilde{x}}(k)$ to V.

- **Verification:** The verifier V first decrypts $\tilde{ct}$ using $\tilde{w} = (y, r)$ and obtains k'. If $f(k') \neq c$, then it aborts; else, it decrypts ct' with k' and obtains y'. It accepts only if $y' = y$.

Theorem 2. *Protocol 3.2 is a three-round witness indistinguishable argument, assuming the existence of witness encryption.*

We show this protocol is a WI argument by showing the following two lemmas.

Lemma 1. *Protocol 3.2 is sound, assuming the security of witness encryption.*

Proof. Towards a contradiction, assume that there exists a PPT adversary P^* that can break the soundness of Protocol 3.2. We use the cheating prover P^* to construct a PPT adversary R^{P^*} breaking the security of witness encryption.

Without loss of generality, we assume P^* is deterministic. For infinitely many $x \notin L$, P^* can generate an accepting transcript for V with non-negligible probability ϵ. Let $f(k)$ be the first message sent by P^*.

After receiving $f(k)$, the reduction R invokes an external witness encryption challenger with plaintexts $y_0 \xleftarrow{\text{R}} \{0,1\}^n, y_1 \xleftarrow{\text{R}} \{0,1\}^n$ and receives back a ciphertext $ct = \text{Enc}_x(y_b)$, where $b \xleftarrow{\text{R}} \{0,1\}$. Then it passes ct to P^* and receives back $\tilde{ct}, ct'$.

Given k as a non-uniform advice, R uses k as private key to ct' and recovers y. If $y = y_\beta$ for $\beta \in \{0,1\}$, then R outputs $b' = \beta$. If $y \neq y_\beta$ for $\beta \in \{0,1\}$, then R outputs a random bit $b' \xleftarrow{\text{R}} \{0,1\}$.

Since P^* outputs an accepting proof with probability ϵ, the advantage of that R^{P^*} outputs $b' = b$ is at least $\frac{1}{2}\epsilon$, which is against the security of witness encryption. $\qquad\square$

Lemma 2. *Protocol 3.2 is witness indistinguishable, assuming the existence of witness encryption.*

Proof. Let V^* be an arbitrary PPT malicious verifier. Game_b denotes the experiment $\langle P(w_b), V^* \rangle (x)$ where the prover completes the proof using w_b, for $b \in \{0,1\}$: The prover uses w_b to decrypt ct sent by V^* and obtains $\tilde{y}_b = \text{Dec}_{w_b}(ct)$; Then P generates the third message $\tilde{ct} = \text{Enc}_{\tilde{x}}(k), ct' = \text{enc}_k(\tilde{y}_b)$, where $\tilde{x} = (x, ct)$. The only difference between the two experiments is the way of generating $\tilde{y}$.

To complete the proof, we show that for any ciphertext ct sent by V^*, it will fall into the following two cases:

- Case 1. $(x, ct) \in \tilde{L}$. In this case, ct is actually an encryption under x. By the correctness of witness encryption of L, it holds that $\tilde{y}_0 = \text{Dec}_{w_0}(ct) = \text{Dec}_{w_1}(ct) = \tilde{y}_1$. The distributions Game_0 and Game_1 are identical.
- Case 2. $(x, ct) \notin \tilde{L}$. This in turn implies that the distributions $\{\tilde{ct} = \text{Enc}_{\tilde{x}}(k)\}$ and $\{\tilde{ct} = \text{Enc}_{\tilde{x}}(0^n)\}$ are computationally indistinguishable. By one-wayness of injective one way function f and the CPA security of hybrid encryption, we have that $\tilde{y}_b$ is computationally hiding. In this case, though $\tilde{y}_0$ and $\tilde{y}_1$ may be not the same value, $\{f(k), ct, \text{Enc}_{\tilde{x}}(k), \text{enc}_k(\tilde{y}_0)\} \overset{c}{\approx} \{f(k), ct, \text{Enc}_{\tilde{x}}(k), \text{enc}_k(\tilde{y}_1)\}$.

Thus, in either case, $\text{Game}_0 \overset{c}{\approx} \text{Game}_1$ as desired. $\qquad\square$

4 Two-Round Witness Indistinguishable Proofs for Specific Languages

In this section, we present a two-round witness indistinguishable proof for specific languages, based on witness encryption technique. We transform a two-round HVZK proof from lossy encryption into a two-round witness indistinguishable proof, using witness encryption techniques.

Let $L = \{pk : (pk, sk) \leftarrow \mathsf{LE.Gen}(1^n, \mathsf{inj})\}$ be the language consisting of all injective public keys. Recall an HVZK proof system using lossy encryption [5] for a specific language that works as follows:

1. V sends to the prover an encryption ct of a random string $y \xleftarrow{\text{R}} \{0,1\}^n$ under pk.
2. After receiving ct, P decrypts the ciphertext using its secret key and sends back $\tilde{y}$.
3. V accepts iff $y = \tilde{y}$.

It's not hard to see this protocol is an HVZK proof. The proof is similar to the proof of the protocol in Fig. 1. In the following, we transform this HVZK protocol into witness indistinguishable, without additional round. We consider an NP language $L_{or} = L \vee L = \{(pk_0, pk_1) : pk_0 \in L \text{ or } pk_1 \in L\}$, since witness indistinguishability is only meaningful for languages whose instance has two or more independent witnesses.

Protocol 4.1. Two-Round Witness Indistinguishable Proof

- **Ingredients:** Let $(\mathsf{LE.Gen}, \mathsf{LE.Enc}, \mathsf{LE.Dec})$ be a lossy encryption scheme and $(\mathsf{Enc}, \mathsf{Dec})$ be a witness encryption scheme.
- **Common input:** $(pk_0, pk_1) \in L_{or}$
- **Private input of P:** sk such that $sk \in R_L(pk_b)$, for $b \in \{0,1\}$.
- **Interaction:**
  1. The verifier selects $y \xleftarrow{\text{R}} \{0,1\}^n$ and computes $ct_0 = \mathsf{LE.Enc}(pk_0, y; r_0)$, $ct_1 = \mathsf{LE.Enc}(pk_0, y; r_1)$. Then it sends $ct = (ct_0, ct_1)$ to P.
  2. After receiving ct, the prover does the following.
     (a) Decrypt ct_b using its witness sk and obtain $\tilde{y}$, where $\tilde{y} = 0^n$ if $\mathsf{LE.Dec}_{sk}(ct_b) = \bot$.
     (b) Use $(pk, ct) \in \tilde{L} = \{(pk, ct_0, ct_1) : \exists(y, r_0, r_1) \text{ s.t. } ct_0 = \mathsf{LE.Enc}(pk_0, y; r_0), ct_1 = \mathsf{LE.Enc}(pk_0, y; r_1)\}$ as statement to encrypt $\tilde{y}$ and obtain $\tilde{ct} = \mathsf{Enc}_{(pk, ct)}(\tilde{y})$.
     (c) Output $\tilde{ct}$.
- **Verification:** The verifier uses (y, r_0, r_1) as witness to decrypt $\tilde{ct}$ and obtains y'. V accepts iff $y' = y$.

Theorem 3. *Assuming the existence of lossy encryption and witness encryption, Protocol 4.1 is a two-round witness indistinguishable proof.*

Proof. Regarding completeness, it's easy to see if both parties follow the protocol, then we have $\tilde{y} = y$ and $y' = \tilde{y}$, by the correctness of lossy encryption and witness encryption respectively. Thus V accepts in the final step.

We now proceed to prove soundness. By contradiction, we assume that for $pk = (pk_0, pk_1) \notin L_{or}$, P^* can generate an accepting proof with non-negligible probability. We can construct an (unbounded) adversary R^{P^*} to break the lossiness of lossy keys in Definition 8.

The reduction R invokes an external lossy encryption challenger C with pk_0 and $y_0, y_1 \xleftarrow{\text{R}} \{0,1\}^n$ and receives back $ct_0 = \text{LE.Enc}(pk_0, y_\beta; r_1)$, for $\beta \in \{0,1\}$. Then it computes $ct_1 = \text{LE.Enc}(pk_1, y_0; r_1)$ and sends $ct = (ct_0, ct_1)$ to P^*. P^* returns a ciphertext $\tilde{ct}$. The reduction R now invokes the LE.Open algorithm on inputs ct_0, y_0 and obtains r'_0. Then it uses (y_0, r'_0, r_1) as witness to decrypt $\tilde{ct}$ and gets y'. If $y' = y_{\beta'}$, for $\beta' \in \{0,1\}$, then it outputs β'; otherwise, it outputs $\beta' \xleftarrow{\text{R}} \{0,1\}$.

Since P^* outputs an accepting proof with non-negligible probability, we have the advantage of R^{P^*} breaking the lossiness of lossy keys (i.e. the advantage of R^{P^*} outputs $\beta' = \beta$) is non-negligible.

Finally, we prove that the protocol is witness indistinguishable. Define Game_b as the experiment in which the prover uses sk_b as witness during the proof. After receiving $ct = (ct_0, ct_1)$ from V^*, the prover uses sk_b to decrypt ct_b and obtains $\tilde{y}_b$, then it encrypts $\tilde{y}_b$ using (pk, ct) as statement: $\tilde{ct}_b = \text{Enc}_{(pk,ct)}(\tilde{y}_b)$. Using the same proof idea as Lemma 2, we can have that $\text{Game}_0 \overset{c}{\approx} \text{Game}_1$. Due to page limitation, we defer to the full version of our paper.   □

5 Three-Round Zero Knowledge Arguments from Two-Message Secure Function Evaluation

Jawurek et al. [22] proposed an efficient zero knowledge protocol for generic languages based on Yao's garbled circuits. Informally, in their protocol, P and V first execute a SFE $(P(w), V(y))$ to compute function f_x^L which on input (w, y) outputs $\hat{y} = y$ if $w \in R_L$ otherwise $\hat{y} = \bot$. At the end of the secure function evaluation, P obtains $\hat{y}$. For zero knowledge against a malicious verifier, they used a standard commitment technique: the prover sends a commitment of $\hat{y}$ to V, and reveals $\hat{y}$ to V only if V sends back a valid opening of the garbled circuit.

Following the above idea, we reduce the round-complexity of zero-knowledge protocols in [22]. Instead of using a standard commitment technique, we use another SFE to ensure that V obtains $\hat{y}$ only if it honestly generates the garbled circuit for $f_x^L(w, y)$. This leads to a three-round zero knowledge protocol.

5.1 Constructions

Let L be an NP language with corresponding relation R_L. $(\text{OT}_1, \text{OT}_2, \text{OT}_3)$ is a two-message OT protocol. $(\text{Garble}, \text{Eval}, \text{Ver})$ is a garbling scheme. Let $\hat{L} :=$ $\{(f_x^L, \hat{E}) : \exists \overline{K^E} \text{ s.t. } \text{Ver}(\hat{E}, \overline{K^E}, f_x^L) = 1\}$ be a language consisting of all legal garbled circuits of f_x^L.

Protocol 5.1. Three-Round Zero Knowledge Arguments

- **Ingredients:** enc is a private key encryption algorithm. f is an injective one way function.
- **Input:** $x \in L$ is common input and $w \in R_L(x)$ is the private input of P.
- **Interaction:**
  1. The prover P does the following:
     (a) Select $k \xleftarrow{\text{R}} \{0,1\}^n$ and compute $c = f(k)$;
     (b) Act as the receiver of OT protocols using its private input w as choice bits: $(ot_{1,i}^E, st^E) \leftarrow \text{OT}_1(w_i)$, for $i \in [\|w\|]$;
     (c) Output $c, ot_1^E = \{ot_{1,i}^E\}_{i \in [\|w\|]}$.
  2. The verifier V does the following:
     (a) Construct a circuit E for f_x^L with $x \in L$ and $y \xleftarrow{\text{R}} \{0,1\}^n$ hardwired in it which on input $w \in \{0,1\}^{|w|}$ outputs y if $w \in R_L(x)$ and $\bot$ otherwise.
     (b) Play the role of function constructor of SFE $(P(w), V(y))\,(x)$: Evaluate the garbled circuit for E, i.e. $(\hat{E}, \overline{K^E}) \leftarrow \text{Garble}(1^n, E)$, where $\overline{K^E} = \{lab_{i,0}^E, lab_{i,1}^E\}_{i \in [\|w\|]}$, and compute $ot_{2,i}^E \leftarrow \text{OT}_2(ot_{1,i}^E, lab_{i,0}^E, lab_{i,1}^E)$;
     (c) Play the role of function evaluator of SFE $\left(V(\overline{K^E}), P(k)\right)(\hat{E})$: For $j \in [l]$, $(ot_{1,j}^D, st^D) \leftarrow \text{OT}_1(\overline{K_j^E})$, where $l = |\overline{K^E}|$;
     (d) Output $\hat{E}, \{ot_{2,i}^E\}, \{ot_{1,j}^D\}$.
  3. The prover P does the following:
     (a) Act as the function evaluator of SFE $(P(w), V(y))\,(x)$ to obtain $\hat{y}$: Compute $\{lab_{i,w_i}^E\}_{i \in [\|w\|]} \leftarrow \text{OT}_3(st^E, ot_2^E)$, and obtain $\hat{y} \leftarrow \text{Eval}(\{lab_{i,w_i}^E\}_{i \in [\|w\|]}, \hat{E})$;
     (b) Compute $ct = \text{enc}_k(\hat{y})$;
     (c) Let D be a circuit with $\hat{E}, k$ hardwired in it, and $D_{\hat{E},k}(\overline{K^E}) = k$ iff $\text{Ver}(\hat{E}, \overline{K^E}, f_x^L) = 1$, otherwise it outputs $\bot$.
     (d) Play the role of function constructor of SFE $\left(V(\overline{K^E}), P(k)\right)(\hat{E})$: Produce $(\hat{D}, \overline{K}_D) \leftarrow \text{Garble}(1^n, D)$, and $\{ot_{2,j}^D \leftarrow \text{OT}_2(ot_{1,j}^D, lab_{j,0}^D, lab_{j,1}^D)\}$;
     (e) Output $ct, \hat{D}, \{ot_{2,j}^D\}$
- **Verification:** The verifier works as the follows:
  1. Act as the function evaluator of SFE $\left(V(\overline{K^E}), P(k)\right)(\hat{E})$ to obtain k': Run $\text{OT}_3(st^D, ot_2^D)$ to obtain the corresponding input labels $\{lab_{j, \overline{K_j^E}}^D\}_{j \in [l]}$, then compute $\text{Eval}(\hat{D}, \{lab_{j, \overline{K_j^E}}^D\})$;
  2. If $f(k') = c$ then use k' to decrypt ct and obtain y'.
  3. Accept iff $y' = y$.

Theorem 4. *This protocol is a three-round witness indistinguishable argument, assuming the existence of two-message OT protocol and Yao's garbled circuits.*

Note that if the underlying two-message OT protocol is instantiated by weak OT [3], then the resulting protocol is zero knowledge with super-polynomial simulation. If the underlying two-message OT protocol is instantiated by an ideal OT protocol like [22], then the resulting protocol is zero knowledge in $\mathcal{F}_{OT}$-hybrid model.

5.2 Security

We prove Theorem 4 by showing the above protocol has soundness and zero knowledge.

Soundness. If there exists a PPT cheating prover P^* breaking the soundness of Protocol 5.1 with non-negligible probability. We can construct a PPT adversary R^{P^*} that breaks the indistinguishable security for the function constructor of SFE $(P(w), V(y))(x)$, using the cheating prover P^*. The proof of soundness is similar to the proof of Lemma 1. For lack of space, we omit the details and the formal proof appears in the full version.

Zero Knowledge. We show this protocol is zero knowledge by constructing a simulator *Sim*.

Proof. Let V^* be a PPT adversarial verifier. The simulator *Sim* does the following:

1. Select $k \xleftarrow{R} \{0,1\}^n$ and compute $c = f(k)$ and $ot_1^E \leftarrow \mathsf{OT}_1(0^n)$.
2. Send c, ot_1^E to V^* and receive back $\hat{E}, ot_2^E, ot_1^D$.
3. Run Ext to extract $\overline{K}^E$ from ot_1^D.
4. Run GC.Ext on inputs $\hat{E}, \overline{K}^E$ to extract the evaluation result $y = \mathsf{Eval}(\hat{E}, \overline{K}^E)$.
   - If y is a valid value such that $\mathsf{Ver}(\hat{E}, \overline{K^E}, f_x^L) = 1$, then it sets $\hat{y} = y$.
   - If y is not a valid value (i.e. y might be a function, $\mathsf{Ver}(\hat{E}, \overline{K^E}, f_x^L) = 0$), then it sets $\hat{y} = 0^n$.
5. Use $\hat{y}$ to compute $ct = \mathsf{enc}_k(\hat{y}), \hat{D}, \{ot_{2,j}^D\}$, where D is a circuit with $\hat{E}, k$ hardwired in it and $D_{\hat{E},k}(\overline{K^E}) = r$ iff $\mathsf{Ver}(\hat{E}, \overline{K^E}, f_x^L) = 1$, otherwise it outputs $\bot$.
6. Output $ct, \hat{D}, \{ot_{2,j}^D\}$.

Here we argue that the simulation is computationally indistinguishable from a real proof, by constructing a hybrid simulator Sim' that has witness w. Sim' works in the same way as Sim except the first simulation message $c = f(k), ot_1^E \leftarrow \mathsf{OT}_1(w)$. By the receiver security of OT protocol, we have the $Sim'^{V^*}(x, w) \overset{c}{\approx} Sim^{V^*}(x)$.

Next, we show that $Sim'^{V^*}(x, w) \overset{c}{\approx} \langle P(w), V^* \rangle (x)$. Note that if V^* "cheats" (i.e. $\mathsf{Ver}(\hat{E}, \overline{KE}, f_x^L) = 0$), then the simulator Sim' generates a ciphertext $ct = \mathsf{enc}_k(0^n)$ together with $\hat{D}_{\hat{E},k}, \{ot_{2,j}^D\}$, while an honest verifier might encrypt a different value y. By a simple hybrid game, we have $\{ct = \mathsf{enc}_k(0^n), \hat{D}_{\hat{E},k}, \{ot_{2,j}^D\}\} \overset{c}{\approx}$ $\{ct = \mathsf{enc}_k(0^n), \hat{D}_{\hat{E},0^n}, \{ot_{2,j}^D\}\} \overset{c}{\approx} \{ct = \mathsf{enc}_k(y), \hat{D}_{\hat{E},k}, \{ot_{2,j}^D\}\}$. The former follows the indistinguishable security for function constructor of SFE, since $D_{\hat{E},k}(\overline{KE}) = D_{\hat{E},0^n}(\overline{KE}) = \bot$, for $\mathsf{Ver}(\hat{E}, \overline{KE}, f_x^L) = 0$. The latter follows the security of the private encryption scheme $(\mathsf{enc}, \mathsf{dec})$, since V^* cannot obtain k conditioned on $\mathsf{Ver}(\hat{E}, \overline{KE}, f_x^L) = 0$.

In the other case, V^* follows the protocol honestly, the view of V^* in the real word and in the simulation is computationally indistinguishable. This is guaranteed by the verifiability of garbled circuit: the extracted string y is equal to $\mathsf{Eval}(\hat{E}, \overline{KE})$ with overwhelming probability. □

6   Conclusion

In this paper, we propose a new conditional verification technique using the idea of witness encryption, and it can be used to transform private coin HVZK protocols into witness indistinguishable/zero knowledge protocols with at most one more round. Following this method, we present the constructions of two-round witness indistinguishable proofs for OR-composition of specific languages possessed of lossy encryption, from witness encryption. Furthermore, we also present the efficient construction of three-round zero knowledge for generic languages under standard assumptions (the existence of two-message SFE), in which the expensive karp reductions are avoided.

Acknowledgements. We thank Yi Deng and Xuecheng Ma for helpful discussions. We also thank the anonymous reviewers for comments and suggestions.

This work was supported in part by the National Natural Science Foundation of China (Grant No. 61772521), Key Research Program of Frontier Sciences, CAS (Grant No. QYZDB-SSW-SYS035), and the Open Project Program of the State Key Laboratory of Cryptology.

References

1. Aiello, W., Bhatt, S., Ostrovsky, R., Rajagopalan, S.R.: Fast verification of any remote procedure call: short witness-indistinguishable one-round proofs for NP. In: Montanari, U., Rolim, J.D.P., Welzl, E. (eds.) ICALP 2000. LNCS, vol. 1853, pp. 463–474. Springer, Heidelberg (2000). https://doi.org/10.1007/3-540-45022-X_39
2. Ananth, P., Jain, A.: On secure two-party computation in three rounds. In: Kalai, Y., Reyzin, L. (eds.) TCC 2017. LNCS, vol. 10677, pp. 612–644. Springer, Cham (2017). https://doi.org/10.1007/978-3-319-70500-2_21
3. Badrinarayanan, S., Garg, S., Ishai, Y., Sahai, A., Wadia, A.: Two-message witness indistinguishability and secure computation in the plain model from new assumptions. In: Takagi, T., Peyrin, T. (eds.) ASIACRYPT 2017. LNCS, vol. 10626, pp. 275–303. Springer, Cham (2017). https://doi.org/10.1007/978-3-319-70700-6_10

4. Bellare, M., Hofheinz, D., Yilek, S.: Possibility and impossibility results for encryption and commitment secure under selective opening. In: Joux, A. (ed.) EUROCRYPT 2009. LNCS, vol. 5479, pp. 1–35. Springer, Heidelberg (2009). https://doi.org/10.1007/978-3-642-01001-9_1

5. Berman, I., Degwekar, A., Rothblum, R.D., Vasudevan, P.N.: From laconic zero-knowledge to public-key cryptography. In: Shacham, H., Boldyreva, A. (eds.) CRYPTO 2018. LNCS, vol. 10993, pp. 674–697. Springer, Cham (2018). https://doi.org/10.1007/978-3-319-96878-0_23

6. Bitansky, N., Paneth, O.: Point obfuscation and 3-round zero-knowledge. In: Cramer, R. (ed.) TCC 2012. LNCS, vol. 7194, pp. 190–208. Springer, Heidelberg (2012). https://doi.org/10.1007/978-3-642-28914-9_11

7. Bitansky, N., Paneth, O.: ZAPs and non-interactive witness indistinguishability from indistinguishability obfuscation. In: Dodis, Y., Nielsen, J.B. (eds.) TCC 2015. LNCS, vol. 9015, pp. 401–427. Springer, Heidelberg (2015). https://doi.org/10.1007/978-3-662-46497-7_16

8. Blum, M.: How to prove a theorem so no one else can claim it. In: ICM 1986 (1986)

9. Cramer, R., Damgård, I., Schoenmakers, B.: Proofs of partial knowledge and simplified design of witness hiding protocols. In: Desmedt, Y.G. (ed.) CRYPTO 1994. LNCS, vol. 839, pp. 174–187. Springer, Heidelberg (1994). https://doi.org/10.1007/3-540-48658-5_19

10. Deng, Y., Song, X., Yu, J., Chen, Y.: On the security of classic protocols for unique witness relations. In: Abdalla, M., Dahab, R. (eds.) PKC 2018. LNCS, vol. 10770, pp. 589–615. Springer, Cham (2018). https://doi.org/10.1007/978-3-319-76581-5_20

11. Dwork, C., Naor, M.: Zaps and their applications. In: FOCS 2000, pp. 283–293. IEEE Computer Society (2000)

12. Feige, U., Shamir, A.: Witness indistinguishable and witness hiding protocols. In: STOC 1990, pp. 416–426. ACM Press (1990)

13. Ganesh, C., Kondi, Y., Patra, A., Sarkar, P.: Efficient adaptively secure zero-knowledge from garbled circuits. In: Abdalla, M., Dahab, R. (eds.) PKC 2018. LNCS, vol. 10770, pp. 499–529. Springer, Cham (2018). https://doi.org/10.1007/978-3-319-76581-5_17

14. Garg, S., Gentry, C., Halevi, S., Raykova, M., Sahai, A., Waters, B.: Candidate indistinguishability obfuscation and functional encryption for all circuits. In: FOCS 2013, pp. 40–49. IEEE Computer Society (2013)

15. Garg, S., Gentry, C., Sahai, A., Waters, B.: Witness encryption and its applications. In: STOC 2013, pp. 467–476. ACM (2013)

16. Goldreich, O., Krawczyk, H.: On the composition of zero-knowledge proof systems. SIAM J. Comput. 25(1), 169–192 (1996)

17. Goldreich, O., Micali, S., Wigderson, A.: How to play any mental game. In: STOC 1987, pp. 218–229. ACM Press (1987)

18. Goldwasser, S., Micali, S., Rackoff, C.: The knowledge complexity of interactive proof systems. SIAM J. Comput. 18(1), 186–208 (1989)

19. Halevi, S., Kalai, Y.T.: Smooth projective hashing and two-message oblivious transfer. J. Cryptology 25(1), 158–193 (2012)

20. Hemenway, B., Libert, B., Ostrovsky, R., Vergnaud, D.: Lossy encryption: constructions from general assumptions and efficient selective opening chosen ciphertext security. In: Lee, D.H., Wang, X. (eds.) ASIACRYPT 2011. LNCS, vol. 7073, pp. 70–88. Springer, Heidelberg (2011). https://doi.org/10.1007/978-3-642-25385-0_4

21. Jain, A., Kalai, Y.T., Khurana, D., Rothblum, R.: Distinguisher-dependent simulation in two rounds and its applications. In: Katz, J., Shacham, H. (eds.) CRYPTO 2017. LNCS, vol. 10402, pp. 158–189. Springer, Cham (2017). https://doi.org/10.1007/978-3-319-63715-0_6

22. Jawurek, M., Kerschbaum, F., Orlandi, C.: Zero-knowledge using garbled circuits: how to prove non-algebraic statements efficiently. In: CCS 2013, pp. 955–966. ACM (2013)

23. Kalai, Y.T., Raz, R.: Probabilistically checkable arguments. In: Halevi, S. (ed.) CRYPTO 2009. LNCS, vol. 5677, pp. 143–159. Springer, Heidelberg (2009). https://doi.org/10.1007/978-3-642-03356-8_9

24. Naor, M., Pinkas, B.: Oblivious transfer and polynomial evaluation. In: STOC 1999, pp. 245–254. ACM (1999)

25. Naor, M., Pinkas, B.: Efficient oblivious transfer protocols. In: Proceedings of the Twelfth Annual ACM-SIAM Symposium on Discrete Algorithms, pp. 448–457. Society for Industrial and Applied Mathematics (2001)

26. Peikert, C., Vaikuntanathan, V., Waters, B.: A framework for efficient and composable oblivious transfer. In: Wagner, D. (ed.) CRYPTO 2008. LNCS, vol. 5157, pp. 554–571. Springer, Heidelberg (2008). https://doi.org/10.1007/978-3-540-85174-5_31

27. Yao, A.C.-C.: How to generate and exchange secrets. In: FOCS 1986, pp. 162–167. IEEE (1986)

Faster Homomorphic Permutation and Optimizing Bootstrapping in Matrix GSW-FHE

Shuai Liu[✉] and Bin Hu

Information Science and Technology Institute, Zhengzhou, China
sssshuai1993@163.com

Abstract. We present a new packing messages strategy for the Matrix GSW-FHE proposed by Hiromasa et al. at PKC 2015. Based on the packing messages strategy, we describe a simpler homomorphic permutation algorithm which just needs one homomorphic multiplication.

By applying this permutation algorithm, we propose an optimizing bootstrapping procedure that can refresh ciphertexts of all known standard LWE-based FHE. Our optimizing bootstrapping procedure needs less homomorphic multiplication operation and outputs refreshed ciphertexts with smaller noise. Alternatively, we give a space-time trade-off to hasten considerably the execution time whilst sacrificing reasonable memory space.

Keywords: Homomorphic permutation · Bootstrapping · Matrix GSW-FHE

1 Introduction

Fully homomorphic encryption (FHE) enables performing arbitrarily-complex function over ciphertexts without knowing the secret key. Almost all known FHE schemes [2–8] followed the same blueprint, namely the first FHE scheme [1] proposed by Gentry in 2009. To date, the fastest (and simplest) FHE scheme based on LWE assumption is GSW-FHE by Gentry, Sahai, and Waters [7].

Packing multiple messages into one ciphertext allows us to evaluate more efficiently by applying SIMD (single-instruction-multiple data) homomorphic operations to all encrypted messages. Smart and Vercautren [9], for the first time, showed that applying the Chinese reminder theorem (CRT) to number fields partitions the message space of the Gentry's FHE [1] scheme into a vector of plaintext slots. At PKC 2015, Hiromasa, Abe, and Okamoto proposed a variant [10] of GSW-FHE, which can encrypt matrices and support homomorphic matrix addition and multiplication. (hereafter, referred to as Matrix GSW-FHE). To implement SIMD homomorphic operations, we need a complete set of operations over packed messages. In general, it's easy to compute homomorphic slot-wise addition and multiplication, but permuting plaintext slots homomorphically is nontrivial. In this paper we will present a new packing messages strategy and a simpler homomorphic permutation algorithm of Matrix GSW-FHE scheme. We have to remind readers that our new packing messages strategy don't support homomorphic slot-wise multiplication though it leads to a

© Springer Nature Switzerland AG 2019
F. Guo et al. (Eds.): Inscrypt 2018, LNCS 11449, pp. 607–617, 2019.
https://doi.org/10.1007/978-3-030-14234-6_32

simpler homomorphic permutation algorithm. We find that the algorithm results in higher efficiency in many applications, specifically we propose an optimizing bootstrapping procedure to bring out the potential of our homomorphic permutation algorithm.

Bootstrapping, originally due to Gentry [1], is currently the only known technique to obtaining a "pure" fully homomorphic encryption scheme from a somewhat homomorphic encryption scheme. The bootstrapping procedure output refreshed ciphertexts with reduced noise by homomorphically evaluating the decryption circuit.

Bootstrapping has received intensive study, with progress often going hand-in-hand with innovations in the design of homomorphic encryption schemes. There have recently been the significant progresses [11, 12] in improving the bootstrapping procedure of LWE-based FHE. Their progresses make use of the asymmetric noise growth in ciphertexts of GSW-FHE. The major milestone is due to Brakerski and Vaikuntanathan [12], who gave a bootstrapping method that incurs only polynomial error in the security parameter λ. The BV method is motivated by the "circuit sequentialization" property of Barrington's Theorem [13], which converts any depth-d circuit into a length-4^d "branching program", which is essentially a fixed sequence of conditional multiplications.

Unlike most previous works, Alperin-Sheriff and Peikert [11] treated the decryption more directly as an arithmetic circuit. In more detail, the decryption function for essentially every LWE-based FHE scheme can without loss of generality (via bit-decomposition techniques) be written as a "rounded inner product" $\lfloor \langle s, c \rangle \rceil_2 \in \{0, 1\}$ between the secret key $s \in Z_q^d$ and a binary ciphertext $c \in \{0, 1\}^d$ for some appropriate rounding function $\lfloor \cdot \rceil_2 : Z_q \rightarrow \{0, 1\}$. The authors observed that the inner product is just a subset-sum of the secret key elements and uses only the additive group structure of Z_q. The additive group Z_q is isomorphic to a subgroup of the symmetric group S_q. The authors rewrote the inner product to the sequence of compositions of the cyclic permutations, which we will introduce in detail in Sect. 2.2. In [10], Hiromasa et al. optimized the bootstrapping procedure of [11]. We find that the bootstrapping procedure in [10] mainly uses many homomorphic permutation operations, and there is some room for improvement.

1.1 Our Results

In this paper, we first present a new packing messages strategy and a simpler homomorphic permutation algorithm of the Matrix GSW-FHE scheme. Then, we optimize the bootstrapping procedure in [10] that can refresh ciphertexts of all known LWE-based FHE scheme. Our bootstrapping procedure is more efficient and outputs refreshed ciphertexts with smaller noise since it needs less homomorphic multiplications.

Finally, we give a space-time trade-off with no need for bit-decomposition technique, which can hasten considerably the execution time whilst sacrificing reasonable memory space.

1.2   Organization

The rest of the paper is organized as follows. In Sect. 2 we introduce the Matrix GSW-FHE and recall some basic facts about symmetric groups. In Sect. 3 we present a new packing messages strategy and a simpler homomorphic permutation algorithm in Matrix GSW-FHE. In Sect. 4 we propose an optimizing bootstrapping procedure and analyze the security, correctness and performance of our optimizing bootstrapping procedure. In Sect. 5, we study a space-time trade-off for further improvement.

2   Preliminaries

For a nonnegative integer n, we let $[n] = \{1, \ldots, n\}$. We let Z denote the set of integers. Vectors are in column form and are written by using bold lower-case letters, e.g., x. We denote the i-th element of a vector by x_i. $\|x\|_\infty$ denote the l_∞ norm (the maximum norm) of the vector x and $\|x\|_2$ denote the l_2 norm (the Euclidean norm) of x. Matrices are written by using bold capital letters, e.g., X, and the i-th column vector of a matrix is denoted by x_i. For a matrix $X \in Z^{m \times n}$, $\|X\|_\infty = \max_{i \in [n]}\{\|x_i\|_\infty\}$ and $\|X\|_2 = \max_{i \in [n]}\{\|x_i\|_2\}$. We denote the concatenation of matrices or vectors by $[X_1\|X_2]$. And we let I_n denote the $n \times n$ identity matrix.

2.1   Subgaussian

A real random variable X is subguassian with parameter s if for all real number t, its (scaled) moment generating function holds $E[\exp(2\pi t X)] \le \exp(\pi s^2 t^2)$. It's easy to see that subguassian random variables have the following two properties:

(1) Homogeneity: If the subguassian random variable X has parameter s, then cX is subguassian with parameter cs.
(2) Pythagorean additivity: For two subgaussian random variables X_1 and X_2 (which are independent from each other) with parameter s_1 and s_2, respectively, $X_1 + X_2$ is subguassian with parameter $\sqrt{s_1^2 + s_2^2}$.

A real random vector $x \in R^n$ is subguassian with parameter s if all coordinates x_i is subguassian with parameter s. For a subguassian vector $x \in R^n$, there exists a universal constant C such that $\Pr[\|x\|_2 > C \cdot s\sqrt{n}] \le 2^{-\Omega(n)}$. And subguassian vectors also have the two properties: homogeneity and pythagorean additivity. By using the notion of the subguassian vectors, we can tightly analyze the noise growth in the Matrix GSW-FHE scheme.

2.2   Matrix GSW-FHE

In this section, we review the Matrix GSW-FHE scheme formally. Let λ be the security parameter and r be the number of bits to be encrypted, which defines the message space $\{0, 1\}^{r \times r}$. The Matrix GSW-FHE scheme is parameterized by an integer dimension n, an integer modulus q, and some error distribution χ over Z which we assume to be subgaussian. Let $l = \lceil \log q \rceil$, $m = O((n+r) \log q)$, and $N = (n+r) \cdot l$. Let ciphertext space be $Z_q^{(n+r) \times N}$. Define $g^T = (1, 2, 2^2, \ldots, 2^{l-1})$ and $G = g^T * I_{n+r}$.

- KeyGen$(1^\lambda, r)$: Set the parameters n, q, m, l, N and χ as described above. Sample a uniformly random matrix $A \leftarrow Z_q^{n \times m}$, secret key matrix $S' \leftarrow \chi^{r \times n}$, and noise matrix $E \leftarrow \chi^{r \times m}$. Set $S = [I_r || -S'] \in Z_q^{r \times (n+r)}$. We denote the i-th row of S by s_i^T. Let

$$B = \left(\frac{S'A + E}{A} \right) \in Z_q^{(n+r) \times m}.$$

Let $M_{(i,j)} \in \{0,1\}^{r \times r} (i, j = 1, \cdots, r)$ be the matrix with 1 in the (i,j)-th position and 0 in the others. For all $i, j = 1, \ldots, r$, sample uniformly random matrices $R_{(i,j)} \leftarrow \{0,1\}^{m \times N}$, and set

$$P_{(i,j)} = BR_{(i,j)} + \left(\frac{M_{(i,j)}S}{0} \right) G \in Z_q^{(n+r) \times N}.$$

Output $pk = (\{P_{(i,j)}\}_{i,j \in [r]}, B)$ and $sk = S$.
- SecEnc$_{sk}(M \in \{0,1\}^{r \times r})$: Sample a random matrix $A' \leftarrow Z_q^{n \times N}$ and $E \leftarrow \chi^{r \times N}$, and output the ciphertext

$$C = \left[\left(\frac{S'A' + E}{A'} \right) + \left(\frac{MS}{0} \right) G \right]_q \in Z_q^{(n+r) \times N}.$$

- PubEnc$_{pk}(M \in \{0,1\}^{r \times r})$: Sample a random matrix $R \leftarrow \{0,1\}^{m \times N}$, and output the ciphertext

$$C = BR + \sum_{i,j \in [r]: M[i,j]=1} P_{(i,j)} \in Z_q^{(n+r) \times N},$$

where $M[i,j]$ is the (i,j)-th element of M.
- Dec$_{sk}(C)$: Output the matrix $M = (\lfloor \langle s_i, c_{jl-1} \rangle \rceil_2)_{i,j \in [r]} \in \{0,1\}^{r \times r}$.
- $C_1 \oplus C_2$: Output $C_{add} = C_1 + C_2$ as the result of homomorphic addition between the input ciphertexts.
- $C_1 \otimes C_2$: Output $C_{mult} = C_1 G^{-1}(C_2)$ as the result of homomorphic multiplication between the input ciphertexts, where $G^{-1}(C)$ is a randomized, efficiently computable function that outputs a matrix X' such that $GX' = C \mod q$ and X' is subgaussian.

2.3 Symmetric Groups and Z_q-Embeddings

To understand our bootstrapping procedure, it is necessary to know some basic facts about symmetric groups, which we can find in most abstract algebra textbooks, e.g., [14].

A symmetric group S_r is the group of all permutations $\pi : \{1,\ldots,r\} \rightarrow \{1,\ldots,r\}$ with function composition as the group operation. S_r is isomorphic to the multiplicative group of r-by-r permutation matrices (i.e., 0–1 matrices with exactly one nonzero element in each row and each column). Every $\pi \in S_r$ is corresponding to a permutation matrix P_π with 1 in the $(\pi(i), i)$-th $(i = 1,\ldots,r)$ position and 0 in the others.

The additive cyclic group $(Z_r, +)$ embeds into the symmetric group S_r: every $x \in Z_r$ corresponds to a cyclic permutation $\pi \in S_r$, defined as $\pi(i) = i + x$. Notice that the permutation matrices in the image of this embedding can be represented by just their first column, an indicator vector with 1 in the $(x+1)$-th position, because the remaining columns are just the successive cyclic shifts of this column. Similarly, such permutation matrices can be multiplied only by multiplying one matrix by the first column of the other.

3 Simpler Homomorphic Permutation in Matrix GSW-FHE

The original Matrix GSW-FHE scheme [10] encrypts matrices and supports homomorphic matrix addition and multiplication. To achieve homomorphic slot-wise multiplication and permutation operation, the authors let plaintext slots correspond to diagonal entries of plaintext matrices. They achieve homomorphic permutation by multiplying the encryptions of a permutation and its inverse from left and right. We find that homomorphic permutation can be achieved just by one homomorphic multiplication operation.

We first introduce a new packing messages strategy in Matrix GSW-FHE.

Packing Messages in Column-Major Order: We let plaintext slots in packed FHE correspond to entries of first column in plaintext matrix with 0 in other columns.

For an r-dimensional vector v and a permutation π, it is easy to permute v by computing $w = P_\pi v$, where P_π is a permutation matrix corresponding to the permutation π. Given a permutation π, we can obtain the corresponding permutation matrix by the following function.

- PerMatrixGen(π): Take as input a permutation π, output the corresponding permutation matrix $P_\pi \in \{0,1\}^{r \times r}$ with 1 in the $(\pi(i), i)$-th $(i = 1,\ldots,r)$ position and 0 in the others.

  Based on our new packing messages strategy, we present a simpler homomorphic permutation algorithm that can permute plaintext slots when packing messages in column-major order as follow.

- PermuteKeyGen(S, π): Input a secret key matrix S of the Matrix GSW-FHE scheme and a permutation π, and generate P_π=PerMatrixGen(π). Output the permute key $C_\pi = \text{SecEnc}_S(P_\pi)$.

- SlotPermute(C, C_π): Given the permute key C_π and a ciphertext C that encrypts a plaintext matrix which packs messages in first column, output $C = C_\pi \otimes C$.

It should be noted that our packing messages strategy don't support homomorphic slot-wise multiplication. However, homomorphic slot-wise multiplication is not necessary for some special applications. In next section we will give an optimizing bootstrapping procedure to bring out the potential of our homomorphic permutation algorithm.

4 Bootstrapping

In this section, we optimize the bootstrapping procedure of [10] by using our packing messages strategy and homomorphic permutation algorithm described in Sect. 3. In Sect. 4.1, we present the optimizing bootstrapping procedure, whose correctness, security and performance are discussed in Sect. 4.2.

4.1 Optimizing Bootstrapping Procedure

Our bootstrapping procedure rely on the instantiation of Matrix GSW-FHE with parameters n, Q, χ. Importantly, the modulus Q is not the modulus q_L of the scheme we are bootstrapping, but rather some $Q \gg q_L$ that is sufficiently larger than the error in the output ciphertext of our bootstrapping procedure.

We follow the framework of bootstrapping procedure in [11] to bootstrap any LWE-based FHE scheme. Assuming that the ciphertext c_1 to be bootstrapped encrypts a plaintext m under a secret key s_1 for modulus q_L. We can make dimension d and modulus q as small as quasi-linear $\widetilde{O}(\lambda)$ in the security parameter via dimension-modulus reduction technique [4], while still providing provable 2^λ security under conventional lattice assumptions. Here, set modulus $q = \prod_{i=1}^{t} r_i$, where r_i are small and powers of distinct primes. We can get the appropriate modulus q by Lemma 1 [11].

Lemma 1 ([11]). For all $x \geq 7$, the product of all maximal prime powers $r_i \leq x$ is at least $\exp(3x/4)$.

Let $d' = d \cdot \lceil \log q \rceil$, then we get a binary ciphertext $c \in \{0,1\}^{d'}$ encrypts m under secret key $s \in Z_q^{d'}$ by Lemma 2 [2] as follows. We first describe two subroutines.

- BitDecomp$(x \in Z_q^n, q)$: Decompose x into bit representation. Namely, write $x = \sum_{j=0}^{\lfloor \log q \rfloor} 2^j u_j$, where $u_j \in Z_2^n$, and output $(u_0, u_1, \ldots, u_{\lfloor \log q \rfloor}) \in Z_2^{n \cdot \lceil \log q \rceil}$.
- Powersof $2(x \in Z_q^n, q)$: Output the vector $(x, 2 \cdot x, \ldots, 2^{\lfloor \log q \rfloor} \cdot x) \in Z_q^{n \cdot \lceil \log q \rceil}$.

Lemma 2 ([2]). For vectors c, s of equal length, we have

$$\langle \text{BitDecomp}(c, q), \text{Powersof } 2(s, q) \rangle = \langle c, s \rangle \bmod q.$$

After above pre-processing, we just need to evaluate the function $\lfloor \langle s, c \rangle \rceil_2 \in \{0, 1\}$ between the secret key $s \in Z_q^{d'}$ and a binary ciphertext $c \in \{0, 1\}^{d'}$ for an rounding function $\lfloor \cdot \rceil_2 : Z_q \to \{0, 1\}$. It is evident that the inner product is just a subset-sum of the Z_q-entries of s indicated by c, and uses only the additive group structure of Z_q.

By the Chinese Remainder Theorem, the ring Z_q is isomorphic to the direct product of rings $Z_{r_1} \times Z_{r_2} \times \cdots \times Z_{r_t}$. Recalling the group embeddings of $(Z_{r_i}, +)$ into S_{r_i}, we get an group embedding from $(Z_q, +)$ into $S_{r_1} \times S_{r_2} \times \cdots \times S_{r_t}$. For all $i \in [t], x \in Z_{r_i}$ corresponds to a cyclic permutation that can be represented by an indicator vector with 1 in the x-th position. Let $\phi_i : Z_q \to \{0, 1\}^r$ be the isomorphism of an element in Z_q into the cyclic permutation that corresponds to an element in Z_{r_i}, where $r = \max_i \{r_i\}$.

Our optimizing bootstrapping procedure consists of two algorithms except for above pre-processing, and we give the detail below.

- BootKeyGen(sk, s): Input the secret key $s \in Z_q^{d'}$ for ciphertexts to be refreshed and a secret key sk for the Matrix GSW-FHE scheme. For every $i \in [t]$ and $j \in [d']$, let $D_{i,j} \in \{0,1\}^{r \times r}$ be a matrix with $\phi_i(s_j)$ in its first column and 0 in the others, and $\pi_{\phi_i(s_j)}$ be the permutation corresponding to $\phi_i(s_j)$. Generate

$$\tau_{i,j} = \text{SecEnc}_{sk}(D_{i,j}),$$

$$C^{i,j} = \text{PermuteKeyGen}(sk, \pi_{\phi_i(s_j)}).$$

  In addition, we generate hints to check the equality on packed indicator vectors. For every $x \in Z_q$ such that $\lfloor x \rfloor_2 = 1$, compute

$$C^{\phi_i(x)} = \text{PermuteKeyGen}(sk, \pi_{\phi_i(x)}) \ (i \in [t]),$$

  where $\pi_{\phi_i(x)}$ is the cyclic permutation that maps the $(x \bmod r_i)$-th row to the first row in the matrix. Output the bootstrapping key

$$\text{bk} = \{(\tau_{i,j}, C^{i,j}, C^{\phi_i(x)})\}$$

- Bootstrap(bk, $c \in \{0,1\}^{d'}$): Given the bootstrapping key bk and a binary ciphertext $c \in \{0,1\}^{d'}$, do the following:
  Inner Product: For every $i \in [t]$, homomorphically compute an encryption of $\phi_i(\langle c, s \rangle)$. Let $h = \min\{j \in [d'] : c_j = 1\}$. For $i \in [t]$, set $C_i^* = \tau_{i,h}$, and iteratively compute

$$C_i^* = \text{SlotPermute}(C_i^*, C^{i,j}),$$

  for $j = h+1, \ldots, d'$ such that $c_j = 1$.
  Rounding: Homomorphically check the equality between $\langle c, s \rangle$ and every $x \in Z_q$ such that $\lfloor x \rfloor_2 = 1$, and sum their results. We can get the refreshed ciphertext as:

$$C^* = \oplus(\bigotimes_{i \in [t]} (\text{SlotPermute}(C_i^*, C^{\phi_i(x)}))) \qquad (1)$$

  where $\oplus$ traverses through all $x \in Z_q$ such that $\lfloor x \rfloor_2 = 1$.
  Output the refreshed ciphertext C^*.

The bootstrapping procedure outputs a refreshed ciphertext C^* that encrypts in the first slot the same plaintext as the ciphertext c.

4.2   Correctness, Security and Performance

Our bootstrapping procedure bases on the Matrix GSW-FHE, so it is secure by assuming the circular security and DLWE. Correctness holds as the following theorem.

Theorem 1 (Correctness). Given a secret key sk for the Matrix GSW-FHE, a ciphertext c and a secret key s described in our bootstrapping procedure, let $bk = \text{BootKeyGen}(sk, s)$. The refreshed ciphertext $C^* = \text{Bootstrap}(bk, c)$ encrypts $\lfloor \langle c, s \rangle \rceil_2 \in \{0, 1\}$ in the first slot.

Proof. From the basic facts about symmetric groups and Z_{r_i}-embeddings, it is easy to see that C_i^* encrypts $\phi_i(\langle c, s \rangle)$. Because Z_q is isomorphic to $Z_{r_1} \times Z_{r_2} \times \cdots \times Z_{r_t}$ by CRT, $\underset{i \in [t]}{\otimes} (C^{\phi_i(x)} \otimes C_i^*)$ encrypts 1 in the first slot if and only if $x = \langle c, s \rangle \bmod q$. So, C^* encrypts 1 in the first slot if and only if $\lfloor \langle c, s \rangle \rceil_2 = 1$.

Here, we will analyze the noise growth of our bootstrapping procedure. Let B be the initial noise such that $\|E\|_\infty < B$, where E is the noise matrix of fresh ciphertext which outputted by SecEnc_{sk}. Recall that n is the LWE dimension, r is the number of encrypted bits, $l = \lceil \log Q \rceil$, $N = (n + r) \cdot l$, $t = O(\log \lambda / \log \log \lambda)$, $d = \tilde{O}(\lambda)$, $d' = d \cdot \lceil \log q \rceil$ and $q = \tilde{O}(\lambda)$. We first introduce two lemmas about noise growth in Matrix GSW-FHE scheme.

Lemma 3 ([10]). Given a secret key matrix S of the Matrix GSW-FHE, let C_1 and C_2 be two ciphertexts that encrypt $M_1 \in \{0, 1\}^{r \times r}$ and $M_2 \in \{0, 1\}^{r \times r}$ with noise matrices E_1 and E_2, respectively. For $C_{add} = C_1 \oplus C_2$ and $C_{mult} = C_1 \otimes C_2$, we have

$$SC_{add} = E_{add} + (M_1 + M_2)SG,$$

$$SC_{mult} = E_{mult} + (M_1 M_2)SG,$$

where $E_{add} = E_1 + E_2$ and $E_{mult} = E + M_1 E_2$. In particular, E has in every row the independent subgaussian entries with parameter $O(\|E_1^T\|_2)$.

Lemma 4 ([10]). For $i = 1, \ldots, k$, let C_i be a ciphertext that encrypts $M_i \in \{0, 1\}^{r \times r}$ such that for any matrix $E \in Z^{r \times N}$, $\|(M_i E)^T\|_2 \leq \|E^T\|_2$, with noise matrix E_i. Let

$$C = C_1 \otimes (C_2 \otimes (\cdots (C_{k-1} \otimes (C_k \otimes G)) \cdots)).$$

For $i = 1, \ldots, k$, let $e_i = \|E_i^T\|_2$. Then the noise matrix of C has in every row the independent subgaussian entries with parameter $O(\sqrt{\sum_{i=1}^{k} e_i^2})$.

In Lemma 4, there is a fixed ciphertext $G \in Z^{(n+r) \times N}$ of the message I_r with noise 0. This makes the noise in the output ciphertext subguassian and independent from the noise in the input ciphertexts. It is easy to see that the Matrix GSW-FHE scheme has the asymmetric noise growth property, so computing a polynomial length chain of homomorphic multiplications incurs the noise growth by a multiplicative polynomial factor. We estimate the noise growth of our bootstrapping procedure in Theorem 2.

Theorem 2. Given a secret key sk, a ciphertext c and a secret key s described in our bootstrapping procedure, let $\text{bk} = \text{BootKeyGen}(sk, s)$. The noise in the refreshed ciphertext $C^* = \text{Bootstrap}(\text{bk}, c)$ has independent subgaussian entries with parameter $O(B\sqrt{Nd't q})$.

Proof. We can write the parenthesized part before the additions in Eq. (1) as a sequence of $O(d't)$ homomorphic multiplications. From Lemma 4, we can get that the noise in the term are subgaussian with parameter $O(B\sqrt{Nd't})$. From Lemma 3 and the Pythagorean additivity of subgaussian random variables, the noise in C^* are subgaussian with parameter $O(B\sqrt{Nd't q})$.

In conclusion, our bootstrapping procedure outputs refreshed ciphertexts with error growth by the $O(\sqrt{Nd't q})$ factor. By choosing a larger modulus Q than the final noise, we can get a pure FHE.

Finally, we compare our optimizing bootstrapping procedure with that in [10] as follows.

From Table 1, our optimizing bootstrapping procedure uses less homomorphic multiplications and outputs the refreshed ciphertexts with smaller noise.

Table 1. Performance comparison.

	PKC15 [10]	Our procedure
Homomorphic multiplications	$2qd't$	$qd't$
Noise growth	$B\sqrt{2Nd't q}$	$B\sqrt{Nd't q}$

5   A Space-Time Trade-Off

To make further improvement, we adopt a space-time trade-off. Here, we no longer use bit-decomposition technique, and evaluate directly a function $\lfloor \langle s, c \rangle \rceil_2 \in \{0, 1\}$ between the secret key $s \in Z_q^d$ and a ciphertext $c \in Z_q^d$ after the dimension-modulus reduction. We store the encryptions of $k \cdot s_i$ for every $k \in \{1, \ldots, q - 1\}$ and $s_i \in Z_q (i \in [d])$ in the bootstrapping key rather than the encryptions of $s_i \in Z_q$, on which we will give the detail explanation in Sect. 5.1.

5.1   The Bootstrapping Procedure

Similarly, given a ciphertext c_1 to be bootstrapped that encrypts a plaintext m under the secret key s_1 for modulus q_L, we first make dimension d and modulus q as small as quasi-linear $\widetilde{O}(\lambda)$ via dimension-modulus reduction technique [4], and get the secret key $s \in Z_q^d$ and a ciphertext $c \in Z_q^d$.

Then we evaluate the decryption function $\lfloor \langle s, c \rangle \rfloor_2 \in \{0, 1\}$ homomorphically as follows.

- BootKeyGen(q, sk, s): Input the modulus q, secret key $s \in \mathbb{Z}_q^d$ and a secret key sk for the Matrix GSW-FHE scheme. For every $i \in [t], j \in [d]$ and $k \in \{1, \ldots, q-1\}$, let $D_{i,j,k} \in \{0, 1\}^{r \times r}$ be a matrix with $\phi_i(k \cdot s_j)$ in its first column and 0 in the others, and $\pi_{\phi_i(k \cdot s_j)}$ be the permutation corresponding to $\phi_i(k \cdot s_j)$. Compute

$$\tau_{i,j,k} = \text{SecEnc}_{sk}(D_{i,j,k}),$$

$$C^{i,j,k} = \text{PermuteKeyGen}(sk, \pi_{\phi_i(k \cdot s_j)}).$$

For every $x \in \mathbb{Z}_q$ such that $\lfloor x \rfloor_2 = 1$, compute

$$C^{\phi_i(x)} = \text{PermuteKeyGen}(sk, \pi_{\phi_i(x)}) \ (i \in [t]),$$

where $\pi_{\phi_i(x)}$ is the cyclic permutation that maps the $(x \bmod r_i)$-th row to the first row in the matrix. Output the bootstrapping key

$$\text{bk} = \{(\tau_{i,j,k}, C^{i,j,k}, C^{\phi_i(x)})\}.$$

- Bootstrap$(\text{bk}, c \in \mathbb{Z}_q^d)$: Given the ciphertext $c \in \mathbb{Z}_q^d$ and bootstrapping key bk, do the following:
Inner Product: Let $h = \min\{j \in [d] : c_j \neq 0\}$. For every $i \in [t]$, set $C_i^* = \tau_{i,h,c_h}$, iteratively compute

$$C_i^* = \text{SlotPermute}(C_i^*, C^{i,j,c_j})$$

For $j = h + 1, \ldots, d$ such that $c_j \neq 0$.
Rounding: Homomorphically check the equality between $\langle c, s \rangle$ and every $x \in \mathbb{Z}_q$ such that $\lfloor x \rfloor_2 = 1$, and sum their results. Get the refreshed ciphertext

$$C^* = \oplus(\bigotimes_{i \in [t]} (\text{SlotPermute}(C_i^*, C^{\phi_i(x)})))$$

where $\oplus$ traverses through all $x \in \mathbb{Z}_q$ such that $\lfloor x \rfloor_2 = 1$.

5.2   Efficiency Comparison

We can prove that the space-time trade-off bootstrapping is secure and correct and analyze its noise growth like in Sect. 4.2. Below we just give the analysis results and efficiency comparison (Table 2).

It is easy to see that the space-time trade-off bootstrapping procedure optimizes the number of homomorphic multiplication and noise growth while increases memory complexity of the bootstrapping key. It is worthy because we can repeatedly use the same bootstrapping key to refresh as many ciphertexts as we want.

Table 2. Efficiency comparison.

	PKC15 [10]	Optimizing procedure	Space-time tradeoff
Homomorphic multiplications	$2qdt \cdot \log q$	$qdt \cdot \log q$	qdt
Noise growth	$B\sqrt{2Nqdt} \cdot \log q$	$B\sqrt{Nqdt} \cdot \log q$	$B\sqrt{Nqdt}$
Memory complexity	$dt \cdot \log q$	$dt \cdot \log q$	qdt

References

1. Gentry, C.: A Fully Homomorphic Encryption Scheme. Stanford University, Stanford (2009)
2. Brakerski, Z., Gentry, C., Vaikuntanathan, V.: (Leveled) Fully homomorphic encryption without bootstrapping. ACM Trans. Comput. Theory **6**(3), 1–36 (2014)
3. Brakerski, Z.: Fully homomorphic encryption without modulus switching from classical GapSVP. In: Safavi-Naini, R., Canetti, R. (eds.) CRYPTO 2012. LNCS, vol. 7417, pp. 868–886. Springer, Heidelberg (2012). https://doi.org/10.1007/978-3-642-32009-5_50
4. Brakerski, Z., Vaikuntanathan, V.: Efficient fully homomorphic encryption from (standard) LWE. In: Foundations of Computer Science, pp. 97–106. IEEE (2011)
5. Brakerski, Z., Vaikuntanathan, V.: Fully homomorphic encryption from ring-LWE and security for key dependent messages. In: Rogaway, P. (ed.) CRYPTO 2011. LNCS, vol. 6841, pp. 505–524. Springer, Heidelberg (2011). https://doi.org/10.1007/978-3-642-22792-9_29
6. van Dijk, M., Gentry, C., Halevi, S., Vaikuntanathan, V.: Fully homomorphic encryption over the integers. In: Gilbert, H. (ed.) EUROCRYPT 2010. LNCS, vol. 6110, pp. 24–43. Springer, Heidelberg (2010). https://doi.org/10.1007/978-3-642-13190-5_2
7. Gentry, C., Sahai, A., Waters, B.: Homomorphic encryption from learning with errors: conceptually-simpler, asymptotically-faster, attribute-based. In: Canetti, R., Garay, J.A. (eds.) CRYPTO 2013. LNCS, vol. 8042, pp. 75–92. Springer, Heidelberg (2013). https://doi.org/10.1007/978-3-642-40041-4_5
8. López-Alt, A., Tromer, E., Vaikuntanathan, V.: On-the-fly multiparty computation on the cloud via multikey fully homomorphic encryption. In: Forty-Fourth ACM Symposium on Theory of Computing, pp. 1219–1234. ACM (2012)
9. Smart, N.P., Vercauteren, F.: Fully homomorphic encryption with relatively small key and ciphertext sizes. In: Nguyen, P.Q., Pointcheval, D. (eds.) PKC 2010. LNCS, vol. 6056, pp. 420–443. Springer, Heidelberg (2010). https://doi.org/10.1007/978-3-642-13013-7_25
10. Hiromasa, R., Abe, M., Okamoto, T.: Packing messages and optimizing bootstrapping in GSW-FHE. In: Katz, J. (ed.) PKC 2015. LNCS, vol. 9020, pp. 699–715. Springer, Heidelberg (2015). https://doi.org/10.1007/978-3-662-46447-2_31
11. Alperin-Sheriff, J., Peikert, C.: Faster bootstrapping with polynomial error. In: Garay, J.A., Gennaro, R. (eds.) CRYPTO 2014. LNCS, vol. 8616, pp. 297–314. Springer, Heidelberg (2014). https://doi.org/10.1007/978-3-662-44371-2_17
12. Brakerski, Z., Vaikuntanathan, V.: Lattice-based FHE as secure as PKE. In: Conference on Innovations in Theoretical Computer Science, pp. 1–12 (2014)
13. Barrington, D.A.: Bounded-width polynomial-size branching programs recognize exactly those languages in NC^1. J. Comput. Syst. Sci. **38**(1), 150–164 (1989)
14. Jacobson, N.: Basic Algebra I. Dover Publications, USA (2012)

Short Papers

A Note on the Sidelnikov-Shestakov Attack of Niederreiter Scheme

Dingyi Pei and Jingang Liu[✉]

School of Mathematics and Information Science, Guangzhou University,
Guangzhou 510006, People's Republic of China
dypei4188@163.com, xy07liu@126.com

Abstract. The terminology "code based public-key cryptosystem" means that the algorithmic primitives of such public-key cryptosystems use error correcting codes. In papers [1,2] methods of building such public-key cryptosystems have been suggested. The Niederreiter's public-key cryptosystem [2] based on q-ary generalized Reed-Solomon codes was proposed in 1986, Sidelnikov and Shestakov [3] presented an attack on this public-key cryptosystem in 1992, showing its insecurity. By examining the attack algorithm, we note that one can change some redundant procedures to simplify the algorithm.

Keywords: Code-based cryptography · Niederreiter encryption ·
GRS codes · Sidelnikov-Shestakov attack

1 Introduction

Many widely-used public key cryptosystems, such as RSA and elliptic curve cryptography, can be broken by a large-scale quantum computer. By the terminology "code based public-key cryptosystem", it means that the algorithmic primitives of such public-key cryptosystems use error correcting codes, as one promising family of public key systems which might still work in a pos-quantum computer environment [4]. In 1978, McEliece [1] proposed the first public-key cryptosystem based on coding theory. McEliece's proposal to use Goppa codes is one of the oldest public-key cryptosystems and remains unbroken for appropriate system parameters. Its security is based on the $\mathcal{NP}$-complete problem of decoding random linear codes. However, the main drawback lies in the large size of the public key. In 1986, H. Niederreiter proposed a different scheme which uses generalized Reed-Solomon (GRS) codes. Unfortunately, Sidelnikov and Shestakov [3] showed in 1992 that Niederreiter's proposal to use GRS codes is insecure. Subsequently, the approach of [3] plays an important role in cryptanalysis regarding code-based cryptosystem, such as distinguisher and filtration attacks [5,6].

In this paper, we will simplify the attack suggested in [3]. As Goppa codes are subfield subcodes of GRS codes over $\mathbb{F}_{2^m}$, this attack has been widely concerned in [7,8]. Furthermore, a different version of this attack was proposed in [9].

© Springer Nature Switzerland AG 2019
F. Guo et al. (Eds.): Inscrypt 2018, LNCS 11449, pp. 621–625, 2019.
https://doi.org/10.1007/978-3-030-14234-6_33

2   Niederreiter's Public-Key Cryptosystem Based on GRS Codes

Let $\mathbb{F}_q$ be a finite field with q elements. The symbol $\mathfrak{A}$ denotes a check matrix of a q-ary GRS code over $\mathbb{F}_q$,

$$
\mathfrak{A}(x_1, x_2, \ldots, x_n; z_1, z_2, \ldots, z_n)
$$
$$
= \begin{pmatrix} z_1 x_1^0 & z_2 x_2^0 & \ldots & z_n x_n^0 \\ z_1 x_1^1 & z_2 x_2^1 & \ldots & z_n x_n^1 \\ \vdots & \vdots & \ddots & \vdots \\ z_1 x_1^s & z_2 x_2^s & \ldots & z_n x_n^s \end{pmatrix} \in \mathbb{F}_q^{(s+1) \times n} \tag{1}
$$

where
$$
s + 1 < n < q; \; x_i, \; z_i \in \mathbb{F}_q
$$
and
$$
z_i \neq 0 \; (1 \leq i \leq n), \; x_i \neq x_j \; for \; i \neq j
$$

Suppose this GRS code has an efficient syndrome decoding algorithm $\mathcal{D}$, which can correct up to t errors. Let $\mathcal{E}$ be a collection consisting of all matrices of the form $\mathfrak{B} = \mathbf{H}\mathfrak{A}$ where $\mathfrak{A}$ is a matrix of type (1) and

$$
\mathbf{H} = (h_{ij})_{0 \leq i,j \leq s}
$$

is a $(s+1) \times (s+1)$ non-singular matrix with the elements in $\mathbb{F}_q$. It follows from the definitions that the matrix $\mathfrak{B}$ of $\mathcal{E}$ has the form

$$
\mathfrak{B}_{(s+1) \times n} = \mathbf{H}\mathfrak{A} = \begin{pmatrix} z_1 f_0(x_1) & z_2 f_0(x_2) & \ldots & z_n f_0(x_n) \\ z_1 f_1(x_1) & z_2 f_1(x_2) & \ldots & z_n f_1(x_n) \\ \vdots & \vdots & \ddots & \vdots \\ z_1 f_s(x_1) & z_2 f_s(x_2) & \ldots & z_n f_s(x_n) \end{pmatrix} = (b_{ij}) \tag{2}
$$

and
$$
b_{ij} = z_j f_i(x_j) = z_j \sum_{k=0}^{s} h_{ik} x_j{}^k \qquad (0 \leq i \leq s, 1 \leq j \leq n) \tag{3}
$$

In Niederreiter's public-key cryptosystem, Bob randomly and equiprobably chooses a matrix

$$
\mathfrak{B} = \mathbf{H}\mathfrak{A}(x_1, x_2, \ldots, x_n; z_1, z_2, \ldots, z_n)
$$

of type (2) in $\mathcal{E}$ with t as his public key, and takes $\mathbf{H}; x_1, x_2, \ldots, x_n; z_1, z_2, \ldots, z_n$ and the decoding algorithm $\mathcal{D}$ as his private key. If Alice wants to send a secret message m to Bob, firstly, the message m must be transformed into a vector $\bar{m} \in \mathbb{F}_q^n$ with not more than $t = \lceil \frac{s}{2} \rceil$ non-zero coordinates, called a plaintext. Then Alice encrypts $\bar{m}$ into a ciphertext $c = \mathfrak{B}\bar{m}^T$. When Bob receives the ciphertext c, he calculates $\mathbf{H}^{-1}c = \mathfrak{A}\bar{m}^T$ and reconstructs the plaintext $\bar{m}$ using the syndrome decoding algorithm $\mathcal{D}$.

3   Simplified Attack

An attack on the public-key cryptosystem based on GRS codes was proposed in [3], which can recover a (alternative) private key $\mathbf{H} = \left(h_{ij}\right)$ and $x_1, x_2, \ldots, x_n$; $z_1, z_2, \ldots, z_n$ by using its public key $\mathfrak{B} = \left(b_{ij}\right)$. More precisely, one solution

$$\left(\mathbf{H} = \left(h_{ij}\right); x_1, x_2, \ldots, x_n; z_1, z_2, \ldots, z_n\right)$$

as unknown of the system of Eq. (3) can be computed. The calculation is accomplished in two steps: first to find the numbers $x_1, x_2, \ldots, x_n$, and then the numbers $z_1, z_2, \ldots, z_n$ as well as the matrix $\mathbf{H}$.

The most space of [3] is devoted to describing the algorithm in the first step, exploiting birational transformations on the projective line $\mathbb{F}_q \cup \infty$, and solutions of several systems of linear equations. It's easy to see that this algorithm can not guarantee to find the real numbers $x_1, x_2, \ldots, x_n$ used in the original private key. In this note, we simplify the attack algorithm by pointing out that the algorithm of the first step may be replaced by "randomly and equiprobably to choose n different numbers $x_1, x_2, \ldots, x_n$ from $\mathbb{F}_q$", which may reduce $\mathcal{O}(s^3 + sn)$ arithmetic operations in the first step (Refer to [3] for detail). There are $\binom{q}{n}$ choices for $x_1, x_2, \ldots, x_n$. The rest of the algorithm is the same as that in the second step of [3]. For completeness, we briefly explain it as follows.

Let $x_1, x_2, \ldots, x_n$ be the numbers randomly chosen in the first step. Since any $s + 1$ columns of $\mathfrak{B}$ are linearly independent over $\mathbb{F}_q$, and any $s + 2$ columns of $\mathfrak{B}$ are linearly dependent over $\mathbb{F}_q$, the system of equations

$$\sum_{j=1}^{s+2} c_j b_{ij} = 0 \qquad (0 \leq i \leq s)$$

has a solution

$$(c_1, c_2, \ldots, c_{s+2}) \in \mathbb{F}_q^{s+2}$$

with each $c_j \neq 0$ $(1 \leq j \leq s + 2)$, otherwise the matrix $\mathfrak{B}$ would contain $s + 1$ linearly dependent columns. Furthermore,

$$\sum_{j=1}^{s+2} c_j b_{ij} = \sum_{j=1}^{s+2} c_j z_j \sum_{k=0}^{s} h_{ik} x_j^k$$

$$= \sum_{k=0}^{s} (\sum_{j=1}^{s+2} c_j x_j^k z_j) h_{ik} = 0 \qquad (0 \leq i \leq s)$$

which implies that

$$(\sum_{j=1}^{s+2} c_j x_j^0 z_j, \; \sum_{j=1}^{s+2} c_j x_j^1 z_j, \ldots, \; \sum_{j=1}^{s+2} c_j x_j^s z_j) \cdot \mathbf{H^T} = 0 \qquad (4)$$

Because $\mathbf{H}$ is a non-singular matrix, it reduces that

$$\sum_{j=1}^{s+2} c_j x_j^k z_j = 0 \qquad (0 \le k \le s) \tag{5}$$

Since for any $\alpha \ne 0 \in \mathbb{F}_q$, we have

$$\alpha^{-1}\mathbf{H} \cdot \mathfrak{A}(x_1, x_2, \ldots, x_n;\ \alpha z_1, \alpha z_2, \ldots, \alpha z_n)$$
$$= \mathbf{H}\mathfrak{A}(x_1, x_2, \ldots, x_n;\ z_1, z_2, \ldots, z_n)$$

We may assume that $z_1 = 1$. Then equality (5) becomes a linear system of $s+1$ equations with $s+1$ unknowns $z_2, z_3, \ldots, z_{s+2}$,

$$\sum_{j=2}^{s+2} (c_j x_j^k z_j + c_1 x_1^k) = 0 \qquad (0 \le k \le s)$$

This system has unique solution because its determinant is the form of Vandermonde determinant. Solving this system yields the unique sought numbers

$$z_1 = 1, z_2, \ldots, z_{s+2}$$

with each

$$z_i \ne 0 \ (2 \le i \le s+2)$$

By (3) we have, for each $(0 \le i \le s)$

$$\sum_{k=0}^{s} h_{ik} x_j^k = z_j^{-1} b_{ij} \qquad (1 \le j \le s+1)$$

This is a system of linear equations with unknown

$$\mathbf{H}_i = (h_{i0}, h_{i1}, \ldots, h_{is})$$

which is the i-th row of the matrix $\mathbf{H}$. Its determinant also is the Vandermonde determinant, the $\mathbf{H}_i$ can be determined uniquely, so does the matrix $\mathbf{H}$.

To find the matrix $\mathbf{H}^{-1}$, we have by (2)

$$\mathfrak{A} = \mathbf{H}^{-1}\mathfrak{B} = \begin{pmatrix} z_1 & z_2 & \cdots & z_n \\ z_1 x_1 & z_2 x_2 & \cdots & z_n x_n \\ \vdots & \vdots & \ddots & \vdots \\ z_1 x_1^s & z_2 x_2^s & \cdots & z_n x_n^s \end{pmatrix}$$

The sought numbers z_j $(s+3 \le j \le n)$ are determined by the first row. The algorithm is accomplished now. The computational complexity of the algorithm is $\mathcal{O}(s^4 + sn)$ as shown in [3]. For a given set $x_1, x_2, \ldots, x_n$, there is an unique solution for $z_1, z_2, \ldots, z_n$ and $\mathbf{H}$, the number of all solutions of the equation system (3) is $\binom{q}{n}$.

4   Conclusion

In this note, we studied Sidelnikov-Shestakov attack of Niederreiter's public-key cryptosystems based on Generalized Read-Solomon codes, and simplified the original attack algorithm [3]. Future work in attempting to apply the improved attack on other related methods, may also be an interesting problem.

Acknowledgments. The authors would like to thank the anonymous reviewers of Inscrypt 2018 for their fruitful comments that improved the presentation of this note. This work has been partially supported by the Guangzhou University project (Project No. 2017GDJC-D04).

References

1. McEliece, R.J.: A public-key cryptosystem based on algebraic coding theory. Deep space network progress report, 42–44, pp. 114–116 (1978)
2. Niederreiter, H.: Knapsack-type cryptosystems and algebraic coding theory. Prob. Control Inf. Theory **15**(2), 159–166 (1986)
3. Sidelnikov, V.M., Shestakov, S.O.: On insecurity of cryptosystems based on generalized Reed-Solomon codes. Discrete Math. Appl. **2**(4), 439–444 (1992)
4. Chen, L., Chen, L., Jordan, S., Liu, Y.-K., Moody, D., et al.: Report on post-quantum cryptography. Technical reports (2016). https://doi.org/10.6028/nist.ir. 8105
5. Couvreur, A., Gaborit, P., Gauthier-Umana, V., et al.: Distinguisher-based attacks on public-key cryptosystems using Reed–Solomon codes. Des. codes Crypt. **73**(2), 641–666 (2014)
6. Couvreur, A., Otmani, A., Tillich, J.P.: Polynomial time attack on wild McEliece over quadratic extensions. In: Nguyen, P.Q., Oswald, E. (eds.) EUROCRYPT 2014. LNCS, vol. 8441, pp. 17–39. Springer, Heidelberg (2014). https://doi.org/10.1007/978-3-642-55220-5_2
7. Engelbert, D., Overbeck, R., Schmidt, A.: A summary of McEliece-type cryptosystems and their security. J. Math. Cryptol. **1**(2), 151–199 (2007)
8. Overbeck, R., Sendrier, N.: Code-based cryptography. In: Bernstein, D.J., Buchmann, J., Dahmen, E. (eds.) Post-Quantum Cryptography, pp. 95–145. Springer, Berlin, Heidelberg (2009). https://doi.org/10.1007/978-3-540-88702-7_4
9. Gabidulin, E.: Public-key cryptosystems based on linear codes. In: Proceedings of 4th IMA Conference on Cryptography and Coding 1993, Codes & Ciphers. IMA Press (1995)

An Efficient Anonymous Authentication Scheme Based on Double Authentication Preventing Signature for Mobile Healthcare Crowd Sensing

Jinhui Liu[1], Yong Yu[1(✉)], Yannan Li[2], Yanqi Zhao[1], and Xiaojiang Du[3]

[1] School of Computer Science, Shaanxi Normal University, Xi'an 710119, China
yuyong@snnu.edu.cn
[2] School of Computing and Information Technology, University of Wollongong, Wollongong, NSW 2522, Australia
[3] Department of Computer and Information Sciences, Temple University, Philadelphia, PA 19122, USA

Abstract. With the widespread growth of cloud computing and mobile healthcare crowd sensing (MHCS), an increasing number of individuals are outsourcing their masses of bio-information in the cloud server to achieve convenient and efficient. In this environment, Cloud Data Center (CDC) needs to authenticate masses of information without revealing owners' sensitive information. However, tremendous communication cost, storage space cost and checking time cost lead to CDC that give rise to all kinds of privacy concerns as well. To mitigate these issues, To mitigate these issues, we propose a data anonymous batch verification scheme for MHCS based on a certificateless double authentication preventing aggregate signature. The proposed scheme can authenticate all sensing bio-information in a privacy preserving way. We then present that the proposed CL-DAPAS scheme is existentially unforgeable in the Random Oracle Model (ROM) assuming that Computational Diffie-Hellman problem is difficult to solve. Furthermore, we provide an implementation and evaluate performance of the proposed scheme and demonstrate that it achieves less efficient computational cost compared with some related schemes.

Keywords: Mobile healthcare crowd sensing · Security · Privacy · Double authentication preventing signature · Elliptic curve discrete logarithm problem

1 Introduction

An increasing interest is growing around Cloud Data Centers (CDC) that allows the delivery of various kinds of agile services and applications over telecommunication networks and the Internet. Mobile crowd sensing (MCS) in the IOT assembles scenario, environmental, and individual data within a specific range

© Springer Nature Switzerland AG 2019
F. Guo et al. (Eds.): Inscrypt 2018, LNCS 11449, pp. 626–636, 2019.
https://doi.org/10.1007/978-3-030-14234-6_34

via the intelligent sensing equipment carried by mobile users, thus providing social decision-making services [1]. As an important application branch of MCS, MHCS furnishes a more convenient healthcare medical services for institutions and individuals [2,3]. In MHCS, participants accept a sensing assignment for specific purpose from cloud sever and they make a collection of relevant health data and upload these data to the cloud sever. At the same time, the cloud sever transmits requested information to a range of special healthcare institutes for further analysis. CDC in MHCS needs to authenticate masses of bio-information without revealing sensitive information of these participants. There exists numerous research findings from data integrity checking protocols and data deletion protocols that were proposed to different requirements of authentication which can be applied to MHCS [4–10].

A representative structure of the MHCS is listed in Fig. 1 [3,11]. Communication process in MHCS can be falled into two aspects. For one thing, participants put up health data which are assembled by mobile intelligent terminals to a CS (Cloud Server). For another, by studying personal health data, anytime anywhere medical service and health information can be offered by remote healthcare system and vital signs of patients which are refered to long distance health applications can be mounted in mobile intelligent endpoints or other monitoring equipment.

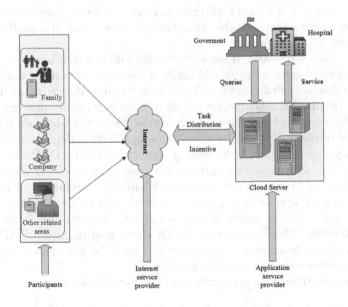

Fig. 1. A typical MHCS framework

By wireless communication model, adversaries against MHCS is easy to manage fairly communication channels, that is to say, adversaries could hold up, alter, replay and erase messages that transmitted in MHCS system. Hence MHCS are susceptible to numberous types of attacks. In practice, sensitive information of participates, such as identity, individual social activities and health status, may be leakaged by the collected health data. These collected health data ought to be managed safely in a actual time mode, else it will reduce health service quality. If health data is eavesdropped or tampered by an adversary, it will cause damage to personal health and estates, so far as to personal lives. Therefore, security and privacy protection of collected health data in MHCS is an indispensable part of many practical applications [12–14].

Several papers have studied related security and privacy of wireless issues [15–18]. Aggregate signature (AS), as one of the most efficient privacy and integrity, resolving the issues of limited resources, privacy, message integrity and authenticity, is applicable to addressing the some issues in MHCS [19–22]. At present, there are many AS schemes which have been put forward for all kinds of practical applications. In 2003, Boneh et al. put forward the first AS (aggregate signature) which enables a signer to construct a valid signatures on their messages to be signed and have a batch verification [19]. After that, most of AS schemes were incurred a complicated certificate management [23,37]. In 2007, Castro et al. [24] provided a general notion of certificateless (CL) AS that made a combination of properties of AS and CLPKC (Certificateless Public Key Cryptography). The same year, Gong et al. standardized a security model for CL-AS [25]. After that many CLAS schemes were designed [3,26–29]. Although previously proposed AS could mitigate privacy preserving authentication for MHCS, there exists many double signature problems and the performance of these schemes is unsatisfactory.

Consider such a scenario, if some special field doctor in a hospital sign twice about a patient of same identity and kinds of diseases, we can consider that the doctor have done some misconducts. To prevent fraud by discouraging users from submitting (signing) duplicates, we use double authentication preventing signatures (DAPS) instead of conventional signatures, where the address a (or its associated space respectively) can be given some application dependent semantics. Unlike group signature and linkable-ring signature [30,31], DAPS are stronger signatures in the sense that signers secret keys can be revealed [32,33]. Revealing the secret key as discouragement to behave fraudulent is related to PKI-assured non-transferability approach in anonymous credential systems. Many instances are shown that a double signer is not enough of a penalty but is enough of a deterable function. There are some research about post-quantum DAPS system [34–36]. Based on these, we provide a new and more higher efficient conditional privacy protection signature scheme for MHCS.

Our main contributions are summarized in the following.

1. We propose a high efficient authentication scheme to verify batch messages received from MHCS participants.
2. We make a security analysis to show that CL-DAPAS fulfil some security needs in MHCS.
3. We present a computation cost analysis to show that our CL-DAPAS scheme has higher efficiency than some related schemes.

2 Preliminaries and System Model

2.1 Hard Problem Assumption

Definition 1 (ECDLP (Elliptic Curve Discrete Logarithm Problem)). *Given two points $P, Q \in G$ on E, it is difficult to calculate an integer $x \in Z_q^*$ to get the equation $P = xQ$.*

Definition 2 (CDHP (Computational Diffie Hellman Problem)). *Given two random points $xP, yP \in G_1$, where x, y are two unknown information in Z_q, it is difficult to obtain xyP in polynomial time.*

2.2 System Model

We define system model of MHCS scenario, which consists of requestors, a Cloud Data Center (CDC), a Management Server (MS), and a MHCS participants.

1. For some specific purposes, requestors refer healthcare sensing tasks to CDC. Then they can study memoir from CDC and then forecast certain health and medical problems in some regions.
2. According to the demands of the requestors, CDC release and manage healthcare sensing tasks. And it can aggregate and verify healthcare data for participants.
3. MS can administer registration for participants, where MS is a trusted third party. MS assignments indexes for participants to substitute for their actual identities and is responsible for issuing a half private keys of legitimate participants. MS is able to verify health data uploaded by participants by using an index.
4. Participants can upload healthcare data for CDC by intelligent terminals.

2.3 Security Requirements

The aim objective of the proposed scheme for MHCS is to provide an efficient privacy preserving to satisfy the following security requirements:

1. **Batch authentication:** The signed health data is able to be aggregated and verified by CDC.
2. **Nonrepudiation:** Participants have sent related health data to CDC that they cannot deny.
3. **Anonymity:** Even if CDC can obtain and check these aggregated messages, CDC is not able to get data provider's real identity.
4. **Deterable-iff-double signature by one signer:** If an participant signs on colliding message (a, p_1) and (a, p_2), he can be linked and his signature keys can be extracted by anyone.

3   The Proposed Data Batch Verification Scheme Based on CL-DAPAS for MHCS

Consider such a scenario in MHCS, if some special field doctor in a hospital sign twice about a patient of same identity and kinds of diseases, we can consider that the doctor have done some misconduct. Due to lack of space, a concrete CL-DAPAS will appear in the full version of this paper.

3.1   The Proposed Scheme

Initialization. In this phase, MS sets up an enrollment system in the following.

1. G is an q order additive group. P is a generator of G. Choose a key s_{MS} and calculate corresponding public key $P_{MSpub} = s_{MS}P$. Elect hash functions $h_1 : \{0,1\}^* \times G \rightarrow G$ and $h_2 : \{0,1\}^* \times G \rightarrow Z_q^*$.
2. Publish parameters $(P, E, G, p, q, P_{MSpub}, h_1, h_2)$ and maintain the master private key s_{MS}. CDC's key pair (Q_{CDC}, s_{CDC}) as its key pair, where $Q_{CDC} = s_{CDC}P$.

Registration. In this phase, a participant C_i computes partial key and MS is to access a CDC.

1. C_i chooses randomly a number $s_{i1} \in_R Z_q^*$ as partial private key and computes $Q_{i1} = s_{i1}P$. C_i obtains psk_{i1} from MS who computes $psk_{i1} = s_{MS}h_1(Id_i, Q_{i1})$ as the other part of private key.
   C_i's public-private keys (s_{i1}, psk_{i1}) and (Id_i, Q_{i1}) as public key.
2. MS chooses randomly a number $w_i \in_R Z_q^*$ and computes
   $Q_{i2} = h_1(Id_i, Q_{i1})$, $psk_{i2} = s_{MS}h_1(Id_i, Q_{i1})$, $index_{is} = w_iQ_{i2}$ and $index_{iv} = w_ipsk_{i2}$. Thus, MS stores serial number $sn_i = (Id_i, Q_{i1}, Q_{i2}, index_{is}, index_{iv})$. Then MS sends $sn_i = index_{iv}$ and $index_{is}$ to the C_i via a secure channel.

Sign. C_i chooses randomly $r_i \in_R Z_q^*$ and $t_i \in_R Z_+$, where t_i is a time stamp which is able to keep freshness of $M_i = (a, p_i)$. C_i performs the following steps:

1. C_i computes $R_i = r_iP$, $K_i = h_2(p_i\|t_i, R_i)$, $S_i = s_{i1} + a \cdot K_ir_i \bmod q$,
   $U_i = psk_{i1} + r_iP_{MSpub}$ and $Enc_{Q_{CDC}}(SN_i\|K_i\|t_i) = SN_i'$
2. C_i uploads $(R_i, K_i, S_i, U_i, M_i, SN_i')$ to CDC who announces the sensing task, where $M_i = (a, p_i)$.

Verify. To ensure the validity of each required sensing data signed by a C_i, the following steps are executed by CDC.

1. CDC calculates $SN_i\|K_i\|t_i = Dec_{s_{CDC}}(SN_i')$. Verify $K_i = h_2(p_i\|t_i, R_i)$.
2. Check whether equations $K_i = h_2(p_i\|t_i, R_i)$, $S_iP = Q_{i1} + a \cdot k_iR_i$ and $e(U_i, P) = e(P_{MSpub}, R_i + h_1(Id_i, Q_{i1}))$ hold.
   If the above equations are true, then the verifier affirms the signature is a valid signature; otherwise, the signature is invalid.

Aggregation. Upon receiving $(R_i, K_i, S_i, U_i, M_i, SN_i')$, CDC computes $SN_i \| K_i \| t_i = Dec_{s_{CDC}}(SN_i')$.

For a set of n participants $C_1, \cdots, C_n$ and the corresponding signatures $(R_i, K_i, S_i, U_i, M_i)$, CDC aggregates all signatures as follows once time T is up:

1. $KR = \sum_{i=1}^{n} a \cdot K_i R_i, \; Q = \sum_{i=1}^{n} Q_{i1}, \; R = \sum_{i=1}^{n} R_i, \; S = \sum_{i=1}^{n} S_i \bmod q,$

   $H = \sum_{i=1}^{n} h_1(Id_i, Q_{i1})$ and $index_v = \sum_{i=1}^{n} index_{iv} \bmod q.$

2. $\sigma = (KR, Q, S, R, H, index_v)$ is the aggregated signature.

Batch Verification. CDC verifies the validity of these equations. Check whether equations $SP = Q + KR$ and $e(U, P) = e(P_{MSpub}, H + R)$ hold.

Extract$_{sk}$ Iff Double Signature by One Signer. C_i: If C_j sign twice, CDC receives two signatures from colliding messages $M_{i1} = (a, p_{i1})$ and $M_{i2} = (a, p_{i2})$ from one signer.

According to $\sigma_{i1} = (M_{i1}, R_i, K_{i1}, S_{i1}, U_i)$ and $\sigma_{i2} = (M_{i2}, R_i, K_{i2}, S_{i2}, U_i)$, Anyone can compute the private key s_{i1}, psk_{i1} of C_j as follows.

1. According to $R_i = r_i P$, $K_{i1} = h_2(ID_i \| R_i \| p_{i1})$, $K_{i2} = h_2(ID_i \| p_i, R_i)$,

$$\begin{cases} S_{i1} = s_{i1} + a \cdot K_{i1} r_i \bmod q \; ; \\ S_{i2} = s_{i1} + a \cdot K_{i2} r_i \bmod q \; . \end{cases}$$

2. Compute

$$s_{i1} = \frac{(K_{i1} S_{i2} - K_{i2} S_{i1})}{(K_{i1} - K_{i2})}, r_i = \frac{(S_{i2} - S_{i1})}{a(K_{i2} - K_{i1})} \text{ and } psk_{i1} = U_i - \frac{(S_{i2} - S_{i1})}{a(K_{i2} - K_{i1})} P_{pub}.$$

3.2 Security Analysis

Theorem 1. *If the adversary $\mathcal{A}_1$ who has the ability of substituting for participants' public keys with MS' private keys can break CL-DAPAS, CDH problem could be solved in a non-negligible probability.*

Theorem 2. *Assuming that CDH problem is hard, our CL-DAPAS is existentially unforgeable under chosen message attack.*

The proof process of the two theorem above will appear in the full version of this paper. By security analysis, we can show that our scheme satisfy the following property.

Batch Authentication and Message Integrity Authentication: The authentication and integrity of individual CL-DAPAS can be reduced to the CDH assumption. So CDC could authenticate identities of participants by their signatures. Furthermore, CDC is able to find any variation of received signatures by checking whether the equation $SP = Q + KR$ holds.

Non-repudiation: The non-repudiation of the individual crowdsensed data depends on the security of underlying Encryption algorithm. MHCS participants can not deny that they have transmitted their health data. CDC can verify their signatures via corresponding public keys.

No Inefficiency Problem of the Double Secret Key: CDC needs to save the master key secretly which can be reduced to the CDH assumption. Therefore, the proposed scheme for MHCS is able to provide no inefficiency problem of the double secret key.

Deterable-iff-double Signature by One Signer: Deterable-iff-double signature by one signer can be reduced to DSE security of the DAPAS [32,33].

4   Performance Analysis

To give practical performance analysis, we get the execution time of different cryptographic processes by Pairing-Based Cryptography library [38], which is a famous and free java library for implementing of pairing-based cryptosystems. For schemes based on bilinear pairings for MHCS, to achieve 80 bits security level, we choose a bilinear pairing $e : G_a \times G_a \to G_m$, where G_a is generated by a q order point P on $E : y = x^3 + x$ mod $\bar{p}$. For the proposed scheme, we use Type-I elliptic curve $E : y^2 = x^3 - x + 1$ over a ternary extension field F_{3^m}. G_1 is a group of points $E(F_{3^m})$. The experiment is executed on a personal calculator, which is equipped with an windows 7 64 OS, intel(R) Core(TM) i7-4710MQ CPU 2.50 GHz, 12 GB RAM With JPBC library for 1000 times. Execution time and related cryptographic operations are shown in Table 1.

Table 1. The definition and execution time of related operations.

Cryptographic operation	Definition	Execution time
T_{bp}	a bilinear pairing process	7.8 ms
T_{sm-bp}	a point multiplication process	14 ms
T_{pa-bp}	a point addition process	0.0005 ms
T_{Z_p-bp}	a map-to-point hash process	0.003 ms
T_{G_1-bp}	a map-to-G_1 hash process	32.8 ms
T_{sm-ecc}	a point multiplication process	2.8 ms
T_{pa-ecc}	a point addition process	0.0005 ms
T_{Z_p-ecc}	a map-to-point hash process	0.003 ms
T_{G_1-ecc}	a map-to-G_1 hash process	0.2 ms

Let P_1, P_2, P_3 and P_4 denote Signing, Verification, Aggregation and Batch Verification phase respectively. We present a comparison analysis of THH [27], Malhi-Batra [28], XGCL [29], Liu-Cao scheme [3] and our proposed scheme.

In the Signing stage P_1, we find that our scheme requires $2nT_{bp}+nT_{HZ_p-ecc}+nT_{sm-ecc}+nT_{pa-ecc} \approx 18.4035n$ ms, while schemes in THH [27], Malhi-Batra [28], XGCL [29] and Liu-Cao's scheme [3] require $2nT_{HZ_p-bp}+2nT_{HG-bp}+3nT_{sm-bp} \approx 107.6006n$ ms, $nT_{HZ_p-bp}+4nT_{sm-bp} \approx 56.003n$ ms and $nT_{HZ_p-bp}+3nT_{sm-bp} \approx 42.003n$ ms, $nT_{HZ_p-bp}+2nT_{sm-bp} \approx 28.003n$ ms respectively. For the total execution time, the percentage improvement for the Signing stage P_1 of CLDAPAS over THH et al.'s scheme is about $\frac{(107.6006n-18.4035n)}{107.6006n} \approx 83\%$. Other percentage improvements can also be computed by similar method, they are 67%, 56%, 34% respectively.

In the verification stage, our scheme needs $nT_{HZ_p-bp}+nT_{HG-bp}+5nT_{sm-ecc}+2nT_{bp} \approx 29.8003n$ ms, while schemes require $2nT_{HZ_p-bp}+3nT_{HG-bp}+4nT_{bp}+2nT_{sm-bp} \approx 157.606n$ ms in [27], $nT_{HZ_p-bp}+nT_{HG-bp}+3nT_{bp}+3nT_{sm-bp} \approx 98.203n$ ms in [28], $nT_{HZ_p-bp}+nT_{HG-bp}+3nT_{bp}+2nT_{sm-bp} \approx 84.203n$ ms in [29] and $nT_{HZ_p-bp}+nT_{HG-bp}+2nT_{bp}+nT_{sm-bp} \approx 62.403n$ ms in [3]. The percentage improvement for P_2 of CLDAPAS are 81%, 70%, 65%, 52% respectively.

In aggregation stage P_3, our scheme needs $5T_{sm-ecc} \approx 14n$ ms scalar multiplications, while the scheme in [3] requires $28n$ ms.

In aggregation verification stage P_4, our scheme needs $2nT_{sm-ecc}+2T_{bp} \approx 21.2n$ ms, while schemes in [3,27–29] requires about $31.2+28n$ ms, $23.4+42n$ ms, $23.4+28n$ ms and $15.6n$ ms respectively. Although the execution time of our scheme in batch verification stage P_4 is higher than the execution time of scheme [3], other stages are much lower than execution time of these schemes.

5   Conclusion

To protect the security and privacy of online health data from the unauthorized entities in MHCS, we construct an efficient anonymous data batch authentication scheme. Our proposed scheme has advantages of certificateless signature, aggregate signature and double signature that can be disincentivized. The security analysis of the scheme is conducted to ensure the data integrity, non-repudiation, no inefficiency problem of the double secret key, batch authentication and deterable function. Performance analysis results of our proposed scheme has higher efficient in time consumption. With rapid development of quantum computers, in the future we will study the design of post-quantum certificateless double authentication preventing aggregate signatures which are suitable for MHCS.

Acknowledgments. The author would like to thank the anonymous reviewers for their constructive comments and suggestions. This work was supported by National Key R&D Program of China (2017YFB0802000), National Natural Science Foundation of China (61772326, 61572303, 61872229, 61802239), NSFC Research Fund for International Young Scientists (61750110528), National Cryptography Development Fund during the 13th Five-year Plan Period (MMJJ20170216, MMJJ201701304), Foundation of State Key Laboratory of Information Security (2017-MS-03), Fundamental Research Funds for the Central Universities(GK201702004, GK201803061, 2018CBLY006) and China Postdoctoral Science Foundation (2018M631121).

References

1. Ganti, R.K., Ye, F., Lei, H.: Mobile crowdsensing: current state and future challenges. IEEE Commun. Mag. **49**(11), 32–37 (2011)
2. Pryss, R., Reichert, M., Herrmann, J., Langguth, B., Schlee, W.: Mobile crowd sensing in clinical and psychological trials – a case study. In: IEEE International Symposium on Computer-Based Medical Systems, pp. 23–24 (2015)
3. Liu, J., Cao, H., Li, Q., Cai, F., Du, X., Gui, M.: A large-scale concurrent data Anonymous batch verification scheme for mobile healthcare crowd sensing. IEEE Internet Things J. (2018). https://doi.org/10.1109/JIOT.2018.2828463
4. Zhang, H., Zhang, Q., Du, X.: Toward vehicle-assisted cloud computing for smartphones. IEEE Trans. Veh. Technol. **12**(64), 5610–5618 (2015)
5. Li, J., Chen, X., Chow, S.S.M., Huang, Q., Wong, D.S., Liu, Z.: Multi-authority fine-grained access control with accountability and its application in cloud. J. Netw. Comput. Appl. https://doi.org/10.1016/j.jnca.2018.03.006
6. Li, T., Li, J., Liu, Z., Li, P., Jia, C.: Differentially private naive bayes learning over multiple data sources. Inf. Sci. **444**, 89–104 (2018)
7. Yu, Y., et al.: Identity-based remote data integrity checking with perfect data privacy preserving for cloud storage. IEEE Trans. Inf. Forensics Secur. **12**(4), 767–778 (2017)
8. Li, Y., Yu, Y., Susilo, W., Min, G., Ni, J., Choo, R.: Fuzzy identity-based data integrity auditing for reliable cloud storage systems. IEEE Trans. Dependable Secur. Comput. **16**(1), 72–83 (2019)
9. Yu, Y., Li, Y., Yang, B., Susilo, W., Yang, G., Bai, J.: Attribute-based cloud data integrity auditing for secure outsourced storage. IEEE Trans. Emerg. Top. Comput. https://doi.org/10.1109/TETC.2017.2759329
10. Xue, L., Yu, Y., Li, Y., Au, M.H., Du, X., Yang, B.: Efficient attribute-based encryption with attribute revocation for assured data deletion. Inf. Sci. **479**, 640–650 (2019)
11. He, D., Chan, S., Guizani, M.: User privacy and data trustworthiness in mobile crowd sensing. IEEE Wirel. Commun. **22**(1), 28–34 (2015)
12. Gisdakis, S., Giannetsos, T., Papadimitratos, P.: Security, privacy, and incentive provision for mobile crowd sensing systems. IEEE Internet Things J. **3**(5), 839–853 (2016)
13. Zhang, K., Ni, J., Yang, K., Liang, X., Ren, J., Shen, X.S.: Security and privacy in smart city applications: challenges and solutions. IEEE Commun. Mag. **55**(1), 122–129 (2017)
14. Ni, J., Zhang, K., Yu, Y., Lin, X., Shen, X.S.: Providing task allocation and secure deduplication for mobile crowdsensing via fog computing. IEEE Trans. Dependable Secur. Comput. 1–12 (2018). https://doi.org/10.1109/TDSC.2018.2791432
15. Xiao, Y., Rayi, V., Sun, B., Du, X., Hu, F., Galloway, M.: A survey of key management schemes in wireless sensor networks. J. Comput. Commun. **30**(11–12), 2314–2341 (2007)
16. Du, X., Xiao, Y., Guizani, M., Chen, H.H.: An effective key management scheme for heterogeneous sensor networks. Ad Hoc Netw. **5**(1), 24–34 (2007)
17. Du, X., Chen, H.H.: Security in wireless sensor networks. IEEE Wirel. Commun. Mag. **15**(4), 60–66 (2008)
18. Du, X., Guizani, M., Xiao, Y., Chen, H.H.: Transactions papers, a routing-driven elliptic curve cryptography based key management scheme for heterogeneous sensor networks. IEEE Trans. Wirel. Commun. **8**(3), 1223–1229 (2009)

19. Boneh, D., Gentry, C., Lynn, B., Shacham, H.: Aggregate and verifiably encrypted signatures from bilinear maps. In: Biham, E. (ed.) EUROCRYPT 2003. LNCS, vol. 2656, pp. 416–432. Springer, Heidelberg (2003). https://doi.org/10.1007/3-540-39200-9_26

20. Xiong, H., Guan, Z., Chen, Z., Li, F.: An efficient certificateless aggregate signature with constant pairing computations. Inf. Sci. **219**, 225–235 (2013)

21. Shen, L., Ma, J., Liu, X., Wei, F., Miao, M.: A secure and efficient id-based aggregate signature scheme for wireless sensor networks. IEEE Internet Things J. **4**(2), 546–554 (2017)

22. Kumar, P., Kumari, S., Sharma, V., Sangaiah, A.K., Wei, J., Li, X.: A certificateless aggregate signature scheme for healthcare wireless sensor network. Sustain. Comput. Inform. Syst. **18**, 80–89 (2018)

23. Zhang, L., Zhang, F.: A new certificateless aggregate signature scheme. Comput. Commun. **32**(6), 1079–1085 (2009)

24. Deng, J., Xu, C., Wu, H., Dong, L.: A new certificateless signature with enhanced security and aggregation version. Concurr. Comput. Pract. Exp. **28**(4), 1124–1133 (2016)

25. Gong, Z., Long, Y., Hong, X., Chen, K.: Two certificateless aggregate signatures from bilinear maps. In: IEEE SNPD 2007, vol. 3, pp. 188–193 (2007)

26. Au, M.H., Yang, G., Susilo, W., Zhang, Y.: (Strong) Multidesignated verifiers signatures secure against rogue key attack. Concurr. Comput. Pract. Exp. **26**(8), 1574–1592 (2014)

27. Tu, H., He, D., Huang, B.: Reattack of a certificateless aggregate signature scheme with constant pairing computations. Sci. World J. **2014**, 1–9 (2014)

28. Malhi, A.K., Batra, S.: An efficient certificateless aggregate signature scheme for vehicular ad-hoc networks. Discret. Math. Theor. Comput. Sci. **17**(1), 317–320 (2015)

29. Bayat, M., Barmshoory, M., Rahimi, M., Aref, M.R.: A secure authentication scheme for VANETs with batch verification. Wirel. Netw. **21**(5), 1–11 (2014)

30. Camenisch, J., Stadler, M.: Efficient group signature schemes for large groups. In: Kaliski, B.S. (ed.) CRYPTO 1997. LNCS, vol. 1294, pp. 410–424. Springer, Heidelberg (1997). https://doi.org/10.1007/BFb0052252

31. Au, M.H., Liu, J.K., Susilo, W., Yuen, T.H.: Secure id-based linkable and revocable-iff-linked ring signature with constant-size construction. Theory Comput. Sci. **469**, 1–14 (2013)

32. Poettering, B., Stebila, D.: Double-authentication-preventing signatures. In: Kutyłowski, M., Vaidya, J. (eds.) ESORICS 2014, Part I. LNCS, vol. 8712, pp. 436–453. Springer, Cham (2014). https://doi.org/10.1007/978-3-319-11203-9_25

33. Bellare, M., Poettering, B., Stebila, D.: Deterring certificate subversion: efficient double-authentication-preventing signatures. In: Fehr, S. (ed.) PKC 2017, Part II. LNCS, vol. 10175, pp. 121–151. Springer, Heidelberg (2017). https://doi.org/10.1007/978-3-662-54388-7_5

34. Boneh, D., Kim, S., Nikolaenko, V.: Lattice-based DAPS and generalizations: self-enforcement in signature schemes. In: Gollmann, D., Miyaji, A., Kikuchi, H. (eds.) ACNS 2017. LNCS, vol. 10355, pp. 457–477. Springer, Cham (2017). https://doi.org/10.1007/978-3-319-61204-1_23

35. Mao, S., Zhang, P., Wang, H., Zhang, H., Wu, W.: Cryptanalysis of a lattice based key exchange protocol. Sci. China Inf. Sci. **60**(2), 028101–028105 (2017)

36. Wu, W., Zhang, H., Wang, H., Mao, S., Wu, S., Han, H.: Cryptanalysis of an MOR cryptosystem based on a finite associative algebra. Sci. China Inf. Sci. **59**(3), 32111 (2016)

37. Huang, X., Mu, Y., Susilo, W., Wong, D.S., Wu, W.: Certificateless signatures: new schemes and security models. Comput. J. **55**(4), 457–474 (2011)
38. He, D., Zeadally, S., Xu, B., Huang, X.: An efficient identity-based conditional privacy-preserving authentication scheme for vehicular ad hoc networks. IEEE Trans. Inf. Forensics Secur. **10**(12), 2681–2691 (2015)

Understanding User Behavior in Online Banking System

Yuan Wang[1,2], Liming Wang[1]([✉]), Zhen Xu[1], and Wei An[1]

[1] Institute of Information Engineering, Chinese Academy of Sciences, Beijing, China
{wangyuan,wangliming,xuzhen,anwei}@iie.ac.cn
[2] School of Cyber Security, University of Chinese Academy of Sciences, Beijing, China

Abstract. Currently, online banking has become extremely popular all over the world and plays a significant role in people's daily lives. However, the user behaviors have yet to be studied carefully in existing works. In this paper, we provide a large-scale, comprehensive measurement study of online banking users based on a two-week long dataset consisting of transactions conducted by personal users in one of the top banks in China. We demonstrate the customer behaviors mostly comply with the heavy-tail distribution which implies abnormal activities. In further analysis of those activities, we figure out that most of them are generated by two types of accounts, i.e., corporate accounts paying salaries and dishonest bank employees plastering the achievement. We extract a set of features to classify the two types of abnormal accounts from the benign ones. The experimental result illustrates that our system can accurately detect them with only 0.5% false positive rate.

Keywords: Online bank · User behavior · Abnormal detection

1 Introduction

Currently, online banking has become extremely popular all over the world and plays a significant role in people's daily lives. Beneficial to online banking, customers can conduct their financial activities like payments, money transfers or investment in a convenient and efficient manner at anytime and anywhere.

The popularity of Internet banking has led to an increase of frauds, perpetrated through cyber attacks, phishing scams and malware campaigns, resulting in substantial financial losses [15]. A lot of researchers dedicate in mitigating those threats [1–4,9,11,14,15]. The most challenging reason for bank fraud detection is its dynamic behavioral characteristics. To outwit online banking defenses, fraudulent behavior is dynamic, rare, and dispersed in very large and highly imbalanced datasets. In addition, different customer habits vary widely, making it more difficult to distinguish fraudulent transactions from normal ones.

Therefore, in-depth understanding the customer behaviors is urgent because (1) It can make our understanding of customer behavior more clear and profound; (2) It can help us portray customer behavior more appropriately; (3) It provides

© Springer Nature Switzerland AG 2019
F. Guo et al. (Eds.): Inscrypt 2018, LNCS 11449, pp. 637–646, 2019.
https://doi.org/10.1007/978-3-030-14234-6_35

reliable knowledge to distinguish between suspicious behavior and good behavior. However, few studies have been carried out on understanding customer behaviors due to existing barriers. Privacy is the first one that leads to the unavailability of the data for researchers, and another one is the competition issue. Therefore, most works on online banking only provide coarse results without detailed analysis. Due to the cooperation with a large Chinese bank, we have the opportunity to investigate online banking customer behaviors based on the anonymized ground-truth dataset that will be addressed in detail in Sect. 2.

In this paper, we systematically studied the customer behavior of online banking. Using the transaction data, we analyzed customer behavior from the access pattern and transaction pattern to characterize how customers access the online banking service and conduct their transaction activities. To deeply understand customer behavior, we compared sessions from thirdparty websites with online banking websites in access pattern analysis and examined the differences between non-transaction and transaction sessions through transaction pattern analysis. Our main contributions are stated as follows:

(1) We first present analysis results of customer behavior from a session perspective. We find that session length (of requests) is a heavy-tailed (also power-law) behavior and that sessions from online banking website have a marked bimodal pattern in working hours, while sessions from thirdparty websites do not perform as well.
(2) We provide insights into the details of transaction behavior. We find that transaction amount follows a lognormal distribution. Our analysis of the number of transactions and payees per session shows that the dishonest internal employees and corporate customers are among the personal accounts.
(3) Based on the analysis, we propose CatchAbs, a supervised method for abnormal activites detection. We show that it can accurately catch these two types of abnormal behaviors.

The remainder of this paper is organized as follows. Section 2 describes the data used in this paper and Sect. 3 estimates the access patterns of online banking customer, especially characteristics of the session perspective. In Sect. 4, we investigate the transaction behavior and summarize the findings we derived and implications. In Sect. 5, we present the detection system and analyze the results. Section 6 discusses the related work, while Sect. 7 concludes this paper.

2   Data Description

With the online banking system, customers log in to access the online banking service through a browser, and they can perform various financial activities, inquiries, money transfers, fee payments, and investments, by using a personal account or corporate account. Each request of a customer will be stored as a record in the data. Our data is collected from one of the top banks in China, whose online banking system provides online services for millions of customers every day. It includes all the records in the duration of 12 days from July 7, 2014 to July 18, 2014. The record contains various information about the customer's behavior, such as time stamp, account ID, payer ID, payee ID, operation (e.g. login, money transfer), amount, login IP, login area, operation status (success or failure).

Personal information was anonymized to meet personal privacy policy. Three types of sensitive information about customer identities are anonymized: (1) customer login ID (or user ID) usually with a unique ID for one customer in the online banking website, (2) customer transaction IDs (payer IDs or query IDs) in the online banking site, one for a card, where sometimes one customer login ID may correspond to a few transaction IDs, (3) payee IDs of the beneficiary account in a transaction. After filtering some error records, we finally have 23,212,800 sessions and 91,002,483 records in total (Table 1).

The characteristics of the authenticated session are that the session retains the user ID of the successfully logged-in user, while the unauthenticated session does not have the user ID. A total of 4,983,518 authenticated sessions include 3,412,869 customers and 23,863,321 total records in our data. Unauthenticated sessions may be created by the crawler and have less value than authenticated sessions, so our analysis in the following sections will focus on authenticated sessions. Operation describes a customer's action like 'login' or 'logout' in the online banking system. We call a session as a transaction session if there exists at least one transaction (money-moving operation) in a session; otherwise call it as a non-transaction session.

Table 1. Summary of the on-line banking data

		Records	Sessions	Customers
Unauthenticated		18,162,843	12,467,088	0
Authenticated	Website	56,249,672	6,457,533	2,707,737
	Thirdparty	16,589,968	4,288,179	1,375,557
Total		91,002,483	23,212,800	3,411,486

Customers can also access online banking services through a thirdparty website. For example, a customer surfs an online shopping website, finds a product of interest, and then logins to an online banking account for payment. To the online banking system, these sessions from thirdparty websites are given a special login API ('PayGateLogin'). In our paper, we use 'thirdparty' to denote these sessions and 'website' denotes those sessions from online banking homepage.

3   Access Patterns

Login frequency is the key metric for the online banking system. We first study the login frequency of customers in term of the number of logins per hour in the duration of 12 days. As shown in Fig. 1, both logins from the online banking

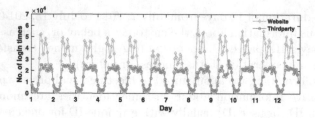

Fig. 1. No. of customer logins over time (interval of 1 h).

website and the thirdparty websites reveal a clear diurnal pattern, i.e. the heavy logins in the daytime and the light logins at night. The logins from online banking homepage (website) are significantly different from those via the thirdparty websites (thirdparty). It is observable that the number of website logins on every day is bimodal. Specifically, one peak appears before lunch time (10 am–11 am), and the other appears at afternoon (3 pm–4 pm), which implies that more people like to access the online banking service at work time.

Unlike the counter service, customers can access the online banking system at anytime via the online banking system and thereby increase the service capability for the bank. As shown in Fig. 1, the online banking system responses to tens of customers every second in the busy hour, while the inter-arrival time even achieves 325 s at night for the online banking system. Also, logins of online banking at weekend are remarkably less than that on weekdays. However, the logins from the thirdparty websites do not reveal the bimodal pattern and the weekend pattern.

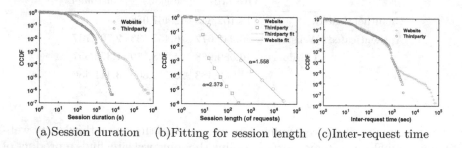

(a)Session duration   (b)Fitting for session length   (c)Inter-request time

Fig. 2. Characteristic of intra-session.

Figure 2(a) shows CCDF as session duration varies. Here, the complementary cumulative distribution(CCDF) is defined as

$$F(x) = P(X > x) \tag{1}$$

which presents more information on the tail-end extreme events. As shown in this figure, customers spent less time from the thirdparty websites (thirdparty) than that from online banking (website). Specifically, the mean and median of session duration of thirdparty sessions are 71.4 s and 34 s, 209.6 s and 87 s for website sessions, which double the time that is spent on the thirdparty sessions on average. Most of thirdparty sessions last for a short time, while some website sessions last for a longtime, even for a few hours. As shown in Fig. 2(a), 85.47% of thirdparty sessions are less than 100 s, while only 58.62% of website sessions last less than 100 s.

In Fig. 2(b), we observe a well fitted power-law distribution of session length of online banking sessions (website) in double-logarithmic plot of CCDF and a power-law tail for the distribution of thirdparty sessions. Here, the power-law distribution has a probability density function (PDF)

$$f(x) \sim x^{-\alpha-1}, \quad x \to \infty. \tag{2}$$

where the complementary cumulative distribution (CCDF) is

$$P(X \geq x) \sim x^{-\alpha}, \quad x \to \infty. \tag{3}$$

The power-law-type distribution is called heavy-tailed or fat-tailed if $\alpha < 2$. In this case, the variance of the random variable is infinite. Furthermore, when $\alpha \leq 1$, the mean of random variable is also infinite [5]. The fitting result of website sessions is shown in Eq. (3) with $\alpha = 1.558$. It reveals that the distribution of website sessions is a heavy-tailed distribution. This implies that the number of long sessions is more than expectation as exponential distribution or normal distribution, e.g., the longest session has 44,187 requests.

We also characterize the inter-request time within a session. The CCDF distribution is shown in Fig. 3(c). Due to the timeout settled by online banking, the distributions present a large change around 900 s (15 m). The inter-requests more than 900 s happen when customer return to the online banking system after timeout, the online banking will still record this request with the session ID kept on customer client cache. However, the online banking system will not respond to this request and will require customers to login again.

4   Transaction Patterns

4.1   Transaction and Non-transaction

We first examine the characteristics of non-transaction activities and transaction activities from the session view. Our data has 1,253,652 transaction sessions in total and most transactions are performed through website sessions.

As shown in Fig. 5(a), non-transaction sessions take less time than that of transaction sessions. 58.58% of non-transaction sessions are performed within the range of [10 s, 100 s], while 72.66% of transaction sessions with falling into the range of [100 s, 1000 s]. The mean and median of session duration of non-transaction session are 119.6 s, and 38 s, respectively, while they are 329 s and 193 s for transaction sessions.

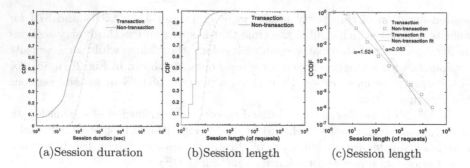

(a)Session duration   (b)Session length   (c)Session length

Fig. 3. Characteristics of non-transaction and transaction sessions.

Also, non-transaction sessions have less requests as shown in Fig. 5(b), 91.25% non-transaction sessions have less than 10 requests, while there are only 36.14% transaction sessions with less than 10 requests. The mean and median of session length are 16.3 and 11 for transaction sessions, respectively, and they are 5.5 and 4 for non-transaction sessions. Most of the non-transaction sessions are query tasks, which usually take less time than that of transaction tasks, as explained in Sect. 4. Figure 5(c) shows that the distribution of session length of non-transaction sessions is fitted to a power-law distribution with $\alpha = 1.524$, which means that it also follows the heavy-tailed distribution. It can be explained that customers with transaction tasks have more clear goals than those with non-transaction tasks.

4.2 Transaction Amount

In order to understand transaction behavior, we first examine the amount per transaction. As shown in Fig. 4, the transaction amount clearly follows a log-normal distribution. The probability distribution function for the lognormal distribution is given by:

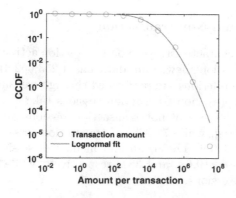

Fig. 4. CCDF of amount per transaction, which follows a lognormal distribution.

With this equation, we fit the log-normal distribution of Fig. 4 as Eq. (4) with $\sigma = 2.11$ and $\mu = 8.83$. The mean, and median of transaction amounts are 22,786 and 1900 (CNY), respectively. Among the transactions, the largest 10% contribute 81.35% of the total transaction amount, which largely follows the 80–20 rule [10].

$$f(x) = \frac{1}{x\sigma\sqrt{2\pi}}e^{-\frac{(lnx-\mu)^2}{2\sigma^2}} \tag{4}$$

4.3   Transaction Times

The distribution of the number of transactions per session is shown in Fig. 5(a), which follows a power-law distribution with $\alpha = 1.922$. 85.46% of transaction sessions have only one transaction in one session. However, the maximum is 3240 transactions in a session.

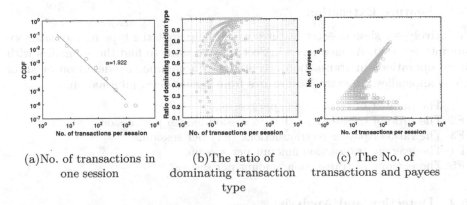

(a)No. of transactions in one session

(b)The ratio of dominating transaction type

(c) The No. of transactions and payees

Fig. 5. Characteristic of transaction sessions.

Then we investigate the dominating transaction type, which contributes the most transactions in the online banking system. Figure 5(b) shows the ratio of the dominating transaction type in a session. We can find that the more transactions there are in a session, the higher the proportion of its dominating transaction type. When a session has more than 10 transactions, the dominating transaction type contributes most of the transactions: the proportion of dominating transaction type for these sessions is all greater than or equal to 0.5; the proportion of dominating transaction type for 90% of sessions exceeds 0.969.

To further examine the transaction behavior, Fig. 5(c) shows the number of transactions and payees per session. We find that sessions follow two trends: One trend is that a large number of transactions accompany a small number of payees; Another trend is that the number of payees increases with the number of transactions. (1) We choose the group of sessions with more than 100 transactions and more than 100 payees. After examining the transaction type and amount for every session, we confirm these sessions are wage payment activities by corporate customers. (2) We choose the group of sessions with more than 100 transactions and less than 10 payees to analyze. These sessions are mainly divided into two transaction types. One type is fee payment transaction, which refers to business behavior. The other type has proved to be fraud behavior of bank employee to obtain better job performance.

5 Abnormal Detection

In this section, we develop a detection system CatchAbs that distinguishes the abnormal accounts described in Sect. 4.3. Since manual tagging takes a lot of time and effort, we only mark sessions with session length greater than 500. In the end, we found 152 anomalous sessions in these 376 sessions, 22 of which were bank employee activities and 130 were corporate events.

5.1 Feature Extraction

Intuitively, we should select features which help spot the type of anomalies we are interested in. As mentioned in Sect. 4.3, we want to find the anomalies with large operations in transaction activities. To accommodate detection of all of these anomalies, we extract 5 features from session-level information.

F1 The number of transactions per session.
F2 The ratio of transactions (F1) to session length per session.
F3 The ratio of payees to transactions (F1) per session.
F4 The average transaction amount per session.
F5 The entropy of transaction amount per session.

5.2 Detection and Analysis

After we extract the sessions, we want to predict whether they are abnormal or normal. We use a random forest, a supervised classifier, using the features described above. The major advantage of using random forest lies in the unexcelled accuracy and efficiency.

We computed values for all 5 features for all sessions in our dataset, input the the data to a random forest classifier, and ran 10 fold cross-validation(CV). In 10-fold CV, the data is randomly splitted into 10 folds, where the classifier is trained on 9-folds and tested on the remaining fold. The classifier repeats this process 10 times, each time a different fold is used for testing.

The resulting classification accuracy was 96.9%, with 0.5% false positives (i.e. classify normal users as abnormal) and 0.0% false negatives (i.e. classify abnormal users as normal). Further, we dig into the false positives (FPs) obtained from the classifier to gain a better understanding into possible classes of abnormal activities that we may have missed in our ground truth data. We manually checked each session incorrectly classified as abnormal. We find that most of them stem from a pay fee service with a very little amount. It is not expected to see these service provider activities among normal personal accounts.

6 Related Work

A few works have been carried out on customer behavior analysis in online banking because of the privacy, secrecy and commercial interest concerns. Their works focused on two aspects: service quality improving and the online banking fraud detecting.

Service Quality Improving: Some works attempted to improve the service quality of online banking services [6,7,12,13]. These works focused on the attitude of customers who use the online banking services and investigated the factors contributing to customer satisfaction [6]. They usually adopted the way of asking the participants and bank customers with a questionnaire. Different to their work, our analysis is based on the transaction data, which comprehensively describes customer behaviors during transaction activities in server side, with the objective to in-depth understand customer behaviors and to improve the quality of online banking services.

Online Banking Fraud Detecting: Some works detected the online banking fraud based on customer behavior analysis [1,2,9,11,15]. Their research usually models the behavior of each customer and monitors whether it deviates from normal behavior [8]. However, these works do not systematically analyze customer behavior based on the real data. Wei *et al.* [15] introduced a systematic online banking fraud detection method using transaction data from a large Australian bank, but they did not provide any analysis for the online banking customer behavior. Carminati *et al.* [2] developed a semi-supervised and unsupervised fraud and anomaly detection method based on a real-world dataset of a large Italian national bank. His system design is guided by data analysis, but his work only describes the distribution of the amount and transaction frequency. Compared to these studies, our research relies on the dataset that includes more details about the transaction, and more online banking patterns are revealed in this paper. Moreover, because of the lack of publicly available and real-world frauds, most these works resort to synthetically generated frauds. Our work based on ground truth data reveals some of the abnormal behavior that is happening.

7 Conclusion

In this paper, we have analyzed the characteristics of online banking customer behaviors based on personal transaction data collected from a large bank in China. To the best of our knowledge, this work is the first attempt to comprehensively understand the usage patterns of the online banking.

We first analyzed the statistical and distribution properties of the important variables of the access patterns from the session level. The analysis showed that most customer behaviors follow a power-law distribution. Then, we investigated the details of the transaction behaviors, e.g., the number of transactions, the transaction amount, and the transaction account. Our analysis also revealed some special accounts, e.g., corporate accounts and dishonest internal employees. Finally, we developed CatchAbs, a supervised method for detection of these two abnormal behaviors. In a word, our work will be helpful to improve the quality and security of the online banking service.

References

1. Cabanes, G., Bennani, Y., Grozavu, N.: Unsupervised learning for analyzing the dynamic behavior of online banking fraud. In: Ding, W., et al. (eds.) ICDM Workshops, pp. 513–520. IEEE Computer Society (2013)
2. Carminati, M., Caron, R., Maggi, F., Epifani, I., Zanero, S.: BankSealer: a decision support system for online banking fraud analysis and investigation. Comput. Secur. **53**, 175–186 (2015)
3. Carminati, M., Valentini, L., Zanero, S.: A supervised auto-tuning approach for a banking fraud detection system. In: Dolev, S., Lodha, S. (eds.) CSCML 2017. LNCS, vol. 10332, pp. 215–233. Springer, Cham (2017). https://doi.org/10.1007/978-3-319-60080-2_17
4. Dhankhad, S., Mohammed, E., Far, B.: Supervised machine learning algorithms for credit card fraudulent transaction detection: a comparative study. In: 2018 IEEE International Conference on Information Reuse and Integration (IRI), pp. 122–125. IEEE (2018)
5. Gao, J., Cao, Y., Tung, W.-W., Hu, J.: Multiscale Analysis of Complex Time Series: Integration of Chaos and Random Fractal Theory, and Beyond. Wiley, Hoboken (2007)
6. Hanafizadeh, P., Keating, B.W., Khedmatgozar, H.R.: A systematic review of internet banking adoption. Telematics and Inform. **31**(3), 492–510 (2014)
7. Herington, C., Weaven, S.: E-retailing by banks: e-service quality and its importance to customer satisfaction. Eur. J. Mark. **43**(9/10), 1220–1231 (2009)
8. Jyothsna, V., Prasad, V.R., Prasad, K.M.: A review of anomaly based intrusion detection systems. Int. J. Comput. Appl. **28**(7), 26–35 (2011)
9. Karlsen, K.N., Killingberg, T.: Profile based intrusion detection for internet banking systems (2008)
10. Kock, R.: 80–20 Principle: The Secret to Success by Achieving More with Less. Crown Business, New York City (1999)
11. Kovach, S., Ruggiero, W.V.: Online banking fraud detection based on local and global behavior. In: Proceedings of the Fifth International Conference on Digital Society, Guadeloupe, France, pp. 166–171 (2011)
12. Pikkarainen, K., Pikkarainen, T., Karjaluoto, H., Pahnila, S.: The measurement of end-user computing satisfaction of online banking services: empirical evidence from finland. Int. J. Bank Mark. **24**(3), 158–172 (2006)
13. Rodrigues, L.F., Costa, C.J., Oliveira, A.: How does the web game design influence the behavior of e-banking users? Comput. Hum. Behav. **74**, 163–174 (2017)
14. Carminati, M., Baggio, A., Maggi, F., Spagnolini, U., Zanero, S.: FraudBuster: temporal analysis and detection of advanced financial frauds. In: Giuffrida, C., Bardin, S., Blanc, G. (eds.) DIMVA 2018. LNCS, vol. 10885, pp. 211–233. Springer, Cham (2018). https://doi.org/10.1007/978-3-319-93411-2_10
15. Wei, W., Li, J., Cao, L., Ou, Y., Chen, J.: Effective detection of sophisticated online banking fraud on extremely imbalanced data. World Wide Web **16**(4), 449–475 (2013)

Privacy-Preserving Remote User Authentication with k-Times Untraceability

Yangguang Tian[1(⊠)], Yingjiu Li[1], Binanda Sengupta[1], Robert Huijie Deng[1], Albert Ching[2], and Weiwei Liu[3]

[1] School of Information Systems,
Singapore Management University, Singapore, Singapore
{ygtian,yjli,binandas,robertdeng}@smu.edu.sg
[2] i-Sprint Innovations, Singapore, Singapore
albert.ching@i-sprint.com
[3] School of Mathematics and Statistics,
North China University of Water Resources and Electric Power, Zhengzhou, China
liuweiwei@ncwu.edu.cn

Abstract. Remote user authentication has found numerous real-world applications, especially in a user-server model. In this work, we introduce the notion of *anonymous remote user authentication with k-times untraceability* (k-RUA) for a given parameter k, where authorized users authenticate themselves to an authority (typically a server) in an anonymous and k-times untraceable manner. We define the formal security models for a generic k-RUA construction that guarantees user authenticity, anonymity and user privacy. We provide a concrete instantiation of k-RUA having the following properties: (1) a third party cannot impersonate an authorized user by producing valid transcripts for the user while conversing during a session; (2) a third party having access to the communication channel between the user and the authority cannot identify the session participants; (3) the authority can trace the real identities of dishonest users who have authenticated themselves for more than k times; (4) our k-RUA construction avoids using expensive pairing operations—which makes it efficient and suitable for devices having limited amount of computational resources.

Keywords: Remote user authentication · Anonymity ·
User privacy · k-times untraceability

1 Introduction

User authentication is typically the first line of defense in most of the secure information systems. In the well-known user-server setting, a user has to authenticate herself to a (possibly remote) authentication server before opting for the services. Moreover, in order to protect a legitimate user's privacy, anonymous

© Springer Nature Switzerland AG 2019
F. Guo et al. (Eds.): Inscrypt 2018, LNCS 11449, pp. 647–657, 2019.
https://doi.org/10.1007/978-3-030-14234-6_36

user authentication is widely studied in the literature and is deployed in numerous real-world applications. Researchers have come up with several solutions that exploit cryptographic techniques, such as group signatures [2], blind signatures and ring signatures [16], to ensure (or enhance) privacy. On the other hand, in some applications, it is required that a legitimate user can authenticate herself (and benefit from the services) for a limited number of times. For example, systems like e-cash, e-coupon and e-voting need such privacy guarantees. In such scenarios, k-times anonymous authentication (k-TAA) [3,13–15] serves the purpose. It is a fine-grained approach for privacy protection which ensures that a legitimate user can be authenticated anonymously only up to k number of times (for a threshold parameter k). On the other hand, if a user tries to authenticate herself beyond the threshold k, then her anonymity is compromised.

Although k-TAA schemes address the issue of restricting a user to bounded number of authentications, k-TAA is not suitable for building an authentication system for a mobile platform due to the following reasons. First, the traditional (and more generic) user authentication system involves an authentication server and multiple independent users, whereas k-TAA requires an extra (trusted) group manager. For example, it is cumbersome for a mobile device user if she has to consult a third party every time she enrolls to (or logs into) a server. Second, a mobile-platform-based system usually employs devices with low-power and limited resources, whereas k-TAA requires certain computation-intensive operations such as pairings (bilinear maps) and proofs of knowledge. Thus, to achieve both anonymity and traceability in a secure mobile setting is a non-trivial task.

In this work, we aim to design an efficient anonymous remote user authentication system suitable for mobile devices with a guarantee that a dishonest user deviating from the correct execution of the protocol can be traced. We explore whether we can exploit an e-coupon[1]/e-cash system to construct an anonymous remote user authentication system with traceability. We observe that an e-coupon system is more suitable than an e-cash system due to the following reasons. Unlike a bank, an e-coupon system, in general, does not involve central authority (group manager), which is required in an e-cash system in order to generate coins for the users. Moreover, e-cash system usually uses more expensive algorithms/protocols than e-coupon system. The deployment of mobile e-coupon systems [9] has showed their viability in practice. In the e-coupon system, the issue[2] protocol between a user and the vendor (service provider) can be applied to the enrollment phase of user authentication. On the other hand, the redeem protocol involves checking the authenticity of coupons, and certain services are redeemed in case coupons are valid. We do not consider whether the services are provided or not; we only focus on checking the authenticity of coupons in the user authentication setting as the goal of authentication server is to authenticate a legitimate (or authorized) user only.

---

[1] An e-coupon is also sometimes named as a multi-coupon as such a coupon can be redeemed more than once [6].

[2] An e-coupon system is usually comprised of issue and redeem protocols [6].

We note that a secure and anonymous remote user authentication with traceability cannot be simply built upon existing e-coupon systems. The main concerns of existing e-coupon systems [1,5,6,10,12] can be listed as follows: unforgeability, double-redemption detection, unlinkability and unsplittability. The e-coupon system proposed by Liu et al. [11] has a new property: "k-times redemption detection" while the basic security requirements mentioned above are also met. Specifically, the real identity of a dishonest user can be traced by the service provider if the user tries to redeem the coupon more than k times—which aligns with our design goal. However, contrary to their claims, their e-coupon system fails to achieve traceability since a dishonest user in their system can misuse coupon without being detected.

1.1 This Work

In this work, we introduce the notion of anonymous remote user authentication with k-times untraceability (k-RUA) that enables authorized users to authenticate themselves to a remote authentication server anonymously and ensures the traceability to detect dishonest users. Our contributions can be summarized as follows.

- We present the formal security definitions for privacy-preserving remote user authentication. In particular, we propose a user authenticity model to capture impersonation attacks, an anonymity model to address an honest-but-curious[3] authentication server and a user privacy to ensure the privacy of protocol participants.
- We present the *first* generic construction of k-RUA, which is built upon a secure e-coupon system. We prove it can achieve user authenticity, anonymity and user privacy. In particular, k-times untraceability enables an authorized user to authenticate herself to an authentication server up to k times without being traced. The real identity of a dishonest user is revealed to the authentication server in case the user tries to authenticate for more than k times.
- We show that the e-coupon system proposed in [11] fails to achieve their claimed k-times redemption detection. We fix their e-coupon system in our proposed k-RUA. In addition, we show that the same attacks are applicable to their previous work [10] and we also fix it accordingly.

1.2 Related Work

k-Times Anonymous Authentication. Teranishi et al. [14] proposed the first authentication scheme which allows users to anonymously perform the authentication at most k times (k-TAA). In particular, a user's identity is fully protected within the k-times authentication, while anyone is able to trace a dishonest user trying to authenticate herself beyond the allowable k times. Later on, dynamic

---

[3] The authentication server is assumed to execute the protocol as specified, just try to learn additional information from the transcript during protocol execution.

k-TAA (denote k-TAA′) schemes were proposed in the literature [3,13] that allow the service provider to independently grant/revoke a user from his access group in order to have better control over their clients. We note that some constructions [3,13] were based on expensive pairings (bilinear maps), which are not suitable for devices with limited resources.

E-coupon System. The privacy-preserving e-coupon system was first proposed by Chen et al. [6] that allows a user purchase e-coupons and redeem them unlinkably. Furthermore, the number of redemptions remaining can be hidden from the vendor (i.e., coupon issuer). To reduce the cost for issuing and redeeming coupons, Nguyen [12] proposed an efficient e-coupon system which has constant communication and computation costs (that does not scale with the redemption limit k). Nguyen's e-coupon system also allows the coupon issuer to revoke an e-coupon. In an independent work [5], Canard et al. proposed an e-coupon system that is more efficient than [6]. They added new features to an e-coupon system that include the following: a user can choose the number of coupons she wants to issue; a user can choose the value of each coupon from a set of pre-defined values.

Armknecht et al. [1] proposed an e-coupon system that takes into account multiple vendors. Specifically, a user can redeem multiple coupons anonymously with different vendors in an arbitrary order. This system prevents double-spending by maintaining a trusted database that records the transaction of each redeemed coupon. Liu et al. [10] proposed a pairing-free e-coupon system that achieves both traceability against dishonest users and anonymity (i.e., untraceable) for honest users without involving any trusted *third* party.

In a recent work, Liu et al. [11] introduced a new notion called "strong user privacy", i.e., the privacy of the service chosen by a user during the redemption process (user redemption privacy). To meet strong user privacy requirements, they rely on an existing oblivious transfer scheme [7]. We also notice that the vendor can easily *link* two redemptions since a single coupon is issued by each user. However, the vendor cannot trace the real identities of honest users as long as the number of redemptions does not exceed k.

2 Security Model

Notation. We define a system with n users. We denote the i-th session established by a user U as Π_U^i, and identities of all the users recognised by Π_U^i during the execution of that session by partner identifier pid_U^i. We define sid_U^i as the unique session identifier belonging to the session i established by the user U. Specifically, $\mathsf{sid}_U^i = \{m_j\}_{j=1}^n$, where $m_j \in \{0,1\}^*$ is the message transcript among users.

We say an oracle Π_U^i may be *used* or *unused*. The oracle is considered as unused if it has never been initialized. The oracle is initialized as soon as it becomes part of a group. After the initialisation the oracle is marked as used and turns into the *stand-by* state where it waits for an invocation to execute a protocol operation. Upon receiving such invocation the oracle Π_U^i learns its partner identifier pid_U^i and turns into a *processing* state where it sends, receives and processes messages according to the description of the protocol. During that phase, the internal state information $state_U^i$ is maintained by the oracle. The oracle Π_U^i remains in the processing state until it collects enough information to finalise the user authentication. As soon as the authentication is accomplished Π_U^i *accepts* and *terminates* the protocol execution meaning that it would not send or receive further messages. If the protocol execution fails then Π_U^i terminates without being accepted.

2.1 System Model

A remote user authentication with k-times untraceability (k-RUA) involves two types of entities: multiple enorlled users and an authentication server. We define a k-RUA protocol that consists of the following algorithms/protocols:

- Setup: The authentication server $\mathbb{S}$ takes the security parameter λ as input, outputs the master public/secret key pair (mpk, msk).
- KeyGen: User takes master public key mpk as input, outputs a public/secret key pair (pk, sk).
- Enrollment: This is an interactive protocol that runs between an enrolled user and an authentication server $\mathbb{S}$ over a public channel. The enrolled user will generate a credential and become an authorized user after enrollment.
- Authentication: This is an interactive protocol between an authorized user and an authentication server $\mathbb{S}$ over a public channel. An authorized user sends her credential and k-size commitments to $\mathbb{S}$, while $\mathbb{S}$ accept it if and only if the credential send is valid.
- k-Times Untraceability: The authentication server $\mathbb{S}$ takes $k+1$ authentication transcripts of one user as input, outputs the user's secret key sk.

2.2 Security Model

User Authenticity. Informally, an adversary $\mathcal{A}$ attempts to impersonate an authorized user and authenticate to an authentication server. We define a formal authenticity game between a probabilistic polynomial-time (PPT) adversary $\mathcal{A}$ and a simulator (i.e., challenger) $\mathcal{S}$ below.

- Setup. $\mathcal{S}$ generates a master public/secret key pair (mpk, msk) for authentication server $\mathbb{S}$ and public/secret key pairs $(\text{pk}_i, \text{sk}_i)$ for n users by running the corresponding KeyGen algorithms. In addition, $\mathcal{S}$ honestly generates credential s_i for n users by running the Enrollment protocol. Eventually, $\mathcal{S}$ sends user's identity/credential $\{ID_i, s_i\}$ and server's identity $ID_{\mathbb{S}}$ to $\mathcal{A}$.
- Training. $\mathcal{A}$ can make the following queries in arbitrary sequence to $\mathcal{S}$.
    - Send: If $\mathcal{A}$ issues a send query in the form of (U, i, m) to simulate a network message for the i-th session of user U, then $\mathcal{S}$ would simulate the reaction of instance oracle Π_U^i upon receiving message m, and return to $\mathcal{A}$ the

response that Π_U^i would generate; If $\mathcal{A}$ issues a send query in the form of $(U', \text{'}start\text{'})$, then $\mathcal{S}$ creates a new instance oracle $\Pi_{U'}^i$ and returns to $\mathcal{A}$ the first protocol message.

- **Secret Key Reveal:** If $\mathcal{A}$ issues a secret key reveal (or corrupt, for short) query to user i, then $\mathcal{S}$ will return the secret key sk_i to $\mathcal{A}$.
- **Master Secret Key Reveal:** If $\mathcal{A}$ issues a master secret key reveal query to $\mathbb{S}$, then $\mathcal{S}$ returns the master secret key msk to $\mathcal{A}$.
- **State Reveal:** If $\mathcal{A}$ issues a state reveal query to (possibly unaccepted) instance oracle $\Pi_{U_i}^j$ $(j \neq i)$, then $\mathcal{S}$ will return all internal state values contained in $\Pi_{U_i}^j$ at the moment the query is asked.

- Challenge. $\mathcal{A}$ wins the game if all of the following conditions hold.
  1. $\mathbb{S}$ accept user i; It implies $\mathrm{pid}_{\mathbb{S}}^s$ and $\mathrm{sid}_{\mathbb{S}}^s$ exist.
  2. $\mathcal{A}$ did *not* issue Master Secret Key Reveal query to $\mathbb{S}$;
  3. $m \in \mathrm{sid}_{\mathbb{S}}^s$, *but* there exists *no* $\Pi_{U_i}^s$ which has sent m (m denotes the message transcript from user i).

Note that $\mathcal{A}$ is allowed to reveal all user's secret keys. We define the advantage of an adversary $\mathcal{A}$ in the above game as

$$\mathrm{Adv}_{\mathcal{A}}(\lambda) = |\Pr[\mathcal{A} \; wins]|.$$

Definition 1. *We say a k-RUA protocol has user authenticity if for any PPT $\mathcal{A}$, $\mathrm{Adv}_{\mathcal{A}}^{k\text{-}RUA}(\lambda)$ is a negligible function of the security parameter λ.*

Anonymity. Informally, an adversary (e.g., authentication server) is not allowed to identify who are the authenticated users, with the condition that authorized users authenticate themselves to authentication server within k times. We define a game between an *insider* adversary $\mathcal{A}$ and a simulator $\mathcal{S}$ below.

- Setup: $\mathcal{S}$ generates a master public/secret key pair $(\mathrm{mpk}, \mathrm{msk})$ for authentication server $\mathbb{S}$ and public/secret key pairs $(\mathrm{pk}_i, \mathrm{sk}_i)$ for n users by running the corresponding KeyGen algorithms. In addition, $\mathcal{S}$ honestly generates a k-size set of credentials $\{s_i\}$ for each user by running the Enrollment protocol. Eventually, $\mathcal{S}$ sends user's identities/credential sets $\{ID_i, s_i\}$ and server's master public/secret key pairs $(\mathrm{mpk}, \mathrm{msk})$ to $\mathcal{A}$. $\mathcal{S}$ also tosses a random coin b which will be used later in the game.
- Training: $\mathcal{A}$ interacts with all users via a set of oracle queries (as defined in the user authenticity model). Eventually, $\mathcal{A}$ outputs two new distinct users (ID_0, ID_1), while $\mathcal{S}$ generates two credential sets $\{s_0\}, \{s_1\}$ for users (ID_0, ID_1) by running the Enrollment protocol.
- Challenge: $\mathcal{A}$ is given one of challenge credential sets $\{s_b\}$, and $\mathcal{A}$ continues to interact with all users (include two new users ID_0, ID_1) via all oracle queries until it terminates and outputs bit b'.

Note that $\mathcal{A}$ is allowed to activate at most k sessions for ID_0 or ID_1 during Challenge stage, and $\mathcal{A}$ is *not* allowed to reveal the secret keys of ID_0 and ID_1. We define the advantage of $\mathcal{A}$ in the above game as

$$\mathrm{Adv}_{\mathcal{A}}(\lambda) = |\Pr[\mathcal{S} \to 1] - 1/2|.$$

Definition 2. *We say a k-RUA protocol has anonymity if for any PPT $\mathcal{A}$, $\text{Adv}_{\mathcal{A}}(\lambda)$ is a negligible function of the security parameter λ.*

User Privacy. Informally, an adversary (e.g., non-authorized user) is not allowed to identify who are the session participants. We define a game between an *outsider* adversary $\mathcal{A}$ and a simulator $\mathcal{S}$ below:

- Setup: $\mathcal{S}$ generates a master public/secret key pair (mpk, msk) for $\mathbb{S}$ and public/secret key pairs $(\text{pk}_i, \text{sk}_i)$ for n users by running the corresponding KeyGen algorithms. In addition, $\mathcal{S}$ honestly generates credential s_i for each user by running the Enrollment protocol. Eventually, $\mathcal{S}$ sends user's identity/credential $\{ID_i, s_i\}$ and server's identity $ID_{\mathbb{S}}$ to $\mathcal{A}$. $\mathcal{S}$ also tosses a random coin b which will be used later in the game. We denote the original n users set as $\mathcal{U}$.
- Training: $\mathcal{A}$ is allowed to issue Send, State Reveal queries and at most n-2 Secret Key Reveal queries to $\mathcal{S}$. In particular, $\mathcal{A}$ is *not* allowed to issue Master Secret Key Reveal query to $\mathbb{S}$. We denote the honest (i.e., uncorrupted) user set as $\mathcal{U}'$.
- Challenge: $\mathcal{S}$ randomly selects two users $ID_0, ID_1 \in \mathcal{U}'$ as challenge candidates, and $\mathcal{S}$ removes them from $\mathcal{U}'$ and simulates ID_b^* by either $ID_b^* = ID_1$ if $b = 1$ or $ID_b^* = ID_0$ if $b = 0$.
  Let authentication server $\mathbb{S}$ interact with user ID_b^*. $\mathcal{A}$ can access all the communication transcripts among them.

$$\mathbb{S} \leftrightarrow ID_b^* = \begin{cases} ID_1 & b = 1 \\ ID_0 & b = 0 \end{cases}$$

Finally, $\mathcal{A}$ outputs b' as its guess for b. If $b' = b$, then $\mathcal{S}$ outputs 1; otherwise, $\mathcal{S}$ outputs 0.
We define the advantage of $\mathcal{A}$ in the above game as

$$\text{Adv}_{\mathcal{A}}(\lambda) = \Pr[\mathcal{S} \to 1] - 1/2.$$

Definition 3. *We say a k-RUA protocol has anonymity if for any PPT $\mathcal{A}$, $\text{Adv}_{\mathcal{A}}(\lambda)$ is a negligible function of the security parameter λ.*

3 Security Risks of E-coupon Systems [10, 11]

We notice that the privacy-preserving e-coupon systems in [10,11] include two important primitives: a new blind signature scheme and an existing oblivious transfer scheme [7]. The blind signature aims to achieve user's anonymity (i.e., untraceability) with respect to service provider, which is the *target* of subsequent attacks. That is, the dishonest users may misuse a valid coupon and successfully avoid the Reveal algorithm. To show the potential security risks of [10] and its extension [11], we just review the extended e-coupon system [11]. Note that the detailed description of extended e-coupon system is referred to [11], and the notation below will mostly *follow* the notation in [10,11].

Concrete Attacks. By summarising the security risks in [11], we classify two types of adversaries. The goal for both of them is to avoid their Reveal algorithm and misuse a valid coupon. Below we present the detailed attacks respectively.

- Type one. The target is user's secret key. In the issue stage, user receives values $(\delta_1 = pk_{\mathcal{U}}^{k'}, \delta_2 = g^{k'})$ from $\mathbb{S}$. However, a dishonest user $\mathcal{U}$ can replace her secret key x to x' and ask $\mathbb{S}$ to blindly sign it. Specifically, a dishonest user computes $\alpha = (g^{x'y})^{x_1}, \beta = (g^{x'})^{x_1}, \lambda = g^{x_1}$, and $m = \mathrm{H}_1(\alpha, \beta, \lambda), r = m \cdot \beta^a \cdot \delta_1'^{b \cdot x_1/a}$ where $\delta_1' = g^{k \cdot x'}$. Eventually, user stores $(\alpha, \beta, \lambda, r, s)$ as a valid coupon after interaction with $\mathbb{S}$. Note that α, β, r are generated using the new secret key x'.
  Notice that a dishonest user is allowed to modify the value δ_1 (to δ_1') and pass the verification of blinded signature successfully: $\mathrm{H}_1(\alpha, \beta, \lambda) \overset{?}{=} \beta^{-s} \cdot \alpha^{\mathrm{H}_2(\mathrm{H}_1(\alpha, \beta, \lambda), r)} \cdot r$. In the reveal stage, the secret value x_1 will be revealed with regard to a misbehaving user. However, $\mathbb{S}$ could not determine the identity of dishonest user in its database since $pk_{\mathcal{U}}^{x_1} \neq \beta(= g^{x_1 \cdot x'})$.
- Type two. The target is the chosen randomness. In the issue stage, a dishonest user computes $\lambda = g^{x_1'}$ (rather than $\lambda = g^{x_1}$) using a different randomness and generates other parameters honestly using the randomness x_1. In the reveal stage, a secret value x_1' will be revealed with regard to a misbehaving user $\mathcal{U}$. However, $\mathbb{S}$ could not determine the identity of dishonest user in its database since $pk_{\mathcal{U}}^{x_1'} \neq \beta(= g^{x_1 \cdot x})$. Note that the randomness in λ is different from the randomness in α, β, r.
  Same attack can be applied to [10]. If a dishonest user redeems a coupon twice, $(R_1 = x_1' + c_1 \cdot x_1 \cdot x, R_2 = x_1' + c_2 \cdot x_1 \cdot x)$, then $\mathbb{S}$ is not able to obtain the secret key x (what $\mathbb{S}$ can obtain is a value $x_1 \cdot x$).

4 Proposed Construction

A user obtains her credential after interacting with an authentication server $\mathbb{S}$ during Enrollment stage. Later, $\mathbb{S}$ acknowledges an authorized user's authenticity during Authentication stage if and only if the user authenticates with a valid credential. In particular, $\mathbb{S}$ is able to *link* the authorized user's credential with commitments at most k times. If an authorized user authenticates herself to $\mathbb{S}$ for $k+1$ times, then $\mathbb{S}$ can *identify* the real identity of the user.

- Setup: The authentication server $\mathbb{S}$ takes the security parameter λ as input and outputs the master secret key $\mathsf{msk} = (y, e, f)$ and the master public key $\mathsf{mpk} = (g^y, g_1 = g^e, g_2 = g^f, g_1^y, g_2^y)$. $\mathbb{S}$ also generates the hash functions $\mathrm{H}_1 : \{0,1\}^* \to \mathbb{G}, \mathrm{H}_2 : \mathbb{G} \to \mathbb{Z}_q$. $\mathbb{S}$ chooses a public key encryption (PKE) scheme (e.g., [8]) for the system.
- KeyGen: The user i chooses the secret key $\mathsf{sk}_i = x \in \mathbb{Z}_q$ and computes the public key $\mathsf{pk}_i = g_1^x$.

- Enrollment: The user i and the authentication server $\mathbb{S}$ interact with each other as described below
  - Upon receiving a request from the user i, $\mathbb{S}$ chooses a random element $\mathcal{K} \in_R \mathbb{Z}_q$, computes $(\delta_1 = g^{\mathcal{K}}, \delta_2 = (g_1^x \cdot g_2)^{\mathcal{K}})$ and sends them to the user i;
  - The user i chooses $x_1, a, b \in_R \mathbb{Z}_q$ and computes $\alpha = (g_1^x \cdot g_2)^{y \cdot x_1}, \beta = (g_1^x \cdot g_2)^{x_1}$. Then, the user i computes $m = \mathtt{H}_1(\alpha\|\beta), r = m \cdot \beta^a \cdot \delta_2^{b \cdot x_1}, m' = \mathtt{H}_2(m\|r)/b$ and sends m' to $\mathbb{S}$;
  - $\mathbb{S}$ computes the *blinded* signature $s' = \mathcal{K} + y \cdot m'$ and sends it to the user i;
  - The user i verifies whether $g^{s'} \overset{?}{=} g^{y \cdot m'} \cdot \delta_1$. If verification fails, it outputs abort; otherwise, the user computes $s = s' \cdot b + a$ and stores (α, β, r, s) as a valid credential.
- Authentication: The authorized user i and the authentication server $\mathbb{S}$ interact with each other as described below
  - The user i computes two k-size sets of commitments $(S_1, S_2, \cdots, S_k) = (g_1^{x \cdot s_1}, g_1^{x \cdot s_2}, \cdots, g_1^{x \cdot s_k})$ and $(\overline{S_1}, \overline{S_2}, \cdots, \overline{S_k}) = (g_2^{s_1}, g_2^{s_2}, \cdots, g_2^{s_k})$, where $s_i \in \mathbb{Z}_q$ for each $1 \leq i \leq k$;
  - The user i generates the ciphertext $C_i = \mathtt{Enc}_{\mathtt{mpk}}(\{S_i, \overline{S_i}\})$ and sends it to the authentication server $\mathbb{S}$ as an authentication request;
  - Upon receiving a request from the user i, $\mathbb{S}$ chooses a challenge nonce c_i and sends it to the user i;
  - The user i computes $R_1 = x_1 + s_1 \cdot c_i + s_2 \cdot c_i^2 + \cdots s_k \cdot c_i^k, R_2 = x \cdot R_1$ and sends message $m_i = (R_1, R_2, \alpha, \beta, r, s)$ to $\mathbb{S}$;
  - $\mathbb{S}$ checks whether $\mathtt{H}_1(\alpha\|\beta) \overset{?}{=} \beta^{-s} \cdot \alpha^{\mathtt{H}_2(\mathtt{H}_1(\alpha\|\beta)\|r)} \cdot r$ and $g_1^{R_2} \cdot g_2^{R_1} \overset{?}{=} \beta \cdot S_1^{c_i} \cdot S_2^{c_i^2} \cdots S_k^{c_i^k} \cdot \overline{S_1}^{c_i} \cdot \overline{S_2}^{c_i^2} \cdots \overline{S_k}^{c_i^k}$. If either of them fails, it outputs abort; otherwise, it outputs accept.
- Trace: We assume that a specific credential (α, β, r, s) is used by a dishonest user for $k + 1$ times. Then, $\mathbb{S}$ gets $k + 1$ shares about the secret x_1 and $x_1 \cdot x$, respectively. Once $\mathbb{S}$ obtains the values of x_1 and $x_1 \cdot x$, $\mathbb{S}$ can successfully compute the user's secret key x.

4.1 Security Analysis

Theorem 4. *The proposed k-RUA achieves user authenticity if the OMDL assumption* [4] *holds over the underlying group* $\mathbb{G}$.

Due to the page limit, the detailed security proof and the subsequent proofs are deferred to the full version of this work.

Theorem 5. *The proposed k-RUA achieves anonymity if the DDH assumption* [8] *holds over the underlying group* $\mathbb{G}$.

Theorem 6. *The proposed k-RUA achieves user privacy if the underlying public key encryption scheme* [8] *is IND-CCA secure.*

5   Conclusion

In this work, we have proposed a generic construction of anonymous remote user authentication with k-times untraceability. We have also defined the formal security models to achieve certain security requirements that include user authenticity, anonymity and user privacy. We leave the construction of anonymous and traceable remote user authentication with designated verifier (where authorized users can be authenticated by a designated authentication server only) as a future work.

Acknowledgements. The work is supported by the Singapore National Research Foundation under NCR Award Number NCR2016NCR-NCR002-022. It is also supported by AXA Research Fund.

References

1. Armknecht, F., Escalante B, A.N., Löhr, H., Manulis, M., Sadeghi, A.-R.: Secure multi-coupons for federated environments: privacy-preserving and customer-friendly. In: Chen, L., Mu, Y., Susilo, W. (eds.) ISPEC 2008. LNCS, vol. 4991, pp. 29–44. Springer, Heidelberg (2008). https://doi.org/10.1007/978-3-540-79104-1_3
2. Ateniese, G., Camenisch, J., Joye, M., Tsudik, G.: A practical and provably secure coalition-resistant group signature scheme. In: Bellare, M. (ed.) CRYPTO 2000. LNCS, vol. 1880, pp. 255–270. Springer, Heidelberg (2000). https://doi.org/10.1007/3-540-44598-6_16
3. Au, M.H., Susilo, W., Mu, Y., Chow, S.S.M.: Constant-size dynamic k-times anonymous authentication. IEEE Syst. J. **7**(2), 249–261 (2013)
4. Bellare, M., Namprempre, C., Pointcheval, D., Semanko, M.: The one-more-RSA-inversion problems and the security of Chaum's blind signature scheme. J. Cryptol. **16**(3), 185–215 (2003)
5. Canard, S., Gouget, A., Hufschmitt, E.: A handy multi-coupon system. In: Zhou, J., Yung, M., Bao, F. (eds.) ACNS 2006. LNCS, vol. 3989, pp. 66–81. Springer, Heidelberg (2006). https://doi.org/10.1007/11767480_5
6. Chen, L., Enzmann, M., Sadeghi, A.-R., Schneider, M., Steiner, M.: A privacy-protecting coupon system. In: Patrick, A.S., Yung, M. (eds.) FC 2005. LNCS, vol. 3570, pp. 93–108. Springer, Heidelberg (2005). https://doi.org/10.1007/11507840_12
7. Chu, C.-K., Tzeng, W.-G.: Efficient k-Out-of-n oblivious transfer schemes with adaptive and non-adaptive queries. In: Vaudenay, S. (ed.) PKC 2005. LNCS, vol. 3386, pp. 172–183. Springer, Heidelberg (2005). https://doi.org/10.1007/978-3-540-30580-4_12
8. Cramer, R., Shoup, V.: A practical public key cryptosystem provably secure against adaptive chosen ciphertext attack. In: Krawczyk, H. (ed.) CRYPTO 1998. LNCS, vol. 1462, pp. 13–25. Springer, Heidelberg (1998). https://doi.org/10.1007/BFb0055717
9. Hinarejos, M.F., Isern-Deyà, A.-P., Ferrer-Gomila, J.-L., Huguet-Rotger, L.: Deployment and performance evaluation of mobile multicoupon solutions. Int. J. Inf. Secur. **18**, 1–24 (2018)

10. Liu, W., Mu, Y., Yang, G.: An efficient privacy-preserving e-coupon system. In: Lin, D., Yung, M., Zhou, J. (eds.) Inscrypt 2014. LNCS, vol. 8957, pp. 3–15. Springer, Cham (2015). https://doi.org/10.1007/978-3-319-16745-9_1
11. Liu, W., Mu, Y., Yang, G., Yu, Y.: Efficient e-coupon systems with strong user privacy. Telecommun. Syst. **64**(4), 695–708 (2017)
12. Nguyen, L.: Privacy-protecting coupon system revisited. In: Di Crescenzo, G., Rubin, A. (eds.) FC 2006. LNCS, vol. 4107, pp. 266–280. Springer, Heidelberg (2006). https://doi.org/10.1007/11889663_22
13. Nguyen, L., Safavi-Naini, R.: Dynamic k-times anonymous authentication. In: Ioannidis, J., Keromytis, A., Yung, M. (eds.) ACNS 2005. LNCS, vol. 3531, pp. 318–333. Springer, Heidelberg (2005). https://doi.org/10.1007/11496137_22
14. Teranishi, I., Furukawa, J., Sako, K.: k-Times anonymous authentication (extended abstract). In: Lee, P.J. (ed.) ASIACRYPT 2004. LNCS, vol. 3329, pp. 308–322. Springer, Heidelberg (2004). https://doi.org/10.1007/978-3-540-30539-2_22
15. Tian, Y., Zhang, S., Yang, G., Mu, Y., Yu, Y.: Privacy-preserving k-time authenticated secret handshakes. In: Pieprzyk, J., Suriadi, S. (eds.) ACISP 2017. LNCS, vol. 10343, pp. 281–300. Springer, Cham (2017). https://doi.org/10.1007/978-3-319-59870-3_16
16. Zhang, F., Kim, K.: ID-based blind signature and ring signature from pairings. In: Zheng, Y. (ed.) ASIACRYPT 2002. LNCS, vol. 2501, pp. 533–547. Springer, Heidelberg (2002). https://doi.org/10.1007/3-540-36178-2_33

Early Detection of Remote Access Trojan by Software Network Behavior

Masatsugu Oya[1] and Kazumasa Omote[2(✉)]

[1] JAIST, Nomi, Ishikawa 923-1292, Japan
s1510008@jaist.ac.jp
[2] University of Tsukuba, Tsukuba 305-8573, Japan
omote@risk.tsukuba.ac.jp

Abstract. APT (Advanced Persistent Threat) attack is increasing in recent years. APT attackers usually utilize malware called RAT (Remote Access Trojan) to access and control computers by stealth. The invasion method of RAT has been refined and it is extremely difficult to prevent its infection beforehand. Hence, an approach to detect RAT infection at the early stage after infection is important. However, there are two drawbacks in the existing early detection methods of RAT; (1) they do not become early detection in some circumstances; (2) they do not consider the RAT-like healthy software (e.g., system related software and antivirus software) for evaluation experiments. In this paper, we propose a detection method of RAT based on the new mechanism of early detection. Our evaluation experiments show that the proposed method can distinguish between RAT and the RAT-like healthy software with great accuracy.

Keywords: Advanced Persistent Threat (APT) attack ·
Remote Access Trojan (RAT) · Machine learning ·
Host-based detection

1 Introduction

Along with the rapid development of networking technologies and information systems, most organizations store information in their computers as digitalized data. At the same time, APT (Advanced Persistent Threat) attack, which is a type of cyber-crime targeting high-value information assets owned by a specific organization, is increasing [11]. Today, APT attack is one of the biggest threat to companies and government agencies. The ultimate objective of APT attacks is to steal high-value information assets such as technical property, financial information, and personal information of customers. Once confidential information is leaked, organization must incur a great loss, therefore, strong protection measures against APT attacks are extremely important.

APT attackers usually use malware called RAT (Remote Access Trojan) to achieve their ultimate goal. RAT is a type of malware that enables the attacker to access and control remote computers by stealth. After a computer in the

F. Guo et al. (Eds.): Inscrypt 2018, LNCS 11449, pp. 658–671, 2019.
https://doi.org/10.1007/978-3-030-14234-6_37

target organization is infected with RAT, it establishes a connection with C&C (Command and Control) server prepared by the attacker. The attacker sends commands through C&C server to control infected computers and RAT conducts intelligent activities such as downloading tools, exploring the network, searching and gathering files in the computers, and sending them to the attacker.

RAT infects computers by targeted emails in most cases [12]. The attacker guides the targets to open the attachments or URLs by utilizing any measures including social engineering. The methods of targeted email has become more and more sophisticated, so that it is extremely difficult to completely block the intrusion of RAT at the entrance. Therefore, an approach to detect infection of RAT at the early stage of post-infection activity is important.

One of the traditional detection methods of malware is signature based detection. In signature based detection method, malicious network communications are judged based on predefined signatures. However, with this method, it is not possible to detect unknown malware or variants of known malware, so that detection can be easily avoided [7]. On the other hand, in behavior based malware detection method, it is possible to detect unknown malware and variants of known malware by modeling behaviors peculiar to malware and different from normal state. Also, malware detection methods are classified into two types depending on the place where the system is introduced: network based detection method and host based detection method. In a host based detection method, it is necessary to consider the influence on the host computer and the operation management of the system since the system is installed in each computer, so that the operation is difficult as compared with network base detection method. However, since the host based detection method is much richer in the amount of information that can be used for malware detection, it is possible to detect malware more accurately. Moreover, the host based detection method has the advantage that it is relatively easy to identify the illegal software on the host when detecting malware.

As a related research on our approach, Adachi et al. [1] proposed a host based early detection method of RAT based on network behavior on a computer. However, this method has a drawback that much time may be required for detection according to behavior of RAT or benign communication. As a result, it does not become early detection in some circumstances. Furthermore, only several specific benign software selected by the authors were used for the evaluation experiments. As a result, it incorrectly detects the communication of system related software and antivirus software as RAT. Therefore, the practicality of this method on a real environment is unclear.

Our contributions are as follows.

- We propose a detection method of RAT based on the new mechanism of early detection. The mechanism is different from the existing methods [1,3]. While the early stage may get longer in the existing methods, our early stage finishes after a fixed period of time. Thanks to this improvement, it achieves true early detection.

- Our method is greatly different from existing researches in that features extracted from multiple connections in the initial stage communication are combined to generate features for one process. As a result, diversity of various communication by the same process can be expressed as a feature, and also, it is possible to learn a more accurate detection model of RAT.
- We perform evaluation experiments considering the RAT-like healthy software such as system related software and antivirus software. The network behavior of such software resembles RAT. As for benign features, we capture the data of communication and process from seven computers in the campus network of JAIST. Nevertheless, our method distinguishes between such software and RAT with great accuracy. Our method is superior to the previous method [1]. More precisely, our method can detect RAT with F-value of 91.5% while the previous method can detect it with F-value of 69.6% in our experiment.

2 Related Work

As related researches on behavior based malware detection method, methods of learning a model classifying malignant behavior and benign behavior using a machine learning algorithm have been proposed. Tang et al. [10] and Ozsoy et al. [4] proposed systems that detect malware by using machine learning techniques for the behavior of hardware such as CPU. In the research by Sangkatsanee et al. [9] and the research by Bekerman et al. [2], techniques for detecting attacks by extracting network features such as the number of packets, the number of destination ports, the number of TCP packets with an ACK flag was proposed. However, it is not clear whether these methods are effective for RAT.

As a research on RAT detection, Li et al. [5] proposed a method of calculating feature values from sessions and learning detection models using clustering method. Liang et al. [6] showed that a highly accurate detection model can be realized by using features, such as the number of destination IP addresses and the number of connections for each application, that can be acquired on each computer. However, these methods use all network packets from the beginning to the end of a session or software to judge whether the communication is generated by RAT or not. It means that confidential information can has been already stolen at the point when the system detects the communication of RAT. Yamada et al. [14] proposed the method to detect reconnaissance activities of RAT. However, it is also unclear whether the method contribute to the prevention of information leakage. Wu et al. [13] proposed the network-based detection framework of human controlled RAT session.

Jiang et al. [3] proposed a method to detect RAT before the information leakage occurs by using the communication data extracted from the early stage of the session. Adachi et al. [1] improved the detection rate of RAT by adding features that can be acquired on the computer to the approach of using the data from the early stage of the session. However, in common with these two studies, they have a drawback that much time may be required for detection according to behavior of RAT or benign communication. As a result, it does not become early detection for many situations. Furthermore, only several specific benign software selected by the authors were used for the evaluation experiments. As a result, it incorrectly detects the communication of system related software and antivirus software as RAT. Thus, these methods [1,3] are not practical.

The existing methods [1,3] of RAT do not become early detection in some circumstances, since the early stage does not finish as long as the packets are transmitted in the existing methods. In other words, the early stage finishes when the observed packets are not transmitted for a fixed period of time. Thus, much time may be required for RAT detection. On the other hand, in our new mechanism of early detection, the early stage inevitably finishes after a fixed period of time.

3   Proposed Method

From the viewpoint of countermeasures against information leakage, detection of RAT should be realized as early as possible after infection. We propose a detection method of RAT based on the new mechanism of early detection. The mechanism is different from the existing methods [1,3]. While the early stage may get longer in the existing methods, our early stage finishes after a fixed period of time. Thanks to this improvement, it achieves true early detection.

Our proposed method consists of two stages: learning phase and detection phase. In both stages, feature extraction is a main of processing. In this section, we first describe the details of the feature extraction processing and then explain the each stage. For simplicity, the detection engine running on the host is assumed to be trustworthy.

3.1   Our Approach

We observed benign and RAT communications, and then discovered the following important innate characteristics of RAT:

- RAT tends to behave secretly, and then the communication data are low.
- Benign communication including the RAT-like healthy software has greater traffic from the beginning because of non-stealthiness. Note that it does not always has greater traffic.

Our results confirm that the above innate feature of RAT practically exists and that the difference of network behavior between RAT and the RAT-like healthy software is obvious during the early stage. If the communication data of RAT are large, much witness are captured by network devices such as IDS. Our approach is based on the above characteristics.

3.2   Feature Extraction

In feature extraction processing, features are calculated from monitored communication for each process and a feature vector of the process is generated. The target network communication is TCP connections that is started from the

Process

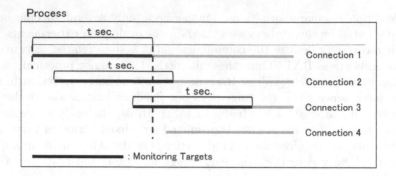

Fig. 1. Monitoring of target communications

target computer to the external network. Therefore, UDP connections, communication from the target computer to a computer in the same network, and connection initialized from the outside are not monitored. This is because most RATs communicate by TCP packets and a connection is established from the infected computer to the C&C server when RAT infects the computer. Also, considering the privacy of users and the scalability of the system, TCP payloads are discarded and only the header parts are acquired.

Since the purpose of this research is to detect RAT at the early stage, features are calculated using only a part of the first few connections for each process. The new definition of the early stage of communication in this research is as follows.

Definition 1 (Early Stage). *The early stage of communication is t seconds from the first packet for same 5-tuple (Source IP address, Destination IP address, Source port number, Destination Port number, and Protocol) network packets.*

For feature extraction, the first few early stage of connections in each process are used. Specifically, for each process, the early stage of connections initiated during the early stage of the first connection of the process are monitored. Thus, the monitoring time in each process is $2t$ seconds at maximum. In the case of the example of Fig. 1, the system monitors the early stage of Connection 1, which is the first connection of the process, and Connection 2 and Connection 3, which are the connections started during the early stage of Connection 1.

From the early stage of monitoring connections, eleven types of features shown in Table 1 are extracted. Then, after obtaining features from all monitoring early stage connections of the process, "Mean", "Standard Deviation (SD)", "Maximum value (Man)", "Minimum value (Min)", and "Range" of each connection features, and also, "Sum" of "PacNum", "OutPac", "InPac", "OutByte" and "InByte" are calculated. Further, "Number of Connections (Conn)" and "Number of Destination IP addresses (DstIP)" are counted. Finally, a 62 dimensional vector is outputted as a feature vector of the process. A specific calculation procedure of feature vectors is as follows.

Table 1. Connection features to extract

Feature	Explanation
PacNum	Total number of packets
OutPac	Number of outbound packets
InPac	Number of inbound packets
OutByte	Data size of outbound packets
InByte	Data size of inbound packets
OutByteSD	Standard deviation of data size of outbound packets
InByteSD	Standard deviation of data size of outbound packets
O/Ipac	Rate of OutPac to InPac
O/Ibyte	Rate of OutByte to InByte
OB/OP	Average data size per one outbound packet
IB/IP	Average data size per one inbound packet

1. Read a packet.
2. Judge whether the packet is TCP and the destination is toward the outside of the network.
3. Identify the connection from the set of source IP address, destination IP address, source port number, and destination port number.
4. If it is a new connection, identify the process ID, the process name, and the path of the executable file from the source port number, and store them in a correspondence table, otherwise, refer the correspondence table and identify the process.
5. Judge whether the packet is monitoring target.
6. If it is a monitoring target, update connection features (PacNum, OutPac, InPac, OutByte, InByte).
7. When all monitoring connections of a process are captured, calculate remaining connection features (OutByteSD, InByteSD, O/Ipac, O/Ibyte, OB/OP, IB/IP).
8. Calculate Mean, SD, Max, Min, Range of each connection feature and Sum of PacNum, OutPac, InPac, OutByte, InByte.
9. Calculate "Conn" and "DstIP".
10. Output a feature vector of the process.

Our proposed method differs greatly from existing researches in the point that the feature vector of a process is generated based on the multiple early stage connections of the process. Therefore, the diversity of connection, such as differences and variations in communication sizes for each connection, by the same process can be captured as features. RAT communication is often single session and single connection, and due to its characteristics, there is a time lag between the establishment of the connection to the C&C server and the attacker who confirms the connection starts attacks. Thus, we can guess that RAT communication in the early stage is monotonous. On the other hand, benign software will generate a wide variety of connections even in the early stage. Therefore, we expect that the difference between RAT and benign software become clear.

3.3   Learning Phase

In this phase, at first, feature vectors of processes of benign software and RATs are collected, and then the detection model of RAT is learned using those data. Feature vectors of benign software are gathered by performing the feature extraction processing described in the previous section on computers which can be guaranteed that they are not infected with malware. Also, feature vectors of RAT are collected by running prepared RAT samples. After that, for each collected feature vector, 0 is assigned if the feature vector is for benign software, and 1 if it is RAT as a label. Finally, the detection model of RAT is generated by applying supervised learning algorithm of machine learning for this dataset.

3.4   Detection Phase

At the detection phase, the feature extraction processing is executed at the monitor target computer, and the calculated feature vector is given as an input to the detection model generated at the learning phase. When the output is 0, it is assumed that the process is generated by benign software, and when the output is 1, the process is judged to be RAT.

When a process of RAT is detected, by referring to the location data of the execution file saved during the feature extraction processing, it is possible to check and analyze the actual substance. Therefore, it becomes possible to quickly respond to attacks in the first place, and it makes a time for implementing countermeasures before information leakage due to APT attack occurs.

4   Evaluation Experiments

4.1   Overview

In this section, we perform two types of evaluation experiments to confirm the effectiveness of the RAT detection method proposed in the previous section. In the first experiment, we mainly evaluate the detection performance of RAT by K-fold cross-validation for feature vectors of RAT and benign software. K-fold cross-validation is a method of dividing data into k groups and verifying each group using a model learned with all data of other groups. K-fold cross-validation enables to evaluate the detection performance against unknown RAT with limited data since RAT used for learning is not used at the time of evaluation. In this experiment, we set $k = 5$.

In the second experiment, the detection model of RAT was learned using all of the feature vectors of RAT and a part of the feature vector of benign software, and we evaluate the false detection of the proposed system by using the remaining

Table 2. List of RAT samples

BX	Bandook	Bozok	Cerberus	CyberGate
DarkComet	DarkNET	Ghost	LeGeNd	Mega
Netbus	NovaLite	Nuclear	OptixPro	Orion
Pandora	PoisonIvy	ProRAT	Turkojan	WiRAT
dalethRAT	deamondRAT	jSpy	njRAT	ucuL

feature vectors of benign software. In the case that many false detections are created by the system, the cost for examining alerts increases during operation, which increases the burden on the system administrators, so that the system is not practical. Therefore, in the second experiment, the practicality of the proposed system is evaluated from the viewpoint of the amount of false detection.

Before these experiments, we perform a preliminary experiment to determine the parameter t of the early stage of communication and the combination of the features to use in the experiments. In all experiments, we use seven type of machine learning classification algorithms: Decision Tree (DT), Random Forest (RF), Support Vector Machine (SVM), Naive Bayes (NB), Gradient Tree Boosting (GTB), AdaBoost (AB), and Multi-layer Perceptron (MLP).

4.2 Evaluation Indices

We use Accuracy (ACC), FPR, FNR, Precision (PRC), Recall (RCL), and F-measure (F1) as evaluation indices of the experiments. ACC is the accuracy of the overall identification, FPR is the false detection rate of the benign process, and FNR is the index showing the overlook rate of RAT. Also, PRC is the reliability of malignancy judgment, RCL means the detection rate of RAT, and F1 is the harmonic mean of PRC and RCL, which is a comprehensive measure of accuracy and completeness.

4.3 Dataset

As a benign dataset, we use daily communications including system related software and anti-virus software from active PCs to generate new dataset. The feature vectors of benign software used in the experiments are generated by collecting logs of communication and processes from seven computers in the campus network of JAIST and then by executing the feature extraction program. We acquired about 24 h (weekday) of communication logs from each computer. The usage purpose of each computer is creation of documents, browsing of emails and Web sites, and access to file servers, so it has no big difference from the usage of most organizations.

Feature vectors of RAT are collected by running RAT samples in a isolated network environment, and executing the feature extraction program. We use 25 kinds of RATs for evaluation. Table 2 shows the list of RAT samples used in experiments.

4.4 Preliminary Experiment

For evaluation, it is necessary to derive the optimum value of t, the parameter of the early stage communication, and the combination of features. However, it is impossible to test all possible combinations from the viewpoint of computational cost. Therefore, we determine t and the combination of features by the following procedure.

Table 3. Evaluation results of Experiment 1

DATA	AO'16[1]						Proposed					
	ACC	FPR	FNR	PRC	RCL	F1	ACC	FPR	FNR	PRC	RCL	F1
PC1+RAT	0.883	0.100	0.200	0.625	0.800	0.702	0.983	0.011	0.040	0.960	0.960	0.960
PC2+RAT	0.733	0.289	0.200	0.476	0.800	0.597	0.970	0.027	0.040	0.923	0.960	0.941
PC3+RAT	0.822	0.185	0.160	0.636	0.840	0.724	0.938	0.054	0.080	0.885	0.920	0.902
PC4+RAT	0.933	0.055	0.160	0.677	0.840	0.750	0.972	0.019	0.080	0.885	0.920	0.902
PC5+RAT	0.894	0.099	0.160	0.538	0.840	0.656	0.984	0.006	0.080	0.958	0.920	0.939
PC6+RAT	0.868	0.126	0.160	0.600	0.840	0.700	0.960	0.020	0.120	0.917	0.880	0.898
PC7+RAT	0.893	0.080	0.200	0.741	0.800	0.769	0.935	0.048	0.120	0.846	0.880	0.863
Total	0.874	0.115	0.177	0.603	0.823	0.696	0.967	0.022	0.080	0.910	0.920	0.915

When t becomes smaller, the earlier detection is possible, but the amount of features is smaller. So we first set the values from 1 to 10 as candidate values of t. For each candidate value, we evaluate the detection performance using 15 useful features determined by F value in analysis of variance. At this time, we consider t at which the evaluation result is the best as the optimum value. Next, we fix t is to the optimum value and find the best combination of features by brute force.

As a result of the above processing, the optimum value of t became 4, and the optimum combination of features became "InByteSDMin + IB/IPMean + IB/IPMax + IB/IPMin + OutByteSDMax + OutByteSDMean + OB/OPMin + IB/IPRange". In the subsequent experiments, we use the value of t and the combination of features obtained.

4.5 Experiment 1

In this experiment, we evaluate the detection performance of the proposed method using collected benign communication and RAT communication. We use feature vectors extracted from each computer and feature vectors of RAT as one dataset, and calculate performance indices by 5-fold cross validation. Table 3 shows the results of this experiment. In evaluation experiments using the method of Adachi et al. [1], the performance was the best on average when SVM was used as a learning algorithm[1] In the proposed method of this research, the best performance was obtained when GTB was used. Note that we implemented the method of Adachi et al. [1] by ourselves for comparison.

---

[1] Naive Bayes was the best algorithm in [1]. But, as a result of our code and feature refining, the result by SVM was the best in our experiment.

Table 4. Evaluation results of Experiment 2

TrainData	TestData	AO'16 [1]		Proposed	
		FP	FPR	FP	FPR
PC1+RAT	PC2+PC3+PC4+PC5+PC6+PC7	77	0.109	49	0.078
PC2+RAT	PC1+PC3+PC4+PC5+PC6+PC7	84	0.112	44	0.068
PC3+RAT	PC1+PC2+PC4+PC5+PC6+PC7	78	0.103	29	0.044
PC4+RAT	PC1+PC2+PC3+PC5+PC6+PC7	108	0.168	26	0.046
PC5+RAT	PC1+PC2+PC3+PC4+PC6+PC7	81	0.126	42	0.075
PC6+RAT	PC1+PC2+PC3+PC4+PC5+PC7	64	0.090	15	0.024
PC7+RAT	PC1+PC2+PC3+PC4+PC5+PC6	99	0.134	14	0.022
Total		591	0.120	219	0.051

Comparing the results, our method is better than the method by Adachi et al. for all evaluation indices. The detection rate (RCL) of RAT in the proposed method is 0.920 as a whole, and it becomes clear that most RAT can be detected. On the other hand, the detection rate by Adachi et al. method is 0.823, indicating that the detection performance of our method is high by about 0.1. As for FPR, the proposed method was 0.022 as a whole, while that of Adachi et al. was 0.115. In PRC which is an index of reliability of RAT detection, the proposed method is about 0.3 better than the method by Adachi et al.

4.6 Experiment 2

In this experiment, the detection model learned using communication of the benign process of one computer and all communication of RAT is tested by the data collected from the remaining computers. At that time, we derive the false detection rate and evaluate whether it can be suppressed to a level that can withstand practical use. Also, the collected environment of data used for learning and data used for testing is different in this experiment, so the versatility of the proposed method can also be evaluated.

Table 4 shows the evaluation result of number of false positives and the FPR. In the method of Adachi et al., the FPR is as high as 0.120 as a whole, and many benign processes are falsely detected as RAT. Note that we implemented the method of Adachi et al. [1] by ourselves for comparison. On the other hand, in the proposed method of this study, the number of processes misjudged as RAT is relatively small, and the FPR is 0.051 as a whole. Therefore, it can be said that the proposed method is more practical in terms of false detection rate. Also, this experimental result shows that the proposed method is effective even when the collection environment of learning data and evaluation data is different.

5 Discussion

5.1 False Detection

In the previous section, we show that the proposed method can detect infection of RAT with high accuracy, and also the possibility of false detection of benign software is greatly improved compared to existing research. However, in a large organization that owns a large number of computers, even if there are few false detection alerts on one computer, the burden on the system administrators becomes large since the number of alerts as a whole increases.

Table 5. Processes frequently judged as RAT (RAT-like healthy software)

Process	Count	Type	Distributor
backgroundTaskHost.exe	40	System	Microsoft
ActionUriServer.exe	30	System	Microsoft
svchost.exe	14	System	Microsoft
McPltCmd.exe	10	Antivirus	McAfee
OneDrive.exe	9	Cloud	Microsoft
explorer.exe	8	System	Microsoft
System	7	System	Microsoft
avgnt.exe	6	Antivirus	Avira
Avira.ServiceHost.exe	6	Antivirus	Avira
Avira.Systray.exe	6	Antivirus	Avira
Dropbox.exe	6	Cloud	Dropbox
OSE.EXE	6	Update	Microsoft
Shogidokoro.exe	6	Other	Individual
TeamViewer_Service.exe	6	Development	TeamViewer
wsqmcons.exe	6	System	Microsoft

Table 5 shows processes that are erroneously detected as RAT many times by our method. From the results, many erroneous detections occurred for Windows system related processes, antivirus software related processes, software update related processes, and cloud storage services. We consider that the characteristics of these processes are similar to RAT since they do not perform vigorous communication at the early stage compared with other benign processes.

We assume that it is possible to avoid false detection by pre-registering processes often judged as RAT in the whitelist. In the proposed method, when an alert occurs, the location of the executable file of the process can be easily specified, so the whitelist can be realized by confirming the digital signature of executable files. Table 6 shows the FPR and the FP, which are calculated based on the experiment in the previous section, depending on the presence

Table 6. False detection without whitelist and with whitelist

	Without WL	With WL: 4 Signatures[a]	With WL: 8 Signatures[b]
FPR	0.051	0.007	0.003
Average FP on 1-PC for 7 days	36.500	5.167	2.167

[a]Microsoft, McAfee, Avira, Dropbox
[b]Microsoft, McAfee, Avira, Dropbox, TeamViewer, Opera, Oracle, ASUS

of the whitelist. Note that the FP is the estimated average value on 1-PC for 7 days. The results indicates that it is possible to reduce the number of false detections by about 90% by registering digital signatures of Microsoft, McAfee, Avira, Dropbox in the whitelist. Also, the FPR decreases to 0.003 when eight publishers, which are Microsoft, McAfee, Avira, Dropbox, TeamViewer, Opera, Oracle, ASUS, are registered in the whitelist.

5.2 Evasion

We discuss whether our method can be avoided by attackers. As a detection avoidance, it is conceivable that attackers make RAT to generate communication similar to the features of a benign process. In this case, RAT needs to establish some connections with different traffic amounts and make each packet size widely varied. However, artificially generating unnecessary communication leads to an increase in the possibility that RAT communication will be detected by another attack detection system. In particular, mechanically generated communication is expected to be regarded as communication of Bots. Also, unnecessary communication increases the amount of traces of the attack. In APT attacks, attackers need to complete tasks without noticing the targets, therefore, we consider that attackers are not willing to attempt such means. Furthermore, since this method learns the detection model by machine learning, the detection criterion is not clear compared with signature based detection methods. Thus, it is extremely difficult to analyze and generate communication that the detection model misses. From the above viewpoint, we conclude that the risk that attackers intentionally avoid the detection model by such a method is low.

As another detection avoidance method, injecting RAT into a running benign process (e.g., cross-process injection) is conceivable. If the RAT program is injected into a process under execution, the RAT apparently functions as the benign process, so it may be excluded from detection by the whitelist. Also, if the injection process already communicates and the monitoring time of the proposed method has passed, the proposed method cannot detect RAT infection. Therefore, it is necessary to detect RAT infected by injection by another method. In this case, since the occurrence of code injection itself can be regarded as suspicious activity, a system that can detect injection can be effective. As measures against injection, there is a method that previously records the address where Windows API call instructions on the software executable file are described, and detects the injection by checking the record when the API is actually called [8].

6   Conclusion

We proposed a detection method of RAT based on the new mechanism of early detection. The mechanism is different from the existing methods [1,3]. While the early stage may get longer in the existing methods, our early stage finishes after a fixed period of time. Thanks to this improvement, it achieves true early detection. This makes it possible for the proposed method to more clearly distinguish between RAT and the RAT-like healthy software communication including system related one. Evaluation experiments show that the proposed method can detect RAT in early stage of post-infection activity with a detection rate of 92%, FPR of 2.2% and FNR of 8.0%. Therefore, we conclude that the proposed method is sufficiently practical as an early detection system of RAT. As a future work, we will conduct the experimental evaluation using new RATs in various networks.

Acknowledgements. This work was partly supported by Grant-in-Aid for Scientific Research (C) (16K00183).

References

1. Adachi, D., Omote, K.: A host-based detection method of remote access trojan in the early stage. In: Bao, F., Chen, L., Deng, R.H., Wang, G. (eds.) ISPEC 2016. LNCS, vol. 10060, pp. 110–121. Springer, Cham (2016). https://doi.org/10.1007/978-3-319-49151-6_8
2. Bekerman, D., Shapira, B., Rokach, L., Bar, A.: Unknown malware detection using network traffic classification. In: CNS 2015, pp. 134–142. IEEE (2015)
3. Jiang, D., Omote, K.: A RAT detection method based on network behavior of the communication's early stage. IEICE Trans. Fundam. **E99.A**(1), 145–153 (2016)
4. Khasawneh, K.N., Ozsoy, M., Donovick, C., Abu-Ghazaleh, N., Ponomarev, D.: Ensemble learning for low-level hardware-supported malware detection. In: Bos, H., Monrose, F., Blanc, G. (eds.) RAID 2015. LNCS, vol. 9404, pp. 3–25. Springer, Cham (2015). https://doi.org/10.1007/978-3-319-26362-5_1
5. Li, S., Yun, X., Zhang, Y., Xiao, J., Wang, Y.: A general framework of trojan communication detection based on network traces. In: NAS 2012, pp. 49–58. IEEE (2012)
6. Liang, Y., Peng, G., Zhang, H., Wang, Y.: An unknown trojan detection method based on software network behavior. Wuhan Univ. J. Nat. Sci, **18**(5), 369–376 (2013)
7. Moser, A., Kruegel, C., Kirda, E.: Limits of static analysis for malware detection. In: ACSAC 2007, pp. 421–430. IEEE (2007)
8. Rabek, J.C., Khazan, R.I., Lewandowski, S.M., Cunningham, R.K.: Detection of injected, dynamically generated, and obfuscated malicious code. In: ACM workshop on Rapid Malcode, pp. 76–82. ACM (2003)
9. Sangkatsanee, P., Wattanapongsakrn, N., Charnsripinyo, C.: Practical real-time intrusion detection using machine learning approaches. Comput. Commun. **34**(18), 2227–2235 (2011)

10. Tang, A., Sethumadhavan, S., Stolfo, S.J.: Unsupervised anomaly-based malware detection using hardware features. In: Stavrou, A., Bos, H., Portokalidis, G. (eds.) RAID 2014. LNCS, vol. 8688, pp. 109–129. Springer, Cham (2014). https://doi.org/10.1007/978-3-319-11379-1_6
11. Tankard, C.: Advanced persistent threats and how to monitor and deter them. Netw. Secur. **2011**(8), 16–19 (2011)
12. Check Point Software Technologies Ltd., Grobal Cyber Attack Treands Report (2017)
13. Wu, S., Liu, S., Lin, W., Zhao, X., Chen, S.: Detecting remote access trojans through external control at area network borders. In: ANCS 2017, pp. 131–141. ACM/IEEE (2017)
14. Yamada, M., Morinaga, M., Unno, Y., Torii, S., Takenaka, M.: RAT-based malicious activities detection on enterprise internal networks. In: ICITST 2015, pp. 321–325. IEEE (2015)

Author Index